A Stephen Birnbaum Travel Guide

Birnbaum's
CANADA
1990

Stephen Birnbaum
Alexandra Mayes Birnbaum
EDITORS

Lois Spritzer
EXECUTIVE EDITOR

Laura Brengelman
Managing Editor

Kristin Moehlmann
John Storch
Senior Editors

Catherine J. Langevin
Julie Quick
Associate Editors

Stephen Coleman
Assistant Editor

HOUGHTON MIFFLIN COMPANY / BOSTON 1989

THE TOWN OF PICKERING PUBLIC LIBRARY

This book is published by special arrangement
with Eric Lasher and Maureen Lasher.

Copyright © 1989 by Houghton Mifflin Company

All rights reserved.

For information about permission to reproduce selections from this book, write to Permissions, Houghton Mifflin Company, 2 Park Street, Boston, Massachusetts 02108.

ISBN: 0-395-51146-1
ISSN: 0749-2561 (Stephen Birnbaum Travel Guides)
ISSN: 0884-1039 (Canada)

Printed in the United States of America

WP 10 9 8 7 6 5 4 3 2 1

Contents

xi   **A Word from the Editor**

1   **How to Use This Guide**

GETTING READY TO GO

A mini-encyclopedia of all the practical travel data you need to plan your vacation down to the final detail.

When and How to Go

  9   What's Where: Canada East to West
13   When to Go
16   Traveling by Plane
29   Touring by Train
30   Touring by Bus
31   Touring by Car
38   Package Tours
41   Camping, Hiking, Biking, Recreational Vehicles

Preparing

47   Calculating Costs
50   Planning a Trip
52   How to Use a Travel Agent
55   Insurance
59   Border Crossings
60   How to Pack
63   Hints for Handicapped Travelers
68   Hints for Single Travelers
70   Hints for Older Travelers
73   Hints for Traveling with Children
77   Hints for Traveling with Pets
79   Staying Healthy

On the Road

81   Credit and Currency
83   Accommodations
86   Dining Out
88   Time Zones, Business Hours, and Bank Holidays

vi CONTENTS

89 Mail, Telephone, and Electricity
90 Medical and Legal Help on the Road
91 Drinking and Drug Laws
92 Religion on the Road

Sources and Resources

94 Tourist Information
95 Notes on Sports
97 Weights and Measures
98 Camera and Equipment

PERSPECTIVES

A cultural and historical survey of Canada's past and present, its people, politics, and heritage.

105 The Canadian Past: A Short History of a Huge Country
123 Contemporary Canada and the Storm of Separatism

THE CITIES

Thorough, qualitative guides to each of the nine cities most often visited by vacationers and businesspeople. Each section, a comprehensive report of the city's most compelling attractions and amenities, is designed to be used on the spot. Directions and recommendations are immediately accessible because each guide is presented in a consistent form.

135	Calgary	203	Quebec City
145	Edmonton	221	Toronto
155	Halifax	242	Vancouver
166	Montreal	261	Winnipeg
190	Ottawa		

DIVERSIONS

A selective guide to 15 active and cerebral vacations, including the places to pursue them where your quality of experience is likely to be highest.

For the Body

275 Downhill Skiing
284 Cross-Country Skiing
288 The Best Tennis Vacations

291	Golf in Canada: A Land of Links
296	Where They Bite: Fishing in Canada
302	Sailing Canada's Many Waters
307	Canoeing and Rafting
312	Mountain Climbing
315	Hiking and Backpacking
319	Hunting
322	Ice Skating

For the Experience

326	Festivals, Fairs, and Fancy Acts
330	National Parks
336	Special Havens
345	Farm and Ranch Vacations

DIRECTIONS

Canada's most spectacular routes and roads, most arresting natural wonders, most magnificent parks and forests, all organized into 45 specific driving tours.

Alberta

356	Lethbridge to Calgary via Waterton Lakes National Park
361	Calgary to Banff and Jasper National Parks
368	Cypress Hills Provincial Park to Edmonton via the Dinosaur Country
373	Edmonton to Slave Lake and Peace River

British Columbia

381	Vancouver Island
387	Fraser River
393	Okanagan Orchard Country
396	The Pacific National Parks
398	Prince George to Prince Rupert
401	Prince George to the Yukon

Manitoba

405	Whiteshell
409	The Wheat Belt
414	Interlake
418	The North

New Brunswick

- 425 The Acadian Trail
- 431 The Fundy Coast
- 438 The St. John River

Newfoundland

- 446 Avalon's Southern Shore
- 449 Central Newfoundland
- 454 The West Coast
- 459 Northern Avalon

The Northwest Territories

- 465 The Hay River to Yellowknife
- 470 The Nahanni
- 472 Dawson City to Inuvik
- 475 Hay River to Fort Smith

Nova Scotia

- 482 Yarmouth to Amherst
- 493 Yarmouth to the Strait of Canso
- 500 Amherst around Cape Breton Island

Ontario

- 510 Windsor to Stratford: Ontario's England
- 523 The Heritage Highways
- 537 The Western Lakeshores
- 548 Yonge Street: Toronto to Thunder Bay

Prince Edward Island

- 566 Blue Heron Drive
- 571 Lady Slipper Drive
- 573 The Kings Byway

Quebec

- 579 The Eastern Townships
- 584 Beaupré/Charlevoix and Saguenay
- 594 The North Shore
- 599 The Laurentians
- 608 The Gaspé Peninsula
- 621 Iles de la Madeleine

Saskatchewan

629 The Trans-Canada across Saskatchewan
635 Estevan to the Northern Lakes
640 The Yellowhead Highway

The Yukon Territory

650 The Dawson Circle Route
659 The Trail of '98

667 **Index**

A Word from the Editor

Most veteran transatlantic air travelers had a less than auspicious introduction to Canada, since the old propeller plane route to and from Europe usually included a stop in Gander (Newfoundland), hardly the Confederation's most scenic spot. A broader recognition of Canada's abundant attractions came somewhat later, and it is really only in recent years — with the coming of a couple of expos and a pair of Olympic extravaganzas — that Canada's travel bounty has even begun to be understood by the rest of the world.

Part of the problem of comprehending all that Canada has to offer is the sheer size of the undertaking. Few countries offer as vast a panorama or as diverse a spectrum of landscapes — to say nothing of the variety of ethnic and cultural influences. To even the most cursory observer, Canada seems at least three countries: the marvelously austere Maritimes of the East, the fiercely French Quebecois nearer the center of the continent, and the vast sweep of the pioneer West that stretches from the province of Ontario (just above the Great Lakes) to the Pacific Ocean. And that doesn't even begin to consider the trackless wilderness of the Yukon and the Northwest Territories.

Canada is one of my own favorite travel destinations, so creating and revising this book has been more joy than toil; even my least pleasant experiences in Canada have enhanced my appreciation of Canadian kindness and the hospitality that are regularly offered to visitors. I recall with some embarrassment the occasion of being stopped by an unmarked patrol car of the Royal Canadian Mounted Police — they call them "ghost" cars in Canada — and getting myself set for the sort of dressing down that my speed would have earned me in any other country. Instead, the RCMP officer was almost apologetic in warning me that driving too fast might well endanger my safety, and I was sent on my way with just that warning — and a very pleasant one at that. It not only made me observe the speed limit thereafter, but made me feel particularly welcome and well cared for in what was, after all, a foreign land.

For visitors from the US, the foreign quality of Canada can take on quite a different cast from place to place. The dour demeanor of the Atlantic provinces is an extension (and occasionally an exaggeration) of the inscrutable mien that is regularly encountered in Maine. In contrast, the Canadian West — from the flat prairies of Saskatchewan and Manitoba to the islands of Vancouver Harbour — are almost unfailingly and heartily friendly; this is the segment of Canada where it is most difficult to realize that you have crossed a national border.

French Canada has come to be a somewhat different matter, and Montreal's advertisement of itself as "the second largest French-speaking city in the world" has lately taken on new meaning. (We won't tell them that they've lately dropped to fourth place, behind Nice and Kinshasa.) As a vacation alternative to Paris, Montreal has substantial appeal both in its ambience and in the fact that the US dollar currently fares far better in Canada than in Europe. But separatist spirit has shown its face in a myriad of small ways, including the reluctance of a number of Montreal cabdrivers to speak English to US visitors. For the visitor, however, this slight inconvenience may prove oddly welcome; it means that the Montreal taxi ranks now more closely approximate the indifference regularly shown foreign visitors in France.

In creating this guide, I've tried as much as possible to offer some insights into a country that I consider vastly underrated as a tourist destination. The genesis of this book was clearly my own increasing interest in the Canadian countryside and urban experience, and my perception that more and more of my sophisticated and knowledgeable traveling acquaintances were reporting extremely pleasant experiences just north of the US border. But I should, I think, apologize for at least one indulgence in this text that is baldly chauvinistic, and that is our constant reference to citizens of the US as "Americans." Strictly speaking, Canadian citizens are just as much residents of the North American continent as US citizens, and we apologize for any slight our Canadian readers may feel about our having appropriated this terminology. It was done strictly in an effort to simplify the narrative, rather than in an attempt to appropriate a common continental distinction.

As I've indicated, part of Canada's appeal is its extremely wide variety of terrain and cultural influence. And although Canada is often referred to as a single destination, it is actually a dazzling blend of ethnic and historic diversity. It's just this diversity that has combined to produce environments and atmospheres that are almost always intriguing and often unique. So in preparing this guide, we have tried to produce a book that accurately reflects all the appeal of this vast country.

In the same way, the increasing and broadening sophistication of US travelers — no matter where they are headed — has made it essential that any Canadian guidebook reflect and keep pace with the real needs of its prospective readers. That's why we've tried to create a guide that's specifically organized, written, and edited for this newly knowledgeable traveler, for whom qualitative information is infinitely more desirable than mere quantities of unappraised data. We think that this book, as well as the other guides in our series, represents a new generation of travel guides, ones that are especially responsive to the needs and interests of today's travelers.

For years, dating back as far as Herr Baedeker, travel guides have tended to be encyclopedic, seemingly much more concerned with demonstrating expertise in geography and history than in any analysis of the sorts of things that more naturally concern a typical tourist. But today, when it is hardly necessary to tell a traveler where Vancouver is located, it is hard to justify devoting endless pages to historical perspective. In many cases, the traveler has been to Canada nearly as often as the guidebook editor, so it becomes the responsibility of that editor to provide new perceptions and to suggest new directions to make his guide genuinely valuable.

That's exactly what we've tried to do in our series. I think you'll notice a new tone to the text, as well as an organization and focus that are distinctive. And even a random examination will demonstrate a substantial departure from standard guidebook orientation, for we've not only attempted to provide information of a different sort, but we've also tried to present it in a context that makes it particularly accessible.

Needless to say, it's difficult to decide what to include in a guide of this size — and what to omit. Early on, we realized that giving up the encyclopedic approach precluded the inclusion of every route and restaurant, which helped define our overall editorial focus. Similarly, when we discussed ways of presenting certain information in other than strict geographical order, we found that the new format enabled us to arrange data in a way that we feel best answers the questions travelers typically ask.

Large numbers of specific questions have provided the real editorial skeleton for this book. The volume of mail I regularly receive seems to emphasize that modern travelers want very precise information, so we've tried to address these needs and have organized our material in the most responsive way possible. Readers who want to know about the best restaurant in Montreal or the best beach on Prince Edward Island will have no trouble whatever extracting that data from this guide.

Travel guides are, above all, reflections of personal taste, and putting one's name on a title page obviously puts one's preferences on the line. But I think I ought to amplify just what "personal" means. I do not believe in the sort of personal guidebook that's a palpable misrepresentation on its face. It is, for example, hardly possible for any single travel writer to visit thousands of restaurants (and nearly that many hotels) in any given year and provide accurate appraisals of each one. And even if it were physically possible for one human being to do so, it would of necessity have to be done at a dead sprint, and the perceptions derived therefrom would probably be less valid than those of any other individual visiting the same establishments. It is, therefore, impossible (especially in an annually revised and updated guidebook *series* such as we offer) to have only one person provide all the data on the entire world.

I also happen to think that such individual orientation is of substantially less value to readers. Visiting a single hotel for just one night or eating one hasty meal in a given restaurant hardly equips anyone to provide appraisals that are of more than passing interest. No amount of doggedly alliterative or oppressively onomatopoeic text can camouflage a technique that is specious on its face. We have, therefore, chosen what I like to describe as the "thee and me" approach to restaurant and hotel appraisal and, to a somewhat more limited degree, to the sites and sights we have included in the other sections of our text. What this really reflects is personal sampling tempered by intelligent counsel from informed local sources, and these additional friends-of-the-editor are almost always residents of the city and/or area about which they have been consulted.

Despite the presence of several editors, a considerable number of researchers, and numerous insightful local correspondents, very precise editing and tailoring keep our text fiercely subjective. So what follows is purposely designed to be the gospel according to Birnbaum, and it represents as much of my own tastes and insights as is humanly possible. It is probable, therefore, that if you like your cities clean and your mountains uncrowded, prefer small hotels with personality to vast high-rise anonymities, and can't tolerate fresh fish that's been relentlessly overcooked, we're likely to have a long and meaningful relationship. Readers with dissimilar tastes may be less enraptured.

I also should point out something about the person to whom this guidebook is directed. Above all, he or she is a "visitor." This means that such elements as restaurants have been specifically picked to provide the visitor with a representative, enlightening, exciting, and above all pleasant experience. Since so many extraneous considerations can affect the reception and service accorded a regular restaurant patron, our choices can in no way be construed as a definitive guide to resident dining. We think we've listed all the best places in various price ranges, but they were chosen from a visitor's viewpoint.

Other evidence of how we've tried to tailor our text to reflect changing travel habits is most apparent in the section we call DIVERSIONS. Where once it was common for travelers to spend a Canadian visit nailed to a single spot, the emphasis today is more on pursuing some active enterprise while seeing the surrounding countryside. Such is the amount of perspiration regularly stimulated by today's "leisurely" vacationer that the by-product of a typical modern holiday is often the need to take another vacation immediately after the first one is over. So we've selected every activity we could reasonably evaluate and organized the material in a way that is especially accessible to activists of either an athletic or cerebral bent. It is no longer necessary, therefore, to wade through a pound or two of extraneous prose just to find the best golf course within a reasonable radius of your destination.

If there is a single thing that best characterizes the revolution and evolution of current holiday habits, it is that Americans now consider travel a right rather than a privilege. No longer is a trip to the far corners of the world necessarily a once-in-a-lifetime thing; nor is the idea of visiting exotic, faraway places in the least worrisome. Travel today translates as the enthusiastic desire to sample all of the world's opportunities, to find that elusive quality of experience that is not only enriching but comfortable. For that reason, we've tried to make what follows not only helpful and enlightening, but the sort of welcome companion of which every traveler dreams.

Finally, I should point out that every good travel guide is a living enterprise; that is, no part of this text is cast in bronze. In our annual revisions, we expect to refine, expand, and further hone all our material to serve your travel needs even better. To this end, no contribution is of greater value to us than your personal reaction to what we have written as well as information reflecting your own experiences while using the book. We earnestly and enthusiastically solicit your comments on this book *and* your opinions and perceptions about places you have recently visited. In this way, we will be able to provide the best information — including the actual experiences of the traveling public — to make that experience more readily available to others. Please write to us at 60 E. 42nd St., New York, NY 10165.

We sincerely hope to hear from you.

STEPHEN BIRNBAUM

How to Use This Guide

? A great deal of care has gone into the special organization of this guidebook, and we believe it represents a real breakthrough in the presentation of travel material. Our aim has been to create a new, more modern generation of travel books and to make this guide the most useful and practical travel tool available today.

Our text is divided into five basic sections in order to present information on every possible aspect of a Canadian vacation in the best possible manner. This organization itself should alert you to the vast and varied opportunities available in this country — as well as indicating all the specific, detailed data necessary to plan a trip in Canada. You won't find much of the conventional "swaying palms and shimmering sands" text here; we've chosen instead to use the available space for more useful and purposeful information. Prospective Canadian itineraries tend to speak for themselves, and with so many diverse travel opportunities, we feel our main job is to explain them and to provide the basic information — how, when, where, how much, and what's best — to allow you to make the most intelligent choices possible.

What follows is a brief summary of the five basic sections of this book and what you can expect to find in each. We believe that you will find both your travel planning and en route enjoyment enhanced considerably by having this book at your side.

GETTING READY TO GO

This compendium of practical travel facts is a sort of know-it-all companion that can provide all the precise information you need to go about creating a trip through Canada. There are entries on more than two dozen separate topics, including how to travel, what preparations to make before you leave, what to expect in the different regions of Canada, what your trip is likely to cost, and how to avoid prospective problems. The individual entries are specific, realistic, and cost-oriented. Except where noted, all prices in this book are in US dollars.

We expect that you will use this section most in the course of planning your trip, for its ideas and suggestions are intended to facilitate the often confusing planning period. Entries are intentionally concise in an effort to get to the meat of the matter with the least extraneous prose. This information is further augmented by extensive lists of specific sources from which to obtain even more specialized information and some suggestions for obtaining travel information on your own.

PERSPECTIVES

A cultural and historical survey of Canada's past and present, its people, politics, and heritage, this section provides a glimpse of the cultural diversity that characterizes Canadian life, and the current conflicts that permeate contemporary economic and social activity.

THE CITIES

Here are individual reports on the nine Canadian cities most visited by tourists and businesspeople, researched and written with the assistance of local experts and journalists to provide insights into their own turf. Although useful in the planning stage, THE CITIES is really designed to be used on the spot. Each report offers a short-stay guide to its city within a consistent format: an essay, introducing the city as a contemporary place to live; *At-a-Glance,* a site-by-site survey of the most important (and sometimes most eclectic) sights to see and things to do; *Sources and Resources,* a concise listing of pertinent tourist information, meant to answer a myriad of pressing questions as they arise — from something simple, like the address of the tourist office, to something more difficult, like where to find the best nightspot, to see a show, to play tennis, or to get a taxi; and *Best in Town,* our cost and quality choices of the best places to eat and sleep on a variety of budgets.

DIVERSIONS

This section is designed to help travelers find the very best locations in which to satisfy their fondest vacation desires without having to wade through endless unrelated text. We have instead prepared this selective guide to the broadest possible range of activities and the best places to pursue them.

Our list of 15 theme vacations is designed to lead the active vacationer to the very best locations throughout Canada at which to pursue a favorite hobby or learn a new sport. Whether our suggestion is for a resort, a particular mountain, or an undeveloped wilderness lake, each is made to take you where the quality of experience is highest. Whether you opt for golf or tennis, fishing or canoeing, visiting battle sites or climbing mountain peaks, each entry is the equivalent of getting a comprehensive checklist to the absolute best in Canada.

DIRECTIONS

This series of 45 Canadian driving itineraries, from Prince Edward Island to British Columbia's Vancouver Island, traverses Canada's most beautiful routes and roads, past its most spectacular natural wonders, through its most magnificent national parks and forests. DIRECTIONS is the only section of the book that is organized geographically, and its routes cover the touring highlights of the entire country in short, independent segments that describe journeys of one to three days. Itineraries can be "connected" for longer trips or used individually for short, intensive explorations. Whether you are planning a major family vacation to cover thousands of miles or simply want to escape to the country for just a day, the format is adaptable to your specific needs.

Each entry includes a guide to sightseeing highlights; a cost and quality guide to accommodations and food along the road (small inns, clean and comfortable motels, country hotels, campgrounds, and off-the-main-road discoveries); and suggestions for activities.

Although each of the sections of the book has a distinct format and function, they have been designed to be used together to provide a complete package of travel information. To use this book to full advantage, take a few minutes to read the table of contents and random entries in each section. This will provide a sense of how it all fits together.

Pick and choose information that you need from different sections. For example, assume that you have always been interested in an outdoor vacation walking through one of Canada's wilderness areas, but you never knew exactly how to organize it or where to go. You might well begin by reading the short, informative section on hiking in GETTING READY TO GO. This would provide plenty of ideas on how to organize the trip, where to go for more information, and what to take along. But where to go? Turn to *Hiking and Backpacking,* DIVERSIONS, for a list of the best hiking trails in Canada, or to *National Parks,* DIVERSIONS, for a survey of every Canadian national park; a look through the selections will direct you to a trail equal to your expertise. Perhaps you will choose as your destination one of the Lake Louise trails in Banff National Park. Turn next to DIRECTIONS for suggestions on what else to see while in Alberta, including the Dinosaur Provincial Park and Blackfoot Indian Preserve. In fact, you may even decide to take a break from hiking in the wilds and visit Alberta's two major cities, Calgary and Edmonton; each is fully covered in THE CITIES.

In other words, the sections of this book are building blocks to help you put together the best possible trip. Use them selectively, as tools, sources of ideas, a reference work for accurate facts, and a guide to the best buys, the most exciting sights, the most pleasant accommodations and delicious food, *the best travel experiences* that you can have in Canada.

MARITIME PROVINCES

GETTING READY TO GO

When and How to Go

What's Where: Canada East to West

Canada, the second largest country in the world, sprawls across the Northern Hemisphere like a silent giant, flinging mountains and plains, tundra, and Arctic islands over 3.8 million square miles. Only the Soviet Union, with a total area of 8.65 million square miles, is larger; yet Canada has only 25 million people, just one-tenth the population of the US. Because of Canada's exceptional geography — the proximity of the Arctic Ocean and vast expanses of virtually uninhabited northern territories where the soil never fully thaws and agriculture is impossible — the huge majority of Canadians live in a temperate belt 200 miles deep that runs just north of the 4,000-mile US-Canada border like an artful seam.

Canada's formidable magnitude is divided into 12 separate political entities. These include ten provinces (east to west: Newfoundland — including Labrador — Nova Scotia, Prince Edward Island, New Brunswick, Quebec, Ontario, Manitoba, Saskatchewan, Alberta, and British Columbia) and two territories (the Northwest Territories and the Yukon Territory). The territories account for 38% of Canada's area but for only a minute fraction of the population.

TERRAIN: The Canadian landmass is shaped roughly like a ship, its bow pointed bravely into the Atlantic, its stern rising high along the country's long Pacific coast and the Yukon Territory. Ontario's southernmost toehold in Lake Erie provides an anchor for this ship, and the ragged sail of islands 2,850 miles to the north — Ellesmere, Axel Heiberg, Perry, Queen Elizabeth — flutters in the Arctic Ocean, the country's northernmost point, facing the permanent polar ice that announces the North Pole. Some 5,780 miles separate Canada's easternmost point, Newfoundland's Cape Spear, from Mt. St. Elias on the Yukon's border with Alaska. If Canada resembles a ship, it is a ship not only surrounded by, but nearly aswamp with, water. Hudson Bay, a vast inland arm of the Arctic Ocean, dips into the landmass like a giant puncture, and more than one-third of the world's known freshwater sources are held within the country's huge, interlocking system of natural inland waterways.

The country forms five distinct geographical regions, each characterized by a dominating physical feature.

Appalachian Region – The finger of land that extends along Canada's eastern shore, like an extension of New England, includes Nova Scotia, Newfoundland, New Brunswick, and Prince Edward Island provinces, bounded on the east by the sea and on the west by the St. Lawrence River. The area derives its name from the mountain system that originates in Quebec and runs south all the way to Alabama. In Canada, this ancient range of folded mountains has eroded to summits less than 5,000 feet high. Most of the mountains have been submerged by the sea, and what remains are predominantly islands and peninsulas: Newfoundland, Anticosti Island, Prince Edward Island, Cape Breton Island, the Gaspé Peninsula, Nova Scotia, and New Brunswick.

The land consists of two parallel highlands of hard, ancient rock separated by lower land. One of the upland areas is in northwest New Brunswick; the other extends through Nova Scotia and Cape Breton Island. In between these two ridges lies a lower area that was once covered with water; eons ago the area was filled in with sediment rich in carbon, and now coal is mined there.

The sea has been instrumental in shaping the geography of this region. In fact, the provinces are known collectively as the Maritime Provinces, indicating their close relation to the sea. Land comes into crashing contact with sea in the Bay of Fundy between New Brunswick and Nova Scotia where massive waves beat against rugged sandstone cliffs. The Gulf of St. Lawrence, from which the St. Lawrence River flows to the Great Lakes, is a large body of water separating Newfoundland, Nova Scotia, and the southeast mainland. Northumberland Strait, in the gulf, lies between Prince Edward Island and the northern coasts of New Brunswick and Nova Scotia. These waters are rich with fish, because the cold waters of the Labrador current from the Arctic Ocean meet the warmer Gulf Stream current and support a wide variety of marine life. Lobsters, clams, oysters, scallops, cod, mackerel, tuna, herring, haddock, and swordfish are among the species found here. Fishermen living in small villages up and down the white or red sand coasts fish in the same waters as did their fathers and grandfathers. The principal cities in the area are all seaports: Halifax, Nova Scotia; Saint John, New Brunswick; and St. John's, Newfoundland.

Inland, the land becomes a series of gently rolling hills and plains, much of which is forest or farmland. Red spruce, balsam, yellow birch, sugar maple, and beech are common in the forest zones. The upland areas, once covered with glacier deposits, now offer no fertile soils. But the lower areas support agriculture, particularly potato fields in New Brunswick and Prince Edward Island and the apple and cherry orchards and cranberry bogs of Nova Scotia.

Canadian Shield – The Canadian (or Precambrian) Shield is Canada's largest geographic region, encompassing 1.6 million square miles, almost half of the country. This shield-shaped region stretches from the coast of Labrador in the northeast through northern Quebec, northern Ontario, northern Manitoba, northern Saskatchewan, and the Northwest Territories to the Arctic Ocean. It surrounds and includes the Hudson Bay. This huge embayment of the Arctic Ocean, 650 miles wide and 850 miles long, was explored and named (none too modestly) by Henry Hudson in 1610 during his search for the Northwest Passage.

Hudson's expedition opened the way to English and French traders and merchants who were attracted by the rich profits of fur trading with the Indians. Two large rival companies, the Hudson's Bay Company and the Northwest Company, were formed to exploit the wealth of the region. Today the area still survives by its rich natural resources, particularly gold, uranium, iron ore, radium, timber, and waterfalls and rapids with potential hydroelectric power. Most of the towns located in the shield revolve around these commercial concerns and are generally centers of lumbering, pulp and paper, or mining.

The terrain itself, one of the oldest sections of the earth's crust, is rough and wild. Ancient Precambrian (prior to Paleozoic) rocks with crystalline form line the surface. During the Ice Age, glaciers rubbed away the top soil; as they retreated, they left the surface strewn with rocks and boulders, which still characterize the area. Forested hills and numerous lakes and streams are also found here. Though you will not encounter too many people, you will probably see some of the shield's other inhabitants: lynx, snowshoe rabbit, wolf, beaver, wolverine, mink, river otter, bobcat, weasel, and, in the far north, the arctic fox.

Most of the shield is agriculturally poor because of the lack of soil and preponderance of rocks. An exception is the area south of James Bay, the southernmost section of Hudson Bay, known as the Clay Belt. A layer of sediment that was once the floor of a lake remains around the bay and supports agriculture. The vegetation in the rest of the shield is restricted to forest and woodland and occurs in three major zones. Just north of the Clay Belt is a stretch of forest where spruce, fir, larch, hemlock, and pine grow. The northern woodland prevails above this zone and looks like open parkland, where widely separate candelabra spruce stand on a deep lichen floor. The northernmost zone of the shield is the forest tundra with permafrost. Strips of white and black spruce dominate the southern edge of this zone.

The shield offers great opportunities for fishermen, hunters, trekkers, and people seeking a rugged solitude. Wilderness camps from which woodspeople launch various expeditions are located in many small towns (see *Where They Bite, Hiking and Backpacking,* and *Hunting,* DIVERSIONS).

St. Lawrence Lowland and Lakes Region – Below the Canadian Shield and to the west of the Appalachian region is the St. Lawrence Lowland, the center of Canada's population and industry. In its two provinces, Quebec and Ontario, live 62% of all Canadians. The lifeline of the area is the St. Lawrence River, which traverses southern Ontario and Quebec through a series of fertile valleys.

The geography of the region itself has spawned development. Eons ago there were many more lakes in the area than there are today. As they dried and contracted, they left deposits of fertile sediments. Consequently, the lands along the St. Lawrence River and between Lakes Huron, Erie, and Ontario are excellent for farming. With the St. Lawrence Seaway providing access from the Atlantic Ocean to the heartland of North America 2,000 miles away, the development of agricultural business, industry, and commerce was inevitable. In these lowlands rose the greatest cities of Canada, Montreal and Toronto, each with populations nearing 3 million; Ottawa, the nation's capital, population 750,000; and the other major urban-industrial centers of Hamilton, Kitchener, London, Sarnia, and Windsor.

On the map, Ontario resembles a bulky leg with the toes pointing southwest. The thigh and upper leg are part of the Canadian Shield, while the lower portion, with footholds in the St. Lawrence River and Lakes Ontario, Huron, and Erie, is the center of population. The climate here is mild, ranging from January temperatures of 25F (-4C) to July highs in the 80s F (30s C). Ontario is Canada's most productive province; the north is a major source of minerals, and the south, of farm and dairy products and tobacco. Toronto, the largest city in Canada, is clean and cosmopolitan, with a significant French-speaking population, a diverse ethnic composition, and the avant-garde architecture of Mies van der Rohe and Viljo Revell. In Ottawa, the nation's capital, the government offices create an interesting juxtaposition of geometric modern and older Gothic architecture. (For complete descriptions of these cities, including their points of interest and best restaurants and hotels, see THE CITIES.)

Quebec is the largest province in Canada and also the largest region in North America where the language, culture, and people are French. The province covers 594,860 square miles, from the temperate south, where the St. Lawrence flows through Quebec City, to the cold Ungava and James bays, where Eskimos live and hunt over vast regions of scrubby bush. Quebec is only slightly less productive than Ontario. Its mines yield iron, copper, and asbestos; its farms fill the dairy needs of Quebec and some of the other provinces.

Quebec City is the heart of Quebec and French Canada. The 17th-century city is the center of French culture in Canada. Its abundance of churches and old ecclesiastical structures emphasizes Quebec's importance as a stronghold of the Roman Catholic Church. But the traditional character of the city belies the fact that it is a fast-growing urban and industrial center. Indeed, it is here in Quebec that the St. Lawrence River meets one of its tributaries, the St. Charles, and narrows to a mere ¾ mile; as a result, the St. Lawrence harbor can accommodate huge tankers.

Farther down the St. Lawrence, 1,000 miles from the Atlantic, lies Montreal, Canada's second-largest city and the world's biggest inland seaport. The metropolitan area sprawls over Montreal Island, one of a group of islands near the confluence of the St.

Lawrence and the Ottawa River, which flows in from the west. Montreal is Canada's major industrial and commercial center and the terminus of international airlines, major rail systems, and several shipping lines. Its port is the most important grain-shipping station in the world. Like Quebec City, the city is predominantly French-Canadian, although there is a significant Anglo-Saxon minority; the two cultures have a history of conflict. In many ways, Montreal is the flagship city of Canada. It has been the point of entry for most overseas visitors and the major destination of many others.

Great Plains and Prairies – To the west of the St. Lawrence Lowlands and the Canadian Shield, extending from the US border northwest to the Arctic Ocean, lies a vast stretch of Canada composed of wide prairies and sweeping plains. This region encompasses the provinces of Manitoba, Saskatchewan, and Alberta as well as a large chunk of the Northwest Territories. Most of the people here live on the prairie in the southern part of these provinces. The countryside is flat, and grass covers the rich, dark soil laid down by the rivers that run into Hudson Bay. The only trees are thin screens of oak, poplar, and birch surrounding the many farmhouses. When the railway opened up these lands at the end of the 19th century, it was used primarily to transport wheat crops at harvest time. Today much of this region is still a calm, gold sea, but erosion due to single-crop farming and the removal of the grass cover have reduced its fertility and hurt farming. Farther west, out of the reach of the Saskatchewan rivers, the climate and terrain are too dry for wheat; these lands are used primarily for cattle ranching. The recent discovery of oil in this area has stimulated additional commercial development. New businesses and industries are locating in the larger prairie cities of Winnipeg, Regina, Saskatoon, Calgary, and Edmonton.

In the north the land is mostly wild. Moose, elk, bear, timber wolves, and deer roam this region, similar to the Canadian Shield. Too cold for agriculture and covered with coniferous forest, lake, and swamp, the north is rich in oil and minerals, including nickel, copper, and zinc. Mining settlements have sprung up on the shores of the three major lakes: Great Bear Lake, Great Slave Lake, and Lake Athabasca. Except for these, the region is desolate; in the far north, the soil is permanently frozen and the forest gives way to tundra.

Province by province, the geography of the prairies changes from east to west. In Manitoba the prairie begins at the edge of the Canadian Shield; most of the population lives in the south in a fertile triangle that is the dry bed of a glacial lake that drained into Hudson Bay 15,000 years ago, leaving rich, black earth in its place. The soil yields great quantities of wheat while the myriad lakes in the north produce millions of pounds of fish. Winnipeg, the capital of Manitoba and the sixth largest city in Canada, is the center of the grain market and home to over 620,000 inhabitants of the province — a blend of British, Indian, Ukrainian, German, Dutch, Icelandic, Polish, and French (concentrated primarily in St. Boniface, across the Red River from the capital).

Saskatchewan is the heart of the prairie provinces. Most of it is farmland, though many of the farms are now owned by agribusinesses rather than families. Regina is the administrative, financial, and commercial center of the province.

In Alberta the wheat fields of the east give way to ranch country in the west. Underneath the surface is a wealth of oil and gas. Edmonton, the northernmost city in North America, is one of Canada's major petrochemical centers and the retail trade center of the province. Large numbers of Ukrainians, French, Germans, and Poles populate this province. Calgary, Alberta's second city, sits at the point where the Rockies meet the prairie flatlands. This old cattle town is now a communications and transportation center, but it recalls its heritage for a few days every summer when several hundred thousand would-be cowboys and cowgirls descend on the city for the *Calgary Stampede,* an orgy of bronco busting, branding, and pony racing.

Western Mountains – Canada's westernmost region begins where the Great Plains merge into the Rocky Mountains and extends across British Columbia to the Coast

Range. It is one of the world's finest fishing, hunting, canoeing, and wilderness camping areas. The region is geographically the most diverse in Canada, encompassing the rugged Rocky peaks, the rain forests of the Coast Range, the great boreal forests and rivers of the interior plains, mild Vancouver, and the frozen tundra of the Yukon Territory. The region stretches north to south from the US border to Alaska.

The northern Rockies march down the eastern side of the region, forming the border between British Columbia and Alberta. Like the Andes in South America, the Alps of Europe, and the Himalayas of Asia, the Rockies were created by a relatively recent upfolding and therefore are very high. The tallest Canadian peaks approach 20,000 feet: Mt. Logan is 19,850 feet and Mt. St. Elias is 18,000 feet. It is an area of alpine lakes, meadows, glacier-studded peaks, and big game. The Rocky Mountain Valley runs from Flathead Lake in Montana to about 1,000 miles up into the Yukon; it varies greatly in terrain, from flatlands to rugged cliffs with steep, sheer walls. Except at great altitudes, the mountains and valleys are forested and provide commercial lumber.

Between the Rocky Mountain Valley on the east and the Coast Mountains on the west lies the Interior Plateau, with boreal forests, a plethora of rivers, and deep, blue lakes (including Babine, Chilko, Morice, Francois, Stuart, and Tatla) inhabited by giant lake trout, rainbow trout, and Dolly Varden trout. On the west the plateau runs into the snow-capped Coast Range, which stretches from the mainland opposite Vancouver to the Yukon Territory. The peaks here are lower than the Rocky summits but are noted for their rain forests, streams stocked with steelhead, and, in the northern reaches, the juxtaposition of glaciers and forests. Beyond the Coast Range lies the shore of the Pacific Ocean, warmed by the mild Japan Current and studded with the numerous islands, bays, and inlets of the archipelago better known as the Inside Passage, through which 19th-century prospectors made their way to the Yukon and Alaska in search of gold.

Most of the population is concentrated around Vancouver and Victoria in the southwest, close to the US border. Winter temperatures seldom drop below freezing, summers are cool, and it rains all year. Vancouver is a modern city with a spectacular island setting, the Pacific to the west and the Coast Range to the north and east, and is the lumbering, mining, industrial, and commercial center of British Columbia. Across the Strait of Juan de Fuca to the southeast lies Victoria, the capital of British Columbia. An extensive network of ferries connects points on the mainland with Vancouver Island.

Compared with the mild climate of southwestern Canada, the Yukon Territory makes a strong contrast. These 200,000 square miles are very mountainous and abound in alpine meadows, lakes, wild rivers (the Yukon River is navigable in summertime from Whitehorse to the Bering Sea), tundra, and snow. In fact, the only time it doesn't snow in the Yukon is during June, July, and August. Most of the year is winter, with average temperatures dropping well below zero F (-17C). People are scarce in these parts, and over half of the territory's 50,000 inhabitants (a mix of Caucasians, Eskimos, and Indians) live in Whitehorse, the largest town. However, there's plenty of big game, including grizzlies, and if you're interested in hunting, camping, backpacking, or mountain climbing, the Yukon is a true frontier, still beckoning with the call of the wild.

When to Go

The decision of exactly when to travel may be imposed by the requirements of a rigid schedule; more likely there will be some choice, and the decision will be made on the basis of precisely what you want to see and do, what activities or events you'd like to attend, and what suits your mood.

14 GETTING READY / When to Go

There really isn't a "best" time to visit Canada. The country is too large and its geography too varied to have tourist seasons in the classic manner of the Caribbean islands. Summer is generally best for touring and sightseeing; winter, obviously, best for snow and ice sports. But even such broad distinctions don't recognize that Canada's major cities — Montreal, Toronto, Vancouver — make wonderful long-weekend winter destinations, even when the snow is piled high and the wind is whistling. And the Canadian climate deals out some significant surprises: Spring in the far north is late but exquisite. So timing a visit to Canada depends far more on your own interests and requirements than on anything inherent in the Canadian weather or tourist facilities.

CLIMATE: It's difficult to generalize about Canadian weather, but the whole country does experience four distinct seasons, and changes in the weather are frequent. Below is a brief description of the climate in various Canadian regions to help in planning. For a city-by-city review of weather, also see the *Climate* entry in each city report in THE CITIES.

More detailed weather information and temperature charts compiled month by month for some 40 Canadian locations are presented in the government tourist office's free brochure *Travel Information*. For a copy, write to Tourism Canada, 235 Queen St., Ottawa, Ontario K1A 0H6, or call 613-954-3852; this brochure is also available from any of the 14 Tourism Canada bureaus in the US listed in this section.

Please note that although temperatures are most often recorded on the Celsius scale in Canada, for purposes of clarity we shall discuss climate and temperature using the more familiar Fahrenheit scale.

The Maritimes: New Brunswick, Newfoundland, Nova Scotia, Prince Edward Island – The seasons are quite distinct: cold, snowy winters with temperatures in the 20s or lower (much lower inland in Newfoundland, New Brunswick, and Prince Edward Island); short, temperate springs; warm summers, in the 60s and 70s; mostly clear, crisp autumns with beautiful red, yellow, and orange foliage, especially in New Brunswick. Prime tourist seasons are summer, for coastal resorts; autumn (especially the last 2 weeks in September and the first 2 weeks in October) throughout the region for foliage. Since the Maritime Provinces are relatively flat, winter sports are limited to cross-country skiing and snowmobiling (see DIVERSIONS). The best foliage route is the Trans-Canada Highway through New Brunswick.

Central Canada: Ontario, Quebec – Again, seasons are distinct; temperatures range from below freezing in winter to the 80s in summer. Winters are cold, damp, and overcast in southern Ontario, drier but colder in Quebec. In the summer, humidity tends to be high throughout Ontario and Quebec — Toronto is also often hotter than Miami. Fall is pleasant, with moderate temperatures, and is the region's best season. A temperate spring begins in April and continues into June. Visitors to the metropolitan areas usually come in summer, when many urbanites spend their weekends in the country, and the cities are, consequently, pleasantly uncrowded.

The Prairies: Alberta, Manitoba, Saskatchewan – Very cold and dry winters and moderate summers are characteristic of this region. Manitoba suffers the harshest winters, with heavy snowfalls and temperatures in the -10 to -15 range. In the more westerly areas, such as southern Alberta, winter temperatures average in the 20s. Summers across the region are comfortable, in the high 60s and 70s, and can be quite dry. With the exception of winter skiing in the Canadian Rockies, summer is the most popular tourist season, when the prairies are at their most attractive. Trees are few and far between due to the weather extremes. Consequently, the short autumn is not as dramatic as in other areas of the country. The most extraordinary weather phenomena are the chinooks in southern Alberta, sudden breaths of warm weather from the west which in the middle of winter can raise the temperature as much as 30 degrees in a few hours. Though short-lived (no more than a few days, and most last only a day or less), chinooks are a looked-for part of winter in cities like Calgary.

British Columbia – This region is a delight year-round, especially in the southwestern corner around Vancouver. The coastal regions get a high rainfall in the winter. The range of temperature is not as great as in other regions, varying between the 30s in the winter and the high 60s and 70s in summer. In general, this region is best seen in late spring, summer, or early fall when the weather is warm. The winters can be damp and therefore colder than temperatures indicate, particularly in the interior of British Columbia. Vancouver and Victoria are almost always warmer than New York in winter: Spring and autumn are pleasant, but again quite damp in coastal areas.

The North: Northwest Territories, Yukon Territory – This region, the coldest in Canada, includes the great expanses of the Northwest Territories and the Yukon Territory in the Arctic Circle. Winter is bitterly cold, with temperatures of -25 quite common even in the region's southernmost city, Yellowknife. Summer heat is quite welcome in the North — though you may have to contend with mosquitoes instead of the cold. The tundra has a beautiful brief, late spring; in summer temperatures reach the 70s and the sun shines late into the night.

SPORTS: The weather dictates the types of sports played in Canada. Golf and tennis begin in May in most of the country and last well into October, but in Vancouver and lower British Columbia, it is possible to play outdoor participant sports year-round.

Backpacking, canoeing, mountain climbing, and wilderness trips are usually pursued in the summer, since this is when lakes and the mountain air are warmer and less equipment is required (see DIVERSIONS). All sections of Canada, except the prairies, are popular for these sports.

Water sports, like yachting and scuba diving, begin in the coastal waters and large lakes of eastern Canada in the late spring and continue through fall. Most regattas and other events are scheduled in July and August. On British Columbia's coast, the season lasts longer, with regattas starting in June and finishing in September.

The country has a full range of winter sports, such as ice skating, snowmobiling, dogsledding, and curling, but skiing — both downhill and cross-country — is the most popular (see DIVERSIONS). There are slopes in every province, but those in Alberta, British Columbia, and Quebec are the best. The season usually starts in earnest around Christmas (although snowfalls as early as Thanksgiving are common) and lasts through early April. Naturally, skiing conditions depend upon snow, so the determined skier should be prepared to make plans around the weather. Newspapers and radio stations in ski areas carry daily ski-condition reports, often updated several times a day. If you are uncertain of the conditions at your destination call the management of the resort to get a complete report. A ski guide published by Tourism Canada is available from any of the 14 Tourism Canada bureaus listed in this section.

PARKS: Canada's national parks are open year-round, though some are in such remote areas they are difficult to get to in winter months. All provide camping facilities year-round, too. As parks are most crowded in the summer, during high season — July and August — there may be as many as 17 different campgrounds open in popular parks such as Banff and Jasper, but during winter, only one or two may be open. A list of campgrounds in national parks can be found in the *National Parks* brochure, available from the Canadian Parks Service, Ottawa, Ontario K1A 0H3 (phone: 819-997-2800). There are also numerous provincial parks, many of which allow camping. Information on these parks is generally contained in travel literature put out by the individual provinces and available from the Tourism Section of Canadian Consulates. (Addresses are listed later in this section. Also see *Camping*, and *Canada's National Parks* in DIVERSIONS.)

CULTURAL EVENTS: As in the US, the Canadian season for concerts, plays, art exhibits, dance, and other cultural events is November through April. Montreal and Toronto are still the two great cultural centers, and the *Montreal Symphony* and the *Toronto Symphony* are Canada's two major orchestras. Toronto is the major theatrical center, with over 25 theaters. Schedules of events are available in local magazines and from the tourism bureaus in most cities (addresses are given in THE CITIES).

Summer activities are less formal, and often held outdoors. The major cities offer full schedules of concerts, exhibits, and theater as well as entertainment for children. Of national (and often international) interest are the *Shakespeare Festival* in Stratford, Ontario; the *Shaw Drama Festival,* Niagara-on-the-Lake, Ontario; *Folklorama,* Winnipeg, Manitoba; and the *Charlottetown Summer Festival,* Charlottetown, Prince Edward Island. (See also "Special Events" in THE CITIES and *Festivals, Fairs, and Fancy Acts,* DIVERSIONS.)

FAIRS AND CELEBRATIONS: Turtle derbies, bathtub races, blossom festivals, provincial fairs, rodeos and stampedes, horse shows, ethnic festivals, and numerous similar events — from the *Chocolate Fest* in New Brunswick to the Yukon's *Sourdough Rendezvous* — bring people together throughout the country. To find out what events are taking place along your itinerary or to get a list so that you can plan your trip around them, write the provincial tourist boards, most of which publish a calendar of events (addresses are given in *Sources and Resources* in this section).

Traveling by Plane

Given Canada's size, travel by air is usually the most efficient way to get to and around the country. It can also be one of the least expensive ways to travel if you have a great distance to cover and if you take advantage of the low fares offered by both scheduled airlines and charter companies. If you do decide to fly, you should know what kinds of flights are available, the rules and regulations pertaining to air travel, and the options for special packages.

SCHEDULED FLIGHTS: Air service to Canada is provided by two Canadian airlines — Air Canada and Canadian Airlines International, both private companies — and several US carriers — American, Continental, Delta, Eastern (we hope), Piedmont, Northwest Orient, United, and US Air. Flights to major Canadian cities depart from a number of US cities, including Atlanta, Baltimore, Boston, Buffalo, Chicago, Dallas, Denver, Detroit, Ft. Lauderdale, Hartford, Houston, Los Angeles, Miami, Minneapolis, New York, Orlando, Philadelphia, Pittsburgh, Portland, Salt Lake City, San Francisco, Seattle, Tampa, and Washington.

In early 1986, Wardair began scheduled service and is now Canada's third-largest scheduled carrier, with daily service from Toronto to six major Canadian cities. It offers business class and economy fares that are competitive with the excursion rates offered by other scheduled airlines.

Tickets – When traveling on one of the many regularly scheduled flights, a full-fare ticket provides maximum travel flexibility (although at considerable expense), because tickets are sold on an open reservation system. This means that there are no advance booking requirements — a prospective passenger can buy a ticket for a flight right up to the minute of takeoff, if seats are available. If your ticket is for a round trip, you can make the return reservation any time you wish, months before you leave, or the day before you return. You are not required to stay at your destination for any specified amount of time. (Tickets are generally good for a year and can be renewed if not used.) You can also cancel your flight at any time without penalty. However, while it is true that this category of ticket can be purchased at the last minute, it is advisable to reserve well in advance during popular travel periods and around holiday times.

No matter what kind of ticket you buy, it is wise to reconfirm that you will be using your return reservations. Some airlines no longer require reconfirmations; others recommend that you confirm your return flight 48 or 72 hours in advance. If you do not call the airline to let them know you will be using the return leg of your reservation, they (or their computer) may assume you are not coming and automatically cancel your seat.

Fares – Air fares are changing so rapidly that even experts find it difficult to keep up with them. This volatile situation is due to a number of factors, including airline deregulation, high labor costs, and vastly increased competition. Before the Airline Deregulation Act of 1978, US airlines had no choice but to set their rates and routes within the guidelines of the Civil Aeronautics Board (CAB), and they could compete for passengers only by offering better service than their competitors. With the loosening of controls (and the elimination of the CAB), airlines are now engaged in a far more intense competition relating to price and schedule, which has opened the door to a wide range of discount fares and promotional offers. Intensifying the competitive atmosphere has been the creation of several new carriers offering fewer frills and far lower prices. These carriers seem to appear and disappear with dismaying regularity. They have, however, served to drive down fares and make older, more entrenched carriers aware that they are in a genuine competition for travelers' dollars.

Now that fares for flights within Canada have also been deregulated, the situation is similar in the Canadian airline industry. Both Canadian and American airlines are still required to file their proposed fares for international flights, however, the former with Canada's Air Transport Committee, the latter with the US Department of Transportation.

In general, the great variety of US domestic fares, Canadian domestic fares, and fares between the two countries can be reduced to three basic categories: first class, coach (sometimes called economy or tourist class), and excursion or discount fares. A fourth category, called business or executive class (an intermediate class between first and coach, with many of the amenities of first class and more legroom than coach), has been added by many airlines in recent years. Air Canada offers first class service from Los Angeles, San Francisco, and Miami (Saturdays only), and also offers executive class from San Francisco, New York, Los Angeles, and Chicago. Canadian Airlines International offers business class on both domestic and international flights and first class service on international and wide-body 767 domestic routes.

A first class ticket is your admission to the special section of the aircraft with larger seats, more legroom, sleeperette seating on some wide-body aircraft, better food (or more elaborately served food, in any case), free drinks and headsets for movies and music channels, and, above all, personal attention. First class fares are about double those of full-fare economy, although both first class passengers and people paying ecomomy fares are entitled to reserve seats and are sold tickets on an open reservation system.

Coach passengers sit more snugly, as many as 10 in a single row on a wide-body jet, behind the first class section and receive standard meal service. Alcoholic drinks are not free, nor are the headsets. Like first class passengers, however, passengers paying the full coach fare are subject to none of the restrictions that are usually attached to less expensive discount fares. There are no advance booking requirements, no minimum stay requirements, and no cancellation penalties. Tickets are sold on an open reservation system: They can be bought for a flight up to the minute of takeoff, if seats are available, and if the ticket is round-trip, the return reservation can be made any time you wish — months before you leave or the day before you return. Both first class and coach tickets are generally good for a year, after which they can be renewed if not used, and if you ultimately decide not to fly at all, your money will be refunded. Stopover privileges on both tickets are unlimited or extremely generous.

Excursions and other discount fares are the airlines' equivalent of a special sale, and usually apply to round-trip bookings. These fares generally differ according to the season and the number of travel days permitted. They are only a bit less flexible than economy tickets and are, therefore, useful for both business travelers and tourists. Most round-trip excursion tickets include strict minimum and maximum stay requirements and reservations can be changed only within the prescribed time limits, so don't count on extending a ticket beyond the prescribed time of return or staying less time than required. Different airlines may have different regulations concerning the number of stopovers permitted, and sometimes excursion fares are less expensive during midweek. Needless to say, these reduced-rate seats are most limited at busy times such as holidays, when full-fare coach seats sell more quickly than usual. Passengers fortunate enough to get a discount or excursion fare ticket sit with the coach passengers, and for all intents and purposes are indistinguishable from them. They receive all the same basic services, even though they have paid anywhere between 30% and 55% less for the trip. Obviously, it's wise to make plans early enough to qualify for the least expensive transportation.

These discount or excursion fares may masquerade under a variety of names and they may vary from city to city, but they invariably have strings attached, whether offered by the major airlines flying between the US and Canada or by the regional Canadian lines. Sometimes the ticket requires only that you fly at night or on a weekend but is otherwise unrestricted — usually, the restrictions are more elaborate. A common requirement is that the ticket be purchased a certain number of days — usually no fewer than 7, 14, or 21 days — in advance of departure, though it may be booked weeks or months in advance (it has to be "ticketed," or paid for, shortly after booking, however). The return reservation usually has to be made at the time of the original ticketing and cannot be changed later than a certain number of days (again, usually 7, 14, or 21 days) before the return flight. If events force a passenger to change the return reservation after the date allowed, the difference between the round-trip excursion rate and the round-trip coach rate will probably have to be paid, though most airlines allow passengers to use their discounted fares by standing by for an empty seat, even if they don't otherwise have standby fares. Another common condition is a miminum and maximum stay requirement: for example 6 to 14 days, or 1 to 6 days, and including at least one Saturday night. Last, cancellation penalties of up to 50% of the full price of the ticket are currently being assessed — check the specific penalty in effect when you purchase your discount/excursion ticket — so careful planning is imperative. Of even greater risk — and bearing the lowest price of all the current discount fares — is the ticket where no change at all in departure and/or return flights is permitted, and the ticket price is totally non-refundable. Even if none of the above conditions apply, prospective passengers can be fairly sure that the number of discount seats per flight at this lowest price is strictly limited or that the fare offering includes a set expiration date — which means it's absolutely necessary to move fast to enjoy the lowest possible prices.

There are also group inclusive tour fares available to many destinations. The requirements vary as to number of travel days, number of stopovers permitted, and number of passengers required for a group. (The last can be as few as two full fares.) The group fare always requires that a specified dollar amount of ground arrangements be purchased, in advance, along with the ticket.

Most major airlines have traditionally offered their most attractive special fares to encourage travel in slow seasons and to inaugurate and publicize new routes. But in today's economic climate, increasingly the stimulus for special fares is the appearance of airlines consistently associated with bargain rates. These tend to be smaller carriers that can offer more for less because of lower overhead, uncomplicated route networks, and other limitations in their service. On these airlines, all seats on any given flight generally sell for the same price, which is somewhat below the lowest discount fare offered by the larger, more established airlines, even after these cut their fares in response. This gap, too, may disappear in the future, but it is important to note that tickets offered by the smaller airlines specializing in low-cost travel frequently are not subject to the same restrictions as the lowest-priced ticket offered by the more established carriers. They may not require advance purchase or mimimum and maximum stays, may involve no cancellation penalties, may be available one-way or round-trip, and may, for all intents and purposes, resemble the competition's high-priced full-fare coach. But never assume this until you know it's so.

The leading carriers now also offer a bonus system to frequent travelers. After the first 10,000 miles, for example, you might receive a first class ticket for the coach fare; after another 10,000 miles you might receive a discount on your next ticket purchase. The value of the bonuses continues to increase as you log more miles.

Given the frequency with which the airfare picture changes, it is more than possible that by the time you are ready to fly, the foregoing discussion may be somewhat out of date. That's why it is always wise to comparison shop, and to do a good job of it, it's necessary to read the business and travel sections of your local newspaper regularly and to call the airlines that serve your destination from your most convenient gateway. The potential savings are well worth the effort.

Ask about discount or promotional fares and about any conditions that might restrict booking, payment, cancellation, and changes in plans. Check the prices from other cities. A special rate may be offered in a nearby city but not in yours, and it may be enough of a bargain to warrant your leaving from that city. If you have a flexible schedule, investigate standby fares. But remember that, depending on your departure point, these may not work out to be the rock-bottom price. Ask if there is a difference in price for midweek travel versus weekend travel, or if there is a further discount for traveling early in the morning or late at night. Also be sure to investigate package deals, which are offered by virtually every airline. They may include a car rental, accommodations, and/or dining or sightseeing features, in addition to the basic air fare. The combined cost of packaged elements is usually considerably less than the cost of the exact same elements when purchased separately.

When you're satisfied that you've found the lowest possible price for which you can conveniently qualify (you may have to call an airline more than once, because different clerks have been known to quote different prices), make your booking. Then, to protect yourself against fare increases, purchase and pay for your ticket as soon as possible after you've received a confirmed reservation. Airlines generally will honor their tickets, even if the operative price at the time of your flight is higher than the price you paid; if fares go up between the time you *reserve* a flight and the time you *pay* for it, you likely will be out of luck. Finally, with excursion or discount fares, it is important to remember that when a reservation clerk says that you must purchase a ticket by a specific date, this is an absolute deadline. Miss the deadline and the airline may automatically cancel your reservation without telling you.

If you don't have the time and patience to investigate personally all possible air departures and connections for a proposed trip, remember that a travel agent can be of inestimable help. A good agent should have all the information on which flights go where and when and which categories of tickets are available on each. Most have computerized reservation links with the major carriers, so that a seat can be reserved and confirmed in minutes. An increasing number of agents also possess fare-comparison computer programs, so they are often very reliable sources of detailed competitive price data. (For more information, see *How to Use a Travel Agent.*)

Reservations – When making plane reservations through a travel agent, ask the agent to give the airline your home phone number as well as a daytime business number. All too often the agent uses his or her agency number as the official contact for changes in flight plans. During the winter, especially, weather conditions hundreds or even thousands of miles away can wreak havoc with flight schedules. Aircraft are constantly in use, and a plane delayed in the Orient or on the West Coast can miss its scheduled flight from the East Coast the next morning. The airlines are fairly reliable about getting this sort of information to passengers if they can reach them — but diligence does little good at 6 PM if the airline has only the agency or an office number.

If you look at the back of your ticket, you'll see the need for reconfirmation of return flights stated explicitly. Some (though increasingly fewer) return reservations from international destinations are automatically canceled after a required reconfirmation period (typically 72 hours) has passed — even if you have a confirmed, fully paid ticked in hand. Reconfirmation is not required on domestic flights, but it is still a good idea, allowing you to make sure in plenty of time that the airline did not slip up in entering your original reservation, or in registering any changes you may have made since, and that it has your seat reservation request in the computer. Every travel agent or airline ticket office should give each passenger a reminder to reconfirm flights, but this seldom happens, so the reponsibility rests with the traveler. Don't be lulled into a false sense of security by the "OK" on your ticket next to the number and time of the return flight. That only means that a reservation has been entered; a reconfirmation may still be necessary.

If you plan not to take a reserved flight, by all means inform the airline of your cancellation. Because the problem of "no-shows" is a consistently annoying one for airlines, they are allowed to overbook flights, a practice that often contributes to the threat of denied boarding for a certain number of passengers (see *Getting Bumped*, below). Let the airline know you're not coming and you'll spare everyone some confusion. Bear in mind that only certain kinds of tickets allow the luxury of last minute changes in flight plans — those sold on an open reservation system (first class and full-fare coach) do, while excursions and other discount fares are often restricted in some way. Even first class and coach passengers should remember that if they do not show up for a flight that is the first of several connecting ones, the airline will cancel all of their reservations unless informed not to do so.

Seating – For most types of tickets, airline seats are usually assigned on a first-come, first-served basis at check-in, although some airlines make it possible to reserve a seat at the time of ticket purchase. Always check in early for your flight, even with advance seat assignments.

Most airlines furnish seating charts, which make choosing a seat much easier, but in general, there are a few basics to consider. You must decide first whether you prefer smoking or non-smoking sections and a window, aisle, or middle seat.

The amount of legroom provided (as well as chest room, especially when the seat in front of you is in a reclining position) is determined by pitch, a measure of the distance between the back of the seat in front of you and the front of your seat. The amount of pitch is a matter of airline policy, not the type of plane you fly. First class and business class seats have the greatest pitch, a fact that figures prominently in airline advertising. In economy class or coach, the standard pitch ranges from 33 to as little as 31 inches — downright cramped. The number of seats abreast, another factor determining comfort, depends on a combination of airline policy and airplane dimensions. First and business classes have the fewest seats per row. Economy generally has 9 seats per row on a DC-10 or an L-1011, making either one slightly more comfortable than a 747, on which there are normally 10 seats per row. Charter flights on DC-10s and L-1011s, however, often have 10 seats per row and can be noticeably more cramped than 747 charters, on which the seating normally remains at 10 per row.

Airline representatives claim that most aircraft are more stable toward the front and midsection, while seats farthest away from the engines are quietest. Passengers who have long legs and are traveling on a wide-body aircraft might request a seat directly behind a door or emergency exit, since these seats often have greater than average pitch, or a seat in the first row of a given section, since these seats have extra legroom. It is often impossible, however, to see the movie from these seats, which are directly behind the plane's exits. Be aware that the first row of the economy section (called a "bulkhead" seat) on a conventional aircraft (not a widebody) does *not* offer extra legroom, since the fixed partition will not permit passengers to slide their feet under it, and that watching a movie from this first row seat can be difficult and uncomfortable. A window seat protects you from aisle traffic and clumsy serving carts, and also allows you a view, while an aisle seat enables you to get up and stretch your legs without disturbing your fellow travelers. Middle seats are the least desirable, and seats in the last row are the most undesirable of all, since they seldom recline fully. If you wish to avoid children on your flight, remember that families generally do not sit in smoking areas. Once in the air, if you find that you are sitting in an especially noisy section, you are usually free to move to any unoccupied seat — if there is one.

If you have a weight problem, you may face the prospect of a long flight with special trepidation. Center seats in the alignments of wide-body 747s, L1011s, and DC-10s are about 1½ inches wider than those on either side, so larger travelers tend to be more comfortable there.

Simply reserving an airline seat in advance, however, may actually guarantee very little. Most airlines require that passengers arrive at the departure gate at least 30 minutes (sometimes more) ahead of time to hold a seat reservation. A far better strategy is to visit an airline ticket office (or one of a select group of travel agents) to secure an actual boarding pass for your specific flight. Once this has been issued, airline computers show you as "checked in," and you effectively own the seat you have selected. This is also good insurance against getting bumped from an overbooked flight and is, therefore, an especially valuable tactic at peak holiday travel times.

Smoking – The US government has adopted minimum standards to ensure that non-smokers will not be "unreasonably burdened" by passengers who smoke. For a wallet-size guide, which notes in detail the rights of non-smokers according to these regulations, send a stamped, self-addressed envelope to ASH (Action on Smoking and Health), Airline Card, 2013 H St. NW, Washington, DC 20006 (phone: 202-659-4310). The US Department of Transportation has determined that non-smoking sections must be enlarged to accommodate all passengers who wish to sit in a non-smoking section. According to a recently added proviso, however, the airline does not have to shift seating to accommodate non-smokers who arrive late for the flight or travelers flying standby. Cigar and pipe smoking are prohibited on all flights, even in the smoking sections. Air Canada has been an industry leader in barring smoking entirely from all of its North American flights and some US carriers are following suit.

Flying with Children – On longer flights, the bulkhead seats are usually reserved for families traveling with small children. Infants under 2 years of age travel free on most domestic flights, provided they do not occupy a seat (a second infant without a second adult would pay the fare applicable to children ages 2 through 11, generally 75% of the adult fare). Most airlines make complimentary bassinets available. Ask about obtaining one when you make your reservation, and, when checking in, request a bulkhead or other seat that has enough room in front to use it. On some planes they hook into a bulkhead wall; on others they are placed on the floor in front of you. Even if you do use a bassinet, babies must be held during takeoff and landing. (For more information on flying with children, see *Hints for Traveling with Children.*)

Meals – If you have specific diet requirements (vegetarian, kosher, low calorie, low sodium, and so on), make sure to let the airlines know well before departure time. There is no extra charge for this option. It is, however, advisable to request special meals when you make your reservations — check-in time is too late. It's also wise to reconfirm that your request for a special meal has made its way into the airline's computer — the time to do this is 24 hours prior to departure.

Getting Bumped – A special air travel problem is the possibility that an airline will accept more reservations (and sell more tickets) than there are seats on a given flight. This is entirely legal and is done to make up for "no-shows," passengers who don't show up for a flight for which they have made reservations and bought tickets. If the airline has oversold the flight and everyone does show up, there simply aren't enough seats. When this happens, the airline is subject to stringent rules designed to protect travelers.

In such cases, the airline first seeks ticketholders willing to give up their seats voluntarily in return for a negotiable sum of money, or some other inducement such as an offer of upgraded seating on the next flight or a voucher for a free trip at some other time. If there are not enough volunteers, the airline may bump passengers against their wishes. Anyone inconvenienced in this way, however, is entitled to an explanation of the criteria used to determine who does and does not get on the flight, as well as to compensation if the resulting delay exceeds certain limits. If the airline can put the bumped passengers on an alternate flight that gets them to their planned destination within 1 hour of their originally scheduled arrival time, no compensation is owed. If the delay is more than an hour — but less than 2 hours on a domestic US flight and less than 4 hours on an international flight — they must be paid denied-boarding compensation equivalent to the one-way fare to their destination (but not more than $200). If the delay is more than 2 hours beyond the original arrival time on a domestic flight or more than 4 hours on an international flight, the compensation must be doubled. The airline may also offer bumped travelers a voucher for a free flight instead of the denied-boarding compensation. The passenger can choose either the money or the voucher, the dollar value of which may be no less than the monetary compensation to which the passenger would be entitled. The voucher is not a substitute for the bumped passenger's original ticket; the airline continues to honor that as well. Keep in mind that the above regulations and policies are for flights leaving the US only, and do *not* apply to charters or to inbound flights from Canada, even on US carriers.

In Canada, each airline is free to determine what compensation it will pay to passengers who are bumped because of overbooking. However, they are required to spell out what that policy is on the airline ticket. Air Canada's policy, for example, is similar to US policy. Passengers involuntarily bumped are paid the price of a one-way ticket (up to $200) if the airline can get them to their destination within 4 hours of the original arrival time, and twice that amount (up to $400) if they reach their destination 4 or more hours late. Keep in mind that this is one airline's policy only. Don't assume every carrier will be as generous.

To protect yourself as best you can against getting bumped, arrive at the airport early, allowing plenty of time to check in and get to the gate. If the flight is oversold, ask immediately for the written statement explaining the airline's policy on denied-boarding compensation and its boarding priorities. If the airline refuses to give you this information, or if you feel they have not handled the situation properly, file a complaint with both the airline and the appropriate government agency (see *Consumer Protection*, below).

Delays and Cancellations – The above compensation rules also do not apply if the flight is canceled or delayed, or if a smaller aircraft is substituted due to mechanical problems. Each airline has its own policy for assisting passengers whose flights are delayed or canceled or who must wait for another flight because their original one was overbooked. Most airline personnel will make new travel arrangements if necessary. If the delay is longer than 4 hours, the airline may pay for a phone call or telegram, a meal, and in some cases a hotel room and transportation to it.

Deregulation of US airlines has meant the traveler must find out for himself what he is entitled to receive. A useful booklet, *Fly Rights, A Guide to Air Travel in the US*, is available for $1 from the Superintendent of Documents, US Government Printing Office, Washington, DC 20402-9325 (phone: 202-783-3238). When ordering, specify the stock number of this publication, 050-000-00513-5, and allow 3 to 4 weeks for delivery.

GETTING READY / Traveling by Plane 23

■ **Caution:** If you are bumped or miss a flight, be sure to ask the airline to notify other airlines on which you have reservations or connecting flights. When your name is taken off the passenger list of your initial flight, the computer automatically cancels all of your reservations unless *you* take steps to preserve them.

Baggage – Travelers from the US face two different kinds of rules. When you fly in on a US airline or on a major international carrier, US baggage regulations will be in effect. Though airline baggage allowances vary slightly, in general all passengers are allowed to carry on board, without charge, one piece of luggage that will fit easily under a seat of the plane or in an overhead bin and whose combined dimensions (length, width, and depth) do not exceed 45 inches. A reasonable amount of reading material, camera equipment, and a handbag are also allowed. In addition, all passengers are allowed to check two bags in the cargo hold: one usually not to exceed 62 inches when length, width, and depth are combined, the other not to exceed 55 inches in combined dimensions. No single bag may weigh more than 70 pounds. Most airlines will allow you to check the 45-inch bag in the hold if you prefer not to carry it with you, but a few require that it be stowed in the cabin under a seat. Airline's policies regarding baggage allowances for children vary and are usually based on the percentage of full adult fare paid. Charges for additional, oversize, or overweight bags are usually made at a flat rate; the actual dollar amount varying from carrier to carrier. If you plan to travel with a bike, skis, golf clubs, or other sports gear, be sure to check with the airline beforehand. Most have procedures for handling such baggage, but you will probably have to pay for transport regardless of how much other baggage you have checked.

In general, baggage allowances follow these guidelines in Canada, but care should be exercised on regional and local airlines. Their smaller aircraft often don't have the same luggage capacity and may also have to carry mail and freight to outpost destinations. When booking flights off the routes of major trunk carriers, verify baggage allowances. Sports equipment is often subject to excess baggage charges.

To reduce the chances of your luggage going astray, remove all airline tags from previous trips, label each bag inside and out, and lock them. If your bags are not in the baggage claim area after your flight, or if they're damaged, report the problem to the airline personnel immediately. Keep in mind that policies regarding the specific time limit in which you have to make your claim vary from carrier to carrier. Fill out a report form on your lost or damaged luggage and hold on to a copy of it and your claim check. If you must surrender the check to claim a damaged bag, get a receipt for it to prove that you did, indeed, check your baggage on the flight. If luggage is missing, be sure to give the airline your destination and/or the telephone number where you can be reached. Also take the name and number of the person in charge of recovering lost luggage. Most airlines have emergency funds for passengers stranded away from home without their luggage, but if it turns out your bags are truly lost and not simply delayed, do not then and there sign anything indicating you'll accept an offered settlement. Since the airline is responsible for the value of your bags within certain statuary limits ($1,250 for a lost bag on a domestic flight; $9.07 per pound on an international flight), you should take some time to assess the extent of your loss (see *Insurance* in this section). It's a good idea to keep records indicating the value of the contents of your luggage. An alternative idea is to take a Polaroid picture of the most valuable of your packed items just after putting them in your suitcase.

Considering the increased incidence of damage to baggage, it's now more than ever a good idea to keep the sales slips that confirm how much you paid for your bags. These are invaluable in establishing the value of damaged baggage and eliminate any arguments. A better way to protect your precious baggage from the luggage-eating conveyers is to try to carry your gear on board wherever possible.

Airline Clubs – US carriers often have clubs for travelers who pay for membership. These are not clubs solely for first class passengers. Membership (which, by law, now requires a fee) entitles the traveler to use the private lounges at airports along their route, to refreshments served in those lounges, and to check-cashing privileges at most of their counters. Extras include special telephone numbers for individual reservations, embossed luggage tags, and a membership card for identification. Two airlines that offer membership in such clubs are: American — the *Admiral's Club,* single yearly membership is $150 for the first year, $100 yearly thereafter, spouse an additional $50, lifetime memberships also available; and Continental — the *President's Club,* single yearly membership is $140 for the first year, $90 yearly thereafter, lifetime membership including spouse also available. However, these companies do not have club facilities in all airports. Lounge privileges are also offered to first class passengers, and other airlines also offer a variety of special club and lounge facilities in many airports.

CHARTER FLIGHTS: By booking a block of seats on a specially arranged flight, charter operators offer travelers air transportation, often coupled with a hotel room, meals, and other travel services, for a substantial reduction over the full coach or economy fare.

Charters were once the best bargain around, but this is no longer necessarily the case. Various promotional fares on scheduled airlines are often just as low, especially on the most competitive routes, and they are usually more flexible. As a result, charter flights have been discontinued in many areas, but to some popular vacation spots, they can still be a good buy. They are especially attractive to people living in smaller cities or out-of-the-way places, because they frequently take off from nearby airports, saving travelers the inconvenience and expense of getting to a major gateway. Where demand persists, charter operators will continue to rent planes or seats from scheduled airlines (or from special charter airlines) and offer flights to the public directly through advertisements or travel agents. You buy the ticket from the operator or the agent, not from the airline owning the plane.

Charter travel once required that an individual be a member of a club or other "affinity" group whose main purpose was not travel. But since the approval of "public charters" years ago, operators have had some of the flexibility of scheduled airlines, making charters more competitive. Public charters are open to anyone, whether belonging to a group or not, and have no advance booking requirements or minimum stay requirements. One-way arrangements are permitted, though charters are almost always round-trip, and it is unlikely that you would be sold a one-way seat on a round-trip flight. Operators can offer air-only charters, selling transportation alone, or they can offer charter packages — the flight plus a combination of land arrangements such as accommodations, meals, tours, or car rental.

From the consumer's standpoint, charters differ from scheduled airlines in two main respects: you generally need to book and pay in advance, and you can't change the itinerary or the departure and return dates once you've booked the flight. In practice, however, these restrictions don't always apply. For instance, it's possible to book a one-way charter in the US, giving you more flexibility in scheduling your return. And if you take a charter within Canada, you can buy a ticket up to the day of departure. Some things to keep in mind about the charter game are:

1. It cannot be repeated often enough that if you are forced to cancel your trip, you can lose much (and possibly all) of your money unless you have cancellation insurance, which is a *must* (see *Insurance*). Frequently, if the cancellation is well in advance (often 6 weeks or more), you may forfeit only a $25 or $50 penalty. If you cancel only 2 or 3 weeks before the flight, there may be no refund at all unless you or the operator can supply a substitute passenger.
2. Charter flights may be canceled by the operator up to 10 days before departure for any reason, usually underbooking. Your money is returned in this event, but there may be too little time to make new arrangements.

3. Most charters have little of the flexibility of regularly scheduled flights regarding refunds and the changing of flight dates; if you book a return flight, you must be on it or lose your money.
4. Charter operators are permitted to assess a surcharge, if fuel or other costs warrant it, of up to 10% of the air fare up to 10 days before departure.
5. Because of the economics of charter flights, your plane almost always will be full, so you will be crowded, though not necessarily uncomfortable.

Charter flights have never been a large part of the air traffic between the US and Canada, with the exception of flights to Florida and Hawaii. Wardair has regular flights between Tampa, Ft. Lauderdale, and several other Florida cities and Montreal and Toronto, as well as regular service between Oahu and Vancouver and Toronto, and it has recently begun offering charter service to Los Angeles, Phoenix, San Francisco, and San Diego. Presumably the charter business to Florida and Hawaii grew because Canadians, like Americans living in the north, like to escape the worst ravages of winter. But because it's possible to originate a trip in Florida or Hawaii, these charters also offer US travelers living in these locales some very attractive fares to Canada.

Wardair offers charter service to Florida and the Caribbean in the winter, to Germany and California in summer, and to Hawaii year-round. For more information on Wardair, see "Scheduled Flights" earlier in this section. Canadian Airlines International also runs charter flights, both within the country and to foreign destinations, but bookings and regulations for these are handled by tour operators. If you're interested in charter flights within Canada, it's best to bear in mind that US travel agents may be unaware of what's available. The Sunday travel section of a major Canadian city newspaper is the best source of Canadian flight opportunities.

Booking – If you do take a charter, read the contract's fine print carefully and pay particular attention to the following:

1. Instructions concerning the payment of the deposit and its balance and to whom the check is to be made payable. Ordinarily, checks are made out to an escrow account, which means the charter company can't spend your money until your flight has safely returned. This provides some protection for you. To ensure the safe handling of your money, make out your check to the escrow account, the number of which must appear by law on the brochure, though all too often it is on the back in fine print. Write the details of the charter, including the destination and dates, on the face of the check; on the back, print "For Deposit Only." Your travel agent may prefer that you make out your check to the agency, saying that it will then pay the tour operator the fee minus commission. It is perfectly legal to write the check as we suggest, however, and if your agent objects too vociferously (he or she should trust the tour operator to send the proper commission), consider taking your business elsewhere. If you don't make your check out to the escrow account, you lose the protection of escrow should the trip be canceled. Furthermore, recent bankruptcies in the travel industry have served to point out that even the protection of escrow may not be enough to safeguard a traveler's investment. More and more, insurance is becoming a necessity (see *Insurance*). The charter company should be bonded (usually by an insurance company), and if you want to file a claim against it, the claim should be sent to the bonding agent. The contract will set a time limit within which a claim must be filed.
2. Note specific stipulations and penalties for cancellations. Most charters allow you to cancel up to 45 days in advance, but some cancellation dates are 50 to 60 days before departure.
3. Note stipulations regarding cancellation and major changes made by the charterer. US rules say that charter flights may not be canceled within 10 days of departure except when circumstances — such as natural disasters or political upheavals

— make it physically impossible to fly. Charterers may make "major changes," however, such as in the date or place of departure or return, but you are entitled to cancel and receive a refund if you don't accept these changes. A price increase of more than 10% up to 10 days before departure is considered a major change; no price increase is allowed during the last 10 days prior to departure.

DISCOUNT TRAVEL SOURCES: An excellent source of information on economical travel opportunities is the *Consumer Reports Travel Letter,* published monthly by Consumers Union. It keeps abreast of the scene on a wide variety of fronts, including package tours, rental cars, insurance, and more, but it is especially helpful for its comprehensive coverage of air fares, offering guidance on all the options from scheduled flights on major or low-fare airlines to charters and discount sources. For a year's subscription send $37 to Consumer Reports Travel Letter, PO Box 2886, Boulder, CO 80322 (phone: 800-525-0643). Another source is *Travel Smart,* a monthly newsletter offering information on a wide variety of trips with additional discount travel services available to subscribers. For a year's subscription, send $37 to Communications House, 40 Beechdale Rd., Dobbs Ferry, NY 10522 (phone: 914-693-8300 in New York; 800-327-3633 elsewhere in the US).

Still another way to take advantage of bargain air fares is open to those who have a flexible schedule. A number of organizations, usually set up as last-minute travel clubs and functioning on a membership basis, routinely keep in touch with travel suppliers to help them dispose of unsold inventory at discounts of between 15% and 60%. A great deal of the inventory consists of complete tour packages and cruises, but some clubs offer air-only charter seats and, occasionally, seats on scheduled flights. Members pay an annual fee and receive the toll-free number of a telephone hot line to call for information on imminent trips. In some cases, they also receive periodic mailings with information on upcoming trips for which there is more advance notice. Despite the suggestive names of the clubs providing these services, last-minute travel does not necessarily mean than you cannot make plans until literally the last minute. Trips can be announced as little as a few days' or as much as 2 months in advance of departure, but the average is from 1 to 4 weeks notice. It does mean that your choice at any given time is limited to what is offered and, if your heart is set on a particular destination, you might not find what you want, no matter how attractive the bargains. Among these organizations are the following:

Discount Club of America, 61-33 Woodhaven Blvd., Rego Park, NY, 11374; (phone: 718-335-9612 or 800-321-9587). Annual fee: $39.

Discount Travel International, Ives Building, 114 Forrest Ave., Suite 205, Narberth, PA 19072 (phone: 215-668-2182 in Pennsylvania; 800-824-4000 elsewhere in the US). Annual fee: $45 per household.

Encore Short Notice, 4501 Forbes Blvd., Lanham, MD 20706 (phone: 301-459-8020 or 800-638-0930 for customer service). Annual fee: $36 per family.

Last-Minute Travel Club, 132 Brookline Ave., Boston, MA 02215 (phone: 617-267-9800 or 800-LAST-MIN). Annual fee: $30 per person; $35 per couple or family.

Moment's Notice, 40 E. 49th St., New York, NY 10017 (phone: 212-486-0503). Annual fee: $45 per family.

On Call to Travel, 14335 S.W. Allen Blvd., Suite 209, Beaverton, OR 97005 (phone: 503-643-7212, members may call collect). Annual fee: $39 per family, first year; $29 yearly thereafter.

Spur-of-the-Moment Tours and Cruises, 10780 Jefferson Blvd., Culver City, CA 90230 (phone: 213-839-2418 in California; 800-343-1991 elsewhere in the US). No fee.

Stand Buys Limited, 311 W. Superior St., Suite 414, Chicago IL 60610 (phone: 800-331-0257 for membership information; 800-848-8402 for customer service; 800-433-9383 for reservations). Annual fee: $45 per family.

Worldwide Discount Travel Club, 1674 Meridian Ave., Miami Beach, FL 33139 (phone: 305-534-2082). Annual fee: $50 per family; $40 per person.

NET FARE SOURCES: The newest notion for reducing the costs of travel services comes from travel agents who offer individual travelers "net" fares. Defined simply, a net fare is the bare minimum amount at which an airline or tour operator will carry a prospective traveler. It doesn't include the amount that would normally be paid to the travel agent as a commission. Traditionally, such travel agent commissions amount to about 10% on domestic fares and from 8% to 20% on international tickets — not counting significant additions to these commission levels that are payable retroactively when agents sell more than a specific volume of tickets or trips for a single supplier. At press time, at least one travel agency in the US was offering travelers the opportunity to purchase tickets and/or tours for a net price. Instead of making their income from individual commissions, this agency assesses a fixed fee that may or may not provide a bargain for travelers; it requires a little arithmetic to determine whether to use the services of a net travel agent or those of one who accepts conventional commissions.

McTravel Travel Services (130 S. Jefferson, Chicago, IL 60606-3691; phone: 800-333-3335 in the US except Illinois; 312-876-1116 in Illinois and throughout Canada) is a formula fee-based agency that rebates its ordinary agency commission to the customer. For domestic flights, an agent will find the lowest retail ticket price, then rebate 8% of that price minus an $8 ticket-writing charge. The rebate percentage for international flights varies from 8% to 20%, depending on the airline selected, and the ticket-writing fee is $20. *McTravel* will rebate on all tickets including max savers, super savers, and senior citizen passes. Available 7 days a week, reservations should be made far enough in advance to allow the tickets to be sent by first class mail, since extra charges accrue for special handling as they do for reservations that require any significant amount of research. It's possible to economize further by making your own airline reservation, then asking *McTravel* only to write/issue your ticket. For travelers who live outside the Chicago area, business may be transacted by phone, and purchases may be charged to a credit card.

One of the potential drawbacks of buying from agencies selling travel services at net fares is that your options may be limited. *McTravel Travel Services* recently lost a court battle with American Airlines, which refused to do business with the discounter. A US District Court in Chicago ruled in the airline's favor, and other carriers are expected to follow suit.

BARTERED TRAVEL SOURCES: Say a company buys advertising space in a newspaper for a hotel. As payment, the hotel gives the company a number of hotel rooms in lieu of cash. This is barter, a common means of exchange among hotels, airlines, car rental companies, cruise lines, tour operators, restaurants, and other service companies. When a bartering company finds itself with excess hotel rooms (or empty airline seats or cruise ship cabin space, and so on) and offers them to the public, considerable savings can be had.

Bartered-travel clubs can often offer discounts of up to 50% to members, who pay an annual fee (approximately $50 at press time) that entitles them to select from the flights, cruises, hotels, that the company obtained by barter. Members usually present a voucher, club credit card, or scrip (a dollar-denomination voucher negotiable only for the bartered product) to the hotel, which in turn subtracts the dollar amount from the bartering company's account.

Selling bartered travel is a perfectly legitimate means of retailing. One advantage to club members is that they don't have to wait until the last minute to obtain room or flight reservations. However, hotel rooms and airline seats are usually offered to members on a space-available basis. Ticket vouchers are good only for a particular hotel and cannot be used at other hotels. The same goes for car rentals, cruises, package tours, and restaurants. The following clubs offer bartered travel at a discount to members:

IGT (In Good Taste) Services, 22 E. 29th St., New York, NY 10016 (phone: 212-725-9600 or 800-444-8872). Annual membership fee of $48 includes $25 credit toward future charges.

The Travel Guild, 18210 Redmond Way, Redmond, WA 98052 (phone: 206-885-1213). Annual membership fee: $48.

Travel World Leisure Club, 225 W. 34th St., Suite 2203, New York, NY 10122 (phone: 212-239-4855 or 800-444-TWLC). Annual membership fee: $50 per family.

CONSUMER PROTECTION: Consumers who feel that they have not been dealt with fairly by an airline should make their complaints known. Begin with the customer service representative at the airport where the problem occurs. If he or she cannot resolve your complaint to your satisfaction, write to the airline's consumer office. In a businesslike, typed letter, explain what reservations you held, what happened, the names of the employees who were involved, and what you expect the airline to do to remedy the situation. Send copies (never the originals) of the tickets, receipts, and other documents that support your claims. Ideally, all correspondence should be sent via certified mail, return receipt requested. This provides proof that your complaint was received.

If you still receive no satisfaction and your complaint is against a US carrier contact the US Department of Transportation. Passengers with consumer complaints — lost baggage, compensation for getting bumped, smoking and non-smoking rules, deceptive practices by an airline, charter regulations — should write to the Consumer Affairs Division, Room 10405, US Department of Transportation, 400 Seventh St. SW, Washington, DC 20590, or call the office at 202-366-2220. DOT personnel stress, however, that consumers should initially direct their complaints to the airline that provoked them.

If your complaint involves a Canadian airline, you can enlist the aid of the Canadian government. Write a formal letter requesting assistance (attaching copies of your correspondence with the airline, if you think it helps explain your case), and address the letter to The Secretary, National Transportation Agency of Canada, Ottawa, Ontario K1A ON9. For further information call 613-997-6567.

To avoid more serious problems, *always* choose charter flights and tour packages with care. When you consider a charter, ask your travel agent who runs it and carefully check out the company. The Better Business Bureau in the company's home city can report on how many complaints, if any, have been lodged against it in the past. As emphasized above, protect yourself with trip cancellation and interruption insurance, which can help safeguard your investment in the event that you or a traveling companion is unable to make the trip and must cancel too late to receive a full refund from the company providing your travel services. (This is advisable whether you're buying a charter flight alone or a tour package for which the air fare is provided by charter or scheduled flight.) Some travel insurance policies have an additional feature, covering the possibility of default or bankruptcy on the part of the tour operator or airline, charter or scheduled.

Should this type of coverage not be available to you (state insurance regulations vary, there is a wide difference in price, and so on), your best bet is to pay for airline tickets and tour packages with a credit card. The federal Fair Credit Billing Act permits purchasers to refuse payment for credit card charges where services have not been delivered, so the onus of dealing with the receiver for a bankrupt airline falls on the credit card company. Do not rely on another airline to honor the ticket you're holding, since the days when virtually all major carriers subscribed to a default protection program that bound them to do so are long gone. Some airlines may voluntarily step forward to accommodate the stranded passengers of a fellow carrier, but this is now an entirely altruistic act.

Touring by Train

Canada's two transcontinental passenger services — the *Canadian National Railway* and the *Canadian Pacific* — were reorganized in 1977 into one overall managing system, *VIA Rail Canada*. The reorganization integrated the two railways and provided more coordinated and economical service. If you have the time — the 3,000-mile trip takes about 4 days and 3 nights — there is no better way to grasp the vastness of Canada than to ride one of the transcontinentals from Montreal to Vancouver. In the course of the journey you'll see the variety of geography that shapes the lives of Canadians from the East Coast to the West Coast, from the St. Lawrence to the Pacific. Prospective train travelers with less time should note that the route segment between Calgary and Vancouver, through the Canadian Rockies, is by far the most beautiful.

In addition to transcontinental routes, *VIA* runs shorter lines between the major eastern cities, and between Winnipeg, Manitoba, and Churchill on the Hudson Bay. Also note that, as we went to press, *Amtrak* had resumed the overnight *Montrealer* service between New York, Washington DC, and Montreal. Information on routes, schedules, fares, and special tours and packages can be obtained from VIA Rail, 2 Place Ville Marie, Suite 400, Montreal, Quebec H3C 3N5 (phone: 514-871-1331). You can also get information on the *Montrealer* and *VIA* — and book tickets — through any *Amtrak* office in the US.

ACCOMMODATIONS AND FARES: *VIA Rail* fares are based on the quality of accommodation the passenger enjoys on the journey. Least expensive is the basic fare, called coach; it means simply that the passenger is entitled to a seat on the train. The "daynighter" is somewhat more luxurious, offering complimentary pillow and blanket, and reclining lounging seats with footrests. Sleeping berths, called "section accommodations," cost a bit more and provide an upper or lower sleeping berth that folds into a seat during the day. Washroom facilities are shared. Roomettes are small rooms with one bed and a private washroom. Most comfortable are double-occupancy bedroom accommodations, with two beds and a private washroom. Roomettes and bedrooms are scarce on transcontinental trains, and in summer especially they should be booked well in advance.

The cost of a coach seat — basic transportation fare — on a train will generally be something more than the cost of a bus ticket to the same destination, and something less than coach fare on a plane, except on such competitive routes, where very inexpensive flights may be available. However, while the plane makes the trip in a few hours, the train can take several days, and it is likely that anyone making the trip by train will want some kind of sleeping accommodation rather than just a coach seat. When comparing costs, however, take into account that the extra expense of accommodations on the train are offset by the comparable cost you would be paying for a hotel room. The cost of a train compared with that of a plane is very much relative to the level of comfort.

VIA has also introduced a number of incentive fares to encourage off-peak, excursion, and group travel. The Canrail Pass, for example, like the Eurailpass and USA Rail Pass, allows unlimited travel in selected areas for specified periods at extremely low rates. Special fares are available to passengers over 60, and children between 2 and 11 travel at half-fare; under 2, free in coach.

BOOKING: Tickets may be obtained from *VIA Rail* offices and stations, from *Amtrak* offices, or from travel agents. Payment can be made in cash or by major credit card. Remember to ask about group, senior citizen, and youth discounts as well as any special incentive fares. Reservations are advised for all club cars (*VIA*'s first class), section accommodations, roomettes, and bedrooms, and on a number of regular short runs. Passengers can usually stop anywhere along their route for as long as they like if they reach their final destination before their ticket expires (tickets are good for a year). If you have a round-trip excursion fare, you must return to your departure point before the ticket expires. Meals or snacks are served on board most trains. Sleeping car attendants should be tipped at least $1 a night, assuming you're pleased with the service.

BAGGAGE: On long-distance trains (ones with baggage cars), bags can be checked through to your destination up to 30 minutes before departure (and should be claimed within 30 minutes after arrival). You are allowed to check free of charge up to 150 pounds for each adult and 75 pounds for each child traveling at half fare. Attendants on the train, or Red Caps in most stations, will help you with your luggage (tip about $1 per bag).

TOURS: *VIA Rail* offers some of the best values in escorted and independent package tours available in Canada. You can take trips to isolated hinterlands, around scenic routes, and into the large cities. At their most basic, these economical packages include rail fare and hotel. For example, at press time, *VIA Rail*'s price for "A Taste of Quebec," a 7-night tour including transportation (sleeping car accommodations), hotel, sightseeing, transfers, and a rail guidebook, was $700 (Canadian) per person, double occupancy. Purchasing transportation and accommodations separately would cost over 30% more.

As these packages are usually heavily subscribed, it is advisable to book as far in advance as possible. And most tours must be paid in full at least 30 days before departure, or your reservation can be canceled. Brochures and details are available from travel agents and *VIA Rail* and *Amtrak* offices. It's best, however, to book through *VIA Rail*, since the price its agents quote will be in Canadian dollars, and given the favorable rate of exchange, that could save you about 20% on the cost of the tour.

Two special train treks will appeal to hikers and backpackers. The *Algoma Central Railway* runs from Sault Ste. Marie, Ontario, to the gorgeous wilderness Agawa Canyon, 114 miles (183.1 km) north of the city. (A complete description of the trip can be found in *Ontario, The Western Lakeshores*, DIRECTIONS.) For information, contact Algoma Central Railway, 129 Bay St., Sault Ste. Marie, Ontario P6A 1W7 (phone: 705-254-4331/2/3/4). The other, the *Polar Bear Express*, ventures into the Arctic watershed from Cochrane to Moosonee in northern Ontario. The express is run by Ontario Northland Transportation Commission, 555 Oak St. E., North Bay, Ontario P1B 8L3 (phone: 705-472-4500).

Touring by Bus

Bus companies still comprise Canada's most comprehensive transport system. Except for the far north, you can get virtually anywhere you want by bus. The system covers almost every populated area of the country and serves many towns without airports or railway connections.

Gray Coach, Greyhound Lines of Canada, and *Voyageur* are the three largest companies. None is truly national: *Voyageur* operates only in Ontario and Quebec; *Gray Coach,* only in Ontario; while *Greyhound Lines of Canada* runs some 415 buses over 14,000 miles, but does not operate east of Toronto. (*Eastern Greyhound* — one of the four companies that were once *Greyhound* in the US — runs an American service from New York to Montreal.) With its head office in Calgary, *Greyhound* is the main operator in western Canada. For further information on *Gray Coach, Greyhound Lines of Canada,* and *Voyageur,* call 416-393-7911.

These three companies, with many smaller lines around the country — such as *SMT (Eastern) Limited* in New Brunswick (phone: 506-458-8350) and *Acadian Lines Limited* in Nova Scotia (phone: 902-454-9321) — offer the most frequent transportation in Canada. They are, however, somewhat slower than trains, planes, or private cars, and there is clearly a trade-off of money saved for time spent en route.

ACCOMMODATIONS AND FARES: In general, the cost of a bus trip is less than half that of a journey by plane. In some cases (like long-distance, return excursion trips), the savings are even greater. Rail clearly offers some competition for the bus lines, but it can't really compete with the buses' unlimited travel tickets, which represent considerable savings over normal fares. *Greyhound*'s unlimited travel program, called Ameripass, allows the ticket holder to travel anywhere in mainland Canada and the US (on both company and non-company routes) for specified time periods (7 days, 15 days, and 30 days).

BOOKING: Reservations are not necessary on most bus routes; companies usually send as many buses as are needed to handle all passengers. Most companies allow passengers to make free stopovers along the route, though some limit the stopovers to cities where passengers must change of bus. Tickets issued by some bus lines have no expiration date. (However, a company might not honor a ticket that's too old.) *Greyhound* one-way tickets are good for 30 days; round-trip tickets, for one year.

SERVICES: Most buses are not equipped for food service. On long trips they make meal stops, and most bus terminals also provide food services. It is not a bad idea to bring some food aboard. Most companies provide air conditioned, heated buses with toilets, even on short runs. Most seats have reading lamps and are both upholstered and adjustable.

FOR COMFORTABLE TRAVEL: Dress casually with loose-fitting clothes. Be sure you have a sweater or jacket (even in the summer, air conditioning can make buses quite cool). Passengers are allowed to listen to radios or cassette players, but must use earphones. Choose a seat in the front near the driver for the best view, or in the middle between the front and rear wheels for the smoothest ride. Avoid the back near the toilet unless you smoke. Smokers are generally restricted to the last rows of any bus; often pipes and cigars are forbidden.

TOURS: In addition to its regular service, *Gray Coach* offers a wide variety of bus tours that include transportation, hotels, and escorted sightseeing. These tours go to such popular destinations as Agawa Canyon, Montreal, Quebec, and Ottawa as well as to Atlantic and Western Canada. *Gray Coach* also offers sightseeing tours of Toronto. Information on the tour program can be obtained from any local *Gray Coach* office and most travel agents, or call 416-979-3511.

Touring by Car

DRIVING YOUR OWN CAR: Automobile travel is the most popular mode of transportation in Canada, just as it is in the US. Canadian roads are generally better, speed limits are higher, and there are fewer toll roads than in the States. But here, too, you pay for the convenience of having the car: on average, the cost per mile to drive is from 5 to 6 times the cost of flying (cost varies with the size and condition of your car, the price of gasoline, and whether you're doing city or highway driving). Driving, however, becomes more economical with more passengers and affords travelers the opportunity to explore inaccessible regions at their own pace and on their own schedule. Rather than just the means to an end, a well-planned driving route can be an important part of the adventure.

Canadians drive on the right, as in the US, and obey similar traffic rules. American, British, and most other European drivers' licenses are recognized by Canadian officials. Canada is on the metric system, so speed limits are posted everywhere in kilometers per hour (kmh). Common speed limits are 100 kmh on freeways, 80 kmh on highways, and 50 kmh on city streets. The "Rule of Six" is a convenient rule of thumb for converting kilometers to miles: Take the figure in kilometers and multiply by .6 (sixtenths). Thus, 100 kmh is approximately equivalent to 60 mph; 80 kmh equals approximately 50 mph; 50 kmh = 30 mph. Road signs and traffic symbols are universally understood graphic designs, so even when you're driving through Quebec where French is spoken, you should have no problem understanding the rules of the road.

Before setting out, make certain that everything you need is in order. Read about the places you intend to visit and study relevant maps. If at all possible, discuss your intended trip with someone who has already driven the route to find out about road conditions and available services. If you can't speak to someone personally, try to read about others' experiences. The automobile clubs listed below also offer a wealth of information regarding specific driving routes.

Car Insurance – US motorists should obtain a Canadian Non-Resident Inter-Provincial Motor Vehicle Liability Insurance Card, which proves the holder has a valid automobile liability insurance policy. This will be required as proof of financial responsibility should you be involved in an accident in Canadian territory. You can only get this card in the US through a US insurance agent.

Automobile Clubs – To protect yourself in case of on-the-road breakdowns, you should consider joining a reputable national automobile club, preferably one that has reciprocal service with affiliates in Canada. The largest of these is the *American Automobile Association (AAA)*, with over 30 million members in chapters throughout the US, as well as branch offices throughout Canada and *Canadian Automobile Association* affiliates. Other clubs offer similar services, but their domain is more limited to the US. Some will reimburse you for towing charges incurred in Canada upon receiving a receipt, but the difference between having *AAA* officers on hand to advise at the time of the trouble and being paid several weeks after your return is substantial. Keep this in mind when choosing a club. If paying for car service in US dollars, be sure that this is clearly indicated on your receipt. Also, when filing a claim, be sure to keep a copy of the claim form and all receipts.

Any club should offer three basic services:

1. On-the-road insurance, covering accidents, personal injury, arrest and bail bond, and lawyer's fees for defense of contested traffic cases.
2. Around-the-clock (24-hour) emergency breakdown service, including reduced rates on (or free) towing to the nearest garage. For instance, *AAA* has a toll-free number for emergency road service; members are referred to the nearest service facility. Other clubs allow members to call any local mechanic and be reimbursed for the cost of towing at a later date.
3. Travel and vacation planning service, including advice and maps.

These are the basic services; specific policies and programs vary from club to club. Before joining one, get information and brochures from several national clubs, and compare benefits and costs to find the services that best match your travel needs. Most clubs cost between $12 and $60 a year and include your spouse in membership. Listed below are the major Canadian and several of the largest US auto and travel clubs:

Allstate Motor Club: A member of the Sears family, run by Allstate Insurance. Will reimburse up to $50 for emergency road service in Canada; does trip routing through the national office. Join through any Allstate agency or contact

Customer Service, PO Box 3096, Arlington Heights, IL 60006 (phone: 800-323-6282).

American Automobile Association: With offices in many Canadian cities, contract stations throughout Canada, and a large network of affiliates through the *Canadian Automobile Association* (a federation of provincial Canadian auto clubs), the *AAA* provides roadside assistance at a wide range of locations as well as a variety of additional services, including a travel agency, trip planning, and traveler's checks. *AAA* publishes a pamphlet called *AAA Offices to Serve You Abroad,* which lists offices in Canada and the US. Although *AAA* members receive a discount, non-members can also order from an extensive selection of highway and topographical maps available. For 24-hour emergency service throughout the US and Canada, *AAA* members can call 800-336-HELP. Join through a local chapter or contact the national office, 8111 Gatehouse Rd., Falls Church, VA 22047 (phone: 703-222-6000).

Amoco Motor Club: Although the organization has no branches in Canada, it is affiliated with *Canadian Tires* which provides service to *Amoco* club members. The US national office provides maps and does routings for Canadian driving tours. Will reimburse for up to $40 on any service call in Canada upon receipt of a claim form. Join at any Amoco dealer or contact the national office, PO Box 9014, Des Moines, IA 50306 (phone: 800-334-3300; for road service in Canada, 800-263-1023).

Canadian Automobile Association: Provides full membership services to *AAA* members. Affiliated visiting members are entitled to travel information, itineraries, maps, tourbooks, bulletins on road and weather conditions, and accommodation reservations, emergency road, and travel agency services upon presentation of an *AAA* membership card. Contact CAA at 1775 Courtwood Crescent, Ottawa, Ontario, Canada K2C 3J2 (phone: 613-226-7631; for emergency road service, both AAA and CAA members can call 800-336-HELP).

Exxon Travel Club: Provides a wide range of services throughout the US and Canada including trip routing, maps and atlases, reimbursement for towing, discounts on car rentals and accommodations, and a variety of insurance packages. Ask for information from the national office, PO Box 3633, Houston, TX 77253 (phone: 713-680-5723).

Ford Auto Club: Provides trip routing services through the national office and reimbursement for emergency towing service up to $50. Contact the Membership Services Division, PO Box 224688, Dallas, TX 75222 (phone: 800-348-5220).

Montgomery Ward Auto Club: Open to (but not limited to) people with a Montgomery Ward charge account. Although the organization has no offices in Canada, it does chart driving routes through Canada and will reimburse members up to $80 for Canadian road service upon receipt of a claim. Join through the credit manager at any Montgomery Ward store, or contact the national office, 200 N. Martingale Rd., Schaumburg, IL 60173 (phone: 312-490-7485 in Illinois; 800-621-5151 elsewhere in the US).

Motor Club of America: No offices in Canada, but does routings for Canadian trips. Reimburses members for the amount of a local tow upon receipt of the bill. Ask for information from the national office, 484 Central Ave., Newark, NJ 07107 (phone: 201-733-1234; 800-222-6288 in New York; 800-435-7622 elsewhere in the continental US).

United States Auto Club: No Canadian offices, but US branches do trip routings. Reimburses members up to $70 for Canadian road service. Ask for information from the national office, PO Box 660460, Dallas, TX 75266-0460 (phone: 215-541-4246 or 800-348-2761).

34 GETTING READY / Touring by Car

Oil Company Credit Cards – Most oil companies offer credit cards that can be used to pay for gas, repairs, and most car parts at their respective service stations throughout the US and Canada. A credit card will reduce the amount of money you must carry on your trip. Applications for cards are available at the respective service stations (Sunoco stations have applications for Sunoco cards only, and so on), and you will be granted a card if you can establish credit-worthiness — another credit card of any kind or an established credit rating. They are issued free, and usually take about a month for processing after application.

Charges are handled in two ways, and it is important to know under which system your card is operated. A few companies — Amoco, for example — allow some cardholders (depending on the kind of account) to carry charges from month to month. The cardholder pays only a minimum amount each month, and the balance is carried over. For this privilege the cardholder is charged an interest rate (usually about 1½% a month, 18% a year — this varies for different cards and from state to state) on the balance carried over. If you spent $300 on gasoline during a 2-week trip, you could spread the payment of this $300 over several months — virtually a "travel now, pay later" system — but you will end up paying more than the basic $300 when the cost of the interest charge is included.

Other companies — an example is Gulf — insist that the cardholder pay the full balance due at the end of each billing period (usually a month) if it's under $50. On any balance over $50, if only partial payment is made, revolving credit is then extended to the unpaid balance, but interest charges will be added. There are advantages to both systems; when you consider a credit card, know which way it works and decide what is best for you.

When you buy gas or pay for car repairs in Canada with a credit card, make sure you are paying in Canadian dollars, and be sure to check the bill you receive at home. There have been cases of people being charged, say, $10 CN (Canadian) in Manitoba, and when they return home being billed $10 US and, depending on the current exchange rate, such an overcharge can be 20% or more.

Maps – Consult road maps. Many automobile clubs offer their members free maps and precise routings. Other travelers can get road maps free by writing to the provincial tourist offices (see *Tourist Information* in this section). Maps are available at Canadian service stations, but due to budget cutbacks in the oil industry, most companies now charge for them (usually about $1 each). The *Rand McNally Road Atlas: US, Canada and Mexico* ($6.95) is excellent.

Preparing Your Car – Before heading off on the road, always make certain that your car is in the best possible condition. Have it thoroughly inspected, paying special attention to brakes and tires, and be sure that your spare tire is in good shape. If you have room, a full-size spare is preferable to the small, solid rubber spares provided with many new cars. The days when every gas station had a mechanic on the premises have given way to self-service gas "stops" with convenience stores or, in Canada, road-side diners — so if you need a tire repaired, ask at your hotel or refer to the local yellow pages to find a service station that provides this service. Always carry liability insurance. Other suggestions include the following:

1. In addition to the spare tire, bring the following equipment: a flashlight with an extra set of batteries, jack, wrench, two wooden blocks; an extra set of keys (well hidden); jumper cables; gloves; a white towel (useful for signaling for help as well as for wiping the car); flares and/or reflectors; a first-aid kit; a container of water for the radiator; and a steel container of gasoline. (Plastic containers tend to break when the car is bouncing over rocky roads. This, in turn, creates the danger of fire should the gasoline ignite from a static electricity spark. Plastic containers also tend to burst at high altitudes.) For driving in Canada, the well-prepared traveler should also carry an ice scraper, anti-freeze, and snow chains.

GETTING READY / Touring by Car 35

If traveling in an isolated area, you may also want to carry a couple of extra fan belts, distributor points, a fuel pump replacement kit, condensers, and spark plugs. If driving at a high altitude, change cold spark plugs for hot, and advance the spark to prevent the engine from stalling. When driving a foreign car through rural areas it is advisable to carry a basic selection of spare parts (ask your local mechanic for a list of essentials), as service stations in small towns are not likely to stock them. This can forestall a wait of up to several days for parts to be sent from a foreign parts distributor in a distant metropolitan area.

2. Make the first days of your trip the shortest, and plan to drive no more than 300-400 miles per day (6-7 hours); this is a comfortable pace for most travelers. When traveling with children, plan on 200-250 miles a day (4-5 hours) at the most. Stop to rest when you are tired.

Breakdowns – If you break down on the road, immediate emergency procedure is to get the car off the highway, raise the hood as a signal that help is needed, and tie a white rag to the door handle or antenna for the same reason. Don't leave the car unattended, and don't try any major repairs on the road.

Mechanics and Car Care – For any but the most simple malfunctions, you will probably need a mechanic. An excellent series of booklets on car care, mileage, and mechanical problems and their sources is published by Shell Oil Company in its *Come to Shell for Answers* series, available from some *Shell* dealers or directly from the company at PO Box 2463, Houston, TX 77252 (phone: 713-241-6161). Other suggestions for breakdowns and on-the-road car care:

1. Have some idea of what needs to be done. Oil needs to be changed approximately every 3,000 miles; a tune-up is needed every 12,000 miles (every 24,000 miles for transistorized ignition cars); spark plugs need to be changed every 25,000 miles; fan and air conditioning belts every 5,000 miles.
2. Get an estimate in writing on major repairs, and make sure there is a firm understanding that the mechanic will call if any other problems arise. The average cost for labor varies substantially between rural and metropolitan areas as well as from station to station.
3. Be aware of dishonest practices. Some mechanics will cheat you. While checking oil they can "short stick" the dipper so the full amount of oil in your engine doesn't register; be sure to watch while oil is being checked. When buying gas, make sure the attendant resets the pump, moving the counter back to zero. The best way to avoid being cheated is to know your car's oil and gas consumption.
4. Recognize the warning signals.
   - Fluid leaks: Spread paper and look for brown or black fluid, which usually means an *oil leak;* straw-colored fluid near wheel is likely to be *leaking brake fluid;* pink or reddish fluid means an *automatic transmission leak;* colorless or greenish fluid near the front, a *radiator or hose leak.*
   - Car has trouble starting: May be a vapor lock caused by hot weather; a cold, wet rag on the fuel line and pump may help.
   - Engine missing after quick acceleration: Could be a fleck of carbon lodged between electrodes of a spark plug. Clean plugs.
   - Rattle in rear: Loose muffler or tail pipe.
   - Rattling noise: Bent fan blade or loose pulley.
   - Loud squealing noise when wheel turns: Low power-steering fluid.
5. If your car needs to be towed, agree in advance on the price and on the station to which it will be towed. If you ask *AAA* or *CAA* clubs, they will often name stations they consider reliable.

SPEED: Watch the speedometer closely. Remember that Canada's speed limits are in kilometers per hour *not* miles per hour. It is all too easy when touring along Canada's open and well-maintained and designed roadways to inch up in speed. Speed traps mean expensive tickets that may also affect your insurance rates. Also, when traveling at dawn and dusk in forested areas, keep in mind the high incident of fatal accidents due to animals crossing the roads. It pays to exercise extra care and drive more slowly at these times; many drivers prefer to limit highway driving in such areas to daylight hours.

GASOLINE: The major oil companies have stations in Canada: Shell, Esso, Gulf, Sunoco, and Texaco, as well as Canadian companies, like Petro-Canada. Gas is generally sold in liters in Canada. At press time, the cost of gas was as much as 50% to 60% more expensive than in the US — so be sure to take into account this rather substantial expense. In the more remote reaches of Canada, gas stations are not very numerous, so fill up when you see a station in the late afternoon before they shut down for the day. (Touring routes described in DIRECTIONS note where gas stations are scarce.)

Considering the inflated cost of gas in Canada at the time of this writing, gas economy is of particular concern. The prudent traveler should begin by doing some preliminary research, planning an itinerary, and making as many reservations as possible in advance, in order to not waste gas figuring out where to go, stay, or eat. Drive early in the day, when there is less traffic. Then leave your car at the hotel and use local transportation within cities.

Make sure that your tires are properly inflated and your engine is tuned correctly to cut gas consumption. Avoid speeding — at 55 miles per hour (approximately 90 kmh) a car gets 25% better mileage than at 70 (approximately 112 kmh). The number of miles per gallon or liter is also increased by driving smoothly. Accelerate gently, anticipate stops, get into high gear quickly, and maintain a steady speed.

RENTING A CAR: Before renting a car in the US for a driving tour through Canada, you should consider the alternative of flying to Canada and renting there; you may well find that the combination of air fare plus Canadian rental is no more than the total cost of renting in the US, especially with the numerous special fly/drive packages that include the cost of rental in air fare to a Canadian gateway city (see below). The major rental companies in the US all have branches in Canada, and there are also numerous national Canadian rental firms as well as local companies in the major Canadian cities.

Whatever you decide to do, you should know that renting a car is rarely as simple as signing on the dotted line and roaring off into the night. If you are renting for personal use, you must have a valid drivers license and will have to convince the renting agency that (1) you are personally credit-worthy; and (2) you will bring the car back at the stated time. This will be easy if you have a major credit card (these are also accepted widely in Canada); all large agencies and most local companies accept credit cards in lieu of a cash deposit, as well as for payment of your final bill. If you prefer to pay in cash, leave your credit card imprint as a "deposit," then pay your bill in cash when you return the car.

If you don't have a major credit card, renting a car for personal use becomes more complicated. If you are planning to rent from an agency near your home, the best thing to do is to call the renting company several days in advance, give them your name, home address, and information on your business or employer; the rental agency then runs its own credit check on you. This can be time consuming, so you should try to have it done before you leave home. If you are paying in cash and are planning to rent a car in Canada, it is best to make arrangements in advance — otherwise you must bring along a letter of employment and go to the agency during business hours so it can call your employer for verification. In Canada, *Avis* honors car rental vouchers, based upon agreements the rental company has with various travel agents in Canada and the US. The voucher enables you to pay for the car rental in advance to the travel agent and eliminates the on-the-spot credit check when picking up the car from the *Avis* branch location.

In addition to paying the rental fee up front, you will also have to leave a hefty deposit when you pick up the car — either a substantial flat fee or a percentage of the total rental cost. (Each company has a different deposit policy; look around for the best deal.) If you return the car on time, the full deposit will be refunded, otherwise additional charges will be deducted and any unused portion of the deposit will be refunded.

Cost and Requirements – Renting is not inexpensive, but it is possible to economize by determining your own needs and then shopping around among the car rental companies until you find the best deal. As you comparison-shop, keep in mind that rates vary considerably, not only from city to city, but also from location to location within the same city. It might be less expensive to rent a car in the center of a city rather than at the airport. Usually, locally based companies are less expensive than the national giants. Ask about special rates or promotional deals, such as weekend or weekly rates, bonus coupons for airline tickets, or 24-hour rates that include gas and unlimited mileage.

It used to be that cars were rented only on a per-day, per-mile basis. Then when the competition among rival companies heated up, several of the upstart outfits began to offer flat rates that included unlimited mileage. Now most American-based car rental agencies, including the giants, offer flat rates on a regular basis or as special packages. Canadian companies, however, seem to prefer a combination of the two rental schemes. Most rent cars for a per-day rate that usually includes a fixed number of free kilometers (generally 100) per day and a per-kilometer rate that applies to distances driven beyond that.

Most Canadian companies have weekly rates that offer a substantial savings over the daily rate. These, too, come with free kilometers, usually 1,000 or 1,500. Unlike car rental companies in the US, Canadian firms generally don't offer unlimited free kilometers. If you intend to cover a lot of ground, consider renting a car in the US, where deals offering unlimited free mileage (though lately being replaced by mileage caps) can still be found. The per-day rates tend to be a bit higher, however.

Another thing to keep in mind when renting a car for touring is one-way fees. In most instances, you must return the car to the point from which it was rented. To leave it elsewhere usually will mean an additional one-way drop-off charge, which can be quite expensive.

Electing to pay for collision damage waiver protection will add considerably to the cost of renting a car. The renter may be responsible for the full value of the vehicle being rented, but you can dispense with the possible obligation to pay even this amount by buying the offered waiver at a cost of about $10 a day. Before making any decisions about optional rental car waivers, check with your own insurance agent and determine whether your personal auto policy covers rented vehicles; if it does you probably won't need to pay for the waiver. Be aware, too, that increasing numbers of so-called "premium" credit cards — gold or platinum American Express cards, gold Visa or MasterCards — automatically provide collision damage waiver coverage if the car rental is charged to the appropriate credit card. However, the specific terms of such coverage differ sharply among individual credit card companies — whose policies may further vary depending on whether rentals are transacted in the US or abroad — so check with the credit card company for information on the amount of coverage provided (also see *Credit Cards* in this section). Considering that repair costs for a rental car have become a real headache of late, and car rental companies are getting away with steep fees (up to the full retail price of the car) for damage to their property — if you are not otherwise covered it is wise to pay for the insurance offered by the car rental company rather than risk traveling without any coverage.

Most rental firms in the US require clients to be at least 21 years of age, although some US and most Canadian firms have an age limit of 18 (this varies somewhat from province to province). *Avis*'s policy varies in different locations and *Hertz*'s minimum-age requirement is 25, unless the renter's employer has a contract with *Hertz* stating that drivers can be under 25. Also *Hertz* reserves the right to charge a rate differential, and luxury models may not be available to young renters. If you rent the car in the US to drive into Canada, also make sure you have a copy of the rental contract stipulating use in Canada.

Major US companies with branches in Canada and the largest Canadian rental firm are as follows:

American International Rent-A-Car: 800-225-2529 in Boston, MA, and Portland, ME; 800-527-0202 elsewhere in the US and throughout Canada

Avis: 918-664-4600 in Oklahoma or 800-331-1212 elsewhere in the US, ask for the international department; 800-387-7600 in Ontario and Quebec; 800-268-2310 elsewhere in Canada

Budget Rent-A-Car: 800-527-0700 in the US; 800-268-8900 in Canada

Dollar Rent-A-Car System: throughout the US and Canada, 800-421-6868

Hertz: 800-654-3131 in the US; 800-620-9620 in Toronto; 800-263-0600 elsewhere in Canada

Sears Rent-A-Car: 800-527-0770 or 800-268-8900 throughout the US and Canada

Thrifty Rent-A-Car: 800-367-2277 in the US and Canada

Tilden Rent-A-Car System: Largest Canadian firm, affiliated with *National* in the States; for *National,* or reservations through them with *Tilden* in Canada: 800-328-4567 in the continental US; 800-CAR-RENT in Alaska, Hawaii, and throughout Canada

Though the cost of gasoline is higher in Canada than in the US, it's something motorists often forget to budget into their car rental expenses. On the road, remember self-serve (where you do the pumping) is usually less expensive than full-serve. Similarly, gas paid for in cash usually costs less than fuel paid for with a credit card. Also, when picking up a rental car, be sure to confirm the policy regarding the gas tank level on return. Some agencies include a charge for the initial tank of gas in the rental fee and suggest that you return the car with a close to empty tank. In other cases, if you do not return the car with a full tank, you will have to pay to refill the tank, and gasoline at the car rental company's pump is always much more expensive than gasoline bought at a service station.

Fly/Drive Packages – Air Canada, Canadian Airlines International, and several Canadian tour wholesalers offer fly/drive packages that include air fare and car rental. These packages allow you to rent cars in many Canadian cities for driving tours, and many include hotel vouchers for participating hotels across Canada. The cost of the package varies according to the size of the car and quality of the hotels; there is usually a drop-off charge if you rent the car in one city and return it in another. For information on available packages, check with the airline or your travel agent.

Package Tours

If the mere thought of buying a travel package conjures up visions of a trip spent marching in lockstep with a horde of frazzled fellow travelers, remember that packages have come a long way. For one thing, not all packages are necessarily escorted tours, and the one you buy does not have to include any organized touring at all — nor will it necessarily include traveling companions. If it does, however, you'll find that people of all sorts — many just like yourself — are taking advantage of packages today because they are economical and convenient, save the purchaser an immense amount of planning time, and exist in such variety that it's

GETTING READY / Package Tours

virtually impossible not to find one that suits at least the majority of any traveler's preferences. Given the high cost of travel these days, packages have emerged as a good buy.

There are hundreds of package programs on the market today. In the US, numerous packages to Canada are offered by the airlines, *VIA Rail,* and hotels, as well as by independent tour operators. Many of these are sports packages, especially ski packages, and one good reason to use a package is to ensure good accommodations where it is difficult to book hotels on your own, such as in wilderness spots. In essence, a package is a combination of travel services that can be purchased as a single booking. It may include any or all of the following: round-trip air transportation, local transportation (and/or car rentals), accommodations, some or all meals, sightseeing, entertainment, transfers to and from the hotel at each destination, taxes, tips, escort service, and a variety of incidental features that might be offered as options at additional cost. In other words, a package can be any combination from a fully escorted tour offered at an all-inclusive price to a simple fly-drive booking allowing you to function totally on your own. Its principal advantage is that it saves money: The cost of the combined arrangements invariably is well below the price that would be paid if all the elements included were bought separately, and, particularly if transportation is provided by charter or discount flight, it could even be less than a round-trip economy airline ticket on a regularly scheduled flight. A package tour provides more than economy and convenience: It releases the traveler from having to make individual arrangements for each separate section of the tour.

The lower prices are possible through package travel as a result of high-volume commerce. The tour packager negotiates for services in wholesale quantities — blocks of airline seats or hotel rooms, group meals, dozens of rental cars, busloads of ground transportation, and so on — and they are made available at a lower per-person price because of the large quantities purchased for use during a given time period. Most packages, however, are subject to restrictions governing the duration of the trip and require total payment by a given time before departure.

Tour programs generally can be divided into two categories — "escorted" and "independent" — depending on arrangements offered. An escorted tour means that a guide will accompany the group from the beginning of the tour through to return. On independent tours, you generally have a choice of hotels, meal plans, and sightseeing trips in each city as well as a variety of special excursions. The independent plan is for people who do not want a set itinerary but who prefer confirmed reservations. Whether you choose an escorted or independent tour, always bring along full contact information for your tour operator in case problems arise, although US tour operators often have Canadian affiliates who are available to give additional assistance or make other arrangements on the spot.

To determine whether a package — or more specifically, which package — fits your travel plans, start by evaluating your interests and needs, deciding how much and what you want to spend, see, and do. Gather whatever package tour information is available for your time schedule and read the brochure carefully to determine what is included. Be sure that you take the time to read the brochure *carefully.* Keep in mind that travel brochures are written to entice you into signing up for a package tour. Often the language is deceptive and devious. For example, a brochure may quote the lowest prices for a package tour based on facilities that are unavailable during the off-season, undesirable at any season, or just plain nonexistent. Information such as "breakfast included" or taxes (which can add up) are important items. Note, too, that prices quoted in brochures are almost always based on double occupancy. The rate listed is for each of two people sharing a double room, and if you travel alone, the supplement for single accommodations can raise the price considerably (see *Hints for Single Travelers*).

Increasingly, in this age of rapidly rising air fares, the brochure will *not* include the price of the airline ticket in the price of the package, though sample applicable fares from various gateway cities will usually be listed separately as extras to be added to the price of the ground arrangements. Before doing this, get the latest fares from the airline, because the samples will invariably be out of date by the time you read them. If the brochure gives more than one category of sample fares per gateway city — such as an individual tour-basing fare, an excursion or other discount fare, or a group fare — your travel agent or airline tour desk will be able to tell you which one applies to the package you choose, depending on when you travel, how far in advance you book, and other factors. (An individual tour-basing fare is a fare computed as part of a package that includes land arrangements, thereby entitling a carrier to reduce the air portion almost to the absolute minimum. Though it always represents a saving over full-fare coach or economy, lately it has not been as inexpensive as the excursion and other discount fares that are also available to individuals. The group fare is usually the least expensive fare, and it is the tour operator, not you, who makes up the group.) When the brochure does include round-trip transportation in the package price, don't forget to add the round-trip transportation cost from your home city to the departure city to come up with the total cost of the package.

Finally, read the responsibility clause (usually in fine print at the end of the descriptive literature) to determine the precise elements for which the tour operator is — and is not — liable. Here the tour operator frequently expresses the right to change services or schedules as long as equivalent arrangements are offered. This clause also absolves the operator of responsibility for circumstances beyond human control, such as hurricanes or forest fires, or injury to you or your property. In reading the brochure, ask the following:

1. Does the tour include air fare or other transportation, sightseeing, meals, transfers, taxes, baggage handling, tips, or any other services? Do you want all these services?
2. If the brochure indicates that "some meals" are included, does this mean a welcoming and farewell dinner, two breakfasts, or every evening meal?
3. What classes of hotels are offered? If you will be traveling alone, what is the single supplement?
4. Does the tour itinerary or price vary according to the season?
5. Are the prices guaranteed; that is, if costs increase between the time you book and the time you depart, can surcharges unilaterally be added?
6. Do you get a full refund if you cancel? If not, be sure to obtain cancellation insurance.
7. Can the operator cancel if too few people join?

One of the consumer's biggest problems is finding enough information to judge the reliability of a tour packager, since individuals seldom have direct contact with the firm putting the package together. Usually, a retail travel agent intervenes between customer and tour operator, and much depends on his or her candor and cooperation. So ask questions about the tour you are considering. For example: Has the agent ever used the package provided by this tour operator? How long has the tour operator been in business? Is the tour operator a member of the *United States Tour Operators Association (USTOA)?* (The *USTOA* will provide a list of its members upon request and also offers a useful brochure, *How to Select a Package Tour;* contact the USTOA, 211 E. 51st St., Suite 12B, New York, NY 10022; phone: 212-944-5727. Also check the Better Business Bureau in your area to see if any complaints have been filed against the operator.) Which and how many companies are involved in the package? If air travel is by charter flight, is there an escrow account in which deposits will be held, and, if so, what is the name of the bank?

This last question is very important. US law requires that tour operators deposit every charter passenger's deposit and subsequent payment in a proper escrow account.

Money paid into such an account cannot legally be used except to pay for the costs of a particular package or as a refund if the trip is canceled. To ensure the safe handling of your money, make your check payable to the escrow account — by law, the name of the depository bank appears in the operator-participant contract; it's usually found in that mass of minuscule type on the back of the brochure. Write the details of the charter, including the destination and dates, on the face of the check; on the back, print "For Deposit Only." Your travel agent may prefer that you make your check out to the agency, saying that it will then pay the tour operator the fee minus commission. But it is perfectly legal to write your check as we suggest, and if your agent objects too vociferously (the agent should have sufficient faith in the tour operator to trust him to send the proper commission), consider taking your business elsewhere. If you don't make your check out to the escrow account, you lose the protection of escrow should the trip be canceled or the tour operator or travel agent fail. Furthermore, recent bankruptcies in the travel industry have served to point out that even the protection of escrow may not be enough to safeguard a traveler's investment. Increasingly, insurance is becoming a necessity (see *Insurance*), and payment by credit card has become popular since it offers some additional safeguards if the tour operator defaults.

Be aware that US laws don't apply if you book a tour in Canada. The Canadian federal government has no jurisdiction over tour operators, and provincial laws vary. British Columbia, Ontario, and Quebec have consumer legislation that will protect a traveler's funds if a tour operator goes bankrupt. However, the other provinces have no such laws, and just what you should do if the operator fails and you're out a trip is distressingly unclear. To protect yourself as much as possible, book a tour only through an established, reputable agent. And remember that tours run in conjunction with the large airlines — Air Canada, Canadian Airlines International, Wardair, for instance — or *VIA Rail Canada* are among the safest bets.

Camping, Hiking, Biking, Recreational Vehicles

CAMPING: One of the major attractions of Canada is its size — vast wilderness areas from east to west. Camping is probably the best way to see the outdoors, and that can mean anything from backpacking with a small tent to living in comfort in a plush recreational vehicle. And, fortunately, in Canada campgrounds number in the thousands, some privately run, but most in national or provincial parks.

Where to Camp – The national and provincial park system has preserved some of Canada's most beautiful areas for the enjoyment of visitors. There are also some 80 historic parks and sites, administered by Parks Canada, in which Canada's cultural heritage can be experienced firsthand. Campsites are located in or near all these parks.

Camping facilities are also located along the Trans-Canada Highway, which stretches from St. John's, Newfoundland, to Victoria, British Columbia. There's a campground approximately every 100 miles and a picnic ground every 50 miles.

A good guide to help you locate campgrounds along your route is the *National Parks* brochure, which, in addition to providing a wealth of other information, details the parks' many and varied campgrounds. It's available free from the Canadian Parks Service, Ottawa, Ontario K1A 0H3 (phone: 819-997-2800). Another useful book is *Campground and Trailer Park Directory,* published by Rand McNally ($12.95). Wider in scope than the National Parks guide, it lists both government-run and privately run campgrounds in Canada. (The Rand McNally directory covers all of North America, including the US and Mexico, as well as Canada.) The provincial governments also publish guides to camping facilities, which are available free from the tourist office of each province or from national tourist offices. (See *Tourist Information* later in this section for addresses of provincial and national tourist offices.)

National parks have a variety of camping facilities, distinguished by the kind of camping experience they cater to and divided into five categories:

1. Tents and RVs: Most of the campgrounds do not have trailer hook-ups, although many have sewage disposal stations.
2. Tents: For tent campers only. Most campsites have level tent pads, picnic tables, fireplaces or grills, parking places for cars, nearby water sources, and toilet buildings with shower facilities.
3. Primitive: Pit privies, potable water, fireplaces and firewood, and, in some cases, wood stoves and communal kitchen shelters. Often these sites must be reached by a good hike or by boat.
4. Group Tenting: Campgrounds for organized groups which must be reserved in advance.
5. Winter Camping: Those campgrounds open for winter use, some with heated toilet facilities and enclosed kitchen shelters.

For general information on Canada's national parks, see *National Parks,* DIVERSIONS.

Campsites in most Canadian parks are all assigned on a first-come, first-served basis with no advance reservations except for group tenting areas. No one may camp longer than 2 weeks in a national park; the maximum allowed at provincial campgrounds varies with the province. All campgrounds in national parks are open from May to September, and because of the increasing popularity of winter camping, there's at least one campground open all winter long in most national parks. Fees range from $6 to $15 (CN), depending on location, services offered, and time of year.

Necessities – Remember, first, that mosquitoes and blackflies are at their worst from early June to July in Canada, so be sure to bring along plenty of insect repellant. The farther north you camp the more annoying the bugs become. When you are in open areas or actually on the water, however, they are not a serious problem.

For outdoor camping, necessities include a tent with flyscreens (the lighter and easier to carry and assemble the better), a sleeping bag, a foam pad or air mattress, a waterproof ground cloth, first-aid kit (including sunscreen), sewing and toiletry kits, backpack stove (building fires is prohibited in many areas, especially during dry periods), fuel (particularly where there is little wood, as in the Arctic), matches, nested cooking pots and cooking utensils, canteen, three-quarter ax (well-sharpened and sheath-protected), jackknife, and flashlight with an extra set of batteries.

Keep food simple. Unless backpacking deep into the wilderness, you will probably be close enough to a store to stock up on perishables; staples such as sugar, coffee, and powdered milk can be carried along. Most parks do not allow glass or tin containers. Dehydrated food has consequently become more popular, but it is also more expensive. An economical option for the more enterprising camper is to dry a variety of food at home; camping supply stores and bookstores carry cookbooks covering this simple process. Keep in mind that many forest rangers warn about the dangers of leaving food in an area accessible to animals, repeating countless stories of scavenging bears and other wildlife invading tents and vehicles. As a basic safety precaution, it is advisable to hang foodstuffs from a tree some distance from your sleeping area.

Organized Trips – Interesting nature interpretation programs are held at all national parks, with walks or car tours, exhibits, and nightly talks or slide shows. If you want to go farther afield with an experience guide and other campers, camping trips are available through a number of organizations including the following:

GETTING READY / Camping, Hiking, Biking 43

Alpine Club of Canada, PO Box 1026, Banff, Alberta T0L 0M0 (phone: 403-762-4481)

Federation of Ontario Naturalists, 355 Lesmill Rd., Don Mills, Ontario M3B 2W8 (phone: 416-444-8419)

REI Adventures, PO Box 8090, Berkeley, CA 94707 (phone: 800-622-2236 nationwide except California; 800-624-2236 in California; 415-526-4005 in Canada). Offers trips to the Yukon only.

Sierra Club of Western Canada, Rm. 314-620 View St., Victoria, BC V8W 1J6 (phone: 604-386-5255)

HIKING: If you would rather eliminate all the gear and planning and take to the outdoors unencumbered, park the car and go for a day's hike. Canada is blessed with beautiful hiking trails. One good guide to them is *The Canadian Rockies Trail Guide: A Hiker's Manual to the National Parks,* by Bart Robinson and Brian Patton (Summerthought Publishing, PO Box 1420, Banff, Alberta T0L 0C0; $11). Also useful is a series of recreation maps detailing hiking, as well as cross-country and downhill skiing trails, put out by the Outdoor Recreation Council of British Columbia, Suite 334, 1367 W. Broadway, Vancouver BC V6H 4A9. (See *Hiking and Backpacking,* DIVERSIONS, for a park-by-park discussion of trails.)

To make outings safe and pleasant, find out in advance about the trails you plan to hike and be realistic about your own physical limitations. Choose an easy route if you are out of shape. Stick to defined trails unless you are an experienced hiker or know the area well. If it is at all wild, let someone know where you are going and when you expect to be back, at least by leaving a note on your car if the hike is impromptu.

All you need to set out are a pair of sturdy shoes and socks, jeans or long pants to protect your legs, a canteen of water, a hat to protect you from the sun, and, if you like, a picnic lunch. It is a good idea to dress in layers, so that you can add or remove clothing according to the elevation and weather. Make sure, too, to wear clothes with pockets or bring a pack to keep your hands free. Some useful and important pocket- or pack-stuffers include trail mix, jackknife, first-aid kit, map, compass, and sunglasses. In areas where snakes are common, include a snakebite kit.

An increasingly popular pastime with hikers is trail riding. Even if you've never ridden a horse before, you can enjoy the outdoor experience of trail riding in the Canadian Rockies. When you book an organized tour from any of the several operators specializing in foothill and mountain trail rides, they'll take your riding experience into account. On a typical trail ride, an experienced guide takes the group along trails opened up by early explorers. You'll see mountain majesty as you've never seen it from the highway or campsite. These trips average about 5 days and are available as packages. Contact the Alberta or British Columbia provincial tourist offices for more information and the names of the tour operators. For more information on all sorts of wilderness experiences, see *Hiking and Backpacking,* DIVERSIONS.

BIKING: In choosing bike routes, long or short, look for ways to escape the omnipresent automobile and its fumes and noise. Stick to side roads; use provincial highway maps which list secondary roads that the gasoline company maps often ignore. An excellent resource is the *Canadian Cycling Association (CCA),* an umbrella organization of provincial cycling groups. The *CCA* is the distributor of *The Great Canadian Bicycle Trail* (available as three regional trail guides for $5.35 each or as a three-volume set for $15). Other useful books published by the association are *The Complete Guide to Bicycling in Canada* ($12.65), *The Canadian Rockies Bicycling Guide* ($8.75), *The British Columbia Bicycling Guide* ($7.80), and *Backcountry Biking in the Canadian Rockies* ($11.70) — these prices all include postage and handling. To order these books or for a copy of *CAA*'s free brochure listing its publications as well as those of its member groups, contact CAA, 1600 James Naismith Dr., Gloucester, Ontario K1B

5N4 (phone: 613-748-5629). For general biking information, try *The Complete Book of Bicycling* by Eugene A. Sloane (Simon & Schuster; $24.95) and *Anybody's Bike Book* by Tom Cuthbertson (Ten Speed Press; $7.95 paperback).

Road Safety – While the car may be the bane of cyclists, cyclists who do not follow the rules of the road strike terror into the hearts of automobile drivers. Follow the same rules and regulations as motor vehicle drivers. Stay to the right side of the road. Ride no more than two abreast — single file where traffic is heavy. Keep three bicycle lengths behind the cycle in front of you. Stay alert to sand, gravel, potholes, and wet or oily surfaces, all of which can make you lose control. Wear bright clothes and use lights or wear reflective material at dusk or at night, and, above all, always wear a helmet.

Choosing and Renting a Bike – Although many bicycling enthusiasts choose to take along their own bikes, in Canada there are five basic types of bicycle available for rent: the children's fun bike, the domestic one-gear bike, the three-gear bike with caliper brakes, the touring bike with dropped handlebars and 5, 10, or even 15 gears, and the lightweight competition bike. A bicycle is the correct size for you if you can straddle its center bar with feet flat on the ground and still have an inch or so between your crotch and the bar. (Nowadays, because women's old-fashioned barless bikes are not as strong as men's, most women use men's bicycles.) The seat height is right if your leg is just short of completely extended when you push the pedal to the bottom of its arc. Experienced cyclists keep the tires fully inflated (pressure requirements vary widely, but are always imprinted on the side of the tire; stay within 5 pounds of the recommended pressure) and pedal at an even pace. For roadside repairs, and especially on longer rides, carry a tool kit that contains a bike wrench, screwdriver, pliers, tire repair kit, cycle oil, and work gloves. All are available in any bike shop.

To be completely comfortable, divide your weight; put about 50% on your saddle and about 25% on your arms and legs. To stop sliding in your seat and for better support, set your saddle level. A firm saddle is better than a soft springy one for a long ride. Do not use top, or tenth, gear all the way; for most riding the middle gears are best. On long rides remember that until you are very fit, short efforts with rests in between are better than one long haul.

If you are planning to travel by plane to Canada with your bicycle, be sure to check with the airline beforehand. The airline may require that the bike be partially dismantled and packaged and, although most carriers have procedures for handling such special baggage, you will probably have to pay for transport regardless of how much other baggage you have checked. As with other baggage, make sure that the bike is thoroughly labeled with your name, a business address and phone number, and the correct airport destination code (for further information see *Traveling by Plane* in this section).

Tours – Cycling is a pleasant way to take in the summer scenery and get some exercise at the same time. In recent years, the cycling scene has considerably expanded in Canada to include everything from competition rallies to 3-week guided tours of Nova Scotia or the mountains of western Canada. *Rocky Mountain Cycle Tours* (PO Box 1978, Canmore, Alberta T0L 0M0; phone: 403-678-6770) offers high-country bikers a full range of tours lasting 1, 6, and 14 days. The 6-day camping tour from Banff to Jasper passes through some of the most spectacular scenery in the Canadian Rockies. Participants have a choice of camping (5 nights in tents, 1 night in a lodge) for $550, or hotels for all 6 nights ($775, per person, double occupancy). Prices include all meals, camping fees, guide service, and all equipment except sleeping bags, which cost an extra $20; bike rentals are also extra and are available for $80 for the 6 days. Most provincial cycling associations either offer tours or have information on what is available. Look under "Associations" in major city yellow pages for addresses, or contact the *Canadian Cycling Association* (address above), which can direct you to provincial groups sponsoring trips.

GETTING READY / Camping, Hiking, Biking 45

RECREATIONAL VEHICLES: The term *recreational vehicle* — RV — is applied to all manner of camping vehicles, whether towed or self-propelled. The level of comfort in an RV is limited only by the amount of money you choose to spend. They range from simple fold-down campers providing shelter similar to a large tent to luxurious RVs, fully equipped homes on wheels, requiring electrical hook-ups at night to run the TV set and kitchen appliances.

RVs will appeal most to the kind of person who prefers the flexibilty of accommodation — there are countless private, state, and national campgrounds throughout the country that provide RV hookups — and enjoys camping with a little extra comfort. An RV undoubtedly saves a traveler a great deal of money on accommodations and, if cooking appliances are part of the unit, on food as well. However, it is important to remember that buying or renting an RV is a major expense; also, any kind of RV increases gas consumption considerably.

Be aware that there are limits on the size of towed RVs (trailers) allowed on Canadian roads, so before you go, it is wise to check the regulations for the provinces you plan to visit. For instance, in Ontario, the maximum length allowed for a trailer is 48 feet (75 feet for trailer plus car). Should your combination of vehicles and load exceed this limit, you must secure an Oversize Permit from the Oversize/Overweight Permit Office of the Ministry of Transportation and Communication, 2680 Keele St., Main Fl., East Building, Downsview, Ontario M3M 1J8 (phone: 416-750-3407). For other provinces, contact the same department in the provincial capital.

US citizens generally need no permit to bring a car or trailer into Canada. If a customs official suspected a vehicle were being brought in for good, he might impose a maximum 12-month stay and require a deposit, which would be refunded when the vehicle left the country. But this happens rarely. You must carry motor vehicle registration forms and, if the vehicle is rented, a copy of the rental contract stipulating use in Canada. If you are driving a car not registered in your name, carry a letter from the registered owner authorizing you to use it.

Vehicles from all countries other than the US, transported directly to Canada by air or sea, must be thoroughly washed or otherwise treated to remove all soil, and an affidavit or declaration to that effect must accompany the vehicle. This mandate includes vehicles arriving by ferry from Newfoundland. (Vehicles arriving in the US must on arrival meet the same requirements and are similarly inspected by US officials.) All drivers' licenses, including international licenses, are valid in Canada.

Towable RVs – Tow vehicles are hitched to cars or trucks and pulled. At their simplest, they are fold-down campers — tents on wheels that unfold into sleeping spaces. Fold-down camping trailers weigh about 1,100 pounds and cost between $1,500 and $8,000, with an average price of $4,000. More elaborate are travel trailers, 10 to 30 feet long (average is about 22 feet), weighing up to 10,000 pounds and costing from $5,000 to $37,000, with an average price of $12,500. Fifth-wheel models, built to be towed by a pickup truck, range in price from $9,000 to $36,000, with an average price of $17,700. The park trailer, designed for seasonal or temporary living, sleeps up to 8 people and costs $14,000 to $26,000, with an average price of $16,900. The trailer should be equipped with brakes unless you expect that the combined weight of the trailer and its load will never exceed 3,000 pounds.

The *Canadian Recreational Vehicle Association* (670 Bloor St. W., Toronto, Ontario M6G 1L2; phone: 416-533-7800) represents manufacturers of all types of Canadian Standards Association-certified RVs. *AAA* and its Canadian equivalents can provide good booklets on trailers.

Motorized RVs – There are two styles of motorized recreational vehicles:

1. The motor home is a recreational vehicle built on or as part of a motorized vehicle chassis. It usually has kitchen, dining, bathroom, and sleeping facilities, all accessi-

ble from the driver's area. Electricity, heat, air conditioning, water, and propane-gas systems are generally included. Prices for compact models average $30,000; larger, more luxurious models cost an average of $51,000.
2. Van conversions are vans manufactured by auto makers and modified for recreation by customization specialists. Among the custom features are side windows, carpeting, paneling, and sofas. These vehicles, which usually sleep 2 to 4 but have no cooking facilities, sell for an average of $20,000.
3. Also in this category are truck-campers — camping units that are loaded onto the bed of a pickup. They sleep 2 to 6, often have kitchen facilities, and range in price from $2,000 to $10,000. This may seem like the most economical option of the three, however, keep in mind that this cost is in addition to the initial investment in the pickup truck.

Gas Consumption – Although an RV does save the traveler a great deal of money on on food and accommodations, the major expense in operating any RV is its high gas consumption. At the time of this writing, this substantial expense is of particular concern when budgeting for travel in Canada, as recent Canadian gas prices have sky-rocketed to as much as 50% to 60% over US prices.

It is most expensive to tow a large trailer camper, which decreases auto mileage by 50%. More economical, because it's smaller, is the fold-down tow camper, which will reduce normal car mileage by only about 10 to 15%. Self-propelled RVs have no better mileage records. A truck camper gets about 20% less mileage than the same truck without a camper, and an average Class A motorhome gets only 7 to 12 miles per gallon of gas. (Remember that gas in Canada is generally sold in liters, and you must adjust calculations accordingly.) Only in a converted van will you find that your gas consumption does not change too drastically.

To reduce gas consumption, travel lightly (for every 100 pounds of weight, you use 1% more gas). Carry only the water you need on the road. Put everything inside your RV to reduce wind resistance, and thereby save on gas.

Renting – RVs are a poor choice for people who do not like to drive. They are also not for people who want to leave housekeeping chores behind when they set off on vacation. They are sure to sour a person who cannot stand to do any maintenance or simple handyman chores, nor are they for people who need lots of privacy. The best way to introduce yourself to traveling by RV is to rent one. Some dealers will apply rental fees to the eventual price of purchase (check the yellow pages, then shop around for the best terms). There are numerous dealers throughout Canada, and some provincial tourist offices, such as Ontario Travel and Tourism British Columbia, publish guides listing these dealers. (See *Tourist Information* later in this section for addresses.)

When renting in Canada, bear the following in mind: Companies often require several months' notice in peak periods, so make inquiries as early as possible. Insurance, mileage costs, and the provincial sales tax should be discussed at the time of booking. Advance deposits and rental costs vary and usually are based on a weekly rate with an additional cost per kilometer, depending on the season and the lavishness of the motorhome. A truck-camper rental may be as much as 50% less per week than a luxury motorhome rental.

A complimentary packet of information on how to operate, maintain, choose, and use a recreational vehicle is available from the *Recreational Vehicle Industry Association,* PO Box 2999, Reston, VA 22090. You might also want to subscribe to *Trailer Life,* published by *TL Enterprises* (29901 Agoura Rd., Agoura, CA 91301; phone: 818-991-4980). A 1-year subscription costs $11.98; *TL Enterprises* also provides discounts on a variety of services for RV owners. For further information on how to operate, choose, and use a recreational vehicle, see Richard A. Wolters' *Living on Wheels* (Dutton; currently out of print; check your library or bookstore).

Preparing

Calculating Costs

The value of the Canadian dollar relative to the US dollar has made Canada an attractive destination for Americans in recent years. Toronto and Montreal, Canada's most expensive cities, have prices approaching, but still less than, those of major US cities; generally speaking, prices in Canada's medium-size cities and small towns also compare favorably to US prices in equivalent places.

Estimating the cost of travel expenses in Canada depends on the mode of transportation chosen, what part of the country you plan to visit, how long you will stay there, and, in some cases, what time of the year you plan to travel. In addition to the basics of transportation, hotels, meals, and sightseeing, you have to take into account seasonal price changes that apply on certain air routings and at popular vacation destinations as well as inflation, price fluctuations, and the vagaries of currency exchange. So, while the price guidelines in this book will remain useful, costs for both facilities and services may have changed somewhat in the months since publication.

DETERMINING A BUDGET: A realistic appraisal of your travel expenses is the most crucial bit of planning you will undertake before any trip. It is also, unfortunately, one for which it is most difficult to give precise, practical advice. Travel styles are intensely personal, and personal taste determines cost to a great extent. Will you stay in a hotel every night and eat every meal in a restaurant, or are you planning to do some camping and picnicking, thus reducing your daily expenses? Base your calculations on your own travel style, and make estimates of expenses from that. If published figures on the cost of travel were always taken as gospel, many trips would not be taken. But in reality, it's possible to economize. On the other hand, don't be lulled into feeling that it's not necessary to do some arithmetic before you go. No matter how generous your travel budget, without careful planning beforehand — and strict accounting along the way — you will spend more than you anticipated.

When calculating costs, start with the basics, the major expenses being transportation, accommodations, and food. However, don't forget such extras as local transportation, shopping, and miscellaneous items such as laundry, taxes, and tips.

There are regional differences in prices in Canada, although they tend to be between rural and urban areas. Based on a national average, which is nonetheless somewhat arbitrary, you can get an indication of the regional differences. Remember that Canada is not a country of averages, since its population is so small relative to that of the US. Also, 90% of the Canadian population lives within 200 miles of the US.

If you spend every night in a hotel or motel and eat every meal in a modestly priced restaurant, you can expect to spend around $75 per person per day traveling. This figure does not include transportation costs, but it does include accommodations (based on two people sharing a room), three meals, some sightseeing, and other modest entertainment costs. The accommodations take into consideration the differences between motels in rural areas (about $40 per night for two) and moderate hotels in urban areas (about $65 per night for two). Meals are all calculated for inexpensive restaurants, and the entertainment normally includes one sightseeing tour and admission to one museum or historic site. These figures are based on averages compiled by travel sources across the country.

Adjusted for regional price differences, the $75-per-person-per-day figure can be useful. For instance, overall prices in rural areas such as the British Columbia interior, the Maritimes, Southern Ontario, the prairies, and Southern Quebec are the lowest in the country — about 10% less than the national figure. Travel in major cities such as Toronto, Montreal, Calgary, Edmonton, and Vancouver costs about 20% more. The travel cost for medium-size cities such as Halifax, Hamilton, Quebec City, London, Regina, Saskatoon, and Winnipeg runs about 10% more than average. In remote areas (more than 250 miles north of the US border) such as the Northwest Territories, Northern Ontario, Northern Quebec, and the Yukon, expect to pay as much as 15% more.

You should be able to use these averages to forecast a reasonably accurate picture of your daily travel costs, based on exactly how you want to travel. As you can see, savings on the daily allowance can occur while motoring in rural areas; budgeting families can take advantage of very inexpensive guesthouse accommodations in the Maritime Provinces. Campgrounds in national and provincial parks and on private land are located across the country and are a particularly inexpensive way to see rural Canada.

In planning your budget, it is also wise to allow a realistic amount for both entertainment and recreation. Are you planning to spend time sightseeing and going to local museums? Do you intend to spend your days skiing at a popular resort? Is daily tennis a part of your plan? Will your children be disappointed if they don't take a whale watching cruise? If so, charges for these attractions and recreations must be taken into account.

When estimating costs for eating out, don't forget to include 15% on your total restaurant bill for tipping. Additionally, most provinces (the Northwest Territories and the Yukon are two exceptions) have sales tax on most items, including food and lodging. Quebec, however, doesn't impose a separate tax on accommodations. If you spend over $100 CN (Canadian) on goods in Ontario, you will be eligible for a refund of provincial sales tax. Forms to use when applying for the refund are available at retail shops throughout the province.

Picnicking is another excellent way to cut costs. Most provinces have major scenic highways with well-maintained rest areas equipped with log tables and benches, trash cans, and sometimes fireplaces, running water, and toilets. A stop at a grocery store or supermarket can save you quite a bit compared to a restaurant lunch.

If at any point in the planning process it appears impossible to estimate expenses, consider this suggestion: The easiest way to put a ceiling on the price of some or all of the above is to buy a travel package. A totally planned and escorted one, with almost all transportation, rooms, meals, sightseeing, local travel, tips, and a dinner show or two included and prepaid, allows you to know beforehand almost exactly what the trip will cost, and the only surprise will be the one you spring on yourself by succumbing to some irresistible, expensive souvenir.

The various types of packages available are discussed under *Package Tours* in this section, but a few points bear repeating here. Not all packages are package *tours*. There are loosely organized arrangements including nothing more than a stay at a hotel, transfers between hotel and airport, baggage handling, taxes, and tips, which leave the entire matter of how you spend your time and where you eat your meals — and with whom — up to you. Equally common are the hotel-plus-car packages, which take care of accommodations and local transportation. On such independent or hosted "tours," there may be a tour company representative available at a local office to answer questions, or a company host may be stationed at a desk in the hotel to arrange optional excursions, but you will never have to travel in a group unless you wish to. More and more, even experienced travelers are being won over to the idea of package travel, not only for the convenience and planning time saved, but above all for the money saved. Whatever elements you choose in your package, the organizer has gotten them for you wholesale, and they are prepaid, thus eliminating the dismal prospect of returning to your hotel room each night to subtract the day's disbursements from your remaining cash.

TRANSPORTATION: In earlier sections of GETTING READY TO GO we have discussed the comparative costs of different modes of transportation and the myriad special travel rates available through package tours, charter flights, and train and bus budget deals. See each of the relevant sections for specific information. Transportation is likely to represent the largest item in your travel budget in a country as vast as Canada, but the encouraging aspect of this is that you will be able to determine most of these costs before you leave. Most fares will have to be paid in advance, particularly if you take advantage of charter air travel or other special deals.

Air fare is really the easiest cost to pin down precisely, though the range and variety of flights available may be confusing initially. The possibilities are outlined fully in *Traveling by Plane*. Essentially the traveler can choose from various types of tickets on scheduled flights, ranging in expense from first class and excursion fares to discount tickets and charters.

Except for breakdowns or repairs (for which you should budget something), car costs can be calculated by figuring mileage, based upon your own experience, and average gas prices. When estimating, remember that in Canada gasoline is now sold metrically, in liters. Also, at press time, gas prices were about 50% to 60% more expensive in Canada than in the US, so be sure to take this substantial expense into account.

FOOD: Meals are a more difficult expense to estimate. If you stay in a condominium or are camping out, you will be able to prepare some meals yourself. Depending on where you're staying, groceries can be more expensive than they are at home, but they will certainly be less expensive than eating out. Independent travelers eating all their meals in restaurants should allow roughly $60 to $80 a day per couple for food. That includes breakfast (about $10 to $15 for two), lunch (about $15 to $20 for two), and an average dinner for two in a moderate, neither-scrimp-nor-splurge restaurant, not including alcoholic beverages or tips. You could easily add a beer and a glass of house wine to the dinner tab without wreaking havoc with these figures, but if you want the pick of the wine list or have a tendency to order lobster, expect the check, even in a moderate establishment, to run much higher. A steady diet of better restaurants will drive the average up higher still, but the figures can be revised downward, too, if you choose fruit for breakfast rather than bacon and eggs, put together your own picnic lunches for the beach, and frequently visit fast-food outlets. In general, however, you can expect to pay less at a Canadian restaurant than at an American restaurant of equal quality. Our restaurant selections, chosen to give the best value for money — whether expensive or dirt cheap — are listed in the *Eating Out* section of each city chapter.

ACCOMMODATIONS: There is a wide range of choice and a substantial difference in degrees of luxury provided among the expensive, moderate, and inexpensive hotels. Generally, the member hotels of international chains in any given city are priced roughly equally. In the larger cities, such as Quebec and Toronto, this ranges from around $120 and up, although similar hotels elsewhere range from about $90 to $110 for a double. There is a big jump from these international class hotels to those in the moderate category in the same cities, and accommodations will generally be about $20 to $45 less per night. Inexpensive, yet acceptable hotels in major cities charge about $50 for a double room. In small towns and rural areas, these price ranges will be substantially lower. Also watch for budget motels designed to offer basic (but acceptable) accommodations at especially economical prices, where a double room may cost as little as $20 to $30. When inquiring about hotel rates, be certain to ask if they include local taxes and service charges. It also is wise to note that rates will likely be quoted in Canadian dollars, so it will be necessary to convert costs to US dollars to budget accurately. For specific information on accommodations throughout Canada, see *Best In Town,* THE CITIES, and *Best En Route,* DIRECTIONS.

In addition to standard hotel accommodations, other alternatives include a wide range of camping facilities, rural inns, bed-and-breakfast establishments, and package options including resorts catering to a variety of special interests and vacations on farms and ranches. For information on these and other adventures across Canada, see DIVERSIONS.

Should you require more advance information on hotels, contact the provincial tourist offices. Each provincial tourist office provides a comprehensive accommodations guide describing all licensed establishments in its territory. The most reliable restaurant listings (detailing costs, menus, and so on) are usually found in the weekly and monthly city magazines that are published in most major Canadian cities. Again, provincial tourist offices can be of some assistance. (For a list of provincial tourist offices, see *Tourist Information* in this section.)

■ **A note on our hotel/restaurant cost categories:** There are a great many moderate and inexpensive hotels and restaurants which we have not included in this book. Our *Best in Town* and *Best en Route* listings include only those places we think are best in their price range. We have rated our listings by general price categories: expensive, moderate, and inexpensive. The introductory paragraph of each listing explains just what those categories mean within the context of local prices.

Planning a Trip

Travelers fall into two categories: those who make lists and those who do not. Some people prefer to plot the course of their trip to the finest detail, with contingency plans and alternatives at the ready. For others, the joy of a voyage is its spontaneity; exhaustive planning only lessens the thrill of anticipation and the sense of freedom.

For most travelers, however, a week-plus trip is too expensive for an "I'll take my chances" type of vacation. Even perennial gypsies and anarchistic wanderers have to take into account the logistics of getting around, and even with minimal baggage, they need to think about packing. Hence at least some planning is crucial. This is not to suggest that you work out your itinerary in minute detail before you go, however, you still have to decide certain basics at the very start: where to go, what to do, and how much to spend. These decisions require a certain amount of forethought, consideration, and planning. So before rigorously planning specific travel-related details, you might want to establish your general travel objectives:

1. How much time do you have for the entire trip and how much of it are you willing to spend getting where you're going?
2. What interests and/or activities do you want to pursue while on vacation? Do you want to visit one, a few, or many different places?
3. At what time of year do you want to go?
4. What kind of geography or climate would you prefer?

5. Do you want peace and privacy or lots of action and company?
6. How much money can you spend for the entire vacation?

Obviously, your answers will be determined by your personal tastes and lifestyle. These will condition the degree of comfort you require; whether you will select a tour or opt for total independence; and how much responsibility you want to take for your own arrangements (or whether you want everything arranged for you, with the kinds of services provided in a comprehensive package trip).

There is a good deal of travel information available on Canada. You can turn to travel agents, who specialize in planning and arranging trips (see *How to Use a Travel Agent*, in this section), to travel clubs such as *AAA* and other motoring organizations that have tour centers, and to general travel sources like books, guidebooks, brochures, and maps. Brochures and maps distributed by city and provincial tourism offices are of inestimable value (for a complete list of provincial tourism offices see *Tourist Information* in this section; city tourist offices are listed in the individual city reports of THE CITIES).

You can now make almost all of your own travel arrangements if you have the time to follow through with hotels, airlines, tour operators, and so on. But you'll probably save considerable time and energy if you have a travel agent make the reservations and arrangements for you. The agent also should be able to advise you of alternative arrangements of which you may not be aware. Only rarely will a travel agent's services cost a traveler any money, and they may even save you some (see *How to Use a Travel Agent*). Well before departure (depending on how far in advance you make your reservations), the agent will deliver a packet that includes all your tickets and hotel confirmations and often a day-by-day outline of where you'll be when, along with a detailed list of whatever flights you're taking.

Make plans early. During the summer season and on American holidays, make hotel reservations at least a month in advance in all major cities. If you are flying at these times, and hope to take advantage of the considerable savings offered through discount fares or charter programs, purchase tickets as far in advance as possible. Ski season — from November to April — is another busy time, especially in the Canadian Rockies and in the mountains north and south of Montreal. The more specific your requirements, the further in advance you should book. Many hotels require deposits before they will guarantee reservations. Be sure you have a receipt for any deposit.

While making vacation arrangements is fun and exciting, don't forget to prepare for your absence from home. Before you leave, attend to these household matters:

1. Arrange for your mail to be forwarded, held by the post office, or picked up daily at your house. Someone should check your door occasionally to pick up any unexpected deliveries. Piles of mail or packages announce to thieves that no one is home.
2. Cancel all deliveries (newspapers, milk, and so on).
3. Arrange for the lawn to be mowed and plants to be watered at regular intervals.
4. Arrange for the care of pets.
5. Etch your social security number in a prominent place on all appliances (television sets, radios, cameras, kitchen appliances). This considerably reduces their appeal to thieves and facilitates identification.
6. Leave a house key, your itinerary, and your automobile license number (if you are driving your own car) with a relative or friend. Notify the police, the building manager, or a neighbor that you are leaving and tell them who has the key and itinerary.
7. Empty the refrigerator and lower the thermostat.
8. Immediately before leaving, check that all doors, windows, and garage doors are securely locked.

To discourage thieves further, it is wise to set up several variable timers around the house so that lights and even the television set go on and off several times in different rooms each night.

Make a list of any valuable items you are carrying with you, including credit card numbers and the serial numbers of your traveler's checks. Put copies in your purse, or pocket, and leave copies at home. Put a label with your name and home address on the inside of your luggage to facilitate identification in case of loss. Put your name and business address — *never your home address* — on a label on the outside of your luggage.

Review your travel documents. If you are traveling by air, check to see that your ticket has been filled in correctly. The left side of the ticket should have a list of each stop you will make (even if you are only stopping to change planes), beginning with your departure point. Be sure that the list is correct, and count the number of carbons to see that you have one for each plane you will take. If you have confirmed reservations, be sure that the column marked "status" says "OK" beside each flight. Have in hand vouchers or proof of payment for any reservations for which you've paid in advance; this includes hotels, transfers to and from the airport, sightseeing tours, car rentals, and special events.

If you are traveling by car, bring your driver's license, automobile registration, proof of insurance, gasoline credit cards and auto service card (if you have them), maps, guidebooks, flashlight, an extra set of batteries, emergency flasher, container of water, jack and spare tire, first-aid kit, extra car keys, and sunglasses. (For more information on preparing your car, see *Touring by Car* in this section.)

If you are traveling by plane, call to reconfirm your flight 72 hours before departure, both going and returning. However, this will not prevent you from getting bumped in case the flight is overbooked; see *Traveling by Plane*.

Finally, you should always bear in mind that despite the most careful plans, things do not always occur on schedule. If you maintain a flexible attitude at all times, shrug cheerfully in the face of postponements and cancellations, you will enjoy yourself a lot more.

How to Use a Travel Agent

A reliable travel agent remains your best source of service and information for planning a trip, whether you have prepared a specific itinerary and require an agent only to make reservations, or need extensive help in sorting through the maze of air fares, tour offerings, hotel packages, and the score of other elements that may be involved in your trip.

You should know what you want from a travel agent so that you can evaluate what you are getting. It is perfectly reasonable to expect your travel agent to be a thoroughly knowledgeable travel specialist, with information about your destination and, even more crucial, a command of current air fares, ground arrangements, and other wrinkles in the travel scene. Most travel agents work through computer reservations systems (CRS) to assess the availability and rates of flights, hotels, and car rental firms, and can book reservations through the CRS. Despite reports of "computer bias," in which a computer may favor one airline over another, the CRS should provide agents with the entire spectrum of alternative flights to a destination and the complete range of fares in considerably less time than it takes to telephone the airlines individually — and at no extra charge to the client.

To make the most intelligent use of a travel agent's time and expertise, you should know something of the economics of the industry. As a client, traditionally you pay nothing for the agent's services; with few exceptions, it's all free, from hotel bookings to advice on package tours and the best hunting lodges. Any money the travel agent makes on the time spent arranging your itinerary — booking hotels, resorts, or flights, or suggesting activities — comes from commissions paid by the suppliers of these services — the airlines, hotels, and so on. These commissions generally run from about 8 to 20% of the total cost of the service, although suppliers often reward agencies that sell their services in volume with an increased commission called an override.

Among the few exceptions to the general rule of free service by a travel agency are the agencies beginning to practice *net pricing*. In essence, travel agencies operating this way return all of their commissions and overrides to their customers and make their income instead by charging a flat fee per transaction (thus adding a charge after a reduction has been made). Sometimes the rebate from the agent arrives later, in the form of a check. Net pricing has become rather controversial, however, since a major airline refused to do business with a leading proponent of it and the courts supported this action (see *Net Fare Sources*).

Net fares and fees are a very recent and not very widespread practice, but even a conventional travel agent may sometimes charge you a fee for such special services as long-distance telephone or cable costs incurred in making a booking, for reserving a room in a place that does not pay a commission (such as a small, out-of-the-way hotel), or for special attention such as planning a highly personalized itinerary. A fee may also be assessed in instances of deeply discounted air fares. In most instances, however, you'll find that travel agents make their time and experience available to you at no charge, and you do not pay more for an airline ticket, package tour, or other product bought from a travel agent than you would for the same product bought directly from the supplier.

This commission system implies two things about your relationship with an agent:

1. You will get better service if you arrive at the agent's desk with your basic itinerary already planned. Know roughly where you want to go, what you want to do, and how much you want to spend. Use the agent to make bookings (which pay commissions) and to advise you on facilities, activities, and alternatives within the limits of your basic itinerary. You get the best service when you are requesting commissionable items. Since there are few commissions on camping or driving-camping tours, an agent is unlikely to be very enthusiastic about helping to plan one. (If you have this type of trip in mind, most automobile clubs provide driving routes through Canada for their members.) The more vague your plans, the less direction you can expect from most agents. If you walk into an agency and say, "I have two weeks in June; what shall I do?" you will most likely walk out with nothing more than a handful of brochures. So do a little preliminary homework.
2. Be wary. There is always the danger that an incompetent or unethical agent will send you to a place offering the best commissions rather than the best facilities for your purposes. The only way to be sure you are getting the best service is to pick a good, reliable travel agent, one who knows where to go for information if he or she is unfamiliar with an area — although most agents are familiar with major destinations throughout Canada.

You should choose a travel agent with the same care with which you would choose a doctor or lawyer. You will be spending a good deal of money on the basis of the agent's judgment, so you have a right to expect that judgment to be mature, informed, and interested. At the moment, unfortunately, there aren't many standards within the travel agent industry to help you gauge competence, and the quality of individual agents varies enormously. At present, only seven states have registration, licensing, or other form of travel agent-related legislation on their books. Rhode Island licenses travel agents; Florida, Hawaii, and Ohio register them; and California, Illinois, and Washington have laws governing the sale of transportation or related services. While state licensing of agents cannot absolutely guarantee competence, it can at least ensure that an agent has met some minimum requirements.

Perhaps the best-prepared agents are those who have completed the CTC Travel Management program offered by the *Institute of Certified Travel Agents* and carry the initials CTC (Certified Travel Counselor) after their names. This indicates a relatively high level of expertise. For a free listing of CTCs in your area, send a self-addressed, stamped, #10 envelope to ICTA, 148 Linden St., Box 82-56, Wellesley, MA 02181 (phone: 617-237-0280).

An agent's membership in the *American Society of Travel Agents (ASTA)* can be a useful guideline in selecting a travel agent. But keep in mind that *ASTA* is an industry organization, requiring only that its members be licensed in those states where required; be accredited to represent the suppliers whose products they sell, including airline and cruise tickets; and be adherents to its Principles of Professional Conduct and Ethics code. *ASTA* does not guarantee the competence, ethics, or financial soundness of its members, but it does offer some recourse if you feel you have been dealt with unfairly. Complaints may be registered with ASTA, Consumer Affairs Department, PO Box 23992, Washington, DC 20026-3992 (phone: 703-739-2782). First try to resolve the complaint directly with the supplier. For a list of *ASTA* members in your area, send a self-addressed, stamped, #10 envelope to ASTA, Public Relations Dept., at the address above. There is also the *Association of Retail Travel Agents (ARTA),* a smaller but highly respected trade organization similar to *ASTA.* Its member agencies and agents similarly agree to abide by a Code of Ethics, and complaints about a member can be made to ARTA's Grievance Committee, 25 S. Riverside Ave., Croton-on-Hudson, NY 10520 (914-271-HELP).

Agencies listed with the *National Association of Cruise Only Agencies (NACOA)* have demonstrated professionalism in the selling of cruises. For a listing of cruise-only agencies in your state (requests are limited to three states), send a self-addressed, stamped envelope to NACOA, PO Box 7209, Freeport, NY 11520. Agencies that belong to a travel consortium, such as *Associated Travel Nationwide* and *Travel Trust International,* have access to preferred rates, as do the huge networks of *American Express* and *Ask Mr. Foster* travel agencies.

A number of banks own travel agencies, too. These provide the same services as other accredited commercial travel bureaus. Anyone can become a client, not only the bank's customers. You can find out more about these agencies, which belong to the *Association of Bank Travel Bureaus,* by inquiring at your bank or looking in the yellow pages.

Perhaps the best way to find a travel agent is by word of mouth. If the agent (or agency) has done a good job for your friends over a period of time, it probably indicates a certain level of commitment and competence. Always ask not only for the name of the company, but for the name of the specific agent with whom your friends dealt, for it is that individual who will serve you, and quality can vary widely within a single agency. There are some superb travel agents in the business, and they can facilitate vacation or business arrangements.

Once you've made an initial selection from those recommended, be entirely frank and candid with the agent. Budget considerations rank at the top of the candor list, and there's no sense in wasting the agent's (or your) time poring over itineraries that you know you can't afford. Similarly, if you like a fair degree of comfort, that fact should not be kept secret from your travel agent, who may assume that you wish to travel on a tight budget even when that's not the case.

Insurance

It is unfortunate that most decisions to buy travel insurance are impulsive and are usually made without any real consideration of the traveler's existing policies. Too often the result is the purchase of needlessly expensive short-term policies that duplicate existing coverage and reinforce the tendency to buy coverage on a trip-by-trip basis rather than to work out a total and continuing travel insurance package that might well be more effective and economical.

Therefore, the first person you should discuss travel insurance with is your own insurance broker, not a travel agent or the clerk behind the airport insurance counter. You may well discover that the insurance you already carry — homeowner's policies and/or accident, health, and life insurance — protects you adequately while you travel, and that your real needs are in the more mundane areas of excess value insurance for baggage or trip cancellation insurance.

To make insurance decisions intelligently, however, you should first understand the basic categories of travel insurance and what they are designed to cover. Then you can decide what you should have in the broader context of your personal insurance needs, and you can choose the most economical way of getting the desired protection: through riders on existing policies; with one-time short-term policies; through a special program put together for the frequent traveler; through coverage that's part of a travel club's benefits; or with a combination policy sold by insurance companies through brokers, automobile clubs, tour operators, and travel agents.

There are seven basic categories of travel insurance:

1. Baggage and personal effects insurance
2. Personal accident and sickness insurance
3. Trip cancellation and interruption insurance
4. Default and/or bankruptcy insurance
5. Flight insurance (to cover death or injury)
6. Automobile insurance (for driving your own or a rented car)
7. Combination policies

Baggage and Personal Effects Insurance – Ask your agent if baggage and personal effects are included in your current homeowner's policy or if you will need a special floater to cover you for the duration of a trip. The object is to protect your bags and their contents in case of damage or theft any time during your travels, not just while you're in flight and covered by the airline's policy. Furthermore, only limited protection is provided by the airline. Baggage liability varies from carrier to carrier, but generally speaking, for domestic air travel in the US, luggage is insured to $1,250 — that's per passenger, not per bag. On international flights on US carriers, the liability limit is $9.07 per pound of baggage (which comes to about $360 per 40-pound suitcase), and up to $400 per passenger for unchecked baggage. Canadian airlines insure baggage for up to a maximum of $750 (CN) on domestic flights and $640 (CN) on flights originating in the US that cross the Canadian border only. These limits should be specified on your airline ticket, but to be awarded even this amount, you'll have to provide an itemized list of lost property, and if you're including new and/or expensive items, be prepared for a request that you back up your claim with sales receipts or other proofs of purchase.

If you are driving your own car or a rental, check the protection necessary from damage or theft with your insurance agent. If traveling by bus or train, you may need more protection than is automatically included in the ticket as *VIA Rail* and Canadian bus companies provide only limited protection. *VIA Rail* takes responsibility for a maximum of $100 (CN) per passenger, as do some bus companies — check the fine print on every ticket.

If you are carrying goods worth more than the maximum protection offered by the airline, bus, or train company, you should consider excess value insurance. Additional coverage is available from the airlines at an average, currently, of $1 per $100 worth of coverage. This insurence can be purchased at the airline counter when you check in, though you should arrive early to fill out the necessary forms and avoid holding up other passengers checking in. You can also buy excess value insurance from *VIA Rail* and some bus lines. But either the cost is too high, as with *VIA Rail,* which bases cost on the ticket price and the baggage weight, or the maximum protection too low, as with *Greyhound Lines of Canada,* which will only accept liability for up to $50 (CN), so you would be wise to buy coverage elsewhere. Excess value insurance is also included in some of the combination travel insurance policies discussed below.

■**A note of warning:** Be sure to read the fine print of any excess value insurance policy; there are often specific exclusions, such as cash, tickets, furs, gold and silver objects, art, and antiques. And remember that insurance companies ordinarily will pay only the depreciated value of the goods rather than their replacement value. The best way to protect the items you're carrying in your luggage is to take photos of your valuables, and keep a record of the serial numbers of such items as cameras, typewriters, radios, and so on. This will establish that you do, indeed, own the objects. If your luggage disappears en route or is damaged, deal with the situation immediately, at the airport or bus station. If an airline loses your luggage, you will be asked to fill out a Property Irregularity Report before you leave the airport. If your property disappears at other transportation centers, tell the local company, but also report it to the police (since the insurance company will check with the police when processing the claim). When traveling by train in Canada, remember that often not all baggage is checked on your train; so your baggage may not be lost, just on the next train!

Personal Accident and Sickness Insurance – This covers you in case of illness during your trip or death in an accident. Most policies insure you for hospital and doctors' expenses, lost income, and so on. In most cases it is a standard part of existing health insurance policies, though you should check with your broker to be sure that your policy will pay for any medical expenses incurred abroad. If not, take out a separate vacation accident policy or an entire vacation insurance policy that includes health and life coverage.

Trip Cancellation and Interruption Insurance – Although modern public charters have eliminated many of the old advance booking requirements, most charter and package tour passengers still pay for their travel well in advance of departure. The disappointment of having to miss a vacation because of illness or any other reason pales before the awful prospect that not all (and sometimes none) of the money paid in advance might be returned. So cancellation insurance for any package tour is a must. Although cancellation penalties vary (they are listed in the fine print in every tour brochure, and before you purchase a package tour you should know exactly what they are), rarely will a passenger get more than 50% of this money back if forced to cancel within a few weeks of leaving. Therefore, if you book a package tour or charter flight, you should have trip cancellation insurance to guarantee full reimbursement or refund should you, a traveling companion, or a member of your immediate family get sick, forcing you to cancel your trip or *return home early.* The key here is *not* to buy just enough insurance to guarantee full reimbursement for the cost of the package or charter in case of cancellation. The proper amount of coverage should be sufficient to reimburse you for the cost of having to catch up with a tour after its departure or having to travel home at the full economy air fare if you have to forgo the return flight of your charter. There is usually quite a discrepancy between a charter air fare and the amount necessary to travel the same distance on a regularly scheduled flight at full economy fare.

Trip cancellation insurance is available from travel agents and tour operators in two forms: as part of a short-term, all-purpose travel insurance package (sold by the travel agent); or as specific cancellation insurance designed by the tour operator for a specific charter tour. Generally, tour operators' policies are less expensive, but also less inclusive. Cancellation insurance is also available directly from insurance companies or their agents as part of a short-term, all-inclusive travel insurance policy.

Before you decide which policy you want, read each one carefully. (Either can be purchased from a travel agent when you book the charter or package tour.) Be certain that the policy you select includes enough coverage to pay your fare from the farthest destination on your itinerary should you have to miss the charter flight. Also, be sure to check the fine print for stipulations concerning "family members" and "pre-existing medical conditions," as well as allowance for living expenses if you must delay your return due to bodily injury or illness.

Default and/or Bankruptcy Insurance – Although trip cancellation insurance usually protects you if you are unable to complete — or depart on — your trip, a fairly recent innovation is coverage in the event of default and/or bankruptcy on the part of the tour operator, airline, or other travel supplier. In some travel insurance packages this contingency is included in the trip cancellation portion of the coverage; in others, it is a separate feature. Either way, it is becoming increasingly important. Whereas sophisticated travelers have long known to beware of the possibility of default or bankruptcy when buying a charter flight or tour package, in recent years more than a few respected scheduled airlines have unexpectedly revealed their shaky financial condition, sometimes leaving hordes of stranded ticketholders in their wake. Moreover, the value of escrow protection of a charter passenger's funds has lately been unreliable. While default/bankruptcy insurance will not ordinarily result in reimbursement in time to pay for new arrangements, it can ensure that you will eventually get your money back, and even independent travelers buying no more than an airplane ticket may want to consider it.

Should this type of coverage be unavailable to you (state insurance regulations vary, there is a wide variation in price, and so on), the best bet is to pay for airline tickets and tour packages with a credit card. The federal Fair Credit Billing Act permits purchasers to refuse payment for credit card charges where services have not been delivered, so the potential onus of dealing with a receiver for a bankrupt airline falls on the credit card company. Do not assume that another airline will automatically honor the ticket you're holding on a bankrupt airline, since the days when virtually all major carriers subscribed to a default protection program are long gone. Some airlines may voluntarily step forward to accommodate stranded passengers, but this is now an entirely altruistic act.

Flight Insurance – US airlines have carefully established limits of liability for the death or injury of passengers. For international flights, they are printed right on the ticket: a maximum of $75,000 in case of death or injury. For domestic flights in the US, the limitation is established by state law, with a few states setting unlimited liability. Canadian airlines, like US carriers, have carefully established limits of liability; for domestic flights in Canada, the limitation varies from province to province. But remember, these limits of liability are not the same thing as insurance policies; they merely state the *maximum* an airline will pay in the case of death or injury, and every penny of that is usually subject to a legal battle.

This may make you feel that you are not adequately protected, but before you buy last-minute flight insurance from an airport vending machine, consider the purchase in light of your total existing insurance coverage. A careful review of your current policies may reveal that you are already amply covered for accidental death, sometimes up to three times the amount provided for by the flight insurance you're buying in the airport.

Be aware that airport insurance, the kind typically bought at a counter or from a vending machine, is among the most expensive forms of life insurance coverage available, and that even within a single airport, rates for approximately the same coverage vary widely. Often the vending machines are more expensive than coverage sold over the counter, even when policies are with the same national company.

If you buy your plane ticket with an American Express, Carte Blanche, or Diners Club credit card, you are automatically issued life and accident insurance at no extra cost. American Express automatically provides $100,000 in insurance; Carte Blanche provides $150,000 and Diners Club provides $350,000. Additional coverage can be obtained at extremely reasonable prices, but a cardholder must sign up for it in advance. With American Express, $4 per ticket buys an additional $250,000 worth of flight insurance; $6.50 buys $500,000 worth; and $13 provides an added $1 million worth of coverage. Carte Blanche and Diners Club each offer an additional $250,000 worth of insurance for $4; $500,000 for $6.50. Both also provide $1,250 free insurance — over and above what the airline will pay — for checked baggage that's lost or damaged. American Express provides $500 coverage for checked baggage; $1,250 for carry-ons.

Automobile Insurance – All drivers in Canada are required by law to have automobile insurance for their car. The minimum coverage is determined by provincial law, but this minimum is usually too low for adequate protection. Your insurance agents can advise you on the proper amount of insurance necessary. There are several kinds of coverage you should have in Canada:

1. *Liability Insurance:* This provides protection if you are sued for injuring someone or his property. US motorists driving in Canada should obtain a Canadian Non-Resident Inter-Provincial Motor Vehicle Liability Insurance Card, which provides evidence of financial responsibility by a valid automobile liability insurance policy. This card is available only in the US through insurance agents. All provinces in Canada require visiting motorists to produce evidence of financial responsibility should they be involved in an accident. Financial responsibility limits vary from $50,000 to $200,000 (CN) depending upon the province or territory. Information and advice regarding auto insurance may be obtained from the Insurance Bureau of Canada, 181 University Avenue, Toronto, Ontario, Canada, M5H 3M7 (phone: 416-362-2031 or 445-5912).
2. *Accident Insurance:* This protects against payments for death or bodily injury and includes loss of pay, medical expenses, and so on. These policies also include coverage against uninsured motorists.
3. *Comprehensive and Collision Insurance:* This protects against loss of or damage to your car. There is usually a deductible amount indicated for this coverage; it is either paid by the policyholder toward the cost of repairs or deducted from the loss settlement.

   When you rent a car, the rental company is required to provide you with collision protection. In your car rental contract, you'll see that for about $10 to $12 a day, you may buy optional collision damage waiver (CDW) protection to relieve you of all responsibility for any damage to the rental car. If you do not accept the CDW coverage, you may be liable for as much as the full retail cost of the car you're renting. Before agreeing to this coverage, however, check your own personal auto insurance policy. It may very well cover your entire liability exposure without any additional cost, or you automatically may be covered by the credit card company (American Express, or premium cards from Visa or Master-Card) to which you are charging the cost of your rental.

Combination Packages – Short-term insurance policies, which include personal accident and medical coverage, trip cancellation insurance, and baggage and personal effects insurance, are available through retail insurance agencies, automobile clubs, and many travel agents. These combination policies are designed to cover you for the duration of a single trip.

Border Crossings

ENTRY REQUIREMENTS: Citizens and legal residents of the US can cross the US-Canada border in either direction without passports or visas. To help speed the process, native US travelers should carry some identification, such as a birth, baptismal, or voter's certificate, that officially verifies their citizenship. Proof of residence may also be required. Naturalized US citizens should carry their naturalization certificate or some other evidence of citizenship. Permanent residents of the US who are not American citizens should have Alien Registration Receipt cards (US Form I-151 or Form I-551). Visitors under 18 years of age not accompanied by an adult should carry a letter from a parent or guardian giving them permission to travel to Canada.

Any visitor to Canada who is not a US citizen must have a valid national passport. In addition, a visa may be required of visitors other than British citizens. Generally speaking, the Canadian government doesn't require visas of citizens of most Commonwealth countries and of Common Market members. But the situation changes frequently, and citizens of countries other than the US and Great Britain would do well to contact the nearest Canadian consulate to find out whether or not a visa is required. These travelers should also be aware that visas are issued in the *home* country of the applicant. Thus, someone planning to travel to both the US and Canada shouldn't wait until arriving in the US to apply for a visa. Citizens of countries with no official Canadian representative in residence should contact the Canadian consulate in a neighboring country. Questions about entering Canada should be addressed to the Employment and Immigration Commission, Phase IV, Place du Portage, Ottawa-Hull, Ontario K1A 0J9 (phone: 613-994-7141).

Visitors to the US who cross into Canada and then return to the US should check with the US Immigration and Naturalization Service to make sure that they have all the papers they need for reentry into the US.

DUTY AND CUSTOMS: Vehicles and trailers can be taken into Canada for tours of up to 12 months without duty; permits, when necessary, are issued at the point of entry. Rental vehicles or trailers of the U-Haul variety are also admissible with authorization from the rental company for use in Canada. All driver's licenses, including international licenses, are valid in Canada.

Sporting equipment, including fishing tackle, boats, outboard motors, motorized toboggans, snowmobiles, and camping equipment, can be brought into Canada duty-free. Occasionally a deposit is requested to ensure that items are being brought into the country for pleasure, not to be sold. Hunting rifles and shotguns can be brought into the country duty-free, but owners must carry their Firearms Transaction Record (Form 4473). Handguns *cannot* be brought into the country, nor can automatic weapons, which are illegal. No permit is required to bring tackle for sport fishing into Canada.

Every visitor is allowed to bring, duty-free, a reasonable amount of food for the length of the stay; otherwise, all food is subject to duty of 17.5%. Up to 22 pounds (10 kilograms) of meats per person can be imported without duty.

Each visitor is allowed to bring into Canada up to 50 cigars, 200 cigarettes, and 2 pounds (0.9 kilograms) of manufactured tobacco. Each visitor over legal drinking age (which varies from province to province and territory to territory; see *Drinking and Drug Laws*) may import 40 ounces (1.1 liters) of liquor or wine, or 24 12-ounce cans or bottles of beer or ale into Canada duty-free as personal baggage.

All plants and plant material must be declared at the border. House plants from the continental US are generally permitted entry, but bonsai and all outdoor plants, including bulbs, require permits. Plants from other countries are only permitted under the authority of the Plant Quarantine Act. Visitors planning to bring plants should write in advance for specific regulations to Plant Protection Division, Food Production and Inspection Branch, Agriculture Canada, 930 Carling Ave., Ottawa, Ontario K1A 0C5.

Direct any further inquiries concerning Canadian customs regulations to Revenue Canada, Customs and Excise, Public Relations Branch, Ottawa, Ontario K1A OL5 (phone: 613-993-0534).

REENTERING THE US: US residents who have spent 48 hours or less in Canada can bring into the US duty-free merchandise worth a total of $25, including any of the following: 10 cigars (not Cuban), 50 cigarettes, 4 ounces (150 milliliters) of alcoholic beverages, or perfume.

American residents who have spent more than 48 hours in Canada may return with up to $400 worth of merchandise for personal or household use once every 30 days without paying duty. Up to one liter of alcoholic beverage (depending on the laws of the state by which you return), 100 cigars, and 200 cigarettes may be imported into the US for personal use. Members of the same family traveling together may combine their duty-free exemptions. Gifts valued at $50 or less may be sent to people in the US duty- and tax-free. The package should be clearly marked "Unsolicited Gift."

US residents are prohibited from bringing certain goods into the US, including items made from whalebone and sealskin, Cuban goods, items from North Korea, Vietnam, and Cambodia. Tourists who want to bring Canadian plants into the US must have a plant certificate from an office of the Canadian Plant Health Division. For more information, contact the Permit Officer, Food Production and Inspection Branch, Agriculture Canada, 930 Carling Ave., Ottawa, Ontario K1A 0C5. To check on the regulations governing the importation of a wildlife product (for example, furs and leathers), contact the US Fish and Wildlife Service, Department of the Interior, Washington, DC 20240 (phone: 202-343-9242).

For more information on any aspect of American customs regulations, write the US Customs Service, 1301 Constitution Ave., Washington, DC 20229, or call 202-566-8195 on a touchtone phone, press code 122, and ask for the free booklet, *Know Before You Go*.

How to Pack

No one can provide a completely foolproof list of precisely what to pack, so it's best to let common sense, space, and comfort guide you. Keep one maxim in mind: Less is more. You simply won't need as much clothing as you think, and although there is nothing more frustrating than arriving at your destination without the very item that in its absence becomes crucial, you are far more likely to need a forgotten accessory — or a needle and thread or scissors — than a particular piece of clothing.

GETTING READY / How to Pack

As with almost anything relating to travel, a little advance planning can go a long way. There are specific things to consider before you open the first drawer or fold the first pair of underwear:

1. Where are you going (city, country, or both)?
2. How many total days will you be gone?
3. What's the average temperature likely to be during your stay?

The goal is to remain perfectly comfortable, neat, clean, and adequately fashionable wherever you go, but actually to pack as little as possible. The main obstacle to achieving this end is habit: Most of us wake each morning with an entire wardrobe hanging in our closets, and we assume that our suitcase should offer the same variety and selection. Not so — only our anxiety about being caught short makes us treat a suitcase like a mobile closet. This worry can be eliminated by learning to travel light and by following two firm packing principles:

1. Organize your travel wardrobe around a single color — blue or brown, for example — that allows you to mix and match clothes. Holding firm to one color scheme will make it easy to eliminate items of clothing that don't harmonize, and by picking clothes for their adaptability and compatibility with your basic color, you will put together the widest selection with the fewest pieces of clothing.
2. Use laundries to replenish your wardrobe. Never overpack to ensure a supply of fresh clothing — shirts, blouses, underwear — for each day of a long trip. Businesspeople routinely use hotel laundries or dry-cleaning services to wash and clean clothes. If these are too expensive, opt for local self-service laundries.

CLIMATE AND CLOTHES: Exactly what you pack on your trip will be a function of where you are going and when, and the kinds of things you intend to do. As a first step, however, find out about the general weather conditions — temperature, rainfall, seasonal variations — at your destination, as a few degrees can make all the difference between being comfortably attired and very real suffering. This information is included in the individual city reports of THE CITIES; other sources of information are airlines and travel agents. The Canadian Government Office of Tourism publishes *Canada Travel Information,* a brochure with a chart of general weather information and suggested clothing (available from the Canadian tourist offices listed under *Tourist Information* in this section).

Keeping temperature and climate in mind, consider the problem of luggage. Plan on one suitcase per person (and in a pinch, remember that it's always easier to carry two small suitcases than to schlepp one roughly the size of the *QE2*). Standard 26- to 28-inch suitcases can be made to work for 1 week or 1 month, and unless you are going for no more than a weekend, never cram wardrobes for two people into one suitcase.

Attire is quite casual throughout Canada; only at the most elegant hotels and restaurants are dressy clothes required. Accessorize everything beforehand so you know exactly what you will be wearing with what. If you are planning to be on the move — either in a car, bus, train, or plane — consider loose-fitting clothes that do not wrinkle. Perishable clothes — pure cotton and linen — are the hard-to-keep-up fabrics and should be left behind. Lightweight wools, manmade fabrics such as jerseys and knits, and drip-dry fabrics travel best (although in very hot weather cotton clothing may be the most comfortable), and prints look fresher longer than solids.

Women should figure on a maximum of five daytime and three late afternoon-evening changes. Whether you are going to be gone for a week or a month, this number should be enough. Again, before packing, lay out every piece of clothing you think you might want to take. Eliminate items that don't mix, match, or interchange within your chosen color scheme. If you can't wear it in at least two distinct incarnations, leave it home.

Men will find that color coordination is crucial. Solid colors coordinate best, and a sport jacket that also goes with a pair of pants from a suit provides an added option. Hanging bags are best for suits and jackets, and shirts should be chosen that can be used for both daytime and evening wear. Double-duty shoes are also preferable.

Finally, prepare for changes in the weather or for atypical temperatures; for instance, if you're going on a day's outing in the mountains, where it is cooler, dress in layers so that as the weather changes you can add or remove clothes as required.

Pack clothes that have a lot of pockets for traveler's checks, documents, and tickets. If your bag gets lost or stolen, you will retain possession of the essentials. It is a good idea to wear loose-fitting clothes that can be rinsed in Woolite or a similar cold-water detergent and hung to drip dry. And be sure to have comfortable shoes. Pack lightweight sandals for beach and evening wear. It is permissible to wear your most comfortable shoes almost everywhere.

Your carry-on luggage should contain a survival kit with the basic things you will need in case your luggage gets lost or stolen: a toothbrush, toothpaste, prescription medications, a sweater, nightclothes, and a change of underwear. With all of your essential items at hand at all times, you will be prepared for any sudden, unexpected occurrence that separates you from your suitcase. If you have many 1- or 2-nighters, you can live out of your survival case without having to unpack completely at each hotel.

Sundries – If you are traveling in the heat of summer and will be spending a lot of time outdoors, pack special items so you won't spend your entire vacation horizontal in a hotel room (or hospital) because of sunburn. Be sure to take a sun hat (to protect hair as well as skin), sunscreen, and tanning lotion, which is available in graduated degrees of sunblock corresponding to the level of your skin's sensitivity. (The quantity of sunscreen is indicated by number: the higher the number, the greater the protection.) A good moisturizer is necessary to help keep your skin from drying out and peeling. The best advice is to take the sun's rays in small doses — no more than 20 minutes at a stretch — increasing your sunbathing time as your vacation progresses. Also, if you are heading for a vacation on skiis, do not underestimate the effect of the sun's glare off snowy slopes, especially in higher altitudes — the exposed areas of your face and neck are particularly susceptible to a painful burn.

PACKING: The basic idea of packing is to get everything into the suitcase and out again with as few wrinkles as possible. Simple, casual clothes — shirts, jeans and slacks, permanent press skirts — can be rolled into neat, tight sausages that keep other suitcase items in place and leave the clothes themselves amazingly unwrinkled. The rolled clothes can be retrieved, shaken out, and hung up at your destination. For items that are too bulky or too delicate for even careful rolling, a suitcase can be packed from bottom up to ensure the most protection for everything. Put heavy items on the bottom toward the hinges so that they do not wrinkle other clothes. Candidates for the bottom layer include shoes (stuff them with small items to save space), a toiletry kit, handbags (stuff them to help keep their shape), and an alarm clock. Fill out this layer with things that will not wrinkle or will not matter if they do, such as sweaters, socks, a bathing suit, gloves, and underwear.

If you get this first, heavy layer as smooth as possible with the fill-ins, you will have a shelf for the next layer, or the most easily wrinkled items, like slacks, jackets, shirts, dresses, and skirts. These should be buttoned and zipped and laid along the whole length of the suitcase with as little folding as possible. When you do need to make a fold, do it on a crease (as with pants), along a seam in the fabric, or where it will not show, such as shirttails. Alternate each piece of clothing, using one side of the suitcase, then the other, to make the layers as flat as possible. On the top layer put the things you will want at once: nightclothes, an umbrella or raincoat, and a sweater.

With men's two-suiter suitcases, follow the same procedure. Then place jackets on hangers, straighten them out, and leave them unbuttoned. If they are too wide for the suitcase, fold them lengthwise down the middle, straighten the shoulders, and fold the sleeves in along the seam.

SOME PACKING HINTS: Some travelers like to have at hand a small bag with the basics for an overnight stay, particularly if they are flying. Always keep necessary medicine, valuable jewelry, and travel or business documents in your purse, briefcase, or carry-on bag, not in the luggage you will check. Tuck a bathing suit into your handbag, too; in case of lost baggage, it's frustrating to be without one. And whether in your overnight bag or checked luggage, cosmetics and any liquids should be packed in plastic bottles or at least wrapped in plastic bags and tied.

Golf clubs and skiis may be checked through as luggage (most airlines are accustomed to handling them), but tennis rackets should be carried onto the plane. Some airlines require that bicycles be partially dismantled and packaged. Check with the airline before departure to see if there is a specific regulation regarding any special equipment or sporting gear you plan to take.

It is always a good idea to add an empty, flattened airline bag or similar piece of luggage to your suitcase; you'll find it indispensable as a beach bag. Keep in mind, too, that you're likely to do some shopping, and save room for those items.

For more information on packing clothes, send your request with a #10 stamped, self-addressed envelope to Samsonite Travel Advisory Service, PO Box 39609, Dept. 80, Denver, CO 80239, for its free booklet, *Getting a Handle on Luggage*.

Hints for Handicapped Travelers

From 35 to 50 million people in the US have some sort of disability, and at least half this number are physically handicapped. Like everyone else today, they — and the uncounted disabled millions around the world — are on the move. More than ever before, they are demanding facilities they can use comfortably, and they are being heard. The disabled traveler will find that services for the handicapped have considerably improved in the Canadian travel industry over the last few years, and though accessibility is far from universal, it is being brought up to more acceptable standards every day.

PLANNING: Good planning is essential: Collect as much information as you can about your specific disability and about facilities for the disabled in the area you're visiting, make your travel arrangements well in advance, and specify to all services involved the exact nature of your condition or restricted mobility, as your trip will be much more comfortable if you know that there are accommodations and facilities to suit your needs. The best way to find out if your intended destination can accommodate a handicapped traveler is to write or phone the local tourist association or hotel and ask specific questions. If you require a corridor of a certain width to maneuver a wheelchair or if you need handles on the bathroom walls for support, ask the hotel manager. A travel agent or the local chapter or national office of the organization that deals with your particular disability — for example, the American Foundation for the Blind or the American Heart Association — will supply the most up-to-date information on the subject. The following sources offer general information on access:

Access to the World, by Louise Weiss, published by Facts on File, 460 Park Ave. S., New York, NY 10016 (phone: 212-683-2244), costs $16.95, and can be ordered by phone with a credit card. Henry Holt also now publishes Weiss' excellent book in paperback; check with local bookstores.

Access Travel: A Guide to the Accessibility of Airport Terminals, published by the Airport Operators Council International, provides information on more than

64 GETTING READY / Handicapped Travelers

200 airports worldwide with ratings according to 70 features, including accessibility to bathrooms, corridor width, and parking spaces. For a free copy, write to the Consumer Information Center, Access America, Dept. 571T, Pueblo, CO 81009, or call 202-293-8500 and ask for "Item 571T-Access Travel." To help travel agents plan trips for the handicapped, this material is reprinted with additional information on tourist boards, city information offices, and tour operators specializing in travel for the handicapped (see "Tours," below) in the North American edition of the *Official Airline Guides Travel Planner,* issued quarterly by Official Airline Guides, 2000 Clearwater Dr., Oak Brook, IL 60521 (phone: 312-574-6000).

The *Canadian Rehabilitation Council for the Disabled* publishes two useful books by Cinnie Noble. The first, *Handi-Travel: A Resource Book for Disabled and Elderly Travelers* ($12.95 CN, plus $1.50 postage, or $12.95 US postpaid) is a comprehensive travel guide full of practical tips for those with disabilities affecting mobility, hearing, or sight. *The Handicapped Traveler* ($12.95; plus $2 for shipping and handling, 50¢ each additional copy), though written for travel agents, also provides a wealth of useful information for the disabled traveler. To order and for other useful information, contact the Canadian Rehabilitation Council for the Disabled, 1 Yonge St., Suite 2110, Toronto, Ontario M5E 1E5 (phone: 416-862-0340).

Information Center for Individuals with Disabilities, Inc. (ICID), Fort Point Pl., 1st Fl., 27-43 Wormwood St., Boston, MA 02210; phone: 617-727-5540/1 or 800-462-5015 in Massachusetts only; both voice and TDD (telecommunications device for the deaf). ICID provides information and referral services on disability-related issues and will help you research your trip. The center publishes fact sheets on vacation planning, tour operators, travel agents, and travel resources.

The Itinerary is a travel magazine for people with disabilities. Published bimonthly, it includes information on accessibility, listings of tours, news of adaptive devices, travel aids, and special services as well as numerous general travel hints. A subscription is $10 a year; write to The Itinerary, PO Box 1084, Bayonne, NJ 07002-1084 (phone: 201-858-3400).

A List of Guidebooks for Handicapped Travelers is a free listing of useful publications for the disabled, compiled by the President's Committee on Employment of People with Disabilities, 1111 20th St. NW, Suite 636, Vanguard Bldg., Washington, DC 20036 (free; published September 1975).

Mobility International/USA (MIUSA), the US branch of Mobility International, a nonprofit British-based organization with affiliates in some 35 countries, offers advice and assistance to disabled travelers — including information on accommodations, access guides, and study tours. Among its publications are a quarterly newsletter and a comprehensive sourcebook, *World of Options, A Guide to International Educational Exchange, Community Service, and Travel for Persons with Disabilities.* Individual membership is $20 a year; subscription to the newsletter alone is $10 annually. For more information, contact MIUSA, PO Box 3551, Eugene, OR 97403; phone: 503-343-1284, voice and TDD (telecommunications device for the deaf).

National Rehabilitation Information Center, 8455 Colesville Rd., Suite 935, Silver Spring, MD 20910 (phone: 301-588-9284). A general information and referral service.

The *Paralyzed Veterans of America (PVA)* is a national organization that offers information and advocacy services for veterans with spinal cord injuries. *PVA* also sponsors *Access to the Skies,* a program that coordinates the efforts of the national and international air travel industry in providing airport and airplane access for the handicapped. Members also receive several helpful publications as well as regular notification of conferences on subjects of interest to the handicapped traveler. For membership information, contact PVA/ATTS Program, 801 18th St. NW, Washington, DC 20006 (phone: 202-USA-1300).

Society for the Advancement of Travel for the Handicapped (SATH), 26 Court St., Penthouse, Brooklyn, NY 11242 (phone: 718-858-5483). To keep abreast of developments in travel for the handicapped as they occur, you may want to join *SATH,* a nonprofit organization whose members include travel agents, tour operators, and other travel suppliers, as well as consumers. Membership costs $40 ($25 for students and travelers who are 65 and older) and the fee is tax deductible. *SATH* publishes a quarterly newsletter, an excellent booklet, *Travel Tips for the Handicapped,* and provides information on travel agents or tour operators in the US and overseas who have experience (or an interest) in travel for the handicapped. *SATH* also offers a free 48-page guide, *The United States Welcomes Handicapped Visitors,* that covers transportation, accommodations, insurance, and customs regulations. Send a self-addressed, #10 envelope to *SATH* at the address above, and include $1 for postage.

The *Travel Information Service* at Moss Rehabilitation Hospital is a service designed to help physically handicapped people plan trips. It cannot make travel arrangements but, for a nominal fee per package, it will supply information from its files on as many as three cities, countries, or special interests. Write to the Travel Information Service, Moss Rehabilitation Hospital, 12th St. and Tabor Rd., Philadelphia, PA 19141 (phone: 215-456-9600).

TravelAbility, by Lois Reamy, is a vast database with information on locating tours for the handicapped; coping with public transport; and finding accommodations, special equipment, and travel agents. It also offers a step-by-step planning guide. Previously published by Macmillan, *TravelAbility* is currently out of print but may be available at your local library.

It should be noted that most of the material published with disabled travelers in mind deals with the wheelchair-bound traveler for whom architectural barriers are a prime concern. For travelers with diabetes, a pamphlet entitled *Ticket to Safe Travel* is available for 50¢ from the New York Diabetes Association, 505 8th Ave., 21st Floor, New York, NY 10018 (phone: 212-947-9707). Another, *Travel for the Patient with Chronic Obstructive Pulmonary Disease,* is available for $2 from Dr. Harold Silver, 1601 18th St. NW, Washington, DC 20009 (phone: 202-667-0134). For blind travelers *Seeing Eye Dogs as Air Travelers* can be obtained free from the Seeing Eye, Box 375, Washington Valley Rd., Morristown, NJ 07960 (phone: 201-539-4425). The library of the *Canadian Paraplegic Association,* 520 Sutherland Dr., Toronto, Ontario M4G 3V9 (phone: 416-422-5644) is another good source of information on travel for the mobility disabled. A few more basic resource directories to look for are *Travel for the Disabled* by Helen Hecker ($9.95) and, by the same author, *The Directory of Travel Agencies for the Disabled* ($12.95). *Wheelchair Vagabond* by John G. Nelson, is another useful guidebook for those travelers confined to a wheelchair (softcover, $9.95; hardcover, $14.95). All three are published by Twin Peaks Press, PO Box 129, Vancouver, WA 98666; to order, call 800-637-CALM. Additionally, *The Physically Disabled Traveler's Guide* by Rod W. Durgin and Norene Lindsay, is helpful and informative. Available from Resource Directories, 3361 Executive Pkwy., Suite 302, Toledo, OH 43606 (phone: 419-536-5353) for $9.95, plus $2 for postage and handling.

When considering traveling to Canada, those who depend on Seeing Eye dogs will be glad to note that Seeing Eye dogs may enter Canada from the US without certification or further restrictions. The only exception to this open policy is in travel to Newfoundland, where an entry permit may be required. For further information contact the Provincial Veterinary Services divisions of the provinces you plan to visit. (Also see *Hints for Traveling with Pets* in this section.)

PLANE: Advise the airline that you are handicapped when you book your flight. The Federal Aviation Administration (FAA) has ruled that US airlines must accept disabled and handicapped passengers as long as the airline has advance notice and the passenger represents no insurmountable problem in the emergency evacuation procedures. As a matter of course, US airlines were pretty good about helping handicapped passengers even before the ruling, although each airline has somewhat different procedures. Canadian airlines are also good about accommodating the disabled traveler, but, again, policies vary from carrier to carrier. Ask for specifics when you book your flight.

Disabled passengers should always make reservations well in advance and give the airline all relevant details of their condition at that time. These details include information on mobility, toilet and special oxygen needs, and requirements for airline-supplied equipment, such as a wheelchair or portable oxygen. Be sure that the person you speak to understands fully the degree of your disability: The more details provided, the more effective the help the airline can give you. On the day before the flight, call back to make sure that all arrangements have been taken care of, and on the day of the flight, arrive early so that you can board before the rest of the passengers. Carry a medical certificate with you, stating your specific disability or the need to carry a particular medicine. (Some airlines require the certificate, and you should find out the rules of the airline you'll be flying with well beforehand.)

Because most airports have jetways (corridors connecting the terminal with the door of the plane), a disabled passenger can usually be taken as far as the plane, and sometimes right on it, in a wheelchair. If not, a narrow boarding chair may be used to take you to your seat. Your own wheelchair, which will be folded and put in the baggage compartment, should be tagged as escort luggage to ensure that it's available at planeside upon landing rather than in the baggage claim area. Travel is not quite as simple if your wheelchair is battery-operated: Unless it has non-spillable batteries, it might not be accepted on board, and you will have to check with the airline ahead of time to find out how the batteries and the chair should be packaged for the flight. Usually people in wheelchairs are asked to wait until other passengers have disembarked. If you are making a tight connection, be sure to tell the attendant.

Passengers who use oxygen may not use their personal supply in the cabin, though it may be carried on the plane as cargo when properly packed and labeled. If you will need oxygen during the flight, the airline will supply it to you (there is a charge) provided you have given advance notice — 24 hours to a few days, depending on the carrier.

Several airlines now have booklets describing procedures for accommodating the handicapped on their flights. For example, United Airlines has a list of travel tips for the handicapped; contact United Airlines, Consumer Affairs Department, PO Box 66100, Chicago, IL 60666 (phone: 312-952-6796).

Useful information on every stage of air travel, from planning to arrival, is provided in the booklet *Incapacitated Passengers Air Travel Guide.* To receive a free copy, write to Senior Manager, Passenger Services, International Air Transport Association, 2000 Peel St., Montreal, Quebec H3A 2R4 Canada (phone: 514-844-6311). For an access guide to over 200 airports worldwide, write for *Access Travel: A Guide to the Accessibility of Airport Terminals* published by the Airport Operators Council International (see listing above). *Air Transportation of Handicapped Persons* is another useful booklet and explain the general guidelines that govern air carrier policies. It is also available free upon written request. Ask for "Free Advisory Circular #AC-120-32" from the Distribution Unit, US Department of Transportation, Publications Section, M-443-2, Washington, DC 20590; for speedy service, enclose a self-addressed mailing label with your request.

GROUND TRANSPORTATION: Perhaps the simplest solution to getting around is to travel with an able-bodied companion who can drive. If you are accustomed to driving your own hand-controlled car and want to rent one, you are in luck. Some rental companies will fit cars with hand controls. Both *Avis* and *Hertz* have some hand-control cars available in Toronto and other major Canadian cities. *Avis* can convert a car to hand controls with as little as 24 hours' notice, though it's a good idea to arrange for one earlier (phone: 800-331-1212). *Hertz* requires a minimum of 5 days to install the controls, and makes the additional stipulation that the car be returned to the office from which it was rented (phone: 800-654-3131). Neither company charges extra for hand controls, but both will fit them only on a full-size car, and both request that you bring your handicapped driver's permit with you. Other car rental companies provide hand-control cars at some locations, but as there are usually only a limited number available, call well in advance.

Taking taxis or hiring a chauffeur-driven car are other solutions to the mobility problem. Contact local transportation authorities for information on special van or bus services for disabled travelers.

TRAIN: On most routes *VIA Rail* accepts wheelchair passengers, although 24-hour advance notice is required. However, on some shorter runs the train has no baggage car, thus no place to store the wheelchair. As *VIA Rail* personnel aren't required to carry a disabled passenger on or off the train and some of the older equipment may present barriers, it's wise to have a companion along. Disabled persons who can't travel by themselves can apply for a two-for-one fare certificate, which allows a companion to travel free on the Canadian railway. The certificate is issued by the *Canadian Rehabilitation Council for the Disabled* (1 Yonge St., Suite 2110, Toronto, Ontario M5E 1E5; phone: 416-862-0340) on receipt of an application signed by a doctor. Blind passengers and their companions are also eligible for the two-for-one fare. (Seeing-eye dogs ride in the passenger cars at no extra charge.) On long distance journeys it's a good idea to reserve a bedroom or a roomette, which have private washrooms and room service.

BY BUS: Bus companies do not have consistent written policies on carrying handicapped people. For wheelchair-bound passengers, the rule essentially is that if the wheelchair can be folded to fit in the baggage compartment, the bus will take you. Make sure to ask about the bus company's regulations when making reservations. Like *VIA Rail, Gray Coach, Greyhound Lines of Canada, Voyageur,* and many smaller lines also honor the two-for-one fare certificates.

TOURS: Programs designed for the physically impaired are run by specialists who have researched hotels, restaurants, and places of interest to be sure they present no insurmountable obstacles. The following travel agencies or tour operators specialize in making group or individual arrangements for travelers with physical or other disabilities. Because of the requirements of handicapped travel, however, the same packages may not be offered regularly.

Access: The Foundation for Accessibility by the Disabled, PO Box 356, Malvern, NY 11565 (phone: 516-887-5684). Travelers referral service which acts as an intermediary with tour operators and agents worldwide. Also provides information on accessibility at various locations.

Accessible Tours/Directions Unlimited, 720 N. Bedford Rd., Bedford Hills, NY 10507 (phone: 914-241-1700 in New York State; 800-533-5343 elsewhere). Arranges group or individual tours for disabled persons traveling in the company of able-bodied friends or family members. Accepts the unaccompanied traveler if completely self-sufficient.

Evergreen Travel Service, 19505L 44th Ave. W., Lynnwood, WA 98036-5699 (phone: locally, 206-776-1184; 800-562-9298 elsewhere in Washington State;

800-435-2288 elsewhere). The oldest company in the world offering worldwide tours and cruises for the disabled (Wings on Wheels) and sight impaired/blind (White Cane Tours). Most programs are first class or deluxe, and include escort by the owner or his family.

Flying Wheels Travel, 143 W. Bridge St., Box 382, Owatonna, MN 55060 (phone: 507-451-5005 or 800-533-0363). Handles both tours and individual arrangements.

The Guided Tour, 555 Ashbourne Rd., Elkins Park, PA 19117 (phone: 215-782-1370). Arranges tours for persons with developmental and learning disabilities, and sponsors separate tours for members of the same population who are also physically disabled or who simply need a slower pace.

Handi-Travel, First National Travel Corporation, 300 John St., Thorn Hill, Ontario L3T 5W4, Canada (phone: 416-731-4714). Handles tours and individual arrangements.

InterpreTours, Ask Mr. Foster, 16660 Ventura Blvd., Encino, CA 91436; phone: 818-788-4118 for voice; 818-788-5328 for TDD (telecommunications device for the deaf). Arranges independent travel, cruises, and tours for the deaf, with an interpreter as tour guide.

Sprout, 204 W. 20th St., New York, NY 10011 (phone: 212-431-1265). Arranges travel programs for mildly and moderately disabled adults, 18 years of age and over.

Travel Horizons Unlimited, 11 E. 44th St., New York, NY 10017 (phone: 212-687-5121 in New York; 800-847-4257 elsewhere). Travel agent and registered nurse Mary Ann Hamm sets up custom-designed trips for individual travelers requiring all types of kidney dialysis and handles arrangements for the dialysis.

Whole Person Tours, PO Box 1084, Bayonne, NJ 07002-1084 (phone: 201-858-3400). Handicapped owner Bob Zywicki travels the world with his wheelchair, and offers a line-up of escorted tours (many by himself) for the disabled. A catalogue of foreign and domestic programs designed for travelers with disabilities is available for $2. *Whole Person Tours* is also the publisher of *The Itinerary,* a bimonthly newsletter for disabled travelers (a 1-year subscription costs $10).

Hints for Single Travelers

Just about the last trip in human history in which the participants were neatly paired was the voyage of Noah's Ark. Ever since, passenger lists and tour groups have reflected the same kind of asymmetry that occurs in real life, as countless individuals set forth to see the world unaccompanied (or unencumbered, depending on your outlook) by spouse, lover, friend, or relative.

There are some things to be said for traveling alone. There is the pleasure of privacy, though a solitary traveler must be self-reliant, independent, and responsible. Unfortunately, traveling alone can also turn a traveler into a second class citizen.

The truth is that the travel industry is not very fair to people who vacation by themselves. People traveling alone almost invariably end up paying more than individuals traveling in pairs. Most travel bargains, including package tours, hotel accommodations, resort packages, and cruises, are based on *double-occupancy* rates. This means that the per-person price is offered on the basis of two people traveling together and sharing a double room (which means they will each spend a good deal more on meals and extras). The single traveler will have to pay a surcharge, called a single supplement, for exactly the same package. In extreme cases, this can add as much as 30% to 50%

GETTING READY / Single Travelers 69

to the basic per-person rate. As far as the travel industry is concerned, single travel has not yet come into its own.

There are, however, countless thousands of indivuduals who *do* travel alone. Inevitably, their greatest obstacle is the single supplement charge, which prevents them from cashing in on travel bargains available to anyone traveling as part of a pair. The obvious, most effective alternative is to find a traveling companion. Even special "singles' tours" that promise no supplements are based on people sharing double rooms. If you are interested in finding another single traveler to help share the cost, consider contacting the travel agents listed below. Some charge fees, others are free, but the basic service offered by all is the same: to match the unattached person with a compatible travel mate. The better established among these agencies are:

Cosmos: This agency offers a guaranteed-share plan whereby singles who wish to share rooms (and avoid paying the single supplement) are matched by the tour escort with like-minded individuals of the same sex. Contact Cosmos at one of their three North American branches: 95-25 Queens Blvd., Rego Park, NY 11374 (phone: 800-221-0090 from the eastern US); 150 S. Los Robles Ave., Pasadena, CA 91101 (phone: 818-449-2019 or 800-556-5454); or call 416-787-1281 for the office in Toronto, Canada.

Grand Circle Travel: Arranges escorted cruise/air packages for "mature" travelers, including singles. Membership, which is automatic when you book a trip through *Grand Circle,* includes a free subscription to its quarterly magazine, discount certificates on future trips, and other extras. Contact Grand Circle Travel, 347 Congress St., Boston, MA 02210 (phone: 617-350-7500 in Boston; 800-221-2610 elsewhere in the US).

Jane's International: This service puts potential traveling companions, in touch with one another. No age limit, no fee. For information, contact Jane's International, 2603 Bath Ave., Brooklyn, NY 11214 (phone: 718-266-2045).

Saga International Holidays: An organization for seniors over 60, including singles. Members receive the club magazine, which includes a classified section aimed at helping lone travelers find suitable traveling companions. A 3-year membership costs $5. Contact Saga International Holidays, 120 Boylston St., Boston MA 02116 (phone: 617-451-6808 or one of the following nationwide toll-free numbers: for reservations, 800-343-0273; for customer service, 800-441-6662; for brochure requests, 800-248-2234).

Singleworld: About two-thirds of this agency's clientele are under 35, and about half this number are women, but *Singleworld* organizes tours and cruises with departures categorized by age group. The annual membership fee is $20. 401 Theodore Fremd Ave., Rye, NY 10580 (phone: 914-967-3334 or 800-223-6490 in the continental US).

Travel Companion Exchange: Every 8 weeks this group publishes a directory of singles looking for travel companions and provides members with full-page profiles of likely partners. Membership fees range from $3 to $11 per month (with a 6-month minimum enrollment), depending on the level of service required. PO Box 833, Amityville, NY 11701 (phone: 516-454-0880).

Travel Mates International, Inc.: Will search for and arrange shares on existing package tours for men and women of any age. The agency will also organize group tours for its own clients. Annual membership fee is $15. 49 W. 44th St., New York, NY 10036 (phone: 212-221-6565).

A special guidebook for solo travelers, prepared by Eleanor Adams Baxel, offers information on how to avoid paying supplementary charges, how to pick the right travel agent, how to calculate costs, and much more. Entitled *A Guide for Solo*

Travel Abroad, previously published by the Berkshire Traveller Press, it's out of print but may be available in your local library.

WOMEN AND STUDENTS: Two specific groups of single travelers deserve special mention: women and students. Countless women travel by themselves, and such an adventure need not be feared. You will generally find people very courteous and welcoming, but remember that crime is a worldwide problem. Keep a careful eye on your belongings while on the beach or lounging in a park; lock your car and hotel doors; deposit your valuables in the hotel's safe; and don't hitchhike.

One lingering inhibition many female travelers still harbor is that of eating alone in public places. The trick here is to relax and enjoy your meal and surroundings; while you may run across the occasional unenlightened waiter, dining solo is no longer an uncommon sight. A book offering lively, helpful advice on female solo travel is *The Traveling Woman,* by Dena Kaye. Though out of print, it may be found in your local library.

Students traveling on a strict budget have a few accommodation options. They can stay at one of the many *YMCA* or *YWCA* residences in Montreal, Toronto and three other major cities. But note that membership is often required if you plan to stay more than a day or two. Students and singles should also keep in mind that youth hostels exist in many cities throughout Canada. Hostels are run by the hosteling associations of some 60-plus countries that make up the *International Youth Hostel Federation (IYHF);* membership in one of the national associations allows access to hostels all over the world. *IYHF* hostels serve travelers of all ages under a self-help system. Visitors carry their own gear, provide their own services, and contribute to the upkeep of the hostel by performing a small domestic chore. To join the American affiliate, *American Youth Hostels, Inc., (AYH),* write to the national office, PO Box 37613, Washington, DC 20013-7613 (phone: 202-783-6161). The cost of membership in *AYH* varies, depending on the type of membership and age category, but generally annual fees are $10 for Youth memberships (17 and under), $20 for Adult (18 to 54), and $10 for Senior (55 and up). A $1 mailing charge should be added to each membership fee cited above. The *AYH Handbook,* which lists hostels in the US, comes with your *AYH* card. Information on international hostels is not included with membership. For additional information, you may also want to contact the *Canadian Hostelling Association,* 1600 James Naismith Dr., 6th Fl., Gloucester, Ottawa, Ontario K1B 5N4 (phone: 613-748-5638) which publishes a free handbook listing Canadian hostels.

Hints for Older Travelers

Special package deals and more free time are just two factors that have given Americans over age 65 a chance to see the world at affordable prices. Senior citizens make up an ever-growing segment of the travel population, and the trend among them is to travel more frequently and for longer periods of time. No longer limited by 3-week vacations or the business week, older travelers can take advantage of off-season, off-peak travel which is both less expensive and more pleasant than traveling in high season. October to mid-November and May and June are good times of the year to travel in Canada to avoid the crowds and still enjoy moderate temperatures for touring and outdoor activities.

When planning a vacation, prepare your itinerary with one eye on your own physical condition and the other on a topographical map. Keep in mind variations in climate, terrain, and altitudes, which may pose some danger for anyone with heart or breathing problems.

An excellent book to read before embarking on any trip is Rosalind Massow's *Travel Easy: The Practical Guide for People Over 50,* available for $8.95 (plus $1.75 postage and handling per order, not per book) from AARP Books, c/o Scott, Foresman, 1865 Miner St., Des Plaines, IL 60016 (phone: 202-728-4313 or 800-238-2300). It discusses a host of travel-related subjects, from choosing a destination to getting set for departure, with chapters on transportation options, tours, cruises, avoiding health problems, and handling dental emergencies en route. Another book, *The International Health Guide for Senior Citizens,* covers such topics as trip preparations, food and water precautions, adjusting to weather and climate conditions, finding a doctor, motion sickness, and jet lag. The book also discusses specific health and travel problems, and includes a list of resource organizations that can provide medical assistance for travelers; available for $4.95 postpaid from Pilot Books, 103 Cooper St., Babylon, NY 11702 (phone: 516-422-2225). A third book on health for older travelers, Rosalind Massow's excellent *Now It's Your Turn to Travel* has a chapter on medical problems. Previously published by Collier Books, it is out of print but available in libraries. Also, see *Medical and Legal Aid* in this section. An excellent guide for the budget-conscious older traveler is *The Discount Guide for Travelers Over 55* by Caroline and Walter Weintz (E.P. Dutton; $7.95).

Travel Tips for Senior Citizens (State Department publication 8970), a booklet with general advice, is available for $1 from the Superintendent of Documents, US Government Printing Office, Washington, DC 20402 (phone: 202-783-3238). The booklet *101 Tips for the Mature Traveler* is available free from Grand Circle Travel, 347 Congress St., Suite 3A, Boston, MA 02210 (phone: 617-350-7500 or 800-221-2610).

HEALTH: Health facilities are generally maintained by individual Canadian provinces, but Blue Cross is usually honored throughout Canada. Be sure to take along any prescription medication you need, enough to last *without a new prescription* for the duration of your trip; pack all medications separately in a carry-on bag in case your luggage is lost or detoured, along with a note from your doctor for the benefit of airport authorities. It is also wise to bring a few common non-prescription over-the-counter medications with you: aspirin and something for stomach upset may come in handy. If you have specific medical problems, bring prescriptions and a "medical file" composed of the following:

1. A summary of medical history, current diagnosis.
2. A list of drugs to which you are allergic.
3. Your most recent electrocardiogram, if you have heart problems.
4. Your doctor's name, address, and telephone number.

■ **A word of caution:** Don't overdo it. Allow time for some relaxing each day to refresh yourself for the next scheduled sightseeing event. Traveling across time zones can be exhausting and adjusting to major climatic changes can make you feel dizzy and drained. Plan on spending at least one full day resting before you start touring. If you're part of a group tour, be sure to check the planned itinerary thoroughly. Some package deals sound wonderful because they include all the places you've ever dreamed of visiting. In fact, they can become so hectic and tiring that you'll be reaching for a pillow instead of your camera.

DISCOUNTS AND PACKAGES: Senior citizens with identification are eligible for a large variety of discounts across Canada. Some discounts are only available to Canadians (like free entry into national parks), but many others are available to anyone over 65. Although the rules change from place to place and from city to city, acceptable proof of eligibility (or age) is, for Canadians, a special card issued by the province; for older people from the US and other countries, a driver's license, passport, birth certificate, a membership card in a recognized senior citizens' organization such as the *American Association of Retired Persons* (see below), or a Medicare card. Because senior citizen discounts are common but by no means standard, always ask about them before you pay — whether it's for a movie in Toronto or a hotel in Vancouver. Discounts are often available for transportation, museums, cultural and sports events, and dozens of other activities. Depending on the local management, discounts of 10% to 25% are often available at a variety of hotel chains, including *Marriott, Holiday Inn, Sheraton, Howard Johnson,* and *Rodeway Inns.* The following are some standard reductions available to all senior citizens in Canada:

Bus: Voyageur offers senior citizens 1/3 off regular one-way or round-trip fares, while *Greyhound* and *Gray Coach* each offer a 10% reduction on regular fares. Many of the smaller Canadian lines also give discounts to older travelers.

Train: VIA Rail offers older travelers 1/3 off regular coach fares at all times.

Plane: Air Canada offers up to 60% reduction on confirmed reservations for flights from the US. Canadian Airlines International also offers special senior citizen rates, as do most smaller regional airlines. Check with the airline or your travel agent for current discounted rates.

Many other travel suppliers offer discounts to older travelers. Some of these discounts, however, are extended only to bona fide members of certain senior citizens organizations. Because the same organizations offer package tours to both domestic and international destinations, the benefits of membership are twofold: Those who join can take advantage of discounts as individual travelers and also reap the savings that group travel affords. In addition, because the age requirements for some of these organizations are quite low (or nonexistent), the benefits can begin to accrue early. Among the organizations dedicated to helping you see the world are the following:

American Association of Retired Persons (AARP): The largest and best known of these organizations, membership is open to anyone 50 or over, whether retired or not. *AARP* offers travel programs, designed exclusively for senior citizens, that cover the globe and include a broad range of escorted tours, hosted tours, and cruises, including packages to the Maritime Provinces and the Canadian Rockies. Dues are $5 a year, or $12.50 for 3 years, and include spouse. For membership information, contact AARP at 1909 K St. NW, Washington, DC 20049 (phone: 202-347-8800); for travel information and reservations, contact AARP Travel Service, PO Box 29233, Los Angeles, CA 90009. (phone: 800-227-7737 in the U.S; or 213-322-7323 in Canada).

Mature Outlook: This organization has replaced the *National Association of Mature People.* Through its *Travel Alert,* last-minute tours, cruises, and other vacation packages are available to members at special savings. Hotel and car rental discounts and travel accident insurance are also available. Membership is open to anyone 50 years of age or older, costs $9.95 a year, and includes its bimonthly newsletter and magazine as well as information on package tours. Contact the Customer Service Center, 60001 N. Clark St., Chicago, IL 60660. (phone: 800-336-6330 throughout the U.S and Canada).

National Council of Senior Citizens: Here, too, the emphasis is always on keeping costs low. The roster of tours offered is different each year and its travel service will also book individual tours for members. Although most members are over 50, membership is open to anyone, regardless of age, for an annual fee of $12 per person or $16 per couple. Lifetime membership costs $150. While the travel service does not arrange group tours to Canada, individual tours can be booked anywhere. For information contact the National Council of Senior Citizens, 925 15th St. NW, Washington, DC 20005 (phone: 202-347-8800).

Certain travel agencies and tour operators around the country specialize in group travel for older travelers. For example, *Gadabout Tours,* operated by Lois Anderson, arranges tours for people 55 and over to Montreal, Quebec, Banff, Jasper, Vancouver, Victoria, Toronto and the Gaspé Peninsula, as well as to New Brunswick, Newfoundland, Nova Scotia, and Prince Edward Island. For information write to Gadabout Tours, 700 E. Tahquitz Way, Palm Springs, CA 92262 (phone: 619-325-5556; 800-521-7309 in California; 800-952-5068 elsewhere in the US). *Grand Circle Travel* and *Saga International Holidays* are two other such operators that cater to the over-50 market (see *Hints for Single Travelers*).

Many travel agencies, particularly the larger ones, are delighted to make presentations to help a group select destinations. A local chamber of commerce should be able to provide the names of such agencies. Once a time and place are determined, an organization member or travel agent can obtain group quotations for transportation, accommodations, meal plans, and sightseeing. Groups of 40 or more usually get the best breaks.

Another choice open to older travelers is a trip that includes an educational element. *Elderhostel,* a nonprofit organization, offers educational programs at a huge number of schools in the US and Canada. Programs run for 1 week and usually feature three different courses of study. Accommodations are in residence halls, and meals are taken in student cafeterias. Elderhostelers must be at least 60 years old (younger if a spouse or companion qualifies), in good health, and not in need of special diets. For information, write to Elderhostel, 80 Boylston St., Suite 400, Boston, MA 02116 (phone: 617-426-7788).

Hints for Traveling with Children

What better way to be receptive to new experiences than to take along the young, wide-eyed members of your family? Their company does not have to be a burden or their presence an excessive expense. The current generation of discounts for children and family package deals can make a trip together quite reasonable.

A family trip will be an investment in your children's future, making geography and history come alive for them and leaving a sure memory that will be among the fondest you will all share someday. Their insights will be refreshing, and their impulses may take you to unexpected places with unexpected dividends. The experience will be invaluable to them at any age.

It is necessary to take some extra time beforehand to prepare children for travel. Here are several hints for making a trip with children easy and fun.

1. Children, like everyone else, will derive more pleasure from a trip if they know something about the country before they arrive. Begin their education about a month before you leave. Using maps, travel magazines, and travel books, give children a clear idea of where you are going and how far away it is. Part of the excitement of the journey will be associating the tiny dots on the map with the very real places they will visit a few weeks later. You can show them pictures of streets and scenes in which they will stand within a month. Don't shirk history lessons, but don't burden them with dates. Make history light, anecdotal, pertinent, but most of all, fun. If you simply make materials available and keep your vacation destination and your travel plans a topic of everyday conversation, your children will absorb more than you realize.
2. Children should help plan the itinerary, and where you go and what you do should

reflect some of their ideas. If they know enough about the sites they'll visit beforehand, they will have the excitement of recognition when they arrive and the illumination of seeing how something is or is not the way they expected it to be.
3. Give children specific responsibilities. The job of carrying their own flight bags and looking after their personal things, along with some other light travel chores, will give them a stake in the journey. Tell them how they can be helpful when you are checking in or out of hotels.
4. Give each child a travel diary or scrapbook to take along. Filling these with impressions, observations, and mementos will pass the time on trains and planes and help them to assimilate their experiences.

PACKING: Choose your children's clothes much as you would your own. Select a basic color (perhaps different for each child) and coordinate everything with it. Plan their wardrobes with layering in mind — shirts and sweaters that can be taken off and put back on as the temperature varies. Take only drip-dry, wrinkle-resistant items that they can manage themselves and comfortable shoes — sneakers and sandals. Younger children will need more changes, but keep it to a minimum. No one likes to carry added luggage (remember that *you* will have to manage most of it!)

Take as many handy snacks as you can squeeze into the corners of your suitcases — things like dried fruit and nut mixes, hard candies, peanut butter, and crackers — and moist towelettes for cleaning. Don't worry if your supply of nibbles is quickly depleted. Airports and bus and train stations are well stocked with such items.

Pack a special medical kit (see *Staying Healthy*), including children's aspirin or acetaminophen, an antihistamine or decongestant, Dramamine, and diarrhea medication. Diapers are available at department stores and children's stores. A selection of baby foods is available in most supermarkets, but in the event that you may not be able to find the instant formula to which your child is accustomed, bring along a supply in the 8-ounce "ready-to-feed" cans. Disposable nursers are expensive but handy. If you breast-feed your baby, there is no reason you can't enjoy your trip; just be sure you get enough rest and liquids.

Good toys to take for infants are the same sorts of things they like at home — well-made bright huggables and chewables; for small children, a favorite doll or stuffed animal for comfort, spelling and counting games, and tying, braiding, and lacing activities; for older children, playing cards, travel board games with magnetic pieces, and hand-held electronic games. Softcover books and art materials (crayons, markers, paper, scissors, glue sticks, and stickers) ward off boredom for children of most ages, as do radio-cassette players with headphones. Take along a variety of musical and storytelling cassettes, extra batteries, and maybe even an extra set of headphones so two children can listen. *Advice:* Avoid toys that are noisy, breakable, or spillable, those that require a large play area, and those that have lots of little pieces that can be scattered and lost. When traveling, coordinate activities with attention spans; dole out playthings one at a time so you don't run out of diversions before you get where you're going. Children become restless during long waiting periods, and a game plus a small snack — such as a box of raisins or crackers — will help keep them quiet. It is also a good idea to carry tissues, Band-Aids, a pocket medicine kit, and pre-moistened washcloths.

GETTING THERE AND GETTING AROUND: Begin early to investigate all available discount and charter flights, as well as any package deals and special rates offered by the major airlines. Booking is sometimes required up to 2 months in advance. You may find that charter plans offer no reductions for children, or not enough to offset the risk of last-minute delays or other inconveniences to which charters are subject. The major scheduled airlines, however, almost invariably provide hefty discounts for children (for specific information on fares and in-flight accommodations for children, see *Traveling by Plane*).

PLANE: When you make your reservations, let the airlines know that you are traveling with a child. On US carriers, generally, infants under 2 years of age fly free if they travel on the lap of an obliging adult. However, on longer flights, this may not be comfortable. (A second infant without a second adult would pay the fare applicable to children 2 through 11, usually 75% of the adult fare.) For children 2 to 11, prices vary for promotions when children with an adult fly free or at a deep discount (usually during the months of January and February), or when family fares extend discounts to spouses as well. On Air Canada and Canadian Airlines International, children under 2 travel free on domestic flights only; from ages 2 through 11, they travel at two-thirds of the adult fare.

If traveling with an infant, request a bulkhead seat, and ask to be provided with a bassinet. Request seats on the aisle if you have a toddler or if you think you will need to use the bathroom frequently. (Try to discourage children from being in the aisle when meals are served.) Carry on the plane all you will need to care for and occupy your children during the flight — diapers, formula, "lovies," books, sweaters, and so on. (Never check as baggage any item essential to a child's well-being, such as prescription medicine.) Dress your baby simply, with a minimum of buttons and snaps, because the only place you may have to change a diaper is at your seat. The flight attendant can warm a bottle for you.

Just as you would request a vegetarian or kosher meal, you are entitled to ask for a hot dog or hamburger in lieu of the airline's regular dinner if you give at least 24 hours' notice. Some, but not all, airlines have baby food aboard. While you should bring along toys from home, you can also ask about children's diversions. Some carriers, such as United and Delta, have terrific free packages of games, coloring books, and puzzles.

When the plane takes off and lands, make sure your baby is nursing or has a bottle, pacifier, or thumb in its mouth. This sucking will make the child swallow and help to clear stopped ears. A piece of hard candy will do the same thing for an older child.

Avoid night flights. Since you probably won't sleep nearly as well as your kids, you risk an impossible first day at your destination, groggily taking care of your rested, energetic children. Nap time is, however, a good time to travel, especially for babies, and try to travel during off-hours, when there are apt to be extra seats. If you do have to take a long night flight, keep in mind that when you disembark, you will probably be tired and not really ready for sightseeing. The best thing to do is to head for your hotel, shower, have a snack, and take a nap. If your children are too excited to sleep, give them some toys to play with while you rest.

■ **Note:** Newborn babies, whose lungs may not be able to adjust to the altitude, should not be taken aboard an airplane. And some airlines may refuse to allow a pregnant woman in her 8th or 9th month aboard, for fear that something could go wrong with an in-flight birth. Check with the airline ahead of time and carry a letter from your doctor stating that you are fit to travel and indicating the estimated date of birth.

CAR: Traveling by car, you can be flexible — making any number of stops at roadside shops or in small towns, and meeting moods and emergencies as they arise. You can also take more with you, including items like ice chests and charcoal grills for picnics. Keep your car supplied with dried fruits, crackers, candy bars, bottled water, and facial tissue and/or toilet paper. Games and simple toys, such as magnetic checkerboards or drawing pencils and pads can also provide a welcome diversion. Frequent stops for children to run around make car travel much easier. Along most major highways, there are well-spaced rest areas where you can pull over and have a meal. If a break is in order between these facilities, the next best alternative is to get off at a local exit and follow the signs to a nearby park or town.

TRAIN: *VIA Rail,* Canada's train network, offers special arrangements for children and families. Children under 2 (accompanied by an adult) are allowed to travel free anytime; a second child under 2 travel at half-fare (half the full adult fare). Children 2 to 11 travel for half fare at all times.

Amtrak, which connects major US East Coast cities with Montreal and Toronto, also offers discounts for families. Children under 2 (accompanied by an adult) are allowed to travel free at any time; children 2 to 12 who accompany an adult traveling on an excursion fare are charged half the adult fare. All long-distance trains with dining car service offer children's dishes. Both *Amtrak* and *VIA Rail* also offer economical family plans — ask about current special packages when making reservations to determine the best deal for your family.

BUS: Major Canadian bus companies offer special discounts for children. For example, children 5 to 11 traveling on *Gray Coach, Greyhound,* or *Voyageur* coach lines pay half fare, although on some *Greyhound* routes they must be accompanied by an adult. Children under 5 who sit on an adult's lap travel free. Be sure your bus has a bathroom.

FAMILY TRIPS: An alternative to long car trips are holidays specifically planned for the family that are based on some adventure or activity exciting for all. A few examples are the following:

> Ice skating on the largest indoor or outdoor rinks in the world — on Ottawa's *Rideau Canal Skating Rink,* 14 million square feet of ice, 5.3 miles (8.5 km), accommodating some 50,000 skaters at once; or in *Columbian Four Rinks,* the year-round facilities in Burnaby, Vancouver, with 68,000 square feet of enclosed ice.
>
> Skiing in the Quebec Laurentians. All the major ski areas have ski schools that offer lessons for all ages. (See *Downhill Skiing,* DIVERSIONS.)
>
> Any one of Canada's many vibrant summer festivals, ranging from the *Shediac Lobster Festival* in New Brunswick (featuring lobster-eating contests and stage shows), to the *Calgary Stampede,* in which the city celebrates its Old West bronco-busting heritage. (See *Festivals, Fairs, and Fancy Acts,* DIVERSIONS.)

These are just a few of the literally hundreds of Canadian vacation possibilities for families. For other ideas, see DIVERSIONS and the individual city reports in THE CITIES.

One book of ideas, with the names and addresses of the companies that feature such adventures, is *Adventure Travel North America* by Pat Dickerman (Holt; out of print, but check your local library). Also see *What to Do with the Kids This Year: One Hundred Family Vacation Places with Time Off for You!* by Jane Wilford and Janet Tice (Globe Pequot Press; $8.95).

Travel With Your Children publishes a newsletter, *Family Travel Times,* that focuses on the child traveler and offers helpful hints for parents. Membership is $35 a year. For a sample copy of the newsletter, send $1 to Travel With Your Children, 80 Eighth Ave., New York, NY 10011 (phone: 212-206-0688).

Libraries, museums, and various organizations like the *YMCA* in major cities have special programs for children; these run the gamut from movies and puppet shows to storytelling hours in city parks. Listings of these events, many of which are free, can usually be found in the Friday and Sunday editions of local newspapers or at the city's tourism bureau or information center. Local or provincial festivals, fairs, rodeos, parades, and other special events capture children's imaginations. For a list of these events, write to the city or provincial tourist bureau where you plan to visit; also, see *Festivals, Fairs, and Fancy Acts* in DIVERSIONS. And ask about discounts; children often get discounts on everything from movies to monuments.

ACCOMMODATIONS: Often a cot will be placed in a hotel room at little or no extra charge. Special rates are sometimes available for families in adjoining rooms. Try to find hotels that welcome children — that don't charge for children under a certain age, for example. In many of the larger chain hotels, the staffs are more used to noisy or slightly misbehaving children. These hotels are also likely to have swimming pools or game rooms — both popular with most young travelers. Write the hotel in advance to discuss how old your children are, how long you plan to stay, and to ask for suggestions on sleeping arrangements.

As is happening in the US, Canadian colleges and universities are opening campuses to travelers during traditional academic vacations and summers. These facilities are generally very modestly priced, an advantage for families on the road. Some offer accommodations only (usually in dormitory rooms); others open recreational facilities and sports centers to visitors.

Guest farms and dude ranches are popular Canadian destinations; lists of them can be obtained from Canadian tourist offices in US cities or Canadian provinces. In the eastern provinces, guest farms are generally under 200 acres and specialize in dairy or mixed farming; in Alberta and Manitoba there are working ranches where visitors are a sideline; also out west are the dude or guest ranches, where guests contribute substantially to the property's income. (For more information see *Farm and Ranch Vacations*, DIVERSIONS.) Theme parks are rapidly expanding family vacation places. They offer entertainment, rides, and games for the whole family. Good examples are *Canada's Wonderland,* about 20 miles (32 km) northwest of Toronto, and *Storyland,* outside Renfrew, Ontario, where over 150 storybook characters come to life to tell their own stories.

Consider trading houses or apartments with people in the area where you would like to vacation. Join an organization that fosters such arrangements, such as the *Vacation Exchange Club,* 12006 111th Ave., Youngtown, AZ 85363 (phone: 602-972-2186). For further information on home exchanges, see *Accommodations* in this section.

■ **A final word of advice:** If you are spending your vacation traveling, rather than visiting one spot or engaging in one activity, pace the days with children in mind; break the trip into half-day segments, with running around or "doing" time built in; keep travel time on the road to a maximum of 4 or 5 hours a day. First and foremost, don't forget that a child's attention span is far shorter than an adult's. Children don't have to see every museum or all of any museum to learn something from their trip; watching, playing with, and talking to other children can be equally enlightening experiences. Also, remember the places that children the world over love to visit: zoos, country fairs, amusement parks, beaches, and nature trails. Let your children lead the way sometimes — their perspective is different than yours, and they may lead you to things you would never have noticed on your own.

Hints for Traveling with Pets

You may wish to bring your pet along on your vacation. Although all animals are subject to inspection by the Animal Health inspectors at the border, there are no substantial obstacles in traveling with your pet throughout Canada. Your pet should be fully vaccinated, however, and you will have to bring along the paperwork described below.

DOGS AND CATS: Dogs and cats from the US may be brought into Canada if the owner has a certificate, signed by a licensed veterinarian of Canada or the US, that clearly identifies the animal and certifies that it has been vaccinated against rabies during the preceding 36 months. Puppies or kittens under 3 months old and Seeing Eye dogs may be imported into Canada without certification or further restriction.

Pet dogs and cats entering Newfoundland must be certified to do so. Entry permits should be obtained in advance from: Provincial Veterinary Service, Government of Newfoundland, PO Box 7400, St. John's West, Newfoundland A1E 3Y5 (phone: 709-576-6886).

BIRDS AND OTHER ANIMALS: Other pets from the US, including monkeys, fish, and reptiles, are allowed to enter without restriction. Turtles and tortoises require a Canadian import permit before admission. Up to two pet birds (of the parrot family and songbirds) per family may be imported provided: 1) the owner accompanies the birds to Canada; 2) the owner makes a declaration on arrival in Canada that certifies that, for the 90 days preceding the date of entry, the birds have not been in contact with any other birds and have been in the visitor's personal possession for this period. Send requests for permits to the Chief of Imports, Animal Health Division, Food Production and Inspection Branch, Agriculture Canada, Ottawa, Ontario K1A 0Y9 (phone: 613-995-5433).

BY PLANE AND CAR: Many US airlines require a health certificate for your pet. United, for example, requires a US Interstate Health Certificate, signed by an accredited veterinarian and dated no more than 30 days before travel. Canadian airlines do not require a certificate, but travelers should follow the procedures listed above to pass the customs inspection upon arrival. As do many US carriers, both Air Canada and Canadian Airlines International require a leak-proof kennel for a dog or cat. In addition, Canadian Airlines International will not accept puppies or kittens under 8 weeks old. Policies and restrictions vary among other carriers — so check with the airline well in advance of your departure.

It's a good idea to buy a traveling kennel if your dog is being transported by plane or car. Most airlines sell them, as do pet stores. Any animal must be boxed for the plane trip; on a car trip a kennel is a good safety measure. The most important features of a kennel are size, comfort, and cleanliness. Your kennel should be large enough to permit room for your pet to walk around, turn around, and lie down; it should be constructed completely of non-chewable materials — metal or high-grade plastic. Chewable materials such as cardboard or fiberboard can be toxic. The kennel should have a sanitized pad on the bottom with a wire mesh floor that is raised at least an inch above the pad. The box should lock, be thoroughly ventilated, and be easy to handle and transport.

If your pet is traveling by plane, label the kennel with your name, address, destination, pet's name, and special handling instructions. Remove the animal's collar before putting it in the kennel. Dogs should not be muzzled. Put a few toys and familiar objects in the kennel to acquaint the animal with its box before the start of the trip.

Airlines will usually allow one kenneled pet to fly in the passenger compartment for a standard fee, if the kennel fits underneath the seat. This space should be reserved when you reserve your own seat. If there is no space in the passenger compartment, or the animal is too large to be brought in, it must fly as cargo, in a special area reserved for live cargo. Charges are established on the basis of weight and size of the animal.

Don't ship your pet during very hot or very cold weather; animals are sometimes left on the runway during the loading of the hold. Afternoon and evening flights are best in hot weather. Fly in off-peak times, when the cargo hold has less baggage and more ventilation and the personnel have more time to watch your pet. Pets should be the last cargo loaded, and the boxed pet should be given to the cargo officer, not to the ticket-counter person, who will place the kennel on a conveyor belt. Avoid flights with stopovers and transfers lest your pet be misplaced.

When you land, retrieve your pet as soon as possible. Return it to its normal feeding schedule slowly.

If you decide to drive with an animal, be aware that animals can suffer motion sickness. You can ascertain if your pet is susceptible by taking it for short trips before you undertake the real journey. Here are a few tips to make your trip with your pet as much fun as possible:

1. Bring along a kennel or sleeping box for a dog or cat.
2. Make plenty of exercise and feeding stops. *You* may want to set a new record for the distance — your pet does not.
3. Take along some of your pet's toys or most adored objects.
4. Don't let your dog ride with its head out of the window. There are cinders, dirt, and rocks that can injure its eyes and head, and the wind can irritate its nasal and respiratory passages. Keep the windows almost closed, allowing enough ventilation for comfort.
5. If you have to leave your pet alone in the car, park in the shade and leave the windows down an inch or two for air. But don't leave the car unlocked. Canadians like dogs, too.

But it is best to leave your pet at home. That way you won't miss the thrill of finding out how glad it is to see you when you get back.

Staying Healthy

The surest way to return home in good health is to be prepared for medical problems that might occur on vacation. Below we've outlined everything you need to think about before you go.

Obviously, your state of health is crucial to the success of a vacation. There's nothing like an injury or illness, whether serious or relatively minor, to dampen or destroy a holiday. And health problems always seem more debilitating when you are away. Most problems, however, can be prevented or greatly alleviated with intelligent foresight and attention to precautionary details.

Older travelers or anyone suffering from a chronic medical condition, such as diabetes, high blood pressure, cardiopulmonary disease, asthma, or ear, eye, or sinus trouble, should consult a physician before leaving home. A checkup is advisable. A pre-trip dental checkup is not a bad idea, either.

FIRST AID: Put together a compact, personal medical kit including Band-Aids, antiseptic, nose drops, insect repellent, aspirin, an extra pair of prescription glasses, sunglasses, or contact lenses (and a copy of your prescription for glasses or lenses), over-the-counter remedies for diarrhea, indigestion, and motion sickness, a thermometer, and a supply of those prescription medicines you take regularly. In a corner of your kit, keep a list of all the drugs you have brought and their purpose as well as duplicate copies of your doctor's prescriptions (or a note from your doctor). These copies could come in handy if you are ever questioned by police or airport authorities about any drugs you are carrying; they are also necessary to refill any prescriptions in the event of loss. It is also a good idea to ask your doctor to prepare a medical identification card that includes such information as your blood type, your social security number, any allergies or chronic health problems you have, and your medical insurance information. Considering the essential contents of this kit, keep it with you, rather than in your luggage.

SUNBURN: Depending on when and where you're vacationing, the burning power of the sun can be phenomenal and can quickly cause severe sunburn or sunstroke. To protect yourself against these ills, wear sunglasses, take along a broad-brimmed hat and cover-up, and use a sunscreen lotion. When choosing a sunscreen, look for one that has a PABA (the para-amino-benzoic acid) base. PABA blocks out most of the harmful ultraviolet rays of the sun.

Some tips on tanning:

1. Allow only 20 minutes or so the first day; increase your exposure gradually.
2. You are most likely to get a painful burn when the sun is the strongest, between 10 AM and 2 PM.

80 GETTING READY / Staying Healthy

3. When judging if you've had enough sun, remember that time in the water (in terms of exposure to ultraviolet rays) is the same as time lying on the beach.
4. A beach umbrella or other cover doesn't keep all the rays of the sun from reaching you. If you are sensitive to light, be especially careful.
5. As many ultraviolet rays reach you on cloudy days as on sunny days. Even if you don't feel hot, you are still exposed to rays.

If, despite these precautions, you find yourself with a painful sunburn, take a cooling bath, apply a first-aid spray or the liquid of an aloe plant, and stay out of the sun. If you develop a more serious burn and experience chills, fever, nausea, headaches, or dizziness, consult a doctor at once.

WATER SAFETY: Canada, particularly in the Maritime Provinces, boasts some beautiful beaches, but it's important to remember that they can also be treacherous. A few precautions are necessary: Beware of the undertow, that current of water running back down the beach after a wave has washed ashore; it can knock you off your feet and into the surf. Even more dangerous is the riptide, a strong current of water running against the tide, which can pull you out toward sea. If this happens, don't panic or try to fight the current, because it will only exhaust you; instead, ride it out while waiting for it to subside, which usually happens not too far from shore, or try swimming away. parallel to the beach.

INSECTS AND OTHER PESTS: Blackflies and mosquitoes can be troublesome, so as we have said, be sure to pack a repellent. If you are bitten by a snake call a doctor immediately. Cockroaches and termites thrive in warm weather, but pose no serious health threat.

WATER: The tap water in Canada is generally quite pure. However, when traveling in rural areas, be aware that the local water supply may not be purified and local residents either have developed immunities to the natural bacteria or boil it for drinking. You should also avoid drinking water from streams or freshwater pools. In campgrounds water is usually indicated as drinkable or for washing only — if you're not sure, ask.

Following all these precautions will not guarantee an illness-free trip, but it should minimize the risk. As a final hedge against economic if not physical problems, make sure your health insurance will cover all eventualities while you are away. If not, there are policies designed specifically for travel. Many are worth investigating. As with all insurance, they seem like a waste of money until you need them.

HELPFUL PUBLICATIONS: Practically every phase of health care — before, during, and after a trip — is covered in *The New Traveler's Health Guide* by Drs. Patrick J. Doyle and James E. Banta. It is available for $4.95, plus $2 postage and handling, from Acropolis Books Ltd., 2400 17th St. NW, Washington, DC 20009-9964; phone: 800-451-7771.

For more information regarding preventive health care for travelers contact *IAMAT (International Association for Medical Assistance to Travelers)*, 417 Center St., Lewiston, NY 14092 (phone: 716-754-4883) or write to the US Government Printing Office, Washington, DC 20402, for the US Public Health Service's booklet *Health Information for International Travel* (HEW Publication CDC-86-8280; enclose check or money order for $4.75 payable to Superintendent of Documents).

On the Road

Credit and Currency

 FOREIGN EXCHANGE: Americans should have little difficulty with matters of exchange in Canada. Both countries have money systems based on 100 cents to the dollar, although the US dollar and the Canadian dollar are not equal in value. In recent years, the Canadian dollar has been worth between 70¢ and 85¢ US. This provides Americans in Canada with a bonus of 15% to 30% in buying power.

Although American money is usually accepted in Canada, travelers would be wise to exchange their funds at federally chartered banks (rather than credit unions or trust companies), where they will receive the best prevailing rate of exchange. By using Canadian money during their travels, travelers will avoid exchange problems and erratic exchange rates at stores and hotels, which are usually far less favorable than those offered by banks.

Money and all types of negotiable instruments, in any amount, may be brought into or taken out of the US. Citizens of any country importing or exporting $10,000 or more between Canada and the US are required to file a report of the transaction with US Customs (US Customs Form 4790). If you have any questions about this regulation, contact the US Customs Service in your city, or at 1301 Constitution Ave. NW, Washington, DC 20229 (phone: 202-566-8005).

TRAVELER'S CHECKS: It's wise to carry traveler's checks on the road instead of (or in addition to) cash, since it's possible to replace traveler's checks if they are stolen or lost; travelers can usually receive partial or full replacement funds the same day if they have their purchase receipt and proper identification. Issued in various denominations and available in both US and Canadian dollars, with adequate proof of identification (credit cards, driver's license, passport) traveler's checks are as good as cash in most hotels, restaurants, stores, and banks. More and more establishments are, however, beginning to restrict the amount of traveler's checks they will accept or cash, so it is wise to purchase at least some of your checks in small — say, $20 — denominations.

To avoid complications should you need to redeem lost checks, keep the purchase receipt and an accurate list, by serial number, of the checks that have been spent or cashed. Always keep these records separate from the checks themselves (you may want to give them to a traveling companion to hold).

Every type of traveler's check is legal tender in banks around the world and each company guarantees full replacement if checks are lost or stolen. After that the similarity ends. Some charge a fee for purchase, others are free; you can buy traveler's checks at almost any bank, and some are available by mail. Most important, each traveler's check issuer differs slightly in its refund policy — the amount refunded immediately, the accessibility of refund locations, and the availability of a 24-hour refund service. Here is a list of the major traveler's check companies whose checks are accepted in Canada and the numbers to call in the event that loss or theft makes replacement necessary:

> *American Express:* To report lost or stolen checks in the US and Canada, call 800-221-7282.
> *Bank of America:* To report lost or stolen checks in the US, call 800-227-3460; in Canada, call collect, 24 hours, 415-622-3800 or 415-624-5400.
> *Citicorp:* To report lost or stolen checks in the US, call 800-645-6556 or 813-623-1709, collect, in the US and Canada.
> *MasterCard:* To report lost or stolen checks in the US, call 800-223-9920 or 212-974-5696, collect, in the US and Canada.
> *Thomas Cook MasterCard:* To report lost or stolen checks in the US, call 800-223-9920 or 212-974-5696, collect, in the US and Canada.
> *Visa:* To report lost or stolen checks in the US and Canada, call 800-227-6811 or 415-574-7111, collect.

CREDIT CARDS: There are two different kinds of credit cards available to consumers in the United States, and travelers must decide which one best serves their interests — although they often elect to carry both types. "Convenience" or "travel and entertainment" cards — American Express, Diners Club, and Carte Blanche — are widely accepted. They cost the cardholder a basic annual membership fee ($35 to $50 is typical for these three), but put no strict limit on the amount that may be charged on the card in any month. However, the entire amount charged must be paid in full at the end of each billing period (usually a month), so the cardholder is not actually extended any long-term credit.

"Bank cards" are also rarely issued free these days (with the exception of Sears' Discover Card), and certain services they provide (check cashing, for example) can carry extra cost. But this category comprises *real* credit cards, in the sense that the cardholder has the privilege of paying a small amount (1/36 is typical) of the total outstanding balance in each billing period. For the privilege, the cardholder is charged a high annual interest rate (currently three to four times the going bank passbook savings rate) on the balance owed. Many banks now charge interest from the purchase date, not from the first billing date (as they used to do); consider this when you are calculating the actual cost of a purchase. In addition, a maximum is set on the total amount the cardholder can charge, which represents the limit of credit the card company is willing to extend. The major bank cards are Visa and MasterCard, with Discover growing rapidly.

Getting any credit card will involve a fairly extensive credit check; to pass, you will need a job (at which you have worked for at least a year), a minimum salary, and a good credit rating.

Note that some establishments you may encounter during the course of your travels may not honor any credit cards and some may not honor *all* cards, so there is a practical reason to carry more than one when you travel. Most US credit cards, including the principal bank cards, are honored in Canada. The following is a list of credit cards that enjoy wide domestic and international acceptance:

> *American Express:* Emergency personal check cashing at American Express or representatives' offices (up to $200 cash in local currency, $800 in traveler's checks); emergency personal check cashing for guests at participating hotels (up to $250 in the US and Canada), and, for holders of airline tickets, at participating airlines in the US (up to $250). Extended payment plan for cruises, tours, railway and airline tickets, as well as other pre-paid travel arrangements. $100,000 free travel accident insurance on plane, train, bus, and ship if ticket was charged to card; up to $1 million additional low-cost flight insurance

available. As we went to press, American Express had announced a 3-hour replacement of lost or stolen traveler's checks. Contact American Express Card, PO Box 39, Church St. Station, New York, NY 10008 (phone: 800-528-4800, throughout the US except New York; 212-477-5700 in New York and Canada).

Carte Blanche: Extended payment plan for air travel (up to $2,000). $150,000 free travel accident insurance on plane, train, and ship if ticket was charged to card, plus $1,250 checked or carry-on baggage insurance, and $25,000 rental car insurance. Contact Carte Blanche, PO Box 17326, Denver, CO 80217 (phone: 800-525-9135 in the US; 303-790-2433 in Canada, cardholders may call collect).

Diners Club: Emergency personal check cashing at participating Citibank branches, and other designated banks worldwide (up to $1,000 in a 14-day period, with a minimum per check of $50 in the US and $250 in Canada); emergency personal check cashing for guests at participating hotels and motels (up to $250 per stay). Qualified card members are eligible for extended payment plan. $350,000 free travel accident insurance on plane, train, and ship if ticket was charged to your card, plus $1,250 checked and carry-on baggage insurance and $25,000 rental car insurance. Medical, legal, and travel assistance available worldwide (phone: 800-356-3448, or collect from outside the US, 214-680-6480). Contact Diners Club, PO Box 17326, Denver, CO 80217 (phone: 800-525-9135 in the US; 303-790-2433 in Canada, cardholders may call collect).

Discover Card: Created by Sears, Roebuck, it provides the holder with cash advances at more than 500 locations nationwide and offers a revolving credit line for purchases at a wide range of service establishments. Other deposit, lending, and investment services are also available. For information, call 800-858-5588 (if you can't reach this number by dialing directly, dial an operator who will be able to place the call).

MasterCard and Visa: Cash advance at participating banks worldwide, and a revolving credit line for purchases at a wide range of service establishments. Interest charge on unpaid balance and other details are set by each individual issuing bank. Check with your bank for information.

No matter what you are using — traveler's checks, credit cards, or cash — plan ahead. Also, carry your travel funds carefully. You might consider carrying your money (cash and traveler's checks) in more than one place. Never put money in a back pocket or an open purse. Money should be kept in a buttoned front pocket, in a money purse pinned inside your shirt or blouse, or in one of the convenient money belts or leg pouches sold by many travel shops. It may be quaint and old-fashioned, but it's safe.

Accommodations

As everywhere else in the world, tourism to Canada has increased, with a concomitant explosion in the Canadian motel and hotel industry. In Vancouver, planners were spurred into action by EXPO '86 and Calgary responded to hosting the 1988 Winter Olympics in much the same way that Montreal reacted to Expo '67 and the 1976 Summer Olympics. Reverberations of the recent international boom also have been felt everywhere in Canada, as virtually every major hotel chain built new hostelries across the country. In this respect, the accommodations situation in Canada is not so different from that in the US. Though there are many independently owned places to stay in varying price ranges — including some fine old hotels and lovely country inns (you will find our pick of them listed in THE CITIES, DIVERSIONS, and DIRECTIONS) — the majority of the hotels in Canada are relatively new establishments that are part of national or international chains, and they are to a great extent standardized in price and quality.

There is at least one benefit to this standardization: The overall level of accommodations is quite high. Thus, travelers arriving in an unfamiliar town can assume that there will be safe, clean, and comfortable accommodations nearby in an acceptable price range.

You can choose for yourself just what price range is acceptable. Some chains — like the *Four Seasons, Hilton International,* and *Westin* — offer accommodations with a broad range of facilities and amenities. The hotels are modern and comfortable, the service competent, the facilities complete, and the prices, as you would expect, are high, comparable to those at similar establishments in the US. More and more, the trend in such top-ranking Canadian hotels is toward year-round convenience: They are built in conjunction with business-residential-shopping complexes, clustered together within short, weatherproof walking distance. Also on the expensive side are Canada's big resort hotels, with extensive first class sports facilities, amenities, and locations — the *Banff Springs* hotel in Alberta and the *Gray Rocks Inn* in Quebec, for example.

RESERVATIONS: It is best to make advance reservations for accommodations in any major Canadian city, even if you are traveling during the off-season. Several Canadian cities have convention centers, and hotel space can be scarce if a large convention is being hosted at the same time you visit. All the hotel entries in the *Best in Town* sections of THE CITIES chapters include phone numbers for reservations. Farm vacation accommodations, and hotels near major summer destinations like Banff and the Maritime Provinces, should be booked as far in advance as possible because these areas do not have as many facilities as the cities. Most major hotel and motel chains list their toll-free (800) reservation numbers in the white pages of the telephone directory, and any hotel within a chain can assure reservations for you at sister facilities.

The advice to make reservations early is always woven into every travel article; making a *late* reservation may be almost as good advice. It's not at all unusual for hotel rooms, totally unavailable as far as 6 months in advance, to suddenly become available 6 days — or even 6 hours — before your arrival. Cancellations tend to occur closer to rather than farther from a designated date, and somewhat flexible travelers recognize that there will almost always be some cancellation on the date they plan to arrive.

OVERBOOKING: The worldwide travel boom has brought with it some abuses that are pretty much standard operating procedure in any industry facing demand that frequently outstrips supply. Anticipating a certain percentage of no-shows, hotels routinely overbook rooms. When cancellations don't occur and everybody with a reservation arrives as promised, it's not impossible to find yourself with a valid reservation for which no room exists.

There's no sure way to avoid all the pitfalls of overbooking, but you can minimize the risks. Always carry evidence of your confirmed reservation. This should be a direct communication from the hotel — to you or your travel agent — and should specify the exact dates and duration of yur accommodations and the price. The weakest form of confirmation is the voucher slip a travel agent routinely issues, since it carries no official indication that the hotel itself has verified your reservation.

Even better is the increasing opportunity to guarantee hotel reservations by giving the hotel (or its reservation system) your credit card number and agreeing that the hotel is authorized to charge you for that room no matter what. It's still possible to cancel if you do so before 6 PM of the day of your reservations (sometimes 5 PM in resort areas), but when you do cancel under this arrangement, make sure you get a cancellation number to protect you from being billed erroneously.

If all these precautions fail and you are left standing at the reservation desk with a reservation the hotel clerk won't honor, you have a last resort: Complain as long and as loudly as necessary to get satisfaction! The person who makes the most noise usually gets the last room in the house. It might as well be you.

What if you can't get reservations in the first place? This is a problem that often confronts businesspeople who can't plan months ahead. The word from savvy travelers is that a bit of currency (perhaps attached discreetly to a business card) often increases your chances with recalcitrant desk clerks. There are less venal ways of improving your odds, however. If you are making reservations for business, ask an associate at your destination to make reservations for you.

There is a good reason to do this above and beyond the very real point that a resident has the broadest knowledge of local hotels. Often a hotel will appear sold out on its computer when in fact a few rooms are available. The proliferation of computerized reservations has made it unwise for a hotel to indicate that it suddenly has five rooms available (from cancellations) when there might be 30 or 40 travel agents lined up in the computer waiting for them. That small a number of vacancies is much more likely to be held by the hotel for its own local sale, so a local associate is an invaluable conduit to these otherwise inaccessible rooms.

BUDGET ACCOMMODATIONS: The budget hotel is designed to offer basic accommodations (a comfortable bed, clean bathroom, central heating and air conditioning) without frills or ancillary services, bar or restaurant, or elaborate lobby. Canada has two budget hotel chains, *Journey's End* and *Relax Inns*. Many other pleasant, clean, and inexpensive independents — motels and guesthouses — can be found often throughout the country. Each of the provincial tourist offices publishes a comprehensive accommodations booklet that gives a complete rundown on all licensed establishments in its territory. Listings include prices, amenities, and, sometimes, nearby attractions. Some provinces, such as Manitoba, Quebec, and Ontario, go a step further and use a star system to rate the standards of comfort found at each hotel; Quebec also rates restaurants in the various establishments.

At hotels and motels in all price ranges, ask about minimum rates, weekend discounts, weekly rates, commercial discounts for business travelers, special promotions, and special rates for children staying in the same room as their parents.

During the summer, major universities and colleges throughout Canada put up travelers in their dormitories for modest prices. There's no one guide that lists all the accommodations offered, but provincial tourist offices should be able to tell you what's available in campus housing. (See *Tourist Information* in this section.) Hostels are another inexpensive choice. The *Canadian Hostelling Association* (1600 James Naismith Dr., 6th Fl., Gloucester, Ottawa, Ontario K1B 5N4; phone: 613-748-5638) publishes a free handbook listing Canadian hostels. For additional information on hostels, see *Hints for Single Travelers* in this section.

BED-AND-BREAKFAST AND OTHER ACCOMMODATIONS: Bed-and-breakfast accommodations (or B&Bs, as they are known in Great Britain) are becoming popular in Canada. Bed-and-breakfast establishments provide precisely what the name implies. The bed may be in an extra room in a family home, in an apartment with a separate entrance, or in a free-standing cottage elsewhere on the host's property, and a private bath often comes with it, as does, occasionally, a kitchenette. The breakfast will probably be a version of the continental breakfast: fruit plus juice, toast or roll or homemade bread and jam or marmalade, and coffee or tea. Or, if you're in a studio with a kitchen, you may be furnished with the makings of a breakfast you'll have to prepare for yourself.

Beyond these two fundamentals, nothing else is predictable about going the bed-and-breakfast route. You may have a patio, garden, pool, and barbecue pit at your door, or only the bare necessities. Accommodations range from private homes and lovely mansions to small inns and guesthouses. A private bath isn't always offered, so check before you reserve. Also, there can be a fine line between "bed-and-breakfast establishment" and "boarding house," so find out as much as you can before you book to avoid disappointment. The big-city version of this type of accommodation are guesthouses, common in Montreal. These are usually well-maintained brownstones that rent rooms on a daily or weekly basis. Both bed-and-breakfast establishments and guesthouses are listed in local newspapers.

A directory of such establishments, *The Complete Guide to Bed & Breakfast, Inns, and Guesthouses in the U.S. and Canada* by Pamela Lanier, covers over 5,000 bed-and-breakfast establishments as well as over 250 bed-and-breakfast reservations services; available for $14.95 from John Muir Publications, Box 613, Santa Fe, NM 87505 (phone: 505-982-4078). Another useful directory is the annual brochure published by the *Bed & Breakfast Reservations Services Worldwide, Inc.* (a trade association), which provides a listing of its members. It costs $3; to order the most recent edition write to Bed & Breakfast Reservations Services Worldwide, Inc., PO Box 14797, Dept. 174, Baton Rouge, LA 70898, or call 504-346-1928.

Farm, seashore, or ranch vacations, including bed-and-breakfast establishments, offer excellent vacation value in a comfortable Canadian home environment. For between $25 and $100 a day, people will put you up and, most times, feed you in their own homes. Provincial and city tourist authorities have lists of participating farms (see also *Farm and Ranch Vacations,* DIVERSIONS). Or contact *Canadian Country Vacations Association,* 525 Kylemore Ave., Winnipeg, Manitoba R3L 1B5 (phone: 204-475-6624), which offers "Meet the People" tours, including a variety of locally hosted vacations in Manitoba and eastern Canada.

HOME EXCHANGES: An alternative for families who are content to stay in one place during their vacation is a home exchange. The home exchange is an exceptionally inexpensive way to ensure comfortable, reasonable living quarters with amenities that no hotel could possibly offer, often including a car. Moreover, it allows you to live in a new community in a way that few tourists ever do: For a little while, at least, you will become something of a local resident. Several companies publish directories of individuals and families willing to trade homes with others for a specific period of time. In some cases, you must be willing to list your own home in the directory; in others, you can subscribe without appearing in it. There is no guarantee that you will find a listing in the area you are interested in, but each of the organizations given below has hundreds or even thousands of foreign and domestic properties.

International Home Exchange Service/Intervac US: Part of the Intervac network of 22 countries, which publishes three books containing 7,000 listings per year. The $35 annual subscription entitles you to the three books and the opportunity to be listed. PO Box 3975, San Francisco, CA 94119 (call collect: 415-435-3497).

Vacation Exchange Club: Through its affiliates in the Directory Group Association, this organization offers some 6,000 listings, in 40 countries. For $24.70 a year, the subscriber receives two directories, one in late winter and one in spring, plus a listing in one of them. The directories without the subscriber's own listing cost $16. For a free brochure describing the program, contact the organization at 12006 111th Ave., Youngtown, AZ 85363 (phone: 602-972-2186).

World Wide Exchange: The $45 annual membership fee includes one free listing (for house, yacht, or motorhome) and three free guides. 1344 Pacific Ave., Suite 103, Santa Cruz, CA 95060 (phone: 408-425-0531).

Dining Out

In the past 15 years, Canadian cities have been experiencing something of a restaurant boom. Part of this is due to the larger change of medium-size cities becoming conscious of their distinctive qualities as urban communities. Another factor that affects these areas as well as the large cities is the recent

GETTING READY / Dining Out

establishment of training programs for cooks, chefs, and restaurateurs in colleges across the country. Although most of these programs are less than 15 years old, they are already making an impact on the dining-out scene.

The change is reflected in a proliferation of restaurants that serve everything from traditional French food with rich sauces to nouvelle cuisine, in which the emphasis is on basic ingredients, carefully and creatively prepared. It is also evident in the international reputation Canadian chefs have earned in recent years, starting in 1983 when Canadian chefs took five first places in the six international culinary competitions they entered, and continuing the next year at the World Culinary Olympics, where Team Canada won a total of 15 gold medals (including one Grand Gold and the title of World Champion of the Nations). In November 1987, the Canadian team picked up seven gold medals at an international culinary competition in Basel, Switzerland. So now travelers have even greater reason to discover the regional specialties reponsible for Canada's gastronomic success.

The four Atlantic provinces — Newfoundland, Prince Edward Island, New Brunswick, and Nova Scotia — specialize in fresh seafood. Lobsters turn up everywhere from traditional country inn lobster suppers to summer beach parties and in various shapes and forms — boiled, broiled, steamed, in casseroles, and in salads. Atlantic salmon and oyster stews are New Brunswick's main dishes, served with baked beans and steamed brown bread. Prince Edward Island's juicy Malpeque oysters are very popular, and large sea scallops, clam chowder, and herring dishes are specialties of Nova Scotia. In Newfoundland cod is king, but the Great Banks also brings salmon, trout, halibut, and hake to the table, served fresh, dried, salted, or in a thick, hearty fish stew. Throughout the provinces, the abundant native fruits and berries find their way into rich desserts — apple, blueberry, cranberry, blackberry, and strawberry pies, puddings, jams, and jellies.

Farther inland lies the traditional gastronomic capital of Canada, Montreal. Like all of Quebec, Montreal is renowned for its French cuisine; in Montreal it's done with a special panache. Restaurants here run the gamut from classic haute cuisine served in austere settings to the provincial French fare of Brittany and Normandy. French Canadians have developed a distinct cuisine similar to the food of Normandy, where many French Canadians originated. Typical dishes include thick pea or cabbage soups; for the main course, meat pies filled with pork (known as *tourtière*) or *cipâte,* a beef pie, and for dessert, fruit pies stuffed with a triple layer of blueberries. Another Quebec specialty served after meals is *trempette,* home-baked bread soaked in maple syrup and topped with whipped cream.

Also special in Montreal is Brome Lake duckling, prepared with a specimen from the famous duck-raising area of Quebec near the Vermont border. The duckling is filled with apple stuffing and cooked in calvados (apple brandy). It's a highly reputed delicacy, available in any number of Montreal's rustic French-Canadian restaurants as well as at the Ritz-Carlton's elegant restaurant, *Café de Paris.* Montreal also has a good selection of ethnic restaurants — Chinese, Vietnamese, Italian, Spanish, and Greek. Quebec City's restaurants are dominated by provincial French kitchens, a pervasive cuisine in its elegant restaurants as well as in the city's many bistros and crêperies.

Toronto is Canada's third East Coast food center. There is a strong French influence here as well as a substantial number of ethnic restaurants which reflect the cosmopolitan atmosphere of the city. In addition to Greek, Chinese, and Italian restaurants, you can sample various Eastern European specialties in the Hungarian, Czechoslovakian, and Polish shops and restaurants of Kensington Market.

Across the prairies and cattle country of Manitoba, Saskatchewan, and Alberta, restaurants serve hearty fare. Thick, tender steaks and freshly baked bread made with Canada's high-quality grains are a mainstay. The myriad lakes yield freshwater fish such as whitefish and pickerel. Menus are enriched by the heritage of the Ukrainian immigrants who populate the prairie cities; stuffed cabbage, potato dumplings, spicy sausage, and borscht are routinely served.

West Coast cuisine is dominated by the sea; the Pacific provides a bounty of seafood — king crab, oysters, shrimp, cod, haddock, and salmon — usually served up with produce grown in British Columbia. Apples, peaches, plums, pears, Bing cherries, and a variety of berries grow here and appear on the table — fresh and unadorned, in fancy desserts, and sometimes as locally produced fruit cordials or wines. Vancouver and Victoria are the best food cities on the West Coast and offer an innovative selection of regional specialties and international cuisine. A good countrywide guide to Canadian restaurants is *Where to Eat in Canada,* by Anne Hardy (Oberon Press, Ottawa; $9.30). Though it leaves a little to be desired in the way of organization, it does provide useful descriptions and informed opinions on the places it covers and is updated annually.

RESERVATIONS: Restaurants vary widely on reservation policies. At some, it is absolutely required (especially at more expensive and popular places in larger cities); other equally fine restaurants refuse to take reservations at all — the patron simply arrives and waits until a table is free. If you are planning a big night out, it certainly is advisable to call the restaurant early in the day (or a few days in advance) to find out its policy. Every restaurant listing in *Best in Town* gives its reservation policy and a telephone number (if the restaurant has a phone).

Time Zones, Business Hours, and Bank Holidays

TIME ZONES: Canada is divided into seven time zones, but because the two most northeasterly zones — Newfoundland Standard Time and Atlantic Standard Time — are only a half-hour apart, there is no more than a 5½-hour difference between its east and west coasts. Traveling west from Atlantic Standard Time, the zones get earlier by hour intervals.

The zones encompass the following areas: Newfoundland Standard Time — Newfoundland and Labrador; Atlantic Standard Time — Maritime Provinces, Gaspé Peninsula, Anticosti Island, Quebec Province east of Comeau Bay, most of Baffin Island, and Melville Peninsula; Eastern Standard Time — Quebec Province west of Comeau Bay and all of Ontario east of 90° longitude; Central Standard Time — Ontario west of 90° longitude, Manitoba, and the Keewatin district of Saskatchewan in the southeastern section of the province; Mountain Standard Time — the remainder of Saskatchewan including Regina, Alberta, those parts of the Northwest Territories directly north of Saskatchewan and Alberta, and the northeastern section of British Columbia; Pacific Standard Time — the remainder of British Columbia; Yukon Standard Time — the Yukon Territory.

Daylight Savings Time begins across the country on the last Sunday in April and extends to the last Saturday in October. It is not observed, however, in most parts of Saskatchewan.

BUSINESS HOURS: Business hours throughout Canada are fairly standard and very similar to those in the US: 9 AM to 5 PM, Mondays through Fridays. While an hour lunch break is customary, employees often take it in shifts so that it rarely interrupts service, especially at banks and other public service operations.

Banks are traditionally open from 10 AM to 3 PM, Mondays through Thursdays, and until 6 PM on Fridays, but as in the US, the trend is toward longer hours. Banks are generally closed on Saturdays and Sundays, although in major cities some banks offer services on Saturday mornings.

Retail stores are usually open from 9 or 9:30 AM to 5 or 5:30 PM. They are usually open until 9 PM on Thursday or Friday nights. Most major stores are open on Saturdays, closed on Sundays. Blue laws, which close some bars and restaurants on Sundays or stipulate that you can only be served an alcoholic drink with a meal, vary from place to place. Delicatessens and supermarkets are open from 9:30 AM to 5:30 PM, although some stay open later. In major cities, you can usually find a drugstore that is open until midnight, or all night, and on Sundays; check the local yellow pages.

HOLIDAYS: National holidays, when banks, post offices, libraries, most stores, and many museums are closed, include: *New Year's Day,* January 1; *Good Friday,* the Friday before Easter; *Easter Monday,* the Monday following Easter; *Victoria Day,* a Monday in late May; *Canada Day,* July 1; *Labour Day,* the first Monday in September; *Thanksgiving,* the second Monday in October; *Remembrance Day,* November 11; *Christmas Day,* December 25; *Boxing Day,* December 26.

There are also several provincial holidays, which may vary by a day or so from year to year. In 1989, Newfoundland residents celebrated *St. Patrick's Day* on March 13; *St. George's Day* on April 24; *Discovery Day* on June 26; *Memorial Day* on July 1; and *Orangeman's Day* on July 10. In Quebec, *Saint-Jean Baptiste Day* was celebrated on June 24; in the Yukon, *Discovery Days* are usually celebrated from around August 19 through August 21. Alberta celebrates *Heritage Day,* which usually falls on August 7, and this date is also observed as *British Columbia Day* in British Columbia and as a civic holiday in Manitoba, New Brunswick, the Northwest Territories, Ontario, and Saskatchewan.

Mail, Telephone, and Electricity

MAIL: Main offices and postal stations in Canada are open from 9 AM to 5:30 PM, Mondays through Fridays. Some offices have Saturday hours. Stamps are also available at most hotel desks. Vending machines for stamps are outside post offices and in shopping centers. The rate for a regular letter posted in Canada to be sent to the US is currently 44¢; a postcard costs about 32¢. All but local or nearby deliveries are air mailed.

To have your first class mail held or forwarded to another US or a Canadian address while on vacation, fill in a change of address card (available at US post offices). Generally, this free service lasts for a month, longer at the discretion of the post office. You can also have your third class mail sent on, but you will have to pay for this service.

It is possible to receive mail directly in Canada even if you plan to spend most of your time traveling. Allow a minimum of 10 days for mail delivery between the US and Canada. Visitors may have mail sent to "General Delivery" by using the following: (Name), c/o General Office, Main Post Office (City, Province, and Postal Code, obtained from the post office). Mail must be picked up by the addressee in person within 15 days, or it will be returned to sender.

If you are an American Express customer (either a cardholder or carrier of American Express traveler's checks) you can have mail sent to their offices in cities on your route. American Express will hold mail for 30 days; letters must be marked "Client Mail Service." Any *American Express Travel Service* office can provide information on its mail service, as well as a directory to American Express offices in Canada.

TELEPHONE: Public telephones are on hand just about everywhere if you are in a city or town. This includes transportation terminals, hotel lobbies, restaurants, drugstores, sidewalk booths, and along the highways. The average price of a local call is 25¢ (CN). US coins cannot be used in pay phones.

Long-distance rates are charged according to when the call is placed: weekdays daytime; weekdays evenings; and nights, weekends, and holidays. Least expensive are the calls you dial yourself from a private phone at night, and on weekends and holidays. It is always more expensive to call from a pay phone than it is to call from a private phone (you must pay for a minimum 3-minute call). If the operator assists you, calls are more expensive. This includes credit card, bill-to-a-third-number, collect, and time-and-charge calls as well as person-to-person calls, which are the most expensive. Check the phone directory of the city you are in for exact rates and reductions.

If you are planning to be away for more than a month, you may be able to save money by asking the telephone company to temporarily suspend your home telephone service. You can also arrange to have your calls forwarded to another number.

Hotel Surcharges – When you are calling from your hotel room, inquire about any surcharges the hotel may have. These can be excessive, but can be avoided by calling collect, using a telephone credit card (free from any US phone company), or calling from a public pay phone.

Emergencies – Dial "O" for the operator, who will connect you directly with the service you need.

ELECTRICITY: Canada has the same electrical current system as that in the US: 110 volts, 60 cycles, alternating current (AC). American appliances running on standard current can be used throughout Canada without adapters or convertors.

Medical and Legal Help on the Road

MEDICAL HELP: You will discover, in the event of an emergency, that most tourist facilities — transportation companies, hotels, and resorts — are equipped to handle the situation quickly and efficiently. All hospitals are prepared for emergency cases, and even the tiniest of Canadian towns has a medical clinic or private physician nearby. Canadian medical service is excellent, with costs comparable to medical care in the US.

If you are on your own, you can get emergency help by dialing "O" for Operator. You will be put into immediate contact with the service you require. If you are staying in a hotel or motel, ask for the house physician, who may visit you in your room or ask you to visit an office. (This service is apt to be expensive, especially if the doctor makes a "house" call to your room.) In larger cities, many hospitals have walk-in clinics designed to serve people who do not really need emergency service, but who have no place to go for immediate medical attention. You can also go directly to the emergency room. A phone call to a local hospital requesting the name of a doctor will usually turn up a name; some hospitals actually have referral services for this purpose. The medical society in most provinces will refer you to a member physician in the specialty you need (listed in the telephone book under the city or provincial medical society).

Emergency assistance is also available from the various medical programs designed for travelers who have chronic ailments or whose illness requires them to return home. The *Medic Alert Foundation* sells identification emblems that specify that the wearer has a health condition that may not be readily apparent to a casual observer. A heart condition, diabetes, epilepsy, or severe allergy are the sorts of things that these emblems were developed to communicate, conditions that can result in tragic errors if not recognized when emergency treatment is necessary and when you may be unable to speak for yourself. In addition to the identification emblems, the foundation maintains a computerized central file from which your complete medical history is available 24 hours a day by telephone call (the telephone number is clearly inscribed on the ID badge). The one-time membership is tax deductible and ranges from $25 to $45, and is based on the type of metal from which the emblem is made, the choices ranging from stainless steel to 10K gold-filled. For information, contact the *Medic Alert Foundation,* Turlock, CA 95381-1009 (phone: 209-668-3333 or 800-ID-ALERT).

International SOS Assistance also offers a program to cover medical emergencies while traveling. Members are provided with telephone access — 24 hours a day, 365 days a year — to a worldwide, monitored, multilingual network of medical centers. A phone call brings assistance ranging from a telephone consultation to transportation home by ambulance or aircraft, and in some cases transportation of a family member to wherever you are hospitalized. The service can be purchased for a week ($15), a week plus additional days ($15, plus $2 for each additional day), a month ($45), or a year ($195). For information, contact *International SOS Assistance, Inc.,* PO Box 11568, Philadelphia, PA 19116 (phone: 215-244-1500 or 800-523-8930).

The *International Health Care Service* provides information about health conditions in various countries, advice on immunizations recommended, and treatment if necessary. A pre-travel counseling and immunization package costs $175; a post-travel screening, $75, plus lab work. Appointments are necessary. The service also publishes *The International Health Care Travelers Guide,* available for $4.50 with a self-addressed envelope. Contact: The International Health Care Service, New York Hospital-Cornell Medical Center, 440 E 69th St., New York, NY 10021 (phone: 212-472-4284).

LEGAL AID: The best way to begin looking for legal aid in an unfamiliar area is with a call to your own lawyer. If you don't have, or cannot reach, your own lawyer, most cities offer lawyer referral services (sometimes called attorney referral services) maintained by provincial legal associations. They are listed in the yellow pages under "Lawyers." In smaller towns, you will usually find a toll-free number that connects you to the service in the nearest larger city. The referral service is almost always free.

Once you have found a lawyer, ask how many cases of this type the lawyer has worked on, and the arrangements to be made regarding fee and additional costs such as medical or ballistics experts, transcripts, or court fees. For most violations, you will receive a citation at most. There are, however, the rare occasions when travelers find themselves in jail. Since obtaining a bond can be difficult away from home, the bail bonds offered by *AAA* and other automobile clubs are extremely useful (see *Touring by Car*). If you do not have this protection, ask to see a copy of the local bail procedures, which differ from province to province. A lawyer will be able to advise you on the alternatives you have in the state in which you are incarcerated.

The *SafeTravel Network* provides 24-hour emergency access to a worldwide network of physicians, lawyers, and other specialists. The service is available to purchasers of Bank America Travelers Cheques for 45 days of coverage. The cost is $8.50. For information, call 800-227-3333; or call collect, 415-624-2222. Some credit card companies offer similar services (see *Credit Cards* and *Traveler's Checks*).

Drinking and Drug Laws

Drinking: The legal drinking age is 19 in Newfoundland, Prince Edward Island, British Columbia, New Brunswick, the Northwest Territories, Nova Scotia, Ontario, Saskatchewan, and the Yukon territory. Only in Alberta, Manitoba, and Quebec is the legal age 18.

Although liquor laws have become more uniform across the country during the last decade, it is still difficult to generalize about what kinds of alcoholic drinks may be sold, at what hours, and to whom. Except in Quebec, which has the most liberal drinking laws in the country, liquor by the bottle is usually sold only through provincial government liquor stores, located in larger cities and most towns. In Quebec, beer and wine are sold at retail grocery stores; hard liquor is available at government liquor stores. In Ontario, domestic beer is sold through large outlets called Brewers' Retail; wine is sold through liquor control stores.

It is possible to find dry towns in all corners of the country. Usually, however, you will find a community just a few minutes away where the sale of liquor is legal.

Licensed restaurants, hotels, lounges, and bars are found across the country, though some may sell only wine or beer (called beverage rooms). Again, hours during which bars and restaurants may serve liquor vary, though traditionally bar closing time is between midnight and 3 AM. Most provinces require liquor stores to close on Sundays and holidays. Some alcoholic beverages may be purchased on Sundays, usually only with meals at authorized dining rooms, restaurants, and private clubs.

Every visitor to Canada may import 40 ounces of liquor or wine, or 288 ounces of beer or ale (twenty-four 12-ounce cans, eighteen 16-ounce cans) as personal baggage, duty-free. Anything in excess of this amount is subject to duties and taxes and requires a provincial permit. If excess liquor is declared, it will be held by Canada Customs at the point of entry for 30 days. A receipt will be issued, and the owner can claim it upon return. People leaving Canada from a point other than their point of entry can make arrangements to have their property returned at the point of departure.

No provinces forbid the import of liquor from one province to another as long as it is for personal use. This is useful to know, since liquor and wine prices vary quite considerably throughout Canada. If you are visiting Alberta and British Columbia, for instance, you will notice an appreciable difference in liquor prices, Alberta being much less expensive. It is worth adding that the prices of beer do not vary as greatly, although it tends to be slightly more expensive in eastern Canada.

DRUGS: The best advice we can offer is: Don't carry, use, buy, or sell illegal drugs. The dangers are clear enough when indulging in your own home; if you take drugs while traveling you may endanger not only your own life but also put your fellow travelers in jeopardy. And if you get caught, you may end up spending your hard-earned vacation funds on bail and attorney's fees — and end up in jail.

Under Canada's Narcotics Control Act, in effect at the time of this writing, if you are charged with possession of marijuana, cocaine, heroin, or PCP, you face 6 months' imprisonment, a fine of up to $1,000, or both *for a first offense.* First offenders convicted of possession for the purpose of trafficking face up to life imprisonment and hefty fines. Similar penalties apply to those caught smuggling illegal drugs into or out of Canada.

Don't assume that you're safe by carrying only small amounts of controlled substances for "personal use." According to a sergeant with the narcotics division of the Royal Canadian Mounted Police in Ottawa, stiff penalties have been imposed on drug offenders convicted of possessing mere traces of illegal drugs. If you value your life and reputation, don't get mixed up in the illegal drug trade.

Religion on the Road

The surest source of information on religious services in an unfamiliar town is the desk clerk of your hotel or motel. You can also check the yellow pages of the phone book under "Churches" and call for more information. Church listings are also often printed as part of general tourist guides provided locally. The local tourist council can certainly provide the information you need on services in the town. Some newspapers also print a listing of religious services in their area in weekend editions.

You may want to use your vacation to broaden your religious experience by joining an unfamiliar faith in its service. This can be a moving experience, especially if the service is held in a church, synagogue, or temple that is historically significant or architecturally notable. You will almost always find yourself made welcome and comfortable.

Certain kinds of services are prevalent in specific areas, depending upon the concentration of religious groups in that area. The Roman Catholic, United Church of Canada, and Anglican churches have the largest followings in Canada, and you will find their services in every province. Since 77% of the Jews in Canada are based in Toronto and Montreal, the largest number of synagogues are found in these two cities. The Presbyterian church is centered in Ontario; Canadian Baptists live primarily in the Maritime Provinces.

Sources and Resources

Tourist Information

Listed below are the addresses of provincial tourism offices. (City tourist offices in Canada are listed in the individual city reports of THE CITIES.) Consult these offices when planning your trip. They can provide a wealth of useful free information. For the best result, request general information on specific provinces or cities you are interested in visiting (several areas have travel kits that include lists of hotels, tourist attractions, maps, and so on) as well as specific information relevant to your interests: facilities for specific sports, tours and itineraries of special interest, accommodations, and restaurants. With the exception of the Yukon, all these offices can be called from the US (except Alaska) toll-free. Where noted, the toll-free number is good for the eastern US only.

PROVINCIAL TOURIST OFFICES

Travel Alberta: Imperial Oil Building, 15th Flr., 10025 Jasper Ave., Edmonton, Alberta T5J 3Z3 (phone: 403-427-4321 or 800-222-6501 from Alberta; 800-661-8888 from elsewhere in Canada and the US)

Tourism British Columbia: Parliament Buildings, Victoria, British Columbia V8V 1X4 (phone: 604-387-1642, or 800-663-6000)

Labrador: See Newfoundland.

Travel Manitoba: 155 Carlton St., 7th Flr., Dept. 7020, Winnipeg, Manitoba R3C 3H8 (phone: 204-945-3777, or 800-665-0040, ext. 20)

Tourism New Brunswick: PO Box 12345, Fredericton, New Brunswick E3B 5C3 (phone: 506-453-2377 or 800-442-4442 from New Brunswick; 800-561-0123 from elsewhere in Canada and the US)

Newfoundland and Labrador Tourism Branch: Department of Development and Tourism, PO Box 2016, St. John's, Newfoundland A1C 5R8 (phone: 709-576-2830 or 800-563-6353 in Canada and the continental US)

TravelArctic: Yellowknife, Northwest Territories X1A 2L9 (phone: 403-873-7200 or 800-661-0788)

Nova Scotia Department of Tourism: PO Box 456, Halifax, Nova Scotia B3J 2R5 (phone: 902-425-5781 or 800-565-7105 from Nova Scotia, Prince Edward Island, and New Brunswick; 800-565-7180 from Newfoundland and Quebec; 800-565-7166 from elsewhere in Canada); Nova Scotia Tourist Information Office, 136 Commercial St., Portland, ME 04101 (phone: 800-492-0643 from Maine or 800-341-6096 from elsewhere in the US)

Ontario Travel: Queen's Park, Toronto, Ontario M7A 2E5 (phone: 416-965-4008 or 800-268-3735)

Department of Tourism and Parks (Prince Edward Island): PO Box 940, Charlottetown, Prince Edward Island C1A 7M5 (phone: 902-368-4444; 800-565-9060 in the US east of the Mississippi; 800-565-0243 from Quebec, Ontario, and Newfoundland; 800-565-7421 from New Brunswick and Nova Scotia, March 15 to October 31)

Tourisme Quebec: PO Box 20,000, Quebec City, Quebec G1K 7X2 (phone: 514-

873-2015 or 800-361-5405 from Quebec; 800-361-6490 from Ontario and the Atlantic Provinces; 800-443-7000 from the eastern US; 800-363-7777 elsewhere in the continental US)

Tourism Saskatchewan: 1919 Saskatchewan Dr., Regina, Saskatchewan S4P 3V7 (phone: 306-787-2300 or 800-667-7538 from Saskatchewan; 800-667-7191 from elsewhere in Canada and the US)

Tourism Yukon: PO Box 2703, Whitehorse, Yukon Y1A 2C6 (phone: 403-667-5340)

Notes on Sports

Both spectator and participatory sports are major activities in Canada. You can take in major seasonal sporting events during your travels whether you're inclined toward skiing in the Quebec Laurentians, watching a hockey game in Montreal, or summer snowmobiling on a huge glacier in the Canadian Rockies. See the individual city reports in THE CITIES for ticket information and the entries on specific sports in DIVERSIONS for complete information.

CURLING: This Canadian game has Scottish origins and is somewhat related to shuffleboard. The big difference is that it is played on a 46-yard long ice rink with 40-pound stones (also known as "granites"). Two players or "curlers" slide eight stones toward a circular target, while assistants vigorously brush the ice with brooms along the path of the stone in an attempt to place a stone nearest the center. Curling is a major winter sport in Canada, and the season extends from October to April. The Labatt Brier tournament highlights the curling season and features, in addition to curling, an opening day parade with Scottish bands. There are many teams throughout Canada; for ticket information, contact the tourist office of the province you visit.

FISHING: Canada is a fisherman's paradise. The hundreds of thousands of lakes and streams teem with all the major freshwater species: all families of trout, Arctic char, maskinonge (muskellunge), walleye, large- and small-mouth bass, Atlantic and Pacific salmon, northern pike, whitefish, Arctic grayling, inconnu, goldeye, perch, and a variety of panfish. On the Atlantic and Pacific coasts, you can go after a variety of saltwater fish: striped bass, bluefin tuna, sharks, and deep-sea fish.

Most of the best fishing spots are accessible by car, rail, or air and are located near comfortable lodges, resorts, hotels, or campgrounds. For the best of Canada's prime places to wet a line, see *Where They Bite* in DIVERSIONS.

FOOTBALL: This popular sport is under the aegis of the Canadian Football League. Though some 50% of the professional players are Americans, the rules are 100% Canadian: The game is played on a 110-yard field (larger than an American field) with 12 players (1 more than American teams) and 3 downs (1 less than in American football). Toronto, Ottawa, Hamilton, Edmonton, Winnipeg, Calgary, Regina, and Vancouver all field professional teams that compete from late August to the end of November. The season culminates in the Grey Cup National Championship. For ticket information, see the *Sports* section of the individual city reports in THE CITIES.

GOLF: Part and parcel with the Canadians' British heritage is their love of golf and a corresponding abundance of first class golf courses. Golf is played at nearly 1,000 courses around the country. The largest number are concentrated in Ontario and Quebec, where the season extends from the end of April to the beginning of November, and in British Columbia, where people play golf all year, but there are even courses in the Northwest Territories. Canada hosts several tournaments on the PGA circuit, including the Canadian Open and the Canadian PGA Championship for male pros. Top female pros compete in the annual Du Maurier Classic, which is held alternately in Toronto and Montreal. For further information on men's tournaments, contact the

Royal Canadian Golf Association, Golf House, RR #2, Oakville, Ontario L6J 4Z3 (phone: 416-844-1800); for the women's competitions, the Canadian Ladies' Golf Association, 1600 James Naismith Dr., Gloucester, Ontario K1B 5N4 (phone: 613-748-5642). For complete details on the best courses in Canada, see *Golf* in DIVERSIONS.

HOCKEY: Hockey is king in Canada and reigns over a broad domain encompassing professional, college, community, and school teams. With its long winters and the preponderance of frozen lakes and rinks, Canada is real hockey country; in fact, many of its citizens learn to skate about the same time they learn to walk. So the ice is hotly contested on all levels, from October through May by professionals in the long-established National Hockey League. The NHL is composed of seven Canadian teams, including the Calgary *Flames*, Edmonton *Oilers*, Montreal *Canadiens*, Quebec *Nordiques*, Toronto *Maple Leafs*, Vancouver *Canucks*, Winnipeg *Jets*, and American teams in Boston, Buffalo, Chicago, Detroit, Hartford, Los Angeles, Minnesota, New Jersey, New York (the *Islanders* and the *Rangers*), Philadelphia, Pittsburgh, St. Louis, and Washington. The NHL's best teams compete for the Stanley Cup in May. The best way to get tickets for hockey games is to get a season schedule from the National Hockey League, 960 Sun Life Bldg., 1155 Metcalfe, Montreal, Quebec H3B 2W2 (phone: 514-871-9220), and then contact the team's home arena box office (see the individual city reports in THE CITIES for addresses for tickets). Tickets may also be bought in advance at various ticket offices in the host city.

College hockey competition takes place throughout the country from October to March. The leading teams are affiliated with the University of Toronto and York in Toronto, Concordia in Montreal, St. Mary's in Halifax, and the University of Alberta in Edmonton. For tickets to inter-collegiate hockey games, contact the universities. The Canadian Inter-Athletic Championship Tournament is the big game at the end of the season.

HORSE RACING: Thoroughbred racing and pari-mutuel betting take place in British Columbia, Alberta, Saskatchewan, Manitoba, and Ontario during the spring, summer, and fall. The oldest continuously run stake event in North America, the 129-year-old Queen's Plate takes place at *Woodbine Race Track* in Toronto each summer. For specifics, check the local newspapers.

LACROSSE: Though lacrosse is officially Canada's national sport, the two attempts to organize professional leagues in the past few years have failed. But the game is played widely on an amateur, minor league, and semi-pro level, particularly in western Canada and Ontario, during the late winter and the summer. At the end of the season, the best teams compete for the Mann Cup.

SKIING: Canadians love to ski and, between ideal snowy climate and extensive mountainous terrain, Canada has some of the finest ski areas in the world for both recreational and competitive skiing. Even near major metropolitan centers, a skier in Canada is seldom very far from a good run. The major regions are Mont Tremblant and Mont-Ste.-Anne in eastern Quebec, Lake Louise and Jasper in Alberta, and western British Columbia, all with breathtaking vertical drops for alpine skiing and extensive cross-country trails as well. The province of Ontario also has a myriad of popular ski slopes. Canada is on the World Cup Circuit, the most prestigious competition for amateur and Olympic-ranked skiers. Big events take place every few years, including the giant slalom and slalom at Whistler Mountain (north of Vancouver) and the World Cup Downhill Championship. For complete information on the best places to ski in Canada, see *Downhill* and *Cross-Country Skiing* in DIVERSIONS.

SNOWMOBILING: Once used primarily for winter transportation in rural areas, snowmobiles are now used mainly for recreation. Located in the heart of the snow belt, Canada has thousands of miles of groomed trails — 38,000 miles in the province of Quebec alone. Ontario is another major snowmobiling region, but snowmobiling tours and concessions are springing up across the country. In the Canadian Rockies, a variation on the snowmobiling tour is offered via large-track vehicle on 5-mile-long and

¾-mile-wide Athabasca Glacier. Canada has a professional snowmobiling circuit known as Sno Pro, where factory team racing pros whiz around the track at speeds greater than 100 mph for cash and prizes. These events are generally held in January at tracks in Beausejour, Manitoba, and Waldheim, Saskatchewan. In order to drive a snowmobile that can exceed 50 mph, one needs a driver's license; children must obtain a special permit.

TENNIS: There's a tennis boom in Canada, as many more people take up the sport and courts spring up to accommodate them. It is played a great deal in Ontario and Quebec from April to October and in British Columbia year-round. Facilities range from public, municipally maintained courts to indoor and outdoor private clubs, to tennis cooperatives. The biggest events in tennis are two professionally sanctioned tournaments: the men's Player's International and the women's Player's Challenge. Both are held annually in August, with one played in Montreal, the other in Toronto, on an alternating basis. For information, contact Tennis Canada, 3111 Steeles Ave. W., Downsview, Ontario M3J 3H2 (416-665-9777). For complete descriptions of the best courts in Canada, see *The Best Tennis Vacations* in DIVERSIONS.

Weights and Measures

When traveling in Canada, you'll find that just about every quantity, whether length, weight, or capacity, will be in a figure unfamiliar to the average US citizen. In fact, this is true for travel almost everywhere in the world, since the US is one of the few remaining countries not using the metric system.

The tables and conversion factors listed below should give you all the information you'll need to understand any transaction, road sign, or map you encounter.

APPROXIMATE EQUIVALENTS		
Metric Unit	**Abbreviation**	**US Equivalent**
LENGTH		
millimeter	mm	.04 inch
meter	m	39.37 inches
kilometer	km	.62 mile
AREA		
square centimeter	sq cm	.155 square inch
square meter	sq m	10.7 square feet
hectare	ha	2.47 acres
square kilometer	sq km	.3861 square mile
CAPACITY		
liter	l	1.057 quarts
WEIGHT		
gram	g	.035 ounce
kilogram	kg	2.2 pounds
metric ton	MT	1.1 tons
ENERGY		
kilowatt	kw	1.34 horsepower

CONVERSION TABLES METRIC TO US MEASUREMENTS

Multiply	by	to convert to
LENGTH		
millimeters	.04	inches
meters	3.3	feet
meters	1.1	yards
kilometers	.6	miles
CAPACITY		
liters	2.11	pints (liquid)
liters	1.06	quarts (liquid)
liters	.26	gallons (liquid)
WEIGHT		
grams	.04	ounces (avoir.)
kilograms	2.2	pounds (avoir.)

US TO METRIC MEASUREMENTS

LENGTH		
inches	25.	millimeters
feet	.3	meters
yards	.9	meters
miles	1.6	kilometers
CAPACITY		
pints	.47	liters
quarts	.95	liters
gallons	3.8	liters
WEIGHT		
ounces	28.	grams
pounds	.45	kilograms

TEMPERATURE

$°F = (°C \times 9/5) + 32 \qquad °C = (°F - 32) \times 5/9$

Camera and Equipment

Vacations are everybody's favorite time for taking pictures. After all, most of us want to remember the places we visit — and show them off to others — through spectacular photographs. Here are a few suggestions to help you get the best results from your travel picture-taking.

BEFORE THE TRIP: If you're taking your camera out after a long period in mothballs, or have just bought a new one, check it thoroughly before you leave to prevent unexpected breakdowns and disappointing pictures.

GETTING READY / Camera and Equipment   99

1. Shoot at least one test roll, using the kind of film you plan to take along with you. Use all the shutter speeds and f-stops on your camera, and vary the focus to make sure everything is in order. Do this well in advance of your departure so there will be time to have film developed and to make repairs, if necessary. If you're in a rush, most large cities have custom labs that can process film in as little as an hour. Repairs, unfortunately, take longer.
2. Clean your camera thoroughly, inside and out. Dust and dirt can jam camera mechanisms, scratch film, and mar photographs. Remove surface dust from lenses and camera body with a soft camel's-hair brush. Next, use at least two layers of crumpled lens tissue and your breath to clean lenses and filters. Don't rub hard and don't use water, saliva, or compressed air on lenses or filters because they are so easily damaged. Persistent stains can be removed by using a Q-tip moistened with liquid lens cleaner. Anything that doesn't come off easily needs professional attention. Once your lenses are clean, protect them from dirt and damage with inexpensive skylight or ultraviolet filters.
3. Check the batteries for the light meter and take along extras just in case yours wear out during the trip. They can be difficult to find while traveling.

EQUIPMENT TO TAKE ALONG: Keep your gear light and compact. Items that are too heavy or bulky to be carried comfortably on a full-day excursion will likely stay in your hotel room.

1. Most single lens reflex (SLR) cameras come with a 50mm, or "normal," lens, a general purpose lens that frames subjects within an approximately average angle of view. This is good for street scenes taken at a distance of 25 feet or more and for full-length portraits shot at 8 to 12 feet. You can expand your photographic options with a wide-angle lens such as a 35mm, 28mm, or 24mm. These give a broader than normal angle of view and greater than normal "depth of field," that is, sharp focus from foreground to background. They are especially handy for panoramas, cityscapes, and for large buildings or statuary from which you can't step back. For extreme close-ups, a macro-lens is best, but a screw-on magnifying lens is an inexpensive alternative. Telephoto lenses, 65mm to 1000mm, are good for shooting details from a distance (as in animal photography), but since they tend to be heavy and bulky, unless you anticipate a frequent need for them, omit them from vacation photography equipment. A zoom, which is a big lens but relatively light, has a variable angle of view so it gives a range of options. Try a 35mm to 80mm; beware of inexpensive models that give poor quality photographs. Protect all lenses with skylight or ultraviolet filters, which should be removed for cleaning only. A polarizing filter helps to eliminate glare and reflection to achieve fully saturated colors in very bright sunlight. It is also effective in removing snow glare. Take along a couple of extra lens caps (they're the first things to get lost) or buy an inexpensive lens cap "leash."
2. Travel photographs work best in color. Good slide films are Kodachrome 64 and Fujichrome 50, both moderate- to slow-speed films that provide saturated colors and work well in most outdoor lighting situations. For very bright conditions, try slower film like Kodachrome 25. If the weather is cloudy, or you're indoors with only natural light, use a faster film, such as Kodachrome or Ektachrome 200 or 400. These can be "pushed" to higher speeds. There are even faster films on the market for low-light situations. The result may be pictures with whiter, colder tones and a grainier image, but high-speed films open up picture possibilities that slower films cannot.

Films tend to render color in slightly different ways. Kodachrome brings out reds and oranges. Fujichrome is noted for its yellows, greens, and whites. Agfachrome mutes bright tones, producing fine browns, yellows, and whites. Anticipate what you are likely to see, and take along whichever types of film will enhance your results. You might test films as you test your camera (see above).

If you prefer film that develops into prints rather than slides, try Kodacolor 100 or 400 for most lighting situations. Vericolor is a professional film that gives excellent results, especially in skin tones, but suffers shifts in color when subjected to temperature extremes; take it along for people photography *if* you're sure you can protect it from heat and cold. All lens and filter information applies equally to print and slide films.

How much film should you take? If you are serious about your photography, pack one roll of film (36 exposures) for each day of your trip. Film is especially expensive at the most popular tourism and travel destinations, and any leftovers can be bartered away or brought home and safely stored in your refrigerator. Processing is also generally more expensive away from home — and not always as good. If you are concerned about airport security X-rays damaging your undeveloped film (X-rays do not affect processed film), store it in lead-lined bags, sold in camera shops. This possibility is not as much of a threat as it used to be, however. In the US, incidents of X-ray damage to unprocessed film (exposed or unexposed) are minimal because low-dosage X-ray equipment is used virtually everywhere. As a rule of thumb, photo industry sources say that film with speeds up to ASA 400 can go through security machinery in the US five times without any noticeable effect. Abroad, the situation varies from country to country, but the trend is toward equipment that delivers less and less radiation. While it is doubtful that one exposure would ruin your pictures, if you're traveling without a protective bag you may want to ask to have your photo equipment inspected by hand, especially on a prolonged trip with repeated security checks. (Naturally, this is possible only if you're carrying your film and camera on board with you; it's a good idea anyway, because it helps to preclude loss or theft or the possibility at some airports that checked baggage will be X-rayed more heavily than hand baggage.) In the US, Federal Aviation Administration regulations require that if you request a hand inspection, you get it, but elsewhere the response may depend on the humor of the inspector. One type of film that should never be subjected to X-rays, even in the US, is the new, very high speed film with an ASA rating of 1000. If you are taking some of this overseas, note that there are lead-lined bags made especially for it. Finally, the walk-through metal detector devices at airports do not affect film, though the film cartridges will set them off.

3. A small battery-powered electronic flash unit, or "strobe," is handy for very dim light or at night, but only if the subject is at a distance of 15 feet or less. Flash units cannot illuminate an entire scene, and many museums do not permit flash photography, so take such a unit only if you know you will need it. If your camera does not have a hot-shoe, you will need a PC cord to synchronize the flash with your shutter. Be sure to take along extra batteries for the flash.
4. Invest in a broad camera strap if you now have a thin one. It will make carrying the camera much more comfortable.
5. A sturdy canvas or leather camera bag, preferably with padded pockets — not an airline bag — will keep equipment organized and easy to find.
6. For cleaning, bring along a camel's-hair brush that retracts into a rubber squeeze bulb. Also, take plenty of lens tissue and plastic bags to protect equipment from dust.

SOME TIPS: For better pictures, the following pointers will help:

1. *Get close.* Move in to get your subject to fill the frame.
2. *Vary your angle.* Shoot from above or below — look for unusual perspectives.
3. *Pay attention to backgrounds.* Keep it simple or blur it out.

4. *Look for details.* Not just a whole building, but a decorative element; not just an entire street scene, but a single remarkable face.
5. *Don't be lazy.* Always carry your camera gear with you, loaded and ready for those unexpected moments.

PERSPECTIVES

The Canadian Past: A Short History of a Huge Country

For two million years, a land bridge between Asia and North America appeared and disappeared as great sheets of ice retreated and advanced across the North American continent. For the last 10,000 to 15,000 years these ice sheets — the word "glacier" hardly conveys their continent-spanning immensity — have been in retreat, and that land bridge, the Bering Strait, has been covered by the icy waters of the Bering Sea. But when the ice moved forward, as it did intermittently for millennia, sculpting the earth with implacable force as it crept south from the Arctic, whole seas were drawn into the frozen advance, and a bridge of some 50 to 60 miles of dry land appeared between Asia and North America.

It was during such a period of advance that the first Asian peoples crossed the land bridge and entered North America about 25,000 years ago. Their progression south is an epic — one that will never be told and never really known — that moved through corridors of thaw in the huge masses of ice. They and the peoples who followed were the antecedents of the spectacular Indian cultures of North America. At the time of the earliest crossings, more than three-quarters of the earth's surface was covered by ice, but by 8000 BC the great glaciers were in abeyance and native American cultures — from the Arctic to Mexico — were developing in astounding profusion and diversity.

The main Indian tribes of the Canadian Northwest were the Tlinglit in what is now Alaska, the Tsimshian, Salish, and Kwakiutl along the coast, and the Chinook and Nootka on Vancouver Island and along the Columbia River. Their cultures were hierarchical; chiefs were rich and powerful men who could command the attention of both slaves and commoners. In return, they were expected to finance the great whale hunts and to provide both fishing and war canoes for the men of the tribe. The chief and his wife had a large part in the religious rituals that ensured good whaling. Life along the coast centered on the incredibly rich waters — fresh water, in the streams running to the sea, and the sea itself — that dominated every aspect of existence. The salmon and whale were treated like respected brothers, brothers of the sea, and seal, beaver, and otter provided food, clothing, and fur for trade.

The Indians of the Canadian plains — stretching from the eastern edge of the Rockies across what is now Alberta, Saskatchewan, and Manitoba — had nowhere near as comfortable an existence. The Blackfoot, Plains, Cree, and Assiniboin were hunters and foragers who spent their lives following the great buffalo herds. It was for only a relatively short time — from the 17th century — that they had horses, the "big dogs" that totally changed their lives. Before that, every move was made by human strength, and the only pack animals were, literally, dogs.

Though most of the East Coast Indians were also hunters and gatherers, their lives were far richer and more comfortable than that of their plains brothers. The Montagnais and Naskapi roamed northeastern Canada; the Algonquin, Abernaki, Maliseet, and Iroquois ranged through lower Canada, the Great Lakes district, and what became the northeastern US. The Huron and other tribes of the Iroquois Confederacy actually farmed portions of their land in addition to hunting; almost all the other northeastern tribes hunted in the huge, rich forests of the area.

As the Huron became increasingly agricultural and established themselves in lower Canada (Ontario), a schism developed that separated the Huron tribes from the more mobile tribes of the Iroquois Nation. By the early 1600s, this had resulted in open hostility between the two groups, and the Hurons not only defended the area called Huronia from Iroquois raids, but forced the Five Nations Confederacy (as the Iroquois Nation was also called) to remain south of the St. Lawrence River.

On the eastern seaboard, across the Great Plains, up and down the Pacific Northwest Coast, groups of Indian tribes crafted lifestyles and practiced religions adapted to the realities of the life they found. By the time the Europeans arrived in North America, these peoples had for eons maintained stable and successful societies, as distinct from one another as the courts of the Renaissance were different from communities of Vikings. Into these delicate cultures stormed the realities of European history.

THE COMING OF EUROPEANS

At the northernmost tip of the huge island of Newfoundland is the tiny fishing village of L'Anse-au-Meadow. It is located in a desolate and remote part of the province, where the European history of Canada and the New World began.

Close to 1,000 years ago, about 500 years before Columbus planted the flag of imperial Spain on the sands of a Caribbean isle, the Vikings from Scandinavia, some of the most intrepid travelers of all time, established a settlement at L'Anse-au-Meadow and called it Vinland. The Vikings, in their longboats, reached this part of Canada by using the Faeroes, Iceland, and Greenland as stepping-stones. Although they attempted to maintain a colony here (the foundation of some of their buildings, unearthed by archaeologist Helge Ingstad and others are still visible), their life in the New World was doomed. Viking men, women, and children suffered from the long, bitter winters and from deadly Indian attacks. Many perished. The survivors fled back to more congenial and familiar lands, to Iceland, Denmark, and Sweden.

Scholars speculate that while the Vikings were in the New World they roamed far to the south, sailing down the coast of eastern North America, possibly establishing other settlements. In Yarmouth, Nova Scotia, for example, there is a strange runic stone that local folklore claims was left by the

Norsemen. But conclusive proof of their presence in other parts of Canada's eastern seaboard is yet to be found, except the very tangible remains at L'Anse-au-Meadow. And even much of what can be seen there today is shrouded in mystery.

It was not until 500 years after the Viking period that a more enduring exploration of Canada took place. John Cabot (actually Giovanni Caboto, a Venetian adventurer using an English name) landed on a desolate Cape Breton Island beach in the summer of 1497. He claimed this "new-found land" for England, where he had moved, some historians say, in the 1480s to live in Bristol, then a major departure point for explorers headed for the New World. His English backers had financed his sail west in hopes of finding a new route to the East Indies. Cabot failed in this quest, but he did make a discovery that would, in due time, provide countless men and several nations with riches beyond expectation. He found one of the most fertile commercial fishing grounds in the world, the Grand Banks off the coast of Newfoundland.

At the time, Cabot's investors thought his voyage largely a loss. However, it was not long before other investors, in France and Portugal, heard about Cabot's exciting Grand Banks find, and they didn't hesitate to send fishing expeditions to exploit the cod fishing there.

The French and the Portuguese were the first to develop the cod fisheries of Newfoundland and to make handsome profits from them. Eventually England sent ships in great enough numbers to compete effectively with the French and Portuguese. And, in a relatively short period of time, England became master of the rich fisheries of this region, in part by exerting its sovereignty over Newfoundland — Britain's earliest colony — based on Cabot's prior discoveries. Cod was not only "king" in its own right, it was the lure that brought more adventurous explorers to open the doors of a vast, unknown continent.

One of these seekers was Jacques Cartier, a Frenchman from St.-Malo. In 1534, Cartier sailed into the Gulf of St. Lawrence, earning the right to name it. He landed on what is now the province of Prince Edward Island, which he called "Ile St. Jean," and on the Gaspé Peninsula, the eastern gateway via the St. Lawrence River into the heartland of Canada. Cartier sailed down the St. Lawrence as far as Montreal, following what he thought was the Northwest Passage. He claimed all he saw for France, and he called his discovery Kannata, an Algonquin word meaning "a settlement."

With England and France entrenched in Canada, the stage was set for an epic conflict between two old rivals. For several decades, the French neither explored nor exploited Cartier's rich discoveries. It wasn't until a craze for beaver hats — started by Francis II — overtook the royal court and forced ambitious hatters to press for a new source of beaver that the French sent expeditions into the St. Lawrence River to trade with the Indians. But they were unaware of the hostility between the tribes of lower Canada and those farther south. Unwittingly they became allies of the Huron tribes against the Iroquois Nation by supplying weapons and other goods to the nearby tribes.

French explorer Samuel de Champlain, the most honored of Canada's early explorers, charted the St. Lawrence River as far as Montreal Island and pushed up the Ottawa River to the point at which the city of Ottawa is presently located. In 1604, Champlain led an expedition to Acadia, the area that today includes Maine, Nova Scotia, and New Brunswick, in order to establish a trading colony. Sieur de Monts, a Huguenot aristocrat, sailed with Champlain as lieutenant governor of the new colony. The expedition spent its first winter on an island in the St. Croix River, losing many of its party to the climate and disease. Champlain moved the group to a more habitable site on Nova Scotia's Bay of Fundy. Here at Port Royal, in 1605, Champlain's Habitation started its life as the first permanent European settlement in Canada.

Three years later, in 1608, Champlain founded what became the most important city in New France and, later, the capital of one of Canada's premier provinces. On an apron of land below a massive rock mesa overlooking the St. Lawrence River, Champlain established the French village of Quebec. This historic event took place one year after the founding of Jamestown, Virginia, and 12 years before the Pilgrims landed at Plymouth, Massachusetts.

During the 17th century, Quebec not only became the locus of the fur trade in New France but also, and equally important, the center of the Roman Catholic church in North America. The fur traders, *les coureurs de bois,* ranged into the interior as far as the Rocky Mountains and the Gulf of Mexico; only a step behind were the "black robe" priests. In many instances they blazed trails ahead of the traders. In the United States, Detroit, St. Louis, Pittsburgh, and New Orleans were discovered and originally settled by French pioneers from Quebec. It was Louis Joliet and Father Marquette who first reached the "Father of Waters," the Mississippi River. Cavelier de La Salle claimed Louisiana for the French. Among the different religious orders that came to New France, three stand out as exceptional in Canadian history: the legendary Jesuits, who brought culture, scholarship, and missionary zeal combined with humane tolerance, uncommon courage, and inquiring minds; the Ursuline sisters, with their grace, compassion, knowledge, and medical skill; and the Société de Notre Dame, largely a lay group. In 1642, they founded the city of Montreal as a utopia of peace and prayer, and it soon replaced Quebec as the center for the fur trade in spite of its purely inspirational origins. (Montreal retained its primacy as Canada's commercial center until this century, when Toronto assumed the dominant position.) As cod enriched the English off the foggy coast of Newfoundland, beaver and other animal pelts filled coffers in France and created a new, politically powerful aristocracy in the North American colony.

THE FRENCH AND ENGLISH WARS

During the 17th century, England established colonies along the American eastern seaboard from Maine to Georgia. In addition, in 1610 Henry Hudson discovered the huge bay in the Canadian north that bears his name. Here, in 1670, the English established a fur trading company (the Hudson's Bay Company, still a very active concern on the Canadian retailing and trading scene), which brought them into open conflict with French interests.

From 1689 to 1815, England and France waged intermittent war in a struggle for commercial and military hegemony over much of the world. This conflict is often referred to as the Second Hundred Years' War. Canada was merely one of several areas at stake. The English fought the French in the Caribbean, in India, in the Pacific, in Belgium and Bavaria, and in Quebec. It is easiest to conceptualize the North American war as one aspect of a much larger global struggle. King William's War in America (1689–1697) was the War of the League of Augsburg in Europe; Queen Anne's War (1702–1713) was the War of the Spanish Succession; America's French and Indian War, which brought about the complete expulsion of the French from Canada, was Europe's Seven Years' War; and the War of 1812 was only a minor episode in the overwhelmingly long conflict known as the Wars of the French Revolution and Napoleon.

Amid this wide-ranging war, a smaller — but equally crucial — conflict was taking place. An offensive by the Iroquois Nation (Mohawk, Oneida, Onondaga, Cayuga, and Seneca) against the Huron Nation began with a series of raids against both the Huron and the French fur traders. The English, who had supplied the Iroquois with guns in exchange for furs, supported this action. Open warfare began in the 1640s and lasted until 1667, creating an environment of terror for all the European settlers caught in its wake. Both Indian nations wanted to control the fur trade with the tribes of the interior, because that was the only way to gain the valued goods of the Europeans. And the two European nations wanted control of the continent.

Nevertheless, the North American war of the 18th century, while nearly always related to European conflicts, displayed an increasingly indigenous character. During the War of the Spanish Succession, the French renewed their border raids, but the shape of the future was foretold when the British sent six men-of-war and a regiment of marines to Boston in 1710. Supplemented by militia raised in New England, this force captured Port Royal in Acadia. By the Treaty of Utrecht, the French recognized the English possession of Hudson Bay, Newfoundland, and Acadia (which the English promptly renamed Nova Scotia).

When the War of the Austrian Succession broke out in Europe in 1740, the challenge was readily accepted in North America. Led by Massachusetts's Governor William Shirley, ambitious Calvinist merchants sponsored an expedition against Louisbourg, in Nova Scotia. Lacking French support, the town fell to the New Englanders. A combination of New England militiamen and British seapower held the town against a French attempt to recapture it the following year. But on the European continent the French had done relatively well, and at the Peace of Aix-la-Chapelle (1748), Louisburg was returned to France — to the dismay and disgust of the men who had taken it.

At the advent of the French and Indian War in the middle of the century, the population of the English colonies was roughly 2 million, whereas in all of North America there were no more than 80,000 French. Even without English superiority on the sea, the struggle would have called for an amazing effort on the part of the French. In the first years of the war the French did quite well. In 1756 they sent substantial reinforcements to the St. Lawrence under a brilliant, well-read general, the Marquis de Montcalm. At first Montcalm overcame his heavy numerical disadvantages by a series of bold strikes. Aided by the disunity of the English colonies and by the inexperience of British leadership in the ways of wilderness warfare, he captured Fort Oswego, destroyed the English outposts in northern New York, and kept the British colonial forces on guard and off balance along the entire frontier. But Montcalm was unable to maintain these advantages.

The corruption and petty intrigue that riddled Quebec society had its effect on Montcalm's campaign. From the outset of his command, Montcalm had been suspicious of his colleagues in the government of Quebec, and they repaid his lack of confidence with hostility. The governor, the Marquis of Vaudreuil, a native of the colony, symbolized an interest that increasingly resented both overseas control and inadequate French support. Vaudreuil and Montcalm never resolved their differences, and the result took its toll on the French effort. Pure avarice further undermined the war effort. Some French merchants were intent on making a private fortune while the colony floundered in a sea of inflation, corrupt influences, and fraud.

In addition, a growing determination on the part of the English to clear the French from their path of expansion crystallized under the new leadership of William Pitt. His government waged a swift and brilliant campaign. In 1758, Pitt dispatched a fresh sea and land force and began a gigantic pincer movement. Fort Frontenac, guardian of the Lake Ontario approaches to the St. Lawrence Valley, fell in the summer of 1758 while a combined force under Generals Wolfe and Amherst smashed its way into the fortress of Louisburg and thereby secured the sea approaches to the St. Lawrence. In June 1759, an even larger assault force sailed up the river to just below Quebec. From July until early September the British played cat and mouse with Quebec, making feints above and below the citadel. As autumn approached, both Montcalm and Vaudreuil became convinced that Wolfe planned a direct attack; the British obviously could not risk an extended campaign during the winter, as the river would be sealed by ice.

During the siege, Quebec's Lower Town was repeatedly shelled by Wolfe's artillery at Lévis, on the south shore of the St. Lawrence. The Lower Town's buildings were either reduced to rubble or left standing as shells. Montcalm had the strategic advantage of Quebec's Upper Town, which was protected by high, steep cliffs, but the hard siege took its toll. The French were running out of ammunition and food. Montcalm's previous efforts to protect New France had been undermined by corruption, and the weaknesses were now growing into bleeding wounds as he desperately tried to keep Quebec — and thus New France — from slipping out of his fingers. In the middle of September, Wolfe had a stroke of good luck. On the dark night of September 12, he led a force of British and Scottish infantry past French river patrols to a point west of Lower Town. Here they bluffed their way past French sentries and climbed up the steep cliffs, where they assembled on the Plains of Abraham on the morning of September 13. An astonished Montcalm rushed his forces out of the fortified walls of Upper Town to confront the British. Within moments the battle was over, won by the British. Both Wolfe and Montcalm were shot. Wolfe died in the midst of the smoke and slaughter on the Plains of Abraham. Montcalm succumbed to his mortal wounds a few hours later inside the walls of Quebec. Although the Battle of Quebec was not the last between the French and British in this campaign, it proved decisive. New France ceased to exist.

According to legend, as New France faded away on the bloody ground of the Plains of Abraham, the cry *"Je me souviens"* ("I remember") was heard. The aristocracy and the affluent bourgeoisie abandoned Quebec and fled back to France, but the farmers, craftsmen, trappers, fishermen, and nuns and priests who stayed never forgot what they had lost on the Plains. They taught "Je me souviens" to the next generation, and it was passed on, generation by generation, down to the present day. *"Je me souviens"* is Quebec's motto; visitors can see it everywhere in the province.

After the defeat of the French, there was a brief lull before an even more serious storm. The campaign in North America had been costly for the British, and the coffers of the national treasury needed replenishing. Since the American colonists had benefited from the war — they could now go about their business with a far greater sense of security — London felt it was only fair for them to bear part of the great cost of the war and of maintaining a standing army. As anyone educated in the US knows, the bitterness over "taxation without representation" was one of the causes of the American Revolution, but few realize that it was far from a one-sided injustice.

Another major issue that exacerbated the problem was the Quebec Act of 1774. The act set aside the policy of uniform colonial growth and placed full authority in Quebec in the hands of the governor and an appointed council. In addition, it provided a string of benefits for the French-Canadian upper class: Roman Catholics were allowed to hold civil office; the seignorial land-holding system was confirmed, as was French civil law; and the Roman Catholic church was allowed to collect tithes. The province's boundaries were extended to include much of the old French empire — the region between the Ohio and the Mississippi rivers in which Montreal fur traders were still the dominant economic force.

To the staunchly Protestant "American" colonists the Quebec Act was a bitter pill to swallow, especially because it closed off the Ohio and Mississippi valleys to expansion, protecting them for the French. On the part of the British, the Quebec Act was simply a graceful acknowledgment that over 60,000 white inhabitants of conquered Canada were French and Roman Catholic. And Britain felt it had a perfect right to control commercial activity in the western territories.

THE AMERICAN REVOLUTION

At the convening of the first Continental Congress in 1774, there was no United States and no Canada as such, only 15 British colonies (Nova Scotia the 14th and Quebec the 15th). Both Nova Scotia and Quebec were invited to attend; both declined. The bishops of Quebec felt threatened by the Protestantism of the English colonies and by the new, revolutionary ideas that were sweeping the western world. There was strong pro-American sentiment in Nova Scotia, but the colony's geographical remoteness and the presence of the British navy, headquartered in Halifax, prevented any action. Thus, 13

English colonies declared their independence while two remained in the imperial fold. The US and Canada came into being as distinct entities.

Whether one thought of suppressing the rebellion or simply of retaining British control of the northern half of the continent, Quebec remained a key. As was also to be the case in the struggle of 1812, the "Americans" moved first. Congress dispatched two hastily organized armies to capture Montreal and Quebec. In November 1775, General Richard Montgomery took Montreal and Trois-Rivières and moved on to Quebec, the keystone to this 15th British colony. Benedict Arnold, who later joined the British side and lived in Saint John, New Brunswick, led a force of men through the wilderness of Maine to join Montgomery at Quebec. It was a classic pincer that might have won Quebec and the rest of Canada for America. Unfortunately, in 1775 Montgomery was killed in an attack on Quebec, and Arnold had to withdraw the American forces south into New York State.

What went wrong with the American plan that almost worked? Although many of the French sided with the Americans and considered them liberators, it was the Americans themselves who, by their conduct in Montreal, soured their potential allies. While occupying Montreal, American troops insulted the Catholic clergy, took over private homes and buildings by force, and tried to buy goods and services with worthless paper money. An American delegation, under the leadership of Benjamin Franklin, went to Montreal to soothe the feelings of the people. But the damage had been done. At Quebec the French fought beside the British against the forces of Montgomery and Arnold. What could have been a relatively short war became a protracted one.

With the British in control of Quebec and Nova Scotia, the English-speaking population on the Canadian mainland and in the Maritimes increased dramatically and in a most unexpected way. Those Americans who remained loyal to the British monarchy fled from the 13 colonies for their personal safety. While many returned to England, over 40,000 went to Canada. Some 35,000 went to Nova Scotia and 7,000 to what is now Ontario. In every sense of the word they were war refugees. A significant portion of these people were well educated (at Harvard and Yale, especially) and had been the affluent ruling elite in the colonies. They fled with only minimal necessities, at best to what was essentially a hostile wilderness, and many did not survive. Some gave up and went to the West Indies and other less severe climates in the British Empire. Others waited out the war, returning to the American states when the new government granted them amnesty. Those who stayed in Canada, however, cut back the thick forests and established cities, towns, farms, and industries. Loyalists living on the north shore of the Bay of Fundy and in that area's interior developed the region and formed their own colony, New Brunswick.

At the conclusion of the war, many other Americans went to Canada, claiming to have been Loyalists. Some were, in truth; others pretended to be so only because they wanted the free land offered to Loyalists. The availability of land attracted many apolitical Americans in general. In 1791, Quebec, which had been extended west of Lake Erie, was divided into Upper Canada (present-day Ontario) and Lower Canada (present-day Quebec). Seventeen years later Upper Canada had a population of around 80,000; 80% were

American. Lower Canada had the larger population: 250,000 in 1806, of whom 100,000 were American in origin. Both Nova Scotia and New Brunswick experienced dramatic population increases in the years immediately following what many called a civil war between Englishmen. In addition to the indigenous French and Indian populations, the Scottish who sought refuge in the Maritimes after the "clearances" of the highlands, the Acadians of the *Evangeline* saga who came back to Nova Scotia, and those British and Hessian soldiers who opted for a freer life in the New World, Canada's population in the early 19th century burgeoned with Americans who either felt more comfortable with a monarchy than with a republican democracy or simply wanted land on their own terms.

The fate of the British Loyalists is a historic footnote with which most US citizens are unfamiliar. Those Americans who could prove their loyalty to the Crown during the American Revolution were decreed by George III "United Empire Loyalists." They were entitled to add the initials *UEL* after their signature and could pass on this honor to future generations. This royal benediction created a new elite in Canada and strengthened its standing with the military, aristocratic, political, and commercial elites that began to pour into Canada from Great Britain. Both as a distinct class and by marriage into the British upper class, the Loyalists not only prospered but came to dominate much of Canada's social and commercial life. Saint John, New Brunswick, Halifax, Nova Scotia, Montreal, and Toronto became their centers of influence. Their power, and that of their descendants, continued well into the 20th century. In today's Canada, however, it is considerably diminished except in certain social circles and a few communities in Ontario and New Brunswick, where the initials *UEL* after one's name still carry some clout.

BRITISH CANADA

Between the signing of the Treaty of Versailles in 1783 and the War of 1812, the people of Canada developed farms, industries, communities, and cultural and political institutions. In Lower Canada, for example, the French professional class gained control of the elected assembly. Great Britain was a good customer for Canadian fur, fish, timber, and grain. However, the Jay Treaty of 1749 initiated a new era of trade between Great Britain and the US, and Canada was faced with serious competition for its chief market. Still, Canadian goods were allowed to enter Great Britain under the system of "imperial preference" duty free — and the US became Canada's second-best market.

The first 15 years of the 19th century saw Great Britain leading the opposition to Napoleonic expansion in Europe. It is doubtful that the English were looking for another fight with the Americans; they had their hands full with France. But interference with American shipping on the high seas and a number of confrontations between the US and Canada precipitated the War of 1812.

In 1813, American forces succeeded in capturing Toronto, then known as York, and burned and sacked it. The British retaliated in 1814 by capturing and burning Washington, DC. The war had reached its nadir.

A number of other battles took place along the border and on Lakes Erie,

Ontario, and Champlain. In 1814 the Treaty of Ghent ended the war, but border disputes continued. And it was not until 1842 that the US-Canadian border at Maine, Quebec, and New Brunswick was finally determined after difficult negotiations and sporadic armed clashes. The Treaty of Ghent did not eliminate the strong British belief that the US would not be content until it finally took Canada, either by force or by seduction. The British were so concerned about the continuing American threat that they built an interlocking waterway of lakes and canals between Kingston and the Ottawa River to the northeast. This — the Rideau Waterway — was an alternate route to move people and goods to the safety of Montreal if the St. Lawrence River, easily accessible from northern New York State, came under American control. The Rideau was never used for the defense of Canada; today it is one of the country's finest recreational boating waterways. And contrary to past expectations, the border between Canada and the US is the longest and oldest *undefended* border in the world, a rare memorial to what is possible between nations when there is mutual goodwill and respect.

With the direct threat of American intervention becoming ever less urgent in 1837 and 1838, the Canadians experienced severe internal struggles, which, had they been successful, might have radically changed the course of Canadian history.

In Lower (French-speaking) Canada an increasing number of French intellectuals and politicians were convinced that English interests in both London and British North America were using their economic power to keep French Canadians in a state of perpetual inferiority (an opinion that is often just as passionately expressed today). Louis Joseph Papineau, a leading French political figure, and his colleagues pressed for a reform of Lower Canada's political system. They wanted to form an independent republic with separate executive and legislative branches of government, patterned after those of the US. Papineau was not only denounced by English-speaking Canadians, which was only to be expected, but also by French-Canadian bishops and conservative professionals. Papineau, in effect, preached the same democratic liberalism that had produced radical change in the governments of America and France. The Roman Catholic clergy felt so threatened that anyone who openly declared himself to be a "liberal" was automatically excommunicated from the Church (a form of political control that persisted long after Papineau). Papineau and his "patriots," as they are remembered in Quebec, launched their rebellion in 1837. It was crushed in 1838, without excessive loss of life. Though Papineau failed, he did set in motion the desire of many to separate French Quebec from British Canada.

Around the same time that Papineau was active in Lower Canada, another rebellion, with somewhat similar goals, was taking place in English-speaking Upper Canada. A fiery, vociferous Scot, William Lyon Mackenzie, editor of the *Colonial Advocate,* sought to reform his government by taking it out of the hands of the conservative power elite and remaking it on the American model. Failing to achieve his goals in the legislative assembly, Mackenzie and his reformers felt that an independent, democratic state could only be forged by the force of arms. In December 1837, the quixotic Mackenzie and a poorly armed, poorly trained band of a few hundred followers marched to capture the capital of Toronto. Within a few hours, the lackluster assault ran out of steam, and Mackenzie had to flee for his life across the American border.

The Papineau and Mackenzie rebellions, although failures in their own right, did enable more moderate reformers, such as Robert Baldwin, to present a stronger case to the British Parliament for the doctrine of responsible government for Canada. The Canadians wanted a greater say in the running of their own political affairs. This doctrine led to the Union Act of 1840, which joined Upper and Lower Canada under a single government with the name of the Province of Canada. It was a big step toward self-rule, but as the bickering between the French and English continued, the union proved to be inadequate to its task.

A COUNTRY EMERGES

Canada in the mid-19th century was maturing and developing in other ways. The Maritime Provinces were prosperous as centers of fishing, lumber, shipbuilding, and trade. The Oregon Territory boundary was fixed on the 49th parallel in 1846 and became one of the longest sections of the border between Canada and the US. In 1856 gold was discovered in the Fraser River in British Columbia, unleashing a stampede of prospectors to the west coast.

Captain James Cook, the English explorer, is reputed to have been the first white man to set foot in British Columbia. He landed at Nootka, west of Vancouver Island, in 1778. Fourteen years later Captain George Vancouver explored the landscape and inlets where the city bearing his name is located. In 1858, its growth due mainly to the gold discovery, British Columbia became a colony of the English Crown. The territories between British Columbia and the western fringe of the Province of Canada were controlled by the great fur trading companies, such as Hudson's Bay. Between 1850 and 1867, Canada increased its railroads from a mere 66 miles of track (6,000 in the US at the same time) to 2,000 miles. This was also the period when slavery was legal in the US. For many black slaves, Canada was the Promised Land — the last stop on the Underground Railroad.

In the east, the population of Canada and the Maritimes continued to grow, in part through immigration. Though the vast majority of immigrants during this period came from the United Kingdom, many arrived from Germany, Switzerland, and other European countries. A large percentage of these new Canadians were Protestant, but there were also many Catholics, primarily Irish fleeing the potato famine, and an increasing number of Jews. Most of these people assimilated easily into the English-speaking mainstream. Through hard work, good sense, and shrewd investment they built successful businesses and created outstanding cultural institutions. This effort eventually loosened the grip of the old upper classes and pushed Canada on the road to becoming a genuinely pluralistic society. The native French, on the other hand, increased their population dramatically through an extremely high birth rate.

Many children were needed to work the farms, to counter the growing number of English-speaking peoples, and to preserve the French language and the Catholic religion in Canada. To English-speaking Canadians, the average

French Canadian was considered an inferior, no more than a "hewer of wood and a drawer of water." In reality, French Canadians were products of a highly insular society that had survived against great odds and that viewed the outside world and new ideas with profound suspicion.

Without the Church, the French Canadians, as a distinct ethnic group, might have disappeared, making Canada more like the English-speaking melting pot of the US. But the Church did its job exceedingly well, and as a result, it became powerful. Huge churches with richly decorated interiors could be found in even small, rural hamlets. Thousands of men and women took religious vows and labored in seminaries, convents, schools, and hospitals owned by the Church. Those laypeople who aspired to be professionals received a "classical education," concentrating on the humanities, theology, and philosophy. Well-educated French-Canadian males went into law, medicine, religion, or politics. The fields of industry, finance, and engineering were left to the English. Thus, French Canadians ensured their cultural survival and gained a large measure of control over their political life.

THE DOMINION OF CANADA

By the middle of the 19th century, political leaders in both British North America and England were talking about the need to establish a stronger union between the provinces. Their concern was based on population growth, westward expansion, political problems between the French and the English, and a possible threat from the US, which by the conclusion of its Civil War had amassed a huge army capable of invasion.

In October 1864, delegates met in Charlottetown, on Prince Edward Island, and drafted plans for a union. In Canadian history, these delegates are called the Fathers of Confederation. On July 1, 1867, the Dominion of Canada was born, with the British North America Act as its constitution. Sir John A. Macdonald, chief architect of confederation and leader of the Conservative party, became Canada's first prime minister. Confederation created a federal union under a parliamentary system of government in the provinces of Ontario, Quebec, Nova Scotia, and New Brunswick. Ironically, Prince Edward Island, the host of the Charlottetown conference, did not join the union until 1873. Newfoundland, the first land in North America to be inhabited by Europeans, did not become part of Canada until 1949. Manitoba joined the confederation in 1870; British Columbia, in 1871; Alberta and Saskatchewan, in 1905; Nova Scotia, not until 1949.

Sir John A. Macdonald, considered by many the greatest Canadian prime minister, launched the new Dominion of Canada with a national policy that promoted western settlement, encouraged the building of a transcontinental railroad, and established high tariffs on foreign goods.

Western settlement presented the new dominion with urgent problems. Over half the 40,000 inhabitants between the Great Lakes and the Rockies were Indians who lived off the seemingly endless herds of buffalo. The rest were French-Canadian trappers, English-speaking traders, and Métis (half French and half Indian). In 1869 the government paid $1.5 million to the Hudson's Bay Company for territory from the Great Lakes to the Red River (in Manitoba). About 6,000 Métis lived along the banks of the Red River, and they felt threatened by the government's policy of expansion. Under the charismatic leadership of Louis Riel, the Métis took Fort Garry, a trading post where the city of Winnipeg eventually rose. Their price for cooperating with the federal government was the protection of their language, religion, and lands, and the establishment of a self-governing province on the pattern of the others in the confederation. Macdonald agreed to negotiate with Riel. Unhappily, just then Riel executed an arrogant white troublemaker from Ontario, which outraged English-speaking Canada. While accepting the Métis' terms, Macdonald also sent an army to the Red River to keep the peace and maintain control of the new lands. (Riel escaped before the troops took Fort Garry.)

The Canadian federal government, seeing how the Indian wars were inhibiting the development of the American West, was quick to sign treaties with its own native people. Its efforts were successful, and most of the Indians surrendered their lands to the government by the end of the 1870s. In 1873 the Northwest Mounted Police (now called the Royal Canadian Mounted Police) began kicking out whiskey traders from the new lands and building forts that later became western cities such as Calgary.

As the transcontinental railroad pushed west across the prairies, bringing hordes of new settlers hungry for land, the Métis again felt that their way of life and very survival were threatened. Riel, who had been living in Montana, came back to Canada to lead the Métis in a new uprising. In addition, the Indians, suffering from starvation resulting from broken treaty promises, took to the warpath against the whites. In 1885 Riel took the Mountie post at Duck Lake (on the southern Saskatchewan River, in what was then the Northwest Territories), killing and wounding policemen in the battle. This success sent the Indians against the town of Battleford, the trading post and mission at Frog Lake, and Fort Pitt. During May 1885, Canadian forces attacked Riel at Batoche, defeating his army of determined Métis.

Riel surrendered. The Métis went home to their destroyed settlements and the Indians to their pitiful reservations, and Riel was hanged. Though the west was secured for continued development, Riel's death stirred up a hornet's nest in eastern Canada. Many people believed that the man was insane (he had spent time in a Quebec asylum) and that his life should have been spared for that reason alone. Most of French Canada was against the execution. They felt that Riel was killed because he was French and a Roman Catholic. Riel became a legend, and his death continues to be a sore point between English and French Canadians.

APPROACHING THE TWENTIETH CENTURY

In 1885, the same year as the Battle of Batoche, the main line of the transcontinental Canadian Pacific Railway was completed. In terms of human effort, engineering skill, and private financing, it was a great accomplishment. One can very well say that the transcontinental railroad was the cement that glued the provinces of Canada into one nation.

Between 1885 and 1914, when Canada entered World War I, new resources were discovered, new lands were settled and made productive, new industries were developed, and new people arrived on the scene. In 1898, for example, gold was discovered in the Yukon, and the Klondike gold rush brought people by the thousands. More significant were the continuing numbers of settlers who arrived. As all of the good, free land was taken up in the US, thousands of Europeans and Americans looked to western Canada. The prairie provinces of Manitoba, Saskatchewan, and Alberta not only produced enough grain to feed Canada but also earned the nation the title the Granary of Great Britain. In time Canada and the US were known as the breadbaskets of the world. Manufacturing, mining, lumbering, pulp and paper, fishing, and hydroelectric power continued to grow and add to the prosperity of the nation. Although Canada had a strong financial community (banks, insurance companies, and trading firms headquartered mainly in Montreal), much of the capital to fund the development of resources and the building of manufacturing plants came from Great Britain and the US. In time, the US dominated much of the nation's economic life. This became — and remains — a source of bitter anti-American feeling on the part of many Canadians.

THE FIRST WORLD WAR AND ITS AFTERMATH

On July 11, 1896, Sir Wilfrid Laurier, leader of the Liberal party, became prime minister of Canada. Laurier was Canada's first French-Canadian, Roman Catholic prime minister, yet he spoke out against the meddling of the Church in Canadian politics. One of Laurier's ideas, which cost him his job in the election of 1911, was to create a Canadian navy rather than give money to Great Britain for the defense of Canada. English Canadians pilloried Laurier as the author of a naval policy designed to isolate Canada from Britain. In Quebec and French Canada, he was portrayed as the fool of British imperialism. French Canadians condemned Laurier because they feared being drawn into a war of Britain's making. They remembered Britain's desire to enlist Canadians to help fight the Boers in South Africa. (Though a volunteer force of French Canadians did join the combat, the majority resisted conscription.) Sir Robert Borden followed Laurier and was prime minister when World War I broke out in Europe. Parliament passed the War Measures Act in order to mobilize the nation to assist the Allies — the prime ally being Great Britain. During the early years of the war, enough Canadians were slaughtered in Europe to cause a serious shortage in the number of additional men the government had promised to send overseas. Conscription was the solution, but many French Canadians would have nothing to do with it. In a climate of hatred and bitterness on both sides of the issue, close to 122,000 men were drafted, only 47,000 of whom were sent to Europe before the war ended. It should be noted that while much of Quebec was against aiding Great Britain, many French Canadians served their country in Europe with exceptional valor and distinction.

World War I greatly increased Canada's capacity to produce. And land and jobs attracted people from all over Europe to Canada after the war. So many Ukrainians emigrated that in time their culture became second only to that of the English in many places on the Canadian prairie. Many Jews also came into the country, settling in Montreal and Toronto as tradespeople and storekeepers or moving west to farm land, which had been denied them by law in Europe.

By the 1920s McGill University in Montreal, Dalhousie University in Halifax, and Trinity College of the University of Toronto were considered among the finest academic institutions in the world. At the University of Toronto, for example, Frederick G. Banting and Charles Best discovered insulin in 1922. Canadian art reached new heights during this time with the Group of Seven landscape painters. Canadian music, drama, and literature were also gaining the respect of international audiences. But by end of the 1920s, the economic prosperity that provided the backbone of all these achievements was quickly evaporating. On the eve of the Great Depression, severe droughts decimated the rich, grain-producing prairie, and the 1930s were ushered in with the chill prospect of hunger and despair.

In 1939 Hitler attacked Poland, Great Britain declared war on Germany, and seven days later, Canada was once again embroiled in war. Before World War I, Prime Minister Laurier could not sell the concept of a Canadian navy to the people. However, at the start of World War II, Canada entered battle with a rather respectable armed force, including the famous Royal Canadian Air Force of 11 squadrons. Many Americans who wanted to fight joined the RCAF, and President Franklin D. Roosevelt allowed American manufacturers to build aircraft on Canadian soil so that he could help Winston Churchill prior to America's official entry into the war. Roosevelt and Churchill had their famous Atlantic Conference off the coast of Newfoundland. Later, they met again at the Citadel, on the heights of Quebec City, to work on the invasion of France. This conference was held on Canadian soil as a gesture to Prime Minister William Lyon Mackenzie King, who insisted that Canada be made a full partner in the war effort.

In the deepwater ports of Halifax, Nova Scotia, and St. John's, Newfoundland, the great convoys formed to bring desperately needed supplies to England and Russia, sailing through Nazi U-boat wolf packs over the North Atlantic route.

In Quebec, conscription was again a passionate issue, and for the same reasons cited during World War I. While many avoided the war, other French Canadians joined Quebec regiments and fought bravely for Canada and the free world. Still other French Canadians — for example, René Lévesque, who later became premier of Quebec — joined the US Army and saw action throughout Europe.

THE CONTEMPORARY CHALLENGE

By the end of the war, 41,814 Canadians had died. Canada had more than paid its dues for membership in any league of nations and could no longer be seen as a mere child of the British colonial system. As a result, the country was one of the founding nations of the UN and became an important part of NATO. As a member of the UN, Canada also fought in the Korean War, its soldiers suffering 1,557 casualties. In 1956, through the genius of Lester B. Pearson, the nation's chief delegate to the UN, Canada won the Nobel Peace

Prize for his efforts. From that day on, Canada became a trusted party in helping to resolve a number of potentially dangerous international disputes.

Being an international leader was only one of many dramatic changes Canada experienced after the war. In 1952 the Right Honourable Vincent Massey was the first native Canadian to be appointed governor-general of the country. In 1959 the St. Lawrence Seaway, a Canadian-American project, opened for shipping from the Great Lakes to the Atlantic. Also during this period, Canada was a strong advocate for establishing the multiracial Commonwealth of Nations out of the old British Commonwealth, and it helped to organize the Colombo Plan to provide aid to underdeveloped nations. Between 1945 and 1957, Canada received over 1.5 million immigrants. These people, mostly skilled and educated, radically changed the complexion of many Canadian cities. Toronto, for example, has been transformed by immigrants from Italy, Greece, Poland, the West Indies, Uganda, Pakistan, and China; it is one of the most exciting multiracial, multicultural cities in North America.

Canada also expanded its government social programs to better the quality of life for its people, such as providing comprehensive health care for all. Its national and provincial health care systems are presently being studied in Washington as models for a US national health care system. A policy of bilingualism was adopted by the federal government, and French became the second official language of the country. Federal business must now be conducted in both French and English, and bilingualism is encouraged in all sectors of Canadian life, including the printing of labels on every kind of product. To strengthen its sense of national identity, Canada adopted a new flag and the theme of "unity through diversity." By its hundredth anniversary, in 1967, Canadian industries were booming, its cities were becoming showplaces, and its people were enjoying one of the highest standards of living in the world. There was an air of general complacency and self-congratulation in centennial celebrations around the country, a spirit only made stronger by the worldwide success of the World's Fair — EXPO '67 — in Montreal.

It was at this international confabulation, however, that France's president, Charles de Gaulle, dropped a verbal bomb that shook Canada to its foundation and set the course of political dialogue for the rest of the century. In a public speech before thousands of people, de Gaulle called for a free Quebec. His words shocked Canadians across the country, but it gave new life to a Quebec separatist movement that had begun to decay into terrorist tactics and hooliganism.

In 1968, inflated by de Gaulle's dictum, separatists gathered around Réné Lévesque, a popular journalist, and formed the Parti Quebecois. That same year Pierre Elliott Trudeau, a French Canadian whose style reminded voters of John F. Kennedy's, became prime minister. Trudeau advocated a better deal for French Canadians, but within the federal system. Canadians all over the country looked to Trudeau as the one person who might be able to save the country from being Balkanized or absorbed into the United States. In the Quebec provincial elections of 1970, Lévesque's Parti Quebecois won only seven seats in the legislature but received 23% of the popular vote.

During the same year, the FLQ, a terrorist organization, kidnapped James Cross, the British trade commissioner, and Pierre Laporte, a Quebec cabinet minister. The Marxist FLQ attempted to foment a revolution in Quebec. Student and worker groups protested in support of the FLQ. At the request of civil authorities in Quebec, the government proclaimed the War Measures Act, giving it virtually unlimited power and in the process denying the civil liberties of those innocent people arrested or held during the period. The FLQ killed Laporte, but freed Cross on the promise of safe passage to Cuba. The invocation of the War Measures Act proved a double-edged sword for the government; many Canadians applauded its use, but it created an aftermath of bitterness and anger in Quebec that remains today.

To the shock of many Canadians, Lévesque and his Parti Québécois won the provincial election of 1976, the year of the Summer Olympics in Montreal. As soon as Lévesque assumed power he was on the road, selling Quebec separatism both inside and outside Canada. His party also passed strict language laws that abandoned the concept of bilingualism and established French as the only official language in Quebec.

There was an immediate effect on Canadian consciousness. Most visible among these changes was the flight, mainly of English-dominated businesses and commercial enterprises, from Quebec to more friendly locations elsewhere in Canada. The competition between Montreal and Toronto for dominance as the most important municipality in Canada has clearly been won by Toronto, and this ascendancy is even discernible in tourist patterns from the US. Air Canada, Canada's government-controlled national flag carrier, now flies nonstop to Toronto from all seven US cities it serves (Boston, Chicago, Los Angeles, Miami, New York, San Francisco, and Tampa), but nonstop to Montreal only from Miami, New York, and Tampa.

Canada's politics took on a rather volatile cast during 1979, and the 1980s did not see any easing of national tensions. The Conservative government of Joe Clark replaced Pierre Trudeau's Liberals in the spring of 1979, but lasted in office a scant 8 months. In February 1980, Trudeau was returned to power with a significant national mandate — a more than interesting irony in view of the fact that Trudeau had personally announced his retirement from politics only three weeks before then-Prime Minister Clark's government fell. In May 1980, all Canada watched as Quebecois finally voted a resounding *"non"* to a separatism proposal that would have given Lévesque the right to negotiate sovereignty for Quebec. This long-debated question of separation — rejected by 60% of Quebec's population — was viewed by some as a personal defeat for René Lévesque, then premier of the province. M. Lévesque's declining status was unceremoniously confirmed when his party lost the next provincial election to the far more conservative Liberals, putting separatism in a descendant position for the rest of the decade.

The overwhelming Quebec support for Prime Minister Brian Mulroney's Conservative party in the 1984 and 1988 national elections, and the triumph of the Liberal party in the 1985 provincial races signaled a further decline in separatist preoccupation. In addition, Mulroney has championed the Canada-US Free Trade Agreement, and in the November 1988 federal elections his Progressive Conservative Party and the Free Trade Agreement were supported by the majority; Quebecers led the way, electing 40% of the 171 Conservatives in the 295-member House of Commons.

The election results seem to indicate that the people of Quebec are more concerned with improving their flagging economy than with insisting on independence, echoing the economic concerns that seem now to preoccupy all of the rest of Canada. Declining oil prices have deflated the oil-fueled boom of Canada's West, and the new free trade pact promises an uncertain period of opportunity and competitive pressure. Canadians remain strongly divided on the advantages and disadvantages of the Free Trade Agreement. At this point, no one can predict who will benefit most from the new trade relationship between the twin giants of North America; everyone agrees, however, that the change is likely to be far-reaching.

Contemporary Canada and the Storm of Separatism

The 1980 Canadian national election brought the debate on provincial independence — especially in relation to Quebec — to an international audience. And despite the declining strength of the Parti Québécois — which still clings to the principle of separatism — US observers still ask the question: How can a province even attempt to secede? The recent voting patterns of the Quebec electorate, as indicated in both the 1984 and 1988 national elections (which went heavily for Conservative Prime Minister Brian Mulroney's party), only increases this confusion.

If US citizens fail to comprehend the true divisiveness and passion of the separatist issue, it is because one of the gravest mistakes we make is to misunderstand — or worse still, simply miss — the profound difference between Canadians and ourselves. To be candid, these differences are not always so readily apparent. Where they are — as in Quebec City and certain other pockets of the province — they are unmistakable, and no one would suggest that Quebecois and New Yorkers are alike. But elsewhere, similarities are more striking than differences, and this is deceptive. But, a first-time visitor might argue, the Canadian people are made up of just about the same mixture of races and ethnic groups as Americans. And the landscape is much the same; we share the Rockies and the Appalachians, the Great Lakes and massive midwestern prairies. So what's deceptive?

The idea is deceptive that Canadians have the same monolithic sense of national identity that characterizes the United States and most other nationalities. (If you doubt that this is an American trait, just remember that we have appropriated the very word "American" to refer to ourselves, effectively disenfranchising every Canadian and Mexican, not to mention millions of South Americans.) Except for French Canadians, this is not true of many of Canada's citizens. Canadian culture is a curious contradiction, a manifestation of several conflicting forces. Not the least of these is that until relatively recently, Canadians were British subjects. Their allegiances and alliances were directed across the Atlantic, and the confederation of provinces was less than a binding psychological reality. And Canada has always been under the economic domination of one or another industrial neighbor — first Britain and then the US.

The building of a national identity has required unceasing effort — the rejection of foreign economic domination, at least in principle, even when in fact it has been impossible; the struggle to establish and maintain a cohesive national political unity that functions effectively in all parts of this huge country. But it has also meant finding a bridge across an even deeper schism in Canadian life. Canadians are keen observers of life in the United States, and early on they rejected the melting pot idea of culture that until 15 or 20 years ago was so dear to American hearts. They saw the price that arriving immigrants had to pay to melt into the American pot, and they foresaw the movement currently under way in the US to regain lost national and racial heritages in the third, fourth, and fifth generations. The Canadian national government adopted a policy of multi-culturalism to encourage Canadians to be proud of their ethnic roots. This policy celebrates Canadian diversity by building acceptance of it into the national system with a wide variety of national, provincial, and local programs. The constant desire by French Canadians to have their culture accepted on a separate but equal status with that of the English was a powerful force in moving the entire country to accept multi-culturalism. Going far beyond paying mere lip service to this ideal, the federal government established the Multi-culturalism Directorate of the Department of the Secretary of State as well as implementing its programs in this area through other federal cultural agencies.

Multi-culturalism has meant, however, that regional and ethnic identity vies with national identity in the Canadian heart. And that means that the threat of separatism is far more real in Canada than it could be in the US. A Canadian would not necessarily find the idea of an independent province, joined in an economic agreement with the other Canadian provinces, an unthinkable idea, especially if that Canadian were part of a strong-minded minority with a powerful tradition of its own, or lived in a province endowed with rich natural resources that spelled out a prosperous future as an independent political entity.

THE PEOPLE AND THE PROVINCES

Like the people of Western Europe and the US, the majority of Canadians — about 75% — dwell in urban centers settled for the most part within 200 miles of the US border. A huge portion of Canada's enormous land mass — the second largest in the world — is uninhabited. The Yukon and Northwest Territories, comprising over 40% of the nation's land, have around 70,000 inhabitants (mostly Inuit and Indian), so the Canada most of us think of is southern, urban Canada: economically modern and socially advanced. Of Canada's 25 million people, over 15 million (nearly two-thirds) inhabit two provinces: Ontario, historically English-speaking Upper Canada, and Quebec, French-speaking Lower Canada. Over 40% of all Canadians are of British origin; 30% are French. The roots of provincial rivalry and separatism lie in this simple yet significant demographic fact.

Canada's modern history has witnessed a persistent effort on the part of its people to establish some kind of distinct identity. In contemporary times, this has crystallized both as a struggle for provincial autonomy and independence at the regional level and as the policy of multi-culturalism at the national level. The result is Canada's growing unwillingness to allow foreign influences to dominate its cultural life and to blur its national character.

But how successful has Canada been in resisting cultural and economic manipulation from abroad? During the 19th century, the dominant cultural and economic factor in Canadian life was British; in our century the US has replaced the UK and has come to symbolize foreign influence. It is hard to alter this picture. American investors control overwhelmingly large percentages of Canadian industry, and what is more, Canada is still primarily a producer and exporter of raw materials. The US remains its chief supplier of finished products. Nor is this true in the industrial world alone. During the mid-1960s, when Ottawa expanded its university system and created thousands of academic positions, most of the professors and instructors were recruited from the US. When Canadians turn on television, what do they watch? "Dallas" and "Family Ties." The Canadian Broadcasting Company has yet to find a national substitute. And with the possible exception of *Maclean's,* there are still no weekly magazines to challenge the stature of *Newsweek, Time,* and *US News and World Report.* The impact of America — from popular music to fast-food chains — tends to lessen the reality of the political border separating the two countries.

In response to Americanization, the federal government has developed strict policies to regulate foreign investment and to check foreign influence on Canadian firms. Federal programs encourage the development of resources and industries by Canadians and create new markets for Canadian goods with countries other than the traditional trading partners. On a cultural level, the government's policies are also designed to limit foreign influence. For example, several years ago *Time* ceased publishing its Canadian edition when certain tax advantages were rescinded by the government and Canadian majority ownership was required. Most notably, large grants to artists, writers, filmmakers, and publishers have energized a truly Canadian contribution to the international arts scene. Still, no government can legislate cultural values, and today's Canada remains a mixture of foreign influences and purely Canadian qualities. The new free trade pact between Canada and the US will doubtless further the blurring of national sovereignties.

Canadians live in ten self-governing provinces: Newfoundland-Labrador, Nova Scotia, New Brunswick, Prince Edward Island, Quebec, Ontario, Manitoba, Saskatchewan, Alberta, and British Columbia. The Yukon and Northwest Territories are under federal jurisdiction.

Ethnically, the majority of groups in the Atlantic area are of English, Irish, Scottish, and German descent. Large numbers of Scots settled in Nova Scotia and Prince Edward Island, and the port of Halifax, significant since the 18th century, has long attracted English immigrants. There is a large population of Irish in the Maritimes, and the Irish brogue is strong in Newfoundland. In Nova Scotia there are significant numbers of blacks, descendants of settlers who originally came to Canada on the Underground Railroad and those who more recently have come from the West Indies. Pockets of Germans, Swiss, and Scandinavians can also be found in Nova Scotia and New Brunswick. And both provinces have sizable populations of Micmac Indians. Of all the peoples of the Atlantic provinces, the Scots are perhaps the most evident, with their Highland games in the summer and their concerts that feature bagpiping, sword dancing, and Celtic songs.

By contrast, the majority of Quebec's population is French and is undergoing rapid change. Prior to World War II, the prevailing image of the Quebec French was unquestionably conservative: a people dominated by their tradition and church, subject to high population growth and low economic status, unwilling to assimilate into the English-speaking mainstream. The postwar years witnessed a profound shift. The power of the Church has rapidly declined, and it now serves mainly in a pastoral capacity. The Church of Quebec, once one of the most conservative in the Roman Catholic world, today is considered one of the most progressive. Quebec families, once the largest in Canada, are now quite consciously the products of one of the lowest birth rates in the nation. Economically, more and more Quebec men and women are entering business and technical careers, areas previously reserved to the English-speaking. No doubt this has contributed to the transformation of Montreal into a world center of fashion, filmmaking, recording, painting, and publishing.

Not long ago, the English in Quebec controlled most of its financial institutions, but with the dynamic growth of the credit union movement, the French have created huge pools of capital under their own control. This economic power is a very real factor in the controversy over French-speaking autonomy, an issue that divides the Quebecois as much as the rest of the country. It is a hotly debated issue. For example, new immigrants living in Quebec must send their children to French schools. This policy has caused great anguish among the large Italian and Greek segments of the population, who see their future in the larger context of English-speaking North America. An underlying racism is causing concern in the substantial Jewish community which has made immense contributions to the economic and cultural life of the province. English-speaking shopkeepers in predominantly English-speaking neighborhoods have been forced by provincial law to change their signs to French. Many of those who could afford to move left for Ontario and other provinces. A severe decline in property values detained others, who waited for better days. On the positive side, the increasing number of both French and English Quebecois who reject cultural extremes and the racism of the few worked hard to retain a just society for all the people of the province. Recent elections — both national and provincial — suggest that sanity and self-preservation have triumphed.

The predominantly English-speaking Protestant province of Ontario has, in recent years, undergone rapid developments as well. For most of its history, Ontario's population has consisted mainly of people from Britain and America; its leading Protestant denominations — particularly the Anglicans — exerted enormous influence on political and social life. Strong family and business ties with the powerful elites of Britain greatly affected the economic development of not only Ontario but all of Canada.

Toronto and Montreal became centers of commercial and financial activity. There was also the influence of the fraternal orders, such as the Masons and the Orangemen. It used to be said in Ontario that a person couldn't get a political office unless he was either a Mason or an Orangeman. Torontonians of today look back on their own past with amusement when they recall what a straight-laced, WASPish society it was in which their forebears lived. It was a time of highly exclusive and restricted WASP neighborhoods, where even Jews or Catholics who had the money to buy homes were denied the opportunity on the basis of religion. The blue laws were so strict that a storekeeper could get fined for selling an ice cream cone on Sunday. Even as late as the 1950s, travelers were warned: "Don't get caught overnight in Toronto; you'll die of boredom."

The three prairie provinces — Manitoba, Saskatchewan, and Alberta — have a combined population of about 4.5 million people. The majority of these are descendants of the pioneers who came west in search of large tracts of inexpensive land for farming and ranching. These early settlers not only survived, but they also turned the prairie into one of the major grain- and meat-producing areas of the world, with usually enough surplus for export to other countries. The original inhabitants were the nomadic Plains Indians, such as the Sioux and the Blackfoot. Their descendants either live on reservations or have become assimilated into the white communities.

The first whites in the area were the French trappers, many of whom married Indian women. The Métis were the offspring of these unions. These descendants of the French have either become assimilated or live in a number of communities that are fairly homogeneous and where the language, religion, and culture of their forebears is kept alive. They consider themselves French Canadians, and they have mixed feelings about the separatist fuss their cousins in Quebec have made. The federal bilingual laws were promulgated just as much for them as for the people in Quebec. Because being a Métis means being part in the Indian's world and part in the white man's world — and not necessarily being accepted in either — this group has formed its own activist organizations and has pressed the provincial and federal governments to recognize its unique status and to provide legal, economic, and cultural services. Many Métis have blended into the population and have done very well for themselves, but for some it has been quite difficult.

Others who have settled in the prairie were Americans, English, Scots, Irish, Scandinavians, Jews, and Germans. One of the largest ethnic groups to flourish in the prairie provinces have been the Ukrainians. Travelers are surprised to suddenly see the onion domes of an Orthodox church sticking up over a broad field of golden wheat. And one of the most unusual groups in this area are the Hutterites, a communal religious society, originally from Germany, that bases its way of life on farming, hard work, strict discipline, and prayer.

For the first few years of this decade, the fastest-growing and most prosperous province in this region was Alberta. Its rapid growth was due to big finds of oil and natural gas. But the worldwide oil glut has slowed Alberta's boom days to a crawl, and many local companies and communities have felt unfamiliar bad times. Provincial officials are even now trying to regulate these domestic pendulum swings so the province can proceed at a more stable pace.

On Canada's Pacific coast is British Columbia, where 1.5 of the province's 2.8 million people live in the Greater Vancouver–Victoria urban area. By contrast, the people of rural British Columbia work in mining, lumbering, agriculture, and tourism. The mountainous interior of British Columbia is probably one of Canada's most beautiful regions. The Okanagan Valley is one of the most productive fruit-growing areas in the country. And though the majority of the province's population is of British origin, there are also unusual groups such as the Dukhobors, who can appropriately be called Russian Quakers.

As mentioned, the Yukon and Northwest Territories together comprise roughly 40% of the total Canadian land mass, but only 70,800 people live here. In recent years, oil and gas production has reached up into the Arctic, where it threatens to transform the traditional Inuit, or Eskimo, way of life. Ever since man can remember, the Inuit have lived in harmony with their often brutal natural habitat; now their transition into our contemporary world is painful and difficult.

In virtually every province some ethnic group is threatened by external forces, and every province boasts its own variety of multi-culturalism.

THE STORM OF SEPARATISM

The constitutionality of separatism has been an extremely subtle bit of business, since Canada is an independent sovereign state and a member of the Commonwealth of Nations. Constitutionally, the Queen of England is also the Queen of Canada and the chief of state, although she exercises about as much influence on policy here as she does in Britain — which is to say, she is powerless. The foundations of modern Canadian government are based upon the British North America Act of 1867, and it is to this act that all debates on the legality of separatism must inevitably be traced.

The creators of the act closely examined the US federal system, but used it more as a warning than as a model (remember, the Civil War had just ended). To avoid issues like states' rights and the problems that might ensue, the central government was made very strong and was given the key role of legislation. The act also established quite explicitly that any unnamed or "residual" powers ought to reside in the central government as well. The provinces were then awarded jurisdiction over roads, direct taxation, municipal affairs, education, and the like.

In the years since then, the provinces began to question the very legality of Canada's constitution. In 1867, the provinces were never considered sovereign entities — as the states, prior to the Constitutional Convention of 1787, considered themselves — nor were "the Canadian people" directly consulted. Clearly the act flowed legally from London's imperial prerogative; it was a gift of the mother country. After much discussion and negotiation, a compromise was finally reached and a constitution of Canada's own making drafted. Despite disagreement and dissent from Quebec (which insisted on a greater degree of provincial autonomy) and arguments over the constitution's new Charter of Rights and Freedom, the constitution was sent to Great Britain, where it was approved by Parliament. In April 1982, Queen Elizabeth flew to Ottawa to sign the proclamation formally transferring constitutional power from Britain to Canada, the result of which was that Canada could amend its constitution without first seeking approval from Great Britain. The major addition to the redrafted constitution has been the Canadian Charter of Rights and Freedom, which is based on the US Bill of Rights and guarantees certain rights and privileges to every Canadian citizen. The charter stirred much controversy in the Canadian Parliament and was passed only after a compromise clause was negotiated, allowing the Canadian Parliament and the provincial legislatures to pass their own laws overriding the provisions of the charter. Despite this addition, Quebec never officially approved the repatriation of Canada's Constitution.

After much storm and debate the spectre of a confrontation on the matter of separatism largely dematerialized after the Quebec provincial election of 1985. The defeat of the Parti Québécois at the polls brought a new feeling of accommodation into office. The Meech Lake Accord of 1987 sought, among other issues, to address the fact that Quebec had not approved the Constitution in 1982; one provision of the accord recognizes "that Quebec constitutes within Canada a distinct society." Yet as we went to press, the accord — which also addresses issues revolving around immigration, the senate, conferences and amendments, and national programs — had still not officially been enacted into law, since New Brunswick and Manitoba have withheld their necessary ratification. And while Quebec's desire to be "a distinct society" legally remains strong, separatism from the rest of Canada no longer seems a realistic alternative to the majority of Quebec citizens.

CANADIAN CULTURE TODAY

One of the most enjoyable aspects of a visit to Canada is the rich panorama of its culture. Only decades ago, both Canadians and foreigners viewed Canada as a cultural wasteland. What culture there was had usually been imported from Great Britain, France, or the US. It was the rule that talented Canadians had to flee the country to achieve fame. But the cultural scene in Canada has changed so since World War II that Canadian talent finds sufficient reward and acclaim working at home, and Canadian cultural offerings have become sought after abroad.

In dance, Canada has received international praise for the *National Ballet of Canada* in Toronto (with which Rudolph Nureyev was associated), for the *Grands Ballets Canadiens* in Montreal, and for the *Royal Winnipeg Ballet* in Winnipeg. Original Canadian and international drama can be seen in playhouses across the country. The plays of Shakespeare and Shaw are beautifully performed at Stratford, Ontario, and Molière is ever popular in Montreal. The federal government sponsors touring companies that perform in even the most remote settlements in the land. There are opera companies in most of the major cities; the *Canadian Opera Company* in Toronto is one of the best, and the Canadian Jon Vickers has achieved international success as one of the great dramatic tenors of our day. Almost every city has its own orchestra and smaller musical ensembles. Toronto, Montreal, and Vancouver boast symphony orchestras of international status.

Generally, Canadians have opted for a competitive rather than a protective approach to cultural independence. Begun as a wartime information service, the National Film Board has been expanded and now produces outstanding short subjects, documentaries, experimental, and animated films. Through private investment, too, the ground has been broken for a feature film industry in Canada; and by the end of the 1950s most provinces and a number of cities had established councils to supplement the work of the federal government. The magnificent artistic and planning success of EXPO '67 is only one example of this cultural advance.

In the field of broadcasting, the Canadian Broadcasting Company (CBC) provides news, entertainment, and educational programs over radio and television. In the north the CBC broadcasts in English, French, Indian, and Inukitut, the language of the Inuit. Radio Canada, the CBC's French-language service, produces and broadcasts programs to the French-speaking people of Quebec and other provinces; it is known for producing elaborate melodramas and musical shows. Radio Canada International, the CBC's shortwave service, broadcasts every day in 11 languages from transmitters in New Brunswick. The CBC also has an armed forces broadcasting service, which provides shortwave programming to Canadian troops around the world.

Canada has come a long way in the visual arts. At one level, an intensive search for identity was clearly seen in the extraordinarily influential group of artists known as the Group of Seven: Tom Thomson, Lawren Harris, J. E. H. MacDonald, A. Y. Jackson, Arthur Lismer, Franz Johnston, Frank Carmichael, and Frederick Varley. These painters went straight to the land, to the magnificent colors of Canadian autumns, to the cool darkness of northern lakes, to a vibrant sense of national image. They were the first group of Canadian artists to achieve international status.

Today, painters and sculptors working in all media are exhibiting their work in private galleries and public museums throughout Canada. Some of the outstanding museums include the *Art Gallery of Ontario,* the *Royal Ontario Museum,* and the *McMichael Museum* in Ontario; the *National Gallery of Canada* in Ottawa; the *Montreal Museum of Fine Arts;* the *Vancouver Art Gallery;* and the *Norman Mackenzie Art Gallery* in Regina. The Royal Canadian Academy serves as the premier professional organization for visual artists, and the federally funded Canada Council supports many individual artists, galleries, and museums as well as activities in other cultural fields.

In addition to the visual arts, Canada boasts many excellent writers. Along with Lucy Maud Montgomery, who made Prince Edward Island's Cavendish area famous in her children's book, *Anne of Green Gables,* there are Margaret Atwood, Mordecai Richler, Robertson Davies, and the economist-humorist Stephen Leacock.

Canada also has a number of exceptional museums and restorations that depict the history of the country. These include the *National Museum of Natural Sciences,* the *National Museum of Civilization,* the *National Museum of Science and Technology,* and the *Canadian War Museum* (all in Ottawa); the *Alexander Graham Bell Museum* in Nova Scotia; the *Glenbow Museum of Calgary; Kings Landing Historic Settlement* and *Village Historique Acadien* (both in New Brunswick); *Fort Louisbourg* and *Champlain's Habitation* restorations (both in Nova Scotia); *Upper Canada Village* and *Black Creek*

Village (both in Ontario); *Place Royale* in Quebec City; and *Vieux Montréal* in Montreal.

Canada has an excellent national library system, with the new Metropolitan Library in Toronto being one of the most comprehensive and stunning facilities of its kind in North America. And, similar in nature to the Library of Congress in the US, the Library of Parliament in Ottawa maintains one of the most complete collections of books in Canada.

THE CITIES

CALGARY

For a very long time, Calgary was Canada's best kept secret. Oh, folks in the cattle business knew it as a railhead, and oil drillers came into town to change clothes on their way to or from the big drilling fields, but for the rest of the world Calgary was known mostly as a town out near the Rockies where they had a hell of a rodeo once a year.

Then, in just 2 weeks during the winter of 1988, Calgary came of age for the entire planet. As tens of millions of sports enthusiasts watched the pageantry and competition of the Winter Olympics, they could not escape noticing that the surroundings were something very special, and that the Calgarians were pretty good at putting on an international party. Suddenly, lots of folks from all over the world wanted to see Calgary for themselves.

What they found was a warm, welcoming metropolis sitting on the vast Canadian prairie, with the jagged, snow-capped peaks of the Canadian Rockies jutting up to the west, and fields of golden grain extending to the east. It was these vast, grassy plains in southern and central Alberta that spawned the development of a huge ranching industry, of which Calgary — then a brash, bustling prairie city — was the center.

Once a year Calgary still puts on the world-famous Calgary Stampede — that Rolls-Royce of rodeos — in an effort to fool itself and everyone else into believing that it remains the simple cowtown of earlier days. Don't believe it for a minute. The Stampede no more represents contemporary Calgary than Will Rogers's deceptively slow-talking stage persona mirrored his rapier wit. Certainly there is historical truth to the cowtown image, but nowadays this prairie city of 658,000 is heavily into oil — and oil money — and the ten-gallon hat, cowboy boots, and saddle have been shed for a business suit and a pocket calculator. More than 600 Canadian oil and gas companies have their head offices here, with ancillary services provided by hundreds of drilling companies. Even the recent stagnation of oil demand and the loss of more than few get-rich-quick fortunes have hardly dampened local enthusiasm.

Much of how modern-day Calgary looks is the result of the oil boom. This era of prosperity saw the city swell well by more than 20,000 newcomers a year and city boundaries expand at a phenomenal rate. Those heady days produced an almost entirely new city core of steel and glass, which led one Canadian author to comment that the city looked as though it had just been uncrated. Many worried that the city's rapid growth would destroy traces of its tradition and history. Happily, public concern has led to the preservation of many examples of pioneer Calgary architecture. While its population has stabilized and construction slowed, the city continues to benefit from several ambitious projects launched during the boom. The impressive *Calgary Olympic Saddledome,* the major facility used during Calgary's stint as host of the 1988 Winter Olympics; a spacious downtown performing arts center that incorporates the historic Burns Building; a new, mirrored-glass municipal building, next door to the quaint sandstone city hall; and an ultra-modern light rail transit system.

This city has literally risen from the prairies. Situated at the western end of the Great Plains that sweep westward across Manitoba, Saskatchewan, and Alberta to wash against the eastern face of the Rocky Mountains, Calgary sits in the foothills of the Rockies at an altitude of 3,440 feet. Though high, the city is a traditional plains city, very flat and spread out. Two small rivers, the Bow and the Elbow, flow through the city to meet near the downtown area. Its altitude assures that Calgary gets lots of sun, and on clear days — that is, most every day — the rugged snow-capped peaks of the Rockies are visible some 50 miles to the west.

Calgary was founded in the late summer of 1875 by a contingent of the Northwest Mounted Police (now called the Royal Canadian Mounted Police) who set up camp near the confluence of the Bow and Elbow rivers. The police had come west to control the whiskey traders, who were creating havoc among the Indians, and to prepare the way for the thousands of eastern Canadians and immigrants who wanted to homestead. Here they subsequently built a fort, named after Calgary Bay in Scotland.

For 8 years after it was established, Calgary was no more than a minor post, overshadowed by Fort Walsh and Fort Macleod to the south and by Rocky Mountain House and Edmonton to the north.

In 1877 the five Indian tribes that roamed and hunted in southern Alberta agreed to sign a treaty ceding all rights to the land except for areas designated by the government. In return, the government agreed to provide the Blackfoot, Stoney, Sarcee, Blood, and Peigan Indians with education, medical care, hunting rights, ammunition money, farm implements, and suits of clothing for the chiefs. The controversy over the terms, and whether the government ever actually fulfilled its end of the bargain, still rages. Nevertheless, the agreement was reached without bloodshed, and the government gained complete access to the lands of southern Alberta for agriculture and for the railroad, which rolled into Calgary in 1883. The young settlement suddenly took on a whole new importance. By the end of the year, its population reached 600, and by 1889 it had risen to 2,000. In the coming years, thousands of people making their way west stopped in Calgary, and many stayed.

The abundance of grassy plains in southern and central Alberta spawned the development of a huge ranching industry, of which Calgary was the center. When the lush grazing lands encouraged US cattle owners to move their tremendous herds north from overgrazed ranges in the American plains, the city's meat packing industry was an inevitable result.

By 1893 enough pioneers had homesteaded in Calgary to allow the city to be granted a charter. Farming and ranching formed the foundation of a thriving but unrepentantly agricultural economy. In 1914, when oil was discovered at Turner Valley, just south of Calgary, an era of new prosperity began. However, not until the big discovery in the Leduc fields, near Edmonton, years later did Calgary really start to make its mark as a focal point of Canada's oil and gas industry.

Calgary became a brash, bustling, prairie city — an atmosphere still apparent today. The city has always attracted a confident, entrepreneurial breed of individual. Many people are drawn here because one needn't belong to an entrenched establishment to get ahead.

During the recent surge of expansion, which resulted in millions of square feet of high-rise office space downtown, city planners managed to maintain a comfortable urban environment. For example, the Stephen Avenue pedestrian mall was created so pedestrians would have priority over traffic. These 6 blocks of open space, trees, benches, shops, restaurants, and cinemas are prime territory for just sitting back and watching the world go by (this activity is restricted to spring, summer, and fall, since Calgary winters often send the mercury down to $-30F$ or $-34C$). Downtown Calgary is also the site of two interconnected shopping complexes, bracketed by the city's two largest department stores — *Eaton's* and *The Bay*. This arrangement allows residents to shop in a variety of stores without ever stepping outside. Calgary also has a number of enclosed overhead walkways that link stores and office buildings — another boon during the cold winters. Devonian Gardens at the top of Toronto-Dominion Square (the largest downtown shopping center) is a completely enclosed garden with 2½ acres of lush tropical plants and fountains. On balmy summer days, workers head to Prince's Island, a park full of trees and running water only 3 blocks from downtown.

Hardly surprising in a city whose prosperity is based on natural resources, the hand of nature is writ large around Calgary. Just 81 miles (129 km) away is Banff National Park in the Canadian Rockies, gateway to some of the best skiing in the world. To the east are the endless plains, and over the western ridge of Rockies, the Pacific Ocean. Should residents be inclined to forget where they are and to what they owe their living, there are the incredible Canadian prairie winters, with temperatures dropping to an average of zero F ($-18C$) to remind them of nature's power. And should they come to think of nature as nothing but a harsh winter mistress, they also have the chinooks, the amazingly warm winds that sweep in from the Pacific on even the most bitterly cold days, bringing the temperature up 30 or 40 degrees in a matter of hours and leaving breathless Calgary residents with a brief, nearly supernatural spring respite.

This phenomenon culminates in a dramatic chinook arch, a layer of white clouds covered by an arch of brilliant blue sky. At sunset, the chinook produces astonishing contrasts of light and dark — lines of long, flat, absolutely black clouds topped by startlingly clear skies. It's a sight to set even the most jaded spirits wandering.

CALGARY AT-A-GLANCE

SEEING THE CITY: The best view of the city is from the top of the newly renovated, 626-foot Calgary Tower. On a clear day, the Rocky Mountains are visible to the west. You can have a meal or drinks in the revolving dining room and cocktail lounge or just admire the scenery from the observation deck (there's a snack bar, should you get hungry). Open daily from 7:30 AM to 11 PM; Ninth Ave. and Centre St. S. (phone: 266-7171).

SPECIAL PLACES: It's easy to get around downtown Calgary because there is no traffic on the downtown mall, and the overhead walkways allow you to cross streets above traffic, where it exists. The streets are numbered and laid out in a north-south, east-west grid pattern. Calgary Transit buses shuttle around downtown and connect it with all other sections. A light-rail transit line (a modern, high-speed version of the old cable-car system) opened in 1981 to link downtown with the southern reaches of the city, and in 1985 the northeast line was completed. The northwest route was completed for the 1988 Winter Olympics.

Olympic Plaza – A $5.6 million downtown park which was the setting for the presentation of the medals during the 1988 Winter Olympics. Just 2 blocks from City Hall on Macleod Trail, between Seventh and Eighth Aves.

Glenbow Museum – The art gallery has permanent and changing exhibits, with carvings and ceramics from all over the world. The highlight is the floor devoted to Indian artifacts from all over Canada and the US, with a strong emphasis on the Indian tribes of southern Alberta. Open daily, 10 AM to 6 PM. Small admission charge, except on Saturdays. 130 Ninth Ave. S.E. (phone: 264-8300).

Calgary Centennial Planetarium – In the star chamber, the wonders of the universe are revealed by 100 special effects projectors and a sophisticated sound system. Or you can view the moon and the planets directly through the telescopes and slide-open roof at the observatory. The aerospace museum has displays of vintage aircraft and their engines, model rockets, and a weather station. Open Wednesdays through Sundays. Admission charge. 11th St. and Seventh Ave. S.W. (phone: 264-4060).

Fort Calgary – On the site of the original Northwest Mounted Police Fort built in 1875, this 40-acre park at the confluence of the Bow and Elbow rivers contains an interpretive center with exhibits and audiovisual presentations recounting Calgary's early days. The recently renovated Deane House, built in 1906 by N.W. MP Captain Richard Deane, offers lunch and afternoon tea and charming views of the Elbow River; guided tours are provided (no admission charge). Interpretive Center open daily in summer, Wednesdays through Sundays in winter (9 AM to 5 PM.) Deane House open year-round. Park open daily. No admission fee. 750 Ninth Ave. S.E. (phone: 290-1875).

Calgary Zoo – Animals live in their natural habitats; no barred cages at this large zoo. There are some innovative exhibit designs, too, which allow viewers to watch polar bears and seals swim from an underwater perspective. There are also expanded North American and Eurasian exhibits, a children's zoo, and interpretive programs for kids. Open daily. Admission charge. 1300 Zoo Rd. S.E. (phone: 265-9310).

Calgary Prehistoric Park – The Calgary Zoo's multimillion-dollar project transports visitors back to when southern Alberta was a land of swamps and volcanoes and hoodoos — those queer, toadstool-like rock formations that still exist in parts of the province. These manmade reproductions are painstakingly realistic, as are the fiberglass-skinned dinosaurs that populate the fern-filled swamps. The park, which is included in the zoo admission fee, is beside its main entrance, on the south side of Memorial Dr. S.E.. Closed in winter.

Inglewood Bird Sanctuary – Just 1½ miles downstream from the zoo, this patch of nature offers visitors a chance to observe some 230 varieties of birds year-round. In summer, wildlife experts give guided tours and visitors bicycle along the riverpath. Ninth Ave. and Sanctuary Rd. S.E. (phone: 269-6588).

Stephen Avenue Mall – A 6-block, traffic-free pedestrian mall lined with trees, fountains, and benches; in summer, especially around noon, it is full of workers taking breaks, shoppers, and street musicians and performers. Outdoor cafes line the mall. Many of the city's original sandstone buildings stand on the block between First and

Second Sts. The second floor of the Lancaster Building, 304 Eighth Ave. S.W., has many restaurants offering international fare.

Downtown Connection – This huge indoor shopping complex consists of two malls (Toronto-Dominion Square and Scotia Fashion Center), the *Bay,* and 200 smaller stores, all connected by a series of skywalks. *Eaton's* is just a block away. A 2½-acre park, the Devonian Gardens, on top of Toronto-Dominion Square is a popular gathering place. The stores carry everything from souvenirs to clothing. There are restaurants (*Earl's Place,* on the third level of Toronto-Dominion Square, the *Dilettante* in Scotia Centre) and several fast-food outlets. Three blocks between First and Fourth Sts. S.W., and Seventh and Eighth Aves.

Kensington – A revitalized, older neighborhood that today is thick with trendy restaurants, pubs, bookstores, craft shops, and tiny stores purveying first-rate ice cream. The area stretches west along Kensington Road for several blocks from Tenth St. N.W. A lovely Bow River pathway follows Memorial Drive, 1 block south of Kensington Road.

SUBURBS

Heritage Park – A pioneer village re-created with buildings transplanted from their original locations in small Alberta towns. Among the structures are a working blacksmith's shop, a bakery where you can buy fresh bread, a small log church still used for services and weddings, and a newspaper office distributing the park's official newspaper. The houses are furnished with period pieces, and the occupants even dress in early-1900s styles. If you really want to journey back in time, the means of transportation are diverse: an old steam train, an electrical streetcar, a carousel, a horse-drawn bus, or the SS *Moyie,* a paddlewheeler that plies the waters of the Glenmore Reservoir. Available refreshments range from ice cream and snack bar fare to great Alberta beef and homemade apple pie served up in the dining room of the *Wainwright* hotel. Open from May to October. Small admission charge. West of 14th St. and Heritage Dr. S.W. (phone: 252-1858).

Fish Creek Provincial Park – These 2,800 acres on the city's southern edge shelter a mixture of grassland, poplar and spruce groves, and native shrubs; a wildlife refuge is also located here. Park interpreters present slide shows and lead nature walks to acquaint visitors with the human and natural history of the area. There's also a small, manmade lake where people swim in the summer. Open daily. No admission charge. More than 5 miles (8 km) long from Canyon Meadows Drive and Bow Bottom Trail S.E. to Canyon Meadows Drive and 24th St. S.W. (phone: 297-5293).

■**EXTRA SPECIAL:** High River, 30 miles (48 km) south of Calgary, has the atmosphere of an authentic small Western town. Several stores carry handicrafts made by local artisans, including ceramics, leatherwork, and wooden carvings. If you're in Alberta during July, check the dates for High River's annual North American Chuckwagon Championship. You'll see the same names and rigs that appear at the Calgary *Stampede.* For more information write to the High River Chamber of Commerce, Box 1258, High River, Alberta TOL 1B0.

Calgary is a major stopover for travelers bound for Banff National Park. Only 75 miles (120 km) west of Calgary along the Trans-Canada Highway, Banff has spectacular Rocky Mountain scenery and some of the best skiing areas in Canada (see *Skiing,* below, and the *Skiing* sections in DIVERSIONS). For complete information on Banff, see *National Parks* in DIVERSIONS.

SOURCES AND RESOURCES

TOURIST INFORMATION: The Calgary Tourist and Convention Bureau (1300 Sixth Ave. S.W.; phone: 263-8510; mailing address: 237 Eighth Ave. S.E., Calgary, Alberta T2G 0K8) supplies maps, brochures, free accommodation assistance, and general information, and publishes an annual visitor's guide that lists city attractions and services (closed weekends).

Local Coverage – The *Calgary Sun* and the *Calgary Herald,* morning dailies; *Alberta Report,* weekly news magazine.

Food – See *My Favorite Restaurants in Calgary and Banff* by John Gilcrest.

Telephone – The area code for Calgary is 403.

Sales Tax – Neither the city of Calgary nor the province of Alberta has sales tax.

Currency – All prices are quoted in US dollars unless otherwise indicated.

TIPPING: At restaurants generally leave 15% of the bill. Taxi drivers should be given 10 to 15% of the fare. Airport porters and bellboys are given about $1 (CN) per bag, and hotel maids should receive about $1 (CN) per day.

CLIMATE: Calgary tends to be sunny and dry during most of the year. Temperatures range from an average of 10F (−12C) in January to an average of 58F (16C) in July. From May to the middle of September, expect warm days and cool nights. During the winter, the city gets about 50 inches of snow and unpredictable chinooks: warm westerly winds that can raise the temperature 20 to 30 degrees in an hour. Anyone who ventures to Calgary in the winter should bring along boots, a heavy coat, gloves, and a hat.

GETTING AROUND: Bus – *Calgary Transit* serves all parts of the city. For detailed route information, call 276-7801, or stop in at the transit information booth, Seventh Ave. and First St. S.W. *Brewster Transportation and Tours, White Stetson Tours, Pacific Western,* and *Cardinal Coach Lines* are among those available for charter bus tours.

Taxi – Taxis generally cannot be hailed on the streets, but are available at hotels, or one can be called. Major companies are *Yellow Cab* (phone: 250-8311), *Prestige Cabs* (phone: 250-5911), and *Checker Cab* (phone: 272-1111).

Car Rental – All major firms are represented at Calgary International Airport as well as downtown: *Avis,* 240 Ninth Ave. S.W. (phone: 269-6166); *Hertz,* 227 Sixth Ave. S.W. (phone: 221-1300); *Tilden,* First St. and Fifth Ave. S. (phone: 263-6386).

SPECIAL EVENTS: During the famous *Calgary Exhibition and Stampede,* during the first or second week of July, the city reclaims its Western heritage with rodeos, chuckwagon races, grandstand shows, exhibitions, displays, and general carryings-on. *Stampede* dates vary slightly every year; check with the CTCB before coming and make reservations for grandstand events well in advance. Most of the action takes place within walking distance of downtown, at *Stampede Park,* but the mall, suburban shopping centers, and parks are also filled with cowboys in wagons, Indians in traditional dress, and Western bands. If you can't make the *Stampede, Rodeo Royale* is held inside the *Stampede Corral* in February and March.

CALGARY / Sources and Resources 141

MUSEUMS: The *Glenbow Museum,* Fort Calgary, the Planetarium, and Heritage Park are described in *Special Places.* Other museums worth a visit:

The Energeum – Oilfield memorabilia and video games tell the tale of energy in Alberta. No admission charge. 640 Fifth Ave. S.W. (phone: 297-4293).

Military Museum – At the Canadian Forces Base on Crowchild Trail between 33rd and 50th Aves. Closed Mondays and Saturdays (phone: 240-7901).

Stockmen's Memorial Foundation – A museum, small gallery of Western art, and library illustrating the province's ranching history. 2116 27th Ave. N.E. (phone: 250-7529).

SHOPPING: Special goods found in Calgary are mostly furs, Western wear and Indian crafts. *Western Outfitters* (128 8th Ave. S.E.; phone: 266-3656) is a good place for cowboy hats, boots, and jeans. *Alberta Boots* (614 Tenth Ave. S.W.; phone: 263-4623) is the province's only cowboy boot manufacturer. For native crafts, try *Cottage Craft Gifts* (6503 Elbow Dr. S.W.; phone: 252-3797) or the *Glenbow Museum*'s excellent gift shop for authentic native-made crafts from western and northern Canada (130 Ninth Ave. S.E.; phone: 264-8300). The *Mount Royal Village* area on 17th Avenue S.W. features trendy clothing shops, antiques stores, art galleries, and bookstores; similar shopping opportunities will be found in the Kensington district (Kensington Rd. and 10th St. N.W.). The *Downtown Connection,* a huge downtown shopping complex, has most anything else you'll want, including furs.

SPORTS: Though Calgary is only 80 miles (128 km) away from the Rocky Mountain skiing areas, it has a fair share of its own diversions.

Auto Racing – The 160-acre *Race City Speedway* hosts major national and international stock car, motorcycle, hot rod, and formula Grand Prix–style competitions throughout the summer. 114 Ave. and 68th St. S.E. (phone: 236-7223).

Baseball – The Calgary *Cannons,* a farm team for the Seattle *Mariners* and part of the Pacific Coast League, play at *Foothills Baseball Stadium* from April through August (phone: 284-1111).

Boating – There's sailing on the Glenmore Reservoir in the southwest section of the city; *Glenmore Boats–Sailboats* rents boats (phone: 266-3055). During the spring and summer many people canoe and kayak on the Bow and Elbow rivers; University of Calgary *Campus Recreation Rentals* supplies equipment (phone: 220-5038).

Fishing and Hunting – The area around Calgary supports upland birds, big game, waterfowl, and freshwater fish. For full information, contact the Department of Fish and Wildlife, Rm. 200, Sloane Square Bldg., 5920 1A St. S.W. (phone: 297-6423). The Bow River, downstream from Calgary, is reputed to be one of the finest fishing grounds in the world for brown and rainbow trout. Consult the "Float Trips" section of the *Adventure Guide* published by Travel Alberta, 10025 Jasper Ave., 15th Fl., Edmonton, Alberta T5J 3Z3 (phone: 403-427-4321 in Edmonton; 800-222-6501 elsewhere in Alberta; 800-661-8888 elsewhere in Canada or in the US). The Travel Alberta office in Calgary Mc Dougall Center is located at 455 Sixth St. S.W. (phone: 297-6574).

Football – The professional *Stampeders* play from June through November at *McMahon Stadium* in northwest Calgary (phone: 289-0258).

Golf – Six municipal courses and numerous private courses will accept transient players. *Shaganappi Golf Course* is the closest municipal course to downtown, Bow Trail and 26th St. S.W. (phone: 249-1212).

Hockey – The Stanley Cup champion Calgary *Flames* compete in the National Hockey League and play at the *Calgary Olympic Saddledome, Stampede Park,* from October to May (phone: 261-0455).

Horseback Riding – Lessons, group trail rides, hayrides, and mountain trips in the summer are available at *Fish Creek Trail Rides,* southwest of Calgary in Fish Creek Provincial Park (phone: 251-6955). *Spruce Meadows Stables,* just southwest of the city (phone: 256-4977), is the site of several annual international equestrian competitions.

Horse Racing – Harness and thoroughbred racing can be enjoyed year-round at *Stampede Park* (phone: 261-0214).

Skating – The Olympic Oval on the University of Calgary campus is the first covered 400-meter speed skating track in North America, and the first ever used in Olympic competition. This $40-million facility is not just for the use of the world's elite speed skaters, however. So, bring your own blades, or rent them here (phone: 220-7890).

Skiing – The newest ski destination in the Canadian Rockies is Nakiska at Mount Allen, about 60 miles (96.5 km) west of Calgary, where the 1988 Olympic alpine comptetition was held. Three big areas near Banff are Sunshine Village, Skiing Louise, and Mt. Norquay. For the novice or the experienced downhill skier who just wants a little practice, there's Canada Olympic Park, Rte. 1 west at Bowfort Rd. (phone: 288-4112). They also rent equipment (see DIVERSIONS).

Swimming – The city-owned *Lindsay Park Sports Centre,* 2225 Macleod Trail S.E. (phone: 233-8619), has three pools and numerous other facilities, including squash courts, running track, sauna, and weight room.

Tennis – There are private and public courts in the city. For information on the public courts, (phone 268-5218).

THEATER: For complete listings, check the publications cited above. Since 1985, two of the city's professional companies, *Theatre Calgary* and *Alberta Theatre Projects,* have been staging plays at the $75-million *Calgary Centre for the Performing Arts* at 205 Eighth Ave. S.E. (phone: 266-8888 for tickets; 294-7444 for information). The *Lunchbox Theatre* also presents short, noontime productions on Mondays through Saturdays in Bow Valley Square, downtown (phone: 265-4292).

MUSIC: The *Calgary Philharmonic* presents concerts from fall through the spring at the *Jack Singer Concert Hall* in the new *Calgary Centre for the Performing Arts* (phone: 294-7420).

NIGHTCLUBS AND NIGHTLIFE: *Electric Avenue* is the name Calgarians have given to a neon-lit strip of bistros and dance clubs along Eleventh Avenue S.W. between Fourth and Eighth Sts. It's heaven for bar-hoppers, and a muscular young rickshaw puller can even be hired to transport revelers from one watering hole to the next. Downtown, along the Stephen Street Mall, is the *Unicorn,* 304 8th Ave. S.W. (phone: 233-2666); it has good food and is a warm pub where locals extend a hearty welcome to newcomers. If you want to listen or dance to Western music in the company of real cowboys and cowgirls, head south of town for the *Ranchman's,* 9615 Macleod Trail (phone: 253-1100), just one of a number of country and western dance hall bars.

BEST IN TOWN

CHECKING IN: Calgary has several first class hotels downtown and a spate of motels on the two primary approaches to the city — along the southern end of Macleod Trail from the south and along 16th Ave. north from the Trans-Canada Highway. Accommodations are often booked solid during the

CALGARY / Best in Town 143

Stampede; the city also hosts many conventions, so reserve rooms in advance. Expect to pay about $76 and up for a double room in the places listed as expensive and $34 to $72 in the moderate range. There are no inexpensive hotels worth recommending in Calgary, though bed-and-breakfast establishments provide a low-cost option. Contact the *Bed and Breakfast Bureau,* Box 7094, Station E., Calgary, Alberta T3C 3L8 (phone: 403-242-5555). All telephone numbers are in the 403 area code unless otherwise indicated.

Delta Bow Valley Inn – Along with 390 rooms, including some that are non-smoking, this place has exercise facilities, a dining room, tavern, pool, sauna, and Jacuzzi. 209 Fourth Ave. S.E. (phone: 266-1980). Expensive.

Palliser – A gracious old hotel constructed in 1914 by the Canadian Pacific Rail Company and still a link in the company chain. The 11-story sandstone structure contains 400 rooms, all of which have been restored. Solid brass doors, original marble pillars and staircases, and a large chandelier decorate the elegant lobby. The *Rimrock* dining room has an Old West flavor in its decor and menu. There are also 2 coffee shops; covered walkways lead to the Calgary Tower complex of 80 shops, movie theaters, and offices. 133 Ninth Ave. S.W. (phone: 262-1234). Expensive.

Skyline – One of the city's newest downtown hotels, in the Convention Centre complex, it has 237 rooms and features an indoor garden and a pool. The *Traders* dining room has a fine menu, and guests can catch a quick bite at the *Wheat Sheaf* coffee shop. Children under 16 can stay free in the same room as their parents, and rooms for non-smokers are available. Ninth Ave. and Centre St. S.E. (phone: 266-7331). Expensive.

Westin Calgary – This 525-room hotel is another of the city's best known. Its *Owl's Nest* restaurant is among the city's finest (see *Eating Out*), and there's also an informal dining room and cocktail lounge. Facilities include a swimming pool, shops in the lobby, underground parking; the rooms are air conditioned. Fourth Ave. and Third St. S.W. (phone: 266-1611). Expensive.

Prince Royal Inn Apartment Hotel – Great for families, it has a dining room, lounge, hot tub, and fully equipped kitchens. 618 Fifth Ave., S.W. (phone: 263-0520). Moderate.

Relax Inn–North – This family-style hotel offers 200 rooms, a pool, hot tub, restaurant, gift shop, and game rooms. 2750 Sun Ridge Blvd. N.E. (phone: 291-1260). Moderate.

Relax Inn–South – A 270-unit motel with air conditioned rooms and some of the most reasonably priced accommodations in the city. Rooms for non-smokers available. 9206 Macleod Trail S. (phone: 253-7070). Moderate.

Stampeder Inn – In south Calgary, this modern hostelry has 150 rooms, air conditioning, a dining room, and a cocktail lounge. Children under 12 may stay in the room with their parents at no charge; rooms for non-smokers are available. 3828 Macleod Trail (phone: 243-5531). Moderate.

Sun Bow Inn – Built around an indoor courtyard with a swimming pool, the hotel has a poolside dining room; rooms for non-smokers are available. 2359 Banff Trail N.W. (phone: 289-1973). Moderate.

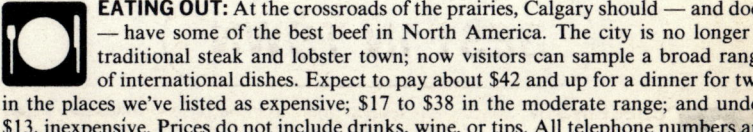

EATING OUT: At the crossroads of the prairies, Calgary should — and does — have some of the best beef in North America. The city is no longer a traditional steak and lobster town; now visitors can sample a broad range of international dishes. Expect to pay about $42 and up for a dinner for two in the places we've listed as expensive; $17 to $38 in the moderate range; and under $13, inexpensive. Prices do not include drinks, wine, or tips. All telephone numbers are in the 403 area code unless otherwise indicated.

La Chaumière – Authentic French food and fine service are this Gallic restaurant's hallmarks. Specialties include breast of duck in brandy, rack of lamb, and scampi Parod. Closed Sundays. Reservations advised. Major credit cards accepted. 121 17th Ave. S.E. (phone: 228-5690). Expensive.

Owl's Nest – Renowned for its beef entrées, British Columbia salmon, Beluga malossol caviar, medallions of venison, and quail, this plush restaurant in the *Westin Calgary* is a Calgary institution. Open daily. Reservations advised. Major credit cards accepted. 320 Fourth Ave. S.W. (phone: 267-2823/4). Expensive.

Traders – Dark paneling, elegant table settings, and fine food distinguish this restaurant in the *Skyline* hotel. Open daily. Reservations advised. Major credit cards accepted. Ninth Ave. and Centre St. S.W. (phone: 266-7331). Expensive.

La Dolce Vita – Lovingly prepared Italian food (veal, seafood, pasta) presented in an elegant yet comfortable setting. The owner makes his own *cassata* — Sicilian ice cream with candied fruit — that is a must. Closed Sundays. Reservations advised. Major credit cards accepted. 916 1st Ave. N.E. (phone: 263-3445). Moderate.

Le Flamboyant – Tiny and unassuming, but the Mauritian-style Créole and curry dishes are exquisite. The bouillabaise, heaped with crab legs and prawns, is a specialty. Open Tuesdays through Saturdays. Major credit cards accepted. 4018 16th St. S.W. (phone: 287-0060). Moderate.

Silver Inn – Though this family-run restaurant is located outside Calgary's Chinatown, it offers the best Peking-style fare in town. The menu is extensive, service is efficient and friendly, and the restaurant is fully licensed. Closed Mondays and holidays. Major credit cards accepted. 2702 Centre St. N.E. (phone: 276-6711). Moderate.

Green Street Cafe – In the heart of downtown, this place has a quiet atmosphere with a pleasant view of the nearby park. The menu features everything from crêpes to steak. Major credit cards accepted. 815 Seventh Ave. S.W. (phone: 266-1551). Moderate to inexpensive.

Café Danois – On the mezzanine floor of the Chevron Plaza, this tiny restaurant serves beautifully presented open-face Danish sandwiches, soups, and entrées such as homemade sausage or sole, as well as non-Danish food. Reservations advised for dinner. Major credit cards accepted. 500 Fifth Ave. S.W. (phone: 263-1114). Inexpensive.

4 St. Rose – Centrally located, this restaurant serves an eclectic menu including soup, salads, sandwiches, pizza, omelettes, and tempting desserts. The decor makes for a cozy atmosphere, and the offbeat clientele is great for people watching. No reservations. Major credit cards accepted. 2116 Fourth St. S.W. (phone: 287-0113). Inexpensive.

EDMONTON

Boom towns are a familiar western phenomenon, well anchored in North American folklore and mythology. The very term evokes dramatic images of towns materializing overnight in the midst of the untamed and uncharted wilderness, of hardy men engaged in a lonely struggle with the elements driven on by the dream of the mother lode, of dingy saloons and dance halls festering with crooked gambling and drunken brawls, and of incredible fortunes made over years and lost in a matter of hours.

From Charlie Chaplin's epic tale of Alaskan misadventure *The Gold Rush,* to Robert Altman's popular classic *McCabe and Mrs. Miller,* the boom town is embedded in our culture as an arena where both the brave and the foolish try to strike it rich — and where they most often fail. And when they fail and the mine or well runs dry, the boom town suddenly finds itself a ghost town.

Consider Edmonton, the capital of the province of Alberta, the largest northerly city in the Americas (with a metropolitan area population of 740,000) and the wiliest boom town in the Northern Hemisphere. Three times it has experienced the frenetic explosion of a boom — in the days of the Hudson's Bay Company and "King Fur," during the Gold Rush of '98, and in the late 1970s to early 1980s with excessive oil and gas development. Each time the tide has passed, the boom dissipated, the prospectors giving up in despair, yet Edmonton has emerged stronger, richer, more stable, and more beautiful than before.

An example is the way the city handled its oil boom. (Just about 25 miles south of Edmonton, at Leduc, are a slew of very lucrative wells.) With more money flowing though provincial coffers than was imaginable 40 years before, it might have been easy for a city to lose its perspective. But not Edmonton. Shortly after the Progressive Conservatives came to power in the early 1970s, they decided it was time to establish a special fund for the wealth the province was amassing from its oil and gas royalties. It's called the Alberta Heritage Savings Trust Fund, and the politicians who sit under the dome in the Legislature Building in Edmonton make the final decisions on how to spend the surplus revenue. And they are very judicious.

Fort Edmonton was established as a fur trading post in 1795 on the mighty North Saskatchewan River, the banks of which rise some 200 feet near the original site. Chief Factor John Rowand was the first commander of the fort in the early 19th century, and as such he was regent of a realm known as Rupert's Land, which consisted of the southern half of Alberta and the southeastern quarter of Saskatchewan. From the very beginning, Edmonton was the seat of power and commerce in north-central Canada.

While Hudson's Bay fur traders roamed the north in search of beaver, muskrat, and mink pelts, a number of missionaries traveled around southern Alberta, attempting to make Christian converts of the local Wood, Cree, and

Blackfoot Indians. The missionaries built schools and churches, but their efforts were subverted when Rupert's Land became part of Canada in 1869, and whiskey traders and other unscrupulous characters moved up from the Montana Territory, founding Fort Whoop-Up and bedeviling the population. Most God-fearing citizens in the new province had to wait 5 years before the Royal Canadian Mounted Police arrived to restore order.

It was in 1871, in the midst of this lawless era, that Edmonton was incorporated as a town with a population of about 600. Soon after, when Canada's first transcontinental railway was laid, Edmonton became an important stop — the crossroads between east and west as well as north and south. (Today Edmonton lies at the heart of the Canadian railway network, with eight different railway lines running through the city.) The railroad has in many ways been the true source of Edmonton's wealth, and it is the reason Edmonton became known as Canada's "gateway to the north."

When gold was discovered in the Klondike in 1898, prospectors and other would-be millionaires prepared for the ordeal in Edmonton; the tiny town of 700 suddenly mushroomed into a respectably sized town of 4,000. A disaster for most of the unfortunate prospectors, the Gold Rush is remembered fondly by Edmonton folks, and their warm nostalgia takes yearly expression in a colorful bacchanalia known as *Klondike Days*. During this giant masquerade, which occurs during the last 2 weeks of July, they take a break from fortune hunting to traipse about town in "Gay Nineties" dress, occasionally panning for gold, often stopping for a drink, and generally attempting to celebrate as long as they can still stand. Unsuspecting tourists who are inappropriately attired are subjected to surprising citizens' arrests and may find themselves in a Klondike clink. Bail is a Klondike dollar that has been specially minted for the occasion.

The oil boom was particularly kind to Edmonton, and perhaps someday in the not too distant future Edmontonians will declare a local holiday to celebrate the invention of the internal combustion engine. The discovery of oil in Alberta early in this century, and the subsequent gusher at Leduc, spurred fantastic local industrial growth. An indication of just how much growth is involved is the fact that Edmonton's population quadrupled between 1939 and 1965.

While wallowing in the profitable wake of this boom, Edmontonians further benefited from the discovery of natural gas reserves at Viking and the development of the Alberta tar sands at Fort McMurray. Hence, the entire province of Alberta has no sales tax.

What may be a pleasant surprise, however, is seeing how intelligently the Edmontonians have used their wealth in city planning and development. Far from being the amorphous hodgepodge of slums and mansions one might expect in a boom town, Edmonton is an extremely well-designed modern city that has made a valiant effort to retain and even reconstruct valuable artifacts of its past while confronting its future.

For example, a replica of Fort Edmonton now stands on a 158-acre park in the suburbs, and replicas of the city in its various stages of development are being constructed in the same park. Other efforts at making the city a pleasant habitat include the recent establishment of a 2,100-acre park —

Capital City Recreation Park — along the spectacular banks of the North Saskatchewan River, which now separates the downtown area of the city from the suburbs. The park is a verdant complement to the already dramatic scenery, and it's a tribute to inspired city planning, as is the fact that Edmonton now has a total of 10,000 acres of city parks. In summer months, when the city often has sunlight until 10 or 11 PM, these parks are filled with people playing, cycling, riding horses, having a baseball game, picnicking, and generally cavorting.

In the winter, Edmontonians are smart enough to get outdoors and use these same parks for skating and cross-country skiing. The winters are very cold, but rather than struggle through unplowed streets and icy sidewalks, Edmontonians can take advantage of an extensive system of underground and overhead walkways that crisscross the downtown area.

Today, a visitor to Edmonton will inevitably be struck by the dynamic high-rise skyline that stands starkly silhouetted against the deep blue western sky; he or she may well marvel at the sleek lines of the massive *Commonwealth Stadium,* built in 1978, or at the ultramodern technological grace of the Muttart Conservatory, a series of four huge glass pyramids near downtown Edmonton.

In spite of its economic enterprises and unabashed emphasis on capital gains, Edmonton has managed to save a lot of sunlight and space for its most important natural resource — its people. As a result, Edmonton is more than just a boom town — it's the boom town that won.

EDMONTON AT-A-GLANCE

SEEING THE CITY: One of the best ways to get a bird's-eye view of Edmonton is from Vista 33, on the 33rd floor of the Alberta Telephone Tower. From an elevation of 388 feet you have a view of 2,500 square miles; you'll see everything from the International Airport to the refinery-petrochemical area to the university. Just as the viewing gallery gives guests an overview of Edmonton, the *Man and Telecommunications Museum,* an integral part of Vista 33, gives them an overview of telecommunications, from the primitive switchboard to modern technology. Vista 33 is open daily year-round, except Christmas and New Year's Day, from 10 AM to 8 PM. Elevation charge. Jasper Ave. and 100th St. (phone: 473-3333).

SPECIAL PLACES: You can walk around downtown Edmonton quite easily, although in the winter the under- and aboveground "pedways" make more sense. Like Manhattan, the streets are laid out in an urban geometric grid and, except for the major routes, are numbered. A public bus system operates from downtown to all the outlying areas of the city; and the Light Rail Transit tramway has a mile (1.6 km) of track downtown and extends more than 6 miles (9.6 km) to the northeast tip of Edmonton's city limits.

DOWNTOWN

Alberta's Legislature Building – Constructed in 1912 on the site of the original trading post, Fort Edmonton, the elegant domed building lies nestled amid manicured lawns and formal gardens overlooking the North Saskatchewan River valley. You can take a guided tour of the building at any time of year, and if you're in town during November or from February to late May, you can watch the Canadian politicians lobby and legislate. 109th St. and 97th Ave. (phone: 427-7362).

Edmonton Civic Centre – One of Edmonton's showcases is a 6-block area containing the *Edmonton Art Gallery,* Churchill Square, City Hall, the Law Courts Building, the new Canada Place complex, the Convention Centre, the Centennial Library, and Edmonton's pride and joy, the spectacular *Citadel Theatre.* The *Citadel*'s five-theater complex is one of Canada's major centers for the performing arts. 100th St. and 102nd Ave.

Muttart Conservatory – A controlled botanical incubator unique in North America, the Muttart is a collection of graceful, pyramid-shaped greenhouses. The small central pyramid is the reception foyer; each of the others contains the flora of a specific climatic zone, with one exception, which is used as a showcase for changing seasonal displays. The Muttart is open daily and has an admission charge. 98th Ave. and 96 A St., south side (phone: 428-5226).

SUBURBS

Fort Edmonton – An authentic reconstruction of the early trading post from which the city grew, this is a nucleus for an entire park that allows visitors to step into the past and reexperience history. You can take a look at the fur press, the stockade, and a clay bake oven. The park also features "1885 Street" — urban Edmonton a century ago — with such highlights as McDougall's General Store and the Northwest Mounted Police Jail, and "1905 Street," with Ernest Brown's Photography Studio and the Masonic Temple. Near the park, which runs along the river, is the *John Janzen Nature Centre,* an interpretive museum that illustrates the geological eras preceding man's recorded history. From the *Janzen Centre* (phone: 428-7900) you can take a nature walk accompanied by a skilled guide and get a firsthand view of the North Saskatchewan River valley around which Edmonton grew. Fort Edmonton is closed in winter, except for some special programs and events; the *Janzen Centre* is open year-round. South bank of the North Saskatchewan off Whitemud Drive (phone: 428-2992).

Provincial Museum of Alberta – An important center for the preservation of Alberta's natural and human history, the museum was completed in 1967 to mark Canada's centennial. Exhibits depict early Indian life, pioneer settlement, and geological and ecological zones of the province. The museum presents regular film festivals and cultural performances and has a bookstore that features the works of Alberta authors. Open daily during summer; closed Mondays, Labour Day to Victoria Day. No admission charge. 12845 102nd Ave. (phone: 427-1730).

Valley Zoo – Expanded from the Storyland theme (fairy tale displays, farm animals, and a miniature train), the zoo now also features buildings for reptiles and nocturnal animals, and winter quarters for tropical birds and animals. Open year-round, daily in the summer and weekends in the winter. Admission charge. Buena Vista Rd. and 134th St. (phone: 483-5511).

Edmonton Space Sciences Centre – Since it opened in 1984, the center has become one of Edmonton's major attractions. It houses a planetarium star theater, western Canada's first IMAX theater (projecting large-format films onto a 60-by-40-foot screen), science exhibit galleries, a public observatory, science shop, and a café. Open daily; shows on Tuesdays through Sundays. Admission charge. 111th Ave. and 142nd St. (phone: 451-7722).

West Edmonton Mall – A shopper's Disneyland, this 5-million-plus-square-foot mall/amusement park (Canada Fantasyland) is listed in the *Guinness Book of World Records* as the largest in the world. It features more than 800 shops and services, the *Fantasyland* hotel, reasonable facsimiles of Bourbon Street and a Parisian boulevard, animal displays, aviaries, aquariums, a 20-ride Fantasyland, an ice palace, a water park with slides, deep-sea adventure submarine rides, and a miniature Pebble Beach golf course. Small charge for rides. Open daily. Shuttle bus service operates from many downtown hotels for a small charge. Admission charge for most attractions. 87th Ave. and 170th St.

■ **EXTRA SPECIAL:** If you're in Edmonton during the last 2 weeks of July, plan on celebrating *Klondike Days,* a remembrance of Edmonton's heritage as the starting point for prospectors heading northward to seek their fortunes. The city regresses to the wild era of the "Gay Nineties" and the Yukon Gold Rush as everyone dresses in the Victorian manner and enjoys the festivities, which include the World Championship Sourdough Raft Race on the North Saskatchewan River, parades, garden parties, sporting events, and more.

SOURCES AND RESOURCES

TOURIST INFORMATION: For general information, brochures, and maps, contact the Edmonton Tourism Visitor Information Centre, #104, 9797 Jasper Ave. (phone: 422-5505).

Local Coverage – *The Edmonton Sun,* a morning daily, except Saturday; *The Edmonton Journal,* morning daily; *Alberta Report,* a weekly news magazine.

Food – For details on restaurants in the Edmonton area, the Edmonton Tourism Visitor Information Centre has two publications available — the *International Guide* and *Billy's Guide.*

Telephone – The area code for Edmonton is 403.

Sales Tax – Neither the city of Edmonton nor the province of Alberta has a sales tax.

Currency – All prices are quoted in US dollars unless otherwise indicated.

TIPPING: At restaurants add 15 to 20% to your bill for service. At hotels, bellboys should receieve $1 per bag and hotel maids, $5 per room. Airport porters are tipped $1 per bag. Taxi drivers should be tipped 10 to 15% of the fare.

CLIMATE: At an altitude of 2,182 feet, the city averages 6.25 hours of sunshine a day. This is the result of Edmonton's extreme northerly position, which gives it daylight past 11 PM and average temperatures of 75F (24C) during the summer. Edmonton's location also accounts for very cold winters, with the mean January temperature averaging 5F (−15C).

GETTING AROUND: Bus – *Edmonton Transit* offers bus service around Edmonton and environs. For detailed information on routes, call 421-4636.

Tramway – The *Light Rail Transit* (LRT), operated by Edmonton Transit, offers tram service in the downtown area and northeastern section of the city. For detailed route information, call 421-4636.

Taxi – Taxis can be hailed on street corners and at taxi stands in front of major hotels. In the middle of the winter, however, you may want to call instead of venturing outside. Try *Yellow Cab* (phone: 462-3456) or *Co-Op Taxi* (phone: 425-8310).

Car Rental – Most major North American firms are represented.

Sightseeing Tours – *Royal Tours* offers guided tours to various attractions. Your hotel front desk can handle reservations, or call 424-8687.

SPECIAL EVENTS: In order to avoid being one-upped by the notorious *Calgary Stampede,* Edmontonians have come up with *Klondike Days,* which they celebrate annually during the last 2 weeks of July (right after the *Stampede;* see *Extra Special*). In June, Edmonton hosts *Jazz City,* a weeklong, world class jazz festival. August brings the *Edmonton Folk Festival,* 3 days on a sunny hill with some of the country's best folk artists. For the *Fringe Theater Event,* which runs for 9 days in August, 650 performances are staged in 12 theaters in the Old Strathcona district. Then there's the *Heritage Festival,* a 2-day celebration in Hawrelak Park that celebrates Edmonton's multi-culturalism. It's only a few years old, but thousands come to partake of the food and cultures of more than 44 nations.

MUSEUMS: The *Provincial Museum* and Fort Edmonton are described in *Special Places.* Other Edmonton museums of note:

Edmonton Art Gallery – 2 Sir Winston Churchill Sq. (phone: 422-6823).

Father Lacombe Chapel – The original log cabin built in 1861 by Father Albert Lacombe, a prairie priest who translated the New Testament into Cree. St. Albert, 12 miles (19 km) north of Edmonton off Hwy. 2 (no phone).

Rutherford House – Alberta's first restored historical home. 11153 Saskatchewan Dr. (phone: 427-3995).

Ukrainian-Canadian Archives and Museum – 9543 110th Ave. (phone: 424-7580).

Ukrainian Cultural Heritage Village – Yellowhead Hwy. 16, 30 miles (48 km) east of Edmonton (phone: 662-3640).

SHOPPING: Edmonton Centre, 100th St. and 102nd Ave., and Eaton Centre, 101st St. and 102nd Ave., both in the heart of downtown; Londonderry Shopping Mall, 137th Ave. and 66th St.; Heritage Mall, 23rd Ave. and 111th St., in the southwest section of the city; and West Edmonton Mall, 87th Ave. and 170th St. For Eskimo crafts and carvings, visit *Canadiana Galleries,* 12306 Jasper Ave. (phone: 482-5471) or *Bearclaw Gallery* (phone: 479-8502); the *Silversmith* has imported silver goods, including jewelry, imported from other parts of the country, 201 Edmonton Centre (phone: 424-8539); for handmade jewelry, pottery, paintings, and more, *Firewood Gallery* at 8118 103rd St. (phone: 433-9551); visit *Birks Jewelers* for a wide variety of sterling goods (phone: 444-1656, West Edmonton Mall; 426-7290, Edmonton Centre); for some of the best chocolate in Canada, *Chocolaterie Bernard Callebut* (phone: 452-3795, 102nd Ave.; 423-3083, Manulise Place, 10180 101st St.; 436-0908, 11004 51st Ave.); for French Canadian foods, *Frenchy's Deli,* 1612 118th Ave. (phone: 477-5958); and for an elegant selection of clothing, perfume, and more, visit *Holt Renfrew* at 10180 101st St. (phone: 425-5300). There are also some 25 shopping malls in the Greater Edmonton area.

SPORTS: Baseball – The Edmonton *Trappers* of the Pacific Coast League play in John Ducey Park, minutes from downtown. Call 429-2934 for schedule information.

Football – Edmonton's professional football team, the *Eskimos,* plays from late July until the middle of November. Ticket information can be obtained from the *Eskimos* box office (phone: 429-2881).

Golf – There are both municipal and private golf courses. Two good municipal ones are *Riverside Golf Course,* on Rowland Rd. and 84th St. (phone: 465-4710); and *Victoria Golf Course and Driving Range,* 99th Ave. and 121st St. (phone: 488-9238, golf course; 488-1438, driving range).

Hockey – The Edmonton *Oilers* belong to the National Hockey League and play from October to the Stanley Cup playoffs in May. Call 474-8561 for dates of games; 471-2191 for tickets.

Riding – *Whitemud Equine Centre,* 7450 Whitemud Rd. (phone: 435-3597).
Skiing – *Rainbow Valley Ski Hill,* 132nd St. and 45th Ave. (phone: 434-4314).
Swimming – There are indoor and outdoor pools. For information, phone 428-3559.
Tennis – Edmonton has a number of municipal and private courts. For more information on the municipal courts, phone 428-3575.

THEATER: Edmonton caters to theatergoers; it has more theaters per capita than any other Canadian city. A few of them include the *Citadel Theatre,* 9828 101 A Ave. (phone: 425-1820), Edmonton's largest with five stages; the *Phoenix Theatre* (phone: 429-4015 for information on what and where they're performing); *Stage West* at the *Mayfield Inn* has dinner theater, Mayfield Rd. and 109th Ave. (phone: 483-4051); *Studio Theatre,* 82nd Ave. between 112th and 114th Sts. (phone: 432-2495), for the University of Alberta's drama department productions; the prominent *Northern Light Theatre* (phone: 471-1586), which performs at the *Jubilee Auditorium;* and *Walterdale Playhouse,* 10322 83rd Ave. (phone: 439-2845), Edmonton's oldest community theater.

MUSIC: The *Edmonton Symphony Orchestra* presents concerts throughout the year (except in the summer) at the *Jubilee Auditorium.* For more information, call 428-1414. The *Jubilee Auditorium* is also home to the *Edmonton Opera,* one of North America's most financially stable opera associations. For more information, call 482-7030.

NIGHTCLUBS AND NIGHTLIFE: There's live jazz at the *Yardbird Suite,* 103rd St. and 86th Ave. (phone: 432-0428). For a singles bar with dancing, try *Barry T's,* 6111 104th St. (phone: 438-2582), or the very lively *Goose Loonie's Party & Playhouse,* 99th St. and Argyle Rd. (phone: 438-5571), where the 18–25 set goes to be seen. *The Rose and Crown Pub* in the *Hilton* hotel (phone: 428-7111) has a piano bar with sing-alongs and attracts a more sophisticated, professional crowd.

Gambling is a favorite pastime of Edmontonians, and as a result there's usually a casino with a temporary government permit operating somewhere in the city. For time and place, consult the local papers.

BEST IN TOWN

CHECKING IN: Edmonton has several first class hotels as well as dozens of more moderately priced and serviceable establishments. Expect to pay about $64 or more for a double room in the hotels we list as expensive; between $42 and $64 in those we categorize as moderate; and inexpensive, under $42. All telephone numbers are in the 403 area code unless otherwise indicated.

Fantasyland – Part of the West Edmonton Mall complex, this hotel features fantasy motifs (Polynesian, Arabian, Victorian, and even Western, where the bed is in the flat-bed of a pickup truck) in a third of its 360 deluxe rooms. Most rooms have a Jacuzzi. Non-smoking rooms; children under 12 free; honeymoon packages; cocktail lounge and dining room; water slide and wave pool in adjoining mall. 87th Ave. and 170th St. (phone: 444-3000). Expensive.

Hilton – Connected by a pedestrian walkway to the Edmonton Centre shopping mall, it has 314 rooms (27 of which are suites), non-smoking floors, a concierge, exercise equipment, indoor pool, sauna, and whirlpool bath. Downstairs, there are lounges, a café, the *Vintage Room* restaurant (with an alternative low-calorie, low-sodium menu), and an old English-style pub, the *Rose and Crown*. Weekend rates available. 10235 101st St. (phone: 428-7111). Expensive.

Westin – This handsome hostelry has become the place where royalty stops: the Queen of England visited in 1978; Prince Charles and Diana, in 1983. There are 413 rooms and suites, a swimming pool, sauna, whirlpool bath, and one of the finest dining rooms in the city. A family plan and special weekend rates are available year-round. 10135 100th St. at 101 A Ave. (phone: 426-3636). Expensive.

Mayfield Inn – Located in the west end of the city, the 232-room property has a Rec Centre with swimming pool, squash and racquetball courts, gym, the *Stage West* dinner theater, dining room, 3 lounges, and a nightclub. Mayfield Rd. and 109th Ave. (phone: 484-0821). Moderate.

Renford Inn at Fifth – Between downtown Edmonton and the Legislature grounds, this hotel has 107 rooms with telephones and color TV sets. There is an indoor swimming pool, dining room, cocktail lounge, and British-style pub. No charge for children under 12. 104th St. and 100th Ave. (phone: 423-5611). Moderate.

Kingsway Inn – Five minutes from downtown and just blocks from the midtown municipal airport, this hotel has 70 rooms with cable TV and phones, banquet and meeting facilities, gift shop, free parking, a restaurant, and pubs. 10812 Kingsway Ave. (phone: 479-4266). Inexpensive.

Klondike Valley Campground – This comfortable campground has 148 camping sites, 64 with sewage, electricity, and water, and 84 with electricity and water. There are flush toilets, showers, a playground, laundry facilities, a barbecue facility, and a small grocery store. Leased by the city of Edmonton, on Hwy. 2 South (phone: 988-5067). Inexpensive.

Relax Inn – Two very reasonably priced motels on the southern and western edges of the city, one just off the highway to Calgary and the International Airport, the other on the highway to Jasper. Each has an indoor pool and whirlpool bath, and all 220 rooms have a color TV set and a telephone. 10320 45th Ave. (phone: 436-9770) or 18320 Stony Plain Rd. (phone: 483-6031). Inexpensive.

EATING OUT: Besides making the city rich, those booms brought folks into Edmonton — all kinds of folks who cook all kinds of food. The result has been to augment regular prairie fare — which centers on Alberta beef, some of the best in the country — with a potpourri of cuisines that is truly delightful. Expect to pay about $34 and up for a meal for two at any of the restaurants we list as expensive; between $17 and $34 in the moderate range; and under $17 in the inexpensive. Prices don't include drinks, wine, or tips. All telephone numbers are in the 403 area code unless otherwise indicated.

Carvery – Known for its mammoth servings, this fine establishment with a woodsy, hunting hall atmosphere serves some of the best beef that Alberta produces, along with wild game such as buffalo. The chicken dishes are also good. At the *Westin*, 10135 100th St. (phone: 426-3636). Expensive.

Hy's Steak Loft – The premier steakhouse in Edmonton, complete with a well-appointed dining room and tuxedoed waiters. Though seafood, fowl, and lamb fill out the menu, steak is what this place does best, and considering that Alberta beef is among the best in the world, it would be a shame to order anything else. Closed Sundays. Reservations necessary. Major credit cards accepted. 10013 101st St. (phone: 424-4444). Expensive.

Un-Heard-Of – The intercom at the entrance gives this small restaurant a speakeasy feel, but the standards are much higher. The six-course prix fixe menu runs from a light pâté that changes with the best ingredients available, through a main course of lamb, beef, or game hen in a maple glaze. Light, delicious desserts. Reservations, as far in advance as possible, are necessary. Open Tuesdays through Saturdays. 9602 82nd Ave. (phone: 432-0480). Expensive.

Walden's – Choose between lunch in a sunlit garden or dinner in a cozy corner. Diners are offered continental cuisine and gracious service in a parklike setting. Highlights of the menu are spinach salad, Alberta rabbit, and quiche Lorraine. A good wine cellar. Open daily. Reservations necessary for dinner only. Major credit cards accepted. 10245 104th St. (phone: 420-6363). Expensive.

La Suisse – This restaurant goes a long way to prove that there's much more to Swiss cuisine than fondue. Rich pâtés, garlic-steamed mussels, freshly made soups, fork-tender veal with local wild mushrooms, and pork tenderloin in a dark, brandy-laden sauce all receive eye-opening presentations. Service is top-notch and never cloying. Open daily. Reservations advised. Major credit cards accepted. 10304 111th St. (phone: 420-6005). Expensive to moderate.

Sushi Tomi – Sushi in a landlocked town can often be iffy, but Edmonton's premier sushi bar has garnered the praise of seafood connoisseurs from both coasts. Perhaps it's because Hiroshi Yoshida, the restaurant's most exacting chef, sees that fish is flown in fresh daily from Vancouver. (The creative Yoshida-san also frequently auditions new off-the-menu dishes.) Open daily. Reservations advised. Major credit cards accepted. 10126 100th St. (phone: 422-6083). Expensive to moderate.

Chef's Table – One of Edmonton's most creative restaurants, in marked contrast to its industrial area location. Hong Kong-born, Edmonton-trained chef Peter Lai prepares delicious California-style dishes. The menu includes a wide variety of seafood, fowl, pasta, and veal — all prepared with unexpected touches; the appetizer of oysters comes stuffed with fresh ginger and chives, lightly breaded and pan-fried; the lobster and pasta entrée has undercooked seafood and crisp asparagus; and the honeydew melon balls are topped with a Tahitian vanilla-riesling sauce. Major credit cards accepted. 11121 156th St. (phone: 453-3532). Moderate.

Smokey Joe's Hickory Smokehouse – Likely the most ethnically American restaurant to be found in this Canadian city, this is a small, family operation that's big on servings and heart, and relatively low on cost. The Goldfeder family smokes chicken, turkey, pork ribs, ham, sausage, beef ribs, and brisket Oklahoma-pit-barbecue style: unseasoned over whole hickory logs for 24 to 30 hours. The result is moist, tender meat and fowl, which can be helped along with the devilish homemade hot sauce (served on the side) and jalapeños pickled in a Cajun brine spiked with a dose of cayenne. Also good are the pecan pies for which mother Marcia Goldfeder returns to the family nut groves in Hugo, Oklahoma. Paterfamilias Smokey Joe himself usually holds court nightly, and children and small animals are happier for it. Open daily. Reservations unnecessary. Major credit cards accepted. 156th St. and 87th Ave. (phone: 489-3940). Moderate.

Vi's – A refurbished house within view of the North Saskatchewan River, this restaurant is known throughout town for its thick homemade soups, good sandwiches, fresher-than-fresh salads, and chocolate-glazed pecan pie. The supper menu changes weekly. Open daily. No reservations. Major credit cards accepted. 9712 111th St. (phone: 482-6402). Moderate.

Mongolian Food Experience – An eclectic mix of cuisines from China, India, and Malaysia makes the experience memorable. Most interesting (and most inexpensive) is the Mongolian barbecue, a serve-yourself buffet groaning with mushrooms, bean sprouts, green onions, cabbage, green pepper, turkey, lamb, and beef, all anointed with hoisin, oyster, curry, or hot sauces, stir-fried on a teppan grill and served with steamed rice. Other notable dishes include *mu shu* pork, B-4 duck (moist chunks of barbecued duck sautéed with bamboo shoots and black mushrooms), incendiary Szechwan beef strips, and delicate lemon chicken. Open daily. Reservations necessary. Major credit cards accepted. 10160 100 A St. (phone: 426-6806). Moderate to inexpensive.

Bul-Go-Gi House – One of several Korean restaurants in town, it started up as a small café, but has undergone steady expansion. Tops on the menu is the Bul-Go-Gi, a mélange of vegetables and marinated beef cooked at your table; the accompanying side dish of hot pickle *kim chee;* and Bee-Bim-Bab, a bowl of vegetables capped by a fried egg. Closed Sundays. Reservations unnecessary. Visa accepted. 8813 92nd St. (phone: 466-2330). Inexpensive.

Harbin – Named after Edmonton's northern-Chinese sister city, the Harbin is known for its creative hand in the kitchen and its light touch on the pocketbook. Particularly good are the Szechuan dishes that appear as benign as grandmother's oatmeal. Those green beans cut on the bias are hot chilies, and woe to the diner who mistakes them for anything else. Of the menu's 84 dishes, 23 are spicy. Diners with less flaming palates should try the sesame chicken (batter-fried, then drizzled with honey and rolled in sesame seeds), the cinnamon-salt prawns (exactly as they sound), or the *king-tu* chicken, which comes sizzling to your table smothered in hoisin and soy, seasoned with five-spice powder. Servings are more than ample, especially with the soups. Open daily. Major credit cards accepted. 10401 Mayfield Rd. (phone: 484-9452). Inexpensive.

HALIFAX

The largest city on Canada's eastern seaboard (with 115,000 people), Halifax has a long and rich military and naval heritage as both a garrison town and naval base, thanks to its strategic location overlooking the mouth of one of the world's great natural harbors. From its earliest days, when it was a tiny Indian summer-fishing settlement in the middle of the southern Nova Scotia coast and known as Chebucto, or "at the biggest harbor," to World War II, when it was the major British naval base in the North Atlantic, Halifax has always been a center of maritime activity.

Today, Halifax is the provincial capital of Nova Scotia and the commercial, administrative, and military center of Atlantic Canada. Still, Halifax retains the feel of a small city. Ask a cross section of Haligonians (that's what they're called) why they like their town, and most will reply that they enjoy all the cultural amenities of bigger metropolises without the disadvantages of size and impersonality. The streets are lined with trees; there are beautiful, relaxing parks; there are fine old buildings; and the downtown is a nicely balanced mixture of modern office towers and older restored shops.

Centuries before the city was founded in 1749 by Colonel Edward Cornwallis, Micmac Indians launched hunting, fishing, and war missions from the harbor. Early French and British explorers failed to convince authorities at home of the strategic importance of the harbor, and for many years the Micmac regularly massacred New England fishermen who had stopped along the coast to dry fish, gather firewood, or take on water. Eventually it became apparent to the British that the Micmac hostility was French-inspired and that there was a constant market for English scalps in the French settlement of Fort Louisbourg, located on the southeastern shore of Cape Breton Island, north of Nova Scotia. A rag-tag group of New England farmers, hunters, and townsmen shocked the world by invading and capturing Louisbourg. The French prepared a counterattack designed to recover Louisbourg, take control of all of Nova Scotia, and go on to destroy Boston. However, the attack ended in disaster without a shot being fired; storms, scurvy, typhus, and dissension verging on mutiny destroyed the mission.

When the Treaty of Aix-la-Chapelle returned Louisbourg to France, the need to establish an English fortress on mainland Nova Scotia was finally recognized, and in 1749 Colonel Edward Cornwallis, with 3,000 others in some 20 ships, landed and founded Halifax. The settlement was successful, and with few exceptions the French settlers were deported. When British control over all of Canada was finally established in 1763, Halifax became the chief station of His Majesty's Army and Navy on the Atlantic seaboard.

Before the fledgling town ever got a chance to establish its civilian identity, it was teeming with British military personnel. Army and navy men outnumbered civilians, and the American Revolution and the War of 1812 left the city with an indelibly military (and predominantly British) complexion. From the first, Halifax has been a port city, with emphasis clearly on the first word. But the superiority of its harbor and the wisdom of building there have been proven in every war Britain has had the misfortune to fight.

From the open ocean to the city, the harbor narrows gradually, a feature that made it easy to defend. The city was built on a shoe-shaped peninsula — the toe facing south to the sea, the heel north into Bedford Basin, and the sole opposite the mile-wide strip of water separating the city from neighboring Dartmouth.

The American Revolution and the 1812 war affected Halifax in other ways as well. The city enjoyed all the benefits of war — military spending, employment, and excitement — and none of the horror. The city thrived and its population grew. In the wake of the Revolutionary War, 25,000 Loyalists fled to Nova Scotia, and after the War of 1812, thousands of blacks escaped from slavery to settle in the Halifax-Dartmouth region.

Wartime prosperity is notoriously ephemeral, however, and when peace came, the Haligonians experienced a sudden depression. However, the gradual development of a civilian shipbuilding industry alongside the traditional military economy led to increased prosperity in Halifax until the outbreak of World War I, when it again became a military base — a vital link in the North American lifeline to the embattled countries of Europe.

Halifax suffered its worst maritime disaster late in the war. In fact, it was the worst recorded manmade explosion before the atomic bombing of Hiroshima in 1945. In December 1917, the munitions ship *Mont Blanc,* laden with 2,500 tons of explosives, collided with the Belgian relief ship *Imo* in Halifax Harbour. The explosion, felt 52 miles away, flattened the north end of the city, leaving 2,000 dead, 2,000 injured, 6,000 homeless, and 199 blinded. Known simply as "the Explosion," this tragic event is commemorated yearly. A monument to those who died is located at Fort Needham.

After swift reconstruction, Halifax assumed its position as a center of Canada's maritime industry. The city played an important role in the early days of World War II, when the German U-boat wolf packs sought to isolate England by cutting it off from Canadian or American supply ships. With its 10 square miles of deepwater anchorage, the Bedford Basin of Halifax Harbour was the natural staging area for the North Atlantic convoys. Some 17,500 ships sailed from here. When the war ended, soldiers and sailors (and more than a few Haligonians) released their pent-up frustrations in the V-E Day riots, a rampage of looting, drinking, and carousing that left the downtown area a shambles.

Superficially, Halifax has changed a great deal in the last decade. Shiny new office towers have sprung up on both sides of the harbor, vast shopping centers have followed the burgeoning population to the suburbs, and new restaurants reflect a far more cosmopolitan taste than before. Yet underneath, the city is much as it has always been: largely dependent on the military branches of government for its income; optimistic about the future (especially since the discovery of natural gas offshore); and still strongly English and Irish in temperament, culture, and tradition.

Fortunately, like many Canadian cities, Halifax has been blessed with cogent and restrained city planning. Newfound wealth has not caused residents to ignore their cultural and architectural heritage, and the city's 19th-century waterfront area reeks of brine, barnacles, and Her Majesty's Royal Navy. Halifax is a paradise for anyone who loves great seaports, the accompanying nautical lore and traditions, the ships, and most of all — the sea.

HALIFAX AT-A-GLANCE

SEEING THE CITY: One of the abiding reminders of Halifax's British origin must be its policy of restoration and protection of historic buildings. The Haligonian passion for preservation even extends to the traditional viewing point of the city. As Halifax expanded, it became apparent that high-rise construction might block out the best view of the city and harbor, as seen from the roadway surrounding Citadel Hill. In 1973 Halifax passed an ordinance prohibiting the construction of any building that threatens certain "view planes." And so today you can see some of the same views that the Loyalists did when they arrived here 200 years ago — downtown Halifax, the harbor, and the Atlantic beyond. At noon every day a cannon is fired from Citadel Hill, as it has been for 150 years, and at the top of the hill, for a small entrance fee, you can visit the Citadel — a fort built in 1828 — and its museums.

SPECIAL PLACES: You can easily see downtown Halifax on foot, although there is a steep grade from the harbor to Citadel Hill. Ferries link downtown Halifax with her sister city of Dartmouth, across the harbor. Motorists are cautioned about the large number of one-way streets.

DOWNTOWN

Historic Properties – On the Halifax waterfront, virtually at the foot of Citadel Hill, is the retail development that has brought life back to buildings constructed in the 18th century. In those days the buildings were the center of activity. After coming within a vote or two of being demolished, the 3-acre site has been saved by a private Halifax company, with assistance from the government, and is now known as the Historic Properties. The area has been expanded to include buildings on two other streets. In the summer, Historic Properties is the dock site for *Bluenose II,* a replica of the original *Bluenose,* the fishing schooner that dominated international racing for close to 2 decades and is depicted on the Canadian dime. The schooner cruises the harbor three times daily in summer, occasionally under full sail. (Information can be obtained on the site or by phoning 422-2678.) The modern vessel, *Haligonian III,* with full bar and cafeteria, has regular tours leaving from the Historic Properties dock. In addition, the *Mar II,* a 75-foot Danish ship, offers 1- and 2-hour sailing tours of the harbor, both in the morning and the afternoon (phone: 423-8471). Charters are available on all three craft. Call *Halifax Water Tours* (phone: 423-1271) for more information.

Province House – The Nova Scotia legislature meets here. Built between 1811 and 1818, Province House was described as a "gem of Georgian architecture" by none other than Charles Dickens. It is one of the finest examples of Georgian architecture on the continent. If the legislature is in session, visitors can hear debates from the Public Gallery. The Legislative Library is handsome, with tall windows, two curving staircases leading to a mezzanine balcony, and alcoves adorned with fine wood carvings and metal tracings. Province House is also the location of the office of the premier of Nova Scotia.

The building is generally open to visitors year-round; the staff usually provides tours on request. 1690 Hollis St.

St. Paul's Church – Built in 1750, St. Paul's is the oldest existing building in Halifax and the oldest Protestant church in Canada. It welcomes visitors daily from June to September. The oak frame and pine timbers for St. Paul's were brought by sea from Boston and Portsmouth, New Hampshire. St. Paul's Cemetery, 3 blocks south, has a unique memorial to two Nova Scotians killed in the Crimean War. General Ross, who burned Washington in the War of 1812, is buried here. Barrington St. (phone: 429-2240).

Citadel Hill – The key to the defense of Halifax, Citadel Hill today contains two museums inside the star-shaped fort built of granite and ironstone quarried at Purcell's Cove, a community on the outskirts of the city. The Citadel is a national historic park. One of the museums is part of the *Nova Scotia Museum;* the other is devoted to military artifacts. A sound-and-light show, called *Tides of History,* reviews 300 years of life in the harbor in 50 minutes. See it before exploring the ramparts. Summertime events include candlelight tours and dinners featuring hosts in historic costumes. Check with staff for times and dates. The Old Town Clock, which stands on the eastern slope of the hill and has clock faces on all four sides, was commissioned by the Duke of Kent, father of Queen Victoria, head of the garrison at Halifax from 1794 to 1800. Guided tours are available. Admission charge.

Halifax Public Gardens – Covering close to 18 acres, these grounds are among the finest in the country and are the oldest formal Victorian gardens in North America. Created in 1867, they were enlarged in 1874 to their present size. Tree-shaded gravel walks wind among the many flower beds, fountains, and a large pond. A bandstand commemorating Queen Victoria's Golden Jubilee of 1887 stands near the center of the gardens and, during summer, acts as a stage for concerts. At Spring Garden Rd., Summer St., Sackville St., and S. Park St.

Point Pleasant Park – The 186-acre wooded park at the extreme southerly end of peninsular Halifax, out of bounds to private automobiles, provides countless trails, picnic areas, a supervised saltwater beach on the harbor side, and several fortresses that are national historic sites, including, most notably, Martello Tower.

Halifax Container Pier – Halterm, Halifax's container pier, one of the busiest in Canada, can be seen closely from the breakwater off the Point Pleasant Park parking lot. You can stand literally within a stone's throw of huge ocean vessels unloading cargoes day and night. Off Hollis St. just before Point Pleasant Park.

Nova Scotia Museum – Near the Citadel and Public Gardens, the museum contains countless displays and exhibits on all aspects of life in Nova Scotia — from its geological formation to the arrival of the first inhabitants 11,000 years ago through European settlement and up to the present day. The spacious foyer is dominated by a 10-foot-high lens from the old Sambro Lighthouse and a stagecoach that operated between Yarmouth and Tusket in the late 19th century. 1747 Summer St. (phone: 429-4610).

SUBURBS

Fleming Park – On the western shore of the North West Arm of Halifax Harbour, Fleming Park is the site of Memorial Tower, or the Dingle, as it is called locally. Built in 1912, the 10-story tower commemorates the 1758 establishment of representative government in Nova Scotia, the first in Canada. You can reach the top of the tower by walking up steps inside; those who do are rewarded by a remarkable view of the North West Arm, its yacht clubs, beautiful homes, Dalhousie University and sections of the city, and the harbor mouth. It is open during daylight hours.

York Redoubt – Just outside Halifax, on the Herring Cove Road, you can visit York Redoubt, a 200-year-old fort overlooking the harbor. A national historic site, the park features old muzzle-loaders, a photographic display, a viewing tower, and picnic facilities. From the park, there is a good view of Mauger's (pronounced Major's) Beach Lighthouse, on a sandspit projecting into the harbor from McNab's Island. The round trip from downtown Halifax to York Redoubt is about 20 miles (32 km). A longer trip on the same road takes you to small fishing communities typical of those around the province — Herring Cove, Portuguese Cove, Ketch Harbour, and Sambro. The shops in Sambro usually have lobsters for sale, a good idea for a delightful seaside picnic. Sandy Cove Road affords a good view of Sambro Lighthouse on Sambro Island. Built in 1759, the 82-foot lighthouse was originally operated by three men with seal oil for fuel. The round trip from Halifax to Sambro is about 50 miles (80 km).

■ **EXTRA SPECIAL:** Peggy's Cove is a photographers' and artists' colony that is well-nigh legendary in Canada, thanks to its status as one of the best-preserved rustic fishing villages in North America. Named for one of its original inhabitants, Peggy's Cove has a number of quaint gift shops, as well as two spectacular murals in St. John's Anglican Church. About 35 miles (56 km) west of Halifax on Rte. 333.

SOURCES AND RESOURCES

TOURIST INFORMATION: For general information, brochures, and maps, contact the Nova Scotia Tourist Bureau, Old Red Store, Historic Properties (phone: 424-4247) or the Nova Scotia Department of Tourism, PO Box 130, Halifax (phone: 424-5000). US residents should write to Nova Scotia Tourism, 129 Commercial St., Portland, ME 04101 (phone: 800-341-6096 outside Maine; 800-492-0643 from Maine). The City of Halifax operates a tourist bureau in City Hall, with an entrance off Duke Street.

Metro Guide is one of the best guides to the city. Published by Metro Guide Publishing Ltd. (phone: 420-9943), it is distributed free in hotels, restaurants, some stores, the Halifax Visitors and Convention Bureau, bureaus of information around the province, the Dartmouth Tourist Bureau, and in Air Canada ticket offices. The book describes a walking tour of historic downtown Halifax and Dartmouth, and outlines the driving tour of Halifax known as the Kingfisher (the official city symbol) Motor Tour and marked by street signs. The book also describes a number of hotels, restaurants, lounges, and other tourist-related services. The *Halifax Visitor's Guide* is published by Art East & Company Ltd. (1652 Barrington St.). This magazine-format publication is a good source of up-to-date information on tours of all types, museums and libraries, parks and recreation, dining out, and shopping. A city and district map produced by the Royal Bank of Canada is also widely available.

Local Coverage – The *Chronicle-Herald,* morning daily tabloid; the *Mail-Star,* afternoon daily (same entertainment listings in both papers); the *Daily News,* morning daily.

Food – The tourist bureau has a list of restaurants, or you can check the *Metro Guide.*
Telephone – The area code for Halifax is 902.
Sales Tax – Meals over $3.50 ($4 CN) and most purchased goods have a 10% sales tax.
Currency – All prices are quoted in US dollars unless otherwise indicated.

TIPPING: At restaurants generally leave 15% of the bill. Taxi drivers receive about $1 (CN). At hotels bellboys are usually given $1 (CN) per bag, but it is usually not customary to tip maids.

160 HALIFAX / Sources and Resources

CLIMATE: Compared with the rest of Canada, Nova Scotia has relatively moderate temperatures, and, thanks to the Gulf Stream, Halifax is a bit more temperate than that. In February, the coldest month of the year, the average low is 16F (−9C) and the average high is 31F (−1C); in July and August, the average daytime high is 74F (23C) and the average nighttime low is 57F (14C); water temperature is rarely above 70F (22C). The climate is not particularly humid; in summer months the rainfall is usually less than 4 inches, although in the rainiest month, December, precipitation can be as much as 7 inches. For weather information, call 835-7277.

GETTING AROUND: Bus – Regular transit service is operated by a metropolitan transit authority. Exact fare is required. For schedule and route information, phone 426-6600.

Taxi – Cabs are hailed in the streets or found at taxi stands at major hotels, shopping areas, and around the city. If you need to call a cab, try *Yellow Taxi* (phone: 422-1551) or the *Y Taxi* (phone: 422-4433). Meters are used on all trips except for some outside the city (to the airport, for example), during which flat rates apply.

Car Rental – All major national firms are represented.

Tours – In addition to water tours available at Historic Properties and the ferry across Halifax Harbour (see *Halifax At-a-Glance*), the best way to see the city is from a city bus tour offered by either the *Gray Line of Halifax* (phone: 454-9321) or *Halifax Transit* (phone: 426-6600). For those who prefer a more offbeat approach to seeing the city, rickshaws are available for both tour and taxi service (phone: 421-8736), or the energetic visitor can join a bicycle tour organized by the *Velo Bicycle Club* (phone: 423-4697). Tours are available in summer months only.

SPECIAL EVENTS: *Halifax Natal Day* is celebrated the first weekend in August. The festivities include a parade, concerts, picnics, and fireworks. *Nova Scotia Festival of the Arts* is held in mid-August and includes a large display of local arts and crafts. The *Nova Scotia International Tattoo* is in late June. The *Tattoo* — a military pageant featuring marching bands, dancing, singing, and athletic displays — is an event worth seeing. It is rated among the top three in the world and is staged indoors at the *Metro Centre*.

MUSEUMS: The *Nova Scotia Museum* and the *Citadel Museum* are described in *Special Places*. Other notable Halifax museums include the following:

Art Gallery of Nova Scotia – 6152 Coburg Rd. (phone: 424-7542).
Maritime Command Museum – Gottingen and Albert Sts. (phone: 426-5210).
Maritime Museum of the Atlantic – Lower Water St. (phone: 429-8210).
The Public Archives of Nova Scotia – On University Ave. at Robie St. (phone: 423-9115).

SHOPPING: Halifax is blessed with a number of native craftspeople who produce a wide range of goods, including pottery, jewelry, ceramics, rugs, quilts, woodwork, and all manner of dolls. If you have the time, it may be worth your while to visit the craftspeople at their shop, which more often than not doubles as their home. Handmade stained glass creations are sold at the *Glass Garden Studio*, 1528½ Queen St. (phone: 422-9172); *Wayne Kelly*, 1378 Robie St. (phone: 422-4132); *T. E. Smith-Lamothe*, 5539 Inglis St. (phone: 423-6662); and the *Stowe/Terris Studio*, 2182 Gottingen St. (phone: 423-0681). Local weaver *V. Louise Whitton*, 6121 North St. (phone: 455-1965), will fashion sale items from her loom. A

HALIFAX / Sources and Resources

list of other weavers is available from the Atlantic Spinners and Handweavers Association, through the *Nova Scotia Museum*. While some of the artisans keep shop hours, others are available by appointment only; it is best to call in advance. For more extensive information, call the Nova Scotia Department of Tourism and Culture, Recreation, and Fitness (phone: 424-7512), or write to the department at Box 864, Halifax B3J 2V2, and ask for a copy of its *Buyer's Guide to Arts and Crafts in Nova Scotia,* a free publication which is also available at tourist bureaus and craft outlets. For more conventional shopping, head to Historic Properties (see *Special Places*).

SPORTS: Halifax's only professional sports franchise is the Halifax *Citadels,* the farm team of the Quebec *Nordiques* of the National Hockey League. *Halifax Metro Centre* (phone: 426-8726).

Cycling – *Velo Halifax* is a non-competitive touring and recreational bicycle club whose members ride together for fun and friendship. Visitors to the city with access to a bicycle are welcome to join club members for Sunday or weekend rides. Weather permitting, members ride 30 to 50 miles (48 to 80 km). For those not up to tackling such an excursion, the club produces a pamphlet suggesting a couple of routes. It is available at the Halifax tourist bureau at Historic Properties. *Down East Bicycle Tours,* RR #2, Kingston, Nova Scotia, organizes weekend, and 6- and 12-day tours that originate in Halifax. Guides and van support are provided, and accommodations are in bed-and-breakfast establishments along the way. Brochures are available at Historic Properties, or call George Dagley (phone: 765-8923).

Fishing – Trout fishing in stocked lakes is available within the Dartmouth city limits. For the true anglers, however, real trout and salmon fishing is available in the lakes and streams along Marine Drive on the road between Halifax and Sherbrooke to the east. Excellent Atlantic salmon fishing can be had in the St. Mary's River near Sherbrooke, which is about 120 miles (193 km) from Halifax.

Golf – Golfers have their choice of five 18-hole courses, all 10 miles (16 km) or less from downtown hotels. There are two *Ashburn* golf courses, the newer one in Fall River (phone: 861-2978), and the older in Halifax (phone: 443-8260). Both allow non-members to play weekdays. *Brightwood Golf and Country Club* in Dartmouth (phone: 466-7688) has a similar policy. *Hartlen Point Forces Golf Course* in Eastern Passage (phone: 465-6353), and *Oakfield Country Club* in Grand Lake (phone: 861-2777) are both open to the public. Four 9-hole courses are also in easy reach.

Jogging – Halifax is a city of joggers, and those looking for companionship should have no trouble finding some. Point Pleasant Park, the 186-acre wooded park in the city's south end, is frequented by joggers throughout daylight hours. The YMCA, 1565 South Park St. (phone: 422-6437), is also a good spot to meet joggers, particularly at noon and shortly after 5 PM, when businesspeople leave the "Y" to jog around the city.

Tennis – Public courts are available on the Halifax Common, near the Halifax *Holiday Inn* and *Château Halifax* hotels. For serious players, the Nova Scotia Open Tennis Tournament is held in late August at the *Waegwoltic Club* (phone: 429-2822).

THEATER: *Neptune Theatre,* 5216 Sackville St. (phone: 429-7070), offers live professional theater in an intimate setting. Check newspapers for performances. Lunchtime shows are sometimes offered. Summer dinner theater is featured around town; check local newspaper listings.

MUSIC: Dalhousie University's *Rebecca Cohn Auditorium* is the center for many visiting performers. It is located in the *Dalhousie Arts Centre;* call 424-2298 for the box office. Other concerts are regularly held at the *Neptune Theatre* and at *Metro Centre.*

NIGHTCLUBS AND NIGHTLIFE: Visitors to the city, particularly during the summer, are often surprised to discover how much of a party town Halifax is. The festive atmosphere is particularly noticeable on Friday and Saturday nights along Argyle St., where pubs seem to be everywhere — as do the patrons. This isn't a rowdy crowd, just one that knows how to have fun. In recent years, there have been so many bars and lounges popping up in the downtown core — and often closing just as quickly — that the scene has become a very fluid one. (To keep up with it, check the *Metro Guide.*) For pub crawlers, it's perfect: Most of the bars and lounges are within walking distance of one another. *Secretary's,* 5184 Sackville St., attracts a young crowd with live bands and rock videos filling out the entertainment schedule when the jive and lip-synch contests aren't happening. The *Thirsty Duck,* upstairs at 5472 Spring Garden Rd., features traditional pub music, with live entertainment on weekends; the good food served here from 11 AM to 10 PM is an added enticement, and the shuffleboard or darts enthusiast won't be disappointed either. Dance to live rock music 6 days a week at *My Apartment,* 1740 Argyle St. It's usually loud and packed. The *Seahorse,* 1665 Argyle St., attracts the young and artsy set. Watch the revelers from the glassed-in patio at *Lawrence of Oregano,* 1726 Argyle, while enjoying something from its menu of standard pasta fare. At the *Lower Deck* in Historic Properties along the waterfront, the entertainment usually features single acts ranging from comedy to Nova Scotia music; upstairs, at the *Middle Deck,* listen to live music that can be anything from R&B to contemporary. If you lose interest, cross the street to *O'Carroll's Oyster Bar,* at 1860 Upper Water St., and enjoy their piano bar; if that doesn't suit you, try the *Up Here Bar,* 1662 Barrington St., where you can gaze at art for sale while having a drink and something to eat (waffles are a big item on this menu). Crave cabaret entertainment? Check out the *Misty Moon,* 1595 Barrington St. (phone: 422-5871), where Canadian and American bands are regularly featured; it's open nightly from 7 PM to 3 AM and there's a cover charge. Alternatively there is the *Palace,* 1721 Brunswick St. (phone: 429-5959). Other popular nightspots include *Thackeray's Pub,* 5435 Spring Garden Rd., and *Maxwell's Plum* at Sackville and Grafton Sts. And to find plenty more possibilities — just follow the crowd.

BEST IN TOWN

CHECKING IN: There was a time not too many years ago when Halifax only had two hotels of distinction, the *Lord Nelson* and the *Nova Scotian.* But as the city began to grow into a major metropolitan area, hotels began to appear. More than 600 first class rooms have been added downtown, all with the basic amenities (phones, color TV sets, and so on). Expect to pay $75 or more for a double at those places classified as expensive; between $40 and $75 for those described as moderate; and under $40 at inexpensive accommodations. A toll-free number (phone: 800-565-7105) is available for reservations throughout the province. All telephone numbers are in the 902 area code unless otherwise indicated.

Delta Barrington Inn – One of the city's newer hotels, belonging to the respected Delta chain, it is part of yet another restoration of the old town. The façade on the Granville Street side, dating back to the mid-19th century, was carefully dismantled and all the stones replaced once the hotel was built. It is situated between the Scotia Square complex and Historic Properties on the waterfront and has 200 rooms, a restaurant, piano bar, heated indoor swimming pool, sauna, and whirlpool bath. Corner of Duke and Barrington Sts. (phone: 429-7410). Expensive.

Halifax Sheraton – A classy low-rise hotel that blends well with the Historic

Properties development next door on the waterfront. Great location, lovely surroundings, and tasteful decoration are its hallmarks. 1919 Upper Water St. (phone: 421-1700). Expensive.

Prince George – Open since 1986, this hotel enjoys a convenient, city-center location, a block from the Grand Parade at City Hall. A handy underground walkway connects it with the World Trade and Convention Centre and the adjacent *Metro Centre,* the 10,000-seat entertainment-sports arena. Guests can enjoy the hotel pool, whirlpool bath, sauna, and exercise room; dine in the restaurant or café; or socialize in its popular lounge. Underground parking. 1725 Market St. (phone: 425-1986). Expensive.

Château Halifax – Operated by Canadian Pacific Hotels, it is ideally situated in the city's downtown Scotia Square complex. The hotel has an enclosed patio garden and a tower with views of the harbor, Citadel Hill, and Bedford Basin; 305 rooms; a heated indoor-outdoor swimming pool; a sauna; and air conditioning. It has a special weekend rate. 1990 Barrington St. (phone: 425-6700). Moderate.

Citadel Halifax – Near Scotia Square and *Metro Centre,* it is not quite as posh as *Château Halifax* but is slightly less expensive. Some of its 278 air conditioned rooms are in a high-rise tower overlooking the harbor. 1960 Brunswick St. (phone: 422-1391). Moderate.

Halliburton House Inn – This bed-and-breakfast establishment in the heart of downtown Halifax occupies a registered 40-room heritage property. Of the 3 buildings that comprise the inn, the oldest was built in 1820 and was once the home of Sir Brenton Halliburton, the first chief justice of the province's Supreme Court. Completely renovated to provide modern comfort and convenience, the period elegance and charm have been carefully preserved with many antique furnishings. The inn has a library, dining room, and private garden, and each room has a private bath and phone. In addition to breakfast, guests are treated to afternoon tea. 5184 Morris St. (phone: 420-0658). Moderate.

Holiday Inn – Don't confuse this with the one in Dartmouth. This hotel overlooks Halifax Common, where hundreds of amateur athletes engage in softball, football, tennis, baseball, field hockey, soccer, and even cricket. There's a heated indoor swimming pool. Quinpool and Robie Sts. (phone: 423-1161). Moderate.

Nova Scotian – Adjoining the Canadian National Railway station, this venerable old hotel has recently been lovingly and tastefully refurbished. Much of its grandeur is back, along with some new touches, such as a pool and tennis court. Although located several blocks from downtown, it provides free shuttle service. Some of the 316 rooms overlook the harbor, and about half have air conditioning. 1181 Hollis St. (phone: 423-7231). Moderate.

Chebucto Inn – Although removed from downtown, this property is situated near the main roads in and out of the city. It has 32 units, all with air conditioning. 6151 Lady Hammond Rd. (phone: 453-4330). Inexpensive.

Lord Nelson – One of Halifax's oldies, a little rundown but still well used, it is across the street from the Public Gardens. It has 320 rooms and free guest parking. At the corner of Spring Garden Rd. and South Park St. (phone: 423-6331). Inexpensive.

EATING OUT: Halifax's restaurants have improved dramatically over the last 15 years. There was a time when those wishing to dine out were restricted to the *Nova Scotian* and one or two other hotels. Today things are better, but one still hears the complaint that, given the city's proximity to some of the world's best fishing grounds, there is not enough high-quality fish available. Expect to pay more than $35 for two in those restaurants we've categorized as expensive; between $15 and $35 in the moderate range; under $17 at those places listed as inexpensive. Prices don't include wine, drinks, or tip. All telephone numbers are in the 902 area code unless otherwise indicated.

Clipper Cay – With an unsurpassed location on the harborfront in the Historic Properties area, this is probably one of the city's best seafood restaurants. Of particular note is the smoked salmon. Downstairs, at *The Cay Side,* inexpensive lunches and suppers are available. Open daily. Reservations advised. Major credit cards accepted. At the end of Water St. (phone: 423-6818). Expensive.

Scanway – Tucked away in a 2-story boutique complex, the menu features Scandinavian fare. Closed Sundays. Major credit cards accepted. 1569 Dresden Row, off Spring Garden Rd. (phone: 422-3733). Expensive.

Mother Tucker's – Close to Historic Properties and the business district, it is a popular spot for seafood and prime ribs, featuring a huge salad bar. During busy periods, patrons wait in an adjoining bar until their table is ready. Open daily. Reservations advised. Major credit cards accepted. 1668 Lower Water St. (phone: 422-4436). Expensive to moderate.

La Perla – This unpretentious pearl of a restaurant has wonderful food plus Old World charm. It's situated almost directly opposite the Dartmouth ferry terminal, and a ferry ride across the harbor is the quickest and most fun way to arrive. Outside the terminal, look for the small canopy over the entryway to a tiny house. Dine downstairs or up; the atmosphere is quiet and intimate, the music low and classical. The menu is primarily Northern Italian, though not limited to mounds of pasta. Salads are especially good here, and the main courses a delight. Reservations necessary. Major credit cards accepted. 71 Alderney Dr. (phone: 469-3241). Expensive to moderate.

McKelvie's – The decor is nautical, dress is informal, and the specialty is fish. The building is a grand old firehall that's been converted; there's also a terrace for summer dining. Conveniently opposite the *Maritime Museum of the Atlantic* on the waterfront, next to Historic Properties. Open daily. Reservations advised. Major credit cards accepted. 1680 Lower Water St. (phone: 421-6161). Moderate.

Old Man Morias – Here Greek food is served up in an original Halifax townhouse. Proprietors Vasilios and Panagiota Migas arrived in Canada without knowing any English and have worked hard to become established. Closed Sundays. Reservations advised. Major credit cards accepted. 1150 Barrington St. (phone: 422-7960). Moderate.

Privateer's Warehouse – The *Lower Deck* is a pub, the *Middle Deck* is a lounge, and the *Upper Deck* is one of the best places to eat in town. There, seafood and steaks are served by a staff that is friendly and efficient. The Shrimps Lady Wentworth are especially good. The dining room's stone walls and wooden beams are decorated with things nautical, as befits the building's history. Closed Sundays. Reservations advised. Major credit cards accepted. At Historic Properties (phone: 422-1289). Moderate.

Sanremo – Seafood is the specialty here, Northern Italian style. A sister restaurant to *La Perla,* patrons are finding it to be every bit as good as its elder sibling. The small dining room is situated in such a way as to present a lovely view of Halifax to every table. Open daily for dinner. Reservations advised. Major credit cards accepted. 67 Alderney Drive, Dartmouth, just across the street from the Dartmouth ferry terminal (phone: 469-3241). Moderate.

Silver Spoon – Its quaint coffeehouse/tearoom has satisfied many a sweet tooth, and its restaurant has delighted patrons with more substantial delicacies. Coffee, tea, and desserts are quite special. Open daily. Most major credit cards accepted. The premises are back-to-back: dessert shop, 1866 Water St.; restaurant, 1865 Hollis St. (phone: 422-1519, for both). Moderate.

Suisha Gardens – One sign of the growing variety of cuisine available in Halifax was the opening of this Oriental eatery, which features teppan cooking, where the meal is prepared at your table, and other Japanese dishes. The cooking has been Westernized from its stricter Japanese roots, but the service is fast and the food good. Weekdays, lunches are a good bet for someone who wants to eat well but quickly. Open daily. Reservations advised. Major credit cards accepted. On the main floor of the Maritime Centre at the corner of Barrington St. and Spring Garden Rd. (phone: 422-1576). Moderate.

Thackeray's – At this pleasant and sophisticated dining spot, located on one of Halifax's most popular streets, the kitchen specializes in meat and poultry dishes, and also produces very good desserts. Open daily. Reservations advised. Most major credit cards accepted. 5435 Spring Garden Rd. (phone: 423-5995). Moderate.

Lawrence of Oregano – Across the street from the Grand Parade, at City Hall, it caters to a youthful clientele of office workers and university students. A good spot to grab a pizza and a beer. Lively, pleasant ambience. Major credit cards accepted. 726 Argyle Street (phone: 422-6907). Moderate to inexpensive.

Midtown Tavern – This is a place for those not concerned about surroundings and who like to drink draft beer at a student hangout. The food is surprisingly good, particularly the fish and chips and the corned beef and cabbage. Closed Sundays. No credit cards accepted. Prince St. at Grafton St. (no phone). Inexpensive.

Soup'er Sandwich – An unpretentious place, popular with office workers looking to grab a quick bite. Homemade soups and chowders made with fresh ingredients have made this fast-food eatery a winner. The fish is always fresh, and there's a daily luncheon special and a quiche of the day. Closed Sundays. Visa accepted. 1820 Hollis St. (phone: 425-3474). Inexpensive.

Camille's, Fries and Company, and *Wilman's* – All are local favorites for take-out fish and chips. Wrapped in brown paper, the deep-fried fish (clams and scallops are usually available) are great for a picnic in one of the city parks or along the waterfront. *Camille's:* Open daily. No credit cards accepted. 2654 Barrington St. (phone: 423-8869). *Fries and Company:* Closed Sundays. No credit cards accepted. Chebucto Rd. at Connolly St. (phone: 455-5250). *Wilman's:* Closed Sundays. No credit cards accepted. 5644 Kane St. (phone: 454-0929). All inexpensive.

Or sample some of the best French fries in town, alfresco, from *Bud the Spud's* popular chip wagon, usually parked at noon outside the Halifax Regional Public Library at Spring Garden Rd. and Grafton St.

MONTREAL

Since 1535 — when Jacques Cartier first laid eyes on the St. Lawrence River village of Hochelaga, climbed with its Indian residents to the top of its 764-foot mountain, took a look at the 50-mile view, and exclaimed "What a royal mount" — the spot has emerged as Canada's second largest city, and just behind Paris, Nice, and Kinshasha, Zaire, as one of the world's largest French-speaking cities.

Yet some of the most dramatic changes on the face of Montreal have been etched in the past 25 years, with the construction of luxury hotels; a vast underground network of shops and services linked by a clean, efficient Métro system; an accretion of fashionable boutiques and excellent restaurants; and careful restorations in the historic quarter. Montreal's new look was sparked by a complete midtown facelift during the 1960s, a renovation that gained momentum during EXPO '67, when over 50 million people visited the World's Fair and brought Montreal to international attention. The increase in tourism continued throughout the early 1970s, and reached a peak in 1976, when Montreal hosted the Summer Olympic Games.

A second building boom has transformed the downtown area now that 12 major construction projects worth $1 million or more have been completed. They include the conversions of the former *Mount Royal* and *Windsor* hotels, both on Peel Street, into chic shopping, condo, and office complexes, along with several showy office towers.

The transformation has been so complete that some residents now claim they can't remember what Montreal looked like before. They exaggerate for effect. One of the first priorities when construction began was the preservation of Vieux Montréal (Old Montreal). No one considered destroying the historic city a reasonable way of effecting change, and as a result preservation and progress proceeded apace. The protection of special buildings extends to modern Montreal as well: The city's *Olympic Stadium* has become a spectacular sports facility open to the public, and the EXPO '67 grounds on Ile Notre Dame (also part of the world's fair acreage) are now the site of the *Palais de la Civilisation,* the former French pavilion, which features one major cultural event each summer.

Compelling and cosmopolitan, Montreal sits on an anvil-shaped island 32 miles long and 10 miles wide in the middle of the St. Lawrence River, some 170 miles (274 km) northeast of Lake Ontario. The river borders the city on the south and east and provides the crucial navigable link between the inland Great Lakes and the Atlantic Ocean. (The other great French city on the St. Lawrence, Quebec City, is 153 miles north of Montreal.) A narrow branch of the St. Lawrence, known as Rivière des Prairies, borders the city on the west and the north. From the top of Mount Royal residents can see all the surrounding river country. Except for Mount Royal, the island is flat.

The most appealing fact about Montreal, especially for Americans, is its Frenchness. Without jet lag and with a minimum of cost and bother, Americans have easy access to what is essentially a European city, providing the very best of the traditional French experience. Two-thirds of Montreal's 2.8 million inhabitants are of French origin. It only takes about two steps into the city to discover that you are truly in a foreign country. Montreal — indeed, all of the surrounding province of Quebec — is proudly French, and it is the French-Canadian patois that is heard all around. Nearly everyone is bilingual, but there is no question of the primary tongue.

What makes a visit to Montreal such a different experience from a visit to Quebec City are its size and sophistication: Montreal is simply more cosmopolitan. In part this is because Montreal benefits from its large minorities representation — from more than 100 ethnic groups. Sixteen percent of the non-French population is Anglo-Saxon; the remainder have far-flung roots in Central Europe, Greece, Italy, Hungary, or China. Montreal has the country's largest Jewish population and a Chinese community of more than 50,000. Groups of Italians, Hungarians, Greeks, Germans, and West Indians have also brought their traditions to Montreal.

And yet Montreal's special character has to be accounted for by more than just the diversity of its population. When large numbers of European settlers moved into Toronto, they managed to break the English-only monopoly on politics, money, and culture that had held the city in thrall since its founding. They made Toronto more livable and changed the nature of life in the city. Not so in Montreal. There is no mistaking that its population is predominantly and profoundly French. But it is accepting of the world. Perhaps because Montreal was never the headquarters of the Catholic Church, or because it passed some part of this century as a "sin city," it seems to live easier with itself. The reasons for this subtle flavor of life — everywhere palpable but rarely tangible — must lie in its history.

When explorer-entrepreneur Samuel de Champlain reached Montreal's shores in 1603, he foresaw the great value of this natural transportation crossroad as an inland port and returned in 1609 to erect a trading post near the foot of the Lachine Rapids. (The ravages of warring tribes had left no trace of the Indian village of Hochelaga, first seen by Cartier.) The spot was christened Place Royale and is still a nucleus of commercial activity.

Champlain was followed by a succession of missionaries determined to convert the Indians to Christianity. In 1642 the permanent community of Ville Marie was founded at Place Royale (in what is now known as Vieux Montréal) by a small group led by the French career soldier Paul de Chomedey, Sieur de Maisonneuve. Shortly after their arrival, the colonists narrowly escaped being swept away in a disastrous flood. As a token of gratitude for their survival, they climbed Mount Royal's eastern slope and planted a wooden cross at the top. Today, the illuminated 100-foot steel cross that stands in its stead — and on a different site — can be seen for miles on clear nights.

While the flood did not obliterate Ville Marie, the Indians very nearly did. During the next 60 years, the rapidly growing colony of traders, explorers, and missionaries was besieged by numerous attacks; an open state of war existed with the Iroquois until an Indian treaty was signed in 1701.

In the 18th century, Montreal (the name Ville Marie was dropped during this period) prospered through its burgeoning fur trade, though not without difficulties. The Indians were quieted, but trouble with the English and Americans took its toll on the French settlement. In 1759, when Quebec City fell to the British as a result of the battle on the Plains of Abraham, the capital of New France moved briefly to Montreal. A year later Montreal, too, fell to the British.

After the Revolution, Americans eyed Montreal and Quebec City as potential extensions of the original 13 colonies. In November 1775, General Richard Montgomery marched on Montreal and occupied it without firing a shot. The American occupation lasted only 7 months, however, until June 1776, when Montgomery failed to capture Quebec City and Montreal returned to British rule.

Montreal's expansion under the British gained momentum during the early 19th century, when fur trading, shipbuilding, and railroading reached a crescendo. In 1832 Montreal was incorporated as a city, and by 1843 it was the capital of the Province of Canada (an 1841 union of Upper and Lower Canada, encompassing today's provinces of Ontario and Quebec).

The city's expansion during the early 1900s began a period when Montreal justifiably bore the reputation of being a "wicked city"; prostitution, illegal gambling, and other vices flourished, mostly under the well-paid protection of the authorities.

By the end of the 1940s, the central section of Montreal was a dreary core of slums and rundown buildings, which has since completely vanished. A war on corruption, mounted during the 1950s by city official Jean Drapeau, wiped out the modern blot on the face of Montreal.

Called to act as public prosecutor in the city's police inquiry in 1950, Drapeau earned a reputation as an uncompromising foe of vice; this reputation got him elected mayor of Montreal for the first time in 1954. Drapeau's administration initiated a time of change in both the face and feeling of Montreal. He remained the city's most famous civic leader until he retired. Jean Doré was elected to a 4-year term as mayor in November 1986.

The first renovation in Montreal was Place Ville Marie, an underground complex of shops, restaurants, and services in the heart of downtown, built to hide the ugly pityards of the Canadian National Railway. Place Ville Marie was only the first of six underground complexes in Montreal, each of which provides weatherproof access to hotels, office buildings, banks, and stores in different parts of the city and is linked by the city's modern, quiet Métro system.

It was no sooner than the Métro began operation in 1966 that more than 50 million visitors flooded the city for EXPO '67, the 1967 World Exposition.

The success of EXPO '67 was part of an explosion of daring construction undertaken by the city. During the 1960s and 1970s Montreal put up a stunning cultural and performing arts center, *Place des Arts;* became one of the two Canadian cities with a major league baseball team, the Montreal *Expos* (Toronto has the *Blue Jays*); and hosted the 1976 Summer Olympics.

At the same time that the city was acquiring its new look, municipal and provincial ordinances wisely assured the preservation of Vieux Montréal, designating the 95-acre waterfront sector a historical site.

The city spreads out in all directions from the peaks on Mount Royal, and probably the best way to appreciate the mountain and its surrounding Mount Royal Park is to hire one of the omnipresent *calèches*. These horse-drawn carriages seem to be stationed at every important tourist area around the city, and they can't be beaten as a means of sightseeing locomotion. (In winter, in Mount Royal Park, the carriages give way to sleighs, and you can huddle down in a furry lap robe and see the city.)

In the course of meandering through Mount Royal Park, it's possible to assimilate a little local sociology along with an appreciation of the scenic beauty and arboreal pleasures. It is certainly no secret that there is no love lost between the descendants of the original French founders and the progeny of the British conquerers. They live in an increasingly cordial coexistence, although former antipathies are still evident in Montreal's neighborhood patterns. To the west is Westmount, the "bedroom" for Montreal's prosperous English community. On the other side of the mountain is Outremont, the turf of the wealthy French inhabitants. Each community is equally affluent but entirely separate, and it is easy to distinguish the lines of demarcation. As you ride along, just note the names of the passing apartment buildings. When the names cease being such Anglophilic gems as "The Trafalgar" and begin to take on the markedly Gallic cast of "Le Trianon," you'll know that you have "crossed the channel."

Museums of various types can be found in Montreal; the performing arts — ranging from concerts by the acclaimed *Montreal Symphony Orchestra* to French-language puppet shows — are heavily patronized; thousands of Montrealers flock to the *Olympic Stadium* to root for the National League *Expos*.

It would probably take about a week's conscientious effort to see just the most important sights of this city, so you may have to be a bit selective your first time around. But no one ever visits Montreal just once, so you can console yourself with the inevitability of there being a next time.

MONTREAL AT-A-GLANCE

SEEING THE CITY: Montreal has several vantage points from which to capture the sweep of the city, its mountain — 764-foot Mount Royal — the St. Lawrence River, and, on a clear day, beyond to the mountains of New York and Vermont. Two lookout points on Mount Royal itself offer spectacular views. To reach the Mount Royal Chalet Lookout, follow the path up from the Mount Royal Park parking lot; in the summertime, you can mount the summit by horse-drawn *calèche* or a mini-train ride that begins at Beaver Lake. If driving, you have access to an impressive view of the north and east at the lookout on the eastern slope of Camillien Houde Parkway, the only road over the mountain on which automobiles are permitted.

The Westmount Lookout, also accessible by car, opens up an excellent view of the southwestern section of the city and surroundings. Arrows on the lookout's ledge indicate 22 points of interest, extending to the Green Mountains of Vermont and New York's Adirondacks.

The old clock tower, recently refurbished and now an interpretative center tracing the old port's past, yields a vista of the harbor from its top story. From St. Joseph's Oratory, 3800 Queen Mary Road, there is an excellent view of the northern part of the city.

Still other panoramas of Montreal can be seen while having lunch, cocktails, or dinner at the *Château Champlain*'s *L'Escapade,* 1050 de la Gauchetière St. W (phone: 878-1688), or at the *Le Grand* hotel's *Tour de Ville,* 777 University St. (phone: 879-1370).

SPECIAL PLACES: The best way to get a feel for Montreal is by walking through its streets and parks. Because of its layout, Montreal is easy to cope with on foot. Though not exactly true in direction, Montreal's street plan is laid out on a north-south, east-west axis. Each block covers approximately 100 numbers. The east-west numbering starts at St. Lawrence Boulevard, so the street number 900 West, for example, is 9 blocks west of St. Lawrence. The north-south numbers start at the river and run north, following the same formula. Most interesting to the visitor is the area wedged between the river on the south and east and Mount Royal on the north and west.

Anyone who wearies quickly or would like to visit places farther afield should head for the nearest Métro station and hop aboard a soundless, rubber-tired train. The city's four subway lines put visitors within proximity of the most important attractions.

UNDERGROUND MONTREAL

Also called *la ville souterraine,* this below-street-level network of commercial-business-residential complexes is for many as vital a part of the city as that aboveground. Conceived by architect I. M. Pei and developer William Zeckendorf during the 1950s, Montreal's first subterranean complex, Place Ville Marie, opened in 1962. Montrealers took to it immediately, moving underground to shop, socialize, and seek refuge from inclement weather and city traffic. Its successful reception prompted a gradual expansion into other sections of the city, and today the network extends some 9 pedestrian miles (14.4 km). All the centers, known as *"places,"* are linked by the Métro system. Plans exist for further development in the next decade.

Because of access to such a wide variety of attractions and services, you could spend days in Montreal without ever going outside. Many Montrealers do just that — especially when winter dumps 100 inches of snow on the city. The complex network gives access to the city's main sports facilities, exhibits, and performing arts centers, about 1,500 shops, 150 restaurants, and apartments, 8 major hotels, the 2 main rail and bus terminals, numerous banks and 25 cinemas and theaters, some 11,000 indoor parking spaces, and even a municipal library branch at the McGill Métro station. Reasonably priced tours of Underground Montreal are conducted by *Les Montrealistes* (phone: 744-3009), *Guidatour* (phone: 844-4021), *Visites de Montréal* (phone: 843-3308), *Gray Line* (phone: 280-5327), and *Hertz Tourist Guide* (phone: 937-6690).

Place Ville Marie – The city's first underground complex has had a facelift and now houses over 85 boutiques and stores as well as an elegant marble and brass fast-food market, *Les Cours de la Place,* with everything from Baskin-Robbins ice cream to Oriental snacks. Interconnecting promenades link Place Ville Marie with Place Bonaventure and Place du Canada, forming an underground core of some 200 shops, 20 restaurants and bars, and entrances to three major hotels — the *Queen Elizabeth,* Hilton's *Bonaventure International* hotel, and *Château Champlain.* Enter Place Ville Marie through the *Queen Elizabeth,* 900 René-Lévesque Blvd.

Place Bonaventure – Linked to Place Ville Marie by walkways leading through Central Station, this 6-acre arcade houses about 100 shops that carry fashions, handicrafts, and furniture from around the world. Above the shopping concourse are a merchandise market, an exhibition hall, and the *Bonaventure International* hotel. Enter the *Bonaventure International* hotel through Place Bonaventure, corner of Lagavchatière and Mansfield Streets, or through *Château Champlain,* 1050 de la Gauchetière W.

Bell-Banque Nationale towers – Joined to the pedestrian passageway between Place Victoria and the Beaver Hall Hill building, these two office towers have increased the underground city's shopping and dining potential with a 2-tiered mall of boutiques and a large restaurant complex on the lower level.

Place Victoria – Facing the just relandscaped Victoria Square, this massive office tower is home to the Montreal Stock Exchange and yet another underground shopping mall. Stock Exchange tours are given by reservation only. Admission charge (phone: 871-2424). The complex is connected to *Le Grand* hotel.

Place Alexis Nihon – A short subway ride away from the central core, this recently redesigned plaza offers more weatherproofed shopping. Some 80,000 people pass through the complex each day en route to the office building, apartment tower, 3-floor shopping mall, and covered parking levels. 1500 Atwater; take the Métro to Atwater.

Faubourg Ste.-Catherine – Near the Concordia Métro station is Montreal's answer to Boston's Quincy Market, a vast and colorful complex stretching one long city block on Ste.-Catherine Street between Guy and St. Mathieu. Rows of boutiques and counters display a tempting array of delicious edibles, and there are a number of specialty stores as well.

Westmount Square – French high-fashion designers are represented in this poshest of Montreal's underground plazas, just a stroll away from Plaza Alexis Nihon. Situated directly beneath three gleaming office towers designed by Mies van der Rohe is a deli and the *Jockey Club,* cinemas, and china and jewelry shops. But the main attractions are the salons of *Jousse of Paris, Guy Laroche,* and *Cacharel.* Take the Métro to Atwater.

Place des Arts – The heart of Montreal's cultural life is its lavish performing arts center, which contains a stunning and acoustically superb concert hall and theater accommodating over 5,000 people. Home of the *Montreal Symphony Orchestra, Les Grands Ballets Canadiens,* and the *Montreal Opera,* it is also the setting for chamber music concerts, ballet recitals, and plays. On Sunday mornings, the lobby of the center hosts *"Sons et Brioche,"* informal concerts served up with a continental breakfast. (Tickets — very reasonably priced ones, at that — are available at Place des Arts half an hour prior to performance.) 175 St. Catherine St. W.; take the Métro to *Place des Arts.* (Call 842-2112 for program and ticket information.)

Complexe Desjardins – Completed in mid-1976 with the opening of the *Méridien* hotel, this impressive complex contains meeting halls, offices, and an enclosed shopping center with some 100 boutiques and specialty stores and 20 restaurants. Sculptures, fountains, plants, and a regular series of entertainment events and special exhibits make it a popular gathering place. It's linked by an underground walkway to *Place des Arts.*

Complexe Guy Favreau – This complex housing offices, apartments, and boutiques, as well as the National Film Board's movie theater, connects to the Complexe Desjardins and the city's convention center, Palais des Congrès. The latter is a favorite with visitors, who enjoy playing with its Telidon computers, which list all of Montreal's attractions, complete with tourist information and helpful graphics. (These computers are now found in most major hotel lobbies.) The convention center mall also melds with the new Chinatown pedestrian plaza, lined with Oriental shops and restaurants.

Alcan Building – The Canadian aluminum company's international headquarters, Maison Alcan, is an award-winning blend of old and new architecture. Noontime concerts are presented and periodic exhibitions held in its marble atrium, which is ringed with various eateries, shops, and an art gallery. Just a few steps from the Peel Métro station, at the corner of Sherbrooke and Stanley Sts.

OLD MONTREAL

Both private enterprise and government funds are contributing to the restoration of important buildings in Vieux Montréal, the city's historic waterfront section. You can drive around it or see it by horse-drawn *calèche,* but the best way to get a feel for it is by strolling through the narrow streets. Arm yourself with a detailed guidebook to the area — get a free copy of *A Walking Tour of Vieux Montréal* from the Greater Montreal Convention and Tourism Bureau, in the Dorchester Square Building (Dorchester Square at Peel St.; phone: 871-1595), or its visitor center (on the corner of Place Jacques Cartier and Notre Dame St. in Old Montreal). If you are visiting in July or August, join the weekly guided walking tour conducted by *Les Montréalistes* (phone: 744-3009), a professional guide company. Highlights include the following:

Notre Dame Basilica – Opened in 1829, this building was designed in neo-Gothic style by New York architect James O'Donnell, whose grave lies in the church basement. In addition to its monumental altar and exquisite wood carvings and paintings, the church houses an organ with 5,772 pipes and a small museum in the sacristy, open on weekends only from 9 AM to 5 PM for a small admission fee. Adjacent to the main church is the newly restored Sacred Heart Chapel. The stained-glass windows depict the early history of Montreal. As you leave, step into the Place d'Armes to glance up at the twin spires and get a true perspective of the church's scale. Open daily. Place d'Armes (phone: 849-1070).

Place Jacques Cartier – This cobblestoned square, the largest in Old Montreal, was once the main marketplace. Now it's the hub of Old Montreal activity and is lined with attractive restaurants and restored houses. Dominating the square is a statue of Horatio Nelson atop a 35-foot column (erected in 1809). In warm weather, there is a flower market at the base of the column, offering blossoms of every conceivable size and hue; in autumn, apples and pumpkins are the fare. Alfresco cafés line both sides of the square, perfect for relaxing and drinking in the flavor of the early 19th century. Between St. Paul and Notre Dame.

Vieux Port – Developed as a government project in 1981, it's now a summertime entertainment center. The port itself has undergone extensive renovation of late with the addition of parkland, flowers, and fountains along the length of the federally owned dock area. Now strollers may rest on a bench and take in the waterfront as it was some 100 years ago, although Great Lakes tankers like the *Maplecliffe Hall* (open for tours all summer) have replaced sailing ships. Encouraged by this government move to bring back the once-neglected harbor, nearby companies and property owners have refurbished their buildings with charming courtyards and outdoor cafés. The *Vieux Port Festival* kicks off the season on Saint-Jean Baptiste Day (June 24), and events continue until Labor Day. Daily activities include puppet shows, clowns, movies, dancing, and theater (all free); at night, the large outdoor stage facing the harbor might host the *Montreal Symphony Orchestra* or various rock groups. There's also an immense flea market with piles of second-hand bargains. The former Louis-Joliet passenger ship terminal hosts exhibitions every summer. A favorite summer stop is the garden restaurant at *Gibby's* (phone: 283-5256), in the Youville courtyard. Near the waterfront, at the foot of Place d'Youville.

Château de Ramezay – The manor, built in 1705, originally served as the residence of French governors in Montreal. It later housed the offices of the West India Company and, still later, was the residence of English governors. During the American occupation between 1775 and 1776, the Continental Army, under Generals Richard Montgomery and Benedict Arnold, established its headquarters here. Today the château is a fine historical museum, with exhibits reflecting its own past as well as that of Montreal. Closed Mondays. Admission charge. 280 Notre Dame St. E. (phone: 861-7182).

Notre Dame de Bonsecours Chapel – The city's oldest church is also called the Sailors' Chapel because of the large number of sailors who worship here. Built originally in 1657, it was destroyed by fire and twice rebuilt and modified. The present chapel dates from 1771, the façade from 1895. Inside, you'll see votive lamps in the shape of model ships, placed there by mariners as tokens of their faith. A series of dolls and miniatures in a small museum upstairs depicts the life of Ste. Marguerite Bourgeoys, foundress of the Congregation of Notre Dame order of nuns and Canada's first saint. More energetic visitors may hike to the spire's summit for an uplifting view of the harbor and historic quarter. Closed Mondays. Admission charge for the museum. 400 St. Paul St. E. (phone: 845-9991).

Place d'Youville – One of the first civic centers built in Montreal, Place d'Youville is now surrounded by monuments and historic sites. An interesting landmark is Fire Station 1, which has been restored and now houses the Montreal History Center, where a synchronized audio-visual presentation leads visitors through 11 display rooms and 400 years of history. Permanent exhibits include an old streetcar, a "talking" telephone booth, and a simulated shoe factory. Periodic expositions feature Quebec's past. Closed Mondays. Admission charge. For information, call 872-3207.

ELSEWHERE IN THE CITY

Angrignon Park – A 262-acre recreational oasis summer and winter, this park is at its busiest from mid-December to late March, when it is the site of Winter Wonderland. Surrounding the Children's Zoo building, Wonderland offers all kinds of free outdoor fun, from cross-country skiing and snowshoeing, and skating on the decorated rink to thrilling slides down the icy toboggan run. Open daily from 10 AM to 10 PM. Admission charge for zoo. 3400 Trinitaires Blvd. Get off at Métro Station Angrinon.

Olympic Park – Having hosted the 1976 Summer Olympic Games, Montreal is now using these spectacular facilities for all types of sports events and exhibits. The Montreal *Expos* play at the stadium which is now topped with its long-awaited tower and retractable roof. A newly opened restaurant and observation deck offer panoramic views of the city. Meets, classes, and public swimming periods are held regularly in the 50-meter pool and 50-foot diving pool. The guided tour that offers a behind-the-scenes look at the facilities is 45 minutes well spent. You'll get an explanation of some impressive, technologically advanced features — like the ripple and bubble machines that diving coaches can use to create air bubbles instantly on the surface of the pool to mitigate the physical impact of a athlete's bad dive. Tours are conducted in English daily, except holidays. Admission charge. 4545 Pierre de Coubertin Ave.; take the Métro to Viau (phone: 252-4646 or 252-4737).

Botanical Garden – Across from the Olympic Park, this noted horticultural showplace was founded by naturalist Brother Marie Victorin. Actually a complex of some 30 specialized gardens and 9 greenhouses, there are more than 25,000 different species and varieties of plants on display, grouped according to use (economical, medicinal, ornamental) and habitat. It also claims to have North America's most complete collection of bonsai trees and the country's largest and grandest exhibition greenhouse. In the midst of expansion, the highly acclaimed Japanese gardens opened during the summer of 1988, and as we went to press the Insectarium scheduled to open this year. The Chinese gardens, also slated for completion in 1990, will make Montreal's botanical gardens the second largest in the world, after London's Kew Gardens. The visitors reception center presents video, art, and photographic displays on the world of botany. A mini-train tour is conducted by bilingual guides. Open daily. Admission charge for greenhouses. 4101 Sherbrooke St. E. (phone: 872-1400).

Mount Royal – Because it dominates the city scene, you can't avoid seeing Mount Royal from one angle or another (the mountain has two major peaks: Mount Royal and Westmount). But lovely Mount Royal Park, planned by the renowned landscape architect Frederick Law Olmsted, of New York City's Central Park fame, is worth a closer look. Not only is it a fine vantage point from which to view the St. Lawrence River, Montreal, and the mountains beyond, it is also a good spot from which to observe Montrealers at their leisure. They use the 500-acre park year-round — especially in winter, for skiing, skating, or horse-drawn sleigh rides (you can hire them in the park). In summer, Beaver Lake is the site of twice-weekly folk dancing, and the audience is invited to participate. The Université de Montréal, the second largest French-speaking university in the world, is located on the north side of Mount Royal; and St. Joseph's Oratory, described below, is on Westmount's north slope. The park is bounded by Park Avenue on the east and, continuing counterclockwise, Mont Royal Boulevard, Camillien Houde Parkway, Remembrance Road, Côte des Neiges, and Pine Avenue.

St. Joseph's Oratory – For more than 2 million people each year, a visit to this shrine is reason enough for a trip to Montreal. Even if you don't make a pilgrimage up the 99 steps to the basilica of this church founded 75 years ago by Holy Cross Brother André for the glorification of St. Joseph, the patron saint of Canada, you will notice the oratory's monumental dome as a distinctive landmark on the city's skyline. Brother André is said to have had great healing power; he is entombed here. Organ recitals are given on Wednesdays during the summer at 8 PM (admission charge), and the children's choir *Les Petits Chanteurs du Mont-Royal* performs Sundays at 11 AM. Crèches from around the world are featured every Christmas. The basilica, the oratory museum recounting the shrine's history, and the art gallery featuring religious works are all open daily from 10 AM to 5 PM. Admission charge. 3800 Queen Mary Rd. (phone: 733-8211).

St. Denis Street – This area, known as Montreal's Latin Quarter, is the site of the Université du Québec campus. It features a pleasant square with an agora, fountains, and an art gallery. The façade of historic St.-Jacques Cathedral has been integrated into the institution's main building. St. Denis Street and its theater (*Théâtre St.-Denis*) were the original hosts to the city's annual *Jazz Festival* in early July, and they still provide the sites for many events in this now much expanded 10-day musicfest (see *Special Events*). The street is also popular for its restaurants and attracts an academic crowd to its bookshops, art galleries, and coffeehouses. St. Denis, above Sherbrooke Street, is gaining a reputation as a fashion hub due to the many up-and-coming Quebec designers who have showrooms and boutiques here.

Westmount – This mountainside "city within a city" was traditionally the enclave of Montreal's wealthy English-speaking population. Today, the residents of this high-rent district must still be wealthy to maintain themselves in Westmount fashion, but the "English only" requisite has eased somewhat as the city's cultures have blended. This is the section of town for house-staring — or, more appropriately, mansion-staring. The palatial stone house West Mount, which gave the area its name and was owned by Beaver Steamship Line's William Murray, has been torn down, but there are a number of other impressive examples of 19th- and early-20th-century homes (and a few even earlier landmarks) to fill the gap. The sturdy of limb can take the Métro to Atwater station, which is linked to elegant Westmount Square, and start a walking tour of the area from there. But because of Westmount's hills, the less hearty may prefer to see it by car. The most interesting sights fall between St. Catherine St. and Edgehill, from Greene Ave. to Victoria Ave.

Outremont – The traditional French-speaking counterpart to English-speaking Westmount is the "ville" of Outremont, hidden on the northeast slope of Mount Royal. Incorporated in 1875, the village was principally made up of large tracts of farmland owned and cultivated by elite residents. While the farms have long since been divided into smaller building lots, some of the original old farmhouses still exist. Outremont's terrain is easily as rugged as Westmount's, so it is best explored by car. The section's main thoroughfare, Côte Ste. Catherine, and the parallel Maplewood Avenue display the best of Outremont's marvelous mansions, and Laurier Ave. is lined with smart boutiques and cafés. Try *Café Laurier,* 394 Laurier W., for a relaxing coffee break. Bounded north and south by Glendale Ave. and Mont Royal Blvd., east and west by Hutchinson and Canterbury Aves.

Museum of Fine Arts – Galleries in this neoclassic building house an impressive permanent collection of European, Canadian, and Eastern art as well as frequent special exhibits. Canada's oldest fine arts museum (1860), it has staged a string of highly regarded international exhibitions, including Picasso, Miró, the Vatican Collection, Leonardo da Vinci, and Chagall. Free guided tours of permanent and temporary exhibitions. Closed Mondays. Small admission charge. 1379 Sherbrooke W. (phone: 285-1600).

McGill University – Chartered in 1821, this prestigious school was built with funds from the estate of Scottish immigrant James McGill, who amassed a fortune as a fur trader and served in Lower Canada's Parliament. The campus is close to the site of the 16th-century Indian town of Hochelaga, discovered by Cartier in 1535. A stroll around the campus and down fashionable Sherbrooke Street reveals a number of interesting architectural façades, including some fine old mansions that now belong to the university. Guided tours of the university grounds can be arranged by phoning 398-3770. The university's *McCord Museum,* which has a collection of Indian artifacts, Eskimo carvings, paintings, furnishings, and photographs that focus on the ethnology of Canada, will be closed until 1992 for major renovations. Museum activities and exhibits will be held at other places in the city. During the summer, McGill provides inexpensive accommodations in its dormitories, with cafeteria service and sports facilities available to guests. Call 398-6367 for information.

MacKay to de la Montagne – A concentration of restaurants, pubs, discos, trendy fashion boutiques, and art galleries ensconced in brownstone and gray stone Victorian houses is centered in this 9-square-block downtown area that you are bound to discover sooner or later. Whether you choose to browse, shop, or bar-hop, you'll know that this is where the action is, and in good weather much of the action is out on the street. *Thursdays,* 1449 Crescent St., is a nice place to eat or have a drink. MacKay, Bishop, Crescent, and de la Montagne (also known as Mountain) Sts. between Sherbrooke St. and René-Lévesque Blvd.

Prince Arthur Pedestrian Mall – Once a quiet residential street, part of McGill's low-cost student ghetto from the 1950s to the early 1970s, today the stretch of Prince Arthur from St. Laurent Boulevard to St. Louis Square has been transformed into an attractive mall. Enhanced by a fountain, overflowing tubs of flowers, and streetlamps, it is currently home to an array of moderately priced restaurants that run the gamut of ethnicities from Greek and Italian to Vietnamese, Polish, and Quebecoise. People watchers will find summer a great time to take advantage of one of the many outdoor cafés that line this lovely street. Most of the restaurants are BYOW (bring your own wine). Summer is also the season for outdoor performances by local musicians, magicians, and acrobats.

Dow Planetarium – Outer space is highlighted in this giant theater of the stars, Canada's first major planetarium, a gift to the city from Dow Brewery Ltd. in the mid-60s. Its special programs change at various times of year and are narrated in French and English on alternate hours (call for times). Closed Mondays, holidays, and for 3 weeks after Labor Day. Admission charge. 1000 St. Jacques W. (phone: 872-4530).

Maison Radio–Canada – One of the world's largest and most modern radio and television centers, the Canadian Broadcasting Company's (CBC's) headquarters of

French and English broadcasting sprawls over 25 acres in downtown Montreal. The 23-story hexagonal building that houses the studios also has galleries where invited guests can watch operations in two television studios and control rooms. The center also has an extensive art collection of paintings, sculptures, and graphics done mostly by artists of Quebec and the Atlantic provinces. Open to the public, but call ahead to make arrangements.. 1400 René-Lévesque Blvd. (phone: 728-1122).

St. Lawrence Seaway – Montreal is the starting point of this modern engineering miracle, which makes it possible for oceanbound ships to travel all the way through the Great Lakes. Often missed by the average visitor, the observatory at the St. Lambert Lock offers a close look at the intricate locking procedures. Ships from the ocean must be raised and lowered some 15 feet as they pass through the lock. The observation tower also commands a fine view of Montreal's skyline across the St. Lawrence River. A scenic bicycle path runs along the lock. Open May to mid-October; weekends only September and October. No admission charge. Take the Victoria Bridge from downtown across to St. Lambert Lock on Rte. 15 on the south shore of the river (phone: 672-4110).

■**EXTRA SPECIAL:** Montreal's largest satellite among its St. Lawrence River islands is Ile Ste. Hélène, which Samuel de Champlain named after his wife, Hélène Boule. It was once the site of a military installation and, more recently, part of the extensive grounds of EXPO '67, which also included its neighboring island, Ile Notre Dame. (When the fair was over, these facilities were renamed *Man and His World,* after the EXPO's main theme.) Besides EXPO '67, there's plenty to do on these two islands, which are linked to the city proper by two bridges — Pont de la Concorde and Pont Jacques Cartier — as well as by the Métro system. Get off at the Ile St. Hélène stop on the Métro.

Ile Notre Dame – Its annual *Floralies* flower show has been so successful that the island has become a popular year-round park. Pedal boat rentals are an ideal way to explore the island's canals in summer while, in winter, the frozen canals become huge ice skating rinks. Snowshoeing, cross-country skiing, and horse-drawn sleigh rides can also be enjoyed. Other sites here include the Olympic rowing basin, which is transformed into a skating rink each winter, the Canadian Grand Prix racetrack, Gilles Villeneuve Circuit, and the *Palais de la Civilisation* exhibition center. Open mid-June to Labor Day; exhibition center open May to October. Admission charge for exhibition center only.

Ile Ste. Hélène – La Ronde, a rollicking amusement park, covers 135 acres of this island. In addition to rides, La Ronde has spirited restaurants and pubs that Montrealers frequent on warm summer evenings (especially from the end of May to mid-June when it's the launching pad for a 10-day *Fireworks Festival*), and an Aquapark with waterslides and swimming and wading pools. Open mid-June to Labor Day. Admission charge (phone: 272-6222).

The *David Stewart Museum* (formerly the *Military and Marine Museum*) in Ile Ste. Hélène's Old Fort (built in the early 1820s by order of the Duke of Wellington) houses historic uniforms, military equipment, and model ships. It features special historical displays June to November (weather permitting); admission charge. In the summer, two colorfully uniformed resident companies of colonial troops — La Compagnie Franche de la Marine (French) and Fraser's Highlanders (Scottish) — perform authentic 18th-century drills and marches. Open year-round; daily from May to September, closed Mondays the rest of the year. Admission charge (phone: 861-6701).

The Montreal Aquarium is home to a wide variety of native and exotic fish and other aquatic animals, but the most popular residents are the penguins. They delight visitors with their antics in a simulated South Pole on the second floor.

Open daily year-round, except on some holidays. Admission charge. In the Alcan Pavilion at La Ronde (phone: 872-4656).

The *Festin du Gouverneur* restaurant in the Old Fort invites diners to enjoy an 18th-century banquet served by costumed performers who sing, dance, and draw patrons into the act. Reservations required (phone: 879-1141). The island is also the site of *Hélène de Champlain* restaurant in an attractive mock Normandy–style building overlooking the river and the rose gardens that remain from EXPO '67 (phone: 395-2424).

Every winter, in late January, Iles Ste. Hélène and Notre Dame play host to *La Fête des Neiges,* a 10-day pre-Lenten snow carnival that includes costume balls on ice, skating races, sledding, and other outdoor sports, all aided and abetted by plentiful refreshments. Imaginative snow sculptures add so much to the fun that they seem to become contagious, often found across the St. Lawrence decorating Vieux Montréal as well. For information call 872-6093.

■ **Note:** The Laurentian Mountains — called Les Laurentides by French Canadians — extend from 20 to 80 miles (32 to 128 km) north of Montreal and contain some of the best ski slopes in eastern North America. Laurentides National Park is described in full detail in the Laurentian tour route of Quebec Province in DIRECTIONS.

SOURCES AND RESOURCES

TOURIST INFORMATION: The Greater Montreal Convention and Tourism Bureau and Tourism Quebec are both under the same roof in the new Infotouriste building at Dorchester Square (phone: 873-2015; from eastern US, 800-443-7000). Visitor information, maps, brochures, and a city guidebook for the handicapped are also available at the tourist bureau kiosks at the international tourist reception center in the Dorchester Square Building off Peel Street and in Place Jacques Cartier (phone: 871-1595).

Local Coverage – There are two daily English-language newspapers, the *Montreal Gazette* and *Montreal Daily News,* available at newsstands every morning, except Sundays. The monthly *Montreal* magazine, available at newsstands, has entertainment and restaurant listings.

Food – The *Shopping, Restaurants and Nightlife Guide,* available free at the tourist office, lists details on many of the city's restaurants.

Telephone – The area code for Montreal is 514.

Sales Tax – The 9% sales tax does not apply to hotel rooms, books, and clothing purchases below about $424 ($500 Canadian); meals above $2.75 ($3.25 CN)) have a 10% tax.

Currency – All prices are quoted in US dollars unless otherwise indicated.

TIPPING: At restaurants leave a 12 to 15% tip. Taxi drivers usually receive 15% of the fare. Airport porters and bellboys are given $1 (CN) per bag, and hotel maids should receive about $2 (CN) per day.

CLIMATE: While there's no getting around Montreal's cold and snowy winters, its summers seem to make up for it, delivering pleasantly mild temperatures that usually range in the 70s F (20 to 25C). June and September evenings can be cooler, however, so a light jacket may come in handy.

Spring temperatures average between the 50s and the mid-60s F (10 to 18C) and in fall drop to the 40s to mid-50s F (5 to 12C). December through March brings frigid temperatures — the low averaging about 10F, the high about 25F (−12 to −4C) — and plenty of snow (a monthly average of 23 inches). Montrealers cope by bundling up in fur couts, boots, hats, and gloves, and by going underground, as we described earlier.

GETTING AROUND: Métro and Bus – *STCUM,* the city transit system, is an efficient network linking various areas of the city with four different underground lines and 150 bus lines. (The same tickets are used on the Métro and the buses.) Métro trains are clean and quiet, whizzing underground on rubber-tired wheels. The price of the Métro ride (85¢/$1.05 CN per ride; $6.35/$7.50 CN for eight tickets) also includes admission to a veritable underground art gallery of murals, sculptures, stained glass windows, enameled steel frescoes, and ceramics built into exhibits in the 60 stations of the system. *STCUM* issues a helpful, complimentary map of the routes, available at hotel desks and all Métro station ticket booths. For 24-hour information about service, call 288-6287.

Taxi – You can hail cabs on the street or at stands at the corner of main intersections near the railway stations and hotels. The drop fee is about $1.70.

Car Rental – Montreal is served by *Avis,* 1225 Metcalfe St. (phone: 866-7906); *Budget,* 1460 Guy St. (phone: 937-9121); *Hertz,* 1475 Aylmer St. (phone: 842-8537); *Holiday,* 1600 Berri St. (phone: 845-5954); *Tilden,* 1200 Stanley St. (phone: 878-2771), and *Via Route,* 1255 Mackay St. (phone: 871-1166).

Harbor Cruises – A scenic and restful way to see the entire island from the St. Lawrence; *Montreal Harbor Cruises* has six different tours departing from Victoria Pier at the foot of Berri St. from May 2nd through October 15th. Ticket prices vary with the cruise (phone: 842-3871). In addition, *Amphibustour* (phone: 386-1298) travels on both the streets and waters of the port; a ferryboat runs from Jacques Cartier Pier to Cité du Havre island park daily, from noon to 10 PM.

Horse-Drawn Carriage – A romantic way to see the town is by *calèche;* these are stationed at Dorchester Square, Place Jacques Cartier, and atop Mount Royal.

Tours – Some taxicab drivers are licensed tour guides (make sure you get a licensed guide); they can be found at stands around Dorchester Square. Sightseeing tours leaving from Dorchester Square are provided by *Gray Line Sightseeing Tours,* 1241 Peel St. (phone: 280-5327) and *Murray Hill Sightseeing Services,* 1380 Barre St. (phone: 937-5311). During the summer, guides from *Les Montréalistes* conduct daily walking tours of Old Montreal. The same group offers tours of Chinatown, downtown Montreal, and De la Commune Street along the Vieux Port. For rendezvous points and information, call 744-3009. Other private companies offering a variety of tours include *Guidatour* (phone: 844-4021), *Step-on-Guides* (phone: 935-5131), *Hertz Tourist Guides* (phone: 937-6690), *Visites de Montréal* (phone: 843-3308), and *Voyages Astral* (phone: 866-1001). For more information on private guided tours call the Greater Montreal Convention and Tourism Bureau (phone: 873-2015), or pick up a free copy of *A Walking Tour of Vieux Montréal* from the tourism bureau and do it yourself.

SPECIAL EVENTS: Montreal hosts several big annual affairs. During the period prior to Lent, the island stages a 10-day snow carnival, *Fête des Neiges* (see *Montreal At-a-Glance, Extra Special*).

The 10-day *International Jazz Festival* draws jazz greats — and more than 400,000 of their fans — every year in early July. The major concerts are held at *Place des Arts,* with many more intimate events happening along St. Denis Street and in the *Théâtre St.-Denis* and the *Spectrum* (call 871-1881 for information).

The *International Cartoon Salon* provides a platform for cartoonists from all over the world to compete for prizes in various categories, as well as an opportunity to exhibit their work throughout the summer at *Complexe Guy Favreau* (phone: 872-6771).

The *Just for Laughs Festival* is a 10-day comedy event attracting stand-up comics from all over the world to test their wits against each other in French and English. It is held in early July at the *Comedy Nest,* 1234 Bishop St., the *St. Denis Theatre,* on St. Denis St., and Place des Arts. For tickets and information, call 845-3155.

The *Palais de la Civilization* on Ile Notre Dame presents an outstanding exhibit every summer. Past exhibits include "China: Treasures and Splendors" and "Gold of the Thracian Horsemen," and *"Cités Ciné,"* in 1989, which was about film. Open daily, except Mondays, from the end of May until mid-October, 10 AM to 6 PM. For more information, call 872-4560.

When they're in town, the unusual *Le Cirque de Soleil* mini-circus performs at Le Vieux-Port (phone: 522-2324).

During the last week in August, *The World Film Festival* brings the latest movies and their stars to Montreal's *Cinéma Parisien* at *Place des Arts* (phone: 848-3883). Another film event, nearly 20 years old, the *Montreal Festival of New Cinema and Video* presents avant-garde filmworks in late October (call 843-4729 for dates and places).

The *Grand Prix du Canada* is a Formula One racing car event held in mid-June at the 4.41-km Gilles Villeneuve track on Ile Notre-Dame. For information, call 392-4731.

The *Montreal International Marathon* draws runners from around the world on the fourth Sunday in September. For information, call 879-1027.

Now in its fourth year, the *Tour de l'Ile de Montréal* is fast becoming one of the most popular bicycle races in North America. Held in early June, the route encircles the island of Montreal via Sherbrooke Street (phone: 251-6949).

Place Bonaventure's exhibition hall is the site of numerous shows throughout the year, ranging from Canada's largest *Antique Show* to boat and camping exhibits. For information, call 397-2222.

MUSEUMS: For complete descriptions of the *Montreal Museum of Fine Arts, Château de Ramezay,* the *David Stewart (Military and Maritime) Museum,* and the *McCord Museum,* see *Special Places.* Other notable Montreal museums include the following:

Bank of Montreal Museum – Early currency and bank memorabilia. Open from 10 AM to 4 PM, Mondays through Fridays; closed weekends. No admission charge. 129 St. Jacques St. at Place d'Armes (phone: 877-6892).

Canadian Center for Architecture – This new museum, an architectural masterpiece in itself, is a study center devoted to architecture. It contains 20,000 prints and drawings, plus 45,000 photographs and important architectural archives, including works by Leonardo da Vinci and Michelangelo. Open Wednesdays and Fridays, 10 AM to 6 PM; Thursdays, 10 AM to 8 PM; Saturdays and Sundays, 10 AM to 5 PM. Admission charge. 1920 Baile St. (phone: 939-7000).

Fur Trade Museum – A historic home displays memorabilia from the area's rich fur-trading past. Open daily, mid-May to September; Wednesdays through Sundays, 9 AM to 5 PM, September to late March. No admission charge. 1255 Saint Joseph Blvd. at 12th Ave., Lachine (phone: 637-7433 or 283-6054).

Marc-Aurèle Fortin Museum – Works and memorabilia of the Canadian artist. Open daily, 11 AM to 5 PM. Admission charge. 118 St. Pierre St. (phone: 845-6108).

Marguerite d'Youville Centre – Motherhouse of the Grey Nuns; guided tours are given of the chapel and crypt where the founder is buried. Open Wednesdays through Sundays from 1:30 to 4:30 PM. No admission charge. 1185 St. Matthew St. (phone: 932-7724).

Montreal History Center – Audio-visual tour through 11 display rooms describing Montreal's history. Open 10 AM to 4:30 PM daily, except Mondays. Admission charge. Place d'Youville at St. Pierre St. (phone: 872-3207).

Montreal Museum of Decorative Arts – International design from 1940 to the present, including glass and textile exhibits. Open Wednesdays through Sundays only, 11 AM to 5 PM. Admission charge. Corner of Piè IX and Sherbrooke St. (phone: 259-2575).

Museum of Contemporary Art – Canadian and international works. Open daily, 10 AM to 6 PM, except Mondays. No admission charge. Cité du Havre (phone: 873-2878).

Redpath Museum – An impressive anthropological collection, including Egyptian mummies and rare fossils. From September through May, open Mondays through Fridays, 9 AM to 5 PM; June through August, Mondays through Thursdays, 9 AM to 5 PM. No admission charge. 859 Sherbrooke St. W. (phone: 398-4087).

Saidye Bronfman Centre – Contemporary works by national and international artists. Closed Saturdays. No admission charge. 5170 Côte Ste. Catherine (phone: 739-2301).

Saint Laurent Museum of Art – This arts and crafts center is housed in the old chapel that once served the Collège St. Laurent school. Open daily, except Saturdays, noon to 5 PM. No admission charge. 615 Sainte-Croix Blvd., St. Laurent (phone: 747-7367).

Sir George-Étienne Cartier House – This national historic park was the Montreal home of one of Canada's founding fathers. Some of the rooms have been restored to their former Victorian glory and others are reserved for various exhibitions. May through August, open daily, 9 AM to 5 PM; September through April, open Wednesdays through Sundays, 10 AM to 5 PM. No admission charge. 458 Notre-Dame St. E. (phone: 283-2282).

Wax Museum of Montreal – Open daily, 9 AM to 5 PM. Admission charge. 3715 Queen Mary (phone: 738-5959).

SHOPPING: Since the duty-free allowance for US citizens returning from Canada has been raised to $338 ($400 CN) and the US dollar is at a premium north of the border, there are some excellent values obtainable on a shopping spree in Montreal. Canadian import tariffs are different from those in the US, so in some cases this may mean even better buys. It also usually means a wider selection of imported products.

The underground shopping areas (see *Special Places*) provide a great variety of shops that could probably satisfy most shopping needs. But Montreal's department stores have fine selections of clothing, china, crystal, and furniture. Four of the best known in Canada are on St. Catherine Street West, between Mountain and Union Streets in the heart of downtown. In general, shopping hours are from 9 or 9:30 AM to 6 PM on weekdays, except on Thursdays and Fridays, when many stores stay open until 9 PM, and on Saturdays, until 5 PM.

Eaton's – This Montreal branch of the Canadian chain was founded by Timothy Eaton and dates back to 1925. Its merchandise runs the gamut from appliances to works of art, and a personalized-shopping service will do all the work for reluctant shoppers. The *Art Deco* restaurant on the ninth floor is modeled after the dining room of the *Ile de France,* the favorite vessel of Lady Eaton. 677 St. Catherine St. W. (phone: 284-8484).

Holt Renfrew – For true chic in furs. The firm traces its heritage to the 1837 furriers Henderson, Holt, and Renfrew. It is still known for its exceptional fur fashions as well as haute couture lines, its Gucci boutique, and stylish men's clothing. 1300 Sherbrooke St. W. (phone: 842-5111).

Ogilvy's – This once tartan-trimmed testament to days gone by has been transformed into a glossy new complex of chic boutiques and elegant counters. However, the columns and grand main-floor chandeliers have been retained, and traditional goods can still be found in many departments. The store's Scottish heritage continues to manifest itself every day at noon when shoppers hear the skirl of the bagpipes played by a kilted piper. Every Christmas since 1947 Montrealers have looked forward to *Ogilvy's* main window display of animated Steiff toys, a spectacle that ushers in the holiday season. 1307 St. Catherine St. W. (phone: 842-7711).

Simpson – A full-line department store begun at the turn of the century as John Murphy Company. China, fur, and a selection of fine fashions are the specialties here. 977 St. Catherine St. W. (phone: 284-4231).

The Bay – Founded in 1845 as Henry Morgan and Company, it was purchased by the Hudson's Bay Company in 1960. It is strong on new trends, French boutique styles, and campus fashions. The variety of dining spots includes a buffet cafeteria, a licensed dining room, and *Le Soupière,* which serves soup, sandwiches, dessert, and coffee. 585 St. Catherine St. W., at Phillips Sq. (phone: 281-4631).

Devotees of fine antiques and delicate craftsmanship head for the fine (and expensive) shops on the aforementioned Sherbrooke Street and its attendant sidestreets, but the bargain hunters frequent the rather unimposing stalls along Notre Dame Street West between Atwater and Guy Streets.

A variety of shops around town carry typical Canadian crafts such as wood carvings, woven products, pottery, jewelry, and Inuit (Eskimo) art. One fine showcase for Canadian crafts is the *Canadian Guild of Crafts,* 2025 Peel St. (phone: 849-6091); it carries crafts from all over Canada, including a notable selection of Eskimo art, and features Indian and Eskimo art galleries open during business hours.

SPORTS: Baseball – The National League *Expos* baseball team plays at the spectacular *Olympic Stadium* (see *Special Places*) with a capacity of 53,858. For information, call 253-3434. Olympic Park is situated in the east end of the city, in the block bounded by Pie IX, Sherbrooke, Viau, and Pierre de Coubertin; take the Métro to Viau.

Biking – The Vieux Port rents bicycles to visitors who want to explore its waterfront trails. In addition, the island of Montreal has 20 bike paths, 12 of them city-run (phone: 872-6211). For information on commercial rentals, call *Vélo-Québec* (phone: 252-3000). Rentals are also available from *Cycle Peel,* 6665 Saint-Jacques St. (phone: 486-1148) and *La Cordec Velo,* 2159 St. Catherine E. (phone: 524-1515).

Golf – The 9-hole *Golf Le Village* is located at Sherbrooke and Viau Sts. (phone: 872-5558, for information). Golfers can find more than 30 courses on the island of Montreal and in the surrounding area.

Hockey – From October through April, the ice is hotly contested at the *Forum* by *Les Canadiens* and their NHL challengers. 2313 St. Catherine St. W. (phone: 932-6131).

Horse Racing – Harness racing takes place nightly, except Tuesdays and Thursdays, at *Blue Bonnets Race Track.* Races begin at 7:30 PM, except on Sundays, when post time is 1:30 PM. 7440 Decarie Blvd. (phone: 739-2741).

Jet-boat Tours – Organized expeditions over the Lachine Rapids, in small hydrofoil-like crafts, leave from Victoria Pier at the foot of Berri St. in Vieux Montreal-daily every other hour from 10 AM to 6 PM. May to late September (phone: 284-9607).

Jogging – Mount Royal Park and Angrignon Park both have paved trails for taking a pleasant run.

Swimming – The stunning Olympic-size pool at Olympic Park is open to the public year-round (phone: 252-4737); the city of Montreal also runs over 50 indoor and outdoor pools and the large public pools at Ile Ste. Hélène (phone: 872-6211). Two of the best indoor pools are the *Cegep du Vieux-Montréal,* 255 Ontario St. E. (phone: 872-2644) and the *Complex Claude-Robillard,* 1000 Emile-Journault (phone: 872-6900).

Tennis – The Player's International Championships alternate between men's and women's events; it's the women's turn this year. From early to mid-August at the *Jarry Tennis Stadium,* Jarry Park (phone: 273-1515). The City of Montreal operates more than 200 municipal courts that are open to the public, either at no charge or for a nominal fee. For information and court reservations, call 872-6763.

Winter Sports – Ice skating, snowshoeing, cross-country skiing, and tobogganing are practiced in parks all over town once winter sets in. All told, the city has 164 skating rinks; 11 cross-country ski areas, each with several trails; 11 large snowshoeing areas; 7 alpine slopes; and 9 toboggan runs among its facilities. From January to March, snowshoeing and cross-country skiing are popular on Notre Dame Island as well as skating along its 1.2-mile-long basin. Close to 1,000 Parks Department employees keep it all in condition. For information, call the municipal recreation department at 872-6211.

THEATER: Both English and French productions are presented at a dozen theaters around town. Local newspapers and in-hotel magazine guides list current attractions. English-language productions are most likely to be found at the *Centaur Theatre,* 453 St. François Xavier (phone: 288-3161).

MUSIC: Since music transcends all language barriers, you can enjoy all that Montreal has to offer, from grand symphony at the *Place des Arts* to French folk music at *boîtes à chanson,* Quebec-style cafés. Again, the guides mentioned above should have up-to-date schedules. The *Montreal Symphony Orchestra* performs at *Salle Wilfrid Pelletier, Place des Arts,* 175 St. Catherine St. W. (phone: 842-2112), as do *Les Grand Ballets Canadiens, L'Opéra de Montreal,* and other guest soloists. Programs of chamber music are given at the *Place des Arts' Théâtre Maisonneuve* and *Théâtre Port-Royale* (same phone number). *Pollack Concert Hall* also regularly schedules varied musical programs, 555 Sherbrooke St. W. (phone: 398-4547). Throughout the year rock stars perform at the *Forum* (phone: 932-6131) and *Olympic Stadium* (phone: 253-3434). Special productions, such as Handel's *Messiah* at Christmastime, are presented at *Notre Dame Basilica,* Place d'Armes (call the *Montreal Symphony* office, 842-3402), and at other Montreal churches.

NIGHTCLUBS AND NIGHTLIFE: Nightlife for the younger set centers around Crescent, Mountain, and St. Denis streets. The supper club crowd can choose from the many hotel and restaurant dining-entertainment spots. Among the more elegant nightspots are *Arthur's* in the *Queen Elizabeth* hotel, 900 René-Lévesque Blvd. W. (phone: 861-3511), a dinner-theater that presents comic skits, shows, and music. The *Château Champlain*'s *Le Caf'Conc'* supper club is reminiscent of Paris' Moulin Rouge; you can go for dinner and the show or for drinks only at showtime. The hotel's *L'Escapade* restaurant on the 36th floor gives a good view along with music. Both are at 1050 Lagauchetière (phone: 878-1688). *Le Stage Dinner Theatre,* at *La Diligence* restaurant, serves up a menu of supper and drama at 7385 Décarie Blvd. (phone: 731-7771). Other spots for entertainment are *Le Portage* at the *Bonaventure* hotel, 1 Place Bonaventure (phone: 878-2332); and *Solmar,* 111 St. Paul St. E. (phone: 861-4562), which has fado music and Portuguese cuisine. *Vieux Munich,* 1170 St. Denis St., features a Bavarian orchestra and dancing every night after 6 PM (phone: 288-8011), while the *Saboyon,* 666 Sherbrooke St. W. (phone: 288-0373), features a dance band as well as Greek music and food.

Dance bands play at the the *Méridien*'s *Le Café Fleurie* restaurant, 4 Complexe

Desjardins (phone: 285-1450); and *Le Grand* hotel's revolving *Tour de Ville* restaurant, 777 University St. (phone: 879-1370). The *Ritz Carlton's Café de Paris,* 1228 Sherbrooke St. W (phone: 842-4212), features piano music.

Disco and bar-hopping abound around Crescent, Mountain, Bishop, and Mackay Streets and a number of sidestreets between Dorchester and Sherbrooke. Currently popular are *Au papillon gourmet,* a piano bar at 2310 Guy St. (phone: 935-4255); *Biddles* for great jazz and ribs at 2060 Aylmer St. (phone: 842-8656); *Le Business* disco at 3500 St. Lawrence Blvd., above Sherbrooke (phone: 844-3988); *Cheers,* 1260 Mackay St. (phone: 932-3138); *Comfort's,* 1195 Crescent (phone: 861-0758); for rock, *Déjà Vu* at 1224 Bishop (phone: 866-0512) as well as the *American Rock Café,* at 2080 Aylmer (phone: 288-9272); *Esprit,* 1234 Mountain St. (phone: 397-1711); *Kick's Bar,* 2051 Mountain St. (phone: 288-2660); *Metropolis,* a turn-of-the-century theater with six bars and dancing on three floors, 59 Ste. Catherine St. E. (phone: 288-5559); *Salsathèque,* for Latin music and dancing, at 1220 Peel St. (phone: 875-0016); *Septembre,* 2015-A Mountain St. (phone: 849-4544); *Tuttles,* 2045 Crescent St. (phone: 288-0144); *Thirsty's,* 1187 Bishop St. (phone: 871-9808); *Sir Winston Churchill Pub* at 1459 Crescent St. (phone: 288-0611); *Winnie's,* 1455 Crescent St. (phone: 288-0623); and *Yesterday's* at 1285 de Maisonneuve Blvd. W. (phone: 282-0220).

Vieux Montréal is fast becoming a hot nightspot area. Favorites include the *Bijou,* 300 Le Moyne St. (phone: 288-5508); *La Cage aux Sports,* a popular hang-out with sports personalities, 395 Le Moyne (phone: 288-1115); *Chez Brandy,* 21 St. Paul St. E. (phone: 871-9178); *L'Air du temps* at 191 St. Paul St. W. (phone: 842-2003); and *Zhivago* for caviar, vodka, and dancing at 419 St. Pierre St. (phone: 284-0333).

BEST IN TOWN

CHECKING IN: With more than 16,000 hotel rooms in the Montreal area, there is no difficulty finding suitable accommodations. Hotels in all categories dot Montreal's downtown center, close to shopping, restaurants, and the city's other attractions. Even some of the luxury hotels offer weekend packages that are real bargains, including the small extras to make a stay more pleasant. Double room rates will run about $90 or more in the expensive category and about $60 to about $85 in the moderate category. A number of firms handle bed-and-breakfast lodgings; they include *Ah! Accommodations as at Home,* 101 Northview Ave. (phone: 486-6910); *Bed & Breakfast de Chez Nous,* 5386 Brodeur (phone: 485-1252); *Bed & Breakfast Downtown,* 3458 Laval Ave. (phone: 289-9749 or 800-361-9935); *Bed & Breakfast Montreal,* 4912 Victoria Ave. (phone: 738-9410); *Bed & Breakfast Mount Royal* (phone: 484-7802); *Relais Montréal Hospitalité,* 3977 Laval Ave. (phone: 287-9635); and *Welcome Bed & Breakfast,* 3950 Laval Ave. (phone: 844-5897).

The downtown *YMCA,* 1451 Stanley St. (phone: 849-8393) and *YWCA,* 1355 René-Lévesque Blvd. W. (phone: 866-9941) as well as the youth hostel at 3541 Aylmer (phone: 843-3317); McGill University (phone: 398-6367; see *Montreal At-a-Glance, Special Places*), Montreal University (phone: 343-6531); MacDonald College in Ste. Anne de Bellevue (phone: 457-5254), and the Collège Français on Fairmont St. W. (phone: 495-2581) all offer inexpensive accommodations. In addition, there are two campgrounds in the immediate area: *Camping Henri* in Pointe-aux-Trembles (phone: 642-5477) and *L'Anse à l'Orme* on Gouin Blvd. in the nearby suburb of Pierrefonds (phone: 626-3268). *KOA* runs a campground on South Shore at St. Philippe (phone: 659-8626). All telephone numbers are in the 514 area code unless otherwise indicated.

Bonaventure International – In a unique 3-story penthouse location — 17 stories above the Place Bonaventure — is Hilton International's 394-room hotel. Standing in the rooftop lobby, looking at the open-air gardens and outdoor pool (used even in winter because it is heated and can be entered from indoors), it is hard to believe that you are right above one of Montreal's busiest office and commercial complexes. The outside rooms have a lovely view of a good portion of the central city (often including the St. Lawrence Seaway). The inside rooms (preferred by many) look out on a contemplative, Japanese-style central garden that contains a brook, a multitude of trees and bushes, and a couple of waterfalls, all there on the roof. *Le Castillion* restaurant is an elegant luncheon or dinner setting. 1 Place Bonaventure (phone: 878-2332). Expensive.

Le Centre Sheraton – This 824-room hostelry has posh suites on the top 5 floors, dubbed appropriately *Le Sommet de la Tour* (the Top of the Tower). The hotel's *Pointe du Vue* restaurant is quickly gaining a reputation for fine nouvelle cuisine. 1201 René-Lévesque Blvd. W. (phone: 878-2000). Expensive.

Château Champlain – The huge, arched picture windows covering the 36-story façade of this Canadian Pacific property make it a distinctive landmark on Montreal's skyline (known to locals as the cheese grater). Its 616 rooms and suites are spacious and elegantly furnished, and a health club and swimming pool have recently been added. 1050 Lagauchetière W. (phone: 878-9000). Expensive.

La Citadelle – An old Quality Inn high-rise has been completely refurbished to create this European-style hotel with 182 comfortable rooms, a health spa, and pool. *C'est La Vie,* the lobby bar, attracts a lively crowd for its happy hour. 410 Sherbrooke St. W. (phone: 844-8851; 800-361-7545 in US). Expensive.

Delta – Here is a luxury high-rise with 453 rooms (most with balconies), a health club, pools, and an innovative "Creativity Center" designed to keep young travelers occupied while their parents are sightseeing. Convenient downtown location. On the corner of Sherbrooke and City Councillors Sts. (phone: 286-1986). Expensive.

Four Seasons (Quatre Saisons) – This superb member of the Four Seasons group has 240 rooms, including deluxe suites and 2 extraordinary split-level penthouses. European touches include the efficient services of a 24-hour concierge and a free nightly shoeshine. Among the facilities are a heated outdoor pool, sauna, whirlpool bath, and exercise room. *Pierre de Coubertin* restaurant is now a private dining and meeting room, though the downstairs café, *Le Restaurant,* is open to the public. 1050 Sherbrooke St. W. (phone: 284-1110). Expensive.

Holiday Inn Crown Plaza – The 1987 top-to-bottom remodeling of this hotel adds splash to the 486 rooms of this, the largest and most convenient of the several *Holiday Inns* in the area. It has an indoor pool. 420 Sherbrooke St. W. (phone: 842-6111). Expensive.

Maritime – Centrally located, this recently renovated hotel has 214 rooms, an indoor pool, and sauna. 1155 Guy St. (phone: 932-1411). Expensive.

Méridien Montréal – This 601-room property is the focal point of the enclosed commercial-business complex at Complexe Desjardins, adjacent to *Place des Arts,* Montreal's performing arts center. The atmosphere is French at this local link in the Air France hotel chain. Has both an indoor and outdoor pool. 4 Complexe Desjardins, enter at 4 Jeanne Mance St. (phone: 285-1450). Expensive.

De la Montagne – This relatively new 120-room hotel is within a stone's throw of the chic boutiques and restaurants in the Crescent Street–de la Montagne Street area. Its rooftop pool and terrace are popular for summer rendezvous, and its dining room, *Le Lutetia,* is highly regarded. 1430 de la Montagne St. (phone: 288-5656). Expensive.

Queen Elizabeth (Reine Elizabeth) – A king-size, 1,045-room property, it is the city's largest. With direct access to underground Place Ville Marie's shops and services and Canadian National's Central Station, it is one of the most conveniently located, too. In addition to the restaurants in the hotel itself, including the well-known *Beaver Club* (see *Eating Out*), the newly refurbished building features an elegant shopping arcade in the lower lobby, separate from the shops of Place Ville Marie. 900 René-Lévesque Blvd. W. (phone: 861-3511). Expensive.

Ramada Inn Centreville – Of the three *Ramada Inns* in the Montreal area, this is the most convenient to downtown. An outdoor pool and complimentary parking are among its attractions; 205 rooms. 1005 Guy St. (phone: 866-4611). Expensive.

Ritz Carlton – In the manner of the grand hotels of Europe, this 240-room hotel on tree-lined Sherbrooke Street caters to a loyal international clientele by providing personalized service (two staff members to each guest) and impeccable decor. This is one of the rare instances where a Ritz hostelry was actually inaugurated by M. Cesar Ritz himself. During the summer, lunch, tea, and dinner are served alfresco at the *Ritz Garden* restaurant, which overlooks the manicured lawn and flower-fringed duck pond in the center court of the hotel. 1228 Sherbrooke St. W. (phone: 842-4212). Expensive.

Le Shangrila – Opened in 1985, this high-rise hotel has a pleasant sidewalk café, *Le Jardinier,* 167 well-appointed rooms, and agreeable ambience. 3407 Peel Street (phone: 288-4141). Expensive.

Le Grand – An ambitious hotel with 737 rooms, a 40-foot-high atrium lobby with glass-enclosed elevators, an indoor pool, sauna, and massage room. *Chez Antoine,* an Art Deco oasis in the corridor linking the hotel to Place Victoria, serves an innovative menu featuring seafood and meat grilled over charcoal flavored with mesquite, applewood, sassafras, and hickory. *Le Tour de Ville* is the city's only revolving rooftop restaurant. 777 University St. (phone: 879-1370). Expensive to moderate.

Manoir LeMoyne – Just a few blocks from the Montreal Forum, this hotel has 286 rooms, most of which are actually apartments with fully equipped kitchens, dining alcoves, and spacious balconies. *Bellamy's* is its fairly good restaurant and piano bar. There's an indoor pool and sauna, too. 2100 de Maisonneuve Blvd. (phone: 931-8861). Expensive to moderate.

Ramada Renaissance Du Parc – The hub of another major office-apartment-shopping complex at the base of Mount Royal, this 465-room hotel, now a member of the Ramada Renaissance chain, has an attractive lobby lounge and piano bar, indoor and outdoor pools, sauna, and indoor tennis. The restaurant called *Puzzles* is a popular spot. 3625 Av. du Parc (phone: 288-6666). Expensive to moderate.

Château Versailles – A small, European-style hotel with 70 deluxe rooms, fast becoming a favorite with repeat visitors. The hotel only serves breakfast, but its advantage is being in an area abounding in good, moderately priced restaurants. 1659 Sherbrooke St. W. (phone: 933-3611). Moderate.

De l'Institut – Located near the University of Quebec, this 42-room hotel is part of the province's School of Tourism and is managed by teachers and students. Meals served here are said to be quite good. 3535 St. Denis (phone: 873-4163). Moderate.

Lord Berri – A relatively new 154-room hostelry close to the Berri Métro station and Voyageur bus terminal in the city's east end. The *Café-Bistro* restaurant offers a reasonably priced menu. 1199 Berri St., near Dorchester Blvd. E. (phone: 845-9236). Moderate.

EATING OUT: For the Gallic gourmandizer, that unique gastronomic malcontent for whom foreign means nothing but French, Montreal provides a cornucopia of delights comparable to anything available on the far side of the Atlantic. Here is truly the opportunity to have your crêpe and eat it too. The predominant cuisines are French and French Canadian, but many of Montreal's ethnic restaurants, as well as seafood and steakhouses, are excellent. Montrealers seem to live to eat and they have high dining standards; the ambience of a restaurant is as important a consideration as its food. Our choices reflect this native concern. Expect to pay $55 or more for a dinner for two in the expensive range; $25 to $50 in the moderate category; and under $25 in the inexpensive category. Prices do not include drinks, wine, or tips. The 10% provincial tax is applied to all meals of $2.75 ($3.25 CN) and up, and the average tip is 12 to 15%. By law, all menus must be posted outside the establishment. All telephone numbers are in the 514 area code unless otherwise indicated.

Beaver Club – As the name implies, this was once a private club, exclusively for those hearty souls who had journeyed to the Northwest Territories in search of furs. Now the public is welcome (at very high prices), though trophies and pelts from the early fur trading days still decorate the dining room. Nouvelle cuisine selections have been added to the already extensive menu. The bouillabaisse — made with a whole Canadian lobster, halibut, scallops, and fish stock thickened with butter — served with fresh greens is delicious. For dessert, don't pass up the delightful fresh fruit sherbets. Open daily. Reservations advised. Major credit cards. In the *Queen Elizabeth* hotel, 900 René-Lévesque Blvd. (phone: 861-3511). Expensive.

Les Chênets – A small, intimate French place, decorated with copper pots. Try the oysters from France (called Portuguese), mussels marinière, fresh Pacific salmon, pheasant with mushrooms — but anything is fine. The wine list is also good and includes 60 kinds of cognac. Pricey, but one of the finest meals in town. Open daily. Reservations advised. Major credit cards. 2075 Bishop St. (phone: 844-1842). Expensive.

Chez Delmo – Well-prepared seafood draws Montrealers to this restaurant in the financial district of Old Montreal. There is dining room service, and at lunchtime seafood is also served up at the Victorian-style mahogany bar. Closed Sundays and some holidays. Reservations advised. Major credit cards. 211 Notre Dame St. W. (phone: 849-4061). Expensive.

Chez St. Desjardins' – A Montreal favorite since 1892, it features a menu inspired by the sea. Open daily. Reservations advised. Major credit cards accepted. 1175 Mackay St. (phone: 866-9741). Expensive.

Chez la Mère Michel – In this fine old stone house converted to an attractive, dark-beamed, candlelit dining spot, French cuisine achieves authentic excellence. The lobster soufflé is a special treat, and don't miss a chance for a drink in the snug downstairs bar. Closed Sundays. Reservations necessary. Major credit cards. 1209 Guy St. (phone: 934-0473). Expensive.

Daberto – Probably Montreal's most sophisticated Italian restaurant, it overlooks the *Museum of Fine Arts* and offers up true culinary artistry of its own. Be sure to try shrimps à la Berci; also fine are any of a multitude of pasta dishes. Open daily. Reservations advised. Major credit cards. 1172 De La Montogne (phone: 866-2191). Expensive.

Gibby's – If you are after good steaks and atmosphere, try this spot in Old Montreal's restored, early-18th-century Youville Stables. While filling yourself on the large portions, you can take your time and enjoy the attractive stone-walled, beamed interior. Though most diners order a beef dish, there are other entrées as well, all accompanied by fresh, hot bread and a generous salad. Open daily. Reservations necessary. Major credit cards accepted. 298 Place d'Youville (phone: 282-1837). Expensive.

Les Halles – A special dining place in a converted, 2-story townhouse that has been divided into several intimate dining areas. You may be greeted at the door by an oversized cherub who will insist on planting the traditional French kiss of greeting on both your cheeks before letting you out of the foyer. That goes for both ladies and gentlemen. He will then lead you into one of several small dining alcoves and present a menu that is both classic and creative. Try the specialties such as *pamplemousse Marie Louise* (grapefruit stuffed with seafood) or the fine *tournedos*. Closed Sundays and holidays. Reservations necessary. Major credit cards accepted. 1450 Crescent St. (phone: 844-2328). Expensive.

La Marée – Owned by the same gentleman who operates *Le SaintAmable*, this establishment specializes in *fruits de mer*, as its name suggests. *Turbot au champagne*, imported French whitefish prepared in champagne, is one of the fine dishes. This restaurant is also housed in a carefully restored Old Montreal house on Jacques Cartier Square. Open daily, but generally closed Sundays during the winter. Reservations necessary. Major credit cards accepted. 404 Place Jacques-Cartier (phone: 861-8126). Expensive.

Le Saint Amable – Located in a lovely old stone house overlooking Place Jacques Cartier in the heart of Old Montreal, this French restaurant owned by Pierre Garcin has long held a high rank for its cuisine, service, and atmosphere. *Tournedos Opera* — filet mignon in a pastry crust — is a specialty. Open daily except Christmas. Reservations necessary. Major credit cards accepted. 188 Saint Amable St. (phone: 866-3471). Expensive.

Les Trois Arches – A highly rated restaurant about 15 minutes from downtown Montreal in suburban Pierrefonds. Located in a century-old graystone mansion, formerly the home of Canadian Army Brigadier General Meighen, its specialty is fine French cuisine. Of particular note are the *canard aux olives*, sorrel salmon, and sweetbread with truffles. Reservations advised. Major credit cards accepted. 11,131 Meighen St. (yes, that's the right street address) in Pierrefonds (phone: 683-8200). Expensive.

Atlantic Pavilion – This seafood establishment, with its classic nautical decor, dominates the atrium of the Alcan building. Service, even on busy Sunday evenings, is friendly and efficient. Among the best dishes are the grilled scampi, lobster thermidor, and Arctic char. Open daily. Reservations advised. Major credit cards accepted. 1188 Sherbrooke St. W. (phone: 285-1636). Expensive to moderate.

Auberge le Vieux Saint-Gabriel – Long favored for its good French Canadian food and old-time ambience, this restaurant rambles through an Old Montreal building that dates from fur-trading days, complete with a tunnel leading to a room (now a cozy bar) used to hide furs from raiding Indians. For a taste of old Quebec, this is the place. Open daily. Reservations advised. Major credit cards accepted. 426 Saint-Gabriel St. (phone: 878-3561). Expensive to moderate.

Bonaparte – An attractive little dining room in the heart of Vieux Montreal, this restaurant specializes in French cuisine and seafood. Ask for one of the balcony tables, overlooking the street. Reservations advised for lunch. Major credit cards accepted. 433 St. François Xavier St. (phone: 844-4368). Expensive to moderate.

Le Fadeau – Seventeenth-century ambience and excellent food and service are the fare at this classic French restaurant in an Old Montreal house. Selections from an excellent wine cellar complement the cuisine. Open daily. Reservations necessary. Major credit cards accepted. 423 St. Claude St. (phone: 878-3959). Expensive to moderate.

Le Mas des Oliviers – If you're gearing up for a night in Montreal's best disco area (Stanley, Mountain, and Bishop Sts.) start off the way Montrealers do — by having dinner here. Try the lamb dishes — they're Chef Jacques Muller's specialty. Open daily. Reservations necessary. Major credit cards accepted. 1216 Bishop St. (phone: 861-6733). Expensive to moderate.

Les Serres du Vieux Montréal – A greenhouse dining room that is always humming, particularly in the summer when cooling ceiling fans spin lazily overhead. Full-course dinners, generous salads, and quiche are the fare. Major credit cards accepted. 417 Saint-Pierre St. (phone: 288-9788). Expensive to moderate.

Arigato – The sushi and sashimi combinations at this Japanese restaurant draw a loyal lunchtime crowd. Reservations advised. Major credit cards accepted. 75 de la Gauchetière St. W., on the Chinatown Mall (phone: 395-2470). Moderate.

Le Caveau – French cuisine is served in this cozy little house in the heart of midtown. Checkered tablecloths and candlelight add an atmosphere of intimacy. The less expensive of the two menus offers good value and has almost the same selection as the regular menu. The *tournedos,* house wine, and crème caramel are all of high quality. Open daily. Reservations advised. Major credit cards accepted. 2063 Victoria St. (phone: 844-1624). Moderate.

Les Copines de Chine – A relatively new Chinese restaurant with an attractive setting in the tropical, plant-filled atrium of Place Dupuis. Its appetizing Szechwan dishes are served by an attentive staff. Closed Sundays and holidays. Major credit cards accepted. 870 de Maisonneuve Blvd. E.(phone: 842-8325). Moderate.

Le Latini – A different pasta dish is featured every day, and the veal specialties are tasty and tender. In summer, guests may dine alfresco on the new terrace. Closed Sundays. Major credit cards accepted. 1130 Jeanne Mance St., near *Complexe Desjardins* (phone: 861-3166). Moderate.

La Mer à Boire – Nestled in a historic house, this eatery serves hearty French-Canadian dishes beside a cozy hearth. The decor is rough-hewn, early Montreal, but the walls display an impressive collection of contemporary Quebec art. Major credit cards accepted. 429 Saint Vincent St. (phone: 397-9610). Moderate.

Le Paris – Yet another fine French restaurant with an atmosphere that is truly Parisian. Closed Sundays and holidays. Major credit cards accepted. 1812 Sainte-Catherine W. St. (phone: 937-4898). Moderate.

Le Petit Havre – A fine French restaurant in Old Montreal with so many faithful followers it's almost like a private club. Closed Sundays and holidays. Reservations advised. Major credit cards accepted. 443 St. Vincent (phone: 861-0581). Moderate.

Les Filles du Roy – Another popular tourist haunt for French-Canadian food in a 17th-century Quebec setting. The waitresses wear costumes fashioned after the period's "daughters of the king" who came to New France to marry eligible settlers. Open daily. Sunday brunch is a special treat. Reservations advised. Major credit cards accepted. 415 Bonsecours St. (phone: 849-3535). Moderate to inexpensive.

Bonsai – A Vietnamese restaurant named for the artistic miniature Japanese trees, it serves light meals accented with tasty soups and spring rolls. Ask for a table in the back dining room, which overlooks the Old Port. Closed Sundays. Major credit cards accepted. 138 St. Paul St. E. (phone: 861-6640). Inexpensive.

Chez Vito – In the Côte-des-Neiges area, near the University of Montreal, this popular place has fine Italian cuisine and a good disco upstairs. Open daily. No reservations. Major credit cards accepted. 5408-12 Côte-des-Neiges (phone: 735-3623). Inexpensive.

Dionysus – One of the better places in Montreal's "Greek ghetto." Authentic Greek food, decor, and atmosphere prevail, down to the bouzouki music playing in the background. Open daily. Reservations advised. Major credit cards accepted. 5301 Park Ave. (phone: 277-8940). Inexpensive.

Lung Fung – This Chinatown restaurant has an extensive Cantonese menu and is fully licensed. House specialties include shrimp on toast as an appetizer; "Great Vegetable Mix," a combination of Chinese stir-fried vegetables; and chicken stuffed with chopped meat in oyster sauce. Open daily. Reservations unnecessary. Major credit cards accepted. 81 Lagauchetière St. W. (phone: 866-2101). Inexpensive.

La Maison Greque – Very reasonable no-frills restaurant featuring *moussaka* and *brochette au poisson.* Diners must bring their own wine, but it's worth a stop at the liquor store when a meal for two costs about $13. Open daily. Major credit cards accepted. 450 Duluth St. E. (phone: 842-0969). Inexpensive.

Montreal Hebrew Delicatessen and Steak House – Known locally as *Schwartz's,* this deli is famous for its smoked meat (a sort of illegitimate product of the mating of corned beef and pastrami) and grilled steaks, and draws a cross section of Montrealers. You'll share a crowded table with other diners, and the French fries may be the best on this continent. No liquor license, but plenty of Dr. Brown's cream soda. Open daily. Closed Yom Kippur. No reservations. No credit cards accepted. 3895 St. Lawrence Blvd. (phone: 842-4813). Inexpensive.

Rotisserie Laurier – Chicken, Quebec style. Major credit cards accepted. 381 Laurier W. (phone: 273-3671). Inexpensive.

Stash's Café Bazaar – Just beside Notre-Dame Church in Old Montreal, this establishment specializes in Polish food. The decor is simple and the atmosphere friendly. Open daily. No reservations. Major credit cards. 461 Saint Sulpice St. (phone: 861-2915). Inexpensive.

Sucrerie de la Montagne – Anyone with a sweet tooth should make the trip to this sugaring-off spot 20 miles (32 km) southwest of the city. The maple sugar feast includes *tourtiere* (meat pie) and baked beans, finished off with the traditional maple syrup pie, more commonly served in Quebec City. A full meal runs about $6.50 per person. Open 11 AM to 8 PM all year. Groups need reservations. 300 Rang St-Georges, off Route 40 (phone: 451-5204). Inexpensive.

Swensen's – An outlet of the San Francisco–based chain of old-fashioned ice cream parlors is serving some of the richest, creamiest ice cream found from the American West to the Canadian East. There are 27 flavors to choose from, including sticky chewy chocolate, black raspberry cheesecake, butterscotch marble, swiss orange chocolate chip — one better than the next. Open daily. At the corner of St. Catherine St. W. and Mansfield Ave. (phone: 861-5017). Inexpensive.

OTTAWA

Ottawa is Canada's national capital. Everything else about the city is merely supporting evidence for that simple but essential fact of Ottawa life.

Ottawa's role as the home base for the national government is so crucial to the city's existence, in fact, that if Queen Victoria had taken the expected course in 1858 and named one of the then more important cities — the front-runners were Toronto and Montreal — as the new capital of the merged colonies of Upper and Lower Canada (present-day Ontario and Quebec), Ottawa today would probably be just another dowdy, over-the-hill lumbering town. Instead, the capricious ruler chose Ottawa, encouraged by some wildly romantic watercolors of the community and fed up with all the petty bickering over which backwoods colonial outpost was more deserving of the honor. Her choice transformed the place overnight from a brawling, sprawling mill town into a reluctantly austere and dignified city. Nine years later, the colonies joined with a couple of Britain's other North American possessions to form Canada. Ottawa remained the capital of the new country because the government buildings, erected at great expense, were already in place and because few in the fledgling nation could stomach the thought of another interminable battle over which city should be the seat of the government.

The city is situated on the southern bank of the Ottawa River at its junction with the Rideau River. The impressive Parliament Buildings rise from a hill above the Ottawa River to dominate the surrounding area and announce Ottawa's federal prominence in Gothic grandeur. Yet, despite its aura of power, Ottawa is very much a city of human proportions, with a population of just over 750,000 (the national capital region encompasses Hull, across the river in the province of Quebec). Because of its national significance, it has amenities other cities of its size might not be able to support. The city's role as the host for foreign embassies means almost unlimited access to the world's cuisines, and for a city of its size, it has a disproportionate number of good restaurants. French and French-Canadian cuisine are the specialties, but visitors can sample ethnic food at an eclectic selection of restaurants, from Russian and Irish to Mexican and Lebanese. Culturally, the city is well set up. The *National Arts Centre* is a first-rate facility with an acoustically superb opera house, a theater, and a studio which draw Canadian and international stars. Cerebral stimulation is available at the *National Gallery of Canada* or at any of Ottawa's several national museums, and there's enough hiking, biking, skiing, and swimming to exhaust even the most physically fit.

Ottawa's current eminence, however, stands in stark contrast to its beginnings. If its selection as Canada's capital is not the stuff of heroic legend, its early history is even less awe-inspiring. The Outaouac Indians (from whom the city takes its name) used the area as a regular stopover on their nomadic jaunts, but the unwelcoming climate — Ottawa can be as hot and muggy in summer as Lagos, Nigeria, and colder in winter than Moscow — discouraged permanent settlement. Samuel de Champlain, the French explorer, paused briefly near the site of the present Parliament Buildings in 1613 to admire the Chaudière Falls, pronounced himself much impressed, then hurried on in search of more interesting and rewarding discoveries.

Finally, in 1796, a hardy, puritanical New Englander, Philemon Wright, dragged along family and friends to a spot on the north side of the Ottawa River (now Hull), where he established a small settlement. Thirteen years later, another group began to hack out sprawling farms from the forests, swamp, and beaver meadow on the site that is now the city of Ottawa.

These settlers were joined in 1826 by Lieutenant-Colonel John By and the Royal Engineers, a rag-tag band of Irish laborers, army engineers, and British veterans of the Napoleonic and American wars who had been assigned the task of constructing a canal from Ottawa to Kingston, Ontario. Although the nearly 125-mile-long system of locks, dams, rivers, and lakes was originally intended to serve as a secure military route from Montreal to Kingston in the event of American attack, the threat never materialized, and the canal became a commercial venture almost as soon as it was completed in 1832. Today it is called the Rideau Canal.

Its good location at the midpoint of the then main water route between Montreal and the growing cities on the Great Lakes briefly gave Ottawa a sense of commercial purpose. That, in turn, attracted a group of American lumber barons, who set up mills, hired workers, and jammed up the Ottawa River with gigantic log booms.

It was this rambunctious wilderness town that Queen Victoria, with the flourish of a royal prerogative, made into a capital city. The choice was not a popular one, and, after the new legislature's first session in 1866, one disgruntled politician wrote to a friend that there was "an almost unanimous desire . . . to get away from Ottawa as soon as practicable."

Despite such carping, the city remained the capital and flourished. Under the watchful eye of a national government anxious to make it a vibrant hybrid of Canada's two founding cultures (35% of Ottawa's residents are of French descent, although most are bilingual), Ottawa has become — as officials like to boast — "a city of urban grace in which all Canadians can take pride."

Partly because it couldn't hope to compete with the elegant European sophistication of Montreal or the bustling cultural diversity of Toronto, Ottawa has staked out its own claim as a living, breathing model of what human-oriented urban planning is all about.

Modern Ottawa is a family place. The city is festooned with parks and open spaces, dotted with six national museums and many historic sites, and crowned with the *National Arts Centre,* a sparkling $36 million cultural showplace. Sprawling right in the middle of the city is a 1,200-acre experimental farm, with real cows and squealing pigs to delight city-bred kids and botanical and ornamental gardens to satisfy quieter tastes. For those who would rather act than observe, 65 miles of bicycle paths meander from the downtown core to the city's residential suburbs; in the winter, a 5-mile stretch of the Rideau Canal, extending from the Parliament Buildings to the thoroughly modern campus of Carleton University, is transformed into the world's longest skating rink. To complete Ottawa's year-round picture, the city is neatly wrapped by a unique 2½-mile-wide greenbelt of dairy and beef farms, open spaces, and hobby gardens for the capital's apartment dwellers.

Ottawa is, ultimately, as much a pleasant state of mind as it is a city in the conventional sense, and the result is an environment that is as rewarding to visit as it is to live in.

From the real-life theater of the daily House of Commons Question Period, which allows opposition politicians to grill the government of the day, to the serene beauty of Gatineau Park just 15 minutes away by car, Canada's capital — once snidely referred to as "Westminister in the wilderness" — measures up to true capital status.

OTTAWA AT-A-GLANCE

SEEING THE CITY: The best place to get an overview of the capital is from the lookout of the Peace Tower, a Parliament building, on Wellington Street, in the center of the city. Just a touch over 300 feet high, the tower opens up a panoramic view extending 40 miles in all directions. To the north stand the new concrete and glass government buildings rising up from the Quebec side of the Ottawa River; beyond lies Gatineau Park, an 88,000-acre wilderness and recreation area popular with locals and visitors alike. To the east, you can catch a glimpse of the Rideau Canal. In the summer, pleasure boats wend their way along the calm channel; in the winter, skaters glide along its frozen length. To the south and west is the city itself, graced here, there, and everywhere by lush green parkland. Free English and French tours of the Parliamentary Centre Block, which include a trip to the top of the Peace Tower, start at the Info-Tent on the east side of the Centre Block. Tours are conducted daily (except Christmas and New Year's Day) from 9 AM to 4:30 PM (in the summer until 9 PM).

SPECIAL PLACES: Many of Ottawa's most interesting sights, including the must-see *National Gallery,* lie within a casual stroll of no more than a couple of blocks from the Parliament Buildings. Any downtown habitué will gladly point you toward the place of your choosing.

DOWNTOWN

Parliament Buildings – These impressive Gothic structures are Canada's single most famous landmark. Erected on a promontory above the Ottawa River, the Parliament Hill complex once housed the entire federal administration but now serves primarily as the meeting place of federal politicians. The East and West Blocks of the Parliament Buildings (the only original, century-old structures remaining are on the Centre Block and were rebuilt after a disastrous fire in 1916) as well as the nearby Confederation Building contain offices for members of Parliament and are not open to the public. Visitors are welcome, however, to tour the Centre Block, which houses not only the chambers for the House of Commons and the Senate but also the opulent, domed Parliamentary Library and the magnificent Peace Tower. (Tour details are given above.) You can also visit the newly renovated East Block, which contains the old cabinet-meeting rooms. When Parliament is in session, you can watch the action from the public galleries overlooking the House of Commons and Senate chambers. At 10 AM daily from the end of June through Labor Day, the lawns in front of the Centre Block are the scene of a Changing the Guard ceremony, involving 125 soldiers dressed in bright scarlet uniforms topped with giant bearskin busbies. In spring the tulip gardens are spectacular. The tulips were given to Canada by Queen Juliana of the Netherlands to commemorate the sacrifices made by the Canadian First Army in the liberation of Holland and to thank Canada for protecting the Dutch Royal Family during World War II. Open daily. Free. Wellington St. between Bank and Elgin (phone: 995-7771).

Rideau Canal – This 123-mile-long canal, linking Kingston on Lake Ontario with Ottawa, was constructed between 1826 and 1832 on the recommendation of the Duke of Wellington to provide safe lines of communication between Montreal and the new settlements on the lake in the event of war with the US. Despite its military origins, this inland waterway is now used as a recreational facility year-round. Much of the old stonework on the original locks and dams remains. Flower gardens, tall trees, and bike paths used by hikers and cross-country skiers in the winter line the 5-mile stretch in central Ottawa. During the summer, many Ottawans sail and canoe on the canal. From spring to fall, a 1½-hour boat tour cruises the central stretch, departing daily between 11:30 AM and 8:30 PM from a landing near the Government Conference Centre. In the winter, the canal is transformed into an excellently maintained 5-mile-long skating rink. South from the Ottawa River between Colonel By Dr. and Queen Elizabeth Driveway.

Rideau Centre – It cost $250 million, covers 14 acres, contains a convention center that can seat 4,000, boasts a 475-room luxury hotel, and has a multilevel shopping complex with over 200 stores, 18 restaurants, and 3 movie houses. On top of it, literally, there's a 5-acre park with winding paths, park benches, and real trees. The center has had an impressive impact on the heart of Ottawa, reversing the trend begun in the 60s when the city bled into the suburbs every night at 5 o'clock. 50 Rideau St. (phone: 236-6565).

Sparks Street Mall – An outdoor mall — five city blocks filled with boutiques, department stores, historic buildings, rock gardens, sculptures, live entertainment, and the best people-watching real estate in the capital — is Canada's first permanent pedestrian-only street, recently spruced up by a major facelift. The *Four Corners,* 93 Sparks St., and the *Davis Agency Canadiana Shop,* 203 Sparks St., are musts for Canadian crafts — everything from handwoven British Columbia blankets to Inuit carvings. During the summer, the mall comes alive with flower peddlers, fruit vendors, musicians, street corner orators, and armies of lunch hour civil servants trying to catch a little sun. 240 Sparks is a giant glass enclosure housing federal government offices, a variety of lunch-on-a-bun spots, and stores selling elegant apparel. Open daily. Sparks St. and Elgin to Lyon.

Byward Market – This market has been an Ottawa institution since the mid-1800s, when local farmers first set up their stalls and began peddling fresh produce to city slickers. In recent years, the farmers have been joined by local artists and craftspeople who display their wares in the renovated market building. The market also houses an impressive array of specialty foreign grocery stores, fish markets, cheese shops, and cozy restaurants. On summer nights, its cobblestone courtyards and side streets become impromptu stages for sidewalk entertainers. The market itself operates daily May through October. Between Clarence and George Sts.

Nicholas Street Jail – Ottawa's last public hanging took place here in 1869, when the country's only political assassin, Patrick Whelan, was strung up for the murder of D'Arcy McGee, a member of Parliament. The forbidding structure served as the local lock-up for more than a century. In 1972 it was converted into a hostel for young travelers (see *Best in Town*). A 40-minute public tour every Sunday at 2 PM lets you view the tiny 3½-by-9-foot cells. Open daily. Free. 75 Nicholas St. (phone: 235-2595).

National Museum of Natural Sciences – With 2 million zoological specimens, from the daspletosaurus (a 4-ton, 28-foot long tyrannosaur) on up the evolutionary ladder, this museum is particularly fascinating for children. The building that houses the exhibits is the castle-like structure where the House of Commons met after the Parliament Buildings burned down in 1916. Metcalfe at McLeod (phone: 996-3102).

National Museum of Civilization – The main hall of this new $225 million museum is the length of a football field and 5 stories tall. Inside are a West Coast Indian village and rain forest, and a domed theater shows IMAX and OMNIMAX movies — the former projects crystal-clear images on a huge screen, while the latter has a 19,000-pound wrap-around screen. The museum also offers changing exhibitions, festivals, a resource center, and a children's museum. Admission charge. 100 Laurier St., next to the *National Gallery* (phone: 995-8287).

National Gallery of Canada – A veritable glass mountain illuminated by natural light, the gallery is a breathtaking work of architecture — a major attraction in itself. It houses more than 25,000 paintings, sculptures, and drawings, including many by the world's great masters; the international photograph collection numbers around 15,000 pieces. The Canadian collection has works by the famous Group of Seven, including Paul Kane's paintings of native people and Cornelius Kreigoff's portrayals of pioneer life. Closed Mondays from November to May. No admission charge on Thursdays. Sussex Drive (phone: 990-1985).

SUBURBS

Government House – Diagonally across the street from the prime minister's home is the 88-acre estate of the governor-general, the Queen's official Canadian representative. In addition to a rambling mansion for the governor-general and a guesthouse for the Queen and other foreign dignitaries, the tree-lined grounds also have gardens, a skating rink, and even a cricket pitch to add a little touch of Britain. Guided tours of the house and grounds are available by appointment only (phone: 992-5473).

Laurier House – Purchased by Canada's seventh prime minister, Sir Wilfrid Laurier, after his election in 1896, this 18-room brick house was also home to the tenth of the country's fifteen prime ministers — Laurier's fellow Liberal, William Lyon Mackenzie King. King was a popular leader and held power longer than any other prime minister, serving from 1921 to 1930 and again from 1935 to 1948. King bequeathed the house to the people of Canada; he died in 1950. Now the house is a showcase of the furniture and personal effects (right down to King's shaving mug in the bathroom) of the two men. Closed Mondays. Free. 335 Laurier Ave. E (phone: 992-8142).

Canadian War Museum – Exhibits here are related to Canada's military history. Displays include skulls taken by the Indians as the spoils of war, a mock-up of a German bunker overlooking Normandy's beaches on D-day, and Goering's staff car. Open daily. Free. 330 Sussex Dr. (phone: 992-2774).

Central Experimental Farm – Established in 1886 as the headquarters of the research branch of the federal Department of Agriculture, the farm sprawls over 1,200 acres within the city limits. The spectacular ornamental gardens are a favorite spot for local wedding photographs, and the Arboretum is a showplace of rare trees. You can take in the display of more than 10 million insect samples in the farm's Neatby Building or visit the dairy barn and piggery. From spring through fall, you can jump aboard a horse-drawn wagon for a free tour of the grounds weekdays at 10 AM and 2 PM, weather permitting. Open daily. Free. Prince of Wales Dr. between the Driveway and Base Line Rd. (phone: 995-5222).

Rockcliffe Park Village – A community of 22,000, set among stately mansions and narrow, tree-lined streets, it is the city's most elegant residential area. The village's first home was Rideau Hall, built in 1838. It has been the residence of all Canada's governor-generals since Confederation. Many of the other residents are also government officials (close to 600 diplomats live here). Most of the ambassadors' residences are identifiable by their country's emblems decorating the entranceways.

National Museum of Science and Technology – This popular museum encourages involvement; visitors can clamber aboard a train and ring the bell of a ship's wheelhouse. Exhibits range from a display of early motor cars to a non-radioactive, charred chunk of the Soviet satellite that crashed in northern Canada in 1978. Closed Mondays during the winter. No admission charge. 1867 St. Laurent Blvd. (phone: 998-4566).

National Aviation Museum – Housed in dilapidated World War II hangars until 1988, this fine collection of aircraft dating back to the turn of the century is now displayed in an $18 million showplace at Rockcliffe Airport. More than 50 aircraft are exhibited in this new building, including the *Silver Dart*, the first plane ever flown in the British Empire, at Baddeck, Nova Scotia, in 1909. Closed Mondays during the winter; open daily the rest of the year. No admission charge. Rockcliffe Airport off St. Laurent Blvd. (phone: 998-4566).

Vincent Massey Park – This spot was named after the first native-born Governor-General of Canada. Offering a pleasant break from sightseeing, these 52 acres of country right in the city provide cycling paths, barbecue pits, picnic tables, ample parking, and plenty of grass and trees in which to frolic. You can also enjoy cross-country skiing and tobogganing in winter. Open daily. Free. Base Line Rd. west of Riverside Dr.

Gatineau Park – An 88,000-acre wilderness and recreation area that has more than 60 miles of hiking and cross-country trails, 40 lakes for fishing, swimming, and boating, plenty of camping and picnic facilities, and a lion's share of the area's beautiful scenery. On the drive that wanders through the rolling hills of the park is Moorside, the summer home of former Canadian Prime Minister William Lyon Mackenzie King. The grounds are decorated with the ruins of old British and Ottawa buildings. Delightful lunches, afternoon tea, and dinners are served here. Open noon to 6:30 PM daily, from mid-May to mid-October. The park is just 15 minutes from the Parliament Buildings on the Quebec side of the Ottawa River (phone: 239-5000).

■**EXTRA SPECIAL:** Every evening at dusk from late May to early September a sound-and-light show, using 600 powerful spotlights and a synchronized sound-track, brings Canada's history to life on the grounds of Parliament Hill. The National Capital Commission spent 3 years and $2.5 million developing the show. Admission is free. From 10 AM to 4:30 PM all summer, actors in period costume mingle with tourists on Parliament Hill and present historical vignettes. Some are controversial, and spectators are encouraged to heckle. Call 239-5000 for more information.

SOURCES AND RESOURCES

TOURIST INFORMATION: Canada's Capital Visitor and Convention Bureau, 65 Elgin St., in the *National Arts Centre* (phone: 237-5158), is where you'll find all manner of maps, brochures, and helpful hints. The National Capital Commission, 7th floor, 161 Laurier Ave. W., maintains two visitor centers where you can pick up maps of the various NCC-operated cycling, hiking, and nature trails in the region. They are located at 14 Metcalfe St. (opposite the Parliament Buildings, phone: 239-5000) and at 25 Laurier in Hull (phone: 819-778-2229). Both centers are open weekdays from 9 AM to 5 PM and in the summer until 9 PM. From May to September, the NCC staffs an Info-Tent on Parliament Hill.

Local Coverage – The *Ottawa Citizen* and the *Ottawa Sun*, both dailies; *Ottawa Magazine*, monthly; *What's On in Ottawa*, monthly magazine. Ottawa also has eight local radio stations, as well as four TV stations and two cable TV centers.

Food – Two area dining guides are *Dining Out in Ottawa-Hull and Environs* by

Marilyn Mannes (Borealis Press, about $3.80, and *The Consumer Guide of Restaurants of the National Capital Region* (SERPA Publications; about $4, which lists nearly 1,200 restaurants. The *Ottawa Citizen* has restaurant reviews and publishes an excellent restaurant ratings list twice a year (available free through hotels).

Telephone – The area code for Ottawa is 613; the area code for Hull is 819.

Sales Tax – The sales tax in the region is 8%. (Note: Visitors from the US are eligible, under certain conditions, for a sales tax refund on accumulated purchases of $100 or more and a rebate of what they may have paid in hotel and motel tax. Stores and tourist centers can provide details.)

Currency – All prices are quoted in US dollars unless otherwise indicated.

TIPPING: Taxi drivers are generally given $2 to $4 (CN), depending on the length of the trip. Leave a 10 to 15% percent tip in restaurants. Hotel maids should usually be given $1 (CN) per day, and bellboys and airport porters get about $2 (CN); if you have more than three bags, give more.

CLIMATE: Ottawa's weather is extremely variable. The temperature has been known to top 98F (37C) at the height of summer and to plummet to −25F (−31C) in the depths of winter. The warmest month is July and the coldest is January; there is rainfall about 100 days a year and snow during another 45.

GETTING AROUND: Daytime downtown parking is notoriously expensive, so look for the less expensive parking lots just outside the core area.

Bus – Although many places of interest are within walking distance, especially in summer, try the bus system anyway. The $450 million high-speed, buses-only Transitway is a novelty as well as a way of beating traffic jams. Regular runs from 6 AM to midnight. OC Transpo, the city bus agency, offers tourists special rates. For information, call 741-4390.

Sightseeing Tours – It's possible to view this lovely city by earth, water, or air. *OC Transpo/Gray Line* (phone: 748-4426) offers excellent sightseeing bus tours of the city, starting near the *Château Laurier* daily on the hour from 10 AM to 7 PM, early May through late October. *Picadilly Bus Tours* (phone: 235-7674) offers tours of the city on London double-decker buses from Confederation Square (near Parliament Hill) from May 1 to October 23. Another wheeled conveyance to consider are the rickshaws of *Velvet Wheels,* pulled skillfully by fit young students who literally provide a running commentary. *Paul's Boat Lines* (phone: 733-5186) cruises the Ottawa River and Rideau Canal all summer; *Ottawa Riverboat Company* (phone: 232-4888) has classy moonlight dinner-dance cruises aboard its Edwardian-style motor vessel, the *Senator,* and party and brunch cruises aboard the larger *Sea Prince II.* Head toward Confederation Square, and ticket sellers for both companies will find you. Riding in hot air balloons has become a popular way of seeing the city from the sky, and five companies offer such excursions: *Alpha* (phone: 234-1221); *Great Canadian* (phone: 833-3101); *High Time* (phone: 745-2936); *Ottawa Balloon Adventures* (phone: 749-5333); and *Windborne* (phone: 233-1232). For those who prefer to keep their feet on the ground, daily walking tours are organized during the summer by the NCC (phone: 239-5000). For a nominal charge these expeditions explore areas of the Lower Town that are off-limits to traffic.

Taxi – All cabs in Ottawa are metered. Cab stands are located at major hotels. Otherwise, call *Blue Line* (phone: 238-1111) or *Capital* (phone: 746-2233). Hailing a cab is an uncommon practice in Ottawa.

Car Rental – All the major North American firms are represented: *Avis,* 320 Queen St. (phone: 238-3421); *Budget,* 443 Somerset W. (phone: 232-1526); *Hertz,* Ottawa International Airport (phone: 521-3294).

MUSEUMS: For complete descriptions of the *National Museum of Science and Technology,* the *National Aeronautical Collection,* the *National Museum of Civilization,* the *National Museum of Natural Sciences,* the *Canadian War Museum,* and the *National Gallery of Canada,* see *Special Places.* If you're not thoroughly exhausted by these, another notable museum is *Bytown Museum* (this is the city's oldest building and has displays of early Ottawa), on the Rideau Canal, under the bridge next to the *Château Laurier* (phone: 234-4570). Open Mondays through Saturdays from mid-May through September. Free. Also worth a visit is the *Currency Museum,* a few blocks west at 245 Sparks Street (phone: 782-8914), and (also nearby) the *National Postal Museum* at 365 Laurier. Both are open year-round. Free.

SPECIAL EVENTS: The 10-day *Winterlude* celebration, held every February on the Rideau Canal, includes a parade, ice sculptures, sleigh rides, harness races on ice, and other events. Begun in 1977, it is one of Canada's biggest winter attractions, capped off on the final day by an international 55-km (88-mile) cross-country ski race in Gatineau Park. During the weeklong *Festival of Spring,* held every May, the city dazzles with millions of colorful tulips as well as crafts exhibits, fairs, concerts, boat shows, and community events. Other summer highlights include *Canada Day* (July 1), the *Jazz Festival,* during the first 2 weeks of July, and the *International Cycling Festival* in Hull, during the first 2 weeks of August. The *Ottawa Exhibition,* featuring an agricultural display, games of chance, rides, entertainment, and craft exhibitions, takes place at the end of August. Autumn brings the *Festival of Arts* for 2 weeks in October.

SHOPPING: In addition to the Sparks Street Mall described in *Special Places,* there are a number of other prime shopping areas. Most notable is the downtown area's Rideau Centre with 220 stores. Place de Ville, 320 Queen, an underground concourse linking the *Skyline* and *Holiday Inn* (Ottawa Centre hotels), houses 20 shops. L'Esplanade Laurier, 181 Bank St., has 12 clothing boutiques, 6 restaurants and delis, and 12 craft and hobby shops as well as a pharmacy and a liquor store. The main suburban malls are Bayshore, at the western end of the Queensway, with 90 stores, including *The Bay* and *Eaton's* department stores; and the St. Laurent Shopping Centre, just off the St. Laurent Blvd. exit of the Queensway, which has 160 shops, including another branch of *The Bay* department store.

SPORTS: Though Ottawa has its share of spectator sports, it is much more a city of doers than watchers.
  Biking – The National Capital Commission maintains more than 65 miles of trails. Bikes can be rented from *Rent-A-Bike* (phone: 233-0268). The best places to ride are on the Colonel By and the Ottawa River Parkways, which wind around the city. On Sunday mornings they are closed to auto traffic.
  Football – The Ottawa *Rough Riders,* a professional team in the Canadian Football League, play home games in Lansdowne Park at the *Civic Centre* (phone: 563-4551).
  Golf – The NCC maintains two public 18-hole courses, the *Champlain* on Aylmer Rd. (phone: 777-0449) and the *Capital Golf Course* on Rte. 31 (phone: 521-2612), while more than 30 private clubs within an hour's drive of downtown Ottawa have greens fees.
  Hiking – Information on trails, including Sasparilla Trail, especially designed for the aged and handicapped, is available from the NCC or the Ontario Ministry of Natural Resources (phone: 992-4231). There are bird-watching trails starting at the *Ottawa-Carleton Conservation Centre* (phone: 828-3620). One trail stretches 125 miles (201 km) from the outskirts of Ottawa to Kingston, Ontario (phone: 828-1679, for information).

Hockey – The Ottawa area has two Junior A teams. The Ottawa *67s* (phone: 232-6767) play at the *Civic Centre* in Lansdowne Park and the *Hull Olympiques* (phone: 819-777-2791) play at *Guertin Arena* in Hull.

Horse Racing – Two racetracks offer harness racing: *Rideau-Carleton Raceway* (from July through November only), on the southern edge of Ottawa (phone: 822-2211); and the *Connaught Park Raceway* (year-round), in Hull (phone: 819-771-6111).

Jogging – Ottawa has many wonderful jogging paths. Among them are two that run along either side of the Rideau Canal, each about 5 miles long. There is also a path that runs parallel to the Ottawa River Parkway.

Skating – During the winter, the Rideau Canal freezes and is transformed into a 5-mile-long outdoor skating rink, stretching south from the Ottawa River between Colonel By Drive and Queen Elizabeth Driveway. During the day and at night, when the rink is lighted, thousands of people skate on what is the world's longest outdoor skating rink; in the morning, some people even skate to work.

Skiing – *Camp Fortune* in the Gatineau Hills is only minutes from downtown Ottawa on the new Hwy. 5 (phone: 819-827-1717). In addition, the region has numerous downhill courses, including *Edelweiss* (phone: 819-459-2859) and *Vorlage* (phone: 819-459-2301), both in Wakefield; *Mont Cascades* on Hwy. 307 (phone: 819-827-0301); and *Mt. Pakenham* on Rtes. 17 and 29 (phone: 624-5290). All of these places rent skis and offer instruction. There are also more than 60 miles of cross-country ski trails in the Gatineau Hills.

Soccer – Now the leading sport in the region, with 14,000 registered players, soccer games are played throughout the city from May to October. The *Ottawa Intrepid* plays in the professional Canadian Soccer League at the *Terry Fox Stadium* on Riverside Drive. See local papers for game times, or phone 722-7774.

Tennis – Free courts are located throughout the city, many of them with floodlights for night play. Call the city recreation department for information (phone: 563-3222).

Water Sports – Canoes and paddleboats can be rented at many locations, including the Rideau Canal on Fifth Ave. and Dows Lake at the southern end of the main stretch of the canal (phone: 232-1001). Sailboat rentals and lessons are available on the Rideau and Ottawa rivers (phone: 733-5100). There's good swimming at Lac Phillippe, Lac Lapeche, and Meech Lake in the Gatineau Hills, though all three tend to get crowded and the NCC has introduced daily fees for cars and motorcycles. Ontario and Quebec require fishing licenses, which are available for a modest fee at most fishing tackle stores.

THEATER: For a complete list of current offerings and performance schedules, check the local publications. The *National Arts Centre* maintains one repertory company that performs in French. Touring companies often appear at one of the *NAC*'s three theaters, 65 Elgin St. (for information, call 237-4440). The *Ottawa Little Theatre* presents amateur productions with a professional flair in a 510-seat modern hall at 400 King Edward Ave. (phone: 233-8948). The *Great Canadian Theatre Company*, 910 Gladstone (phone: 236-5192), has a reputation for doing strong theme plays. *Théâtre de L'Ile*, 1 Rue Wellington in Hull (phone: 819-771-6669), stages popular works in French.

MUSIC: Canada's *National Symphony Orchestra*, the local *Ottawa Symphony Orchestra*, and many guest artists perform at the *National Arts Centre*, 65 Elgin St. (phone: 237-4440). The *Orpheus Operatic Society* stages musicals at the High School of Commerce Auditorium, Rochester St. at the Queensway. (phone: 729-4318).

NIGHTCLUBS AND NIGHTLIFE: No more jokes about Ottawa rolling up the sidewalks at 6 PM. The city after dark has changed beyond recognition in recent years, with nightclubs offering everything from the big band sound to hot jazz, from male strippers to Second City–style comedy. The once dreary Elgin and Somerset streets downtown are now stretches of chic sidewalk restaurants and boutiques, competing with the lively Byward Market area for attention, particularly on warm summer nights. *Barrymore's,* at 323 Bank has the happy knack for booking biggies before they become expensive (Tina Turner and the rock group *U2,* for example), and the *Beachcomber Room* at the *Talisman Motor Inn* has live groups as well as a DJ most nights. Piano bars proliferate: *Perrier's* (*Delta* hotel); *Amoretto's,* 366 Lisgar; *Lautrec's* (*Holiday Inn,* Kent St.); *Lynn's,* 85 O'Connor; and *Tramps,* 53 William St. For the latest information on jazz anywhere in the city, call the Jazzline (phone: 232-7755). The *Downstairs Club,* 207 Rideau St., and the *Rainbow Bistro,* 76 Murray, are lively blues spots. Folk and country can be heard live on different nights at the *Bank Café,* 294 Bank St.; *Bayshore* hotel, 2980 Carling Ave.; *Blackburn Arms* restaurant, 2586 Innes Rd.; *Butler* hotel, 112 Montreal Rd.; *Caps Pub,* Eastview Shopping Centre; and at least 15 other spots. Dance bars include *Friends and Company* at 221 Rideau St.; *Grand Central,* 141 George St.; *Impressions,* 3700 Richmond; and *Stoney Monday's* at 62 York St. *Astralight* on St. Laurent Blvd. is a no-alcohol dance spot for teens and is — to the surprise of many adults — enormously popular. Top dinner-dance spots in town include the *Canadian Grill* at the *Chateau Laurier* hotel; *Talk of the Town,* 50 Gloucester St.; *Villa Lucia Supper Place,* 3430 Carling Ave.; and *La Ronde* at the *Holiday Inn,* Kent St. *Skit Row* (292 Elgin) and *Yuk Yuk's* (88 Albert St.) present wild comedy.

BEST IN TOWN

CHECKING IN: Because Ottawa is almost always playing host to conventions and conferences, there are plenty of hotels and motels. But be warned — if there are a number of conventions in town at once, you may have trouble finding a room downtown. Expect to pay $72 or more for a double room (sometimes less on weekends) in the establishments listed as expensive; between $47 and $72 for a moderately priced room; and under $47 (as low as about $8 at the hostel) in those places classed as inexpensive. All telephone numbers are in the 613 area code unless otherwise indicated.

Château Laurier – This is the flagship hotel of the venerable Canadian National hotel chain. Named for former Prime Minister Sir Wilfrid Laurier, the hotel opened its doors in 1912. Its 500 rooms, including a number of ornate suites, have the comfortable feel of aged whiskey and fine cigars. Naturally, this is the favorite Ottawa hotel of Canada's Establishment, and you'll probably spot Canada's movers and shakers being very sedate and dignified over lunch in the hotel's ritzy *Canadian Grill* or cocktails in the elegant *Zoe's* lounge. The hotel has an indoor pool. On Confederation Sq. at Rideau and Elgin (phone: 232-6411). Expensive.

Four Seasons – Built by an innovative local millionaire-developer in the late 1960s, this hotel is the epitome of modern comfort, and its 236 rooms are the city's most expensive. A fashionable dining room and an indoor-outdoor wine bar compete for attention. It also has a small indoor pool, whirlpool bath, and sauna. 150 Albert St. (phone: 238-1500). Expensive.

Radisson – Formerly the *Holiday Inn Ottawa Center,* this revised edition is more upscale than its predecessor. A modern high-rise, the hotel has 504 spacious rooms that come equipped with such high-tech novelties as TV sets that will display your bill at the touch of a button and mini-bars that can be locked by a computer at the front desk (for times when the kids are by themselves). Other amenities include a pool and fitness club; *La Ronde,* the revolving rooftop restaurant; and an underground shopping concourse. *Café Toulouse* is a popular lunch spot, with outdoor tables in summer, and *Lautrec's* piano bar is a pleasant place for cocktails. 100 Kent (phone: 238-1122). Expensive.

Skyline – Overshadowed somewhat by the opening of several new hotels in the late 70s, the 450-room *Skyline* is now enjoying renewed popularity. One reason is its special July-August rate (roughly two-thirds the regular rate). Another is its proximity to Parliament Hill and the center of things. A third is its restaurants, *Henry VIII* and *Le Trianon,* both popular for lunch and dinner; the *Light Affair* serves breakfast, lunch, and dinner. 101 Lyon St. (phone: 237-3600). Expensive.

Westin – Opened in the fall of 1983 as part of a vast new shopping and convention complex, this 24-story hotel has 475 rooms (10 specially equipped for the handicapped), in addition to a pool, gym, hot tub, and squash courts. Its restaurants serve good, moderately priced food as well as expensive haute cuisine. At lobby level, the hotel connects with Rideau Centre. 11 Colonel By Dr. (phone: 560-7000). Expensive.

Beacon Arms – Dropped from our listings a few years ago because it had become seedy and rundown, this 158-room Ottawa landmark has bounced back thanks to a top-to-bottom renovation. Considering its location, only a few blocks from Parliament Hill, the rates are a bargain. 88 Albert St. (phone: 235-1413). Moderate.

Cartier Place – One of an increasing number of apartment hotels springing up in Ottawa and offering good facilities at rates below those of the major hotels. There are 132 apartments (studios and 1- and 2-bedrooms) available for any length of stay; maid service included. 180 Cooper St. (phone: 236-5000). Moderate.

Talisman – A 10-minute drive from downtown Ottawa, this motor hotel is a very attractive spot with 2 pools, pleasant restaurants (with live entertainment most nights), and nearly 300 rooms equipped with "honor" bars. Guests have free access to the facilities at a nearby health club. 1376 Carling Ave. (phone: 722-7601). Moderate.

Roxborough – Though small (150 rooms), its European-style intimacy and location (400 yards from Parliament Hill) make it quite an attractive choice. Civilized amenities include a morning newspaper delivered with a continental breakfast and a shoeshine. All are complimentary. There is also a good lunch bar and a restaurant. 123 Metcalfe St. (phone: 237-5171). Moderate to inexpensive.

Journey's End – Located on the main freeway at the east and west ends of the city, these 2 no-frills motels offer clean, pleasant, air conditioned accommodations with easy access to downtown. The west-end motel also has housekeeping units. East-end: take St. Laurent Blvd. exit (phone: 744-2900); west-end: exit at Eagleson Rd. (phone: 592-2200). Inexpensive.

Nicholas Gaol International Hostel – Sleep in a 19th-century jail cell, complete with bars (not locked) and bunk-style beds. Twentieth-century guests enjoy creature comforts, like carpeting, lockers, a laundry room, kitchen access, and enlarged cells. There are 160 beds in separate male-female dormitories, with a few family rooms available by reservation. Bike, canoe, and skate rentals. Open to everyone, though hostel members get reduced rates and discounts at about 20 stores and entertainment centers in the city. 75 Nicholas St. (phone: 235-2595). Inexpensive.

EATING OUT: Ottawa is a great place for almost any kind of food you fancy because of the city's role as a host for foreign government missions. French and French-Canadian fare are specialties in this bilingual, bicultural city, but there's also a strong showing of other ethnic foods, ranging from Russian to Chinese. Expect to pay $35 or more for a meal for two in restaurants classed as expensive; between $20 and $30 at those places listed as moderate; and under $20 in establishments categorized as inexpensive. Prices do not include drinks, wine, or tips. All telephone numbers are in the 613 area code unless otherwise indicated.

Chez Jean Pierre – Former US Embassy chef Jean Pierre Muller works culinary wonders in his own French restaurant. The prices are steep, but patrons usually don't mind asking for the check after such a pleasurable meal. Reservations necessary. Closed Sundays and Mondays. Major credit cards. 210 Somerset St. (phone: 235-9711). Expensive.

Le Jardin – Widely acknowledged for its excellent food and consistent quality, it specializes in French cuisine and pledges never to use canned or frozen products. The decor is pleasing: an 1875 stone house that recently won a Heritage Canada award for its renovation. Though the restaurant no longer serves lunch, it is open nightly for dinner. Reservations recommended. All credit cards. 127 York St. (phone: 238-1828). Expensive.

L'Oree du Bois – A 15-minute drive across the river from Ottawa and up into the Gatineau Hills, near the Camp Fortune ski slopes, this restaurant enjoys a beautiful wooded setting and a reputation for excellent French cuisine. Specialties include *pavé au poivre vert, pot-au-feu de la mer, saumon a l'oseille,* and *canard au cidre.* Lunch for groups by reservation. Closed Mondays from April to October, Sundays and Mondays November to March. Major credit cards. Kingsmere Rd., Old Chelsea (phone: 819-827-0332). Expensive to moderate.

Bay Street Bistro – Though the waiters here can be a bit brusque at times, the "Italian-Californian" food is usually excellent. A sidewalk patio is open during the summer. Open daily; dinner only on Sundays. Reservations necessary for weekday lunches. Major credit cards accepted. 160 Bay, near the Public Archives (phone: 234-1111). Moderate.

GuadalaHarry's – A Mexican village lurking behind a 19th-century stone façade. Incongruous, yes, but the noisy, harmonious atmosphere makes this a great place to go with the gang. Reservations accepted. Open daily. Major credit cards. 18 York St. (phone: 234-8229). Moderate.

Haveli – This Indian restaurant has grown in size and popularity, with its much-talked-about specialties, including marinated leg of lamb and Ghandi's favorite — a complete vegetarian dinner. The decor is opulent dark wood and burnished brass. Lunch menu changes daily. Closed Sundays. Major credit cards. 87 George St., Market Mall upstairs (phone: 230-3566). Moderate.

Mamma Teresa – This firmly ensconced Italian restaurant has fine food and a comfortable atmosphere. Veal is the specialty, and dishes are served with homemade pasta, plenty of fresh bread, and deep-fried zucchini. There's a good selection of Italian wines. Open daily. Reservations advised. Major credit cards. 300 Somerset St., W. (phone: 236-3023). Moderate.

Moroccan Village – Once a tiny, popular restaurant on the outskirts of the city, it's now moved to larger premises in the busy Byward Market area. The atmosphere is as appealing as the traditional Moroccan food. 77 Clarence (phone: 230-2421). Moderate.

The Place Next Door – Tom Jones and Shirley MacLaine are among the celebrities who have eaten here, but the restaurant is also loved by locals who line up on weekends to get in. It's all on account of some very good steaks and seafood and the personable owner Dave Smith and his brother Scottie. Ample free parking in an area where parking is expensive. Open daily. Major credit cards. 320 Rideau St. (phone: 232-1741). Moderate.

Ritz 3 – There are five of them, actually, and each one is different and first rate. For example, the one on Clarence Street has pizza with unusual toppings — everything from scallops and mustard on watercress to figs and shrimp. Demand is so great, however, that they won't take reservations at some locations. So call first: 15 Clarence St. (phone: 234-3499); 274 Elgin (phone: 235-7027); 1665 Bank (phone: 238-3270); 226 Nepean — known as *Tidbitz* (phone: 238-8752); and on the Driveway at the canal (phone: 238-8998). Moderate.

Brokerage – There are two of these eateries, and each has a very good reputation for salads and light, interesting meals at modest prices. No reservations, and lines usually form by 11:45 AM for lunch. Closed Sundays. Major credit cards. 90 Sparks (phone: 232-6385), and Rideau Centre (phone: 230-8001). Inexpensive.

Crystal Dragon – Popular with the Chinese community, the place has a very plain decor, so the obvious appeal is the astonishing variety of Cantonese food. It takes 20 minutes just to read the menu, but the service is fast and the dishes always good. Open daily. All credit cards. 704 Somerset St. W. (phone: 234-9416). Inexpensive.

Hurley's Roadhouse – The menu is straightforward — burgers, chicken, steaks — but the atmosphere is special. Another Byward Market fun spot; the rooftop patio is popular in summer. Open daily. Major credit cards. 73 York St. (phone: 230-9347). Inexpensive.

Khyber Pass – Noted for its authentic Afghan dishes (including vegetarian specials) and ample servings, this Byward Market restaurant has grown in both size and reputation. Open daily. Major credit cards. 271 Dalhousie St. (phone: 235-0881). Inexpensive.

Zak's – The 1950s are back. Highlighted by vinyl-swathed banquettes, metal paper napkin dispensers, and "Wake Up Little Susie" playing on the jukebox, the food at this real diner is exactly what you'd expect, with such "specialties" as burgers (great) and deep-fried clams. Open daily until midnight, at least. Major credit cards. Reservations for groups of 15 or more. 14 Byward Market (phone: 233-0433). Inexpensive.

QUEBEC CITY

The key battle that determined the fate of French Canada lasted only about 20 minutes. It occurred on the morning of September 13, 1759, on the Plains of Abraham in Quebec City, the capital of New France. The city had been under siege by the British general James Wolfe since July and was surviving nicely. But on the evening of September 12, Wolfe led a group of soldiers up the steep hill from Anse au Foulon (formerly called Wolfe's Cove) and assembled the force on the Plains of Abraham. That is where the astonished and horrified French found them the next morning when the Marquis de Montcalm, the commander of the city's defenses, rushed his troops into battle. In the ensuing fight, both Wolfe and Montcalm were killed (Wolfe died on the battlefield, Montcalm shortly after in the city) and the French were decisively defeated. Canada was to be British. But according to legend, as smoke obscured the battlefield and the dream of New France died with its last defenders, a voice was heard across the Plains, crying: "*Je me souviens*" — "I remember."

Those words have become the motto of Quebec Province, and nowhere do they resound with more conviction than in Quebec City, itself the most vivid and tangible remnant of New France in Canada. Rising on the massive cliff of Cape Diamond some 350 feet above the St. Lawrence River, Quebec City is the foundation of French culture and the rock upon which Canadian federalism has come close to foundering. Though the English won control of Canada, Quebec City retained its French language, culture, and heritage. And through subsequent invasions by the British and Americans in the course of its history and the contemporary French-English controversy concerning the independence of Quebec, the city survives as a stronghold of French culture on an English-speaking continent.

Quebec City was the first French settlement in North America. And despite 2 centuries of English rule, it is French today. Of the metropolitan population of 576,000, 95% is of French stock, primarily from Normandy and Brittany on the northwest coast of France. These Quebecois have a deeply rooted heritage. They are a family-oriented, provincial people; their city reflects this attitude toward life.

Most everyone here speaks French; newspapers, plays, and conversations are generally in French, though many people can speak English, particularly those who work in businesses catering to tourists.

Many of the buildings in the old section of the city are restored 17th- and 18th-century stone houses, similar to those in the villages of provincial France. The cuisine is French or hearty Quebecois — thick pea soups, meat pies, and rich maple syrup pies for dessert. Street signs, store names, and customs attest to the city's French character. Even the walls that surround the Old City of Quebec (Quebec City is the only walled city on the continent) seem to protect its insular culture, and they demarcate historic Quebec from the newer parts of the city, where modern hotels, shopping malls, and office buildings acknowledge the 20th century.

The French architecture and the dramatic natural setting of Quebec City combine to make it one of the most beautiful cities in North America. Sometimes called the Gibraltar of America, Quebec City is carved into the 350-foot cliff of Cape Diamond.

At the foot of Cape Diamond is the St. Lawrence River, caught midway on its long journey from Lake Ontario to the Atlantic Ocean at the Gulf of St. Lawrence. As huge as the St. Lawrence is — and it is miles wide at points both above and below Quebec City — Cape Diamond seems almost to tame it, lunging eastward toward its confluence with a small tributary, the St. Charles, at the point where it narrows to a mere three-quarters of a mile.

To the southeast stands another promontory that forms the foundation of the town of Lévis. Some 25 miles (40 km) to the northeast, the hills culminate in the high peak of Mont-Ste.-Anne, one of the finest ski areas in eastern Canada. Quebec City is a city on a hill, and its view is wide. Turn to the right and you're on your way to the Gaspé Peninsula, with its poor but picturesque villages; turn left and you are soon at Montreal, a mere 153 miles (246 km) away; go straight north and you bump into the fabulous Laurentian slopes, which the Quebecois call the Laurentides.

The history of Quebec City seems to be stratified, starting at the foot of Cape Diamond and progressing up the hill as the young settlement developed. Its history flows from the river. The Amerindians inhabited this area for thousands of years, using the river as their main source of transportation. Jacques Cartier sailed by Cape Diamond in 1535 and gave the great rock its name. When Samuel de Champlain sailed down the St. Lawrence in the early 17th century, he was attracted by the strategically located site and founded the city in 1608. Champlain established his first "habitation" here, a trading post comprised of a store, a few houses, and surrounding fortifications. The site of this development, now known as Place Royale, is located at the foot of Cape Diamond near the river. Place Royale became the center of a fur trading colony — a meeting place for the merchants who governed the community as well as a commercial center and residential area where wealthy Quebec merchants built their homes. As more colonists and missionaries arrived, the settlement grew up the hill. In 1647, the Château St. Louis was built as a governor's residence at the top of the cliff (today the spectacular *Château Frontenac* hotel occupies this site.)

The Canadian headquarters of the Roman Catholic Church was also established in Old Upper Town soon after Bishop Laval settled in Quebec City in 1659. The Church had a major influence on the development of the province. For more than 3 centuries, the Church acted as a cultural force in the city, initially conservative, more liberal in recent years.

Quarrels between the Church and the trading company motivated the King of France to send over a royal *intendant* — a royal overseer of sorts — to administer the province in 1663. Jean Talon, the first intendant, and Comte Louis de Buade de Frontenac, the governor, dealt with this conflict and also settled problems with various Indian tribes that had been attacking the young settlement. Together they fostered an atmosphere of peace and security during which the town developed as the center of New France.

This period was cut short by a much more significant struggle for power — between the two major colonizing forces, France and England. In 1690, Frontenac subdued an attack on the city led by Sir William Phipps, the British governor of Massachusetts. Three years later, walls were constructed to fortify the city's defenses. In 1759, during the Seven Years' War, Quebec City fell to the British as a result of the Battle of the Plains of Abraham. Today a plaque under the monument honoring both Montcalm and Wolfe reads: "Their courage gave them the same lot." The fate of Canada, however, took a different turn, and the period of English rule began. But this battle had a profound effect on the Quebecois psyche. Many of the aristocratic French returned to France. Those who stayed taught their children what had been lost on the grounds of the Plains of Abraham: "Je me souviens."

Quebec City remained the political and military center of Canada, with timber and shipbuilding as its two main industries. During the 19th century the town was quiet, its growth interrupted only by natural disasters, a few destructive landslides and fires. But with the growth of Montreal and Toronto in the mid-19th century, Quebec City's economic supremacy began to recede; Montreal and Toronto became the commercial centers of Canada.

But Quebec City remains the most important historical center of Canada. In order for a community to flourish, it must have a sense of its past; to visit Quebec City is to know that all was not lost on the Plains of Abraham. The old city walls, which the United Nations declared a historic site in 1985, have been restored, and they surround the most historic section of the city, Old Quebec. The Quebec government declared the area around Place Royale a special zone in the 1960s, and more than twenty 17th- and 18th-century houses and buildings have been restored. Museums, cultural centers, and restaurants now occupy authentically restored houses. The Old Upper Town is a well-preserved area of narrow cobblestoned streets lined with historic buildings. You haven't really tasted Old Quebec until you go to one of its oldest buildings, now *Aux Anciens Canadiens* restaurant, for a hearty Quebecois meal topped off with maple syrup pie served with heavy cream.

Beyond the city walls, farther up the hill, lies 20th-century Quebec. Here is a concentration of all the amenities found in any other modern provincial capital — a convention center, an underground shopping gallery, Place Quebec, adjoined by the *Québec Hilton International;* several other luxurious high-rise hotels; and the stately National Assembly, as the legislature is called. Beyond spreads the suburb of Ste. Foy, rapidly developed in the past 25 years to accommodate a growing population. Many Quebecois work in Ste. Foy at the suburb's two major shopping malls or at Laval University, a major employer and, with 26,000 students, also a big draw to the city. The largest employer of all is the provincial government, with more than 40,000 civil servants.

Around Parliament Hill you find that Quebec City's present is inextricably bound with its past. Sculptures of historically prominent Canadians are carved into niches on the National Assembly. These figures and the nearby Plains of Abraham and Citadelle — the star-shaped fortress that won the city the sobriquet "Gibraltar of America" — record Quebec City's struggle to become what it is today.

And in many ways the struggle still continues, though its form has changed. The weapons are words rather than cannons, but the French-English controversy in Canada still simmers. Many Quebecois feel they have been excluded from the mainstream of Canadian political-economic life because of their language and culture. During the late 1950s and early 60s, what historians refer to as a "quiet revolution" swept Quebec. Coinciding with growing Quebec nationalism, a liberal government headed by Premier Jean Lesage introduced major education and social reforms which gave rise to a new political party, the Parti Quebecois. Headed by Réné Lévesque, it was determined to lead the province to political independence from English-speaking Canada, while still maintaining an economic link. The PQ was elected to power in 1976 and re-elected in 1981, though a provincial referendum on independence in 1980 was rejected. In the 1985 provincial election, the PQ was defeated by the less separatist-oriented Liberal Party, which strongly favors Quebec staying within the existing Canadian political system.

There will probably always be some resentment between French and English Canada, and Quebec City, as the capital of the only French-speaking province in Canada, will most likely remain firmly rooted in its heritage. Through almost 4 centuries and six invasions, Quebec City has remained authentically French. The strength of its collective memory ("*Je me souviens*") has transformed it into a vibrant survivor.

QUEBEC CITY AT-A-GLANCE

SEEING THE CITY: *L'Astral*, the *Loew's Le Concorde* hotel's revolving rooftop restaurant-bar, situated on the highest point of Cape Diamond, has the best panorama of Quebec City and surrounding areas, day or night. On a clear day, you can see as far as Ile d'Orléans, the most picturesque island of the St. Lawrence River, and, some 25 miles away, a chain of mountains dominated by Mont-St.-Anne, one of the region's best ski slopes. *L'Astral* is open from 11:45 AM to 3 PM and 6 to 11 PM daily except Sundays, when it is open from 11:45 AM to 3 PM. 1225 Place Montcalm (phone: 647-2222).

There are many fine views of the river, but two of the best are from Dufferin Terrace, a boardwalk flanking the *Château Frontenac* hotel, and Earl Grey Terrace, an observatory adjoining the Plains of Abraham, between Wolfe and Montcalm streets, in Parc des Champs de Bataille.

SPECIAL PLACES: The best way to see Quebec City is by strolling down its streets and alleys. You'll definitely want to ride the *funiculaire*, the outdoor elevator that links the Lower and Upper Towns. But Quebec City is more a feast for feet, a people-size place where the scale of sites is that of an easy day's perambulation. The rewards for lazy, languid strolls are quaint cobbled streets, historic houses, and the sort of secure claustrophobia conferred by a city that you can almost drape around your shoulders. But first arm yourself with a map. The streets are laid out in a haphazard fashion, particularly in the older sections. Old Lower Town centers around Place Royale at river level. If you walk north and west, you'll find a new cluster of cafés, boutiques, and antiques stores in what used to be the city's financial district. The stock exchange and the old banks closed after Quebec's importance as a trading center waned. But just a few more blocks north, you'll find the spruced up port area, with old warehouses reincarnated as fashionable boutiques. Old Upper Town revolves around Place d'Armes, at the top of the funicular next to the *Château Frontenac.* Parliament Hill, farther up the hill, is the site of government buildings abutting sleek high-rise hotels. Beyond them all are the suburbs. The Plains of Abraham have been made into a lovely park, with miles of walking and jogging paths, picnic tables, bird-feeding stations, and great river views.

OLD LOWER TOWN

Place Royale – This small, cobblestoned square is known as the Canadian "cradle of French civilization." It was here that Champlain built his first "habitation" in 1608, which included buildings for lodging, a store, a stockade, and gardens. During the French regime, the square was used as a marketplace, and successful merchants built their homes here. In the center of the square is a bronze bust of Louis XIV. The area has been declared a special historic zone by the Quebec government and is presently undergoing restoration. Despite the destruction of some of the houses, the place and the streets leading off it are lined with the greatest concentration of 17th- and 18th-century buildings in North America. Most of the buildings clustered around the Church of Notre Dame des Victoires are architectural gems that began life as the houses of wealthy merchants. As the centuries slipped by, the area went downhill and the townsfolk simply forgot its history. Then, in 1960, a fire bared some strange brick walls. "They don't build walls like that anymore," noted assorted passersby until some of them realized that these were genuine historic treasures. The main floors of some of these homes are open to the public as museums, cultural centers, art galleries, and restaurants, while some of the upper floors are residential. Off Notre Dame at the foot of Cape Diamond near the river.

Place de Paris – In 1984, France paid tribute to this city and province by inaugurating the Place au Quebec in Paris. To reciprocate, a monument was erected on the exact spot where the French first set foot on Quebec soil — at the corner of today's Rue de la Place and Rue de l'Union — and dubbed it Place de Paris.

Maisons Bruneau, Drapeau, and Rageot – The multimedia production, "Place Royale: Business Center of New France," which describes the business activities of the area during colonial times, is presented here daily. No admission charge. 3A Place Royale, beside La Maisons des Vins.

La Batterie Royale – Built in 1691, this royal artillery, one of the oldest in Quebec City, has been entirely restored. On the corner of Rue sous le Fort and St.-Pierre.

Entrepôt Thibodeau – This house is now the Place Royale tourist reception center. Stop here first to pick up the Place Royale brochure, which describes points of interest in the area. Open daily from 10 AM to 6 PM June 24 to Labor Day; in winter, with reservations only (phone: 643-9314). No admission charge. Place Marché Finlay (phone: 643-6631).

Maison Fornel – With foundations dating back to 1658 and vaulted cellars constructed in 1735, this restored house is now an atmospheric exhibition center. Its reconstruction in 1964 initiated the Place Royale restoration project. The exhibition "Place Royale: 400 Years of History," provides a good perspective on the area's past and ongoing restoration; a brochure in English is available. No admission charge. Rue St. Pierre just south of Ruelle de la Place.

Notre Dame des Victoires – Our Lady of Victories was built in 1688 and renamed to commemorate the triumph of the French over the English during the attacks of 1690 and 1711. The small stone structure was rebuilt in 1759, after the bombardment, in accordance with the original design. The exterior is quite modest, yet inside there is exquisite woodwork, including a main altar minutely carved in the shape of an old fort, paintings from the School of Rubens, and old battle flags. Mass is still held every Sunday. Open daily. No admission charge. Place Royale (phone: 692-1650).

Maison des Vins – This restored home now houses an excellent wine store with an extensive selection of imported wines. This establishment is worth a visit for a look at its exposed brick walls, vaulted candlelit wine cellars, and its array of bottles ranging from a Mouton Rothschild 1879 (valued between about $13,000 and $21,000), to the local specialty, Caribou, a mixture of wine and alcohol that is stronger than wine and, according to some Quebecois, more effective for getting through the long, cold winters. Open Tuesdays through Saturdays. Reservations are required for guided tours. 1 Place Royale (phone: 643-1214).

Maison Chevalier – Three buildings, constructed in the 17th and 18th centuries for several merchants, including Jean Baptiste Chevalier, that have been linked to form an interesting ethnographic museum. Exhibits vary, but include old toys, costumes, furniture, and folk art. No admission charge. Corner of Cul de Sac and Notre Dame (phone: 643-9689).

Maison Jolliet – This restored house was the home of explorer Louis Jolliet, who, accompanied by Jacques Marquette, discovered the Mississippi River in 1672. His house now contains the entrance to the *funiculaire,* which for 60¢ saves you the trouble of having to climb back up to Upper Town. In operation daily from 7 AM to 10:45 PM. Opposite Sous le Fort at the foot of Escalier du Petit Champlain.

Musée de la Civilisation – Located between Place Royale and the Old Port near the St. Lawrence River, this new building designed by architect Moshe Safdie won an award for the way in which its modern architecture is integrated into the historic neighborhood of the Old Port. Along with galleries, a stone house built in 1732 is enclosed in this large museum. Open Tuesdays through Sundays, except during the summer (June 15 to September), open daily. Admission charge for adults over 16. 85 Rue Dalhousie, near Place Royale (phone: 643-2158).

OLD UPPER TOWN

Place d'Armes – A small square that served as a meeting place and parade ground during the French regime. In the center of the square stands a Gothic fountain surmounted by the granite and bronze Monument of Faith, constructed in 1916 in memory of the Récolets (Franciscan) missionaries who arrived in 1615. Today the square is a good orientation point in Old Upper Town, the section of Old Quebec built above the cliff, where military, religious, and residential buildings from the 17th, 18th, and 19th centuries have been restored. One of the loveliest, La Maison Vallée (which dates from 1732), has become the home of the Tussaud-like wax museum *(Musée de Cire).* Many of Quebec's most interesting restaurants and stores at the L'Empire shopping arcade (phone: 692-2470) are up here, too. For traditional Canadian fare and decor, check out *Aux Anciens Canadiens* (see *Eating Out*) in a house built in 1677 and named after the classic Canadian volume whose author, Philippe Aubert de Gaspé, once lived on the premises.

Château Frontenac – This grand hotel owned by C.P. Hotels, Ltd., in all its classic French glory, is Quebec City's most recognizable landmark. Everything about this structure, built in 1892, announces its grandeur, from its broad, slanting copper roof, its turrets and towers, and its imposing red brick walls to its magnificent setting high above the St. Lawrence River. Champlain lived on this site until his death in 1635; then the Château St. Louis, residence of the governor of New France, was built in 1647, destroyed, and then rebuilt regally by Governor Frontenac in 1694, only to be completely razed by fire in 1834. Spend some time strolling around the lobby, the inner courtyard, or taking in the excellent river view from the circular cocktail lounge. The terrace is a favorite spot for relaxing on summer nights. At the north end of the terrace there's a statue of Samuel de Champlain, watching over the city he founded in 1608. 1 Av. des Carrières (phone: 692-3861).

Jardin des Gouverneurs – Originally the private garden of Château St. Louis, it was opened to the public in 1838. Here stands the Wolfe-Montcalm monument, erected in 1828. It is one of the few monuments in the world commemorating both the triumphant and the defeated: "Their courage gave them the same lot; history, the same fame; posterity, the same monument." Open daily. No admission charge. Next to *Château Frontenac* at Av. des Carrières and Rue Mont Carmel.

Musée du Fort – This museum is a good place to get your bearings historically. A 30-minute sound-and-light show presented on a 450-foot-square model of the 18th-century city recreates the most important battles and sieges of Quebec, including the Battle of the Plains of Abraham and the attack by Arnold and Montgomery during the American Revolution. There's also a wide variety of guides and history books in English. Open daily (call for hours), except December 1 through Christmas. Shows alternate in English and French. Admission charge. 10 Rue Ste. Anne (phone: 692-2175).

Notre Dame Basilica – First built in 1647, this Roman Catholic church of the cardinal archbishop of Quebec once served the diocese of all French North America. The façade is unusual for its two unequal towers; the vaulted interior contains interesting devotional paintings. Open daily. No admission charge. Rue Buade and Côte de la Fabrique.

Quebec Seminary – Beyond the iron gates lies a group of 17th-century buildings that were part of a training school for Catholic priests founded in 1663 by François de Montmorency Laval, the first bishop of Quebec. The main chapel is worth a visit for a look at its marble altars, valuable relics, and the sarcophagus of Bishop Laval; the sundial over the door dates back to 1773. The museum here has been recently renovated and has a collection of religious and secular art from both Quebec and Europe as well as some early scientific instruments. The museum is closed Mondays. 9 Rue de l'Université (phone: 692-2843). Visits to other parts of the seminary must be arranged in advance; call 692-3981 for information.

Anglican Cathedral – This stately structure was the first Church of England cathedral ever built (1804) outside of the British Isles. The pews, including the Royal Pew — which may be occupied only by the British sovereign or her representative — are composed of solid English oak; the large stained glass windows are awe-inspiring. Open daily except Mondays, 1 to 3 PM. 31 Desjardins (phone: 692-2193).

Ursuline Convent – Founded in 1639, it is the oldest school for women in North America. The convent itself was twice destroyed by fire, but some original walls still stand. A few of the present buildings date from the 17th century. The chapel contains a number of interesting relics and valuable paintings; its votive lamp, first lit in 1717, has never been extinguished. The defeated General Montcalm is buried in a tomb in the chapel. (His skull is preserved under glass at *Musée Marie des Ursulines,* 12 Donnaconna.) Open daily except Mondays. Admission charge. Rue du Parloir and Donnaconna (phone: 694-0694).

Montmorency Park – Named in honor of Bishop Laval — François de Montmorency Laval — this park, straddling the hill between the Old Upper Town and Old Lower Town, affords good views of the Lower Town, the harbor, and the surrounding area. A monument to Sir Georges Etienne Cartier, a French-Canadian political leader, and another to Louis Hébert (the first farmer to settle in Quebec City), stand in the center of the park. On the hill, off Côte de la Montagne.

Laval Monument – An impressive statue honoring Bishop Laval, Canada's first bishop, who arrived in 1659 and was one of the most prominent citizens of New France.

He founded the Quebec Seminary, the predecessor of Laval University. The work, sculpted by Philippe Hébert, was unveiled in 1908. At Côte de la Montagne across from Montmorency Park.

PARLIAMENT HILL AND THE PLAINS OF ABRAHAM

La Promenade des Gouverneurs – This 2,200-foot-long walkway leads from Dufferin Terrace up Cape Diamond, beside the Citadelle, all the way to the Plains of Abraham. As you stroll, you have excellent views of the river upstream to the Quebec Bridge and downstream to the Ile d'Orléans. Open daily from late May to October (closed the rest of the year). No admission charge. Begins at the end of Dufferin Terrace

Citadelle – A massive star-shaped fortress that commands a strategic position at the highest point on Quebec's promontory, 350 feet above the St. Lawrence. The French built previous fortifications on this site, but the present citadel was constructed between 1820 and 1832 by the British government as a defense against American attack following the War of 1812. The fortress was never subjected to enemy fire. It was first occupied by British troops, then by the Royal Canadian Artillery, and now by the Royal 22nd Regiment. From mid-June to the first Monday in September, the Changing of the Guard is performed daily at 10 AM, and the Ceremonial Retreat is enacted at 7 PM on Tuesdays, Thursdays, Saturdays, and Sundays. Closed December through February except to groups with previous reservations (write Musée de la Citadelle, CP 6020, Haute-Ville, Quebec G1R 4V7), and weekday mornings in November and during *Carnaval*. Admission charge. Reached by Côte de la Citadelle (phone: 648-3563).

Plains of Abraham – Named for Abraham Martin, the first St. Lawrence River pilot, this is where Canada's French-English struggle was decided in 1759. Now part of 230-acre Parc des Champs de Bataille, this was the scene of the battle between the British forces led by General James Wolfe and the French under General Montcalm that sealed the fate of New France. Both generals lost their lives in the struggle and the British gained control of Canada. Many Quebec residents returned to France; those who remained kept alive the idea of a French identity in North America, from which sprang the motto of the province: "Je me souviens." There is an observation post affording excellent river views and various monuments and statues. The *Quebec Museum* (see below) is also on the grounds. Open daily from June 15 to September 15, closed on Mondays for the rest of the year. Beyond the Citadelle to the west, off Grande Allée.

Quebec Museum – Dedicated to Quebec's history and its accomplishments in the fine arts, the museum contains the most significant collection of Quebecois paintings, sculptures, and decorative arts from the late-17th century to the 1980s. Open daily. No admission charge. In Parc des Champs de Bataille, off Grande Allée (phone: 643-2150).

Regimental Museum – This 1750 structure holds an interesting display of ancient weapons and uniforms. Closed January and February, except to groups reserving ahead, and during *Carnaval*. Admission included in the entrance charge to the Citadelle. Côte de la Citadelle off Rue St. Louis (phone: 648-3563).

National Assembly – Also known as the Parliament Buildings, these imposing French Renaissance buildings were constructed between 1877 and 1886. The 12 bronze statues in niches on the façade, commemorating people prominent in Quebec and Canada's history, were executed by the Quebec sculptor Hébert. Guided tours are conducted daily in July and August and on weekdays from September to November and from January to May. The Assembly is not in session from June 24 to October. Bounded by Rue Dufferin, Blvd. St. Cyrille E., St. Augustin, and Grande Allée (phone: 643-7239).

Complex G – This is an example of new Quebec, right down to its straightforward, no-nonsense name. At 31 stories, it is the city's highest building. It houses various ministries and provincial government services. An observation gallery on top is open daily in summer and weekdays in winter. No admission charge. Bounded by Blvd. St. Cyrille E., de la Chevrotière, St. Amable, and Conroy.

Grand Théâtre de Québec – Another work of modern architecture, this sleek structure built in 1970 comprises a music conservatory and two entertainment halls. 269 Blvd. St. Cyrille at the corner of Rue Claire Fontaine (phone: 643-8131).

SUBURBS

Ste. Foy – This town has grown up quickly in the last 25 years to become Quebec's major bedroom community. In addition to rows of neat wood and brick houses, the town supports two large shopping malls, Place Laurier and Place Ste. Foy (see *Shopping*, below). Follow Grande Allée about 2 miles (3 km) west of the National Assembly.

Laval University – An outgrowth of the Quebec Seminary founded by Bishop Laval, it is the oldest French-language university on the continent. The construction of a sprawling 465-acre campus was begun in 1948 to accommodate the growing numbers of students. One of the school's 25 modern buildings is the physical education and sports complex. Its excellent facilities, including an Olympic-size pool, are open to the public at certain hours, mainly weekends. Off Blvd. Laurier (Rte. 175) and bounded by du Vallon, Myrand, and Chemin Ste. Foy (phone: 656-2131).

Ile d'Orléans – This island in the St. Lawrence River below Quebec was relatively isolated until a suspension bridge connecting it with the mainland was built in 1935. Because of this, the island retains a great deal of its 18th-century French-Canadian influence. Most of the islanders are of Norman or Breton stock, and, like their ancestors, most are farmers. (Island apples and strawberries are especially good.) The island is only 21 miles (34 km) long and about 5 miles (8 km) wide. You can easily make a complete driving tour in a grand circle, stopping in village after village of 17th- and 18th-century houses and churches. (Route 368 is a 42-mile — 68-km — route that circles the island.) Ste. Famille has the most interesting church on the island — a triple-spired structure built in 1742. On the east side of the island are some summer cottages and Ste. Pétronille, a summer resort village. 10 miles (16 km) northeast of Quebec. Take Autoroute Dufferin down the hill near the National Assembly, then Rte. 138.

■ **EXTRA SPECIAL:** *Ste. Anne de Beaupré* is a small village near Mont-Ste.-Anne dominated by a massive cathedral, which is an internationally renowned Catholic shrine. Millions of people have made pilgrimages here, and the piles of crutches, canes, and folding wheelchairs in the cathedral attest to healings that the faithful believe take place. The present basilica (1922) can accommodate 10,000 people. The fountain of Ste. Anne in front is said to have the healing powers. The sanctuary has a marble statue of Ste. Anne, as well as other venerable religious items. An information bureau has been set up, and guides are available to lead tours.

Mont-Ste.-Anne is also a popular winter sports center. Its downhill runs, night skiing, cross-country ski tracks, and lift facilities attract a different breed of pilgrim — in search of miraculous skiing (see below). To reach the ski area, head 5 miles (8 km) beyond the village on Rte. 138 and turn north onto Rte. 360.

Just east of Mont-Ste.-Anne is the *Réserve nationale de la faune du Cap Tourmente*, developed by naturalists to protect the Greater Snow Goose, which stops here during its seasonal migrations. The noisy October gatherings can easily attract 100,000 screeching birds. In May, ducks, herons, swallows, and red-winged blackbirds build their nests in the many pounds of the region. The reserve also offers a nature-interpretation center. To visit, head east on Route 138 after leaving Ste. Anne de Beaupré and watch for signs for *Cap Tourmente*.

En route to Ste. Anne de Beaupré or on the return to Quebec City, stop off at the 274-foot-high Montmorency Falls. In 1759, the English general Wolfe established his headquarters near the top. These old buildings have been made into a beautiful, old hotel, the *Manoir Montmorency,* with a dining room offering a fantastic view over Ile d'Orléans in Quebec City (phone: 663-2877).

SOURCES AND RESOURCES

TOURIST INFORMATION: For tourist information, maps, and brochures, contact the Quebec City Region Tourism and Convention Bureau, 60 Rue d'Auteuil (phone: 692-2471), or the reception office of the Quebec Department of Tourism, 12 Ste. Anne (phone: 643-2280 or 800-443-7000 in the Eastern US). The Place Royale restoration has its own information center in Entrepôt Thibodeau, open during summer only; Place Marché Finlay (phone: 643-6631).

English-language city guidebooks are hard to find; most are written in French. *Librairie Garneau,* a bookstore at 47 Buade, and *Musée du Fort* at 10 Rue St. Anne have a fair selection.

Local Coverage – *Le Soleil,* French morning and afternoon daily; *Le Journal de Québec,* French morning daily; *Québec Chronicle-Telegraph,* English weekly that hits the newsstands on Wednesdays. *Voilà Québec* is a bilingual quarterly entertainment, sightseeing, and dining guide distributed free in hotels. For English television programs, tune to CKMI, Channel 5; the English radio station is CBVE at 104.7 FM.

Food – *Les Restaurants,* published by the Quebec Urban Community, lists restaurants in both the city and suburbs (free). Also check *Voilà Québec.*

Telephone – The area code for Quebec City is 418.

Sales Tax – In Quebec City there is a 9% sales tax only on clothing purchases above about $424 ($500 CN). There is also a 10% sales tax on meals above $2.75 ($3.25 CN).

Currency – All prices are quoted in US dollars unless otherwise indicated.

TIPPING: Waiters and waitresses should get 10% of the total bill, including tax. Hotel maids should be given $1 to $2 (CN) per day, and bellboys, $1 (CN) per bag (although some hotels do not allow tipping). Taxi drivers usually receive 10% of the total fare. It is unneccessary to tip airport porters.

CLIMATE: Quebec City is generally clear and sunny and has relatively low humidity because of its altitude — about 350 feet above sea level. Summertime temperatures average in the low to mid-70s F (mid-20s C) and edge up to 90F (32C) highs; during the winter, temperatures average around 20F (−6C), though they can plummet down to −10F (−23C) in January and February. In addition to cold weather, winter brings snow, and lots of it — 150 to 200 inches for the season. July has the most rainfall, with an average of 4.5 inches. For a 24-hour weather reporting service, call 872-2859; for winter road conditions, 643-6830.

GETTING AROUND: Bus – The *Quebec Urban Community Transit Commission (CTCUQ)* operates buses that serve the metropolitan area from 5:30 AM to 1 AM. Exact change $1.15 ($1.35 CN) is required. For route information, call 627-2511. During the winter, *CTCUQ* also runs *Skibus,* which serves several ski areas around Quebec. Look for the red and white snowflake symbol at bus stops throughout the city. *Dupont Transport,* leaving from major hotels, takes skiers to Mont-Ste.-Anne (phone: 529-0616).

Taxi – Generally cannot be hailed in the streets. There are cab stands at the major hotels and in Old Quebec at Place d'Armes and at d'Youville Square. The principal cab companies are *Taxi Co-op* (phone: 525-5191); *Taxi Quebec* (phone: 522-2001); *Taxi Co-op* in Ste. Foy (phone: 653-7237). The 20-minute trip from downtown to the airport should run about $14. There's limited shuttle bus service to the airport from major hotels for about $5; check ahead, since service may not begin early enough for some morning flights.

Car Rentals – Major firms that serve the city are *Avis,* at the *Québec Hilton International,* 3 Place Quebec (phone: 523-1075), 2785 Blvd. Laurier (phone: 651-5087), and the airport (phone: 872-2861); *Budget,* at the *Château Frontenac,* 1 Av. des Carrières (phone: 694-9551), 29 Côte du Palais (phone: 692-3660), and Place Quebec, 5 Place Quebec (phone: 529-0966); *Hertz,* 1136 Rue Fournier, Ste. Foy (phone: 658-6785), 44 Côte du Palais (phone: 694-1224), and the airport; *Tilden,* 295 Rue St. Paul (phone: 694-1727) and the airport (phone: 871-1224).

Ferry – Year-round service links Quebec and Lévis, operating every half hour from 6 AM to midnight, then less frequently. The ferry ride affords panoramic views of both cities.

Cruises – You can take a cruise on the Saint Lawrence aboard the *M/V Louis Jolliet.* The boat leaves from Chouinard Pier, 10 Dalhousie, in the Place Royale section of the city from June through September and by request only from May to mid-June and early September to October (phone: 692-1159). Also available is a St. Lawrence excursion combined with fine dining on Ile d'Orléans. From early June through mid-September, the boat leaves from its dock at Ile d'Orléans five times daily; contact *Beautemps Mauvaistemps* (phone: 828-2275).

Calèche – Horse-drawn carriages tour Old Quebec, the Parliament area, and the Plains of Abraham year-round. The fare for the 45-minute tour is about $25 for up to five people. A tip is customary for the driver. The *calèches* line up at Rue d'Auteuil near Rue St. Louis (phone: 667-9029).

Walking Tours – Quebec City is best seen on foot. To enrich your stroll, rent a tape-recorded tour tracing the city's history from *Sonore Tours* at Place d'Armes (phone: 694-0665); summers only. Or pick up a free copy of *Quebec City Region* — which includes walking tours — at the tourist office, and do it yourself. The Quebec Ministry of Cultural Affairs publishes this folder about Place Royale, which can be obtained at the Place Royale information center in Entrepôt Thibodeau, Place Marché Finlay. *Baillairgé Cultural Tours Inc.* (phone: 658-4799) offers 2¼-hour walking tours of the old town, leaving from *Musée du Fort,* across the street from the *Château Frontenac,* at 9:30 AM and 2 PM daily. The tour guides, who are also in charge of protocol for diplomats and dignitaries visiting Quebec City, are especially interesting and knowledgeable. Tours available from late June to mid-October. Fee: about $8.50.

Note: You can walk down several flights of wooden steps from Dufferin Terrace, the 80-foot-wide boardwalk flanking the *Château Frontenac* in the Old Upper Town, to Place Royale in Old Lower Town. On the way back, rest your feet by returning on the *funiculaire,* an enclosed elevator–cable car that whisks you back and commands a splendid river view — for about 50¢.

SPECIAL EVENTS: Next to New Orleans's *Mardi Gras,* the *Carnaval de Québec,* a 10-day affair starting this year on February 2nd, is the biggest blowout in North America. Over half a million people from all over Canada and the US flood the city to celebrate winter. A 7-foot snowman — Le Bonhomme Carnaval — presides over the festivities, which include two parades (one in Upper Town, one in Lower Town), snow sculpture contests, ice-skating shows, fireworks, a queen's coronation, and lots of winter sports and events — hockey, skiing, and a canoe race on the frozen St. Lawrence River. The biggest events are scheduled over two weekends. Hotels are generally booked solid during *Carnaval,* so if you want to go, make arrangements several months in advance. Your best bet for last-minute reservations is through the *Carnaval*'s lodging committee, which can sometimes book rooms in motels or guesthouses (phone: 524-8411, from December 15 to *Carnaval* time). For general information, contact the Québec Carnaval, 290 Joly, Quebec City (phone: 626-3716).

The *Quebec Summer Festival* is a more sedate event that celebrates Quebec's national cultural heritage through songfests, theatrical presentations, and concerts during the first 2 weeks of July. For information, contact the festival office at PO Box 24, Station B, Quebec City G1K 7A1 (phone: 692-4540).

MUSEUMS: For complete descriptions of the *Musée du Fort, Musée du Quebec, Musée de la Civilisation,* and Maison Chevalier, see *Special Places.* Other interesting museums include the following:

Musée de Cire – Wax museum. 22 Rue Ste. Anne (phone: 692-2289).

Musée du Québec – Showcase for Quebec arts and crafts. Parc des Champs de Bataille (phone: 643-2150).

Musée des Ursulines – An interesting permanent exhibition of very rare embroideries, some 500 years old. 12 Donnaconna (phone: 694-0694).

Parc Cartier-Breboeuf – A replica of Jacques Cartier's ship. On St. Charles River, at 175 de l'Espinay near Parc de l'Exposition (phone: 648-4038).

SHOPPING: Shops are generally open from 9:30 AM to 5:30 PM Mondays through Wednesdays; until 9 PM on Thursdays and Fridays; and until 5 PM on Saturdays. Shops are shuttered on Sundays except for some in Old Quebec. One of Canada's largest shopping centers, Place Laurier, is in the suburb of Ste. Foy and houses over 300 shops and boutiques in a 4-story complex; Place Ste. Foy next door tends to have more sophisticated clothing stores.

Near the National Assembly is Place Québec, another shopping complex with myriad shops. This multilevel shopping promenade connected to the *Québec Hilton International* contains many smart boutiques, two cinemas, and a few restaurants. Near Place d'Armes there is a new shopping arcade with all sorts of stores. The *Maison des Vins,* 1 Place Royale, carries an extensive assortment of imported wines. For Quebec handicrafts, try the stores along Rue Champlain and Rue de Petit Champlain. They are usually open Sundays.

The best places to find Eskimo or Indian art are the boutiques on St. Louis, Desjardins, or Quartier Petit Champlain. Authentic Huron Indian craftwork, including snowshoes and moccasins, can be found at Huron Village in Loretteville, a suburb of Quebec en route to the airport (about 15 minutes from downtown). Try *Artisanat Gros-Louis,* 125 Rue Maurice Bastien (phone: 843-2503), or *Artisans Indiens du Québec,* 540 Rue Max Gros-Louis (phone: 845-2150).

Antiques collectors should visit Old Lower Town and the shops on St. Paul Street. Best bets are *L'Heritage,* 109 and 111 St. Paul; and *La Galerie 141,* 145 St. Paul.

SPORTS: Quebec City has an active sports scene for both spectators and participants.

Golf – Ten 18-hole and an equal number of 9-hole courses are within a 19-mile (30-km) radius of the city. Among the best are *Club de Golf Royal Québec,* Bedard St. in Boischatel, near Montmorency Falls (phone: 822-0331); *Lorette Golf Club,* on Cook St. in Loretteville (phone: 842-8441); *Club de Golf Mont Tourbillon* in Lac Beauport, 12 miles (19 km) north of the city (phone: 849-4418); and the course at Mont-Ste.-Anne, 25 miles (40 km) northeast of the city (phone: 827-4561).

Harness Racing – They're off and running at the *Quebec Hippodrome* on the Exhibition Grounds. Follow Dorchester Blvd. until you see signs for Parc de l'Exposition (phone: 524-5283). Check ahead for days open during the winter.

Hockey – The National Hockey League team, the *Nordiques,* faces challengers at the *Coliseum* on the Exposition Grounds (tickets, phone: 647-1211; schedule information, phone: 529-8441).

Skating – Join the locals in Parc d'Esplanade, off Rue d'Auteuil. Other popular spots are the 3-kilometer circuit on the St. Charles River, between the Samson and Marie de l'Incarnation bridges and Place d'Youville, just outside the St. Jean Gate in Old Quebec. Village des Sports in Valcartier (Autoroute de la Capitale, then Rte. 371) offers skating paths through the woods, and L'Anneau de Glace de Ste. Foy (see *Suburbs*) is an outdoor Olympic-size skating track made of artificial ice. Skating begins mid-October and usually lasts to the end of March (phone: 654-4462).

Skiing – Downhill skiing is best at Mont-Ste.-Anne, a World Cup complex 25 miles (40 km) northeast of the city. The most direct route follows Route 138. You can also get there via the new Route 440. A more scenic route leaves 138 at Beaupré and continues along Route 360. Lac Beauport and Stoneham also have good slopes only a short drive from the city. All of them offer good night skiing. For information on buses to the ski areas, see *Getting Around.* For cross-country skiing and snowshoeing, try Plains of Abraham or the nearby provincial parks with marked trails, and Réserve Faunique des Laurentides, northwest via Rte. 175. Mont-Ste.-Anne, Lac Delage, and Duchesnay also have miles of groomed cross-country trails.

Swimming – Some of the hotels have pools; the *Physical Education and Sports Pavilion* at Laval University in Ste. Foy, off Rte. 175 (phone: 656-2807), has an Olympic-size pool open to the public weekends; the *YMCA,* 835 Blvd. St. Cyrille W (phone: 527-2518), also has a pool the public can use for a fee at certain hours; call ahead.

Tennis – Indoor and outdoor tennis courts as well as squash courts are available from 7 AM to 11 PM daily at the *Montcalm Tennis Club,* 901 Champlain Blvd. (phone: 687-1250). Courts are also available for rent at *Club de Tennis Avantage, Inc.,* 1080 Bouvier, Charlesbourg W. (phone: 627-3343) and at *Tennisport,* 4230 Blvd. Hamel (phone: 872-0111).

Tobogganing – There are slides at the Village des Sports, near Valcartier, north of the city.

THEATER: A variety of plays is offered in French, rarely in English. Major theaters include the *Grand Théâtre du Québec,* 1100 Rue Claire-Fontaine at the corner of St. Cyrille (phone: 643-6976); *Palais Montcalm,* 975 Place d'Youville (phone: 670-9011 or 694-7110); and the French-language *Théâtre du Trident* plays in the *Grand Théâtre* (phone: 643-5873); *Bibliothèque Gabrielle Roy,* 350 Rue St. Joseph E (phone: 529-0924); and *Salle Albert-Rousseau,* CEGEP Ste. Foy, 2410 Chemin Ste. Foy (phone: 659-6629). Student productions are presented at the *Conservatoire d'Art Dramatique,* 11 St. Stanislas (phone: 643-9833), and at the *Théâtre de la Cité Universitaire* on the Laval Campus in Ste. Foy (phone: 656-2765). Summer theaters are *Théâtre de l'Ile,* Ile d'Orléans (phone: 828-9530); *Théâtre Beaumont-St. Michel* on Rte. 2 between Beaumont and St. Michel (phone: 884-2839); and *Théâtre du Bois de Coulonge,* Blvd. Laurier (phone: 681-4679). Among the small theaters are *Théâtre Petit Champlain,* 68 Petit Champlain (phone: 692-4398) which often hosts folk-singing *chansonniers; Théâtre de la Bordée,* 1091½ Rue St. Jean (phone: 694-9631); *Théâtre de la Fenière,* 1500 de la Fenière, Ancienne Lorette (phone: 872-1424); and *Théâtre Paul Hébert,* 1451 Av. Royale, St. Jean, Ile d'Orléans (phone: 829-2202).

MUSIC: The *Quebec Symphony Orchestra* performs at Louis-Frechette Hall in the *Grand Théâtre de Québec,* 1100 Rue Claire-Fontaine (phone: 643-6976). Touring groups usually play at *Palais Montcalm,* 975 Place d'Youville (phone: 670-9011 or 694-7110). The small pubs along Rue St. Jean between Rue d'Auteuil and Côte de la Fabrique, on Grande Allée, and in the Old Port area (see *Nightclubs and Nightlife*), have live music, ranging from Quebecois folk music to rock and blues. The bar in the *Clarendon* hotel, 57 Rue Ste. Anne (phone: 692-2480), has jazz.

NIGHTCLUBS AND NIGHTLIFE: The pubs along and around St. Jean attract a young crowd. One popular place is *Bar Elite,* 54 Rue Couillard (phone: 692-1204). The bars and discos along Grande Allée near the National Assembly and in the Old Port area tend to be more sophisticated.

BEST IN TOWN

CHECKING IN: Quebec City has a wide range of hostelries, from the magnificent *Château Frontenac* — a landmark since it was built in the 1890s — to small family-run guesthouses. Four modern high-rise hotels dramatically altered the city's skyline during the 1973-1974 period, when the Municipal Convention Center was being completed. The city now has more than 3,500 rooms in major convention hotels and motels plus more than 4,000 others in motels and inns in the region. The best bet for motoring visitors is to check into one of the motels in Ste. Foy. If you are planning to visit Quebec City during *Carnaval* in early February or during the summer, make reservations as far in advance as possible. During the winter, rooms are generally available, and some places even have discount rates. Expect to pay $100 to $170 and up per night for a double room in the expensive range; $70 to $100 in the moderate range; and about $65 in the inexpensive range. All telephone numbers are in the 418 area code unless otherwise indicated.

Auberge des Gouverneurs – Adjacent to the *Québec Hilton International,* this modern high-rise has 361 nicely appointed rooms, an elaborate dining room, and an outdoor swimming pool. 690 St. Cyrille E (phone: 647-1717). Expensive.

Auberge des Gouverneurs Ste. Foy – A suburban motor hotel, it has 318 attractive rooms, a sophisticated restaurant, a piano bar, and a heated outdoor pool that's open only in summer. 3030 Blvd. Laurier (phone: 651-3030). Expensive.

Le Château Frontenac – The grand dame of Quebec City hotels, this stunning 1892 French Renaissance structure is beautifully situated above the St. Lawrence River. It is no longer the best hostelry in town, but what the Champs-Élysées is to Paris and Red Square is to Moscow, this venerable hotel is to Quebec City — the point to which tourist tracks are inevitably drawn. The 500-room Canadian Pacific property continues to be refurbished, so modern comforts have been added without compromising its Old World appeal. Rooms are air conditioned and many have river views. *Le Champlain* is an excellent dining room; there's also an attractive circular cocktail lounge overlooking the St. Lawrence; café-style restaurants; and a small gallery of shops. (For more information on its history, see *Special Places*). 1 Av. des Carrières (phone: 692-3861). Expensive.

Loews Le Concorde – A dramatic pyramidal structure distinguishes this 424-room hotel. *L'Astral,* this city's only revolving restaurant, sits atop the 29-story pyramid. Other restaurants are available, too, and there is an outdoor pool. During the winter, guests may use the indoor pool at an adjacent club. 1225 Place Montcalm (phone: 647-2222). Expensive.

Québec Hilton International – With one of the best addresses in the city, this striking, modern high-rise has 563 rooms and 36 suite-combinations. Service is attentive and friendly. Facilities include a wide variety of restaurants; a heated outdoor pool (closed in winter); a health club; and small liquor-vending machines.

In addition, the hotel is connected by underground passages with an extensive shopping arcade and the *Convention Centre.* 3 Place Quebec (phone: 647-2411). Expensive.

Auberge Ramada Inn – This 99-room hotel, formerly known as *la Nouvelle-Orléans,* is a rustic-looking lodge done up in Canadiana. Rooms have all amenities and there are 28 split-level suites. It offers a choice of restaurants: *Mon Patelin* for Quebecois and Italian specialties, *Le Vivier* for seafood. It has an outdoor pool. Near the Quebec bridge in Ste. Foy. 1200 Av. Lavigerie (phone: 651-2440). Expensive to moderate.

Clarendon – Within the old city walls, just opposite City Hall — very convenient for sightseeing — this hotel was built in 1870 but was recently refurbished. The rooms have private baths, color TV sets, and phones but no air conditioning. The 4-star *Charles Baillargé* restaurant serves dinner accompanied by performances of classical music; a cocktail lounge is also on the premises. 57 Rue Ste. Anne, near Desjardins (phone: 692-2480). Expensive to moderate.

Auberge du Tresor – Formerly the *Hôtel Le Homestead,* this 300-year-old building has been renovated recently and now its 21 guestrooms — most overlooking Place d'Armes — are equipped with private bath, TV set, and air conditioning. Conveniently situated for those whose main objective is sightseeing, the hotel also has a cocktail lounge, a fine dining room with an extensive, multi-ethnic menu, and a café in summer. 20 Rue Ste. Anne at Rue du Tresor (phone: 694-1876). Moderate.

Le Château de Pierre – This 15-room English-style mansion (1853) was converted from a private residence to a guesthouse in 1960 and has much repeat business. The 15 rooms are decorated with contemporary furniture; all have color TV sets, and air conditioning; most are large enough for 2 double beds. 17 Av. Ste. Geneviève, a few steps from Rue Laporte (phone: 694-0429). Moderate.

Fleur de Lys – Renovated in 1985, in the heart of Old Upper Town, 16 of the 33 units are equipped with kitchenettes. All have color TV sets, air conditioning, and direct-dial phone. Continental breakfast served in the rooms; other facilites include a laundromat and parking garage. 115 Rue Ste. Anne, near Desjardins (phone: 694-0106). Moderate.

Le Germain des Prés – Decorated in European Art Deco, this new 127-room hotel offers personalized service. Rooms include TV sets, remote control AM-FM cassette radios, bathrobes, and fresh fruit. The hotel has a continental breakfast room and is near shopping centers. Transportation to the airport is complimentary. 1200 Ave. Germain des Prés Ste. Foy (phone: 658-1224). Moderate.

Hotel Chateaubriand – Formerly the *Holiday Inn–Ste. Foy,* it has 342 spacious rooms, a heated outdoor swimming pool (closed in winter), and a good restaurant. 3225 Hochelaga (phone: 653-4901). Moderate.

Manoir Ste. Geneviève – One of the best things about this 9-room guesthouse is Marguerite Corriveau, the friendly proprietress. The house was built in the early 1800s and was one of the first in the Jardin des Gouverneurs. All the rooms are furnished with old English furniture but have modern baths, and three have kitchenettes. 13 Av. Ste. Geneviève at Rue Laporte (phone: 647-9377). Moderate.

Château Laurier – Near the National Assembly, this 55-room hotel is quiet and convenient, with a dining room and coffee shop that's open until 5 AM — a rarity in Quebec City. 695 Grande Allée (phone: 522-8108). Moderate to inexpensive.

Mercure – Though slightly out of the way, this is a well-run 56-room hostelry with real Quebecois atmosphere and good food. 638 St. Vallier W. (phone: 529-3787). Moderate to inexpensive.

Belley – Situated in the Old Port area, this new small hotel has 8 rooms decorated with stylish, black-lacquered Oriental furniture and Quebecois artwork. Showers (but no baths) in every room. No restaurant on the premises, but continental breakfast is available at the *Tavern Belley* next door. 249 Rue St. Paul (phone: 692-1694). Inexpensive.

EATING OUT: Even if you don't know the difference between flambé and soufflé, Quebec City awaits you. At the myriad French restaurants here you can try both, as well as a broad selection of other Gallic dishes. Quebecois food is the regional specialty, and several restaurants serve generous portions of hearty pea soup, meat pie, and maple sugar-based desserts. For a change of taste, there's excellent Greek food at *Mykonos* or fondue at *Chalet Suisse.* An added bonus is the relatively modest prices of the restaurants. Expect to pay $85 and up for a very expensive dinner for two; between $70 and $85 in the expensive range; $40 to $60 in the moderate range; and under $40 in the inexpensive range. Note that a provincial sales tax of 10% is added to your tab for meals costing more than $2.75 ($3.25 CN). Prices given do not include drinks, wine, or tip. All telephone numbers are in the 418 area code unless otherwise indicated.

L'Âtre – The pride of Ile d'Orléans is this 1680 farmhouse-turned-fashionable-restaurant. The menu is Quebecois. Open daily from mid-June to early September only. Reservations necessary. Major credit cards accepted. 4403 Royal (Rte. 368) near Ste. Famille, east of the island bridge (phone: 829-2474). Very expensive.

Le Croquembroche – This elegant, provincial-style restaurant has emerged as one of the top two or three dining rooms in town. It features beautifully prepared French nouvelle cuisine and Quebec City specialties. For starters, try the snails baked in grape leaves and puff pastry or the creamed Arctic char soup with orange zest. Grilled meats and fish, roasted on a spit in the dining area and served with suave sauces, are commendable entrées. Open weekdays for lunch; daily for dinner. Reservations advised. Major credit cards accepted. Lobby level of the *Québec Hilton,* 3 Place Quebec (phone: 674-2411). Very expensive.

Le Paris-Brest – Art Deco combined with stained glass windows and brass fittings creates an engaging decor in which to dine on the specialty here, French food. Open daily. Major credit cards accepted. 590 Grande Allée E. (phone: 529-2243). Very expensive.

A la table de Serge Bruyère – Possibly the best in town. Monsieur Bruyère constantly experiments with nouvelle cuisine and has come up with such dishes as *feuilletée de langoustine à la tomate fraîche* (prawns in puff pastry with tomato) and scallops with leek purée. Only one seating each evening, so reservations are necessary, about a week ahead. Closed Sundays and Mondays. Major credit cards accepted. 1200 Rue St. Jean (phone: 694-0618). Very expensive.

Le Marie Clarisse – A very good seafood restaurant near the bottom of the *funiculaire.* Closed Sundays and Mondays. Reservations advised. Most major credit cards. 12 Petit Champlain (phone: 692-0857). Very expensive to expensive.

Aux Anciens Canadiens – This house was built in 1675, and was at one time the home of Philippe Aubert de Gaspé. It's a wonderful place for a large lunch or brunch (dinner is served, too). Specialties include thick Canadian pea soup, *tourtière* (meat pie), meatball ragoût, and, for dessert, sinfully delicious maple syrup pie served with heavy cream. Open daily. Reservations advised. Major credit cards accepted. 34 Rue St. Louis (phone: 692-1627). Expensive.

Le Champlain – The *Château Frontenac*'s dining room has changed over to nouvelle cuisine. Try the Brome Lake duckling with cassis vinegar, or the Dover sole soufflé with lobster sauce. Quiet harp and flute music adds to the serenity. Closed Mondays in winter. Reservations advised. Major credit cards accepted. In the *Château Frontenac,* 1 Av. des Carrières (phone: 692-3861). Expensive.

Le Continental – The cuisine could hardly be a surprise — an extensive menu of European specialties ranging from sweetbreads Madère to steak flambé au poivre. The oak-paneled dining room is attractive and spacious and the service usually very good. For starters, try the Gaspé en crêpe (seafood crêpe). Closed Sundays from November to February. Open daily the rest of the year. Reservations advised. Major credit cards accepted. 26 Rue St. Louis (phone: 694-9995). Expensive.

Apsara – A good place for adventurous eating in Quebec, it serves Thai, Cambodian, and Vietnamese foods. The plate of assorted appetizers is a wise and flavorful selection for the uninitiated. Open daily. Reservations advised. Major credit cards accepted. 71 d'Auteuil (phone: 694-0232). Expensive to moderate.

Auberge Louis Hébert – Offers friendly service and an attractive setting, with calico lampshades dangling above the tables. Specialties include fresh Quebec lamb and *confit d'oie*, a goose pâté. The outdoor terrace is open for summer dining. Open daily. Major credit cards accepted. 668 Grande Allée E. (phone: 525-7812). Expensive to moderate.

Café d'Europe – French and Italian dishes are served in cheery and cozy surroundings in Old Quebec. The café also has great little one-person pizzas and a good dessert cart. Closed Sundays. Major credit cards accepted. 27 Rue Ste. Angèle (phone: 692-3835). Expensive to moderate.

Café de la Paix – This is a small, friendly place with French food. The seafood plate, rack of lamb, and, in the fall, various kinds of game like bison and wild boar, are all good bets. Open daily. Reservations advised. Major credit cards accepted. 44 Desjardins (phone: 692-1430). Expensive to moderate.

L'Echaudé – This is one of several restaurants that opened in the Old Lower Town in 1984 when the port area was renovated. Its Art Deco interior is cool and relaxing, its nouvelle cuisine menu intriguing, and its desserts sumptuous. Try the *bavaroise aux framboises*, a raspberry custard with a tangy sauce. Open daily. Reservations advised. Major credit cards accepted. 73 Sault-au-Matelot (phone: 692-1299). Expensive to moderate.

Gambrinus – Just half a block from the *Château Frontenac*, this is a fine Italian restaurant. The pasta dishes with seafood sauces are especially noteworthy, as is the cheesecake for dessert. Open daily. Reservations advised. Major credit cards. 15 Rue du Fort (phone: 692-5144). Expensive to moderate.

Kyoto – The place to go if you've a yen for Japanese food, it's decorated in bamboo, with Japanese prints on the wall, and has long tables that seat eight. On a gas burner right on your table, the cook — who loves to show off and make people laugh — prepares authentic Japanese chicken, steak, shrimp, or lobster dishes, with all the traditional accompaniments. Open daily; no lunch on weekends. Reservations advised on Saturday and Sunday. Major credit cards accepted. 560 Grande Allée E. (phone: 529-6141). Expensive to moderate.

La Ripaille – This long-established, well-run, small restaurant specializes in French and Italian food. The things to try here are the crab dishes and veal escalopes. It's a good place for lunch. Open daily. Reservations advised. Major credit cards accepted. 9 Rue Buade (phone: 692-2450). Expensive to moderate.

Le Saint-Amour – An easy 5-minute walk from all the major hotels, this fine French restaurant specializes in nouvelle cuisine. Try the *lotte*, a white fish, in vinegar and honey sauce. There's also a better-than-average wine list. Open daily. Reservations advised. Major credit cards accepted. 48 Ste. Ursule (phone: 694-0667). Expensive to moderate.

Balico – Off the usual tourist trail, this intimate little restaurant specializes in the food of the Provence region of France. The fish soups are quite delicious, and the *aïoli* (garlic mayonnaise) unforgettable. Closed Mondays. Reservations advised. Major credit cards accepted. 935 Rue Bourlamaque (phone: 648-1880). Moderate.

Le Chalet Suisse – For a change of pace, try the fondues at this festive, multistoried place. Some suggestions: the Chinese fondue — thinly sliced beef served in a heated beef bouillon — grilled cheese *raclette*, or a traditional Swiss cheese fondue. One of the few restaurants in town open past 11 PM, hence its regulars include provincial politicians when the National Assembly is in session. Open daily. Reservations advised. Major credit cards accepted. 26 Rue Ste. Anne (phone: 694-1320). Moderate.

Le Fiacre – For a congenial atmosphere, good service, and down-to-earth food — charcoal-broiled steaks or seafood — this large restaurant in Ste. Foy fits the bill and the budget. Open daily. Reservations advised Wednesdays through Saturdays. Major credit cards accepted. 1156 Av. Fournier at Blvd. Laurier (phone: 651-4055). Moderate.

Fleur de Lotus – Near City Hall, this Cambodian restaurant serves Vietnamese and Thai food. Open daily. Major credit cards accepted. 50 Rue de la Fabrique (phone: 692-4286). Moderate.

Mykonos – The total Greek population of Quebec City numbers 150, so it's surprising that there's a Greek restaurant here at all, let alone such a fine one. The menu features a wide variety of Greek dishes, but *agneau* (lamb) is the specialty — you can have a generous portion of roast lamb or shish kebab with lamb or beef. Accompanying the lamb is *briam*, fresh string beans, onions, potatoes, zucchini, and eggplant, baked in layers. *Galactobouriko*, custard served in *phyllo*, a thin pastry crust, tops off the meal. Open daily. Reservations advised. Major credit cards accepted. 1066 Rue St. Jean (phone: 692-2048). Moderate.

Le d'Orsay – A restaurant-pub with a good location and an excellent selection of European beers. Open daily. Reservations advised. Major credit cards accepted. 65 Buade St., just across from City Hall (phone: 694-1582). Moderate.

Le Biarritz – It's an intimate restaurant that can accommodate groups or twosomes for cozy dining. The escargots are a good choice for starters, and any of the many veal dishes will make a satisfying entrée. Open daily. Reservations advised. Major credit cards accepted. 136 Ste. Anne (phone: 692-2433). Moderate to inexpensive.

Café Latin – A lovely place to dawdle over an espresso, sandwich, quiche, or salad to the accompaniment of taped classical music. It also has the best maple sugar pie in town. Outdoor dining on the terrace in summer. Open daily. No credit cards accepted. 8½ Ste. Ursule (phone: 692-0919). Inexpensive.

La Campagne – This small Vietnamese restaurant serves a delicious house soup and unusual dishes like chicken with pineapple and squid stuffed with port. Bring your own wine. Closed Mondays. Reservations unnecessary. Major credit cards accepted. 555 St. Jean (phone: 525-5247). Inexpensive.

Les Delices du Maghreb – Good and inexpensive Mediterranean and Provençal food in unpretentious surroundings. It's in a less than fashionable, but still interesting, part of downtown, surrounded by shops and cafés that seem left over from the 1960s. Bring your own wine. Open daily. Reservations unneccessary. 798 Rue St. Jean (phone: 529-9578). Inexpensive.

Marie Antoinette – For fast food, Quebec-style. Breakfast is especially recommended. Open 24 hours daily. Reservations unneccessary. Major credit cards accepted. There are ten of these restaurants in the area, including ones at 2813 Laurier Blvd. (phone: 653-5993) and 44 Kennedy St. Lévis (phone: 837-5809). Inexpensive.

Le Trompe L'Oeil – This small restaurant is a wonderful lunch stop on a visit to the Old Lower Town. Daily fixed menus provide complete lunches including soup, main dish, and dessert at very reasonable prices. Open daily for lunch and dinner. Reservations unnecessary. Major credit cards accepted. 89 Sault-au-Matelot (phone: 694-0152). Inexpensive.

TORONTO

There was a time when Toronto was content with its position as the second city of Canada and willingly deferred to Montreal as the spicier, more intriguing Canadian travel destination. Toronto even accepted and embraced its longtime image as the squarest city in Canada — if not in all of North America. But anyone who visits the city today knows that the so-called Queen City's former lethargic attitude has changed dramatically. A vibrant rhythm has replaced the old puritanical chord, and a new spirit flows through the city's bustling streets. After-dark entertainment has a vital, exciting beat; restaurants have grown in number and variety; and modern structures are being built as rapidly as old neighborhoods are being restored. Toronto has truly developed a strong cosmopolitan personality.

The dreams of farm kids and immigrants and a surprising combination of economic and sociological factors have transformed Toronto from a minor North American city to the financial, commercial, and communications center of Canada. This change is reflected in the ethnic composition of the population, the character of the city, and even in its physical profile. Dominating the skyline are two structures built in 1975 and 1976, the CN Tower — an 1,815-foot communications tower that is the tallest free-standing structure in the world — and Royal Bank Plaza, two triangular towers that appear to be solid gold (actually, there's 2,500 ounces of gold in the windows). The construction and eminence of both structures symbolize the city's ascendancy, a rise that occurred during the past 2 decades.

One of the fastest growing cities in North America, Toronto has surpassed Montreal as the Canadian city with the largest metropolitan population (Toronto's is about 3 million). The rapid rate of growth was initially spurred by the large influx of immigrants from the war-ravaged countries of Western and Central Europe, who came in a great wave during the early 1950s. Some 500,000 Italians now live here, as well as large communities of Germans, Portuguese, Ukrainians, and others from Asia and the Caribbean. What was once a predominantly white Anglo-Saxon Protestant population is now 43% British and 57% a diverse ethnic mosaic. For a city its size, Toronto has proportionately the largest Italian population in North America and substantial other minority communities with their own newspapers and traditions.

The immigrants came to Toronto because it was where the jobs were. And the jobs are still here; 6,200 industrial plants in and around the city account for one-fifth of all manufacturing in Canada. A third of the country's purchasing power is located within a 100-mile radius of Toronto; most national companies are headquartered here, and most international companies maintain offices here. Jobs brought people and people brought more jobs. Thus mass-scale immigration was responsible for Toronto's evolution as an international city.

Rising on the north bank of Lake Ontario, Toronto covers 244 square miles, six municipalities that stretch from the flat, central downtown section to numerous hills in the sprawling suburbs. The city is laid out on a rectangular grid, but the neat order of the plan is interrupted by a greenbelt of wooded ravines created by two small rivers — the Humber and the Don — that cut through the city with miles of wooded parkland. These stretches of green are regarded by residents as one of Toronto's prime recreational areas; summer and winter, they use the space to hike, jog, and cross-country ski.

The lake has a wide, deep harbor that can accommodate oceangoing vessels, making Toronto a major port on the St. Lawrence Seaway, the more so since a $10 million construction-dredging program completed in 1974 established a new harbor entrance. The waterfront area close to downtown has been renovated and is now the site of Harbourfront, a government-funded complex that includes recreational, cultural, and crafts centers, restaurants, and residential and commercial complexes. Also bordering the lake are Harbour Square, exclusive, modern high-rise apartments, and the *Harbour Castle Westin,* a spectacular double-towered luxury hotel. Beaches, walkways, and marinas stretch along the lakefront.

Downtown rises to the north. Innovative architecture characterizes the city — the banking towers; a new city hall, with two curved towers surrounding a lower rotunda; Eaton Centre, the spacious shopping gallery that looks like nothing so much as a huge greenhouse (inside are some of the best shops in Canada); the public library, designed by Raymond Moriyama; and numerous other avant-garde buildings.

All this has contributed to the transformation of a city that only 30 years ago was an almost provincial, essentially British town. The Huron Indians set up camp at the end of their portage connecting Lake Huron to Lake Ontario. They called the site Toronto, the Indian word for "meeting place." French fur traders discovered it in the early 18th century and built a fort here in 1720. The fort was burned to the ground in 1759, and from that time Toronto's history and character were predominantly British.

In 1796 the site was proclaimed the capital of Upper Canada and welcomed Loyalist refugees from the US. They named the settlement York, after the Duke of York, the son of George III and the major opponent of the American Revolution.

During the War of 1812 between Britain and the US, the town was occupied by American troops who destroyed the Parliament buildings and archives and stole the mace, the symbol of British sovereignty and authority. The British retaliated by marching on Washington and burning all of its public buildings. (Before setting fire to the presidential mansion, a regiment of Scottish soldiers finished off a fine dinner prepared for the President, then proceeded to burn as much of the house as possible, leaving only a scorched outer shell. It was rebuilt quickly and painted white in such a hurry that it became known as the White House.) In 1934, President Franklin D. Roosevelt returned the mace to the government of Ontario as a gesture of international goodwill.

When the city was incorporated in 1834 and its name reverted from York to the original Toronto, the most remarkable thing about it was its growth.

By 1901 its population reached 200,000, and its business extended throughout Canada. It was very much an English town — English-speaking, Anglophilic, its character heavily influenced by and indebted to classic English traits. People were civil (and still are, which may explain the disproportionately low number of violent crimes committed here in relation to cities of comparable size), reserved, helpful when asked for help, but hardly gregarious. Its business world was run like a very select British club, with the reins of financial and corporate power held tightly in a few hands. The view of what made a good and satisfying life was vividly perceived and rigidly maintained. Life in Toronto was a long series of blue laws. Until World War II, Toronto was a WASP town — white, Anglo-Saxon, and Protestant — and so immersed in the work ethic that anything that even looked like fun was assumed to be harmful, sinful, prideful, or all three. In the words of the late Gordon Sinclair, Toronto's outspoken radio and TV broadcaster, "Everyday life was dreary enough, but Sundays were murder. Everything but the churches shut down tight. *Eaton's* [the major department store] even drew its curtains to prevent the small enjoyment of window-shopping on the Sabbath."

What turned Toronto the Good into Toronto the Human was the infusion of cultures from several continents over the last 40 years. More than a million Toronto residents today have roots in non-English-speaking countries. These groups have brought their customs, cultures, and cuisines with them, and they have utterly changed the city's character. Toronto has become a city of neighborhoods. Thousands of Greeks live in the East End around Danforth Avenue at the end of Bloor Street, and elsewhere there are large communities of Italians, Ukrainians, and Hungarians. Bordering Chinatown is a Portuguese neighborhood distinguished by its houses painted in lovely pastels. Toronto is home to a sizable German population as well, although its members tend not to live in any easily defined ethnic enclave. In nearby Kensington Market, most of these cultures meet to buy from and sell to one another. Strongly Portuguese and Caribbean, with some Italians and Jews, this market is where everyone can get everything. And as inexpensive as the goods always are, they get even less expensive if the buyer speaks the native tongue of the seller.

Toronto celebrates its ethnicity every year at the end of June in a 10-day blowout known as *Caravan*. Various groups set up pavilions in churches and community centers and offer the public food and drink, handicrafts and art, songs and dances, from the old country. Visitors buy a "passport" and go from pavilion to pavilion on an around-the-world tour, stopping here for some Greek baklava, there for a demonstration of Ukrainian folk dancing, around the corner for a taste of Caribbean steel band music. In the course of a day's ramble, you can have Italian pasta washed down by Irish coffee or a potent Polish liqueur.

Caravan is a short-lived phenomenon, though a lot happens in its brief appearance each year. A more lasting gift from Toronto's newer residents has been the proliferation of theaters, clubs, and ethnic restaurants and, even more important, the effect such variety has had on living habits in the city. With so much to choose from, Toronto has opened up at night. Residents are determined that the city center should not be a daytime-only experience, and a good deal of the most recent construction — the last wave of which added so many of the buildings that now make the city's skyline unique — fosters and encourages this feeling. Mixed development downtown — commercial and residential complexes — keeps people in the heart of the city. So instead of becoming a ghost town after working hours, downtown Toronto remains vibrant, drawing people to its nightlife.

A concomitant movement has awakened in the city's neighborhoods. Until 30 years ago, Toronto appeared to be following the American model: a city center for business in the day, with rings of ever more affluent suburbs around it. When the great numbers of immigrants arrived, they moved into the older neighborhoods, where they established communities with strong bonds and natural cohesion. This movement has been extended to downtown commercial neighborhoods in recent years by young middle class people who years ago might have moved to the suburbs.

The phenomenon that sparked the revival of the decaying neighborhoods was the election in 1972 of a reform city council, which reversed developers' plans for massive demolition to make way for inner-city high-rises and instead promoted city-run nonprofit housing, rent control, and tenants' rights. (Today it seems inconceivable that old City Hall was almost torn down to make way for an earlier version of ultra-posh Eaton Centre, but it's true.) The mood of the residents changed, and with the support of the city, the restoration of the old neighborhoods began in earnest. One small group of 200 people managed to save their historic church — Church of the Holy Trinity — from destruction during the construction of Eaton Centre. Not only did developers revise their plans to protect the sanctity of the lovely little church, one of the oldest houses of worship in the city, but they changed the plans to ensure that sun would shine on the building.

Toronto residents created and maintain a lively and livable city. Toronto has its showplaces, like the spectacular Ontario Science Centre, the Toronto Zoo, where you can ZooSki — cross-country ski — around the building that houses the zoo's major indoor complexes, and the new SkyDome stadium (see below). But the city is worth a visit for even more fundamental reasons. Its number one tourist attraction is its healthy urban environment. As Canada's leading metropolis, it has achieved a balance between progress and preservation. Wherever Toronto's heading, much of the rest of urban Canada is likely soon to follow. And much of the rest of urban North America might do well to take note.

TORONTO AT-A-GLANCE

 SEEING THE CITY: The best way to grasp the lay of the land is from the CN Tower, Toronto's most visible and famous landmark. The property of Canadian National, the publicly owned railway, this communication tower is the world's tallest free-standing structure. From the base of the reflecting pool, the tower stretches 1,815 feet and 5 inches. (There are taller TV antennas, but they're supported by guy wires and thus are not free-standing.) Four exterior glass elevators whisk visitors 1,122 feet up to the Sky Pod, which has an outdoor observation deck, an indoor deck with zoom lens peritelescopes, the world's highest revolving restaurant, *Top of Toronto,* and a nightclub called *Sparkles.* On a clear day, Buffalo and Niagara Falls and everything in between is visible. The Sky Pod level also contains a broadcasting studio and communications equipment. Another elevator leads to the 1,500-foot level, where you can look up at the transmission mast and down on everything else, except the jets approaching Toronto International Airport. Open daily. Admission charge. 301 Front St. W. (phone: 360-8500).

SPECIAL PLACES: Toronto is designed on a straightforward grid system, which makes it easy to walk around downtown. The north-south reference points are Highway 401 and Lake Ontario. Yonge Street is the main north-south artery, and cross streets are numbered east and west from Yonge. Bloor Street is the city's principal east-west thoroughfare. Downtown extends from Bloor south to Lake Ontario, between Jarvis Street and Spadina Avenue. Midtown covers the area north of Bloor to Eglinton Avenue. The Toronto Transit Commission (TTC) is one of the safest, cleanest, and most efficient public transit systems in North America. If you avoid the buses and subways at rush hour, the system is also one of the most comfortable. The TTC has an extensive route structure and will get you anywhere you want to go in metropolitan Toronto for a single fare.

DOWNTOWN

SkyDome – Set on 8 acres, this 31-story amphitheater is one of the world's largest, with a capacity for 60,000 spectators and many other facilities. Home of the *Blue Jays* baseball team and football's Toronto *Argonauts,* it also hosts other major league sporting events, plus concerts, exhibitions, and more. The new amphitheater has a retractable dome roof that covers the stadium during inclement weather and opens up when the weather is good. The stadium also boasts the world's largest scoreboard/replay machine, SkyVision (35 by 115 feet), along with an 800-seat restaurant overlooking the football end-zone, several bars, a health club, a 364-suite hotel with 70 rooms overlooking the stadium, a *Hard Rock Café,* and a *McDonald's* with seating for 500 people. Parking at the SkyDome is limited, and most fans will have to reach it through public transportation. 277 Front St. W. (phone: 341-3663).

Royal Ontario Museum – Affectionately referred to as the *ROM,* it's Canada's largest public museum — recently made even larger after an $83-million renovation and expansion project — which features collections drawn from 20 science, art, and archaeology departments. The *ROM* is well known for its Chinese collections, and the Bat Cave and Dinosaur Gallery are popular with kids of all ages. As we went to press, several new galleries were scheduled to open, including the European Galley, Gallery of Birds, and the Ethnology Gallery of Native Peoples of North America. Also, mummies were slated to be on exhibit in the Egypt-Nubia Gallery by 1990, and an Earth Sciences gem hall promises to dazzle visitors. The adjacent McLaughlin Planetarium presents Laserium shows Wednesdays through Sundays (call 586-5750 for show times and admission prices; children under 6 not admitted). Original star shows are also presented every few months; for more information call 586-5736. The museum's Sigmund Samuel Building houses furniture, ceramics, and silver (14 Queen's Park Crescent; open daily; no admission charge). The main museum building is open daily and there is an admission charge. The *ROM* Shop is a cornucopia of gifts from around the world. 100 Queen's Park (phone: 586-5549).

Provincial Parliament Buildings – As you leave the museum, turn right. That pile of pink Romanesque rock is the back of the provincial parliament buildings; from the front they are striking brownstones. They're located in Queen's Park, which has become synonymous with the provincial legislature. Enthroned beside the buildings is regally resplendent Queen Victoria. Her equally regal son, Edward VII, astride his sturdy steed, has become a shrine for local pigeons. Sir John A. Macdonald, Canada's first prime minister and the chief architect of Canadian Confederation, and his political as well as personal adversary, George Brown, are also represented here. Here's a bit of Canadiana to put these two characters in proper perspective: Once, during a legislative debate, Brown accused Macdonald of being drunk — a fairly safe accusation. Macdonald's reply was immortalized in the annals of Canadian history: "Better Sir John A. drunk," he said, "than George Brown sober." Queen's Park with its sweeping lawns and old trees is a favorite picnic ground. Outdoor musical evenings are held regularly during the summer. Free guided tours on weekdays during the winter (call for times); in summer, tours are conducted daily, every hour. The legislature convenes on Mondays through Wednesdays from 1:30 to 6 PM and on Thursdays from 10 AM to 12 PM. Queen's Park Crescent at University Ave. (phone ahead to book a tour: 965-4028).

Ontario Hydro – From the steps to Queen's Park look up to the right. That mirrored, concave building is the headquarters of Canada's largest power-producing and distributing organization. It employs a radical heating system, eliminating the traditional boiler: Heat provided by interior lighting and old-fashioned body warmth is recirculated throughout the building. Technical tours only (not for the general public) are by appointment only. 700 University Ave. (phone: 592-3345).

University of Toronto – Before continuing south on University Avenue, detour one block west to one of North America's better universities, dating from 1827. The campus sprawls over several city blocks; the best route for a short tour is around King's College Circle. Take a look inside Hart House, the Gothic student center built with Massey money (the family of Hollywood actor Raymond and his brother, Vincent, former governor-general of Canada). Among the other buildings are the Old Observatory, University College, Knox College, and the Medical Sciences Building. Many scientific firsts have happened in this last building: Dr. Frederick Banting and Dr. Charles Best discovered insulin in 1922; the first electric heart pacemaker was developed; and Pablum, the first precooked vitamin-enriched cereal, was formulated. Student guides lead free walking tours Mondays through Fridays during June, July, and August. Hart House (phone: 978-2452).

Tour of the Universe – For those who've always wondered what it's like to be an astronaut, this futuristic attraction is a must-see. The year is 2019. "Astronauts" are checked in by security, insert their 3-D pass into a computer terminal, and pass through customs. Then it's blast-off time, so fasten your seat belts for a bumpy ride through outer space. Upon returning from the solar system, reenter the earth with a visit to the gift shop. Open daily year-round. Admission charge. At the base of the CN Tower (phone: 363-TOUR).

Mary Pickford's Birthplace – Along stately University Avenue, with its wide, flowered median, you will find the city's most famous hospitals — Toronto General, Mt. Sinai, and Hospital for Sick Children. In the gardens of the "Sick Kids" on the east side of University Avenue is a plaque and bronze bust commemorating the birthplace of Gladys Marie Smith, better known as Mary Pickford, America's Sweetheart. Incidentally, Miss Pickford requested her Canadian citizenship back, which was granted in October 1978. 55 University Ave.

Chinatown – Several blocks downtown are the focal point of Toronto's Chinese, Korean, and Japanese communities: here you'll find many interesting grocery stores and restaurants. The best places to eat are the *Macay Court* restaurant, 405 Dundas St. W. (basement) and *Young Lok*, 122 St. Patrick St. University Ave. and Dundas St. W. (see *Eating Out* for more information).

City Hall and Nathan Phillips Square – This distinctive modern complex was designed by Finnish architect Viljo Revell. Two curved towers of unequal height focus on the low-domed Council Chamber, which, from an aerial view, resembles a giant eye. Surrounding the buildings is a square named for Toronto's longtime mayor Nathan Phillips, who initiated plans for a new city hall back in 1957. The square is a popular gathering place and the site of special events during the summer. The reflecting pool and fountains circulate 12,000 gallons of water a minute. In summer, office workers dip their toes in the pool; in winter they skate on its frozen surface. *The Archer,* a bronze Henry Moore sculpture, was purchased by public donation to adorn the square after the city council refused to buy it. Free tours are conducted daily (call for times). Bay and Queen Sts. (phone: 392-7341).

Eaton Centre – A modern 4-level shopping gallery, it has a high glass roof, lots of space and light, marble floors, trees, plants, flowers, and benches. *Eaton's,* an institution in Canadian merchandising (whose founder, Timothy Eaton, first set up shop in Toronto in 1869), has its plush flagship store here. In addition, the center houses another 300 shops, boutiques, and restaurants. For a bite or a beer, drop into *Elephant and Castle.* You'll find the best ice cream in the city at *Swensen's.* The gallery was constructed in accordance with the city's policy for architectural preservation and was built around two of the city's oldest buildings, Trinity Church and Scadding House, the former home of an early Toronto historian. Shops are closed Sundays; some restaurants open daily. 220 Yonge St. (phone: 598-2322).

Bank Towers – Canada's five major banks have offices in these high-rise office-commercial complexes that dominate the Toronto skyline. All four complexes are linked underground by concourses that house shops, cinemas, and restaurants. The tallest of the buildings is the white marble, 72-story Bank of Montreal building, known as First Canadian Place because it was Canada's first chartered bank. Most striking is the Royal Bank Plaza, two triangular towers of 41 and 26 stories respectively with serrated walls and windows covered with 2,500 ounces of gold. Inside there's a cascading fountain and an international art collection featuring Venezuelan Jesús Soto's sculpture composed of 8,600 20-inch-long aluminum tubes. You can't miss it — the work is 100 feet high and 60 feet wide and occupies more than half the space in the hall. Commerce Court is a stainless steel skyscraper with 7,400 windows of double-glazed reflective glass. The three jet black buildings are the Toronto Dominion Centre; the lobby often has art exhibits. King and Bay Sts. The fifth major bank tower is the Bank of Novia Scotia or "Scotia Bank" tower.

Art Gallery of Ontario – The highlight here is the *Henry Moore Sculpture Centre,* the largest public collection of his work, displayed with related drawings, prints, studio material, and photography donated by Moore. Of the gallery's permanent collection, over half is the work of Canadian artists, including a wide variety of paintings and sculpture from the early 19th century through the present. Old Masters, Impressionists, and early-20th-century artists are also represented. (As we went to press, the gallery was undergoing a $35 million expansion.) Connected to the gallery by an underground walkway is the *Grange,* a charming museum that is Toronto's oldest remaining brick house, circa 1817. Some say it's haunted, but the atmosphere is cheery and the furnishings delightful. Vera, the upstairs maid, often greets guests; and goods baked fresh from the hearth are sold to visitors on Tuesdays, Thursdays, and Saturdays. Faces the front lawn of Grange Park. Closed Mondays. Admission charge covers entrance to the gallery and Grange. Gallery on Dundas St. W., between McCaul and Beverley Sts. (phone: 977-0414).

Yorkville – Once a hangout for the Toronto hippie generation before they headed west, this area is now the most chic in the city. Renovated townhouses, boutiques with designer fashions and expensive jewelry, quiet courtyards, wrought-iron lampposts, and art galleries flank the narrow streets. There are several cafés where you can sit by a window box sipping an aperitif and watch the world. Yorkville Village was incorporated in 1853, and eagle-eyed explorers will find the original coat of arms — brewer, smith, brickmaker, carpenter, and farmer — outside many of the specialty stores. Hazelton Lanes, 55 Avenue Rd., is a classy commercial-residential complex with some 70 boutiques and an outdoor café that is transformed into an ice skating rink in winter. Some of the most expensive chocolate around is sold at *Teuscher of Switzerland,* which imports its chocolates from Zurich; try the champagne truffles — you'll go broke happily. Bounded by Bloor St., Avenue Rd., Bay St., and Scollard St.

Queen Street West – The up-and-coming cousin to Yorkville, this once-moribund stretch just west of city hall now hums with colorful street life, sidewalk jewelry vendors, and an assortment of shops selling everything from new and used furniture and books to state-of-the-art computers. Nearby is the Ontario College of Art, the proximity of which played a big role in the development of this area: When graduates from the acclaimed art school needed places to show their wares, they began opening shops along this street. High-fashion highlights include *Twinkle Toes* (#320) for men's and women's footwear; *Next* (#348) for boots; *Club Monaco* (#403) for sportswear, plus an inexpensive lunch counter offering sandwiches, salads, and cappuccino; and *Marilyn Brooks Boutique* (#383) for fine clothing from a top Canadian designer. From John St. to Spadina Ave.

Kensington Market – The complete antithesis of Yorkville, this is the place to get everything from salted fish and fresh produce to deals on stereos. This outdoor market has character — lots of it — and a heavy ethnic flavor. Jewish, Portuguese, Caribbean, and Italian influences are apparent. The food sold here is 10% lower in price and probably better tasting than anywhere else in the city. Closed Sundays. No admission charge. College and Dundas Sts., west of Spadina.

St. Lawrence Market – If you're into markets, this is another good one. Erected in 1844 to serve as Toronto's first City Hall, it's now a clearinghouse for farmers, butchers, and fishmongers. Saturday's the big day here, when the area farmers truck their produce to the Farmer's Market across the street. Open Tuesdays through Saturdays. 95 Front St. E.

Casa Loma – This magnificent, rambling, eccentric, turreted mansion — a 98-room mock medieval castle — was built by Sir Henry Pellatt between 1911 and 1914 to house the collection of massive furniture and grandiose art he had collected from the greatest galleries of Europe during his career as one of Toronto's most successful financiers. The mansion must be the ultimate expression of Sir Henry's idiosyncratic pursuit of the grand and grandiose. He imported European craftsmen to build the house, then filled it with his pieces of European art and furniture. You will be fascinated by its splendor — the conservatory, with elegant bronze doors; Peacock Alley, running the length of the house, copied and named after the Peacock Alley in the royal residence of Windsor Castle; the Great Hall, with a 60-foot ceiling; the Oak Room, where three artisans worked for 3 years to chisel the French oak paneling; as well as the 15 bathrooms, 23 fireplaces, and a wine cellar with space for 1,700 bottles. In the 1920s, Sir Henry found the cost of upkeep beyond even his ample means; Casa Loma was taken by the city for back taxes, and Sir Henry had to auction most of his Chippendales and Reynoldses to keep body and soul together. For a while the place fell to the mice and disrepair. In 1937, the Kiwanis Club of West Toronto restored the castle and still runs it today as a tourist attraction. Proceeds go to community projects. There are guided tours; the castle is equipped for the handicapped. As we went to press, the Garden Club of Toronto was renovating Casa Loma's 10 acres of gardens, with completion slated for 1991. Be sure to climb the two towers; the Norman Tower is open and the Scottish Tower is enclosed. Open daily. Admission charge. 1 Austin Terrace (phone: 923-1171).

Fort York – This restored fort from the War of 1812 re-creates the atmosphere of an early-19th-century garrison. Open daily. Admission charge. On Garrison Rd. off Fleet St. between Bathurst St. and Strachan Ave., near Exhibition Pl. (phone: 392-6916).

Mackenzie House – The mid-Victorian home and print shop of William Lyon Mackenzie, first mayor of Toronto, has authentic 1850s furnishings. Open daily. Admission charge. 82 Bond St. (phone: 392-6915).

Colborne Lodge – An 1836 Regency country cottage, it was the home of John G. Howard, a city surveyor and architect. He donated his estate to the city, and now it's part of High Park. The lodge is furnished in period pieces, and there are some fine examples of early Canadian art. Open daily. Small admission charge. Colborne Lodge Dr. in High Park (phone: 392-6827).

OUTDOORS

Ontario Place – This 96-acre theme park on the edge of Lake Ontario is part playground, part exposition and cultural center, and mostly lush green park. The cinesphere is a giant structure shaped like a dimpled basketball and spiked with luminous eyeballs. Inside there's a curved movie screen, 6 stories high. At the *Forum* (capacity 10,000), you can listen to the *Toronto Symphony*, to jazz, or to popular performers. Children's Village is an imaginative area for kids up to 12 (there's even a height restriction of 58 inches). The Pavilion, a series of interconnected pods built right in Lake Ontario, houses good restaurants and exhibits. The west island features a wilderness flume ride and water stage facility showcasing Ontario talent. Open daily from mid-May to Labor Day. Films shown in winter. Admission charge. 955 Lakeshore Blvd. W. (phone: 965-7711).

Harbourfront – The federal government restored this 92-acre waterfront area and built a recreation/culture complex. At the Queen's Quay Terminal and in the surrounding park you can listen to jazz, make crafts, participate in sports, examine old steam engines, feed the ducks, or just watch the ships go by. The area is divided into several sections: York Quay, with an art gallery, theater, and café for jazz and poetry readings; Spadina Quay, with a marina and picnic facilities; and Bathurst Quay, with a park and cooperative housing projects. There's also a year-round antiques and flea market, and in the summer there's a sailing school. Open daily. No admission charge, although sometimes there's a charge for specific events. 235 Queen's Quay W. (phone: 973-3000).

Toronto Islands – This group of islands off the Toronto shore of Lake Ontario encompasses Hanlan's Point, Ward's Island, Centre Island, Algonquin Island, and four small islands. The 15-minute ferry ride to the islands is the least expensive and quickest escape from the intensity of city life. You can't take your car; bicycles (bring your own on weekdays only) and legs are the standard modes of transportation. Centre Island, the most popular, has 612 acres of park, picnic grounds, restaurants, boating, a barnyard zoo, and Centreville, a child-size replica of a 19th-century Ontario village with lots of rides (open May 24 to Labor Day). Ward's Island and Hanlan's Point have fewer facilities and attract fewer people, but swimming is good at Ward's Island, and public tennis courts are available at Hanlan's Point. There are also boat rentals.

THE SUBURBS

Ontario Science Centre – A spectacular facility that was built in 1967 at a cost of $30 million as Ontario's contribution to Canada's Centennial. Since then, it has attracted millions of visitors from all over the world for its scientific and technological exhibits, which stress interaction and participation and show that science can be fun. Designed by Raymond Moriyama, the structure itself is extremely well integrated with its environment. It is built into a ravine; visitors enter at the top of a cliff and work their way down on glass-enclosed escalators that open up a view of the natural surroundings in the lush, wooded valley. Inside, there are many different exhibits — Food/Earth Hall, Exploring Space, Hall of Communication, Hall of Life, Hall of Transportation, Science Arcade, Hall of the Atom — as well as demonstrations, films, and theaters with multimedia shows. There are far too many things to see and do to cover everything, even in several visits. There are no tours, so plot your own course from the Science Centre's map and set your own pace. Wherever you head, you'll find numerous opportunities to participate: Pit your wits against a computer in a game of Hangman; make a machine talk; make your hair stand on end with a charge of static electricity; test your fitness, your reflexes, or your perception. Hosts knowledgable about science are around to help you experiment if you want guidance. Open daily. Admission charge. 770 Don Mills Rd. (phone: 429-4100).

Metro Toronto Zoo – This impressive zoo is one of the largest in the world. Stretched between two arms of the Rouge River, these 710 acres of river valley and 8 pavilions have been shaped to simulate the natural habitats of the zoo's nearly 4,000 animal residents. The geographic regions represented include Africa, Australia, Eurasia, Indo-Malaysia, North America, and South America. The African Pavilion is the largest and is equipped with ponds and a jungle atmosphere to keep the gorillas, hippos, bongos, and monkeys feeling right at home. Orangutans and gibbons swing through trees in the rain forest environment of Indo-Malaysia. Other settings accommodate polar bears, alligators, zebras, Japanese macaques, and South African fur seals. A slow, rubber-wheeled train negotiates the 3½-mile path though the Canadian Domain, where deer, Arctic wolves, caribou, moose, and antelope play. The zoo can easily take up a full day. There are several ways to approach it: You can ride the train, take a variety of walking tours including the Round the World Tour, or in the winter try it by ZooSki — go cross-country skiing on trails through Africa and Eurasia (ski rentals are available at the zoo). Open daily. Admission charge. Just north of Hwy. 401 on Meadowvale Rd., 10 miles (16 km) east of the Don Valley Pkwy. (phone: 392-5900, or 392-5901 for recording).

Black Creek Pioneer Village – This restored 19th-century town depicts life in a rural Ontario village over a hundred years ago. The buildings include a homestead and farm, a general store, a blacksmith's shop, a town hall, and a flour mill. Costumed folk in last century's fashions perform tasks such as shoeing horses, making butter, and weaving rugs. Open daily in summer; buildings closed in January and February, but there's a sports program with skating, and horse-drawn sleigh rides. Admission charge. Jane St. at Steeles Ave. W. (phone: 736-1733 or 661-6610 for recorded message).

McMichael Canadian Art Collection – These attractive galleries built of handhewn logs and fieldstone, set amidst 100 acres of breathtaking conserved land overlooking the Humber River Valley, shelter many works of the Group of Seven, an informal school of artists who broke away from traditional British painting early in the 20th century and immortalized the Canadian landscape. There are also exhibits of Northwest Coast, Inuit, and contemporary Indian art. Closed Mondays, November through April. Lively weekend programs include tours, talks, films, and Sunday afternoon jazz concerts. There's a full service restaurant and book and gift shop with exclusive, Canadian handcrafted goods. Admission charge. In Kleinburg, north of Toronto (phone: 893-ARTS).

Canada's Wonderland – Canada's major theme park is just 20 miles (32 km) northwest of downtown Toronto. The park features five live stage shows and some 30 thrilling rides, including the only stand-up looping roller coaster in Canada. Shops and restaurants line International Street, which leads to six theme areas. Top entertainers perform in the Kingswood Music Theatre (capacity 15,000). The children's and adult's pay-one-price passports allow unlimited use of the park for the day (Kingswood not included). Open daily June to September, weekends in May and September to mid-October. On Hwy. 400 between Rutherford Rd. and Major Mackenzie Dr. (phone: 832-7000).

■ **EXTRA SPECIAL:** Just 82 miles (132 km) southwest of Toronto is Niagara Falls, one of the most powerful waterfalls in the world, as well as one of the Western

Hemisphere's major tourist attractions. The falls are formed as the waters of Lake Erie race downhill to join Lake Ontario, becoming the Niagara River en route. The river gathers strength and power in the narrows and then plunges almost 200 feet to form the famous falls. A small island in the river splits this whitewater juggernaut at the point of its mighty dive, dividing it into two falls instead of one — the Horseshoe (Canadian) Falls, 176 feet high and 2,100 feet wide; and the American Falls, 182 feet high and 1,076 feet wide. There are several ways to see the falls — from a tower or helicopter ride; on the *Maid of the Mist* sightseeing boat that carries visitors to the base of the Horseshoe Falls; or from one of the restaurants that overlook them.

SOURCES AND RESOURCES

TOURIST INFORMATION: For general information, brochures, and maps, contact the Metropolitan Toronto Convention and Visitors Association, 207 Queen's Quay W., Suite 509 (phone: 368-9821). The association maintains several outdoor kiosks that provide quick information, and a permanent Visitor Information Centre outside the Eaton Centre at Yonge and Dundas Sts. Its city map has plenty of helpful information and an insert on the subway routes.

The *Toronto Guidebook,* edited by Alexander Ross (Grey de Pencier Publications; $4.95), is the best local guide. The *Toronto Book,* edited by William Kilbourn (Gage Publishing Co.; $35), is a good anthology of Toronto literature past and present.

Local Coverage – The *Globe* and *Mail,* morning daily except Sundays; the *Sun,* morning daily; the *Toronto Star,* morning and afternoon daily except weekends, when it comes out in the morning; *Toronto Life,* monthly magazine; *T.O. Magazine,* published ten times a year; *Metropolitan Toronto Events Guide,* a quarterly booklet with lists of what's going on in town. *Key to Toronto* is a monthly magazine distributed free to hotel guests by the Hotel Association of Metropolitan Toronto. CBC Radio (740) is the national network; CFRB (1010) was the home base of the late popular commentator Gordon Sinclair; CHUM (104.5 FM) is the most popular rock music station.

Food – *Toronto Life* and *Metropolitan Toronto Events Guide,* list most of the established restaurants and many newcomers.

Telephone – The area code for Toronto is 416.

Sales Tax – There is an 8% tax on the sale of most goods.

Currency – All prices are quoted in US dollars unless otherwise indicated.

TIPPING: Taxi drivers are generally given 10% of the fare. At restaurants tip 15 to 20% of the bill. Bellboys and airport porters usually receive 50¢ (CN) to $1 (CN) per bag, and hotel maids should be given about $1 (CN) per day.

CLIMATE: Toronto gets a lot of sunshine all year. Summers are warm, with average temperatures around 71F (21C); winters are cold, with average temperatures around 23F (−5C) and a fair amount of snowfall. For the latest weather information, call 676-3066, 24 hours a day.

GETTING AROUND: Public Transit – The *Toronto Transit Commission* (*TTC*) operates an efficient, modern system covering over 700 miles of routes. The *TTC* publishes a handy pocketsize *Ride Guide* available free from station collectors, the *TTC* Center at Bloor-Yonge subway station, by phoning 393-INFO, or by writing to them at 1900 Yonge St., Toronto, M4S 1Z2. The

232 TORONTO / Sources and Resources

guide will help you easily find your way around. Subways are clean and safe. Some 2,300 vehicles — buses, trolleys, streetcars, and subways — make up this interconnecting system. The exact change or a token is required for the first fare, but additional transfers along the same route are free (including subway-bus transfers). Special family fares are available on Sundays and holidays. For information on routes and fares, contact the TTC information line between 7 AM and 11:30 PM at 393-4636.

Taxi – Cabs are easy to hail on the street. Major cab companies are *Co-op Taxi* (phone: 364-8161) and *Diamond* (phone: 366-6868).

Car Rental – All major North American firms are represented: *Avis,* 80 Bloor St. E. (phone: 964-2051); *Budget,* 141 Bay St. (phone: 364-7104); *Hertz,* 39 Richmond St. W. (phone: 363-9022); and *Tilden,* at Union Station, Front St. (phone: 364-4191).

Sightseeing Tours – *Gray Coach,* 610 Bay St. (phone: 979-3511), has excellent bus tours of the city with passenger pickups at all major hotels and the bus terminal.

SPECIAL EVENTS: In May, the *International Children's Festival* features over 100 performances by international companies. Free activities include jugglers, mimes, and more. Harbourfront, 235 Queen's Quay W. (phone: 973-3000). At the end of June, the *Caravan* festival is held, and 50 of Toronto's ethnic communities set up national pavilions in church basements, school gyms, and public halls for a 10-day orgy of international cuisines. For information, contact the *Metro Caravan,* 263 Adelaide St. W. (phone: 977-0466).

The *International Picnic,* an annual free bash sponsored by the multilingual radio station CHIN, features free eating contests and games. For the exact date, check the publications noted above or contact CHIN, 637 College St. (phone: 531-9991).

Caribana is a 10-day West Indies carnival in mid-summer; for information, refer to *Metropolitan Toronto Happenings* or *Key to Toronto.*

The *Canadian National Exhibition* is the city's big fair, running for 3 weeks, mid-August to Labor Day; there's fine bandstand entertainment nightly. For information, contact Canadian National Exhibition, Lakeshore Blvd. (phone: 393-6000).

The *Royal Agricultural Winter Fair* at Exhibition Park on Lakeshore Boulevard is the showcase for what is billed as the largest agricultural fair under one roof (27½ acres). The fair runs for a week in mid-November, and its *Royal Horse Show* attracts international competition.

MUSEUMS: The *Royal Ontario Museum,* the *Ontario Science Centre,* the *McMichael Canadian Art Collection,* Fort York, Casa Loma, and the *Art Gallery of Ontario* are described in detail in *Special Places.* At the *Art Gallery of Ontario* you can pick up an excellent guidebook to the art scene at more than 30 galleries around the city. Three other interesting museums to visit are

Gibson House – A restored 19th-century home. 5172 Yonge St. (phone: 225-0146).

Marine Museum of Upper Canada – History of shipping and waterways. Lakeshore Blvd., Exhibition Pl. (phone: 392-6827).

Museum of History of Medicine – Known for its Egyptian mummy, on which an autopsy has been performed, and for the Drake Collection of pediatric artifacts, this museum's exhibits span 5,000 years of health care, from the ancient world to the 20th century. No admission charge but donations requested. Academy of Medicine, 288 Bloor St. W. (phone: 922-0564).

SHOPPING: Toronto is a good shopping city with stores carrying imported goods and native crafts — everything from Swiss chocolate to Eskimo soapstone sculpture. There's a broad selection of shopping areas as well, ranging from the exclusive Hazelton Lanes, which houses the biggest names in fashion and design, to Kensington Market (see *Special Places*).

TORONTO / Sources and Resources

Antiques – The ideal spot for browsing in myriad antiques-cum-kitsch shops is on Queen St. West, between University Ave. and Bathurst St. *Pao & Moltke Ltd.,* 118 Yorkville Ave. (phone: 925-6197), has an unusual assortment of Chinese antiques.

China – *Ashley China,* 50 Bloor St. W. (phone: 964-2900), carries the finest and most distinctive English bone china dinnerware.

Chocolate – Swiss chocolates are air-expressed weekly from Zurich to *Teuscher Switzerland* in Hazelton Lanes at 55 Avenue Rd. (phone: 961-1303).

Cigars – *Winston & Holmes,* 138 Cumberland St., is Toronto's foremost tobacconist. Here you'll find Cuban cigars (phone: 968-1290).

Crafts – The *Guild Shop,* 140 Cumberland St. (phone: 921-1721), is a nonprofit retail outlet for Canadian craftspeople. Returning US residents do not have to pay duty on original works of Inuit art and are also reimbursed the Ontario sales tax of 8% (ask for the special form you must fill in and mail from home). *The Pottery Shop,* 140 Yorkville Ave. (phone: 923-1803), specializes in handcrafted clay and glass pieces. *Yonge at Art* offers reasonably priced goods, including jewelry and toys, handcrafted by Canadians; the shop is run by the Inner City Angels, and proceeds support their charity programs. Scadding House, 6 Trinity Square, next to Eaton Centre (phone: 598-0242).

Eskimo Art – *The Inuit Gallery of Eskimo Art* features primitive Eskimo carvings, sculptures, prints, and wall hangings. 9 Prince Arthur Ave. (phone: 921-9785).

Fashion – *Holt Renfrew & Co.,* 50 Bloor St. W. (phone: 922-2333) carries high-style clothes and accessories for men and women. *Chez Catherine,* at 20A Hazelton Lanes (phone: 967-5666), is a big name in fashions for women.

Jewelry – Both casual shoppers and connoisseurs call at the *Gold Shoppe,* 25 Bloor St. W. (phone: 923-5565), for antique jewelry and silver. At *European Jewellery,* 390 Bay St. (phone: 369-0009), and 111 Bloor St. W. (phone: 967-7201), you can purchase elegant and distinctive pieces. *Fraleigh Jewelers & Gemologists,* at 1977 Yonge St. in the *Four Seasons* hotel has lovely estate and antique jewelry (phone: 924-2296).

Leather Goods – *Lanzi of Italy,* 123 Yorkville Ave. (phone: 964-2582), and *Hermès,* in Hazelton Lanes at 55 Avenue Rd. (phone: 968-8626), carry leather accessories.

Tweeds and Linens – *Irish Import House,* 444 Yonge St. W. (phone: 595-0500), has Irish goods at lower-than-usual prices; 15% off Waterford and Belleek.

Wool – *Norma,* 116 Cumberland St. (phone: 923-5514), carries pure wool sweaters, jackets, and suits by Canadian designer Norma Lepofsky.

Women's clothing – *Canadian Signatures* features clothing and accessories, made exclusively by Canadian designers. 138 Cumberland (Old York Lane), store #7 (phone: 975-0400).

SPORTS: Toronto is the home of baseball's American League *Blue Jays,* the National Hockey League *Maple Leafs,* and the Canadian Football League *Argonauts.* The Metro Parks Department maintains good facilities around the city for participatory sports.

Baseball – The new *SkyDome* is home base for the Toronto *Blue Jays,* 277 Front St. W. (phone: 595-0077 or 341-3663).

Bicycling – There are some excellent bike paths around the Toronto parks. If you're really keen on biking, check *The Great Toronto Bicycling Guide,* by Elliot Kats (Great North Books, $3.95), which describes many of them. *Boardwalk Cycle,* 748 Markham Rd. (phone: 431-1961), provides the wheels.

Football – The *Argonauts* play from June until early November. The *SkyDome* is their new home (phone: 595-1131 or 341-3663).

Golf – There are many pay-as-you-play courses in and around Toronto. *Lakeview Golf Course,* 1190 Dixie Rd., ¾ mile (1.2 km) south of the Queen Elizabeth Way (phone: 278-4411), is a good, narrow 18-hole course with pro shop, lockers, showers, and a snack bar. *Don Valley Golf Course,* 4200 Yonge St., south of Hwy. 401 (phone: 392-2465), is one of the most challenging public courses around.

Hockey – Hockey in Toronto means large crowds every time the *Maple Leafs* defend their home ice at *Maple Leaf Gardens.* Since 1927, when the team was established, the *Leafs* have won the Stanley Cup, the symbol of hockey supremacy, 11 times — a record second only to that of the Montreal *Canadiens.* Tickets for *Leaf* games are not as hard to come by as they used to be. For tickets, head to the *Gardens,* 60 Carlton St. (phone: 977-1641).

Horse Racing – At *Greenwood Race Track,* 1669 Queen St. E. (phone: 698-3131), thoroughbreds and standardbreds take turns on the turf. There's an enclosed grandstand and dining room. *Woodbine Race Track,* Rexdale Blvd. at Hwy. 27 (phone: 675-6110), is exclusively for thoroughbred racing. Every summer it is the scene of the *Queen's Plate* — the oldest continuously run stake event in North America at 128 years and the highlight of the Canadian racing season for Canadian-bred 3-year-olds.

Jogging – In downtown Ontario, City Hall has a jogging track. In central Ontario, jog at the University of Toronto or Queens Park. The Martin Goodman Trail along the harborfront is also pleasant, as are the stretches of wooded green cutting through the city along the Humber and Don Rivers.

Skiing – Cross-country skiing is a way of life in Toronto, and you can do it around the Toronto Zoo, the Toronto Islands, or along the greenbelted ravines that run through the city from downtown to the Ontario Science Center. Rental equipment is available at *Rudy's Sport Centre Ltd.,* 1055 Eglinton Ave. W. (phone: 781-9196), and at the zoo (phone: 392-5900). The downhill picture right around the city is rather bleak — just some overcrowded mini-hills. Collingwood, 90 miles (144 km) north of Toronto, is the area's main ski resort. *Gray Coach* buses make weekend departures from the terminal, Bay and Dundas Sts. (phone: 979-3511).

Tennis – The Metro Parks Department (phone: 392-8184) maintains public courts in at least two parks, but the best courts are in private clubs, like the *Toronto Lawn Tennis Club,* to which you must be invited by a member. Hanlan's Point, one of the Toronto Islands, has good public courts, as does Ramsden Park on Yonge St.

THEATER: For complete listings of current performances, check the publications listed above. Toronto has a large variety of theatrical offerings ranging from its own repertory groups to stagings of London shows by English performers. An organization called *5 Star Tickets* (phone: 596-8211) sells half-price tickets to events given by selected professional performing arts companies on the day of performance (tickets to out-of-town events are available the day before the performance). Outside Eaton Centre at Yonge and Dundas Sts. (open daily; cash only), or at the *Royal Ontario Museum.*

Two major theater festivals, focusing on the works of Shaw and Shakespeare, are held at theater centers within 2 hours of the city. Among the most prominent of the city's more than 30 theaters are the *O'Keefe Centre,* Front and Yonge Sts. (phone: 872-2262), home of the *Canadian Opera Company* and the *National Ballet of Canada;* the *Royal Alexandra Theatre,* 260 King St. W. (phone: 593-4211), for Broadway, London, and local productions; the newly renovated *Pantages Theater* which opened with *Phantom of the Opera,* 263 Yonge St. (phone: 872-2222); the *St. Lawrence Centre for the Performing Arts,* 27 Front St. E. (phone: 366-7723), for Toronto repertory groups. *Second City,* Canada's version of "Saturday Night Live," presents a satirical revue in a nightclub-supperclub setting at the *Old Fire Hall,* 110 Lombard St. (phone: 863-1111). *Toronto Workshop Productions,* 12 Alexander St. (phone: 925-8640), and *Tarragon Theatre,* 30 Bridgman Ave. (phone: 531-1827) stage new Canadian plays.

The *Stratford Shakespeare Festival,* in Stratford, Ontario, 98 miles (157 km) southwest of Toronto, is one of the foremost theater centers in Canada. The main *Festival* theater performs Shakespeare's masterpieces, as well as other productions; two smaller stages — the Avon and the Third stage — present a variety of plays. The festival runs from May through October. The *Visitors' Guide to Stratford* lists attractions, accommodations, and facilities and is available from the Stratford Shakespeare Festival, PO Box 520, Stratford, Ontario (or for more information call the Toronto box office at 364-8355).

The *Shaw Festival* is presented by one of the few professional theater companies concentrating mainly on the works of George Bernard Shaw and his contemporaries. The plays are supplemented with concerts, seminars, lectures, and exhibits, all in a country setting, at Niagara-on-the-Lake, 82 miles (131 km) from Toronto. The festival runs from April 26 to October 15. For information, contact the Shaw Festival Theater, Niagara-on-the-Lake, Ontario (Toronto box office phone: 361-1544).

MUSIC: The *Toronto Symphony* performs in the *Roy Thomson Hall,* 60 Simcoe St. (phone: 593-7769). Musical performances are also given in the Edward Johnson Building by the University of Toronto music faculty (phone: 978-3744), and at Convocation Hall, also on campus (phone: 978-2100); Ontario Place (phone: 965-7711); and Nathan Phillips Square, downtown (phone: 392-7341). Classical concerts are also performed in the city's churches and schools.

NIGHTCLUBS AND NIGHTLIFE: The city has a growing number of night spots catering to every taste. *Bamboo* serves Thai food from noon to closing and features live reggae, salsa, and Latin music for dancing at 312 Queen St. W. (phone: 593-5771). Three of the largest and liveliest discos are *The Copa,* 21 Scollard St. (phone: 922-6500); *RPM,* 132 Queen's Quay E. (phone: 869-1462); and *The Diamond Club,* 410 Sherbourne St. (phone: 927-9010). *Celebrities* is a disco in the *Harbour Castle Westin,* 1 Harbour Sq. (phone: 869-1600). *Beaton's,* in the *Westbury* hotel, 475 Yonge St. (phone: 924-0611), is a chic lounge and bar. The city's most impressive big-name supper club is the *Imperial Room* in the *Royal York* hotel, 100 Front St. W. (phone: 368-2511), where top-name entertainers perform. Reservations necessary. *Barrister's Bar* in the *Hilton International* hotel, 145 Richmond St. W. (phone: 869-3456), is a quiet, elegant library lounge. For jazz aficionados, there's *Chick 'N' Deli* at 744 Mt. Pleasant Ave. (phone: 489-3313); and *Café des Copains,* 48 Wellington St. E. (phone: 869-0148). Try the new piano bar, *George's,* at *Bigliardi's* restaurant and mingle with hockey players after a game, 463 Church St. (phone: 922-9594). *Sparkles* is a nightclub located two thirds of the way up the CN Tower, 301 Front St. W. (phone: 362-5411). Since 1977, when the Rolling Stones recorded at *El Mocambo,* 464 Spadina Ave. (phone: 961-2558), it has become the place for rock in Canada. The *Lounge* at the *King Edward* hotel is a popular meeting spot, 37 King St. E. (phone: 863-9700).

BEST IN TOWN

CHECKING IN: As the up-and-coming major metropolis of Canada, Toronto has a proliferation of hotels to accommodate its large numbers of visitors. Even so, reservations are recommended. You can choose from a very wide selection, from the modern, luxurious *L'Hotel* downtown or the elegant *King Edward.* The Hotel Association of Metropolitan Toronto offers information about room availability and makes free reservations (call 596-7117). Expect to pay $130 and up for a double room in the places listed as expensive; from $95 to $125 in the moderate range; and under $90 in the inexpensive category. All telephone numbers are in the 416 area code unless otherwise indicated.

Four Seasons Toronto – Nicely positioned right in the heart of Yorkville, a colorful area of boutiques, galleries, sidewalk cafés, and clubs. The hotel has 381 beautifully appointed guestrooms and suites. Special touches include 24-hour concierge and room service, health club, indoor-outdoor pool, twice daily maid service, and a multilingual staff. There's good French dining in *Truffles* and continental dishes in *Le Café,* while *La Serre,* the hotel's cocktail lounge, is a nice choice for lunch. 21 Avenue Rd. (phone: 416-964-0411). Expensive.

Harbour Castle Westin – This sleek twin-towered structure dominates the Toronto waterfront. Its architecture is well integrated with its surroundings, creating a luxurious yet comfortable atmosphere. Its revolving *Lighthouse* restaurant has panoramic views of the area, and all 977 rooms have views of either Lake Ontario and the islands or the city skyline. The health club has an indoor swimming pool, whirlpool bath, sauna, steam room, gym, squash courts, and an outdoor track specially equipped to melt snow. In addition to the *Lighthouse,* the *Châteauneuf* restaurant serves French food (see *Eating Out*), the *Poseidon* has seafood, and there are 2 lobby lounges. Free shuttle bus service between the hotel and Eaton Centre, City Hall, and other downtown locations. 1 Harbour Sq. (phone: 416-869-1600). Expensive.

King Edward – Warmly referred to by locals as "The King Eddy," this hotel is everything a first class establishment should be — from the elegant marble-columned lobby to the spacious and tastefully furnished rooms. The hotel's *Lounge Bar* has greeted the Rockefellers and royalty; Prime Minister Margaret Thatcher even made her own tea in the Royal Suite. The *Café Victoria* is fine for breakfast or pre-theater dining; lunch and dinner are served at *Chiaro's.* 37 King St. E. (phone: 863-9700). Expensive.

L'Hotel – A first class business hotel next to the CN Tower, it has 588 rooms and suites in a variety of styles — some specially designed for handicapped guests. *Entrée Gold,* the super service-oriented "hotel within the hotel," on the 8th and 9th floors, provides separate check-in and check-out facilities, complete concierge services, continental breakfast, limousine service, cocktails, hors d'oeuvres, and complimentary local calls and newspapers. *Chanterelles* offers nouvelle cuisine, and the *Orchard Café* serves continental food; for lighter fare try one of the lounges, the *Skylight,* or *Le Bar.* Other facilities include a heated pool, whirlpool bath, saunas, squash courts, and exercise room. (phone: 416-597-1400). Expensive.

Park Plaza – Situated at the crossroads of Toronto chic — Avenue Road and Bloor Street — this landmark property, built in the 1930s, has been newly renovated. The *Prince Arthur Lounge* has soft piano music and an intimate atmosphere as well as good food. The *Prince Arthur Dining Room* serves continental food. 4 Avenue Rd. (phone: 416-924-5471). Expensive (but with less expensive rates weekends and in midwinter).

Sutton Place – A member of the Leading Hotels of the World group, it has attracted such celebrities as Al Pacino, Faye Dunaway, Paul Newman, and Kim Basinger. Guests who seek extra special service stay in Regency Floor suites, where 24-hour butler service is provided. All guests have access to the exercise, business, and banquet facilities. Visit *Alexandra's Piano Bar,* the hotel's chic lunch spot, filled with photos of stars who have eaten there. 955 Bay St. (phone: 924-9221 or 800-268-3790). Expensive.

Toronto Airport Marriott – This 423-room property is just 5 minutes from the airport and 20 minutes from downtown Toronto. For dining and entertainment, try the *Mikado* steak house, a Japanese steak and seafood restaurant with Teppanyaki-style display cooking. The *Terrace* is a large café, and *Toucans* is an entertainment lounge. For recreation, an indoor swimming pool, a hydrotherapy pool, weight room, and saunas are provided. 901 Dixon Rd. (phone: 416-674-9400). Expensive.

Hilton International – A striking Canadian showpiece, this hotel has 601 large and lovely rooms and is conveniently located downtown near theaters, shopping, and most of the major office buildings. There's a good selection of restaurants on the premises: *The Garden Court* has complete meals or light dining; *La Cour* has fine dining; *Trader Vic's* has Polynesian drinks and food; and the *Barrister's Bar* has hearty snacks and nightly entertainment. There is a sauna and indoor and outdoor pools. 145 Richmond St. W. (phone: 416-869-3456). Expensive to moderate.

Royal York – With 1,438 fully renovated guest rooms, it is not only the largest hotel in Toronto, it's the largest hotel in the British Commonwealth. This grande dame of Toronto hotels has been a landmark since it was built in 1929. While its rooms may be a trifle cramped, its service facilities still remain among the best in Canada, with two floors for conventions. The hotel plays host to royalty, prime ministers, and visiting celebrities. The *Imperial Room* offers dinner and dancing. There is an underground gallery of stores, airline offices (airport buses are at the west door of the hotel), and eating spots like the *Acadian Room, Dick Turpin's,* and *Benihana of Tokyo.* As we went to press, a new pool was slated to be open in early 1990. 100 Front St. W. (phone: 416-368-2511). Expensive to moderate on weeknights; moderate to inexpensive on weekends.

Sheraton Centre – A city within a city, this hotel has 396 rooms, a waterfall cascading three stories into the lobby, gardens and paths on the grounds, over 60 stores and boutiques, 2 theaters, 8 restaurants, including the *Winter Palace* (see *Eating Out*), and 5 bars. This is also home to *Good Queen Bess,* an intimate English pub literally shipped from England. The square shape of the hotel contrasts nicely with the curved structure of City Hall, to which it is linked by a footbridge. It has a sauna and an indoor-outdoor pool. 123 Queen St. W. (phone: 416-361-1000). Expensive to moderate.

Windsor Arms – Opened in 1928 as an apartment hotel, today it is owned by Canadian entrepreneur George Minden and is a popular choice with the film, theatrical, and literary crowd. Each of the 81 rooms and suites still reflects the residential concept and is individually decorated. The *Three Small Rooms* restaurant (see *Eating Out*) has an elegant dining room serving haute cuisine, an informal grill, and a wine cellar. The *Courtyard Café* is a favorite venue for spotting famous actors, artists, and musicians. No recreational facilities. 22 St. Thomas St. (phone: 416-979-2341). Expensive to moderate.

Westbury – The twin towers house 545 spacious rooms, each of which has a color TV set, phone, and first-run movies. *Creighton's* serves French food in an elegant setting; *Beaton's Lounge* is for nightly entertainment, Mondays through Saturdays; and the coffee shop is for light fare. 475 Yonge St. (phone: 416-924-0611). Moderate.

Delta Chelsea Inn – An ideal place for families, because some of the rooms have kitchen facilities. The property is conveniently located just 2 blocks north of Eaton Centre. There are 2 good restaurants (with special children's menus; children under 6 eat free), a lounge, a health club, sauna, a children's creative center, and an indoor pool. 33 Gerrard St. W. (phone: 416-595-1975). Moderate to inexpensive.

Bond Place – Very close to Eaton Centre, its 285 rooms are small, clean, and inexpensive. There is a coffee shop and lounge but no recreational facilities. 65 Dundas St. E. (phone: 416-362-6061). Inexpensive.

Carlton Inn – This establishment is right next door to *Maple Leaf Gardens*. Most of the 536 modern rooms have a small refrigerator, and there's also a dining room, 2 pubs, a pool, and sauna. 30 Carlton St. (phone: 416-977-6655). Inexpensive.

EATING OUT: The postwar immigration boom coupled with Toronto's flourishing economy has stimulated a proliferation of ethnic eating places, and today the city has over 4,000 restaurants. The choices of food, which formerly ran the gamut from roast beef to Yorkshire pudding, now include a host of cuisines — Chinese, French, Moroccan, Indonesian, Greek, Japanese, and Italian. The quality is generally high. Expect to pay $60 and up for a dinner for two in the expensive category, $35 to $60 in the moderate category, and under $35 in the inexpensive range. Prices do not include drinks, wine, or tips. All telephone numbers are in the 416 area code unless otherwise indicated.

Châteauneuf – Rich burgundy tones and lovely tapestries decorate this intimate dining place in the *Harbour Castle Westin* hotel. The menu is French, and favorites such as fresh lobster medallions and crêpes filled with golden caviar and sour cream are prepared and presented with care. For dessert, try cassis or raspberry sorbet. Closed Sundays. Major credit cards accepted. Reservations advised. Harbour Castle Westin, 1 Harbour Sq. (phone: 869-1600). Expensive.

Fenton's – This restaurant was begun in a small refurbished house, near the busy Yonge-Bloor intersection, and has grown to include another room and an enclosed garden. A staple of the ever-changing menu is the caviar — both Russian and Iranian — and there's an extensive wine list. Open daily. Reservations advised. Major credit cards accepted. 2 Gloucester St. (phone: 961-8485). Expensive.

Glossops – The 3 dining areas in this renovated house are nicely decorated in soft pastels brightened by fresh flowers. Specialties are veal, lamb, and seafood, all served by a very attentive staff. Closed Sundays. Reservations advised. Major credit cards accepted. 39 Prince Arthur Ave. (phone: 964-2440). Expensive.

Scaramouche – Imaginative continental dishes featuring salmon, veal, and lamb are served in this elegant dining room with a lovely view of the city. There's also a pasta bar. A must for dessert is the bittersweet chocolate and praline truffle. Dinner only; closed Sundays. Reservations necessary. Major credit cards accepted. 1 Benvenuto Pl. (phone: 961-8011). Expensive.

Stelle – The hottest spot in the trendy Queen Street West area, the atmosphere — distinctly "artistic" — aims to capture the feel of a 1950s kitchen with a 1980s twist. Toward that end, diners sit on white vinyl chairs (which match one of the walls in color and material), and the waitresses are shod in white sneakers. The menu is an eclectic mix of Southern Asian, Northern Italian, and Latin American fare. Try the chicken Bangkok cloaked in ginger, shallots, chilies, and an orange-peanut sauce. Open daily for dinner. Reservations necessary. Major credit cards accepted. 807 Queen St. W. (phone: 868-0054). Expensive.

Three Small Rooms – The three dining rooms in the *Windsor Arms* hotel offer a variety of dining experiences. The *Restaurant* serves cuisine naturelle and privately imported wines in elegant surroundings. The *Grill* has a warm, cozy atmosphere and specializes in grilled meats and seafood. It's a great place for lunch. The *Wine Cellar* offers cheese fondue, supreme of grouper amandine, and a variety of wines poured into massive goblets. The *Restaurant* is closed Sundays; the others, open daily. Reservations advised. Major credit cards accepted. 22 St. Thomas St. (phone: 979-2212). Expensive.

23 St. Thomas Street – Fashioned after the *Palm* steakhouse in New York, this spot is a basic upscale beef and seafood place in a very pretty setting. Menu includes live lobster and veal chops, plus an excellent wine list. Portions here are plentiful. Has a copper bar, along with a warm lounge furnished with antiques and

Persian carpets. Across from the *Windsor Arms* hotel at 23 St. Thomas St. (phone: 922-1340). Expensive.

Winston's – A tip of the hat to Paul Bocuse; this establishment serves rich haute cuisine in a flamboyantly grand setting. The city's patricians come here to see and be seen, and tourists may have to compete with the important regulars here for good tables and service. Specialties include duckling with fresh papaya, mango, rum, and wine, and Dover sole with shrimp, pine nuts, and green peppercorns. For dessert, don't pass up the Grand Marnier soufflé. Jackets and ties are mandatory for gentlemen. Closed Sundays. Reservations necessary. Major credit cards accepted. 104 Adelaide St. W. (phone: 363-1627). Expensive.

Winter Palace – Atop the 43-story Sheraton Centre complex, this restaurant commands an excellent view of City Hall and Nathan Phillips Square. The interior is elegant, and the menu features French dishes with a Russian flair. Sample the *zakuska,* a dish of seven different hors d'oeuvres, including caviar, partridge pâté, and smoked salmon, followed by the veal tenderloin or scampi Fabergé. Dining is enhanced in the summer by the multicolored lights that shimmer from the reflecting pool 43 stories below, and in winter, by the soft glow that bathes the skaters on the frozen pool in front of City Hall. Closed Sundays. Reservations necessary. Major credit cards accepted. 123 Queen St. W. in Sheraton Centre (phone: 361-1000). Expensive.

Chanterelles – Superb food, thoughtful service, and a handsome setting off the lobby of *L'Hotel* make this a fine dining choice. The menu includes everything from oysters and caviar to rack of lamb. There's a pre-theater dinner, but you may want to go after the performance just to try the *Chanterelles* cake — sinful but heavenly. 225 Front St. W. (phone: 597-8142). Expensive to moderate.

Courtyard Café – Also in the *Windsor Arms* hotel, this café is a good place for a late night nibble where guests go to see and be seen. An award-winning chef prepares continental dishes served amid lots of brass railings and potted plants. The service is impeccable. Open daily. Reservations advised. Major credit cards accepted. 22 St. Thomas St. (phone: 979-2212). Expensive to moderate.

Gatsby's – For elegant and intimate dining amidst late Victorian decor, try this classy eatery. There's a huge selection of good continental cuisine. Closed Sundays. Reservations advised. Major credit cards accepted. 504 Church St. (phone: 925-4545). Expensive to moderate.

George Bigliardi's – Popular with the hockey crowd and high-powered business types, this elegant dining lounge serves steaks, seafood, pasta, and sausages — all with that special Italian touch. Enjoy the house cocktail, the "Midnight George," at the brass-railed bar or the new piano bar. Open for dinner only. 463 Church St., 2 blocks north of Maple Leaf Gardens (phone: 922-9594). Moderate to expensive.

Old Fish Market – A casual and comfortable place where the specialties are all kinds of fresh fish and seafood. There's also an oyster bar. Open daily. Major credit cards accepted. 12 Market St. (phone: 363-0334). Expensive to moderate.

Bellair Café – Serving pasta, salads, seafood, and great homemade ice cream in a light, airy, contemporary dining room, this place is a popular spot for business lunches and shopping breaks. Celebrities are sometimes seen during dinner hours. Open daily. 100 Cumberland St. at Bellair (phone: 964-2222). Moderate.

Doctor's House and Livery – Located 40 minutes north of dowtown Toronto, this 19th-century home has gone through several transmutations — from a doctor's house and barn to a tearoom to the gift shop and the restaurant it is today. The atmosphere is very homey. The menu includes Canadian specialties like salmon and duckling with sweet plums and maple syrup. The Sunday brunch features a wide range of light and heavy fare, from omelettes to prime ribs. Children's portions available. Closed Mondays in winter. Reservations advised. Most major credit cards accepted. Nashville Rd., Kleinburg (phone: 893-1615). Moderate.

Jacques Omelettes – This Yorkville restaurant, with a French à la carte menu, is frequented by devotees of the classic French omelette. Chef Jacques Sorin prepares fresh garnishes every morning and cooks omelettes to order perfectly. The Niçoise omelette is highly recommended. Closed Sundays. Reservations advised. Major credit cards accepted. 126a Cumberland Ave. (phone: 961-1893). Moderate.

Old House on Church Street – In a historic Toronto home, super atmosphere and delicious huge portions are offered. Guests may dine upstairs, or downstairs in the garden during summer months. Lamb, pasta, and seafood are all expertly prepared by the Greek chef–owner. Try the famous cheesecake for dessert. Open for lunch, dinner, and Sunday brunch. 582 Church St. (phone: 925-5316). Moderate.

Pink Pearl – Specializing in Hong Kong-style Cantonese food, the surroundings and service are distinguished, and dining is a leisurely affair. Highlights of the extensive menu include Rainbow Chopped in Crystal Fold — chopped meats and vegetables sautéed together and served with crispy noodles; Peking Supreme Beef Filet — sliced beef tenderloin sautéed with oyster sauce and served sizzling hot; and braised lobster prepared in black bean and garlic sauce. Open daily. Reservations advised for dinner. Major credit cards accepted. 120 Avenue Rd. (phone: 966-3631). Moderate.

Le Select – With a French bistro atmosphere on trendy Queen Street, this spot has a real zinc bar, small tables set closely together, a super wine list, and baskets filled with homemade bread which are suspended on pulleys above diners' heads. The service is inconsistent, and the food varies from being super to mundane, but the music (jazz and classical tapes) and Canadian art posters on the walls still make it one of this town's favorites. Be prepared to wait in line. 328 Queen St. W. (phone: 596-6405). Moderate.

Top of Toronto – This revolving restaurant at the top of the CN Tower has incredible views and is best for Sunday brunch. Open daily; Sunday brunch from 10 AM to 2 PM. Reservations advised. Major credit cards accepted. 301 Front St. W. (phone: 362-5411). Moderate.

Ed's Warehouse – When entrepreneur Ed Mirvish bought and restored the *Royal Alexandra Theatre,* he also started a restaurant empire, seating 1,500 guests, next door. Garish, with Tiffany lamps and plush old-time autos, this restaurant is great for beef. Jackets are a must; no blue jeans allowed. Open daily. Reservations unnecessary. Major credit cards accepted. 270 King St. W. (phone: 593-6676). Moderate to inexpensive.

Filet of Sole – Fishing scenes of Peggy's Cove in Nova Scotia line the walls of this informal, top-rated seafood restaurant. Remarkably varied menu is printed twice daily. Try the shellfish platters. It caters to a theater crowd that likes to linger at their tables. Open weekdays for lunch and dinner; dinner only on weekends. Reservations necessary. Major credit cards accepted. 11 Duncan St. (phone: 598-3256). Moderate to inexpensive.

Masa – The focus here is on authentic Japanese food. Diners can sit in a standard booth or dine in traditional Japanese style on mats in partitioned lounges. Open daily; weekends, dinner only. Reservations advised on weekends. Major credit cards accepted. 195 Richmond St. W. (phone: 977-9519). Moderate to inexpensive.

Sultan's Tent – For an intriguing change, try some authentic Moroccan cuisine in the Yorkville shopping district. The decor looks genuine — rich tapestries, low round tables, and comfortable divans and brass vases. Specialties include lamb with honey and almonds, chicken with lemon and olives, and couscous — cracked wheat steamed and served with various meats and vegetables. For dessert try the pastries — dense combinations of honey, nuts, and layers of pastry —

and some strong Moroccan coffee or mint tea. Arabic music and belly dancers. Closed Sundays. Reservations advised. Major credit cards accepted. 1280 Bay St. (phone: 961-0601). Moderate to inexpensive.

Church Street Café – Paintings by local artists hang on the walls, adding a bohemian touch to this informal, diner-style establishment. Continental fare includes rack of lamb, beef tenderloin medallions, and poached salmon. Open daily. Reservations necessary for groups of six or more. Major credit cards accepted. 485 Church St. (phone: 925-1155). Inexpensive.

Crooks – If you're looking for a burger or a bowl of pasta served in a local saloon, try this cozy, casual eatery with red-checkered tablecloths and good tunes on the jukebox. Popular with journalists and cops. 106 Front St. E. (phone: 396-8906). Inexpensive.

Groaning Board – The gimmick here is the showing of award-winning commercials from the *Cannes International Advertising Film Festival*. While you're watching, pick something from a menu of hearty meat and vegetarian dishes, soups, salads, and sandwiches and homemade desserts. Open daily. Reservations advised for four or more. Major credit cards accepted. 131 Jarvis St. (phone: 363-0265). Inexpensive.

Ilie's – All dinners are *table d'hôte* in this Romanian restaurant. Don't miss the *bors* — navy bean, bacon, and vegetable soup. For an entrée, try the crispy duckling or breaded veal cutlet in tomato and garlic sauce. Fully licensed. Closed Mondays. Reservations advised. Major credit cards accepted. 300 Eglinton St. W. (phone: 483-2654). Inexpensive.

Just Desserts – Virtually all manner of baked goods from oversized butter tarts to hefty pieces of an entire realm of cheesecakes as well as salads and quiche. The desserts are the cream of the crop of the best bakeries across town. The colorful assortment contrasts nicely with the tiled black and white decor. Sample one of the many coffees, teas, or juices. Open daily until 3 AM, 24 hours on Fridays and Saturdays. No reservations. No credit cards accepted. 306 Davenport Rd. (phone: 922-6824). Inexpensive.

Korea House – The specialty here is succulent barbecued beef with pickled sesame leaves and cabbage. Fully licensed. Open daily. Reservations unnecessary. Most major credit cards accepted. 666 Bloor St. W. (phone: 536-8666). Inexpensive.

Silver Rail – It's Toronto's original tavern, the first bar to serve liquor legally in 1947. Here you'll see native Torontonians — including judges and shoppers — sipping beer at the "mile-long" bar, and eating plain, simple, mashed-potatoes-and-gravy style grub in booths. Across from the Eaton Centre at 225 Yonge St. (phone: 368-8697). Inexpensive.

Vines – Across the street from the St. Lawrence Centre and the O'Keefe Centre, this wine bar is an ideal place to spend an hour or two dissecting the latest play or opera. Bistro-style hot dishes and light fare — cold roast beef, pâtés, and cheese plates — complement a wide variety of international wines. Wine is sold by the glass or by the bottle and a special vintage is featured daily. Closed Sundays. No reservations. Major credit cards accepted. 38 Wellington St. E. (phone: 869-0744). Inexpensive.

Young Lok – Peking and Szechwan regional cuisines along with a tasty Mongolian grill, are the specialties served here, in what looks like an Oriental garden. Open daily. Reservations necessary for six or more. Major credit cards accepted. 122 St. Patrick St. (phone: 593-9819). Inexpensive.

VANCOUVER

In Vancouver, life is dominated by the elements — the sea, the mountains, and the weather that the two brew up between them. Pale buildings gleam in the marine air like opals set against varied hues of green — the green of the sea and the darker, truer green of the fir-covered slopes east of the city. The skyline is high-rise steel and glass, with snowcapped mountains for a backdrop. Around almost any corner is a glimpse of water, usually streaked by the white wake of an oceangoing freighter or dotted by white triangles of sailboats trailing colorful spinnakers.

Tucked into the southwestern corner of British Columbia, Canada's Pacific province, Vancouver is just about as close to the sea as it can be without leaving continental Canada. Downtown Vancouver sits on a peninsula bounded by English Bay to the west, the Fraser River to the south, and Burrard Inlet on the north. Across Burrard Inlet is the more securely landlocked residential suburb of North Vancouver. Flanking its lovely neighborhoods are the tall peaks of the Coastal Range — Grouse Mountain, Mt. Seymour, and Hollyburn. These 3,000-to-4,000-foot peaks do more than provide a magnificent background to the city; by capturing the storms that sweep in from the sea and down from the Alaskan panhandle, they create Vancouver's foggy, rainy climate, the gardener's delight and sun-worshiper's despair.

So the city spends its days between the towering certainties of mountain and the omnipresent sea. It would be tempting to say after a glimpse at the map that the mountains almost seem to be pushing the city into the waiting fingers of the sea, except that most residents embrace the surrounding elements and there is no hint of hostility in the relationship. They've *come* to Vancouver for the sea and the mountains, and those fingers of Pacific Ocean tickle their fancy and fill their leisure time with a diversity of activities unavailable anywhere else in Canada.

The sea, mountains, and moderate climate are prime forces in the city's development as part of Canada. Several thousand miles lie between Vancouver and Canada's other major cities, Toronto and Montreal (Vancouver, with just over a million residents in its metropolitan area, is Canada's third largest city and home to half of British Columbia's population.) This distance is further augmented by the Rocky Mountains, 400 miles (644 km) east of Vancouver, a psychological as well as physical barrier that isolates the city from eastern, urban Canada. Toronto and Montreal are 5 and 6 hours away by air. As a result, the city more resembles the US West Coast than the rest of Canada (the US border is only 30 miles (48 km) south; San Francisco is 2 hours away by air). It is as if the bonds of sea and mountain, which the city shares with the entire American Pacific coast, are stronger than the weight of culture and politics it shares with the rest of Canada.

The impact of the sea on life in Vancouver is enormous. The city has an excellent natural harbor that is active year-round. Wheat, timber, lumber, oil, and manufactured goods flow through the port in a steady stream, providing a crucial economic and transportation link with the rest of the world and maintaining an especially active trade relationship with Japan. Ships transport grain and lumber from Vancouver, returning with cars, appliances, and other Japanese consumer goods. The many rivers that flow from the Coastal Range into the sea along the Vancouver coast make the area prime salmon country. You'll be offered salmon everywhere — smoked or fresh, or frozen and packed to travel. It's part of the menu in many of the city's restaurants, from salmon sushi at the Japanese places to salmon Wellington in others. And if you fish, you may very well see it face-to-face.

When residents aren't on the sea or in it, they spend a good deal of their time over it. Because the city stretches over peninsulas and islands, most people have to cross water at least twice a day on one of the city's 20 bridges. And everywhere are seagulls — vying with pigeons for a place in the sun (or rain) on apartment ledges; scrambling after scraps at hamburger drive-ins; and battling with ducks and swans in the ponds of Stanley Park.

Still, with just over a million people, Vancouver is not any larger than a medium-size city by most standards. In the shadows of the aggressively new high-rise office buildings, there is a pulse of money and youth and drive. At the same time, the people — in full view of all these high-rises — stroll along the waterfront development at the foot of Granville Street and eat lunch on the grass at Stanley Park, all the while speaking of that balance between work and leisure that gives life a certain grace.

Vancouver offers almost an embarrassment of riches for recreational activity, from boating and sailing out of Burrard Inlet or English Bay to skiing on Grouse Mountain. The thousand acres of Stanley Park offer miles of walking and biking trails through silent woodlands and over rolling lawns; cricket, tennis, lawn bowling, and putting; and less active sports, such as bird-, water-, and people-watching.

The city itself is very much the product of the 20th century. The residents' interest and concern with the environment are reflected in the cleanliness of downtown streets. The newness of the city is reflected in its slick-as-glass skyline, a forest of high-rise buildings pricking the sky. The city's historic buildings are predominantly in the older sections of town — Gastown, where the city started, and Chinatown. Residential areas consist of nicely laid out streets with apartment buildings in the west end on the southern shore of English Bay; large, spectacular homes in Shaughnessy and Kerrisdale, south of downtown; sprawling contemporary homes in the southwestern suburbs of Richmond and Burnaby as well as in West Vancouver, on the north shore, where residents enjoy the highest per capita wealth in Canada.

Growth came quickly to Vancouver. Just over 100 years ago it was little more than tall trees stretching from the mountains to the sea. The Indians who lived here fished salmon and whale and traded furs with the white men, who first entered the area in June 1792, when explorer George Vancouver charted Burrard Inlet. Simon Fraser reached the Pacific from an inland route in 1808. But there was no permanent white settlement here until 1866, when a pioneer named "Gassy" Jack Deighton built a saloon and set up business near a very small sawmill where liquor was forbidden. A community grew up around the establishment, and two more saloons opened to serve the thirsty lumberjacks. The town lacked refinement, but it was certainly lively. Occasional sprees turned into community bashes that closed down the mill for days at a time. The area was so rich in potential resources, however, that the town kept growing. In 1886, with a population of 2,500 and 350 wooden buildings, it was incorporated as a city and named Vancouver. To celebrate, it ordered a brand-new fire wagon, but the city burned down 3 months later, 1½ months before the new wagon arrived.

The city was soon rebuilt and began to thrive with the construction of the transcontinental railroad. A large influx of Chinese workers also came with the railroad, and thus began a number of ugly incidents between whites and the Chinese. When the city forcibly deported the Chinese from work camps to Victoria on Vancouver Island, the provincial government stepped in with constables to restore order. The deportation so outraged provincial officials that the city's charter was revoked for a period of time. As a result of such rabid racism, Vancouver's Chinese community segregated itself in Chinatown and established something of a parallel community.

The Canadian Pacific Railroad finally arrived in 1887, and Vancouver was on its way. Within the next few years several hotels and department stores were established. The first, the *Vancouver,* opened its doors in 1887, and *Hudson's Bay Company* opened the city's first department store. They're both still open for business.

In the 20th century, Vancouver has grown by leaps and bounds. The opening of the Panama Canal in 1914 strengthened the city by providing easy access to Europe for grain shipments from the western prairies. During US Prohibition, shipping took a new twist and rum-runners plied the coast for intrepid entrepreneurs who smuggled spirits southward. Today the situation is somewhat reversed. Because of lower liquor prices in the US, Vancouver residents often stash fifths of Jack Daniels in their glove compartments when they cross the border from Washington State at Blaine.

Metropolitan Vancouver includes Burnaby, Richmond, New Westminster, Delta, and Surrey as well as North and West Vancouver. About 28% of the population are of British extraction; the others come from diverse backgrounds: some 100,340 Chinese, 60,435 Germans, 45,710 Indo-Pakistanis, 29,395 Italians, as well as smaller numbers of French, Japanese, Greeks, Scandinavians, Ukrainians, and Russians. Many of these groups have their own newspapers, magazines, and clubs. Radio station CJVB caters exclusively to the ethnic community, with programming in many languages.

In spite of all the variety, though, you're always aware of Vancouver's basic Scottish-English heritage, on which the city was built. Labor and honor here are spelled with a "u"; the final letters of words like theater and center are transposed. People queue up and are almost universally polite.

The ethnic community has made an impact on the restaurant scene, with representative cuisines of almost all the various national groups. Vancouver also has all the accoutrements of a major city — a symphony orchestra, an opera company, and several dance companies. The shopping is good here. West Vancouver's Park Royal Shopping Centre was the first big shopping mall in Canada. Malls have since become a Canadian rage, opening under, over, and alongside city streets and in suburban spaces from downtown Vancouver all the way to Underground Montreal. Old office buildings and warehouses have been converted into boutiques and studios. And there are antiques stores and galleries on South Granville Street, Oriental crafts stores and vegetable markets in Chinatown; and delis, boutiques, and specialty stores in Gastown. But when you've had your fill of all these, there's plenty left of where Vancouverites spend their free time — the outdoors.

Leisure activity focuses on the sea year-round. From virtually any point in the city, it's a matter of minutes to the sandy beaches or rocky bays. Many people own boats and go sailing and fishing. During the summer, people swim in English Bay (every New Year's Day hundreds of hardy souls brave a dip in the cold depths, called the Polar Bear Swim).

Those more attuned to seasonal changes head for the mountains in wintertime. Grouse, Cypress, and Seymour Mountains are approximately 20 minutes away, provides challenging slopes and equipment rentals. Other world-famous ski areas, such as Whistler and Blackcomb, are only 90 minutes from downtown.

Vancouver has a typical West Coast atmosphere in its high priority on outdoor activities. Perhaps this has something to do with the slower-paced, low-key feel of the whole city. Though business does get done in Vancouver, the pace is less hectic than that of eastern urban centers. Standing shoulder to shoulder with the wilderness and mixing races and nationalities, skyscrapers and ski runs, Vancouver is a delight to the imagination and the eye of the discerning visitor.

VANCOUVER AT-A-GLANCE

SEEING THE CITY: Grouse Mountain, rising 3,974 feet in North Vancouver, commands a spectacular view of the city and the surrounding coastal area. You can reach the top of the mountain and enjoy panoramic views along the way on the Grouse Mountain Skyride, an aerial tramway that runs from the parking lot to the summit. Open daily. Admission charge. At the top of Capilano Rd. in North Vancouver (phone: 984-0661).

Some 500 feet above the harbor, the Harbour Centre Observation Deck opens up a vista of waterfront activities. You can spend an hour or two watching the ships go by — oceangoing cruise ships, freighters, sailboats, yachts, seaplanes, and even rowing teams in training. Powerful telescopes are on hand for a closer look; staff members answer questions and point out special sights. After you've seen the city, take a half hour to view *Vancouver,* a marvelous panoramic film shown on a huge screen by a number of computer-directed projectors that produce stunning effects. Open daily. Admission charge. 555 W. Hastings St. (phone: 689-0421).

And as if to emphasize what a beautiful town this really is, the drive from the airport along tree-lined Granville Street, with the North Shore mountains in the background, is a wonderful introduction.

SPECIAL PLACES: Walking is the best way to get a feel for certain sections, including Gastown, Chinatown, the Granville Island complex, Canada Place, and Stanley Park. But many of the area's attractions lie in the suburbs and outlying areas, to which it is most convenient to drive.

DOWNTOWN

Chinatown – The second largest Chinese quarter in North America (only San Francisco's is larger or more energetic) encompasses a fair-size piece of downtown. This area has been the nucleus of the Chinese community for almost a century, first as a self-imposed ghetto in which the Chinese protected themselves from discrimination and physical abuse, today as a vibrant commercial community. Restaurants offer authentic Cantonese, Mandarin, and Shanghai cooking as well as Chinese-Canadian, which is virtually indistinguishable from Chinese-American. The stores range from large import emporiums to holes in the wall, with Mah-Jongg sets, jade and ivory carvings, dried lychee nuts, and dozens of items you never thought you wanted until you saw them. The groceries feature smoked duck, bok choy, ginger root, and squid. At the Chinese newspaper office, the latest edition is posted in the window. Herbalists promise cures with roots and leaves and powdered bones. On Pender Street you can buy a cricket cage for a dollar or a cloisonné vase for a hundred. There are also jade figurines of Kuan Yin, the goddess of mercy, or soapstone Foo dogs to guard your temple. Some highlights are the world's thinnest office building, at Pender and Carrall; the Dr. Sun Yat-Sen Classical Chinese Garden at 578 Carral St.; the Kuomintang Building, 529 Gore; the Chinese Cultural Centre, 50 E. Pender St.; and Wong's Benevolent Society, 121-125 E. Pender St., exemplary of the balcony style. Two good places to eat are *Yen Lock,* 67 E. Pender St., and *Sun Tung Lock* seafood restaurant, 127 E. Pender St., both with appetizing dim sum and other Cantonese specialties. On Pender St. between Gore and Carrall Sts.

Stanley Park – Surrounded by the sea on three sides, this city park is one of the most beautiful in the world. The 1,000 acres are bespeckled with tall evergreens, gardens, lakes, lagoons, 50 miles of trails, tennis courts, a miniature golf course, bowling greens, restaurants, coffee shops, snack bars, a zoo, and the Vancouver Aquarium (see below). Residents use the park for hiking, jogging, biking, concerts, picnicking, and simple relaxing. The Seawall flanks the water for 5 miles and makes a lovely walk. Open daily. No admission charge. At the foot of W. Georgia St.

Vancouver Aquarium – With 8,000 aquatic inhabitants, this is Canada's largest and most famous aquarium. Attractions include the H. R. MacMillan Gallery of Whales, the Marine Mammal Center, and IMAQ, the Arctic Sea display. Popular exhibitions are the Amazon Gallery and the British Columbia Hall of Fish, displaying local sealife. There are killer whale shows throughout the day and public feedings of sharks, sea otters, and harbor seals. The gift shop features local craftwork. Open daily. Admission charge. In Stanley Park (phone: 685-3364).

Gastown – Named for "Gassy" Jack Deighton, first citizen and saloonkeeper, this is where Vancouver began as a rowdy milltown. Later it was the city's Skid Row and, still later, home of the drug culture. Today it is a living example of successful urban renewal. Extensive renovation has transformed the warehouses into antique stores, boutiques, galleries, and restaurants with lovely brick façades and gaslight fixtures. *The Landing,* at the Cordova St. entrance to Gastown, is the latest trendy shopping center. The only steam clock in the world is at Cambie and Water streets. *Umberto Al Porto,* 321 Water St., has homemade pasta and a harbor view from the upstairs lounge. Bounded by Water, Alexander, Columbia, and Cordova Sts.

Granville Island Market – Just under the south end of the Granville Bridge, this large indoor market has become the prime gathering spot for those in search of the freshest seafood and produce. You can get salmon packed to go, and a number of the stalls sell snacking food that you can consume while watching the tugboats glide to and fro. Take any Granville Street bus and change at Broadway for the #51. Two independent ferry services, *Granville Island Ferries* and the *Aquabus,* run daily between Vancouver's West End and the Island. Granville Island itself is growing in importance each day — the complex is now home to two theaters, galleries, assorted shops, and a number of restaurants.

Robson Street – Once a charming, old European neighborhood with numerous small shops, Robsonstrasse has become Robson Street, a name change echoed by its metamorphosis into a fashion magnet for upscale boutiques. A few of the old-time businesses remain, however, and you can still buy knockwurst in bulk. The *Heidelberg* restaurant continues to harken back to a bygone era and still serves up hearty cooking. *European News* is another survivor and, although it has recently had a bit of a facelift, this week's copy of *Der Spiegel* (or today's edition of the *The New York Times*) are still available here. But the street where shopkeepers once knew their customers by name is now primarily a haven for shops with names well known to the world at large: *Ralph Lauren, Alfred Sung, Rodier Paris, Ferragamo,* and the list goes on. A few bargains are still available but, in general, shopping here will require a well-stocked wallet.

Robson Square – The innovative complex designed by Arthur Erickson houses the provincial government offices, the courthouse, and shopping facilities in a multilevel galleria. The key attractions are a skating rink, food fair, cinemas, and a theater. Robson at Hornby.

Vancouver Art Gallery – The old courthouse is now the new Art Gallery, the dramatic centerpiece of the Robson Square complex. There are four well-designed floors of exhibit space and numerous traveling shows; one entire room is devoted to the late Emily Carr, British Columbia's best-known artist. Closed Tuesdays. Admission charge, except Thursday evenings, when it's free. 750 Hornby St. (phone: 682-4668).

Canada Place – Built for Expo '86, this building is known for its ship-like appearance and five sails on the roof. It houses the Trade and Convention Centre, the *Pan Pacific* hotel, and *CN IMAX* (Canadian National Image Maximum) *Theatre;* The special IMAX screen makes viewers feel as if they are in the picture (phone: 682-6422).

BEYOND DOWNTOWN AND THE SUBURBS

Van Dusen Botanical Gardens – Gardening is such a passion in Vancouver that it has been called the city's religion. If that's the case, Van Dusen must be the answer to a communal prayer. Its 55 acres of formal gardens and lakes are given over to displays of native and exotic plants. The fountain at the entrance is a gift from the Swedish Society and depicts the contribution of Swedish Canadians to the economic and cultural life of British Columbia. Open daily. Admission charge. 37th Ave. and Oak St. (phone: 266-7194).

Simon Fraser University – Sitting atop Burnaby Mountain, this campus commands beautiful views of the city and the surrounding coastal areas. Most of its striking modern buildings were designed by Arthur Erickson. Hourly tours of the campus are conducted from July 1 to Labor Day and on weekends during the rest of the year (no charge). The campus theater has frequent programs that may interest visitors. Open daily. No admission charge. In Burnaby on Burnaby Mountain (phone: 291-3111).

Museum of Anthropology – The University of British Columbia campus museum has fine collections of art and artifacts from British Columbian coastal Indians, and from elsewhere in the Americas, the Pacific Islands, Asia, and Africa. The entire collection is displayed in public galleries, with striking visible storage galleries designed around computerized data books for browsing or serious research. There's also a unique group of totem poles in the Great Hall. Closed Mondays. Admission charge, except Tuesdays. On N.W. Marine Dr. (phone: 228-3825).

Bloedel Conservatory – Under this ultramodern dome, you'll find some 500 exotic plants and flowers thriving in simulated desert, rain forest, and tropical environments. There are also 30 varieties of birds from throughout the world. Open daily. Admission charge. In Queen Elizabeth Park at 33rd and Cambie (phone: 872-5513).

H. R. MacMillan Planetarium – An unusual building that has sophisticated projection and sound equipment essential to its imaginative visual presentations of astronomical themes. The shows change frequently, and you should make reservations in advance. Here, too, is the *Centennial Museum,* depicting Vancouver's early history as well as native British Columbian cultures, and the *Maritime Museum,* permanent berth of the *St. Roch,* the first vessel ever to navigate the treacherous Northwest Passage in 1928. The Royal Canadian Mounted Police schooner has been restored and is now a national historic site. There's also a restaurant and gift shop. Closed Mondays. Admission charge. 1100 Chestnut St. in Vanier Park (phone: 736-7765).

Nitobe Memorial Gardens – This traditional Japanese garden on the University of BC campus is a serene, tranquil setting for contemplation. Though the gardens are small, you'll probably want to linger. There's a teahouse for ceremonial occasions. Open daily from April to early October; otherwise, closed on weekends. Admission charge. On the campus at N.W. Marine Dr. (phone: 228-3928).

Lighthouse Park – Eight miles of trails lead through virgin forest, one of the most beautiful in the southwestern corner of British Columbia. The park is named for the 60-foot Point Atkinson Lighthouse, to which a short, half-mile hiking trail leads. It ends at a rocky bluff overlooking the beautiful Gulf of Georgia. Open daily. No admission charge. 5 miles (8 km) west of Lions Gate Bridge on Marine Dr., West Vancouver.

Old Hasting Mill Store – This small museum, with its collection of Indian artifacts, is one of the few buildings that survived the great fire of 1886. Originally built on Burrard Inlet, the store was relocated to its present site in 1930. Open daily June to September 15 and weekends only September 16 through May. Admission by donation. 1575 Alma Rd. at Point Grey Rd. (phone: 228-1213).

Grouse Mountain – In addition to the Skyride and stunning views of the city from the summit (see *Seeing the City,* above), this 3,974-foot mountain is only 20 minutes from downtown and has good ski runs with chair lifts, a chalet, a lounge, rentals, and a variety of slopes. In summertime its many paths are great for hiking. The *Grouse Nest* dining room serves lunch and dinner and has excellent views. Open daily. Admission charge. At the top of Capilano Rd. in North Vancouver (phone: 984-0661).

Capilano Suspension Bridge – One of the world's longest suspension foot bridges, hanging 230 feet above the Capilano River and stretching 450 feet across the canyon. The original bridge was erected in 1899; the bridge that stands now was built in 1956. If you walk the bridge you will feel its movement underneath. There's a gift shop and totem pole park. Open daily until dark, with illumination in July and August until 10:30 PM. Admission charge. 3735 Capilano Rd., North Vancouver (phone: 985-7474).

Capilano Salmon Hatchery – A working fish farm built to increase the declining salmon run in the Capilano River, and so far it has been extremely effective. You can see salmon in glass tanks and study the life cycle of this amazing fish as it is described in illustrated diagrams. Open daily. No admission charge. 4500 Capilano Rd., North Vancouver (phone: 987-1411).

Cypress Provincial Park – This mountain park overlooking the city has meadows, lakes, and forests spanning 7,037 acres of the North Shore Mountains. Hiking, snowshoeing, and cross-country and downhill skiing are favorite activities here. Open daily (phone: 929-1291).

FARTHER OUT

Reifel Bird Sanctuary – Home and nesting ground of swans, geese, and ducks, this wild bird sanctuary has footpaths and observation towers for viewing. The 850-acre site is open daily. Admission charge. Take Hwy. 99 south to the Ladner exit, then River Rd. west; cross the Westham Island Bridge and continue to the end of the road (phone: 946-6980).

Vancouver Game Farm – Lions and tigers and bears, monkeys, zebras, and giraffes, are among the 80 species from all over the world that inhabit these 120 acres of farmland. You can amble around the grounds or tour by car. The amiable elephants give rides during the summer. There are also picnic facilities and a gift shop. Open daily. Admission charge. 5048 264th St., Aldergrove (phone: 261-0225).

Fort Langley National Historic Park – Built in 1827 as the Hudson's Bay Company's fort, this park includes the original company store and restored gates, palisades, officers' quarters, and shops. The fort is historically quite interesting if for no other reason than it predates Vancouver by a good deal. Open daily. Admission charge. 30 miles (48 km) east in Fort Langley (phone: 888-4424).

BC Farm Machinery Museum – Just a short jaunt away from the fort, this museum has a collection of restored antique balers and tractors, including a 1902 Case traction engine. There's also a 1930 black and yellow Tiger Moth crop-spray plane. Closed November through February; open daily the rest of the year. Admission charge. King St. in Fort Langley (phone: 888-8386).

Royal Hudson Steam Train – A must for train buffs, this is a journey into the past aboard a genuine steam engine. Day trips aboard the *Royal Hudson Steam Engine 2860* leave from North Vancouver, follow Howe Sound, with its magnificent ocean and mountain views, and proceed up the coast to the logging community of Squamish. The train is replete with a bar car and several refurbished passenger cars. The round trip takes a good 6 hours, including a lunch stop in Squamish. Another option provides what is perhaps the best way to see Howe Sound and to have a trip on this train. The boat-train day trip transports travelers one way on the train and they return by means of the M.V. *Britannia,* Canada's largest sightseeing vessel. Trips are made throughout the spring and summer. Reservations are mandatory. Tickets and details from Harbour Ferries, 1782 W. Georgia St. (phone: 687-9558).

■**EXTRA SPECIAL:** Just a 90-minute ferry ride through the spectacular Gulf Islands, and you're on Vancouver Island, 24 miles across the Strait of Georgia from the mainland. Some 285 miles in length, it is Canada's largest Pacific island and quite spectacular. Actually the top of a partially submerged mountain system, much of the island is heavily forested and mountainous. This is most dramatically apparent in the Pacific Rim National Park on the western coast. Here seals, sea lions, and shore birds inhabit 250 square miles of craggy headlands, white sandy beaches, interior lakes, and estuaries. There are campgrounds in the park and accommodations nearby.

From the terminal at Swartz Bay, it's a 45-minute drive to Victoria, the provincial capital. Victoria is beautifully situated on the shores of the Juan de Fuca Strait, surrounded by sea, with snowcapped mountains forming an impressive backdrop. This is the most English community on the continent, a haven of Sunday afternoon games of lawn bowling, well-loved gardens, and proper English high tea. The wealth of its 250,000 residents is reflected in the lovely residential districts of fine homes and carefully tended gardens. The main attractions are the dignified Parliament Buildings and the renowned Butchart Gardens (phone: 652-5256) — 50 acres developed from an old quarry with six gardens, including the Sunken Lake with its fountains, an English rose garden, the lush Italian gardens, and a delicate Japanese garden. At night they're illuminated. There's a restaurant, coffee shop, and gift shop, and live entertainment during July and August.

Shops in Victoria offer good values in woolens, china, crystal, jade, antiques, and handicrafts. If you are staying over, reserve a room at the *Empress* (phone: 384-8111), the castle by the sea that is the grande dame of Canadian Pacific hotels (as we went to press it was closed for restoration, but slated to reopen by 1990); or if you prefer something smaller and a bit out of town, try the charming *Oak*

Bay Beach hotel (1175 Beach Dr.; phone: 598-4556). For more details on Victoria, see the Vancouver route in DIRECTIONS.

SOURCES AND RESOURCES

TOURIST INFORMATION: For general information, brochures, and maps, contact Tourism Vancouver, 562 Burrard St. (phone: 682-2222). The office is conveniently located just down the street from the *Hyatt Regency* hotel. City street maps are available at most newsstands and department stores.

For maps and general information on Victoria, contact the Tourism Victoria, 812 Wharf St., in front of the *Empress* hotel (phone: 382-2127).

Local Coverage – The *Province,* morning daily and the only Sunday paper; the *Sun,* afternoon daily except Sundays. *Vancouver; Western Living,* and *V* are monthly magazines concerned with the West Coast lifestyle; another monthly, *Key to Vancouver,* includes maps and information on shopping and entertainment.

Food – *Vancouver* contains short items on some of the city's restaurants, and the *Sun* and *Province* both have restaurant reviews. Vancouver *Gastronomique* ($9.95) describes a full range of options.

Telephone – The area code for Vancouver is 604.

Sales Tax – The basic sales tax is 6%.

Currency – All prices are quoted in US dollars unless otherwise indicated.

TIPPING: At a restaurant generally leave 15% of the bill. Taxi drivers are usually given 10 to 15% of the fare. Airport porters and bellboys are given about $1 (CN) per bag. Hotel maids' service fee is usually included in the bill, but if you want to tip, leave $1 (CN) per day.

CLIMATE: Rain is a fact of life in Vancouver, so an umbrella and a raincoat are good ideas no matter what time of year you visit. Some snow usually falls during the winter months, although it rarely stays on the ground very long. Winter mornings can be nippy, but on a few days the mercury dips below 32F (zero C); the average winter temperature is around 39F (4C). Summers are warm and pleasant, with temperatures averaging in the 60s and 70s F (15-23C).

GETTING AROUND: Airport Transportation – *Airport Express* runs a mini-bus service every 15 minutes from 5:45 AM and calls at major downtown hotels. For information, call 273-0071.

Bus – The *BC Hydro* bus system covers most of Greater Vancouver with extensive downtown service; exact fare is required. Service is greatly reduced after midnight. For route information, call 261-5100.

Ferry – *Sea-Bus* is a ferry system that links the North Shore with downtown Vancouver. Ferries depart every 15 minutes from the downtown terminal at the CP Rail station and from the North Vancouver terminal at the foot of Lonsdale. Transfers are available to connect with *Sea-Bus.* For information, call 261-5100.

For information on service to Vancouver Island, contact *BC Ferries* (phone: 669-1211) which sail to Victoria and Nanaimo, farther north on the Island.

Taxi – Major companies are *Yellow Cab* (phone: 681-3311); *Black Top Cabs* (phone: 681-2181); *Maclure's* (phone: 731-9211); and *Advance* (phone: 876-5555). Taxi stands are located throughout the city and at most hotels. Hailing cabs in the street is difficult.

VANCOUVER / Sources and Resources 251

Almost any fare within the city will be under $10; a trip to the airport from downtown runs about $13.50.

Car Rental – All major North American firms are represented: *Avis,* near the *Vancouver* hotel, 757 Hornby St. (phone: 682-1621); *Hertz,* 666 Seymour St. (phone: 688-2411); and *Budget,* 450 W. Georgia St. (phone: 685-0536).

Sightseeing Tours – *Gray Line* (phone: 681-8687) operates tours from most of the downtown hotels, and in summer, colorful British doubledeckers join the fleet.

SPECIAL EVENTS: For exact dates, check with the Visitors Bureau. At the *Polar Bear Swim,* held every New Year's Day since 1919, hardy souls of all ages dip into the Pacific at English Bay.

Considered one of the best of its kind in North America, the annual *Children's Festival* in May has a lively program of puppet shows, mime, dancers, singers, and plays — all performed under colorful tents in Vanier Park.

The *Vancouver Sea Festival* in mid-July is a series of parades, concerts, salmon barbecues, and sports events, topped off by a gigantic fireworks display over English Bay. Another highlight is the Nanaimo to Vancouver *Bathtub Race,* which draws contestants from around the world.

The *Vancouver Folk Music Festival* is a long weekend in mid-July filled with performances by musicians from all over North America; there are workshops and jam sessions as well.

The *Abbotsford International Air Show* features aerobatics and aircraft displays by everything from Piper Cubs to 747s. (You can fly your own plane in and take part.) It's held on a weekend in early August at the Abbotsford Airport, 30 miles (48 km) east of Vancouver. For information, call 859-9211.

Every year in late August, a grand parade through downtown Vancouver kicks off the *Pacific National Exhibition,* featuring concerts by renowned artists, logging sports exhibitions, livestock and agricultural displays, horse races, food fairs, and a good midway. For information, call 253-2311.

In December the *Christmas Carol Ship,* with a troupe of carolers on board, leads a flotilla of ships, all lit up for Christmas, around Vancouver Harbor from December 9th through the 18th. For information, call 683-2000.

MUSEUMS: The *Museum of Anthropology,* the *Vancouver Art Gallery,* the *MacMillan Planetarium,* the *Maritime Museum,* the *Centennial Museum,* and the *Vancouver Aquarium* are described fully in *Special Places.* Other interesting museums include the following:

Cap's Cycle Museum – Antique bicycles. 420 E. Columbia St., New Westminster (phone: 524-3611).

BC Sports Hall of Fame – Medals and memorabilia from Olympic Games, focusing on BC athletes. In the BC Pavilion of Exhibition Park (phone: 253-5655).

Arts, Sciences & Technology Centre – Exhibits geared toward children. 1455 Quebec St. (phone: 687-8414).

SHOPPING: Vancouver is a good city to shop in, with almost everything you need and some things you never even thought of buying. The four major downtown department stores — *Eaton's, The Bay, Woodward's,* and *Sears* — carry a full line of standard merchandise, and numerous shops have regional goods and unusual specialties — everything from salmon packed to travel to Indian and Eskimo art to railway paraphernalia. The following is a highly eclectic guide.

Antiques – *Deeler's Antiques,* 832 N. Park Royal, West Vancouver (phone: 922-

0213), is one of the largest importers and a good place to browse. *Uno Langmann Ltd.,* 2117 S. Granville St. (phone: 736-8825), specializes in pre-1830 quality items. *Vancouver Antique Centre,* 422 Richards St., features 20 shops (phone: 669-0089).

Art – *The Marion Scott Gallery,* 671 Howe St. (phone: 685-1934), carries a notable collection of Indian and Eskimo carvings, hangings, and baskets. *Leona Latimer,* 1590 W. 2nd Ave (phone: 732-4556) carries Northwest Coast Indian jewelry, wood and stone carvings, and original paintings.

Books – *Duthie's* is Vancouver's foremost bookstore, with several locations. *The Paperback Cellar,* 919 Robson St. (phone: 684-4496), has a broad range of titles.

Coffee – *Murchie's,* 970 Robson St. (call 662-3776 for additional locations), is an old-fashioned coffee and tea shop that sells fresh-roasted coffee and a variety of teas.

Fashion – The *Pacific Centre* and *Vancouver Centre* shopping malls run underground for more than 2 square blocks and connect places such as the *Four Seasons* hotel and *Eaton's* department store. You'll find many shops in both complexes including *Holt Renfrew,* which features high quality men's and women's clothing and accessories. Robson Street has become a major fashion center, with elegant designer — as well as fun — fashion boutiques. Fine shops such as *Leone* can be found at the *Sinclair Centre,* a restored building at 757 W. Hastings.

Furs – *Pappas Designers Ltd.,* 449 Hamilton St. (phone: 681-6391), has a terrific array of high-fashion furs and a clientele from rock stars to jet setters. A classic selection is offered at *Amante Furs,* 480 Granville St. (phone: 689-5929).

Games – If there's a game going, *Good Stuff Games* — at four locations around town, including one at Pacific Centre — has got it, from backgammon to computer chess and everything in between. Proprietor John Pozer will sit down and take challengers on in any game at just about any time.

Jewelry – *Brinkhaus,* 705 Hornby, features fine gems and Swiss watches (phone: 689-7055). *Le Must de Cartier Boutique* is in Pacific Centre (phone: 689-9411). *Birks,* 710 Granville St. (phone: 669-3333), Canada's major jewelry and silver supplier, has nine locations in town. Luxurious jewelry, sterling silver, and Royal Copenhagen china are available at *Georg Jensen,* 648 Hornby (phone: 688-4744). For gold and silver jewelry handcrafted by a European master, try *Toni Cavelti,* 692 Seymour St. (phone: 681-3481).

Leather – *Neto Leathers,* in Gastown at 347 Water St. (phone: 682-6424), features well-crafted garments in leather, suede, and fur.

Pipes – *Pipe Den,* 714 West Hastings St. (phone: 688-5023), has a wide selection of pipes, a pipe reconditioning service, and more than 40 blends of tobacco. They also do custom tobacco blending.

Quilts – At *Down 'n Under,* at Park Royal in West Vancouver (phone: 926-2821), they have an excellent selection of European-style eiderdown quilts.

Railway Paraphernalia – *Railway World,* 150 Water St. (phone: 681-4811), is heaven for the train buff, with items ranging from models to books and calendars.

Sailing Supplies – The *Quarterdeck,* 375 Water St. (phone: 683-7475), has everything for sailors and their vessels.

Salmon – Some of the world's best salmon comes from BC waters, and fresh or smoked salmon can be bought packed to go at *Longliner Seafoods,* on Granville Island (phone: 681-9016), or at *Jet Set Sam,* at the airport (phone: 273-9917).

Tuxedos – If you get an unexpected invitation to a formal occasion, *Black & Lee,* 1110 Seymour St. (phone: 688-2481), can supply everything you need, including shirts, shoes, and accessories.

Woolens – *Edward Chapman Ltd.,* 833 W. Pender St. (phone: 685-6207), for men; *Chapman's Collectibles,* Pacific Centre (phone: 688-6711) and *Edward Chapman Ladies Shop,* 2596 Granville St. (phone: 732-3394), for women.

SPORTS: Vancouver has become a major sports city in recent years, with plenty to participate in and watch.

Baseball – The *Canadians* have brought pro baseball back to the city with their home games at *Nat Bailey Stadium,* 4601 Ontario St. (phone: 872-5232).

Bicycling – Riding around Stanley Park is a good way to see this attraction or work off a big lunch. Rent 1- to 5-speeds, mountain bikes, and tandems (2-seaters) from *Stanley Park Bike Rentals,* 676 Chilco St. (phone: 681-5581).

Fishing – Vancouver is special in having easy access to both freshwater and deep-sea fishing. Take your pick — from the Capilano River, where you can catch trout, steelhead, and Dolly Varden, to any of the bays surrounding the city. The main catch is salmon. Fishing charter companies include *Westin Bayshore Yacht Charter,* 1601 W. Georgia St. (phone: 682-3377), and *Malibu Yacht Charters,* at the foot of Bute St. (phone: 685-8468).

Football – The *BC Lions,* Vancouver's contenders in the Canadian Football League, take on all comers at the city's domed *BC Place Stadium,* 777 Pacific Blvd. S. (phone: 669-2300).

Golf – Eight excellent private golf courses, plus a dozen or more public links, dot the area. *Gleaneagles* in West Vancouver (phone: 921-7353) is the best, with *Langara,* 290 W. 49th Ave. (phone: 327-4423), a close second. Upgraded to one of the best public facilites in the entire country is the *University Golf Club,* 5185 University Blvd. (phone: 224-7513).

Hockey – The National Hockey League Vancouver *Canucks* defend the ice at *Pacific Coliseum* in Exhibition Park (phone: 254-5141).

Horse Racing – The horses run at *Exhibition Park,* on the Pacific National Exhibition grounds, from April through October. For information and reservations, call 254-1631.

Jogging – Stanley Park has a 7-km (4.3-mile) path that circles around the beautiful park. Jogging along the 1-mile West Vancouver Seawall is also nice.

Motor Racing – You can catch national and international race car action at Westwood, 12 miles (19 km) from downtown, from March to September.

Sailing – There are several yacht clubs, including the venerable *Royal Vancouver Yacht Club* (phone: 224-1344). Among the boat charter outfits are: *Admiralty Yachts,* 1666 Duranleau St. (phone: 685-7371) and *Pacific Quest Charters,* 1521 Foreshore Walk (phone: 682-2205).

Skiing – At Grouse, Seymour, and Cypress Mountains, you can ski down splendid slopes overlooking the city. For information and weather reports, call 926-5612. Some of the finest skiing in North America is at Whistler and Blackcomb Mountains, about 1½ hours drive from Vancouver. For information, call 687-6761. Dozens of ski packages are available, ranging from one-day jaunts to week-long ski-ins. The Vancouver Visitors Bureau has full details.

Tennis – The city maintains an extensive number of municipal courts. Most popular are those in Stanley Park.

THEATER: The dailies and some city magazines give complete listings of what's on where and when. Among the most prominent theaters, repertory groups, and box offices are: *Arts Club Theatre,* Granville Island (phone: 687-1644); *Theatre Sports/Back Alley Theatre,* 751 Thurlow St. (phone: 688-7013); *Concert Box Office,* 1304 W. Georgia St. (phone: 280-4444); *Metro Theatre,* 1370 S.W. Marine Dr. (phone: 266-7191); *Orpheum Theatre,* Granville Mall (phone: 665-3050); *Punchlines,* 15 Water St. (phone: 684-3015) for stand-up comedy; *Queen Elizabeth Theatre,* 649 Cambie St. (phone: 665-3050); *Studio 58,* 100 W. 49th Ave.

(phone: 324-5227); *Vancouver East Cultural Centre,* 1895 Venables St. (phone: 254-9578); *Vancouver Opera Association,* 1132 Hamilton St. (phone: 682-2871); *Vancouver Playhouse,* 543 W. 7th Ave. (phone: 872-6622); the *Waterfront Theatre,* Granville Island (phone: 685-6217).

MUSIC: Almost any evening, there's some musical entertainment in Vancouver, from resident ensembles and orchestras to soloists and singers to visiting superstars. Rock concerts frequently take place in the *BC Place Stadium,* the *Pacific Coliseum,* and sometimes at the *Queen Elizabeth Theatre.* Here, too, an active program of dance performances offers some world class troupes, including the *Joffrey Ballet, Royal Winnipeg Ballet,* and BC's own troupe, Ballet British Columbia. The recently revitalized Vancouver Symphony Orchestra offers a full season of music. The *Vancouver Opera Association* presents classic operas each year. A good reference for musical events is the *Canadian Music Centre* (phone: 734-4622).

NIGHTCLUBS AND NIGHTLIFE: Vancouver has an eclectic after-hours scene offering something for everyone. The *Pelican Bay Bar* in the *Granville Island* hotel (phone: 683-7373) is very lively and attracts a crowd ranging in age from early 20s to late 40s. Another big attraction is *Richard's on Richards,* 1036 Richards St. (phone: 687-6794), which has 4 bars, videos, and dancing to both live and recorded music. In the same vein, *Systems,* 350 Richards St. (phone: 687-5007), has an 1,800-foot dance floor. Other spots include *The Luv-A-Fair,* 1275 Seymour St. (phone: 685-3288), where straights and gays meet to see rock videos and dance to live and recorded sounds.

Among the hotel meeting places are: the *Mardi Gras* in the *Century Plaza* hotel, 1015 Burrard St. (phone: 687-0575), and the *Bacchus Lounge* in the *Wedgewood* hotel, 845 Hornby St. (phone: 689-7777).

The newly renovated *Commodore Ballroom,* 870 Granville St. (phone: 681-7838), is another place to keep in mind for a wide variety of entertainment, ranging from the *New Glenn Miller Orchestra* and Cajun rocker Clifton Chenier to bluesman John Mayall.

Down in Gastown, the *Town Pump,* 66 Water St. (phone: 683-6695), has brick walls and lots of brass trimmings, and features live bands that run from rhythm and blues to folk. *Hot Jazz Society,* 2120 Main St. (phone: 873-4131), is where live Dixieland, swing, and big band sounds are produced by local and visiting musicians.

BEST IN TOWN

CHECKING IN: Vancouver has a good choice of accommodations, from comfortable, old-fashioned smaller hotels to modern, luxury high-rises. During the past decade, especially in preparation for the wildly successful 1986 World's Fair, numerous major hotels were constructed downtown. All hotels listed have room phones and color TV sets. Expect to pay $130 and up per night for a double room in the expensive range; $75 to $120 in the moderate range; and from $55 to $72 in the inexpensive category. All telephone numbers are in the 604 area code unless otherwise indicated.

Delta Place – Formerly the *Mandarin Oriental* hotel, this top downtown hotel is now operated by the Delta Chain. Amenities include two elegant restaurants, squash and racquetball courts, a library, and a billiard room. 645 Howe St. (phone: 687-1122). Expensive.

Four Seasons – This leading hotel in the center of the city soars above Pacific Centre. Everything is located right here or just an enclosed walk away. Among the features are three restaurants, including the popular *Chartwell*. The 385 rooms and suites have spectacular city and mountain views. The *Garden Lounge,* with its piano bar, is a favorite meeting spot. 791 W. Georgia St. (phone: 689-9333). Expensive.

Hyatt Regency – An elegant, lively hotel that sits atop the *Royal Centre* shopping mall. There are lots of luxurious touches in the rooms, 3 restaurants, lounges, and Sunday brunches which have become a Vancouver habit. 655 Burrard St. (phone: 687-6543). Expensive.

Méridien – The newest luxury hotel in town; gracious, appealing, and entirely satisfying. Although the rooms tend to be on the smallish side, they are exceptionally well done. Marble bathrooms are very luxurious, and corner rooms that end in the number 25 have especially good views. There's a substantial health and beauty center, plus a swimming pool and sundeck on the adjacent apartment building. Super service and extremely personal attention for a property with almost 400 rooms. 845 Burrard St. (phone: 682-5511 or 800-543-4300). Expensive.

Pan Pacific – Right on the harbor at Canada Place — the city's new downtown waterfront development, which is the legacy of Expo '86 — this hotel provides a view of harbor activity nearly as spectacular as the view in Hong Kong. A member of the Leading Hotels of the World group, it blends artfully with its location since the design includes a pierlike wing jutting into the water. There are 505 luxurious rooms and suites, including some classed as ultra-deluxe (with special amenities such as a private concierge). The three restaurants here include one with casual dining and a harbor view, another with Japanese cuisine, and the more formal *Five Sails,* with continental fare and panoramas of both the water and the North Shore mountains. Another highlight is the fitness club, with squash and racquetball courts, sauna, and aerobics classes. 999 Canada Place (phone: 662-8111; in the US, 800-663-1515). Expensive.

Vancouver – Now operated by Canadian National, this hotel has long been a landmark on the downtown skyline. Stately, comfortable, and elegant throughout, it is not without its own informal touches. *The Roof* is a favorite weekend restaurant stop, with good food, entertainment, and a nice view. 900 W. Georgia St. (phone: 684-3131). Expensive.

Westin Bayshore Inn – It's in the heart of the city, but the ocean is at your doorstep; in fact, you can moor your yacht at the hotel dock. The late Howard Hughes once rented the top floors for a brief stay. There's a selection of elegant shops in the lobby, Beefeater-costumed doormen, a pool, a *Trader Vic's* restaurant and the *Garden Restaurant* on the lobby level. 1601 W. Georgia St. (phone: 682-3377). Expensive.

Coast Georgian Court – Many of the 180 rooms afford magnificent panoramic views, and if you intend to go to any of the sporting events or trade shows at the BC Place Stadium, this is your best bet. The lounge is at once dignified and homey, and there is also a dining room. Of the 12 floors, 4 are designated for non-smokers. 773 Beatty St. (phone: 682-5555). Expensive to moderate.

Delta's Airport Inn – Convenient to the airport, this inn is just 20 minutes from downtown. Facilities include covered tennis courts, pools, patios, and saunas. Rooms are modern, spacious, and comfortable. A courtesy bus will meet you at the airport. 10251 St. Edward's Dr., Richmond (phone: 278-9611). Moderate.

Georgia – The *Beatles* once stayed here, and if that's not enough, there's also plenty of Old World charm. Though the rooms are air conditioned, you can open the windows if you're a fresh-air fan. A streetside restaurant, *Night Court,* is busy at lunchtime and open to the wee hours. 801 W. George St. (phone: 682-5566). Moderate.

Granville Island – Situated near the city's popular covered market, this waterfront hotel has a total of 54 rooms or suites. Also within are a popular nightspot and a restaurant; without are many seawall pathways on which to stroll. 1253 Johnston St. (phone: 683-7373). Moderate.

New World Harbourside – Close to the downtown core, this sleek 19-story hotel has a revolving restaurant on top and good views of seaplanes and tugs from some rooms that overlook the water. 1133 W. Hastings St. (phone: 689-9211). Moderate.

Westbrook – Once host to many of the international participants at Expo '86, it boasts 193 studio suites, each with a queen-size bed, separate sitting area, and a kitchenette. Other amenities include *Page's Café,* a sports complex, and a good location. 1234 Hornby St. (phone: 688-1234). Moderate.

Park Royal – This small, quiet hotel is nestled below the mountains on the banks of the Capilano River, across the Lion's Gate Bridge, 15 minutes from downtown. Beaches, golf, and ski lifts are nearby, as is the Park Royal Shopping Center. There's a lovely terrace, surrounded by flowers and trees, where lunch, cocktails, and light evening meals are served. The *Tudor Dining Room*'s Sunday brunch is quite popular among the locals, as is the cozy pub. 440 Clyde St. at Sixth Ave., West Vancouver (phone: 926-5511). Moderate.

Ramada Renaissance – The primary attractions at this West End complex are a close proximity to the beach activity at English Bay and a 2-block stroll from the delights of Stanley Park. All rooms come with a refrigerator and coffeemaker; a small kitchen can be plugged into service for an additional $17 per day. *Humphrey's* restaurant graces the 35th floor, and there is a shopping complex on the lower level. 1733 Comox St. (phone: 688-7711). Moderate.

Wedgewood – Right across from the Robson Square complex, this intimate hotel has just 94 rooms, but each is attractively decorated and the price includes a continental breakfast. 845 Hornby St. (phone: 689-7777). Moderate.

Royal Garden – Accommodations here offer good value. The 210 rooms are quiet, comfortable, and attractive; there's an indoor pool, dining room, coffee shop, and cocktail lounge. 1110 Howe St. (phone: 684-2151). Moderate to inexpensive.

Barclay – Situated in the heart of the West End within strolling distance of most of the attractions of the city core, this small European-style hostelry has 90 comfortable suites. *Barclay's,* the house restaurant, has notably reasonable prices. 1348 Robson St. (phone: 688-8850). Inexpensive.

Sylvia – Just a stone's throw from the Pacific, this 9-story West End hotel offers great value. The ivy-covered building has recently been updated and its facilities now include a nicely presented restaurant and bistro. Make reservations in advance, particularly in the summer. 1154 Gilford St. (phone: 681-9321). Inexpensive.

EATING OUT: Vancouver has undergone something of a restaurant boom in the past decade. Seafood is still king here, and it's available in a variety of forms. But there's been a proliferation of ethnic restaurants. These, added to Vancouver's already good supply of French and Italian restaurants, steakhouses, and Chinatown dining spots, now give the city a wide range of cuisines to choose from. Expect to pay $40 and up for two for a dinner in the expensive range; $30 to $45 in the moderate range; and under $30 (in some cases, a lot under) in the inexpensive category. Prices do not include drinks, wine, or tip. All telephone numbers are in the 604 area code unless otherwise indicated.

Cannery – This dockside restaurant looks as if it has been around for a very long time, with its weathered woods, old brass, and nautical artifacts, but it's actually just about 15 years old. It's the seafood and the views of the harbor and mountains that make this a favorite spot in town. Open Mondays through Fridays for lunch; dinner daily. Reservations necessary. Major credit cards accepted. 2205 Commissioner St., about a 10-minute drive from city center (phone: 254-9606). Expensive.

Le Gavroche – Located in a charming West End house, this restaurant offers an interesting — and changing — menu. The game dishes are particularly notable, and the seasonal specialties are all good bets. Desserts are geared to send a weight watcher back to the drawing board. Closed Sundays. Major credit cards accepted. 1616 Alberni St. (phone: 685-3924). Expensive.

Umberto's – What began as an Italian eatery in an old yellow house has grown into three adjacent restaurants — the original; a dining room specializing in game (*Il Giardino di Umberto*); and a seafood restaurant (*Umberto's Fish House*). Umberto Menghi, the affable and energetic proprietor, divides his evenings between the restaurants. The food is decidedly Italian and eminently elegant, with close attention to detail. Desserts are identical in the three places (and the orange cake is marvelous), but specialties differ significantly — from pheasant and reindeer in a pepper sauce at *Il Giardino* to fresh salmon, sturgeon, halibut, red snapper, and crab at *Umberto's Fish House*. Closed Sundays. Reservations necessary, even for lunch. Major credit cards accepted. 1376, 1380, and 1382 Hornby St. (phone: 687-6316 for *Umberto's;* 669-2422 for *Il Giardino;* 687-6621 for *Umberto's Fish House*). Expensive.

William Tell – Known as "the special occasion place," this restaurant serves haute cuisine in a luxurious atmosphere of traditional elegance. The delicious fare draws heavily on local delicacies, complemented by the chef's contemporary touch. Open daily. Major credit cards accepted. 765 Beatty St. (phone: 688-3504). Expensive.

Bridges – In a bright yellow building on a highly visible corner of Granville Island, this place offers a prize view of marine activities, the city skyline, and the bustle that makes the island such a lively spot. Seating is on numerous levels to take advantage of the view, and the menu of mostly seafood changes every day. A wine bar fills the lower floor, and a wide deck is popular for fair-weather dining. Open daily. Reservations necessary. Major credit cards accepted. 1696 Duranleau St. (phone: 687-4400). Expensive to moderate.

Jonathan's Seafood House – Since it's next to a row of Granville Island houseboats, the seafood menu seems appropriate; thankfully, the kitchen staff is capable of not overcooking the fare. Guests have a lovely view from almost all the tables. Open daily. Reservations advised. Major credit cards accepted. 1333 Johnston St. (phone: 683-7373). Expensive to moderate.

Pelican Bay – Nesting on the east side of burgeoning Granville Island is a waterside eatery that's part of the new *Granville Island* hotel. The menu is continental, with a slant toward seafood, and the view of houseboats, barges, and birds forms a very pretty picture. Open daily. Reservations advised. Major credit cards accepted. 1253 Johnston St. (phone: 683-8155). Expensive to moderate.

Prow – An aptly named place, it sits on the northeastern corner of Canada Place, surrounded on three sides by the waters of Vancouver harbor. The entire range of maritime activity can be observed from most tables: seaplanes, tugs, freighters, and the occasional seal all contribute to the scene. The food is creatively prepared, and the handling of vegetables an added plus. Open daily; no lunch served on Saturdays. Major credit cards accepted. 999 Canada Place (phone: 684-1339). Expensive to moderate.

Quilicum – The only restaurant in town featuring authentic dishes of Indians native to Canada's northwest coast. Try the salmon cooked over alderwood and garnished with cedar. Patrons sit at tatami-like tables, and Indian artwork (for sale) lines the restaurant walls. Reservations advised. Open daily. Major credit cards accepted. 1724 Davie St. (phone: 681-7044). Expensive to moderate.

Bandi's – Located in a nice little clapboard house, it has an atmosphere that one might expect to find in a country inn — Hungarian style. The food is hearty and very tasty, the soups delicious, and the homemade peasant bread addictive. Open for lunch Mondays through Fridays; dinner daily. Major credit cards accepted. 1427 Howe St. (phone: 685-3391). Moderate.

Bishop's – John Bishop is a true perfectionist and the output of his kitchen wins wide applause for its superior presentation and taste. While the place is small and located in residential Kitsilano, it is well worth the 10-minute taxi ride from downtown. Open for lunch Mondays through Fridays; dinner daily. Reservations advised. Major credit cards accepted. 2183 W. 4th Ave. (phone: 738-2025). Moderate.

Café de Paris – The music, the decor — marble-topped tables and brass fixtures — and the French waiters all lend this convivial place an authentic Gallic bistro mood. The café has a menu that caters to various appetites, and it is a popular stop after a stroll in nearby Stanley Park. Closed Sundays. Major credit cards accepted. 751 Denman St. (phone: 687-1418). Moderate.

Café Splash – Tucked into a corner of a waterside apartment complex, the two main features here are a good view of Granville Island water activities and the superior efforts of a female chef. The menu offers a variety of fresh, grilled seafood, steaks, veal, chicken, duck, and pheasant. There is alfresco dining during the summer. Open Tuesdays through Fridays for lunch, Tuesdays through Saturdays for dinner. Major credit cards accepted. 1600 Howe St. (phone: 682-5600). Moderate.

Caffè de' Medici – Classic fixtures, paintings, and attractive furnishings make this Italian restaurant look as if it has been part of the scene for years. In reality, it's part of the modern Galleria complex near the central corner of Burrard and Robson streets. The pastas are standouts, and the chef is known for handling seafood with care. Open for lunch Mondays through Fridays; dinner daily. Major credit cards accepted. 1025 Robson St. (phone: 669-9322). Moderate.

Christopher's – An imaginative eye for decor and an inventive menu are two of the strong points at this place. Fresh herbs are grown outside, and the chef has a light touch with sauces. Open daily. Major credit cards accepted. 510 Nelson St. (phone: 688-7722). Moderate.

Delilah's – Famous with the locals for serving the best martinis in town, this hotel restaurant blends modern comfort with Old World charm. Prix fixe menu with two- or five-course dinners. Open for dinner daily; Sunday brunch. Since reservations are not accepted (and it's a very popular place), try to get there early and, if necessary, remember that it's worth the wait. 1906 Haro St. (phone: 687-3424). Moderate.

English Bay Café – Once a beachfront fish and chip shop, this is now an elegant restaurant with a fabulous ocean view. The lower level bistro offers casual dining, and on warm evenings dinner is also served on the outdoor deck. Specialties include rack of lamb and Dungeness crab in béarnaise sauce. Sunday brunch is also served. Open daily. Reservations necessary. Credit cards accepted. 1795 Beach Ave. (phone: 669-2225). Moderate.

Jean Pierre's – In the Bentall Centre office complex, this elegantly appointed restaurant serves continental dishes and attracts a healthy crowd at lunchtime and during cocktail hours when there's live piano music. For a quieter setting, opt for dinner. Reservations advised. Closed for dinner Sundays. Major credit cards accepted. 1055 Dunsmuir St. (phone: 669-0360). Moderate.

Joe Fortes' Seafood & Chop House – In Vancouver's early days, Mr. Fortes was a well-loved character who lived on the beach and taught many youngsters to swim. Named in his honor, this attractive restaurant, decorated with mahogany, brass, and greenery, is a favorite with young executives. Reservations advised.

Open daily. Major credit cards accepted. 777 Thurlow St. (phone: 669-1940). Moderate.

Kamei Sushi – Many city sushi fans feel that this is the leading spot for the Japanese delicacy. You may sit at the counter to watch the chefs artfully construct the various dishes or in the dining room. The non-sushi items on the menu are also very good. Open daily. Reservations advised. Major credit cards accepted. 811 Thurlow St. (phone: 684-5767). New branches at 1414 W. Broadway (phone: 732-0112) and 601 W. Broadway (phone: 876-3388) provide both more room and a higher level of energy. Moderate.

A Kettle of Fish – The type of seafood place that people are always searching for — a restaurant committed to serving *really* fresh seafood, not the ubiquitous "fresh frozen" kind. It has a convivial greenhouse feeling with skylights, lots of plants, and objects that would be at home in an English garden. The menu changes daily, as the owner never knows just what's going to be fresh. Open daily. Reservations advised. Major credit cards accepted. 900 Pacific St. (phone: 682-6661). Moderate.

Koji – Although the chef for whom this place was named no longer works here, other sushi experts have stepped up to his counter and continue to turn out superior dishes. The decor is attractive and there's a nice view of the downtown cityscape. Open daily. Reservations advised. Major credit cards accepted. 601 W. Broadway (phone: 876-9267). Moderate.

O'Doul's – Rebuilt for the 1986 World Exposition, this restaurant remains the perfect place for an affordable Saturday brunch. Open daily. Major credit cards accepted. 1300 Robson St. (phone: 684-8461). Moderate.

Prospect Point Café – Nearby Prospect Point has one of the best views in Stanley Park, and it is shared by this café. An inventive menu and imaginative decor increase its appeal. Outdoor dining is available in good weather. Closed Mondays. Reservations advised. Major credit cards accepted. Stanley Park (phone: 669-2737). Moderate.

Salmon House on the Hill – Salmon is the specialty, but roast prime rib and Cornish game hens are also served. The restaurant's magnificent view of the city, park, mountains, and sea lures tourists and locals alike. Open daily. Reservations advised. Major credit cards accepted. 2229 Folkestone Way, West Vancouver (phone: 926-3212). Moderate.

Santa Fé Cafe – Fresh, innovative Southwest-California dishes are prepared in this open-air kitchen. Open for lunch Mondays through Fridays; dinner daily. Reservations advised. Major credit cards accepted. 1688 W. 4th Ave. (phone: 738-8777).

Teahouse – In Stanley Park at Ferguson Point, this airy and attractive spot has blossomed on a site that formerly housed a very British teahouse. Now the interior is all white and leafy green, and there's a separate conservatory, where the nicest tables are set. The menu changes often, and the seafood specials are usually the best choices. The sunsets here are breathtaking. Open daily. Reservations necessary. Major credit cards accepted. In Stanley Park overlooking the bay at Ferguson Pt. (phone: 669-3281). Moderate.

Tsui Hang Village – Crowded and congested and very friendly, this Chinese restaurant is thought by many to be one of the best of its kind in town. Seafood is the specialty, and diners can pick their own right out of the bubbling fish tanks. The crab with black bean sauce is sloppy, but well worth the mess. Open daily. Most major credit cards accepted. 615 Davie St. (phone: 683-6868). Moderate.

Umberto al Porto – Homemade pasta and an array of Italian specialties are served at this Gastown establishment, and if seated on the upper level, you can get a terrific glimpse of the harbor and the distant mountains. Located in one of Gastown's most attractive buildings, it's close to most of the area's best shops. Open

Mondays through Fridays for lunch; Mondays through Saturdays for dinner. Major credit cards accepted. 321 Water St. (phone: 683-8376). Moderate.

Vassilis Taverna – At this family-run spot, a favorite with Grecophiles, all the usual favorites are offered, along with a few interesting adaptations. The Greek salad and roast chicken are special treats. Open daily. Major credit cards accepted. 2884 W. Broadway (phone: 733-3231). Moderate.

The Kegs – The original of what is now an international chain. The fare is hearty, with an emphasis on steak, plus a few seafood dishes. There's also a salad bar. It's good family value, although some people find the joviality a little taxing. Open daily. Major credit cards accepted. Three locations: *The Keg,* on Granville Island (phone: 685-4735), and *Keg Coal Harbour* (phone: 682-5608) and the *Keg Boathouse* (phone: 669-8851), both at the foot of Cardero St. Moderate to inexpensive.

Sun Tung Lock Seafood – Right in the heart of Chinatown, this place serves a delightful dim sum lunch that consists of about 40 items; the dinner menu is also quite extensive. Tiny local shrimp, kept in massive tanks, are delicious, as are seasonal specials like fried quail and stuffed oysters. Closed Thursdays. Major credit cards accepted. 127 E. Pender St., 2nd floor (phone: 682-3804). Moderate to inexpensive.

Afghan Horseman – Off the beaten track, diners may sit at tables or on the floor, Afghani style, while enjoying their meals. The Horseman's Platter provides a way for a couple to sample the best of Afghani cuisine. Open for lunch Mondays through Fridays; dinner, closed Sundays. Major credit cards accepted. 445 W. Broadway (phone: 873-5923). Inexpensive.

Flamingo House – This Chinese restaurant isn't anywhere near Chinatown but serves great *dim sum* at lunch. Dinner items are well seasoned and freshly prepared. Open daily. Major credit cards accepted. 7510 Cambie St. (phone: 325-4511). Inexpensive.

The Only (Seafood Café) – Firmly ensconced in the steambath and pawnshop district, this longtime restaurant serves some of the freshest seafood around. Inside are a few booths, a serpentine counter, dozens of gas burners, and huge frying pans. The menu includes clams, oysters, pickled herring and boiled potatoes, salmon, and sole. Every few minutes someone will truck a cartload of salmon through the place (mind your jacket). No frills, no sauces, no appetizers, no liquor, no restrooms, no parking, no reservations, no credit cards accepted. Just incredibly fresh seafood. Closed Sundays. 20 E. Hastings St. (phone: 681-6546). Inexpensive.

Pink Pearl – Just about the most authentic Chinese restaurant this side of Taiwan. The Sunday morning *dim sum* brunch is crowded, chaotic, noisy, and absolutely irresistible. The fresh local crab in black bean sauce is reason in itself to visit Vancouver. If you have time for only one Oriental meal, make this your stop. Open daily. Major credit cards accepted. 1132 E. Hastings St. (phone: 253-4316). Inexpensive.

Tony Roma's – A great place for family or informal dining, there are three versions of ribs, good hamburgers, a full range of beers, and, in general, a menu geared to just about every appetite. Open daily. No reservations. Major credit cards accepted. 801 Pacific St. (phone: 669-7336). Inexpensive.

Yang's – One of the best Chinese restaurants in town; small, very plain, and informal, but the chef is a master. Just place yourself in your waiter's hands and say how much you want to spend per person. Closed Wednesdays. Major credit cards accepted. 4186 Main St. (phone: 873-2116). Inexpensive.

WINNIPEG

No matter how you approach Winnipeg, it is hard to shake the impression that the city is no more than a small ship on a vast prairie ocean and, given a good, hard wind, could simply float away in all that space. The impression is certainly unfair to a city of Winnipeg's substance — 625,000 people, the provincial capital of Manitoba, and a city of no mean cultural and economic attainments — but it has the ring of psychological truth to it.

The nearest urban centers of any size are Toronto, 1,200 miles to the east, and Calgary, 800 miles west; north of Winnipeg stretch the immense reaches of Manitoba and to the west the equally huge prairie provinces of Saskatchewan and Alberta. Manitoba is a vast province of a quarter of a million square miles — 20% larger than France, stretching from Hudson Bay to the US border, from the eastern pine forests of Minnesota to an upland rise that leads eventually to the foothills of the Rockies. The capital of all this land is just 60 miles north of the US border at the conjunction of the Red and Assiniboine rivers.

In 1612 Captain Thomas Button, an English seafarer, spent the winter with his ships at what is now the site of Port Nelson on Hudson Bay. Button and other explorers had been looking for a northern passage to the Orient through the Arctic Ocean. They found their way blocked by the landmass of mid-Canada and discovered an area so rich in forest, streams, fish, and fur-bearing animals that the news they brought back of potential riches more than made up for the loss of easier access to the spice trade.

In 1670 King Charles II granted a franchise for all the lands draining into Hudson Bay to the Hudson's Bay Company, then a fur trading syndicate. (Today the company — popularly called *The Bay* — still operates fur trading posts in northern Canada and runs a chain of major department stores throughout Canada as well.) To sustain its operation, the Hudson's Bay Company decided to develop an agricultural settlement at the junction of the Red and Assiniboine rivers, a floodplain north of what would become the US border. The deeply silted, rich soil of the Red River basin soon became an asset more important than the fur trade, and the agricultural industry of western Canada was born. By 1870, when Manitoba became part of the Confederation of provinces comprising Canada, there were 12,000 settlers in the Red River Colony.

The union of Manitoba with Canada was, however, not without strife. The entire province had been the domain of several Indian tribes. In the course of the long years of trade between the Indians and the French voyageurs, a culture of French and Indian people called Métis developed. By the late 19th century, the Métis were relatively isolated from both the Indians and the white settlers who were coming to the area in increasing numbers. Louis Riel, a French-speaking Métis, opposed Manitoba's entry into the Confederation of Canada, but his opposition was brutally crushed by the Conservative (Tory) government of Prime Minister Sir John A. Macdonald. Riel's movement, in armed resistance to the government, was eventually put down and Riel himself was hanged. Today, the Riel Rebellion is one of the reasons that Quebec and French-speaking peoples in Canada usually vote for the Liberal party in preference to the Conservative.

The bitterness of the struggle was overlooked but never really resolved in the next decade, when the Canadian Pacific Railroad was under construction. The railroad changed life in every way on the prairies; nothing was the same afterward. It brought gangloads of immigrant Eastern European and Chinese laborers into western Canada, changing forever the demographics and ethnic politics of the provinces, and it turned small agricultural centers into boom towns, awash with prosperity and under siege by the gaudy ladies who decorated the bars and bedrooms of shanty hotels. The West opened up with a splash. And while the laborers laid track, the CPR laid its plans, becoming a colossus of land, mining, and transportation interests.

Winnipeg was affected as deeply as any other city in the West and, because of its location as a gateway to the prairies, more than many. Laborers came with the railroad and stayed on; settlers from the East took the first trains out and did the same. The city that exists today in all its sophistication still carries the mark of that early development. And the center of Winnipeg's business and cultural life remains the settlers' crossroads, Portage Avenue and Main Street, only a few blocks from the junction of the Red and Assiniboine rivers.

For a city its size, it has an extraordinary spectrum of community-supported cultural activities. Opera, a highly acclaimed ballet, a symphony orchestra, several chamber music groups, two universities, professional sports, several legitimate theaters, and hundreds of restaurants feed the vitality of this city.

Not far from the Portage and Main crossroads are the Manitoba Theatre Centre and the Warehouse Theatre, venues for stage plays; the *Centennial Concert Hall,* home of both the *Winnipeg Symphony Orchestra* and the *Royal Winnipeg Ballet;* the Civic Centre, headquarters for the city's council and administration; the financial district; and the Commmodity Exchange, where Canada's crops are sold to the world. On the downtown mile of Portage Avenue, Portage Place, a spanking new shopping center and office/residential complex, is linked by heated skybridges to virtually every major building on or near the thoroughfare, making it possible to visit almost every major downtown building in winter without getting cold.

Winnipeg remains, from its railroad boom town days, a city of great ethnic diversity. The leading population groups are English-Scottish, German, Ukrainian, French, native North American, Jewish, Polish, Dutch, and Italian. People of Icelandic descent make up a small but vital force in the city's business and government life. The newest wave of immigrants comes from the Far East. The Filipino community is close to 25,000, and more than 2,500 Vietnamese boat people have been resettled here, adding spice to Winnipeg's ethnic salad.

Some clustering of the ethnic groups has taken place through the circumstances of historical development and economic change. Winnipeg's North

End was the traditional stopping place for newly arrived immigrants; today it is slowly turning into a corridor of high-rise developments and senior citizens' housing projects stretching several miles north on both sides of North Main Street. To the southeast, the suburb of St. Boniface is the home of Winnipeg's French-speaking citizens; to the northeast, the town of Transcona is a bedroom community for employees of the Canadian National Railroad and other working people.

Winnipeg's most prosperous suburbs lie south of the Assiniboine River. Winding along and leading from Wellington Crescent, home of some of the the city's wealthiest and best-known families, River Heights, with old, stately homes, and Tuxedo, with sprawling mansions and enclosed grounds, remain the most prestigious addresses. Farther west, the suburb of Charleswood has recently attracted young families. Along both shores of the Assiniboine lies the pleasant suburb of St. James, with its picturesque homes and quaintly named streets.

The long, snowy months of winter take their toll, but residents take an almost perverse pride in their ability to handle whatever the Manitoba winter cares to dish out. When temperatures drop to the point that frostbite is an imminent danger on even the shortest outing, residents walk. When blizzards that in other places would shut down cities for weeks batter Winnipeg, residents take it in stride: they claim to have the best snow-removal system in western Canada, spending $10 million a year to plow the snow and repair the streets. Perhaps this stoic bravery harkens back to those early settlers standing at the crossroads of Portage Avenue and Main Street. Though today it is lined with banks, in those days it was quite desolate, and then as now it is the coldest intersection in Canada (winter temperatures can drop to −40F). If that didn't discourage their predecessors, it isn't going to discourage contemporary residents, though the underground shopping mall — Lombard Place — now makes it easier to traverse that infamous intersection. And so there is a common tradition of muddling through that reflects the city's survival of frontier hardships. Isolated on the vast Canadian prairies, Winnipeg has a sense of self-reliance that has given it financial and cultural vigor. That's the most remarkable thing about this very cosmopolitan urban island.

WINNIPEG AT-A-GLANCE

SEEING THE CITY: For a panoramic view of Winnipeg, visit the two *Royal Crown* revolving restaurants in the gothic high-rise, Fort Garry Place. In Canada's only bi-level, revolving dining rooms, European food is served. Lunch daily from 11 AM to 3 PM, and dinner from 5 PM to midnight. 83 Garry St (phone: 947-1990).

SPECIAL PLACES: Winnipeg's downtown commercial center is a crazy quilt of odd-shaped blocks defined by streets, originally laid out more or less parallel to the meandering rivers that meet near the city's center. If you want to walk through this area of Victorian office blocks and soaring modern towers, it's best to park in a commercial lot. (City parking meters cost 50¢ an hour and often there's a 1-hour limit; parking violators are sometimes towed and heavily fined.)

Downtown public transportation is frequent and excellent. A free weekdays-only bus called DASH rings the downtown area and connects the Legislative Building and its grounds with the many shopping areas near Portage Avenue. DASH runs every few minutes from 11:00 AM to 3:15 PM.

DOWNTOWN

Legislative Building – The legislative chambers and executive offices of the Manitoba government are open to the public year-round and serve as an excellent starting point for a tour of the city. The neoclassical architecture is set off by well-groomed, statue-filled lawns that surround the building. Atop the capitol's 255-foot dome stands *Golden Boy,* a 5-ton, 13½-foot gilded bronze statue holding a sheaf of wheat under his arm, a hardly demure symbol of the importance of this grain to Winnipeg's economy. Adjacent to the Legislative Building is the Woodsworth Building (405 Broadway). Off the lobby is an excellent cafeteria open to the public with just about the least expensive lunch in town — about $2.50 for several courses. Open from about 9 AM to about 4 PM, it's best to get there before or after the noon to 1 PM rush. Closed weekends and all government holidays. Broadway and Osborne Sts. (phone: 945-3700 for guided tours).

Winnipeg Commodity Exchange – This is one of the largest grain exchanges in the world and the only commodity futures market in Canada. Visitors can view the trading from a gallery overlooking the floor. Open weekdays 9:30 AM to 1:15 PM; guided tours are available by calling 949-0495. Trizec Building at Portage and Main Sts.

Winnipeg Art Gallery – From small beginnings at the turn of the century, this museum has emerged as one of Canada's finest art showplaces. This triangular building, constructed in the early 60s, houses the work of Canadian and European artists as well as the largest collection of contemporary Eskimo sculpture in Canada. The comprehensive collection of Eskimo work makes the gallery a must on any Winnipeg visit. The gallery also hosts frequent traveling shows. Closed Mondays. No admission charge. Portage Ave. and Memorial Blvd. (phone: 786-6641).

Portage Place – A swanky, friendly center joined by skywalk to major downtown stores, such as the *Hudson Bay* store. On the third level, the spectacular *IMAX Theatre,* with a 5½-story-high, 71-foot-wide screen, shows stunning wildlife and other films custom-made for its huge 70mm format.

Exchange District – During the day on summer weekends, the square teems with produce vendors and antiques peddlers. At night, the action shifts to the discos, nightclubs, and restaurants bordering the square; this is also one of the city's red-light districts, so you'll see ladies of the evening here as well. King St. and Bannatyne Ave.

SUBURBS

Osborne Village – This is Winnipeg's best shopping district. On each side of Osborne Street are small shops selling wicker furniture, books, Tiffany lamps, imported Pakistani carvings, handmade gold jewelry, records, fine clothing for women and children, and a variety of other exotica. Several excellent tea shops and restaurants are in the area, including the *Tea Cozy, Victor's,* and *Basil's* (see *Eating Out* for more information). Osborne St., just across the Osborne St. Bridge from the Legislative Bldg.

Assiniboine Park and Zoo – A 376-acre complex of recreational grounds, botanical gardens, a zoo, a miniature ride-along train, and ornate pavilions, this excellent park is just minutes from downtown. In the summer you can rent bicycles, including tandems, for a few dollars a day. But beware: Eating facilities within the park are limited to snack bars at the botanical gardens, the zoo, and a midpark pavilion; the food served is in the category of "only as a last resort." Located 4 miles (6 km) west of the city center off Wellington Crescent or Corydon Ave. Free (phone: 888-3634).

Kildonan Park – One of Winnipeg's most interesting entertainment complexes, Kildonan has summer swimming pools, Canada's only outdoor theater (the Rainbow Stage, open July and August), a dining pavilion with adequate luncheons, and a Hansel and Gretel Witches' Hut. In the summer, you can walk or cycle along the Red River through the dense trees of the park; in the winter, you can toboggan or skate. Approximately 5 miles (8 km) north of the city center on Main St.

St. Boniface Basilica – The original basilica was gutted by fire in 1968. The ruins of the building were left standing, and within them was built another cathedral of handsome contemporary design. Also of interest here is the gravesite of Louis Riel, the Métis resistance leader. Rue Taché, on the eastern side of the Red River.

Manitoba Museum of Man and Nature – This, the largest of Winnipeg's museums, recreates life on the prairies and in the north. Adjacent to the museum is a planetarium with science shows, dioramas, specimens, and a replica of a 17th-century fur trading ship. Open daily. Admission charge. 190 Rupert Ave. (phone: 956-2830).

Lower Fort Garry – Built in the early 1830s by the Hudson's Bay Company, this is the only stone fur trade fort still intact in North America. In 1951 it was presented to the Canadian government and is now a national historic site. Costumed characters reenact the days of Lower Fort Garry's glory. Open daily from late May to late August and weekends in September. Admission charge. 20 miles (32 km) north of Winnipeg on Rte. 9 (phone: 983-3600).

Manitoba Children's Museum – The hands-on exhibits here include a model grain elevator, railroad switching yard, and a television studio. Open Tuesdays through Saturdays, 9:30 AM to 5 PM; Sundays and holidays, 11 AM to 5 PM. 109 Pacific Ave. (phone: 957-0005).

Royal Canadian Mint – Purported to be one of the most modern facilities in the world, the mint produces coins for a number of countries as well as Canada. It is laid out so visitors can see just how the money is made. Open weekdays from 9 AM to 3 PM for guided tours. Lagimodière Blvd. and the Trans-Canada Hwy. (phone: 257-3359).

Dugald Costume Museum – Canada's only historical display of clothing from 1765 to modern times. Open April to November, 10 AM to 5 PM. On Highway 15, 30 minutes east of downtown (phone: 853-2166).

■ **EXTRA SPECIAL:** Oak Hammock Marsh is a 8,705-acre wildlife management area in which you can view over 50,000 Canada and snow geese resting on their migratory flights. Spring and fall are the best viewing times. Guided tours are available except in winter (phone: 945-6784 for schedules). The area is also home to a plethora of mammals, including minks, weasels, deer, and coyotes. On Hwy. 67 between Stonewall and Selkirk.

SOURCES AND RESOURCES

TOURIST INFORMATION: For general information, brochures, and maps, contact Travel Manitoba, 155 Carlton St., 7th Floor, Winnipeg, Manitoba R3C 3H8 (phone: 945-3777; in the US, 800-665-0040). The best Winnipeg city map is the *City of Winnipeg Tourist and Street Guide,* available free from Travel Manitoba. *The Manitoba Vacation Planner* is the best guide to the city. It is distributed at no charge by Travel Manitoba.

Local Coverage – The *Free Press,* daily; the *Sun,* daily (except Fridays).

Food – The *Free Press* publishes restaurant reviews on Saturdays.

Telephone – The area code for Winnipeg is 204.

Sales Tax – The basic sales tax is 7%.
Currency – All prices are quoted in US dollars unless otherwise indicated.

TIPPING: Leave 15 to 20% of the bill at most restaurants. Taxi drivers aren't necesarily always tipped, but when you do, give 10% of the fare. Airport porters and bellboys generally receive $1.50 per bag, and hotel maids, $1.50 per day.

CLIMATE: Winter, from November through March, is a challenge. With average temperatures hovering around −11F (−24C) during December, January, and February, with readings of −20F (−29C) not uncommon, precautions against the cold are absolutely necessary.

Winnipeg averages a substantial 50 inches of snow each winter. Drivers should carry a shovel, battery booster cables, and a tow rope at all times, and anyone driving in outlying areas or on the rural roads, including the Trans-Canada Highway, should carry some emergency rations, extra gasoline, and flares (if snowplows approach with their roar and blinding lights). Nevertheless, from about 10 AM to 2 PM during the remarkably sunny days of midwinter, it is possible to walk outside with only light winter wear. It's very sunny and very cold — that's the paradox of Manitoba's winters.

GETTING AROUND: Bus – *Winnipeg Transit* operates bus lines throughout the city and suburbs. Maps of the system are available at gas stations, and additional information can be obtained directly from *Winnipeg Transit* at 284-7190.

Taxi – Cabs can be hailed in the street; taxi stands are located at the larger hotels throughout the city.

Car Rental – All major national companies are represented.

Riverboats – Three companies conduct river cruises on the Red and Assiniboine Rivers during spring, summer, and early fall. The MS *Paddlewheel Queen*, a replica of the old sternwheelers, brings an air of the Old South to Winnipeg. Evening cruises feature dining and dancing. The MS *Lady Winnipeg* and *Paddlewheel Princess* make sightseeing cruises down the Red River to Lower Fort Garry, a scenic 20-mile (32-km) trip. Contact *Paddlewheel–Gray Line Tours*, PO Box 3930, Station B, or 1048 Main St. (phone: 339-1696); *River Rouge Ltd.*, 312 Nairn Ave. (phone: 669-2824); or *Lord Selkirk II*, 69 Birchbark Bay (phone: 582-2331).

SPECIAL EVENTS: Every August, Winnipeg hosts the week-long international festival *Folkorama*. More than 40 ethnic groups celebrate their diverse heritages in colorful pavilions throughout the city with native dances, songs, displays, and food. China, Greece, the Philippines, and the Ukraine are only a few of the many countries represented in addition to the pavilions dedicated to Canada's Indians. A *Folkorama* passport costs $8.50 ($4 for those over 65 or under 13) and provides access to all the pavilions, which are connected by frequent shuttle bus service provided by the city.

Another annual July event is the *Winnipeg Folk Festival*, a 4-day affair held at Birds Hill Park, about 20 miles (32 km) northwest of the city. The festival attracts top names in folk music and has an international reputation.

For children and the young at heart, Winnipeg offers an annual carnival, the *Red River Exhibition*. Held during late June and early July, the "Ex" site sprawls around the Winnipeg Arena. There are many roller coasters and other rides, numerous games of chance, and casino games.

Special seasonal festivals with an ethnic accent are the *Oktoberfest*, a German party for beer and sausage fans, and the *Festival du Voyageur*, a late winter event held in the

French suburb of St. Boniface, featuring dogsled races, ice sculpture competitions, and hearty food.

MUSEUMS: The *Manitoba Museum of Man and Nature* and the *Winnipeg Art Gallery* are described in *Special Places*. Also of interest is Manitoba's Provincial Archives Building, which houses frequently changing exhibits of historical information, maps, and other memorabilia. The archives are open weekdays only. 200 Vaughan St. (phone: 945-3971).

SHOPPING: Winnipeg's two largest department stores, *Eaton's* and *The Bay*, are located on Portage Avenue; both offer comprehensive services, dining facilities, and can provide tickets to sporting and theatrical events. Both are connected to most major downtown buildings and to each other by an enclosed skybridge.

The *Crafts Guild of Manitoba* carries the work of Manitoban carvers, weavers, and jewelers and specializes in the leatherwork and carving of local Indians and Eskimos. Open Mondays through Fridays from 10 AM to 4:30 PM; Saturdays in July and August from 10 AM to 1 PM. 183 Kennedy St. (phone: 943-1190).

St. Vital Shopping Center is a 10-minute drive southwest of Portage Ave. and Main St. Osborne Village and the Exchange District are interesting centers mentioned in *Special Places*. Note that most stores are closed Sundays in Winnipeg. Polo Park, an upscale shopping mall, is 10 minutes west of the city center on Portage Ave.

SPORTS: Bicycling – A popular summer diversion in Winnipeg. City parks have marked bicycle paths, and bicycles may be rented in Assiniboine Park.

Boxing – Matches are held in the *Winnipeg Arena*, 1430 Maroons Rd. (phone: 780-7328).

Cross-Country Skiing – Most city parks support some cross-country skiing and snowshoeing, but the best for both activities are Assiniboine and Kildonan parks.

Curling – This Canadian game has Scottish origins and is somewhat related to shuffleboard. Played on an ice rink by teams of four, two players, or "curlers," slide squat, circular stones, each weighing 40 pounds, at goals 46 yards apart. Two "assistants" skate ahead of the curlers, vigorously sweeping the ice with brooms along the path of the stone — one of the eyecatching features of the game. A team scores by getting the stones within the 6-foot circle surrounding the "button" (goal), and as close to it as possible. Curling is played at all city ice facilities from September to June.

Fishing – Good fishing is available at Lockport, 20 miles (32 km) north of Winnipeg.

Football – The Canadian Football League's *Blue Bombers* make their home in Winnipeg. Their stadium is adjacent to the Polo Park shopping center, just south of Portage Ave. (phone: 775-9751).

Golf – Municipal courses dot the city; perhaps the best of the 7 public courses is *John Blumberg*, 4540 Portage Ave. (phone: 888-8860).

Hockey – The *Winnipeg Jets*, part of the NHL, confront their opposition at the *Winnipeg Arena* (phone: 772-9491).

Horse Racing – Thoroughbred and harness racing are held year-round at *Assiniboia Downs*, 3975 Portage Ave. (phone: 885-3330).

Ice Skating – At any of the public ice facilities.

Jogging – Residents do it anytime, anywhere, even in midwinter. In the summer, many jogging paths are open in city parks.

Lacrosse – A sport more common to eastern Canada, lacrosse is nevertheless played in Assiniboine Park on summer Sundays.

Snowmobiling – Restricted in Winnipeg proper, it can be enjoyed at Birds Hill Park, 20 miles (32 km) northeast of Winnipeg.

Squash – City athletic clubs have courts as does the *YMHA,* 370 Hargrave St. (phone: 947-0601).

Swimming – Public municipal pools, mostly indoor, are located at Sinclair and Dufferin Sts. (phone: 589-8315), Dalhousie and Baylor drives (phone: 269-7416), 25 Poseidon Bay (phone: 284-4030), 999 Sargent Ave. (phone: 783-7111), 381 Sherbrook St. (phone: 786-8475), and 644 Parkdale St. (phone: 832-1348).

Tennis – Both public and private courts around the city. In summer, championship matches are held at the *Winnipeg Canoe Club,* 47 Dunkirk Pl. (phone: 233-4928).

Wrestling – Matches are held once a month during fall and winter at the *Winnipeg Arena* (phone: 783-7328).

THEATER: Most of Winnipeg's live performances — legitimate and musical — take place during the fall and winter months. The *Manitoba Theatre Centre,* 174 Market St. (phone: 942-6537), has a season of serious and comic drama. A companion theater, *The Warehouse,* 140 Rupert St. (phone: 942-6537), offers experimental drama with modest ticket prices. The *Prairie Theatre Exchange,* 160 Princess St. (phone: 942-7291), features dramas for both children and adults and provides minimal audience comforts for moderate ticket prices. *Le Cercle Molière,* 340 Provencher, in the French-speaking suburb of St. Boniface, presents plays and revues in French (phone: 233-8053). Avant-garde theater and plays for children are presented at the *Gas Station Theatre,* 445 River Ave. (phone: 284-2757).

MUSIC: Major performances by the *Winnipeg Symphony Orchestra* and the *Manitoba Opera Association* take place in the *Centennial Concert Hall,* 555 Main St. (phone: 956-1360). During the summer, musicals are performed at the *Rainbow Stage* in Kildonan Park (phone: 943-2929 or 338-4702).

The very fine *Royal Winnipeg Ballet* has four major performances at the *Centennial Concert Hall,* 555 Main St. (phone: 956-1360), and offers a free summer performance at Assiniboine Park. The *Contemporary Dancers* perform at the *Playhouse Theatre,* 180 Market St. (phone: 986-3003).

NIGHTCLUBS AND NIGHTLIFE: Winnipeg's night scene has gone through a renaissance and has emerged sophisticated and exciting. The poshest nightclub is *Desoto's,* 173 McDermot (phone: 943-4444), a moderately expensive establishment with 2 bars, 2 dance floors, and frequent dance exhibitions by comely waitresses. There is a piano bar at *Hy's Steak Loft,* 216 Kennedy St. (phone: 942-1000). Along Osborne St., between River Ave. and Stradbrook St., several bars and nightclubs offer entertainment. The latest meeting place is the cavernous *Rorie Street Marble Club,* 65 Rorie St. (phone: 943-4222), in the financial district. Be prepared to wait in line to get in. Comedians perform at *Yuk-Yuk's,* 108 Osborne (phone: 475-9857) and at *Rumor's,* 2025 Corydon Ave. (phone: 453-8216).

BEST IN TOWN

CHECKING IN: Winnipeg's accommodations range from turn-of-the-century establishments to ultramodern complexes. Many are located in the city center, within easy walking distance of Winnipeg's finer shopping, dining, and entertainment facilities. All the hotels listed are well managed, have phones in every room, and accept major credit cards. Expect to pay $50 to $105 for a double in those hotels we've classed as expensive; between $35 and $50 at places in the moderate category; between $15 and $30 at the inexpensive places. All telephone numbers are in the 204 area code unless otherwise indicated.

Birchwood Inn – One of Winnipeg's major hotels, it is in the rapidly expanding western suburb of St. James. Ample shopping opportunities exist at the nearby Unicity Shopping Center. The 200-room hotel has several restaurants and bars. 2520 Portage Ave. (phone: 885-4478). Expensive.

Delta Winnipeg – With 272 rooms atop a high-rise garage, this hotel has excellent parking and an indoor pool with a view of much of Winnipeg. 288 Portage Ave. (phone: 956-0410 or 800-268-1133). Expensive.

Fort Garry – Winnipeg's grande dame, built to resemble a French chateau, has 242 guestrooms, suites, 2 stunning dining rooms, and French-Canadian management. 222 Broadway Ave. (phone: 942-8251 or 800-665-8088). Expensive.

Holiday Inn Downtown – This new structure is part of a complex of office buildings and apartments, with an indoor swimming pool fringed by pinball machines. Several restaurants are available within the hotel, but knowing diners will visit either *Ichi Ban Japanese Steak House* or the *Garden Crêperie* (see *Eating Out*), both located elsewhere in the complex. St. Mary's Ave. and Carlton St. (phone: 942-0551 or 800-465-4329). Expensive.

Sheraton Winnipeg – Near *Eaton Place Shopping Centre* and the *Winnipeg Convention Centre,* this 1985 renovation of an apartment building features 286 expansive rooms with balconies, a pool, sauna, whirlpool, and outdoor sundeck. *Options* restaurant has an extensive continental menu, leaning on the Italian side. There is live entertainment nightly in *Windows* lounge. 161 Donald St. (phone: 942-5300 or 800-325-3535). Expensive.

Westin – In the middle of Winnipeg's financial district, near major department stores, the inn is attached to an elaborate shopping and office complex, with ample parking nearby. 2 Lombard Pl. (phone: 957-1350 or 800-228-3000). Expensive.

Marlborough Inn – Carefully renovated to retain its grand architectural features, the hotel has an elegant restaurant, *Churchill's* (see *Eating Out*) and a coffee shop, *Flanders,* built in carefully detailed, gothic style. Close to many nightspots and the city's financial district. 331 Smith St. (phone: 942-6411). Expensive to moderate.

Viscount Gort Flag Inn – Conveniently located near most places in Winnipeg. The Polo Park shopping center is a 5-minute walk, and the *Winnipeg Stadium and Arena* — home of many competitive sporting events — is only a 2-minute drive. 1670 Portage Ave. (phone: 775-0451 or 800-661-1460). Expensive to moderate.

Grant Motor Inn – A modern, well-managed, 65-room hotel with a passable dining room. 635 Pembina Hwy. (phone: 453-8247). Moderate.a

Journey's End – Located just inside the city limits, this recently opened, no-frills motel is close to the University of Manitoba. Pembina Hwy. at Perimeter Hwy. (phone: 800-668-4200). Moderate.

Norlander – Near the University of Manitoba. An attractive Scandinavian-style decor. 1792 Pembina Hwy. (phone: 269-6955). Moderate.

Relax Plaza – Centrally located, this medium-size hotel with 160 rooms has a pool and special facilities for handicapped guests. 360 Colony St. at Portage Ave. (phone: 786-7011). Expensive.

TraveLodge – Near the point at which the Trans-Canada Highway enters Winnipeg from the east, the motel is adjacent to a small shopping center. 20 Alpine, in St. Vital (phone: 255-6000 or 800-255-3050). Moderate.

There are also various bed-and-breakfast accommodations — from modest homes to mansions — available in the Winnipeg area. For more information phone 256-6151 or write to B&B of Manitoba, 93 Healy St., Winnipeg, Manitoba R2N 2S2.

EATING OUT: For a seemingly isolated prairie town, Winnipeg boasts a large variety of restaurants that reflect its multi-culturism. Among the offerings are French, Italian, Danish, and Vietnamese cuisine, in addition to native Canadian fare. The restaurant cited as very expensive can run $85 or more for a meal for two, not including drinks; those in the expensive category will charge $40 and over; in the moderate range, $25 to $40; and in the inexpensive range, $15 to $20 without wine or drinks. (Inexpensive dining places in Winnipeg often have no liquor service.) All telephone numbers are in the 204 area code unless otherwise indicated.

Dubrovnik – Yugoslavian and continental dishes are the specialties of this restaurant, which is housed in an old mansion along the Assiniboine River. Closed Sundays. Reservations necessary. Major credit cards accepted. 390 Assiniboine Ave. (phone: 944-0594). Very expensive.

Le Beaujolais – Located in the French-speaking suburb of St. Boniface, this elegant restaurant offers nouvelle cuisine, elegant pastries, and deft service. Open daily. Reservations necessary. Major credit cards accepted. 131 Provencher (phone: 237-6276). Expensive.

Beefeater – This restaurant is popular with fans of charcoal-broiled steaks. Decor, to the chagrin of any self-respecting Beefeater, is Napoleonic. Open daily. Reservations advised for lunch and dinner. Major credit cards accepted. 437 Stradbrook at Osborne St. (phone: 475-8745). Expensive.

Churchill's – An elegant dining room in the *Marlborough Inn* that has been magnificently restored in the grand European castle tradition, but the menu remains basic steakhouse, with some elaborate soups and desserts added. Deft service and a good wine list. Closed Sundays. Major credit cards accepted. 331 Smith St. (phone: 947-1526). Expensive.

Cibo's – Housed in what used to be a cellar, this elegant Northern Italian restaurant features veal and seafood. Closed Sundays. Reservations necessary. 282 Bannatyne (phone: 943-4922). Expensive.

Ichi Ban Japanese Steak House – A beautifully decorated restaurant, this place has, among other things, a small artificial meandering river. *Ichi Ban* offers just what the name implies — steaks in the Japanese fashion — as well as sukiyaki, tempura, and a small selection of more exotic dishes. Open daily. Reservations necessary. Major credit cards accepted. 189 Carlton St. (phone: 942-7493). Expensive.

Rae and Jerry's – Located west of the downtown core, this place has good steaks, chicken, fish, and roast beef. Open daily. Reservations necessary. Major credit cards accepted. 1405 Portage Ave. (phone: 775-8154). Expensive.

Royal Crown – Located on top of Fort Garry Place, which has ancient Greek, Romanesque, and Renaissance-style architecture, this remarkable restaurant has two levels revolving in opposite directions. Dine on continental specialties while enjoying the superb view. Open daily. Reservations necessary. Major credit cards accepted. 83 Garry St. (phone: 947-1990). Expensive.

Victor's – On a well-restored block in Osborne Village, this restaurant offers good European cuisine and excellent service. Interesting stained glass windows in the main dining room. Closed Sundays. Reservations necessary. Major credit cards accepted. River and Osborne Sts. (phone: 284-2339). Expensive.

Amici – A Northern Italian *ristorante* with a luxuriously formal upstairs, and a café downstairs. Superb service. Closed Sundays. Major credit cards accepted. 326 Broadway (phone: 943-4997). Expensive upstairs; moderate downstairs.

Philippe's – It's a good choice for elaborate European fare served in an ornate setting, made even more pleasant on weekends when there's the additional attraction of dancing. Open daily. Reservations advised. Major credit cards accepted. 2583 Portage Ave. (phone: 837-9428). Expensive to moderate.

Basil's – A charming, European-style coffeehouse in the Osborne Village. Open daily for late afternoon coffee and dinner; lunch Mondays to Saturdays only. Reservations unnecessary. 117 Osborne St. (phone: 453-8440). Moderate.

Edohei Sushi – Recline on tatami mats to read the menu choices, which include sushi and excellent tempura. Lunch from 12 to 2 PM on Mondays, Wednesdays, Thursdays, and Fridays; dinner from 5 to 10:30 PM daily. Closed Tuesdays. Reservations advised. Major credit cards accepted. 355 Ellice Ave. (phone: 943-0427). Moderate.

Fork & Cork – Swiss fondues and Dutch cuisine are the staple of this intimate restaurant. Open daily. Major credit cards accepted. 218 Sherbrook St. (phone: 783-5754). Moderate.

Garden Crêperie – A large, attractive restaurant in an office building complex, it has an extensive menu of anything and everything that can possibly be rolled or squeezed into a pancake. Open daily. Reservations unnecessary. Major credit cards accepted. 349 York, in the Lakeview Square complex (phone: 957-0221). Moderate.

Krønborg – You can take your pick from among about 150 Danish sandwiches or enjoy a hearty dinner here. Closed Sundays. Reservations unnecessary. Major credit cards accepted. 1875 Pembina Hwy. (phone: 261-1448). Moderate.

Oliver's Old Bailey – A popular Winnipeg steakhouse, decorated in the manner of a fine mansion. Closed Sundays. Major credit cards accepted. 185 Lombard Ave. (phone: 943-4448). Moderate.

Tea Cozy – In Osborne Village, this shop serves tea and coffee, late breakfast, and lunch in a very English manner. The gingerbread cake with whipped cream is a favorite. Open daily. Reservations unnecessary. Major credit cards accepted. 99 Osborne St. (phone: 475-1027). Moderate.

Vidoni's – Classic Romanian cuisine is served in a plushly contemporary dining room. The menu emphasizes roasted meats prepared with massive infusions of garlic. Chicken Dracula (no kidding) is intoxicating; make sure your friends and loved ones partake. Closed Sundays. Reservations necessary for dinner. Major credit cards accepted. 715 Ellice Ave. (phone: 786-2122). Moderate.

Yamato – Japanese cuisine — everything from sushi and sashimi to teriyaki and tempura. Open daily. Reservations advised. Major credit cards accepted. 667B Stafford St. (phone: 452-1166). Moderate.

Bistro Bohemia – Bright by day, intimate by night, this small establishment serves superb Czech food, as well as a more varied, authentic European menu. Desserts are superb. Closed Sundays. Reservations advised. Visa and MasterCard accepted. 159 Osborne St. (phone: 453-1944). Moderate to inexpensive.

Bistro Dansk – A frequently changing Danish menu and knowing service keeps this one of Winnipeg's favorite restaurants. Closed Sundays. Reservations advised. Visa only. 63 Sherbrook St. (phone: 775-5662). Moderate to inexpensive.

Carlos and Murphy's – Built to resemble a Wild West saloon, this Mexican restaurant and bar has good food, a devoted clientele, and an atmosphere conducive to mingling. Open daily for dinner. Reservations unnecessary. Major credit cards accepted. 129 Osborne St. (phone: 284-3510). Inexpensive.

Le Croissant – A French bakery, butcher shop, and cheese shop in one, this Gallic spot is a great place to stop for picnic food. Serving take-out food only. 268 Blvd. Taché in the French suburb of St. Boniface (phone: 237-3550). Inexpensive.

D'8 Schtove – The name is a Low German pun and the food is Mennonite peasant fare. Sausages are homemade and desserts are undeceivingly rich. Open daily.

Reservations unnecessary. MasterCard and Visa accepted. 1842 Pembina Hwy. (phone: 275-2294). Inexpensive.

The King's Head Tavern – This authentic British pub serves endless kegs of ale, along with superb fish and chips, sausages prepared in several ways, and excellent desserts. 120 King St. (phone: 957-1470). Inexpensive.

Nibbler's Nosh – A Jewish delicatessen with delicious, authentic fare and very tasty pastries. 973 Corydon at Stafford (phone: 284-0310). Inexpensive.

Old Spaghetti Factory – This restaurant is an old warehouse restored with many turn-of-the-century antiques, including a genuine cable car. The bar serves inexpensive lunches. Open daily. No reservations. Major credit cards accepted. 291 Bannatyne (phone: 957-1391). Inexpensive.

Thanh Huong – Fine Vietnamese food, including soups, noodle dishes, authentic beverages, and desserts, served in an informal setting. Open daily for lunch and dinner. Major credit cards accepted. 534 Sargent Ave. (phone: 774-8888). Inexpensive.

DIVERSIONS

For the Body

Downhill Skiing

Canadians can probably be classified in two major groups: Those who ski and those who intend to learn. That's not surprising, considering the usually abundant quantities of snow north of the international border, the mountainous terrain up there, and the number of mountains developed for skiing.

Natural snowfall can be expected from late November to late March, but sometimes — particularly in eastern Canada — the "Great White North" is not quite white enough, so many of the major ski areas have installed supplementary snowmaking machinery to ensure good ski conditions even during periods of light snowfall.

In any case, a skier in Canada is seldom very far from a good run. There's skiing in Newfoundland or in the Maritimes, for instance — though the atmosphere may be better than the ski slopes. In Ontario, the picture is brighter, with large ski areas close to both Ottawa and Toronto. Even the prairie provinces of Manitoba and Saskatchewan have some lift-serviced verticals. All of these places are of principal delight to skiers from the cities nearby. But Canada has many more ski areas that are worth traveling a long distance to savor — some because of their unique ambience, some because of the world class slopes. Quebec is undoubtedly the queen of eastern Canada skiing with Parc du Mont-Ste.-Anne, a giant area outside Quebec City; the Eastern Townships, a quartet of mountains with first class runs for all levels of ability and with a less hectic pace than at some of the older, more popular resorts; and the grand Laurentians, mountains that offer a vacation experience as notable for the excitement quotient of the nearly 1,000 slopes and runs of its 125-odd ski areas as for the elegant cuisine and the regional specialties (meat pies, vinegar-splashed French fries) served in the restaurants of the quaint villages at the lift base. That the Laurentians must be one of the few ski areas in the Western Hemisphere where the chef is held in as much regard as the head ski instructor is more important for many skiers than the fact that the runs are shorter and conditions frequently icier and rockier than those in Canada's other great ski region, the ineffably beautiful Rocky Mountains.

In the Rockies, powder-drenched bowls and trail-cut forests provide skiing so dazzling, runs so unique, that Europeans forsake the cozy slopeside villages of their own Alps to enjoy it. The scenery inspires awe; the snow quality and the variety of slopes are equaled in few other places in the world. Yet in Alberta and British Columbia, more than a few Canadian ski areas — particularly the ones in British Columbia's interior — have long been considered just local operations. Opening up the mountains with lifts, and attracting skiers from outside the area with extensive lodging facilities and nightlife, has been a relatively new endeavor, and only in the last few years has money gone into development programs that have brought the mountains the fame they deserve. The ultimate dollop of recognition was acquired in February 1988, when the Winter Olympics were held on the slopes surrounding Calgary. Meanwhile, helicopter skiing, in ranges of the Rockies known as the Cariboos, Bugaboos, and others has soared in popularity, and the seemingly endless runs and the fluffy, untrammeled powder snow of a number of nearby mountain ranges (which have never known the hum of a ski lift) have been discovered by thousands of brave and hardy skiers. Skiing of the sort found here is quite simply unavailable anywhere else in the world.

For more information about helicopter skiing and for rundowns of the facilities of all the major Canadian resorts, consult the regional ski directories published by the Canadian Government Office of Tourism and available from its offices in major US cities. The various consulates can provide further information. Or browse through issues of the magazine *Ski Canada* (277 Front St. E., Suite 100, Toronto, Ontario M5A 1E8; phone: 416-368-0185). The *White Book of Ski Areas, US & Canada* (Inter-Ski Services, Inc., PO Box 3635, Georgetown Station, Washington, DC 20007; phone: 202-342-0886) lists all the ski areas in both countries, with brief descriptions. It's revised annually and can be found in ski shops and bookstores ($13.95) or by mail through the publisher ($16).

EAST

OUTAOUAIS (OTTAWA VALLEY), near Ottawa, Ontario, and Hull, Quebec: Ski-O, a complex of ski centers that together boast some 69 slopes within commuting distance of the nation's capital, can't boast world class skiing, but there is something for every ability in the Gatineau area. The maximum vertical drop available at its biggest area, Mont Ste. Marie, near the town of Lac Ste. Marie, is only 1,250 feet. And the others are even less: 650 feet at Edelweiss Valley and 465 feet at Vorlage, both in Wakefield, Quebec; 650 feet at Camp Fortune, in Old Chelsea, Quebec; and 550 feet at Mont Cascades, near Cantley, Quebec. The longest run in the area is at Mont Ste. Marie, and it's just a little over 2 miles long. All the areas make snow and offer night skiing, ski and instruction packages, and rentals. Athough Mont Ste. Marie is the only destination ski resort, the other areas — with the exception of Mont Cascades and Camp Fortune — offer accommodations near the base. Basically these are typical city ski areas. School kids are bused in on weekdays, and ski clubbers and other recreationists in vastly greater numbers arrive on weekends. There's little of the camaraderie found at a full-fledged destination resort, but especially on weekdays, it's possible to cram in quite a lot of mileage and have a good time at that. And for those who want to combine a ski vacation with a trip to Canada's capital and a tour of the Parliament buildings, the Outaouais will be just the place. Information: Canada's Capital Visitors and Convention Bureau, 222 Queen St., 7th Floor, Ottawa, Ontario K1P 5V9 (phone: 613-237-5158).

LAURENTIANS (LES LAURENTIDES), near Montreal, Quebec: Beginning about 35 miles (56 km) from the city, along the high-speed Laurentian Autoroute leading into the hills to the northwest, there is a succession of ski communities one after another — more than 20 major ones in all, each the center of a cluster of ski areas situated just minutes apart. If only for the sheer number of runs in the area — some 300 in the space of 40 square miles, a concentration greater than that of any other area of comparable size in the world — the Laurentians would be unique. But the frills of a skiing vacation here also stand out. The region's charming French villages are full of lovely inns, pleasant resorts, and small hotels so close to the skiing that it's easy to schuss right to your doorstep — or, more to the point, to your dining room, where good food is the order of the day. (Especially endearing are local specialties like *tourtière,* a meat pie, and the sweet, maple-sugar-flavored pie known as *tarte au sucre.*)

Every one of the ski areas has its special charm. At the northern end of this string of resorts is Mont Tremblant, the dowager queen of Canada's winter resorts, which, with a vertical drop of 2,100 feet and runs that extend up to 2 miles in length, offers plenty of good skiing for experts and intermediates. A new detachable quad chairlift and jet T-bar have been erected; restaurants on top and at the base of the mountain have been renovated; the beginner's area has been relocated; a nursery has been installed; and snowmaking facilities have been extended to the very top of Mont Tremblant's south side. It has a number of first-rate hotels, including the big *Station Mont Tremblant Lodge* and the smaller *Cuttle's Tremblant Club.* Some 3 miles (5 km) away in St. Jovite is the *Gray Rocks Inn,* a friendly sprawl of a 252-room Victorian hostelry on 2,600 acres with its own ski hill, *Sugar Peak,* a hundred yards from the inn. The vertical here is a mere 620 feet, but the proprietors never wasted time deluding themselves that they had the Matterhorn on their hands. Instead, they touted the mountain as ideal for learning and, in 1938, developed the *Snow Eagle Ski School,* with a teaching program so thorough that there are even a couple of instructors whose sole job is keeping the others on their toes. Consequently, there are hundreds of graduates who will testify that the school is North America's best. Among the many aspects that make the lodge outstanding are its new sports complex, indoor swimming, whirlpool bath, saunas, its nightlife (which is vigorous enough to make the place a good bet for the solo vacationer), and its lunches (served on white-linen-covered tables in a dining room practically at the lift base). Other ski areas offer similar delights. Belle Neige in Val-Morin, a small hill with a vertical of only about 520 feet and 2 T-bars and 2 chair lifts, is distinguished by the proximity of the *Hôtel la Sapinière,* a member of the Relais & Châteaux hotel association and the proud possessor of one of Canada's finest kitchens (see *Special Havens*).

And so it goes. The Laurentians are far from being Canada's biggest mountains, but the plenitude of amenities goes a long way toward taking the sting out of foregoing, for the moment, the steeper-and-wilder-and-more-dazzlingly beautiful slopes Canada offers in such abundance. For general information and lists of small hostelries: Association Touristique des Laurentides, 14142 Rue de Lachapelle, RR1, St. Jérôme, Quebec J7Z 5T4 (phone: 514-436-8532). The following resorts can be contacted in Mont Tremblant, Quebec J0T 1Z0: Station Mont Tremblant (phone: 819-425-8711 or 800-567-6761); and Cuttle's Tremblant Club (phone: 819-425-2731). Write the Gray Rocks Inn at PO Box 1000, St. Jovite, Quebec J0T 2H0, or call 819-425-2771. Also see *Special Havens* and *Ice Skating.*

EASTERN TOWNSHIPS (ESTRIE), Montreal, Quebec: Unlike the Laurentians, which were initially built up to serve as summer resorts and were then strung with lifts to help the communities make it through the winter, the mountains in this northern extension of the Appalachians, 44 miles (71 km) southeast of Montreal and just north of the Vermont border, were developed primarily for skiing, because of the suitability of the terrain. Each one is the peer of Mont Tremblant or any comparable Vermont resort. Mont Sutton, near Sutton, has 54 trails, 9 chair lifts, a 1,509-foot vertical, and unique glade skiing. Owl's Head, near Mansonville, has a 1,770-foot vertical. Mont Orford, near Magog, has a 1,772-foot vertical and 32 trails. Bromont, with a 1,328-foot vertical and 26 trails, is the fourth member of the quartet of major mountains in the area. Headquarter at any one of the four mountains, ski there, and then use your interchangeable lift ticket to sample the other three. Wherever you go, you're going to find runs to suit everyone in the family, varied terrain, and good lift service; each area has its own unique character.

Where should you lodge? That will depend on the kind of town you like best. Owl's Head has a small lodge right at the base, and new apartment-hotels and condominiums with ski-in/ski-out access to lifts and trails. It will be interesting to see what effect Owl's Head's multimillion-dollar expansion project will have on the tenor of the place (with not much of anything around it, Owl's Head has been valued by people who enjoy making their own après-ski entertainment). The expansion includes more snowmaking, 2 new trails, and a detachable quad chairlift. Those who go for Owl's Head usually go for it in a big way and return year after year after year. The *Auberge Bromont* at Bromont is a cozy place with views of the night-lighted runs. The areas around Mont Sutton and Mont Orford are livelier; they're both close to a couple of other small towns that boast restaurants and other nighttime activities. (Among the more interesting hostelries in this area are *Village Archimède* at Sutton, *Hovey Manor* at North Hatley, and Magog's *Cheribourg Resort.*) Although the Eastern Townships don't bustle with as much activity as the Laurentians, and although this is still very much the farming area that it was before the lifts went in just over 20 years ago, these mountains offer an abundance of amenities for those who've come first and foremost to ski. What's more, the quality of the skiing is among the best in the East.

General information: Quebec Ski East, 2883 W. King St., Sherbrooke, Quebec J1L 1C6 (phone: 819-564-8989). For reservations and local information: Mont Orford Resort Center, Box 248, Magog, Quebec J1X 3W8 (phone: 819-843-6548); Owl's Head, Mansonville, Quebec J0E 1X0 (phone: 514-292-5592); Sutton Tourist Association, for lodging: CP 418, Sutton, Quebec J0E 2K0 (phone: 514-538-2646 or 514-538-2537), for skiing: CP 280, Sutton, Quebec J0E 2K0 (phone: 514-538-2339); and Bromont Ski Area, CP29, Bromont, Quebec J0E 1L0 (phone: 514-534-2200).

QUEBEC CITY: The Old Capital is so close to good skiing that many of the city's major hotels offer ski packages. Mont-Ste.-Anne, mountain enough to have hosted the first Canadian Winter Games in 1967 and now a regular stop on the World Cup circuit, is the biggest of the local areas. Located at Beaupré, a rather nondescript one-street town about half an hour's drive east of the city, it boasted terrain that was already considerable before development of its north and west sides a few years ago doubled the skiable area; today 40 slopes and 14 lifts of varying types allow for an uphill capacity of over 17,150. Consequently, there's now the option of enjoying the sunny conditions on the southern slopes (the top three-quarters of them as challenging as any of Vermont's steepest and hairiest), or the intermediate and novice north-facing runs, or even the intermediate and expert trails of the mountain's western exposure. Every year more runs are being backed up by an elaborate new snowmaking system; well over 85 percent of the skiable terrain is currently covered. With the addition of 8 lighted trails, Mont-Ste.-Anne now claims to have the highest vertical night skiing in Canada. It also offers the cross-country skier over 110 miles of double-track, groomed and patrolled trails equal to the very best in North America. As we went to press, a base village incorporating hotel-condos, a shopping plaza, conference and health facilities, a second 18-hole golf course, equestrian center, and an aquatic park was slated to be operational by early 1990.

The region's next most extensive skiing is to be found at Stoneham, with a 1,380-foot vertical. In addition, it's possible to ski the two areas at longtime favorite vacation center Lac Beauport — Le Relais and Mont St. Castin, whose verticals measure 750 and 550 feet respectively. As is inevitable due to these areas' proximity to the city, every one of them is busier still on weekends; only Mont-Ste.-Anne would, in its own right, warrant traveling a long distance to ski. But the city's food, lodging, and lively après-ski activity is as exceptional as Aspen's; and for beginners, intermediates, and even experts for whom what goes après is as important as what happens right on the slopes, Quebec City is hard to equal, providing an all-around vacation that includes some skiing. The attractions are such, in fact, that it's probably best to headquarter in the city and schlep to the ski area every day, rather than the other way round.

A number of hotels in its eastern districts are most convenient to Mont-Ste.-Anne, but the historic old *Château Frontenac* in the center of town has the most atmosphere, while the *Québec Hilton International* is more modern and rather elegant. The *Quebec Winter Carnival* turns the city upside down in February. Enjoy it — or avoid it if you hate hubbub and crowds. Information: Quebec City Region Tourism and Convention Bureau, 60 Rue d'Auteuil, Quebec City, Quebec G1R 4C4 (phone: 418-692-2471); and Parc du Mont-Ste.-Anne, PO Box 400, Beaupré, Quebec G0A 1E0 (phone: 418-827-4561; a Central Reservation Service for Quebec City and the Charlevoix region, RESERVOTEL, can be reached at 800-463-1568). Also see *Quebec City,* THE CITIES, and *Festivals, Fairs, and Fancy Acts.*

WEST

So special and inclusive are the opportunities for winter recreation in the Canadian Rockies that the province of Alberta was chosen to host the 1988 Winter Olympics. But much fine skiing can be found in other parts of western Canada.

The heart of the Canadian Rockies offers just about everything a skier could want — great slopes, deep powder, some of the continent's most glorious scenery, and a ski season that consistently extends into June. Mount Norquay is known as Banff's challenge to advanced skiers, but it does offer some easy skiing for beginners as well. At Sunshine Village, an alpine resort in a bowl above the treeline, you'll find tons of powder, the longest season in the area, and on-hill accommodations. Canada's largest ski location is Lake Louise, with a variety of terrain — bowls, moguls, open runs, and forested slopes.

With shuttle buses linking the three big ski complexes, and the availability of interchangeable lift tickets, mountain-hopping is a common practice here. It's probably more convenient to set up a base in the town of Banff and travel to each of the three ski areas. Mt. Norquay, site of the celebrated mile-long chute known as the North American, as well as a couple of other hair-raisers that are nearly as steep, also boasts some of the finest novice terrain anywhere — acres of broad fields covered with ultralight, carefully groomed powder. Accommodations are available in a variety of more than 30 hotels in 4-mile-distant (6.4 km) Banff, including the modern and very comfortable *Banff Park Lodge*, or the spired-and-turreted *Banff Springs* hotel, one of the dramatic hotels that the Canadian Pacific Railway built in the late 19th century in its efforts to develop traffic on the line. "The Springs," as it's called, boasts a good breakfast buffet, an Olympic-size indoor swimming pool, a heated outdoor pool, skating rink, innumerable places to eat, a health club with three Jacuzzis and a sauna, a new Presidential Suite with luxurious amenities, and more. For slopeside resort life, look to Sunshine Village, a complex of forest runs and above-timberline snowfields with a 3,420-foot vertical that is served by just under a dozen lifts. All resort facilities are in a complex of buildings at the lift base (at 7,200 feet), which is accessible by gondola from the parking lot at the end of an access road branching off the Trans-Canada. There's also plenty of programmed après-ski activity. The most extensive terrain in the area, however — indeed, the nation's largest lift-serviced downhill ski area, our northern neighbor's answer to Aspen and Squaw Valley — is to be found at Skiing Louise, 35 miles (56 km) and 45 minutes down the Trans-Canada from Banff. There, skiers find 17 square *miles* of mogul fields, steep chutes, vast glacial bowls, gentle trails through the glades — and just about any other kind of ski terrain imaginable — on four mountain faces. Some 43 designated runs, ranging up to 5 miles in length, are draped down 3,250 vertical feet of hillside and served by a panoply of lifts. Here all lodgings are about 2 miles (3.2 km) from lift base; for charm, the best bets are the newly expanded *Post* hotel (Box 69, Lake Louise, Alberta T0L 1E0; phone: 403-522-3989), known for its kitchen, and the winterized *Château Lake Louise*, the grandest of all the Canadian Pacific hotels. Banff is also the jumping-off place for some of the finest helicopter skiing in the world.

Information: Banff/Lake Louise Chamber of Commerce, Box 1298, Banff, Alberta T0L 0C0 (phone: 403-762-3777), and Banff Club Ski, Box 1085, Banff, Alberta T0L 0C0 (phone: 403-762-4561). Also see *Wilderness Skiing, Special Havens,* and *Ice Skating.*

NAKISKA AT MOUNT ALLAN, Kananaskis Village, Alberta: The Kananaskis-Nakiska area, site of the 1988 Olympic alpine competition, is the newest ski destination in Canada. It boasts trememdous fall-line skiing, first class facilities, state-of-the-art snowmaking, Western Canada's first two detachable quad chair lifts. Kids have their own ski area, with a handle tow and a day-care center. Kananaskis Village includes a general store, ski rental shop, post office, and a new complex of restaurants, shops, and three hotels. The *Hotel Kananaskis* is a 69-suite luxury hotel. The *Lodge at Kananaskis* is a 255-room hotel with a health club; guests can swim from the pool area to the hot tub located outside under the stars. There's also a sauna outside and plenty of snow to roll in. For more moderately priced accommodations, try the *Kananaskis Inn*, a 90-unit hotel. Other winter activities there include horsedrawn sleigh rides, tobogganing, ice skating, and cross-country skiing. For more information, write or call Kananaskis Village Resort Association, Box 100, Kananaskis Village, Alberta TOL 2HO (phone: 402-591-7555).

MARMOT BASIN, Jasper, Alberta: The Canadian Rockies' third largest downhill center provides some of the West's finest open slope and bowl skiing off its 7,930-foot summit and delights skiers of all levels. Thirty-five of the trails are gentle enough that even the most fearful novice can snatch a look at the scenery, and there are sunny bowls that make intermediates feel like hotshots. A memorable 30% are rated expert, including an extraordinary deep-powder run accessible via the Knob Chair. With the recent addition of a high-speed T-bar, the area now offers 7 varied lifts, which means less waiting and more skiing. Marmot Basin also offers a nursery for children from 19 months to 5 years of age, a skier improvement center with ski week vacation packages, and a rental and retail ski shop. But for all that, Marmot Basin would be just another wonderful ski resort were it not for its location inside the boundaries of spectacular Jasper National Park. When you've had enough of the vast downhills, join a cross-country ski tour, snowshoe tour, "canyon crawl," or walking tour guided by park naturalists — or take a day off from skiing altogether for the 60-mile (96-km) drive down the Columbia Icefields Parkway, right through the middle of one of the most gorgeous parts of the awe-inspiring Rockies, to the Columbia Icefield. Marmot Basin's lodging is all of 12 miles (19 km) from lift base in Jasper, a family-oriented community of 4,000, offering a satisfying lineup of après-ski activities. But for those who want to sample the skiing and activities at Banff, a weekly bus service provides transportation, offering the chance to take in the scenery on the 172-mile (275-km) round trip. Information: Marmot Basin Ski-Lifts Ltd., PO Box 1300, Jasper, Alberta T0E 1E0 (phone: 403-852-3816); Jasper Park Chamber of Commerce, Box 98, Jasper, Alberta T0E 1E0 (phone: 403-852-3858); or for ski packages, Marmot Experience, Box 1570, Jasper, Alberta T0E 1E0 (phone: 403-852-4242, or 800-661-1931, in Western Canada).

TOD MOUNTAIN, Kamloops, British Columbia: One of a number of Canadian Rockies ski areas in the interior, with 3,100-foot-plus verticals and slopes, Tod Mountain, 33 miles (53 km) from British Columbia's third largest city, a lumber-and-mining center that some 65,000 souls call home, has stepped over the threshold into the big time with the initiation of a major development that will soon put it in a league with only a few other ski areas in North America. The deep, dry powder snow, a specialty of the BC interior, the extra-long beginner and intermediate runs (5 and 7 miles, respectively), the steep mogul fields that shoot toward the base, and the "Challenger," which ranks among North America's steepest slopes, are as satisfying as ever. Tod has as close to an ideal distribution of terrain for skiers of all ability levels as any other mountain anywhere, and it can comfortably handle 12,600 skiers a day. But with just 5 lifts, it hasn't even come close to maximizing its potential. However, its current construction program promises much, much more in the future. Until on-hill accommodations are built, buses are available to carry skiers between the mountain and Kamloops, which is accessible by rail, air, bus, or car. The season is late November until May. Information: Tod Mountain Development, Ltd., PO Box 869, Kamloops, BC V2C 5M8 (phone: 604-372-5757).

OKANAGAN VALLEY (BIG WHITE SKI RESORT, APEX-ALPINE, SILVER STAR), Kelowna, British Columbia: The region of pine-clad, lake-dotted mountains whose valleys yield the prodigious harvests of fruit for which the province is so famous is blessed in winter with what some people call Canada's best snow — the famed, fast-and-fluffy Okanagan Powder. A good deal of it falls at night, especially during the month of February, so days seem to be almost predictably sunny and the valleys stay green almost the winter long. Kelowna, a town of some 60,000, is at the midpoint of a trio of good-sized ski resorts that stretch up and down the valley: Big White Ski Resort, Apex-Alpine, and Silver Star. Silver Star, an area 14 miles (23 km) from Vernon, has a total of 32 runs — some narrow and tree-lined, some wide-open alpine slopes — with a vertical drop of 1,600 feet; each lift gives access to skiing of all degrees of difficulty. On-mountain accommodations are relatively new and include 3 hotels (with Swiss, railway, and saloon themes) and 3 new apartment-style condominiums. *Big White,* a resort not unlike Colorado's fine *Keystone,* is also a favorite with families, but the variety of runs wrapping around the mountain down its 2,050 feet of vertical is somewhat greater; it's 34 miles (58 km) from Kelowna. Meanwhile, Apex-Alpine, located about 20 miles (32 km) west of Penticton, offers 36 runs (something for every level of skier, with more advanced terrain than many areas) ranging down 2,000 vertical feet; there are on-mountain accommodations for up to 500. Information: Okanagan Similkameen Tourist Association, 104515 Hwy. 97 S., Kelowna, BC V1Z 3J2 (phone: 604-769-5959); Silver Star, Box 7000, Vernon, BC V1T 8X5 (phone: 604-545-2236); Big White Central Resort Ltd., PO Box 2039, Station R, Kelowna, BC V1X 4K5 (604-765-3101); Apex-Alpine, PO Box 488, Penticton, BC V2A 6K9 (phone: 604-292-8222).

KIMBERLEY, Kimberley, British Columbia: Before 1972, the community 2 miles (3 km) from this British Columbia ski resort in the East Kootenays — 50 miles (81 km) north of the international border — was just another mining town. Then the citizens got together and put Bavarian façades on their shop fronts and converted the downtown area into a pedestrian mall, now known as the Platzl. Condominiums at the base of the lifts were designed to carry out the theme. But the mountain that rises 2,300 vertical feet above needed no such cutesification. Kimberley management instead threw its energy into extensive summer grooming of the 34 major runs (which are served by a pair of chairlifts, a trio of drag lifts, two pony tows, and a T-bar); combined with extensive snowmaking early in the season, this manicure assures good conditions around the heavily trafficked lift base area, where all runs converge, through season's end in mid-April. The careful year-round slope preparation also makes Kimberley such a joy for novices and intermediates that many of them can't get enough, and after dark, they go out to ski some more on one of North America's longest lighted ski runs (vertical, 1,800 feet). Other facilities include lodges at the top of the hill and at the base, winterized campsites, two racquetball courts, and 5 tennis courts (2 indoor, 3 outdoor). Information: Kimberley Ski & Summer Resort, Box 40, Kimberley, BC V1A 2Y5 (phone: 604-427-4881).

RED MOUNTAIN, Rossland, British Columbia: Named for the color of the tailings of the old Rossland gold mines, this relatively uncrowded mountain a few miles beyond the Washington State border in the southern Monashees is where 1968 Olympic gold medalist Nancy Greene went from snowplow to slalom. As a result, it was pegged for many years as a hotshot's mountain; ski weekers who had grappled with the terrain, a good many of them from 120-mile-distant Spokane, went back home to confirm the truth of the locally popular saying that if you could master Red, you could handle any other slope in the world. In 1965, 18 years after the first trails were cut on Red itself, lifts were strung up on nearby Granite, which, after the opening up of the Paradise area on its upper southwest flank in 1977, now provides 25 runs for beginners and intermediates ranged down 2,800 vertical feet. The mountain's Main Run is one of Canada's World Cup downhill race courses. All trails from both Granite and Red converge at the lift base, where you'll find a day lodge and, nearby, overnight accommodations in chalets, cabins, and one of the most charming ski hotels anywhere, the 9-room *Ram's Head Inn* (Box 636, Rossland, BC V0G 1Y0; phone: 604-362-9577). Still other lodging places as well as the area's nightlife are in Rossland proper; the fanciest spot is the 67-room *Uplander* hotel (Box 1510, Rossland, BC V0G 1Y0; phone: 604-362-7375). Night skiing is available, and ski races are scheduled throughout the season, which runs from late November through mid-April. Every year in late January there's a lively winter carnival. Information: Red Mountain, Box 939, Rossland, BC V0G 1Y0 (phone: 604-362-7384; 604-362-7700 for central reservations).

VANCOUVER, British Columbia: The three Coast Range ski areas situated just a half hour's bus ride from this lovely city offer urban skiing at its most fantastic: thousand-foot verticals, unbelievable accessibility, spectacular views. Grouse Mountain, the best-developed of the trio, has a 1,200-foot vertical and some satisfyingly steep expert skiing. There are also fine runs for beginners and intermediates, along with snowmaking to ensure top conditions throughout the mid-December-to-March season, and long hours — that is, from early every morning until 10:30 PM. More recently developed Cypress, 5 miles (11 km) from the Upper Levels Highway in West Vancouver, has 18 runs (the longest is 1,700 feet) and night skiing on its expert and intermediate runs. Some people like it best — but Seymour Ski Country specializes in family skiing. It features one of the largest ski schools in the Pacific Northwest, the highest base elevation of the three areas, night skiing, and four double chair lifts. Seymour is about 10 miles (16 km) from the Upper Levels Highway in North Vancouver in an area known for its sunshine and winter warm spells. For those who like skiing hard-pack, Vancouver can provide some pleasant slope time. Information: Grouse Mountain Resorts, Ltd., 6400 Nancy Greene Way, North Vancouver, BC V7R 4N4 (phone: 604-984-0661 for ski conditions); Cypress Bowl Recreations, Box 91252, West Vancouver, BC V7V 3N9 (phone: 604-926-6007 or 926-5612 for ski conditions); Mt. Seymour Resorts, 1700 Indian River Rd., North Vancouver, BC V7G 1L3 (phone: 604-986-2261); and Tourism Vancouver, Pavilion Plaza, 4 Bentall Center, 1055 Dunsmire St., PO Box 49296, Vancouver, BC V7X 1L3 (phone: 604-683-2000 for lodging and après-ski details).

WHISTLER RESORT, Whistler, British Columbia: Nestled in the mountains 75 miles (120 km) north of Vancouver, along the spectacular Sea-to-Sky Highway, this resort has long been one of the giants of North American skiing. Yet, surprisingly enough, it was long known mainly to locals and day-trippers and Whistler Village was the sort of unspoiled Western place frequented by youths investigating alternative lifestyles. This situation has changed — dramatically. Thanks to a multimillion-dollar development program, Whistler Village is full of shops, restaurants, nightspots, hotels, galleries, and more. The skiing remains unparalleled. The resort's two ski mountains boast North America's longest lift-served vertical drops — 5,280 feet at Blackcomb and 5,006 feet at Whistler Mountain. Side by side, this pair offers close to 2,000 acres of world class ski terrain with over 180 trails up to 5 miles long served by more than two dozen lifts, and every type of skiing from forest-edged trails and paths through the glades to broad groomed slopes and breathtaking high alpine powder bowls. Whistler's snowfall often tops 450 inches a year. Open year-round, with a special ski camp in summer. Information: Whistler Resort Association, Box 1400, Whistler, BC V0N 1B0 (phone: 604-932-4222).

WILDERNESS SKIING

Austrian-born skier and mountain guide Hans Gmoser fell in love with the wild, untamed mountains of Western Canada when he came here in 1951 and almost immediately began to explore on skis some of the peaks and slopes that no one before him had ever seen in winter. Before long he was leading tours on a commercial basis.

But getting uphill involved such arduous climbs that, for a dozen years, one run a day was the norm — two at the most. Gmoser was continually frustrated by being unable to take full advantage of the immense concentrations of skiable terrain in the area, until he began using helicopters to get his skiers uphill. Heli-skiing was born, and it boomed. In some ways, heli-skiing's popularity is surprising. Prices are high — from a little more than $1,440 to around $3,000 for a week-long, all-inclusive package, around $170 for a day trip. Then, too, not every skier is strong enough, advanced enough, or gutsy enough to handle the wide-ranging conditions — everything from rain to neck-deep powder to corn snow. Three quarters of the time the snow is very good — of a quality about which most mortal skiers can only dream — but sometimes it is even worse than anyone might imagine. There is also the ever-present danger of skiing in terrain where avalanches are apt to occur.

But for all that, heli-skiing outfits do their best to keep their guests happy and safe. Guides not only seek out the best snow but also lead skiers around crevasses on the glaciers, keep them out of areas of probable avalanche danger, and lend their experienced help to first-time deep-snow skiers to turn what could be a frightening and frustrating day into an unforgettable experience. (*Canadian Mountain Holidays* even offers a week-long program for first-time heli-skiers who would like to build up their confidence in skiing this type of terrain.) Guests always ski with others of similar ability and can rent special powder skis that will make the going easier. As for safety, avalanche rescue transceivers are carried by every member of the heli-skiing parties, and radios linking the skiing groups to the helicopters, the base, and the outside world are standard equipment for the guides.

All of which makes a good case for the contention made by Mike Wiegele, operator of *Mike Wiegele Helicopter Skiing*, that his brand of operation is as safe as any well-established, efficiently operated, lift-serviced ski resort.

And besides, the lure of the mountains themselves is powerful. They offer absolutely extraordinary ski terrain. For instance, along the skiable part of the Columbia Mountains' Purcell Range known as the Bugaboos, in the southeasternmost segment of the Canadian Rockies, the skiable area encompasses some 600 square miles. And if you have your fill of skiing there, there are always the Cariboos, the Monashees, Valemount, Revelstoke, and the Bobbie Burns to tackle. *Each one* of Hans Gmoser's six operations is bigger than 40 conventional resorts combined, and optimum snow conditions prevail from December until May. There is none of the heavy, wet snow found at times on the West Coast. Nor are there the dry, cold, and fierce winds of the Rockies' eastern slopes. The flakes come in generous quantities — some 1,200 centimeters, or about 39 feet, every year — but there's rarely too much at any one time, and for the most part it is the lightest, driest powder imaginable.

Moreover, it's not necessary to be Billy Kidd to tackle it. Advanced intermediates experienced with a variety of terrains should find heli-skiing slopes within their abilities — even if they've never before skied powder. Consequently, for anyone with an adventurous spirit and a little loose cash, heli-skiing is certainly an option. Some good operations include the following:

CANADIAN MOUNTAIN HOLIDAYS, Banff, Alberta: Hans Gmoser's operation, staffed by experienced guides, runs 7-day helicopter ski tours to six areas in British Columbia. Sometimes skiers headquarter at an isolated mountain lodge; sometimes in a facility in a nearby town. Information: Canadian Mountain Holidays, PO Box 1660, Banff, Alberta T0L 0C0 (phone: 403-762-4531).

MIKE WIEGELE HELICOPTER SKIING, Banff, Alberta: Mike Wiegele's operation offers 3-, 5-, and 7-day packages in the Cariboos and the Monashees, covering an area of 3,000 square miles of wilderness. Accommodations are in Blue River, 130 miles (209 km) from Kamloops, where a new lodge and chalets are being built. Ski weeks can also be arranged for private parties. Information: Mike Wiegele Helicopter Skiing, Ltd., PO Box 249, Banff, Alberta T0L 0C0 (phone: 403-762-5548 or from the continental US, 800-661-9170).

MOUNTAIN CANADA (Purcell Helicopter Skiing Ltd.), Golden, British Columbia: This company has 3-, 5- and 7-day heli-skiing packages, as well as day trips into the Purcell Mountains. Skiers lodge at the *Golden Rim Motor Inn,* which has a great view of the Purcells and the Columbia River Valley. Information: Rudi Gertsch, Mountain Canada (Purcell Helicopter Skiing Ltd.), Box 1530, Golden, British Columbia V0A 1H0 (phone: 604-344-5410).

SELKIRK WILDERNESS SKIING, Meadow Creek, British Columbia: Those with a helicopter phobia can still experience this unique brand of deep-powder skiing. Selkirk Wilderness Skiing transports skiers to the top of the mountain via deluxe heated snowcat. A limited number of guests per week are accepted, and they share 20 square miles of varied terrain. Information: Selkirk Wilderness Skiing Ltd., Meadow Creek, British Columbia V0G 1N0 (phone: 604-366-4424).

Cross-Country Skiing

It's not necessary to be an Olympic-caliber athlete to enjoy ski touring — cross-country skiing. Nor is it necessary to go anywhere special in Canada to enjoy the sport. You can ski in city ravines, suburban vest-pocket parks, farmers' fields, and on frozen lakes. But with a long weekend or a week to spare, you'll want to head for the more attractive trails on Canada's hundreds of square miles of public lands. There, given some wisdom in the ways of the winter wilderness, it's a great adventure to break your own trails through the powder. Or tackle one of the many areas where special cross-country ski trails are marked, groomed, and patrolled. The latter can be found at a variety of hostelries: downhill ski resorts; luxury resorts (where après-ski means swimming in a big pool and relaxing in a sauna); dude ranches and guest farms; simple housekeeping cottages in the woods; cozy country inns; and rustic mountain lodges heated by wood stoves and lit by kerosene lanterns. Or you might want to try a lodge-to-lodge or hut-to-hut (tents, actually) tour with accommodations that are a day of skiing apart, on an interconnecting trail (luggage is transported separately by road). For the truly adventurous, there's even helicopter cross-country skiing. Interesting articles dealing with various areas where cross-country skiing is big are published in *Ski Canada* ($24 CN, about $20 US, annually), 227 Front St. E., Suite 100, Toronto, Ontario M5A 1E8 (phone: 416-368-0185).

EAST

Because of Canada's current cross-country skiing boom, most provincial and municipal parks have developed at least one trail and try to keep campgrounds open for die-hard winter lovers. Even the Atlantic provinces have gone in for the sport. Mactaquac Provincial Park, 15 miles (24 km) from Fredericton, New Brunswick, keeps locals happy on its small network of trails. There are 40 miles more at Poley Mountain, north of Saint John, not far from Sussex. In Nova Scotia, the *Old Orchard Inn Ski Touring Centre* (Box 1090, Wolfville, NS B0P 1X0; phone: 902-542-5751) at Annapolis Valley caters exclusively to cross-country skiers. Wentworth Valley, the wooded area surrounding the Canadian Hostelling Association's handsome, century-old *Wentworth* hostel (RR1, Wentworth, Cumberland Co., NS B0M 1Z0; phone: 902-548-2379) is a delight. The hostel accommodates 45 people (bring your own sleeping bag) and has a cross-country ski rental shop. Reservations are necessary.

In Quebec, the Gaspé Provincial Park and the Forillon National Park attract a trickle of experienced skiers looking for a superior wilderness experience. There's an extensive trail network at Parc du Mont-Ste.-Anne — known for its downhill runs — and at a few other areas just outside Quebec City. Quebec's Eastern Townships, also usually thought of for fine alpine skiing, are sprinkled with lodges catering to kick-andgliders. The massive and elegant *Château Montebello,* at Montebello, 40 miles (64 km) east of Ottawa, has gained an international reputation as the annual operational headquarters for the 160-km Canadian Ski Marathon — a giant, anyone-can-enter Nordic competition. (For hotel information, contact Le Château Montebello, Montebello, Quebec J0V 1L0; phone: 819-423-6341. Also see *Special Havens.*)

Meanwhile, in Ontario, there are myriad resorts in the Huronia district, around Barrie. There's wilderness skiing in the glorious Algonquin Provincial Park, while the nearby *Deerhurst Inn and Country Club* (described in *Special Havens*) and the *Bear Trail Inn* (Box 158, Whitney, Ontario K0J 2M0; phone: 613-637-2662) both have good touring trail systems.

In addition to these areas, most of the inns and resorts described in *Special Havens,* and many of the guest farms sketched in *Farm and Ranch Vacations* either maintain their own cross-country ski trail networks or have access to terrain in nearby provincial and national parks. For more ideas, in every case, contact the various province tourist offices. A number of areas in eastern Canada merit special attention for the unique experiences they offer.

ALGOMA COUNTRY, north of Sault Ste. Marie, Ontario: Northward from this city at the junction of Lake Superior and Lake Huron, there is a vast wilderness full of cross-country skiing opportunities, many of them in four provincial parks and one national park. The forests are deep and silent and bring to mind the days when Indians roamed the land. Establish a base at a hotel in Sault Ste. Marie and then head out for day trips into these preserves or to the big *Hiawatha Lodge II* (RR5, Landslide Rd., Sault Ste. Marie, Ontario P6A 6J8; phone: 705-949-9757). There are no overnight accommodations at the lodge, which is home base for the famous *Sault Finnish Ski Club,* but cross-country skiers can stop here for the cocktail lounge and other day facilities. In addition to about 21 miles of immaculately groomed trails, there is a 2-km loop lighted for night skiing. Alternatively, it's possible to headquarter at any one of a number of small, secluded cabins and lodges north and east of Sault Ste. Marie and north of Thessalon in the Mississagi River valley. The trail networks are not extensive, but the lodges themselves are long on charm. (For details, contact the Algoma-Kinniwabi Travel Association, 616 Queen St. E., Suite 203, Sault Ste. Marie, Ontario P6A 2A4; phone: 705-254-4293).

LAURENTIANS, Quebec: Ten years ago, cross-country skiing here had the reputation of being for kamikaze-types only. Trails were severe, with frequent cliff-like descents. Today, most of the trails have been redesigned, upgraded, and mechanically tracked. This vast sweep of mountains may well be the ultimate cross-country ski resort area, the Aspen of cross-country skiing. The main attraction, besides the skiing, is the abundance of wonderful restaurants and lodging places. But when you consider their diversity and the variety of the skiing terrain, putting together a Laurentians ski vacation can become terribly confusing. A few basic facts about the area may be helpful. To wit: The northern Laurentians' trails are not quite so well marked as those in the south; and the farther east or west you travel from the Laurentians Autoroute, which bisects the region from north to south, the wilder and less well marked are the ski routes. The trails at the better-known hostelries of the more northerly St. Jovite–Mont Tremblant area — the *Tremblant Club,* the *Station Mont Tremblant Lodge,* and the *Gray Rocks Inn* (all described in *Special Havens*) — are enjoyable. Most people make their headquarters at one establishment, then spend their vacations exploring its trails and those of its neighbors, accessible via interregional trails. But the very concentration of inns and the proliferation of long-distance trails also suggest the possibility of inn-to-inn touring, and in the south, where the hostelries are situated practically on top of each other, innkeepers are generally quite obliging about transporting your luggage via hotel bus or taxi to your next overnight stop.

Regional trail maps are available from local hotels and ski shops, as is the interregional trail map published by the Laurentian Ski Zone. The Laurentians are also well known for hosting the Canadian Ski Marathon, a mammoth, anyone-can-enter 2-day cross-country ski event, usually held in mid-February, that ranks among the biggest of its kind in the world. Entrance fees range from about $38 to $55, depending on your age group. (For details, contact the Canadian Ski Marathon, P.O. Box 98, Montebello, Quebec J0V 1L0 (phone: 819-423-5157). Information: Association Touristique des Laurentides, 14142 Rue de Lachapelle, RR1, St. Jérôme, Quebec J7Z 5T4 (phone: 514-436-8532). Also see *Downhill Skiing* and the *Laurentians*, DIRECTIONS.

QUEBEC CITY, Quebec: One of the great charms of this endlessly fascinating city is its proximity to the great out-of-doors. You can spend days pursuing your favorite sports — and your nights in the comfort of the city's splendid hotels, sleeping off the effects of a bountiful French-Canadian repast eaten in one of its cozy restaurants. Cross-country skiers will find some of the province's best skiing within an hour's drive of the city. Quebecois themselves take to the Plains of Abraham — like New Yorkers to Central Park — to keep in shape; and though the skiing isn't the best, the views are fine. However, Quebec's best ski terrain — more than what's possible to explore in a 2-week vacation (let alone a 2-week vacation that leaves time to enjoy the delights of the metropolis) — is at Mont-Ste.-Anne, 25 miles (40 km) to the east; at Duchesnay Forestry Station, 25 miles (40 km) northwest; and at Camp Mercier, just inside Laurentides Park, 36 miles (58 km) from downtown. At Mont-Ste.-Anne, the trails are beautifully laid out so that the uphills, the downhills, and the flats follow each other in quick and varied succession, through lovely hardwood forests. (But beginners won't find much within their ability.) Duchesnay's more varied woods trails, through mixed hardwood and fir, are better suited to beginners, while the trails at Camp Mercier, far less windy than at either of the other areas, are flatter still; the snow is also better there. Inexpensive group overnight trips are also available. Information: Quebec City Region Tourism and Convention Bureau, 60 Rue d'Auteuil, Quebec City, Quebec G1R 4C4 (phone: 418-692-2471).

WEST

The cross-country skiing mania means, in Manitoba, Saskatchewan, and Alberta, that scarcely a snowy weekend passes without swarms of skiers descending on municipal and provincial parks near the cities and every ski lodge in sight. Guest farms in the area get some of the traffic, and not a few have reported repeat business all the way from Europe. The woodland trails in Prince Albert National Park, smack in the center of Saskatchewan, are also popular. In Manitoba, the major magnets are Duck Mountain Provincial Park, a major wintering ground for elk; Riding Mountain National Park, near Wasagaming; and Whiteshell Provincial Park, where ski trails lead through black spruce woods, aspen groves, and such. In Alberta some 24 miles of double track have been added at Nakiska. Canadians casting about for a really special cross-country skiing vacation often look to several quite distinctive mountain ranges in the west, where they can base themselves in luxury resorts and backcountry lodges and go out for tours in the valleys or the mountains, with or without guides, depending on the extent of their wilderness savvy. For high-country trips, some skiers rent alpine skis with special touring bindings; others tackle the long downhills with their own skinny skis — and they keep up just fine.

ROCKIES, western Alberta: These high and rocky glaciated mountains are well known for the wealth of downhill skiing opportunities they offer — but some of the continent's most dazzling cross-country skiing can be done here as well, in Banff and Jasper National Parks and in outlying regions. Relatively inexperienced skiers can stick to the marked and mapped trails in the more accessible areas of the parks and consult local ski shops and park personnel for help in planning other day trips — and never run out of new trails to explore. The dramatic *Banff Springs* hotel and the equally imposing *Château Lake Louise* offer good access to the best of all levels of skiing. For information on ground packages, including lift tickets and accommodations, contact Banff Club Ski (Box 1085, Banff, Alberta T0L 0C0; phone: 403-762-4561). Long-celebrated *Skoki Lodge* — a group of half-century-old log structures situated in a mountain-rimmed valley 8 miles (13 km) from the nearest road, lit by lanterns and candles and heated by fireplaces — makes a wonderful retreat. Guests ski all day in the serene woods and meadows in the immediate area and in valleys above timberline and then come back to delicious meals prepared on real wood stoves and friendly conversations with other guests around the fireplace. (For information on this lodge as well as all the others in the Lake Louise area, contact Skiing Louise, PO Box 5, Lake Louise, Alberta, T0L 1E0; phone: 403-522-3555) There are a half dozen such cozy places in the Rockies — though the setup varies a little from one to the next. You will have to ski into the *Lake O'Hara Lodge,* so pack light. The timbered lodge, about 7 miles (11 km) west of Lake Louise, was built by the Canadian-Pacific Railroad company in 1925 (Box 1677, Banff, Alberta T0L 0C0; phone: 403-762-2118 or 604-343-6418); and beautifully situated *Mt. Assiniboine Lodge,* built of logs in about 1928 (Box 1527, Canmore, Alberta T0L 0M0; phone: 403-678-2883). In Jasper National Park, the spectacular Tonquin Valley — edged and overlooked by the renowned "Ramparts," rock cliffs that soar up to 10,000 feet in height — is home to *Tonquin Valley Ski Tours,* a 14-mile back-country trip from Jasper to the lodge (Box 550, Jasper, Alberta T0E 1E0; phone: 403-852-3909). The *Alpine Club of Canada* (Box 1026, Banff, Alberta T0L 0C0; phone: 403-762-4481) operates 15 back-country huts within easy reach of Banff or Jasper, including the *Wates-Gibson Hut* in the Jasper park's Eremite Valley. They also offer accommodations for 67 people in their clubhouse at Canmore. The *Sunshine Village Inn,* perched at the top of the gondola, is the single source for on-slope accommodations at one of Banff's big-time ski resorts (PO Box 1510, Banff, Alberta T0L 0C0; phone: 403-762-2791). There are a number of marked loop trails in the area and some longer overnight tours. Organized tours are available from *Banff Alpine Guides,* Box 1025, Banff, Alberta T0L 0C0 (phone: 403-678-5468); For details about skiing in the parks, contact Banff National Park, PO Box 900, Banff, Alberta T0L 0C0 (phone: 403-762-3324) and Jasper National Park, Box 10, Jasper, Alberta T0E 1E0 (phone: 403-852-6161).

CARIBOOS, British Columbia: This province's Interior Ranges — the Cariboos, Purcells, Selkirks, and Monashees — are well known for the heli-skiing operations found there. But the area is also liberally sprinkled with operations that specialize in cross-country skiing and mountain touring; in fact, the 100–108 Mile area (yes, that's its name) alone hosts a ski trail network of approximately 124 miles. The Cariboos, the most westerly of these four groups of peaks, are most like the Rockies in their relatively smooth contours, but snowfall — though it varies considerably from valley to valley — is generally higher. Of the resorts and lodges in the area that offer cross-country skiing, the fanciest are the *Hills Health and Guest Ranch,* with indoor swimming pool, whirlpool bath, saunas, and chalets that sleep six (Compartment 26, 108 Ranch, 100 Mile House, BC V0K 2E0; phone: 604-791-5225); and, across the road, the *108 Golf and Country Inn Resort,* a modern 62-room motor lodge with all the trimmings (Compartment 2, 108 Ranch, RR1, 100 Mile House, Cariboo, BC V0K 2E0; phone: 604-791-5211; also see *Farm and Ranch Vacations*). Eight miles (13 km) south, in 100 Mile House — the cross-country capital of BC — the *Red Coach Inn* (PO Box 760, 100 Mile House, BC V0K 2E0; phone: 604-395-2266) and many other motels offer fine facilities (including lighted night skiing) and are particularly packed the first weekend in February, when the town hosts the annual 50-km Cariboo Marathon. There are also a number of smaller, more rustic places here. The *Circle H Mountain Lodge* (Box 7, Jesmond Rd., Clinton, BC V0K 1K0; phone: 604-459-2565), situated at the base of Mt.

Bowman, 25 miles (40 km) outside of a blink-and-you-miss-it town called Clinton, is among them. Installed in an old log-and-frame hunting lodge and a number of outlying log cabins, it has about 46 miles of trails with a good mix of terrain for every level of skier. For a list of other lodges in the area, contact the Cariboo Tourist Association, PO Box 4900, Williams Lake, BC V2G 2V8 (phone: 604-392-2226).

WILDERNESS MOUNTAIN SKIING IN THE PURCELLS AND THE SELKIRKS, British Columbia: The Purcells, just west of the Rockies, and the Selkirks, just west of the Purcells, are some of British Columbia's most rugged mountains. Compared to the Rockies, the slopes are steeper, the tops more pointed, the rocks more jagged, the snow much deeper. This is not the sort of terrain easterners envision when they think of cross-country skiing. Yet once you've mastered the turns, your skis can take you all sorts of places, and the high mountains are as beautiful as any. Most of the activity in this particular area centers on a handful of tiny mountain lodges of varying degrees of rusticity and remoteness, from which guests go out on guided day trips with the host, who is invariably a confirmed mountain lover. A rustic and rugged experience is offered by *Valhalla Mountain Touring* (PO Box 284, New Denver, BC V0G 1S0; phone: 604-358-7714). Skiers are transported by heated snowcat to a cozy subalpine cabin, the base for the daily ski tours. Similar alpine hut tours, for skiers equipped with wider mountain touring skis, are available from *Northern Lights Alpine Recreation* (Arnör Larson, Box 399, Invermere, BC V0A 1K0; phone: 604-342-6042). The first day is spent skiing, with full pack, to a secluded hut or cabin with wood-burning heaters. Then there are day trips through meadows and forest and along rivers and lakes, ending back at the cabin, where skiers rest up for the next day's trek. *Mountain Canada* (Box 1530, Golden, BC V0A 1H0; phone: 604-344-5410) offers both guided ski tours and heli-cross-country ski tours of the one-day variety, as well as a seven-day package that also includes 1 day of heli-cross-country skiing. Accommodations and meals are included with the package.

The Best Tennis Vacations

For many years, Canadians simply weren't interested in tennis. The climate didn't help. Building courts was an expensive proposition. Long, hard winters that precluded play for much of the year wrought havoc even on all-weather surfaces; expensive indoor courts were the only alternative, and there was little demand. Promoters, sensing an uncertain return on their investment, steered clear of tennis, at least as far as vacation facilities went.

But gradually tennis has been taking hold north of the US border. Rare indeed is the area without tennis facilities. Courts are now found in all resort hotels and many big-city hotels, as well as in just about all the country's townships and municipalities. (Write to the chamber of commerce or local tourist authority of the area you intend to visit for a list.) And bit by bit, the number of resorts devoted exclusively to tennis has been increasing. Most are located in marvelously scenic country, and most offer private lessons or clinics and other facilities — which you can enjoy even if you've never held a racket in your life. Clinics and intensive instruction programs will teach you the correct way to play right from the beginning; and even experienced players can benefit from a little additional coaching once in a while.

Far more common in Canada than the tennis-only resort, however, is the resort with a few courts and a pro — and these are, in any case, far more relaxing places to spend a vacation. Just check in, sign up for a couple of lessons here and there, play tennis when you want, and spend the rest of your time taking advantage of the resort's saunas, shops, whirlpool baths, swimming pools, golf courses, and waterfront activities.

BANFF SPRINGS HOTEL, Banff, Alberta: The tennis season runs from May, when the weather clears, until October, when temperatures begin to drop, here in the heart of the Canadian Rockies where this turreted 850-room château of a hostelry is situated. The 5 plexi-pave hard-surface courts are used by guests from all over North America as well as by members of a Banff Springs club (whose members pay an annual fee for the privilege), so the setup is exceptionally convivial — somewhat less transient in feeling than at most hotels, but not so stuffy as a good many country clubs. A ball machine and pro are available to help perfect your strokes, and, though the courts aren't lighted, you can play until 10 almost every night — because that's when the sun sets in these parts. Consequently, this establishment is one of your best bets for a tennis vacation that involves pursuing other activities as well. There are plenty to enjoy: fishing in mountain streams, canoeing and rafting, climbing, golf on one of North America's most scenic courses (bar none; see *Golf*), as well as swimming in either of 2 pools. You can relax after all this activity in one of the health club's 3 Jacuzzis or its sauna. Information: Banff Springs Hotel, PO Box 960, Banff, Alberta T0L 0C0 (phone: 403-762-2211).

JASPER PARK LODGE, Jasper, Alberta: Here, the same situation prevails: a great hotel (really a lodge surrounded by old-fashioned log cabins and modern cedar chalets), a fine golf course (see *Golf*), lots of climbing (see *Mountain Climbing*), good fishing, hiking, canoeing and rafting, and all the other Rocky Mountain highs as off-the-court entertainment — plus wonderful tennis. There are 4 hard-surface courts at your disposal. No clinics are offered, but you can take lessons from the pro. Information: Jasper Park Lodge, Box 40, Jasper, Alberta T0E 1E0 (phone: 403-852-3301).

LAKE OKANAGAN RESORT, Kelowna, British Columbia: This is a 300-acre condominium resort hotel on the shores of 90-mile-long Lake Okanagan. There are 7 courts here (3 lighted), and two teaching pros to help you improve your game. You get about 3 hours on the court every day (including work with ball machines and video equipment). Accommodation (for up to 350) is in guestrooms, suites, studios, and 2- and 3-bedroom apartments in Bavarian-style chalets scattered widely around the wooded grounds and at the edge of the 9-hole, par-3 golf course. Access to local championship courses is available through the pro shop. There's also a stadium court with seating for 300 on the property. All sorts of other activities are available in the area, which is Canada's fruit-growing center. (See *Okanagan Orchard Country*, DIRECTIONS.) Information: Lake Okanagan Resort, PO Box 1321, Station A, Kelowna, BC V1Y 7V8 (phone: 604-769-3511).

ELGIN HOUSE, Port Carling, Ontario: There are 4 tennis courts at this 640-acre turn-of-the-century resort in the Muskoka Lakes district, and there's a pro who holds clinics. But clinics here are not like those you find anywhere else. Most guests come to stay a week, with the express purpose of playing and studying tennis. Just after they've all checked in, the pro gathers them together to find out their strengths and weaknesses, then groups them accordingly. Private lessons are available at any time you and the pro deem mutually desirable. Flexibility, in other words, governs the program, and the high percentage of return business would indicate that the guests are happy with the arrangement — and with the resort's other features. Spread out as it is on a lawns-and-woods-blanketed peninsula poking into one Lake Joseph, this is a relaxed sort of place, and even when the house is full — that is, with all 350 guests who can be divided between the various balconied hotel rooms, suites, and 4-bedroom cottages — you don't feel hemmed in by people. In fact, sometimes the management looks around and wonders where everybody has gone. The answer: They're swimming in the pool, wielding their irons on the 9-hole golf course, sailing, canoeing, water skiing, windsurfing on the lake, playing shuffleboard or field games — or, after dinner, enjoying movies, bingo games, pool parties, a popular dinner theater with professional actors, or other social programs cooked up by the full-time recreation director. The resort also offers a nursery with a complete children's program. Information: Elgin House, RR2, Port Carling, Ontario P0B 1J0 (phone: 705-765-3101).

DEERHURST INN AND COUNTRY CLUB, Huntsville, Ontario: This Muskoka Lakes resort grew like Topsy after its birth in 1896, and now, in addition to all the aquatic pursuits you'd expect to find at a country resort with over 200 rooms in a well-developed region such as this one, there's tennis on 5 Har-Tru courts. Lessons are available from a pro. Again, it's not so much for the diehard player as it is for the holidaymaker who just wants to hit some tennis balls on vacation. Information: Deerhurst Resorts Ltd., RR4, Huntsville, Ontario P0A 1K0 (phone: 705-789-5543).

HIDDEN VALLEY RESORT, Huntsville, Ontario: The best surprise here is that this inn sits all by itself at the end of a small road in an area of private cottages and year-round summer homes by the shores of a lake, affectionately known as "Pen" Lake — short for Peninsula. The 4 courts are right on the lake; 2 are lighted. Other diversions — they're what you come for, too — include racquetball, squash, a Universal gym, swimming in outdoor and indoor pools overlooking the lake, relaxing in an oversized whirlpool bath or in the sauna, or playing around in the lake. In winter, the ski slopes of Hidden Valley Highlands terminate at the hotel entrance. Information: Hidden Valley Resort, RR4, Huntsville, Ontario P0A 1K0 (phone: 705-789-2301).

CLEVELANDS HOUSE, Minett, Ontario: Tennis is the major attraction at this handsome older lodge — a 175-room families' delight on a hundred lakeside acres in the Muskoka Lakes district, about 140 miles (225 km) north of Toronto. You'll find 16 courts here and a structured program — available for rank beginners, novices, intermediates, advanced and team players, and children under 14 — which give you court time and time for viewing indoor films, learning the rules of the game, and discussing tactics and strategies. You use ball machines and video equipment when appropriate. Other activities include golf on the challenging 9-hole course, plus boating, fishing, swimming. Rooms are located in 5 lodge buildings and a scattering of bungalows. Information: Clevelands House, Minett, Muskoka, Ontario P0B 1G0 (phone: 705-765-3171).

INN AND TENNIS CLUB AT MANITOU, McKellar, Ontario: This small, ultra-luxurious Relais & Châteaux resort located on a semi-wilderness shore of a north central Ontario lake, not far from the beautiful Georgian Bay area and some 160 miles (258 km) north of Toronto, offers a solid program of 3-, 4-, and 7-day clinics that stand out particularly because of their high teacher-pupil ratio: A staff of 16 pros is always on hand to provide instruction for the 60 guests who can be accommodated at any given time. Facilities include 12 outdoor courts and an indoor court, a complement of ball machines and video equipment, a heated pool, sauna and spa, and boats for sailing on the lake. The suites each have a wood-burning fireplace (and many have whirlpool baths and saunas). The food is delicious, featuring nouvelle cuisine. This is one of North America's best-established tennis resorts, well worth traveling a long distance to experience — and a lot of first-rate tennis players do just that. A "value season" prevails from late May to late June and from Labor Day to mid-October; if your budget is average, you will probably want to time your visit accordingly. Information: Inn and Tennis Club at Manitou, 251 Davenport Road, Toronto, Ontario M5R 1J9 (phone: 416-967-3466).

LAURENTIANS, Quebec: St. Jovite's *Gray Rocks Inn,* a complete tennis resort destination, is the grand old lady of the Laurentians. Well known to skiers for many years for its outstanding teaching program, it offers tennis clinics on a par with those of the *Inn and Tennis Club at Manitou,* described above. However, management here goes for volume as well as quality; the resort, situated on some 2,600 acres on the shores of Lac Ouimet, can accommodate close to 500 guests. Tennis clinics follow the methods developed by Billie Jean King's former coach Dennis Van der Meer — that is, plenty of stroke work. Usually, this means 20 hours of instruction (4 hours per day, for 5 days) with a pair of instructors for each student on the court at any given time. If you don't want to throw yourself entirely into the game, you don't have to: A fee of approximately $30 entitles you to a week's unlimited use of the resort's 22 Har-Tru courts. And when you're not lobbing balls, you can golf on the 18-hole course, enjoy water sports and a fitness center, play badminton and other lawn games, go riding, or, more to the point in this gourmand's paradise, indulge in good French Canadian food in a lovely dining room practically paved with white linen. There's live entertainment nightly. The main lodge includes rooms and small suites, some with fireplaces or balconies and patios. More than fifty 1-, 2-, and 3-bedroom condominums are also available. *Le Chantecler* in Ste. Adéle and *Villa Bellevue,* on Lake Ouimet, both offer tennis weeks and weekends, private lessons, and clinics. *Villa Bellevue* also has a pro available for lessons and guests have access to four new clay courts and can take full advantage of the resort's lakeshore setting and watersports. The resort has recently added an indoor pool, spa, exercise room, and 14 deluxe rooms. *Station Mont Tremblant Lodge* at Mont Tremblant has a half dozen Har-Tru courts, and both private and group lessons and seminars for children are available. You lodge in a variety of deluxe rooms or in chalets of varying sizes, some with fireplaces. *Cuttle's Tremblant Club,* on the edge of Lac Tremblant, has 4 courts and a tennis pro located at its beach club. Information: Gray Rocks Inn, PO Box 1000, St. Jovite, Quebec J0T 2H0 (phone: 819-425-2771); Station Mont Tremblant Lodge, Mont Tremblant, Quebec J0T 1Z0 (phone: 819-425-8711 or 800-567-6761 in the US and Canada); Cuttle's Tremblant Club, Mont Tremblant, Quebec J0T 1Z0 (phone: 819-425-2731); Villa Bellevue, Mont Tremblant, Quebec J0T 1Z0 (phone: 819-425-2734 or 800-567-6763).

MONT STE. MARIE RESORT AND CONFERENCE CENTER, Lac Ste. Marie, Quebec: This ski-and-summer resort in the Gatineau Hills some 55 miles (88 km) north of Ottawa offers tennis on 4 courts that are available daily from 8 AM to 10 PM. When you've had enough on the courts, you'll find plenty of other sports to enjoy on the resort's 4,500 acres, such as a round of golf on the 18-hole course. Lac à la Truite here is reserved for fishing. You can windsurf, swim, canoe, and kayak on Lake Fourniere (canoe and windsurfing equipment can be rented.) There's a health club with sauna, gym equipment, and a full complement of after-dark activities — a must for any complete destination resort that is as relatively remote from the bright lights as this one. Information: Mont Ste. Marie, Quebec J0X 1Z0 (phone: 819-467-5200).

Golf in Canada: A Land of Links

Canada's British heritage is nowhere more obvious than in its abundance of first class golf courses. That they have not exactly reached international renown is much more a by-product of a relatively short grass-growing season than any inadequacy in design, and though the overall playing season may be similarly short, there are more good golfing challenges within Canada's borders than the average golfer could conquer in a lifetime.

As in the US, there are many private golf clubs that bar transient players. But even these enclaves are more pleasant to tourists than their stateside counterparts, especially if you show up on slack days — that is, during the week. A letter from your own golf club president or home course professional requesting playing privileges at a Canadian club, together with your own membership card, often provides more ready access to private clubs than you might suppose.

You needn't go to such trouble, however, for the courses listed below. Most are located at resorts or in public parklands — and they're some of Canada's finest.

EAST

EDMUNDSTON GOLF CLUB, Edmundston, New Brunswick: The main 18-hole championship layout stretches 6,666 yards and plays to par 73, with one long par 3 over a railway spur. There's also a 5-hole par-3 junior course for youngsters or adult practice. This semi-private course also features a clubhouse and pool overlooking the river and the city. Information: Edmundston Golf Club, PO Box 263, Edmundston, NB E3V 3K9 (phone: 506-735-7266 or -3086).

ALGONQUIN GOLF COURSE, St. Andrews, New Brunswick: Part of one of Canada's traditional summer resort hotels, the course borders on Passamaquoddy Bay, due east of Calais on the Maine border. There are a total of 27 holes here, set in rolling seaside terrain. The name of the town in which the course is situated is hardly gratuitous since it's quite reminiscent of its famous namesake on the east coast of Scotland. The 9-hole course has narrow fairways and the 18-hole stretch is very scenic with 13 holes along the bay. Information: Algonquin Golf Club, St. Andrews, NB E0G 2X0 (phone: 506-529-8823).

BALLY HALY GOLF AND CURLING CLUB, St. John's, Newfoundland: Its narrow fairways, side-hill lies, and well-contoured greens would make this 5,800-yard, par-71 course difficult enough, but because of its coastline location, rigorous winds add to its toughness. The course has 18 scenic holes, many with views of the North Atlantic from the tees and fairways. Information: Bally Haly Golf and Curling Club, PO Box 9185, St. John's, Newfoundland A1A 2X9 (phone: 709-753-6090).

BRIGHTWOOD GOLF AND COUNTRY CLUB, Dartmouth, Nova Scotia: Located smack in the center of the city, looking much like Central Park in the center of New York City, this 18-hole course is perched high on a hill on what must surely be the choicest site in the area, and the views are as beautiful as the golf holes are difficult. Information: Brightwood Golf and Country Club, 227 School St., Dartmouth, NS B3A 2Y5 (phone: 902-466-7688).

PINES GOLF CLUB, Digby, Nova Scotia: This club is owned by the provincial government and operated by the Nova Scotia Department of Tourism, which also runs the fine adjacent hotel. At least as appealing as the course's rolling acreage are the famous scallops caught hereabouts, and this is one of the best places in Canada to combine good golf and gastronomy. Information: Pines Golf Club, c/o The Pines Resort Hotel, PO Box 70, Digby, NS B0V 1A0 (phone: 902-245-2511).

OAKFIELD GOLF AND COUNTRY CLUB, Grand Lake, Nova Scotia: With Ashburn, this is one of the prime sites for golfers who live in and around Nova Scotia's capital of Halifax. It's as wide open as Ashburn is wooded but no less difficult. The constant breeze that blows over the lakeside setting makes each hole a bit trickier than it initially appears. The fourth hole here is unique, since the scene off the tee seems to indicate no green immediately at hand. But one *is* tucked in just beyond the far left corner of the seemingly empty square in front of you, and a caddy's advice as to the direction of your drive is indispensable. Information: Oakfield Golf and Country Club, Enfield Post Office, Enfield, Hants County, NS B0N 1N0 (phone: 902-861-2777).

HIGHLAND LINKS, Cape Breton Highlands National Park, Ingonish Beach, Nova Scotia: One of the great adventures in golf, the course is one you play many times to savor its true challenge. The setting is superb, combining seaside, valley, and mountainous terrain in perfect proportion. Tees and greens are placed only in the most perfect positions, and architect Stanley Thompson included walks as long as a half mile between holes to assure maximum enjoyment of this unique layout. Anyone considering a round on this course should enjoy walking; motorized golf carts are prohibited in order to maintain the physical challenge and spirit of the old Scottish links. Information: Cape Breton Highlands National Park, Ingonish Beach, Victoria County, NS B0C 1L0 (phone: 902-285-2600 May through October, or 902-285-2270).

DIVERSIONS / Golf in Canada

LINGAN COUNTRY CLUB, Sydney, Nova Scotia: Golf pros who really know Nova Scotia consider this one of the hardest tracks in all of the Maritimes on which to score. The course measures 6,657 yards and you play every foot of it, for the distances on the scorecard are deadly accurate — your short iron game had better be also. Definitely not for the timid. Information: Lingan Country Club, PO Box 1252, Grand Lake Rd., Sydney, NS B1P 6S9 (phone: 902-562-5100).

UPPER CANADA GOLF COURSE, near Morrisburg, Ontario: Operated by The St. Lawrence Park Commission, the course boasts unusually large greens and rather rolling fairways. The setting is especially picturesque. A driving range, dining facilities, and a pro shop are also on the premises. Information: Upper Canada Golf Course, The St. Lawrence Parks Commission, PO Box 740, Morrisburg, Ontario K0C 1X0 (phone: 613-543-2003).

GLEN LAWRENCE GOLF AND COUNTRY CLUB, Kingston, Ontario: Don't let the rather flat front 9 here lull you into a false sense of security. The back 9 are considerably more rolling, and the course represents a fine test. (There's water to conquer on 7 holes.) Information: Glen Lawrence Golf and Country Club, RR1, Kingston, Ontario K7L 4V1 (phone: 613-545-1021).

WHIRLPOOL GOLF COURSE, Niagara Falls, Ontario: The course gets its name from the famous Niagara Whirlpool, and the scenery includes a view of the Niagara Gorge. There are many trees, many traps, and very challenging green positions. Information: Whirlpool Golf Course, Niagara Parks Commission, PO Box 150, Niagara Falls, Ontario L2E 6T2 (phone: 416-356-1140).

DON VALLEY GOLF COURSE, Toronto, Ontario: Actually 6.5 miles (10 km) from the center of downtown Toronto, this difficult municipal course has the Don River as its main hazard. This winding brook traverses the course and comes into play on at least 11 holes. Information: Metropolitan Toronto Parks and Property Dept., 365 Bay St., 8th Floor, Toronto, Ontario M5H 2V1 (phone: 416-392-2465).

BRUDENELL RIVER PROVINCIAL GOLF COURSE, Roseneath, Prince Edward Island: Part of Brudenell River Provincial Park, this course, built in 1969 and the site of five Canadian National Championships, was designed to open this area to tourism. The seaside setting is well used, with fully half of the 18 holes requiring some passage over a portion of the watery landscape. It is just one of the features of a major recreation complex that also includes a marina, tennis, swimming, canoeing and boardsailing, horseback riding, camping, and 50 chalets. Information: Brudenell River Provincial Golf Course, c/o Harry Simmonds, Department of Tourism and Parks, PO Box 2000, Charlottetown, PEI C1A 7N8 (phone: 902-652-2342 for the pro shop; or, between October and June, 902-652-2356).

GREEN GABLES GOLF COURSE, Cavendish, Prince Edward Island: One of the oldest courses on the island (opened in 1939), it owes its name to PEI's leading literary light, Lucy Maud Montgomery. Early in this century, Miss Montgomery's story of a young orphan girl in *Anne of Green Gables* entranced the world, and the house in which her fictional heroine lived is adjacent to the golf course. Literary lives notwithstanding, the course itself is a rare blend of rolling terrain with seaside dunes and ponds. The course opens each year in mid-May and closes at the end of October. Information: Green Gables Golf Course, Island Coastal Services Ltd., PO Box 151, Charlottetown, PEI C1A 7K4 (phone: 902-892-1062); or Environment Canada, Parks-PEI, PO Box 487, Charlottetown, PEI C1A 7L1 (phone: 902-672-2211).

MILL RIVER PROVINCIAL PARK GOLF COURSE, Woodstock, Prince Edward Island: Here's another course that's part of a larger provincial park-and-recreation complex. The course is absolutely superb, and if you have only one round of golf to play on PEI, this is the place to tee off. It's worth the trip just to play the eighth hole, where a bubbling brook boils down the middle of the fairway all the way from tee to green. Information: Mill River Provincial Golf Course, Department of Tourism and Parks, Woodstock RR3, O'Leary, PEI C0B 1V0 (phone: 902-859-2448).

CARLING LAKE GOLF CLUB, Lachute, Quebec: Designed by Harold Watson, this challenging course occupies a rolling site in the foothills of the Laurentian Mountains. Though it's not the longest course in Canada (at 6,650 yards), it boasts many difficult holes that will challenge the talents of even the lowest-handicap player. Information: Carling Lake Golf Club, PO Box 670, Brownsburg, Quebec J0V 1A0 (phone: 514-437-4653).

LE CHÂTEAU MONTEBELLO, Montebello, Quebec: The resort courses of the Outaouais area have one thing in common — their challenging, rolling terrain. Naturally sculpted ravines and valleys make the most forbidding hazards here, and the entire course is surrounded by dense pine and spruce woods. Information: Le Château Montebello, 392 Rue Notre-Dame, Montebello, Quebec J0V 1L0 (phone: 819-423-6341).

MANOIR RICHELIEU GOLF CLUB, Pointe-au-Pic, Quebec: The precipitous high and low points of this site overlooking the Laurentians make the course both scenic and challenging. Information: Manoir Richelieu Golf Club, 19 Rang Terrebonne, Pointe-au-Pic, Charlevoix, Quebec G0T 1M0. Out of season, write to 181 Rue Richelieu, Pointe-au-Pic, Charlevoix, Quebec, G0T 1M0 (phone: 418-665-3703, year-round).

LE CHANTECLER GOLF CLUB, Ste. Adèle, Quebec: Again, part of a sizable Laurentian resort with abundant mountain scenery to provide a spectacular golfing backdrop. The 18-hole, par-72 course is next door to the *Chantecler* hotel. Information: Le Chantecler Golf Club, 2520 Chemin du Golf, PO Box 165, Ste. Adèle, Quebec J0R 1L0 (phone: 514-229-3742 or, in Montreal only, 800-363-2587).

GRAY ROCKS GOLF CLUB, St. Jovite, Quebec: Part of the large *Gray Rocks Inn* complex, the 18-hole course covers gently rolling, wooded terrain not far from Mont Tremblant. Information: Gray Rocks Golf Club, PO Box 1000, St. Jovite, Quebec J0T 2H0 (phone: 819-425-2771).

WEST

BANFF SPRINGS GOLF CLUB, Banff, Alberta: Set in a valley more than a mile high, this course is surrounded by snowcapped mountains, and you often aim shots at one of the cloud-shrouded peaks. The baronial *Banff Springs* hotel provides a striking background, and every fairway is framed in tall, deep green pine and spruce. The Bow River winds its way down the length of the valley, occasionally throwing up freshets of white water. This is perhaps one of the most beautiful (to say nothing of one of the most difficult) golfing sites in all Canada. Information: Banff Springs Golf Club, c/o Banff Springs Hotel, PO Box 960, Banff, Alberta T0L 0C0 (phone: 403-762-2211).

JASPER PARK LODGE GOLF COURSE, Alberta: This course is as beautiful in its own way as Banff Springs. Both were designed back in the 1920s by Stanley Thompson and are of indisputable quality. The fairways are carved into and out of the slopes of the Canadian Rockies, and despite the course's northerly location, the greens are as manicured and lush as any in this hemisphere. Many fairways have been designed specifically to align themselves with one of the surrounding mountain peaks. Information: Jasper Park Lodge Golf Course, c/o Jasper Park Lodge, Box 40, Jasper, Alberta T0E 1E0 (phone: 403-852-3301).

WATERTON PARK GOLF CLUB, Waterton Park, Alberta: The rolling fairways are a by-product of the Rocky Mountain location, with the surrounding peaks serving as a spectacular background. Information: Waterton Park Golf Club, Waterton Lakes National Park, Box 128, Waterton Park, Alberta T0K 2M0 (phone: 403-859-2383).

FAIRMONT HOT SPRINGS GOLF CLUB, Fairmont Hot Springs, British Columbia: Beyond the condominiums surrounding the course, the mountains compete with the Columbia Lake and Valley to provide the most compelling vista and views. Information: Fairmont Hot Springs Resort Ltd., PO Box 10, Fairmont Hot Springs, BC V0B 1L0 (phone: 604-345-6311).

108 GOLF COURSE, 100 Mile House, British Columbia: This spread in central

British Columbia's Cariboo country, transformed in the 1970s into a 1,500-home development with one of the most luxurious of all Canadian guest ranches, offers magnificent golfing among its many other activities. There is an 18-hole, 6,800-yard, par 71, CPGA-approved golf course that has been the site of one of western Canada's largest tournaments in the past few years as well as a pro, a putting green, chipping green, and outdoor driving range. You can take some time away from your golf game to play tennis, volleyball, or horseshoes; go horseback riding; swim in a heated pool; or relax in a sauna or whirlpool bath. Information: 108 Golf & Country Inn Resort, Compartment 2, RR1, 100 Mile House, BC V0K 2E0 (phone: 604-791-5211).

RADIUM BEST WESTERN GOLF COURSE, Radium Hot Springs, British Columbia: The Canadian Rockies provide an impressive backdrop for this 18-hole, 5,271-yard, par 69 course, at the southern edge of Kootenay National Park, just minutes from the mineral waters of Radium Hot Springs. (The 90-room *Radium Best Western* is between the 16th and 18th fairways.) After a challenging round, guests can repair to the resort's well-equipped sports complex, which offers tennis, racquet ball, squash, an indoor swimming pool, hot tub, exercise gym, sauna, and a massage therapist for those who overdo it. Information: *Best Western* Radium Resort, Box 310, Radium Hot Springs, BC V0A 1M0 (phone: 604-347-9311) or Rocky Mountain Visitors Association of British Columbia, PO Box 10, 495 Wallinger Ave., Kimberley, BC V1A 2Y5 (phone: 604-347-9311).

UPLANDS GOLF CLUB, Victoria, British Columbia: The wind always blows off the surrounding Pacific around here and probably provides the most difficult resident hazard. The course was the site of the Canadian Senior Championships in 1972 and 1985. Information: Uplands Golf Club, 3300 Cadboro Bay Rd., Victoria, BC V8R 5K5 (phone: 604-592-7313); Pro Shop (phone: 604-592-7313).

VICTORIA GOLF CLUB, Victoria, British Columbia: The oldest course in the province, founded in 1893, it has about 75 bunkers and is set beside the Pacific Ocean. Information: Victoria Golf Club, 1110 Beach Dr., Victoria, BC V8S 2M9 (phone: 604-598-4322).

WASAGAMING GOLF COURSE, Riding Mountain National Park, Wasagaming, Manitoba: This province is best known for its rather flat terrain, but this 6,072-yard, par-72 course overlooking the 9.5 square miles of central Canada's beautiful Clear Lake is unusually testing, because of the rolling terrain. Then, too, there are the difficult lies, the blind approaches to the greens, and the fairway-crossing ravines and creeks you have to contend with. It's about 175 miles (280 km) northwest of Winnipeg. Information: Wasagaming Golf Course, c/o Jim Dudman, Box 52, Wasagaming, Manitoba R0J 2H0 (phone: 204-848-2925).

FALCON BEACH GOLF COURSE, Whiteshell Provincial Park, Manitoba: A creek running through this fine 7,000-yard championship course provides a severe hazard on four of the holes. Fairways are tree-lined and bunkered, greens are large, undulating, and well-trapped, and the eighth hole was voted the best par 3 in the province. Information: Falcon Beach Golf Course, c/o Department of Natural Resources, Falcon Lake, Manitoba R0E 0N0 (phone: 204-349-2201).

WASKESIU LAKE GOLF CLUB, Waskesiu Lake, Saskatchewan: Well-trapped and famed for its rolling, wooded terrain, a new irrigation system makes this course, designed by Stanley Thompson in the 1930s, a jewel of the North. It's located in 1,496-square-mile Prince Albert National Park, some 143 miles (229 km) north of Saskatoon. Information: Lobstick Golf & Tennis Club, Inc., P.O. Box 1134, Prince Albert, Saskatchewan S6V 557 (phone: 306-663-5322).

MURRAY MUNICIPAL GOLF CLUB, Regina, Saskatchewan: This hilly public course is kept in top shape through an extensive watering system. You'll find it 7 miles (11 km) northeast of downtown Regina. Information: Murray Municipal Golf Club, c/o City of Regina Community Services and Parks Department, PO Box 1790, Regina, Saskatchewan S4P 3C8 (phone: 306-777-7767).

Where They Bite: Fishing in Canada

 This immense land of bays, lakes, streams, and rivers has the most plentiful and prolific fishing grounds in the world. There are lakes in the northern wilderness that no one has fished, streams flush with brook trout where no line has fallen. With a little patience, more than a little cash, and some generous help from the outfitters listed below (or any of the hundreds of others whose names are on file with provincial tourist authorities), you can arrange a fly-in wilderness fishing expedition to virtually virgin fishing grounds.

But that isn't the only lure of fishing in Canada. The true splendor of Canada's waters is that you can have superior fishing without flying anywhere. Within driving access of any major Canadian city are splendid fishing grounds; a 2-day drive will take you into country that feels as untouched as wilderness, where you will nonetheless find guides, fishing lodges of every degree of comfort and luxury, all the back-up facilities you need, and, best of all, hundreds of thousands of fish. Every area of the country has its own specialties: Atlantic salmon in the rivers of the Maritimes (and bluefin tuna in the ocean), muskie and pike in Ontario, Arctic char in the Northern Territories, steelhead trout and salmon on the Pacific coast, and lake trout everywhere. The fishing is unlimited.

Each province has its own licensing requirements, bag limits, and fishing seasons. Regional tourist offices provide this information (for addresses, see *Tourist Information,* GETTING READY TO GO), as do the fishing bureaus of the provinces (addresses in this section).

EAST

Atlantic salmon, the classic game fish of the East, is called the king of fish in this part of the country, and they are most abundant in the rivers of New Brunswick. Salmon also can be caught in Nova Scotia, Newfoundland, and Labrador. Prince Edward Island has them as well, although in smaller numbers. Catches are strictly controlled almost everywhere.

The fishing in eastern Canada is hardly limited to the king; there are plenty of less regal but equally exciting inland river and lake fish running. New Brunswick's rivers and lakes are one of North America's best resources for small-mouthed bass. Brook trout and lake trout are common on the seaboard and inland; oaunaniche (pronounced *wah-nah-nish,* a breed of landlocked salmon) in Labrador; and walleye and the hard-fighting pike in Ontario and Quebec. Because of the chill of its fresh water, Prince Edward Island has great brook trout fishing. Brook trout is also popular in Nova Scotia, but the waters most accessible by car are fished pretty heavily, so you'll do better scouting out the wilds. Early in the season (in spring), try bait and lures or streamers; later on, wet and dry flies are more effective.

The Maritimes used to be known for huge bluefin tuna; however, their numbers have diminished in the last 5 years. Throughout the Maritimes, charter boats aren't readily available until the end of the lobster season, usually around mid-July, and the fishing gets richer as the summer progresses. Other saltwater fish caught in numbers are halibut, hake (off Prince Edward Island), cod, and haddock.

The regulations on licenses and bag limits change yearly from province to province; for current regulations check with the provincial tourism department.

MIRAMICHI RIVER, near Fredericton, New Brunswick: The Miramichi is a classic salmon stream, one of the very best salmon rivers on the continent, and its name alone conjures up images of quiet mornings on serene pools and that fabled fish, the Atlantic salmon. The season for spring salmon — black salmon — lasts from mid-April until mid-May, while the Miramichi is still high, and fishing is done from a boat. Bright salmon, freshly run from the sea, can be taken from mid-June until the end of September. The waters have receded by then and the river can be waded in most places. Almost needless to say, the only way a salmon can be taken on any New Brunswick river is with a fly rod; and that's as it should be since only a fly rod is appropriate for such an elegant fish. (Anglers should be sure to check the latest regulations on catching large salmon. Immediate release is required for any salmon of at least 2 feet (63 cm) from the tip of the snout to the fork in the tail, measured along the side of the fish.) There are a number of excellent fishing lodges on the Miramichi, each with its own "beat" on the river. To mention a few: *Wilson's Sporting Camp,* Ltd., McNamee, NB E0C 1P0 (phone: 506-365-7962); *Pond's Chalet Resort,* PO Box 8, Ludlow, NB E0C 1N0 (phone: 506-369-2612); and *Wade's Fishing Lodge,* Blackville, NB E0C 1C0 (phone: 506-843-2288) from April through mid-October, or 143 Main St., Fredericton, NB E3A 1C6 (phone: 506-472-6454) the rest of the year. Information: Tourism New Brunswick, PO Box 12345, Fredericton, NB E3B 5C3 (phone: 506-453-2377 or 800-561-0123); and the Department of Natural Resources and Energy, Fish and Wildlife Branch, PO Box 6000, Fredericton, NB E3B 5H1 (phone: 506-453-2440).

HUMBER RIVER, near Corner Brook, Newfoundland: The most productive salmon river on the island, this stream full of vast pools annually gives up, between early July and late August, some 4,000 salmon averaging around 5 or 6 pounds, with 20-pounders not uncommon. The river empties into the Bay of Islands and can be fished upstream by boat or from the shore for about 20 miles from its mouth. Information: Department of Development and Tourism, PO Box 2016, St. John's, Newfoundland A1C 5R8 (phone: 800-563-6353).

GANDER RIVER, near Gander, Newfoundland: This is one of Newfoundland's top salmon rivers, and more than 3,000 salmon, averaging about 6 pounds, are landed annually; fish up to 18 pounds have been netted. The fishing, best from early July to September, is mostly done out of riverboats with outboard motors, but some of the pools on the Gander can be fished from shore. Information: Department of Development and Tourism, PO Box 2016, St. John's, Newfoundland A1C 5R8 (phone: 800-563-6353).

EXPLOITS RIVER, near Grand Falls, Newfoundland: Here is another of Newfoundland's biggest salmon rivers, emptying into Exploits Bay of Notre Dame Bay. There are about 30 miles of fishable water on the Exploits, and about 1,800 salmon are taken annually, their size running up to 18 pounds. Enhancement projects may eventually produce annual returns of 100,000 salmon. The best fishing period runs from early July to late August. Information: Department of Development and Tourism, PO Box 2016, St. John's, Newfoundland A1C 5R8 (phone: 800-563-6353).

RIVER OF PONDS, near River of Ponds, Newfoundland: Here is yet one more lure for salmon fishermen, and about 2,500 salmon are landed annually between early July, when the first run of fish enters the river, and the end of August; best fishing is usually from about July 10 to August 10. A good run of sea trout enters the river in early August. Of the many excellent pools in the River of Ponds, wide and island-dotted Hayward's Pool and Highway Pool are notable, but good fishing can also be had in the Steady, between River of Ponds Lake and Barrister's Pool, and in Island Pool, Rock Pool, Flat Pool, Dashwood Pool, Cran's Pool, and Mid-Dam Pool. Information: Department of Development and Tourism, PO Box 2016, St. John's, Newfoundland A1C 5R8 (phone: 800-563-6353).

EAGLE RIVER, near Goose Bay, Labrador, Newfoundland: This river — a hundred miles of foaming rapids, spectacular waterfalls, placid riffles, and beautiful still pools — sees its peak salmon run beginning about mid-July. It's accessible only by float plane. The nearby White Bear River, which also empties into Sandwich Bay, gets a good run of salmon as well, though somewhat later in the summer. The tidal waters at the mouths of both these rivers are noted for their abundance of big sea-run brook trout. Information: Department of Development and Tourism, PO Box 2016, St. John's, Newfoundland A1C 5R8 (phone: 800-563-6353).

ALBANY WATERSHED, north of Geraldton, Ontario: The wilderness streams and lakes that are part of the Albany River watershed offer a combination of brook trout, walleye, and northern pike fishing. Walleye and brook trout average 2 to 4 pounds — and the hard-fighting northern pike from these cold, clean waters occasionally weigh in at 25 pounds. The guides here are Ojibway Indians from the Indian villages of Fort Hope, Webequie, and Lansdowne House. They still live largely off the land by trapping and hunting and are master woodsmen. Information: Canada North Outfitting, PO Box 1230, Waterdown, Ontario L0R 2H0 (phone: 416-689-7925) or the Ministry of Natural Resources, Geraldton District, PO Box 640, Geraldton, Ontario P0T 1M0 (phone: 807-854-1030).

NORTH CHANNEL, near Little Current, Ontario: When Franklin Delano Roosevelt wanted to go on a Canadian fishing trip after the historic Quebec Conference in 1943, Canadian government officials took him to the North Channel, a rock-studded passage of water between Lake Huron's Manitoulin Island and Ontario's mainland, where FDR reportedly caught as many as 36 bass a day. Though the creel limit is now a mere half dozen daily, splake (a lake trout–brook trout hybrid) are rapidly growing in population, and the limit is 3 per day. North Channel also has good pike, muskie, and excellent jumbo perch fishing in spring and summer, plus magnificent scenery. A family vacation here will keep even non-anglers happy. Information: Espanola District Office, Ministry of Natural Resources, Box 1340, Espanola, Ontario P0P 1C0 (phone: 705-869-1330); and for a list of fishing lodges, the Northern Ontario Tourist Outfitters Association, PO Box 1140, North Bay, Ontario P1B 8K4 (phone: 705-472-5552).

GEORGIAN BAY, north of Midland, Ontario: This large bay, part of Lake Huron, which stretches some 200 miles (320 km) from Wasaga to Great Cloche Island off Little Current, offers some of the province's best fishing — not so much because of its size as its irregular shoreline and the profusion of rocky reefs, bars, and deep channels creating an excellent habitat for smallmouth bass, northern pike, walleyes, muskies, and trout. The eastern shoreline, where the water is especially shallow, offers the most productive smallmouth and pike fishing on the Bay. Parry Sound, on the eastern shore, provides good fishing for lake trout and lake trout backcross (a hybrid that is 80% lake trout and 20% brook trout); daily limit was reduced for Parry Sound from 3 to 2 in January 1988. Honey Harbour, Moon River–Woods Bay, Twelve Mile Bay, Sturgeon Bay, and Magnetawan River areas provide good to excellent muskie action. Largemouth bass are plentiful in select areas along the eastern shore. Severn Sound, to the south, is important for smallmouth, northern pike, and black crappie throughout the summer, and, in the spring and late fall, for walleye. Still farther west, the southwestern section from Wasaga Beach to Wiarton offers good rainbow and lake trout backcross angling during the spring, late summer, and fall; in winter, you can fish for them through the ice from Lion's Head to Collingwood. The northeastern area, where the French River enters the bay — accessible only by boat — provides the best walleye action. In winter, there's good ice fishing for black crappie in the Honey Harbour and Twelve Mile Bay areas, and for walleye (in February and March) in the Port Severn, Waubaushene, area.

For information, contact the Ministry of Natural Resources: Huronia District Office, Midhurst, Ontario L0L 1X0 (phone: 705-728-2900); Owen Sound District Office, 611 Ninth Ave., E, Owen Sound, Ontario N4K 3E4 (phone: 519-376-3860); Sudbury District Office, Box 3500, Station A, Sudbury, Ontario P3A 4S2 (phone: 705-522-7823);

and Lloyd Thurston, District Biologist, Parry Sound District Office, 7 Bay St., Parry Sound, Ontario P2A 1S4 (phone: 705-746-4201). For information about guides, contact the Band Manager, Shawanaga Indian Reservation, PO Box 17, Nobel, Ontario P0G 1G0 (phone: 705-366-2526).

EAGLE LAKE, near Vermilion Bay, Ontario: Until recently, the angler who wanted to fish for big muskellunge considered Eagle Lake an absolute must. Although its rocky reefs and bars with sudden drop-offs are a perfect habitat for these fish, the lake has been so heavily fished for the muskies, lake trout, and walleyes, that the fish are no longer as plentiful as they once were. Outfitters, anglers, and the Ontario Ministry of Natural Resources are working together to implement regulatory changes and undertake habitat improvements that should help return Eagle to its former status as an ideal fish habitat. Information: Dryden District Office, Ministry of Natural Resources, PO Box 730, Dryden, Ontario P8N 2Z4 (phone: 807-223-3341); for a list of lodges on the lake, the Patricia Regional Tourist Council, Box 66, Dryden, Ontario P8N 2Y7 (phone: 807-223-6792).

NORTH LAKE, Prince Edward Island: Hoping to land one of the behemoths of the sea, big-game fishermen from all over the world have fished out of this small seacoast community, and it has won a reputation as the bluefin tuna capital. Until recently, 200 to 300 fish were boated off the coast of PEI, and some years it was as many as 1,200, a catch consistently higher than that from anywhere else in Atlantic Canada, often weighing in at 900 to 1,000 pounds per fish. (The largest tuna caught here to date weighed about 1,400 pounds.) But the number of bluefin tuna is declining, and lately the catch has fallen to 150. Some epic battles between anglers and bluefin have lasted over 10 hours. Once boated, the tuna by custom becomes the property of the boat captain. But there's always time for photographs at the weigh-in ceremony before the fish is taken to the processing plant. About ten tuna charter boats cater to big-game fishermen out of North Lake, as well as several other ports. Information: *North Lake Tuna Charters,* South Lake, PEI (phone: 902-357-2055).

TUNELIK RIVER, near Kuujjuaq, formerly Fort Chimo, Quebec: The battling Arctic char is king of this stream running through the sub-Arctic tundra country of the northern part of the province, and fishing can sometimes be so good that anglers get tired of reeling them in. The average catch runs up to 10 to 15 pounds, and in August, when the spawning season is on, the males are bright red — spectacular. Tunelik also has lake trout and brook trout. The guides are Inuit, and they know the river like a Montrealer knows restaurants. Information: Tourism Quebec, CP Box 20,000, Quebec, Quebec G1K 7X2 (phone: 800-443-7000 from the eastern US; 800-361-6490 from Ontario and the Maritimes; 800-361-5405 from Quebec; 514-873-2015 from Montreal and elsewhere).

CEDAR LAKES, near Messines, Quebec: For a mixed creel, it's hard to beat the easily accessible Cedar Lakes — 4-mile-long, 2-mile-wide Big Cedar and 3-mile-long, mile-wide Little Cedar. Smallmouth bass, which pound for pound fight harder than just about any other species, are abundant here; in fact, they are the mainstay of summer fishing. Most catches weigh in at around 3 pounds, but bigger ones, ranging up to 5¾ pounds, are not unknown. The Cedars also offer good lake trout fishing (best in May and June) and fairly lively northern pike action (especially in May and June and again from July through September). Lake trout fishing in Cedar Lakes can be combined with a spring black bear hunt in the surrounding wilderness. *Moosehead Lodge* is the only establishment on the lakes. Information: Moosehead Lodge, PO Box 61, Messines, Quebec J0X 2J0 (phone: 819-465-2050) or Tourism Quebec, CP Box 20,000, Quebec, Quebec G1K 7X2 (phone: 800-443-7000 from the eastern US; 800-361-6490 from Ontario and the Maritimes; 800-361-5405 from Quebec; 514-873-2015 from Montreal and elsewhere).

GEORGE RIVER, northeast of Schefferville, Quebec: One of the world's great, barely fished salmon rivers, this spectacular stream flows from Michikamau Lake north through the sub-Arctic wilderness and finally drains into Ungava Bay. The season's first angling, right after ice-out when the streams are swollen with melt water, is for "black" salmon; silvers appear, fresh from the sea, in late July and run through August and September. Resident brook trout and lake trout can be taken all summer. In September, the salmon fisherman can combine a fishing trip with a hunt for caribou, which migrate through the George River valley by the thousands at that time of year. During July and August, only fly fishing is allowed on Quebec's designated salmon rivers (the George among them). Information: Gabriel Biron, Ministry of Tourism, 800 Square Victoria, 2nd Floor, Room 260, Montreal, Quebec H4Z 1C3 (phone: 514-873-7977).

WEST

Western Canada can fulfill an angler's greatest expectations. Great Bear and Great Slave lakes in the Northwest Territories have become legendary for trout fishing. British Columbia's superabundance of trout and salmon have made bass seem run-of-the-mill to local anglers. Lake trout thrive in the Yukon, while the prairie provinces are rich with walleye and northern pike as well as big lake trout and, in Manitoba, even trophy brook trout.

KNIGHT INLET, Minstral Island, near Campbell River, British Columbia: From April to September, spring salmon are the rule here rather than the exception, but there's a limit to the number of large spring you can catch. Big tyees are regularly caught from May through August, while coho are taken from July through September. April and May are the best months to go after trout and steelhead. And given the plentiful population of Dungeness crab, anglers and their families can go crabbing in the bays. Accommodations, and fishing guides who know the best spots intimately, are available at the *Hoeya Hilton* (accessible only by float planes from Vancouver or Campbell River), and at *Spring Island.* Information (for both Hoeya Hilton and Spring Island): Blair McLean, Hoeya Hilton, Box 818, Campbell River, BC V9W 6Y4 (604-286-6016).

DISCOVERY PASSAGE, Quadra Island, near Campbell River, British Columbia: The Inside Passage, from the Queen Charlotte Islands to Vancouver, is salmon country, and there are concentrations around Rivers Inlet to the north and the Vancouver-Victoria area to the south. But if big chinook salmon is your game, the Discovery Passage — the 15-mile-long, mile-wide stretch of water that runs from the bottom of Quadra Island to Seymour Narrows — is where you should fish. Chinooks of up to 77 pounds — which the area Indians call tyee, or big salmon — have been taken. Bucktailing — trolling a bucktail fly with fly-fishing tackle — is generally the method to use from April through June, and fly casting is the sport in September and October. Some locals say that the best time for tyee is during August and the first week in September. Most fishermen, however, go for the ferocious coho, which hit hard and then run, leaping like acrobats as the end approaches; it's not uncommon to see schools of them slashing through herring and shrimp from April to October. The best time for casting to them, both from the shore and from boats, is September and October.

Almost as outstanding as the fishing is the scenery — miles and miles of fir-clad mountains that rise majestically from the ocean, hundreds of islands tucked away in inlets and bays, tiny beaches where you can dig for clams and oysters and cook your catch. And there are miles of rivers and streams full of steelhead and cutthroat. The area is well known for its killer whales, seals, and sea lions, and the population of bald eagles is one of the world's largest. The celebrated April Point Fly Fishing Club makes its headquarters at *April Point Lodge and Fishing Resort,* a first class operation owned and operated by the Peterson family for 40 years. The fresh seafood in the dining room is one of the great après-fishing bonuses of a fishing excursion here. Information: April

Point Lodge and Fishing Resort, PO Box 1, Campbell River, BC V9W 4Z9 (phone: 604-285-2222).

UPPER SUSTUT AND FINLAY WATERSHEDS, northwest of Fort St. John, British Columbia: For wilderness fishing, with both fly tackle and spinning gear, nothing can beat the mountain streams, rivers, and lakes of the rugged Cassiar Mountains. The Dolly Varden and rainbow trout run big here. The best time for trout is from May to mid-September; Dolly Varden are plentiful from spring through summer. There is a feeling of remoteness here that is seldom found farther south. The striking scenery and abundant wildlife — including moose, caribou, mountain goats, stone sheep, and grizzly bear — are an added bonus. Information: Ministry of Environment, Information Services Branch, 810 Blanshard St., Victoria, BC V8V 1X5 (phone: 604-387-9422).

NUELTIN LAKE, north of Thompson, Manitoba: On this 120-mile-long lake astride the Manitoba–Northwest Territories border, you'll find superb angling for Arctic grayling averaging a good 3 pounds, and, in the many secluded, underfished bays, fine northern pike action. But the lake trout you pull in are what really put this place on the map. There are strains of lakers here that have learned to use river currents so that they fight like fish twice their size — and when you have a fish on the line as big as the ones in Nueltin, commonly up to 45 pounds, you have a real battle on your hands. Nueltin has outclassed every other Manitoba lake in the lake trout Master Angler Award. The place to stay is *Nueltin Fly-In Lodge,* Manitoba's most northerly lodge. Located on the fringe of the province's last stand of black spruce, only 20 miles (32 km) from the Northwest Territories border, it can be reached only by air. Information: in winter, *Nueltin Fly-In Lodge,* P.O. Box 1561, Morden, Manitoba R0G 1N0 (phone: 204-822-4143); in summer, Box 1229, Thompson, Manitoba R8N 1P1 (phone: 204-284-3247); or Travel Manitoba, Dept. 9269, 155 Carlton St., 7th Floor, Winnipeg, Manitoba R3C 0V8 (phone: 800-665-0040 ext. 269 or 204-945-3777 collect).

BRABANT ISLAND, Mackenzie River, near Hay River, Northwest Territories: This section of the Mackenzie River, not far from Great Slave Lake, is outstanding for northern pike and walleye fishing, with superb Arctic grayling angling in both the river and local feeder streams. For pike fishing, you should bring a good selection of big Red Devil and Pixie spoons; for walleyes, an assortment of jigs and spinners. Arctic grayling, a fly fisherman's delight, are best attracted with black ant or black gnat fly patterns and small Mepps lures. The area's *Brabant Lodge* has modern, fully equipped cabins. Information: Brabant Lodge, 7821 22nd St. S.E., Calgary, Alberta T2C 1Y8 (phone: 800-661-9255 or 403-279-5286), or PO Box 1095, Hay River, Northwest Territories X0E 0R0 (phone: 403-874-2600); and TravelArctic, Government of the Northwest Territories, Yellowknife, Northwest Territories X1A 2L9 (phone: 403-873-7200), or its Tourism Industry Association (phone: 800-661-0788).

GREAT BEAR LAKE, north of Yellowknife, Northwest Territories: For many North American anglers, any mention of this small ocean, 150 miles long and 250 miles wide, is going to conjure up visions of giant lake trout — as well it should. Great Bear Lake has produced more trophy lakers on rod and reel than any other lake on the continent, and the world records for lake trout (65 pounds), as well as those for grayling and lake whitefish, were set in the area. Most lake trout that are taken — and you can expect to catch hundreds in a week — weigh in at 8 to 12 pounds, while grayling run in the 1- to 2-pound class, with 3½- and 4-pounders not all that uncommon. Arctic char is found a short hop away in the Tree River, accessible through *Plummers Great Bear Lodge* (phone: 204-774-5775), an outpost camp. Reaching any of these fishing grounds is not that difficult, and most lodge owners offer transportation from Alberta as part of their package price. Information: TravelArctic, Government of the Northwest Territories, Yellowknife, Northwest Territories X1A 2L9 (phone: 403-873-7200), or its Tourism Industry Association (phone: 800-661-0788).

GREAT SLAVE LAKE, near Yellowknife, Northwest Territories: Great Slave was the first of the great far northern lakes to be discovered by fishermen and is now famous for excellent lake trout and northern pike. Arctic grayling abound in many feeder streams. Fly fishermen can test their skill trying to land whitefish, which can be as challenging as trout. Information: TravelArctic, Government of the Northwest Territories, Yellowknife, Northwest Territories X1A 2L9 (phone: 403-873-7200), or its Tourism Industry Association (phone: 800-661-0788).

LAC LA RONGE AREA, north central Saskatchewan: This massive lake and surrounding waters, including the Churchill River system, provide northern pike, walleye, lake trout, whitefish, and grayling. Lac la Ronge Provincial Park, Saskatchewan's largest (931,000 acres), encompasses 100 lakes. Drive in to this center of northern aviation on an excellent paved highway. Fly-ins are available to 200-plus outfitting camps in the province. Information: Tourism Saskatchewan, 1919 Saskatchewan Dr., Regina, Saskatchewan S4P 3V7 (phone: 800-667-7191).

HANSON LAKE ROAD AREA, northeastern Saskatchewan: Winding some 240 miles through magnificent Canadian Shield country, this route takes anglers to some of the best fishing in the north. Lakes like Little Bear, Deschambault, Jan, and Big Sandy offer some of the most diverse fishing in the province. The route also provides access to the Churchill River system. Many parks, campsites, resorts, and outfitters provide excellent services and access to remote fly-in camps. Information: Tourism Saskatchewan, 1919 Saskatchewan Dr., Regina, Saskatchewan S4P 3V7 (phone: 800-667-7191).

Sailing Canada's Many Waters

With its literally thousands of miles of coastline, Canada offers more good sailing than almost any other country in the world. Not only are there the fjordlike shores of British Columbia and the salt-scented Maritimes, but there are also hundreds of lakes, holding as much as half of the world's fresh water. As you might expect, Canadians are enthusiastic sailors, particularly around Halifax, Vancouver, and Toronto, where there are delightful sails to be had through the channels and lagoons of the idyllic Toronto Islands at the harbor's mouth, and in the area around Vancouver Island and the nearby Gulf Islands. Either area offers immense variety, so if you like to sail, these could well keep you happy. But depending on your inclinations, you might look farther afield, at areas more remote from population centers such as those described below. For a list of the provincial yachting associations, contact the Canadian Yachting Association, 1600 James Naismith Dr., Suite 504, Gloucester, Ontario K1B 5N4 (phone: 613-748-5687).

And when you do begin planning in earnest, be sure to contact the following: the provincial tourist authority for lists of marinas; and Transport Canada, Public Affairs, Tower C, Place de Ville, Ottawa, Ontario K1A 0N5 (phone: 613-990-2309) for a copy of the *Canadian Coast Guard Safe Boating Guide*, the *Directory of Nautical Information*, and other useful brochures. Canadian Hydrographic Service offices have chart catalogues showing chart coverage, related nautical publications, and an international dealership list. You can contact them at either the Chart Distribution Office, Department of Fisheries and Oceans, PO Box 8080, 1675 Russell Rd., Ottawa, Ontario K1G 3H6 (phone: 613-998-4931), or the Department of Fisheries and Oceans, Institute of Ocean Sciences, Patricia Bay, 9860 W Saanich Rd., PO Box 6000, Sidney, BC V8L 4B2 (phone: 604-356-6358). Also, *Canadian Yachting* magazine (227 Front St. E., Suite 100, Toronto, Ontario M5A 1E8; phone: 416-368-0185) and *Pacific Yachting* (202-1132 Hamilton St., Vancouver, BC V6B 2S2; phone: 604-687-1581) both publish cruising and charter guides in every issue.

GREAT CRUISING, EAST TO WEST

NOVA SCOTIA'S COAST: The shipbuilders of this ocean-washed province were famous for making square-riggers; today, they build smaller boats — both fishing and pleasure craft — and rent many of them by the day or the week, with or without crew, for cruises along the province's over 4,500 miles of coastline. There's good cruising all along the rocky bay- and inlet-notched headlands and among the scattered off-lying islands from Halifax to Shelburne, particularly around St. Margaret's and Mahone Bay just west of Halifax. But during the summer, fog rolls in with regularity, and because of the numerous rocks and shoals, you have to know what you're doing. The Northumberland Strait between Pugwash and Canso Strait is another good bet. There's no fog to speak of and very little tide; the water is warm — warmer, in fact, than anywhere else on the Atlantic coast north of the Carolinas — so you can take a dip after you drop anchor. The Bras d'Or Lakes offer the area's most sheltered saltwater cruising and lovely scenic shoreline without the problems of fog or tide. Throughout Nova Scotia's cruising area, anchorages are generally just a few hours' sail apart, and a dozen or more yacht clubs welcome visitors. Information: Nova Scotia Department of Tourism, PO Box 130, Halifax, NS B3J 2M7 (phone: 902-424-4247).

COASTAL NEW BRUNSWICK: The coasts of Prince Edward Island, Nova Scotia, and New Brunswick — so compactly arranged to shelter each other from the blustery Atlantic — together offer some of Canada's finest cruising waters, and sailors head with equal readiness for destinations such as Summerside on Prince Edward Island; Mahone Bay, Nova Scotia; and Pointe-du-Chêne, New Brunswick. Here, the prime cruising area is up and down the Northumberland Strait between New Brunswick and PEI, where you can tie up in tiny fishing villages or little coves, or just cruise along and enjoy the view — mainly of flat-to-rolling countryside occasionally punctuated by a pier or a wharf and a spiky cluster of fishing boats. Information: Tourism New Brunswick, PO Box 12345, Fredericton, NB E3B 5C3 (phone: 800-561-0123 from mainland US and Canada).

ST. JOHN RIVER SYSTEM, New Brunswick: This is unusual cruising for the Maritimes — ideal for families, for dinghy sailors who want to cruise, and for just about anybody else who wants to see what it's like to charter before getting into really big craft. Twenty- and thirty-foot craft are fine on these inland streams. They're tree-lined for the most part — pastoral on the upper reaches, fjordlike lower down. Charters can be arranged. Information: Maritime Bareboat Charters, Ltd., PO Box 99, Grand Bay, NB E0G 1W0 (phone: 506-454-3525).

SHORES OF PRINCE EDWARD ISLAND: The most fantastic thing about the view of this 150-mile-long, 25-mile-wide island, as seen from the water, is the patchwork quilt effect of the fields — bright red when they're freshly plowed — and the forests and the grasslands, whose greens, especially in early June, will dazzle you with their brightness. The land is relatively flat to low and rolling; here and there you'll pass a cluster of farm buildings or a little fishing village, a conglomeration of white houses, piers, wharves, masts, and hulls. The north shore, sparsely settled and relatively barren, is characterized by longer stretches of beaches and more heavily breaking seas than the south shore; there are fishing harbors in the north, but navigation there is tricky because shifting sands often fill them up. Because of the protection afforded by New Brunswick and Nova Scotia to the south, such difficulties plague the south shore less frequently; this is where you'll probably do most of your sailing. The Magdalen Islands, some 80 miles (129 km) to the north, are another favored destination. Information: PEI Sailing Excursions, Victoria By-The-Sea, PEI C0A 2G0 (phone: 902-658-2227); the Charlottetown Yacht Club, PO Box 1024, Charlottetown, PEI C1A 7M4 (phone: 902-892-9065); and the Silver Fox Curling and Yacht Club, 110 Water St., Summerside, PEI C1N 1A9 (phone: 902-436-2153).

THOUSAND ISLANDS AND THE BAY OF QUINTE, Ontario: This province has its fair share of lakes and waterways, from the Great Lakes north to Hudson Bay. Toronto citizens are such wildly enthusiastic sailors, in fact, the harbor is so full on weekends that some locals assert they'd rather contend with a highway. But for vacation cruising, one of the prime destinations is this area at the eastern end of Lake Ontario, where the lake flows into the St. Lawrence River. The Thousand Islands — over 1,700 pink granite or limestone outcroppings ranged between Kingston and Brockville — offer good fishing, fine swimming, delightful scenery. St. Lawrence Islands National Park provides mooring, camping, picnic facilities, and interpretive programs throughout the Islands (see listing later in this section). The Bay of Quinte — long, narrow, and irregular — ranks among the province's prettiest backwaters, and some people prefer it to the Thousand Islands nearby because of the near absence of commercial and power-cruising traffic. The bay, in the heart of historic Prince Edward County, is flanked by prosperous farmlands, wooded slopes, limestone escarpments, sandy beaches, and several of Ontario's oldest towns; occasionally, you'll sense yourself in the heart of the Canadian North. To get to the Bay of Quinte from the west, you can travel around the Isthmus of Murray or, like most boaters, traverse the straight-as-an arrow, 7-mile Murray Canal, near Trenton — a lovely trip. The bay is also the southern terminus of the Trent-Severn Waterway, a 240-mile inland waterway connecting Lake Ontario to Georgian Bay through the heart of central Ontario. Most services are to be found in Kingston. Information: Eastern Ontario Travel Association, 209 Ontario St., Kingston, Ontario K7L 2Z1 (613-549-3682); Ontario Tourism (phone: 800-268-3735, from continental US and Canada, except Yukon); St. Lawrence Islands National Park, Box 469, RR3, Mallorytown, Ontario K0E 1R0 (phone: 613-923-5261); Venture Yacht Charters, Portsmouth Olympic Harbour, 53 Yonge St., Kingston, Ontario K7M 1E4 (phone: 613-549-1007); the Portsmouth Olympic Harbour, 53 Yonge St., Kingston, Ontario K7M 1E4 (phone: 613-544-9842); and the Murray Canal, c/o the Trent-Severn Waterway, PO Box 567, Peterborough, Ontario K9J 6Z6 (phone: 705-742-9267).

ONTARIO'S GEORGIAN BAY AND NORTH CHANNEL: For fine vacation cruising, a Toronto sailor is apt to travel to Lake Huron's spectacular Georgian Bay, which lies about 60 miles (96 km) northwest of Toronto across the neck of land that separates the city from the lake. The vast, bay- and cove-notched, island-dotted expanse of water known as the North Channel — contained to the south by hundred-mile-long Manitoulin Island and to the north by the Ontario mainland — ranks among the prime cruising areas of the world. You can sun yourself on a lonely rock, pick blueberries the size of grapes, fish, swim, explore long fjordlike bays, and spend your nights anchored in the lee of an island or tied up in a tiny cove where it's just you, the water, and the stars. Or you can dock at one of the many resorts and marinas concentrated around Killarney, on the mainland, and Little Current, on Manitoulin Island, for a good meal and some friendly conversation. Powerboating has always been popular, but sailing is taking over, as it is costly to gas up engines; a few 25-to-35-foot sailboats are available for charters. Information: Ontario Travel, Queen's Park, Toronto, Ontario M7A 2E5 (phone: 800-268-3735 or 416-965-4008); and Ontario Sailing Association, 1220 Sheppard Ave. E., Willowdale, Ontario M2K 2X1 (phone: 416-495-4240).

LAKE OF THE WOODS, Ontario-Manitoba: Discovered by Jacques de Noyon in 1688, this longtime section of the fur traders' canoe route between Montreal and the prairies, the largest link in an intricately interconnected chain of lakes, is a mere 70 miles in length and 50 miles in width. But when you figure the multitudinous zigs and zags in the ragged shoreline of the mainland and the over 14,000 scattered islands, the coastline measures 65,000 miles. So complex is the layout that you could sail for an entire season and still be a stranger to the many winding bays, cinched channels, and unexplored landfalls and still not have had your fill of the marvelous scenery —

spruce forests scattered with handsome boulders, clear waters: classic Canadian Shield country. Sailing is extremely popular, and there are wide-ranging facilities for boaters in Minnesota at Warroad, along the north shore of Lake of the Woods and in Kenora, Ontario. The latter, a handsomely sited town of about 10,000, which was once known as Rat Portage because of the muskrats that lived in the area, is the home of a museum devoted to local history and the like; during the summer, there's a lively schedule of fairs, festivals, and regattas, including LOWISA, one of North America's biggest regattas (probably the very biggest staged on an inland lake). There are also cruises on the M.S. *Kenora* four times a day, covering about 18 miles in and around the islands of the north end of the lake. Fishing — for muskies, lake trout, pickerel, and bass — is almost as productive as it was back in fur trading days. In addition, if Lake of the Woods isn't enough for you, travel farther down the Winnipeg River to the west. The Keewatin Boatlift will put you into the Winnipeg River system in a matter of minutes. Information: Kenora Sailing Club, c/o R. H. Aitken, 1511 Beach Rd., Keewatin, Ontario P0X 1C0 (phone: 807-547-2533); the Publicity Board of Kenora Information Centre, 1500 Hwy. 17 E., Kenora, Ontario P9N 1M3 (phone: 807-468-8233 or 807-468-9441); Stephen MacPhee, Canadian Hydrographic Service, Department of Fisheries and Oceans, PO Box 8080, Ottawa, Ontario K1G 3H6; and the Ontario Ministry of Natural Resources, PO Box 5080, Kenora, Ontario P9N 3X9 (phone: 807-468-9841).

LAKE WINNIPEG, Manitoba: This 9,416-square-mile lake, 450 miles long and cinched at the center like a Gibson girl's corseted waist, is the largest body of water lying entirely inside Canada south of the sub-Arctic; and though you won't spot all that many sails in the northern basin even on a sunny day, that's mostly owing to the relatively small size of the province's population — just over a million. The lake's potential for cruising is practically unlimited. The waistline is the site of a cluster of islands, a number of beautiful natural harbors, the handsome Hecla Provincial Park, and the modern *Gull Harbour Resort and Conference Center.* South of these, the lake's western shore is flat and prairie-like enough that you think immediately of Big Sky country; east of there, and north of Hecla Island, you're in Canadian Shield country again. But here, unlike at Lake of the Woods, the shoreline is smooth rather than jagged, and there are long sails between anchorages. The fact that there are few settlements in the north only heightens the sense of isolation you can feel as a result, and brings home most strongly how it must have been for the earliest trappers who settled here in the days of the founding of the Hudson's Bay Company. The few communities that you encounter nowadays are, for the most part, connected with the several reservations that border the lake, except in the south. There are marinas and yacht clubs at Winnipeg Beach, Selkirk, Victoria Beach, Silver Harbour, and Gimli, site of North America's largest Icelandic settlement and, in early August, of a riotous celebration of this heritage. A good deal of the history of Canada — and, indeed, of all of North America — was played out around Lake Winnipeg, and you can't fail to get interested when you come for a visit. Information: Manitoba Sailing Association, 1700 Ellice Ave., Winnipeg, Manitoba R3H 0B1 (phone: 204-985-4000), and Travel Manitoba, Dept. 9269, 155 Carlton St., 7th Floor, Winnipeg, Manitoba R3C 0V8 (phone: 800-665-0040 ext. 269 or 204-945-3777 collect).

KOOTENAY LAKE, British Columbia: Snow-capped mountains plunge right to the water's edge, and sandy beaches edge the shoreline. The scenery is indescribably dramatic. This area is growing, albeit slowly, and many people have just begun to take a look at sailing as a boating option. Kootenay Lake is a place whose time has come, and one of the local marinas has opened a branch at Woodbury, which is one of the largest facilities of its kind on any inland lake in the country. You can sail the lake year-round here, because Kootenay never freezes; and the kind of winter day when the mercury hits 50F (10C) and the wind blows from the south is more than a sometime thing. In summer, a number of the owners of the 120 sailboats moored here head for Crawford Bay and its popular beach; anyone can join the informal good times. But if you want to keep to yourself, there's no dearth of tiny coves within a quarter hour's sail — or, for that matter, of productive fishing holes: The cold, clear waters are full of lingcod, Rocky Mountain whitefish, kokanee (landlocked sockeye salmon), Dolly Varden, and world-famous trophy rainbow trout. Because of the cross valleys that cut through the mountains at frequent intervals, the prevailing northwest-southeast breezes are occasionally interrupted by squallish winds, sometimes doing a complete reversal in a matter of minutes. Most facilities are in Kaslo, Balfour, and Nelson. For information on regattas: West Kootenay Sailing Club, John Stephens, Commodore, 2050 Georgia St., Rossland, BC V0G 1Y0 (phone: 604-362-9446); or Kootenay Lake Yacht Club, Dave Simpson, Secretary-Treasurer, RR1, Nelson, BC V1L 5P4 (phone: 604-825-9337). For information on chartering a sailboat: Kokanee Yacht Charters, RR3, Nelson, BC V1L 5P6 (phone: 604-825-9235 or 825-9364). For general information: Kootenay Country Tourist Association, Site 2-11, Castlegar Airport, RR1, Castlegar, BC V1N 3H7 (phone: 604-365-8486); Kaslo Marina, Box 700, Kaslo, BC V0G 1M0 (phone: 604-353-2341).

COASTAL BRITISH COLUMBIA: Here, along some of the province's 4,390 miles of coastline, there's scenery on a grand scale, like practically nowhere else on earth, in spades, all the way from Victoria on Vancouver Island, and Tsawwassen, in the south, to the Queen Charlottes and Prince Rupert, which face them across Hecate Strait just south of the Alaska border: some 2,000 square miles of water in all. The mountains plunge practically to the water's edge; the shores of the little bays and inlets and the literally thousands of islands are upholstered with forests of primeval evergreens. Then there's the sky: Blue. Bluer. Bluest. You can stop to sun yourself on pebbled beaches, go for a swim, fish for salmon or other finny creatures in the channels, dig for clams, play the rockhound in the coves. You can travel for hundreds of miles and never see a soul. But you've only to detour a little to hit a settlement — a yacht club, a government marina, a fishing village, or any one of a couple of dozen provincial marine parks. And because of the moderating influence of the Pacific Ocean, you can enjoy all of this year-round; sometimes your views take in white-blanketed ski slopes with little skiers moving around like microbes above and water skiers down below. Though the number of pleasure craft owners in British Columbia, some hundred thousand in all, pretty much ensures that there will be activity all up and down the coast, there are some areas that seem to be favorites: the Gulf Islands in the Strait of Georgia around Vancouver; the hundred miles or so beyond that; the Juan de Fuca Strait around Victoria; and the very isolated Queen Charlotte Islands, 400 miles (640 km) to the north, a superb cruising ground in their own right. Information: Ministry of Parks, 1610 Indian River Dr., North Vancouver, BC V7G 1L3 (phone: 604-929-1291) for a list of marine parks, and the British Columbia Sailing Association, 1300 Discovery St., Vancouver, BC V6R 4L9 (phone: 604-222-8155).

CRUISING SCHOOLS

There are nearly 600 establishments that teach sailing of a small boat or dinghy — but learning to cruise is a lot more complicated, and there are proportionately fewer organizations willing to train the novice. A complete list can be obtained from the Canadian Yachting Association, 1600 James Naismith Dr., Suite 504, Gloucester, Ottawa, Ontario K1B 5N4 (phone: 613-748-5687). Here is one of the best:

ATLANTIC YACHTING ACADEMY, headquartered in Dartmouth, Nova Scotia: At the school's various locations, good sailors (with experience on the Great Lakes and other fresh waters) can learn to deal with ocean currents and tides; beginners can get acquainted with the difference between port and starboard; and Pacific coast dwellers and Midwesterners alike can experience the waters of Atlantic Canada. These include small, secluded coves, where people can anchor and never see another boat, and the pretty fishing villages — not to mention the wonderful Bras d'Or lakes — where it's possible to tie up in a cove, within arm's reach of a stand of spruce trees whose scent fills the air with an aroma you won't soon forget. Ken Isles, the school's founder and representative of the Cruise Training of the Nova Scotia Sailing Association, has been active in the movement to standardize sailing instruction in the US and Canada, and he uses these national guidelines in his day- and week-long courses as well as in his navigation and seamanship programs. Registered and certified by the *Canadian Yachting Association,* the academy's instructors are certified by the *CYA* and the Department of Transport. The academy is affiliated with the *International Sailing Schools Association* and awards national and international certification. Information: Atlantic Yachting Academy, PO Box 972 DMPS, Nova Scotia B2Y 3Z6; or at the academy's location, Dartmouth Marina, 1 North St., Dartmouth, Nova Scotia B2Y 1H1 (phone: 902-464-0160).

Canoeing and Rafting

Eons ago, when the glaciers crawled across Canada, they scraped the bedrock bare of soil, gouged out great gaping holes and filled them with water, polished giant boulders and scattered them willy-nilly across the land. The so-called Canadian Shield, the 1.6-million-square-mile horseshoe-shaped expanse of rock that was created in this way is Canada's single most characteristic geological feature. Its vast network of river- and stream-linked lakes has been shaping history here since the days of the Indians.

The rivers, streams, and lakes were the highways along which the French and the English explored the land. Later, to facilitate shipping in strategic areas where rapids or waterfalls made navigation difficult, canals and lock systems were added. When thus combined, Canada's network of waterways ranks among the most extensive in the world. In the Northwest Territories alone, there are enough streams that 100,000 people could canoe through 100,000 lifetimes and still not cover them all. The Mackenzie River — Canada's Mississippi, the trunk of the nation's longest river system — flows some 10,071 miles from its source into the Arctic Ocean. The Quetico area of southern Ontario seems immense when you're paddling through, but it's hardly more than a freckle on a map compared to even such relatively small areas as the Algonquin Provincial Park in southeastern Ontario, or Quebec's La Vérendrye Provincial Park. Of Ontario's 250,000 lakes and 20,000 miles of streams, the Ministry of Natural Resources has documented some 14,000 miles of the most practical water routes.

No two areas are quite alike. In the southernmost parts of Ontario and Quebec, the Canadian Shield is upholstered with the northernmost reaches of the deciduous forests, which present a striking contrast to the so-called boreal forests of conifers that you find farther north, which differ yet again from the tundra of northern Quebec, Labrador, and the Northwest Territories. The farther you go from the cities, the fewer people you'll see.

The canoeing waters described below are only representative of those detailed voluminously elsewhere. *Canoe Canada,* by Nick Nickels, covers some 600 canoe routes, their water conditions and history, and the outfitters that serve them. (Although the book is now out of print and no longer available from its publisher, Van Nostrand Reinhold, you may be able to find it in your local library.) Just where you decide to go will depend ultimately on the kind of fishing you enjoy, the time of year you're going, your own canoeing and camping experience, the time you have to spend, and your desire or reluctance for rapids and portages. Once you've fixed on a route or an area, the provincial tourism offices can furnish you with lists of canoe outfitters and rental agencies whose brochures usually provide excellent descriptions of what you'll find when you get there. A note to a few of them will yield stacks of material.

Most outfitters can provide maps, but in some areas you may find it necessary to order the special Canadian National Topographic Survey Maps — cartographic reproductions of aerial photographs that pinpoint lakes, rivers, roads, buildings, bridges, and some 90 other manmade and natural features. Those scaled at 1:250,000 will give you the general location, while the 1:50,000 series, each map covering approximately one day's paddle, is good for details. To order them and the map indexes that tell you which maps you need, contact the Canada Map Office, 615 Booth St., Ottawa, Ontario K1A 0E9 (phone: 613-952-7000). Also, ask for their two useful brochures, *How to Use a Map* and *Maps and Wilderness Canoeing,* free of charge.

ONTARIO'S VAST PROVINCIAL PARKS: The hardwoods in the forests that cover the ridges and hills of this part of the Canadian Shield just across the US border give the area a look and smell all its own, and for many people canoeing here and canoeing in Canada are one and the same. The Algonquin, Killarney, and Quetico provincial parks are immensely popular, yet there is plenty of room to roam even in the busy summer months. Algonquin Provincial Park, which occupies some 2,925 square miles of highlands between the Ottawa River and Lake Huron's Georgian Bay, boasts over a thousand miles of canoe routes and good fishing for lake and brook trout. Some of the notable destinations here include ultra-deep, cliff-ringed Lake Eustache; the breathtaking Natch Rapids on the Petawawa River (towered over by 300-foot-high cliffs); and Hailstorm Creek, where you may see moose browsing. But that's not the end of it. To the northwest, there's Quetico Provincial Park, with 900 miles of its own water routes that are essentially as the Ojibwa Indians and the voyageurs found them; the portages you use (generally speaking, shorter than those in Algonquin) are often the same ones trod by the famous fur trade governor Sir George Simpson, the explorer La Vérendrye, and the itinerant artist Paul Kane. Additional routes are found in 118,600-acre Killarney Provincial Park, near Georgian Bay. Day trips are possible here, but the area is more appropriate for outings of about 3 days or longer, and the scenery is stunning: white quartzite ridges and crystal-clear waters. Outfitting services are in Atikokan and Thunder Bay for trips into Quetico and the lakes to the west and north outside the park; in Dwight, South River, and Whitney for Algonquin Park trips; in Killarney Village for trips into the Killarney park (due to Killarney Park's popularity, visitors are encouraged to make reservations); and, for paddles in the park proper, at the Portage and Opeongo stores (Algonquin Park, Ontario P0A 1B0; phone: 705-633-5622 in summer only), which have been equipping canoeists for decades. For overviews of canoe routes in the three parks, write to Ministry of Natural Resources at the Algonquin Park District Office, Box 219, Whitney, Ontario K0J 2M0 (phone: 705-633-5572); the Atikokan District Office, 108 Saturn Ave., Atikokan, Ontario P0T 1C0 (phone: 807-597-2735) for Quetico details; and, for Killarney information, the Sudbury District Office, Box 3500, Station A, Sudbury, Ontario P3A 4S2 (phone: 705-522-7823). For listings of outfitters, contact Ontario Travel, Queen's Park, Toronto, Ontario M7A 2E5 (phone: 800-268-3735 or 416-965-4008). Guided trips are offered by Black Feather Wilderness Adventures, 1341 Wellington St. W., Ottawa, Ontario K1Y 3B8 (phone: 613-722-9717) or 40 Wellington St. E., Toronto, M5E 1C7 (phone: 416-861-1555).

NORTHERN ONTARIO: The northern reaches of this 412,582-square-mile province, south of James and Hudson bays, lie in Canadian Shield country. There are literally hundreds of thousands of lakes and as many more streams here, and the huge expanses of cool silent forests, patched here and there with outcroppings of polished rock and scattered with huge glacial boulders, are often impenetrable except by canoe. Many of the waterways are virtually unexplored, and there are areas where you can paddle through clear streams that are seen by only a handful of people in a year. Some 53,000 square miles are drained by the swift-flowing Albany River and its tributaries. Among the province's great wilderness waterways, the Albany was once a major fur trade route between York Factory on Hudson Bay, Lake of the Woods, and Winnipeg. On the upper reaches of the river, which flows through the middle of northern Ontario from its headwaters at Lake St. Joseph, you can still portage the many rapids and falls on wide pathways used by the oversize canoes known as York boats. The pools at the base of the rapids and falls make for some of the river's best fishing. Tributaries include the Kabinakagami, Kenogami, Little Current, Nagagami, and Ogoki rivers. But there are hundreds of routes you can follow. Most canoe trips here are fly-in propositions. Outfitters are located in the areas around Geraldton, Hearst, Longlac, Nakina, Armstrong, and Sioux Lookout. For a list, contact Ontario Travel, Queen's Park, Toronto, Ontario M7A 2E5 (phone: 800-268-3735 or 416-965-4008). The Ministry of Natural Resources Public Information Centre (Room 1640, Whitney Block, 99 Wellesley St. W, Queen's Park, Toronto, Ontario M7A 1W3; phone: 416-965-3081) publishes the helpful *Canoe Routes of Ontario* ($9.95), which gives an overview of the principal watersheds and canoeing possibilities. For information about both guided and unguided trips, contact Wildwaters Nature Tours & Expeditions, 119 N. Cumberland St., PO Box 2777, Thunder Bay, Ontario P7A 4M3 (phone: 807-345-0111).

RIDEAU CANAL, Kingston to Ottawa, Ontario: This 123-mile-long waterway between Lake Ontario and the Ottawa River was built in the early 19th century as a part of Canada's defense against the US. It now is in use as a recreational waterway, as gradually increasing numbers of boats cruise its waters every summer. Above all, the trip is a pleasant one. You'll go through 45 locks, masterpieces made of hand-hewn stone blocks, all but three of which are still operated by hand. Everyone stops at Jones Falls for the awe-inspiring view of the massive horseshoe dam built more than 150 years ago by the British army under the supervision of Lt. Colonel John By. The lockmasters can tell you about the odd-shaped buildings at some of the lock stations, originally designed as fortified structures, and fill you in on other points of interest in the area. Newboro Lock brings you to the full height of the canal where you begin a gradual descent through the Rideau Lakes. One of Ontario's fine cruising and fishing grounds, with a wealth of tree-tufted islands, it is surrounded by forests, fields, weedy shallows, sleepy little villages and towns, cottages, and marinas. At the canal's northern extremity, the Ottawa Locks, you begin a fascinating 79-foot descent through 8 flight locks to the Ottawa River. Information: Superintendent, Rideau Canal, 12 Maple Ave. N., Smiths Falls, Ontario K7A 1Z5 (phone: 613-283-5170), and, for rental information, Ontario Travel, Queen's Park, Toronto, Ontario M7A 2E5 (phone: 800-268-3735 or 416-965-4008).

OTTAWA RIVER, near Pembroke, Ontario: Canada has bigger rivers than this tributary of the St. Lawrence, which was once used by the voyageurs on their journeys between Montreal and Lake Huron, and many of the paddle-snapping rapids that challenged the early Canadians have been tamed by hydro dams. But the island-sprinkled Rocher-Fendu area, 1½ hours west of the nation's capital and just east of Algonquin Park, is a stretch of water so rough you'd want to run it only in a large rubber raft — even when it's at summer levels. When the river is at flood stage during May and June, the towering explosion waves are the equal of wild water anywhere in the world. If you can't sample Canada's whitewater in the West, don't miss the 1- and -2-day trips on the Ottawa. There's also lots of off-water activity. Information: Wilderness Tours, Box 89, Beachburg, Ontario K0J 1C0 (phone: 613-646-2241 or -2291).

BRITISH COLUMBIA'S THOMPSON, FRASER, AND CHILCOTIN RIVERS BY RAFT: Raft tour operators on these three dynamic streams have been turning city slickers into river rats for years. The big, swift-flowing Fraser, the granddaddy of

Canadian streams and one of the largest and deepest in all of North America, flows at an average of 150,000 cubic feet per second, as compared to the mighty Colorado, whose maximum flow is regulated at 25,000 cubic feet per second. In some areas, the Fraser dips and dives past the ruins of Gold Rush towns, and sometimes it roars through deep canyons over roller-coaster rapids. Those at Hell's Gate, below Boston Bar, are the most famous, and sometimes have the rafts practically airborne, but the Moran and Bridge River rapids are even wilder. Alone, the Fraser would make an exciting trip.

But most operators in the area offer floats that combine a number of miles on the big streams with sections on one or more of its tributaries and interconnected lakes. One such trip, on the upper reaches of the Fraser system, takes you from turquoise, 54-mile-long Chilko Lake, ringed on all sides with hanging glaciers and mountains, to its outlet and the crystal-clear Chilko River, then down the Chilko and into the Chilcotin, which flows into the Fraser; scenery ranges from arid benchlands to cool forests of evergreens, and in canyons you'll see rare California bighorn sheep, moose, bear, deer, and more. Shorter versions of this trip, which begin on the Chilcotin, about 20 miles upstream from its confluence with the Fraser, just above the lower of the Chilcotin's two best stretches of whitewater, are also available. Or you can sign up for still shorter trips on the powerful Thompson, a more southerly Fraser tributary that flows roughly southward from Savona via Ashcroft to Lytton through an arid sagebrush-and-bunchgrass land dotted by abandoned mines and cabins. The climate here was aptly described by one tripper as "hotter than a devil's esophagus" — but the whitewater spray will keep you cool enough. Information: Kumsheen Raft Adventures, PO Box 30, Main St., Lytton, BC V0K 1Z0 (phone: 604-455-2296) and Canadian River Expeditions, 845 Chilco St., Suite 400, Vancouver, BC V6G 2R2 (phone: 604-738-4449).

BOWRON LAKES PROVINCIAL PARK, near Barkerville, British Columbia: Located in the northernmost Cariboos near the Fraser River some 70 miles (112 km) east of Quesnel, this rectangularly shaped, 304,000-acre preserve offers one of Canada's classic wilderness canoe trips — a 73-miler that takes in a chain of mountain lakes and portions of the Bowron and Cariboo rivers, past meadows and through thick forests of spruce, lodgepole pine, western hemlock, western red cedar, and occasional deciduous trees, which make the area especially beautiful in the fall. Moose feed in the marshes, beavers build dams in the flats, bears feed on abundant salmon in the streams, and your chances of seeing them all as you paddle silently along are quite good. The clear waters, which flow roughly in a clockwise direction, offer good fishing for Dolly Varden, Kokanee, rainbow trout, whitefish, and lake trout. One of the chief beauties of this trip, however, is that there are only about 5 miles of portaging on the whole circuit, with no single portage longer than 1.5 miles. Early June through October is the season; insects are least prevalent beginning in September. Canoe rentals are available from *Becker's Canoe Outfitters,* Box 129, Wells, BC V0K 2R0 (604-492-2390 or Prince George radio operator N698552, Wells channel); and *Bowron Lake Lodge and Resorts Ltd.,* 672 Walkem St., Quesnel, BC V2J 2J7 (phone: 604-992-2733). Other information: Ministry of Parks, 540 Borland St., Williams Lake, BC V2G 1R8 (phone: 604-398-4414).

SOUTH NAHANNI RIVER, southwestern Northwest Territories: One of the continent's finest wild streams takes in incredible vertical-walled canyons 4,000 feet high, karst landforms and caves, high mountains sprinkled with hot springs, and larger-than-life Virginia Falls, which shows a 4-acre face of white spray and foam where it plunges about 300 feet — over twice the distance of Niagara. Unusual plants, luxuriant growths of grasses, balsams, poplar, and spruce, and all manner of wildlife — including grizzlies and Dall's sheep, golden eagles and trumpeter swans — can be seen here. The ridge walking that some canoe-trippers undertake for a break from their paddling is some of Canada's finest. And the local history, which concerns aboriginal peoples, mysterious murders, and Gold Rush characters, is as fascinating as the landscape. The 1,840-square-mile Nahanni National Park, through which the river flows, publishes a booklet detailing a 183-mile-long section of the South Nahanni, which takes in waters ranging in difficulty from Grade I to Grade IV, and a 78-mile-long section of the Flat River — mostly Grades I and II, except for the Cascade of the Thirteen Steps, which must be portaged. Outside the park, the South Nahanni flows into the Liard, which joins the Mackenzie at Fort Simpson; both of these former fur-trade arteries can be canoed, and the tributaries of the Liard, particularly the Beaver, Grayling, Rabbit, Red, and Toad rivers, offer fine Dolly Varden and Arctic grayling fishing. If you feel that waters of this level in such a true wilderness are beyond your abilities, sign up for a group raft or canoe trip run by outfitters on shorter sections of the stream. Information: Nahanni River Adventures, PO Box 8368, Station F, Edmonton, Alberta T6H 4W6 (phone: 403-439-1316); Black Feather Wilderness Adventures, 1341 Wellington St. S.W., Ottawa, Ontario K1Y 3B8 (phone: 613-722-4229); Nahanni Wilderness Adventures, Box 879, Nanton, Alberta T0L 1R0 (phone: 403-646-5768); TravelArctic, Government of the Northwest Territories, Yellowknife, NWT X1A 2L9 (phone: 403-873-7200); and the Nahanni National Park, Postal Bag 300, Fort Simpson, Northwest Territories X0E 0N0 (phone: 403-695-3151).

GREAT BARREN GROUND RIVERS, Northwest Territories: Canada's northernmost region — the more than 1 million square miles of tundra between the forest-clad Mackenzie Valley and Hudson Bay to the east, plus the Northern Yukon and the Ungava Plateau of northern Quebec and Labrador — are so finely veined with hundreds of thousands of miles of rivers and so liberally dotted with lakes that the area is as much water as land. During the brief summer, you have a canoeing ground that is unequaled anywhere else on earth. Much of the land is rolling tundra, upholstered with dwarf shrubs, mosses that are sometimes emerald in hue, plus lichens, grasses, and sedges; here and there, this palette of greens is spattered with the brilliant blues, reds, and yellows of tiny Arctic flowers. Stunted spruce trees huddle together along the shores of some of the rivers. This is all as you would expect. But occasionally, too, you'll spot trees standing tall along the eskers (ridges of gravel deposited by rivers that flowed underneath the glaciers so many ages ago). In the hundred or so miles south of tree line, you'll find forests of widely spaced spruce, pine, and birch. The wildlife is every bit as abundant as you'd expect. Herds of caribou file across the tundra every spring and fall on their way to and from the tree line in a mysterious migration that, even now, no one understands thoroughly. The tens, or even hundreds, of thousands of caribou often seen traveling together constitute the largest herds of wild animals left on earth. Ducks, geese, and wading birds breed in the kettle ponds and lakes. Canada geese, grizzlies, white tundra wolves, loons, musk oxen, falcons, and tundra swans are commonly seen. Because man is unknown to many of the wild creatures here, they are more readily approached than elsewhere. The fishing can be spectacular. In midsummer, you can paddle through the wee hours of the morning, if you're so inclined, by the eerie half-light of the midnight sun. In late summer the northern lights play magically across the sky. All in all, a trip in the Barren Grounds will be one you won't ever forget — whether you take it on the well-known Coppermine; the Thelon, which flows through a wooded game sanctuary; the Thelon's tributary, the short, swift Hanbury; the furious 615-mile-long Back River, which flows into the Arctic; or the Anderson, Burnside, Dubawnt, Horton, or Kazan. All these rivers are described in some detail in materials available from TravelArctic, Box 1320, Yellowknife, Northwest Territories X1A 2L9 (phone: 403-873-7200). For information on guided trips — and, because of the remoteness of the Barren Grounds, this is the only way to go if you're not an expert canoeist and outdoorsperson — contact Alex Hall, Canoe Arctic Inc., PO Box 130, Fort Smith, Northwest Territories X0E 0P0 (phone: 403-872-2308).

Mountain Climbing

Stunning as they are from the ground, Canada's mountains are still more bewitching when seen up close. Vast expanses of glaciers, whitish-blue icefalls, and breath-stopping peak-behind-peak views are things that some people can't get enough of. And, while well-trained climbers with good judgment and a sound understanding of their own limitations usually encounter little real danger, there is still an element of daring in every meeting with the mountains. That's also part of the attraction.

MOUNTAIN CLIMBING SCHOOLS

Good training at the hands of a competent guide can make the difference between life and death in the mountains when you go on a climb. Good training gives you the solid knowledge of skills and instills a mountain sense and the judgment that will keep you from getting into scrapes to begin with — and help you get out of them safely when they do occur unexpectedly.

But you don't really have to plan to make real climbs to sign up for a course at one of Canada's several mountaineering schools. They can be a lot of fun in their own right, and, believe it or not, even for acrophobics. A good way to see for yourself is to join one of the several day-long beginning rock-climbing courses that are widely available. These will teach you the basics.

If the experience pleases you, you might consider a climbing week where you'll cover more of the same in lecture-practice sessions and on several peak ascents in the area of the base camp. The cost can be $420 or more, including accommodations and meals. Rental equipment is usually extra. Or you could go for 1-day intermediate programs, or 1-day or 2-day snow-and-ice courses aimed at intermediates and beginners with some experience.

The organizations listed below offer a good variety of programs.

ALPINE CLUB OF CANADA, Banff, Alberta: Canada's only national mountaineering club, established in 1906, annually sponsors a variety of week-long mountain-lovers' get-togethers. Training weeks are organized to teach snow-, rock-, and ice-climbing skills to beginners and leadership skills to those with experience. General mountaineering camps, set up in areas that offer a variety of exceptional mountaineering opportunities, give you the chance to go out on daily climbs or form your own climbing parties with kindred spirits. At family camps, parents take turns organizing their own excursions out of the base and squiring each other's youngsters on hikes or scrambles. Venues for all Alpine Club of Canada programs change from year to year. Information: Alpine Club of Canada, Box 1026, Banff, Alberta T0L 0C0 (phone: 403-762-4481).

BANFF ALPINE GUIDES SCHOOL OF MOUNTAINEERING, Banff, Alberta: Between May and September, a group of certified professional mountain guides offer a huge variety of rock and ice climbing schools and private guided climbs. Information: Banff Alpine Guides School of Mountaineering, Box 1025, Banff, Alberta T0L 0C0 (phone: 403-762-2791).

MOUNTAIN CANADA, Golden, British Columbia: This summer school offers 1- to 4-day courses for beginning, intermediate, and advanced climbers in snow-and-ice work, rock-climbing, and rope-leading. Private guiding and mountaineering weeks are also available. Information: Mountain Canada Mountaineering School, PO Box 1530, Golden, BC V0A 1H0 (phone: 604-344-5410).

DIVERSIONS / Mountain Climbing 313

CANADIAN SCHOOL OF MOUNTAINEERING, Canmore, Alberta: CSM recently celebrated its 16th year in operation. Chief Guide Ottmar Setzer, is also part-time proprietor of the *Haus Alpenrose Lodge,* which bills itself as 'the first no-smoking lodge in the Rockies,' and is where most students are housed. Summer courses include: rock climbing weeks or weekends, snow and ice climbing, mountain discovery weeks, Rockies challenge weeks, and special mountaineering weeks. Winter courses include a winter challenge week and waterfall ice-climbing weekend, among others. Information: Canadian School of Mountaineering, 629 9th St., PO Box 723, Canmore, Alberta T0L 0M0 (phone: 403-678-4134).

SOUTHERN ALBERTA HOSTELLING ASSOCIATION, Calgary, Alberta: Among the varied outdoor programs presented in collaboration with area operators, the *SAHA* offers mountaineering, hiking, and trekking with the University of Calgary's Campus Recreation Department. Information: Southern Alberta Hostelling Association, Suite 203, 1414 Kensington Rd. N.W., Calgary, Alberta T2N 3P9 (phone: 403-283-5551).

JASPER CLIMBING SCHOOL AND GUIDE SERVICE, Jasper, Alberta: Hans Schwarz, the local authority on Mt. Robson, shares his knowledge and experience at his climbing school for summer and winter courses. Information: Jasper Climbing School, Box 452, Jasper, Alberta T0E 1E0 (phone: 403-852-3964).

CANADA'S CLASSIC CLIMBING

You'll begin to grasp the incredible scope and variety of the climbing available here when you flip through the pages of the climbing guides published by the Alpine Club of Canada. The books are thick, the details multitudinous, the descriptions concise, and the type small. The possibilities are mind-boggling.

Canada's loftiest peak, 19,850-foot Mt. Logan, and the surrounding St. Elias Mountains — within Kluane National Park — generally fall into the category of expedition climbs.

But the sheer number of mountains in Canada also guarantees the general mountaineer an abundance of peaks to assail — substantial peaks with many routes to the top; peaks which have had a special allure from Canada's earliest days. While the kind of extremely difficult north face routes that challenge very experienced climbers can be found, the summits of these giants are also accessible by easier routes that vary in difficulty from perhaps a scenic route that is ultimately little more than a walk involving some scrambling to the standard routes that pose satisfying mountaineering challenges.

Novice climbers should always go out with a more experienced person or a registered guide. Otherwise, you can discuss routes with climbers from a local club. There are no age limits at hostels; everyone is welcome. The Canadian Hostelling Association, Northern Alberta District, 10926 88th Ave., Edmonton, Alberta T6G 0Z1 (phone: 403-439-3089), and the Southern Alberta Hostelling Association, Suite 203, 1414 Kensington Rd. NW, Calgary, Alberta T2N 3P9 (phone: 403-283-5551), can be very helpful. They maintain a number of hostels just off the Icefields Parkway within walking distance of the starting points for several of the great climbs. (For information on informally organized outdoor trips and mountaineering resources in the southern Alberta area, contact the Calgary Area Outdoor Council, 1111 Memorial Drive N.W., Calgary, Alberta T2N 3E4 (phone: 403-270-2262). The council will forward queries to an organization that can offer assistance.

MT. TEMPLE, MT. VICTORIA, AND MT. LEFROY, next to Lake Louise, Alberta: Ascents of these three 11,000-foot-plus peaks — the ones you see in standard postcards of Lake Louise — mean a long climb that most mountaineers prefer to make in 2 days. First climbed in 1897, Lefroy's summit is accessible via several routes. The Mouse Trap Route to Abbot's Pass (where you camp overnight in a stone structure that accommodates 30 and was built by Swiss guides in 1922; you'll cross Abbot's Pass on both the

Victoria and Lefroy climbs), a snow route known for its changing glaciers, is moderately difficult but fairly straightforward. Behind the hut, there is a 2½-mile (4-km) traverse to the north peak of Mt. Victoria. The three peaks (southern, center, and northern) of Mt. Victoria make a spectacular ridge, popular for climbing and photographing. Temple, one of the bigger of the Rockies' 11,000-foot peaks, is most frequently climbed by the moderately demanding route up its southwest face from Sentinal Pass. Its particular challenges arise from the regularity with which you encounter deceptively dangerous snow patches. When you make it to the top, and if the weather holds, you see an unforgettable view of Paradise Valley below and the scattering of tiny lakes surrounded by wave after wave of mountains. Consult Alpine Club of Canada, (P.O. Box 1026, Banff, Alberta T0L 0C0) publications for detailed information, or contact Banff National Park, Box 900, Banff, Alberta T0L 0C0 (phone: 403-762-3324).

MT. ROBSON, near Jasper, Alberta: Located in eastern British Columbia alongside the Alberta border in Mt. Robson Provincial Park, this 12,972-foot giant, the highest in the Canadian Rockies, is so big that it creates its own weather. Clouds so often hang over Robson when the skies are clear for miles around that some locals quip they've never yet seen the summit. The climb would be difficult for that reason alone, but there are other problems. There's the huge difference in altitude between the 2,800-foot base and the summit, so most climbs last from 3 to 10 days. The standard route, up the south face, is heavily glaciated and leads over a series of ledges; here the climber will encounter many séracs and crevasses in unstable icefalls, unique frosted cornice formations called the Gargoyles, and ice and snow that can be very dangerous. Most of the mountain is raked by avalanches. To climb Robson by any route is a major mountaineering challenge — even experienced climbers frequently turn back. There is no easy way to the top, nor local certified guides for this mountain — Banff is the nearest place to hire one — however, Willi Pfisterer, recently retired from Parks Canada, and Hans Schwarz of Jasper are two recognized authorities on the mountain's idiosyncrasies. Information: Hans Schwarz, Jasper Climbing School and Guide Service, Box 452, 806 Connaught Dr., Jasper, Alberta T0E 1E0 (phone: 403-852-3964); Mt. Robson Provincial Park, PO Box 579, Valemount, BC V0E 2Z0 (phone: 604-566-4325 or 604-565-6340).

MT. EDITH CAVELL, near Jasper, Alberta: The summit of this namesake of a British nurse, which has been famous since the early days of exploration, gives you views over the Tonquin Valley that are especially fine because, at 11,033 feet, the peak is by far the highest in the Jasper townsite vicinity. Getting there is within the skills of most competent mountaineers in good shape, weather permitting. The western slopes, for instance, are technically easy, requiring little more than scrambling with an ice axe, and perhaps crampons. The East Ridge, known for the exposed position it often puts you in, with sheer drop-offs on either side, is a mixed snow-and-ice route, not technically difficult but requiring rock, snow, and ice work in quickly changing sequences, so that you can count on spending 16 to 18 hours round-trip. Expert mountaineers tackle several routes on the North Face. Information: Jasper National Park, PO Box 10, Jasper, Alberta T0E 1E0 (phone: 403-852-6161).

COLUMBIA ICEFIELD, near Jasper, Alberta: Shaped somewhat like a saucer and rimmed with some of the highest peaks in the Rockies, this tremendous, 120-square-mile accumulation of ice lying astride the Continental Divide in Jasper and Banff National Parks sends its melt water to three oceans — the Arctic, 765 miles (1,224 km) away via the Athabasca, the Slave, and the Mackenzie rivers; the Atlantic, by way of the Saskatchewan River, Lake Winnipeg, and Hudson Bay; and the Pacific, via the Columbia River through British Columbia and Washington State. The 11,340-foot Snow Dome, a bland-looking peak where all these river systems originate, is, in specialists' terms, the hydrographical apex of the continent. But the Snow Dome takes a back seat, in the popular mountaineering imagination, to a number of other peaks in the area, among them 12,294-foot Mt. Columbia, the highest in Alberta, and Mt. Athabasca. The latter gets special attention because, though only 11,452 feet high, it is so accessible from the Icefields Parkway, and probably, too, because the North Glacier route, the standard route to the summit, is fairly straightforward for someone experienced in glacier travel and snow climbing. The Silverhorn Route is also particularly pleasant and only moderately difficult. A score of other popular peaks also offer fine challenges. Information: Jasper National Park, PO Box 10, Jasper, Alberta T0E 1E0 (phone: 403-852-6161).

AUYUITTUQ NATIONAL PARK, Baffin Island, Northwest Territories: Baffin Island, above Hudson Bay, is home to some of the most unusual and demanding of Canada's climbs, and big-wall climbers from Yosemite, Europe, and Japan, come here to test themselves on the extremely difficult rock walls and just to get away from it all. In most cases, it's not that the peaks are so technically tough (although a recent American expedition rated the direct west face of Mt. Thor Peak 5.10 A4 Grade 7). Rather, climbing here poses problems simply because of the isolation. The park's outstanding features are Mt. Ascard, with its beautiful peak and the spiky 7,000-foot Penny Highlands, and their 2,200-square-mile ice cap. Information: Superintendent, Auyuittuq National Park, Pangnirtung, Northwest Territories X0A 0R0.

Hiking and Backpacking

One of the best ways to explore Canada's great mountains and forests is on foot. Even on short nature trails you see more than you would from a car — tiny flowers hidden under broken tree trunks, lush growths of ferns whose laciness you can't quite appreciate until you stop — and longer trips take you farther away from the crowds. Most national and provincial parks offer good opportunities for hiking; some have really extensive trail systems. In addition, Canada offers a number of scenic long-distance trails. Consult Elliot Katz's *Complete Guide to Backpacking in Canada* for a comprehensive look at what's available (about $11, $12.95 CN, from Doubleday Canada, 105 Bond St., Toronto, Ontario M5B 1Y3; phone: 416-340-0779). Here's a sampling of some of the nation's hiking hot spots, from west to east:

BANFF NATIONAL PARK, Banff, Alberta: Some 950 miles of trails cut through this 2,500-square-mile preserve and take you through forests of spruce and pine, over high alpine meadows filled with delicate colored flowers, and under high peaks ribboned with waterfalls. Some lead to areas of scenic beauty known around the world — Lake Louise, Skoki Valley, Sunshine Meadows, Egypt Lake, and Moraine Lake and the Valley of the Ten Peaks. Information: Banff National Park, Box 900, Banff, Alberta T0L 0C0 (phone: 403-762-3324). Also see *The Canadian Rockies Trail Guide* (about $11, or $12.95 CN, plus $5 postage and handling, from the Book and Art Den, P.O. Box 1420, Banff, Alberta T0L 0C0).

WATERTON LAKES NATIONAL PARK, near Cardston, Alberta: The 108 miles (180 km) of trails in this 204-square-mile preserve explore the prairies-to-mountains transitional country that gives the area its distinctive character. Most of the trails can be hiked in a day, but backcountry camps are available. There are three main trail systems, one radiating from the town of Waterton Park, one from the Akamina Highway and Cameron Lake, and one from the Red Rock Canyon area. Information: Waterton Lakes National Park, Waterton Park, Alberta T0K 2M0 (phone: 403-859-2262). Also see *National Parks*.

JASPER NATIONAL PARK, Jasper, Alberta: With some 4,200 square miles, and a network of over 600 miles of trails, the hiking possibilities here make your head spin. Some of the more famous take in Brazeau Lake, Jonas Pass, and Amethyst Lake in the Tonquin Valley, with its towering ramparts. The three national parks — Banff, Kootenay, and Yoho — double the available terrain. Information: Jasper National Park, Box 10, Jasper, Alberta T0E 1E0 (phone: 403-852-6161); and Information Services, Parks Canada, Western Region, Room 522, 220 4th Ave. S.E., P.O. Box 2989, Station M, Calgary, Alberta T2P 3H8 (phone: 403-292-4440).

TWEEDSMUIR PROVINCIAL PARK, near Bella Coola, British Columbia: This 2.4-million-acre wilderness is British Columbia's largest provincial park. The South Park lies some 229 miles (369 km) by gravel road from the nearest town of any size. Consequently, much of the south area of the park has changed little since the area's first explorations, over a century and a half ago, affected the landscape. For the hiker, this means that self-sufficiency is paramount. You will not find a dense network of trails like those of the Alberta national parks, but there is plenty of space for wilderness travel. Nearly every North American landform is to be found somewhere within the park boundaries — glaciers and snowfields, lakes and rivers, plains and forest-clad hills. With its large lake system, the northern area is a marine park, accessible only by boat, helicopter, or floating plane. The brightly tinted peaks of the Rainbow Mountains, in the east central part of the park, are especially striking. Licensed guides are available — hiring one is advisable unless you're a very experienced outdoorsperson. Information: Parks and Outdoor Recreation Division, 540 Borland St., Williams Lake, BC V2G 1R8 (phone: 604-398-4414) or the Ministry of B.C. Parks, Bag 5000, Smithers, BC 10J 2N0 (phone: 604-847-7320).

CHILKOOT TRAIL, from Dyea, Alaska, to Bennett, British Columbia: From the winter of 1897 until the fall of 1898, some 30,000 men and women trekked the 33 often-steep and usually rocky miles between these two towns: The promise of gold lured them on. Today's motivations seldom grip hikers with the same force, but the trip remains more magical than most. In addition to the sweeping views of rocky peaks and mirror-still lakes, the trail also turns up traces of the Gold Rush days. The hike is a demanding one, so hikers should come well prepared. The White Pass & Yukon Railway, with service between Skagway and Carcross, comes within 2 miles (3 km) of the trail's end at Bennett, allowing hikers to use it to return to their starting point. From May to September, bus service is also available between Whitehorse and Skagway. Information: Klondike Gold Rush National Historical Park, PO Box 517, Skagway, AK 99840 (907-983-2921), or Superintendent, Yukon National Historic Sites, Parks Canada, Box 5540, Whitehorse, Yukon Y1A 5H4 (phone: 403-668-2116).

YOHO NATIONAL PARK, Field, British Columbia: In the heart of the Rockies, this park is famous for its towering peaks, alpine valleys, thundering waterfalls, and turbulent streams. A network of trails, some 250 miles of them, takes you into the high country, where the views go on forever, and through the valleys, threaded with glacial streams. Backcountry lodges within the park boundaries can be incorporated into your walks. Information: Superintendent, Yoho National Park, PO Box 99, Field, BC V0A 1G0 (phone: 604-343-6324).

MT. ASSINIBOINE PROVINCIAL PARK, near Invermere, British Columbia: Matterhornlike 11,870-foot Mt. Assiniboine dominates the scenery in this fine 96,500-acre expanse of jagged peaks and shining lakes, blue-white glaciers, and wildflower-dotted meadows. Although the preserve is one of the Rockies' loveliest, it's also among the wildest. You can get there only on foot or, by permission, on horseback, or by helicopter from Banff. Although supplies and equipment are not available, there is a concessionaire-operated resort, *Mount Assiniboine Lodge,* and four alpine shelters known as the *Naiset Cabins.* Reservations are required at the lodge (Box 1527, Canmore, Alberta T0L 0M0; phone: 403-678-2883). The wilderness experience you can have here ranks among Canada's finest. Banff and Kootenay national parks adjoin Assiniboine. Information: Ministry of Parks, Southern Interior Region, 101-1050 W. Columbia St., Kamloops, BC V2C 1L2 (phone: 604-828-4501).

MANNING PROVINCIAL PARK, Manning Park, British Columbia: This 176,000-acre (71,400-hectare) preserve, situated some 140 miles (225 km) east of Vancouver just north of the international border, is somewhat more developed than many BC parks. Several self-guiding nature trails, many guided walks, and a variety of day hikes are available in the area. The park itself is the southern terminus of the Canadian leg of the Pacific Crest Trail, which ends in Mexico. Information: Ministry of Parks, 1610 Indian River Dr., North Vancouver, BC V7G 1L3 (phone: 604-929-1291).

KOKANEE GLACIER PROVINCIAL PARK, near Nelson, British Columbia: Preserving some 158,000 acres of rugged Selkirk Mountains country, and accessible only by gravel road and by trail, this park's craggy peaks, canyons, glaciers, and jewellike tarns are well worth the effort it takes to reach them. The main trail, from Gibson Lake to Joker Mill, winds through some of the most spectacular countryside past five crystal-clear lakes. Another trail, beginning at the Slocan Chief hut, takes you up to 9,000 feet and the Kokanee Glacier. This is not the wildest of BC's parks, but some degree of expertise is required to handle the terrain, even in summer. Information: Parks and Outdoor Recreation Division, 101-1050 W. Columbia St., Kamloops, BC V2C 1L4 (phone: 604-828-4501).

GLACIER NATIONAL PARK, near Rogers Pass, British Columbia: Most trails here begin at or near the Trans-Canada Highway, which bisects the park, and then climb steeply into jagged mountains covered with lovely forests of conifers below and spectacular glaciers and snowfields above. Its immensity overwhelms you. Trails lead you near the 10-square-mile Illecillewaet Icefield, one of the park's most awe-inspiring, and to Mt. Abbott, Mt. Sir Donald, and the Asulkan Glacier. Most are short enough for a day's hike, but overnight trips are also possible. A visit to the Rogers Pass Information Centre is well worth a break in the day's hiking. Here, exhibits and movies are offered about the world's largest active avalanche control program, or about the park and people. Park staff members are on hand to help plan hikes and answer questions. Information: Glacier National Park, PO Box 350, Revelstoke, BC V0E 2S0 (phone: 604-837-6274).

WEST COAST TRAIL, PACIFIC RUN NATIONAL PARK, Vancouver Island, British Columbia: The western shore of this island is rocky and cliff-bound, and it often happened in days gone by that storms drove ships onto the rocks and that the sailors who survived later died because they couldn't get up the cliffs. Indeed, the area was once known as the Graveyard of the Pacific. The 45-mile-long West Coast Trail, carved out as an escape hatch, has become one of the nation's most popular hiking trails. Now a part of Pacific Rim National Park, it is also one of the most spectacular for the fine views it gives of foamy surf and sky. The northern terminus is at Bamfield, on Pachena Bay; the southern trailhead is in Port Renfrew. Information: West Coast Trail Information Centres, open mid-May through September (phone: at Pachena Bay 604-728-3234, or at Port Renfrew 604-647-5434); or Pacific Rim National Park, PO Box 280, Ucluelet, BC V0R 3A0 (phone: 604-726-7721).

RIDING MOUNTAIN NATIONAL PARK, Wasagaming, Manitoba: Part of the Manitoba Escarpment, Riding Mountain is actually a plateau rising up from the surrounding prairie, with undulating hills, meadows, lakes, and streams accessible via over 30 hiking trails in summer and over 20 cross-country ski trails in winter. Information: Superintendent, Riding Mountain National Park, Wasagaming, Manitoba R0J 2H0 (phone: 204-848-2811).

DOBSON TRAIL, near Moncton, New Brunswick: Meandering for 37 miles from Riverview into Fundy National Park, this is one of the more beautiful of Canada's long trails because of the primitive Albert County woods-and-valleys landscape it covers. In the park, the trail becomes the Cross Fundy Hiking Trail and gives you access to other trails that lead to the bold, irregular coastline and along quick-flowing streams. The Dobson Trail, marked with blue blazes, is recommended only for experienced hikers. Information: Outdoor Enthusiasts, PO Box 254, Moncton, NB E1C AK9 (phone: 506-855-5089).

BRUCE TRAIL, near Hamilton, Ontario: This 430-mile hiking trail winds over the scenic Niagara Escarpment from Queenston on the Niagara River to the village of Tobermory on the tip of the Bruce Peninsula between Lake Huron and Georgian Bay. A complete guide and maps are available. Information: Bruce Trail Association, Box 857, Hamilton, Ontario L8N 3N9 (phone: 416-529-6821 or 416-529-6823).

ALGONQUIN PROVINCIAL PARK, near Huntsville, Ontario: This immense preserve has long been known for its extensive canoeing. But the Ministry of Natural Resources, which is responsible for the area's administration, has begun cutting trails into the dense forests of hardwoods and conifers that cover the Canadian Shield in the area. Two of these are the Western Uplands Backpacking Trail, made up of three loops of 19, 33, and 42 miles; and the Highland Backpacking Trail, whose two loops are 11 and 22 miles long. Some trails skirt the edges of the lakes, some meander around boggy areas, and some climb ridges. The scenery is always lovely, and a permit system preserves the isolated feeling. Information: Algonquin Park District Office, Ministry of Natural Resources, Box 219, Whitney, Ontario K0J 2M0 (phone: 705-633-5572).

RIDEAU TRAIL, at Kingston, Ontario: A 235-mile-long system that follows trails and secondary roads on its meandering way from the shores of Lake Ontario, through marshes, forests, and fields, to Chaudière Falls in Ottawa, to the north. The scenery varies from serene to spectacular, and historic sites and wildlife are widely in evidence. Come prepared for mosquitoes, which you may find in the swampy areas in late spring and early summer. For about $8.50 ($10 CN) plus $2 postage, you can buy a copy of the new *Rideau Trail Guidebook*. Information: Rideau Trail Association, Box 15, Kingston, Ontario K7L 4V6 (phone: 613-545-0823).

GATINEAU PARK, near Hull, Quebec: This preserve's 88,000 acres are crowded between the Gatineau and Ottawa rivers, not far from Ottawa, a region well known for its hills. They rise as high as 1,367 feet from the valleys, which are at about 600 feet, and most are crisscrossed with hiking trails — more than 120 miles of them. Meandering to waterfalls and beaver ponds, to historic ruined buildings and overlooks of the valleys to the south, some trails loop back to Lac Philippe, where you'll find beaches, picnic grounds, a campground, and semi-wilderness campsites. Zero-impact canoe-camping is possible at Lac La Pêche. Information: Gatineau Park Division, National Capital Commission, 161 Laurier Ave. W., Ottawa, Ontario K1P 6J6 (phone: 819-827-2020).

GUIDED TRIPS

Guided trips provide good opportunities for acquiring camping skills if you don't already have them. They are offered by a number of organizations, among them the following:

SKYLINE HIKERS OF THE CANADIAN ROCKIES, based in Calgary, Alberta: Once a year this independent group of mountain enthusiasts sets up a base camp in the mountains and organizes a variety of day hikes in the area from mid-July to mid-August. Information: Skyline Hikers of the Canadian Rockies, PO Box 3514, Station B, Calgary, Alberta T2M 4M2 (no phone).

STRATHCONA PARK LODGE, near Campbell River, British Columbia: A variety of accommodations and adventure holiday packages for all ages are offered by this wilderness resort on the edge of Strathcona Provincial Park. Information: Strathcona Park Lodge, Box 2160, Campbell River, BC V9W 5C9 (604-286-3122 or Campbell River radio phone, Strathcona One H688568).

BLACK FEATHER WILDERNESS ADVENTURES, Ottawa, Ontario: Guided hikes and canoe trips in many areas of Canada. Information: Black Feather Wilderness Adventures, 1341 Wellington St., Ottawa, Ontario K1Y 3B8 (phone: 613-722-9717); or 40 Wellington St. E., Toronto, Ontario M5E 1C1 (phone: 416-862-0881).

Hunting

Canada's untracked wilderness is just about any hunter's dream. Modern man can return to a more primitive age to stalk big game, such as elk, moose, caribou, and bear, or smaller prey, like grouse, partridge, geese, and ducks. Canadians view their wildlife as a precious natural resource. Game species are professionally managed to ensure their future well-being, and government regulations strictly control hunting seasons. Each province has its own licensing requirements, and the federal government restricts the hunting of migratory birds (a permit can be obtained from any post office for about $8.50; a mandatory habitat stamp for about $5.50). It is absolutely essential that the hunter contact the province and/or the Ministry of Natural Resources to obtain hunting regulations for specific areas. Hunting regulations and license requirements vary from province to province, and they can be quite complicated.

In general, hunting is an autumn activity, when game populations are at their peak. (Sunday hunting is prohibited in many areas.) Bag limits for small game and birds are generous across the country, but the numbers of larger game are strictly limited. Non-resident hunters have no problem bringing rifles, shotguns, and hunting dogs into Canada, provided they observe the regulations outlined in *Travel Information,* available from the provinces, Ministry of Natural Resources, or Canadian Customs (for addresses, see *Tourist Information,* GETTING READY TO GO).

EAST

Hunting in eastern Canada centers around upland game birds, such as partridge, grouse, and woodcock, but some areas are also outstanding for moose, caribou, whitetail deer, and black bear. Hunters from all over the world are drawn to the picturesque province of New Brunswick in pursuit of woodcock. These long-billed game birds are especially common in Kent, Charlotte, Albert, Westmorland, Kings, Queens, York, Victoria, and Northumberland counties; guides with good dogs are available.

NEW BRUNSWICK: Charlotte County (which includes Grand Manan Island) as well as Victoria, Kings, and Queens counties are some of the best spots in eastern Canada to hunt whitetail deer. While the length of the deer season varies from area to area (either 3 or 4 weeks), it generally opens in late October or early November. Non-resident hunters must be accompanied by a guide. Information: Fish and Wildlife Branch, PO Box 6000, Fredericton, NB E3B 5H1 (phone: 506-453-2440).

CHAPLEAU AREA, in Chapleau, Ontario: This expanse of rugged, lake-dotted, boreal forest, is one of the top hunting spots in eastern Canada. Black bear hunting is excellent in both the spring and fall, and hunting for moose and small game is best in the fall. Several lodges and outfitters in the area handle fly-in trips, accommodations, and equipment rentals. There are also six Ontario provincial parks, four with developed campsites and two waterway parks. The Town of Chapleau is the gateway to the Chapleau Crown Game Preserve, the largest wildlife preserve in the world. Information: Ministry of Natural Resources, 190 Cherry St., Chapleau, Ontario P0M 1K0 (phone: 705-864-1710).

WILDERNESS AROUND FORT HOPE, near Nakina, Ontario: A still-wild northern region, it is one of the best places in eastern Canada to hunt moose, especially from mid-September on, during the rut (breeding) season, when bull moose will respond to calls on a birchbark horn, vastly increasing your chances of bagging a fine one. The area's Ojibway Indians are expert moose hunters and guides. Information: Ojibway Country Wilderness Camps, PO Box 1230, Waterdown, Ontario L0R 2H0 (phone: 416-689-7925).

PELEE ISLAND, in Lake Erie, Ontario: Among sportsmen who prize pheasants above all other game birds, this island is justly famous. The pheasant season is split into two periods of two days each during the fall. An additional season is scheduled during winter. Pelee Island takes on an almost holiday-like atmosphere as all the islanders welcome visiting hunters. There are some guides with hunting dogs on the island, but hunters are advised to bring their own if possible. Information: Township Clerk-Treasurer, Township of Pelee, Pelee Island, Ontario N0R 1M0 (phone: 519-724-2931); and the Chatham District Office, Ministry of Natural Resources, Box 1168, Chatham, Ontario N7M 5L8 (phone: 519-354-7340).

JAMES AND HUDSON BAY, Moosonee, Ontario: Snow geese, blue geese, and Canada geese breed and rest in huge numbers along the rugged, unspoiled western shores of James and Hudson Bay. In September and early October during migration, when geese and ducks mass along the coastal flats to feed, the hunting is superb. Cree goose hunting camps operate during this peak season and have cabins and canoes. Based in these comfortable spots, hunters go out with Cree Indian guides. For details about hunting here, contact the Moosonee District Office, Ministry of Natural Resources, PO Box 190, Moosonee, Ontario P0L 1Y0 (phone: 705-336-2987).

ILE AUX GRUES (Crane Island), near Quebec City, Quebec: This split of grass and mud in the St. Lawrence River is one of the best hunting grounds for water fowl in eastern Canada. When greater snow geese by the thousands stop over on the tide flats during their southward migration in October, hunting conditions are ideal. The area is also rich in black ducks, teal, and snipe. Information: Tourism Quebec, PO Box 20,000, Quebec City, Quebec G1K 7X2 (phone 800-443-7000 from the eastern US; 800-361-6490 from Ontario and the Maritimes; 800-361-5405 from Quebec, and 514-873-2015 from Montreal and elsewhere). Questions of a more technical nature can be directed to the Recreation, Hunting and Fishing Department: Ministère du Liosir de la Chasse et de la Pêche, 150 Boul. St-Cyrille E., Quebec City, Quebec G1R 4Y3 (phone: 418-643-3127).

UNGAVA, near Kuujjuaq (formerly Fort Chimo), Quebec: The rolling, tundra-covered hill country south of Ungava Bay is the best caribou area in Canada, thanks to careful management that has allowed the herds to grow to some 700,000 strong. As a result, the number of available hunting licenses has been increased (but there's a two-caribou-per-license limit), and several Inuit from Kuujjuaq have started outfitting hunters. An adult bull caribou makes a magnificent trophy, and a hunt with the Inuit is a supreme outdoor adventure. Hunting season is August 1 through October 31, but most lodges close by the end of September. Information: Tourism Quebec, PO Box 20,000, Quebec City, Quebec G1K 7X2 (phone: 800-443-7000 from the eastern US; 800-361-6490 from Ontario and the Maritimes; 800-361-5405 from Quebec, and 514-873-2015 from Montreal and elsewhere); Louis Brousseau, Marketing Director, Quebec Inuit and Indian Outfitters, 2525 Watt St., Local 12, Ste.-Foy, Quebec G1P 3T2 (phone: 418-659-6009).

WEST

Western Canada is stocked with an unparalleled variety of game. The mountains of Alberta, British Columbia, the Yukon, and the Northwest Territories are internationally famous for their big-game hunting, while the prairies of Manitoba and Saskatchewan have abundant waterfowl and upland game, such as grouse, pheasant, Hungarian partridge, and snipe.

WILLMORE WILDERNESS, north of Jasper National Park, Alberta: This vast Rocky Mountain wilderness is one of the largest strongholds of trophy bighorn sheep on the continent. What makes a mountain hunt here such an unforgettable experience is that, because no motorized transport is allowed in the area, you either hike in or trek in on horseback, with a string of pack horses in tow, much like the country's earliest explorers. About one-third of the bighorns harvested in Alberta every year come from the Willmore Wilderness. Information: Alberta Forest Service, 9920 108th St., 6th Floor, Bramalea Building, Edmonton, Alberta T5K 2M4 (phone: 403-427-3582), or Fish and Wildlife Extension Services, 9920 108th St., 3rd Floor, Bramalea Building, Edmonton, Alberta T5K 2M4 (phone: 403-427-6757).

SPATSIZI PLATEAU, near Kinaskan, British Columbia: Together with the Level Mountain Range, located west of Dease Lake, this area just east of the Stewart Cassiar Highway, a provincial park that allows hunting within its boundaries (though by special permit only) offers some of the province's best hunting for mountain goat and caribou. The season starts early to mid-August and runs through mid-October, but the best time to hunt is from mid-September on, after the animals have acquired their thick winter coats. *Spatsizi,* an Indian term meaning red goats, refers to the color the normally white goats' fur takes on when they roll around in the area's red volcanic dust to protect themselves from insects. Information: Ministry of Environment and Parks, Fish and Wildlife Branch, Information Services, 780 Blanshard St., Victoria, BC V8V 1X5 (phone: 604-387-4573).

QUEEN CHARLOTTE ISLANDS, off the coast of British Columbia: The blacktail deer are abundant on these islands because they have no natural predators here, except for the occasional black bear. In an effort to control the population, the British Columbia Fish and Wildlife Branch allows hunters to bag ten deer per year with a possession limit of three. Information: Ministry of Environment, Fish and Wildlife Branch, Information Services, 780 Blanshard St., Victoria, BC V8V 1X5 (phone: 604-387-4573).

INTERLAKE REGION, between Lake Manitoba and Lake Winnipeg, Manitoba: Sharp-tailed and ruffed grouse have always been a primary hunting attraction in this area, and they are still. In good years, the sharp-tailed grouse are unbelievably abundant, especially during peak season in late September and through October. (The town of Ashern, so enamored of the sharp-tailed grouse that it has erected a 17-foot, 3,800-pound statue of the creature alongside Provincial Highway 6, annually stages its celebrated International One-Box Sharp-tail Hunt, in which teams of selected VIP guests race to bag the largest number of birds with one box of shells.) In 1989, the population of ruffed grouse peaked. Lately, however, because of a resoundingly successful habitat management program, the Interlake Region has become one of the nation's best spots for goose hunting. An estimated 750,000 to 1 million snow geese and 500,000 to 750,000 Canada geese migrate through Manitoba, and the two lakes act as a funnel, so that most of the birds stop to feed and rest in the area; around Grant's Lake and Oak Hammock Marsh, within sight of the Winnipeg skyline, several hundred thousand birds can be seen at any given time. As a result of the healthy population, bag limits are liberal — much to the delight of hunters from more restrictive, more southerly areas. Information: Department of Natural Resources, 1495 St. James St., Box 22, Winnipeg, Manitoba R3H 0W9 (phone: 204-945-6784).

POTHOLE COUNTRY, from Minnedosa to the Assiniboine River, Manitoba: Thanks to an abundance of sloughs, potholes, and other wetlands, this area has been a prime place for duck hunting; however, the number of mallard and pintails has declined annually, and hunting is good only in isolated spots. A habitat management program is being introduced, so with hope the birds' population will multiply in the near future. Goose hunting is excellent throughout much of southern Manitoba. The province's snow goose and Canada goose populations are healthy and expanding. Roughly 1.5 million snow geese and 1 million Canada geese wing their way through southern Manitoba each fall. Information: Department of Natural Resources, 1495 St. James St., Box 22, Winnipeg, Manitoba R3H 0W9 (phone: 204-945-6784).

MACKENZIE MOUNTAINS, near Norman Wells, Northwest Territories: Sheep still die of old age without ever having seen a human being in the rugged Mackenzies — probably among the best Dall's sheep ranges on the continent — and rams with full-curl horns measuring 35 to 38 inches are common, while trophies with 40- to 42-inch horns are bagged in season, between July 15 and October 31. The snow white Dall's ram has to be the most regal trophy a hunter can take. Information: TravelArctic, Government of the Northwest Territories, Yellowknife, NWT X1A 2L9; or call the Arctic Hotline at 1-800-661-0788.

Ice Skating

Canadian winters and ice go together. From December until May, ponds, lakes, rivers, and streams turn into natural rinks. The tradition of bundled-up businessmen skating to their offices originated with the French traders who skated over the frozen waterways from one trading post to another with their goods. Then, inspired by the ingenuity of the French, the Iroquois strapped bones to their feet and joined the sport, and English soldiers in turn began holding competitions for the most creative and intricate patterns cut into ice. Indoor rinks first appeared in Quebec City and Montreal in the 1880s.

Today, skating is enormously popular all over the country. Hockey tends to dominate the scene, and aspiring professionals begin early: There are leagues for tykes aged 7 and 8, atoms aged 9 and 10, peewees aged 11 and 12, bantams aged 13 and 14, midgets aged 15 and 16, juveniles aged 17 to 19, juniors aged 15 to 20, intermediates over 20, and seniors over 21. (Players are delegated to the last four categories on the basis of their ability.) In the last 15 years, the sport of ringette — a fast team sport played by girls with bladeless sticks and a rubber ring — has taken off; there are some 40,000 players in Ontario, the sport's home province, and in a pair of recent exhibition games played against boys' hockey teams, the girls came out ahead. Figure skating is also booming. The Canadian Figure Skating Association has 157,000 members, and some 1,400 clubs based in municipalities nationwide stage seminars for skaters and interclub competitions, sending the winners on to sectional, divisional, national, and international contests. A top Canadian skater in training usually winters in Toronto and summers in the Rockies or England, buying private ice time (usually to the tune of $15,000 annually).

You'll find fine recreational skating in just about every province, in literally hundreds of rinks. But one of the joys of skating in Canada is the preponderance of lakes and rivers that freeze over and the fact that, because of the sport's popularity, warming huts and hot sandwich stands pop up here and there along the shores.

CANADA'S UNIQUE OPEN-AIR SKATING

BANFF SPRINGS HOTEL, Banff, Alberta: Like many big mountain resort hotels, this one provides its guests with an ice-skating facility. But this is a special hotel with a very special setting, and though the rink isn't of Olympic caliber, it's worth taking a few spins just to enjoy the grand scenery: Jagged, snow-capped peaks rising steeply at the edge of the mile-wide Bow River Valley, where the hotel sits. And after a respectable few minutes of invigorating exercise, reward yourself by heading over to the hotel's winterized golf clubhouse, a Tudoresque mini-château, and sit by one of those enormous fieldstone fireplaces and warm up over a hot buttered rum or a bowl of soup. Information: Banff Springs Hotel, PO Box 960, Banff, Alberta T0L 0C0 (phone: 403-762-2211). Also see *Downhill Skiing, Special Havens,* and *Calgary to Banff and Jasper National Parks,* DIRECTIONS.

VANCOUVER, British Columbia: The climate here is so delightful that pleasure boaters can explore the islands offshore all winter long; when snow falls, it never stays around very long. So you might not expect to find much of an outdoor ice-skating scene here. But every November, the city fathers install a rink in the big bubble-covered sunken plaza at the Provincial Courthouse Complex downtown. From then until April, everybody ice skates. Office workers twirl and whirl on their lunch hours and after 5 PM; the rink is open every day until midnight. And there are more than usually interesting places to snack or have a meal — a pub-restaurant called the *Old Bailey* and the European-style *Mozart Konditori* on one side and, on the other, the informal *Food Fair* (closed evenings) where you can prowl for Mexican, Ukrainian, Chinese, and other exotic food (or, if you must, hot dogs), then take it to a pleasant area nearby to eat. Information: Tourism Vancouver, Pavilion Plaza, 4 Bentall Center, 1055 Dunsmire St., PO Box 49296, Vancouver, BC V7X 1L3 (phone: 604-683-2000).

OTTAWA, Ontario: The 5 miles of the 125-mile-long Kingston-to-Ottawa Rideau Canal between Colonel By Drive and Queen Elizabeth Driveway, south of the Ottawa River, becomes the world's longest skating rink every winter, and you'll find hot chocolate stands, skate-sharpening operations, benches, safety patrols, even changing rooms — not to mention thousands of skaters. Students, their packs full of books, skate to school. Office workers skate to work. Friends head for the canal instead of the movies, and kids haul their parents out on the ice on weekends. Information: Canada's Capital Visitors and Convention Bureau, 222 Queen St., 7th Floor, Ottawa, Ontario K1P 5V9 (phone: 613-237-5158), or visit the information center at 65 Elgin St., in the National Arts Centre. Also see *Festivals, Fairs, and Fancy Acts.*

TORONTO, Ontario: Nathan Phillips Square, the huge forecourt of the city's controversial clamshell-like City Hall, is home to concerts and art shows in summer; in winter, the reflecting pool is turned into a skating rink 182 feet by 98 feet, and the brown-baggers of summer give way to assorted school kids, office workers, and other Torontonians every day between 9 AM or so until after 10 PM. Down by the lakeside, Harbourfront's 32,000 sq. ft. open-air rink offers invigorating skating daily from 10 AM to 10 PM. Information: Details: Metropolitan Toronto Convention & Visitors Association, Queens Quay Terminal at Harborfront, PO Box 126, 207 Queens Quay W., Toronto, Ontario M5J 1A7 (phone: 416-368-9990).

LAURENTIANS, Quebec: You're in luck if you arrive after a spell of weather long enough and cold enough to ice over the myriad ponds, lakes, and streams of this lovely area — but before the snow. Then you can skate for miles, play hockey to your heart's content, or trace figures large enough that giants might have made them. The great outdoors is one vast skating rink. But even after the snowfall, there's no dearth of places to skate in this skate-happy region. Almost every village has its rink — if not a man-made oval set up in the schoolyard, then a section of a nearby lake kept plowed for the season. Sections of the lakes at several of the area's best resorts (among them *Gray*

Rocks at St. Jovite and the *Hôtel la Sapinière* at Val David) are usually kept clear, for instance, as are the lakes at Ste. Adèle and Ste. Agathe. The former has a half-mile oval to speed around as well as the regular rink-sized area. And there are indoor rinks as well. The delight of skating here also derives from what goes après: the unique "European flavor" of the après ski in the Laurentians; long sessions at the hearthsides of cozy inns; satiation of galloping appetites in one of the many fine restaurants in the quaint villages, not to mention the gayer-than-Paris-in-springtime nightlife — some of the happiest to be found at any winter resort on earth. For more information contact: Association Touristique des Laurentides, 14142 Rue de Lachapelle, RR1, St. Jérôme, Quebec J7Z 5T4 (phone: 514-436-8532).

MONTREAL, Quebec: Canadians are as enthusiastic about their skating as they are about their sailing, and they don't reserve their ice time exclusively for weekends out of town: Throughout the week, by day and by night, they throng to open-air rinks that the city government maintains for their pleasure — in Montreal at La Fontaine Park and Parc Mont-Royal (both lighted at night and near downtown), and on Ile Notre Dame, where you can skate along its 1.2-mile-long canal. Parc Mont-Royal, whose 530 acres wrap around the sides of a former volcano, is as terrific in winter as it is for summer strolls and calèche rides. The skating all takes place on Beaver Lake (Lac des Castors), and there are fine views of the city. After you've unlaced your skates, you can go cross-country skiing, slide down one of a couple of slopes in a toboggan, ride a horse-drawn sleigh, or warm up over an interesting meal. Information: Greater Montreal Convention and Tourism Bureau, 1010 Ste.-Catherine St. W., Room 410, Montreal, Quebec H3B 1G2 (phone: 514-871-1595).

QUEBEC CITY, Quebec: Beautiful as it can be under a hot summer sun, Quebec occasionally appears to have been built to look its best swathed in a cloak of snow. Québécois put on skates almost as soon as they learn to walk, and there are hundreds of free skating rinks throughout the region on which to practice. To see for yourself, you've only to step into your skates and head for the St. Charles River between Samson and Marie de l'Incarnation bridges, where you'll sail along beside one of the city's many parks, serene under its mantle of white. Those who stay at one of the many hotels and motels in the suburb of Ste. Foy, can enjoy skating at the new *Gaétan Boucher Speed-Skating Rink.* About 20 miles (32 km) north of the city, in Valcartier, you can have another sort of skating experience entirely. An unusual family business, known as the *Village des Sports* (Valcartier Village; phone: 418-844-3725), has cut a circle-trail through the woods, then iced it over. It's 1½ miles long, about as wide as a country road, and lighted at night; speakers concealed in bird houses provide MUZAK to skate by (or rock music, depending on the crowd). The complex is open every day in winter, and rentals are available. There are still other trails for tobogganing, cross-country skiing, and snowshoeing. In summer, the ice rink is given over to roller skating. Information: Quebec City Region Tourism & Convention Bureau, 60 Rue d'Auteuil, Quebec City, Quebec G1R 4C4 (phone: 418-692-2471).

HOCKEY MUSEUMS

INTERNATIONAL HOCKEY HALL OF FAME AND MUSEUM, Kingston, Ontario: People have been playing hockey in Kingston ever since it was called shinney, back in the 1880s, and the collections here record the history of the game through the present. There's the stick used in the big game between Queen's and Royal Military College on Kingston harbor ice around 1886, the first colored hockey cards (1906–1909), an early NHA player contract signed by Alf Smith of Ottawa for $500 a year, the famous No. 9 sweaters of Rocket Richard and Gordie Howe, and Dit Clapper's No. 5, retired by the Boston *Bruins* in 1947 — not to mention the battered skates of Scotty Davidson and referee Mike Rodden, Gordie Howe's gloves, and much more. Open year-round; admission charge. Information: Doug Nichols, Executive Director, *International*

Hockey Hall of Fame and Museum, York and Alfred Sts., PO Box 82, Kingston, Ontario K7L 1X4 (phone: 613-544-2355).

HOCKEY HALL OF FAME AND MUSEUM, Toronto, Ontario: For the serious hockey fan, a visit to this historical museum is a must. The Stanley Cup, the oldest of North America's professional sports trophies, is housed here. So are most of the sport's other famous trophies — Challenge Cup, Canada Cup, and all of the National Hockey League's major trophies. Officially endorsed by the NHL, the CAHA, and the International Ice Hockey Federation, the Hockey Hall of Fame has sections devoted to famous goalies, famous hockey skates and sticks, and other celebrated impedimenta of the sport; a number of audiovisual presentations and regular programs are also part of the show. Information: Hockey Hall of Fame and Museum, Exhibition Pl., Toronto, Ontario M6K 3C3 (phone: 416-595-1345).

For the Experience

Festivals, Fairs, and Fancy Acts

No matter where or when you travel in Canada, you're apt to find the citizenry celebrating — always with spirit and panache. Some festivities honor a town's European heritage. Others — like the rodeos, the lobster festivals, and even the mining festivals — fete the local industry. Some are meant to build up the community's public image, to put it on the map, or to indulge the citizenry's fondness for music, dance, and the other arts. As you would expect, there are plenty of winter festivals, many of them in February.

Provincial tourist authorities can provide you with lists of the various fairs, exhibitions, and festivals taking place at any given time. Even the smallest is worth a detour. Here are a few suggestions.

EAST

FESTIVAL BY THE SEA, St. John, New Brunswick: Some 500 entertainers, many representing other Canadian provinces, perform over 1,200 shows during 2 weeks in August in this festival honoring New Brunswick's marine heritage. Information: Festival by the Sea, P.O. Box 6848, Station A, St. John, NB A2L 4S3 (phone: 506-632-0086).

ACADIAN FESTIVAL, Caraquet, New Brunswick: Centers around the Acadian National Holiday on August 15, the day of the "tintamarre" — the rushing noise that ducks and geese make as they swoop over the marshes. Custom has it that at 6 PM, everybody stops work and makes noise with drums, horns, bells. The festival includes dance performances, the blessing of the fleet, and folk singing — all in French. Information: Acadian Festival, Town of Caraquet, Box 420, Caraquet, NB E0B 1K0 (phone: 506-727-3423).

MIRAMICHI FOLK SONG FESTIVAL, Newcastle, New Brunswick: The oldest festival of its kind in North America, this 5-day event is a gathering of old-timers who indulge in enthusiastic accompanied and unaccompanied singing of lumber camps and days at sea, in French and in English and occasionally in other languages as well. Sometimes there's some clickety-clackety spoon playing and tap dancing, but each night a noted entertainer from the province appears. The festival offers a good opportunity to gather some knowledge of New Brunswick folkways and soak up the atmosphere of this unusual province at the same time. Held annually the first week in August. Information: Susan Butler, PO Box 13, Newcastle, NB E1V 3M2 (phone: 506-773-4469).

SHEDIAC LOBSTER FESTIVAL, Shediac, New Brunswick: One of the hot spots of coastal sailing, this community, long famous for the lobsters brought ashore by its fishermen, is called the "Lobster Capital of the World." So the annual 6-day, mid-July bash celebrating the delectable crustaceans seems entirely appropriate. You'll find all the goings-on that are usual at such small-town festivities — as well as lobster-trapping and boiling exhibitions, lobster-eating contests, and, well worth the trip, plenty of lobsters for all. Information: Shediac Lobster Festival, PO Box 969, Shediac, NB E0A 3G0 (phone: 506-532-2421).

DIVERSIONS / Festivals, Fairs, and Fancy Acts 327

ANTIGONISH HIGHLAND GAMES, Antigonish, Nova Scotia: The Scottish yearning to link arms with kith and kin, near and far, under the shield of the family clan is expressed at this colorful gathering that takes place for a few days annually in mid-July. The oldest Scottish games in North America are held here, but you don't have to be a Scot to enjoy the fun: There are competitions in caber tossing and weight throwing and Highland dancing and piping, and plenty of refreshments, including tea and oatcakes. Information: Nova Scotia Department of Tourism (phone: 902-424-4247).

MUSKOKA WINTER CARNIVAL, Bracebridge, Gravenhurst, and Huntsville, Ontario: This 4-day festival held each February in the Muskoka Lakes district 100 miles (161 km) north of Toronto, is known for the assortment of wild and wacky contests that are on the agenda — motorcycle races, bed races, Wreck-um Derby, snow sculptures, and a talent contest, just to name a few. Information: Ursala Babcock, Box 1749, Gravenhurst, Ontario P0C 1G0 (phone: 705-687-3412) and Ontario Ministry of Tourism and Recreation, Box 1410, 114 Main St. E., Huntsville, Ontario P0A 1K0 (phone: 705-789-4448).

KITCHENER-WATERLOO OKTOBERFEST, Kitchener, Ontario: The German and Pennsylvania Dutch settlers who founded this town around 1800 and named it Berlin never would have imagined that the settlement would give rise to anything like this event, which attracts some 600,000 and ranks among the biggest celebrations of its kind in North America. German clubs and area service groups sponsor nearly 25 festhalls groaning with sausage, sauerkraut, and beer, and, while diners and guzzlers partake, oompah bands merrily entertain. There are concerts, folk-dance shows, performances by brass bands and drum corps, sports tourneys, Canada's largest *Thanksgiving Day* parade, and more — even *Thanksgiving* church services. The event starts the weekend of the Canadian *Thanksgiving.* King Ludwig's Castle at Speakers' Corner is the information center. Information: Kitchener-Waterloo Oktoberfest, Inc., 77 Ontario St. S., PO Box 1053, Kitchener, Ontario N2G 4G1 (phone: 519-576-0571).

SHAW FESTIVAL, Niagara-on-the-Lake, Ontario: With some help from an energetic citizenry instrumental in restoring the many old buildings and homes of this historic Upper Canada capital, George Bernard Shaw has done for Niagara-on-the-Lake what Shakespeare did for Stratford. Every year, from May to October, three separate theaters are given over to productions of ten plays by the celebrated Victorian playwright and his contemporaries. What began as a small community of devoted actors has become one of the most successful professional theaters in North America. Information: Shaw Festival, PO Box 774, Niagara-on-the-Lake, Ontario L0S 1J0 (phone: 416-468-2172). Also see *The Heritage Highways,* DIRECTIONS.

WINTERLUDE, Ottawa, Ontario: No matter how scenic, around about February snow and cold can wear on the nerves of even the most stoic. So Ottawa has created *Winterlude* to help lift the spirits of citizens and winter visitors alike. The second week of February finds this lovely capital alive with harness races on ice, skating shows, music races, and contests of many descriptions. Elaborate ice sculptures delight the eye and fireworks quicken the blood. Hot air balloons provide one mode of transportation, but then so do the ubiquitous skates — everyone in Ottawa, it seems, skates on the Rideau Canal. And, what's more, 1990 marks *Winterlude*'s 13th anniversary. Information: Canada's Capital Visitors and Convention Bureau, 222 Queen St., 7th Floor, Ottawa, Ontario K1P 5V9 (phone: 613-237-5158), or visit the information center at 65 Elgin St., in the National Arts Centre. Also see *Ice Skating.*

FESTIVAL OF SPRING, Ottawa, Ontario: To commemorate the enforced exile of the Dutch royal family in Ottawa during World War II, the people of the Netherlands presented the capital city with 100,000 tulip bulbs in 1945. An additional 20,000 tulip bulbs have been sent every year since, making the Ottawa display the largest of its kind in North America. The blossoming of these Dutch flowers, spectacular enough to bring you from afar to begin with, occasions a 10-day, mid-May program of outdoor entertainment for all ages, including the 10-kilometer National Capital Marathon, a procession of decorated boats on the Rideau Canal, a huge craft market, aerial events, firework displays, and more. Information: Festival of Spring, 1743 St. Laurent Blvd., Suite 226, Ottawa, Ontario K1G 3V4 (phone: 613-238-2345).

NIAGARA GRAPE AND WINE FESTIVAL, St. Catharines, Ontario: Some 25,500 acres are given over to viniculture around this southern Ontario town, so it's only appropriate that at harvest time — in late September — the citizenry celebrates. Over 200 events are planned each year, ranging from winery tours and wine-and-cheese parties to gala balls and gourmet wine tastings, as well as athletic competitions, arts and crafts shows, and concerts. The Grande Parade is one of North America's best. Information: Niagara Grape and Wine Festival, 145 King St. (Carlisle St. entrance), St. Catharines, Ontario L2R 3J2 (phone: 416-688-0212).

STRATFORD FESTIVAL, Stratford, Ontario: This event, held from May to October, produces some of the best theater in the world. Originally known for its fine star-studded productions of Shakespeare, the festival now presents a fine program including plays by other classical writers, world premieres, musicals, and modern contemporary classics; the fame of the *Festival* has attracted actors like Maggie Smith and Peter Ustinov, and the conception brought Alec Guinness and Irene Worth here in the early years. Guest celebrity lectures and other related events are also part of the program. A trio of performing halls houses productions running in repertory throughout the season — so much theater that you could stay for days and still not see everything. The *Festival Theatre,* with a thrust stage, which seats 2,262 within 66 feet of it, presents four or five plays per season; the *Avon Theatre,* with a traditional proscenium arch stage, features contemporary works and classics; the *Third Stage* (another thrust), spotlights the work of the *Young Company.* Information: Stratford Festival, PO Box 520, Stratford, Ontario N5A 6V2 (phone: 519-271-4040).

CANADIAN NATIONAL EXHIBITION, Toronto, Ontario: The world's largest annual exposition, this enormous Canadian version of a state fair keeps over 2 million visitors entertained with everything from a mile-and-a-half midway to agricultural displays and competitions. Artisans compete for prizes with their quilts and other handiwork. There are grandstand shows with name performers, an air show, daily water shows, and many major league sports events. The CNE, founded in 1879, runs from mid-August to Labor Day. Information: Canadian National Exhibition, Exhibition P1., Toronto, Ontario M6K 3C3 (phone: 416-393-6000).

CHARLOTTETOWN FESTIVAL, Charlottetown, Prince Edward Island: Devoted primarily to showcasing large-scale musical productions, this festival also presents the long-running *Anne of Green Gables,* as well as children's entertainment, arts and crafts exhibits, and art classes (some of which can be joined on a single-lesson basis). The June-through-September program was begun by the Confederation Centre of the Arts in 1964. Information: Public Relations, Confederation Centre of the Arts, PO Box 848, Charlottetown, PEI C1A 7L9 (phone: 902-566-2464; box office, 902-566-1267).

LOBSTER CARNIVAL AND LIVESTOCK EXHIBITION, Summerside, Prince Edward Island: Every year the population of this small town of 10,000 swells eightfold as former residents come home and tourists throng here to watch the Miss PEI Beauty Pageant and enjoy daily harness races (the highlight is the Governor's Plate), a mammoth parade, talent contest, daily stage entertainment, and delicious lobster suppers. Held in July. Information: PEI Tourism, Visitors Services Division, PO Box 940, Charlottetown, PEI C1A 7M5 (phone: 902-368-4444).

TYNE VALLEY OYSTER FESTIVAL, Tyne Valley, Prince Edward Island: If you like oysters, this 4-day event, held in early August in an old, picture-pretty community, is for you. In addition to all the fiddling, step dancing, songfests, and parades found in similar fairs in the area, you get oysters — fried, raw, in chowder, and prepared just about any other way you can imagine. Oysters are served at down-home oyster dinners,

Friday and Saturday, and Sunday is the day for harness racing. Information: PEI Tourism, Visitors Services Division, PO Box 940, Charlottetown, PEI C1A 7M5 (phone: 902-368-4444).

QUEBEC WINTER CARNIVAL, Quebec City, Quebec: Quebec fairly explodes for 10 days early each February. Tens of thousands of visitors jam the hotels and crowd the twisted streets of the old town. Parades, ice-carving exhibitions, and snowshoe races fill the calendar, not to mention the crazy canoe race across the ice-choked St. Lawrence River. Information: Quebec Winter Carnival, 290 Rue Joly, Quebec City, Quebec G1N 1L8 (phone: 418-626-3716); or Quebec City Region Tourism & Convention Bureau, 60 Rue d'Auteuil, Quebec City, Quebec G1R 4C4 (phone: 418-692-2471).

WEST

CALGARY EXHIBITION & STAMPEDE, Calgary, Alberta: Canada's self-styled "Greatest Outdoor Show on Earth" draws people from all over the world for 10 days annually, around the first or second week of July. The Half Million Dollar Rodeo, which takes place daily, ranks among the top events on the circuit, and cowboys compete hard for prize money in bareback-bronc riding, saddle-bronc riding, bull riding, steer wrestling, calf roping, barrel racing, wild-horse racing, wild-cow milking, and Indian-buffalo riding. But there are also World Championship Chuckwagon Races, live entertainment, a casino, Indian dance competitions, rock concerts, agricultural exhibits, a midway, a big parade, a vast array of free entertainment, and much more. This is the Wild West at its 20th-century best. Information: Calgary Stampede, PO Box 1860, Calgary, Alberta T2P 2M7 (phone: 403-261-0101 or 800-661-1260) for tickets; Calgary Tourist and Convention Bureau, 237 8th Ave. SE, Calgary, Alberta T2G 0K8 (phone: 403-263-8510) for details on accommodations.

KLONDIKE DAYS, Edmonton, Alberta: The fact that Edmonton is on the map today is almost exclusively owing to the turn-of-the-century Gold Rush in the Yukon, when the community became a supply depot and departure point for north-bound fortune seekers. So when the town fathers were casting around for a theme for a community celebration, this colorful heritage was a natural choice. Everyone dresses in Gay Nineties garb, and buildings all over town disappear behind 19th-century storefronts. All very colorful. What makes the festival so much fun — for the residents as well as the tourists — is the lively program of activities that features everything from marching bands and flapjack breakfasts to river raft and bathtub races, street entertainment, community dances, and sporting events, as well as a midway — Canada's biggest. *Klondike Days* takes place during the last half of each July just after the *Calgary Stampede*. Information: Edmonton Klondike Days Association, 1660-10020-101A Avenue, Edmonton, Alberta T5J 3G2 (phone: 403-426-4055).

WORLD CHAMPIONSHIP OUTHOUSE RACE AND LAC LA HACHE WINTER CARNIVAL, Lac La Hache, British Columbia: This one-of-a-kind affair, featuring one- and two-holers mounted on runners, skis, or skate blades and fitted out with doors (for the sake of modesty), keeps Lac La Hachians thinking outhouses all year-round. Losers can compete in grudge matches; and, lest outsiders feel left out, race planners have included a borrow-an-outhouse match. All sorts of other winter activities are also on the agenda for the 4 days of this February event. Information: Visitor Information, PO Box 252, Lac La Hache, BC V0K 1T0.

WORLD CHAMPION BATHTUB RACE, Nanaimo to Vancouver, British Columbia: The madcap race across the 34 miles of the Strait of Georgia, under the aegis of the Loyal Order of the Bathtub Society, is one of those things you have to see to believe. Why would anyone want to watch a bathtub race, you ask? Suffice it to say that this contest, held every July in conjunction with the *Vancouver Sea Festival,* in "The Bathtub Capital of the World," has spawned dozens more, and, to this day, every bathtub race follows Nanaimo rules. Information: Tourism Vancouver, Pavilion Plaza,

4 Bentall Centre, 1055 Dunsmire St., PO Box 49296, Vancouver, BC V7X 1L3 (phone: 604-683-2000).

VERNON WINTER CARNIVAL, Vernon, British Columbia: This Okanagan Valley community, 110 miles (176) from the international border near Penticton, hosts one of Canada's wildest and wackiest events annually in February — 10 days of old-fashioned skating parties for kids, competitions in broomball, snowgolf, jogging, bed-racing, ice sculpture, and racquetball. In the evening, there are parties given over to Mardi Gras–type merriment, Hawaiiana, Ukrainiana, Klondikiana, MASH-mania, and the like. Some hundred-odd events are staged, but despite the scope, there's a friendliness and a homespun feeling here that you won't find at similar events in the big cities in the East. While you're here, you can stay to ski the lovely Silver Star Mountain with fine dining and on-hill accommodations for 600 (phone: 604-545-2236). Information: Vernon Winter Carnival, 3303 35th Ave., Vernon, BC V1T 2T5, or phone the Tourist Information Center, 604-545-0771. Also see *Downhill Skiing*.

NATIONAL UKRAINIAN FESTIVAL, Dauphin, Manitoba: Cabbage rolls and pirogi, painted Easter eggs and intricate hand-carvings: The culinary and artistic traditions brought by this group of immigrants is extraordinarily rich, as you'll see at this 4-day event which takes place annually during the last weekend in July and the first weekend in August. The events include music, dance, workshops, authentic Ukrainian foods, displays, four grandstand shows, and a colorful parade. It ought to give you a new appreciation for Canada-as-melting-pot. Information: National Ukrainian Festival, 119 Main St. S., Dauphin, Manitoba R7N 1K4 (phone: 204-638-5645); or Dauphin Chamber of Commerce, 107 Main St., N., Dauphin, Manitoba R7N 1C1 (phone: 204-638-4838).

FESTIVAL DU VOYAGEUR, St. Boniface, Manitoba: Every year during the third week in February, this district of Winnipeg stages 10 days of parades, concerts of French-Canadian music, and all manner of contests (in snow sculpture, jigging, fiddling, hockey, ringette, and dog-sled racing) in an effort to beat the midwinter blahs. And it seems to work. Information: Festival du Voyageur, 768 Taché Ave., St. Boniface, Manitoba R2H 2C4 (phone: 204-237-7692).

NORTHERN MANITOBA TRAPPERS' FESTIVAL, The Pas, Manitoba: The oldest festival in western Canada — originated in 1916 — the *Trappers' Festival* is a celebration of the heritage and traditions of the northern pioneer. This five-day event takes place in the third week of February and includes the World Championship Dog Race, a 105-mile, 3-day-long dog sled race that carries over $24,000 in prize money. Events in the King Trapper category include contests in bannock baking, flour packing, log climbing, animal calling, and a marathon snowshoe race. Other goings-on include craft shows, beerfests, ice fishing, and more. Information: Northern Manitoba Trappers' Festival Inc., PO Box 475, The Pas, Manitoba R9A 0N2 (phone: 204-623-7745 or 204-623-2912); or Travel Manitoba, Dept. 8269, 155 Carlton St., 7th Floor, Winnipeg, Manitoba R3C 3H8 (phone: 800-665-0040 ext. 269 or 204-945-3777 collect).

National Parks

A visit to one of Canada's national parks gives you a glimpse into a world of natural beauty that exists scarcely anywhere else on earth: From the rainy coast of the Pacific Rim, with its dense vegetation, to the imposing Canadian Rockies, from rolling prairies to storm-pounded Atlantic shores, the Canadian park system preserves the precious and sometimes fragile ecology of some of the nation's most distinctive regions. Its 70,000 square miles are a vast playground for nature lovers and a rich example of Canada's diverse natural and cultural heritage.

But the system is also designed to please anglers, boaters, golfers, hikers, skiers, campers, swimmers, and photographers. All but the most remote have campgrounds, hiking trails, scenic driving routes, and lively interpretive programs that everyone can enjoy. Details are available from Environment Canada, Parks, Ottawa, Ontario K1A 0H3 (phone: 819-997-3736), or from the individual park offices. A checklist of all the parks follows. For more detailed information about your visit, consult the appropriate section in DIRECTIONS.

EAST

FUNDY NATIONAL PARK, near Alma, New Brunswick: Some of the world's highest tides rise and fall here and, retreating, leave behind vast tidal flats full of periwinkles, limpets, and other sea creatures that make a stroll in the area a delight. The cave-pocked, 200-foot cliffs that the surf pounds elsewhere and the rolling terrain inland, cut by deep valleys whose steep rocky walls are ribboned with waterfalls, are among the park's other features. You can see it all on some 80 miles of hiking trails, which range from a 30-minute loop trail to a 4-day backpacking adventure. Information: Fundy National Park, PO Box 40, Alma, NB E0A 1B0 (phone: 506-887-2000).

KOUCHIBOUGUAC NATIONAL PARK, Kent County, New Brunswick: The name means "River of the Long Tides," and the water — among the warmest north of the Carolinas — is shallow and gentle. There are also a multitude of environments: rivers, beaches, bogs, salt marshes, lagoons, fields, forests, and sand dunes. The area hosts a profusion of migrating waterfowl in spring and fall, and also features trout, flounder, and striped bass (anglers need a park fishing license). Fees are modest and attention has been given to providing considerable access for the physically challenged. At the visitor reception center, you can view an award-winning slide presentation about the park. Information: Kouchibouguac National Park, Kouchibouguac, Kent Co., NB E0A 2A0 (phone: 506-876-2443).

GROS MORNE NATIONAL PARK, near Rocky Harbour, Newfoundland: Situated on the province's west coast at the base of the Great Northern Peninsula, this 703-square-mile preserve dominated by the 2,644-foot Gros Morne Mountain is home to some of the nation's most spectacular scenery — fjordlike ponds, barren expanses of volcanic rock, heavily wooded forests and alpine meadows, bogs and beaches, tide pools and surf-washed headlands, and waterfalls that cascade for such long distances that the stream turns to spray before it hits bottom. The plant and animal life is equally diverse, and the fishing is good. There are several miles of hiking trails to show it all off. Information: Gros Morne National Park, PO Box 130, Rocky Harbour, Newfoundland A0K 4N0 (phone: 709-458-2066 or 709-458-2417).

TERRA NOVA NATIONAL PARK, near Glovertown, Newfoundland: Canada's easternmost national park, this 153-square-mile expanse of ponds, peatlands, spruce, and fir rolls westward from the rugged, rocky coastline adjoining Bonavista Bay and the Labrador Sea, punctuated by natural arches, notched by inlets, and fronted by steep cliffs, from which you can often spot bluish-white icebergs, carried south by the Labrador Current in spring and early summer, or you may spy some of Terra Nova's inhabitants, such as moose, lynx, and bald eagle. Virtually all the outdoor pursuits — bird-watching, hiking, camping, swimming, sailing, snorkeling, scuba diving, cross-country skiing, snowshoeing, golfing, fishing, and canoeing — are available. Information: Terra Nova National Park, Glovertown, Newfoundland A0G 2L0 (phone: 709-533-2801).

AUYUITTUQ NATIONAL PARK, Baffin Island, Northwest Territories: The 8,290 square miles of this national park ("the land that does not melt") are dominated by the spiky, 7,000-foot-high Penny Highlands and their 2,200-square-mile ice cap. Plants have a tenuous hold on existence in such terrain, but the bright blossoms that polka-dot the meadows in June and July, when the May-through-July midnight sun has worked its magic, are among the park's real beauties. And though there are 40 species of birds, and other wildlife abounds, rocks and mountains are what people come here to enjoy. The celebrated Pangnirtung Pass trek is a must for experienced hikers. April, May, and early June are perfect for winter activities such as snowmobiling, cross-country skiing, and snowshoeing; in July and August, there's excellent fishing for the prized Arctic char in the tidewater of Cumberland Sound. Information: Superintendent, Auyuittuq National Park, Pangnirtung, Northwest Territories X0A 0R0 (phone: 819-473-8962). Also see *Mountain Climbing.*

CAPE BRETON HIGHLANDS NATIONAL PARK, near Ingonish Beach, Nova Scotia: One of the most scenic of the Canadian national parks, this one occupies a stretch of tundra-, bog-, and forest-covered highlands between the Gulf of St. Lawrence and the Atlantic Ocean. The 180-mile-long Cabot Trail winds along a famous stretch of coastline, where the mountains meet the sea in awe-inspiring cliffs dotted by bizarrely twisted spruce trees. Equally lovely sights greet those who wander down the park's hiking trails. Stay at the charming *Keltic Lodge,* near the *Cape Breton Highland Links,* one of Canada's best 18-hole courses. Information: Cape Breton Highlands National Park, Ingonish Beach, NS B0C 1L0 (phone: 902-285-2270). Also see *Special Havens* and *Golf.*

KEJIMKUJIK NATIONAL PARK, near Maitland Bridge, Nova Scotia: These rolling, forested 147 square miles are a paradise for backcountry campers and canoeists, thanks to a good system of canoe routes and hiking trails. There's a variety of activities available year-round. The hospitable climate and abundance of wetlands make survival possible here for many species not found elsewhere in Atlantic Canada. Information: Kejimkujik National Park, PO Box 36, Maitland Bridge, Annapolis County, NS B0T 1N0 (phone: 902-682-2772).

GEORGIAN BAY ISLANDS NATIONAL PARK, near Honey Harbour, Ontario: Lake Huron's immense Georgian Bay is only about 2 hours north of Toronto, but its waters are sparklingly clear and island-dotted. Fifty-nine islands in the southeastern part of the Bay belong to this preserve, a favorite of swimmers, fishermen, boaters, hikers, and campers. If you don't have your own boat, you can hire a water taxi or join a tour boat in nearby mainland towns. Information: Georgian Bay Islands National Park, Box 28, Honey Harbour, Ontario P0E 1E0 (phone: 705-756-2415).

POINT PELEE NATIONAL PARK, near Leamington, Ontario: The most southern point on Canada's mainland is a huge sandspit jutting into Lake Erie. Internationally known for its spring and autumn concentrations of migrating birds and stunning monarch butterfly migration each fall. There are miles of sandy beaches, marshes to explore by canoe, and a theater program at the visitor center. Information: Point Pelee National Park, RR1, Leamington, Ontario N8H 3V4 (phone: 519-322-2365).

ST. LAWRENCE ISLANDS NATIONAL PARK, between Brockville and Kingston Ontario: Canada's smallest national park is scattered over 21 of the famous Thousand Islands in the region between Brockville and Kingston, Ontario. Major activities include boating, hiking, camping, fishing, and plain old relaxing. Wide-ranging facilities include individual and group campsites, beaches, and interpretive trails. The mainland base at Mallorytown Landing has parking, campsites, playground, and general day-use facilities. Access to the islands is by private boat, boat rental, or water taxi, and faciliities are available at most of the many local marinas along the river. Information: St. Lawrence Islands National Park, Box 469, RR3, Mallorytown, Ontario K0E 1R0 (phone: 613-923-5261).

PUKASKWA NATIONAL PARK, near Marathon, Ontario: Located 15 miles east of Marathon, Ontario, and accessible by Highway 627, Pukaskwa encompasses a boreal wilderness of 725 square miles on the rocky landscape of the Canadian Shield. The major reception area at Hattie Cove offers 67 semi-serviced campgrounds (with showers), a visitor center, and walking trails on the nearby headlands and beaches of Lake

Superior. The coastal hiking trail (40 miles long) provides opportunities for day and overnight hikes. The bays, harbors, and coves of the park coastline afford limited protection to sea kayakers, canoeists, and boaters. Information: Pukaskwa National Park, Hwy. 627, Hattie Cove, Heron Bay, Ontario P0T IR0 (phone: 807-229-0801).

PRINCE EDWARD ISLAND NATIONAL PARK, near Charlottetown, Prince Edward Island: A prime example of the kind of sandy Atlantic shoreline that Americans prize on Cape Cod, this stretch of northern PEI is all scalloped bays and inlets, sand dunes, sandy beaches, and salt marshes. More than 200 species of birds have been recorded along the park's 25 miles of coast. There are also eight supervised beaches, three campgrounds, lots of recreational activities, and the farmhouse immortalized in Lucy Maud Montgomery's *Anne of Green Gables*. Information: Prince Edward Island National Park, PO Box 487, Charlottetown, PEI C1A 7L1 (phone: 902-672-2211).

FORILLON NATIONAL PARK, Gaspé Peninsula, Quebec: The foghorns moan and the gulls wheel and cry as Quebec meets the sea at this splendid preserve set on a needle-headed, 92-square-mile triangle of land that pokes roughly southeastward into the Atlantic. In the easternmost section, 600-foot-high limestone cliffs slice into the sea. The wildlife here is abundant and varied: some 200 species of birds live in the park, and thousands of sea birds visit annually in summer; whales can usually be spotted off the coast from mid-May to around October; and gray and harbor seals are year-round residents. Inland, there are forests, peat bogs, dunes, lakes, and dozens of streams. Besides the camping, hiking, biking, scuba diving, and sightseeing cruises that keep summer visitors busy, there's snowshoeing, winter camping, and cross-country skiing in winter months. A park interpretation center and an interpretive program help visitors to discover the treasures and beauties of the park. Information: Forillon National Park, PO Box 1220, Gaspé, Quebec G0C 1R0 (phone: 418-368-5505).

LA MAURICIE NATIONAL PARK, near Shawinigan, Quebec: The scenic St. Maurice River flows along the eastern border of this 210-square-mile expanse of glacier-scoured, forest-covered wilderness, and the interconnected lakes and streams forming the river's watershed make for some very good canoeing. Thirteen-mile-long Lake Wapizagonke, contained between two high rocky escarpments, is a principal beauty spot. Hiking, camping, canoeing, canoe-camping and fishing, and cross-country skiing are popular. Two winter shelters provide 44 beds for cross-country skiers. Information: La Mauricie National Park, PO Box 758, Shawinigan, Quebec G9N 6V9 (phone: 819-536-2638).

WEST

BANFF NATIONAL PARK, Banff, Alberta: Established in 1885 on the site of hot sulfur springs discovered by three railway construction workers, this park takes in 2,500 square miles of Canada's most spectacular mountains, alpine meadows, glaciers, forested slopes, rivers, and lakes. And, though the springs are still there — delightful for soaks — getting out into the mountains is the real attraction. The park's network of hiking trails is well developed, and you can go canoeing, riding, skiing, fishing, boating, sailing, scuba diving, and climbing as well. Information: Banff National Park, Box 900, Banff, Alberta T0L 0C0 (phone: 403-762-3324). Also see *Golf, Tennis, Downhill* and *Cross-Country Skiing, Mountain Climbing, Ice Skating,* and *Special Havens.*

WATERTON LAKES NATIONAL PARK, near Cardston, Alberta: It's been said that this Canadian section of the Waterton-Glacier International Peace Park crams a maximum of scenery into a minimum of space. For while the park is only 204 square miles, its scenery varies greatly as a result of its location in a transitional zone between the prairie and the peaks. There's good hiking on 108 miles of prairie and mountain trails, plus riding, biking, fishing, tennis, golf, swimming, and boating (rentals are available at Cameron Lake). Waterton has three campgrounds. In addition, nightly interpretation programs are offered at Townsite and Crandall campgrounds. Information: Waterton Lakes National Park, Waterton Park, Alberta T0K 2M0 (phone: 403-859-2445).

ELK ISLAND NATIONAL PARK, near Edmonton, Alberta: In the early 1900s, when the elk in the Beaver Hills were in danger of extinction, a few conservationists banded together and successfully lobbied for the government to establish a fenced-in preserve to save the animals from hunters. Now, some 1,200 elk, as well as 500 plains bison and 250 rare wood bison, make the park their home. Summer activities include camping, canoeing, sailing, hiking, picnicking, and golf (9 holes); in winter, hiking trails are trekked by snowshoers and cross-country skiers. Information: Elk Island National Park, Attention: Visitor Services, Site 4, RR1, Fort Saskatchewan, Alberta T8L 2N7 (phone: 403-992-6380).

JASPER NATIONAL PARK, Jasper, Alberta: Named for Jasper Hawes, a fur trader of the early 1800s, these 4,200 square miles of lofty peaks and alpine valleys, clear lakes and thundering falls are a backpacker's paradise, thanks to the extensive trail system. On horseback treks, riders often spot all manner of big game. All-weather parkways provide access to such scenic highlights as Maligne Lake, Athabasca Falls, and the renowned Columbia Icefield area. Information: Jasper National Park, Jasper, Alberta T0E 1E0 (phone: 403-852-6161).

WOOD BUFFALO NATIONAL PARK, near Fort Smith, Northwest Territories: One of the world's largest national parks, with some 17,300 square miles, this wilderness preserve is home to the largest extant herds of free-roaming bison in the world and is the only natural nesting ground of the whooping crane. Named a UNESCO World Heritage Site in 1983, it also contains most of the spectacular Peace-Athabasca Delta, one of the planet's biggest freshwater deltas, a staging area for millions of waterfowl. Salt flats with beautiful and unusual vegetation extend throughout the northeastern part of the park. Access is by car or boat, and regularly scheduled flights land at Fort Smith, NWT, and Fort Chipewyan, Alberta. Information: Wood Buffalo National Park, PO Box 750, Fort Smith, Northwest Territories X0E 0P0 (phone: 403-872-2349).

YOHO NATIONAL PARK, Field, British Columbia: Named by the Cree Indians ("Yoho" is an expression meaning *awe*), this 507-square-mile preserve near the top of the Rockies takes in about 25 peaks over 10,000 feet, countless cascading streams and spectacular falls, plus lush forests. The 250-odd miles of hiking trails take you through areas inhabited by the park's abundant wildlife. Or you can take in the park's glories from your car as you drive along the Trans-Canada Highway. Information: Superintendent, Yoho National Park, PO Box 99, Field, BC V0A 1G0 (phone: 604-343-6324).

KOOTENAY NATIONAL PARK, Radium Hot Springs, British Columbia: The Banff-Windermere Highway, the focal point of this long, skinny preserve, makes its beauties remarkably accessible. There in front of you are towering peaks by the score, the 128-foot depths of Marble Canyon; the rusty-colored paint pots whose iron-rich mud the Indians used as body paint; and all manner of wildlife. In May and October, as many as 300 elk may congregate alongside the road at any given time. A complex of swimming and soaking pools is also available. Information: Kootenay National Park, Box 220, Radium Hot Springs, BC V0A 1M0 (phone: 604-347-9615).

GLACIER NATIONAL PARK, near Rogers Pass, British Columbia: A trip to this 521-square-mile preserve in the rugged Selkirk and Purcell ranges is a fascinating geography lesson where you learn that glaciers are dynamic, ever-moving forces, able to slice off whole sections of mountains and carve out their peaks, dig valleys, and polish rock faces as smooth as glass. Evidence of eons of this slicing, carving, and polishing is what makes Glacier so special. But there are wonderful wildflowers as well. Be sure to visit the information center at Rogers Pass. Information: Glacier National Park, PO Box 350, Revelstoke, BC V0E 2S0 (phone: 604-837-5155 or 6274).

MT. REVELSTOKE NATIONAL PARK, near Revelstoke, British Columbia: The views in this 99-square-mile park — particularly from the lookout atop Mt. Revelstoke itself — are what will astound you, because the mountains, which surround the area, are exceptionally rugged and the forests unusually dense. Alpine meadows bloom bright in late summer — as you'll see when you head out on the park's hiking trails that cover over 39 miles. Information: Mt. Revelstoke National Park, PO Box 350, Revelstoke, BC V0E 2S0 (phone: 604-837-5155).

PACIFIC RIM NATIONAL PARK, near Ucluelet, Vancouver Island, British Columbia: This is a wet world. Heavy rains and salt spray produce dense vegetation on the mountains that rise abruptly from the sea on the western edge of this 150-square-mile park. Tidal pools trap clusters of hermit crabs, starfish, limpets, and mussels. But inland the peaks are often snow-capped. The West Coast Trail, chopped out of the storm-pounded sea cliffs, is one of the nation's great hiking adventures, and 14-mile-long Long Beach among its finest strands. Offshore, you can fish, canoe, and camp — in utter solitude — at the Broken Group Islands. Information: Pacific Rim National Park, PO Box 280, Ucluelet, BC V0R 3A0 (phone: 604-726-7721 or 4212).

RIDING MOUNTAIN NATIONAL PARK, near Dauphin, Manitoba: Riding Mountain isn't a mountain at all, but a huge, 2,000-foot-high plateau. Covered with the kind of thick forest more commonly found in the east, as well as the grasslands that are typical of the surrounding prairies, the park's 1,150 square miles are laced with hiking and cross-country ski trails, and a spectrum of wildlife can be spotted. Many visitors come to battle the feisty, voracious northern pike, which is the main game fish, but pickerel, trout, perch, and whitefish can also be caught. Information: Riding Mountain National Park, Wasagaming, Manitoba R0J 2H0 (phone: 204-848-2811).

NAHANNI NATIONAL PARK, near Fort Simpson, Northwest Territories: The first area to be named to UNESCO's World Heritage List of natural sites that form part of our collective heritage, this 1,840-square-mile wilderness surrounding the South Nahanni River is spectacularly beautiful. Unusual plants, high mountains, and incredible canyons manage to dazzle you as much as Virginia Falls — an immense cataract that plunges about 400 feet to the river and shows a 4-acre face of whiteness in the process. Access is by chartered aircraft from Fort Simpson, Fort Liard, Fort Nelson, or Watson Lake; you can run the river and its tributaries in canoes or rafts, on your own or with groups, and explore the mountains and valleys on foot. Since this area is very remote, you must book ahead if you plan to use the services of an outfitter. Information: Nahanni National Park, PO Box 300, Fort Simpson, Northwest Territories X0E 0N0 (phone: 403-695-3151).

PRINCE ALBERT NATIONAL PARK, near Prince Albert, Saskatchewan: Wildlife — moose, deer, elk, caribou, black bear, bison, and beaver — is abundant, and over 200 species of birds have been recorded (one of Canada's largest white pelican colonies being located at Lavallee Lake in the park's secluded northwest corner). Located 30 miles (48 km) north of Prince Albert — the Waskesiu Lake Visitor Services Center is an additional 30 miles (48 km) north — this million-acre wilderness park is near the geographical center of the province. Here, a rolling glacial terrain dotted with spruce bogs, large, cold lakes, and aspen uplands is preserved. Interpretive programs explain the fascinating ecosystems you'll see if you go hiking or canoeing. Information: Prince Albert National Park, PO Box 100, Waskesiu Lake, Saskatchewan S0J 2Y0 (phone: 306-663-5322).

KLUANE NATIONAL PARK, near Haines Junction, Yukon Territory: A good deal of this park's 8,500 square miles is given over to glaciers and mountains, including 19,520-foot Mt. Logan, Canada's highest peak. The world's largest ice fields outside the polar regions are here. Consequently, Kluane is a mountaineer's dream — even though climbing in the Icefield Ranges always means an expedition. But the park's eastern section is unglaciated, and using the old mining roads and some newly constructed trails, you can get a good feeling for a less forbidding Kluane, a preserve that boasts an amazing variety of flora, fauna, and terrain. Kluane's interpretive program, based at a fine visitors center, includes a number of special events and campfire talks at the Kathleen Lake and Congdon Creek campgrounds. Information: Kluane National Park, Haines Junction, Yukon Territory Y0B 1L0 (phone: 403-634-2251).

Special Havens

Since standardization has begun to overtake the Canadian hotel industry, finding acceptable accommodations is usually not a problem. But a question arises: Where are all the hostelries with unique atmosphere, distinctive personality, style, and histories all their own? Not to worry. They're still around, though scattered, from the Maritimes to the Pacific Coast; and sometimes hard to find. A few resorts in this class are better advertised, but putting your finger on one with the facilities and activities that suit you can be a taxing chore.

The Canadian havens described here — our favorites — are places you'll want to visit when the locale is as important as what you do there. Among them are both resorts and inns. Most of the resorts feature stables, championship golf courses, biking and hiking paths, swimming pools, beaches, and often nightclubs and similar after-dark diversions. The inns, usually tucked away in some beautiful part of the country for which the innkeeper has a special affinity, are quieter and smaller. In either case, accommodations will cost more than at a less interesting establishment. If money is an important consideration, ask about off-season rates, normally offered in spring or fall; summers are always busy, and many properties fill to the rafters with skiers just after the first snowfall. Some hostelries also offer lower rates during the week. It's also wise to inquire whether activities will cost extra at resorts, and don't forget to budget for tips.

EAST

MARATHON INN, Grand Manan Island, New Brunswick: The bird life that Audubon admired when he visited here in the early part of the 19th century is as rich as ever, and some 300 species feed on the wild strawberries, blueberries, and blackberries that fairly blanket the island — the largest of the trio of Bay of Fundy isles — in summer. You'll certainly want to watch the birds, but you'll also want to gather the berries to eat with cream at the inn, admire the lupine and other wildflowers that polka-dot the meadows, and join one of the whale-watching tours conducted from August 1 to mid-September. Other activities include: tennis, swimming, beachcombing, hiking, and bicycling. The hotel itself, built in 1871 atop a hill so that there's almost always a breeze, is a delight — well kept, from the wide hallways that lead to the 32 gleaming, lofty-ceilinged guestrooms to the widow's walk that tops the three-story structure; all but six rooms have views over the harbor (and most rooms share a bath). The package is well worth the little extra effort it takes to get to the island, which is accessible only by ferry from Black's Harbor, east of Calais, Maine, on the Canadian side of the border. Open May to October. Information: Marathon Inn, North Head, Grand Manan Island, NB E0G 2M0 (phone: 506-662-8144).

MARSHLANDS INN, Sackville, New Brunswick: Built between 1850 and 1860 and owned by the same family from 1895 until a few years ago, the huge house has been a hostelry for only 5 decades — plenty of time to mellow a place, and when you visit this 16-room establishment, you'll feel as if you've stopped in someone's exceptionally wonderful private home. Before you're packed off to bed at night, they'll ply you with hot chocolate and gingersnaps. Later, if you get chilly, you've only to reach for the fluffy down comforter lying at the foot of your bed. In the morning, you're stuffed like a Périgord goose with goodies like baked apples and porridge, country sausage patties and buckwheat pancakes, and homemade breads and gooseberry jam. For lunch and dinner, you have a choice of all manner of specialties — steak-and-kidney pie, grilled Atlantic salmon (often with an egg sauce), boiled salt cod and pork scraps, and fiddleheads, the top portion of the ostrich fern, a New Brunswick specialty. As for the rooms, they vary. One of the nicer ones has a high four-poster and Oriental rugs. The Tantramar marshes, the summering site for thousands of Canada geese whose honks fill the air during spring and fall migrations, are on the nearby isthmus connecting New Brunswick and Nova Scotia. No wonder Queen Elizabeth took tea here when she toured New Brunswick. Open February through November. Information: Marshlands Inn, 73 Bridge St., PO Box 1440, Sackville, NB E0A 3C0 (phone: 506-536-0170).

ALGONQUIN, St. Andrews-by-the-Sea, New Brunswick: One of the loveliest of the Canadian Pacific hotels, this rambling English country manor of a hostelry, ringed by immaculately manicured lawns and well-tended flower gardens, sits on the edge of Passamaquoddy Bay on a hill overlooking the town, a short walk from the main street. Golfers make pilgrimages to the *Algonquin*'s 9- and 18-hole courses. Guests can swim in Katy's Cove or in the hotel's heated outdoor pool, play tennis or croquet, or go cycling. After such physical exertion, there are several restaurants and evening entertainments from which to choose for unwinding. Another way to relax is to visit the town for some of Canada's most interesting shopping or for a walking tour of the many late-18th- and early-19th-century houses built by the Loyalists who first settled the area. Information: Algonquin Hotel, St. Andrews, NB E0G 2X0 (phone: 506-529-8823). Also see *Golf* and *The Fundy Trail,* DIRECTIONS.

ROSSMOUNT INN, St. Andrews-by-the-Sea, New Brunswick: Victorian England must have been a lovely place, or so you would judge from spending the night at this century-old inn nestled in the woods at the foot of Chamcook Mountain. The inn is British to the core, from the delightful manners of the owners to the lovely carved-and-gleaming furnishings and the portraits of kings and queens hanging on the walls. There's even a dartboard in the taproom. The 16 bedrooms, all with private bath, are comfortable but plainer than the public rooms, and the menu features fresh fish, fruits and berries from the inn's gardens, and breads and desserts baked with whole grains, raw sugar, and honey. Vegetarian meals are offered. Walking, hiking, jogging on trails on the private 87-acre wildlife sanctuary, shopping in town, and playing golf on the nearby course are the favored pastimes. There's also a swimming pool. (Smoking is confined to certain areas, with none permitted in the dining room.) Information: Rossmount Inn, RR2, St. Andrews, NB E0G 2X0 (phone: 506-529-3351).

KELTIC LODGE, Cape Breton Island, Nova Scotia: The lonely site of this provincial government resort in magnificent Cape Breton Highlands National Park, on a rocky peninsula, assures each room a marvelous view over a landscape of rugged, heavily wooded highlands reminiscent of the Scottish Hebrides. That alone, or the hotel's proximity to the Cabot Trail, the scenic highway that rings the island, would make *Keltic Lodge* worth a visit. But it is a relaxing place for far longer stays. You can swim in the large pool or in a fresh water lake, or soak up the salt air on a mile-long beach not far away. The surrounding woods are full of hiking trails, ideal for peaceful rambles. And there's the epic Stanley Thompson–designed golf links and a tennis court. And when you've worked your appetite up to monstrous proportions, you can satisfy it in a big way: The fresh seafood caught by local fishermen and prepared by French chefs can't be beat. Accommodations are offered in the sedate *Main Lodge* with its 32 rooms, the modern 40-room *White Birch Inn,* or in one of the well-appointed cottages (2 or 4 bedrooms, plus a sitting room, in each). Information: Keltic Lodge, PO Box 70, Ingonish Beach, NS B0C 1L0 (phone: 902-285-2880). Also see *Golf* and *National Parks.*

KILMUIR PLACE, Cape Breton Island, Nova Scotia: This lovely little country house just off the Cabot Trail on Nova Scotia's Cape Breton Island is the kind of place to which we would all retire if life were fair. Since it is not, we can only hope to visit, and with only five guestrooms, you'd better book a place early if you hope to do even that. Once you get there, innkeepers Nancy and Guy Parry will make you abundantly welcome, whether you are having a salmon dinner in the dining room or sampling freshly baked goods in the friendly kitchen. The real reason for a visit — besides the utter peace of the place and the beauty of the island — is salmon fishing. The house is filled with family heirlooms, and the atmosphere is warm and loving. Open from end of June to mid-October. Information: Kilmuir Place, Northeast Margaree, Cape Breton Island, NS B0E 2H0 (phone: 902-248-2877).

MILFORD HOUSE, South Milford, Nova Scotia: Located in the province's lake district just 15 miles (24 km) from Kejimkujik National Park, this 600-acre country resort was founded in the 1860s as a stopping-off place for travelers. The main lodge, site of the dining room and the parlors, is a comfortable sort of place with polished wood floors and old-fashioned fireplaces. Guests stay in 27 scattered waterside 2- to 5-bedroom, fireplace-equipped cottages; each comes with its own dock. Hearty country fare — home-baked bread and pastries, fresh vegetables and native berries, homemade soups and fresh fish and roasts — is the specialty of the house. Though you'll find clean linen and fresh flowers on your table every day, *Milford House* is a very informal establishment. Families can bring their squalling babies and find themselves welcomed with open arms, so many return year after year until the children are grown. In fact, when the original owners sold it in 1969, it was to some longtime guests who have continued the traditions they'd grown to love. Canoeing, swimming, and fishing have always been the popular activities, but the tennis courts are starting to catch on, too. Golf is nearby. To get the space you want, you must count on having your reservations confirmed by season's opening in mid-June. The dining room closes in mid-September, but two off-season cabins are equipped for housekeeping and are open year-round. Information: Milford House, South Milford, RR4, Annapolis Royal, NS B0S 1A0 (phone: 902-532-2617). Also see *National Parks.*

MILLCROFT INN, Alton, Ontario: This has to be one of the continent's best examples of adaptive use of an old building. The structure is an 1881 knitting mill, a stone version of the kind that glowers resentfully at municipalities like New Bedford, Massachusetts, and Providence, Rhode Island, which have all but forgotten them. The Toronto movers and shakers behind the Millcroft project restored the mill, installed a bayed, glass-walled "dining pod" to provide guests with a profoundly stomach-churning view of the falls below, and then furnished the whole from stem to stern with a delightful blend of the contemporary and the antique. Lodgings are in rooms in the mill or in "crofts" (contemporary condominium-type loft units that can accommodate four). And the dinners include specialties like warm rabbit and guinea fowl salad, hot goat cheese with sesame seeds and vinaigrette, breast of capon with leeks and Stilton, and poached beef tenderloin with horseradish and mint. On the 100-acre property, you can also take advantage of a heated outdoor pool, sauna, whirlpool bath, Jacuzzi, tennis courts, and ice skating on the mill pond. And the cross-country skiing here in winter is great. Information: Millcroft Inn, Alton, Ontario L0N 1A0 (phone: 519-941-8111).

AROWHON PINES, Algonquin Park, Ontario: Smack in the center of a 3,000-square-mile wildlife preserve, this resort's draw is its natural beauty and tranquility. Seclusion is prized, as guests must travel a 5-mile private road to reach Arowhon, which is situated on the shore of its own lake. Each of the 2- to 12-bedroom cabins, furnished in Canadiana, has a communal lounge with a fireplace; or you can opt for one of three suites in a private cabin with a stone fireplace. Moose, deer, red fox, wolf, bear, and over 100 species of birds call the preserve home, and many hours can be spent seeking out these creatures while hiking the marked trails, picnicking in the woods, or boating. At night there are movies in the main lounge, or you can listen to the call of the loon in front of a blazing bonfire. A member of the Relais & Châteaux group, and known for its fine food fresh from the Canadian North Woods, *Arowhon Pines* is open from May 16 to October 10. Information: Arowhon Pines, Algonquin Park, Ontario P0A 1B0 (phone: 705-633-5661/2), in summer; 297 Balliol St., Toronto, Ontario M4S 1C7 (phone: 416-483-4393), in winter.

BENMILLER INN, Goderich, Ontario: Like so many inns, this one was the result of the owners' love affair with the locality — in this case, a London, Ontario, man and his sister fell in love with an area near Lake Huron, on the banks of the Maitland River, where they used to come as children. They acquired the area's woolen mill, then followed that with the purchase of a flour mill. When both mills had been restored and furnished with antiques, the mill owners' homes were bought, refurbished, and expanded to include 48 rooms. The complex now occupies some 70 acres of rolling woodlands by the river. Each of the four buildings has its own character, and each room is different; but the whole is furnished with antiques and items ingeniously crafted from the old mill machinery. Spindles, for instance, are used for room dividers, and wheels for the bases of coffee tables. The old beams and barnboard add to the rustic charm. There's great fishing in the surrounding stream and on the river during spring and fall, when the salmon run, and you can go trout fishing in the pond on the premises, swim in an indoor pool, play tennis (there are 2 outdoor courts). Stratford is only 45 miles (72 km) away. Information: Benmiller Inn, RR4, Goderich, Ontario N7A 3Y1 (phone: 519-524-2191; 800-265-1711).

PINESTONE INN AND COUNTRY CLUB, Haliburton, Ontario: The fact that you never have to travel very far in Canada to get away from the urban rat race is proved once more at this year-round resort hotel, with a total of 104 rooms in the hotel, villas, chalets, and executive suite. Although it is modern and almost citified — with tennis courts, indoor and outdoor swimming pools, 18-hole golf course, sauna, whirlpool bath, and 2 fancy restaurants with a long wine list — the atmosphere is decidedly low key. Flanking either side of the hotel are a pond and a lake (great for swimming, fishing, boating); and surrounding it all are more woods than you could possibly explore on foot even in a whole summer. In winter, there's cross-country skiing on a 150-mile trail network on the golf course and in the forests along with snowmobiling, sleigh rides, and ice skating. Downhill skiing is within a half-hour drive. Information: Pinestone Inn and Country Club, Box 809, Haliburton, Ontario K0M 1S0 (phone: 705-457-1800).

DEERHURST INN AND COUNTRY CLUB, Huntsville, Ontario: A favorite with summer guests since the turn of the century, this friendly resort on the shores of Peninsula Lake in the heart of the Muskoka tourist area (or Muskoka lakes district) will give you good reasons to join the applause: a fine 18-hole golf course, heated indoor and outdoor pools, five tennis courts, just about any kind of boat rental you could wish for, wooded hiking trails, horseback riding, saunas and whirlpool baths, and a big living room fireplace for quiet nights at the end of busy days. Sixty miles of interconnecting waterways in the area make for great fishing. Then, once the snow falls, the *Deerhurst* is transformed into "The Complete Cross-Country Skier's Resort," with over 17 miles of double-track set trails traversing the rolling pine forests. Also available are snowmobiling, skating on the new rink, dog-sledding, and snowshoeing, with alpine skiing just a half-mile away. Accommodations — many with fireplace and whirlpool bath — are in the main lodge, two modern buildings, separate cottages, or timeshare villas and condominiums. You may dine in any of a number of dining areas, and there's also nightly live entertainment in three different sections of the inn year-round. Information: Deerhurst Inn and Country Club, RR4, Huntsville, Ontario P0A 1K0 (phone: 705-789-5543).

WINDERMERE HOUSE, Muskoka, Ontario: This stately, 78-room resort, with all the charm of a country inn, has been a fixture on Lake Rosseau since it was built in the 1870s. Overlooking the lake, the "Grand Lady of the Muskoka Lakes" has recently been renovated and refurbished. There are fine views of the beach and the water from the verandah of the main house, many of its rooms, and from the Settlers Bay units. (Other rooms overlook charming gardens.) A wealth of diversions include fine dining, dancing, and theater and lounge entertainment. The social director stays busy organizing games, movies, and special children's programs. Sports enthusiasts can enjoy tennis, canoeing, windsurfing, sailing, and the 18-hole championship golf course. Open mid-May to mid-October. Information: Windermere House, Windermere, Ontario P0B 1P0 (phone: 705-769-3611).

SHAW'S, Brackley Beach, Prince Edward Island: The proximity of Brackley Beach, Canada's best strand, to this onetime farm run as a hotel since the mid-19th century by the Shaw family, is among its prime attractions — and for good reason: The beach is 5 miles long, pinkish-tawny, hard-packed, dune-backed — and, more to the point, lapped by waters warm enough for swimming. When you've had enough of the sand and sea, you can golf, play tennis, take in horse races or a play, or go fishing, swimming, or sailing nearby. From June through September, the *Charlottetown Festival* is in full swing not far away. Accommodations are in 28 rooms, some with private bath, and 18 cottages, and there's a main dining room (the food here is a draw in itself). Reservations well in advance are a must. Information: Shaw's Hotel, Brackley Beach, PEI C0A 2H0 (phone: 902-672-2022). Also see *Festivals, Fairs, and Fancy Acts, National Parks,* and *Blue Heron Drive, Prince Edward Island,* DIRECTIONS.

DALVAY-BY-THE-SEA, Dalvay Beach, Prince Edward Island: This small resort hotel, with its pine-paneled, fireplace-warmed, 2-story foyer, has a lot to offer in the way of Victorian charm — which will probably come as a surprise. Since it was designed around a lovely mansion constructed in 1895 by a partner in the Standard Oil Company, most visitors expect a more formal and elegant interior decor. But it's not a bit stuffy. There are no planned activities, since guests always manage to make their own good times — a fact that gives immense pleasure to the management, the Canadian-born grandsons of the Swiss couple who ran the place beginning in 1959. There are two cottages, but two dozen of the resort's 26 rooms, most paneled in island pine, are in the mansion proper. The ones on the second floor are the loveliest, and some have views over both Dalvay Beach, situated on the least-crowded part of Prince Edward Island National Park some 200 yards away, and Dalvay Lake, which is at the hotel's doorstep. You can swim or splash in either one, go canoeing or rowing on the lake, play tennis on the hotel's two courts, or try your hand at lawn bowling on its green. The attractions at Cavendish, setting for native author Lucy Maud Montgomery's *Anne of Green Gables,* and its golf course are nearby. Closed mid-September until June. Information: Dalvay-by-the-Sea Hotel, PO Box 8, Little York, PEI C0A 1P0 (phone: 902-672-2546 in winter; 902-672-2048 in summer). Also see *Golf, National Parks,* and *Blue Heron Drive, Prince Edward Island,* DIRECTIONS.

LA PINSONNIÈRE, Cap à l'Aigle, Quebec: A lovely setting for a lovely inn: in the heart of Charlevoix, a mere fathom from Murray Bay, between the St. Lawrence River and the mountains. A crisp, white mansion that was once a private home, *La Pinsonnière* has 28 rooms and suites, some with fireplace and canopied bed, most with a river view. Whale safaris, cruises on the Saguenay fjord, swimming in the new indoor pool, riding, sailing, tennis, sleigh rides, downhill and cross-country skiing fill your days; theater, concerts, and dining, fill your nights. Like other Relais & Châteaux group properties, the owners rely on fresh produce and foodstuffs to produce their fine cuisine. Closed in November. Information: La Pinsonnière, Cap à l'Aigle, Charlevoix, Quebec, G0T 1B0 (phone: 418-665-4431).

CUTTLE'S TREMBLANT CLUB, Mont Tremblant, Quebec: Facing Mont Tremblant, the highest peak in the Laurentians, this resort on the shores of Lac Tremblant has immediate access to some of Canada's best cross-country ski terrain, snowshoeing trails, and downhill skiing. It even has its own live-in ski instructors to accompany students to the slopes every morning. The various incarnations of the main inn as private home, boarding house, and drinking establishment have given a patina to an already lovely structure — a typically Canadian mix of big stones and massive beams centered upon a gigantic fireplace — one that is carried through to its 15 rooms and 16 suites. Having added 70 condominiums, the present owners have now fixed its place firmly up at the top among Laurentians resorts — the year round. For though the decor seems as if it was arranged to warm the soul when the winds of winter hurled themselves at the windowpanes, *Cuttle's* sparkles in summer as well. It's small enough to be cozy but large enough to give you plenty of things to do: There's swimming, sailing, boating, windsurfing, and fishing on the lake; 4 tennis courts and a beautifully situated swimming pool are also available. Golf and riding are nearby, and the forest around the lake is great for walks and hikes. For the kids, the club has a playground and hosts a social program. The award-winning dining room speaks with a definite French accent — impeccably. Information: Cuttle's Tremblant Club, Mont Tremblant, Quebec J0T 1Z0 (phone: 819-425-2731). Also see *Tennis, Downhill* and *Cross-Country Skiing,* and *The Laurentians, Quebec,* DIRECTIONS.

STATION MONT TREMBLANT LODGE, Mont Tremblant, Quebec: This old, well-established resort, with 50 rooms in small chalets and condominiums, the only one actually on Mont Tremblant, is still the favorite it used to be, and now and then you'll spot a famous face — no surprise since a complement of the kind of facilities that are required by the rich and famous await them. There's plenty of privacy (most lodgings are in a scattering of cottages), and the hotel sets a good table. And you can ski to the slopes. Information: Station Mont Tremblant Lodge, Mont Tremblant, Quebec J0T 1Z0 (phone: 819-425-8711; 800-567-6761). Also see *Downhill* and *Cross-Country Skiing* and *The Laurentians, Quebec,* DIRECTIONS.

LE CHÂTEAU MONTEBELLO, Montebello, Quebec: The brochures describing this Canadian Pacific-owned hotel 40 miles (64 km) east of Ottawa in the Ottawa River Valley as a magnificent playground aren't stretching the point. The baronial 210-room log palace was once a private club, and when you step across the threshold, you feel just a little bit grander, a little bit more important, for being there. The scenes are impressive indeed: Fires that burn in the massive six-sided, three-story stone fireplace cast their flickering light over rafters that look as if they've come from the 15th century. You've never seen anything like it before, and won't for a while to come. Outside, there are 65,000 acres of dense woodlands dotted by over 70 lakes. There's golf, tennis, hiking, fishing, horseback riding, croquet, indoor and outdoor swimming, cross-country skiing, skating, snowshoeing, sleigh riding, and curling — and on and on. The fitness area, complete with squash courts, exercise room, saunas and whirlpool baths, rounds things out. New this year are the executive suites. This is a *seigneurie,* as the French Canadians say, on a very grand scale. Information: Le Château Montebello, Montebello, Quebec J0V 1L0 (phone: 819-423-6341). Also see *Downhill* and *Cross-Country Skiing.*

HOVEY MANOR, North Hatley, Quebec: The story is told often enough that it's probably true, sad though it may be: After the US Civil War, the small groups of Southerners who had summered up north in antebellum days continued to head for Yankeeland — but when the trains arrived there, the travelers pulled the blinds, kept going, and didn't stop until they had crossed the international border. Summer homes were eventually built by a couple of these Southerners, including one Henry Atkinson of Atlanta, who always showed up in North Hatley with two private railway cars, ten horses and several carriages, and 18 servants. The turn-of-the-century home he had built for himself — broad of verandah and white of pillar, inspired by George Washington's Mount Vernon — now lends its very considerable charm to Hovey Manor. All of its 35 rooms — installed not only in the main house but also ingeniously fitted into the former servants' quarters, Ice House, Pump House, and Electrical House — are furnished with Canadian antiques. All rooms have private bath, most face the lake, and many have fireplaces. Each has its own special decor. The Tap Room, where you'll find a vast, 10,000-brick fireplace which is one of 16 of varying sizes scattered throughout the inn, used to be the stables. Sitting atop an 18th-century diamond-pointed Quebec pine armoire in the reception lobby is the inn's celebrated haunted clock, a Gothic-style 80-day chimer that rings only when someone mentions Plumley LeBaron, an early North Hatleyite known for having worn a raccoon coat in the summertime. The site itself is lovely — along a sloping garden down to a private beach facing 10-mile-long Lake Massawippi, surrounded by maples, birches, beeches, and evergreens. In summer, you can canoe, sail, windsurf, water-ski, fish, swim, play tennis on the inn's single court, or golf on any of five courses within a 20-minute drive. In winter, skiers schuss the substantial Eastern Townships slopes or take on the manor's 22 miles of cross-country trails. All year-round, you'll enjoy the creations of the inn's Belgian chef. Information: Hovey Manor, PO Box 60, North Hatley, Quebec J0B 2C0 (phone: 819-842-2421). Also see *Downhill Skiing.*

AUBERGE HATLEY, North Hatley, Quebec: A romantic country inn overlooking Lake Massawippi, this 1903 hostelry is a charming reminder of the colonial grandeur created by 19th-century Confederates who, following their defeat by the Yankees (see *Hovey Manor,* above), summered here with their entourages. Each of its 24 rooms is individually appointed in period antiques, floral wallpaper, quilted bedspreads, and, in some rooms, fireplaces. Original artwork, leather sofas, beamed ceilings, and an old brick fireplace furnish the spacious living room. Guests work up an appetite playing tennis or golf, boating, sailing, boardsailing, or fishing on beautiful Lake Massawippi. Guy Bohec, a 1985 gold medal winner for nouvelle cuisine at the Grand Salon Quebecois d'Art Culinaire, creates magic with his Duck Aiguillettes with Morriolo cherries. The inn, a member of the prestigious Relais & Châteaux group, is closed November 15–30. Information: Auberge Hatley, PO Box 330, North Hatley, Quebec J0B 2C0 (phone: 819-842-2451).

GRAY ROCKS INN, St. Jovite, Quebec: This massive 252-room inn, opened in 1906 when the surrounding Laurentians were still virgin forestlands, occupies 2,600 acres on the shores of Lac Ouimet, with a commanding view of Mont Tremblant, and it is almost as lively as it is large: There are facilities for swimming and diving on the lake, a complete marina that rents sailboats, windsurfing, and canoes, a 5,000-foot airstrip, 22 Har-Tru tennis courts, a fine 18-hole championship golf course, a complete health club, all manner of other sporting facilities, and exceptionally varied nightlife. Tennis clinics by Dennis van der Meer are a big drawing card in summer, and the program is among Canada's best. In winter, the Snow Eagle Ski School, based on the hotel's own Sugar Peak, 100 yards from the main inn, attracts guests from all over the states, and graduates will tell you without equivocating that the school (begun in 1938) is one of North America's best. Big-mountain skiing at Mont Tremblant is only a short drive away. In the capacious dining room, international cuisine is the order of the day. Information: Gray Rocks Inn, PO Box 1000, St. Jovite, Quebec J0T 2H0 (phone: 819-425-2771). Also see *Downhill* and *Cross-Country Skiing, Tennis, Golf,* and *The Laurentians, Quebec,* DIRECTIONS.

AUBERGE HANDFIELD, St. Marc-sur-Richelieu, Quebec: Accommodations at this charming hostelry in the heart of the peaceful Richelieu River Valley not far from Montreal are in nine old Canadian farmhouses rescued from destruction at the hands of local farmers who were modernizing, then transported to the Auberge Handfield's woods-rimmed property and fitted out with Canadian antiques. There is a total of 55 rooms in the establishment. The main lodge — where you'll find the dining room — is charming as well, with a big stone fireplace in the lobby. The inn is just the right size — small enough so you don't get lost, large enough to give you some privacy and to support a goodly number of facilities, including a kidney-shape swimming pool, a marina, and an activities program that includes corn-on-the-cob parties in fall and sugaring-off parties (at the inn's own sugar shack) from the beginning of March to the end of April. The restaurant is noted for both its nouvelle cuisine and its French-Canadian dishes. In winter, there's cross-country skiing, and in summer, summer theater (mainly comedies, performed in French, on a steamboat moored nearby). Information: Auberge Handfield, 555 Chemin du Prince, St. Marc-sur-Richelieu, Quebec J0L 2E0 (phone: 514-584-2226). Also see *Canoeing and Rafting.*

HOSTELLERIE LES TROIS TILLEULS, St. Marc, Quebec: Overlooking the Richelieu River, a 20-minute drive from Montreal, this property was originally a 19th-century mansion. A 21-room rustic inn has been added, and the whole is a member of Relais & Châteaux, the exclusive association of hostelries who abide by the following criteria: courtesy, calm, comfort, cuisine, and character. To that list can be added warmth and relaxation. In each air conditioned room, guests find a color TV set, radio, and balcony from which they can plot the day's activities in the marina or the pool, on the links or the courts. The inn's highlight is its French cuisine; the outstanding menu becomes self-explanatory once you know that both owners are French. Information: Hostellerie les Trois Tilleuls, 290 Rue Richelieu, St. Marc-sur-Richelieu, Quebec J0L 2E0 (phone: 514-584-2231).

HÔTEL LA SAPINIÈRE, Val David, Quebec: In this Laurentians hotel and restaurant, the first Canadian member of France's prestigious Relais & Châteaux group, the primary distinction is the kitchen. Between meals, there's canoeing and rowing on a private lake, swimming in an outdoor heated pool, tennis, badminton, shuffleboard, miniature golf, and, in winter, cross-country skiing in the maple, pine, and fir woods that surround the hotel and downhill skiing at myriad nearby areas. The 70 rooms are large, clean, and comfortably appointed — and must be reserved several months in advance. There are also several private "salons" with fireplaces, 5 meeting rooms with air conditioning, and audio-visual and sound equipment. Information: Hôtel la Sapinière, PO Box 190, Val David, Quebec J0T 2N0 (phone: 819-322-2020 or 514-866-8262). Also see *Downhill* and *Cross-Country Skiing* and *The Laurentians, Quebec,* DIRECTIONS.

WEST

BANFF SPRINGS, Banff, Alberta: Imagine a snow queen's castle rising at the base of an evergreen-covered mountain slope with ice-capped peaks all around in the distance. This hotel with 835 rooms and suites, situated in Banff National Park, is like that. As the focus of tour groups and conventions, the interior accommodations and amenities haven't always been the equal of the exterior architecture, but a major renovation of its guestrooms and eating facilities, along with its new health club, have made the inside more appealing — albeit more modern. And the site remains remarkable: It's surrounded by hundreds of square miles of lofty mountains, deep valleys, stunning glaciers, and crystal lakes. In addition to the hotel's 4 dining rooms, it has a café and deli, sushi and wine bars, an outdoor heated pool, an indoor Olympic-size pool, a health club with 3 Jacuzzis and a sauna, a demanding par-71 golf course, and 5 tennis courts. In winter it's a skier's delight, and there's also ice skating, ski touring, and snowshoeing on the property. Information: Banff Springs Hotel, PO Box 960, Banff, Alberta T0L 0C0 (phone: 403-762-2211). Also see *Downhill Skiing, Ice Skating, Golf, Tennis,* and *Calgary to Banff and Jasper National Parks, Alberta,* DIRECTIONS.

NUM-TI-JAH LODGE, Bow Lake, Alberta: Situated between Jasper and Banff national parks, amidst the mountains and overlooking a lake, this rustic log lodge has a crusty, western flavor, with its chairs crafted of antlers, huge stone fireplaces, and good simple food. Horseback riding and hiking are favored pastimes. Closed November through March. For reservations and information: Num-Ti-Jah Lodge, Bow Lake, Box 39, Lake Louise, Alberta T0L 1E0 (phone: 403-761-7020). Also see *Calgary to Banff and Jasper National Parks, Alberta,* DIRECTIONS.

JASPER PARK LODGE, Jasper, Alberta: Towering snowcapped peaks surround this alpine lodge on the shores of Lac Beauvert deep inside Jasper National Park. Guests stay in what amounts to a small village of modern cedar chalets and original log cabins — there are 400 rooms in all, many with patios and fireplaces. For recreation the choices are golf, tennis, horseback riding, cycling, white-water rafting, boating, fishing, or going for a guided tour of sections of the park. Excellent cuisine is served in several dining rooms or in the comfort of your own cabin, and a variety of evening entertainment, including dancing, is offered. During the summer months, a daily social and cultural program is made available, as is one for children. Open year-round. Ski packages available. Information: Jasper Park Lodge, Box 40, Jasper, Alberta T0E 1E0 (phone: 403-852-3301).

CHÂTEAU LAKE LOUISE, Lake Louise, Alberta: This large, French-style château, one of the Canadian Pacific hotels, has a breathtaking setting on the shores of world-famous Lake Louise — blue-green, beautifully clear, rimmed by mountains, and backed by the blue-white Victoria Glacier. The setting alone would recommend the hotel. But like its fellows, this Gallic beauty is no garden-variety establishment. The resplendence of the interiors almost matches the beauty of the scene outside. Witness the regal pillars in the palatial lobby and the soaring arches of the Victoria Room. The front desk is of carved oak, the lobby furniture is carved and heavy, and the lobby itself is cavernous. Yet it manages to be warm and welcoming. The recently opened Glacier Wing added 140 bedrooms and suites, for a total of 530, and renovation of many of the older rooms has made them fresh and new as well. Though there is no golf course, the excellent layout at the *Banff Springs Hotel* is only 39 miles (63 km) away. On-site diversions include an indoor pool, tanning salon, Jacuzzi, and a steam room, as well as a pub, pizza parlor, and a rooftop restaurant. Also available are ice skating, sleigh rides across frozen Lake Louise, pony trekking in the mountains, canoeing and hiking in pollen-free woods, and downhill and cross-country skiing. Open year-round. Information: Château Lake Louise, Lake Louise, Alberta T0L 1E0 (phone: 403-522-3511). Also see *Calgary to Banff and Jasper National Parks, Alberta,* DIRECTIONS.

FAIRMONT HOT SPRINGS, Fairmont Hot Springs, British Columbia: This hostelry — a long-established resort now housed in a handful of newish buildings — is a delight for families. Kids, especially, love the 10,000 square feet of steaming natural mineral pools. And then there's the setting — on the side of a mountain in the lovely Kootenay district of the Rockies, surrounded by woods, lawns, and gardens, with nice views over the valley below. There's skiing in winter on its own slopes, which have a 1,000-foot vertical, or nearby at big Kimberley and Panorama. In summer, you can play tennis (there are 4 courts), golf on two 18-hole courses, or go riding. The resort also has a recreation center with a pool, Jacuzzis, racquetball and squash courts, work-out room, and sauna. Additional accommodations are provided at the property's 250-site campground (30 spaces are open in winter). Information: Fairmont Hot Springs Resort, Box 10, Fairmont Hot Springs, BC V0B 1L0 (phone: 604-345-6311).

HARRISON HOT SPRINGS, Harrison Hot Springs, British Columbia: Nestled in the Coast Range, in the upper Fraser River Valley some 90 miles (144 km) east of Vancouver, this impressive old 280-room resort sits on the shores of Harrison Lake, in a rural area dotted by farmhouses and speckled with lakes. Though the economics of modern hotelkeeping have touched the *Harrison Hot Springs,* many of the traditions begun in the hotel's early days are intact. Tea and homemade cakes are still served every afternoon in the upper lobby. Dancing to live music in the well-loved Copper Room is as spirited as ever; the band leader, a fixture here for years, has retired — but the band plays on. And a prime attraction is still the hot springs. A circular sulfur indoor pool heated naturally to 100F, a curved indoor swimming pool kept at 90F, and an outdoor pool, with a combination of fresh and mineral water, surrounded by a large sundeck are available. There are Roman and whirlpool baths, a Universal gym and an outdoor fitness course, and registered masseurs and masseuses are on duty at the plush health pavilion. (And the sauna and two of the pools are open around the clock.) Sports facilities abound: You can play tennis, shuffleboard, golf on a 9-hole course; and go bicycling, water skiing, fishing, boating, or boardsailing. Off the property are scenic boat cruises, helicopter trips, and tours of the area's many attractions. Information: Harrison Hot Springs Hotel, Harrison Hot Springs, BC V0M 1K0 (phone: 604-796-2244).

Farm and Ranch Vacations

Holidays at a Canadian farm or ranch can take you back quickly to a childhood you wish you had had — if not to your own youth. They can help introduce your youngsters to a way of life that city and suburban kids simply don't encounter elsewhere. They'll milk a cow, talk to the small animals that many farmers keep, prowl through the woods with a dog at their heels, learn to ride, swim in a creek, and explore to their hearts' content without getting into trouble. For them, as for you, the long summer days fill up quickly with berry picking, riding, haying and combining, visits to auctions in tiny towns you'd otherwise have no reason to visit, or just hanging out in the kitchen while the bread is being baked or the red raspberries, harvested by the gallon from the garden, are being turned into jam. (A farm visit can be a regular cooking school.) The food that shows up on the table — usually simple fare — is meant to satisfy the hearty appetite so easily worked up wherever the air is fresh. Your hosts are friendly folk who learn from you as much as you do from them. They like the stream of strangers that passes through their homes, and they have almost infinite tolerance for the ignorance of people from the city. Among them, you'll find more than a few who speak English with an accent — not just the French Canadians, but also the new Canadians from Germany, the Ukraine, and other parts of the world: Canada is still a melting pot.

The nature of the farms changes with the landscape. In the east, you'll find smaller, old-fashioned places of around 200 acres that specialize in dairy or mixed farming, some owned by French-Canadian families who can teach you a little of their language. In the Maritimes, you'll find farms of 200 to 2,000 acres specializing in apples, potatoes, or beef and dairy cattle. On Prince Edward Island, as an added bonus, you can wake up to a view of the ocean. The larger spreads out west fall into two basic categories: guest (or dude) ranches, where the guest business contributes substantially to the property's income; and working ranches, where guests are a sideline. Guest ranches may offer more luxurious surroundings, a more extensive roster of planned activities, and a wider variety of facilities. Working ranches are make-your-own-fun places, although since they're generally smaller as well, your hosts will always give you plenty of personal attention and many suggestions to keep you busy. Prices can run anywhere from $20 to $85 per night, depending on whether meals are included and on the size and facilities of the farm or ranch; there is usually a discount for children.

Provincial tourism departments can give you information about dude ranches in their province. Farms are also represented by associations. All the members of these associations are inspected regularly and thoroughly and then listed in provincewide directories that are updated annually. When you're picking a farm or ranch, first determine the province you want to visit, then write for the listings, and phone the farms that interest you to get a more specific idea of what they're like and to see how you like your potential hosts. Farms and ranches without children at home tend to be a little quieter than those with children at home, and you may prefer them if you and your spouse are coming alone. Otherwise, you'll probably want to stay with a family whose children are about the same ages as your own. For a complete listing of approved farms in Canada, contact these provincial offices:

ALBERTA: Travel Alberta, 15th Floor, 10025 Jasper Ave., Edmonton, Alberta T5J 3Z3 (phone: 800-661-8888).

MANITOBA: Manitoba Farm Vacations Association, 437 Assinoboine Ave., Winnipeg, Manitoba R3L 1B5 (phone: 204-475-6624).

NEW BRUNSWICK: Tourism New Brunswick, PO Box 12345, Fredericton, NB E3B 5C3 (phone: 800-561-0123 or 506-453-2377); and Olive Allen, President, New Brunswick Farm Vacations, RR3, Port Elgin, New Brunswick E0A 2K0 (phone: 506-538-2597).

NOVA SCOTIA: Jane Reid Stevens, Nova Scotia Farm & Country Vacations Association, Newport Station, Hants Co., NS B0N 2B0 (phone: 902-798-5864).

ONTARIO: Sharon Grose, Ontario Vacation Farm Association, RR2, Alma, Ontario N0B 1A0.

PRINCE EDWARD ISLAND: Prince Edward Island Department of Tourism and Parks, Visitor Services, PO Box 940E, Charlottetown, PEI C1A 7M5 (phone: 902-368-4444).

QUEBEC: Fédération des Agricotours du Québec, 4545 Ave. Pierre-de-Coubertin, CP 1000, Succ. M, Montreal, Quebec H1V 3R2 (phone: 514-252-3138 or 800-361-3585). This organization will help you find the kind of farm you have in mind in the area you want to visit; it also runs a rural bed-and-breakfast program.

SASKATCHEWAN: Doreen Gullagher, President, Saskatchewan Country Vacations Association, Box 204, Clavet, Saskatchewan S0K 0Y0 (phone: 306-933-4936).

FAMILY FARMS

LIIVAM FARMS, Eckville, Alberta: A lot of the Liivams' visitors just stop at bed-and-breakfast accommodations on their way to the mountains, which are not far away. But when they see what there is to do, they exclaim that if they'd only known, they would have planned to stay longer. Many return on their way home, even though that usually means backtracking. The attraction of the place is not hard to understand. The Liivams are an older couple, without any children in the nest, and their home is a very peaceful place, with its berry patch, its fruit trees, and its beautiful lawns planted with big trees 40 or 50 years old — not so common in this part of the province; in mid-July, the blooming of the rapeseed, an oil-producing grain that is common in these parts, turns the fields beyond the house bright yellow for months. There's haymaking in July, harvesting in mid-August or so, and, any time, riding on the farm horses, swimming in a fine pool, fishing in three lakes nearby, plus biking and motor biking, with cross-country skiing in winter. Information: Mr. and Mrs. A. Liivam, RR1, Eckville, Alberta T0M 0X0 (phone: 403-746-5438).

GWYNALTA FARM, Gwynne, Alberta: With 400 acres, this central Alberta dairy farm about 40 miles (64 km) from the provincial capital at Edmonton is not tiny, but it's not particularly big and wealthy either. Yet, when you visit, you never seem to be able to get around to reading the books you brought along, thinking there'd be nothing to distract you. When you sit on the banks of the farm's own lake, you won't see a single car or house — but the fishing is fine and the water, hills, and forests are too lovely to ignore; cutting into the trees, you spot the bare trace of an old buffalo trail. The place is secluded, but every morning there are deer in the yard. Nights are quiet, too — you often spend them sitting out on the big deck of the Glasers' comfortable old house; it might be nice to turn in early and read — but then the northern lights begin to dance across the sky. Hiking and bird-watching are popular in summer, and in winter you can go cross-country skiing, snowmobiling, or ice fishing. And whenever you have a mind to, you can taste the milk collected from the herd of very contented black-and-white cows. The farmhouse can accommodate up to four adults, or two youngsters and two adults. Information: Mr. and Mrs. A. Glaser, Gwynne, Alberta T0C 1L0 (phone: 403-352-3587).

ASPEN RIDGE, Clear Lake, Manitoba: Robert Sopuck has not been taking in guests for very long, partly because he spent just over three years building the house where he lives with his guests — a log structure that one visitor dubbed a log palace, complete with beamed ceilings and a big stone fireplace. That each of the dozen beds has its own down comforter begins to explain the "palace's" appeal to cross-country skiers, though you can't ignore the attraction of heavy snow accumulations and the vastness of the available terrain — Sopuck's 320 rolling acres adjoin government and private land that is also available to skiers, and Riding Mountain National Park is just 2 miles (3 km) away. From mid-May through late June and from late August to early October, the area is equally fine for bird-watching, since the farm lies right on the Central and Mississippi flyways. And there's always horseback riding at nearby stables. Meals are prepared using indigenous ingredients — geese, ducks, garden vegetables — and include specialties like kielbasa and cabbage rolls, typical fare of the area's large Ukrainian population. Sopuck is also knowledgeable about wild foods and is willing to teach any guests who are interested. Information: Robert Sopuck, Aspen Ridge, General Delivery, Lake Audy, Manitoba R0J 0Z0 (phone: 204-848-2964).

DEERBANK FARM, Morris, Manitoba: If you arrive at this 320-acre spread in early July, you can ride atop sweet-smelling bales of hay, fresh from the baler, as the wagon creaks its way through the fields. If you come in August, you can watch the farm's wheat, barley, and oats being combined to separate grain from straw, which is then baled and stacked; and you don't have to be a strong man to help stack those straw bales, as many a past guest has done, or to drive the farm truck from field to bins, where the grain is stored. Whatever chore you choose, you'll work up an appetite for the noon feast — usually a roast with lots of vegetables and a filling dessert — and again for supper, a more modest repast, usually of hash browns, cold sliced beef, salad, more vegetables from the garden, fruit, and cake. The beef is butchered on the property. Accommodations are in the 3 clean, simply furnished spare rooms in the modern farmhouse or in a camper outside; campsites with some hook-ups are also available. Information: Kathleen and Ed Jorgenson, Box 23, RR2, Morris, Manitoba R0G 1K0 (phone: 204-746-8395).

LA FERME DES ERABLES, Aroostook, New Brunswick: This 1,200-acre grain-and-potato farm and cattle ranch not far from the Maine border, a couple of miles off the Trans-Canada Highway in the province's northwest corner, belongs to a family that numbers around 41, when you figure all the sons, daughters, wives, husbands, and grandchildren — and though they don't all live in the farmhouse, there are always quite a few of them around, making the place very lively. The entire family is bilingual, and the kids will babysit or take you around to see the various neighborhood sights — among them the photogenic 225-foot-high Grand Falls and, in Hartland to the south, a 1,282-foot-long covered bridge, the world's longest. Recently added to the farm is a heated indoor swimming pool. Catered bus tours, which place guests in different well-organized homes in the neighborhood, can also be arranged. There are plans for a campground to accommodate both tents and trailers. Information: Aurèle and Fernande St. Amand, Aroostook, NB E0J 1B0 (phone: 506-273-3112). Also see *The Saint John River, New Brunswick,* DIRECTIONS.

ALLEN'S HOLIDAY FARM, Port Elgin, New Brunswick: The three television sets in Mrs. Allen's big, early-19th-century white frame farmhouse aren't turned on much in summer, simply because there are so many other things to do: helping out in the garden, day-tripping to a nearby beach or to PEI via ferry (20 minutes away), chowing down on big meals of roast meat or fish fresh from the not-too-distant sea, or helping with farm chores; in the evenings, there's usually a session of country-and-western music with their friendly neighbors. One Montreal woman managed to find time to put up some raspberry jam, using the fruit from Mrs. Allen's garden. Information: Olive Allen, Allen's Holiday Farm, RR3, Port Elgin, NB E0A 2K0 (phone: 506-538-2597).

BROADLEAF FARM, Hopewell Hill, New Brunswick: This 1,400-acre beef cattle farm — a big one by New Brunswick standards, operated by the horse-happy Hudsons, their married daughter, her husband, the Hudson's married sons, and their wives — is a lively, spic-and-span place. The main attractions are the 80 horses. Western riding lessons, hayrides, and trail rides that take you out by the water and through the woods are all available. But because the farm's marshy sections attract migrating geese and ducks, the place is also good for bird-watching. It also makes a good base for trips to nearby Fundy National Park and Moncton, for tours of the coastline, and for antiques-hunting trips. The old-fashioned country house is comfortable, and the food is good and simple, though occasionally you'll be treated to harvests from the marshes — cranberries and mushrooms as well as exotica like samphire and goosetongue greens. Relax at *Broadleaf Too,* the new home of Vernon and Joyce Hudson, which is right next door and also has guestrooms. A small area for tents and 8 trailer hook-ups is available; reservations for these sites are necessary. And there's a week-long summer camp for the kids. Open year-round. Information: Phyllis and Danny Hudson, Hopewell Hill, Albert Co., NB E0A 1Z0 (phone: 506-882-2349); Joyce and Vernon Hudson, Broadleaf Too, Hopewell Hill, Albert Co., NB E0A 1Z0 (phone: 506-882-2803). Also see *The Fundy Trail, New Brunswick,* DIRECTIONS.

ANDERSON'S HOLIDAY FARM, Sussex, New Brunswick: There are sheep, beef cattle, and a variety of fowl on this 200-acre farm in the heart of dairy country about an hour's drive from Fundy National Park. But kids love the farm's menagerie of ducks, Canada geese, rabbits, ornamental pheasants, and even peacocks. Nearby golf and curling, as well as swimming, tennis, and sightseeing, can keep you so busy you'll need a rest when you get home. They also offer bed-and-breakfast arrangements. Information: Tom and Laura Anderson, RR2, Sussex, NB E0E 1P0 (phone: 506-433-3786). Also see *The Fundy Trail, New Brunswick,* DIRECTIONS.

GLENALBY FARMS, New Hamburg, Ontario: This 200-acre farm, settled five generations ago, in 1861, by Scottish ancestors, raises registered Holsteins, black-and-white cows best known among the dairy breeds, and Lassie collies — and, as you would expect, the animals provide a good deal of the farm entertainment. If your timing is right, you may see the birth of a calf, then bottle-feed the newborn; but you can always wander through the woods with the friendly dogs at your heels. There's berry and cherry picking, haying in July, and more haying and combining in August. The silos are filled in September. Mrs. McMillan bakes the dinner bread, and nearly everything else on the table — from the maple syrup and apple cider and honey to the cheese and crackers — comes from the farm. In the farmhouse, built in 1861, there are large, modern, carpeted guestrooms to accommodate up to 15. You're just 10 minutes from the *Stratford Festival* (among other events, it features Shakespeare productions), in the heart of Mennonite country, convenient to picturesque farmers' markets and antiques auctions where crafts and handmade quilts are sold. Closed November through March. Information: Alex and Ruby McMillan, New Hamburg, Ontario N0B 2G0 (phone: 519-625-8353; telephone inquiries preferred). Also see *Ontario's England,* DIRECTIONS.

ROEWOOD FARM, Wallenstein, Ontario: At this century-old farm in the horse-and-buggy area of southern Ontario, just a half-hour's drive from Stratford and 15 minutes from Kitchener-Elmira, St. Jacos, the old woodshed bell calls you to tempting meals cooked by Austrian-born Anne Roe — anything from apple strudel and Wiener schnitzel to roast capon or turkey and Christmas pudding, even in the middle of July. There are hayrides and hayloft parties, corn roasts (in season), and lots of lawn games for those who don't join in the milking or feed the cows and calves. You can help with the haying in July and August, watch the calves being born in the fall and spring. (A

DIVERSIONS / Farm and Ranch Vacations

few years ago, Mrs. Roe and her son delivered twin calves in the field with a dozen guests looking on.) Swimming, skiing, fishing, and other outdoor activities are all available in the area, and the beautiful, pine-floored rooms house up to 14. Make a friend in the Sociable Room. Shower facilities are communal, but other bathroom facilities are private. Open year-round. Information: Jim and Anne Roe, Roewood Farm, RR3, Wallenstein, Ontario N0B 2S0 (phone: 519-698-2278).

MOLDENHAUERS, Allan, Saskatchewan: You can ride one of the farm's horses when visiting here, but not on trail rides: Guests are on their own to strike out across the pastures or wend down one of the nearby country roads on the farm's six horses. There's no worry about traffic, since Allan, the nearest settlement — 4½ miles (7 km) away — is too small to generate very many vehicles. After a ride, there are rabbits and goats and sheep to be fed and petted, eggs to be gathered, beautiful fields to be photographed, vegetables to be picked and weeds to be pulled in the garden, and more. As soon as guests find out about the old wooden churn, most can hardly wait to make butter. Some courageous souls try milking the cows by hand. Then there are those big meals — traditional country food like fried chicken, home-baked bread and homemade jam, fresh apple pies juicy with the fruit of the farm's own apple tree, topped with whipped cream courtesy of the farm's own cows. Information: Moldenhauers, Box 214, Allan, Saskatchewan S0K 0C0 (phone: 306-257-3578).

WORKING RANCHES

POPLAR BLUFF STOCK FARM, Chauvin, Alberta: At this working farm in east central Alberta, near the Saskatchewan border, the land rolls into the distance in great swells, as far as the eye can see; the skies above are bigger than you ever remember them when you're confined in the city. Oats and barley are the primary business here, but there are some 50 head of beef cattle as well. It makes a fine setting for a relaxing, country vacation. The trails through the small hills near the place are good for hiking, as is nearby Dillberry Provincial Park. Trail rides are also on the activities roster in summer, and there's help if you need it; in winter, cross-country skiing and snowmobiling keep you busy. Year-round, you can visit the communal Hutterite colony 25 miles (40 km) distant, and the hosts often take guests to see the oil field with its little pumps and the big grain elevator not far away. Open all year. Information: Polar Bluff Stock Farm, Harold and Georgina Taylor, RR1, Chauvin, Alberta T0B 0V0 (phone: 403-858-2234).

TL BAR RANCH, Trochu, Alberta: This central Alberta horse and cattle ranch, located between the towns of Red Deer (pop. 36,000) and Drumheller (pop. 6,000) along the Red Deer River in the "Valley of the Dinosaurs," offers accommodations in a log ranch home and a private cottage. Fishing and swimming are as popular as helping out with the ranch chores, but the surrounding Drumheller Valley, carved over the ages by the Red Deer River, is such a fascinating place that exploring — in canoes, on foot, or on horseback — can be the most interesting activity of all. Sometimes, for instance, you'll find dinosaur bones, fossils, and petrified wood that the river has uncovered. The new *Tyrrell Museum of Paleontology,* named for the geologist who found the first dinosaur bones in the area in 1884, explores the prehistory of the area with films and please-touch computer terminals; it's just a 45-minute drive away. June is the month for cattle branding on the ranch, July for the Calgary Stampede not far away. Open May through October. Information: Tom and Willie Lynch, TL Bar Ranch, PO Box 217, Trochu, Alberta T0M 2C0 (phone: 403-442-2207). Also see *Festivals, Fairs, and Fancy Acts* and *Cypress Hills Provincial Park to Edmonton via the Dinosaur Country, Alberta,* DIRECTIONS.

K J 5 RANCH, Rapid City, Manitoba: At this 320-acre spread, you'll find some 150 head of Appaloosas and quarter horses, and there are plenty of trail rides, picnics, and, for those who need them, riding lessons. Boating, water skiing, swimming and golf are nearby, and this is another place where the produce in the garden in the afternoon is on the table at dinner. When the farm begins its 4-month season in June, newborn colts are still wobbly legged. The family's Dalmation is very fond of guests, and you'll be able to tell right away that she enjoys having company. Information: Ken and Janie Bridgeman, K J 5 Ranch, PO Box 209, Rapid City, Manitoba R0K 1W0 (phone: 204-826-2078).

GUEST RANCHES

BLACK CAT GUEST RANCH, Hinton, Alberta: This is a wonderful place, just big enough to give you some privacy — but not too big. It's also beautifully situated so that each of the 16 guestrooms faces the first range of the Rockies. A large, central living room also has a view, plus a fireplace, library, many comfortable chairs, and a pine floor for dancing; the coffee pot is always on. In summer, you can go out for riding, hiking, and fishing at places like Solomon Creek and the Wild Hay River or canoeing on the Athabasca River; or you can go sightseeing to nearby areas like the Columbia Icefield. Upon return, unwind in the new outdoor hot tub with a view of the mountains. Winter's main attraction is cross-country skiing on some 40 miles of poplar- and spruce-lined trails that surround the lodge, sometimes along old logging roads. The ranch is better suited for singles and couples than for families. Information: Gerry and Mary Bond, Black Cat Guest Ranch, Box 976, Hinton, Alberta T0E 1B0 (phone: 403-865-3084 or 4357).

RAFTER SIX RANCH RESORT, Seebe, Alberta: A good-sized operation in the mountainous Kananaskis country, about 25 miles (40 km) from Banff, it can accommodate about 60 guests in its solid-log lodge and cabins. Ordinarily, an establishment of this size doesn't nurture spontaneity. But here, the staff numbers around 25 in the summer, so when a few guests decide they want to go out on a trail ride or take a nature walk or play volleyball, there's always someone from the ranch available to make sure they do it — and have the best time ever. Breakfast rides, hayrides, and barbecues are regular activities, and occasionally a group of the local Stoney Indians (the owner is a blood brother) drops by just to visit or, by request, to dance, in full-dress regalia, for guests. There's also a licensed dining room, cocktail lounge, swimming pool, whirlpool bath, and a game room, and the surrounding mountains are appealing enough to have been chosen — not once, but several times — as movie locations. Open May 1 through October. Information: Rafter Six Ranch Resort, Seebe, Alberta T0L 1X0 (phone: 403-673-3622 or 403-264-1251).

SUNDANCE GUEST RANCH, Ashcroft, British Columbia: This 31-room ranch in the Thompson River Valley is living proof that the wild west is not so wild anymore. Though there's sagebrush for miles around, things at the ranch are eminently civilized. Everything is air conditioned, and swimming in the well-kept heated pool, enjoying hot showers, and sampling mealtime creations of the accomplished chef are as much a part of your experience here as the trail dust and sounds of coyotes howling at night. But horseback riding is still the *Sundance's* raison d'être, and there are daily trail rides (the ranch usually runs about 100 horses), gymkhanas (athletic equestrian events), cookouts, barbecues, and hayrides. Open year-round. Information: Cynthia Rowe, Sundance Guest Ranch, PO Box 489, Ashcroft, BC V0K 1A0 (phone: 604-453-2554/2422).

CHILKO LAKE WILDERNESS RANCH, Williams Lake, British Columbia: It takes a four-wheel-drive vehicle about 4 unforgettable hours to drive the 180 miles (300 km) from Williams Lake to this spread bordering glacier- and stream-fed, 52-mile-long Chilko Lake. But it's easier and even *more* scenic to arrive by plane, across the ice-covered Coast Mountains wilderness. Once at the rustic timber lodge, there's more of the same, either on day-long horseback, hiking, fishing, or canoeing trips or on longer overnight trips in the area. But unless you're a glutton for real wilderness, you may opt for the former. The area immediately surrounding the ranch, covered with dense bush, is wild enough, but the lodge and outlying cabins are most comfortable. Inside the lodge you'll find an indoor pool, sauna, outdoor Jacuzzi, table tennis, pool tables, and a lounge. The food is Canadian style, with terrific picnic lunches, and there's usually fish or meat from the ranch's own smoker. The fishing and hunting are exceptionally good here. Heli-skiing, cross-country skiing, and snowmobiling are available in winter. Maximum 60 guests. Information: Chilko Lake Wilderness Ranch, PO Box 4750, Williams Lake, BC V2G 2V7 (phone: 604-398-8828 or, if you can't get through, radio phone H678596 on the Chilanko 55 channel).

DIRECTIONS

Alberta

Perhaps the most beautiful drive in western Canada starts at Calgary, Alberta's second largest city (pop. 658,000; Edmonton, the provincial capital, has 572,000 people) and follows the spine of the Rocky Mountains north through Banff to Lake Louise and Jasper National Park. These mountains, shared with the Pacific province of British Columbia, are part of the diversified geography that distinguishes Alberta from its sister prairie provinces, Saskatchewan and Manitoba. Covering 255,285 square miles, Alberta is the largest and most westerly of the prairie and plains provinces, but it is the least prairie-like. In the west, on the Alberta-British Columbia border, are the Rocky Mountains; in the southeast corner of the province are badlands and desert; and along the border with the Northwest Territories (of which the province was a part until 1905) are wildernesses of forests, lakes, and rivers.

Nor is the economy devoted exclusively to the traditional prairie concerns of farming and ranching. Oil discoveries in central and southern Alberta, especially the Leduc Fields find in 1947 propelled the province into a period of soaring growth. Although the prosperity Albertans enjoyed during the 1970s has dimmed somewhat with the slide in oil prices, residents are confident of the prospect of steady — if slower — growth in the future. Not the richest of Canada's provinces, Alberta's oil business grew to such proportions that the provincial government set up a trust fund to assure future development as oil reserves wane. Edmonton and Calgary are the centers of the province's oil industry. Some 75% of Alberta's 2.3 million people live in its cities, and the two major oil centers account for the greatest proportion of them. Alberta is the only province with no sales tax, affording its residents one of the lowest tax rates in the country.

Where there is oil there are fossil remains, and, true to form, archaeological excavations in Alberta's badlands earlier in this century turned up more than 100 dinosaur skeletons, four of which have been completely reassembled and put on display in Dinosaur Provincial Park, near the southeastern town of Brooks. In the same part of the country is the Blackfoot Indian Reserve, one of the largest communities of native North Americans in Canada.

Visitors with a yen to enjoy Alberta's natural beauty up close can take advantage of the province's numerous opportunities for trail riding, river rafting, cycling, mountain climbing, and even dog sledding. Farm and ranch vacations offer families a chance to milk cows, ride horses, gather farm-fresh eggs, and smell the country air. Consult Travel Alberta's excellent accommodations guide and its adventure guide; also available from this agency is a comprehensive guide to campgrounds and parks in the province. For complete reports on Calgary and Edmonton, their hotels, restaurants, sights, and activities, see the appropriate chapters of THE CITIES.

The following pages outline four distinct driving routes, each lasting 3 or

4 days, that take you to the most compelling sights and dramatic scenery of this varied, vast western province. Southern Alberta is thoroughly explored in the Lethbridge-Calgary drive, which includes beautiful Waterton Lakes National Park. The high point of any Alberta trip is Banff and Jasper national parks, and the drive through them from Calgary is described in the second Alberta route. Edmonton is the ultimate destination of the third route, from Cypress Hills Provincial Park through the dinosaur-ridden badlands and the Blackfoot Reserve. Finally, for a taste of northern Alberta, we have included the circular Edmonton-Slave Lake journey, a long and exciting trek into Alberta's more northerly wilderness.

Information: Travel Alberta, 10025 Jasper Ave., 15th Floor, Edmonton, Alberta T5J 3Z3 (phone: 403-427-4321 in Edmonton; 800-222-6501 elsewhere in Alberta; 800-661-8888 elsewhere in Canada or the US).

Lethbridge to Calgary via Waterton Lakes National Park

This 250-mile (403-km) route begins at the prairie city of Lethbridge, swings through southwestern Alberta, then heads north to Calgary. It crosses Waterton Lakes National Park in the Rocky Mountains at Alberta's southwestern corner and passes several places of interest elsewhere along the route. Cardston, on the way to Waterton Lakes, has Canada's only Mormon temple, the Alberta Temple. North from Waterton Lakes, fishing is good around Pincher Creek, and at Fort Macleod stands an original prairie fort. The route is easily traveled, and you can take it at your own pace. The whole area enjoys bright blue sky and clean air. The best times for traveling this route are from spring to fall; many attractions close down for the winter. A map of Alberta may be obtained from Travel Alberta (address above). For maps specifically of Waterton Park, Lethbridge, and other parts of this area, write Chinook Country Tourist Association, 2805 Scenic Dr., Lethbridge T1K 5B7.

LETHBRIDGE: This city of 60,300, the commercial center for the surrounding farm and ranch country, sits on the banks of the Oldman River. A pleasant, orderly place, it has blossomed over the last 20 years and is now a far cry from its first days in the 1860s, when Fort Whoop-Up was set up by whiskey traders from the US to sell liquor to whites and Indians, often with tragic results. A reconstruction of the fort stands in Indian Battle Park, in town on the riverbank. All that is missing is the rotgut. The park, which is not on the original site of Fort Whoop-Up, was the site of a battle between the Cree and Blackfoot Nations in 1870 that lasted for days. Details of the epic battle are explained in exhibits inside the fort. The park also has a coal train that will carry you through a simulated entrance to a mine tunnel.

Cross the Oldman River just south of Indian Battle Park and continue south on the bypass road to gain an excellent view of the University of Lethbridge campus. The university's unusual buildings were designed to complement the coulees (deep, sharp, trench erosions in rock) in the surrounding terrain. From the western end of the bypass road, the university looks like a large ship nestled in the folds of the surrounding hills.

On the east side of town, on Mayor Magrath Drive, Exhibition Park offers a variety of diversions, including a golf course and Henderson Lake, with swimming, boating, and fishing. On the shore of the lake is Lethbridge's premier attraction — Nikka Yuko Garden, a beautiful Japanese garden, designed and constructed in Japan under expert supervision and shipped in pieces and assembled without nails in Lethbridge. Nikka Yuko guides are Japanese women in traditional dress who explain the philosophy of the intricate pebble designs, the manicured trees and shrubs, and the miniature pools and waterfalls. The centerpiece is a replica of a Japanese teahouse, but, alas, it does not serve refreshments.

If you're hungry, head south on Mayor Magrath Drive for one-half mile to *Sven Ericksen's* restaurant on the east side of the road. The large, family-style dining room serves home-style cooking at moderate prices.

En Route from Lethbridge – Mayor Magrath Drive becomes Route 5, the direct road to Waterton Lakes park 81 miles (130 km) southwest of Lethbridge. You will cross rolling prairie and coulees beneath an incredibly blue, seemingly infinite sky on the way to the next major town, Cardston, 48 miles (77 km) south of Lethbridge.

CARDSTON: This small town is the home of the Alberta Temple, the country's only Mormon temple, dedicated in 1923. At press time, the visitors center was being remodeled. On Main Street, the *C. O. Card Home and Museum* preserves the house of the leader who first brought the Mormons from Utah to Alberta in the 1880s. The interior accurately reflects the decor and furnishings of early Alberta pioneer homes, providing a fine sense of the atmosphere of a Mormon household. If the temple and the Card home don't make the point that the town is Mormon, note that Cardston is also "dry." Look elsewhere for a cold beer.

Cardston also marks the southern border of the Blood Indian Reserve, with 6,800 residents, the largest reserve in Canada. Every June, the Blood perform the Sun Dance religious ritual; it is one of the few plains tribes maintaining this tradition. However, this dance is not a tourist attraction, nor a public event.

If you need gas, fill up in Cardston. Gas stations are few and far between on the next stretch of highway.

En Route from Cardston – Except for a couple of small towns, Leavitt and Mountain View, this is mostly open country, the approach to the foothills of the Rockies. Thirty-one miles (50 km) after leaving Cardston, you arrive at the gate of Waterton Lakes National Park.

WATERTON LAKES NATIONAL PARK: This little sister of Banff and Jasper shows little family resemblance to the two larger, more popular parks. A more ancient part of the Rockies, Waterton has jagged mountains and ridges; layered rock of contrasting purple, red, and green; chains of connected valleys; and innumerable mountain streams, waterfalls, and lakes. The four largest lakes, connected by small streams, run across the middle of the park. The center of many of its recreational activities, they are the Maskinonge, the Lower Waterton, the Mid-Waterton, and the Upper Waterton. A few miles farther west is Cameron Lake, apart from the other four. The Waterton Lakes townsite is on the northern shore of the Upper Waterton, several miles in from the park gate at Route 5. Waterton Lakes National Park joins the US's Glacier National Park at the US border in Montana. The two parks have been named the International Peace Park, commemorating and celebrating the long open border shared by the two countries.

The town of Waterton is an active park center of motels, restaurants, stores, and campgrounds. *Shoreline Cruise* boats offer leisurely 2-hour cruises of Upper Waterton Lake, crossing the international border and stopping briefly at Goat Haunt, Montana (phone: 403-859-2362). *Shoreline Cruise* also rents boats. The town has docking facilities and a boat launch. (Motorboats are restricted to the main lakes.) Just north of town is the starting point of the Red Rock Canyon hiking trail, which leads through successive stages of canyon rock, a living exhibition of the geology and ecology of this part of the park. Before heading into the wilds, however, visit the *Bayshore Inn* in town; its beautiful view of the area is surpassed only by its old-fashioned dining room and the mountain trout served there. Alberta beef is on all local menus. The *Prince of Wales* hotel, a château-like hostelry up the hill from town, is worth a visit (see *Best En Route*). It has a magnificent view of the lake, huge fireplaces, and an open foyer that rises six floors. A great, formal dining room overlooks the lake. Meals are expensive, but if you want to splurge, this is the place to do it. Waterton has a golf course, tennis courts, riding stables, fishing, an outdoor swimming pool, a lakefront campground, and lake swimming. If you do swim in the lake, be prepared: It is fed by mountain glaciers and is extremely cold.

A short drive from the townsite brings you to Cameron Lake. Apart from the parking lot and picnic spots, the lake is almost in its original pristine state. There are driving and hiking trails that give access to park wilderness and its wildlife — buffalo, elk, deer, moose, bear, Rocky Mountain sheep, cougar, coyote, badger, and skunk. The usual rules about letting the animals go about their own business apply.

During the winter, snowdrifts often block the roads to Waterton Lakes National Park. But if the roads are open and you don't mind that many facilities are closed, the snow-covered mountains are a wonderful sight. If you do visit in the winter, bring food with you, and be sure that you arrive with enough gas in your car to get you to the nearest service station outside the park. You can enjoy a stay at the *Kilmorey Lodge* (see *Best En Route*), open year-round and offering cross-country skiing in winter. It is located near the *Bay Shore Inn.*

En Route from Waterton Lakes – To continue the journey to Calgary, take Route 6 north from the northern exit of the park. After 30 miles (50 km) you will reach the town of Pincher Creek, reputed to be the windiest spot in Alberta. The chinook (the prevailing strong westerly wind from the Rockies) hits Pincher Creek full force as it whistles off the mountains. In town, the *Pincher Creek Museum* and Kootenai Brown Historical Park, at James Ave. and Grove St. (phone: 403-627-3684), have several restored pioneer log cabins, one of which was built in 1889 by Kootenai Brown, the area's most illustrious pioneer. The trout fishing is good in the rivers around Pincher Creek and in Beauvais Lake Provincial Park, just west of town. Open summers only.

A detour west at Pincher Creek on Route 3 will provide a peek into an interesting chapter of Alberta's past. About 20 miles (30 km) west of the Pincher Creek junction lies Crowsnest Pass, birthplace of the province's earliest coal mining and the scene of one of its greatest tragedies, the Frank Slide. The Frank Slide Interpretive Center (also on Route 3) tells the story of the night in 1903 when 90 million tons of rock broke off Turtle Mountain and buried part of the mining town of Frank and an estimated 75 people. The nearby Leitch Collieries stone ruins are now an interpretive center depicting the history of the coal mining industry. The center is open year-round; the collieries are open in summer only.

Returning eastward on Route 3, the road heads northeast of Pincher Creek toward Fort Macleod, 29 miles (47 km) away. On the way, the road passes through part of the Peigan Indian Reserve and its main town, Brocket. In Brocket, you can visit the *Peigan Crafts* store. From here, Fort Macleod is a half-hour drive.

FORT MACLEOD: The authentic reconstruction of the original Fort Macleod stands on 25th Street and gives a glimpse into early frontier life that is thought-provoking. The first fort was built in 1874 by the Northwest Mounted Police. The Mounties were the umpires of the territories, standing between the settlers, Indians, whiskey traders, ranchers, and immigrants. They were hardly impartial, being essentially forces of eastern expansionism, but they represented what law existed. Exhibits in the fort museum detail the history of the NWMP and local Indian cultures, and Mounties in the uniform of the period perform original horseback drills.

Be sure to take a stroll through downtown Fort Macleod, where the streets are lined with historic buildings dating back to the turn of the century. The downtown core has been declared a provincial historic site — the first such designation in Canada — and protected buildings include an old sandstone hotel, a Roman Catholic church, a town hall, and a post office.

The Fort Macleod Rodeo is one of the better small-town rodeos. It usually takes place during the first 10 days of July.

En Route from Fort Macleod – About 9 miles (15 km) northwest of Fort Macleod on Route 516, nestled in the Porcupine Hills, is Head-Smashed-In Buffalo Jump. Named a World Heritage Site by UNESCO, the 5,700-year-old jump was used by Blackfoot Indians, who would stampede buffalo herds over the cliffs and then slaughter them for food. Open early May to early September. A new interpretive center, open year-round, has five display galleries, an audio-visual presentation, and guided tours (phone: 403-553-2731).

Route 2 heads north from Fort Macleod on a direct line to Calgary, 103 miles (166 km) away, and passes through several interesting small towns. About 23 miles (37 km) north of Fort Macleod, Claresholm, a town of just over 3,400, is mainly a service community for area farmers and ranchers. Its small museum in the old Canadian Pacific Railroad station on the main highway is worth a stop.

At this point, you can continue north on Route 2 or take Route 520 west for a winding, 80-mile (129-km) tour of the foothills that will eventually return you to Route 2 at Nanton, 24 miles (39 km) north. Most of the roadway is unpaved and passes through remote territory, but you will see real ranching country and fantastic scenery. Take Route 520 until it meets Route 517. Go north on Route 517, and it will join the Forestry Trunk Road in the Rocky Mountains Forest Reserve. Traveling north on the Trunk Road, you will pass the spectacular Livingstone Falls. Shortly beyond Livingstone Falls, turn east on Route 532, which takes you out of the forest reserve. At the junction with Route 922, head south for a few miles to Chain Lakes Provincial Park, which has 140 picnic sites, cooking shelters, fishing, and a boat launching in an isolated, relaxing environment. From Chain Lakes, Route 533 takes you directly to Nanton in about 45 minutes. Nanton is famous for its sparkling, ice-cold water, available from taps beside the highway. Fifteen miles (24 km) north on Route 2 is High River.

HIGH RIVER: Many Albertans believe this little town typifies western life. Always a center for ranchers, it has also become home for many people who work in Calgary but want to live in a small town. Many of its shops carry arts and crafts made in the area, so if you're looking for a special souvenir, High River might be able to supply it. The unique Western articles produced by *Eamor's Saddlery* and *Olson's Silversmithing* are prized around the world. Each August, the town hosts the North American Chuckwagon Championships. These races attract the same drivers and rigs that appear in the famous Calgary Stampede, but here you get a much closer view of the action. During the championships, there are also horse races, a midway, and a country dance and beer hall. The Little Britches Rodeo, the last 2 weeks of May, features junior cowboys and cowgirls, as young as 7 years, bronco busting, steer wrestling, and calf roping. The *Museum of the Highwood*, on First Street, open year-round, has a good geological collection and exhibits on local history.

En Route from High River – It is a simple, 24-mile (39-km) drive on Route 2 to Calgary. For a bit of homey sustenance, head west on Highway 7 (off Route 2) about 5 miles (8 km) until you reach the small town of Okotoks. On the main street you'll find the *Ginger Tea Room* serving Saskatoon berry pie, cream cheese and cucumber sandwiches in season, and their own blend of Okotokian tea. Open for lunch and afternoon tea (403-938-2907). Back on Route 2, just before Calgary, turn west on Route 22 to see Spruce Meadows, one of the finest equestrian facilities in the world. For a complete report on Calgary, its hotels, and restaurants, see THE CITIES.

BEST EN ROUTE

There are plenty of motels and campgrounds along this route, but except for those in Waterton and Lethbridge, quality is limited. Waterton's *Prince of Wales* hotel is the best in the area. Most motels are simple, functional, and little else. Similarly, the overnight campsites meet only basic needs. There's also little difference in room rates. Expect to pay $50 or more per night for a double in a hotel listed as expensive; $30 to $50 in the moderate range; and $20 to $30 in the inexpensive category. All prices are quoted in US dollars.

LETHBRIDGE

Lethbridge Lodge – This modern, 190-room lodge has a a plant-filled atrium, a spectacular view of the Oldman River valley and features a dining room, country-western tavern, pool and Jacuzzi. 320 Scenic Dr. (phone: 403-328-1123). Expensive.

Sandman Inn – With 138 rooms with color TV sets, and telephones, facilities here include an indoor swimming pool, dining room, cocktail lounge, gift shop, and tavern. Holiday Village, 421 Mayor Magrath Dr. (phone: 403-328-1111). Expensive.

Lodge – This 94-room motel features a dining room, outdoor pool, hot tub, sauna, and satellite TV. Mayor Magrath Dr. and 7th Ave. (phone: 403-329-0100). Moderate.

Park Side Inn – Just a few blocks from the Japanese gardens and Henderson Lake Park, this 64-room hotel has a dining room, cocktail lounge, coffee shop, telephones, and color TV sets. 1009 Mayor Magrath Dr. (phone: 403-328-2366). Moderate.

Sundance Inn – Telephones, color TV sets, an indoor swimming pool, kitchenettes, and complimentary coffee are found in this 54-unit motel. 1030 Mayor Magrath Dr. (phone: 403-328-6636). Moderate.

Henderson Lake Campground – Just across the road from the park and the lake, at the east end of the lake, this campground has 100 camping sites, many with sewer, electric, and water hook-ups. There are also stoves, fireplaces, tables, showers, flush toilets, and laundry facilities. Privately owned (phone: 403-328-5452). Inexpensive.

CARDSTON

Flamingo – At the south end of town, this 38-unit motel has color TV sets, telephones, kitchenettes, and an outdoor pool. All units feature queen-size beds. Major credit cards. 848 Main St. S., or PO Box 92 (phone: 403-653-3952). Moderate.

Lee Creek Campground – Twenty-six camping sites, no hook-ups, but cooking facilities, tap water, and flush toilets (no phone). In the town of Cardston. Inexpensive.

Police Outpost Campground – This campground, operated by the provincial department of recreation and parks, has 46 camping sites, no hook-ups, cooking facilities, pump water, and pit toilets. 10 miles (16 km) west and 11 (18 km) miles south of Cardston (phone: 403-653-2522). Inexpensive.

WATERTON

Bayshore Inn – This 70-unit motel overlooks the lake and has a dining room, cocktail lounge, and color TV sets. Open May 1 to October 1. 111 Waterton Ave. or PO Box 38, Waterton Park (phone: 403-281-9259). Expensive.

Prince of Wales – A château on a hill with a splendid view of the mountains and the lake, this is a perfect headquarters for a park visit. There are 82 rooms, a dining room, cocktail lounge, and telephones. Open June 5 to September 8. Waterton (phone: 403-859-2211). Expensive.

Crandell Mountain Lodge – With 11 units, some kitchenettes, and family units, this motel is open from April to November. 102 Mount View Rd. or PO Box 114, Waterton Park (phone: 403-859-2288). Moderate.

Kilmorey – Right on the lake at the entrance to Waterton townsite, this motor lodge has 25 rooms, dining room, cocktail lounge with fireplaces. Open year-round. Major credit cards. 117 Evergreen Ave. or PO Box 124, Waterton Park (phone: 403-859-2334). Moderate.

Crooked Creek Campground – Seven miles (11 km) east of Waterton Park, it's a small campground, but it's free and open year-round. Operated by Alberta Transportation (no phone). Inexpensive.

Waterton Homestead Campground – Here are 250 camping sites, including 70 trailer spots with electric, sewer, water hook-ups, showers, flush toilets, and laundry facilities. Two miles (3.2 km) north of the park on Route 6 (phone: 403-859-2247). Inexpensive.

PINCHER CREEK

Foothills – A 30-unit motel, it has color TV sets, whirlpool bath, sauna, and telephones. On the east side of Route 6. 1049 Waterton Ave. or PO Box 2347 (phone: 403-627-3341). Moderate.

FORT MACLEOD

Sunset – At the west entrance to town, this motel has 22 units, color TV sets, kitchenettes, and air conditioning. PO Box 398 (phone: 403-553-4448). Moderate.

CLARESHOLM

Sportsman – This inn has 42 units with dining room, direct-dial phones, cable TV sets, and plug-ins for cars; some units have queen-size water beds. PO Box 1328 (phone: 403-625-3347). Moderate.

Calgary to Banff and Jasper National Parks

Immense as they are, stretching from the Yukon Territory to New Mexico, the Rocky Mountains are only part of a much larger chain that reaches deep into Mexico, sending two arms of peaks along Mexico's eastern and western coasts, gathering the country into a stony embrace that comes to fingerpoints of peaks cupped protectively around Mexico City. This huge mountain chain — from the Arctic to the jungles of Chiapas — tells the story of creation; and one of the most revealing and beautiful chapters of that story is open for the reading on the drive between Banff and Jasper national parks, the showpieces of the Canadian West.

These two vast, adjoining parks cover 200 square miles of the Rocky Mountains on the Alberta-British Columbia border, some of the finest mountain scenery in the world. Like fingers caressing a backbone, the 259-mile (417-km) road from Calgary to Banff, past the beautiful Lake Louise, the Columbia Ice Fields, and to Jasper follows the spine of the Continent. Whether for summer or winter sport or because it is simply one of the most wonderful drives in North America, this is the most popular destination in the West.

Banff is a nature sanctuary as well as a major resort. Around the town itself are luxurious hotels, elegant restaurants, galleries, craft shops, ski resorts, and entertainment centers. Since it is one of Canada's most popular vacation areas, be prepared for crowds at the major attractions and considerable traffic on the park's winding roads.

Jasper is somewhat less commercially developed, although the town of Jasper has creature comforts aplenty. And for those who want to commune with nature in peace and quiet, both parks have miles of uncrowded hiking trails, secluded riverside picnic sites, and wilderness paths into the raw, undeveloped Rockies.

A map of Alberta may be obtained from Travel Alberta, 10025 Jasper Ave., 15th Floor, Edmonton T5J 3Z3. For maps of Banff and Jasper, write Banff-Lake Louise Chamber of Commerce, PO Box 1298, 93 Banff Ave., Banff T0L 0C0 (403-762-3777), and Jasper Park Chamber of Commerce; PO Box 98, 632 Connaught Dr., Jasper T0E 1E0 (403-852-4932).

> **En Route from Calgary** – The entrance to Banff National Park lies about 70 miles (113 km) west of Calgary. Both the four-lane, divided Route 1 (the Trans-Canada Hwy.) and the parallel Route 1A lead directly to the park entrance. If you take the TransCanada highway, stop at Canada Olympic Park, on the west edge of the city, site of the 1988 Olympic games. Route 1A passes through several small towns and the Stoney Indian Reserve. If you have time, it's a relaxing way to go. Our route follows Route 1A.
>
> The Crowchild Trail in Calgary becomes Route 1A as you head west. Just outside Calgary, the small town of Cochrane is worth a stop if you want to ramble over the grassy site of the first large ranch in Alberta, established in 1881, and climb to the rocky perch of the Cochrane Ranche's famous horse and rider statue. Cochrane has several new housing developments, built mainly for people who work in Calgary but who prefer to live in Cochrane's small-town atmosphere.

THE STONEY INDIAN RESERVE: About 10 miles (16 km) from Cochrane, on Route 1A, is the Stoney Indian Reserve. You may recognize some of the surrounding landscape from films. *Little Big Man,* with Dustin Hoffman, and *Buffalo Bill and the Indians,* starring Paul Newman, were filmed here. Located on the highway, the main village on the reserve is Morley, settled in the 1800s by Methodist missionary George McDougall. It is the site of the tribe's schools, administrative office, and recreation center. While there are no restaurants, or major retail stores here, it is possible to purchase leather goods, feather and bead work, and jewelry made by the men and women of the reserve at the Nakoda Lodge, a large cedar-log facility built by the Stoney on the shore of Hector Lake, 10 miles (16 km) west of Morley. An addition to the lodge includes 50 motel units. The building is the site of workshops and educational retreats for anyone interested in native culture. Sunday brunches are offered in summer and fall (phone: 403-881-3949). The Stoney value their privacy. While you are welcome to visit the town and other places open to visitors, don't wander off the main highway. The residents have the right to ask you to leave; the reserve is their property.

A few miles west of Morley, near the banks of the Bow River, the Stoney have set aside land for a public campground. The facilities are rudimentary (fire pits, picnic tables, and outhouses), but they include some beautifully wooded camping spots. And the scenery is spectacular. Some of the sites overlook a fenced buffalo paddock, and, to the west, the mountains seem close enough to touch. During the summer, more than a dozen teepees set up in the park make the area feel even more removed from the present day.

Each August the Stoney host a conference of Native Americans interested in the preservation of their religious tradition (by invitation only).

Stoney Indian Park and Morley can also be reached from the Trans-Canada.

En Route from the Stoney Indian Reserve – Route 1 and Route 1A draw closer together as they approach Banff National Park. Just past the town of Exshaw — its large Canada Cement factory visible from both highways — the two roads join and continue a few miles to Canmore. Within a mile or two of this intersection are two guest ranches, *Kananaskis* (see *Best En Route*), and the *Raffer 6*. Originally a coal mining town, Canmore has become a thriving center, with many grocery stores, shops, motels, and fast-food outlets serving Banff's overflow tourist industry. For a leisurely meal, try *Gallagher House,* downtown. It offers fireside tables, afternoon tea, lunch, and dinner in an old-world atmosphere.

KANANASKIS COUNTRY: From Canmore, it's easy to explore Kananaskis Country, a year-round recreational area developed by the provincial government. This 2,400-square-mile mountain wilderness has facilities for hiking, biking, horseback riding, cross-country skiing, fishing, and snowmobiling. The *Canmore Nordic Centre,* on the town's outskirts, hosted the 1988 Winter Olympic cross-country and biathlon events. The center's 34 miles (56 km) of skiing and hiking trails are open to the public (phone: 403-678-2988).

If you follow Route 1 east of Canmore to Route 40 and travel 13 miles (22 km) south, you come to Mount Allan, site of the 1988 Olympic alpine events. Call Ski Nakiska (phone: 403-591-7777) for public skiing information. Only 2 miles (3.2 km) farther south on Route 40 is the challenging and beautiful 36-hole *Kananaskis Country Golf Course* (phone: 403-591-7070).

BANFF NATIONAL PARK: The gates to Banff National Park are just beyond Canmore. The entrance fee depends on which park facilities you plan to use. Although you may drive nonstop through the park or a portion of it, you will have a more enjoyable trip if you view the sights at leisure and participate in some of the activities. Plan at least an overnight stay; 2 days is even more desirable. Campers will find sites throughout the park. (And remember, all national park campsites are first-come, first-served.) For those who prefer motels or hotels, there are adequate accommodations in the town of Banff; at Lake Louise, 35 miles (56 km) beyond; and along the longer stretch of road between Lake Louise and the boundary of Jasper National Park (see *Best en Route,* below). Reserve rooms well in advance; this is a popular area.

The town of Banff, about 10 miles (16 km) beyond the park entrance, is the center of the park's attractions and the home base for exploring the southern portion of the park.

Banff is the fount of the area's tourist industry. In 1841, Sir George Simpson, governor of the Hudson's Bay Company, was the first white man to explore the area. It remained untouched until the 1880s, when the Canadian Pacific Railway prepared to lay track nearby and businessmen decided to exploit the hot springs at Sulphur

Mountain by building a hotel and spa. As the resort gained popularity, the town grew.

Today, Banff is a major tourist center in the summer and the winter ski center, and its stores, bookshops, art galleries, and restaurants are often crowded, but endlessly intriguing. The *Banff National Park Natural History Museum* (93 Banff Ave.) has exhibits explaining the area's geological structure and wildlife.

The *Whyte Museum of the Canadian Rockies,* housed in the Public Library on Bear Street, shows the work of both local and national Canadian artists. The library also houses the Archives of the Canadian Rockies, a collection of rare books and photographs.

The Canadian Pacific's *Banff Springs* hotel (see *Best En Route*) on Spray Avenue is the descendant of the original resort hotel that first established Banff as a vacation spot. It was built between 1910 and 1928, but 18 years was apparently not enough time to complete the job, because when the new hotel was opened to the public, one room still had no door. Three architects worked on the hotel's design, creating a style that can only be described as 16th-century French château with touches of Scottish manse. Part of the 850-room property was recently renovated. The hotel can arrange rafting trips and sleigh rides, in season. Amenities also include indoor and outdoor swimming pools. Fossilized stone used throughout the structure emphasizes its castle-like appearance. Nearby, on Mountain Avenue, you can still take a dip in the Upper Hot Springs Pool. The pool is not intended for swimming but for soaking in the soothing natural sulfur waters. The water — not just warm, but hot — is especially relaxing after a day of hiking or skiing. The outdoor pool is open year-round. The Cave and Basin Hot Springs, discovered 100 years ago by three railway workers, are open from June to September. Special displays reveal the springs' effect on local flora and fauna.

A number of quality stores sell clothing, ceramics, weavings, paintings, and sculptures. But a word of warning: Some of the items are overpriced and can often be found for less money in Calgary. Check the labels if you buy Indian handicrafts; some of them may be made in Japan. Authentic Canadian Indian handicrafts are identified with a label. The *Quest* on Banff Avenue has a good collection of Inuit prints and soapstone carvings.

Banff is also the home of the Banff Centre, one of the best fine arts schools in North America. The original theater school is now only one division of an education complex serving more than 1,600 students annually. The Banff Centre offers instruction in dance, music, writing, and management. All year, in two modern theaters, films, concerts, theater, dance, and recitals are offered. Its annual *Banff Festival of the Arts* is held June through August and features a variety of concerts, exhibitions, and other productions. For information on current events, phone 403-762-6300.

Despite Banff's many attractions, the real interest lies in the mountains, lakes, and forests that surround it. A good way to begin exploring the countryside is to take either of the gondola lifts on the two mountains near town. To the northwest, the Mount Norquay Scenic Lift goes to the top of Mt. Norquay, providing an opportunity to enjoy its commanding view of several mountains; picnic tables and a restaurant at the summit station are open from mid-June to September 1. Even if you don't take the cable car to the top, it's worth driving to the base station. This road goes high on the mountain, with great views and stopping points along the way. To the southeast, the *Sulphur Mountain Gondola* runs much the same operation, with a teahouse and hiking trails at the top. It operates year-round.

Several short hiking trails lead out from Banff. A fascinating 1½-mile loop in Sundance Canyon crosses streams and climbs rocks. Behind the parking lot at Upper Hot Springs is a 2½-mile climb that takes about an hour and brings you back to the hot springs. Two miles down Spray Avenue, you can walk around the sulfur springs at Cave and Basin Pool. Guided horseback trail rides are available from *Warner and MacKenzie Guiding and Outfitting* on Banff Avenue.

Rocky Mountain Raft Tours offers — on a large rubber raft — a 3-hour tour of the Bow River. Tickets may be obtained at the bus station or at the *Banff Springs* hotel. A few miles west of town, at Lake Minnewanka, are 2-hour motorboat tours of the lake, and canoe rentals. For skiers, Mt. Norquay has excellent downhill slopes. *Sunshine Village,* 14 miles (23 km) south of town, has full ski facilities and overnight accommodations.

One of the easiest ways to enjoy the park's splendid scenery is simply to drive through it. A number of major peaks, like Cascade Mountain, Castle Mountain, and Mt. Brett, are short distances away, and there are plenty of seldom-traveled trails throughout the area for easy hikes. Park personnel will help you to find them. A word of caution that can't be repeated too often: The constant presence of human beings has made the animals unafraid of people. Nevertheless, they are still wild; they can be dangerous and unpredictable. Also, in feeding or attempting to play with wild animals, you risk harming them. It is cruel and stupid to feed park animals, here or in any park. Don't do it.

Lake Louise, 35 miles (56 km) northwest of Banff, must not be missed. You can make it a separate overnight stop, a day's round-trip journey from Banff, or the first stop in a full day of driving northward. Lake Louise early in the morning is a special treat. It is a beautifully clear, blue-green lake, surrounded by mountains and backed by the Victoria Glacier. As the sun rises, the mountains and the glacier are mirrored on the lake's surface. Since sunrise can be as early as 4 AM, it helps to stay overnight. The only hotel right on the lake is the *Château Lake Louise* (see *Best En Route*), the Canadian Pacific's landmark hotel, which has recently added a new wing and undergone major renovation. Guests can leave a wake-up call to see the sunrise spectacle. (The hotel serves coffee to those who get up to watch.) Rooms with a view of the lake (as opposed to the mountains) are slightly more expensive.

For years, the lake was an undisturbed preserve of the rich and the powerful, but over the years democracy (and economics) caught up with it. Lake Louise is now accessible to all, and remains beautiful at any time, sunrise or midday. And if you want to get away from other people, rent a canoe or a horse. There is ample privacy and serenity around here for everyone.

The *Lake Louise Inn* and the *Post* hotel, a few miles from the lake, are both charming. Although neither is inexpensive, both are more reasonable than *Château Lake Louise.*

En Route from Lake Louise – From Lake Louise, Route 93 heads north toward Jasper through the large remaining section of Banff park and some of the most striking scenery you will ever see. This section of Route 93 is called the Ice Field Parkway. From the road you will be able to see 12 of the 25 highest peaks in the Rockies and glaciers up to 1,000 feet thick. Be prepared to take your time, because the highway winds and climbs. It's also a good idea to switch drivers once in a while so everyone can get a good look at the scenery. About 22 miles (35 km) past Lake Louise, you can stop for coffee and a meal at *Num-Ti-Jah Lodge* on Bow Lake. You should also stop to absorb the views at Hector Lake, Peyto Lake (which has a mysterious blue tint), and Bow Summit. Forty-six miles (74 km) north of Lake Louise, you reach the boundary with Jasper National Park.

JASPER NATIONAL PARK: Less crowded than Banff, Jasper emphasizes its natural wonders, which complement rather than repeat those of Banff. It's a long 92 miles (148 km) from the park entrance to the town of Jasper, but the sights along the way are amazing.

Immediately after crossing into Jasper you are still in glacier country. Directly inside Jasper's boundary is the Columbia Icefield, from which the Saskatchewan, Columbia, and Athabasca rivers rise. The ice field, covering 160 square miles, lies across the Continental Divide. One toe of the Athabasca Glacier, which is 600 to 1,000 feet thick, spills down the mountain; visitors can ride across the ice in specially-equipped vehicles at the mountain, or park their car and follow the foot trail leading to an excellent view of the mountain's cliffs and the abutting Angel Glacier. Back on Route 93A, it is a short drive to Jasper.

Although the town of Jasper has been growing rapidly in recent years, it still has a more relaxed, less formal atmosphere than that of Banff. One of the first objects to attract your attention will be the large totem pole in the center of the open square near the railway station. From the Queen Charlotte Islands of British Columbia, it is one of the finest examples of a nearly extinct art. Elsewhere in Jasper are many activities similar to those in Banff. The Jasper Tramway Ltd. ascends Whistler Mountain, 7,500 feet. There is a café at the top station and hiking trails leading even higher. Since this is the treeline, there are lovely specimens of rock flowers and moss. Numerous marmots — a type of groundhog — scurry from burrow to burrow. *Jasper Raft Tours* and *Jasper Mountain River Guides* offer whitewater excursions on the Athabasca in large rubber rafts. *Pyramid Riding Stables* on Pyramid Lake Road and the *Jasper Park Riding Academy* at the Jasper Park Lodge provide guided trail rides. The town has a luxurious golf course. And if you want a quiet picnic and an opportunity to appreciate the scenery, there's a tiny island in Pyramid Lake you can reach by footbridge. For a plain but satisfying meal, try *Becker's Bungalow* at *Becker's Roaring River Chalets* on the Jasper-Banff Highway. Its reputation has spread far beyond Jasper.

The Miette Hot Springs, 25 miles (40 km) away, near the park's eastern boundary, has three naturally hot pools, including the hottest one in the mountains. Marmot Basin, 13 miles (21 km) from town, is one of the finest ski areas in the Rockies. A worthwhile trip is to take the side road from Jasper south to the Maligne Lake for the popular 2-hour motor cruise. Fishing is good and boats are for rent. Nearby, Maligne Canyon is one of the best examples of canyon landscape. Trails lead part of the way into the gorge. Like Banff, Jasper has many hiking trails and lots of pristine nature.

BEST EN ROUTE

Although motels, hotels, and campgrounds are plentiful along this route, during the summer you should make reservations. The Chambers of Commerce in Banff (403-762-3777) and Jasper (403-852-3858) can recommend a reservations service. Campsites operate on a first-come, first-served basis. Room rates here are higher than elsewhere in Alberta, but this is the only area in Alberta where you have a real choice of accommodations. Expect to pay $75 to $165 per night for a double room in the expensive range (and even more than this in the high season); $40 to $70 in the moderate category; and up to $35 in the inexpensive range. Following are just a few of the accommodations available; in Banff alone, there are more than 30 hotels, motels, and apartment-style accommodations to choose from. All prices are quoted in US dollars.

CANMORE

- **Cee-Der Chalets** – The 7 individual cozy cabins have kitchenettes and sleep two, four at the most. Some have fireplaces, TV sets, and mountain views. At Harvie Heights, 1 mile (1.6 km) east of the Banff park gates. PO Box 525 (phone: 403-678-5251). Inexpensive.
- **Rocky Mountain Chalets** – Fireplaces, bedroom lofts, and kitchenettes are found in these alpine lodgings. Box 725 (phone: 403-678-5564). Inexpensive.
- **Spray Lakes Campground** – This campground, 20 miles (32 km) south of Canmore, has 50 tent sites with stoves, tables, and outdoor toilets. It's run by the provincial recreation and parks department (phone: 403-678-5533). Inexpensive.

KANANASKIS COUNTRY

The Lodge at Kananaskis – This luxurious new facility in a pristine wilderness setting has 255 rooms, some suites with fireplaces, indoor pool, whirlpool bath, and sauna. Located near Mount Allan's Nakiska ski resort, 13 miles (22 km) south of Rte. 1 on Rte. 40 (phone: 403-591-7711 or 800-268-9411). Expensive.

Mount Engadine Lodge – An alpine lodge that sits alone in primal forest and mountain country. Amenities include a dining room, living room, lounge, and fireplace. You get your choice of dormitory or private accommodations, plus wholesome meals and opportunities for alpine hiking, cross-country skiing, mountain climbing, and wind-surfing. Take Smith-Dorrien Rd. south of Canmore to Mount Shark turnoff (phone: 403-678-4080). Moderate.

BANFF

Banff Park Lodge – The downtown area is only 2 blocks from this modern, quiet, 210-room lodge, with dining rooms, cocktail lounge with live entertainment, heated indoor pool, saunas, and a whirlpool bath. All rooms have queen- or king-size beds. 222 Lynx St. (phone: 403-762-4433). Expensive.

Banff Springs – This castle of a hotel has 850 rooms, indoor and outdoor swimming pools, exercise room, sauna, three public Jacuzzis, ice skating, sleigh rides, a golf course, tennis courts, riding stables, several dining rooms and cocktail lounges, and a posh Presidential Suite. Spray Ave. (phone: 403-762-2211). Expensive.

Homestead Inn – A small basic motel off the main drag where you can get a good night's sleep. With 27 units, color TV sets, and telephones. 218 Lynx St. (phone: 403-762-4471). Moderate.

Mount Royal – A pleasant hotel in the center of town, it has 92 rooms, color TV sets, a dining room, and a cocktail lounge. 138 Banff Ave. (phone: 403-762-3331). Moderate.

Rundle Ridge Chalets – There are 37 cedar chalets with fireplaces here, just a half mile east of the Banff park gates. PO Box 1847, Banff (phone: 403-678-5387). Moderate.

Swiss Village – On the eastern outskirts of Banff, this lodge has 47 motel units with color TV sets and telephones, some with kitchenettes and fireplaces; 22 bungalows. 600 Banff Ave. (phone: 403-762-4581). Moderate.

LAKE LOUISE

Château Lake Louise – In addition to its spectacular Lake Louise setting, there is a new wing — bringing the hotel's total number of rooms to over 530 — outdoor and indoor swimming pools, a tanning salon, Jacuzzi, exercise room, dinner and dancing, cocktail lounges, and a tavern. Reservations are necessary (phone: 403-522-3511). Expensive.

Lake Louise Inn – This 186-unit motel has 38 kitchen apartments, 56 standard rooms, laundry facilities, a tennis court, pool, Jacuzzi, sauna, and an exercise room. Open all year. PO Box 209 (phone: 403-522-3791). Expensive.

Post – A charming, Bavarian-style jewel, this log-constructed hotel was remodeled in 1987. The original *Post* was renovated and now houses an excellent dining room. There is also a pool, Jacuzzi, and sauna. The 95 rooms include suites with lofts, kitchens, and fireplaces. 200 Pipestone (403-522-3989). Expensive to Moderate.

JASPER

Jasper Park Lodge – This sprawling lodge on Lac Beauvert has 400 rooms with adjoining sitting rooms, color TV sets, a golf course, tennis courts, boating, fishing, stables, saunas, whirlpool baths, and car rentals. Open year-round. Ski packages available. Rates soar during peak season — May 20 to September 15 (phone: 403-852-3301). Expensive.

Lobstick Lodge – Five blocks from the center of town, this 138-unit motel has kitchenettes, sauna, executive suites, game rooms, telephones, and TV sets. Geikie St. or PO Box 1200 (phone: 403-852-4431). Moderate.

Pyramid Lake Bungalows – A terraced lakeside property, 3½ miles (5 km) northwest of Jasper, with 10 units, each with a kitchenette, as well as fishing and boating facilities. Ski packages available. Open early April to mid-October. PO Box 388 (phone: 403-852-3536). Moderate.

Whistler's – This 40-room motel with a dining room, cocktail lounge, telephones, and TV sets, is across the street from the Jasper train station. Open year-round. PO Box 250 (phone: 403-852-3361). Moderate.

Cypress Hills Provincial Park to Edmonton via the Dinosaur Country

Modern technology has taken the bad out of badlands. These marginal desert areas were places where, years ago, a man on foot or horseback could well die without due precaution, native intelligence, and desert savvy. Today there is nothing bad about them. In the distances a car can cover, they need hardly be dangerous, and chances are, unless you've done desert driving, the image you carry in your mind of an area named "badlands" doesn't begin to account for its color, the striking rock formations, or its severe beauty.

All the better reason to make this drive from Cypress Hills Provincial Park in southeastern Alberta across the province's badlands and plains to Edmonton, in the center of the province. It is a drive of about 400 miles (644 km) and in its course you will encounter all the surprises, all the grave beauty, all the harsh splendor referred to so cavalierly as "the badlands."

Alberta's badlands contain many surprises. Cypress Hills Provincial Park, in the middle of a desert, is a teeming, green forest with a crazy-quilt ecology. Northwest of Cypress Hills, the city of Medicine Hat provides a variety of urban attractions. West through the badlands, at the towns of Brooks and Drumheller, are the skeletons and fossils of dinosaurs and other extinct creatures discovered in this area. There are excellent opportunities to see these remains and to explore the fossil beds yourself.

At the Blackfoot Indian Reserve, between Brooks and Drumheller, you can look back into Indian history and also see something of present Indian culture. In Alberta's midlands, the desert gives way to rich farm country. Near Red Deer, several lake resorts well equipped for recreation provide a welcome contrast to the arid terrain. North from Red Deer, an easy trip through Alberta's farm communities brings you to the major city of Edmonton. While there is much driving on this route — and in the summer the weather is apt to be hot — there are excellent facilities all along the way, including many farms offering bed-and-breakfast services, and the sights make the driving worth it. If necessary, you could travel the whole route in two crowded days, just glimpsing at the scenery. But since the best attractions lie slightly off the main roads, a more leisurely pace makes sense. A three- or four-day drive allows you to see each sight thoroughly and to stay overnight at spots you find particularly attractive.

A map of Alberta may be obtained from Travel Alberta, 10025 Jasper Ave., 15th Floor, Edmonton T5J 3Z3. For more detailed maps of the Cypress Hills-Medicine Hat-Brooks area, write Southeast Alberta Travel and Convention Bureau, PO Box 605, Medicine Hat T1A 7G5; for the Drumheller area, write Big Country Tourist Association, PO Box 2308, Drumheller T0J 0Y0; for the Red Deer area, write David Thompson Country Tourist Council, 4811 48th Ave., Red Deer T4N 3T2.

CYPRESS HILLS PROVINCIAL PARK: Cypress Hills Park lies just west of Saskatchewan and north of Montana. From the US, take Montana's Route 232; this will become Canada's Route 41. Cypress Hills is 50 miles (80 km) beyond the border. West from Saskatchewan on the Trans-Canada Highway (Rte. 1) is a turnoff south onto Route 41, shortly after you enter Alberta. Another 21 miles (34 km) brings you to Cypress Hills.

This is one of nature's startling oddities. Surrounded by the prairie's rolling hills, Cypress Hills is a wide plateau, 2,000 feet higher than the surrounding countryside and nearly 5,000 feet above sea level. It is covered by a heavy pine forest, supports a wide variety of wildlife, and contains three lakes, the largest of which is Elkwater. This landscape should, by all reason, exist only hundreds of miles farther south. Here in abundance are mountain and woodland orchids, hawthorne, violets, and crocus. Coyotes, moose, deer, and all manner of birds are found in the forest. (As in all Alberta's provincial parks, hunting is forbidden.)

Near the park's northern boundary are Elkwater Lake and the town of Elkwater. The lake has swimming, boating, windsurfing, and bicycling and canoe rentals. The town has a service station and one motel, the *Green Tree,* with 19 units. The campgrounds have 540 sites for both trailers and tents. During the winter, there are facilities for cross-country skiing and Hidden Valley, a downhill course, with a lodge and quad-chair lift.

En Route from Cypress Hills Provincial Park – Take Route 48 north to Route 1 (Trans-Canada Hwy.). Head west on Route 1, and within 45 minutes you will arrive at Medicine Hat.

MEDICINE HAT: Medicine Hat is a tree-filled city (population 43,000), its prosperity based on being built on 780 billion cubic feet of natural gas. The city is said to have "all hell for a basement." This gas reserve, the largest in Canada, is 99% pure and pumped directly into the turn-of-the-century gas lamps that light the revitalized downtown area. Legends concerning the origin of the city's name abound. According to one story, a Cree medicine man lost his headdress during a battle with the Blackfoot, and the Cree consequently lost the battle. Medicine Hat contains more than 70 parks connected by 67½ mile (108 km) of trails for hiking, biking, and cross-country skiing. The Cultural Center is on the Trans Canada Highway at College Drive. The Clay Interpretive Center on Industrial Avenue depicts the history of clay products native to Medicine Hat. The *Medicine Hat Museum and Art Gallery* (1302 Bomford Crescent S.W.) provides a history of the Canadian West through exhibits, reconstructions, and photographic displays. The Tourist Information Center on the Trans Canada Highway at Southridge Drive includes an interpretive center and dump station. Medicine Hat boasts three excellent golf courses, including one that is a par 3.

En Route from Medicine Hat – Continue west on Route 1. For the most part, it is open country until you reach the town of Brooks, 70 miles (113 km) west of

Medicine Hat. This stretch of highway gives you a chance to appreciate the scenery of Alberta's badlands. Prominent here and throughout much of southern Alberta are coulees, sharp trenches worn by wind and water into masses of rock. You will see a few of the formations of curiously columned rock called hoodoos. There are plenty more of them farther along. In Brooks, the Alberta Horticultural Research Center conducts tours of its gardens. The *Brooks and District Museum* takes you back in time, as you walk through an old church and schoolhouse with maps, schoolbooks, and inkwells intact. The main attraction, however, is Dinosaur Provincial Park, containing the largest dinosaur fossil bed in the world, northeast of Brooks.

DINOSAUR PROVINCIAL PARK: The park lies about 15 miles (24 km) outside Brooks. Take Route 873 north at Brooks and follow the signs. Located on the banks of the Red Deer River, the park, named a world heritage site in 1979, was once lush seaside swampland, the home of 11 species of duck-billed dinosaurs. Although its valleys and hills are now covered with juniper, sagebrush, and prickly pear cactus, it is Canada's — and one of the world's — richest fossil grounds. The action of the river has gradually eroded the rock bed, creating spectacular hoodoos and revealing layer upon layer of colored minerals. In the process, the river uncovered the remains of the dinosaurs.

Be sure to stop at the Field Station of the *Tyrrell Museum of Paleontology* in the park. There is an interpretive center where visitors can watch paleontologists at work and visit a nearby winter campground.

Scientists began excavations here late in the last century, ultimately finding the skeletons of 120 dinosaurs, which were duly distributed to museums around the world; only four skeletons remain in the park — three duck-billed dinosaurs and one horned dinosaur, all of which were recovered and restored by Dr. H. C. Sternberg, the world-famous paleontologist. The park has been kept as natural as possible, with the skeletons on display in the badlands, housed in protective buildings. You are welcome to roam around the parkland, and although access to certain areas is restricted, tours are available. Note that all fossils and bones are protected by law; you are not allowed to keep any you may find.

The park is also the site of John Ware's cabin, a museum depicting life on an early Alberta ranch. A former slave from South Carolina, Ware settled here in the late 1800s, when little was known of this valley. He eventually ran a thousand head of cattle on the Red Deer River.

En Route from Dinosaur Provincial Park – The next major destination is Drumheller, to the northwest, where there are more dinosaurs. Pick up Route 1 again at Brooks and continue west. You will be traveling gradually out of the badlands. After about 48 miles (77 km), the highway passes the Blackfoot Indian Reserve. The towns of Cluny and Gleichen on the reserve are well worth your attention. Off the Trans-Canada Highway, a few miles south of Cluny, is Blackfoot Crossing. Here, in 1877, Crowfoot, chief of the Blackfoot Nation, signed Treaty No. 7, which provided peace between the Indians and white settlers. On the way back to the Trans-Canada you will pass a marker indicating Crowfoot's grave. Up the ridge from the marker is an Indian burial ground containing the graves of many Indians who died of starvation and poverty after the treaty was signed. At the edge of the graveyard, surrounded by a black fence, is the grave of Crowfoot. Eight miles (12.8 km) past Cluny on Route 1 will be a turnoff for Gleichen. For locally made Indian crafts, visit the *Blackfoot Craft Society* in Gleichen, or ask for directions to *Early Thunder Creations,* about 10 miles (16 km) east of town. On the south side of town are the buildings of Old Sun College. Here the Blackfoot operate a new museum of Indian history and culture intended to be a major center for the study of Indian civilization. Many exhibits are already completed, and work is continuing to bring back artifacts dispersed throughout Canada over the past century. To view the museum's collections, write or phone the Blackfoot Cultural Studies Department, Old Sun College, Gleichen T0J 1N0 (phone: 403-734-3862) in advance. To continue on to Drumheller, return to the Trans-Canada Highway. A turnoff to Route 21 appears 18 miles (29 km) later. Head north on Route 21 for 23 miles (37 km) and turn east on Route 9. Another 29 miles (47 km) will bring you to Drumheller. Over the course of this route, you will have reentered the badlands.

DRUMHELLER: This city of 6,300 boasts an excellent museum and spectacular landscape. Here, over the ages, the Red Deer River has carved the Drumheller Valley deep into the plains. The region is filled with hoodoos and exposed layers of stone, gullies, and canyons. And, as at Brooks, the river has uncovered the remains of prehistoric animals.

Drumheller's other major attraction is the Dinosaur Trail, a 29-mile (47-km) tourist road that begins at the outskirts of town, travels through the badlands north and west of the city, and brings you back to town. Despite its name, the Dinosaur Trail contains a mixture of attractions relating to local life and history and is more commercial than Dinosaur Provincial Park. Entering through the north gate, you come first to the *Homestead Antique Museum,* a collection assembled by local farmers of just about anything that relates to life in the Drumheller area. The road travels through badlands to the new *Tyrrell Museum of Paleontology* (phone: 403-823-7707), a $30-million provincial museum and research center where you can wander among some 45,000 dinosaur specimens and watch scientists preserving and mounting fossil skeletons. One of the museum's prize pieces is the Albertosaurus skull that geologist Joseph Tyrrell (for whom the center is named) discovered in the area in 1884. The museum also boasts a garden of tropical plants similar to those that thrived in Alberta between 70 and 300 million years ago. The facility is open year-round, and admission is free. Next, you come to the Little Church, a universal house of worship that accommodates six worshipers at a time. Somewhat beyond the Little Church is Horsethief Canyon. From the road you have an excellent view of the canyon's fine desert landscape. After Horsethief Canyon, a ferry takes you across the Red Deer River, and on the opposite bank you pass by thousands of fossilized oysters.

The road has now turned south and continues through more badlands terrain. Drumheller Prehistoric Park contains life-size replicas of dinosaurs and a rock and fossil shop.

Six miles (9.6 km) southwest of town, off Route 9, Horse Shoe Canyon is an excellent example of desert landscape. From the canyon floor the rock piles rise in strange shapes, and the canyon's walls are layers of contrasting green, red, and gold. There are fine vantage points along the canyon's rim, and trails lead down into the canyon itself. You can also take an hour's drive east from Drumheller, along Route 10, to East Coulee. This route goes deeper into the river valley, passes some abandoned coal mine shafts, and reveals more hoodoos and some mushroom-shaped rock formations. There is an interpretive center and a walking trail around the mine site. Near East Coulee, a swinging bridge spans a deep portion of the valley. At East Coulee you will find the Atlas Mines. Although closed now, they were once the region's major working coal mine. Some East Coulee citizens are now working to revive the old 1940s mine as a museum. *The East Coulee School* (ca. 1930) has been restored and is now a museum. There is also a crafts store, tea room, and art gallery. Motel rooms and campsites are readily available in Drumheller.

En Route from Drumheller – To reach the city of Red Deer and, from there, the highway to Edmonton, head north and west. The quickest way is Route 9 west from Drumheller, which becomes Route 72, and 72 miles (116 km) west of Drumheller, intersects Route 2. Go north on Route 2, a four-lane highway, another 57 miles (92 km) to Red Deer. One worthwhile detour along the way is Stephansson House, the historic residence of Iceland's national poet. It's just north of Markerville (turn west off Route 2 onto Route 592). It is also possible to make the trip to Red Deer by way of secondary roads through countryside that lacks any major tourist attractions but does have interesting scenery. Follow Route 56 north from Drumheller for about 25 miles (40 km) and then cut west on Route 585. After 22 miles (35 km), Route 585 intersects Route 21 at Trochu. Head north on Route 21 for 19 miles (31 km) until it intersects Route 42. Take Route 42 west for 24 miles (39 km), and it crosses Route 2 just south of Red Deer.

RED DEER: This city of nearly 55,000 and its vicinity are worth a visit, perhaps an overnight stay. It is the convention capitol of the province and a fast-growing industrial center. Although Red Deer is not a major toursit attraction, there is a museum worth seeing; the *Red Deer and District Museum* (47th Ave. and 47th St.) is devoted to pioneer history. There's a franchise of the *Phil's Steaks and Pancakes* chain in Port O'Call Shopping Center as well as *Smitty's* — a new, attractive alternative to the standard gas station restaurants — on Route 2 south of the city. The *Red Deer Lodge* (49th Ave.) and the *Black Knight Inn* (50th Ave.) both have dining rooms (see *Best En Route*).

Of greater interest to a vacationer is the area just west of the city on Highway 11. Here in wooded countryside is the town of Sylvan Lake, a resort popular with Albertans, with six commercial campgrounds and a public beach, on the south shore of the lake. This area is popular and may be crowded, so those in need of some serious solitude should drive around to the north shore of Sylvan Lake, where Jarvis Bay Provincial Park has been established. Less crowded and more peaceful, the park has trailer sites, picnic facilities, swimming, fishing, and boat rentals.

En Route from Red Deer – From Red Deer it's an easy 93 miles (150 km) north to Edmonton on either Route 2, the major highway, or Route 2A, which passes through towns along the way. The countryside is pleasant, at times spectacular. Sights include two more lake resorts west of the highways. Red Deer can also be the starting point for a trip west on Route 11, the David Thompson Highway. Rocky Mountain House on Route 11, the only national historic park in western Canada, is built on the site of several former trading posts. This 154-mile (248-km) road crosses unspoiled country through the Rocky Mountain Forest Reserve and terminates at the boundary of Banff and Jasper national parks.

Fifteen miles (24 km) north of Red Deer is the town of Lacombe, home of the Canadian Agriculture Department's research station, where scientists develop new varieties of wheat and grain. The station is open to visitors. Seven miles (11 km) west of Lacombe, at Gull Lake, is Aspen Beach Provincial Park, the best of the area's lake resorts, with more than 400 campsites in two campgrounds, swimming, fishing, and boat rentals. Continuing north for another 19 miles (31 km), Routes 2 and 2A both cross Route 13. Follow Route 13 west from Route 2, and you will shortly arrive at Pigeon Lake Provincial Park, with campsites, swimming, fishing, and boat rentals. Route 13 east from Route 2 leads to the town of Wetaskiwin, at the junction of Route 2A. Here, the *Reynolds Museum* (403-352-1351), an agricultural and transportation museum, has assembled one of North America's largest collections of antique and classic cars, fire engines, and airplanes. The final 42 miles (68 km) north take you through farmland, past the town of Leduc, to Edmonton. For a complete account of Edmonton, its hotels and restaurants, see *Edmonton,* THE CITIES. From Edmonton, you can take Route 16 west to Jasper or you can head north and explore the Slave Lake-Peace River region.

BEST EN ROUTE

Medicine Hat, Brooks, Drumheller, and Red Deer have good motels and there are several good campgrounds. There are no truly luxurious or major resort motels, but most are pleasant and comfortable, with the fanciest at Red Deer. Expect to pay $55 to $75 per night for a double room in the expensive range; $40 to $50 in the hotels we list as moderate; $35 and under in the inexpensive range. All prices are quoted in US dollars.

MEDICINE HAT

TraveLodge – At the junction of Routes 1 and 3, this 92-unit motel has both outdoor and indoor swimming pools, telephones, and color TV sets, as well as a dining room and cocktail lounge. 1100 Redcliff Dr. S.W. (phone: 403-527-2275). Expensive.

Imperial – This motel has 104 units, telephones, exercise room, an indoor pool, sauna, and whirlpool bath. At the east entrance to the city on Hwy. 1. 3282 13th Ave. S.E. (phone: 403-527-8811). Moderate.

Gas City Campground – Open May-September with 97 sites. Considered one of the best in the province. (403-526-0644). Inexpensive.

BROOKS

Heritage Inn – Color TV sets, telephones, and air conditioning in all of its 64 rooms. Restaurant and cocktail lounge. Main St., just off the Trans-Canada Hwy., or PO Box 907 (phone: 403-362-6666). Moderate.

Tillebrook Provincial Park – On 344 acres, its 120 tent and trailer sites have electrical hook-ups, showers, flush toilets, and piped water. Open year-round. Five miles (8 km) southeast of Brooks on Rte. 1 (phone: 403-362-4525). Inexpensive.

DRUMHELLER

Drumheller Inn – Features include an indoor pool, whirlpool bath, color TV sets, 100 rooms, executive suites, dining room, and lounge. 100 Railway Ave. S.E. (phone: 403-823-8400). Expensive.

RED DEER

Red Deer Lodge – Considered the best in Red Deer. Built around an indoor courtyard featuring many plants and a swimming pool, this 240-room motel has color TV sets, telephones, hot tub, a surprisingly good dining room, tavern, poolside coffee shop, and cocktail lounge. There are also a number of lovely duplex suites. 4311 49th Ave. (phone: 403-346-8841). Expensive.

Black Knight Inn – A newly renovated 100-room hotel with an indoor swimming pool, sauna, dining room, cocktail lounge, color TV sets, and telephones. 2929 50th Ave. (phone: 403-343-6666). Moderate.

Edmonton to Slave Lake and Peace River

This long route, 717 miles (1154 km), may not suit everyone's taste. Forming a great circle, it begins at Edmonton, heads north to Athabasca, then turns northwest along the edge of Alberta's northern wilderness past the shores of Lesser Slave Lake until it reaches the town of Peace River. At Peace River the route turns southwest until it reaches the town of Grande Prairie, where it heads south and east back to Edmonton. Although this northern area has few major tourist attractions, it has plenty of farmland and open country, with good hunting and fishing. The area is also rich in history; the first European explorers came here in the 1700s. It is a good place to escape to the serenity of unspoiled nature. The population is small, but the residents are friendly. There are numerous points from which the adventurous traveler can venture farther north, deeper into the forest wilderness. However, the route here outlined remains well within the bounds of civilization and can be comfortably traveled by anyone. The roads usually remain passable during the winter, and the area is good for ice fishing, skating, and cross-country skiing.

A map of Alberta may be obtained from Travel Alberta, 10025 Jasper Ave., 15th Floor, Edmonton, Alberta T5J 3Z3. Consult Travel Alberta's *Adventure Guide* for the names of companies offering rafting trips, nature treks, dog-sledding, canoeing, and fishing experiences in Alberta's northern wilderness. For specific maps on the St. Albert–Slave Lake region, write Midnight Twilight Tourist Association, 1 Sturgeon Rd., St. Albert, Alberta T8N 0E8; for the Peace River region, write Land of the Mighty Peace Tourist Association, PO Box 3210, Peace River, Alberta T0H 2X0; for the Grande Prairie region, write Game Country Travel Association, PO Box 1254, Grande Praire, Alberta T8V 4Z1. For a list of outfitters and guides serving the area, write Fish and Wildlife Division, Department of Energy and Natural Resources, Main Floor, North Tower, Petroleum Plaza, 9945-108 St., Edmonton, Alberta T5K 2C9 (phone: 403-427-8580).

ST. ALBERT: Just beyond Edmonton on Route 2 north is St. Albert. Here in 1861 Father Albert Lacombe, one of the great figures in Alberta's history, founded a mission in a log cabin. Lacombe's ministry was, for his time, both progressive and visionary. He aided the Métis (Canadians of European-Indian ancestry) in their efforts to develop the first farms in this area. He worked for peace between the Blackfoot and the Cree nations, and he gave of himself tirelessly during smallpox epidemics. Lacombe's mission still exists, in the Father Lacombe Mission, on St. Vital Avenue off St. Albert Trail. The museum's exhibits include many tools and relics from frontier days as well as material on the history of the Oblate missionary order, to which Father Lacombe belonged.

En Route from St. Albert – North from St. Albert, Route 2 follows the route of an old forest trail, the St. Albert Trail, which dates back to the early 1800s. Unfortunately, no signs of this early trail exist. The road passes by several French-Canadian towns — Villeneuve, Rivière Qui Barre, and Vimy — until it arrives at Clyde, 40 miles (64 km) north of Edmonton. From Clyde, Route 2 follows the path of the old Landing Trail north to the town of Athabasca. Along this stretch, efforts are being made to recreate the historical trail: A parallel trail exists for certain stretches, and there are historical markers, historical collections, playgrounds, and modern recreational facilities along the way. Soon you notice fewer and fewer towns and houses and more and more pine trees. At Athabasca, you are beyond the edge of the great northern forests.

ATHABASCA: Located at the southernmost point of the winding Athabasca River, this town has traditionally been both a crossroads and jumping-off point for travelers.

DIRECTIONS / Alberta

In days gone by, Athabasca saw hundreds of fur traders, gold seekers, and missionaries board the sternwheelers heading north or west. The coming of the railway put an end to all that, and today Athabasca is of interest because of several beautiful lakes nearby. For fishermen, two large lakes containing perch and pike can be reached from Athabasca. Lac la Biche lies 54 miles (87 km) east on Route 55. It has several commercial campsites and Sir Winston Churchill Provincial Park, with campsites. Swimming is allowed, and the Owl Hoot commercial campground has boat rentals. About 40 miles (64 km) north of Athabasca on Route 813 is Calling Lake Provincial Park, a far less developed, quieter locale, with about 25 tent and trailer sites. If the extra driving does not appeal to you, consider three smaller but excellent lakes just off our main route leaving Athabasca, discussed below.

En Route from Athabasca – Leaving Athabasca, Route 2 swings west for 10 miles (16 km) to Baptiste Lake. You can fish and swim in the lake, and boating is allowed, although there are no boat rentals. As the road turns north from Baptiste Lake, it changes from pavement to a packed surface for about 30 miles (48 km), but it remains easily travelable. Ten miles (16 km) north of Baptiste Lake is Island Lake, another fishing spot. And another 10 miles (16 km) north is Lawrence Lake, with fishing, a beach, swimming, and a boat launch but no boat rentals. Island Lake and Lawrence Lake both have small campgrounds.

The next point of major interest is the town of Slave Lake, on the shore of Lesser Slave Lake. When Route 2 becomes paved once again, several miles past Lawrence Lake, you are about 35 miles (56 km) away from Slave Lake. On the way you may want to stop and see the village of Smith, a bustling river town until the railroad passed it by. Some forlorn examples of the original cabins are still standing.

SLAVE LAKE: Slave Lake and its vicinity are essentially places to relax and to enjoy the lake and the woods. The town, with a population of 5,400, sits at the southeastern corner of Lesser Slave Lake. The lake itself is a vast expanse of water over 40 miles (64 km) long. Unlike many of the lakes of southern Alberta, which are fed by the icy waters of mountain glaciers, Lesser Slave warms up during the summer and is quite comfortable for swimming. It also has fine sandy beaches and, during the summer, daylight lasts late into the evening hours, making for great late-night picnics. The shoreline is thick with berry bushes — raspberries, wild strawberries, Saskatoon berries — as well as delicate wild flowers and ferns. There are several motels in town and at least two commercial campgrounds in the area. On the eastern shore of the lake, north of town, Lesser Slave Lake Provincial Park covers 18,000 acres. There are picnic facilities, a beach, and a hiking trail, and swimming and fishing are permitted. From the top of Mt. Marten to the east of the park, you have a commanding view of the length of the lake and of the Swan Hills, a nearly untouched wilderness area out to the south.

If you are a serious hunter or angler, or just a wilderness buff, you may enjoy a side trip from Slave Lake to Desmarais and Wabasca, deeper in the wilderness. To get there, drive north through the provincial park and head northeast on Route 754, for some 40 miles (64 km). There is virtually nothing but unsettled land until you arrive at the two small townsites, located between North and South Wabasca lakes. This is primarily a fishing area — for perch and pike in the lakes and trout in the streams. Write in advance to Eugene Cardinal, General Delivery, Desmarais, Alberta T0G 0T0, to inquire about fishing, hunting, and tour guiding services in the area. Again, this is not a trip for everyone. And once at Desmarais you will be literally in the middle of nowhere; there are no connecting routes or other towns. Therefore, it is advisable to write to or phone the guide service well in advance of your trip.

En Route from Slave Lake – Route 2 travels westward along the southern shore of Lesser Slave Lake. After 25 miles (40 km) a turnoff onto Route 33, an unpaved road, leads down into the Swan Hills. Humans have left the Swan Hills pretty much alone, and the area is full of deer, moose, duck, elk, bear, trout, and pike. It can make an interesting side trip, but keep in mind that much of the area is inaccessible by car.

Returning to Route 2, the road continues west for another 70 miles (113 km). It passes the western end of Lesser Slave Lake at mile 40 (64 km) of this distance. Throughout this area it passes by towns rooted in the early history of the white man in the province. The town of Joussard near the southwestern end of the lake was named after Bishop Joussard, a respected, 19th-century missionary in the Northwest Territories and Alberta. Grouard, near the lake's northwestern corner, bears the name of another missionary. The town's history goes back to 1801, when it was a fur trading outpost. It became a bustling city in the late 1800s, when it gained a large Métis population and the Hudson's Bay Company made it its district headquarters. But after the railroad went well south of the town, Grouard's glory faded. While you may want to visit these towns out of curiosity, you will find little that calls to mind their lively pasts.

At High Prairie, directly on Route 2 about 15 miles (24 km) past the western shore of Lesser Slave, displays showing the area's history can be seen at the *High Prairie and District Centennial Museum*. However, the best museum lies farther along the route at Girouxville (see below). Also at High Prairie is a turnoff onto Route 749, which takes you to Winagami Lake Provincial Park, a few miles to the north. The park has swimming, fishing, and tent and trailer sites. About 15 miles (24 km) west of High Prairie, Route 2 turns north and intersects Route 49 after 18 miles (29 km). A side trip west for 8 miles (13 km) and a turn north on Route 744 will bring you to Girouxville.

The *Girouxville Museum* has exhibits on virtually all aspects of the area's history. In addition to remarkably good and complete collections of tools, household items, Indian artifacts, old books, and documents, the museum has a reconstruction of a trapper's cabin, a chair used in the first meeting of the Alberta legislature, and a 1914 version of a snowmobile. From Girouxville, continue north on Route 744 for a scenic drive to Peace River, or backtrack to Route 2. If you wish, you can stop at Falher, considered to be the honey capital of North America, and tour a honey plant. Once back on Route 2, it's another 38 miles (61 km) north to the town of Peace River.

PEACE RIVER: The Peace River itself and local history are the attractions in this town of about 6,500, located at the point where both the Smoky and the Heart rivers flow into the Peace. Its history reaches back to the days when the Cree called it Sagitawa — the place where one views the meeting of the waters. The fur traders knew it as the Forks, and many a fort was built here. In 1792 Alexander Mackenzie fashioned a shelter and spent the winter here while making his pioneering journey across North America.

An excellent view of the confluence of the waters can be seen from Sagitawa Lookout on Judah Hill on the southeast bank. The confluence is an impressive sight, a vista of calm beauty. You can watch the Peace River, nicknamed "the Mighty Peace," emerge from far back in the countryside. At the points of confluence the river is interspersed by sandbars and green islands. The waters then draw together into a narrower channel and flow north. The sight is all the more impressive if you keep in mind that the Peace rises in British Columbia and flows far to the northwest to join the Slave River. Another excellent spot from which to view the confluence is the top of an 800-foot hill on the east side of town. That hilltop is also the gravesite of the local folk hero, Twelve-Foot Davis. Davis came here during a gold rush in the 1840s. Finding that the best claims had been staked, he took advantage of a surveying error and staked a claim on a 12-foot strip that had been missed between two lots. Thus he won both his fortune and his name.

The *Peace River Centennial Museum*, open from May through October, is in many ways similar to Alberta's other small historical museums, although its collection emphasizes the fur trade. In addition to displays of a fur press and animal traps, there are several Hudson Bay journals kept by early traders and a replica of a paddlewheel boat.

We urge you to think twice before renting a boat. WARNING: The waters at the confluence of the rivers are treacherous; don't take out a boat unless you are expert in boating on rivers. A safer way to travel the Peace is to take the *Tar Island River Cruise*. The Tar Island boat crew will take you on a scenic overnight cruise downriver, fix you a barbecue dinner, let you fish, take you ashore for trail hikes, and bring you back to town. The cruises only operate during the summer. Write ahead for reservations to: Tar Island River Cruises, Box 2070, Peace River T0H 2X0 (phone: 403-624-4295).

En Route from Peace River – Head west on Route 2. In about 16 miles (26 km) you will reach Grimshaw. Just west of town is Queen Elizabeth Provincial Park. There are 200 acres with 56 sites for overnight camping and swimming and boating (no boat rentals) at Cardinal Lake. The junction of Routes 2 and 35 just north of Grimshaw offers another side trip for hunters. The town of Manning, 47 miles (76 km) north on Route 35, is a center for wilderness hunting. There is also good trout fishing in the rivers.

From Grimshaw, Route 2 heads southwest for 42 miles (68 km) and reaches Fairview, another good spot from which to launch hunting trips. South of Fairview on Route 2, the town of Dunvegan has restored the St. Charles Mission, a log church and rectory built by missionaries in 1884. The interior has been turned into a museum and interpretive center depicting the town's history as one of the earliest fur trading posts. A small campground is next to the mission. About 22 miles (35 km) farther south on Route 2 is the town of Rycroft. From Rycroft, Route 2 travels through mostly open country to Grande Prairie, 42 miles (68 km) to the south.

GRANDE PRAIRIE: With a population of about 26,200, Grande Prairie is the chief city of an area of farms, ranches, and forests. It has most of the urban amenities that may be welcome after a succession of small towns; these include a golf course, an Olympic-size swimming pool, and a large shopping plaza. The *Pioneer Museum* in Muskoseepi Park in town has, along with the usual artifacts and fossils, a good display of the wildlife that abounds in the region. Twelve miles (19 km) west of town on Route 2, Saskatoon Island Provincial Park has campsites and allows swimming in its lake. Part of the park has been set aside as a nesting area for trumpeter swans.

The area all around Grande Prairie and that stretching from Valleyview to Whitecourt to the southeast is good hunting country, and there are many hunting and fishing guides in this region. Contact the Fish and Wildlife Division in Edmonton for a list of names.

En Route from Grande Prairie – To return to Edmonton, backtrack on Route 2 and turn east on Route 34 just north of Grande Prairie. You will again be driving through sparsely populated farmland and forests. About 48 miles (77 km) along Route 34, you will reach Williamson Provincial Park, on Sturgeon Lake. The park has swimming and fishing and contains 62 campsites. Another 11 miles (18 km) will bring you to Valleyview, a good spot from which to begin a hunting trip into the countryside. From Valleyview, head south on Route 43. The 97 miles (156 km) to Whitecourt are virtually open wilderness. Along the way you will see the Swan Hills reappearing in the east. There is a road, Route 32, into the hills just before you reach Whitecourt. At Whitecourt, pause to see the McLeod River join the Athabasca River in a roar of waters. Beyond Whitecourt, Route 43 travels for 72 miles (116 km) past the small towns of central Alberta until it joins Route 16 outside Edmonton. At the junction, you can either turn east for the 19-mile (31-km) drive to Edmonton or head west on Route 16 toward Jasper.

BEST EN ROUTE

This route has few motels and campgrounds, although most of the moderate-size towns on the major roads have motels. And there is overnight camping near most of the major scenic attractions. There's little elegance about the motels, but they are comfortable and have the usual amenities. One or two do have more elaborate facilities. The campgrounds tend to be a little more primitive than many in the US. Expect to pay $40 and up per night for a double room in the expensive range; $20 to $40 in the moderate range; $15 to $20 in the inexpensive range. All prices are quoted in US dollars.

ATHABASCA

Athabasca Inn – A 65-room hotel with TV sets, telephones, a dining room and cocktail lounge, and a tavern. No charge for children under 12 occupying the same room as their parents. 5211 42nd Ave. or PO Box 1526 (phone: 403-675-2294). Expensive.

Athabasca Lodge – This motel has 22 units, some with kitchenettes and all with telephones, plug-ins, and color TV sets, and a refrigerator in every room. On Hwy. 25, PO Box 1560 (phone: 403-675-2266). Moderate.

Athabasca Municipal Campground – A city-run spot that has 15 tent and trailer sites, showers, flush toilets, a boat launch, and fishing. Open May 1 through October 15. PO Box 450 (phone: 403-675-2967). Inexpensive.

SLAVE LAKE

Nash's Cabins – Three log cabins near a private beach, 3 miles (4.8 km) north of Slave Lake. Open May to October. PO Box 86 (phone: 403-849-3977). Expensive.

Sawridge – A relatively new 183-room hotel featuring color TV sets, telephones, a dining room, and coffee shop. There is also a gift shop. PO Box 879 (phone: 403-849-4101). Expensive.

PEACE RIVER

Crescent – This motel has 95 units, some with kitchenettes and all with color TV sets, telephones, and plug-ins. Close to the center of town. Major credit cards. 9810 98th St. or PO Box 670 (phone: 403-624-2586). Expensive.

Traveller's – Another motel, this one has 150 rooms with telephones and color TV sets. There's a tavern, dining room, a cocktail lounge, coffee shop, sauna, and the use of an exercise room a block away. Major credit cards. 9510 100th St. (phone: 403-624-3621). Expensive.

GRANDE PRAIRIE

Grande Prairie Inn – This hostelry has 212 rooms, an indoor swimming pool, tropical garden, winter plug-ins for warming up car engines when the weather is cold, telephones, a dining room, and cocktail lounge. Major credit cards. 11633 100 St. (phone: 403-532-5221). Expensive.

Alpine – There are 62 units, some kitchenettes, telephones, color TV sets, and an outdoor swimming pool. Major credit cards. 10901 100th Ave. (phone: 403-532-1680). Moderate.

British Columbia

The third largest province in Canada, British Columbia is also the wettest and most westerly. (Neighboring Yukon juts a few miles farther west, but it is a territory.) BC is bordered on the south by the state of Washington and bits of Montana and Idaho, to the east by Alberta, to the north by the Northwest and Yukon territories and Alaska, and to the west by the Pacific Ocean and the Alaskan Panhandle. The province covers 366,255 square miles, enough land to make 73 Connecticuts or 300 Rhode Islands. Despite the highly visible — to tourists — fruitlands of the Okanagan Valley, the trim pastures of Vancouver Island's east coast, and the truck farms of the Fraser River delta east of Vancouver, less than 10% of the land is now or ever will be arable or grazeable. The rest is covered by virgin forests, towering mountains, and vast expanses of semi-arid sagebrush land.

That immense wilderness is most sparsely inhabited, for three-quarters of the province's population lives at the southwest tip in two cities, the provincial capital of Victoria (population over 260,000) and the Pacific port city of Vancouver, the third largest Canadian city with more than 1 million inhabitants. (For a detailed report on Vancouver see THE CITIES.) Overall population density averages about 13 to every 2 square miles, scarcely more than thinly populated Alaska.

Motoring routes that provide the most sightseeing with the greatest comfort include a drive up Vancouver Island, a trip up the Fraser River road, a tour of the Okanagan fruit country between Kamloops and the US border, another from Kamloops eastward through the stunningly beautiful mountain parks on the Alberta border, and two wilderness routes starting in midprovince at Prince George, one going to the Pacific Ocean at Prince Rupert, the other to the Alaska Highway and the Yukon.

Running between Vancouver Island and the mainland is a protected channel the length of the mainland's coast, protected from the Pacific's rollers by a chain of barrier islands. The channel is called the Inside Passage and is crisscrossed by routes of comfortable automobile ferries that make possible linking the Vancouver Island drive to several of the mainland routes. The ferry rides — around the forested Gulf Islands and through the densely wooded fjords of the northern reaches — are themselves among the province's most picturesque and pleasant voyages. Eagles and sea birds abound. Porpoises, killer whales, seals, and sea lions swarm in those waters. With luck, occasional ferry passengers see the rare humpback whale, and, on the shore, bear and deer. (For routes and fares, write: British Columbia Ferry Corporation, 1112 Fort Street, Victoria, BC V8V 4V2.)

The island drive begins at Victoria. (To clear confusion: Victoria is on Vancouver Island, but the city of Vancouver is across the Strait of Georgia on the mainland.) That pretty little capital city at the island's southernmost tip has a climate strikingly like that of southern England, and the locals exploit their supposed English way of life as a prime tourist draw. The road runs northwest on Route 19 through some of the province's rare farmland. Impeccably kept pastures and barns, manicured row crops, and blooded stock make as pretty a bucolic scene as Kentucky's bluegrass or Pennsylvania's Amish country. On the Inside Passage side of the drive, tugs tow immense log rafts through whitecaps whipped up by a spanking breeze, and fishing boats putter about the sparkling waters on mysterious errands. The drive from Victoria to Port Hardy encompasses more than 300 miles of this rugged picturesque island that has captured the hearts of countless travelers ever since Captain Cook first met the native people off Nootka Sound in 1778. At Port Hardy, the *Queen of the North* loads cars and passengers for an 18-hour trip to Prince Rupert, terminus of one of the wilderness drives through northern British Columbia. Equipped with a dining room, lounge, and staterooms, the ferry makes a comfortable crossing. Reservations are advisable. Contact BC Ferries, 1112 Fort Street, Victoria, BC (604-656-0757), well in advance.

The Fraser River route runs east from Vancouver on the Trans-Canada Highway, Route 1. In its lower reaches, the Fraser River runs serenely through a flat delta of its own building, an alluvial bottomland that supports rich truck and dairy farms. About 75 miles (121 km) east, the delta runs out and mountains close in on the road. The Trans-Canada turns sharply northward here to Yale, the head of navigation on the Fraser. From here on, the river loses its peaceful nature and becomes one of the most turbulent, brawling streams in North America, trying to ram a full-sized river through gorges barely wide enough to accommodate a babbling brook. The route runs through former gold-mining country and ends in Bowron Lake Provincial Park, where the forests teem with moose, bear, and trout.

The Okanagan Valley drive is through fruit orchard country transformed from a sagebrush desert to lush farmland by irrigation. With the grape industry utilizing much of the land, this area now boasts 13 wineries and is sometimes known as Canada's "Napa Valley."

The national park route eastward on Trans-Canada from Kamloops runs through the Rockies in a cluster of national parks of majestic beauty. The highest peaks in Canada, great ice fields and glaciers, cobalt blue lakes, and virgin forests make the mountain section of the route a strong competitor for the most beautiful drive in North America.

Starting at Prince George, Route 16 (the Yellowhead route) runs through a sparsely settled wilderness to the terminal at Prince Rupert. From there, the BC ferry will carry travelers to Vancouver Island so they can make the island drive to Victoria. Alaskan ferries also call at Prince Rupert, making possible a side trip further up the Inside Passage to Alaskan ports like Sitka, Juneau, and Skagway.

From Prince George north on Route 97 and the Alaska Highway to the Yukon border, the road runs through a magnificent game-filled wilderness.

Information: Tourism British Columbia, 1117 Wharf St., Victoria, BC V8W 2Z2 (phone: 604-387-1642 or 800-663-6000).

Vancouver Island

Some Americans still grumble about the Oregon treaty, ratified by Britain and the US in 1846, which established the 49th parallel as the line of demarcation for most of the US-Canada border. The complaint is the little blink in the Far West where Vancouver Island drops just below the 49th, putting the beautiful town of Victoria firmly into what should be — but is not — American territory. It makes some Americans nostalgic for Manifest Destiny.

This island of sunken mountains and soaring, snowcapped peaks gives way to sandy beaches carved out by coves, inlets, and fjords. The waters of the Pacific and the Juan de Fuca Strait splashing against the beaches and rocky edges of this island are so gentle and clear that what a US navy lieutenant said more than 100 years ago is still valid: "Nothing can exceed the beauty of these waters... I venture nothing in saying there is no country in the world that possesses waters equal to these."

For some, long white beaches, waters teeming with salmon, fine deep harbors, and a year-round mild climate (in the southeast, summer temperatures rarely rise above 90F, or 32C, and winter temperatures seldom fall below freezing) are reason enough to travel the eastern edge of the island. But this 310-mile (499-km) trip from Victoria to Port Hardy reveals more than the soothing sands of the coastal resort towns of Qualicum Beach and Parksville, the salmon runs in the renowned Campbell River, and the stately harbor in Victoria. This island also has a history stretching back to the Haida, Kwakiutl, Sooke, and Cowichan Indians who lived in fishing villages along its coasts. Although their populations have been nearly wiped out by disease, war, and treaties, the Cowichan Indians still fish for salmon in the Cowichan River in much the same way as did their ancestors for thousands of years. But, for the most part, you will feel the spirit of the Indians in the giant totem poles (Thunderbird Park, Victoria), in the petroglyphs on the edges of evaporating pools, and in the legends surrounding geographical landmarks like Forbidden Plateau in Courtenay.

In contrast to the Indian spirit is the very real presence of the Canadians — many of English descent — living in the provincial capital. Although you won't see a bobby on every corner, afternoon tea at the *Empress* hotel is a tradition, not just a show the natives put on for tourists. You could easily spend days visiting Victoria's museums and ornate castles or sampling its very English pubs. Victoria is known as the most British city in Canada, and if it is a little bit stuffy and formal, it sets a tone to the journey along the island's Route 19 that is distinct. The road shoots the full length of the island along its eastern shore, with various side trips across the island. It's a favorite drive of residents.

VICTORIA: This provincial capital jutting into the Juan de Fuca Strait is named after Queen Victoria, and true to her memory, it is perfectly, immaculately British. Victorian architecture, spacious parks, manicured gardens with flowers blooming year-round, and its people (many of British descent) make this harbor city the most British in all Canada.

Established as a Hudson's Bay Company post in 1843, the city went through a rowdy boom-town period almost two decades later when fortune seekers stopped on their way to pan for gold in the Fraser River. Bastion Square downtown — with its renovated criminal courthouses, a supply center for miners, a maritime museum, and shops with modern items but mid-19th-century architecture — recaptures the years from 1843 to 1889.

But thousands of years before any white person set foot on the North American continent, Indians on the island used deer antlers to chop down the cedars growing nearby to build homes and canoes. A visitor to Thunderbird Park (across from the provincial buildings) will not only see a Kwakiutl Dance House but will feel the awesome power of the mythical thunderbird, thought to be a representation of the huge California condor. Carvings of this creature crest totem poles (some are originals, some copies) throughout the park. Indians believed the bird created thunder by fluttering its wings and lightning by flashing its eyes.

A visitor to the nearby *Royal British Columbia Museum* (675 Belleville St.) can see one of the best collections of Northwest Coast Indian art and replicas of buildings, fish canneries, and boats from 1740 to the present day.

For a recent rendering of the landscape and people of the Pacific Northwest, visit the *Art Gallery of Greater Victoria* (1040 Moss St.), featuring the paintings of Emily Carr. Although her work became quite famous after her death, during her life she was forced by poverty to paint some of her best work on brown wrapping paper.

The *Royal London Wax Museum* (470 Belleville St.) contains many suprisingly realistic likenesses of some of the prominent people in history and fantasy, a cast of characters ranging from Queen Victoria to Pinocchio.

As the museums and art gallery symbolize the city's past, the Parliament Buildings (501 Belleville St.) exemplify the future of the province. These ornate Victorian structures are built of andesite and native granite. You can visit during working hours.

More of the English influence is evident in the city's Victorian residences; some are far more luxurious than others. Craigdarroch Castle (1050 Joan Crescent) was once the home of a wealthy matron lured to Victoria by her husband's promise of a palatial abode. Robert Dunsmuir, a coal baron, built the castle for his Scottish wife but died before its completion.

Protocol is the name of the game at another posh residence, Government House (1401 Rockland Ave.), the residence of the lieutenant governor of British Columbia, the Queen's official representative. The lawns and hall of the mock-Tudor building are open to visitors. And any visitor who signs the guest book in the hall receives an invitation to join the lieutenant governor and his wife for a tea party each July. One recent guest said women are not required to wear a hat and gloves, but they may feel out of place if they don't.

In an old English setting complete with a Chaucer Lane and a 17th-century Plymouth Tavern stands a replica of William Shakespeare's birthplace and his wife Anne Hathaway's thatched cottage (429 Lampson St.). Bring a copy of the master's sonnets, spread a blanket on the lawn, and you've got the perfect setting to wonder about Shakespeare's "Dark Lady."

Although the city's English influence is well preserved, it is not completely frozen in architecture or buried in museums. A visitor to the *Empress* hotel (721 Government St.) can partake of one of the most British and genteel customs, afternoon high tea. The *Empress* (see *Best En Route*) was closed for renovation at press time; it is scheduled to reopen in early 1990.

If you want something more substantial after your spot of tea, head for *Barb's Place*

(Fisherman's Wharf) or *Old Victoria Fish & Chips* (1316 Broad), where you can get heaping helpings of this moderately priced meal. Other restaurants cater to every whim — *Taj Mahal* (679 Herald St.) for Indian food; *Japanese Village* (734 Broughton St.) for genuine Japanese cuisine; and *La Petite Colombe* (604 Broughton St.) for French fare. Or, instead of eating indoors, order a box lunch from *Sam's Deli* (805 Government St.) and picnic under oaks in Beacon Hill Park. Although any place in the city is good for bird-watching (sparrows and purple finches perch on apartment windowsills downtown), in the park you can watch native wild ducks and black (Australian) swans sail serenely across the ponds. From this 183-acre city park, you may hear the distant clanging of the Carillon, a 62-bell gift from the people of the Netherlands for the 1967 Canadian Centennial.

From the leisurely pace of the people you may get the impression that little work goes on here, but a trip to the inner harbor will put such thoughts to rest. This is a fishing and lumbering center, and ships from all over the world use the harbor as a port of call. For a view of what goes on under the harbor without getting your toes wet, descend to the bottom of the sea at the Underseas Gardens (490 Belleville St.) and watch Pacific salmon, wolf eels, and octopi through windows.

SEALAND: From Victoria, head east on the Marine Drive through a district of modern and mid-Victorian homes on the cliffs overlooking the Haro Strait. About 10 miles (16 km) along this road, you will reach Sealand (Oak Bay Marina, 1327 Beach Dr.), where killer whales perform with seals, sea lions, and porpoises.

Nearby, anglers can rent a boat at Oak Bay and have a fine day of fishing for rockfish, lingcod, sole, and flounder. It is also possible to cast a lure off the rocks for the salmon and black sea bass that thread their way through the kelp beds in search of small herring or needlefish.

BUTCHART GARDENS: Take Route 17 or 17A north from Victoria, then pick up Benevenuto Ave. to Butchart Gardens, where on 50 acres of manicured lawns, ponds, and lakes bloom exotic and native flowers. More than 85 years ago the estate of Robert Pim Butchart was a limestone quarry. Through the years Butchart and his wife transformed this dismal scene into a horticulturist's dream: an English garden with thousands of rose beds, arches, and arbors; a Japanese garden with maple trees, hydrangeas, bamboo, and the rare Tibetan blue poppy; and a formal Italian garden with a cross-shaped lily pond and sculptured trees and hedges. A restaurant on the estate offers lunch and afternoon tea, and the *Seed and Gift Store* offers seeds of many of the flowers on the site. Often, on summer evenings, concerts are held at the Gardens. Follow Route 1 to Duncan.

DUNCAN: On the banks of the Cowichan River, this small, bucolic town survives on lumbering — its traditional industry — and farming and fishing. The river is known for European brown trout and Pacific and Atlantic salmon. Surrounding Cowichan Valley is lumbering country, and the economics and ecology of lumbering are the underpinnings of Duncan's prosperity. All of this, and a great deal more, is explained in the *British Columbia Forest Museum* just a mile outside town, open May to late September. The museum is organized around the theme "Man in the Forest: Yesterday, Today, and Tomorrow," and exhibits explore all aspects of the industry, from the raw beauty and power of forests of 250- and 350-year-old Douglas firs to reseeding and replanting operations in contemporary forests. In addition, the museum has a wonderful collection of early lumbering equipment, including donkey engines, hand carts, and various kinds of saws used when the industry got under way here in 1860.

En Route from Duncan – About 4 miles (6 km) west on Route 18 is Cowichan Bay. Once a prime (and still reasonably good) area for sport fishing, the bay is now covered with log booms to feed nearby mills. You can rent a boat and fish for salmon in late summer and early fall. But the best fishing is off limits to visitors. Local Indians, within whose reserve most of the Cowichan River runs, expelled white anglers from the stretch of the river where steelhead, cutthroat, and brown trout swim.

From Cowichan Bay, you can head back to Route 1, north to the town of Chemainus. Once sustained by its lumber mill, Chemainus seemed doomed when the mill closed. But in a project involving many of the residents, artists took over the sides of stores and buildings to turn the main street into a festival of murals. Each mural depicts an aspect of the area's history from steam locomotives and general stores to loggers and seamen.

Beyond Chemainus, the mountains and sea close together again, funneling travelers through Ladysmith. This town lies on the 49th parallel, the Canada-US border for mainland British Columbia. Continue on Route 1 to Nanaimo.

NANAIMO: More than a century ago, seven tribes of Indians lived in harmony along the shores of the Georgia Strait. The discovery of coal in 1852 and the arrival of countless British miners destroyed that peace. Less than a decade after an Indian showed the coal and its whereabouts to a Hudson's Bay Company employee trading in a fort here, the company added a turreted bastion with cannons to protect the workers from Indian attacks. A visitor can follow a narrow cowpath-like road uphill to view the bastion, now a museum. Forest products have since replaced coal mining as Nanaimo's main industry.

Recently, tourism has become important to Nanaimo, and the city's waterfront facilities have been redeveloped. The latest addition is Swy-a-Lana Lagoon, the world's only mammal tidal lagoon, which draws observers four times daily. Nanaimo also boasts its own professional theater company with a summer program featuring BC playwrights.

In mid-July, the harbor is the site of one of the wackiest races in Canada. Contestants race, or in some cases float, 35 miles over the often stormy Strait of Georgia to the mainland in motorized bathtub-like contraptions. This popular event, the World Champion Bathtub Race, attracts entrants from around the world (see *DIVERSIONS*).

Those who forgo the tub trip can use the strait for the more traditional sport of fishing. (Salmon, trout, and steelhead proliferate here all year.)

En Route from Nanaimo – Just north along the waterfront on Route 19 is Departure Bay, with marina facilities for boats and yachts. At Parksville, follow Route 4 over a small mountain pass descending into the Alberni Valley and running west to Port Alberni. Along the way the mountain pass cuts through MacMillan Park, one of the best examples anywhere of virgin forest. It's also the home of Cathedral Grove, a cluster of tall west coast cedars and Douglas fir rising high above the forest floor.

PORT ALBERNI: Visitors to this mill city are usually more interested in the sport fishing than the city life. Near here, an angler can find chinooks and cohos in the harbor or follow a narrow paved road 6 miles (10 km) northwest to Sproat Lake, noted for its trout. From Sproat Lake, take Highway 4 to the Pacific Rim National Park. Miles of curving, sandy beaches greet you in this national park with some of the best beachcombing in North America.

En Route from Port Alberni – At the end of Route 4 is Tofino, a pretty little fishing village, which is the site of the annual whale watching festival (late March to April). Retrace Route 4 to Parksville, a resort town with long sandy shores splashed by shallow warm water. Rathtrevor Beach Park, just south of town, has camping and picnic facilities. North of Parksville on Route 19 is Qualicum, with more beaches. West of Qualicum on Route 4A, at the Hamilton Swamp Bird Sanctuary, visitors can circle a natural woodland and swamp where waterfowl and other birds abound.

From Qualicum, head north on Route 19 to Courtenay, the southeastern portion of the Comox Valley. Bounded by high mountains and carved out by clear lakes and the river, this area is home to grouse, duck, geese, and pheasant.

COURTENAY: The British established this town as a major farming community in the late 1880s. (It's now a popular recreational area, with golf courses, lodges, and restaurants.) Before this, Indians lived here atop a mountain known as the Forbidden Plateau, haunted by the legend of a mysterious monster, still feared today. While the tribe's braves were away, the legend says, an enormous monster slew every squaw and child on the plateau. It is believed no Indian has ever returned.

Those not frightened by the legend may make the trip up the plateau by foot or on horseback. Both Forbidden Plateau and Mt. Washington offer challenging ski runs during the winter months.

En Route from Courtenay – Head 14 miles (25 km) north along the coast to Miracle Beach Park, a public campsite for 193 tents and a great beach to comb for driftwood. Take Route 19 north to Campbell River.

CAMPBELL RIVER: Although this town is a mining and lumbering port, its fame comes from its excellent salmon fishing. In fact, the most sought-after honor among the fishing fraternity here is membership in the *Tyee Club*. Only those who have caught a tyee salmon weighing more than 30 pounds from a rowboat, on light tackle, in one of two local ponds can become members.

The town enjoys the advantage of the largest river on the island. If you want to rent a boat, tackle, or any other fishing equipment, just walk to the shores of the river, which flows through Strathcona Provincial Park (head west on Rte. 28). Mountain climbers will be challenged by Mt. Albert Edward and Mt. McBride, both over 6,000 feet tall.

About 100 miles (160 km) north on Route 19 is Port McNeill, known for its Vanishing River, a river that disappears into the earth, indicating the existence of a vast subterranean maze of caves and tunnels. Continuing on this portion of Route 19, you'll reach Port Hardy, where visitors can board the *Queen of the North* ferry for a 274-mile (441-km) voyage through the Inside Passage to Prince Rupert on the mainland (British Columbia Ferries, 1112 Fort St., Victoria, for information). Completion of this highway has opened up North Island all the way to Cape Scott and San Josef provincial parks.

BEST EN ROUTE

This island is one of the most popular vacation spots in Canada, with a wide variety of accommodations from basic modern motels and numerous clean campsites to elaborate hotels. This also means that during the peak season (May to October) it is wise to book ahead. Prices range from a few dollars for a place to pitch your tent in a campsite to the expensive hotels (from $110 to $265 for a double) in Victoria. Between these are the moderately priced hotels, bungalows, and cottages ($60 to $110 for a double). Bed-and-breakfast establishments and inexpensive inns are another lodging alternative ($30 to $40 for a double). For a complete listing of accommodations, write Tourism BC, 1117 Wharf St., Victoria, BC V8W 2Z2 (phone: 604-387-1642). All prices are quoted in US dollars.

VICTORIA

Empress – Built in 1906 on the harbor, this Gothic giant reigns as the largest and best-known hotel on the island. In 1988, this bulwark of British custom began extensive renovations, but it still retains its old charm. Amenities include 3 bars, a dining room, a new pool, an exercise room and 480 rooms. 721 Government St. (phone: 604-384-8111). Expensive.

Laurel Point Inn – An addition to the inner harbor that offers plush, modern facilities, including an indoor/outdoor pool, tennis, dining room and bar, and balconies with views. Recent expansion has added banquet facilities and 70 additional rooms. 680 Montreal St. (phone: 604-386-8721). Expensive.

Captain's Palace – This converted mansion has a Tudor exterior, hand-painted fresco ceilings, and antique furniture. The dining room, overlooking the inner harbor, specializes in seafood and steaks. 309 Belleville St. (phone: 604-388-9191). Expensive to moderate.

Oak Bay Beach – A short drive from downtown, this Victorian seaside resort hotel showcases its priceless antiques throughout. Afternoon tea with scones and Devonshire cream is served each afternoon in the lobby. Gardens, golfing, and a marina are nearby. 1175 Beach Dr. (phone: 604-598-4556). Expensive to moderate.

Olde England Inn – In a renovated 17th-century English village, this gabled Tudor hotel offers rooms with furnishings similar to those in an old carriage house. The hotel, on acres of lawns, is a tourist attraction but not a typical one. It's a rare hostelry that offers a guest sleeping accommodations in the same bed that King Edward VII supposedly used in Warwick Castle, England. The hotel serves breakfast, lunch, and dinner, and tea in the lodge. In the suburb of Esquimalt at 429 Lampson St. (phone: 604-388-4353). Expensive to moderate.

LADYSMITH

Yellowpoint Lodge – After a fire destroyed this popular resort a few years ago, the owners didn't take long to rebuild, preserving the original form. It remains one of the island's top getaway spots, on 180 acres overlooking the sea. Book one of the rustic log-and-sandstone cottages or a room in the main lodge. Walking trails, swimming pool, dining area, and rumpus rooms with fireplaces will all still be found here. RR #3 (phone: 604-245-7422). Expensive to moderate.

NANAIMO

Coast Bastion Inn – Part of the town's revitalized waterfront, this 15-story hotel features a well-equipped health club with Universal gym, a whirlpool bath, sauna, and an outdoor deck. Full dining facilities as well as a popular nightclub. 11 Bastion St. (phone: 604-753-6601).

PARKSVILLE

Bayside Inn – Just minutes off the highway on sandy Parksville Bay, this full-service hotel offers ocean and mountain views. Dining room, lounge, indoor pool and whirlpool bath, aerobics room, tennis, racquetball, squash available. 240 Dogwood St. (phone: 604-248-8333). Expensive to moderate.

QUALICUM BEACH

Best Western College Inn – A modern resort with a pool, whirlpool baths, sauna, and lounge entertainment. The dining room was once an English-style boys' school. Despite the resort atmosphere, this sprawling 4-acre vacation site is reminiscent of its original incarnation. PO Box 99 (phone: 604-752-9262). Moderate.

CAMPBELL RIVER

Painter's Lodge – The oldest and the best-known fishing lodge in town, its guest list includes celebrities and plain folk drawn to the great salmon fishing. A main lodge, cottages with fireplaces, a heated pool, boats, guides, access for float planes, a dining room, and a lounge. PO Box 460 (phone: 604-286-1104). Expensive to moderate.

QUADRA ISLAND

April Point – This fishing resort with a view of the fjords and snow-fringed mountains on the island has a tackle shop, boats, guides, swimming, water skiing, and sailing. (From Campbell River, take a 10-minute ride on the Quadra car ferry, May to October.) April Point Lodge and Fishing Resort, PO Box 1, Campbell River (phone: 604-285-2222). Expensive.

Fraser River

From the time Indians were the sole inhabitants of this continent to the last century, when prospectors were struck with gold fever, the Fraser River, with its deadly whirlpools, jagged shoals, and white rapids, blocked the road to the promised land — the deer and elk hunting grounds, fur trading routes, and gold mines of the Cariboo Mountains. Though still as wild and fierce as in earlier days, the Fraser is no longer an obstacle to the modern explorer's promised land of calm rivers and lakes stocked with trout and salmon and of rolling sagebrush hills where ruggedly independent folk tend dude and cattle ranches. In fact, the Fraser, boiling rapids and all, may be the choicest oasis in the promised land. This 850-mile (1,368-km) journey is dominated by the narrow, twisting flow of the Fraser: from the Fraser Valley delta around Hope, rich in fur trading history and alive with farm fairs and festivals, through the scenic but perilous Fraser Canyon slashed out by the raging river, to the cattle ranching country north of Cache Creek, where the spirit of the Wild West is as alive today as it was when gold fever hit more than 100 years ago.

In the farmlands to the south, the Fraser is calm, a source of water that makes the countryside lush with vegetation; but farther north at Hell's Gate and Devil's Cauldron (names worthy of the river's wrath), the river puts on its splashiest performance as it winds its way through narrow cliff walls. Although most people watch this show from an aerial tramway at Yale, others, in defiance of Simon Fraser's caution — "It's so wild I cannot find words to describe it" — don life jackets, cling tightly to a rubberized raft, and hurtle over and through the boiling cauldron.

Each July, the river is the site of another spectacular show. Millions of salmon streak the water red as they force their way upstream through rapids and over rocks to spawn and die. For anyone who prefers salmon smoked and filleted at reasonable prices, a trip farther north may be in order.

Here is cowboy country, where the locals act as if it were only yesterday that the West was unsettled and law and order meant each man dealt with transgressors on his own terms. Here the beer flows freely on a Saturday night, when a clean white shirt and red bandanna dress up the usual pair of jeans. But for all its wild spirit, this region's pace is slow, its tensions few. As expressed by one wrangler, a descendant of a man who outfitted prospectors in the mid-1850s: "Our biggest fear is that a moose will break our fences — we've got miles and miles of the barbed wire — and eat our hay. So big deal. No one's ever been mugged by a moose."

A trip through prairie country is a trip through the living West — cattle rustlers and wrestlers are not just movie stereotypes here — you can live on a ranch, pitch hay in the stables, round up the cattle, or just ride through the bush. And it's also a trip through gold rush country, where a reconstructed village (Barkersville) puts you in the heart of the West when the mountains of the Cariboo and the banks of the Fraser promised, with one lucky gold find, a lifetime of easy living.

En Route from Vancouver – Travel east on Route 1 to Langley, a dairy and truck farming community overlooking the Fraser River. Nearby is Fort Langley, now a national historic park, a restored Hudson's Bay Company fort located on the last point on the Fraser River that seagoing vessels can navigate. A visit here brings back days of this site's boom period in 1859, when gold seekers spent as much as $1,500 daily outfitting themselves. At that time the camp was dominated by the Hudson's Bay Company, which even organized dances for the prospectors. But this was more than a company town; it was the site of the founding of British Columbia. Each November 19, Langley sponsors a banquet and historical program in tribute to the day in 1858 when Governor James Douglas signed the decree making British Columbia a province.

Heading southeast on Route 1, the road passes Abbotsford, noted for its international air show (one of the biggest on the continent), held here each August.

Traveling east on Route 1, the road skirts the Vedder River, where anglers fish for spring salmon in May and June, coho in the fall, and steelhead trout from December to July. A few miles east, the road cuts through Chilliwack, a small farming town on the Fraser delta abutting the cliffs at the foot of the Coastal Range. From the snowcapped peaks of Mt. Slesse and Mt. Clemme, melting snow cascades over the dark green pines of the range, veiling the rocks and trees underneath and inspiring the name Bridal Falls. Near the town runs the 35-mile (56-km) Chilliwack River, swimming with Dolly Varden trout. Although the town is in the heart of dairy farming, cattle ranching, and deep river country, it's most noted for its horses. Visitors and residents often parade through the streets and surrounding countryside on the backs of every type of horse, from Arabian stallions to old nags. And each May the town hosts an elaborate International Horse Show.

South of Chilliwack is Sardis, where Salish Indians sell handwoven mats, aprons, and other garments in old Indian designs. Farther south is Cultus Lake, within a provincial park with camping sites and picnic areas. Each June, crews race war canoes across the 3-mile-wide lake as part of the *Indian Festival*.

Continue east on Route 1 to Hope.

HOPE: This small town, surrounded by mountains and alongside the Fraser River (at this point still calm), is known as the entrance to the Fraser River Valley. Here in 1848 the Hudson's Bay Company established Fort Hope — a fitting name, considering the dangers of the Fraser River just upstream. The name stuck until the town was incorporated in 1965, becoming just Hope. Although the site enjoyed a burst of growth in 1858, when miners stopped before paddlewheeling up the river to the gold fields, it has since shrunk (it has 4,000 residents today). Visitors often stop to stock up on supplies and get a good night's rest before venturing into the interior.

The town has a museum with relics of pioneer days, two of the oldest churches in the province, and a major festival celebrating settlement days. On the second weekend in September, tourists are invited to join the populace in 3 days of logging sports, parades, and motorcycle races commemorating *Brigade Days*.

The area around Hope offers first-rate hiking and climbing, and, due to the updrafts caused by the mountainous terrain, soaring and hang gliding are also popular.

From this town, 5,400-foot Mt. Ogilvie is visible. Goats scamper on its ledges, and black bear, deer, and raccoon live within its forests.

En Route from Hope – The opening of a new highway gives travelers a choice of two routes to Kamloops. The faint of heart can head northeast on the new Coquihalla Highway for a shorter and less adventurous trip to the interior city of Kamloops. While wildlife and scenery abound, gas stations do not. Fill up in Hope. Or head north on Route 1 to Yale, the gateway to Fraser Canyon, where the Fraser rages in all its power. It is such a twisting, treacherous run of water because the mountains in the center of the continent (the Rockies, Selkirks, Cariboos) receive extraordinary amounts of snow. And when the warm Pacific breezes waft eastward, the vast snow fields melt, unleashing a fierce torrent flowing in one direction, carving sheer canyon walls and craggy mountain bluffs. At Yale, the water, squeezed between the reddish bluffs of the Cascade Mountains and the Coastal Range, forms swirling, churning rapids.

These bluffs and rapids mocked the dreams of gold-struck prospectors in the last century. Genteel storekeepers and farmers from eastern Canada and the US forsook families and friends; sailors jumped ships; soldiers deserted regiments. They joined priests, prostitutes, and even shiploads of refined English ladies lured here by the promise of marriage to prospectors, making their way up the Fraser on rough-hewn log rafts. These adventurous, courageous, avaricious (take your pick) people arrived at Yale and found the natural barrier of cliff and water almost insurmountable — almost, but not quite, for their ingenuity was fired by lust. Prospectors used rope ladders to hoist themselves and their horses, mules, and camels over sheer cliff walls that at some points rise 7,000 feet. (An enterprising outfitter introduced camels to lug heavy loads of mining gear. But the beasts' stench so repelled the mules, horses, and prospectors that they were let out to pasture in fields and valleys along the way.) They also built a makeshift road (Cariboo Rd.) along the bedrock of the canyon. Although still precipitous in parts, today's route is made infinitely easier by paved highways overlooking the Fraser and by the tunnels drilled through the canyon walls. When the river is quiet, a traveler can still see an occasional contemporary gold seeker, with manual sluices and gold pans, searching for pay dirt below.

A few miles north of Yale, the canyon constricts to form Hell's Gate, where visitors can board an aerial tramway (open April to November) and peer down at the federal fisheries (constructed by the US and Canada after blockages in the river threatened the lives of the sockeye salmon). Each July, battered and exhausted salmon make their tortuous 24-day journey over rocky riverbeds, through fierce rapids, and over the federal fishway steps to spawn and then die at the mouth of the Adams River.

North on Route 1 is Boston Bar, noted for its gold mining in the last century and for its jade today. Nineteen miles (31 km) north is Jack Ass Mountain, a precipitous ridge on the canyon cliffs where (so the story goes) a donkey laden with heavy gold-mining gear jumped 1,500 feet to the river below rather than carry his burden to Cariboo. A few miles farther north is Lytton, where the Fraser Canyon ends and the Thompson River valley begins.

The Thompson and Fraser rivers converge here, and at their banks fortune seekers still pan for gold and search for jade. But a more reliable quest is for the steelhead trout swimming in these fast-flowing waters from late October to spring.

The Thompson River knifes through mountains, revealing 10,000-year-old rocks and nurturing semi-arid terrain of sagebrush, bunch grass, and prickly pear cactus. An exciting way to experience both the tranquillity and the turbulence of the river is to board a motorized rubber raft in Lytton.

Either rafting the Thompson or traveling Route 1 will lead you to "Gold Pan Campsite" on the banks of the Thompson. From here you can see mountain sheep scampering along the stratified edges of the cliffs.

From Lytton, travel north to Spences Bridge. During the summer, vendors sell honey, fruit, and apple juice along the highway. The town is an Indian reserve, where remains of the "wikiups" (houses used by nomadic Indians) still stand. In a ravine stand apricot trees, part of the orchards an early settler planted. Although chukar, partridge, deer, and grouse still inhabit this region, avid hunting has greatly reduced their numbers. From Spences Bridge, Route 1 rises to what was once a sagebrush plain but is now irrigated ranching country. Some 27 miles (43 km) north is Ashcroft, the entrance to the Bethlehem Copper Pits. A mile out of town is Ashcroft Manor, a pioneer ranch settled by the first lieutenant governor of British Columbia, Clement Cornwall. Although Cornwall was the very personification of the pioneer spirit — his courage and energy were indomitable — his Englishness was equally indelible. When he led guests on "modified" foxhunts, everyone wore traditional garb. (Hunts were modified because the quest was coyote, not fox, of which few exist in BC.) The riding habits and hunt gear are on display in the manor, now restored and open to the public.

A few miles north is Cache Creek, at the junction of Routes 1 and 97.

CACHE CREEK: A stopover for prospectors seeking gold in the Cariboos in the last century, today this city acts as a halfway point between the lower Fraser and Cariboo region. Surrounded by the semi-arid ranching country of the Thompson Flats, Cache Creek is a center for cattle ranching and copper mining. It is also often a base for freshwater sport fishermen.

Although no gold is found here today, the legends of the boomtown era live in the town's name. An ignominious (and perhaps fictional) bandit stole 80 pounds of gold from a successful miner and cached it here before disappearing. It's never been found. Some tell of disbanded camel caravans grazing on the Thompson Flats after an unfortunate run on the Cariboo Trail, where they frightened both man and beast.

En Route from Cache Creek – Follow Route 97 north through the dry hills surrounding Cache Creek. Take a side trip east to Loon Lake for small rainbow trout or follow a dirt road farther northeast to Lake Bonaparte for the bigger trout.

Route 97 runs through Clinton, an up-to-date version of the Old West.

CLINTON: Although its name comes from a British duke, the character of this spunky settlement comes from its history as a roadside stop on the trail to the Cariboo gold fields — 47 Mile House on the Gold Rush Trail.

If you're looking for quiet times in the North, head for Deadwood Gulch Wildlife Display and Art Gallery, the headquarters for tours of Big Bar Provincial Park. Travel 5 miles (8 km) north and 22 miles (35 km) east to 808 acres of wooded and rolling terrain interspersed with lakes for fishing and swimming.

En Route from Clinton – North on Route 97 about 10 miles (16 km) you pass through Painted Chasm. Amid heavily forested areas and grassy meadows with cattle grazing is the chasm, a multicolored gorge rising out of the lowlands with rocks thought to be 10,000 years old.

North of the chasm, a road leads east to Bridge Lake, surrounded by lakes for fishing and waterfowl hunting. In season, grouse and small game thrive here.

Driving farther north on 97 brings you to 100 Mile House.

100 MILE HOUSE: The men who blazed the Cariboo wagon road from Lillooet to the gold fields of Cariboo were paid by the mile. This may explain why 100 Mile House is a good deal short of 100 miles from the start of the trail. Although 100 Mile House (an official designation) is preserved as a testimony to man's chicanery, greed, and ingenuity, it is a sprawling ranch that sets the tone of the town. In 1912, the Marquis of Exeter purchased a ranch here. His son, Lord Martin Cecil, ran it and the Emissaries of the Divine Light, a religious group, until his recent death. The town is known for its annual 50-kilometer Cariboo Marathon, which draws upward of 2,000 hale and hearty cross-country skiers every February.

En Route from 100 Mile House – North of town is T-Bar Ski Hill, with a 4,000- and 1,000-foot drop with good weekend skiing from December to March.

Back on Route 97, the road runs through rolling, wooded country dotted with lakes, where waterfowl live on the marshy borders. One of these lakes, Lac La Hache, beside the highway, has some of the best kokanee (landlocked salmon) fishing in the province.

Drive north on 97 (watch out for chipmunks and squirrels crossing the highway) to Williams Lake.

WILLIAMS LAKE: During the Chilcotin Indian War of 1864, Willy'um, chief of the Shuswap Indians (now the Sugar Cane tribe) saved the white settlers here from being massacred. To show their thanks, the settlers named the town after him. Although a stone marks the spot where the Indians held their tribal meetings (Colunetze, "gathering place of lordly ones"), the Indian spirit has been violated here (as in most other towns) by the rowdier and more aggressive culture of the western gold panners. Typical of the Wild West atmosphere is the Williams Lake Stampede each July, in which top riders, many of them Indian ranch hands, compete in such traditional rodeo events as bronco riding and cattle wrestling.

Running parallel to this hillside town is Williams Lake, 6 miles long and teeming from April to November with rainbow trout, some 14 inches long.

En Route from Williams Lake – Head east on a series of dirt roads to the forested rolling terrain around Horsefly and Quesnel lakes, surrounded by the mountains of Big Timoth and Mt. Stevenson, both over 7,000 feet. You'll find lake trout and kokanee, and a hiker may sight a moose, deer, or black bear roaming through the cottonwoods.

Head north on Route 97, which leads through about 75 miles (121 km) of ranching, logging, and mining country along the edges of the Fraser River to Quesnel, a former Cariboo gold rush town, now a booming lumbering center. During the summer months the main streets are lined with colorful petunia blossoms. Salmon fishing is good where the Quesnel River enters the Fraser.

Head east from here on Route 26 to Barkerville, a restored gold mining boom town near 1,300-acre Bowron Lake Provincial Park.

BARKERVILLE: In 1862, a Cornish fortune seeker named Billy Barker jumped ship, came here, and staked a claim on a small parcel of land. After digging 40 feet down and finding nothing but dirt, Barker was almost ready to give up and head north. But he and his mates persisted and 2 feet deeper they found a pocket of gold nuggets worth $600,000 ($9 million by today's standards). Attracted by Barker's find, thousands of prospectors swarmed here, making this town the biggest city north of San Francisco and west of Chicago. Like the city named for him (now a ghost town restored for tourists), the fate of Billy Barker was sad. He married a more successful gold digger than himself and died penniless in a Victoria nursing home.

A visitor can pan for gold nearby, ride a stagecoach, or watch a period melodrama at the *Theatre Royal*.

A few miles east is Bowron Lake Provincial Park Wilderness Area, where moose, beaver, caribou, mountain goat, grizzly bear, and wolf live in a wildlife sanctuary. In the lakes and streams swim Kamloops, Dolly Varden, and lake trout. If not the most satisfying activity in the park, certainly the most strenuous is canoeing on such lakes as Bowron, Indianpoint, and Isaac; and portaging equipment among them.

BEST EN ROUTE

Sagebrush ranges and wooded plateaus are the backdrop for some of the best vacation bets in the region: ranch holidays. Here are working cattle ranches, where hundreds of head of branded cattle graze on the short grasses of the arid ranges. When cattle hands round them up, you're usually more than welcome to help. One ranch owner describes it as riding like the wind, circling and circling the cattle. Or you can stay on a ranch where expensive, sleek Arabian horses are the main attraction. Here you ride on blazed trails and live in up-to-date accommodations. Wherever you stay, the food is fresh and plentiful. For example, there's roast beef off the range (a freshly slaughtered specialty you're not about to find at your supermarket). The nightly entertainment is usually a gathering of cowpokes — both urban and authentic — sitting around the fireplace listening to cowboy music. The range of prices is wide, from luxury accommodations for $1,300 a week (expensive!) to less fancy ones for about $400 a week (moderate). Although most ranches are open all year, the horseback riding is sometimes replaced by cross-country skiing during the bitterly cold winters.

ASHCROFT

Sundance Guest Ranch – A luxury dude and working cattle ranch for people who like to go out on the trail and rough it up, then have a nice hot bath or a swim in the heated pool when they return. Early every morning, wranglers wake up the guests and take them out to the trails, riding everything from Arabian to quarter horses. Guests are divided according to their riding abilities, some galloping over small rivers, others trotting or walking on the sagebrush prairies on half-day or day-long supervised trail rides. The nightlife is centered around the giant stone fireplace and bar. (Bring your own liquor; mixers, glasses, and ice are supplied.) Each room, with wall-to-wall carpeting, bath, and TV set, is located in the main lodge on the Thompson Flats within view of the river snaking below. Open year-round. Five miles (8 km) south off Highland Valley Rd. PO Box 489 (phone: 604-453-2554/2422). Expensive.

100 MILE HOUSE

108 Golf and Country Inn Resort – Fans of cross-country skiing, horseback riding, swimming, golfing, or tennis should know about this 62-room motor lodge, the *108 Resort.* For riding the open range, late August, September, and October are best. Let them know you're coming and they'll take you along on a real cattle roundup. After a hard day's ride, relax in the whirlpool bath and sauna. Walks and drives will take you to some incredible bird-watching, and there's fishing right on the property. The resort's 62 rooms all have private balconies or patios, color TV sets, and private baths. As for wintertime, the Canadian Olympic team called the ranch's rolling Cariboo rangelands some of the greatest cross-country ski terrain in the entire world. And there's skating, sleigh rides, tobogganing, and ice fishing as well. For those guests whose taste in food is also more basic, European cuisine often takes a back seat to west coast favorites like smoked salmon. Open year-round with a 4,800-foot paved airstrip. Box 2, RR 1 (phone: 604-791-5211). Moderate.

Okanagan Orchard Country

If you rode a horse through British Columbia's Okanagan orchard country in the mid-1850s, you would have galloped through tall green grass and patches of sagebrush, forded rivers and streams, and passed azure lakes. From low mountain plateaus you would have viewed a variety of grouse feeding beside the lakes. Although much of the terrain has changed little in centuries, this valley sandwiched between the Cascade Range and the Monashee Mountains now supports countless apple, pear, and apricot orchards.

The best time to travel this route (a 184-mile/296-km trip from Kamloops south to Osoyoos) is spring, when the direct rays of the sun have not yet singed the grass. Spring is also the best time of year to head from Osoyoos north 117 miles (177 km) to Vernon, through a fairyland of pink peach blossoms misting the borders of lakes and mountains.

You will drive through Kelowna, where in 1869 the Oblate Father Pandosy landscaped his Indian mission with a tiny orchard fed from nearby lakes by a crude irrigation system. Farther south is Penticton, now known as the fruit capital of the region, but little more than a one-horse town before Thomas Ellis, a former Oregonian, buried some peach pits here in 1874. Here, farmers and the cattle ranchers are further exploiting their natural resources of sun (it shines almost daily in the spring and summer), water, and land by setting up boating and fishing facilities and resorts around the lakes, renting horses for prairie rides, and holding fairs to celebrate the fruit harvests.

The route starts in Kamloops, then goes southward into Okanagan country, which is dotted with roadside stands where vendors sell cool fruit drinks that taste as if they have come straight from the tree. They have. The valley is also one of Canada's few wine-producing regions.

KAMLOOPS: This city, sprawled across the sagebrush hills and dry brown mountains is a major junction for motorists driving on Highways 1 and 92. But more significant to the visitor is the name the Indians gave this site — Cumcloups, "the meeting of the waters" — where the north and south branches of the Thompson River converge, creating Kamloops Lake. (A strain of trout that jumps a few feet into the air after being hooked, Kamloops trout, is found in the lake.)

The pioneering spirit of the Overlanders who, struck by gold fever, crossed the Rockies, journeyed through forests, and rafted the rapids of the North Thompson to reach Kamloops is commemorated in many of the city's festivals and celebrations. Kamloops has an indoor rodeo, a bluegrass country music festival, a sunfest, and an international air show in spring and summer.

Nearby mountains are rife with deer, moose, grizzly bear, caribou, and elk, and the lakes teem with trout. For hunting, fishing, and other tourist information, contact the Kamloops Visitors and Convention Bureau (phone: 604-374-3377).

En Route from Kamloops – Follow Route 5 south and turn east on a gravel road to Douglas Lake. Here, in the center of miles of prairie grass broken by cactus and an occasional cottonwood, is Douglas Lake Cattle Ranch, the largest in Canada. A few miles south, the road skirts Nicola Lake, one of the roughest and deepest in the province and noted for good trout and kokanee fishing. Nearby is an entrance to the *Quilchena* hotel (see *Best En Route*), built in 1908 and a fine example of the architecture of the era. South on Route 5 is Merritt, home of the Nicola Valley Rodeo (September) and a spring rodeo (May). Although copper and molybdenum mining is a multimillion-dollar industry here, amateur rockhounds can explore the nearby Coldwater River and Mill Creek for everything from intrusive batholiths and stream gravels to jade, agate, gold, and platinum.

Head south to Princeton and northwest along a dirt road to Coalmount, a mining ghost town. Before the mountains were gouged out in 1860, the town was known as Vermillion Forks because of the red ocher outcroppings, used by the Indians for paint.

Return to Princeton and take Route 3 southeast to Hedley, once the site of an enormously rich base metal and gold mine. Hummocks of stone and bricks lie where buildings were once a hive of activity; now the only signs of life are the grouse and mountain sheep on the surrounding mountains.

Farther southeast, separated from the Okanagan Valley by a small mountain range, is Keremeos. The road through town is edged with blossoming fruit trees in spring and roadside stands selling fruit, apple cider, and honey during the summer. Head south on Route 3 to Osoyoos, a combination ranching-fruit growing town. From Anarchist Mountain Lookout along the road, you can see orchards and deep Osoyoos Lake contrasting with "Desert Gardens," 1 mile (1.6 km) south of town, an arid area of semidesert. This is a resort town where you can fish for trout and bass along the lakeshore or swim among the painted turtles. The town holds a variety of festivals, including the Bowling Jamboree (April/May); Warm Water Open Ski Tournament (May 24); the *Cherry Fiesta* (July); and the International Powerboat Races (September).

As you head north on Route 97 toward Penticton, plains dotted with lupine and some fruit trees give way to the orchards of the Okanagan Valley.

PENTICTON: Since the first orchard was planted here in 1874, this settlement has grown from a few fruit picking, cattle grazing families to a city of some 24,000 people. Located on the southern shores of Okanagan Lake and surrounded by orchards of peach trees, the site of a large fruit packing plant and winery, Penticton is known as the city of beaches and peaches. In fact, each July and August the city celebrates a *Peach Festival,* during which peach brandy is consumed in quantity and visitors and natives alike are coaxed into dancing in the streets.

Besides, with almost 150 miles of shoreline, Lake Okanagan is home to rainbow trout and an old sternwheeler, the SS *Sicamous,* once the only means of transportation on the lake. And, like so many large lakes, the Okanagan has its yet-to-be-seen monster, Ogopogo.

Follow route 97 north across a bridge floating on Lake Okanagan to Kelowna, where Father Pandosy planted the first peach pit in front of his mission house. This city of parks, beaches, gardens, and broad streets is partly encircled by terraced orchards. It's a well-water greenness thanks to lakes hidden in the mountains ringing the valley. A combination of virtually unlimited water resources and nearly 2,000 hours of sunshine a year makes Kelowna not only a major fruit and wine producing region, but also a playground for both tourists and residents.

Heading north to Vernon, the road ascends over Kalamalka Lake (Indian for "lake of many colors"), whose waters change color with every passing cloud. A few miles farther is Vernon, a town with more orchards, sunshine, and lakes, the end of the Okanagan journey.

BEST EN ROUTE

Accommodations range from modern hotels and motels in a big city to dude ranches and beach bungalows. Prices for a double in the expensive category range from $100 to $195; moderate, from $50 to $95; and for an inexpensive room, from $30 to $45. All prices are quoted in US dollars.

KAMLOOPS

Coast Canadian Inn – This hotel recently underwent major renovation and continues to offer the most modern facilities available in this interior city. There's a heated outdoor swimming pool (seasonal), lounge, and dining room. 339 St. Paul St. (phone: 604-372-5201). Expensive to moderate.

QUILCHENA

Quilchena – A hotel on the shores of Nicola Lake that was built in 1908 and has retained its turn-of-the-century decor. Facilities include a licensed dining room, golfing, horses, and boating on Nicola Lake (phone: 604-378-2611). Open May to October. Inexpensive.

PRINCETON

Riverside – On the Tulameen River, the motel offers a cluster of rustic log cabins. Open year-round. PO Box 368 (phone: 604-295-6232). Inexpensive.

NARAMATA

Sandy Beach Lodge – Nestled among peach trees, the cottages here overlook Okanagan Lake. The resort has a swimming pool and tennis courts. Open mid-May to mid-September. PO Box 8 (phone: 604-496-5765). Moderate.

PENTICTON

Delta Lakeside – On the shores of Okanagan Lake, this first class hotel has become a favorite get-away for discriminating Vancouverites. Each of the 200 rooms has a private balcony, and there's outdoor dining, an indoor pool, whirlpool bath, sauna, tennis court, and exercise room. Boardsailing, parasailing, and water skiing facilities are on the lake. 21 Lakeshore Dr. (phone: 604-493-8221). Expensive to moderate.

KELOWNA

Lake Okanagan Resort – A half-hour drive from Kelowna proper, this lakeside resort has both suites and housekeeping units. Recreation facilities abound: a par-3 golf course, horseback riding, water skiing, boardsailing, sailing, 3 heated pools, and the warm waters of Lake Okanagan. Open May to October. 2751 Westside Rd. (phone: 604-769-3511). Expensive to moderate.

VERNON

Tiki Village Motor Inn – This motor hotel has a Polynesian decor, a 1-acre garden courtyard, heated outdoor pool, sauna, and restaurant. 2408 34th St. (604-545-2268). Moderate to inexpensive.

The Pacific National Parks

One hardly thinks of national parks coming in groups, like an exaltation of larks or a clowder of cats, but on British Columbia's eastern border that is exactly what happens. Several mountain chains tumble together — the Purcell, Selkirk, and Rockies — and the result is a jagged tangle of glaciers, chasms, peaks, and snow fields unparalleled in the Western Hemisphere. The Trans-Canada Highway cuts like a blade through this wondrous knot, connecting Kamloops in the west with Banff across the Alberta border. To protect the sanctity of these mountains, huge areas have been made national parks, with access through Revelstoke on the Trans-Canada.

The mountains themselves — Mt. Revelstoke, Glacier, Yoho, Kootenay, and Bugaboo — make up parts of the long chain that separates British Columbia from the rest of Canada, creating its unique weather systems and that touch of isolation responsible for its Pacific coast culture. The 280-mile (451-km) trip from Kamloops on Route 1 (the Trans-Canada) skirts Mt. Revelstoke, bisects Glacier National Park and Yoho National Park, and passes near the entrance to Kootenay Park.

For thousands of years the mountains of the Continental Divide stood in splendid isolation. Few Indians ventured into them, awed by the size of the glacier-torn peaks and chasms. Certain lakes were fished, and ocher beds in the Kootenay Mountains were used for their natural paint. Oddly, early fur traders approached the mountains with the same circumspection, and it wasn't until the railroad came through that the mountains were even partially explored by white men. An expedition of explorers, construction workers, and engineers threaded the railroad over precarious mountain passes, through the densely wooded forests at lower altitudes, and beside lakes and rivers.

This conglomeration of mountains was considered quite special, and the federal government was persuaded to preserve these lands as national parks. Preservation, however, does not preclude the human presence. There are luxurious baths near the hot springs of Kootenay and numerous well-maintained hiking trails linking the most interesting spots in the parks.

En Route from Kamloops – (For more on Kamloops, see the *Okanagan Orchard Country* route.) Head west along Route 1 to the world's richest 300 acres (or so the roadside sign says). Here are the Adams River spawning beds, where in late October millions of salmon spawn and die after fighting their way up the Fraser and Thompson rivers. When the early settlers arrived, the salmon were pitchforked out of the water and used for fertilizer.

Traveling east, the road follows the Columbia River through the mountains of the Monashee Range to Revelstoke. The town, a stop on the Canadian Pacific Railroad, is near the eastern entrance to Mt. Revelstoke park.

MT. REVELSTOKE NATIONAL PARK: So enchanted were the citizens of Revelstoke with the variety of natural rock formations, trees, and animals in the nearby Clachacudainn Mountains that they persuaded the government to designate 100 square miles of it a national park. Thanks to their efforts, a visitor can walk 40 miles of trails, including one 16-mile trail meandering through valleys cloaked in trembling aspen, black cottonwood, and Rocky Mountain maple and over hillsides covered with rain forests of western white pine, western red cedar, western hemlock, Douglas fir, and spruce below the timberline. Other trails lead to mountain meadows of blazing Indian paintbrush, arnica, and valerian to Eva Lake, teeming with trout, and to masses of colorful rock, thought to be 500 million years old.

Although the extensive snowfalls (between 30 and 40 ft.) scare off most of the big animals, a variety of birds, including the wren, finch, Canada jay — and even the golden eagle — fly above.

Before you climb the peaks, including Mt. La Forme (8,400 ft.) and Mt. Cyr (8,520 ft.), or camp in the wild, contact the Superintendent of Parks in Revelstoke.

GLACIER NATIONAL PARK: Between Revelstoke and Golden on Route 1, high up in the Selkirk and Purcell ranges, is this 521-square-mile park, where huge snowfalls occur each year. While some of this snow melts and cascades down waterfalls and rivers or evaporates, much of it never melts. Earlier snows compact, harden, and through their sheer weight create glaciers that crawl down the mountainside. Ragged summits, including the 10,818-foot Mt. Sir Donald, and steep canyon walls have been carved out and polished by the slow-motion flow of countless rivers of ice, forming and descending to the plains over thousands of years.

If you've always wanted to see a glacier nose-to-ice this is the place. There are more than 400 glaciers here, with trails leading to two of them, Illecillewaet and Asulkan. Another trail leads to the Nakimu Caves of Cougar Valley, a seemingly endless maze of limestone passages underground. While trekking through the dense forests of western red cedar and hemlock on any of the hundreds of miles of trail, be careful: Avalanches sometimes close the highway, and the underbrush is too thick to pass in places. Although the snowfall limits the growth period below the timberline to 2 months, the glacial lily, alpine anemone, and heather grow well during summer.

For a map of trails, lakes, glaciers, and campgrounds, contact Parks Canada Administration Offices, Yoho National Park, Box 99, Field, BC V0A 1G0 (phone: 604-343-6324).

En Route from Glacier National Park – Head east on Route 1 to Golden, the gateway to Yoho National Park and the beginning of the Rocky Mountain Range, looming high above the east. This city changed its name from the Cache to Golden after a silver rush in nearby Cathedral Park panned out.

YOHO NATIONAL PARK: Even after other mountain ranges in the province had been smoothed by wind, snow, and rain, the Rockies still had not erupted from the earth. This may explain why the younger range (when the Selkirks were 105 million years old, the Rockies had not yet been born) has 28 peaks soaring more than 10,000 feet into the air. The astounding heights of these peaks have given the park its name, Yoho — "awe" in Cree. Long before the Palliser expedition penetrated Kicking Horse Pass, the Crees had plied the pass from east to west, camped around Emerald Lake, and fished for cutthroat, brook, and lake trout.

More than 250 miles of hiking trails crisscross this 507-square-mile region in the heart of the Rockies. A trip on the Yoho Valley Trail extends from the evergreen forests surrounding the Laughing Falls to the Yoho Glacier.

From the twin-spired Mt. Goodsir, more than 11,000 feet high, to the craggy ridges where mountain goat, hoary marmot, and pika graze, and below, to the wet regions inhabited by ducks and Canada geese, the park is an untamed wilderness.

KOOTENAY NATIONAL PARK: On the southern end of Yoho is this 543-square-mile park, running parallel to the Continental Divide on the western slopes of the Rockies. Marked and wilderness trails lead to Marble Canyon, created by the power of the waterfall at Tokumm Creek; to glaciers on the sides of the mountains; and to grassy alpine meadows dotted with wild flowers, marshes, and lakes.

Other trails lead to the ocher beds southwest of Marble Canyon. Kootenay, Stoney, and Blackfoot Indians dipped into these natural paint pots to stain their bodies, decorate their teepees, and draw pictures on rocks. Near Sinclair Canyon at the southwest end of the park paintings of elk, bighorn sheep, bear, and horses adorn the limestone ledges.

At the base of Redstreak Mountain in the valley carved out by Sinclair Creek is the source of the Radium Best Western, one of the more developed, popular places in the park. Water seeps through faults deep in the earth where the rock masses are hot. When it meets this hot mass, it turns to steam and quickly rises through fissures to meet the cool air. The steam condenses to water at a temperature of 113F (45C) and is channeled to the Aquacourt, which is a modern bathing pool.

BEST EN ROUTE

All of these establishments are near the national parks and range in price from about $45 for an inexpensive room or cottage for two people to $70 for a moderately priced establishment, and $160 for an expensive one. Glacier, Yoho, and Kootenay national parks offer developed campsites on a first-come, first-served basis. For wilderness camping in Revelstoke, check with the park supervisor. All prices are quoted in US dollars.

REVELSTOKE

Three Valley Gap Motor Inn – This sprawling lakefront resort is a ghost town — and a place to sleep. From the gold mining towns of Canada, owner Gordon Bell transported bits and pieces of gambling halls, gin mills, and cabins and reassembled them here to preserve a slice of the Wild West. The structures are filled with authentic furnishings of the period — a long bar, roulette wheels, and spittoons. Open April to October. PO Box 860 (phone: 604-837-2109). Moderate.

YOHO NATIONAL PARK

Emerald Lake Lodge – A rustic lodge overlooking the lake, it is 5 miles (8 km) north of Highway 1. Open year-round, there's a licensed dining room, game rooms, outdoor hot tubs, and a sauna. Box 10, Field (phone: 604-343-6321). Expensive to moderate.

KOOTENAY NATIONAL PARK

Radium Hot Springs Lodge – Overlooking the hot springs, this motor hotel is built on solid rock in the midst of dense pine forests. The lodge has dining facilities, whirlpool baths, sauna, and in-room movies. Ski and whitewater rafting packages are available. PO Box 70, Radium Hot Springs (phone: 604-347-9622). Moderate.

Blakley's Bungalows – Each secluded cottage has its own fireplace and bath or shower. PO Box 190, Radium Hot Springs (phone: 604-347-9918). Inexpensive.

Prince George to Prince Rupert

This region was one of the last in the province to be penetrated by the white man, and it has yet to fall prey to modern "civilization" and development. The Rocky Mountains (which separate this area from the rest of British

Columbia) have always posed a natural, almost insurmountable barrier to explorers, traders, and loggers.

Although there are some large, modern cattle ranches and mining and lumbering operations, this 456-mile (734-km) trip from Prince George — the crossroads of the province — west to Prince Rupert — dubbed the Halibut Capital of the World — takes in a string of small fishing and hunting villages that seem frozen in time. These settlements and the surrounding area are almost as unspoiled as when the Indians hunted moose on the densely wooded foothills and speared salmon in the deep rivers years ago.

Heading west from Prince George, you will drive through river canyons with semiprecious stones at the base to parks where driftwood lines the bottom of deep canyons. You will enter the village of Hazelton, where the Indians have erected a Kwakiutl longhouse to commemorate their past. North of this town is Fort St. James, settled as a Hudson's Bay fort by Simon Fraser when he explored the region. Around the fort are dense evergreen forests and some of the best big-game hunting in the province. The area's large lakes (Burns and Babine are just two) offer boating and fishing.

As the tour proceeds west to the Pacific Ocean, the climate changes drastically. In the interior, 15 to 25 inches of rain fall in a year, but the coastal city of Prince Rupert gets more than 100. As one native remarked, "It's a great place when it's sunny."

PRINCE GEORGE: Before railway and road workers extended the Canadian Pacific Railroad and paved Routes 97 and 16 through the heart of the city, this site was a slumbering Hudson's Bay Company trading post. Today, however, it is the crossroad of the north, south, east, and west. Truckloads of timber, farm produce, and minerals cross the heart of this city daily. To the visitor, all this activity means modern hotels, restaurants, museums (*Prince George Art Gallery*), historic sites (Fort George Stockade), and a taste of city life with emphasis on recreational facilities.

One of the main attractions is the par-71 golf course at the *Prince George Golf Club*. During the summer and spring, golfers ply the course in the usual manner, but come February, ingenious enthusiasts dress up in costumes and whack purple golf balls across the snow-covered course in the World Championship of Snow Golf.

But it is the city's location near the confluence of the Nechako and Fraser rivers that gives this town its special appeal. From here, anglers can travel to nearby lakes swimming with rainbow and steelhead trout or hike to the backwoods to bag the big game — grizzly bear, black bear, caribou, deer, and moose.

For all tourist information, including a list of hunting guides, visit 1198 Victoria St. (phone: 604-562-3700).

En Route from Prince George – Drive west along Route 16 to Vanderhoof, noted for its Nechako Bird Sanctuary, a stopover for Canada geese in the spring and fall. Then head north on Route 27 to Fort St. James, founded in 1806 by Simon Fraser and the original capital of New Caledonia, which was the name of the territory before it became British Columbia. Several of the old Hudson's Bay Company buildings are still standing on the banks of nearby Stuart Lake. There's excellent moose and grouse hunting.

Head back south to Vanderhoof and west on Route 16 through forests of poplar to Fraser Lake, the site of Endako Mines and Fraser Lake Sawmills. At nearby Stellako River, the rainbow trout fishing is excellent.

Head west to Burns Lake, noted for the Pinkut artificial salmon-spawning grounds. The back roads radiating from this town lead to good hunting territory and fishing lakes.

Tschesinkut Lake, 10 miles (16 km) south of town with some of the cleanest water in the province, supports lots of lake and rainbow trout. Another nearby lake is Francois Lake, 80 miles long and teeming with freshwater fish. The area around Burns Lake is also fine moose hunting country.

TWEEDSMUIR PROVINCIAL PARK: Follow Route 35 south to Tweedsmuir Provincial Park, a mixture of semi-arid prairie lands, icecapped mountain peaks, and lush meadows sprouting purple lupine and yellow black-eyed Susans. Running through the park are such rivers as the Bella Coola and Dean, where Dolly Varden and cutthroat swim all year. In the undeveloped thick forests of spruce, moose, mountain caribou, and grizzlies roam.

Return to Route 16; head west toward Hazelton and its Indian village of Ksan.

HAZELTON: Before a Hudson's Bay Company employee renamed the village after the abundant hazelnut trees covering this fertile farmland, Indians called the site Kiran-maksh, "where people fish by torchlight." Beside this modern Indian town is a replica of the Gitksan Indian village (Ksan) that stood there before the white man arrived. It has six Indian longhouses, birchbark canoes, and numerous totem poles, including one carved in 1850.

Continue southwest on Route 16 to its terminus at Prince Rupert.

PRINCE RUPERT: Because of its position on the western coast of the province, this site was chosen as the terminus of the Grand Trunk Pacific Railway. It was also chosen by urban planners to become a city as large and developed as Vancouver. Although, like many artificially created cities, it failed to fulfill the ambitions of its founders, it is still worth a visit.

Situated on lightly hilly terrain in the midst of thick pine forests, Prince Rupert overlooks an ice-free harbor, and its economy is centered around its halibut and salmon canning industry. You may visit these canneries (if you can stand the smell). The city also has a museum (*Museum of Northern British Columbia,* with Tsimpsian and Haida Indian artifacts). In June it celebrates an annual *Sea Fest.*

There is car and passenger service to Port Hardy on Vancouver Island.

BEST EN ROUTE

Although this part of British Columbia is one of Canada's more remote areas, you don't need to suffer the pains of primitive accommodations. In fact, most hotels seem to go out of their way to make sure their facilities match those of the busier tourist areas. You'll find that each hotel is really a self-contained visitors center. The price range in the area is pretty established, with most of the hotels falling into the moderate category — charging around $60 per night, double occupancy. Very few places are inexpensive — under $40 per night for two people — and almost none of the hotel facilities are expensive, charging more than $70 per night, double occupancy. All prices are quoted in US dollars.

PRINCE GEORGE

Coast Inn of the North – Offers everything a traveler could possibly want, from restaurant and lounge to pool and health club. 770 Brunswick St. (phone: 604-563-0121). Expensive to moderate.

Sandman Inn – An inn that provides a wide range of facilities in a modern building, including restaurant, pool, and sauna. 1650 Central St. (phone: 604-563-8131). Moderate.

Yellowhead Inn – Let the management know in advance, and they'll have a waterbed waiting for you. There's a pub on the premises as well as a lounge, so you have a choice of atmospheres in which to relax from driving. 1445 W. Central St. (phone: 604-562-3171). Moderate.

TERRACE

Inn of the West – A fairly small establishment with very nice rooms; the management provides a full range of creature comforts and really cares about its guests. 4620 Lakelse Ave. (phone: 604-638-8141). Moderate.

Sandman Inn – Located in the downtown area of western Terrace, across from the Skeena Mall, with spacious rooms, a restaurant, pool, and other niceties. 4828 Hwy. 16 W. (phone: 604-635-9151). Moderate.

PRINCE RUPERT

Drifter – Overlooking the harbor, this soundproofed motel guarantees a quiet night's slumber and a hearty breakfast in the morning in its restaurant. 1080 W. Third Ave. (phone: 604-624-9161). Moderate.

Prince Rupert – Also overlooking the harbor, and room service and nightly entertainment in the cabaret are offered. Second Ave. and Sixth St. (phone: 604-624-6711). Moderate.

Prince George to the Yukon

For thousands of years, the northern part of British Columbia has been wilderness — snowcapped mountains; forests of spruce and pine alive with caribou, moose, and grizzlies; deep lakes choked with Arctic grayling and Dolly Varden trout; and churning rivers carving out mountain passes. It's a great place for hunters, fishermen, and hikers who believe the farther away from cities and towns the nearer to heaven.

However, civilization is following the gravel and the blacktop of the Alaska Highway, creeping north and south, east and west, into the wilderness. Within this rough, awesomely beautiful mixture of mountain, prairie, and wood lies the raw stuff of commercial interests — oil, minerals, and lumber. Explorers have already dug for oil and found it. Mining companies have begun to extract minerals. Lumber companies have cut forests. This means instant towns, more modern accommodations, more restaurants, and more people — mostly in boom towns hugging the highway. What this will do to the wilderness is anybody's guess. It is doubtful that in this age of ecological sensitivity the wilderness will be mortally threatened, but there is a pristine purity to BC's northern expanses right now that is as delicate as it is virginal. This is a good time to make the 860-mile (1,385-km) trip from Prince George up Route 97 to Dawson Creek and north along the Alaska Highway.

This is a region of extremes: from the valleys of the Peace River region with rich farmlands to the 7,536-foot peak of Mt. St. George in Stone Mountain Park; from the cold waters of Muncho Lake swimming with Arctic grayling to the 120F (49C) Liard Hot Springs, soothing stiff tendons; from dense forests of spruce and pine to oceans of wheat near Dawson Creek; from 20 hours of darkness in cruel, frigid winters to 20 hours of sunlight in pleasant, mild summers.

But before you journey to the northern part of the province, some words of caution. The Alaska Highway is not the New Jersey Turnpike, though 90% of it is now paved. And whether you go in the winter, when the highway is a frozen, snow-covered surface, in the summer, when it's muddy, or during autumn, when the roadbed is fairly good, never wander far from the road unless you've got a guide or have extensive wilderness training. The area beyond has few trails and few facilities for the trekker.

This trip may not be for everybody, but it is for those who prefer the hush accompanying the kaleidoscope of colors as the Northern Lights streak across the unpolluted black sky to the blare of the jukebox and the flashing strobes of a discotheque.

For complete hunting, fishing, and touring information, and for road condition reports to the Yukon border, contact the Peace River Alaska Highway Tourist Association, P.O. Box 6850, Fort St. John V1J 4J3 (phone: 604-785-2544). To fly into the wilderness, contact Air B.C., Dawson Creek Airport (phone: 604-782-1661). Guides, licenses, and tourist information are available year-round from the chambers of commerce in towns along the Alaska Highway.

En Route from Prince George – (For information about Prince George, see the Prince George to Prince Rupert route.) Follow Route 97 (John Hart Hwy.) from Prince George north 32 miles (52 km) to Summit Lake, on the Continental Divide. From this Rocky Mountain ridge, water flows either north to the Arctic Ocean or south to the Pacific or Atlantic. Follow Route 97 north and take Route 39 to MacKenzie, established in 1966 to process the dense forests nearby. Those interested in the lumber industry may tour the town's two pulp mills. But its prime attraction is the 5,960-foot lookout on Morfee Mountain. From here, Williston Lake (the largest manmade lake in the province) and its miles and miles of wilderness can be seen. The lake is rich in lake trout, while within the jackpine forest roam black bear and moose. Return to Route 97.

After cutting through the lowest crossover point in the Rockies, the road passes Chetwynd, on the slopes of the Rockies. Following the wave of prospectors who searched for gold here in 1861, the site slumbered for more than 100 years until a new wave of explorers found coal and natural gas. Beyond the coal mines are good moose and deer territory and fine grayling and jackfish lakes. For hunting and fishing information, contact the Chetwynd Chamber of Commerce, PO Box 1000 (phone: 604-788-3345).

From Chetwynd, Route 97 stretches from the foothills of the mountains to the vastness of the prairies. Dawson Creek is the center of the province's most vital grain-producing region and is also on the edge of fine moose grazing terrain dotted with lakes stocked with northern pike, Arctic grayling, whitefish, and Dolly Varden and rainbow trout. All wilderness information is available from the Dawson Creek Tourist Centre, 900 Alaska Ave., V1G 4T6 (phone: 604-782-9595).

Dawson Creek is also the start (Mi 0/Km 0) of the Alaska Highway, a paved road built during World War II by the US Army Corps of Engineers as a defense measure.

Follow the highway to Fort St. John (Mi 49/Km 79).

FORT ST. JOHN: Although the town is a busy lumbering, oil exploration, and cattle ranching center, tourists are drawn to the fine hunting, fishing, hiking, and canoeing in the environs, rugged mountainous terrain topped by forests of spruce. But before venturing far from the Alaska Highway to seek mountain caribou, mountain goat, and black bear, to blaze your own wilderness route, or to canoe the boiling rapids of the

Peace River, stop at the chamber of commerce to hire a guide or get a map. Hunting, fishing, and all tourist information is available from the Tourist Information Centre, 9323 100th St. (phone: 604-785-3033).

For many years after this site was settled as a fur trading center (Rocky Mountain House, now an Indian reserve, was the fort), these Northerners depended upon fishing and hunting for their livelihood. A few years back, oil was discovered nearby and this northern community went through a building boom, with new restaurants and hotels going up almost daily.

Although the oil discovery brought a new degree of sophistication to the wilderness, the town still stages some traditional events. In February the *Charlies Lake Winter Carnival;* in July, a rodeo; and in August the *Fall Fair.*

En Route from Fort St. John – About 8 miles (13 km) north of town is Charlie Lake, filled with Arctic grayling and gray trout. As the road winds through forested hills and valleys to Pink Mountain (during autumn the multicolored leaves take on a pinkish hue from a distance), do not be surprised to see a moose, black bear, or grizzly parade across the gravel road. Also, stargazers rave about the view of the Northern Lights in the late fall and early winter.

Head northwest to the last fairly large city on the highway, Fort Nelson (Mi 300/Km 483). Beyond this gas-processing and shipbuilding center on the river of the same name is the wilderness, inhabited by grizzlies and olverines. For information, contact the Fort Nelson Bag Service 399, V0C 1R0 (phone: 604-774-2541).

Continue west over Summit Pass, the highest elevation on the highway, through Stone Mountain Provincial Park. From the highway, hikers can follow a 4-mile trail (one of the few improved ones) alongside the North Testa River to Flower Spring Lake, where caribou graze in meadows around the banks. Although the towering peaks of Mt. St. George and Mt. St. Paul may be too taxing for any but the most experienced climber, smaller neighboring mountains may appeal to others. Summit Lake, by the side of the road, is the park's biggest lake and has boating facilities and lake trout and Arctic grayling.

MUNCHO LAKE PROVINCIAL PARK: At Mile 456 (Km 734) this provincial park, 218,476 acres of white spruce and lodgepole pine forests, thins to scrub alpine spruce, lichen, and moss above the timberline. Dominating the park is Muncho Lake (Indian for "big water") ringed by forests inhabited by moose. A hike along an 8-mile trail following Nonda Creek (near the northeastern boundary of the road) will reveal goat, beaver, black bear, and Stone sheep.

A few miles north of the park is the Liard River, Mile 496 (Km 798). From here you can rent equipment and hire a guide to canoe the river, once a prime trade artery for the fur traders and named Liard (French for "poplar") for the trees lining its banks. Here, too, are the Liard Hot Springs, soothingly hot no matter how cold the air. During the winter, visitors don bathing suits and slip into the thermal waters. In the summer, bathers soak in the waters within view of the miniature orchids growing wild on the nearby hills. Near the springs is an 80-unit free campsite; lodging and guide service is available from *Muncho Lake Lodge* (phone: 604-776-3456), Mile 463 (Km 745).

BEST EN ROUTE

As one government tourist official put it: "You're not beating a path through one of the last wilderness regions in the world to find a luxury hotel." But what most of the establishments along the route lack in luxury (and for that matter, character, too, since most are concrete, boxy structures) they make up for in cleanliness and efficiency. New hotels and motels were added to this northern stretch of BC at an astonishing rate a few years ago, after black gold was found in the wilderness. While the oil boom no longer has BC in its grip, the wise traveler will make reservations.

The establishments listed below range from inexpensive ($30 to $40 for a double room) to moderate ($40 to $55 for a double). All prices are quoted in US dollars.

For those purists who scoff at hotel and motel accommodations, there are plenty of campsites in and around the towns on the tour. Check with the chambers of commerce in the towns for locations. The sites are rented on a first-come, first-served basis.

MACKENZIE

Alexander MacKenzie – This hotel has just about everything — a shopping center, laundromat, beer parlor, dining facilities, and nightly entertainment. PO Box 40 (phone: 604-997-3266). Moderate.

Powder King Ski Village – Within walking distance of the slopes, the resort features a 55-room hotel, with 2 dining rooms, a bar, day-care facilities, and triple-chair and T-bar lifts. PO Box 2405 (phone: 604-561-1776). Moderate.

DAWSON CREEK

Peace Villa – This motel has carpeted rooms, a sauna, color TV sets, complimentary coffee, and water beds. At Mile Point Zero. 1641 Alaska Ave. (phone: 604-782-8175). Moderate.

FORT ST. JOHN

Alexander MacKenzie Inn – A 7-story, modern motel that has an indoor pool, a sauna, and nightly entertainment. 9223 100th St. (phone: 604-785-8364). Moderate.

FORT NELSON

Fort Nelson Motor Hotel – This hotel-motel complex has dining facilities, color TV sets, and indoor pool, and a shopper's arcade. But what places this establishment a notch above the others is its main dining room, where 70 stuffed beasts, from moose to grizzlies, keep an eye on the diners. PO Box 240 (phone: 604-774-6971). Moderate.

Manitoba

Rugged, sparsely settled, and vast, the province of Manitoba covers 251,000 square miles of diverse terrain. Bordered by the US state of North Dakota to the south, the Canadian province of Saskatchewan to the west, Ontario to the east, and the Northwest Territories to the north, Manitoba is home to 1 million inhabitants, many of whom make their living by farming or mining.

Manitoba got its name from its original inhabitants, the Ojibwa Indians, who believed in the spirit Manitou, whose drum was the voice of rushing water. White people came through in the early 17th century in search of the Northwest Passage. The first settlers were French, but in the 19th century communities of Mennonites, Icelanders, and Ukrainians built settlements through the plains.

Although there is plenty of wilderness that will appeal to outdoor sportspeople, the climate in Manitoba is certainly a factor to consider before planning a visit. Bone-chilling winters drop the mercury well below −40F. In the southern part of the province, summers can get as hot as the 90s.

The four driving routes in this chapter are: Whiteshell, which takes you from Winnipeg east on the Trans-Canada Highway through the Mennonite village of Steinbach, Whiteshell Provincial Park, Falcon Lake, Winnipeg River, and Pinawa; the Wheat Belt, which runs west on the Trans-Canada Highway across Whitehorse Plain to Brandon, south through Turtle Mountain Provincial Park to the International Peace Garden; Interlake, which takes you north from Winnipeg along the western shores of Lake Winnipeg past Netley Marsh, Gimli, and Hecla Provincial Park; and the North, which goes west from Winnipeg on the Trans-Canada Highway to Portage La Prairie, northwest to Neepawa, a fur trading post of old, then north through picturesque river valleys to Riding Mountain National Park, The Pas, and Flin Flon, home of the *Flin Flon Trout Festival*.

Information: Travel Manitoba, 155 Carlton St., 7th Floor, Winnipeg, Manitoba R3C 3H8 (phone: 800-665-0040, or in Winnipeg, 945-3777).

Whiteshell

Millions of years ago, glaciers covered the high mountains and plains in the eastern part of Manitoba. The movements of the huge ice sheets eroded deep craters and gullies that were eventually filled with crystal-clear water. The ice, sliding through the mountains, exposed quartz and granite layers and ground them down to form gentle hills. Later, the exposed rocks were covered with a thin layer of soil supporting thick forests of barely rooted evergreens. This is the topography of the Canadian Shield.

The Whiteshell tour begins in Winnipeg and runs 209 miles (336 km) east on the Trans-Canada Highway. In this region — the Canadian Shield — the hills, valleys, forests, lakes, and streams provide some of the best fishing, hunting, hiking, and recreation in the province. You will see a replica of a Mennonite village near the town of Steinbach, where villagers still grind grain in a grist mill. An hour's drive east are the resort communities of Falcon Lake and West Hawk Lake, which have fine beaches, sailing, and water skiing, and Whiteshell Provincial Park, where the wilderness has been tamed by the fast-flowing Winnipeg River. In fact, most of this tour winds through the park, where you'll find hiking trails alongside moose, deer, and black bear territories and deep lakes where trophy-sized northern pike, walleye, and smallmouth bass can be caught. To the north are granite bluffs topped with precariously balanced evergreen and spruce trees. Within the park are the remains of those glacier days — shallow marshy lakes, now speckled with nesting geese and ducks. In the winter, tobogganists and downhill skiers careen down the park's snow-covered hills; cross-country skiers slide along the forest trails; and anglers drill holes in the lakes' frozen surfaces to ice fish.

En Route from Winnipeg – As you head east on Route 1 from Winnipeg, the rich, expansive farmlands of the southwest gradually give way to the jagged granite outcroppings of the Precambrian Shield. At the junction of Routes 1 and 12, take a short side trip south for a glimpse of two towns — Ste. Anne and Steinbach — as different from each other in lifestyle as this century is from the last.

Ste. Anne, one of the few predominantly French-speaking communities outside of Quebec, is the first town south of Route 1. The *Musée Pointe des Chênes* exhibits the cultural artifacts of the ancestors of these people.

Ten miles (16 km) south brings you to Steinbach, the center of thriving grain farms where Mennonites, escaping religious persecution in Russia, have lived and farmed since 1873.

STEINBACH: Strictures based on religious teachings are the rule of the town. But religion does not ban an annual festival — *Steinbach Pioneer Days* — in which these people demonstrate for visitors such old-time farming methods as reaping, flailing, and plowing and such homemaking chores as spinning, weaving, and churning butter. It's held during August Long Weekend, the weekend preceding the first Monday in August, in the Mennonite Heritage Village, 1½ miles (2.5 km) north of Steinbach on Route 12. Regardless of when you visit this museum, you can watch and talk to the Mennonites — who are mostly bilingual (English and a Low German dialect) — as they grind whole-wheat grains in one of Canada's few wind-powered grist mills. You can also buy the flour here to bake your own bread. Or forgo the baking and eat bread and other Mennonite food (try the *varenyky*, a cheese- or potato-filled dumpling) at the livery barn, part of the blacksmith shop and houses that make up the museum complex.

En Route from Steinbach – Return to Route 1. Traveling east, you soon reach Sandilands Provincial Forest, filled with acres and acres of pine, spruce, and other evergreens. Its nursery raises trees to landscape parks throughout the province.

Beyond the forest, a bit north of Route 1 on Route 11 and 51 miles (82 km) from Winnipeg, is Hadashville, an excellent spot to reel in northen pike while canoeing on the Whitemouth River. Then continue east on Route 1 to Falcon Lake, the southern entrance to Whiteshell Provincial Park.

WHITESHELL PROVINCIAL PARK: Here are 1,065 square miles of one of Canada's best wilderness, canoeing, fishing, hunting, and vacation lands. The park stretches from Falcon Lake to the south to the swiftly flowing Winnipeg River on the north, and east to the fjord-like streams and granite hills of the Canadian Shield. Dramatic waterfalls — such as Rainbow Falls on the northeastern tip of White Lake — splash and crash over granite and snowy quartz before tumbling into rivers, lakes, and streams edged by forests of jackpine, spruce, and elm. Ruffed grouse feed in the vast wild rice beds encircling small lakes, and Canada geese and ducks make the marshes around Hart, Betula, White, and Jessica lakes their home. Atop a layer of caribou moss and spots of muskeg (decayed vegetation), hunters search in spring and fall for the black bear, in recent years the only big game allowed to be taken in the park. For those who prefer driving a golf ball, smashing a tennis ball, or catching the rays on a beach, the resorts of Falcon Lake and West Hawk Lake are the places to stay. For a rundown on everything the park offers, read *The Manitoba Vacation Planner,* free from Travel Manitoba, 155 Carlton St., 7th Floor, Winnipeg, Manitoba R3C 3H8.

FALCON LAKE: In Falcon Lake's less wild sections are sophisticated sailing and water-skiing facilities and a guarded swimming beach; a major shopping center; an 18-hole golf course on rolling hills; and tennis courts. But the Beaver Creek circular hiking trail (at the entrance to Falcon Beach) penetrates the more pristine wilderness of the Canadian Shield, where beavers construct dams and an occasional deer whizzes through the spruce. Despite the popularity of this resort, an angler can still find an isolated inlet on the lakes in which to reel in a smallmouth bass, northern pike, and walleye.

During the winter, travel east on Route 301 to *Falcon Lake Ski Resort,* where you can ski down 14 slopes of beginner and intermediate trails.

WEST HAWK LAKE: Thousands of years ago, a meteor fell to earth and formed this lake (also known as Crater Lake), the deepest in Manitoba, at 365 feet. No matter how hot the summer day, this lake is spine-tingling cold. The swimmers may mind, but it certainly doesn't bother the smallmouth bass that inhabit this rockbottomed lake. If you don't care to try to land one of these fighting fish (and then fry it up at one of the area's 150 campsites), you can still savor it at one of the resort's restaurants.

En route from West Hawk Lake – Leave the Trans-Canada Highway and head northwest on Route 44. Just west of Caddy Lake, where you can rent canoes and boats to fish for its smallmouth bass, is the Lily Pond. A small, shallow lake lined with hard rock visible on all shores, it gets its name from the yellow and white water lilies floating on the surface. Across the road is a cliff consisting of light-colored "lenses" of granite formed about 2½ million years ago, when molten rock forced its way in between layers of the harder, older stuff.

At the junction of Route 307 near the town of Rennie (the site of hunting and drive-in fishing lodges) is the Alf Hole Goose Sanctuary. In 1937 a trapper named Alf Hole nursed four sick, abandoned Canada goslings back to health in his home. These four returned the next year, bringing more of their flock. Now, 200 geese return here each spring. At the sanctuary's center are exhibits on the life cycle of the Canada goose.

Return to the junction with Route 307 and head north, driving in between Jessica Lake and White Lake, with its Rainbow Falls cascading over the granite ledge.

Continuing along the route, you come to the Bannock Point petroforms about 2 miles (3 km) north of Betula Lake. Archaeologists believe the petroforms of people, turtles, snakes, fish, and birds were arranged by the Ojibwa in configurations to track the movement of the sun and the moon. Cree, Saulteaux, and Ojibwa Indians once rode over and through these hills and valleys, but all that remains of them in the area are their weapons and stuffed replicas of the bison and elk they once pursued.

From here, the highway cuts through Precambrian country at its best — sparkling lakes, verdant evergreen forests and towering granite cliffs. At the end of Natalie Lake is Seven Sisters Falls on the Winnipeg River. This is not the same river on which trappers, adventurers, and Indians canoed. That river was treacherous — filled with rapids, sudden swirling pools of water, and dangerous obstacles like decaying evergreen trees felled by lightning storms. Today the river is calmer, its rapids tamed by several power dams, of which the largest is in Seven Sisters Falls . . . and there are fewer mosquitoes. Even though canoeing on these waters is not like paddling the uncharted wilderness waters in the northern bush, it does have its moments: You glide on cool fresh water teeming with sturgeon and smallmouth bass, through sheltering forests of birch, bur oaks, and evergreens. Along the rugged cliffs are granite and rock formations that geologists believe to be among the oldest in the world — 2½ billion years. When you've had enough canoeing for the day, you can camp at one of the many sites dotting the Winnipeg River from here to Lake of the Woods in Kenora, Ontario, and dine on some fried smallmouth bass filets.

PINAWA: Ten miles (16 km) west on the Winnipeg River is the Whiteshell Nuclear Research site. During the summer months, general tours of the plant (including a portion of the reactor building and laboratories) are conducted at 10 AM and 1:30 PM. Off limits to pregnant women and children under 11 years old. Open Mondays through Fridays year-round, and Saturdays in July and August.

En Route from Pinawa – Returning to Route 44, the road meanders through tall cliffs of dolomite limestone. (Chunks of it were used to build the Legislative Building in Winnipeg.) If you're making this trip in late February, stop at Beausejour for the Canadian Power Toboggan Championship. The race is a commercial event in which major snowmobile manufacturers from the US and Canada demonstrate their sophisticated equipment in heart-stopping races.

At the junction with Route 59 at Lockport (see the *Interlake* route), turn south toward Winnipeg. On the last leg of this journey you drive past Birds Hill Provincial Park — 8,300 acres of aspen, poplar, and cedar groves and thickets of strawberries and blueberries. The park offers opportunities for camping only half an hour from the big-city bustle of Winnipeg.

BEST EN ROUTE

Most of the hotels, inns, and camping sites along this route take advantage of the beautiful natural settings of pine and spruce forests and clear lakes. In some of the expensive resorts, expect to pay between $40 and $70 for a room. The moderate-priced will range from $25 to $40 for a room. Camping will cost from $5 to $9. On summer weekends, some of the more popular camping sites fill up fast. You can't make reservations, so get there early on Friday. All prices are quoted in US dollars.

STEINBACH

Frantz – A 20-unit modern motel with color TV sets and full baths was built outside the town limits to avoid a former ban on alcoholic beverages. Facilities include a cocktail lounge and bar. South of Rte. 52 (phone: 204-326-9831). Moderate.

WHITESHELL PROVINCIAL PARK

Falcon Lake – Close to Falcon Lake, the resort is open year-round, but most units are condos. However, 16 rentals are still available and each has a full bath and a color TV set. There's also a cocktail lounge, restaurant, and swimming pool. Falcon Lake (phone: 204-349-8400). Expensive to moderate.

Tallpine Lodge – Near the 13 rustic housekeeping units — some with baths and fireplaces — is a quaint souvenir shop selling Indian crafts and jewelry. Open year-round. West Hawk (phone: 204-349-2209). Moderate.

Caddy Lake Campground – If you crave peace and quiet, camp here in one of 26 sites near Caddy Lake, with a playground, store, and boat ramp. West of West Hawk on Rte. 44 (no phone). Inexpensive.

Falcon Beach Campground – On summer weekends this is one of the most popular campgrounds in the park. There are 175 tent sites and 117 trailer sites. From here you can rent equipment and boats for fishing on the lake. Falcon Lake (phone: 204-349-2201). Inexpensive.

West Hawk Campground – The 84 campsites and 73 trailer sites are close together, but the tall pines give each a degree of privacy. Often noisy on summer weekends, this provincial government camping facility has picnic shelters and boat rentals. West Hawk (phone: 204-349-2245). Inexpensive.

RENNIE

Inverness Fall Resort – This resort offers 6 deluxe cottages and 4 spartan cabins in a spacious, wooded setting. The complex has a coffee shop and store, tackle and bait shop with fishing and hunting licenses for sale, fly-out fishing service, and canoe, boat, and motor rentals. Closed December. Brereton Lake (phone: 204-369-5336). Moderate.

The Wheat Belt

Just as the fertile black soil of these prairies attracted the first settlers to Manitoba, so the beautiful farm and ranch lands beckon vacationers today. The following 500-mile (805-km) route — stretching from Winnipeg west to the Brandon Hills and south to the International Peace Garden on the Canada–North Dakota border — cuts through the heart of the wheat belt, thousands and thousands of acres devoted to wheat, barley, oilseeds, and oats. This "breadbasket of the world" is also fast becoming an important center of dairy farming and cattle ranching.

The breadbasket appeals to city dwellers seeking a change of pace — vast fields of wheat waving in the breeze, cows grazing in green pastures and, in fall, combines sweeping across the plains. Many farmers and ranchers invite visitors to share their homes, their work (pitching hay, milking cows), and their natural resources: lakes, rivers, streams, and countryside.

Spring, the busy season for farmers, is the best time to see how a farm works. In high summer — June, July, and August — the temperature often rises to 100F (38C), and you're likely to be more comfortable visiting an agricultural fair or putting in hard time under an elm tree fishing for perch or walleye. Yet even in winter, when the mercury drops to 20F (and below) at night, many of the province's farms welcome travelers, offering a place by the family fire and tales of the early prairie days.

En Route from Winnipeg – Leaving Winnipeg on the Trans-Canada Highway (Rte. 1), the road cuts through the Whitehorse Plain, which Indians believed was haunted by the spirit of a murdered Assiniboine Indian maiden. Just off the highway, in the town of St. François Xavier, a statue of a horse immortalizes the white stallion that the maiden and her equally hapless Cree bridegroom rode to escape the arrows of her jealous suitor, a Sioux. Although the lovers were killed, the ghostly white horse escaped with the soul of the maiden and is believed to roam the plains today.

The route continues along Route 26 to Portage la Prairie, 52 miles (84 km) from Winnipeg, passing several small prairie towns. Along this route is the town of Poplar Point, site of St. Anne's Church. Built about 1864, it is one of the oldest log churches in continuous use in western Canada.

PORTAGE LA PRAIRIE: Many of the early French explorers carried canoes through this area on their way to Lake Manitoba in unsuccessful searches for northwest trade routes to the Far East and its riches. More than a century later, a different type of explorer settled here after discovering that the rich black soil of the prairies nourished wheat. The transient life of explorers — such as Pierre Gaultier de La Vérendrye, who built Fort La Reine here in 1738 — and the more settled ways of farmers — such as John Sutherland Sanderson, who established the first homestead in western Canada here — are dramatically and effectively revealed at *Fort La Reine Museum* and Pioneer Village. A trading post, blacksmith shop, and stable make up the museum, and the village includes an early log homestead, a trapper's cabin, and a "farm of the century" home. Open mid-May to mid-September; small admission charge.

There is much more to Portage la Prairie than its past. In July, the town puts on the lively Portage Fair. A permanent attraction is Island Park and Crescent Lake, a preserve with a horseshoe-shaped lake, sanctuaries for deer, one of the largest captive flocks of Canada geese, hiking trails, tennis courts, and a golf course. The park is on Saskatchewan Avenue at Royal Road, and is open only during summer months.

En Route from Portage la Prairie – Travel west on Route 1 to Austin and its Fort Ellice–Edmonton Trail. Just south of town on Route 34 is the *Manitoba Agricultural Museum* and Homesteaders Village, with its large collection of steam engines, three log buildings, and a grist mill. At the end of July, the Threshermen's Reunion and Stampede is marked on the museum grounds with a rodeo and agricultural fair. From Austin, follow the Trans-Canada west to Carberry, where artist, naturalist, and writer Ernest Thompson Seton once lived. This is the center of a unique, desert-like region (see Spruce Woods Provincial Heritage Park, below). The town of Glenboro, south of here, erected a fiberglass camel to give visitors a larger-than-life hint of the terrain (but not the creatures) that awaits them.

SPRUCE WOODS PROVINCIAL HERITAGE PARK: Assiniboine Indians once rode bareback through forests of elm, oak, and trembling aspen (west of the park) to the sloping plains of the Assiniboine River basin. They rode over huge beds of moss, through clumps of fern, and among hazelnut bushes and grapevines to hunt bison, antelope, and mule deer. Like scientists today, they were mystified by the Spirit Sands, a region so similar to a desert that the Canadian Armed Forces simulate desert fighting on it, much to the dismay of environmentalists. (The site of the artillery and tank maneuvers, Camp Shilo, is off limits to tourists.) This region, also known as the Carberry Sandhills, was formed 12,000 years ago when the Assiniboine River flowed into glacial Lake Agassiz, leaving sandy sediment in its wake. Winds whipped the sands into constantly shifting dunes where today rare and endangered desert creatures — the prairie skink and hognose snake — live among the barrel cactus. Although it may appear to be a desert, topographically speaking, it's not. When rain falls in the surrounding countryside, it rains here as well. Spongy sands trap the water and humidity beneath a drier top layer, creating a fascinating phenomenon of sudden springs and thick pots of quicksand. Because of the unique, fragile topography in the park, be careful along the 1-mile (1½-km) Isputinaw and Oxbow Lake trails. Don't expect to see the mainstay of Assiniboine life (bison, antelope, and mule deer). They were slaughtered years ago, mostly by the pioneers.

The park is open year-round, with an extensive winter program. Return via Highway 5 north to Route 1 west to Brandon.

BRANDON: "The Wheat City" lies in the Pembina Valley surrounded by the blue hills of Brandon and divided by the Assiniboine River. On the borders of some of the main streets, golden wheat grows on experimental farms. In the summer the eastern bluebird is an annual visitor. Just outside the city limits, farmers wake at 5 AM to milk cows, beekeepers care for their hives, and children ride their horses before school. But for all this, Brandon — the central terminal for shipping grain — is the second largest city in the province, with a population of 39,000. There are creameries, packing plants, and even oil refineries here. And recently Brandon has become a recreational and cultural center, with good, if not grand, hotels, restaurants, and night spots (see *Best en Route*). Athletes (even the armchair variety) should visit the 84-acre *Keystone Sports Complex,* built for $5 million as a site for the 1979 Canada Winter Games. The *Sportsplex* has an indoor regulation-size swimming pool, racquetball courts, a speed-skating oval, and a hockey arena. It is also the site of three agricultural fairs — the *Royal Manitoba Winter Fair* the last week in March, the Provincial Exhibition in mid-June, and the *Ag-Ex* in late October.

For good classical music and ballet, make reservations for programs playing at Brandon University's West Man Auditorium (270 18th St.). The *Royal Winnipeg Ballet* and the *Winnipeg Symphony* perform here occasionally.

Also at Brandon University is the *B. J. Hales Museum of Natural History,* featuring Sioux and Plains Indian artifacts — pipes, pottery, arrowheads, and tools made of bone — and 250 indigenous species of birds set in displays of prairie grass and simulated snow and ice. Long-time curator of the museum, the late Dr. Jack Lane was the legendary Bluebird Man who saved the eastern bluebird from extinction. By the 1930s their numbers had dwindled to a couple of dozen. Dr. Lane organized children in birdhouse-building brigades and set the houses up around the city. Thanks to him, more than 15,000 of the creatures now nest in birdhouses dotting the city and countryside.

In most grain markets of the world, Manitoba No. 1 Hard means fine wheat. A tour of the Agriculture Canada Research Station may show you there's more to good wheat than hard work and rich soil. The station conducts research in plant nutrition, herbicides, barley genetics, and the controlled breeding and feeding of beef, cattle, swine, and poultry. Tours available weekdays upon request.

En Route from Brandon – Heading west from Brandon on Route 1, you come to Griswold, a Sioux Indian reserve, the home of the ancestors of the Indians who fought General George Armstrong Custer in the Battle of Little Bighorn in 1876. In the reserve is a crafts store.

A worthwhile side trip is Virden, less than 25 miles (39 km) west on Route 1. In 1951, California Sun Oil struck black gold here and the place has never been the same. Pump-jacks in surrounding fields and in the town itself draw crude oil from the natural subterranean reservoirs.

From either Virden or Griswold swing back toward Winnipeg. Head south on 21 from Griswold and pick up Route 2 east to Souris, at the junction of provincial highways 2 and 22.

SOURIS: In this small, hilly town is perhaps the most famous wedding gift in Canada. Seventy-five years ago, a homesteader built a 582-foot suspension bridge across the Souris River for his bride. A huge flood tore it apart in 1976, but the town repaired it. The brave can still cross the Souris River by walking the swaying footbridge, but the acrophobes in the crowd had better stick to photographing the longest suspension bridge in Canada. Nearby is the *Hillcrest Museum,* an early settler's spacious home filled with pioneer heirlooms.

A mile from town are the Souris Agate Pits, where rockhounds will have no trouble collecting agates (from clear to red), petrified wood (beige, brown, or black), and jaspers (mostly red and green). Although scarce, an emerald green epidote veined in pink may be found, too. Before you go to the pits, which are open year-round, stop at the *Souris River Gem Shop,* 8 First St. S., for directions, digging equipment, and a license (about $4), allowing each family to take home 10 pounds of rock. The shop sells natural stone jewelry and guides to identifying your finds.

En Route from Souris – Head south on Route 22 to Route 23. Head east to Route 10 and then south to Boissevain, home of the zany Turtle Derby, an annual event held one weekend in mid-July. A few years back, a North Dakota turtle named Watergate crept his way to glory, winning the $100 prize for his owner. He did even better for those who wagered on him — a $1,000 sweepstake prize.

TURTLE MOUNTAIN PROVINCIAL PARK: The park gets its name from the western painted turtle that lives in the many shallow lakes — ranging from pothole size to massive — on these 47,000 acres. Here, too, are a variety of waterfowl, such as ducks, grebes, coots, herons, and cormorants, which feed on the grassy shores. In the spring and fall, migratory waterfowl swell their numbers. Hikers can pace the park's rolling hills through trembling aspen, black poplar, ash, and birch, and at the edge pick chokecherries, cranberries, and pinchberries in clearings perfumed by wild plum trees. Max Lake has excellent perch and walleye. And nearby William Lake has produced trophy-size catches of rainbow trout. There are campgrounds at Max Lake, Adam Lake, and William Lake Recreation Park. Open year-round.

INTERNATIONAL PEACE GARDEN: Just south of the park on the North Dakota–Manitoba border is this park dedicated to peace and goodwill between the US and Canada. Formal gardens, conceived half a century ago by a Canadian horticulturist, include beautiful flower beds and sunken pools surrounded by rosebushes. Visitors in winter snowshoe and ski on the trails that lead to a series of lakes connected by ornamental spillways and surrounded by terraced panels. Also in the garden are the All Faith Peace Chapel, available to any religious group for services, and the International Music Camp, held each summer. Students from the camp perform concerts and plays each summer Sunday in an open-air amphitheater.

En Route from the Peace Garden – Heading north from the border on Route 10, you'll reach Route 3. Traveling east, you can see Killarney Lake, a pleasant spot for a quick dip, an afternoon of boating, or a picnic. On the shore is Killarney, where the Irish-Canadian community stages a spirited St. Patrick's Day parade. But if you miss it, don't despair — you can still kiss a Blarney stone and photograph the leprechaun perched on top of the shamrock-shaped fountain in Erin Park — or maybe even catch a glimpse of the town's green fire engine. Just north of town on Route 18 is the Pelican Lake Recreation Area, pleasant for camping. Continuing east on Route 3, the road leads to Pilot Mound, whose Assiniboine burial mound dates back 11,000 years. Exhibits at the *Pilot Mound Museum* explain the 1908 excavation that uncovered the site; the museum is open Tuesday, Thursday, and Saturday afternoons.

Back on Route 3, you reach La Rivière and the *Holiday Mountain Ski Resort* (204-242-2172). Expert skiers will find the gentle hills no challenge, but beginners and intermediates will get a workout. Continue east to Morden, where the Agriculture Canada Research Station has a 627-acre farm dedicated to developing new strains of early-maturing crops, fruit trees, and grains. In the spring the town hosts *Blossom Week* (the date changes each year, as fruit trees flower), and in late August the *Corn and Apple Festival,* with free corn on the cob and apple cider. Southwest of town lies Lake Minnewasta, one of the few spots in the province where you can catch largemouth bass. Camping and picnicking facilities can be found at Colert Beach.

From Morden, head east on Route 3, then north at the junction of Route 75; 12 miles (19 km) away is the town of Morris, home of the Manitoba Stampede and Agricultural Exhibition, the second largest rodeo in Canada, held in mid-July. Besides bronco riding, bareback riding, and steer wrestling, the rodeo features toga-clad racers (even before the film *Animal House* made toga parties popular) who compete in the unique Ben Hur Suicide Chariot Race. From Morris continue north to Winnipeg.

BEST EN ROUTE

If pitching in with farmwork or just savoring the rural life attracts you, spend a night, week, or summer on a farm. Some of the farms along the route are listed below, but for a complete roster write the Manitoba Farm Vacations Association, 525 Kylemore Ave., Winnipeg (phone: 204-475-6624). Be sure to make reservations because most farms accommodate only a few guests. If you live in the family's house and share their meals, the most this will cost adults is about $30, children, $13.

If you decide to use public lodging, a night's stay in a double room in an expensive hotel will cost from $35 to $40 (a few dollars more in Brandon), and a moderately priced establishment will cost between $17 and $35. In the moderate range, many bed-and-breakfast accommodations can be found throughout Manitoba. Contact B & B of Manitoba, 93 Healy Cr., Winnipeg (204-256-6151). All prices are quoted in US dollars.

GLENBORO

Hiwin Glen Farm – Ron and Mazo Black run this working dairy farm that accommodates 20 guests in a separate farmhouse. Not far from Spruce Woods Provincial Heritage Park, it features an outdoor pool, and meals can be taken with the family on advance notice. Associate member of Canadian Hostelling Association. Open year-round. On Provincial Trunk Highway 2, 2½ miles (3.5 km), west of the junction with Provincial Trunk Highway 5, Glenboro (phone: 204-827-2891). Moderate, with meals; inexpensive, for lodging only.

SPRUCE WOODS PROVINCIAL HERITAGE PARK

Kiche Manitou Campground – This is a provincial government camping facility with 76 tent sites and 45 trailer sites at the foot of a hill in the park. Open May to October (phone: 204-827-2458). Inexpensive.

BRANDON

Victoria Inn – The newest and plushest in the city, this inn has an indoor swimming pool surrounded by tropical plants and trees. Within the hotel are lounges, small shops, a sun deck, sauna, and the *Tropical Garden Café*. The hotel offers babysitting services and accommodates wheelchairs. 3550 Victoria Ave. (phone: 204-725-1532, or 800-852-2710, from anywhere in Manitoba). Expensive.

Royal Oak Inn – This 100-room luxury hotel boasts a liquor-serving restaurant, *Winsor's*. The indoor swimming area, decorated with tropical plants, has a sauna and whirlpool bath. 3130 Victoria Ave. (phone: 204-728-5775, or 800-852-2709, from anywhere in Manitoba). Expensive.

Redwood TraveLodge – With a fairly central location, this hotel has 60 rooms and a coffee shop. 345 18th St. N. (phone: 204-728-2200, or 800-255-3050, from anywhere in Manitoba). Moderate.

Little Chalet – Here you'll find 27 air conditioned A-frame cabins with color TV sets, an outdoor swimming pool, and coffee shop. At the junction of Rte. 1 and 18th St. (phone: 204-725-1574). Moderate.

TURTLE MOUNTAIN PROVINCIAL PARK

Adam Lake Campground – This government camping facility has 65 tent and 25 trailer sites. Open May to September. Rte. 10 (phone: 204-534-7204). Inexpensive.

MORDEN

Valley View Farm – Help a family of six with milking cows and feeding chickens on this farm in the Pembina Hills. The farm also has horses for riding and a yard in which to park campers. Contact Virginia McKerlie, PO Box 140, RR 1 (phone: 204-822-3731). Moderate to inexpensive.

Interlake

In 1875, Iceland suffered severe and destructive volcanic eruptions, and many Icelanders fled their beautiful but harsh and unpredictable home to seek a land similar but more hospitable where they could continue their lives as fishermen and farmers. When they arrived, these pioneers thought Manitoba promising, with its vast fertile plains and many lakes. So they traded the cold rough waters of the Atlantic Ocean — teeming with saltwater catches — for the gentle, shallow waters of Lake Winnipeg and Lake Manitoba — both brimming with goldeye, whitefish, and walleye. And instead of fjords lashed by harsh waves, the settlers found grassy marshes alive with ducks and geese. Most important, instead of active volcanoes, the immigrants found deep, silent pine forests and fertile land.

The first leg of this 190-mile (175-km) trip from Winnipeg, along the western coast of Lake Winnipeg to an archipelago of wilderness islands, encompasses a region that was once New Iceland — an independent country in the heart of Canada, governed and inhabited by the descendants of the Icelandic settlers. The Icelandic people and their traditions still live here. In Gimli, the area's unofficial capital, the fishermen and farmers may talk to each other in their native tongue, but they will welcome you to festivals of Icelandic poetry and plays, with native food and costumes. And you can stay at an Icelandic-style resort, built smack in the middle of spruce, aspen, and jack pine forests alive with deer and beaver. (On smaller islands, where no cars may penetrate, moose and black bear also thrive.)

The roads are open in the Interlake region all year unless a winter storm closes them. (In winter, when temperatures plunge below −18F, −28C, it's wise to pack extra blankets, food, and a flashlight into your car.) In spring, geese and ducks flock to this well-watered region from the south to feed and mate. In summer, numerous festivals and fairs are held, and the lakes are splendid for sailing and swimming. But autumn is the time of most special scenic beauty. The trees change to a myriad of colors — gold, orange, brown, and rust; the farmer's crops are ripe; and the villagers sponsor fowl suppers, where you'll find tables heaped high with turkey, chicken, fish, vegetables, and such calorie-filled Icelandic desserts as *vinarterta* (prune cake) and *ponnukukur* (sweet pancake).

En Route from Winnipeg – Leave Winnipeg by way of Main Street north to the Perimeter (a route skirting the city) and continue on it as it becomes Route 9. Follow this road 9 miles (14 km) north to Lockport, noted for its locks, historic Anglican church, and, some say, the best hot dogs in Canada.

LOCKPORT: Near the St. Andrews Locks, which are used for the passage of freight and pleasure vessels along the Red River, try your luck at catching some of the many species of fish. (One angler caught a 33½-pound trophy-rating catfish here.)

If you prefer something other than the white, tender, and flaky meat of the catfish for supper, pick up a *Skinner's* hot dog, voted the best in the country by national magazines. Underneath the usual sauerkraut and mustard lurks a unique blend of meat, creating a wiener that people praise from Quebec to British Columbia. (*Skinner's* is on River Road, south of St. Andrews Locks.)

Just south of town is the oldest stone church in western Canada that is still in use — St. Andrews-on-the-Red, built in the 1800s. Worshipers still use the original prayer kneelers, covered with buffalo hide.

Down the road from the church and overlooking the Red River is the *Kennedy House Museum* (1866), once the home of Captain William Kennedy, the first Canadian-born person and the only Métis (son of a Cree mother and Scot father) to command an Arctic exploration.

Return to Route 9 and proceed northeast toward Selkirk. Just outside town, at Lower Fort Garry National Historic Park, is the only stone fort of the fur trade era still intact in North America. Selkirk, north of the fort, is known for its beautiful homes and excellent marina on Lake Winnipeg (see *Winnipeg,* THE CITIES). Head north on Route 9 to Petersfield and the base of Netley Marsh, one of the continent's great waterfowl nesting areas.

NETLEY MARSH: This 100 square miles of briny green marsh grass, bullrush, cattail, and tall cane grass is home to duck, tern, western grebe, and goose. The best way to tour the narrow channels is by canoe, but with a strong gust from Lake Winnipeg, you'll be wading instead of paddling. If an occasional dunking alarms you, take your gear and board the MS *Lady Chesley,* a sightseeing boat. Or if you've left your sea legs in Winnipeg, hike along the dike road skirting the edge of the marsh. Early (4 to 6 AM) risers who venture into the marsh will spot many of the 100 species of aquatic birds eating breakfast. Common terns dive for minnow, great blue herons swoop down and carry off silver fish, and pelicans skim the marsh for surface fish. Throughout the feeding, each bird adds its individual sound to the ear-splitting cacophony. The season for jump, pass, or decoy shooting opens in mid-September. From early spring, when transients swell the bird population, to early fall, when marsh foliage bursts with gold, red, and orange, the marsh is the turf of hunters and birders. Conventional hunting weapons must be declared to Canada Customs. Hunting licenses can be obtained from the Manitoba Department of Natural Resources, 1495 St. James St., Winnipeg R3N 0W9 (phone: 204-945-7257). Dogs may be brought into Canada only if they have rabies innoculation certificates that are no more than 36 months old. See "Border Crossing" in GETTING READY TO GO.

En Route from Netley Marsh – Return to Petersfield and follow Route 9 for 43 miles (69 km) to Winnipeg Beach, a revived family summer vacation spot with a large marina, beaches, and boardwalk. Nine miles (14 km) north, you enter Gimli, the gateway to Icelandic country.

GIMLI: This harbor town by the sandy southwestern shores of Lake Winnipeg so enchanted its Icelandic settlers a century ago that they named it after the home of the mythological Norse gods. If fishing for whitefish, walleye, and goldeye; sailing on a windswept lake near an excellent marina; or soaking up some Icelandic culture appeals to you, summertime in Gimli may be your corner of heaven. (More than half the population of 1,600 is of Icelandic descent. A huge statue of a Viking with his back to the lake never lets you forget it.)

Gimli Historical Museum on the waterfront of Gimli Harbor displays Icelandic and Ukrainian pioneer material and relates the history of fishing on Lake Winnipeg. Open Wednesdays through Sundays 10 AM to 5 PM; June through August, daily 11 AM to 7 PM. Small admission charge.

Many people still fish and farm here, the largest town of Icelanders outside of Iceland. On the weekend before the first Monday of August, the August Long Weekend, they doff their fishing and farming apparel and don colorful Icelandic costumes to host the *Islendingadagurinn,* or *Icelandic Festival,* as a tribute to their ancestors. At the festival, you can feast on smoked *rulla pilsa* (lamb) and *vinarterta* (torte with prune filling); watch or join a 10-mile walking race called *glima;* enjoy the water sports from the harbor; choose an ethnic artifact from the arts and crafts display; and look for the Maid of the Mountains, called *Fjalkona.* She's not your average teenage festival queen, but a respected woman of outstanding merit whose physical appearance is immaterial.

En Route from Gimli – North on Route 9, the road passes (never far from Lake Winnipeg) through the Camp Morton Provincial Recreation Park, with its beaches, picnic tables, and 12 rustic log cabins. Farther north you pass through more lakefront communities settled by Icelanders. The first is Arnes, birthplace of Vilhjalmur Stefansson, the first explorer to report on Arctic climatic conditions (a commemorative statue in town honors him). Beyond this point, Route 9 degenerates to a gravel roadway, and although construction is expected to improve the roadway (and maybe pave the area), switch over to Route 8 to continue north. When Route 8 ends, pick up 234 north to 233 and Hecla Provincial Park.

HECLA PROVINCIAL PARK: This is a vast archipelago of wild and wooded islands thoroughly rimmed by reedy marshes, of which only Hecla Island, the largest, can be reached by car. Canoes will take you to see wildlife preserves where deer, elk, and moose thrive in island habitats isolated from one another and their predators. The rare western grebe, the bald eagle, the blue heron, and the black tern give even the most seasoned bird-watcher an eyeful. Hecla Island is a year-round resort community, named by the Icelandic immigrants for Mt. Hecla, the volcano whose eruption drove them from their homeland. Breathtakingly beautiful granite and limestone cliffs buttress the shores of this largely uninhabited island, offering some of the finest hiking and camping in the province. Badger, fisher, deer, and moose live in the dense forest of spruce, aspen and jack pine surrounded by miles of prairies. In winter, snow buffs don showshoes or cross-country skis to hike through well-mapped and maintained trails. At the north end of the island is *Gull Harbour Resort* hotel (see *Best En Route*), an Icelandic-style luxury hotel with large picture windows overlooking the great outdoors. During the summer, 50,000 ducks, Canada geese, and snow and blue geese make the surrounding marshes home. *Gull Harbour* has facilities for hunters searching out the upland game and waterfowl. But the big attraction on the island is the 18-hole golf course. Duffers beware of the notorious par-4 *Longa Tjo* (Long Pond) and par-5 *Grjotagja* (rocky ravine) holes that make even the pros sweat.

En Route from Hecla – Return to the junction of Routes 8 and 68 and proceed west on Route 68 through sparsely settled "cowboy country." The terrain is slightly rolling, with short, scrubby grasses and wild strawberries and blueberries near enough the road to pick. (Before you eat any, check carefully the free booklet *Edible and Poisonous Berries,* available from Manitoba Department of Natural Resources, Room 201, 1495 St. James St., Winnipeg R3H 0W9.) Where Routes 68 and 6 join, 121 miles (195 km) along, is Eriksdale, an outfitting center for anglers who fish in the Manitoba Narrows and for hunters seeking upland waterfowl and game. The many shops specialize in fishing, hunting, and camping equipment and will also provide licenses.

From Eriksdale, follow Route 417 west to Route 418, then north to Route 235. From Route 235, proceed west along the southern portion of Dog Lake, following the road to Oakview, within walking distance of the Narrows.

MANITOBA NARROWS: Waves crashing against the limestone shores of the narrowest part of the lake gave the province its name. The Ojibwa Indians believed that Manitou, the spirit of good and evil, banged his drum during stormy weather to create the resounding sound.

In these narrow, often rough straits, a skilled angler can haul in a 14-pound walleye and a 35-pound fierce, northern pike. And hunters bag many Canada geese feeding by the marshy shores of the numerous inlets.

Return to Eriksdale.

En Route from Eriksdale – Travel south on Route 6 to Lundar, another Icelandic community. As you drive, you can't miss an 8-foot Canada goose pointing the way the wind blows. With several towns vying for the title "goose capital of Canada," the Lundar folk erected this giant Fiberglas statue to stake their claim — and with good reason. Every spring and fall, flocks of Canada geese pause during their migrations at a wild goose sanctuary in Lundar. There you can feed them; north of town, you can shoot them and eat them. Many shops in town provide equipment and licenses.

Follow Route 6 along the southeast shore of Lake Manitoba to Twin Lake Beaches, a popular swimming, picnicking, and camping spot. From here, follow Route 6 to Winnipeg, the last leg of your Interlake odyssey.

BEST EN ROUTE

Lodgings on this route range from the plush *Gull Harbour Resort and Conference Center,* with just about every recreational facility you can think of, to the spartan lodges where hunters snatch a few hours of shut-eye before rising at 5 AM to fish and stalk game. For a double room, expect to pay $50 to $70 for hotels we list as expensive, $25 to $45 for moderate, and $15 to $20 for inexpensive. All prices are quoted in US dollars.

PETERSFIELD

Chesley's – On the fringes of Netley Marsh, these 7 units and cottages provide comfortable all-service accommodations for avid duck and upland game hunters. The lodge supplies guides and a trip up the Netley River in the MS *Lady Chesley.* After a duck dinner, sportsmen gather in the cedar lodge to discuss the day's hunting. For reservations, write PO Box 220, Petersfield, Manitoba ROC 2LO (phone: 204-738-2250). Inexpensive. Weekly rates available.

GIMLI

Shoreliner – The 18 spartan units provide a spectacular view of the harbor and the Viking statue. 39 First Ave. (phone: 204-642-5992). Moderate.

HECLA ISLAND

Gull Harbour Resort and Conference Center – This modern complex epitomizes Icelandic architecture, with its large picture windows, welcoming *setustofa* (lobby), and wooden furniture. Facilities include 93 comfortable rooms, a gymnasium, indoor swimming pool, and sauna. During the winter, the hotel is a perfect base from which to cross-country ski, skate, and snowmobile. Open all year. Reservations essential. Hecla Island (phone: 800-475-2354). Expensive.

Gull Harbour Campground – After a day of fishing, swimming, or hiking, camp out in this 213-site provincial government facility. Open May to September. Hecla Island (phone: 204-378-2945). Inexpensive.

LUNDAR

Lundar – The main attraction at this 23-unit motor inn is its bar, where local hunters may enlighten a transient about the best hunting spots. Rte. 6 (phone: 204-762-5855). Moderate.

The North

Where the dark, dense forest meets the clear blue lake, rabbit, deer, and fox peep from the bush; a fish leaps in the lake; a bird calls; the scent of pine is in the air; a campfire crackles as bacon and eggs sizzle on the grill; and a cushion of lichen feels soft underfoot. From the sight of the blue sky on the horizon to the taste of the fried, just-caught walleye on your tongue, this is the northern wilderness.

And then there's that other world of the north — the shouts and whoops at the *Flin Flon Trout Festival;* the crack of the mushers' whips over the heads of the lead dogs during the World Championship Dogsled Derby at The Pas; the clatter of chain saws and the crunch of trees felled in the pulp and paper operations; the delicate embroidery and brightly colored Easter eggs in the Ukrainian town of Dauphin; and the camaraderie of a people more than willing to share their good times with visitors.

The tour route outlined below takes you from the wheat farming communities of the interior to the flatlands of Hudson Bay. En route you will visit Riding Mountain National Park, its extensive wilderness preserves, and the lumber and mining towns of Flin Flon and The Pas. From The Pas you may want to hop a plane and visit *real* pioneer country, the subarctic seaport of Churchill.

After The Pas, the trip is no luxury excursion. As you go north, you'll find cedar bogs with a few spindly dwarfed spruce clinging to gray rocks and tundra. This region's frigid winter extends from mid-October to June 15. But the cold climate and pitifully short summer are no reason to skip this leg of the journey.

En Route from Winnipeg – Leaving Winnipeg, head west on the Trans-Canada Highway, Route 1, to Portage la Prairie, where a fair is held each July in remembrance of Thomas Spence, a settler who was a strong advocate of confederation (see Portage la Prairie in the *Wheat Belt* route). From Portage, follow the Yellowhead Route 16 northwest to Neepawa, where a plaque commemorates the 900-mile (1,449-km) road that fur traders trod from the Red River settlement to Fort Edmonton, Alberta.

Neepawa is noted for its salt mines; the Canadian Salt Company once pumped brine out of an underground salt lake near the center of town; the lake still exists. During July, Neepawa culture buffs (14 years and older) paint, sing, or play instruments under the tutelage of top-notch teachers in the week-long *Holiday Festival of Arts*. Students and teachers (some from the *Winnipeg Symphony and Ensemble*) perform concerts and plays.

Continuing west, in the Minnedosa River valley — an area of rolling hills decked with oak trees — lies the small town of Minnedosa (population 2,500).

Hunters flock here each autumn for the fine goose and duck hunting. For those not interested in the sporting life, there's Minnedosa Lake, northeast of town, offering delightful swimming, picnicking, and camping. Each July Minnedosa puts on the *Country Fun Festival,* a family fair at which local musicians stage everything from square dances (fiddlers and all) to rock concerts.

North on Route 10, the road climbs from the valley into sandy, hilly country, then through grassy plains onto the plateau of Riding Mountain National Park.

RIDING MOUNTAIN NATIONAL PARK: Surrounded by the prairies of the Canadian plains, this is a recreational park and nature preserve of prairies and rolling hills, hardwood and evergreen forests, and crystal-clear lakes and streams.

Northern pike and rainbow trout swim in the park's deep cold lakes — Clear Lake, Lake Katherine, and Deep Lake, to name a few — while beaver build dams in marshy, shallow creeks. On the meadow to the west bloom the bright yellow blossoms of shrubby cinquefoil and the purplish Gaillardia. On the prairies around Audy Lake, herds of buffalo roam through the scrubby grasses. An exhibit nearby relates the history of the bison — almost extinct except for one species. Throughout the park are wolves, elk, whitetail deer, and moose. A walk along one of the numerous hiking paths will bring you to the log cabin of Archibald Belaney — more commonly known by his Indian name of Grey Owl — a British naturalist who, in the early 20th century, drew and wrote about the creatures living in the forest around him.

During the winter, you can don cross-country skis and follow several trails through the park. If the prospect of schussing down the steepest downhill ski slope in the province attracts you, take a trip to Mt. Agassiz, on the east side of the park near McCreary.

Adjoining the park is the *Elkhorn Resort* (see *Best En Route*), where horses may be rented for trail rides through the park.

The southeastern entrance to the park is at the resort community of Wasagaming (Indian for "clear water") on the shores of Clear Lake. The lake, regularly stocked with trout, has facilities for fishing, boating, and sailing. Wasagaming also boasts an 18-hole, par-72 golf course (so near Clear Lake that a misguided long drive may cost you a ball), tennis and badminton courts, a roller skating rink, dance pavilion, and cinema.

For information about overnight and day hikes and trails (including one for the blind), visit the Interpretive Center at Wasagaming. Most of the park's facilities are accessible to people in wheelchairs. The information center is open from mid-May to mid-September and on weekdays during the ski season.

From the park, follow Route 10 to Dauphin.

DAUPHIN: After the transcontinental railroad was finished in 1896, Ukrainian immigrants moved north with visions of fertile farming land and homesteading grants. They were not disappointed. Over the years the rich soil of the Dauphin Valley nurtured their crops of wheat, barley, and potatoes. Today, the town is noted for its flour and lumber mills as well as its farming.

Each August Long Weekend, the town holds the annual *Ukrainian Festival* as a tribute to its ancestry. The festival offers much to see and do. Ukrainian Cossack riders in traditional garb ride through the valley; artisans demonstrate *pysanka* (Easter egg decorating); and people gather for Ukrainian dancing, singing, and eating delicious home-cooked foods. These last include *pirogi* (boiled or fried pastry stuffed with potatoes and/or cheese), borscht (beet soup), and kielbasa (sausage). If you miss the festival, you may treat yourself to these dishes at the *Dauphin Allied Arts Center* (in the old town hall).

Another Dauphin attraction includes the 5 professional horseshoe pits in *Dauphin Memorial Community Club,* where anyone can have a fling with a horseshoe.

En Route from Dauphin – Follow Route 10 as it veers west and then north.

At the junction with Route 367 in Garland, head west to Duck Mountain Provincial Park for wilderness camping and excellent fishing. In 1961, a forest fire ravaged much of the park's jack pine and spruce. But as you hike the several well-mapped trails, you will see numerous shrubs, part of the continuing process of forest renewal. The highest point in Manitoba is Baldy Mountain (2,727 ft.), where in late fall you can hear the bugling of elk. The Nicholas Copernicus Observance Committee has mounted a sundial on this mountain to help those hiking the Copernicus Hill Trail keep track of the hour.

Back on Route 10, head north and west to the town of Swan River, where between 1787 and 1821 the Hudson's Bay Company tried to compete with the Northwest Company's franchise to trade with the Plains Indians. The *Swan River Museum,* a mile north of town on the banks of the Swan River, depicts the history of that era through its collection of old photographs and Plains Indian artifacts.

At the end of July, the town sponsors the Northwest Roundup, when farmers exhibit beef cattle, cowboys rope steer, and everybody eats pancake breakfasts at sidewalk buffets.

From Swan River, the road runs through miles of evergreen forests and skirts clear lakes, including the second largest in the province, Lake Winnipegosis. If you stop to fish, you may catch great northern pike; you may also hear black bear, moose, or deer rustling the leaves of the trees behind you.

On Route 10 north of Lake Winnipegosis you'll pass a stretch of floating muskeg (partially decayed vegetable matter) known as "the bog." It's 143 miles (229 km) from Swan River to The Pas.

THE PAS (pronounced "pah"): The Pas not only has the finest fishing and hunting but also some of the liveliest festivals in the country.

In mid-February the town puts on the 5-day *Trappers Festival,* when mushers from all over Canada and the US race teams of Canadian huskies and other breeds through a 105-mile course. (The fastest dogs win $3,500 for the musher.)

Townspeople compete in log-wrestling and log-felling events as well as in the less-rugged contests of moose and goose calling. There's even a muskrat-skinning contest.

For both spectators and participants, there are buffet dinners with continuous entertainment, beerfests, and pancake breakfasts. Lumberjacks, miners, fishermen, trappers, and all other Pas citizens get in the festival spirit by wearing beads and buckskin while hunting the mythical "ice worm" (visitors can buy the album *When the Iceworms Nest Again*) and by crowning one woman Miss Fur Queen of the North.

For a fur of your own, stop at *Roger's Furs,* 120 Main St. (204-687-7729). Also sold here are handmade mukluks (warm furry boots), Eskimo parkas, and coonskin hats.

In mid-August, the Opasquia Indians host the *Opasquia Indian Days Festival.* One of the most popular events is a race in which contestants carry heavy bags of flour and canoes on their backs. Visitors are welcome to compete or, if less energetic, to browse in the reservation shopping mall and buy beaded moccasins and jackets.

En Route from The Pas – Continue north on Route 10. The road skirts Clearwater Lake Provincial Park, known for its crystalline, blue, unpolluted water (bush pilots flying 1,500 feet above have reported spotting rocks lying 35 feet below the surface). The trout living in these waters are so healthy that experts use the lake water as an index by which to measure pollution in other waters. The shores of the lake are home to ducks and geese; moose and other big game roam in the nearby woods.

FLIN FLON: In 1915, gold miners here found an old, tattered novel about Josiah Flintabbatey Flonatin, the discoverer of a city of gold. They named this town after him, soon shortening it to Flin Flon. A statue of Flonatin, designed by cartoonist Al Capp, welcomes visitors. Although little gold is found here now, the industry of the town is dominated by the Flin Flon mine, where visitors can visit the surface operations of the nonferrous metal mines.

Flin Flon is now much more than a mining community. Lumbering has become the other major industry; in the vicinity, the sounds of lumberjacks sawing large evergreens can be heard. And Flin Flon is also a great place for fishing (the town claims to be the "fishing capital of Manitoba"). The first weekend of July, the town hosts the *Flin Flon Trout Festival,* with cash prizes for the biggest lake trout and northern pike. A festival queen presides over the event, which includes pancake breakfasts and a canoe race.

En Route from Flin Flon – Return south on Highway 10 to the junction with Route 391 and follow the road as it enters Grass River Provincial Park. Here you will be awed by the truly untouched wilderness: The terrain is composed of layers of limestone bedrock, Precambrian granite, and permafrost, and is covered with somewhat stunted, dense evergreen forests. You may even see caribou darting about with their young. The park is open from mid-May to the end of September.

CHURCHILL: This subarctic seaport lies on the southwestern shore of Hudson Bay, a vast arm of the Atlantic Ocean extending deep into Canada's north. A town of 1,200 winter-hardened people, Churchill has no road connection to the south and can be reached only by rail, air, or, in summer, ocean-going ship. Along the bleak shore of the bay, trees grow to be little more than wind-worn stumps, yet a thriving world of wildlife, some that cannot be seen anywhere else in the world, dwells near — and even in — the town. In the long subarctic night, the Aurora Borealis, or northern lights, are vivid, illuminating the town with the brightness of street lamps. In spring, which comes in mid-June, arctic flowers create a riot of color.

Though Inuit or native peoples lived in the Churchill region as early as 1700 BC, European settlement began in the winter of 1619–1620 when the Danish seafarer Jens Munck wintered near the present townsite during his fruitless search for the Northwest Passage. Of the original crew of 65, only Munck and two sailors survived to return to Denmark. In 1717, the Hudson's Bay Company established a trading post at Churchill. Later in the 18th century, Fort Prince of Wales (now a national historical site that can be reached by tour boat) was built to defend British colonial fur trading interests.

Today, vast numbers of snow geese, Canada geese, sandhill cranes, and 200 other species of birds migrate through Churchill on their way to and from summer breeding grounds in the high arctic and along the shores of Hudson Bay. Four species of fur seals visit Churchill harbor, fishing for abundant char, grayling pike, and cisco. Beluga whales, now protected against commercial hunting, frolic in the Bay's waters near Churchill from June to early September. And polar bears, which migrate to the frozen ice of the Bay from surrounding land in the fall, often roam Churchill's streets from September to November, making it the only town in the world with an itinerant population of *Ursus maritimus.* At the peak of the bear migration, which occurs around Halloween, the beasts, drawn by smells of food and garbage, are kept under control by Royal Canadian Mounted Police patrols and environment officials armed with tranquilizer dart guns. Tundra buggies, huge vehicles with immense tires and tracks, provide tours to the polar bears' haunts. Souvenirs, including 8-foot-long narwahl tusks, eskimo-carved tombstones, and moosehair earrings, can be bought at the *Arctic Trading Company,* Kelsey Blvd. and Bernier St. (phone: 800-665-0431).

To get to Churchill by air, take Canadian Airlines International from Winnipeg (phone: 204-632-1250), The Pas (phone: 204-624-5219), or Thompson (phone: 800-592-7303). Three days a week, a 2-night, 1-day train journey begins in Winnipeg. Accommodations range from coach to bedrooms and a dining car offers spirits and sustenance. Contact *VIA Rail,* 123 Main St., Winnipeg R3C 2P8 (phone: 204-949-7477). Organized tours are operated by the *Great Canadian Travel Company,* 245 Bell Ave., Winnipeg R3L 0J2 (phone: 204-284-1580).

BEST EN ROUTE

Lodging for doubles ranges from expensive ($25 to $40) hotels and inns with restaurants and cocktail lounges to the more moderately priced ($15 to $25) bungalows and hunting/fishing lodges. Camping in provincial or federal campsites averages about $5 per night and is on a first-come, first-served basis. If you want a truly rustic experience, grab your sleeping bag and camp out under the stars near Audy Lake, home of the bison. It's free, and it might be the most memorable night of your trip. All prices are quoted in US dollars.

RIDING MOUNTAIN NATIONAL PARK

Thunderbird Bungalows – These 22 log cabins surround a spacious lawn and are separated from one another by thick clumps of pine trees. Although within walking distance of Clear Lake, the complex has a heated outdoor swimming pool. Open May to October (phone: 204-848-2521). Expensive.

Elkhorn Resort – An ideal spot for those who want to combine ranch living with all the accoutrements of a resort. Besides horseback riding, hayrides, and horseshoe pits, this ranch, with 60 rooms in the lodge and 16 chalets, has a dining room, cocktail lounge, indoor pool, and sauna. Open year-round. Near Clear Lake and *Clear Lake Golf Course* (phone: 204-848-2802). Expensive.

Wasagaming Campground – Not far from the bustling resort community of Wasagaming is this federal government campground with space for 379 tents and 158 trailers. The facilities include barbecue pits, wood stoves, a playground, store, laundromat, and boat and motor rentals. Open May to mid-September. Near Clear Lake (phone: 204-848-2811). Inexpensive.

Frelo Farm – Just a half-mile away from Riding Mountain National Park is the 624-acre farm of Fred and Lore Roeper, from northern Germany, who welcome guests to their handsome European-style house for a country holiday. Although Mrs. Roeper serves plenty of delicious German food, she also turns out wonderful French dishes and sometimes a Ukrainian feast. Guests keep busy at the national park, at a nearby beach, or by fishing and hiking in the area. Box 142, Angusville (phone: 204-773-2956).

Aspen Ridge – Another farm close to Riding Mountain National Park, this one is very popular with cross-country skiers. The attraction is not only in the farm's 320 rolling acres but also because accommodations are in a lovely log home complete with beamed ceilings, a huge stone fireplace, and puffy down comforters on every bed. Lake Audy (phone: 204-848-2965). Moderate.

DUCK MOUNTAIN PROVINCIAL PARK

Blue Lakes Campground – Thick forests of pine and spruce shelter and create privacy for the 89 tent sites. At night, the dark, dense forests, unlit by electricity or trailer lights, make the provincial campgrounds pitch black. The grounds have a boat ramp and store. Open May to October. Near Blue Lake. Inexpensive.

THE PAS

Wescana Inn – The newest hotel in town has 80 deluxe units and a sauna, but no pool. 425 Fischer Ave. (phone: 204-623-5446). Expensive.

CLEARWATER LAKE PROVINCIAL PARK

New Vickery Lodge – With modest accommodations for serious fishers, the lodge has a guide service, canoes, boats, and a fly-out fishing service. Write to PO Box

2670, The Pas, Manitoba R9A 1K8 (phone: 204-624-5439). Open May to October. Rates on request.

Carpenter's Clearwater Lodge – This simple lodge caters to hunters and fishers who get their licenses here. Write to PO Box 695, The Pas, Manitoba R9A 1K7 (phone: 204-624-5467). Open year-round; weekly rates available. Moderate.

FLIN FLON

Kelsey Trail – This modern, 76-unit motel, near a park in which stands the statue of Josiah Flintabbatey Flonatin, has an indoor swimming pool, sauna, dining room, cocktail lounge, and airport limousine service. Off Rte. 10 (phone: 204-687-7555). Expensive.

CHURCHILL

Seaport – A full-service facility with 21 rooms, licensed dining room, and satellite TV. Can be noisy. Munck St. and Kelsey Blvd. (phone: 204-675-8807). Expensive to moderate.

Tundra Inn – Comfortable accommodations with full bath, satellite TV, radio, and a dining room. 34 Franklin St. (phone: 800-661-1460).

New Brunswick

Tucked under the Gaspé Peninsula and sharing a long western border with Maine is New Brunswick. Its maritime status is firmly established by its extensive seacoast on the Gulf of St. Lawrence and reiterated in the Bay of Fundy, where 50-foot tides crash against the southeastern shore. This land of forested hills is crossed by rivers, which enrich the earth and encourage agriculture. Potato farming is the major industry after lumbering and mineral production.

Conservation is vital to a province so dependent for survival on its natural resources, and a strict program has been enacted to protect the forests from depletion. The province's real natural wonder, the Fundy tide, is in no danger of depletion. Tides in the Bay of Fundy are the highest in the world and are the primal force behind the province's main water-linked phenomena — the reversing falls at Saint John and Hopewell Rocks, a striking formation carved by water out of indigenous limestone.

This land of woods and water was settled by French-speaking Acadians in the early 18th century. The French built forts to protect these settlers, but when the British captured the forts in 1755, the Acadians were expelled. Some returned 30 years later and were given land. In fact, over 35% of the current population of 710,600 is French-speaking. The other early settlers were New Englanders, British immigrants, and Loyalists who came from the US during and after the American Revolution.

Much of New Brunswick is rural, but its major urban areas are Moncton (pop. 103,084 in the metropolitan area), a distribution center; Saint John (pop. 121,265), a manufacturing center; and Fredericton (pop. 65,2768), the provincial capital and gathering place of artists and craftspeople who produce and sell wares.

New Brunswick is a paradise for hikers and bird-watchers. The *New Brunswick Travel Guide* details hundreds of miles of hiking trails, trail lengths, and things to see along the way. (The guide is available from Tourism New Brunswick, PO Box 12345, Fredericton NB E3B 5C3; phone: 800-561-0213). Some 250 species of birds are to be found in the province.

The Acadian Trail follows the eastern coast through fishing, farming, and lumbering villages. In the summer you can start this trip out with a bang at the mid-July *Shediac Lobster Festival,* which celebrates the homely crustacean. The Fundy Coast links the cities along the southern coast of New Brunswick, where the Loyalist heritage is still devoutly maintained. At Saint John, Canada's oldest incorporated city, you can watch the river run upstream, forced by the strength of the Fundy tide. The St. John River route includes Fredericton, Grand Lake (the province's largest freshwater lake), and the beautiful rolling hills of the region's low-tide farming area.

Information: Tourism New Brunswick, PO Box 12345, Fredericton, NB

E3B 5C3 (phone: 506-453-2377; in the US or Canada; 800-561-0123, outside of New Brunswick). Any New Brunswick tourist information center can make reservations for your stay in the province during the high season, from June 1 to mid-September. Many places close from mid-September through May, and the phones may be disconnected during that time.

The Acadian Trail

Acadia, the name France gave its holdings on the Atlantic seaboard in the 17th century, suffered bitterly a hundred years later at the hands of the British.

Acadian residents of Nova Scotia and southern New Brunswick who refused to pledge allegiance to the British Crown fled to northeast New Brunswick in 1755, when British soldiers burned settlements under orders from colonial Governor William Shirley in Massachusetts. The Expulsion routed thousands of French settlers, making Nova Scotia and New Brunswick "safe" for the British Loyalists. This saga is immortalized in Henry Wadsworth Longfellow's *Evangeline, A Tale of Acadia*. The tenacious French slowly drifted back to their northeast corner, establishing settlements in the forest, out of sight of marauding British soldiers. Without help from the Micmac Indians, many Acadians could not have survived the harsh winters. The people on the eastern coast of New Brunswick still rely largely on fishing, farming, lumbering, and mining, despite the growth of new industry nearby.

The climate of eastern New Brunswick is tempered by the Gulf Stream, a stark contrast to the Bay of Fundy. Long sandbars at several points along the coast create some of the best and warmest beaches north of Virginia.

The 270-mile (435-km) drive starts at Shediac, host of an annual lobster festival, and follows Route 11 to Bathurst on the northern coast. Cocagne, a tiny village on the other side of the Caissie Cape, comes alive in summer, when hydroplanes speed down the Cocagne River estuary at 200 miles per hour in an annual regatta.

Two small communities, Rexton and Richibucto, were once the home of a flourishing shipbuilding company. At Big Cove Indian Reserve, 5 miles (8 km) inland, some of the remaining Micmac Indians still make canoes. Nearby Kouchibouguac National Park, one of the richest ecosystems in the world, has been set aside to preserve a coastal timberland that harbors moose, black bear, and a variety of waterfowl. The park features a 16-mile-long beach.

The people of Chatham and Newcastle are proud of their British past, especially of Lord Beaverbrook, the British newspaper magnate who grew up in the area. Chatham and Newcastle sit on opposite sides of the Miramichi River, famous for its Atlantic salmon and trout. If you take the 80-mile canoe trip down the Miramichi, you will not be welcomed by riverside fishermen; a canoe can scare off salmon for hours.

Along the northeastern coast of New Brunswick is some of the best deep-sea fishing in the province. A world-record bluefin tuna, 1,200 pounds, was caught off Miscou Island in Chaleur Bay in 1976.

The Acadian Trail ends at Bathurst, a wood pulp and paper industry center on Chaleur Bay. Route 11 continues to the Quebec border at Matapedia.

SHEDIAC: One of the province's most hospitable communities, this town of 4,370 claims to be the "lobster capital of the world," hosting a 6-day *Lobster Festival* annually in mid-July. A lobster-eating contest, bicycle and 10-km foot races, entertainment, and a big parade, with the requisite fireworks, are all part of the festivities. (For details, see *Festivals, Fairs, and Fancy Acts,* DIVERSIONS.)

Nearby is Parlee Beach Provincial PARK, with a 142-site tent and trailer campground, close to the province's largest beach. If you've tested the icy waters of the Bay of Fundy on the south shore, these waters will seem ideal. The long sandbars and shallow water make it perfect for children.

Shediac also has some of the best seafood spots in the province. *Fisherman's Paradise,* on Main St., is exceptional both in food and service. The unforgettable lobster rolls make a complete dinner; eat in one of the three lavish dining rooms, or take your food out. The chowder is considered the best in the region, portions are gigantic, and prices moderate. (phone: 506-532-6811). *Chez Françoise,* (93 Main St.) is another excellent seafood restaurant, located in an old mansion, now an inn.

COCAGNE: This picturesque fishing village is 13 miles (21 km) north of Shediac on Route 11. Cocagne (pronounced ko-*kann*) was settled in 1767 by Acadians expelled from Nova Scotia by the British. Even today most residents speak French as well as English.

The International Hydroplane Regatta is held here in early August in the wide Cocagne River estuary. The regatta annually draws entries from all over the US and Canada and over 40,000 spectators.

From Cocagne, drive north on Route 530 to Caissie Cape, where there are several lighthouses and a good beach, less crowded than Parlee in Shediac.

About 11 miles (18 km) north of Cocagne on Route 11 is Bouctouche.

BUCTOUCHE: It's pronounced *book TUSH.* If you haven't sampled oysters yet, try some in "the oyster bed of New Brunswick," as this small fishing village and busy port is known. Some of the best are at the *Bouctouche Bay Inn.* (See *Best En Route*).

There are several good beaches on the coastline north of Bouctouche. Also nearby is the Bouctouche Indian Reserve, with a small handicrafts shop, open by appointment. Route 11 goes directly to Rexton; Route 134, however, is the prettier drive, winding close to the coast and through small communities along the way.

REXTON: This pretty coastal village was settled by a group of Scots early in the 19th century. Among the earliest residents were the Jardine brothers — Robert and John — from Dumfriesshire, Scotland, who established one of the first shipbuilding companies in the town and built Kent County's first squarerigger in 1820. Rexton's relationship to the sea has never faltered. John Jardine, incidentally, returned to Great Britain in 1844 to settle in Liverpool, where his son David became chairman of the Cunard Line some years later. A small museum, open daily in summer in the town hall of nearby Richibucto, traces the history of wooden shipbuilding in the area. Rexton is also the birthplace of Andrew Bonar-Law, who became Prime Minister of Britain in 1922. His home is now a museum. *L'Habitant,* in Richibucto, is one of the best places to eat between Shediac and Bathurst. The cooking is plain but reliable, and fish is the best bet.

KOUCHIBOUGUAC NATIONAL PARK: New Brunswick's "other national park" offers a mixture of forest, open fields, and beach. An offshore sand bar, the primary swimming area, runs the entire length of the shoreline. With sand dunes dotted with tufts of sea grass, the area resembles Cape Cod, but without the crowds and commercialization.

Three rivers flow through the park into the Kouchibouguac Bay, forming tidal estuaries and quiet lagoons on the coast.

The park is a flat coastal plain with no stunning vistas, except along the shore at low tide, but the spruce, pine, and birch forests have a varied wildlife population. On the hiking and nature trails, watch for black bear, moose, and deer. Some of the smaller streams have beaver dams. And if you run short of provisions during your stay, try your hand at clam digging. The Northumberland Strait is free of the poisonous red tides that occasionally plague the Bay of Fundy. If you prefer to have your dinner caught for you, try the lobster suppers at *Bon Accueil,* a restaurant in the park. Open June through September, noon to 10 PM daily.

Kouchibouguac has 218 sites for tents and trailers, and 4 wilderness campgrounds for backpackers and canoeists (free). Canoes, boats, sailboards, and bicycles can be rented; sailboarding lessons are also available. At 93 square miles, this park is slightly larger than Fundy National Park, and because it is off the heavily traveled route to Nova Scotia, it's not as crowded. Open May to October. For more information, write to the Superintendent, Kouchibouguac National Park, Kouchibouguac, NB E0A 2A0, or phone 506-876-2443.

En Route from Kouchibouguac – The trip to Chatham via Route 117 through the seaside Acadian villages — Point Sapin; Escuminac, where there is a monument to lost fishermen; and Baie Ste. Anne — home of world champion boxer Yvon Durelle, who still lives there — is twice as long as the more direct Route 11, but more enjoyable. The coastal road has lighthouses, several good beaches, and, occasionally, home-cooked Acadian food; the 22-mile (35-km) drive on Route 11 passes through wilderness forest.

CHATHAM: This area provided timber for Joseph Cunard's shipbuilding industry in the early 19th century, before the invention of the steamship led to the demise of wooden ships in the late 1800s. There are relics of the Cunard empire in the *Miramichi Natural History Museum* on Wellington Street.

The Miramichi River, runs into the Miramichi Bay at Chatham. Jacques Cartier landed here in 1534, when Micmac Indians ruled the area. Micmac means "river of the long tideway." Doaktown has a fascinating Atlantic salmon museum explaining the history of the Atlantic salmon and conservation policies necessary to protect the fish, a lovely historic inn (*Inn by the Pond,* see *Best En Route*), and outfitters to help plan your trip, whether you want to canoe, fish, or hunt. For a list of outfitters, write for the *Outfitters* brochure from Tourism New Brunswick, PO Box 12345, Fredericton, NB E3B 5C3.

Before you leave Chatham, see Middle Island, which, according to legend, was lifted from the forest (forming a lake there) and dropped into the river. Sure enough, just a mile away is a lake the exact size and shape of Middle Island. In 1847, Irish immigrants fleeing the potato famine were quarantined on Middle Island after an outbreak of cholera on their ship. The island became first a hospital and then a burial ground for most of the ship's passengers and crew. It is now a pleasant recreational park with a beach for swimming.

NEWCASTLE: Just up the river from Chatham on Route 8 is Newcastle, a wood pulp- and lumber-exporting center, with some lovely old homes that reflect its booming shipbuilding days under the Cunards. Max Aitken, who became Lord Beaverbrook, was a British newspaper magnate and New Brunswick's great benefactor. He was raised here in the Old Manse (225 Mary St.), the parsonage of his Presbyterian minister father. When Aitken was made a peer in 1917, he took his new name from the Beaver Brook stream north of Newcastle. He restored the Old Manse in 1950 as a library and donated it to the town, along with a copious collection of books. He also donated the town hall, theater, and town square, where his ashes rest.

En Route from Newcastle – Route 8 north intersects Route 11 at Ferry Road. Continue north on Route 11 on the shore of Miramichi Bay. At Bartibog Bridge, you can visit the MacDonald Farm Historical Park, a restoration of an early-19th-century farm. The sandstone farmhouse, built around 1820 by Alexander MacDonald, is decorated with period furnishings and houses a museum.

Burnt Church, 22 miles (35 km) north on a tiny side road off the main highway, is now an Indian reserve. It was the site of a French church burned in 1759 by British troops on their way to Quebec. Excellent sandy beaches are found all along the shore.

Continue north to Tracadie.

TRACADIE: Although the name sounds French, Tracadie is a Micmac Indian name meaning "a good place to camp." Many French settlers, divested of everything during the infamous Expulsion, moved back to this area in the 1780s. This corner of New Brunswick is almost entirely French-speaking, but communication is rarely a problem. Fish are plentiful. There are salmon in the Tracadie River and deep-sea fishing charters are available. Or if a charter is too ambitious, just go down to the beach and dig up some clams. If you come up empty-handed, try one of the local takeouts, which are often very good. A leper colony once existed here, and an odd museum recalls those days.

The small Val Comeau Provincial Park, 5 miles (8 km) south of Tracadie, has 55 campsites, a beach, and a picnic area.

From Tracadie, Route 11 wanders away from the coast to Pokemouche. Take Route 113 east to Shippegan.

SHIPPEGAN: The fishing industry in the northeast corner of New Brunswick employs many people, but there is another industry as well: Peat moss is harvested out of the earth and piled to dry in the sun to reduce its weight. The government is experimenting with a peat-burning electrical plant in the area. The Marine Centre, a tribute to the fishing industry, illustrates sea life in the Gulf of St. Lawrence and the Northumberland Straits. It features a replica of a lighthouse, a "touch tank" and displays of live fishes and seals (506-336-4771). On Lamèque Island, accessible by bridge from Shippegan, the village of Lamèque hosts the *International Baroque Music Festival* in early July and the *Peat Moss Festival* in late July.

MISCOU ISLAND: From Little Shippegan, on the northern tip of Lamèque Island, take the toll-free ferry to Miscou Island, where you'll find endless white sand beaches and a fish restaurant. Deep-sea fishing boats can be chartered in the quest for giant bluefin tuna, averaging 800 pounds. *Miscou Island Camping* has 56 campsites and a few cabins (phone: 506-344-8638).

Returning to Route 11 at Pokemouche, drive north 10 miles (16 km) to Caraquet.

CARAQUET: On Chaleur Bay, this small fishing community is rich with Acadian tradition. Caraquet, which was settled in 1757, is home to one of the largest commercial fleets in New Brunswick. You can buy reasonably priced fresh seafood at the wharf. Small wooden fishing boats bob in the water as their owners sit on the wharf preparing lobster traps. Just east of Caraquet is a wooden shipbuilding company, one of the last of its kind.

In mid-August Caraquet hosts the *Acadian Festival,* with a traditional Blessing of the Fleet (to protect the fishermen) conducted by Catholic priests. Residents will tell you of a fiery ghost ship often seen in Chaleur Bay on stormy nights. Sightings of the ship with sails ablaze have also been reported across the bay in Quebec. The town's small *Acadian Museum* will introduce you to the Acadian way of life.

The dining room of the *Paulin* hotel (143 Blvd. St. Pierre; phone: 506-727-9981) has some of the best scallops on the north coast (see *Best En Route*). By calling ahead, you can arrange to have an authentic Acadian meal, such as chicken *fricôt,* a thick, savory stew, or in season, a fresh-from-the-sea lobster feast.

ACADIAN VILLAGE: This 500-acre village was built in 1977 to commemorate the hardships endured by French settlers expelled by the British. Early Acadian homes, a working tavern, a school, and a blacksmith's ship were dismantled piece by piece from other parts of the province and reassembled here. Craftsmen demonstrate how to make cedar shingles, soap, and candles. All clothing worn by staff is produced on site.

Since there was little arable land in the Caraquet area, the tenacious French exiles created an ingenious alternative. They built a system of dikes to recover swampy marshland from the sea, a skill they brought from their homeland on the coast of Brittany. The site for the re-creation was chosen, in part, because it has a number of these 18th-century engineering marvels. Other features include a restaurant serving Acadian fare — such as *poutine rape,* grated potatoes wrapped around pork and then steamed or fried. The Acadian Village is open daily from 10 AM to 6 PM, early June to early September. Admission charge. In nearby Grand Anse, the unique *Pope's Museum* features portraits of all the popes, a replica of St. Peter, and nuns' and priests' habits. Open daily, 10 AM to 6 PM; admission charge.

BATHURST: Until the mid-1950s, Bathurst's economy was shackled to pulp and paper production. When zinc and copper deposits were discovered in 1953, Bathurst's faltering economy boomed. Because of this heavy industry, much of Bathurst is not particularly attractive, but there are several good beaches nearby on Nepisiguit Bay at Youghall, Caron Point, and Chaleur, and the city has lively discos and taverns. A free tour of the world's largest zinc mine can be arranged by calling 506-456-6671.

Five rivers tumble off the plateau into the Nepisiguit Bay.

Another of New Brunswick's top eating places is in Nigadoo, 9 miles (14 km) north on Route 134. *La Fine Grobe* is 1,000 feet off Route 134, by the Nigadao River Bridge, with a pretty view of the Nepisiguit Bay. The fine menu is mainly French with some Acadian dishes. The restaurant usually closes in September, and then the owners of *La Fine Grobe* begin their "real" work: Georges and Hilda Frachon are artists specializing in pottery, painting, and silk screening; fine examples of their work are on display in the restaurant. *La Fine Grobe* is relatively expensive because the table is yours for the evening. During the summer a more affordably priced luncheon menu is served on the terrace. Dining room hours: 6 PM to whenever. It is advisable to make reservations at least a day in advance (phone: 506-783-3138).

Route 11 goes to the Quebec border at Matapédia, 81 miles (130 km) to the west. Again, Route 134, following the coast, is more scenic. At Petit-Roc, northwest of Bathurst, the new *Mining and Mineral Museum* gives visitors "hands on" experience with geologic resources of the area (506-783-8714).

Continuing on Route 11 or 134, the Eel River bar is one of the longest natural sandbars in the world, with salt water on one side and fresh water on the other. A few miles away on Route 134 is Dalhousie, an attractive town known for processing wood products; its shoreline boasts interesting rock formations that attract rock hounds. The *Restigouche Regional Museum,* 437 George St., depicts the area's pioneering days, as well as the development of fishing and farming (506-684-4685). The *Chaleur Phantom* departs daily for tours of the beautiful Bay of Chaleur and there is a ferry from Dalhousie to Misquasha, Quebec. Chaleur Provincial Park and Inch Arran Municipal Park and are popular for swimming and camping.

Campbelltown, at the western end of the Bay of Chaleur, is an important outfitting and service center for sport fishermen. In the city's waterfront park, you can see a lighthouse and a 28-foot long model of an Atlantic salmon. The *Restigouche Gallery,* 39 Andrew St., is a national exhibition center for regional artists (506-753-5750). The last naval engagement of the Seven Years' War was fought offshore at Campbelltown in 1760. The city was founded 13 years later and named after Sir Archibald Campbell, the lieutenanat governor of the province.

Sugarloaf Provincial Park features camping, tennis, hiking, downhill skiing and Canada's only alpine slide. Visitors can ride up a chairlift and make the downhill run on sleds.

BEST EN ROUTE

Moncton has the best accommodations at the beginning of this route (see *The Fundy Coast* for a complete report on Moncton). You should note festivals and other special events before deciding whether reservations are necessary. For example, the International Hydroplane Regatta draws 40,000 spectators, but Cocagne is so tiny that residents take in guests during the festival. It's a good way to meet the Acadians. Contact the Festival Committee, Hôtel de Ville, Cocagne, NB E0A 1K0.

In French-speaking northeastern New Brunswick, most hotel and motel staff members are bilingual. They are good sources of information on restaurants, shops, and events. For two, expect to pay $40 for accommodations listed as expensive, $25 in the moderate category, and $15 in the inexpensive range. All prices are quoted in US dollars.

BOUCTOUCHE

Bouctouche Bay Inn – The main building here is over 100 years old, and some of the 18 rooms are furnished with antiques. The dining room serves lobster and shrimp in season. Rte. 11 (phone: 506-743-2726). Moderate.

DOAKTOWN

Inn by the Pond – Five beautifully restored rooms in a gracious old home with rustic grounds. Shared bath (phone: 506-365-7492). Moderate.

CHATHAM

Morada – A pleasant motel that features 28 rooms, and serves breakfast in its dining room daily. 64 King St. (phone: 506-773-4491). Moderate.

NEWCASTLE

Wharf Inn – This modern inn has 70 units including 16 executive units, indoor pool and saunas, and a dining room with live entertainment. 1 Jane St. (phone: 506-622-0302). Expensive to moderate.

Governor's Mansion – A historic country inn and motel (built in 1850), with 21 charmingly decorated rooms, it is across from Newcastle on the Miramichi River. (phone: 506-622-3036). Moderate.

CARAQUET

Auberge de Baie – Highlighted with oak and brass trim, this 53-room motel is *the* most convenient to the beach in Caraquet. Recent additions include a new lobby, restaurant, lounge, and conference room. The moderately priced restaurant specializes in seafood. 139 Blvd. St. Pierre W. (phone: 506-727-3485). Expensive.

Hotel Paulin – Built in 1890, it has a homey decor; however, the bath is down the hall. Nonetheless, its 12 old-fashioned rooms and fine service provide an unusual, pleasant atmosphere. The unpretentious dining room is noted for its fresh seafood, gigantic steaks, and daily house specials. The owner/chef will prepare special Acadian or lobster dishes for groups, with advance notice. 143 St. Pierre Blvd. W. (phone: 506-727-9981). Inexpensive.

BATHURST

Atlantic Host – Here are 105 attractive, modern rooms, an indoor pool, sauna, Jacuzzi, racquetball courts, game room, restaurant, lounge, and craft shop. Rte. 11 (phone: 506-548-3335). Expensive.

Fundy Line – Formerly a seminary, this hostelry features sandstone construction with beautiful woodwork and heavy beams. It offers 52 units and a splendid dining room with genuine down-home seafood dishes. 855 St. Anne St. (phone: 506-548-8805). Moderate.

The Fundy Coast

When open warfare broke out between Great Britain and the American colonies in April 1775, not all of George III's American subjects grabbed a musket to fight for independence. Some salvaged what they could of their estates and dashed across the border into New Brunswick. The Fundy Coast follows the path of those who fled the rebellious colonies. These were the Loyalists — or British Loyalists — who remained loyal to the Crown. Along the southern coast of New Brunswick, you will explore cities where this proud heritage is maintained.

This route runs beside the Bay of Fundy, whose 50-foot tides dash the coast with awesome power. At Hopewell Cape and at St. Martins, it has sculpted giant "flowerpots" out of sandstone. In fact, the tide plays such an important role in this area that upon request, the provincial tourism office will send you a timetable to help plan your vacation. A word of caution about swimming in the Bay of Fundy: High tides mix the water so that the temperature never gets much above 65F (16C). Swimming in New Brunswick is much better on the eastern coast, along the Northumberland Strait, where the water is shallow and warm (see *The Acadian Trail*).

The small communities along the coast developed a strong shipbuilding industry in the early 1800s. The famous *Marco Polo,* the fastest sailing ship of the mid-19th century, was built in Saint John. When wooden sailing ships became obsolete, deep-sea fishing became the main industry of smaller coastal centers.

Even though commercial fishing is the fourth largest industry in the province (behind forestry, mining, and agriculture), the Bay of Fundy still yields cod, halibut, flounder, herring, crab, scallops, lobster, and sardines in abundance. Deep-sea fishing enthusiasts can hire boats in St. Andrews. For a real taste of the sea, try the Fundy Isles, all of which are accessible by sea. Grand Manan and Deer Island from the mainland by ferry; and Campobello by ferry from Deer Island and by bridge from Lubec, Maine.

The Fundy Coast is also a farming and dairy region; a land of covered bridges; a place to catch speckled trout or landlocked Atlantic salmon; and it goes by Fundy National Park, for canoeing, backpacking, and 50 miles of hiking trails. The route begins at St. Stephen, on the US-Canada border, and winds for 210 miles (338 km) to Moncton near the Nova Scotia border. The route does not have four-lane highways, although the roads are excellent. Nor does it have a boisterous nightlife, though Saint John is fairly sophisticated. When you explore the Fundy Coast, you enter a region where life is not only touched by the dignity of the sea, but by a long and proud history.

ST. STEPHEN: Your introduction to colonial history begins immediately across the border. Residents of the two border communities — St. Stephen and Calais, Maine — ignored the War of 1812, which Canadian historians regard as an attempt by the US to annex Canada. The atmosphere was so doggedly nonviolent that gunpowder sent by the British to defend St. Stephen was loaned to Calais for their July Fourth festivities. You can visit a landmark named after the war's local peacekeeper, the Duncan McColl United Church. The friendship is renewed each August at the *International Festival*.

A popular British Loyalist settlement in the 1780s, it is now known for its chocolate, lumber, and canning industries. Arthur Ganong invented the chocolate bar here in 1910, and Ganong Brothers Ltd. is still turning out candy. Stop in at *Ganong's Chocolatier,* on Water Street, for some delicious bites. A chocolate festival is held here in early August.

The Crocker Hill Herb Garden, on the St. Croix River, is a pleasant stop for a cup of herbal tea.

British Loyalist memorabilia are on display at the *Charlotte County Historical Society Museum* in the James Muerchie Building, open daily from June to September.

Those who can't wait to sink their hooks into some of the famous landlocked salmon in the Chiputneticook Lakes region to the north of St. Stephen should plan ahead with outfitters in that area (for the booklet *Accommodations,* see *Best en Route*).

En Route from St. Stephen – Oak Bay Provincial Park is only 8 miles (13 km) from the US-Canada border. Oak Bay has 112 campsites, with services for trailers. It also has an excellent saltwater beach on the bay.

Take Route 127 south for 10 miles (16 km) to St. Andrews. Along the way, stop for the exceptional view of Dochet's Island, where in the winter of 1604, Champlain lost half his temporary settlement to scurvy.

ST. ANDREWS: At the close of the Revolutionary War in 1783, British Loyalists in Castine, Maine, were horrified to learn that the US-Canada border had been moved to the other side of the St. Croix River. Almost the entire community moved across the Bay of Fundy to the havens of British protection. Those who could afford it moved their homes — lock, stock, and barrel — along with their possessions, and some are still standing in the center of town. Fourteen of the 280 buildings in St. Andrews erected before 1880 date back to the 1700s.

The local Canadian Club organizes walking tours of the historic homes every odd-numbered year, one afternoon in late July. The Historical Society arranges limited tours for conventions at the famous *Algonquin* hotel. Information on walking tours is available from the St. Andrews Civic Trust, PO Box 484, St. Andrews. Local boat cruises, whale watching, bird watching, and diving can be arranged through an environment-conscious operation, Osprey Travel and Promotion, 222 Water St. (phone: 506-529-8844).

Other historic sites within easy walking distance include: the Blockhouse, which is the last of 12 built to defend St. Andrews during the War of 1812, and the Greenock Church (1822) on Montague Street, with a pulpit built without using a single nail, copied from one in Greenock, Scotland. St. Andrews is a great place to tour by bicycle; several places offer rentals, including the *Algonquin* hotel (phone: 506-529-8823).

Since St. Andrews is an extremely popular resort area, reservations are advisable in midsummer at most hotels and restaurants. Four excellent seafood restaurants are the *Evening Star Dining Room* in the *Tara Manor* (Rte. 127), *Conley's Shore House* (Conley's Wharf), *Whale of a Café* (173 Water St.), and *The Gables* (143 Water St.). Just outside town is *The Rossmount Inn* (see *Best En Route*), noted for its Victorian decor and pleasant dining. It offers elegant rooms for bed and breakfast in historical surroundings. The town boasts some of the best shopping in New Brunswick. *Sea Captain's Loft* (211 Water St.) features handblown glass and woolens; *Cottage Craft* offers locally made and imported woolens; *St. Andrews Woolens Handweaving Ltd.* (22 Douglas St.) weaves 100% virgin wool blankets and sweaters in its own shop; *Tom Smith's Studio* (Water St.) has fine quality pottery; *The Canadian Trading Co.* (224

Water St.) offers a good selection of crafts; and the *Pansy Patch* sells unusual antiques and rare books.

The Sunbury Shores Arts and Nature Center, on Water Street, sponsors shore walks and gives presentations on marine ecology (506-529-3386).

If you enjoy antiques, don't miss the *Ross Memorial Museum,* a restored home at 188 Montague St., with one of the finest collections in eastern Canada (506-529-4270).

The *Huntsman Marine Laboratory Museum* is a 15-minute walk from town. The laboratory itself is a large oceanographic institute that is, unfortunately, closed to the public. Its aquarium, however, is open from May to September, and has tanks with sturgeon, salmon, sea cucumbers, and other local marine life. There is also an excellent film on the area's sealife and a playful group of seals in residence. The nonprofit research and educational institute charges a small admission fee to cover expenses.

The *Algonquin* hotel (see *Best En Route*) has two golf courses open to the public: a 9-hole woodland course and an 18-hole, par-71 course, with 13 fairways near Passamaquoddy Bay.

Five of New Brunswick's 76 covered bridges are near St. Andrews. Ask for directions before rejoining Route 1 toward St. George.

Letete, reached through St. George, is the jumping-off (or floating-off) point for the first major side trip from the Fundy Coast: a chain of beautiful islands nestled between the US and Canadian shores.

FUNDY ISLES: A trip to these little-known islands in the Bay of Fundy takes time and planning (which explains why they remain little known and unspoiled). Each is reached from a different point of embarkation: all from the Canadian coast, including Campobello, which is also accessible by the International Bridge in Lubec, Maine. During late summer, it's very common to see whales in this area. Most of the 350 Right Whales (also called Greenland Whales) are thought to migrate to the Bay of Fundy in August and September. Other varieties of whales here include the humpback and finback. This is also a popular bird-watching area.

Grand Manan – The largest of the Fundy Isles can be reached by ferry from Black's Harbour, 6 miles (10 km) south of St. George on Route 778. The reasonably priced MV *Grand Manan* ferry leaves Black's Harbour five times daily (three times on Sundays) from July through September; less frequently the rest of the year. Often dolphins will ride the bow waves in a watery escort.

Grand Manan is just the place if you want to see whales cavorting offshore and can appreciate the beauty of a delicate wildflower. Or pick up a copy of the *Hiking Guide to Grand Manan,* available in gift shops, and enjoy some of the island's 19 trails, many of which wind near spectacular seascapes.

The island's 2,000 residents live off the sea. Its fishermen take tons of herring, scallops, clams, and lobsters daily. A paved road runs the 15-mile length of the island. The village of North Head boasts the *Shorecrest Lodge,* run by two naturalists, and the *Compass Rose,* a smaller inn with highly regarded food (see *Best En Route*). Additional accommodations can be found at Grand Harbour and Seal Cove. Stop at the island's only beer and liquor store in Castalia, 5 miles (8 km) south of Grand Harbour, if you plan to provide your own entertainment.

Dark Harbour on the west coast is the "dulse capital of the world." Dulse is edible seaweed sold for its high iodine content in health food stores all over the continent. You can pick your own dulse and dry it on the beach — just ask a local resident how to do it. Dulse production is now the second most lucrative industry on the island. The dried product is an acquired taste, and while most New Brunswick residents swear by it, expect mixed reviews on your first bite. But certainly give it a try. The *Manan Island Inn and Spa,* in North Head (phone: 506-662-8624), uses dulse in its pricey health treatments.

People come from all over to photograph the tall, spiky wildflowers called lupens. Other wildflowers, strawberries, blueberries, and blackberries can be found in the meadows and near the picturesque lighthouses at either end of the island.

A free government ferry takes you from Ingall's Head Village to White Head Island. Residents claim that a 33-foot great white shark, the largest catch ever recorded, was landed just off White Head. Boats can also be chartered at Ingall's Head for trips to the Three Islands, home of the Bowdoin Scientific Station, a sanctuary for many of the 250 species of birds on Grand Manan. Boats can also be chartered for a 2-hour trip to Machias Seal Island, where you can see seals, puffins, and an occasional whale. Inquire at the *Shorecrest Lodge* about whale watching expeditions; sightings are practically guaranteed in the mating season.

Deer Island – From St. George, take Route 772 south to Letete, and hop on the free government-run ferry to Deer Island. There is a quiet campground on the island and the world's three largest lobster pounds. From July to *Labor Day,* a private ferry makes the journey to Campobello Island. From the ferry you can see the Old Sow, the second largest whirlpool in the world. *West Isles World* offers rooms, cottages, and whale watching cruises (phone: 506-747-2946).

Campobello Island – You can get to Campobello either by the ferry just mentioned or from US Route 1 at Lubec, Maine. The island features good hiking and walking trails, a lighthouse, and a great 9-hole golf course.

Like most other Fundy Coast history, the island was originally settled by the French and later by British Loyalists from New England. Campobello was given to Captain William Owen in 1767 in exchange for an arm he lost in battle. Benedict Arnold and his wife lived at Snug Cove for a while, but the island draws its fame from an American president who spent many summers here, Franklin Delano Roosevelt. The Roosevelt-Campobello International Park on the southern end of the island encompasses the former 11-acre Roosevelt estate. Many of Roosevelt's artifacts are on display, including the leather chair he used for Washington cabinet meetings, and a childhood letter to Santa Claus. Open year-round; guided tours are available from May to October. *Sunrise at Campobello* was filmed here, and Greer Garson, its star, stayed in the *Owen House,* an ancient inn. Her bedroom can be rented (phone: 506-752-2977).

When you return to the continent from Grand Manan or Deer Island, rejoin Route 1 toward Saint John.

NEW RIVER BEACH: If you cross the border too early in the day to stop at Oak Bay, perhaps this 835-acre provincial park will sound attractive. From New River Beach, facing the Bay of Fundy, there are spectacular ocean views, and the park has 115 campsites, as well as services for trailers.

Lepreau Falls is 3 miles (5 km) beyond New River Beach on Route 1. The falls is 80 feet high, but can be significantly shorter at high tide. It is not one of the seven wonders of New Brunswick, but it is a good place to stop and relax for a few minutes. Another peaceful spot is Dipper Harbour, just off Rte. 1 toward Saint John, where you'll find *Fundy Haven,* an excellent little restaurant.

As you approach Saint John from the west, note that Route 1 merges with Route 7 and becomes the Saint John Throughway. By the way, Saint in the name of the *city* is always spelled out; Saint in the name of the *river* is not. The most serious offense, however, is adding "'s" to "John." St. John's is the capital of Newfoundland.

SAINT JOHN: This is New Brunswick's largest city (pop. 113,000), and one of its most historic. Its harbor is open year-round, so a bulk of the activity in its commercial port comes after the St. Lawrence Seaway freezes in winter. It has been a shipping center since British Loyalists built a shipbuilding center here in the early 19th century. Although similar maritime cities failed with the obsolescence of wooden sailing ships, Saint John thrived. At the Saint John Drydock you will see tankers under construction. A special observation booth overlooks the work area. The drydock is the largest facility of its kind in North America. The Irving Oil refineries are also located here. A good way to see New Brunswick's oldest city is to obtain a brochure at the tourist information center detailing walking tours of the area's many historic buildings.

Relics of the shipbuilding era can be seen at the *New Brunswick Museum* (277 Douglas Ave.). In the 1880s, detailed models were built before the actual construction of the ship. These replicas are displayed in a special exhibition at the museum. Don't miss the miniature of the 1,625-ton *Marco Polo,* the fastest sailing ship of its time. In August, the city's *Festival by the Sea* draws more than 1,000 song-and-dance performers from all over Canada.

For lunch, head toward the recently restored Market Square Complex. Inside you'll find *Grannan's,* as well as a series of international snack bars with quick, tasty, and inexpensive fare. *Café Creole,* on King Square, serves authentic New Orleans-style food (phone: 506-633-8091). *Incredible Edibles,* on Princess Street, a short walk from Market Square, features good pasta, salads, and seafood (phone: 506-633-7554).

Saint John is the heart of Loyalist country. Thousands arrived in this port in 1783 after the US was officially recognized by the Treaty of Paris. Most of the Loyalist sites are within easy walking distance of King's Square on the west side of the harbor: the Loyalist House (1810), the Old Country Courthouse (1828), the Old Loyalist Burying Ground (1783), and the *Barbour's General Store,* with staff in period costumes. The original landing place, Market Slip, is now a colorful restoration with sidewalk cafés, harborfront walk, a maze of interesting shops, and the Hilton chain's smallest hotel, the *Saint John.* The film *Children of a Lesser God* was shot in Saint John and Rothesay, a charming suburban town. The city celebrates *Loyalist Day* in July.

The Old City Market (enter from either Charlotte or Germain Street — it's a whole block long) has been in operation since 1876. Vegetables, meats, fresh lobster, and fish, as well as local handicrafts, are sold here, giving the market the air of an old trading post.

There is the obligatory trip to see the "reversing falls" on the St. John River at Reversing Falls Bridge. Twice a day, the 50-foot Fundy tide comes rushing up the river, reversing its flow at its 15-foot rapids. Cherrybrook Zoo, in a wooded locale, features indigenous and exotic animals. A short drive east on Route 111 leads to unspoiled St. Martins, with its dramatic seacoast, covered bridges, and the *Quaco Inn* (see *Best En Route*).

Direct ferry service to Nova Scotia from Saint John begins at the foot of Lancaster Street. The trip takes almost 3 hours. The *Princess of Acadia* plies the bay three times daily in summer, twice on Sundays.

En Route from Saint John – The most direct road to complete the Fundy Coast is Route 1 toward Sussex. However, a short drive through the farming district of the Kingston Peninsula and the Kennebecasis River valley is recommended. You will see many of New Brunswick's remaining covered bridges as well as some of the best countryside the province has to offer. A complete list of covered bridges can be obtained from Tourism New Brunswick.

Take Route 100 through Rothesay to Gondola Point and cross the Kennebecasis River by ferry (free, year-round, 24 hours) to Reeds Point. Follow Route 850 north to Route 124 east and rejoin Route 1 at Norton. Continue along Route 1 for 12 miles (19 km) to Sussex, through the heart of the dairy district. Try a stay at *Anderson's Holiday Farm Bed and Breakfast,* (phone: 506-433-3786) to experience dairy life. If you don't have time for that, try the tasty ice cream cones from the *Sussex Dairy.* Or for a delicious snack, try the *Broadway Café* directly across from the train station in the middle of town. From Sussex, pick up the Trans-Canada Highway (Route 2) toward Moncton. Drive 10 miles (16 km) to Route 114, also known as the Fundy Tidal Trail, and take the road south to Fundy National Park.

FUNDY NATIONAL PARK: Most of this 80-square-mile park sits on a plateau 1,000 feet above sea level. Its thick forests are laced with 50 miles of hiking trails used by the resident moose, black bear, fox, deer, bobcat, and beaver as well as by two-footed visitors. Its interior streams are excellent for trout and salmon fishing. Guides are available for the nature trails, but you can explore for yourself with relative ease.

The entrance from the northwest on Route 114 is through dense forests, but 2½ miles (4 km) before Alma, a small city at the southeastern corner and home of park headquarters, stop at Hastings Hill for the view, for the road opens suddenly for a vista of the Chignecto Bay. Campers can stock up on supplies at Alma (lobster is plentiful), and you can get a good meal at the *Fundy Park Chalets and Coffee Shop*. For a snack, try the sticky buns at the aptly named *Sticky Bun Shop* in Alma.

A heated, saltwater swimming pool is close to the chalet for those who have tried the icy waters of the Bay of Fundy. Visit the beach, however, even if you don't plan to swim. The coastline is dotted with caves cut into the side of the 200-foot cliffs by the pounding surf. This exploration can be dangerous: Park officials warn that should you lose track of the time, the tide will rise faster than you can climb to safety. Check at park headquarters for a timetable.

A 9-hole golf course, tennis courts, and a lawn-bowling green are available for use through the provincial government. For more information write to the Superintendent, Fundy National Park, Alma, NB, or call 506-887-2000.

En Route from Fundy National Park – Follow Route 114 east from Alma to Hopewell Cape, where the mighty tides have created sculptures from sandstone known locally as the "flower pots." You can take Route 915, which follows the coast and offers great bird watching. From Hopewell Cape, proceed north on Route 114 for 50 miles (81 km) to Moncton, "the hub of the Maritimes." At Hillsborough, you can board a train on the Salem and Hillsborough line for an hour-long dinner excursion through picturesque marshlands (phone: 506-734-3195).

MONCTON: The second largest city in New Brunswick, Moncton is an important distribution center for the other Maritime Provinces. Rail connections to Montreal, Nova Scotia, Prince Edward Island, and the Northumberland coast pass through the city. It has been an important rail center since its designation as maritime headquarters for the Intercolonial Railway in 1872.

The Free Meeting House (Steadman St. and Mountain Rd.) was built in 1821 as an interdenominational place of worship until churches could be built. *Moncton Civic Museum,* just across the street, has displays on the city's history as a rail center. From the museum, walk down King Street toward the Petitcodiac River to Boreview Park. The action of the Fundy tide creates a phenomenon similar to the reversing falls in Saint John: Twice daily a wave — known as the Tidal Bore — rushes upstream as the tide rises in the Bay of Fundy 25 miles (40 km) away. But for all this activity, the wave is usually only one foot high. At Magnetic Hill, cars seem to be pulled uphill. For the most part, though, Moncton's manmade attractions prevail — its plenitude of large shopping malls, and a huge water theme park, Magic Mountain, which has boats, wave pools, and slides.

For a taste of the sea, try *Cy's Seafood* restaurant (170 Main St.; phone: 506-382-0032; closed Sundays), where meals are consistently good. For sophisticated, but expensive, dining *à la française,* splurge at *Chez Jean Pierre,* 21 Toombes St. (phone: 506-382-0332).

BEST EN ROUTE

Most of the accommodations listed here are older establishments, with a friendly staff and homey atmosphere. In heavily traveled areas, we also note some standard accommodations where you have a better chance of getting a room without reservations. In the popular resort areas, you must have a reservation for July and August — with the exception of the *Algonquin* in St. Andrews, where reservations are advisable during the entire summer season. Unless otherwise noted, hotels are open year-round.

The price range is based on double occupancy and follows these general guidelines: expensive, $30 and up; moderate, $15 to $30; inexpensive, below $15. All prices are quoted in US dollars.

The government publication *New Brunswick Accommodations and Campground Guide* lists hundreds of smaller hotels, cabins, guesthouses, and bed-and-breakfast establishments. These generally have between 5 and 15 rooms with fewer but less expensive facilities. For a copy of the *Accommodations Guide,* write to Tourism New Brunswick, PO Box 12345, Fredericton NB E3B 5C3.

ST. STEPHEN

Wandlyn Motor Inn – This hostelry has 50 modern rooms and a dining room specializing in seafood and steaks. 90 King St. (phone: 506-466-1814). Expensive.

ST. ANDREWS

Algonquin – One of the best hotels in the Canadian Pacific chain, it has 188 rooms, a restaurant, coffee shop, 2 lounges, and a clubhouse adjoining the 2 golf courses — one 9-hole and one 18-hole. Special facilities include free golf, tennis, and bicycles for touring the city. It is open from late May to early October. Reservations are a must during the entire summer season. 184 Adophus St. (phone: 506-529-8823). Expensive.

Pansy Patch – Bed and breakfast in this eye-catching house is an experience, with charming hosts, authentic decor. 56 Carleton St. (phone: 506-529-3834). Expensive.

Rossmount Inn – St. Andrews is as English as a town can be without crossing the Atlantic, and its heart could well be this Victorian gem. The decor is eclectic in exactly the fashion of a well-traveled Victorian gentleman's home: Persian rugs, French art, colorful English wallpaper in the parlor and 16 guestrooms. Dining, 6:30 to 9:30 PM. For information, simply write to the *Rossmount* in St. Andrews (phone: 506-529-3351). Expensive.

GRAND MANAN

Shorecrest Lodge – This old-fashioned country inn with 15 guestrooms, a lounge, and dining room, is run by two naturalists who give plenty of direction and information on exploring Grand Manan. North Head (phone: 506-662-3216). Expensive.

Compass Rose – A small, 9-room inn with a delightful ambience. North Head (phone: 506-662-8570). Moderate.

SAINT JOHN

Delta Brunswick – This modern motel is centrally located and has a pool, sauna, whirlpool bath, game room, lounge with live entertainment, bars, and a good, moderately priced dining room. 39 King St. (phone: 506-648-1981). Expensive.

Saint John Hilton – Here is a luxury hotel nicely situated in the renovated historic harborfront area — the best rooms overlook the bay. The *Turn-of-Tide* dining room is first class. Market Sq. (phone: 506-693-8484). Expensive.

ST. MARTINS

Quaco Inn – An old sea captain's home, lovingly restored. There are 6 guestrooms with great beds. The dining room serves excellent local foods for breakfast and dinner (phone: 506-833-4772). Moderate.

ROTHESAY

Shadow Lawn Inn – This fine, old atmospheric inn, built in 1871 and recently refurbished, has 8 guestrooms and a moderately priced restaurant which serves breakfast, and dinner by reservation. Rte. 100 (phone: 506-847-7539). Moderate to inexpensive.

SUSSEX

Maples – This motel has been expanded to include a new pool, lounge, restaurant, a log-constructed convention center, and 36 air conditioned rooms. 1019 Main St. (phone: 506-433-1558). Moderate.

FUNDY NATIONAL PARK

Fundy Park Chalets – The 29 housekeeping units are right in the park (phone: 506-887-2808). Moderate.

MONCTON

Beausejour – Reservations are a must at New Brunswick's finest hotel. The 316 rooms are decorated in early Acadian style; also featured are a lounge, 2 restaurants, and an outdoor pool. Special rates are available with vouchers from the Tourist Information Centers. The *Windjammer Room* specializes in steaks and seafood, and *L'Auberge* serves Acadian dishes. 750 Main St. (phone: 506-854-4344). Expensive.

Canadiana – In contrast to the *Beausejour,* the *Canadiana* offers the same gracious service at half the cost. This century-old house contains 20 rooms, a dining room, and cable television. 46 Archibald St. (phone: 506-382-1054). Moderate.

SACKVILLE

Marshlands Inn – Some 25 miles (40 km) southeast of Moncton, in the neck of land that connects New Brunswick and Nova Scotia, are the Tantramar marshes, the launching pad for thousands of Canada geese each year. On the edge of the marshes is the *Marshlands Inn.* Built in the late 1800s, it's the launching pad for people traveling between the two provinces or bird-watchers and naturalists haunting the marshes. The inn has 20 rooms in a lovely old home, and even if you can't stay overnight, come for a meal (breakfast: 7-10 AM; lunch: noon-2 PM; dinner: 6-9 PM). Treat your tastebuds to a fiddlehead (the top portion of the ostrich fern), a local delicacy cooked until it's fork-tender, then served with lemon juice and butter. Other taste treats are local mushrooms, and rhubarb punch. Write to: PO Box 1440, 73 Bridge St., NB E0A 3C0 (phone: 506-536-0170). Expensive.

Different Drummer – This bed-and-breakfast establishment has 8 rooms and loads of charm. 146 Main St. (phone: 506-536-1291). Moderate.

The St. John River

The St. John River once served as a major Indian waterway between the St. Lawrence River and the Bay of Fundy. This was the territory of the powerful Maliseet, the nomadic tribe that wandered throughout the northernmost Allegheny Mountains. Their swift canoes carried them all the way to Nova Scotia in the warm months. In fact, most of the canoes in use today are based upon the Maliseet design. There are six Indian reserves along the route.

This drive along the St. John River valley, from the busy commercial port of Saint John to the pulp and paper center at Edmundston, is 264 miles (425 km) long. It starts in the rolling hills and agricultural region of the Kingston Peninsula, passes New Brunswick's largest freshwater lake and the provincial capital of Fredericton.

The river turns north at Meductic toward Hartland — with the world's longest covered bridge — and continues through New Brunswick's potato growing district (where you can enjoy a farm vacation at Aroostook — see *Best En Route*) to Perth-Andover. A pleasant sidetrip to the undeveloped 43,000-acre Mt. Carleton Provincial Park returns to Route 2 at Grand Falls.

One of the two best Atlantic salmon and canoeing rivers in North America is the Restigouche — accessible from St. Leonard — which leads to Chaleur Bay on New Brunswick's northern border. Other spots for canoeing and fishing are pointed out along the way. Tourism New Brunswick can send you a free fishing guide (phone: 800-561-0123). Topographical maps of any section of the province are available at modest prices. The *Outfitters* brochure will help plan a fishing or canoeing expedition. It's available from Tourism New Brunswick, PO Box 12345, Fredericton E3B 5C3.

The drive starts in Saint John (described in detail in *The Fundy Coast*).

En Route from Saint John – There are two options at the beginning of this route, depending on how you entered Saint John. If you came from the east through the dairy district surrounding Sussex, take Route 7 directly to Fredericton to avoid repetition. From there, you can do some of the things listed in the area as side trips, such as camping and boating on Grand Lake. If you came from the west along the Fundy Coast, a trip through the Lower St. John River valley on the Kingston Peninsula is recommended. Many of the province's 133 covered bridges can be found on the peninsula. The rolling countryside has not yet been touched by industrialization.

KINGSTON PENINSULA: From Saint John, take Route 100 north for 12 miles (20 km) to Quispamsis. The road is well marked to Gondola Point, where you take the ferry (free, year-round, 24 hours) to Reeds Point. Take Route 850 north for 18 miles (29 km) to a second ferry across the Belleisle Bay (free, year-round, 24 hours). Route 124 west will take you to the ferry at Evandale.

Don't be afraid to ask residents for directions to the covered bridges or to the best place to stop for a leisurely picnic. This drive through the pastoral countryside of New Brunswick seems to make the hours fly by.

THE LOWER ST. JOHN RIVER: From Evandale take Route 102 north for 17½ miles (28 km) to Gagetown, home of the *Queens County Museum* and many crafts studios and antiques nooks, as well as the Loomcrofters, world-famous weavers whose workshop is in a blockhouse dating from the late 18th century. Also in Gagetown: Colpitt's Marina and old-fashioned general store; the old *Steamers Stop Inn,* on Front St. (phone: 448-2903), with seven uniquely decorated rooms and a good restaurant; and the *Loaves and Calico Tearoom,* which features tasty homemade treats.

Look for cattle grazing on the interval islands in the middle of the St. John River. If you pass at the right time of day, you can see the cattle being transported back and forth on wooden flatboats, as they have been for over 100 years. Apple orchards dot the meadowlands.

Route 102 skirts the southern bank of the river as it bends to the west toward Fredericton. At Oromocto, 24 miles (39 km) from Gagetown, the Canadian Forces

Base Gagetown (open to the public) has an army museum. There are some fine craft, gift, and antiques shops in the area.

Route 102 joins Route 7 into Fredericton.

GRAND LAKE: Lakeside Provincial Park at Jemseg has 132 campsites, services for trailers, and a beach. Grand Lake seems to have fallen into disfavor since the completion of Mactaquac Park on the west side of Fredericton. But so much the better: The facilities around Grand Lake — several bed-and-breakfast inns and farm vacation accommodations — are relatively uncrowded.

FREDERICTON: The French were the original settlers here until driven out by British troops in 1759. British Loyalists sailed up the St. John River in 1783 and promptly established a British city. Fredericton was the first major settlement in the "interior" and is still a prosperous city, with many small industries in addition to the major employers, the University of New Brunswick and Provincial Government offices. Officer's Square, part of the original British military compound, has been restored, complete with soldiers in red coats and an hourly changing of the guard, accompanied by a piper, in summer.

This "city of the stately elms" was designated the provincial capital in 1785 by Governor Thomas Carleton to the chagrin of Saint John. The Old Government House (1828) on Woodstock Road, until 1893 the official residence of provincial governors, was the headquarters of the district's Royal Canadian Mounted Police.

Other sites of note are centrally located on Queen Street. The Anglican Christ Church Cathedral (1853) is considered one of the best examples of Gothic architecture in North America. The cathedral's east stained glass window was donated by Trinity Church in New York City.

The Legislative Building's silver dome dominates the skyline. Its Assembly chamber has two giant Reynolds portraits of King George III and Queen Charlotte (the provincial capital was named after their second son, Frederick). A 1783 edition of the *Domesday Book* and a complete set of king-size Audubon bird books are displayed in the Legislative Library annexed to the rear of the main building.

You can't visit Fredericton without being aware of the city's admiration for Lord Beaverbrook (1879–1964). Born William Maxwell Aitken in Maple, Ontario, and raised in Newcastle, New Brunswick, Lord Beaverbrook became a self-made millionaire before the age of 30, making his fortune in the merger of Canada Cement from 13 smaller companies. Beaverbrook owned London's *Daily Express,* was a member of British Parliament from 1910 to 1916, and served in Winston Churchill's cabinet during World War II.

Lord Beaverbrook's legacy in Fredericton is in the buildings he left the town, including several on the University of New Brunswick campus such as the University Library; the Playhouse, home of *Theatre New Brunswick* (on Queen St.); and the *Beaverbrook Art Gallery* (also on Queen St.).

The *Beaverbrook Art Gallery* has works by Botticelli, Sir Joshua Reynolds, Thomas Gainsborough, Constable, Turner, and Hogarth. Its pride and joy is the 10-by-13½-foot *Santiago El Grande,* by Spanish surrealist Salvador Dali.

The Fredericton area has become a center for craftspeople working in materials of various kinds. You'll find batik, pewterware, stained glass, hooked rugs, handwoven clothing, sterling silver jewelry, enamelware (such as miniature paintings on copper buttons), wooden toys, candles, and fine pottery. A list of handicraft studios throughout the province is available from Tourism New Brunswick. In Fredericton, visit *Aitken's Pewter,* 81 Regent Promenade, for goblets and other classy items; *Joan Shaw,* Woodstock Rd., turns out lovely pottery and tea sets; *Shades of Light,* 228 Regent St., presents a smorgasbord of New Brunswick crafts; and *Regent Craft Gallery,* 72 Regent Promenade, also has some lovely pieces.

Just behind the art gallery is the "Green," a massive landscaped park between Queen

Street and the St. John River. *The Pioneer Princess,* a riverboat replica, docks here and offers daily cruises and dinner cruises.

A few of the best places to eat are nearby: *Eighty Eight Ferry* (88 Ferry St.; phone: 506-472-1988), although expensive, is worth it. Probably the city's best restaurant, it is set on the sunny porch of an old-fashioned farmhouse. It has lots of greenery, chintz, and genuine hospitality. In summer, cocktails are served on the lawn beside the garden and the brook. *The Barn,* a trendy spot at 540 Queen St. (phone: 506-455-2742), has good food at moderate prices; and *Mai's,* on Regent St., is a good, small Chinese restaurant. Fredericton's farmers' market on Saturday mornings (on George St. between Regent and St. John, 6 AM to noon) is a must for crafts, produce, and local color — especially for breakfast afterward. For this, visitors should make a beeline to *Goofy Roofy's.* This restaurant, which is part of the market complex, has become something of an institution for its informality and affordability, and is popular with the artistic and political crowds.

From Fredericton, the Trans-Canada Highway (Rte. 2) runs beside the St. John River almost to the Quebec border. Follow Route 2 west 15 miles (24 km) to Mactaquac Provincial Park.

MACTAQUAC PROVINCIAL PARK: This "super park" is one of the newest and largest of the provincial parks. Because of its wide range of facilities and close proximity to Fredericton, it is also crowded most of the summer. In the late 1960s, the New Brunswick Electric Power Commission built the hydroelectric dam from which the park takes its name. The dam's headwaters flooded the St. John River valley for 60 miles (97 km), all the way to Woodstock.

Boating, water skiing, swimming, and fishing are among the popular pastimes at this mammoth, 1,400-acre park. Pickerel, smallmouth bass, and trout are among the fish in the 34-square-mile headpond of the dam. Sailboat and powerboat marinas serve the lake, which has two long beaches.

There are guided nature trails, programs for children, playgrounds supervised by qualified counselors skilled in arts and crafts instruction, and 296 campsites with kitchen shelters, heated washrooms, and showers. The *Park Lodge* has both a bar and restaurant. The lodge also rents clubs for its championship 18-hole golf course, one of the best in the province. *Chickadee Lodge* (phone: 506-363-2759), nearby, offers a bed and a hearty country breakfast, a great view of Mactaquac Headpond, and a proprietor who acts as a hunting guide during hunting season.

En Route from Mactaquac – Continuing on the Trans-Canada Highway, the route intersects with Route 3 to the US border at St. Stephen. Route 3 also leads to Harvey Station. A farmer's market is nearby, and, in addition to fruits and vegetables in season, the market offers patchwork quilts, canned goods, and freshly baked bread. Kings Landing is only 10 miles (16 km) away.

KINGS LANDING: This is the last example of Loyalist tradition along the St. John River Route (3 mi/5 km west of the Route 3 intersection on the Trans-Canada Hwy.). Kings Landing Historical Settlement was constructed when the rising waters of Mactaquac Dam threatened to wash away several sites of historic value along the river. Over 50 buildings, including a school, church, carpenter's shop, and forge, were moved to higher ground. In historic shops, costumed staff of the settlement are busy making horseshoes, planing lumber, and practicing other early crafts. Children will enjoy an hour-long, behind-the-scenes tour, where they can don period costumes, see how buildings were constructed, and eat cookies made on the premises (phone: 506-363-3081).

The *Kings Head Inn* offers wholesome meals from 1800-vintage recipes. The settlement is open from June 1 to mid-October. A family-maximum rate is available. Just past the entrance to Kings Landing Historical Settlement is the *Old Road B & B* (phone: 506-363-2758), which has friendly hosts and first-rate food and lodging.

En Route from Kings Landing – Route 2 runs east along the south bank of the river for 29 miles (47 km) and turns north at Meductic. Just before Meductic, Route 122 leads to the Chiputneticook Lakes region, with landlocked salmon and trout. When you get to Canterbury on Route 122, ask outfitter Albert Conklin of *Skiff Lake Inn Sporting Camps* about canoeing on Eel River. Depending on the time of year, Eel River is the penultimate whitewater in New Brunswick.

MEDUCTIC: This is the site of a Maliseet Indian fort built for protection against the raiding Mohawks. Until recently, excavations were made of the ancient Maliseet burial grounds. Living Maliseets petitioned the Department of Indian Affairs to cease this digging and the excavations were brought to a halt. Indian crafts are available at some reserves along the way. There is an excellent German restaurant in the *John Gyles* motel on Rte. 2 (Trans-Canada Hwy., toward Woodstock).

WOODSTOCK: The streets of this quiet town on the St. John are lined with elms. Its primary activities are agricultural. Visit the restored Old Courthouse (1833) in Upper Woodstock, which doubles as the *Carleton County Historical Society Museum*. If you return to the US at the Woodstock-Houlton, Maine border, note that there are comprehensive duty-free shops here with English woolens, china, and crafts from Canada and all over. Open daily in summer, 24 hours a day.

En Route from Woodstock – Route 2 leads to Hartland, site of the world's longest covered bridge (1,282 ft.). Hartland is where many of the New Brunswick potatoes come from and is a popular resort for salmon and trout fishing. Route 2 crosses to the east bank of the St. John River above Hartland for 12 miles (19 km), returning to the west bank at Florenceville. The Tobique Indian Reserve, near Perth-Andover, is another good place to buy Indian handicrafts and is home to *York's* restaurant. Take Route 109 north to Plaster Rock, home of several outfitters for canoeing, hunting, and fishing on the Tobique River, and the gateway to New Brunswick's largest park.

Strange as it may seem, one of Canada's more famous restaurants is located in Perth-Andover on old Highway 2. *York's* draws people back again and again for its simple, hearty — indeed immense — fixed-price (moderate-price) meals. The waitress offers a choice of lobster, duck, crab, turkey, steak, clams, scallops, chicken, or pork chops, and with it you get five kinds of bread, soup, salad, and either strawberry shortcake or pie for dessert. Second helpings are free and are literally pushed at you — even the steak. Open May to October, there's no menu, no credit cards, no liquor, and no reservations, but it's a great treat. Just be sure to arrive with an empty stomach.

MT. CARLETON PROVINCIAL PARK: This new 43,000-acre park is reserved for wilderness campers. Be forewarned: There are no accommodations in this park, aside from its 88 campsites. There are, on the other hand, moose, deer, otters, muskrat, brook trout, and Atlantic salmon. Mt. Carleton is the highest peak (2,690 ft.) in New Brunswick. A canoe set down on one of the Nepisiguit Lakes will take you all the way to the Bathurst Power Dam by way of the Nepisiguit ("Angry River").

The drive into the park from Plaster Rock takes about an hour. There is a 30-mile (48-km) stretch of gravel road, but even here speeds of 50 to 60 miles per hour are safe except in the early spring. Interior roads are plentiful — although not marked on most maps — thanks to extensive logging in the area. The logging trucks also travel 50 miles per hour on the narrow road, so be careful.

To plan your trip through this wilderness, write Park Superintendent, Box 180, St. Jacques, NB E0L 1K0, or contact a local outfitter in Plaster Rock.

When you return to Plaster Rock, take Route 108 north to Grand Falls. En route, drive through scenic New Denmark, the largest settlement of Danish people in Canada. Spectacular scenery surrounds New Denmark. The *Valhalla* restaurant serves good Danish food (phone: 506-553-6614).

GRAND FALLS: The 75-foot Grand Falls are among Canada's highest cataracts. The best view is from the newly constructed walkway along the gorge, higher than Niagara's. Tours are available of the hydro-electric powerhouse.

En route from Grand Falls – Route 2 runs north from Grand Falls. Just in case you haven't had your fill of canoeing and fishing on this route, the best is last. The Restigouche River winds for almost 100 miles (161 km) to Chaleur Bay on the Quebec border. After the Miramichi River on the east coast, this is the best salmon river in the province.

Route 17 leads to Campbellton on Chaleur Bay. Edmundston is 25 miles (40 km) north on Route 2.

ST. LEONARD: This hamlet between Grand Falls and Edmundston is home to *Madawaska Weavers,* producers of fine hand-woven products, who boast that Princess Anne is a customer (phone: 506-423-6341). Hours: 9 AM to 5 PM.

EDMUNDSTON: The inhabitants of the northern part of the province are predominantly of French origin, since British soldiers drove them out of southern New Brunswick in 1784. Although logs are no longer floated to the pulp and paper mills, the St. John River is polluted for many miles below Edmundston (from mills on the US side, locals will tell you). If you visit in August, don't miss the *Foire Brayon Festival* — the largest Canadian French festival outside of Quebec.

The spires of the Roman Catholic Cathedral of the Immaculate Conception (145 Pine St.) can be seen from all over the city. Lac Baker and Les Jardins provincial parks are nearby. The *Laporte Art Museum* at the St. Louis Maillet College is excellent.

Whitewater canoeing on the St. John River above Edmundston is the best in the province. There is excellent skiing at Mont Farlagne, along with some good restaurants and motels. Worth special mention in the eating department is *La Tulipe Blanche* (9 Hill St.; phone: 506-739-9008), a modern little café with an unusual black and white decor. It has excellent food with regional specialties such as *ployes* (a buckwheat pancake) and *créton* (a chopped-pork paté). *Le Baron,* at 174 Victoria St. (phone: 506-735-3329), is a fine restaurant with a touch of haute cuisine.

BEST EN ROUTE

Except for Fredericton and Edmundston, there are no large cities on this route. Many small lodges and tourist homes can be found along the way. This route follows the Trans-Canada Highway, which means reservations are necessary during July and August. If you find the motels full, consult the *New Brunswick Travel Guide,* available from Tourism New Brunswick, PO Box 12345, Fredericton NB E3B 5C3 (phone: 800-561-0123). For hotels we list as expensive, expect to pay between $30 and $40; for moderate, $15 to $35; and for inexpensive, $15 or less. All prices are quoted in US dollars.

Accommodations in Saint John are listed in the *Best en Route* section at the end of *The Fundy Coast.* There are no accommodations in Mt. Carleton Provincial Park.

PRINCE WILLIAM

Chickadee Lodge – Fine bed-and-breakfast accommodations are found in this 5-room facility. There are 2 lounge areas with fireplaces and a dining area. It also boasts a spectacular view of Mactaquac Headpond. The proprietor acts as a guide during hunting season. Closed late November through April. Route 2 (phone: 506-363-2759). Inexpensive.

FREDERICTON

Wandlyn Motor Inn – This 115-room family motel features a dining room, lounge, pool, sauna, and conference rooms. 58 Prospect St. (phone: 506-452-8937). Expensive.

Lord Beaverbrook – With 165 rooms, this is part of the Keddy's Motor Inn chain and has an indoor pool with a bar, hot tub, and sauna. The hotel's *Maverick Room* (open 5 PM to midnight) is a popular restaurant. 659 Queen St. (phone: 506-455-3371). Expensive.

Carriage House Bed and Breakfast – Built in 1875 for the then-mayor of Fredericton, this 2-story, 32-room mansion includes 2 balconies, a ballroom, and 7 guestrooms. 230 University Ave. (phone: 506-452-9924). Moderate.

WOODSTOCK

Wandlyn Motor Inn – Located on Route 95 near the US-Canada border, this motel has 50 rooms, a dining room, and is usually crowded during July and August. PO Box 1191 (phone: 506-328-8876). Expensive.

AROOSTOOK

La Ferme des Erables I and II – Watch a real potato farm in action, fish for trout, hike, see beef cattle, swim in an indoor pool, or golf nearby. Just 2 rooms. On Rte. 1 (phone: 506-273-3112). Moderate to inexpensive.

GRAND FALLS

Près du Lac – Noted for its hospitality (it received a special award for service), this motel has 100 attractive rooms, indoor pool, whirlpool baths, sauna, gym, and miniature golf. It also features some non-smoking rooms and a non-smoking section in its restaurant. Trans-Canada Hwy. (phone: 506-473-1300). Expensive.

EDMUNDSTON

Howard Johnson's – Located in the heart of town, this motel features 103 rooms, a pool, sauna, whirlpool baths, family restaurant, and a dining room. 100 Rice St. (phone: 506-739-7321). Expensive.

Le Brayon – A hospitable and attractive motel, it has 22 rooms, 7 chalets, and a dining room serving breakfast and dinner. Ste. Basile, Rte. 2 E (phone: 506-263-5514). Moderate.

Lynn – This motel is centrally located in City Centre and has 49 rooms. It is within walking distance of shopping and restaurants, and a mile from the ski slopes. Ski packages are available. 30 Church St. (phone: 506-735-8851). Moderate.

Newfoundland

When Newfoundland finally joined the Canadian Confederation in 1949, it ended a long, on-again, off-again flirtation with that larger political entity. Like many an island, Newfoundland prides itself on self-sufficiency and independence, and for decades that pride kept it at arm's length from the confederation of provinces. It was the tenth — and so far the last — region to become a province of Canada.

The province includes the island of Newfoundland, numerous smaller islands around it, and the huge mainland territory of Labrador. It is the most easterly of the Canadian provinces, with an area of 156,185 square miles, almost three-quarters of which is Labrador. The island is the political and population center of the province, and when people refer to Newfoundland (unless they add "province") they usually mean the island; Labrador is generally referred to simply as Labrador. Some 600,000 people live in the province, all but 30,000 or so on Newfoundland. What is most unique about this population is its homogeneity; 99% of Newfoundland's residents speak English, and something over 95% were born on the island. This says much about the singular cohesiveness of its culture and society, still British to the core.

Newfoundland is in the Atlantic just off the northeastern coast of Canada, separated from the northern tip of Nova Scotia by the Cabot Strait and from Labrador by the narrower Strait of Belle Isle. From the beginning it has been a fishing island, living off the Grand Banks' rich schools of cod. The island, the tenth largest in the world, was discovered in 1497 by John Cabot, sailing under the British flag, who found an opening into a protected harbor that he promptly named St. John's. The port city is the provincial capital today, with 160,000 people. The Grand Banks have been one of the richest fishing grounds in the world and have supported the island for centuries as it was settled and colonized by Irish, Basques, and West Men — settlers from the west of England. (Recent disoveries in the Grand Banks, however, have shown massive oil deposits, which are expected eventually to displace the fisheries as the main source of provincial income.) In 1855, the island was made a self-governing dominion of the British Commonwealth, but it reverted to colony status when it went bankrupt in the Great Depression. It remained aloof from Canada until the debate over joining the Confederation was finally settled in 1949, on April Fool's Day.

The island is a series of mountains and forests dropping precipitously to the sea — a rugged, rocky landscape of hard splendor and icy power. Labrador is even more isolated. It is part of the oldest section of the Canadian Shield, that underpinning of ancient rock that surrounds immense Hudson Bay; it has huge spruce and fir forests, intercut with many lakes and streams, and incredibly good fishing and hunting, although much of it is accessible only by bush plane. The northern coast is home to several Indian and Inuit communities. Western Labrador, the deep interior, handles the bulk of Canada's iron ore mining. The climate here is what's called "temperate Maritime," meaning winters are usually mild, with the average temperature at 32F (0 degrees C); the average summer temperature is 68F (20C). Labrador is much colder.

Our routes follow the natural configuration of the island, which is essentially a large central section with a prominent, nearly separate area on the east called the Avalon Peninsula. Small in comparison to the rest of the island, Avalon nonetheless claims a disproportionate share of attractions for the traveler, including St. John's, headquarters for any excursions in Eastern Newfoundland. The routes that follow are divided into a tour of Avalon's southern shore; a drive across the central part of the island and its west coast on the Trans-Canada Highway, the only road to cut clean across the island's width (this route includes a tour of the more navigable parts of Labrador); and a tour of northern Avalon. To reach Newfoundland by car, you have to go to North Sydney, Nova Scotia, where *Marine Atlantic* operates car ferries to the island. The 6-hour trip to Port aux Basques, on the southwest tip of Newfoundland runs year-round. The 18-hour trip to Argentia, near St. John's, is available only in summer. The speed limit on the highway is 55 mph (90 km/hour); in cities and towns it's 30 mph (55 km/hour). For information and reservations, call *Marine Atlantic,* in Maine, 800-432-7344; in the continental US, 800-341-7981; hearing impaired, call 800-794-8109 in US and Canada. For further information, contact the Newfoundland Department of Development and Tourism, PO Box 2016, St. John's, Newfoundland A1C 5R8 (phone: 709-576-2830 or 800-563-6353).

Avalon's Southern Shore

This tour of the Avalon Peninsula follows the eastern and southern shore from St. John's to the ferry landing at Argentia. Two sanctuaries, at Bay Bulls and Cape St. Mary's, are among the most important seabird sanctuaries in the world. The tour starts on Route 10 south of St. John's and circles a large wilderness area. The trout fishing is excellent, and caribou thrive on the southern shore.

CAPE SPEAR NATIONAL HISTORIC PARK: This is the easternmost point of land in North America. Seven miles (11 km) south of St. John's on Route 11, it is bare, windswept, surf-washed, and wildly picturesque.

Cape Spear derives an unearthly atmosphere from its immense World War II gun emplacements in a state of semiruin. The barrels of two 10-inch guns, weighing 30 tons each, remain on-site. They were originally mounted on "disappearing" carriages and had a firing range of 8 miles. The park service has restored a 19th-century lighthouse, the oldest in Newfoundland, where two lightkeepers and their families lived year-round in dramatic isolation. The sea is spectacular here, but if high seas are running, heed the posted warnings and stay within the prescribed area; visitors who have ventured too close to the breakers have been washed off and drowned.

En Route from Cape Spear – Petty Harbour, 10 miles (16 km) south of Cape Spear on Route 10 (access from Rte. 11), is a compact, busy fishing village and a favorite of photographers for its quaint houses, which cling to steep hills.

Continuing south on Route 10 (the Southern Shore Road, as Newfoundlanders call it), you first reach Bay Bulls. Cannons used for fighting off French raiders in the 18th century are now gateposts for a local church.

BAY BULLS: From here you can visit the great seabird sanctuary offshore. The three islands just offshore are world-famous among birders and ornithologists for their immense colonies of petrels, dovekies, guillemots, puffins, razor-billed auks, murres, terns, kittiwakes, and gulls.

A permit is required if you intend to land on the islands, but none is needed to visit them in a boat. *Bird Island Charters* offers a 2½-hour tour of the islands (phone: 709-753-4850). *Gatherall's Sanctuary Boat Charters* also operates out of Bay Bulls. The sanctuary offers a 5-room hospitality center with home-cooked meals (even homemade jam). Proprietor Rosemary Gatherall can arrange whale watching excursions, cod and squid jigging, and tours of the bird colony. There are thousands of nesting seabirds almost within arm's reach, and the air is filled with birds in flight. A visit to this great nesting colony is unforgettable and especially rewarding for the amateur photographer. The islands are at their best before mid-August, with colonies of puffins, murres, northern gannets, black guillemots, kittiwakes, and Leach's storm petrels. Later in the summer the bird population decreases rapidly, and by autumn the islands are almost deserted.

En Route from Bay Bulls – Every cove along this section of Route 10 south to Cape Race figures in at least one story of high adventure, complete with pirates, wrecks, and buried treasure. Interestingly, the people of the area are of almost pure Irish descent. The eastern shore, once inhabited by outlaws known as "the masterless men," later became a favorite haunt of rum runners bringing tax-free booze from the French islands of St. Pierre and Miquelon. Many ships, carried off course during transatlantic runs, have been wrecked along this shore, and many of their remains are visible still.

FERRYLAND: This was once the English capital of Newfoundland, attacked repeatedly by both the French and the Dutch. Isle au Bois, which plugs the mouth of its harbor, still has the remains of forts and movable guns that rolled from the cliffs into a rocky gulch now washed by the sea. Relics of battles going back to the 17th century litter the area. The old courthouse overlooking Ferryland harbor houses a charming community museum with exhibits on shipwrecks and fishing.

The Ferryland Downs is perfect for leisurely hiking (bring a sweater), and there's always a chance you'll spot a minke whale as you picnic. The Downs provided artistic inspiration for nationally known Newfoundland painter Gerry Squires, who lived for a while in the lighthouse poised over the dramatic harbor entrance.

En Route from Ferryland – The southern shore, especially from Ferryland south, is one of the best trout fishing areas in Newfoundland. The most plentiful species is the eastern brook trout, but landlocked salmon and sea-run salmon are also found here, especially in the rivers running into Trepassey Bay, just west of Cape Race.

THE TREPASSEY BARRENS: The great sweep of barren land at the southern tip of the Avalon Peninsula is remarkably like the inhospitable lands of the Canadian Arctic. Until 1987, this wild area was thought to be the most southerly caribou habitat in the world, but since then, a herd of about 20 Avalon caribou have made their home in the high and remote ranges of the state of Maine, transplanted from these barrens in a dramatic cooperative effort by US and Canadian wildlife officials. From the high road crossing the Trepassey Barrens, you might see as many as 100 of these magnificent animals at once; the whole herd in this region numbers about 3,000.

Another attraction is the great flocks of curlews that pause here briefly during migration. These storklike Arctic birds with sickle-shaped beaks are often found by the hundreds beside the road.

En Route from Trepassey Barrens – You come to the sea at Holyrood Pond, an inlet of the ocean crossed by Route 10 on a causeway. Route 10 becomes Route 90 at St. Vincent's, leading back to the Trans-Canada Highway 30 miles (48 km) west of St. John's.

On St. Mary's Bay shore, Route 90 passes through a number of lovely fishing villages. The landscape along this drive heading north into the bay is lush and gentle — an unexpected respite from the raw power of the scenery that precedes it. Midway to the Trans-Canada is the Salmonier Nature Park, with its 1.2-mile woods walk, unique in Canada, along which you can see moose, caribou, beaver, otter, and other wildlife of Newfoundland and Labrador in spacious, natural enclosures. Butter Pot Provincial Park is just off the highway between the junction of Route 90 and St. John's. Besides excellent camping and swimming, this park offers fine hiking trails to the crest of Butter Pot Mountain, another barrens with a splendid view of Conception Bay.

This loop drive on southern Avalon has a counterpart to the west by way of Routes 91, 92, and 100. About half of this 120-mile (192-km) route is gravel road. Pavement extends from the Trans-Canada Highway to St. Bride's, approximately 9½ miles (15.2 km) from Cape St. Mary's. The access road to the seabird sanctuary from Route 100 is rough and requires careful driving.

The sanctuary is one of two outstanding attractions on the loop: Cataracts Park, on Route 91 west of Colinet, a series of waterfalls in a small rocky gorge with platforms and bridges for viewing; and the lovely sand beaches along the Placentia Bay Shore on Route 100.

BIRD ISLAND: The province's only major seabird sanctuary that is accessible by land. Because of a natural cleft that protects the birds from visitors, you can walk right to the edge of the colony from the parking lot and see such splendid birds as the goose-size gannets incubating eggs and raising chicks almost under your nose.

Few experiences can be more impressive than a visit to the colony during the nesting season in July. There are also kittiwakes, remarkable for their courage to live among the much larger gannets, and murres, duck-size black and white birds.

PLACENTIA: In the late 17th century, this was the base for the French fishery in Newfoundland. For 50 years the French built numerous fortifications around the harbor as they extended their hostilities with Britain (based in St. John's) to the new world. Fort Royal, the centerpiece of Castle Hill National Historic Park, was built in 1693 but ceded to the British 20 years later. Its ruins have been preserved, and an interpretation center provides some of the history of the area. At nearby Argentia, a plaque commemorates the Atlantic Charter, signed by Roosevelt and Churchill in 1941 aboard a British warship anchored in the bay. From Argentia, you can return to St. John's via routes 100 and 1.

BEST EN ROUTE

Accommodations are not plentiful on the Avalon Peninsula's south shore, so you may have to settle for whatever you are near at the end of the day. Plan ahead by consulting the brochure *Newfoundland and Labrador Accommodations Guide,* available from the Department of Development and Tourism, PO Box 2016, St. John's, Newfoundland A1C 5R8. For motels and tourist homes along this route listed as moderate, expect to pay $45 to $55; for inexpensive, $20 to $30. All prices are quoted in US dollars.

CALVERT

Sullivan's – Mrs. Sullivan runs this comfortable guesthouse and provides home-cooked meals. Near Ferryland, 1¼ mile (2 km) from Rte. 10 (phone: 70432-2474 or 2372). Inexpensive.

TREPASSEY

Trepassey – Handy to superb salmon fishing rivers, the evening meal here often centers on fish or local wild game. An expanded "hospitality home," it now offers wheelchair access. Pets allowed. Rte. 10 (phone: 709-438-2934). Inexpensive.

PLACENTIA

Harold – Located near 17th-century French fortifications, the hotel has 23 quiet, clean rooms. Rte. 91 (phone: 709-227-2107 or 2108). Moderate.

Central Newfoundland

This 420-mile (676-km) drive cuts across the island almost to the isthmus of Avalon, then swings south to the Burin Peninsula. The Trans-Canada Highway, the only east-west road across Newfoundland, skirts Notre Dame Bay at Springdale, with access to scenic fishing villages.

Gander is a prime salmon fishing area just south of Notre Dame Bay. Outfitters take you to the interior by float plane, but reservations should be made in advance. The town, an important air base during World War II, has an aviation exhibit at the airport.

Terra Nova National Park, on Bonavista Bay, can be easily reached from St. John's if you ferry to Newfoundland's eastern port at Argentia. The 153-square-mile park has a variety of facilities including boat rentals for exploration of the shoreline. The Burin Peninsula, dotted with beautiful fishing villages, is the jumping-off point for St. Pierre and Miquelon, French territorial islands where a taste of France can be had at modest expense.

En Route from Deer Lake – Route 1 skirts the north shore of Grand Lake and Sandy Lake between two arms of the Long Range Mountains. Lobster House (1,916 ft.) and Mt. Sheffield (1,640 ft.) loom in the distance on the other side of the lakes. Route 410 leads to the Baie Verte Peninsula, 60 miles (97 km) east of Deer Lake.

NOTRE DAME BAY (WEST): This vast network of waterways and islands was created 7,000 years ago, when the last great ice sheet tilted Newfoundland to the northeast, causing deep depressions at the same time. Route 1 makes a wide bend past the bay, touching at it only two points — Halls Bay and Norris Arm. The rest of the bay is served by 800 miles of secondary roads.

On the western side of the bay, the Baie Verte Peninsula has been a major center for mining copper, silver, gold, lead, zinc, cadmium, and asbestos. Because of its unique geological formation, the whole peninsula is a rockhound's delight, with thousands of noncommercial outcroppings of collectible rocks. However, major mining companies have recently staked claims throughout the peninsula following the promising discovery of gold deposits.

A more scenic trip for the motorist is a beautiful drive around landlocked waters on Route 390 (13 mi/21 km farther east on Rte. 1) and Route 391, to such lovely villages as King's Point and Rattling Brook. If you head east on 390, past the area's commercial center, Springdale, you can pick up Route 392, which is mostly unpaved but will take you, in only a few miles, to the ferry to Little Bay Islands. Just 8 miles (13 km) further east on Route 1, Route 380 leads to Roberts Arm, Pilley's Island, Brighton, Cards Harbour, and the ferry to Lushes Bight. Lovely, wooded islands are linked by causeways which span calm channels of clear water filled with shellfish and other marine life.

En Route from Notre Dame Bay (West) – From the Route 380 intersection at South Brook, Route 1 swings inland 49 miles (79 km) to Grand Falls. Less than 2 miles (3.2 km) west of this paper-mill town, there is an entertaining logging museum at Beothuck Provincial Park; ask the park interpreter about "G'arge's Bullet Proof." At the new *Mary March Museum and National Exhibition Centre* in Grand Falls, visitors learn the sad story of the museum's namesake and her now extinct race, the Beothuck Indians. From Grand Falls, Route 1 continues east 32 miles (51 km) to Notre Dame Junction, where you'll find Notre Dame Provincial Park. With 100 campsites and swimming, fishing, and boating facilities, it is an ideal stopover before heading north to Notre Dame Bay (East). Only 7 miles (11 km) from the junction along Route 340 is Lewisporte, home of the By the *Bay Museum* and its craft shop, run by the local Women's Institute. You can go "down" (north) to Labrador by taking the Lewisporte–Goose Bay ferry, the new *Northern Ranger,* which makes a stop at Cartwright on the Labrador coast. The sojourn takes the better part of two days and is probably the closest one can get to the long coastal steamer trips that were once the only transportation to numerous isolated outports. Coastal trips can be booked only from within Newfoundland. For information contact *Marine Atlantic* at the numbers listed above.

NOTRE DAME BAY (EAST): The eastern end of Notre Dame Bay is a beautiful place to spend a few days. Several chains of islands large and small are easily accessible from Boyds Cove on Route 340.

Route 340 crosses Dildo Run, known to be confusing for boatmen who try to negotiate the maze of islands, to Chapel and New World islands. The most attractive settlements on New World Island are Herring Neck and Cobb's Arm. Dildo Run Provincial Park, on Route 340 just across the road from Virgin's Arm, has more than 30 picnic sites overlooking the bay.

TWILLINGATE: New World Island is connected by causeway to Twillingate, the fishing and well-known sealing capital of bygone days. A bell cast in 1862 commemorates the Great Haul of Swiles ("swiles" are seals in local parlance), when an iceberg carrying a large herd of harp seals came so close to shore that the townspeople walked across the ice pans and killed 30,000 of the animals. During summer, icebergs can often be seen floating in the bays and coves surrounding Twillingate. In fact, Newfoundland's northeast coast is one of the very few places in the world where the awesome natural phenomena of icebergs can be viewed from accessible and populated areas.

A burial ground of the Maritime Archaic People, nearly as old as the site at Port au Choix, was found in nearby Back Harbour. The community museum is in the enchanting restored home of Georgina Sterling, who at the turn of the century won world acclaim in opera houses as Madame Toulinguet, "the Nightingale of the North," and of whom the museum tells all. Its shop sells quality local crafts and souvenirs. Jasper, one of the gems mentioned in the Bible, is plentiful in gravel pits near Twillingate. Return to the Trans-Canada Highway at Gander via Routes 331 and 330.

GANDER: The first thing that strikes most visitors to Gander is that there seem to be too many shopping centers, parking lots, and hotels for a town of its size. Such surprise disappears, however, when they discover that it is a center of commerce for the whole northeast coast, an important international airport location serving numerous transatlantic flights, and that it is a popular outfitting station for anglers and hunters heading inland by floatplane. Gander's history is closely tied to the pioneer days of aviation. Because of its proximity to Europe, many early transatlantic flights originated here, and the Allied forces maintained an important airstrip in Gander during World War II. An aviation exhibit has mementos of early flights.

The Gander River, one of the island's most important salmon rivers, flows under Route 1 at Glenwood, 14 miles (23 km) west of the airport town. A beautiful river, passing through idyllic boreal wilderness, it is known for its deceptive shoals and rapids. Many canoeists owe their lives to the guides who work these waters. *Gander River Tours* is one of many guide services that are equipped to provide safe and pleasurable excursions for anglers, sightseers, canoeists, or photographers. River tours of any duration are available, with package deals that include all the wilderness comforts you desire.

Campers can replenish supplies at stores in town, but, as in the rest of Newfoundland, the dining facilities are very limited. Two good restaurants are the *Albatross* motel on Route 1, and *Sinbad's,* in town on Bennett Dr. Avoid the airport cafeteria; the food is institutional in character and overpriced.

TERRA NOVA NATIONAL PARK: The older of Newfoundland's two national parks is 48 miles (77 km) east of Gander on Route 1. Terra Nova's specialty is sea beach, tidal flats, and abundant wildlife. The provincial flower, the carnivorous pitcher plant, grows in inland peat bogs. Black bear and moose can frequently be seen from the road (be very alert for moose crossing the highway); and beaver, muskrat, red fox, lynx, and Canada geese can be seen along the 50 miles (80 km) of nature trails. Maps of the walking trails are available at park headquarters.

Terra Nova hosts a variety of activities, including a nine-hole seaside golf course (slated for expansion) in a beautiful wilderness setting. Cabin, canoe, and bicycle rentals are available at park headquarters. Besides many primitive campsites, there are serviced campgrounds at Newman Sound and Malady Head with over 550 camping sites total, and there is free winter camping at Newman Sound with heated washrooms and an enclosed kitchen. From a boat launch at Salton's Brook on Newman Sound, visitors can explore miles of coastal inlets. Whales and seals cavort among the icebergs in Bonavista Bay in early summer. For more information, write to the Superintendent, Terra Nova National Park, Glovertown, Newfoundland A0G 2L0.

Before leaving this beautiful park, take a short drive on Route 310 to Salvage and Eastport. Salvage, a small fishing village, is situated on a harbor ringed by white houses among bare headlands and surf-washed islands. The *Lane House* has been converted into a fishermen's museum, where you can purchase locally made, traditional handicrafts. *Happy Adventure,* just south of Eastport, has a lobster pool from which you can buy live lobsters in July.

BONAVISTA PENINSULA: From Clarenville, 55 miles (89 km) south of the Terra Nova exit on Route 1, Route 230 leads to Bonavista, the site of a crucial 18th-century battle between the French and English. Michael Gill, a fishing master from Charlestown, Massachusetts, held off French raiders with only two armed ships and assistance from local fishermen. The lighthouse at nearby Cape Bonavista dates back to 1843 and is a provincial historic site. Port Union, one of the neighboring communities, is named for Newfoundland's first Fishermen's Union. There is an imposing monument to William Coaker, organizer of the union and founder of the town. Trinity, 20 miles (32 km) south of Port Union, is an old fishing and mercantile town, first visited by the Portuguese João Vas Corte Real in 1500. It is considered a showcase in Newfoundland for its success in preserving its historic character. The Ryan Premises (a provincial historic site), a blacksmith shop (privately owned but open to visitors upon request), and other buildings now look much as they did in the 19th century, when Trinity was the commercial center of Bonavista Bay. At Hiscock House, guides in costumes from 1910 interpret the life and times of a local merchant household of the area.

BURIN PENINSULA: Route 210 to the Burin Peninsula leaves the Trans-Canada Highway (Rte. 1) at Goobies, 100 miles (161 km) west of St. John's. Most of the road runs inland with short access roads to beautiful coastal villages.

Swift Current, 15 miles (24 km) from the turnoff, has beautiful sea beaches and a very fine river, Piper's Hole.

Pass up Route 211 to Terrenceville and English Harbour East; it has little to offer. Route 212, paved for most of its length, runs out to Bay l'Argent and Little Bay East, settlements of enduring beauty. Bay l'Argent has no silver, despite its name, but has long stretches of silvery rocks and water. Along this shore you may see inshore fishermen splitting and cleaning their catch as it comes out of the water.

Baine Harbour and Rushoon, on the opposite side of the peninsula, are beautiful villages with strong ties to the sea. Still farther south you come to the best of them all — Jean de Baie, Little Bay, and Beau Bois. Beau Bois is one of those places almost too good to be true: Photographs of it have appeared around the world.

MARYSTOWN: Most of Newfoundland's large fishing vessels are constructed in the Marystown Shipyard. Picturesque and placid Mortier Bay, together with neighboring Burin Bay and Burin Bay Arm, turn the area surrounding Marystown into an intimate mixture of land and sea. Burin is a collection of villages scattered among coves and inlets. No single piece of land anywhere in the area is big enough for a town. It is so rugged and hilly that villages only a few hundred yards apart are hidden from one another.

A shipbuilding center, the region is also home to great fleets of trawlers and some of the largest fish processing plants on the island. Millions of pounds of fish are produced annually by the towns that ring the bottom of the peninsula.

The country's quest over the past decade for secure oil and gas reserves has brought imposing symbols of a new industry to the area. Lovely Spanish Room Peninsula, across the bay from Marystown, is now the site of a maintenance and repair facility for the huge semi-submersible oil rigs that probe deep into the earth's mantle on Newfoundland's Grand Banks.

> **En Route from Marystown** – Using Marystown as an anchor point, take Routes 210 and 220 to circle the "boot" of the peninsula, stopping at the other outports — Burin, St. Lawrence, Fortune, and Grand Bank.
>
> Much of the 99-mile (159-km) drive around the boot goes through barren, windswept countryside. The surf on the south shore at Allan's Island, High Beach, and Point au Gaul can be spectacular. The *Golden Sands* resort (see *Best En Route*), near Salt Pond, has 18 cabins and 86 campsites with a fine swimming beach.

ST. PIERRE ISLAND: From Fortune, 34 miles (55 km) west of Marystown on Route 210, you can visit the French islands of St. Pierre and Miquelon. Information on daily ferry service is available from the Department of Development and Tourism in St. John's or by calling 709-832-1955. There are flights between St. John's and St. Pierre three times weekly. Eight passengers can fly on the small plane (phone: 709-576-4100).

Since the islands are French territories, you must clear customs during your visit. But passports are unnecessary: All you will need is the identification used to cross the US-Canadian border.

St. Pierre is one of the most European towns in North America: From its wrought-iron balconies to the tips of its Parisian sandals, it radiates the quiet charm of a slightly seedy French provincial town. Until recently, the islands were famous for their terrific duty-free eating and drinking bargains that made bootleg liquor St. Pierre's major export. Since losing that special tax status, prices have gone up considerably, although most liquor is still less expensive than in Canada and French wines remain an attractive buy.

If you have more than a day to spend in St. Pierre, stay in a pension and plan a short visit to the nearby islands of Miquelon and L'Anglade. You can charter a boat or take one of the tours arranged by the St. Pierre tourist office. *SPM Tours* also offers packages that include daily boat services in the summer (phone: 722-3892). At the northern tip of Miquelon is a small fishing settlement inhabited by pure Basques. Miquelon is joined by 10 miles (16 km) of sand dunes to wild and picturesque L'Anglade Island. The toll in lives and ships the dunes have taken over the centuries is one of the saddest chapters in North Atlantic sailing history. By contrast, the lagoon at the northern end of the dunes is a haven for a large colony of seals.

Going through customs at St. Pierre takes but a moment; upon your return, the delay may be as long as half an hour, especially if you arrive at Fortune with a full shipload. You will have to stand in line to declare your purchases and perhaps open your bags for inspection.

BEST EN ROUTE

On Notre Dame Bay, there are accommodations in many of the coastal fishing villages, and since the Trans-Canada Highway was constructed, these are becoming even more tourist-oriented. Public and private campgrounds are listed in the *Newfoundland and Labrador Accommodations Guide,* which can be obtained from the Department of Development and Tourism, PO Box 2016, St. John's, Newfoundland A1C 5R8.

Grand Falls and Gander are outfitting centers for excursions to the interior. Outfitters in Newfoundland are listed in the *Hunting and Fishing Guide,* available from the address listed above. This brochure includes up-to-date hunting and fishing regulations.

Expect to pay $70 to $80 and up per night for a double room in the expensive range; $45 to $65 in the moderate. Under $45 is inexpensive. All prices are quoted in US dollars.

SPRINGDALE

Pelley Inn – This modern, 23-room motel is 4 miles (6 km) off Route 390. It's a good access point for the ferries to Little Bay Islands and Lushes Bight. Cyril Pelley will arrange boat or land tours of the area. Little Bay Rd. (phone: 709-673-3931). Moderate.

GRAND FALLS

Mount Peyton – A contemporary motel with 150 immaculate rooms, it has a pretty good steakhouse. Rte. 1 (phone: 709-489-2251 or 800-563-4894). Expensive.

TWILLINGATE

Anchor Inn – Directly overlooking the harbor; the owner has added 4 housekeeping units to the original 14 rooms. Rte. 340 (phone: 709-884-2776). Moderate.

GANDER

Albatross – One of the best hotels in central Newfoundland, this 105-room facility is 187 miles (301 km) from Deer Lake, making it a good place to stop the first night of the tour. Facilities include a lounge, convention room, and babysitting services. There is also a restaurant with excellent service, which specializes in delicious local seafood. On Rte. 1 (phone: 709-256-3956 or 800-563-4894). Expensive.

TERRA NOVA NATIONAL PARK

Weston's Terra Nova National Park Chalets – If roughing it in the park's campgrounds is not for you, here are 24 self-contained cabins at a reasonable rate. Extra charges for more than two people. Rte. 1 (phone: 709-533-2296; off-season, 709-651-3434). Moderate.

TRINITY

Village Inn – The proprietors describe themselves as "publicans," the British term for innkeepers. The hotel has only 8 rooms and serves very good meals. Whale watching excursions can be arranged. Rte. 239 (phone: 709-464-3269). Moderate.

LEWIN'S COVE

Golden Sands – This fine resort has 18 cabins and 86 semi-serviced and unserviced trailer sites, with excellent swimming nearby. Just off Rte. 222 (phone: 709-891-2400). Moderate.

ST. PIERRE

Robert – Breakfast comes with a night's stay in this modern 56-room hotel which offers Old World hospitality. Call ahead and someone will meet you at the boat. (Phone: Ask operator for St. Pierre 2419.) Expensive to moderate.

The West Coast

Contrary to popular belief, Newfoundland is not a wasteland enshrouded in fog (although approaching Port aux Basques on the gulf ferries will seem to confirm such preconceptions); this North Atlantic island has splendid wilderness areas, as this 444-mile (711-km) route along the western shore proves. It is an awesome combination of wild surf, rugged mountains, and quiet rivers teeming with salmon.

The tour starts at Port aux Basques, the ferry landing from North Sydney, Nova Scotia. Just up the road at Cape Ray, the surf pounds the shore in a relentless effort to reclaim the entire island. As you drive north along the Trans-Canada Highway, St. George's Bay and then the Gulf of St. Lawrence are on the left and, in striking contrast, the barren Long Range Mountains are on the right.

Halfway between Port aux Basques and Corner Brook is the Port au Port Peninsula. Corner Brook is a popular outfitting center for excursions to the interior and connections to Labrador. The Humber River, which flows into the gulf at Corner Brook, is famous for salmon.

Also between Port aux Basques and Corner Brook is the Barachois Provincial Park, on Route 1, 30 miles (48 km) south of Corner Brook. It's one of the largest and most lovely of the provincial parks, with 158 sites, swimming, and hiking. It's also one of the few places in Newfoundland where chipmunks live.

The next stop is 697-square-mile Gros Morne National Park, with the most spectacular fjords in North America. The park's interior has peat bogs, pristine lakes and streams, and a variety of wildlife, including bald eagles and Arctic hare.

From Gros Morne, Route 430 hugs the shore of the Great Northern Peninsula. At Port au Choix, a 5,000-year-old burial ground of the Maritime Archaic People is on display, and at the northern tip of the peninsula is a Viking settlement thought to have been established around AD 1000.

All waterfront in Newfoundland is open to the public. You will appreciate this, especially on the northern coasts, where you may stop suddenly and head for the beach to better photograph a drifting iceberg. Although there are no private beaches, be sure to ask anyway should you appear to be encroaching on someone's privacy.

Dining facilities on this tour are mediocre, but seafood is the best bet. Be sure that "fresh" fish on the menu does not merely mean not salted, but also not frozen.

CAPE RAY: The ferry from Nova Scotia lands at Port aux Basques, named for the Basque fishermen who began making annual voyages to Newfoundland as early as 1500. The Basques were gradually supplanted by Norman and Breton French, who also fished the waters of Cabot Strait. Until the 19th century, this area was exclusively French-speaking. Today, Port aux Basques and neighboring Channel are important fishing centers.

When you disembark, drive west from Channel along the Cape Ray shore on Route 1. Exit at Cheeseman Provincial Park for a look at the spectacular surf. Waves move swiftly along the smooth, shallow ocean shelf in Cabot Strait and crash against the rocky shoreline.

A word of caution: The surf can be extremely dangerous. On several occasions, people have been swept into the sea by the impact of an unexpectedly high wave. The thrilling spectacle is best watched from a safe distance.

TABLE MOUNTAIN: From Route 1, the hale and hearty can climb 1,700 feet above the ocean to the plateau of Table Mountain, just a few miles north of Cheeseman Provincial Park. Even in midsummer you may find snow fields in its crevasses. Caribou graze on the plateau. On rare occasions the gyrfalcon can be spotted — the only place south of Labrador the great Arctic bird of prey is known to hunt. Hiking boots are recommended for the arduous climb, as are a sweater and lightly packed rain gear, for weather on the plateau is very changeable.

Table Mountain is the first of the Long Range Mountains, once part of the Appalachian chain on the eastern seaboard of North America. Successive ice ages have worn down the Long Range Mountains to less than 3,000 feet.

GRAND CODROY RIVER: The region between Cape Ray and Corner Brook — a 136-mile (219-km) stretch of wooded hill and valley — is the best area in Newfoundland to find moose, caribou, and Atlantic salmon.

The Grand Codroy River, with its two tributaries — the North Branch and South Branch — is 25 miles (40 km) from Port aux Basques on Route 1. Approximately 1,000 salmon are taken annually from the river and its 30 miles of accessible pools.

Seasons vary from river to river, but the best salmon fishing on most rivers is from late June through July. There is no limit on the number of licenses issued, and arrangements with outfitters should be made well in advance. Fishing lodges and cabins have surprisingly modest rates — often lower than those of motels — but few outfitters accept credit cards. There are extra charges for guides. All rivers in the province are subject to closure to anglers on short notice, depending on water depths and temperatures that can affect salmon migration. In recent years, there have been limits on the maximum as well as minimum size of salmon that fishermen are allowed to keep (12 in. to 24.8 in.). It is hoped that when they spawn, the larger salmon's greater egg volume will help maintain one of the healthiest stocks in the world. The rivers of Labrador, being more remote, have no upward limit on the size of fish that may be kept. For current conservation regulations, write Department of Fisheries and Oceans, Newfoundland Region, PO Box 5667, St. John's, Newfoundland A1C 5X1, or call 709-772-4421 and ask for that season's *Angler's Guide*. (For more information, see *Where They Bite: Fishing in Canada*, DIVERSIONS.)

The western coast is also one of Canada's prime moose, black bear, and caribou hunting areas. Hunters with local guides are virtually guaranteed success because big-game populations in Newfoundland have been well managed by the government.

The Newfoundland caribou is the largest of its species in the world. Hunters from the island claim all the world record heads (measured in spread and number of points to the antlers). The season opens in mid-September for both moose and caribou. Licenses must be obtained well in advance from outfitters listed in the brochure *Newfoundland and Labrador Hunting and Fishing Guide,* issued by the Newfoundland Department of Development and Tourism.

PORT AU PORT PENINSULA: With its sea-battered cliffs along its southern shore (Route 460 via Route 490 from Route 1), and sandy beaches in the north (Route 463), Port au Port Peninsula is one of the island's best kept secrets. It is home to descendents of Channel Island French fishermen who jumped ship during the 18th and 19th centuries to take up a free life, away from the hardships of conscripted seamen. They inherited a place of beautiful seaward vistas, particularly that from Piccadilly Head, the site of a provincial park which is known for its lack of flies (a point worth noting) and sandy saltwater beach. To the west, an ancient raised reef projects 14 miles northward. At its tip, Long Point is a resting spot for numerous bird species during their spring migration. To the east, the Lewis Hills rise near vertically to 2,674 feet (815 m), the highest point on the island of Newfoundland and home to bald eagles and osprey.

CORNER BROOK: This city of 30,000 is set on an arm of the sea among mountains. It was transformed from a small coastal village to a busy industrial center in the 1920s, when a pulp and paper mill was built. A recently opened Fine Arts College is also here.

Near Corner Brook are scenic drives on both shores of the Bay of Islands. Route 450 follows the south shore 40 miles (64 km) to the public beach at Bottle Cove and Blow Me Down Provincial Park, with 27 campsites and a hiking trail into the Blomidon Mountains. A lookout tower offers a magnificent view of the bay. Route 440 tours the north shore of the bay to Cox's Cove.

On both shore routes you may visit fishing villages and see fishermen at work. For a small fee, you can usually rent a boat to go angling for codfish. Cod in the Bay of Islands average between 5 and 20 pounds.

The Humber River, which empties into the Bay of Islands at Corner Brook, is another famous salmon river. Catches as large as 20 and 30 pounds have been landed in the pools of the Lower Humber. Besides salmon rivers and hunting areas accessible by car, Corner Brook is an outfitting center for excursions to the interior lodges that can only be reached by small plane.

The *Glynmill Inn* on Cobb's La., off Rte. 1 (see *Best En Route*) is a beautiful old hotel in the European style. Its dining room features seafood in season.

MARBLE MOUNTAIN SKI RESORT: Newfoundland's only major ski area with modern tows and lifts is 5 miles (8 km) east of Corner Brook. Marble Mountain has consistently good snow surfaces from January to early April on a range of slopes from easy to difficult. Cabins are available at Steady Brook but are not a good buy, considering the superior accommodations available at lower rates in nearby Corner Brook.

En Route from Marble Mountain – At Deer Lake, 30 miles (48 km) east of Corner Brook, you leave Route 1 for the 275-mile (443-km) drive to St. Anthony and L'Anse aux Meadows. This coastal road — now entirely paved — offers some of the most scenic driving in the province. Except for the first 20 miles (32 km), Route 430 hugs the shore all the way to the northern tip of Newfoundland. As you drive north, the Gulf of St. Lawrence is on your left and the Long Range Mountains, on your right. Every so often awesome fjords cut into the mountains.

GROS MORNE NATIONAL PARK: The results of 400 million years of continental drifting and of the successive ice ages that ended 12,000 years ago are dramatically evident in this 697-square-mile park on Route 430. The most spectacular park in Eastern Canada, its hiking trails pass through the habitats of Arctic animal and plant species rarely found this far south.

The 2,644-foot slopes of Gros Morne end in a 2,000-foot plateau whose cliffs drop to deep fjords on the Gulf of St. Lawrence. (Gros Morne is French for "big knoll," with connotations of dismal and bleak.) A rugged 2½-mile climb to the top of Gros Morne on the James Callaghan hiking trail is rewarded by a magnificent view of the sea and windswept tundra. Be prepared for climatic changes during the ascent, even in summer.

At the Wiltondale entrance to the park, an alternate road, Route 431, skirts the south shore of beautiful Bonne Bay. The road then skirts a massive flat-topped and desolate mountain of orange rock, named the Tablelands, which resembles a Martian landscape on its descent through ancient uplifted beaches to the existing Trout River shoreline.

Returning from Trout River, proceed to Woody Point, perhaps the most picturesque village on the west coast. Do not return to Wiltondale without first checking the status of the Woody Point–Norris Point ferry. The exquisite 15-minute ride used to be an alternate link to Route 430 on the far side of Bonne Bay. It was curtailed in 1985 when its provincial government subsidy was withdrawn. If it is running, the trip is an unequalled opportunity for photographers and whale watchers. If it is not in service, never mind; the stretch on Route 430 from Wiltondale north to Rocky Harbour, through the fjord of East Arm, is no less spectacular. Continue north along the shore to St. Paul's Inlet, a rock-girt fjord with cliffs rising more than 2,000 feet from the water. En route, you will see a parking lot marking the hiking trail into Western Brook Pond. By all means take it. Round-trip, it's a 5-mile hike on a boardwalk through beautiful woods and open marshy fields. When winds from the upland plateau are not too severe, a tour boat plies the 9 miles to the end of the land-locked fjord. On the way, waterfalls pour over the lip of the plateau 2,000 feet above and turn into a fine mist before reaching the pond. Boat trips should be arranged in advance; inquire at the park information center. The dining room of the *Ocean View* motel in Rocky Harbour has good food. Be sure to ask if fresh salmon and lobster are available.

Swimming in the Gulf of St. Lawrence is for the hardy only: water temperatures at the Shallow Bay and Western Brook beaches rarely exceed 59F (15C). However, the beaches are their own attraction. Their dunes engulf the coastal forests to the treetops and threaten the delicate marshland ecology inland. Berry Hill has 156 serviced campsites, and there are other unserviced campgrounds in the park. On the hiking trails, you should look for black bear, moose, otter, beaver, caribou, bald eagle, osprey, rock ptarmigan, and Arctic hare.

En Route from Gros Morne – On the remainder of Route 430, you are rarely more than a stone's throw from the sea. Remember: All beaches are public and have public access. There is no such thing as a private seafront in Newfoundland; feel free to stop wherever to swim, picnic, or beachcomb.

The beaches on the western shore of the Great Northern Peninsula hold a special fascination for beachcombers, because prevailing winds and currents wash ashore natural flotsam (starfish, shells, and false corals) and manmade artifacts (nets, net floats, and deck gear from ships).

Genuine primitive handicrafts can be purchased on this section of Route 430: individually designed Newfoundland hooked mats as well as "workshop" handicrafts produced under the supervision of the International Grenfell Association. The Straits Development Association sells local knitting, sealskin goods, and embroidered duffel parkas at Flowers Cove, 90 miles (153 km) north of Daniels Harbour.

RIVER OF PONDS: This salmon fishing region is 50 miles (81 km) north of Gros Morne. The salmon run a bit later here than those farther south: The best fishing is between July 10 and August 10. Sea trout up to 30 pounds enter the river in early

August. Sadie House rents inexpensive river cabins (House's Cabins, River of Ponds, Newfoundland A0K 4M0); reserve in advance.

The 150-acre River of Ponds Provincial Park has 40 campsites on a long sand beach with facilities for boating.

PORT AU CHOIX: The Maritime Archaic Indians flourished here in 2340 BC, contemporary with the Pyramid Age in Egypt. The Dorset Eskimos, whose stone tools are among the most delicate and beautiful ever made, lived here for 2,000 years until they were supplanted by the Beothuck Indians in about AD 1100.

Three Maritime Archaic cemeteries were excavated in 1962. Along with the remains of 100 individuals, weapons and other artifacts were found. Relics are on display in the visitor center, open from June to *Labor Day*.

As you drive north past St. John Bay, the Long Range Mountains melt into the coastal flatlands of the northern peninsula.

LABRADOR COAST: St. Barbe Bay, 60 miles (96 km) north of Port au Choix, has ferry service to Labrador. The 22-mile run is made twice daily during the summer; reservations are not necessary. If you take the first ferry in the morning, it's possible to explore the 50 miles (81 km) of Labrador coastline with some wide, white-sand beaches, which can be reached by road, and return the same evening.

There are accommodations at L'Anse au Clair and L'Anse-au-Loup and a provincial park at Pinware River, if you choose to stay overnight in Labrador. Fishing and hunting excursions to the interior of Labrador are arranged by outfitters on the coast.

From St. Barbe Bay, Route 430 continues along the shore for another 21 miles (35 km) and then crosses the tip of the Great Northern Peninsula. Take Route 436 north after you pass Pistolet Bay for 10 miles (16 km) to L'Anse aux Meadows National Historic Park.

L'ANSE AUX MEADOWS: In 1978, this park was declared the first UNESCO World Heritage Site. The distinction derives from the 1960 discovery of a tiny Norse settlement established on this site around AD 1000, the only confirmed Norse settlement in North America and possibly the one founded by the Icelandic trader Thorfinn Karlsefni. If so, then this is the birthplace of North America's first European child, Snorri Thorfinnson, mentioned in the Viking sagas.

Three sod-roofed buildings, of the original six, have been reconstructed, and other artifacts are on display in the visitor center. Open June 1st through September.

En Route from L'Anse aux Meadows – The northern tip of Newfoundland is known for its icebergs. Every summer, numerous icebergs, towering up to 300 feet above the water, float south along Labrador from their birthplace on the west coast of Greenland. Many ground in shallow water for weeks until dislodged by a storm.

This area is close to the ice floes where harp seals deliver their young each spring and an annual seal hunt follows. Beginning in the mid-1950s, several groups have tried to halt the yearly kill of seal pups and have won wide support. Since then, stiff rules have been imposed to ensure that the seals are killed humanely, and quotas have successfully reversed the decline of the herd, which now stands at 1.4 million. In some recent years, the hunt has been suspended because of poor markets in Europe, where the protest is centered. Newfoundlanders regard the hunt as economically essential and resent the protest. To them, life is a matter of wresting a precarious living from the resources of the sea and land around them.

ST. ANTHONY: Only a short drive south of L'Anse aux Meadows, St. Anthony is the headquarters of the famous Grenfell Mission, established in the late 1800s. Dr. Wilfred Grenfell tried, with partial success, to improve the poor living conditions of Newfoundland and Labrador fishermen. Although he built hospitals and missions, his vision and fanaticism, compassion and dictatorial ways, made him both loved and hated on the Labrador coast.

Upon his retirement, Dr. Grenfell founded the International Grenfell Association, which today is involved in community work.

The Grenfell workshop and store at St. Anthony sell a wide range of handcrafted products from postcards to parkas. The parkas, made of strong "Grenfell cloth" and embroidered by hand, are an exceptional buy. Grenfell also promoted Labradorite jewelry, which can be purchased at many Newfoundland craft outlets. Labradorite is a beautiful opalescent stone with green, bronze, and blue highlights (a similar stone is mined in Madagascar). Some inferior stone is polished; you should examine many pieces to find a really good one.

Dr. Grenfell and his successor Dr. Curtis are buried on a hill above St. Anthony. The shrine, overlooking Hare Bay, can be reached by a trail through the woods.

BEST EN ROUTE

For many years the scarcity of paved roads in western Newfoundland depressed tourism. The construction of the Trans-Canada Highway spurred the development of some accommodations, but there is still a dearth of high-quality hotels and motels. Expect to pay $60 to $75 and up per night for a double room in the expensive range; $45 to $55 in the moderate category. All prices are quoted in US dollars.

PORT AUX BASQUES

Port aux Basques – A fairly modern hotel with 50 rooms, all with TV sets and radios, a lounge, and a restaurant specializing in regional seafood. Pets allowed. Grand Bay Rd. and Trans-Canada Hwy. (phone: 709-695-2171). Expensive.

CORNER BROOK

Glynmill Inn – Overlooking a pond and its resident swans in a quiet section of town, this inn provides 92 rooms in a Tudor-style building dating back to 1924. Among the facilities are a lounge, a restaurant specializing in seafood, and a romantic wine cellar serving steaks with an extensive wine list. 1 Cobb La. (phone: 709-634-5181 or 800-563-4894). Expensive.

GROS MORNE NATIONAL PARK

Parsons Hospitality Home and Harbour View Cabins – Florence Parsons rents 2 rooms in her home, 3 housekeeping cabins, and 3 motel units. Her cooking and friendliness are renowned. Pets on leashes allowed. Just off Rte. 430 in Rocky Harbour (phone: 709-458-2544). Inexpensive.

ST. ANTHONY

Viking – On Pistolet Bay, 5½ miles (3.5 km) from the airport and 14 miles (22 km) from town, this motel provides 11 standard rooms, a restaurant, bar, and dancing on Saturday nights. At the intersection of Rtes. 430 and 437 (phone: 709-454-3541). Moderate.

Northern Avalon

This short tour of the Avalon Peninsula can be covered in a day or two. Beginning at St. John's, the provincial capital and one of the oldest cities in North America, the drive follows Avalon's northern shore through picturesque fishing settlements.

St. John's was the reception point for the first transatlantic wireless signal in 1901. Its annual regatta in August is the most popular event of the year. St. John's is also the cultural center of Newfoundland, with several art galleries, museums, and outdoor concerts.

Routes 20 and 30 follow the shore to Flat Rock and Pouch Cove, whose surf is equal in violence to that of Cape Ray, in Newfoundland's southwestern corner. Farther west, via the Trans-Canada Highway and Route 70, Harbour Grace is the only place in the world with a monument to a pirate.

ST. JOHN'S: This city is a gem. Its small harbor, surrounded by high, protective hills, is one of the best in the world. A slim channel, called the Narrows, gives access to the sea and it's a rare moment that there isn't a ship or a fishing boat gliding in or out of the harbor's mouth. Fishermen have been coming to St. John's since the late 15th century, but today their vessels are joined by an incredibly diverse fleet that seeks refuge or engages in commerce in the harbor. On any given day, a visitor may walk along the waterfront (more like an esplanade than a harbor service area) and examine a variety of fishing boats from half a dozen countries. These are docked among oceanographic research ships, sleek and imposing navy vessels, giant US and Soviet satellite tracking craft, cruise ships, oil drilling ships, offshore supply ships, and the boats of transatlantic adventurers (which seem to get tinier and tinier with each record-breaking crossing). Through much of its history the town was ruled by ruthless fishing admirals. Savage fires in the 19th century wiped out the town several times, so the oldest buildings in the city date back only to the Victorian period. Square, flat-topped, wooden houses, painted in a variety of colors, cling to each other as they staircase up the hills leading away from the harbor.

Signal Hill National Historic Park is a good place to begin a tour of St. John's because it offers a splendid panorama of the city to the west. Best known as the site of the first transatlantic reception of a wireless signal, sent by Marchese Guglielmo Marconi on December 12, 1901, Signal Hill actually got its name centuries earlier when company flags were raised to alert merchants, dockworkers, and customs officials of ships approaching the harbor. Time is still marked by a cannon fired at midday on the hill. From mid-July to the end of August, visitors can see — and hear — a military tattoo on Signal Hill which commemorates the last battle between the French and the English in Canada. The event takes place 4 days a week at 3 and 7 PM, weather permitting. Call the Newfoundland Tourism Office, 800-563-6353, for specifics.

Nearby Quidi Vidi Village, reached by car 2 miles (3 km) north of Signal Hill, has a restored fort and a small cottage built around 1740. The cottage, possibly the oldest in English Canada, was used as a dressing station for the English forces at the Battle of Quidi Vidi. The town has a pocket-size harbor enclosed by hills and is a good place to buy fresh fish and lobster in season.

A regatta is held every year during the first week of August at Quidi Vidi Lake. *Regatta Day* has been held every year since 1828, making it the longest running annual sports event in North America. It is a gala event with sideshows, gambling, games, food, drink, and other entertainment that attracts as many as 50,000 people. The course record on Quidi Vidi Lake, set in 1901 by a crew of fishermen from Outer Cove, stood for 80 years.

Prince Phillip Drive, the eastern extension of Route 1 through St. John's, leads to Confederation Hill and Confederation Building, the seat of the provincial government. Half a mile west of Confederation Building are the Arts and Culture Centre and the campus of Memorial University. While the foyers, halls, and grounds of the Confederation Building display the finest examples of works by Newfoundland's traditional and experimental artists as part of its permanent collection, the art gallery of the neighboring facility hosts new works as well as visiting exhibitions.

The *Newfoundland Museum,* directly across Duckworth Street from the Anglican cathedral, has both prehistoric and colonial exhibits. In its annex at the *Murray Premises* (a building on the waterfront which includes gift shops and a liquor store), the museum covers the marine, military, and natural history of the province.

Duckworth Street hosts two commercial art galleries — *The Gallery* and *Pollyanna Gallery* — and, like the *Murray Premises* on Water St., is known for its luxury shops and cafés. (Keep in mind there is no provincial sales tax on locally made crafts; also, tourists who purchase Newfoundland artwork are exempt from the tax.) Across from the *Pollyanna Gallery* is the War Memorial, on the site where Sir Humphrey Gilbert took possession of the colony in the name of Queen Elizabeth I on August 5, 1583. This is the central area for craft shops: The *Cod Jigger* is at 252 Duckworth, and *The Salt Box* is at 194 Duckworth. *Livyers,* also at 194 Duckworth, just downstairs from *The Salt Box,* is filled with beautiful and unusual antiques. *Duckworth Lunch,* at 191 Duckworth, serves fresh bagels, healthy soups, and the best chocolate chip cookies in town.

The dining room at the *Battery Inn,* which looks down on the harbor, has the best view in the city. The *Stone House* restaurant is a restored early-19th-century cottage at 8 Kenna's Hill near Quidi Vidi Lake. Fresh fish and produce are turned into such wonders as iced crab and ginger soup and cod tongues with chive and cream sauce. It probably has the best wine list in St. John's. For quality dining on a restricted budget, the *Continental Café* on George St. offers an international menu, with something for vegetarians, in a casual but intimate atmosphere. The pan-fried cod is choice; for breakfast, the freshly baked muffins are the best in town. A favorite local spot is the *Woodstock Colonial Inn,* 7 miles (11 km) out of town on Route 60. The cooking is superb, the atmosphere pleasing, and you can get such rarities as game dishes and seal flipper pie. The prices are reasonable, the portions generous. The *Kenmount* is a good Chinese restaurant, and for Mexican fare, try *Casa Grande,* a small, charming restaurant on the east end of Duckworth Street, near the *Newfoundland* hotel, or *Zapata's* at 10 Bates Hill.

Until recently, George Street, in the heart of downtown, was a service lane for businesses fronting on major commercial streets on either side. However, the City Fathers decided it should be developed as a major downtown attraction. Now, it is the social hub of the city, with a diverse selection of pubs, nightclubs, restaurants, and the new *Emma Butler Gallery,* at 111 George St.

Several major construction projects are reshaping the downtown skyline. Chief among recent new buildings is the *Radisson Plaza* hotel and convention center, a 276-room hotel operated by Commonwealth Holiday Inns of Canada, with a convention facility that can accommodate 2,000 people. See *Best En Route.*

The grand old Longshoreman's Protective Union Hall, at the foot of Victoria St., is now home to Newfoundland's flourishing indigenous theater. This lively downtown cultural center is known simply as "The Hall," and is the theatrical home of the comedy troup *CODCO.* During the summer it stages free, outdoor concerts.

The *Arts and Culture Centre,* a beautiful modern structure with a truly exceptional theater, hosts a summer festival of the arts that includes both professional and amateur theater, professional and amateur concerts, and crafts shows. There are free outdoor concerts by musical groups playing traditional Newfoundland music. The center also has two art galleries, a maritime museum, and three libraries. In even-numbered years, St. John's features The Sound Symposium, an international exhibit of sound, art, and concerts. Some events are free, including a daily harbor symphony.

Hilly downtown St. John's is a crowded city in the style of Queen Victoria, full of fanciful buildings clustered around the harbor guarded by Signal Hill. You need no directions to reach Duckworth and Water streets, the heart of downtown: Head downhill till you get there.

Apart from Signal Hill and the *Arts and Culture Centre,* downtown St. John's is where everything is located — good restaurants, craft shops, the principal museum, the magnificent old churches, and the best specialty food store in the Atlantic provinces.

Mary Jane's (377 Duckworth St.) is a 2-story establishment purveying anything from dried Chinese lily flowers to vine leaves pickled in Lebanon, brown rice, soy beans, fresh-baked cookies, and every herb and spice known sold in bulk.

St. John's has two major churches, both with splendid interiors — the Roman Catholic basilica (no one can miss its twin towers, built deliberately on the most conspicuous spot in the city) and the Anglican cathedral (straight downhill from the basilica). The cathedral is one of the finest examples of pure Gothic architecture in North America.

En Route from St. John's – The Marine Drive, one of Newfoundland's oldest roads, following the cliffs of the Atlantic shore past Logy Bay, starts from St. John's on Route 30 and joins Route 20 at Torbay. Middle Cove, 8 miles (13 km) from St. John's, has a public beach.

FLAT ROCK: The surf at Flat Rock is so violent at times that it damages houses on the far side of the highway. A huge flat stone, acres in area, forms a natural rock pier and beach. Mass is celebrated in summer at an outdoor shrine built into the rocks of a cliff beside the village church. Pope John Paul II said Mass here during his visit to Canada.

POUCH COVE: The surf at Pouch Cove also displays impressive violence. In this important fishing community, boats have to be winched out of the water on skids because there is no safe place to anchor them.

The lighthouse at Cape St. Francis can be reached only by a narrow, one-lane dirt road from Pouch Cove. It is a wild and picturesque spot.

The road between Pouch Cove and Portugal Cove on the west shore of the peninsula is very poor. You might return to St. John's and drive to Portugal Cove on Route 40.

PORTUGAL COVE: One of the oldest fishing settlements in Newfoundland, Portugal Cove is 16 miles (26 km) south of Pouch Cove. Trap boats and oceangoing fishing boats unload their catches on the wharf, where you may buy fresh salmon and cod.

A ferry connects Portugal Cove to Bell Island, an immense, cliff-ringed rock rising out of the bay, once the site of Canada's most productive iron mine. Though the supply of iron ore has been exhausted, thousands of people still live on the barren island.

En Route from Portugal Cove – Route 41 continues south through scenic Beachy Cove to St. Phillips, a small boat harbor, and Topsail, a town with a stony beach that is a popular Sunday drive destination for area families. At this point, you can return to St. John's within 20 minutes via Route 60, or continue south on Route 60 to the western shore of Conception Bay. The first stop on the west shore is Brigus, almost directly across the bay and 37 miles (60 km) from Topsail.

BRIGUS: If you look, you may find a plaque commemorating Captain Bob Bartlett (1875–1946), Newfoundland's greatest explorer, who made 30 Arctic expeditions, including three attempts to reach the North Pole with Robert Peary. Mementos of the expeditions are preserved in Bartlett's house, Hawthorne Cottage, which Parks Canada has declared a National Historic Site.

PORT-DE-GRAVE PENINSULA: A short drive beyond Brigus via Routes 70 and 72, the Port-de-Grave Peninsula has several small fishing villages worth visiting. At Hibbs Cove, on the eastern tip of the peninsula, the *Fisherman's Museum* is filled with artifacts of the colonial fishing industry.

HARBOUR GRACE: This crusty fishing and mercantile town is 10 miles (16 km) north of the Port de Grave Peninsula on Route 70. Harbour Grace is probably the only town in Canada with a monument to a pirate, Captain Peter Easton, who established his headquarters here in 1610 and built a private navy by enlisting hundreds of Newfoundlanders. In 1611, his navy of pirate ships defeated a French squadron in the harbor. After amassing vast wealth by preying on international shipping, Easton retired as a marquis in Savoy, France, with a fortune estimated at more than $50 million. Four miles (6.4 km) north of Harbour Grace is Carbonear, said to be the home and burial palce of Sheila Na Geira. This Irish princess was en route to the New World when her ship was captured by the adventurer Gilbert Pike. Happily, they fell in love and settled in Carbonear.

En Route from Harbour Grace – Route 74 leads across the peninsula to Trinity Bay and joins Route 80 at Hearts Content. The first transatlantic cable was landed at Hearts Content in 1866; by the turn of the century, it carried 3,000 messages a day to Europe. Route 80 south from Hearts Content passes through Hearts Desire and Hearts Delight, rejoining Route 1 at the head of Trinity Bay for the 50-mile (81-km) drive back to St. John's.

BEST EN ROUTE

Using St. John's as an anchor point, with the best hotels and motels on the Avalon Peninsula, you can cover most of this route in a day's drive. If you go farther along the north shore, there are inexpensive motels on the way. This is the most heavily traveled tourist route in Newfoundland, so reservations are advisable. Expensive lodging runs from $70 to $140; moderate from $35 to $65; inexpensive rooms, under $35. All prices are quoted in US dollars.

ST. JOHN'S

Radisson Plaza – A new 11-story property overlooking the harbor, it is swathed in pastels and marble and has 278 rooms, 9 suites, concierges on 3 floors, non-smoking floors, 24-hour room service, a casual restaurant, specialty dining room, and entertainment lounge. Fitness facilities include a health club, squash courts, indoor pool, sauna, and whirlpool bath. New Gower and Casey Sts. (phone: 709-739-6404 or 800-228-9822). Expensive.

Newfoundland – The grandest hotel in Newfoundland, it has 288 rooms and 14 suites on Cavendish Square, within easy walking distance of most downtown attractions. The elegant new building has a wide range of modern hotel services including a family restaurant, formal dining room, lounge, indoor pool, sauna, and gym. Duckworth St. (phone: 709-726-4980; 800-268-9143). Expensive.

Battery – This is a lovely hotel with 150 rooms and a splendid view of the harbor. Signal Hill (phone: 709-726-0040; 800-267-STEL). Expensive to moderate.

Prescott Inn – Only steps away from the elegant residence of the province's lieutenant governor, this is an award-winning heritage property. The proprietors have produced a wonderful blend of turn-of-the-century architecture, the best of contemporary Newfoundland art, and various modern amenities, including a whirlpool bath. The three large bedrooms, with period furniture, are available year-round. Smoking allowed on balconies only. Military Rd. (phone: 709-753-6036). Moderate.

Parkview Inn – Ensconced in a pleasant downtown residential area, this 15-room property has a fair dining room and reasonable prices. Military Rd. (phone: 709-753-2671). Inexpensive.

The Northwest Territories

To grasp the elemental fact of the Northwest Territories, consider a couple of simple but eloquent statistics: The Territories account for one third of the total area of the world's second largest country; that means they cover a little over 1.3 million square miles from east to west, north to south, stretching from Ellesmere Island, just off Greenland's northern coast, to the Mackenzie Mountain range at the Yukon border. The human population of this immense area is 52,000, nearly 25% of which lives in the capital, Yellowknife, with another 18 percent living on the other shores of Great Slave Lake.

If those figures speak to you of huge expanses of untouched wilderness, of life-and-death encounters with nature, of hunting and fishing for survival, of caribou and bear, moose and walrus, whale and trout, you are quite right. But it is not unexploited, and it is not an unpeopled paradise where modern life has had no impact. The most marginal areas of the Territories are hunted and fished by tribes of Métis, Dene, and Inuit. The life and livelihood of these native North Americans are under greater and greater pressure as new areas open up for development and wildernesses are explored for mineral deposits — especially for oil — by mining companies. So far, much of this human traffic of business and enterprise spins around the Yellowknife area near the Alberta border (which is by far the best route for entering the province and visiting its most accessible areas). But when new roads cut into the wilderness, they carry with them modern life.

Of this huge area, we have chosen to concentrate on Great Slave Lake, circled by smaller and larger towns, providing a wonderful introduction to both the human and natural environment of the Territories; a side trip to Nahanni National Park in the southwestern corner of the province, north of British Columbia (now more accessible since the building of the Liard Highway); and the Dempster Highway, the 460-mile (741-km) route between Dawson City in the Yukon and Inuvik in the Northwest Territories, a road cutting through what had been virgin territory previously unmarked by roadway, crossing the traditional wandering grounds of one of the largest herds of wild caribou in the world.

Information: TravelArctic, Box 1320, Yellowknife, NWT X1A 2L9 (phone: 403-873-7200, or 800-661-0788 to reach the Arctic hotline).

The Hay River to Yellowknife

To journey in the Northwest Territories is to travel between two cultures — one driven by the needs and technologies of contemporary society, the other a traditional, native way of life fast disappearing. The northern frontier is a land of bustling towns and cities not so very different from those towns farther south, with most of the amenities and some of the worries of any even slightly urban environment. The northern Homelands, however, are the small settlements scattered in the North and elsewhere where native people still rely on the traditional pursuits of hunting, fishing, and trapping to live, even while incongruous aspects of modern life appear and impinge on their society. Here traditional arts and crafts exist in the face of increasing pressure to urbanize a way of life that has changed little in thousands of years. And yet, in the last 20 years, the deep currents of change have undercut traditional lifestyles in a way unimaginable to the grandparents of the Inuit alive today. (Inuit — pronounced *in*-oo-it — means "the people" and is the proper term for native Americans of the Far North. The term Eskimo is a derogatory appellation picked up by early settlers, and which today is discouraged by the Inuit.)

Nowhere are all these forces more evident than around the Northwest Territories' mighty Great Slave Lake. The Chipeweyan people live here, a tribe of the Dene (pronounced de-*nay,* also meaning "the people") of the large Mackenzie district. Here too is thriving Yellowknife, the capital of the Territories since 1967. And the drive around the lake from Hay River to the capital crosses the Mackenzie River and gives the visitor a glimpse of the majesty of the area. And through it all run the winds of change, as gas and oil discoveries, in the wake of the Alaska pipeline project, bring to the relations between government and people — especially native people — a new edge and urgency.

A good outfitter is *North Horizon Tours,* run by Norm Zigarlick, a former Arctic bush pilot. Tours include wildlife, photography, fishing, and visits to Arctic communities. Write to PO Box 5896, Station L, Edmonton, AL T6C 4G5 (phone: 403-461-9583).

En Route from Hay River – Drive 27 miles (43 km) south on Highway 2 to Enterprise. There is one gas station and one restaurant in case you need a break. Turn west on Highway 1 to start the 307-mile (494-km) drive skirting Great Slave Lake, the third largest lake in North America, to the NWT capital of Yellowknife. Gas up either in Hay River or Enterprise — it's a 125-mile (201-km) drive to the next gas station in Fort Providence. You should also check to see if the ferry is running across the Mackenzie River to Fort Providence.

The highway is gravel, but the driving is good. Here the road follows a ridge overlooking a wide, wooded plain covered with the familiar jack pine. In the distance, you can see the wide expanse of Great Slave Lake. For a spectacular view — and a look at one of the North's many paradoxes — turn off into the Hart Lake fire tower access road, 29 miles (47 km) from Enterprise. The well-marked road leads to a picnic site, 500 yards beyond which, along the marked path, is a 250-foot escarpment, the remains of a coral reef.

Another 23 miles (37 km) brings you to the well-marked turnoff to Kakisa and the Lady Evelyn Falls campsite, with 10 tent sites and 5 RV pads. Drinking water and firewood are available. Fishing is good below the 48-foot falls and grayling are common. A 10-minute drive past the campsite is the small (pop. 30) village of Kakisa, where the Slavey still live off the land, hunting moose, fishing for pike and whitefish, and trapping muskrat and beaver. The small but well-kept log cabins are nestled in groves of pine and birch. There are no services here. Inquire first if you want to launch a boat because fishing nets are strung out around the lake. Keep your eyes open for the net floats when boating to avoid tangling your outboard in the nets and damaging both.

Eleven miles (18 km) from the Kakisa turnoff on Highway 1 is the junction of Highways 1 and 3. Turn north on Highway 3 for the Mackenzie River ferry crossing, Fort Providence, and Yellowknife. Highway 1 takes you to Fort Simpson and access to Nahanni National Park (see *The Nahanni*).

At the ferry crossing, 15 miles (24 km) from the junction, the *Merv Hardie* takes vehicles across the mile-wide river. The free service is available after break-up and before the freeze-up. Winter travelers drive right across the river on the 4-foot-thick ice, which supports up to 55 tons. When highway communications are interrupted during break-up and freeze-up, perishable goods must be flown into Yellowknife. Before the road to Yellowknife was built, goods were freighted across the ice of Great Slave Lake from Hay River to Yellowknife.

Free ferry service is provided during the summer; in winter, ice bridges make safe crossings possible. There are delays each spring and fall during break-up and freeze-up when these rivers cannot be crossed at all. For information on ferry operations, call 800-661-0751. For information on the Mackenzie or Yellowknife Highway call 800-661-0750 or ZENITH-2010.

FORT PROVIDENCE: Across the river, a 5-mile (8-km) drive takes you to the Fort Providence access road. A motel, restaurant, bar, gas station, and store are located between the junction and the settlement of 663, 3 miles (5 km) up the road. Two excellent craft shops in the village produce some of the best Dene handiwork in the valley. You can buy made-to-measure parkas, moosetufting, porcupine quill, and beadwork designs. Each settlement in the valley has its own style of artwork. One craft shop is in the *Snowshoe Restaurant,* across the street from the motel. The other is in the Dene Band office. If it's closed, inquire around, and someone will open it for you.

At the west end of the village is a monument to Sir Alexander Mackenzie, who passed through here in 1789 in his search for the Pacific Ocean. He didn't find the Pacific, but he was the first white man to get his baggage wet in the Arctic Ocean: He had camped on a beach in the Mackenzie Delta, just out of sight of the ocean. Everyone was sleeping when the tide came in, flooding out the camp. But this had no bearing on Mackenzie calling this, the river that now bears his name, the River of Disappointment. The Dene along the river call it the Mother River or the River of Life.

Father Henri Grollier, a Catholic priest, built a mission on Big Island in 1858, but after he moved it here three years later, the settlement gradually grew around it.

You can rent boats at either of the service stations for some excellent grayling and pike fishing, but watch out for the blackflies. These pesky bugs love to bite anywhere; bring a good insect repellent or head net. A mile from the junction of the access road, a beautiful campsite on the top of the river bluffs has secluded tenting and RV pads and a dumping station for RVs. You can watch tugs pushing laden barges downriver, heading for the High Arctic.

En Route from Providence – Head north on Highway 3 for the 144-mile (232-km) drive to Rae-Edzo, where you can gas up for the additional 62-mile

(100-km) drive into Yellowknife. On the east side of the highway is the Mackenzie Bison Sanctuary. The government transplanted 19 wood buffalo here from the Fort Smith area in 1963. Now the herd numbers well over 500, the only pure herd of wood buffalo left in North America. You probably won't see any near the highway since the animals tend to range closer to the shores of the lake. But you will see an occasional moose browsing in the numerous lakes and sloughs along the highway. And if you're lucky, you'll see a sandhill crane.

There is a picturesque view of Great Slave Lake's North Arm, dotted with numerous islands, at North Arm picnic site, 112 miles (180 km) north of Fort Providence.

There is a popular fishing spot on Mosquito Creek, 7 miles (11 km) south of Edzo on the highway. Pickerel (walleye) and grayling run in springtime. Black bear are also common in the area at that time. Extra care should be taken then, because bears just out of hibernation, still not quite awake, are particularly hungry.

RAE-EDZO: This is the largest Dene community in the NWT (pop. 1,378). The Dogrib tribe was mostly a nomadic people following the migratory caribou in winter and fishing the plentiful lakes in summer. At the turn of the century, this area produced tons of dried meat for Hudson Bay traders. Dr. John Rae established a post on the North Arm, 5 miles from the present settlement in 1852. It was moved in 1906 to its present site, where you can see some log cabins, the only remains of old Fort Rae.

Edzo was intended as a replacement community when it was built in 1965 on the south side of Frank's Channel. The government established this model community with a modern school, a nursing station, and housing at the same time the Mackenzie Highway was being built to Yellowknife. However, the residents refused to move to the new community, even though it was built at a higher, drier, and more sanitary location. They refused to abandon their homes built on the rocks and muskeg, where they could launch canoes into Marian Lake from their own backyards. Some finally did move, but the old community survives, strong as ever. There are no services in Edzo, but there are two gas stations in Rae. Walking around the village you see snowmobiles, dogs tied up waiting for winter snows, and fish hung up on drying racks.

Edzo was named after a famous Dogrib chief who brought peace to the area in the mid-1800s. His antagonist was Chief Akaitcho of the Yellowknife Indians, who ranged from Yellowknife Bay north almost to Coppermine. The Yellowknife preyed on the Dogrib, chasing them out of hunting and fishing grounds. In a confrontation between the two, according to legend, Edzo spoke so long and eloquently that Akaitcho was afraid to wage war again. Akaitcho helped Captain John Back in his trek to the Arctic Ocean up the Back River in 1832. The Yellowknife Indians disappeared as a distinct tribal unit after their ranks were decimated by a great flu epidemic in 1928. The survivors gradually moved into other settlements and were assimilated into other tribal groups.

Frank's Channel, between Rae and Edzo, also marks the geological dividing point between the sedimentary basin, an extension of the Canadian prairies, and the Precambrian Shield. The highway takes on a few more curves as it skirts lakes and sloughs nestled among hard rock outcrops. The familiar spruce and pine grow shorter here as they struggle for footholds in any dip and crevice that can hold a few inches of soil. This is also the area of permafrost, where only a few top feet of ground thaw in summertime.

Proceed north on Highway 3 and drive 62 miles (100 km) to Yellowknife.

YELLOWKNIFE: This city of 1,200, the capital of the Northwest Territories, owes its existence to two gold mines, and owes its growth to government offices administering a territory comprising one third the landmass of Canada. Nearly 25% of all NWT residents live in this city (the population of the entire territory is 52,000).

This city of high-rises and office buildings sprouting out of the surrounding taiga is the most cosmopolitan of all NWT communities. It's come a long way since Laurent Leroux, a Northwest Company trader, first built his trading post on Yellowknife Bay in 1789. Alexander Mackenzie passed through here in his roundabout search for the river that now bears his name. And John Franklin, famous for discovering the Northwest Passage, traveled up the Yellowknife River to the Arctic coast via the Coppermine River in 1819. Franklin later triggered one of the biggest manhunts in British naval history when he disappeared during his exploration in 1848.

The Hudson's Bay Company closed down the Yellowknife trading post in 1823, after the Bay amalgamated with its longtime fur trading rival, the Northwest Company. Little attention was given to the area for the next 75 years. Prospectors on their way to the Klondike via the Mackenzie River found traces of gold in the hard rock in 1896. In 1930, a major discovery precipitated a boom in the area. Con Mines, on the southern edge of Yellowknife, became the first mine to produce in the area in 1938. The second, Giant Yellowknife Mines, began production in 1945. Surface tours can be arranged by phoning the mine office (phone: 403-873-6301). Those who come at the right time may even see molten gold being poured into 70-pound bricks.

Take a walk around Old Town Yellowknife on the peninsula where, in the 1930s and 1940s, shacks fought for space on the bare rocks. Today, the Bush Pilot's Monument is perched on one of these rocks, overlooking the waters of Great Slave Lake. The shacks are long gone, but a cairn commemorates the legendary bush pilots who opened the North with their daring exploits in rickety planes. From the vantage point offered by the Bush Pilot's Monument, visitors can watch the floatplanes take off, flying tourists to remote fishing lakes and prospectors to another potential bonanza. Below the monument on the Back Bay side is the restored *Wild Cat Café,* one of the few surviving landmarks in Old Town.

On your drive into Yellowknife, you will probably notice the Bristol Monument, a Bristol freighter set atop a prominent rock outcrop. This plane made aviation history in May 1967, when Wardair pilot Don Braun touched it down on the North Pole, the first wheeled aircraft to do so. The Bristol, a relic of World War II, helped open many an isolated camp and mine in the NWT by freighting in construction materials, even bulldozers.

The Prince of Wales Northern Heritage Centre on the shore of Frame Lake is just a three-block walk from downtown. Opened in April 1979, it houses extensive displays of northern artifacts, ranging from Inuit carvings to dioramas of northern wildlife. Also in this well-rounded collection is a piece of Cosmos 954, the Soviet satellite that crashed into the Barrenlands 300 miles (483 km) east of Yellowknife on January 24, 1978.

And for something really different: Golf buffs arriving in Yellowknife around the longest day of the year, June 21, can participate in the Midnight Golf Tourney at *Yellowknife Golf Club.* This annual event draws participants and celebrities for a teeoff under the light midnight sky. The course is unique — the turf, sand; the greens, oiled sand; and the biggest hazards, ravens. The large plucky birds have been known to steal a golf ball from under the nose of a golfer. Contestants get a special repallant, liquid refreshment, and extra golf balls, among other things. This event is held in conjunction with *Raven Mad Days,* when stores remain open past midnight and the *Daughters of the Midnight Sun* carry on their tradition of zany entertainment wherever they can find a crowd, be it in a bar or on the street. The *Folks on the Rocks* music festival is held in mid-July.

Yellowknife has numerous hotels and motels that cater to a wide service and price range. Its stores can fill just about every need, but it's well to remember that prices in far-off Yellowknife are about 30% higher than in southern Canada because of the transportation costs. Many stores sell soapstone carvings and handicrafts. The largest collections can be found in *Northern Images* in the YK Mall (corner of Franklin and 48th Sts.) and the *Toa Chen's Art Gallery* in the Scotia Centre (corner of Franklin and

51st Sts.). Both stock the internationally famous Holman Island and Cape Dorset prints and etchings.

There's a large number of campsites within easy reach of Yellowknife. The Fred Henne Park across from the airport, the closest to town, has drinking water, tenting sites, and pads for RVs, with dumping facilities. Also, while at Long Lake consider taking the interesting "Trail of the Early Prospector," a self-guided, 2-hour interpretive hike that explains the area's unique geology as well as some of its flora and fauna. Fred Henne Park can get crowded on weekends because it has the only sandy swimming beach close to town, attracting residents enjoying the short but sunny summers.

Those wishing to get away from the crowds can drive the 50-mile (81-km) Ingraham Trail, named for the Yellowknife hotelier Vic Ingraham. The trail was to be the start of the ambitious Roads to Resources, skirting Great Slave Lake and linking many potential minesites. However, the project was abandoned in the late 60s.

Along the Ingraham Trail you'll now find hiking paths, boat launches, picnic sites, and camping (with drinking water and firewood) at Prelude Lake and Reid Lake territorial parks. Fishing is a popular area pastime, with lake trout, Northern pike, walleye, whitefish, and Arctic grayling the primary catches in the waterways off the trail. It's also a very good place for canoeing. If you venture out here in winter, you might see the Bathurst Caribou herd, which migrates as far south as this road. You can also engage in activities like ice fishing, cross-country skiing, and snowshoeing. (Fishing licenses are necessary; they are available at the Northwest Territories border information booths, most sport fishing lodges, sporting goods and hardware stores, and the RCMP district offices of the Northwest Territories Wildlife Service and the Department of Fisheries and Oceans offices.)

En Route from Yellowknife – Drive 2 miles (3 km) past the Giant Mines property on Highway 4. The first site is the Yellowknife River Park across the bridge. A boat launch provides access to the northern pike-rich river. Or you can fish for grayling and whitefish at Tartan Rapids, 7 miles (11 km) upstream, where Prosperous Lake empties into the river. There are plenty of pike in the shallows and weed beds that will rise to a homemade lure, but red devils are a favorite.

There are three other picnic sites over the next 12 miles (19 km), each providing hiking trails and fishing. Prelude Lake Territorial Park at the end of a 1-mile (1½-km), well-marked turnoff has a boat launch, a beach, and good trout fishing. The *Prelude Lake Lodge* provides commercial accommodations, boat and motor rentals, and a café. Fishermen should watch for sudden shifting winds when boating on the larger lakes. If you get into difficulty, make for the nearest land and wait out the weather; even the smaller lakes kick up sizable waves, and the water here is extremely cold.

At Kilometer 48 you'll find a parking area at the beginning of the well-marked scenic trail leading to the Cameron River Falls. The ¾-mile trail leads to a 45-foot waterfall, and side trails lead to another, smaller waterfall downstream.

Another 8-mile (13-km) drive takes you to Reid Lake Territorial Park, the best along the Ingraham Trail. Water, wood, and a boat launch are available, plus plenty of good fishing. This 27-site camping area is only 7 miles (11 km) from the end of the road at Tibbet Lake.

BEST EN ROUTE

Due to the scarcity of accommodations in the Northwest Territories, make reservations as far in advance as possible. In addition, you should expect to pay between $50 and up per night for a double in the hotels we've listed here. All prices are quoted in US dollars.

Yellowknife has more than 25 dining establishments; some are licensed premises.

YELLOWKNIFE

Discovery Inn – This downtown establishment has 41 rooms, a family-style restaurant, a lounge, and conference facilities. Box 784, Yellowknife, NWT X1A 2N6 (phone: 403-873-4151).

Explorer – A modern hotel with 110 guestrooms, all with color TV sets and air conditioning, the facilities include the *Treeline Café*, fine dining in the *Factors Club*, a cocktail lounge, and game room. Postal Service 7000, Yellowknife, NWT X1A 2R3 (phone: 403-873-3531).

Northern Lites – Located 1 block from downtown, Yellowknife's newest motel has 20 guestrooms, all with cable-equipped color TV sets. Box 2532, Yellowknife, NWT X1A 2P8 (phone: 403-873-6023).

Twin Pine – This motel halfway between Old and New Towns accommodates 100. There is no café, but breakfast is available. Some rooms also have kitchen facilities. Franklin Ave. Mailing address: PO Box 596, Yellowknife, NWT X1A 2N4 (phone: 403-873-8511).

Yellowknife Inn – A 150-room hotel, conveniently located downtown, it has a café, bar, lounge, newsstand, and one of the best dining places in town, the *Mackenzie Dining Room*. The menu includes a selection of Northern dishes such as arctic char, caribou steaks, and musk ox. The café is a crossroads of the North, frequented by businessmen, travelers, and by the mining and aviation fraternity. The inn is the site of the Annex Conference Centre and home of the NWT Legislative Assembly. Franklin Ave. Mailing address: PO Box 490, Yellowknife, NWT X1A 2N4 (phone: 403-873-2601).

YWCA – Here are 32 rooms, many with kitchenettes, for men and women. Weekly and monthly rates are available. 5004 54th St, Yellowknife, NWT X1A 2R6 (phone: 403-920-2777).

The Nahanni

The 450-mile (720-km) journey from Great Slave Lake's western shore to Nahanni National Park in the southwestern corner of the Northwest Territories is a trip that will appeal primarily to hard-core wilderness trekkers, for the main purpose of a visit to Nahanni, besides the lure of burying oneself in its 1,840 square miles of mountains, lakes, and wilderness, is South Nahanni River, one of the purest, wildest, roughest stretches of white water left in the world. The Liard Highway, which opened in 1983, provides easy access to Nahanni National Park for the first time. The highway starts at Fort Nelson, British Columbia, and runs through the fabled Liard Valley to Fort Simpson in the Northwest Territories. To get to Nahanni National Park, drive the Liard Highway from Fort Nelson up to Fort Liard and on to Blackstone Territorial Campground from where you make the 40-mile boat trip into the park.

The usual route into the park is by charter aircraft from Fort Liard or Fort Simpson. *Liard Air Ltd.* (PO Box 3190, Fort Nelson, BC V0C 1R0; call 604-774-2909 in summer; and 604-986-8941 in winter); *Deh Cho Air Ltd.* (Liard Valley Band Development Corp., Fort Liard, NWT X0G 0A0; phone: 403-770-4103); and *Simpson Air* (Box 260, Fort Simpson, NWT X0E 0N0; phone: 403-695-2505) will transport both you and your canoe into Nahanni National Park. *Simpson Air* also has a canoe rental service.

En Route to Nahanni National Park – From the junction of Routes 1 and 3 near Fort Providence, it's a 180-mile (289.7-km) drive to Fort Simpson on the well-graveled, all-weather highway. If you're going straight through, figure on 4 to 5 hours' driving. The park at Whittaker Falls, 93 miles (150 km) from Fort Simpson, has a nice view of Coral Falls, a short hike away. The well-laid-out campsite has wood supplies but no drinking water. Trees are much taller in this area, a favorite moose hunting region. The road is relatively level and straight. A free ferry takes you across the Liard River into Fort Simpson, 10 miles (16 km) away.

FORT SIMPSON: The Northwest Company established the Fort of the Forks here in 1804 to trade for the rich beaver and marten furs that fashion-hungry Europe demanded. This town of 987 at the confluence of the Liard and Mackenzie rivers is named for Sir George Simpson, governor of the Hudson's Bay Company when it amalgamated with its rival Northwest Company in 1812. If you walk around town, you'll see an occasional small, steam river tug lying on the shores, a remnant of the day when Simpson was an important stopping point for river barges that loaded up here with food, fuel, and furs for their voyages up and down the Mackenzie. Simpson has great potential for agriculture, and for many years the church missions grew their own potatoes and grains and raised cattle. The federal government established an experimental farm here but closed it in 1969. When the highway was built, it cost less to import all the food needed from outside.

NAHANNI NATIONAL PARK: The Liard Highway leads to Blackstone Territorial Park, on the Liard River outside Nahanni National Park. Here you'll find an information center, campsites for tents and RVs, and a boat launch. Nahanni National Park is accessible from here only via the Liard River (it's a 40-mile boat trip) and no boat rentals are available; if you don't bring your own craft, an outfitter based here provides trips into the park. Those wishing to fly in can charter an aircraft costing from about 85¢ a mile and up, depending on the aircraft type, the number of passengers, and the weight of gear. Or you may rent a boat and guide for the trip along the Mackenzie River, up the Liard, and into the Nahanni River and its legend-shrouded canyons. At 312 feet, Virginia Falls is twice the height of Niagara Falls, and some of the canyons are twice as deep as those in the Grand Canyon. Legends tell of a lost tribe of Indians (Nahanni means "the people over there"), tropical valleys, and sightings of Sasquatch, the legendary Bigfoot.

The legends arose from prospectors traveling up the Liard on their way to the Klondike gold rush in the Yukon. In 1904, three McLeod brothers entered the Nahanni Valley looking for gold. Rumor had it that they found gold nuggets the size of grapes. The following year, two of the brothers returned to the valley and disappeared. Three years later their headless bodies were found, giving the name to Headless Valley, where they had their cabin. Their fate remains a mystery, with legends mushrooming — of cabins mysteriously burning, of murders, and many tall tales. Others have followed, looking for the McLeod brothers' mother lode, but no one has found it. Albert Faille spent his life looking, making more than 30 trips into the valley; as you portage around Virginia Falls, you use the route he cut on his travels.

You can find orchids growing around the falls, take a dip in sulfur hot springs, hike the trails into the mountains, or stalk wildlife with your camera. Dall's sheep can be seen on the mountainsides, moose and bear in the valley, and woodland caribou in the upper valleys.

Those planning to canoe the river must be experienced in white water. Register your travel plans with the national parks warden at the Fort Simpson headquarters or the Nahanni Butte warden station at the entrance to the park. The Royal Canadian Mounted Police also offer a wilderness travel registration service throughout the North. If you're heading into the bush, tell them where you're going and when you expect to return. If something happens, help will be on the way once you're reported overdue.

Good outfitters that offer canoeing and rafting trips on the Nahanni River in summer months are *Nahanni River Adventures*, PO Box 8368, Station F, Edmonton, AL T6H 4W6 (phone: 403-439-1316) and *Black Feather Wilderness Adventures*, 1341 Wellington St., Ottawa, Ontario K1Y 3B8 (phone: 613-722-9717).

If you decide to canoe yourself, first study the literature on canoeing this valley.

BEST EN ROUTE

Due to the scarcity of accommodations in the Northwest Territories, you should make reservations as far in advance as possible. Expect to pay $40 and up per night for a double in the hotels listed here. All prices are quoted in US dollars.

FORT SIMPSON

Maroda – A 15-room motel with TV sets and kitchenettes, it also has a gift shop. Open year-round. PO Box 67, Fort Simpson, NWT X0E 0N0 (phone: 403-695-2602).

Nahanni Inn – This sturdy hotel that sleeps 70 is open year-round. All rooms have private bath, cable TV, and telephone; 4 suites are equipped with kitchens. A restaurant and cocktail lounge are on the premises. The hotel overlooks the Mackenzie and Liard rivers. PO Box 248, Fort Simpson, NWT X0E 0N0 (phone: 403-695-2201).

Nahanni National Park – For information on accommodations, campsites, and outfitters, contact the Superintendent, Nahanni National Park, Postal Bag 300, Fort Simpson, NWT X0E 0N0 (phone: 403-695-3151).

Dawson City to Inuvik

The Dempster, one of the newest of NWT highways, snakes 475 miles (765 km) from the rolling hills around historic Dawson City, Yukon, to above the Arctic Circle. The road ends at Inuvik, NWT, on the eastern edge of the majestic Mackenzie River delta, so it is necessary to drive out on the same route you came in on. The highway, named after a Royal Canadian Mounted Police corporal who found the ill-fated Dawson patrol, is the only public access highway reaching this far north in North America.

Since the highway is in such a remote area, facilities are scarce, and drivers should carry enough fuel to reach the next gas pump. Although only two places between Dawson and Inuvik provide accommodations, there are plenty of campsites to pitch a tent.

The drive takes you to the top of the world, from the forested slopes of the Yukon across the Eagle Plain wintering grounds of the Porcupine caribou herd to the alpine tundra of the Richardson Mountains. There will be plenty of opportunity to photograph and observe wildlife along the route, so have your camera ready.

Before making this trip, inquire about the state of the highway, whether the ferry is operating across the Peel and Mackenzie rivers, and whether the gas and lodge facilities at Eagle Plains are open. For information on ferry operations, call: toll free, within the Northwest Territories, Zenith 2022; in Inuvik, 403-979-3828. For information on the Dempster Highway., call 800-661-0752 (in NWT and Alberta).

The migration of the 150,000 head of Porcupine caribou across the highway may also temporarily close the road. But since this massive movement coincides with freeze-up and break-up periods, when the ferry is not in operation, the highway will probably be closed anyway. Check with either the Yukon or NWT Department of Highways before proceeding.

The Dempster Highway is also open from December to late April; however, travelers should be well prepared for adverse driving conditions on this road in winter months.

Make sure your tires are good, and carry extra gas in the trunk. In case of breakdowns, there are garages in Dawson and Inuvik; one has recently opened in Fort McPherson. It's wise to have a down-filled jacket as well. The nighttime temperatures can get chilly in high altitudes and near lakes and rivers. A wide variety of food and supplies is available in both Dawson and Inuvik, and you can get the basics in Fort McPherson and Arctic Red River.

En Route to Dawson Creek – From Whitehorse in the Yukon, take Routes 1 and 2 to Steward Junction, 214 miles (345 km) away. Instead of following Route 2 here, turn off to Highway 3 and follow it 114 miles (184 km) to the gold rush town of Dawson Creek. The turnoff to the Dempster is 26 miles (42 km) back, but since you've driven all the way up here, Dawson is worth seeing too (see "The Dawson Circle Route," *The Yukon*).

En Route from Dawson – Drive east on Route 3 to its intersection of Route 11 and turn north. There is a gas station at this junction where you can fuel up and you can stay at the *Eagle Plains* hotel (mi 123/km 371). The next gas available beyond Ogilvie River is at Fort McPherson, 337 miles (543 km) past the lodge. Also check to see if the ferries at Arctic Red River and Fort McPherson are operating.

The Tombstone campgrounds, on a ridge above the Klondike River 45 miles (72 km) north of the junction, offer minimal conveniences. Another 78 miles (126 km) through rolling, forested hills takes you to the Ogilvie River (named for the Yukon commissioner at the time of the Yukon gold rush) campsite. The lodge is across the river.

Caribou stragglers are sometimes visible on the Eagle Plains. The Porcupine herd migrates from the North Slope of Alaska into the Yukon interior. This herd was the subject of much debate during Judge Thomas Berger's public inquiry into the building of the Mackenzie Valley gas pipeline and will also affect the building of a gas pipeline down the Dempster, linking gas reserves in the Mackenzie Delta with the Alaska Highway gas pipeline. As you near the NWT border and the Richardson Mountains, you might see Dall's sheep. In June, snowbanks will still line the side of the road. Once you hit the NWT-Yukon border, the cable-operated ferry across the Peel River is only 47 miles (76 km) away.

FORT McPHERSON: This is a Dene settlement of 760 people on the Peel River. The Loucheux rely on hunting, trapping, and government work for survival. The area is rich in mink, muskrat, lynx, and beaver. The present site, originally called Fort Bell, was established in 1840 by Alex Isbister and John Bell, Northwest Company fur traders. Later its name was changed to honor Murdoch McPherson, chief trader for the Hudson's Bay Company. The RCMP established this as one of their main patrol posts in the early 1900s to bring justice to whalers wintering on Herschel Island off the Yukon's north coast.

In the winter of 1910–1911, Inspector F. J. Fitzgerald of the RCMP attempted a patrol from McPherson to Dawson with three companions. Usually the patrols came from Dawson over the Richardson Mountains; reversing the route would have been a historic first. The patrol, without competent guides, lost its way. With heavy snows and bad weather obscuring landmarks, they missed the turn that would have taken them through a pass. Hopelessly lost, they turned back after running low on food. Starvation and cold took their toll, although two made it to within 20 miles of home. The bodies were found by Corporal W. D. Dempster, en route from Dawson to McPherson in search of the lost patrol. Fort Fitzgerald, formerly Smith's Landing (south of Fort Smith), was renamed to honor the inspector.

For provisions, stop at *Al's General Store* (phone: 403-952-2417).

En Route from Fort McPherson – The Arctic Red River lies just east of Fort McPherson, and between the two communities are two picnic areas that offer excellent views of the river rapids; both are real hot spots for whitefish and grayling. As you approach the ferry crossing at Arctic Red River, you'll come to a ridge with a splendid view of the Arctic Red River pouring into the MacKenzie River. Unbelievably, swans nest in this area.

ARCTIC RED RIVER: This is a traditional fishing camp for the Loucheux, who catch their winter supply of northern pike and whitefish for themselves and their dogs here. You can see fish drying on racks around the town. The settlement gained some permanence when Father Jean Seguin, OMI, established a Roman Catholic mission here in 1868. Eventually, the Hudson's Bay set up a trading post here. Only three families lived here 40 years ago. Now the population is 108.

En Route from Arctic Red River – A government-run ferry takes passengers across the mile-wide river. Across the mighty Mackenzie are four sites in the next 84 miles for picnics, fishing, shutterbugging, and relaxing before you arrive at the next territorial campground, Chuk Park, with the basic conveniences of territorial parks. To view the scenery along the highway, most travelers just pull off on the shoulder of the road.

INUVIK: This Inuvialuit word means "place of man." The Inuvialuit are the Delta and Western Arctic Eskimo, or Inuit. Located in the Mackenzie Delta, this is a modern town as towns in the North go. Construction began in 1955, and it officially opened on July 18, 1958, as a replacement community for Aklavik, on the western side of the delta. Government engineers thought Aklavik would be swept into the Mackenzie because of the constant erosion of the riverbanks. Aklavik's motto is "The Town that Wouldn't Die," so few moved to the new center despite promises of better services and housing. Aklavik is still alive and well, but all government offices moved to the new site, 35 miles (58 km) west. Inuvik, mainly a government town of 3,400, enjoyed a boom period when oil companies were drilling into the delta to find oil and gas reserves. Most of the petroleum exploration now is in the Beaufort Sea, centered out of Tuktoyaktuk (more commonly known as Tuk), 70 miles (113 km) to the north, a modern town with most conveniences. Inuvik is a good example of how people adapt to a frigid northern environment. Until the main street was paved in 1978, wooden boardwalks protected one's boots from the thick, springtime mud. (Vestiges of these wooden sidewalks can still be found in some areas of town.) Buildings are built on piles driven into the permafrost — ground permanently frozen to depths of 300 feet. (If they were built on top of the ground, heat from the building would melt the permafrost; soon the ground would settle and the building sink.) It's impossible to bury sewer and water lines for the same reason. Digging through permafrost is like digging through rock, and if you did bury the lines, they would have to be heated to prevent them from freezing. Instead, service lines are laid on top of the ground in utilidors, insulated corridors connecting buildings.

Permafrost has some advantages. The hunters and trappers association tunneled into a ridge to make a community freezer. Thirty feet underground, meat stays frozen no matter how hot the summer. Summer temperatures may reach the high 80s F (30s C); the summer mean is in the 50s F ('teens C).

The Inuvik branch of *Northern Images,* the retail arm of the northern cooperatives, is housed in an octagonal building. Here you'll find soapstone carvings by internationally recognized Inuit carvers; silkscreens and soapstone lithographs from Holman Island and Sachs Harbour, 400 air miles (644 km) to the northeast; wolf, muskrat, and coyote parkas and coats made in the shops of Tuk and Aklavik. Or you can purchase the finely made Inuvik duffle parkas. Inquire at *Northern Images* about seeing the native craftswomen at work.

Boats and guides are available for fishing the twisting channels of the resource-rich Mackenzie Delta. The fishing is splendid in nearby lakes, accessible by chartering a small plane. *Inuvik's Happy Valley Campground* is a good choice if you'd like to pitch your tent where there are views of the lakes and channels of the Mackenzie Delta.

Inuvik is the transportation center for the delta and western Arctic region, providing regularly scheduled flights to such Inuit centers as Sachs Harbour, Holman Island, Tuk, Aklavik, and Coppermine. Each of these has accommodations if you want to spend a day or two watching how Inuit live off the land, sealing, whaling, and hunting.

BEST EN ROUTE

Due to the scarcity of accommodations in the Northwest Territories, it is necessary to make reservations as far in advance as possible. Expect to pay at least $60 per night for a double in the hotels we've listed here. All prices are quoted in US dollars.

INUVIK

Eskimo Inn – A downtown establishment with 78 rooms and a wide range of services, including a café, lounge, and dining room. Mailing address: PO Box 1740, Inuvik, NWT X0E 0T0 (phone: 403-979-2801).

Finto – This 51-room motel is between the airport and downtown. Mailing address: PO Box 1925, Inuvik, NWT X0E 0T0 (phone: 403-979-2647).

Inuvik Inn – Now 5 rooms, but in the process of expanding to 30: Progress is slow when building is possible only a few months each year. The inn features a café, banquet facilities, catering service, gift shop. On airport road. Box 1557, Inuvik, NWT XOE 0T0 (phone: 403-979-2631).

Mackenzie – This hostelry has 33 newly renovated rooms, 2 licensed lounges, coffee shop, large dining room with fireplace, and a 150-seat nightclub. Box 1618, Inuvik, NWT XOE 0T0 (phone: 403-979-2861).

Hay River to Fort Smith

The 174-mile (280-km) drive along Highway 5 from Hay River to Fort Smith and the Wood Buffalo National Park delights photographers and naturalists. You won't find polar bears this far south, but in the thickets of birch and poplar alongside the road you can photograph the last free herd of buffalo roaming in their natural habitat. The park is the home for migratory birds after their winter vacations in warmer climates. Bird-watchers can count 200 varieties, including the whooping crane whose wild population now numbers nearly 200. Once thought to be extinct, "whoopers" are making a slow comeback. In late August and September the numerous lakes, sloughs, and lush deltas are alive with birds gathering in flocks for their flight south, but it is unlikely that motorists will see them.

Travelers driving here can do so in relative comfort. The all-weather gravel highways from the NWT border are well maintained, wide, relatively straight — and sometimes dusty. For more information on road conditions, call 403-874-3780 (Hay River) or, toll-free, ZENITH-2018 or 800-661-0751 for communities in the NWT on the southern Mackenzie road system (Fort Smith, Pint Point, Fort Resolution, Enterprise, Fort Liard, Fort Simpson, Fort Providence, Yellowknife, Rae Edzo).

The Southern Mackenzie may not be far enough north for you to enjoy the pleasure of the sun overhead 24 hours a day. But during the summer there is more daylight than dark for you to pack more sightseeing into your day. For instance, in June in Fort Smith the sun rises at 3 AM and sets at 10 PM — and it hardly gets dark during the 5-hour nights.

Dress as you would for camping in the mountains. Mean summer temperatures range from the upper 30s F ('teens C) to the low 60s F ('teens C). Highs in the 90s have been recorded in many areas — and most also have records of summer freezes, so bring along a warm jacket. It will also help keep away the mosquitoes. Since the bugs can be a nuisance, take steps to avoid discomfort: Camp in dry, open areas where breezes can sweep them away. A long-lasting mosquito coil is effective if you burn a couple upwind.

All of the camp and picnic sites along this route have drinking water and are well stocked with firewood. The towns of Hay River and Fort Smith can meet most of your needs. If you're not camping, there are hotels and motels with restaurants.

On the banks of the Slave River, Fort Smith developed from a portage around a series of four rapids. This was the favorite and easiest route for early explorers and traders penetrating the Far North.

The gently rolling countryside is an extension of the prairies. Near Fort Smith, approaching the Precambrian Shield, the terrain becomes more rocky.

En Route from Edmonton, Alberta – There are two routes through Alberta to the NWT.

The quicker one is via the Yellowhead Highway 16. Drive 25 miles (40 km) west out of Edmonton and turn north on Highway 43. At Valleyview turn north on Highway 34 to Donnelly. As you go north the road becomes Highway 2. Follow this through the rolling countryside to Peace River, then 16 miles (26 km) farther to Grimshaw. This is Kilometer Zero of the Mackenzie Highway. A monument and plaque just north of the village commemorate the explorer Alexander Mackenzie and the construction of the highway. It's 300 miles (483 km) from Edmonton to Grimshaw and 340 miles (547 km) farther to Hay River, hub of the NWT. Poplar and birch gradually crowd out the farmland as you drive north, with balsam, pine, and spruce taking over near the NWT border.

The second route, via Lesser Slave Lake, is only 25 miles longer, and more picturesque. (You'll also find excellent northern pike fishing in the lake.) Follow Highway 2 north out of Edmonton through the towns of Slave Lake, High Prairie Peace River, and on to Grimshaw.

The well-kept Mackenzie Highway, paved all the way north to Hay River, is wide and straight, unlike the twisting Alaska Highway. Maps, information, and a detailed *Explorers' Guide* are available at the border tourist information center.

Driving and passing other cars on gravel highways require extra caution. Dust, which can impair your view of oncoming traffic, is a special problem. There are 2-mile stretches of straight highway that are oiled and spread with a dust suppressant to make passing safer. Watch for these areas; they are well posted. If you get caught in dust from an oncoming or passing vehicle and you can't see the road, slow down, but don't stop.

NWT drivers are courteous and willing to help those stranded by the roadside. It's more than goodwill; in winter, when temperatures hit 40F below (-40C), it's a matter of survival.

HAY RIVER: This junction community of 3,000 on Great Slave Lake provides access to all the settlements on the Mackenzie Highway system. The Hudson's Bay Company built the first trading post here in 1868, but the population didn't grow until the Mackenzie Highway system was completed and oil and gas exploration begun. A railway finished in 1964 to carry lead-zinc ore from Pine Point to smelters established the town as a transportation center. Freight bound for High Arctic settlements is transhipped here onto barges for the 1,200-mile voyage down the Mackenzie River to the Arctic Ocean, a precarious lifeline depending heavily on the weather: Mackenzie River and High Arctic communities depend for survival on these once-a-year supply drops of food, fuel, and construction material.

Drive past the airport into Hay River's Old Town, where wharves of the barging companies are piled high with supplies for exotic places like Holman Island, Fort Good Hope, and Tuktoyaktuk. Old Town is also the home of the commercial fishermen who ply the waters of Great Slave Lake, winter and summer, bringing in trout, whitefish, northern pike, and inconnu. Some of the pike is shipped to France, where it's made into pâté.

Old Town is an area of small, old frame houses built on the flood plain of the Hay River delta. After two disastrous floods, the townsite was moved to high ground upriver. New Town is dominated by a 14-story high-rise, built in anticipation of a gas pipeline down the Mackenzie Valley. Hay River would then have become a staging area for the project. The Diamond Jenness School, across the street from the high-rise, is a striking example of northern-flavored architecture. Students were given their choice of color for the building, thus, a shocking purple building has become a landmark. Disconcerted at first, everyone is now quite proud of it. (The school was named after the anthropologist who first studied northern native culture around 1910.)

Although relatively small, the town provides most amenities. Several motels and hotels offer good, clean service, and some have restaurants and bars. The *Back Eddy* restaurant (phone: 403-874-6680), just a block from downtown, has the best steaks in town. Unleaded gas is available in the gas stations and garages, and tourists can find just about any camping supplies.

En Route from Hay River – Travel south on Highway 2 for 5 miles (8 km) and turn east onto Highway 5 for the start of the 174-mile (280-km) drive to Fort Smith and Wood Buffalo National Park. Two miles (3 km) from the junction, a road turning north leads to the Hay River Indian Reserve. At the end of the 6-mile (10-km) road, at the original site of Hay River, old churches and the remains of the Hudson's Bay post offer quiet testimony to the two major influences on early northern life.

Highway 5 forks 34 miles (55 km) past the reserve turnoff. Turn south on Highway 5 for 130 miles (209 km) to Fort Smith.

Take Highway 6 to Fort Resolution, 41 miles (66 km) east, where you will find a fur trapping center of 550, most of the inhabitants of Chipeweya descent. This is the last band of North American Indians to hunt wild buffalo as a food source. A sawmill provides employment, but many still support themselves by hunting, trapping, and fishing in the fur-rich Slave delta. Fort Resolution was an important center at one time, when barges plied the Slave River, bringing goods from Fort McMurray. The large mission hostel and school are no longer used.

WOOD BUFFALO NATIONAL PARK: With more than 17,300 square miles, this is Canada's largest national park. Straddling the Alberta-NWT border, it's the home of the world's last free-roaming buffalo herd, the last refuge for the endangered whooping crane, and the world's only river rookery of white pelican. These birds normally nest in lakes, but in a deviation of the evolutionary process some birds adapted to the white waters of the Slave River rapids.

The park was created in 1922 to protect the estimated 1,500 surviving wood buffalo, a longer-legged, darker, and hardier cousin of the plains buffalo. Six years later the government herded 6,000 plains buffalo from Wainright, Alberta, into the park when their grazing grounds became a military range. The park is also home to the Sweetgrass Naturalist camp, an area where Canadian Wildlife Service staff and park staff rounded up buffalo to inoculate them against anthrax, tuberculosis, and other diseases. Although it was to protect the animals, the effort caused them stress and was discontinued during the mid-1970s. At one time, the area had a human population approaching 4,000, supported in part by a large logging operation nearby. Today, it's possible to walk about 9 miles of trail that was once built as an access road from the Sweetgrass Landing to the Sweetgrass Station. An alternative is to paddle in on canoes on Sweetgrass Creek. In addition, some of the buildings on the edge of the corral are still standing, and can be rented by contacting the park service: Superintendent, Wood Buffalo National Park, Box 750, Fort Smith, NWT X0E 0P0 (phone: 403-872-2349). The buildings provide a site from which it's still possible to view the buffalo, wolves, and bison in their native habitat.

The wood and plains buffalo interbred to produce a hybrid that adapts well to the cold. They are frequently visible lounging beside the road or wallowing in the dust to get rid of flies and mosquitoes. Photographers should be prepared: Buffalo and black bear normally will dash out of view when they see a car (buffalo may merely ignore you); nevertheless, don't get out of your vehicle.

When camping, keep your food in the vehicle, never in your tent, unless you want unwelcome visitors. There are special regulations for camping and hiking in national parks. If you're hiking one of the many trails in the park for a couple of days, you'll need a special campfire permit (free), available from a park officer or park headquarters in Fort Smith. Schedules for hikes, lectures, and films are available at the park office. For further information contact: Superintendent, Wood Buffalo National Park, Box 750, Fort Smith, Northwest Territories X0E 0P0 (phone: 403-872-2349).

A variety of features are rare to the area — northern areas of the park are dotted with sinkholes typical of Karst topography, and south there are expansive salt plains encompassing some 250 square miles. Early traders and natives used the salt in their diets and as a medium of trade.

On the highway near the Angus fire tower, 6 miles (10 km) inside the park, there's a sinkhole 80 feet deep and 120 feet across. Sinkholes are created by the collapse of underground caves. Pine Lake, south of Fort Smith, is composed of three adjoining sinkholes 70 feet deep filled with water. If spelunking is what you're after, the park office can direct you to little-explored caves.

Highway 5 takes you into Fort Smith, 1 mile north of the Alberta-NWT border. Five miles (8 km) south of town the highway splits into the 185-mile (298-km) loop road through the southeastern portion of the park. Forty miles (64 km) south of the junction on the west fork of the loop road is the Pine Lake campground, with graveled tenting pads and services for RVs. (A special permit required for fishing in national parks is available for a nominal fee at the warden's station, 1 mile from the campground.)

The west fork of the loop road continues south 50 miles (81 km) to Peace Point on the Peace River. If you want to travel the entire loop, check first at the warden station — the section past Peace Point can become impassable after heavy rains.

Starting back at the junction of the loop road, the east fork takes you on a 15-mile (24-km) drive along Slave River past Mountain, Pelican, and Cassette rapids to Fort Fitzgerald, the southern terminus of the portage around this navigation bottleneck. The road is in good shape for another 40 miles (64 km), to the Hay Camp forest fire control base. Inquire before proceeding farther.

Goods shipped on barges from Fort McMurry once portaged 23 miles from Fort Fitzgerald, more commonly known as Fitz, to Bell Rock, just north of Fort Smith. The four rapids have taken the lives of several unwary travelers who thought they could shoot the white water. The name Rapids of the Drowned speaks for itself. Goods stopped coming through Fort Smith after terminal facilities were built in Hay River in the mid-1960s. Fitz is almost a ghost town now, although some people live here. The town, originally called Smith's Landing, was renamed in honor of RCMP Inspector F. J. Fitzgerald, who died in 1911 along with three companions attempting a patrol by dog team from Fort McPherson to Dawson City. (See Fort McPherson in the *Dawson City to Inuvik* route for more about Fitzgerald.)

The Mountain Rapids are also the nesting site for the northernmost rookery of white pelicans. You can see these graceful birds in the rapids, although they feed mostly in the surrounding lakes. Many trails lead from the road to the bluff overlooking the rapids and the pelican's nesting site, which may be endangered if plans go ahead for a mammoth hydroelectric project on the Mountain Rapids south of Fort Smith.

For information on hiking, paddling, rowing, or dog sledding into Wood Buffalo National Park, contact *SubArctic Wilderness Adventures,* PO Box 685, Fort Smith, NWT X0E 0P0 (phone: 403-872-2467).

FORT SMITH: This town, like many other northern settlements, started out as a Hudson's Bay post in 1874. Its strategic position on a portage contributed to its growth. Everyone traveling north on the main water route of Peace River passed through here. The federal government established Smith as the main administrative center for all the NWT in 1911. In 1967, when the government decided to administer out of the North instead of Ottawa, Yellowknife was chosen as the NWT capital. Many residents were upset by this at the time but now feel it was the best thing to happen to the town. It is now a regional administrative center for the NWT government as well as the territory's academic and vocational training center.

Fort Smith was named after Donald Alexander Smith, the first Baron of Strathcona, who drove the last spike in Canada's transcontinental railroad in 1885. Ironically, the railroad was built to Hay River, which stunted the growth of Fort Smith. The major barge company, Northern Transportation Ltd., moved its transshipment point to Hay River so barges no longer had to make the trip from Fort McMurray, Alberta, to Great Slave Lake via the Slave River.

The town of 2,500 is large enough to meet most travelers' needs. There's a motel, a hotel, and two restaurants for those who are not camping. Food supplies are available at either the Hudson's Bay or Kaeser's general store. Several gas stations sell both leaded and unleaded gas. All stores are clustered in a two-block section of downtown.

Visit the *North of 60 Books,* 71 Portage Ave. (phone: 403-872-2606), where Ib and Lillian Kristensen sell northern handicrafts, gifts, and carvings. The workshop-bookstore features the largest and best collection of books about the North. A big attraction is the mounted head of a "muffaloose," a cross between moose and buffalo that has become the town's symbol. This rare animal was discovered under curious circumstances after a year of bad forest fires — but you can hear the story for yourself at the workshop. Open year-round.

Another must for visitors is the *Northern Life Museum* (110 King St., 403-872-2859) which houses one of the best collections in the North of traditional native crafts, photographs, and artifacts of a disappearing way of life. Open year-round.

There's a public campground beside the Slave River on the northern side of town. Drinking water and showers are available, and there is a dump station for RVs.

BEST EN ROUTE

Due to the scarcity of accommodations in the Northwest Territories, make reservations as far in advance as possible. Expect to pay $40 and up per night for a double in the hotels listed. All prices are quoted in US dollars.

HAY RIVER

Caribou – In the new section of Hay River, this motel features 29 rooms, kitchenettes, phones, TV sets, steam baths, whirlpool baths, and car plug-ins. Licensed dining, lounge. Open year-round. Box 1114, Hay River, NWT X0E 0R0 (phone: 403-874-6706).

Cedar Rest – Right on the highway, this 31-room motel has 16 kitchenettes, waterbeds, and satellite TV. Box 540, Hay River NWT X0E 0R0 (phone: 403-874-3732).

Harbour House – A bed-and-breakfast establishment with 6 rooms, boats, canoes, surf boards. Take out food. Crafts. Box 54, Hay River, NWT X0E 0R0 (phone: 403-874-2233).

Hay River – On Hay River in Old Town, this cedar-log hotel has 22 newly renovated rooms available in winter, 38 in summer. TV sets, phone, licensed dining, café, lounge, entertainment, and convenience store. Small banquets. Box 487, Hay River, NWT X0E 0R0 (phone: 403-874-2951).

Migrator – This motel has 24 rooms, and if you prefer to do your own cooking, 6 have kitchenettes. On the main highway between the Old and New Towns. Mailing address: PO Box 1847, Hay River, NWT X0E 0R0 (phone: 403-874-6792).

Ptarmigan Inn – A 41-room hotel that is in a complex housing a restaurant, dining lounge, downstairs bar, barbershop, and bank. Downtown. Mailing address: PO Box 1000, Hay River, NWT X0E 0R0 (phone: 403-874-6781).

FORT SMITH

Pelican Rapids Inn – Some of the 50 rooms are equipped with kitchens; all have private bath, radio, a TV set, and carpets. In the center of town. For information: PO Box 52, Fort Smith, NWT X0E 0P0 (phone: 403-872-2789).

Pinecrest – Most of the 28 rooms have TV sets and private baths. Cocktail lounge, restaurant, and showers on the premises. Near Wood Buffalo National Park. PO Box 127, Fort Smith, NWT X0E 0P0 (phone: 403-872-2104).

■ **Note:** For half the price of hotels in the Fort Smith area, you can enjoy bed and breakfast in the home of a NWT family. A dozen families lease out their rooms and, by arrangement, will prepare extra meals and do laundry. Contact *SubArctic Wilderness Adventures,* PO Box 685, Fort Smith, NWT (phone: 403-872-2467).

Nova Scotia

Nova Scotia is a province of two parts: the peninsula of Nova Scotia, which is connected to the mainland by a narrow isthmus over the Bay of Fundy, and Cape Breton Island, the northern extreme of the province, linked to the rest of the peninsula by a mile-long causeway. The Atlantic Ocean beats against the long eastern shore of this Maritime Province while the Bay of Fundy and Gulf of St. Lawrence lie to the west. With the sea all around, this long, narrow strip of land naturally has an economy based largely on the fishing trade. From its southern tip in the Bay of Fundy to the northern St. Lawrence Gulf coast, Nova Scotia encompasses 21,425 square miles of fishing villages, ferry towns, and cities with excellent harbors. The Bay of Fundy slope in the southwestern section, the isthmus, and southern Cape Breton are the most lush and fertile parts of the island, while the rural and rocky northeastern reaches of Cape Breton support coal mining and steel production.

Nova Scotia is a mosaic of half a dozen cultural influences. The French and the English struggled for decades to control the land that some 18th-century cynics called "Nova Scarcity." During the 1600s, settlement by both countries was sporadic. In 1720, when the French built their strategic Fortress of Louisbourg on Cape Breton Island, the tussle over Nova Scotia began in earnest. Twenty-five years later, a band of New Englanders captured the fort. Rather than rejoice, Britain handed it back to France in return for French opposition to Bonnie Prince Charlie's claim to the British throne. Enraged, the New Englanders demanded an English base in Nova Scotia — the result was Halifax. As Britain's control over the peninsula tightened, they expelled the French-speaking Acadians and destroyed Louisbourg. These moves helped to steer the rest of Canada into the arms of the British empire.

Other groups began arriving in Nova Scotia: Germans settled on the Atlantic shore, southwest of Halifax, turning Lunenburg into a thriving port; waves of Loyalists rushed in after the American Revolution; shiploads of Irish came, seeking relief from the potato famines of the 1840s; Scots, displaced by the Highland Clearances, landed at Pictou County on the northwestern shore and at Cape Breton with its highlandlike glens; and blacks settled near Halifax after the War of 1812.

Halifax is the capital of Nova Scotia and the commercial, administrative, and military center of the four Maritime Provinces. Its metropolitan population of about 290,000 (including Dartmouth and surrounding communities) encompasses almost one-third of Nova Scotia's 884,300 people. Even so it retains its small-town flavor — shady, tree-lined streets, stately Georgian buildings, and active pubs. For a complete report on *Halifax,* see THE CITIES.

Although Halifax and Dartmouth (facing one another across Halifax Harbour), midway on Nova Scotia's long Atlantic coast, are the province's largest urban centers, many people start their tours of the area from Yarmouth, on the southwestern coast where the Atlantic and the Bay of Fundy meet. This is the docking point of ferries from both Portland and Bar Harbor, Maine. We have divided the province into three routes: from Yarmouth along the Bay of Fundy to Amherst, through Nova Scotia's Acadian country; from Yarmouth south and east along the Atlantic shore to the Strait of Canso, through the Atlantic coast uplands scenery and a series of ever more fascinating fishing villages; and from Amherst across the Strait of Canso through Cape Breton Island, including a stop at the restoration of Fort Louisbourg and a drive along the beautiful Cabot Trail. This last route goes through Scottish Nova Scotia, an area settled by Scots and so filled with lochs and glens that it is almost a miniature of Scotland.

Information: Nova Scotia Tourism, 129 Commercial St., Portland, ME 04101 (outside Maine within the Continental US, 800-341-6096; from Maine, 800-492-0643); or Nova Scotia Department of Tourism, Box 456, Halifax, Nova Scotia B3J 2R5 (phone: 902-424-5000).

Yarmouth to Amherst

The 324-mile (523-km) drive from Yarmouth to Amherst along the Bay of Fundy shore is a ramble through French Nova Scotia along the stunning coastline forged by the powerful tide of the Bay of Fundy. It passes through Acadian villages where the daily language is still the odd French dialect brought by the region's first French settlers. Crossing Annapolis Valley, it skirts the province's most prosperous farmlands. Near the end of the route stands tragic Springhill, where a 1958 mining disaster claimed 76 lives; the town's survival is a testament to the determination and character of the townspeople. The Bay of Fundy is always within easy access.

The route virtually traces the province's history. Here you can walk through the first settlements established in the early 1600s; view the battlegrounds where the French and the English vied for new lands; and remember Longfellow's star-crossed lovers, Evangeline and Gabriel, whose story represents the fate of the Acadians.

Along the route, there's a gradual change of atmosphere that coincides with the changing landscape. As French turns into English, rocky, wind-blown fishing villages are replaced by thriving agricultural communities. The 170-mile (274-km) Bay of Fundy, always nearby on the left, gradually narrows as its bottom imperceptibly rises. This results in the highest tides in the world at the bay's eastern end, the Minas Basin. Generations of Nova Scotians have watched these tides with fascination, some dreaming of the day when that enormous power might be harnessed to provide inexpensive energy for industry.

Although the roads along the Bay of Fundy are sometimes narrow and winding, they are generally good. The road most often follows Routes 1 and 2 and the Evangeline Trail and the Glooscap Trail, signposted routes set up by the Nova Scotia Department of Tourism. The gastronomic attractions of the route are enormous, featuring fish and Acadian dishes in French Nova

Scotia and, a bit farther on, fresh fruit and vegetables in abundance from roadside stands in the Annapolis Valley. And there are countless opportunities to pull over and watch the fishing boats in the weirs, see the gulls diving, or simply to enjoy the cool bay breeze.

To get to Yarmouth, you can take a ferry from either Portland, Maine, or from Bar Harbor. Some ferries have rooms for cars and overnight berth accommodations. Reservations on the Bar Harbor–Yarmouth run can be obtained by calling 800-423-7344 (from Maine) or 800-341-7981 (in the continental US). The Portland-Yarmouth ferry, the *Scotia Prince,* also includes cruise features such as duty-free shopping, a casino, formal dining room, and nightclub with live entertainment; for bookings, call 800-482-0955 (from Maine) or 800-341-7540 (from the rest of the US). Advance reservations on both the Bar Harbor–Yarmouth ferry and the *Scotia Prince* are subject to cancellation if not picked up 1 hour before sailing. Air Canada also has direct flights to Yarmouth from Boston.

At Yarmouth, a major gateway, arrange for membership in the Order of the Good Cheer, the oldest social club in North America. Samuel de Champlain, the great explorer and historian, formed the club more than 375 years ago in an attempt to cheer up his men in the face of the loneliness, disease, and harsh weather of the New World. Today, the order is open to all those who visit Nova Scotia for at least 3 days. There are no initiation fees or dues, and members of the order never meet formally. Members are, however, required to have a good time, remember Nova Scotia pleasantly, speak of the province kindly, and come back again. You can join the club at the Nova Scotia government tourist bureau located at the ferry dock. You might as well; you're bound to fulfill club requirements in any case.

YARMOUTH: This attractive town's narrow, lighthouse-guarded harbor serves as a haven for ferries and herring seiners. (The latter are boats named for seines, the large, weighted nets used by fishermen to trap their catch.) These craft can be seen as they come and go in the harbor or docked below MaiStreet. With a population of 7,600, Yarmouth is the largest community in the province west of Halifax. It is a transportation, commercial, and shopping center for much of western Nova Scotia. A former global shipping capital — with the world's highest per capita ship tonnage — Yarmouth today relies on fishery and fish processing plants, two textile mills, machine shops, and a woodworking plant. The town also features the *Fire Fighters Museum* of Nova Scotia (451 Main St.), with some equipment over 100 years old. At the *Yarmouth County Historical Society Museum* (22 Collins St.), a runic stone linked to the Norse explorations of AD 1000 is on display. This relic is cited as evidence that visitors came to North America long before Columbus.

Yarmouth offers some fine seafood restaurants. A noteworthy example is *Harris' Seafood,* Hwy. 1 (in Yarmouth). Its delicious fish, lobster, and fresh vegetables are popular with Nova Scotians and visitors alike.

En Route from Yarmouth – Travel along Route 1 through the Hebron area's "lupine trail," named for the wild herbs growing on both sides of the road. In June, a blanket of white, pink, and blue spreads back from the road into the fields. Passing by Port Maitland, you might see oxen. On the rocky but highly successful commercial dairy farms, they were more suitable than horses in the days when draft animals were used. Located just 4.3 miles (6.9 km) east of Route 1, the Lake George fish hatchery annually provides millions of trout and salmon for release in the lakes and streams of western Nova Scotia. Thousands of black-backed gulls nest on the islands in Lake George. As you cross into the municipality of Clare, you enter the district settled by Acadians, the early French settlers who named Nova Scotia "Acadie." They were expelled from the province in 1755 by the British; later they returned. In fact, 335 Acadian families are said to have walked from Boston to Digby in the summer of 1768. In Clare, you'll feel as if you've entered a different country. The residents still speak a French quite different from that spoken in Paris or Quebec. And just as the language has been preserved, so have the culture and traditions. Even the smallest communities along the "French shore" are dominated by a large Catholic church; wooden homes and farmhouses all look out to sea. As you follow Route 1, consider a side trip to North Bear Cove and South Bear Cove, where cliffs meet the ocean. After returning to Route 1, you soon reach Clare Park at Smuggler's Cove. During prohibition, when liquor was shipped illegally to the US, the maze of coves here provided rum-runners with hideaways. You'll find their lair at the bottom of the footpath leading down to the picnic area.

METEGHAN: This small town of about 900 people is typical of communities along the coast. It was settled in 1785 by the Acadians; La Vieille Maison, one of the oldest homes, has been preserved. (Privately owned, the home is occasionally open to visitors.) This is a shipbuilding town, and Meteghan's skilled craftsmen gained international recognition in 1966, when they built a 165-foot, three-quarter-size replica of Donald McKay's famous American clipper ship *Flying Cloud* for Arthur Johnston of Philadelphia. The original was built in East Boston in 1851 and destroyed after going aground in 1874.

En Route from Meteghan – Upon entering the community of Saulnierville, look for the Acadian bakery, *Le Pain de Chez Nous,* and turn right to St. Benoni. Along the road you will see waterwheels and, perhaps, a logjam in the river. The jams still serve as bridges for the local lumbering industry.

CHURCH POINT: This tiny village has the tallest wooden church in Canada. On the campus of Université Ste. Anne, the church and its small museum are open to visitors. The province's only French degree-granting institution, the college was founded in 1891 by Eudist (the Congregation of Jesus and Mary) priests from France and has traditionally attracted local students or those of Acadian descent from neighboring Canadian provinces and American states. Lately, however, the college has begun to interest larger numbers of English-speaking students eager to learn Canada's other official language. The *Acadian Festival of Clare,* held annually at Church Point, usually in July, features local crafts, music, and French-Canadian specialties such as *rappie pie* (grated potatoes and chicken or rabbit baked in a crust).

En Route from Church Point – Less than a mile from Church Point is Grosses Coques, meaning "large clams." It's said that the clams in this district are the largest on the North American coast. Reportedly, they were so plentiful that the first settlers lived on them throughout their first winter. Just a 1½-mile (2.5-km) drive to the left of Grosses Coques bridge takes you to Major's Point and its long, blue slate beach. The site of the first Acadian cemetery, this driftwood-studded beach is thick with clams. And it's a great spot for bird-watching. In the village (pop. 357), a stone memorial marks the place of the first chapel. There's also a tablet on the site of the first frame house built in the town of Clare.

ST. BERNARD: Even though its population is only 322, St. Bernard supports a large stone cathedral with a seating capacity of 1,000. Construction of the church was started in 1910 and finished in 1942, and all material and work was supplied by local laborers. It is an interesting example of local conviction, if nothing else. Visitors are welcome.

En Route from St. Bernard – As you leave St. Bernard, look for a road off to the left that takes you to New Edinburgh, 2.3 miles (3.7 km) away. A loop will return you to Route 1, but along the way are beautiful views of the rustic seashore and countryside. Traces of the first townsite, settled by three Scottish Loyalists in 1783, still remain.

WEYMOUTH: Continuing along Route 1 (which becomes Route 101 in several miles) you come to Weymouth, settled by Loyalists in 1783 and named after Weymouth, Massachusetts. Colonel Moodie of North Carolina, a famous Loyalist, settled in this district and wrote an interesting diary of his experiences in the American Revolution. Weymouth is situated on St. Mary's Bay at the mouth of the Sissiboo River (an Indian name meaning "big river"); trading schooners formerly loaded there. Stores in the town are built on logs to allow the river's tides to pass underneath. Periodically, the first floors of the stores flood.

Just past Weymouth, at Weymouth North is a wharf off Fort Point Road; it's frequented by lobster and herring fishermen. Foreign ships load logs here for ports around the world. From the wharf you can see New Edinburgh across the Sissiboo River and Sandy Cove across St. Mary's Bay.

En Route from Weymouth – Five miles (8 km) from Weymouth North is Plympton, with an interesting variety of antiques and crafts shops. Just past Plympton is Savary Park, a provincial picnic site with a fine tidal pool beach and large groves of white birch and evergreen.

Five miles (8 km) farther is Marshalltown, former home of the late Maud Lewis a primitive painter who won international acclaim. The Lewis residence, decorated with her work, has been removed for restoration by the *Nova Scotia Museum*, in Halifax. To the right off Route 101 is Acaciaville (pop. 141). From the Acaciaville hills there are fine views of Digby on the east and the Bay of Fundy on the west.

DIGBY: Like Yarmouth, Digby is a ferry town, served by Canadian National's MV *Princess of Acadia*, which carries cars and passengers to and from Saint John, New Brunswick, three times a day. Digby was named after Robert Digby, a British admiral who commanded the HMS *Atlanta*, the ship that conveyed 1,500 Loyalists from New England in 1783. Digby is one of Nova Scotia's more popular summer resorts, offering horseback riding, canoeing, and swimming. It is also the center of the highly profitable scallop fishery in the Bay of Fundy. (In recent years, the provincial scallop fishery has become more profitable than the lobster fishery.) Take a few minutes to walk to the end of the government wharf downtown to get a close look at the scallop draggers; perhaps you'll also see pulpwood and lumber being loaded onto ocean vessels for export. If you climb to the top of the hill by the high school, you'll get a beautiful view of Annapolis Basin. The *Pines Resort* hotel (see *Best En Route*) serves breakfast, lunch, and dinner. This government-owned establishment is open only in summer. Digby Scallop Days are held in August, and deep-sea fishing and whale-watching excursions are available; check with municipal or provincial tourist bureaus.

En Route from Digby – It's a good idea to take a scenic side trip along the spit of land known as Digby Neck to its end at Brier Island. The trip, on Route 217, includes two short ferry rides, a distance of about 86 miles (138 km). Depending how often your ferry stops (it varies), it could take as long as 7 hours. Heading out on Digby Neck, you'll pass a number of sheep farms. Make a right turn downhill toward the Bay of Fundy into Centreville, one of the prettiest fishing villages in the province. There are several beautiful old churches along the road. In Centreville, *Les Raymond* sells smoked fish and other sea treats from his roadside smoke shop. Back on Route 217, just past Centreville, there is a well-kept picnic park at Lake Medway — a good spot for a swim. The lake water is usually 15 to 20 degrees warmer than that of the numbingly cold Bay of Fundy. (The lake is also stocked with trout.) Sandy Cove, 4 miles (6 km) farther down the road, is at the bottom of a big hill.

SANDY COVE: Leaving Route 217, take the road to the right and follow its meandering path to the long sandy beach on the Bay of Fundy side. At this beach you can have the best view of weir fishing, a style of fishing common only in the Bay of Fundy area. The weirs are long, thin trees driven into the seabed and lined with fishnet. Stretching out from the shore in a straight line, the weirs form a semicircle at the end. Fish are trapped in the large, rounded area after meeting and following the straight section of the weir to its end. If you are lucky, you might see the fishermen enter the weir with their boats to scoop up the fish. For good seafood and homemade bread in a dignified setting, try the *Olde Village Inn,* a restored 1890 inn.

Sandy Cove is also the setting of the mysterious story of Jerome. This man was found on the beach one summer morning in 1854 with both legs freshly amputated above the knees. Two fishermen carried the man to a home, where he was made warm and given hot drinks. But he remained unresponsive and only muttered something that sounded like "Jerome." Since people believed he did not understand English, Jerome was later taken to Meteghan to converse with John Nicholas, a man who spoke to him in French, Italian, and German. Still he did not answer. Living with Nicholas and his family, Jerome eventually learned to walk on his stumps. And occasionally he had brief conversations with children. But most of the time Jerome crouched behind the kitchen stove with his head in his hands. Jerome's case was eventually brought to the attention of the provincial government, and an allowance of $2 per week was established for his keep and given to the Nicholas family. In 1912, 58 years after he was found on Sandy Cove beach, Jerome died, taking his mysterious past with him forever.

En Route from Sandy Cove – Continuing on Route 217, you pass Mink Cove and Little River, two prosperous fishing villages. Mink Cove is well known for its amethyst and quartz, often sought by rockhounds. The next village is East Ferry, where you can board the Joshua Slocum ferry for the 10-minute trip to Tiverton on Long Island. The round-trip fare is about 85¢ ($1 CN) per car. A 10-mile (16-km) trip brings you to Freeport and the second ferry ride to Brier Island.

BRIER ISLAND: Brier Island was the home of Joshua Slocum, who in July 1895 bade good-bye to his mother and set off to become the first man to single-handedly circumnavigate the earth. He accomplished this feat in his 36-foot, 9-inch sloop, *Spray,* which he had built himself. Slocum sailed for 3 years to complete his journey, arriving finally at Gloucester, Massachusetts. A plaque on the southern end of the island memorializes the solitary navigator. From here, follow the short walking trail along the cliffs with the waves crashing below.

You'll also want to wander about Westport, the small community where the ferry docks. Stained glass windows grace many of Westport's more well-to-do homes; these were brought from faraway lands long ago by seamen of the community. The waterfront is lined with fishing shacks and wharves on which lobster traps and orange floats are piled high, and to which bright Cape Island boats are moored. In the late afternoon, fishermen clean their catch along the wharf. If you want an easy opening gambit for conversation, ask any Brier Islander about the Groundhog Day storm. On February 2, 1976, a violent and largely unexpected storm devastated buildings along the waterfront and caused millions of dollars' damage. The memory has not easily faded. Birdwatchers will be impressed with the many species of both land and sea birds that concentrate in the area during migration periods. For advice on the province's best birding spots, check with the Nova Scotia Bird Society, through the *Nova Scotia Museum,* Halifax.

Before heading back on the ferry (which runs 24 hours a day), you may want a snack from the takeout counter by the ferry wharf, which features fish and chips — naturally, the fish are right out of the water.

En Route from Digby – When you return to Route 1, consider stopping at Smith's Cove. Here you can see the St. Anne's Birchbark Chapel on the grounds of Harbourview Inn. The chapel, nearly 60 years old, was built by a local craftsman in honor of a longtime summer visitor, an Anglican bishop. Nearby on Route 1 is the old *Methodist Church Museum* (1885).

The better restaurants on this leg of the journey are all located in the vicinity of Route 1 at Smith's Cove. *Hedley House* (phone: 902-245-2585), on the grounds of the *Hedley House* motor hotel, offers fresh fish and vegetables; the atmosphere is on the formal side. *Harbourview Inn* (phone: 902-245-5686) is well known for its Saturday night lobster boil around the swimming pool and its Sunday buffets. *Mountain Gap Inn* (phone: 902-245-2277, in summer) also offers good meals.

BEAR RIVER: Route 1 crosses Route 101, the road to the river town of Bear River, known as the Switzerland of Nova Scotia (by the time you have crossed Acadian Nova Scotia, Scottish Nova Scotia, English Nova Scotia, and Swiss Nova Scotia, you may well feel it is the most international spot in the Maritimes). The river itself fronts the charming street of 100-year-old shops, each built on stilts as a precaution against untimely floods. The town's fondest folly is a full-scale, wood Dutch windmill, built a few miles out of town. It has a pleasant view of the river and a tearoom from which to enjoy it. Bear River is especially beautiful during the annual *Cherry Carnival* in July.

En Route from Bear River – Head back to Route 1 and Deep Brook. You'll pass Canadian Forces Base Cornwallis on the way to Clementsport. This community was settled by United Empire Loyalists in 1784. Many of its homes were formerly occupied by sea captains. The old Loyalist church of St. Edward, consecrated in 1788, houses many relics and is worth a visit. In a few miles you arrive at Fort Anne National Historic Park at Annapolis Royal.

FORT ANNE NATIONAL HISTORIC PARK: This 28-acre park was the first national historic park in the country. A section of the first fortress, built here in 1635 by d'Aulnay de Charnisay, is still maintained. Since its construction, the fort (then known as Port Royal) has been the scene of attacks by the English, the French, New Englanders, Indians, and even pirates.

In 1690, brigands burned the church and destroyed 28 homes, cremating a mother and her children in one fire. During the winter of 1709, after three attacks by New Englanders had been repulsed in the previous 5 years, three privateers sheltered at Port Royal. They had with them 55 Boston ships that they had seized during the summer. Stung by this latest outrage, the New Englanders launched another expedition in 1710, and in 8 days the fort was captured. It was renamed Annapolis Royal after Queen Anne. The key to the fort was carried to Boston (it was returned in 1922 and placed in the *Fort Anne Museum*). After its capture in 1710, it was attacked many more times, and England maintained a garrison of soldiers here until 1854.

Things have been preserved pretty much as they were then. The British officers' quarters, erected by the Duke of Kent, father of Queen Victoria, originally consisted of 30 rooms, each with a fireplace and a view of the fort and Annapolis Basin. Now the officers' quarters are a museum open to the public. An Acadian room with its original wall beams and ceiling and a complete collection of Acadian kitchen utensils and clothing is part of the museum's displays. There is also a historic library. Fort Anne is open year-round. The museum is open mid-May to mid-October, 9 AM to 6 PM; remainder of the year, weekdays 9 AM to 5 PM. No admission charge.

Two miles (3 km) from Annapolis Royal, turn left for the 7-mile (11-km) drive to Port Royal National Historic Park.

PORT ROYAL NATIONAL HISTORIC PARK: The tiny village of Port Royal is the oldest permanent white settlement north of Florida in North America. A replica of the original Port Royal Habitation that Samuel de Champlain and Pierre du Gua de Monts built in 1605 is on the original site. The replica is exact in size and detail. The building's timber framing was mortised, tenoned, and pinned together in the old manner; no spikes or nails were used. It was here that Champlain founded the Order of the Good

Cheer. The park is open year round, but the buildings are open only from June to mid-October, 9 AM to 6 PM.

En Route from Port Royal – Drive back to Route 1 and continue to Bridgetown, traveling into the Annapolis Valley, framed by the North and South Mountains. As you proceed farther into the valley, you'll probably note an increase in the temperature; the mountains protect the area from the winds and the fog off the Bay of Fundy. The warmer weather has helped make the valley an area that's famed for its produce, particularly apples. The region is probably most beautiful at apple blossom time in late May or early June. Bridgetown (pop. 1,037), a pleasant dairying and fruit farming community, is situated at the head of the Annapolis River. Paradise, at the junction of the Paradise and Annapolis rivers, marked the eastern limit of French settlements in the Port Royal region. Near Paradise is the 9-hole *Eden Golf and Country Club.* Greens-fee players are welcome. As you explore the area, keep an eye open for signs of fairs and church suppers. They have terrific home-cooked food.

LAWRENCETOWN: This is the regional headquarters for sport fishing and hunting. Signs in the town direct you to where you can hire guides with canoes. The town also has a land surveying and photogrammetry school, the only such school in the country. The 5-day Annapolis County Agricultural Exhibition is held here in August.

En Route from Lawrencetown – The next main community along the way is Middleton, so named because it stands about halfway between Annapolis Royal and Kentville. Just 5 miles (8 km) off the road from Middleton, at Mt. Hanly, there is a scenic view of the Annapolis Valley. Passing into Kings County, you enter the best farmland in the province. In addition to apples, plums, pears, and cherries, the area supports a substantial dairy industry. Along the rivers flowing into the Minas Basin great stretches of diked marshes yield roots, grain, and hay. Kingston, a key agricultural service area, hosts the province's largest steer barbecue on the second Saturday in July. The *Paragon Golf Course* is also located in Kingston. Canada's largest antisubmarine air base is located at Greenwood, just off Route 1. The military community totals about 9,000 and has what amounts to its own village, including schools, churches, and recreational facilities. Alfred C. Fuller, who founded the Fuller Brush Company, was born in this region; his home, near Berwick, is a private residence. Berwick, just off Route 1, has two fruit- and vegetable-processing plants, a bakery serving all of mainland Nova Scotia, large fruit packing warehouses, and a meat-processing plant.

KENTVILLE: This shire of Kings County is the home of the *Apple Blossom Festival,* held in late May or early June. The town is also headquarters for the Dominion Atlantic Railway, a subsidiary of the Canadian Pacific Railway. The *George Warden Railway Museum* has hundreds of rail-related items. Memorial Park has tennis courts, baseball diamonds, a public swimming pool, and a football field. Between Kentville and Wolfville, there is a lovely side trip for rockhounds, photographers, and hikers. Route 358 winds through several attractive communities before coming to The Lookoff, a spot which offers a spectacular view of Minas Basin, the valleys of six rivers, and parts of five counties. Further down the road is Scots Bay, with a broad rocky beach and low cliffs, where agates and other stones continually wash up on shore, particularly in spring and early summer. From the end of the road, a hiking trail leads to Cape Split, one of the best walks in the province. Much of the trail is inland, but it emerges at the tip of the cape and ends with a breathtaking panorama from 150-foot cliffs.

WOLFVILLE: This town, the center of Henry Wadsworth Longfellow's Land of Evangeline, is also the home of Acadia University, which was founded by the Nova Scotia Baptist Education Society in 1838. Wolfville is the closest town to Grand Pré and is a convenient base for explorations in this historical area. Nearby Evangeline Beach offers saltwater bathing that is almost warm.

GRAND PRÉ: The name Grand Pré ("great meadow") refers to the large number of dikes in the area, but the community is better known as the site of one of the oldest French settlements in the province and the setting for Longfellow's famous poem "Evangeline." Between 1755 and 1763, nearly 14,000 Acadians were expelled by the British, who feared that the peaceful Acadians would challenge their military authority. On September 5, 1755, standing on the steps of Grand Pré's Acadian church, Lieutenant-Colonel John Winslow announced the Expulsion. In the next 4 months, 6,000 Acadians were torn from their homes and deported. Longfellow imagined that among those sent away was a girl named Evangeline, and her lover, Gabriel. Separated by the Expulsion, Evangeline spent the rest of her life searching unsuccessfully for Gabriel.

Grand Pré National Historic Park, a memorial to the deported Acadians, features a statue of Evangeline. Viewed from the right side, the bronze statue depicts Evangeline as a young girl, but as the viewer moves left, the face seems to change to that of an old woman, still searching. The story of the Acadians is recounted by the park staff in a reconstructed Acadian church serving as a museum and interpretation center. Although the park is open year-round, its buildings are open to the public only from June to mid-October. No admission charge.

Following the subsequent peace, many of the exiled Acadians came back to Nova Scotia. But most residents of Grand Pré are descendants of New Englanders.

Be sure to visit the *Grand Pré Pottery* shop, then treat yourself to *Evangeline Snack Bar*'s luscious strawberry shortcake, pies, and other good food.

Also see the Church of the Covenanters, constructed by New England planters in 1790, with its quaint box pews and pulpit halfway to the ceiling. Worth a visit, too, are the estate vineyards of Grand Pré Wines, which are open to visitors, preferably by appointment.

HANTSPORT: You soon pass into Hants County, where agricultural land changes into a lumbering and light industry area. In the middle of the last century, Hantsport, along the Avon River, served a large number of oceangoing clipper ships. Today it is a major shipping port for the gypsum quarried near Windsor. Observation Lookoff provides an excellent view of the river tides and the loading of the gypsum boats. William Hall, the first black to win the Victoria Cross for heroism, died in Hantsport. The son of an escaped Virginia slave, Hall was rewarded for heroism during the relief of Lucknow during the Indian Mutiny.

WINDSOR: The remnants of Fort Edward, built by the British in 1750, are here. Off King Street and Fort Edward Street stands the oldest blockhouse in Canada. The *Haliburton Memorial Museum* on Clifton Avenue is the former residence of Judge Thomas Charles Haliburton, known as the founder of North American humor, who created the fictional character Sam Slick. The Hants County Exhibition is held here annually in September. Started in 1765, it's believed to be the oldest fair in Canada. King's College School, the oldest educational institution outside the United Kingdom in the British Commonwealth, is also located here.

En Route from Windsor – Take Route 1 to Three Mile Plains before turning left onto Route 14 toward Brooklyn. At Brooklyn, take Route 215 toward Summerville along the Glooscap Trail. This route parallels the drive from Grand Pré to Hantsport and Windsor on the other side of the Avon River. The area, like Hantsport, has active gypsum and barite mines and an anhydrite quarry. As you pass Tennycape, look to your left to Economy Point, on the other side of Minas Basin. Plans for a dam between Economy Point and Burntcoat Head to harness the power of the Bay of Fundy high tides are under discussion. The tides here have been measured at 54 feet — the highest in the world. The small town of Noel, settled by families from Northern Ireland in 1762, is farther along the shore. Local lore has it that the legendary Captain Kidd brought his pirate ship to Noel to be remasted. It's said that although he threw bars of silver to those who supplied timbers, the locals would not touch the pirate's ill-gotten gains. The road then follows the path of the Shubenacadie River to South Maitland, where a pronounced tidal bore appears twice each day. This wall of white water advances over the muddy bottom, signaling the advent of another high tide. From Shubenacadie, pick up Route 2 north. Head for Stewiacke's provincial wildlife park, which contains a large variety of native Nova Scotian animals and birds. The area around Shubenacadie and Stewiacke — located halfway between the Equator and the North Pole — is headquarters for the Micmac Indians of Nova Scotia.

TRURO: This town (pop. 12,500) is a major service community for the surrounding area. Victoria Park, a 1,000-acre natural playground, has two picturesque waterfalls. At the Nova Scotia Agricultural College on Bible Hill, there's a demonstration farm open to visitors. In August, Truro hosts the Nova Scotia Provincial Exhibition, the largest attraction of its kind in the province. From June through October, visitors can also take in harness racing at Truro. *Glengarry House* in the *Glengarry* motel (138 Willow St.) serves good food, especially fish, in a colonial atmosphere. Equally good is the food at the *Palliser* restaurant in the *Tideview* motel on Tidal Bore Road; it also offers a view of the tidal bore. To check on the arrival of this natural phenomenon, which rolls into the Salmon River at the rate of a foot a minute, call Dial-A-Tide at 902-426-5494.

En Route from Truro – Take Route 2 west following the Glooscap Trail through Masstown, where a number of dikes built by the Acadians still function. There's also good striped bass fishing near the mouth of the Bass River. Continuing on Route 2, you climb Economy Mountain. From the peak, there is a spectacular view of Minas Basin. At Five Islands (pop. 199), you can see the five pieces of land the town is named for. According to Indian tradition, the god Glooscap hurled these great chunks of earth at a beaver in anger. Moose Island, one of the five, is supposed to be the hiding place of pirate treasure; the others are called Egg, Diamond, Pinnacle, and Long. Still on Route 2, you now pass through a narrow gorge between two wood-covered hills to Parrsboro.

PARRSBORO: A port town, Parrsboro is across the Minas Basin from Cape Blomidon ships lumber and pulpwood. Until recently, it was also used to ship coal out of the province. Weir fishing, like that done in the Bay of Fundy near Digby, is carried on here. In August, amateur geologists from across the continent gather for the annual Rockhound Roundup. Amethysts, agates, and other attractive minerals may be found along the shores. Follow the main street through Parrsboro and, about 1 mile from town, on the left, you'll see Ottawa House, once the summer home of Sir Charles Tupper. Born in Amherst, Tupper became prime minister of Canada in 1896.

There's a museum and tourist bureau at the three-way intersection near the center of Parrsboro. Check here for tide times and get a complimentary guide for a beach tour and rockhounding. Outside the museum, a cairn commemorates the plane that left Parrsboro in 1919 to fly the first airmail service between Nova Scotia and the US. A giant statue of Glooscap stands nearby. By pushing a button, you can hear the legend of the Indian god.

The *White House* (Upper Main St.) is open all year and serves home-cooked dinners from 5:30 to 7 PM.

En Route from Parrsboro – Take a short side trip to Advocate Harbor along Route 209. This winding road, rising from sea level to 750 feet, unveils a series of extraordinary vistas. At Fox River you can see the picturesque rock formation of Cape Split across Minas Channel. The high hills on the right are known as Woods Mountain. Port Greville was at one time a great shipbuilding center, and yachts and motorboats are still built here. Pollock, haddock, and halibut are caught along this shore, and charter boats are readily available.

SPENCER'S ISLAND: This tiny community is misnamed — it's not, in fact, an island. One of the world's great mystery ships, the *Mary Celeste,* was built here in 1861.

Eleven years later, on October 27, Captain Ben Briggs and ten others, including his wife and their 10-year-old daughter, left New York for Genoa in the 100-foot-long brigantine. Twenty-seven days later the Nova Scotian brigantine *Del Gratia,* sailed by Captain Morehouse of Bear River, Digby County, came upon the *Mary Celeste,* sailing erratically. It was soon found that there was nobody aboard and its one lifeboat was gone. Although there were no signs of violence, the compass was knocked out and ruined, and the navigation instruments had been removed. There had not been any storms, and the last entry in the log was marked for 8 AM, two days earlier. No trace of any of the 11 people or of the lifeboat was ever found.

En Route from Spencer's Island – At nearby Advocate, there's a rock formation known as the Three Sisters; legend claims it is the spot that Glooscap's three sisters were all turned into stone. Turn back to Parrsboro to rejoin Route 2 toward Springhill. Mapleton is the center of the local maple sugar industry. It's said that Indians of the area discovered that maple sap becomes sweet and thick through boiling while cooking potatoes in the sticky substance. Maple sugar and superior maple cream are sold in most candy stores.

SPRINGHILL: This town of 4,900 holds a special place in the hearts of all Nova Scotians. Coal mining began here in 1872, and the 4,000-foot Number 2 mine was the deepest in Canada. In 1891, 125 miners lost their lives in a mining accident. In October 1956, an explosion occurred in Number 4, trapping 118 miners; 39 eventually died in the pits. Just after Christmas the following year, fire destroyed half of the downtown business district. Then, on October 23, 1958, a "bump" (a great disturbance of the earth in a mine) in Number 2 trapped 174 men. A desperate attempt to reach the men began, and 81 were found alive in the first few days. After 6 days of searching, the rescuers had almost abandoned hope, when 12 more miners were found alive; 2 days later, 7 more were rescued. In all, 76 miners died. And in the 2 years following the disaster, 2,400 people left the town to seek employment elsewhere. The tragic events of 1958 are told in "Springhill Mine Disaster," a song made popular by the Brothers Four. Springhill's suffering did not end there: On July 20, 1975, another fire destroyed 75% of the downtown business district. The mines are now closed.

En Route from Springhill – The next town is Amherst, 22 miles (35 km) northwest, the inland gateway to Nova Scotia and the geographical center of the Maritime Provinces. It is built on rising ground above the famous Tantramar marshes. Set in a 187-year-old house with period decor, the *Drury Lane Steak House* is 3 miles (5 km) from Amherst just across the border in New Brunswick, at the junction of Routes 2 and 16. Some claim it's one of the best restaurants in Canada.

BEST EN ROUTE

The road from Yarmouth to Amherst includes a variety of interesting accommodations: a grand old hotel that used to be run by a railroad, an inn tucked away in an apple orchard, and a motel built by Nova Scotian Indians. And equally as various are the prices of these establishments. We've rated places charging over $35 for a double room as expensive; from $17 to $35 as moderate; and below $17 as inexpensive. All prices are quoted in US dollars.

YARMOUTH

Rodd's Colony Harbour Inn – This has a lovely view of Yarmouth Harbour and facilities that include a licensed lounge and dining room with entertainment, a sauna, and mini-bars in the rooms. Complimentary coffee is served in the lobby from 7 to 9 AM. Children under 16 stay free in the same room as their parents. Open year-round. At the ferry terminal (phone: 902-742-9194). Expensive.

Rodd's Grand – One of the most modern hotels in Yarmouth, it has 138 rooms, each with bath and color TV set. Some rooms have lovely views of the harbor. Open year-round. 417 Main St. (phone: 902-742-2446). Expensive.

Gateway Farms Bed & Breakfast – Accommodations available in 3 rooms and 2 shared baths, open May 1 to November 1. Breakfast 7 to 8:30 AM. Chegoggin Rd., off Rte. 1 (phone: 902-742-9786). Moderate.

DIGBY

Pines – By far the best-equipped hotel in the area, this is a grand old place. Originally operated by the Canadian Pacific Railway, it's now run by the provincial government. There are 90 rooms, 60 cottages, an excellent golf course, tennis courts, and shuffleboard. The hotel is open only in summer. PO Box 70 (phone: 902-245-2531). Expensive.

Harbourview Inn – Located 6 miles (10 km) from Digby, this mini-resort has 9 rooms with bath in the main house, 7 efficiency motel units, and 7 housekeeping cottages. It's only open in the summer; be sure to make reservations. Tennis courts and badminton are among the attractions. Smith's Cove, PO Box 35 (phone: 902-245-5686). Moderate.

SOUTH MILFORD

Milford House – Very close to Kejimkujik National Park, due south of Port Royal in the center of the province, is this country lodge devoted primarily to the joys of canoeing, fishing, swimming, and the like. There is a main lodge and lakeside cabins, each of which has a dock. Open June 5 to September 16. RR 4, South Milford, Annapolis Royal B0S 1AO (phone: 902-532-2617). Expensive.

WOLFVILLE

Old Orchard Inn – Nestled in an apple orchard, overlooking the university town of Wolfville, this inn has 110 rooms and 30 rustic chalets. There is also nightly entertainment, cross-country skiing, an indoor swimming pool, saunas, tennis courts, bicycle rentals, and a children's playground. Open year-round. Take Exit 11 off Highway 101 or Route 358 off Route 2. PO Box 1090 (phone: 902-542-5751). Expensive.

TRURO

Best Western Glengarry – This 115-unit motel has spacious grounds, a heated outdoor swimming pool, and complimentary use of cribs. 150 Willow St. (phone: 902-893-4311 or 800-528-1234). Expensive.

Palliser – This resort's flood-lit view of the tidal bore is a main draw. Hotel facilities include a licensed restaurant, 41 units, and 1 cottage. Rte. 102 (phone: 902-893-8951). Expensive.

Walker House – A bed-and-breakfast establishment with 5 rooms, 1 full bath. No pets. Open year-round. 74 Walker St. (phone: 902-895-0198). Moderate.

PARRSBORO

Glooscap – An 11-unit motel with a children's playground, fishing, boating, swimming, and hunting nearby. Open May 1 through November 30. Crossroads, PO Box 640 (phone: 902-254-3135). Moderate.

BRIDGETOWN

Bridgetown – Part of the Friendship Inns organization, the 33-unit motel is well situated for excursions around the Annapolis Valley. Facilities include a dining room, lounge, heated outdoor pool, sauna, and games room. 83 Granville St. (phone: 902-665-4491). Expensive.

Yarmouth to the Strait of Canso

Traveling along the southern and eastern shores of the province, you'll pass through dozens of quaint, hospitable fishing villages. These communities have held great significance for Nova Scotia's economy since the province was first settled, and they could become even more important as Canada asserts greater control over its offshore waters. In addition, the route offers some most impressive scenery. But don't be too put off if, just as soon as you start, you run into fog. All of Nova Scotia's Atlantic coast can be foggy. Yet it rarely lasts long, often burning off before noon. And if you do run into fog, it will help you appreciate the dangers faced daily by the fishermen of the villages you pass on your journey. Certainly mist creates the right mood for this drive; as you explore Oak Island, for instance, where the infamous Captain Kidd is thought to have hidden treasure, wraiths of mist and fog only increase the drama and plausibility of the story. (Look for the treasure if you want, but be warned, you won't be the first. Lives have been lost and fortunes spent in fruitless search.)

Starting at Yarmouth, the 477-mile (768-km) route weaves along Atlantic coastal highways, then proceeds via the well-forested eastern shore to Cape Auld on the Strait of Canso. The area's economy is profoundly affected by its proximity to the Grand Banks fishing grounds off Canso in the Atlantic Ocean. The first part of the journey, appropriately named the "lighthouse route," includes several stretches of good white sand beach. The second part — or "marine drive" — begins on the other side of the Halifax-Dartmouth metropolitan area, an area of brooks, streams, sheltered coves, and forests. Throughout the trip, you'll sense a New England influence in the architecture, a reminder of the thousands of New Englanders who came here after the American Revolution because of their loyalty to England. You'll pass through areas where descendants of Scottish, French, and German settlers maintain their cultural heritage.

YARMOUTH: To get to this gateway port, you can take a ferry from either Bar Harbor or Portland, Maine, or one of Air Canada's daily direct flights from Boston.

Yarmouth itself is a resort attraction, and you can swim, go salmon or trout fishing, or take a boat trip here. Formerly the town was one of the world's shipping leaders; it's still a commercial center for western Nova Scotia. Marked by a lighthouse, Yarmouth's harbor is a good place to watch the ferries and fishing boats cruise by. Other attractions are the *Fire Fighters Museum* and the *Historical Society Museum*. (For information on the town's restaurants, see the Yarmouth entry in the *Yarmouth to Amherst* route.)

En Route from Yarmouth – Take Route 3 to Tusket, a community settled in 1785 by Dutch United Empire Loyalists from New York and New Jersey. Passing through Argyle and Central Argyle, you'll see rugged coast and largely uninhabited countryside. Located at the head and on both sides of Pubnico Harbour are the Pubnico communities. Middle East Pubnico and Lower East Pubnico both have herring plants capable of processing 1,000 tons a day. Crossing into Shelburn

County, you soon come to Shag Harbour. Here, at the top of Chapel Hill near the United Baptist Church, there's a splendid view of the water and Cape Sable Island. At night five lighthouses are visible from this point.

Past Shag Harbour, at Barrington Passage, you'll find the only tourist bureau in the province with a Cape Island fishing boat tied alongside. From here take Route 300 toward Clark's Harbour, crossing over the 4,000-foot Cape Sable Island Causeway built in 1949. Continue along Route 220 through Newellton to West Head, turning right to the government wharf. On the right, just before the wharf, the Cape Sable Island Fisherman's Cooperative has a lobster pound capable of storing 50,000 crustaceans and a salt fish processing operation. Visitors are invited to tour the plant. Continue on Route 330 to Clark's Harbour.

CLARK'S HARBOUR: As you drive into this town, look for a road on the right to K. D. Smith and Sons Boatbuilders. It was in Clark's Harbour that the Cape Island boat, a particularly seaworthy craft, was designed in 1907. The broad-beamed wooden vessel is quite popular with fishermen because it doesn't tip over. Keith or George Smith will be happy to explain the intricacies of the boat's construction.

En Route from Clark's Harbour – Continue on Route 330 past Lower Clark's Harbour and South Side. You'll see countless lobster traps stacked on the shore (it's open season here from November to May) before coming to Barrington Passage and Route 3.

BARRINGTON: Buildings here are preserved as museums. The Old Meeting House, built in 1765 and used by settlers for public meetings and later as a place of worship, is now the oldest nonconformist church in the country. It is located on Route 3 just to the west of the bridge in Barrington. The Old Woolen Mill is just to the east of the bridge. Built in the early 1880s, the mill dyed and spun its own yarns from the wool of sheep raised on the neighboring headlands and islands. After yarn was prepared and dyed, the clattering looms produced yards and bolts of twills and flannels to be used for blankets and suits. It was the last water-powered woolen mill to operate in eastern Canada and was in private use until 1962.

En Route from Barrington – As you head north, you will see the Clyde River. It passes through the villages of Upper and Middle Clyde, hamlets that once consisted of homesteads for lumbermen. Today, the homesteads are used as summer residences or hunting and fishing lodges. Just before Shelburne is Birchtown, first settled by 1,000 black servants who came to Shelburne with their Loyalist masters in 1783.

SHELBURNE: This town was founded in 1783 by a contingent of United Empire Loyalists, many of whom were members of the New York aristocracy. To a great extent it retains the feel and atmosphere of its origin, especially in the *Ross-Thompson House* (Charlotte La.), both a house and a shop — the only extant shop from the 18th century in the province. At one time the store sold necessities — yard goods, rum, china; today it sells items especially associated with the Loyalist period. The rest of the house is also open, filled with period furniture and the delicious odor of pungent spices from around the world, exactly what an enterprising and wide-ranging sea captain might bring home to amuse his patient and long-suffering wife. The town has always been associated with the sea. It was here that many of the world's great yachts have been built, and here that Donald McKay, one of the greatest yacht builders, learned his trade. Appropriately, one of the oldest lighthouses in Nova Scotia, Cape Roseway Light, is here, on McNutt's Island in the entrance to Shelburne's harbor. The island is a lovely place for summer picnics, but only sailors need apply — you must get there by boat. The route so far may have put you in the mood for a fishing expedition of your own.

En Route from Shelburne – Continue on Route 3, also called Route 103 in this area. You'll pass through Jordan Falls, a tiny community where the novelist Zane Grey once caught a record tuna.

From Jordan Falls take Route 3 to Lockeport.

LOCKEPORT: Founded in 1755 by settlers from Plymouth, Massachusetts, Lockeport is known for its crescent beach, more than a mile of hard sand. Near the beach is the *Little School Museum* (1845), the town's first schoolhouse. The school has been refurbished by the Lockeport Garden Club and contains many artifacts of the time.

En Route from Lockeport – Proceeding on Route 103, you soon enter Queens County and travel past Port Joli. In the winter and spring this area, with its plentiful supply of eel grass, lures large numbers of beautiful Canada geese. Shooting — in season — is allowed only when the birds fly over the hills that separate the Port Joli and Port Hebert harbors. A few miles farther is White Point Beach, a popular resort area. There's an attractive beach near *White Point Beach Lodge,* but the water is usually cold. Nearby is the 9-hole seaside course of the *Liverpool Golf and Country Club.* Greens-fee players are welcome.

LIVERPOOL: Situated on the banks of the Mersey River, Liverpool, once the site of an Indian village, was founded in 1760 by New Englanders of Pilgrim stock. The town has an exciting history. It was visited by Samuel de Champlain and Pierre du Gua de Monts in 1604, and was the home of the privateer Joseph Barss, Jr. In the War of 1812, Barss captured more than 100 American vessels. The Barss home is still standing. On the grounds of Old Fort Point there are monuments to the exploits of Barss and others. The Simeon Perkins House on Main Street was built in 1766 by Colonel Perkins, a famous Nova Scotia merchant and diarist. Today the Cape Cod-style home contains rare artifacts, books, and furniture of that fascinating period of trading, Yankee privateering, and the American Revolution. Perkins's dairy, on display at the Royal Bank of Canada, gives an account of the town between 1766 and the War of 1812.

BROOKLYN: This town near Liverpool is the site of the 125,000-ton Mersey paper plant, owned partly by the *Washington Post.* The Nova Scotia Power Corporation on the Mersey River supplies power for the plant, which employs 1,000 people.

En Route from Brooklyn – Take Route 331 just past Mill Village and pass through the delightful fishing villages of Vogler's Cove and West Dublin. Farther along the road, in a major provincial park, you'll find Risser's Beach, one of the many excellent beaches in this area. The water's warm enough for a summer swim. There are many summer homes in the region. You'll see some of them as you begin to follow the LaHave River toward Bridgewater. This river is called the Rhine of Nova Scotia, both for its beauty and because the surrounding area was settled by people of German descent. The area is of particular historic interest as the scene of numerous attempts by the French to build settlements in the 1600s.

BRIDGEWATER: The *DesBrisay Museum* (Jubilee Rd.) was completed in 1967 as a project honoring Canada's Centennial. It contains a collection of old coins, possessions of the early settlers, Indian artifacts, and curios from the sea. Also worth seeing is the Dean Wile Carding Mill (1860), a water-powered wool operation that cleans and untangles fibers before spinning. Bridgewater is situated on the LaHave, a river noted for its good salmon fishing. The town's name refers to the bridge over the river. The South Shore Exhibition and International Ox Pull, featuring oxen from the US competing against local champions, is held here annually in early July. If you have time to spare and are serious about learning how to sail, consider contacting Brian Stokes (phone: 902-543-3658) for boat rental and instruction. If you have no experience, Stokes offers a 5-day, 20-hour shore/afloat course designed to enable you to sail singlehandedly. For the less enthusiastic, short cruises of 1 to 6 hours and a cruise of 2 days are offered.

Just past Bridgewater take Route 332, following the LaHave toward the ocean.

RIVERPORT: The Ovens, Feltzen South Road, is a series of caverns worn into the rocky cliffs by the pounding surf, twisted by the incessant work of the water into fascinating geological formations. A park at the Ovens marks the site of a brief but furious gold rush. For 6 months in 1861, the Ovens yielded $120,000 worth of gold without the aid of machinery (most of the gold was washed from the beach). A town developed, but was soon abandoned; almost as quickly as the gold appeared it disappeared. The park contains old pits and workings, and there is a good lookout point.

LUNENBURG: Probably the most important fishing port in North America, Lunenburg is the home of the Highliner Division of National Sea Products, a Nova Scotia company with fish plants from Florida to Newfoundland. Here you're certain to get an indication of the enormous part fishing plays in the economic and cultural life of the province. According to estimates, national sea-related companies employ 10,000 people, with twice that number indirectly dependent on the firms. In Lunenburg, you'll be able to trace the industry's progress. The town is the home of the original fishing schooner *Bluenose,* which went undefeated in international schooner races between 1921 and 1946 and is remembered with pride by all Nova Scotians and depicted on the back of the Canadian dime. It's honored in Lunenburg with a monument that reads: "1921-1946 Champion of International Schooner Races and symbol of the transformation of an inland people into leading deep-sea fishermen of the North Atlantic. Planted here as farmers in 1753, the German, French, and Swiss immigrants, after clearing the wilderness and practicing the coastal fisheries, gradually went onto the Banks where they vied with the fishermen of Gloucester, their competitors in the International Schooner Races."

A replica of *Bluenose, Bluenose II,* was constructed at the Smith and Rhuland yard in Lunenburg and launched in 1963. Built by a brewery for promotional purposes, the replica is an exact duplicate of the original except for the addition of some modern conveniences. It is now owned by the provincial government. Although it tours around the province and goes to coastal cities of the US, *Bluenose II* spends most of the summer in Halifax, from where it makes daily cruises. The Smith and Rhuland yard also built the *Bounty* for use in the film *Mutiny on the Bounty,* starring Marlon Brando. In addition, the Lunenburg *Fisheries Museum* is at the water end of Duke Street. The museum is housed in two ships, the *Theresa E. Connor,* the last Lunenburg schooner to fish the Grand Banks with dories, and the *Cape Sable,* a steel-hulled trawler. The museum also has an aquarium. The Nova Scotia Fisheries Exhibition and Fishermen's Reunion is held in Lunenburg in early September. Among the annual exhibition events is the international two-person dory race in which the US *Gloucester* fishing fleet challenges that of the Lunenburgers. Have dinner at the *Boscawen Inn* (150 Cumberland St.), a restored Victorian mansion. It specializes in fresh local seafood and home-cooked meals.

MAHONE BAY: Founded in 1754, Mahone Bay is a scenic town at the head of a bay sprinkled with no less than 365 islands. During the War of 1812 an American ship, the *Young Teazer,* was chased into Mahone Bay by a British man-of-war. On board the American vessel was a British deserter. Realizing that the *Young Teazer* couldn't escape and that he would be hanged if captured, the Briton threw a torch into the powder magazine and blew the ship apart. Legend has it that on the anniversary of the explosion, June 27, a ghost ship, engulfed in flames, can be seen in the bay. Three pretty churches standing side by side at the head of the bay make an attractive photograph. Stop for lunch at *Zwicker's Inn,* a refurbished 1805 posthouse, or take tea at *Tingle Bridge Tea House.* Both serve a fine array of made-on-the-premises specialties that certainly won't disappoint.

OAK ISLAND: According to another legend, an enormous treasure is buried here. Some say it's the plunder of Captain Kidd. But the treasure has also been linked to British military engineers attempting to hide valuables during the American Revolution as well as to pirates who used the island as a communal bank. In any event, millions of dollars have been spent, and six men killed, trying to unearth the cache. But nothing of consequence has been found. The search for the treasure began in 1796, when three hunters from Chester noticed a depression in the land and thought someone had been digging there. The next day they began their own excavation. At 10 feet they discovered a layer of planks; at 20 feet they found a second layer. And more layers were found at a depth of 90 feet. Using more sophisticated methods, the diggers went to 96 feet. Then water rushed in and flooded the pit. Subsequent drillings met the same fate, although oak casks and loose metal were encountered. It was later discovered that an ingeniously constructed shaft stretches from the pit to the ocean. This apparently permitted water to enter the main shaft. The original pit has long since collapsed. But the hunt goes on. In the most recent attempt, in late 1978, a private treasure hunter tried to hit paydirt by drilling a new shaft, 8 feet in diameter, 180 feet away from the pit. The island, now pockmarked by drilling, is accessible by car, and tours are offered at a small charge.

CHESTER: A scenic town popular with the many American families who have summered here for generations, Chester was settled in 1759 by New Englanders. Graced with both back and front harbors, Chester also has tennis courts and a golf course open to visitors. A yacht club hosts some of the province's most spirited regattas. *Race Week* in late August features dozens of yachts, many flying beautiful spinnakers — a delightful sight, even for the landlubber. From Chester a ferry travels to Big and Little Tancook islands, famed for cabbages and sauerkraut; the ferry can be picked up at Water Street. Check locally for schedules. The *Captain's House* restaurant has good meals, and the view of the Back Harbour is splendid. Others of note are *The Rope Loft*, in an old fish shack on Water Street, and *Windjammer*, attached to the motel on Route 3 at the southern turnoff to the town. Both have quite good seafood at reasonable prices. For fresh take-out seafood try *Hilchie's*, on Water Street.

HUBBARDS: The pleasant community of Hubbards has a small fish plant and is the home of many summer residents. There is a nice private beach to which you can have access for a small fee. It has a snack bar and picnic facilities.

En Route from Hubbards – As you head toward Halifax on Route 3 you will see many attractive sea views and clean, supervised beaches. Queensland Beach is particularly popular because the water usually reaches 70F (21C) by late summer. At Upper Tantallon look for the turn to your right on Route 333 toward Glen Haven and Peggy's Cove. At one time, many of the houses here were occupied by a species now disappearing — the lone fisherman. Now, commuters travel from their homes here to jobs in Halifax, and summer homes dot the roadside. Even so, old fishing villages, like Indian Harbour and Paddy's Head, are still thriving.

PEGGY'S COVE: This rustic fishing village is probably the most photographed spot in the province. A barren landscape of granite projections and piled boulders stands in stark contrast to the brightly painted homes of Peggy's Cove. Although few of the townspeople are actually engaged in fishing, the provincial government has sought legislation to preserve the maritime character of the village. In St. John's Anglican Church at the entrance to Peggy's Cove are two murals painted by the late William deGarthe, a town resident and one of the province's best-known artists. To enter the church, get the key from the house next door. If you walk on the rocks near the water, don't go too close to the edge. Particularly after storms and during an advancing tide, the waves can crash unexpectedly high up the rocks. In recent years a couple of wave-watchers have been drowned. Visit the post office in the lighthouse. The *Sou' Wester* nearby features hearty chowders and delicious gingerbread.

En Route from Peggy's Cove – It seems as if giants have dropped the huge boulders you'll see as you head toward Halifax through the bare countryside on Route 333. They are the result of glacial movements; the boulders lie where they were when the ice melted. Weeping Widow's Island in Shad Bay has been the scene of several unsuccessful treasure hunts. At White's Lake, take the short drive out to Prospect, a hardy fishing village facing out to sea from a spit of land. Each July the village has a chowder-ama, with lots of hearty fish chowder and baked goods.

When you reach the end of Route 333, look for signs to Route 102. This will take you, via the Bayer's Road Exit, into Halifax. This city, the largest on the east coast of Canada, merits a tour of its own. (For complete details, see *Halifax*, THE CITIES.) While in Halifax, amble down to the waterfront to Historic Properties. The selection of quality specialty shops is good, but more enticing is the atmosphere on a warm, sunny day. It's definitely a stroller's paradise. Lots of people congregate to watch the scenery, have an ice cream, or just pass the time. If time allows, take a trip into the harbor aboard one of the tour boats. For the budget-minded, even a trip on the ferry that runs between the twin cities of Halifax and Dartmouth can be a welcome experience; it's less than the cost of a city bus ride.

Just after you pass Halifax Shopping Centre on the right-hand side of Bayer's Road, look for Connaught Avenue, and make a left turn at this corner. Continue on Connaught until you see signs to the A. Murray MacKay Bridge. Cross the bridge (toll 25¢) and follow Route 111 to the Micmac Rotary, with its lakes on both sides. From the rotary continue on Route 111. Now you've begun the marine drive, which is marked with distinctive signs. At Woodlawn, near the Penhorn Mall shopping center, look for Route 207 to Cole Harbour and Lawrencetown. There's good shooting for Canada geese and other sea birds in the Cole Harbour Dike area. Lawrencetown has a fine sandy beach; although the beach is supervised in season, bathers are warned of a sometimes strong and dangerous undertow. Waves are sometimes adequate for surfing, though hardly challenging to an expert. Three Fathoms Harbour, Seaforth, and West Chezzetcook are all picturesque villages. Early in the morning, the villagers go to sea in small boats; in the afternoon you can see them cleaning their catch on the wharves. At Musquodoboit Harbour you enter a lumbering area, the center of which is Head of Jeddore. Lake Charlotte is one of the province's best hunting and fishing districts.

TANGIER: This was one of the province's first gold mining areas. Nearby, at the Moose River Gold Mines, one of the most famous dramas in Nova Scotia history was acted out on April 12, 1936, the day before Easter, when three Toronto men were trapped in the 141-foot shaft of the gold mine they were inspecting. Six days later, signals indicating that the three were alive came through a hole drilled by rescue crews. Five days later, the men were finally reached. One of them had died. The story received worldwide attention.

At Tangier, look for signs to *Willy Krauch's Smoke Shop.* Krauch is internationally known for the quality of his smoked fish. (He has supplied smoked salmon to Queen Elizabeth II.)

En Route from Tangier – On the way to Sherbrooke, you'll pass through Sheet Harbour, a thickly wooded area known for deer. Inland from Sheet Harbour is the 200-square-mile Liscomb Park Game Sanctuary where moose, mink, muskrat, and other animals roam the forests; it's an ideal spot for camera buffs. Trout fishing is also excellent, but fishermen must be accompanied by registered guides. Port Dufferin, named after the Marquis of Dufferin, is another area where gold has been found. Farther along the route is Necum Teuch, Indian for "a beach of fine sand." Before reaching Ecum Secum, "red bank," you'll cross into Guysborough, mainland Nova Scotia's easternmost county. At Liscomb Mills, look for *Liscombe Lodge* (see *Best En Route*). The restaurant at this government-owned riverside lodge is attractive yet informal. The lodge owners are also complete outfitters for trout and salmon fishing (phone: 902-779-2307).

SHERBROOKE: While you're here, be sure to visit the Sherbrooke Village restoration. Seventeen buildings, including a post office, drugstore, jail, school, church, blacksmith's shop, and sawmill have been restored to their appearance between 1860 and 1880, when Sherbrooke boomed with gold mining, shipbuilding, and lumbering activity. Costumed guides provide tours.

En Route from Sherbrooke – At the junction of Routes 7 and 276, take Route 276 right to Goshen. Then proceed on Route 316 south toward 15-mile (24-km) Country Harbour, with Harbour Island at its mouth. Although its magnificent waters are virtually unspoiled by commerce, the harbor has been mentioned as a possible site for marine industrial development. From Country Harbour you pass through numerous other small fishing towns of rugged beauty. At the junction of Routes 316 and 16, take a swing east to Canso, the closest mainland point to the rich Atlantic fishing grounds. First inhabited by the French in the 1500s, Canso has always been heavily dependent on fishing for its prosperity. Return on Route 16 to Guysborough, an important lumber and pulpwood center. Then take 344 to Mulgrave on the Strait of Canso. Mulgrave faces Port Hawkesbury across the strait; the two towns have benefited from the ice-free, deepwater harbor resulting from the construction of the Canso Causeway, the world's largest, which was built from 1952 to 1955. Auld Cove, the mainland end of the causeway, is also the last stop on this route.

BEST EN ROUTE

The hotels and motels on this route provide generous facilities for the region's favorite forest and sea sports: canoeing, camping, fishing, and swimming. You'll pay $17 to $25 for accommodations we've listed as moderate and over $25 for those we've rated expensive. Prices are subject to fluctuation and are based on the cost for two persons for one night. All prices are quoted in US dollars.

SHELBURNE

Ox Bow Village – On the shores of Lake George, this hotel has 50 spacious rooms, a heated swimming pool, game room, and an enclosed children's playground. RR #2 (phone: 902-875-3000). Expensive to moderate.

LIVERPOOL

Lanes Privateer – At the east end of the Liverpool Bridge spanning the Mersey River, this 28-room motel comes with all the usual conveniences. Lounge and licensed dining room. PO Box 509 (phone: 902-354-3456). Expensive.

White Point Beach Lodge – Open year-round with 47 rooms and 40 cottages, this resort offers daily beach parties and barbecues on a white sandy beach. A freshwater lake, boats, tennis courts, golf course, nature trails, and horseback riding are also available. Off Hwy. 103, Exit 20A or 21 on Rte. 3 (phone: 800-565-5068). Expensive.

Pat's Overnight Guests – Three rooms, one shared bath. Breakfast 7:30 to 9:30 AM. Open May 1 to October 15. 388 Main St., Milton (phone: 902-354-4071). Moderate.

BRIDGEWATER

Auberge Wandlyn Inn – Part of an eastern Canadian motel chain, it has an indoor swimming pool and a sauna. 50 North St. (phone: 800-561-0006). Expensive.

Best Western Bridgewater – This 50-unit motel has a heated indoor swimming pool. 35 High St. (phone: 902-543-8173). Expensive.

WESTERN SHORE

Oak Island Inn Best Western – Overlooking Oak Island and Mahone Bay, this 74-unit inn has a full-service marina, boat and sailboat rentals, and deep-sea fishing charters. Western Shore, Lunenburg County (phone: 902-627-2600 or 800-565-5075). Expensive.

CHESTER

Windjammer – A 15-unit motel located west of town on Route 3 near Chester; the landscaped grounds are set back from the highway. PO Box 240 (phone: 902-275-3567). Expensive.

Big Oaks Inn B & B – Four rooms, 1 shared full bath/shower, and a private powder room. Full breakfast 7 to 8:30 AM. Open May 15 to October 15. No pets. Located in Chester Basin, 3 miles (5 km) west of Chester (phone: 902-275-4542). Moderate.

HUBBARDS

Anchorage House and Cabins – Gordon and Judy Morrison are the friendly proprietors of this lovely, old house with 4 snug guestrooms decorated with homemade quilts and antique furnishings. There are also 3 cabins and 5 housekeeping cottages. Trout ponds, fishing charters, and small boat and bicycle rentals are all available. 6612 Shore Club Rd. (phone: 902-857-9402). Expensive.

LISCOMB MILLS

Liscombe Lodge – The best accommodations on the eastern shore are provided at this government-owned facility on the Liscomb River. The attractive lodge has 35 units, including cottages and cabins. Boating and freshwater and saltwater fishing are nearby. Tennis, marina boat and canoe rentals, playground, lawn games, freshwater fishing, guides and equipment, yacht mooring, hiking trails — all on the premises. Open May to late October. Liscomb Mills, Guysborough County (phone: 902-779-2307). Expensive.

Amherst around Cape Breton Island

Beginning in Amherst, this 530-mile (853-km) route passes through farmlands bordering the warmest salt water north of the Carolinas, crosses the Strait of Canso, then swings around Cape Breton Island to its terminus in Port Hawkesbury. Alexander Graham Bell, who spent his summers on the island, thought this was the most beautiful scenery in North America: rolling hills plunging into verdant valleys, stony cliffs overlooking the ocean, and inland lochs and glens that are purely Scottish. The trip culminates in Louisbourg, where Canada's largest historical restoration project is in progress, offering an authentic picture of a major French military stronghold in the New World.

The first part of the route leads through lands mostly settled by Scots. It was at Pictou that the *Hector* landed in 1773 with 33 families and 25 unmarried men, all refugees from the Highlands of Scotland. On the 11-week journey across the Atlantic, 18 passengers died. But *Hector*'s voyage was just the start of the migration; thousands more followed, giving the area its decisively Scottish character. One of the first communities outside Amherst is Pugwash, birthplace of the great American industrialist Cyrus Eaton. Although Cape Breton has Nova Scotia's highest unemployment rate, you'll see people here who seem to thrive, with a way of life that is fulfilling and comfortable.

Along the way, keep an eye out for good meals in out-of-the-way places. Along Route 6, bordering the Northumberland Strait, look for signs advertising lobster suppers, often sponsored by church groups. The waters around the island contain some of the world's richest lobster grounds, and during the summer months local groups sponsor community suppers of absolutely fresh lobsters. Of particular note is the *Pictou Lobster Carnival* (usually in early July). Watch also for the Chowder Houses sponsored by the government-financed Cape Breton Development Corporation. These very simple places offer chowders, fish dishes, and breads baked by residents who prepare traditional recipes. If you're from a big city, you're likely to find the island's rural simplicity quite refreshing.

AMHERST: This town is named after Lord Jeffrey Amherst (1717–1797), the English baron and governor-general of British North America from 1760 to 1763 who also gave his name to the Massachusetts town and college as well as to Amherstburg and Amherst Island in Ontario. Amherst is the first community on the Nova Scotia side of the Nova Scotia–New Brunswick border. The major provincial tourist bureau is on Route 104 on the New Brunswick side of Amherst.

En Route from Amherst – Take Route 6 on the Sunrise Trail, a stretch of highway following the Northumberland shore to the Canso Causeway. Head for Heather Beach on Northumberland Strait, where you'll find a saltwater beach typical of many along Route 6.

PUGWASH: In Pugwash — with street signs in English and Gaelic — you'll feel the first tangible evidence of the Scottish influence in the area. Pugwash is the site of a major salt mine, which produces 1,000 tons of salt a day. The salt is moved out by ship from Pugwash Harbour, one of many in Nova Scotia capable of handling large ocean vessels. The town of 640 is known internationally as the site of the annual Thinkers Conference sponsored by the late American industrialist Cyrus Eaton, who was born in Pugwash in 1883.

En Route from Pugwash – Continue on Route 6 to Wallace, known for over 100 years for sandstone quarries that have provided material for such famous buildings as the Houses of Parliament in Ottawa and Province House in Halifax. Wallace is the birthplace of Simon Newcomb, the great American scientist and astronomer, who immigrated to the US at the age of 18.

From Wallace, you'll pass Malagash Peninsula, known for its lobsters and oysters and for a salt mine discovered in 1916. The discovery was a key one for Nova Scotia, since the fishing industry required thousands of tons of salt yearly. Most of the province's salt mining is now done in Pugwash.

TATAMAGOUCHE: Anna Swan, an 8-foot-tall giantess, was born near this village (pop. 553) in 1846. She went on to star in P. T. Barnum's show and marry Captain Martin Van Buren Bates, who was also 8 feet tall. In Tatamagouche, you can see Anna Swan's skirt and other mementos at the *Sunrise Trail Museum*.

From Tatamagouche, take a side trip on Route 311 to Balmoral Mills.

BALMORAL MILLS: The *Nova Scotia Museum* operates a grist mill here dating from 1830. Privately owned until 1966 and now completely restored, the mill still grinds grain into flour with old-fashioned water wheels providing the power. You can buy the products of the mill. The *Balmoral* hotel has pastries and pies made from the mill's stone-ground flour, as well as huge helpings of hearty country food. The 23-foot Drysdale Falls, with a marvelous swimming area below, is nearby.

En Route from Balmoral Mills – Travel back to Route 6 and head for Brule, known for its warm water, sandy beaches, golf course, and campgrounds. As you cross into Pictou County, you enter an increasingly industrialized area; people rely more on factories than on the sea or farmlands for their livelihood. At Toney River you might see Irish moss being bailed and dried.

PICTOU: This small city, along with four surrounding towns, forms the third largest industrial area in the province, ranking behind Halifax-Dartmouth and Sydney. It has a shipbuilding yard, a lobster cannery, and a knife manufacturer. In 1773, the *Hector* brought the first settlers from Scotland. In 1973, major ceremonies were held in Pictou to mark the bicentennial of the arrival. One of the key participants was former US Supreme Court Justice William O. Douglas, a descendant of people who traveled on the *Hector*. Pictou is the site of the annual 3-day *Lobster Carnival* early in July. It also hosts the Pictou County–North Colchester Exhibition early in September. Thomas McCulloch's house, overlooking the junction of West River and Pictou Harbour, was built in the early 19th century and today is a museum devoted to tracing the lives of prominent Pictonians of Scottish ancestry. On Shore Road, 2 miles (3 km) east of Pictou, is the *Micmac Indian Museum*. Open during daylight hours in summer, the museum has Indian relics from a nearby 17th-century burial ground.

Continue on to Route 104 (the Trans-Canada Highway) and turn west briefly.

STELLARTON: Coal was discovered in Stellarton in 1798; the Foord Seam here, at 48 feet, is believed to be the thickest seam of coal in the world. A small miners' museum and an 1854 steam locomotive, *Albion,* located near the center of town in Albion Park, commemorate the history of the area.

Continue back east on Route 104 to New Glasgow.

NEW GLASGOW: Named after Glasgow, Scotland, this town was originally the center of Pictou County coal mining. Today it's known for its steel foundries, clay works, and machine shops. The first settlers along the banks of the East River were mostly bachelors. It's reported that once, when a ship bearing new settlers docked in Halifax, three of the single men trekked all the way there on foot to find brides. After the Halifax weddings, the new couples hiked the entire distance back. Along nearby Abercrombie Road, you'll find the Abercrombie Country Club, featuring an 18-hole golf course and a curling rink.

En Route from New Glasgow – At Sutherland's River, take Route 245 north toward Merigomish. At Malignant Cove (named for a British man-of-war wrecked here), follow Route 337 to Cape George. Beautiful sea views grace the road here, and there's a lighthouse at the tip of the cape.

ANTIGONISH: Each year, around the middle of July, this pretty town hosts the Highland Games. This traditional celebration — a kind of Olympics of the clans — features tests of the Scots' brawn like the caber toss (in which hefty competitors heave a large pole as far as they can). In addition to track and field events, there's even a kilted golf tournament. Marching bagpipe bands, a Gaelic choir, a Highland dance competition, and a whiskey-tasting event are part of the week-long festivities.

Antigonish is also the home of St. Francis Xavier University and its sister institution, the Coady Institute. The university won recognition in 1920 for the Antigonish Movement, a self-help program for community development that stressed the use of cooperatives and credit unions. Today, students from more than 80 countries study community development at the Coady Institute on the Antigonish campus. Antigonish, halfway between Halifax and Sydney, was founded by Loyalist soldiers and their families after the American Revolution. *The Lobster Treat,* a converted schoolhouse at 241 Post Road, has fresh, well-prepared food, and the kitchen serves only what's in season.

En Route from Antigonish – Continue east on Route 104 to the Strait of Canso and the Canso Causeway. Completed in 1955, the causeway replaced the ferry service that used to operate from Auld Cove. The causeway, almost a mile long, took 3 years to build and required over 10 million tons of fill, mostly from Cape Porcupine on the mainland side of the Strait of Canso.

STRAIT OF CANSO: Canso Causeway is an ice-free "superport" that permits the world's largest ships to enter the 13 mile long Strait of Canso and dock with ease. The strait area was once considered as a possible site for huge petrochemical developments to handle liquefied natural gas being shipped out of the high Arctic.

En Route from the Strait of Canso – Take Route 19 north along the western shore of Cape Breton Island through Inverness County. At the start, at Creignish, the road rises to 850 feet, a good point from which to see the whole Strait of Canso and St. George's Bay; then it's down again past the farms that support most residents, who farm and fish for a living. The Judique communities were once known in this region for the size and violence of their male residents. These huge Highlanders challenged each other at dances and other social events with the call: "Judique on the floor. Who'll put him off?"

Port Hood (pop. 500) used to be much larger during its coal mining days. The pits have been closed for some time since the mines flooded. From Port Hood, you pass through the farming and sheep raising area of Mabou and Strathlorne. Then the road proceeds through Inverness, a coal mining center since 1865. Farther along, at Margaree Forks, you join the Cabot Trail, a highway named after explorer John Cabot, who's said to have landed here just after Columbus discovered America.

Before heading off to Cape Breton Highlands National Park, you can visit the *Salmon Museum* at North East Margaree. *Margaree Lodge* (phone: 902-248-2506) offers dignified country dining — good fresh fish and vegetables in an attractive setting (see *Best En Route*). The *Margaree Salmon Museum,* only a stone's throw from the river, has marvelous displays of old fishing equipment, legal and illegal. Operated by the Margaree Anglers' Association, the museum also has a display depicting the life cycle of that king of fish, the salmon. The Margaree River, by the way, yielded the largest salmon ever caught in the province: a 45-pounder nabbed in 1933.

As you leave Margaree Forks, you enter an area of the province where French is the first language. Belle Côte might be called the Acadia of Inverness County, for the inhabitants retain the language and tradition of their Norman ancestors. At St. Joseph du Moine there are large, undeveloped deposits of limestone and extensive, untrammeled cranberry bogs. At Grand Etang there is a cooperative lobster canning plant controlled by local fishermen.

CHÉTICAMP: Opposite St. Peter's Church at the south end of the village is the *Acadian Museum,* with frequent demonstrations of spinning and weaving. Crafts, including hooked rugs, are on sale. Acadian meals are also served. *Laurie's* motel (phone: 902-224-2400), on Main St., has homemade mincemeat and fresh fish. Three miles (4.8 km) past Chéticamp you enter Cape Breton Highlands National Park.

CAPE BRETON HIGHLANDS NATIONAL PARK: Forming part of a vast tableland, this 370-square-mile area contains the island's most spectacular scenery. It's a landscape reminiscent of the coast of Scotland: steep cliffs, often hundreds of feet high, loom over a stony shore. Barrens give way to deep, green valleys crisscrossed with rivers and streams. Fox, lynx, and bear roam the park's forests, and over a hundred bird species nest here. Facilities include many hiking trails and a number of campgrounds and picnic parks. And golfers can test their skills on an 18-hole course that is quite challenging.

Although it often climbs mountains only to drop suddenly back to sea level, the road is good and an alert driver will have no difficulty. The curves are sharp and the grades steep, though. French Mountain, at an elevation of 1,492 feet, is the highest point on any highway in the province. The road also climbs MacKenzie Mountain (1,222 ft.), descending, by a series of switchbacks, to Pleasant Bay. Three rivers — the MacKenzie, the Pond, and the Red — converge here. From the bay, the road swings to the east up the side of North Mountain, climbing 1,460 feet. You'll have good views of the park's spectacular gorges as you descend into Sunrise Valley. Heading south for the first time on the Cabot Trail, turn left to Neil Harbour.

Named after an early settler, Neil Harbour is an English-speaking fishing village; it's one of the best spots on the island to plunge into a way of life as dependent on the sea as it was a century ago. Steep grades and more dramatic sights are on the Cabot Trail before Ingonish.

Local legend says that the name "Ingonish" is Portuguese, and that the Portuguese had a fishing base here as early as 1521. Early in the 17th century, the French established an active settlement here, and by 1740, 54 fishing vessels were sailing out of Ingonish. From here continue to Ingonish Beach, the site of the administrative quarters for the park. The community is also a major provincial resort area, with the impressive, provincially owned *Keltic Lodge* (see *Best En Route*) as its centerpiece. The lodge, with a swimming pool, tennis courts, championship golf course, superb cuisine, and spectacular setting, is well worth a visit. Stroll along the nearby beach, with its large breakers and cold water. *Keltic Lodge* (phone: 902-285-2880) lays one of the best tables in the province.

En Route from Ingonish Beach – The road passes Cape Smokey, a winter ski area, from which a chair lift is available in the summer if you want to take in the view from the mountaintop. From this peak, you can clearly see the results of a disastrous forest fire that occurred in June 1968.

The villages of Wreck Cove, Skir Dhu, Briton Cove, and North Shore are next along the trail. In Wreck Cove is the last major hydroelectric power source that can be developed in the province; the lack of this power forces reliance on imported crude oil and coal-fired thermal generating plants, the main reason for Nova Scotia's high electrical costs.

Just south of Indian Brook, take Route 312 toward Jersey Cove. From here, a short ferry trip (it operates 24 hours a day) takes you to Englishtown. Just to your right as you disembark is the grave of Angus MacAskill, the fabled Cape Breton giant who died in 1863 at the age of 38. MacAskill grew to a well-proportioned height of 7 feet, 9 inches and weighed 425 pounds. His boot, on display at the *Nova Scotia Museum* in Halifax, is 14½ inches long. From Englishtown you can soon pick up Route 105 to Sydney, Nova Scotia's steel center. But instead of going directly to Sydney, make a side trip to Baddeck.

BADDECK: This is the community where Alexander Graham Bell summered the last 35 years of his life. During that time, he worked on a host of experiments. Bell's descendants still live in the area, occupying the home at Beinn Bhreagh (Gaelic for "beautiful mountain") where Bell and his wife lived. (Although visible from the government wharf in Baddeck, his home is not open to visitors.) Nearby are the Bells' graves. The fascinating *Alexander Graham Bell Museum,* at the east end of town on Route 205, is open, however. The building itself is tetrahedral in design, a form of four triangular faces used by Bell in his huge man-carrying kites. Inside the museum are photos and artifacts donated by the Bell family. These give an indication of the extraordinary range of Bell's interests, including sheep breeding, medicine, aeronautics, and — the telephone. Aided by Bell, J. A. D. McCurdy flew the *Silver Dart* across icy Bras d'Or Lake near here on February 23, 1909. It was the first flight made in the British empire. This fishing and sailing center is extraordinarily picturesque, especially when the harbor is filled with summer yachts.

En Route from Baddeck – Take Route 105 back to Sydney. Passing over Kelly's Mountain (again), you'll have excellent views of St. Ann's Bay and Bras d'Or Lake. Cross the Bras d'Or Bridge, completed in 1961, and proceed to North Sydney, where ferries travel to Newfoundland. Route 125 leads to Sydney.

SYDNEY: On its deep natural harbor facing Newfoundland across the Cabot Strait, Sydney is a center of shipping and industry. Its first settlers were Loyalists from New

York led by Abraham Cuyler, a former mayor of Albany, New York. Scottish Highlanders were the next group to put down roots. The third largest city of Nova Scotia, Sydney has a population of 29,400; the College of Cape Breton here has over 1,000 students. Steel production, the main industry, is dominated by the Sydney Steel Corporation (SYSCO), owned by the provincial government since the previous owners abandoned the mill in 1967 — and no blessing. The plant has created difficult economic and social problems for three provincial administrations, losing hundreds of millions of dollars but crucial to the whole economy of Cape Breton, where generations of men have worked at steel-related jobs.

FORTRESS OF LOUISBOURG: Just a few miles outside the town of Louisbourg on the Atlantic coast is the largest restoration project ever undertaken in Canada. Originally built by the French between 1720 and 1745, the Fortress of Louisbourg was the headquarters of the French fleet. It became an important trading community and was the most formidable French military establishment on the Atlantic. In 1745 Colonel William Pepperell, enraged over the constant, French-inspired Indian massacres of New England fishermen stopping in Nova Scotia, led a volunteer force of New Englanders in an attack on Louisbourg. The success of the New England force shocked the world. But shortly after it became meaningless, for the fortress was returned to France as part of a treaty with the English. In 1758, hostilities again broke out and the fort was captured by the British, who reduced it to rubble. From that mess, one-quarter of the huge fort has been restored. Comfortable shoes are advised, along with a sweater or jacket to cope with the cool temperatures. The modern site resembles the 18th-century French fort as much as possible. Guides dressed in period costume give the place particular authenticity: even the untidy dress of certain soldiers seems true to the times. The imposing château, a 365-foot-long building with walls 2 feet thick, is topped by a 250-pound wrought-iron fleur-de-lis. The object was made in the fortress's present forge from early French designs. Inside the walls, four periods of furniture — Louis XIII, Louis XIV, Regency, and Louis XV — are displayed in the governor's sumptuous apartments. After touring the fort, drive to Lighthouse Point, Careening Point, and Royal Battery — other areas of scenic beauty and historical importance in the 20-square-mile Fort Louisbourg park. A trip to Kennington Cove, constructed by American volunteers during the siege of 1745, is also a worthwhile stop.

En Route from Louisbourg – A loop diversion from Route 22 proceeds through Main à Dieu. This small, quaint fishing village was almost wiped out by a huge forest fire in the summer of 1976. As you approach the town, you'll see the charred trunks of trees in the surrounding forest. It's easy to imagine the terror the villagers felt as the fire advanced from the woods toward the town. Although flames destroyed a beautiful old church — long a landmark for mariners — and several homes, the fire was extinguished before it could destroy Main à Dieu.

On the road back to Sydney, look for the exit to Route 125 that quickly takes you to Route 4 heading south. Route 4 passes along the shore of saltwater Bras d'Or Lake, a favorite yachting site on the Atlantic coast. At Chapel Island, near Soldier's Cove, is an Indian shrine where Micmac Indians hold an annual 3-day religious festival in July. Next, you pass through St. Peter's across St. Peter's Canal, which was built in 1869 to connect the 400-square-mile Bras d'Or Lake and St. Peter's Bay on the Atlantic.

ST. PETER'S: The first Europeans to occupy this area were the Portuguese. They called the community San Pedro and used it as a fishing base between 1521 and 1527. In the next century, Nicholas Denys exploited the fishing grounds and exported lumber to France. Located on the west side of St. Peter's Canal, the *Nicholas Denys Museum* contains Micmac Indian artifacts and mementos of the early French and British settlers. Until 1745 the port, known first as St. Pierre and later renamed Port Toulouse, was a stronghold of French power. But in that year New Englanders attacked Louisbourg and sank four warships. Louisbourg fell for the second time in 1758, at which time British settlers ousted the French and changed the town's name to St. Peter's. Visit the 90-acre provincial picnic and camping park on the east side of St. Peter's Canal. Here you can hike to the top of Mt. Granville, the original site of Fort Granville, built in 1793. The remains of its ramparts are still visible.

En Route from St. Peter's – Before reaching Port Hawkesbury, take a short side trip to Isle Madame, linked to the mainland by a bridge. The paved loop passes through several scenic Acadian villages. One of these, Arichat, features a cathedral (1838), the century-old Bishop's Palace (now a hospital), and *Le Noir Forge Museum*. Returning to the mainland, take Route 4 through Cleveland, a tiny lumbering community named after US President Grover Cleveland, to Port Hawkesbury.

BEST EN ROUTE

An interesting alternative to hotels and motels is overnight accommodation at one of Cape Breton Island's bed-and-breakfast houses. As part of a Cape Breton Development Corporation program, local residents hang out a "Bed and Breakfast" shingle and open their doors to visitors. To make a reservation at one of these homes, contact any Cape Breton Tourist Information Bureau.

Some of the accommodations listed below offer an American Plan (meals included) and/or a Modified American Plan (dinner and breakfast) in addition to the conventional European Plan (no meals). Expect to pay about $17 per night for two at the hotels listed as inexpensive, $18 to $25 as moderate, and $35 to $70 as expensive. All prices are quoted in US dollars.

ANTIGONISH

Best Western Claymore – Almost anywhere along the route will be within striking distance of Antigonish and its midsummer Highland Games. There are some very attractive inns and lodges on Cape Breton Island with more atmosphere, but to be in the center of the action, try this comfortable motel near the town's shopping center. Nearby Georges Bay can be chilly, making the motel's heated pool all the more attractive. Church St. (phone: 902-863-1050). Expensive.

PORT HASTINGS

Skye – On the Canso Causeway, connecting Cape Breton Island with the rest of Nova Scotia, this place is most interesting for its kitchen—specifically, the simple seafood prepared there. Catches from the Gulf of St. Lawrence and the Atlantic end up on its table. At the junction of Rtes. 105, 4, and 19 (phone: 902-625-1300). Expensive.

INVERNESS

Inverness Beach Village – There are 40 fully equipped cottages with kitchens and a total of 52 bedrooms. Open June 15 to September 15. A quarter-mile north of Inverness on Rte. 19 (phone: 902-258-2653). Expensive.

MARGAREE FORKS

Kilmuir Place – The real reason to visit this tiny farmhouse just off Cape Breton's Cabot Trail (besides its utter peace) is salmon fishing, and the innkeeper can tell you where the salmon are running in the nearby salmon river as well as make judicious suggestions on the most effective fly. There are only 5 guestrooms, so book early in season (June–October 15). Northeast Margaree (phone: 902-248-2877). Expensive.

Margaree Lodge – Overlooking the Margaree Valley, this 46-unit establishment can arrange deep-sea fishing trips, salmon and trout fishing excursions, and guides. Facilities include a dining room and swimming pool. Open early June to mid-October. Junction of Route 19 and Cabot Trail, Margaree Forks (phone: 902-248-2297). Expensive.

MARGAREE VALLEY

Normaway Inn – Besides the charming 9-room country inn on this lovely estate there are 14 comfortable cabins. Good food and hospitality are to be found; the owner often shows films about the local area, and sometimes there's live entertainment—one or two local Cape Breton fiddlers. In the inn lobby are listings of local concerts and square dances. Facilities include badminton, tennis courts, bicycle rentals, and equipment for salmon fishing. Situated 2 miles (3.2 km) off the Cabot Trail on Egypt Road (phone: 902-248-2987).

CHÉTICAMP

Park View – With rooms looking over the Gulf of St. Lawrence and the Cape Breton Highlands, there are facilities here for both deep-sea and freshwater fishing. And if you prefer your water contained, the motel has a pool. Open May 24 to mid-October. At entrance to Cape Breton Highlands National Park, PO Box 117 (phone 902-224-3232). Expensive.

PLEASANT BAY

Beachside – A motel with 20 units that are available on a daily and weekly basis. Fishing, hiking trails, swimming, playground, and barbecue (phone: 902-224-2467). Expensive.

INGONISH AND INGONISH BEACH

Glenghorm – This resort has two parts: "Complex 1" comprises 15 acres of landscaped property, including beach frontage, with 36 motel units, 5 efficiencies, and 11 cottages; "Complex 2" spreads over 6 adjacent acres, also with some beachfront property, plus a swimming pool and 32 more motel units. Guests have access to all facilities. PO Box 39, Ingonish (phone: 902-285-2604). Expensive.

Keltic Lodge – The provincial government runs this resort set on a peninsula sticking out into the Atlantic. The surrounding country looks astoundingly like the Scottish Hebrides. A tough, long 18-hole golf course, superb dining, and a spectacular setting are featured, as are nature trails, tennis courts, and other activities. Open year-round, except from mid-October to late December; reopening depends on snow conditions since alpine and cross-country skiing are offered. Near the east gate of Cape Breton Highlands National Park. Herman Falls, Ingonish Beach (phone: 902-285-2880). Expensive.

BADDECK

Inverary Inn – A charming inn with 24 rooms, 14 cottages, 50 motel units, and lots of room for children to play. Good food is served in a dignified dining room. Shore Rd., Rte. 205 (phone: 902-295-2674). Expensive.

Silver Dart – Overlooking Bras d'Or Lake on a hill above the road, this motel has 82 modern units, waterfront area, walking trails, and bicycle rentals. It's just across the road from the *Inverary Inn*. PO Box 399 (phone: 902-295-2340). Expensive.

LOUISBOURG

Fleur-de-Lis – Just 2 miles (3 km) from the fortress and the national historic site, this motor inn is hardly historic, but it is convenient, with 46 units. Main St. (phone: 902-564-9253). Moderate.

PORT HAWKESBURY

Auberge Wandlyn Inn – Five miles (8 km) west of Canso Causeway, near a small shopping center, it has 74 units, a heated swimming pool, sauna, whirlpool bath, suntan bed, badminton, volleyball courts, and exercise facilities. 717 Reeves St. (phone: in the US, 800-561-0006; in central and eastern Canada, 800-561-0000). Expensive.

Ontario

More than any other province, centrally located Ontario offers a cross section of Canada's past and present, its dual heritage, and its diverse appearances. Its coastal areas, lying on four of the five Great Lakes, were explored in the early days of the fur trade and provided access to the trapping lands of the North and West. The coastal settlements that began as trading posts have become the industrial heart of Canada — and have brought the province's population to over 9 million, the largest in Canada.

The industrial and commercial center of Ontario is that odd peninsula of land surrounded by three Great Lakes — Ontario, Erie, and Huron — that seems to be anchored with a kiss to New York State at Niagara in the east and to Detroit in the west. The peninsula dominates the economic life of the province and is itself dominated by Toronto, the provincial capital, on Lake Ontario. With 2.8 million people, Toronto is the country's most populous metropolitan area (for a detailed report, see *Toronto*, THE CITIES). Above Toronto, in a small nubbin of Ontario jutting into neighboring Quebec, sits Ottawa, the national capital (for a complete report, see *Ottawa*, THE CITIES). This corner of the province is exceedingly fertile, and most of Ontario's vegetables come from its gardens.

Ontario, with 412,000 square miles, is Canada's second largest province. (Quebec is the largest; the Northwest Territories — which cover more than a million square miles, or one-third the total area of Canada — is not a province.) The Great Lakes Peninsula is just a small part of Ontario: The province reaches above the lakes all the way to Hudson Bay, from rich lake districts and mining and lumber country to wilderness accessible only by foot, canoe, or plane.

Culturally, geographically, and historically, Ontario divides rather neatly into four driving routes. First is certainly a tour of the peninsula's "little England": from Windsor, on the Canadian side of the Detroit River, to Stratford, through the heart of Canada's English culture, where architecture, historic sites, and even the green, green gardens conspire to be as much like an English shire as possible. French Ontario is not far away. The traditional "heritage highway" of the voyageurs starts at Niagara and follows the western shore of Lake Ontario north to Hamilton and Toronto and ultimately to the St. Lawrence and its Thousand Islands. The third route leads north and west, along Ontario's compelling Great Lakes' shores: across to Manitoulin Island to Sault Ste. Marie and around the beautiful northern shore of Lake Superior. And following the shape of this shore in a broad inland arc is the fourth route, Toronto's Yonge Street — reputed to be the longest street in the world. Yonge (pronounced "young") Street starts in downtown Toronto and wanders over 1,000 miles north and then west, the only link between civilization and Ontario's vast wilds.

Camping is offered in 220 provincial parks, 3 national parks, and in some of the 304 conservation areas, as well as in hundreds of private sites. Fishing licenses for nonresidents are available at sporting goods stores, resorts, and provincial government offices. Visitors from the US are eligible under certain conditions for a sales tax refund on accumulated purchases of $100 (CN) or more and a rebate on their hotel and motel tax. Stores and tourist centers have details.

Remember that highway distances (and speed limits) are measured in kilometers, not miles, and gas is sold by the liter (roughly one US quart).

Information: Ontario Travel, Queen's Park, Toronto, Ontario M7A 2E1 (from the continental US and Canada, except Alaska, Yukon, and Northwest Territories, 800-268-3735).

Windsor to Stratford: Ontario's England

Just as Quebec is the guardian of Canada's French culture, the southern tip of Ontario — that odd foot of land that drops into the Great Lakes like an anchor — is the citadel of British culture and tradition in Canada. On the route from Windsor, across the river from Detroit, the place names tell the story: Chatham, London, Woodstock, Brantford, Stratford, Waterloo, Kitchener, and on and on. The route ends at Stratford on the River Avon, the site of the summer-long *Shakespearean Festival,* the best presentation of the playwright's work in North America, an undertaking so ambitious that one pleased critic commented that Shakespeare himself would blush were he to know the number and the stature of people who devote their time, talents, and energy to this grand festival every year.

Certainly Stratford and its festival make a fitting culmination to this ramble through British Canada, but there is much else to see in this populous and busy section of Ontario. In counterpoint to other areas of the province, the cities and sites are close to one another. The entire route is only 160 miles (258 km) long; it could be driven in a few hours.

Here, in the most southerly part of Canada, where the fertile land is threaded with grass-banked streams, quiet creeks, and flowing rivers for picnicking, swimming, or fishing, is Canada's vegetable garden. This is one of the most temperate areas of the country, and the miles of flat farmland form a vast prairie, washed on all sides by lakes and rivers. This unusual bit of Canadian geography lies between Lake Erie on the south, Lake Huron on the north, and Lake St. Clair and the Detroit River on the west. To the east is Hamilton and the shores of Lake Ontario. The sandy soil of Elgin and Norfolk counties (southeast) is Ontario's tobacco belt, and the clay soil of Essex and Kent counties (southwest) yields corn and sugar beets. In this area the Indians grew pumpkins, beans, and maize; contemporary gardeners have added a tremendous variety of fruits, vegetables, and flowers.

This is the southernmost portion of what were the lands of the Huron

Nation before their agricultural development led them to leave the more violent Iroquois Confederacy and turn to farming as a way of life. Their withdrawal from that alliance turned this area into a no-man's-land, crossed frequently by warring Indian nations. Only a tribe called the Neutral Indians, who supplied tools and weapons of flint to all combatants, were able to dwell in this embattled area.

Settlers began occupying the area shortly after the British took control in 1763, but not until the 1820s, when the Canada Company was formed to promote development of the Huron Tract, did the "land between the lakes" really begin to thrive. Windsor itself began as the first agriculturally based European settlement in Ontario, and today some of the country's most beautiful gardens thrive in its rich soils.

The route we outline below is designed to take a couple of days and to include the most interesting sites and cities on the peninsula. From Windsor, you travel through Amherstburg and around the point of the peninsula to the north shore of Lake Erie, lined with small fishing villages and farming communities, like Leamington and Port Stanley, before turning north.

Farther inland are the rural metropolitan towns of London and Stratford. Each of these cities grew as a farming center and still has the aura of a giant farmers' market, as if a bustling marketplace had been imposed on a quiet village. The effect is of a rural English town: acres of farmland punctuated by inns, taverns, and hostelries, all marked by their English origins.

WINDSOR: On a small peninsula surrounded by Lake Erie and Lake St. Clair, the sheer beauty of Windsor's position belies its place as the hub of Canada's automotive industry, one of the country's busiest points of entry from the US, and the southernmost city in all of Canada, across the Detroit River from the automotive capital of America. This busy city, with its shops, parks, and recreational areas, is actually *south* of Detroit, connected via the only international underwater tunnel as well as by conventional bridges.

Windsor's little corner of land has been crucial to the area's development and economy ever since European explorers first sailed up the St. Lawrence River and it became a major passage for fur traders penetrating deeper into the new continent. They could portage across the Niagara Peninsula and continue by water past Windsor and Amherstburg on the Detroit River. From such beginnings, Windsor developed into an industrial city closely interlocked with American industries in Detroit.

The city is filled with spacious, colorful parks like Dieppe Gardens, overlooking the river at Ouillette Avenue and Riverside Drive. Here, in 1749, French settlers began the first agriculturally based European community in Ontario. Nearby plaques also establish Windsor's involvement in the Mackenzie Rebellion (1838) and in the growth of the Great Western Railway, which connected Windsor with Niagara Falls in 1854.

Whether or not you're an avid gardener, you will thoroughly enjoy a stroll in Jackson Park Sunken Garden (Tecumseh Rd. and Rte. 3B). With its formal garden and sunken rectangular pool, the park is lovely at all times, but it is especially bewitching in the evenings, when it is transformed into its own world of light and color. Some 400 custom-designed lights have been installed among the flower beds and shrubs, highlighting the most exquisite blooms and delicately sculptured floral designs. Underwater lights turn fountains into rainbow machines; the focal point of the display is the unique sculpture *Coordination,* donated by Windsor artist Hans Hennecke. Residents come mainly for the shady picnic areas, to play tennis, or to visit the Memorial Rose Test

Gardens immediately adjacent, but the park is an absolute bonanza for ambitious photographers. The gardens are laid out in the shape of a compass and contain 12,000 rosebushes of 450 different varieties. This certainly explains why Windsor is called the City of Roses and attracts rose lovers from all over North America. A Lancaster bomber plane, in tribute to the 398 RCAF flyers who died during World War II, is in the center of the garden. No admission charge.

The *Art Gallery of Windsor* (445 Riverside Dr. W.; closed Mondays) only came to roost in this 3-story, $2.25-million structure converted from the old Carling Brewery and Warehouse in recent years. A permanent collection of Canadian paintings and sculpture tracing various styles and themes from the 18th century is on display as well as traveling exhibits and a children's gallery of pioneer toys and furniture. A notable collection of Inuit sculpture is also on exhibit. There is an outdoor sculpture court and a dramatic view of the Detroit River and skyline. No admission charge.

You can balance all this serene beauty with a trip to the Farm Fun Park, a rural theme park with rides, farm animals, an old-fashioned corn broom factory — and fresh seasonal fruits and vegetables, just what the kids need after all that road food (9009 Howard Ave., open daily, except Mondays, from May to mid-June; daily, from mid-June to *Labor Day;* weekends, *Labor Day* to October). Windsor goes wild from June 19 to July 5 with a series of weekend festivals leading up to and following *Canada Day* (July 1) and — because of its proximity to Detroit — *Independence Day.* Don't miss the *Highland Games,* sponsored by Windsor firefighters during the last weekend in June. And visit the *Oktoberfest,* held on 2 weekends in October (phone: 519-966-3815).

If you like "sight-sipping" tours, visit the Hiram Walker distillery, open May through September (phone: 519-254-5171, ext. 537); Colio Wines at nearby Harrow (phone: 519-738-2241) on Wednesdays at 1 PM and Saturdays, on the hour, noon to 4 PM; reservations necessary for 10 or more; and Pelee Island Winery at Kingsville (phone: 519-733-6551), open daily except Sundays, May through December; January through April, open Saturdays only.

Golfers have a choice of numerous public courses, including *Little River* (phone: 519-945-3912), *Roseland* (phone: 519-969-3810), *Fox Glen* (phone: 519-726-6076), *Dominion* (phone: 519-969-4350), *Belleview* (phone: 519-839-4372), and *Lakewood* (phone: 519-735-9171). The nearby countryside is fairly lined with places where horseback riding can be arranged. Less strenuous, but much more exciting, are the harness races at the *Windsor Raceway* — with completely enclosed and heated seating areas since they're mostly winter events (6 mi/10 km south on Rte. 18; late October to June, Tuesdays, Thursday through Sunday evenings, and Saturday afternoons; phone: 519-969-8311).

A magnet for US visitors in downtown Windsor is a 4-block area boasting 13 fur stores. Not only are furs less expensive than at home, but the stores pay the duty and Ontario refunds the 8% provincial tax.

Two of the city's most pleasant restaurants are *Casa Bianca,* offering Italian fare with elegance (345 Victoria; phone: 519-253-5218), and *Sir William's Steakhouse,* an English-style inn that also serves seafood (650 Ouellette Ave., phone: 519-254-5119). *Sir William's* has a lounge with live entertainment.

En Route from Windsor – Amherstburg is only 15 miles (24 km) south of Windsor via Route 18, through a section of Essex County deeply involved in the short war between British Canada and the US. A plaque about 5 miles (8 km) north of the town marks the site of the first major battle.

AMHERSTBURG: Fort Malden, erected here in 1797 by the British after they lost Detroit to the Americans, rapidly became a strategic point in the defense of Canada and was involved in both the War of 1812 and Mackenzie's Rebellion. It was here that General Isaac Brock met with Shawnee Chief Tecumseh to plan the capture of Detroit, which was accomplished by a joint expedition. However, their loss of control over Lake

Erie forced the British to abandon and burn the fortifications at both Detroit and Amherstburg. The fort was partially rebuilt following the war, then converted into a government asylum for mental patients in 1857. The property was used by a private company after the asylum was moved some 13 years later, and in 1939, Fort Malden, some of its original earthworks intact, was declared a national historic park. (Open year-round.)

Dalhousie is one of Amherstburg's best shopping streets, and the proliferation of stores couldn't be more charming. You'll find art, antiques, and unusual gifts at *Down River* (278 Dalhousie), lush greenery and wickerwork at *Plants and Things* (273 Dalhousie), books at *Past and Present* (269 Dalhousie), and *Preservation Hall* (271 Dalhousie) carries pine furniture reproductions and English china.

Also on Dalhousie is the *Park House Museum* (212 Dalhousie), a doubly interesting structure because of its pre-1800 construction and because it was moved here from Detroit in 1799. The house interior is done in 1850s style.

The *North American Black Historical Museum* (277 King St.) traces the black heritage from its origins in Africa through slavery to emancipation and settlement in Essex County. Open Wednesdays through Sundays.

Nearby Bob-Lo Island Amusement Park is a 240-acre island located in the Detroit River slightly south of Amherstburg and is served by three 250-passenger ferries. One of Canada's best amusement parks, it features an arts and crafts colony, a miniature golf course, a safari zoo trail, rides, a spacious dining room, and 6,000 picnic tables and benches. Open daily, late May to Labor Day. All rides and shows included in admission price (phone: 519-252-4444).

En Route from Amherstburg – Take Route 18A due south to Holiday Beach Provincial Park. Here you can camp overnight, enjoy the sandy beach, the picnic area, and stocked fish pond — or simply watch the boats go by. During the migration seasons, this is one of the best places in Ontario for viewing hawks and waterfowl.

Returning to Route 18, you will pass through the small agricultural town of Harrow, where a research station has been established that specializes in crop studies of tobacco, hybrid corn, white beans, peaches, and apricots. You'll see dozens of fruit and vegetable stands along the way.

Continue east until you reach Kingsville, 35 miles (56 km) southeast of Windsor and the home of the world-famous Jack Miner Bird Sanctuary.

KINGSVILLE: This is Canada's most southerly town, 35 miles (56 km) south of Detroit. Its dominant landmark, founded in 1904 by naturalist Jack Miner, OBE, is the Jack Miner Bird Sanctuary (phone: 519-733-4034), which continues under the guidance of his son, Jasper, and grandson, Kirk.

The sanctuary and its founder have become internationally recognized for one of the earliest and most successful efforts in conservation. When Jack Miner began banding birds with his name and address, hunters would return the bands to him, giving the location of their kill. Miner was then able to follow the birds' migratory flight patterns. Most of what is known about migration routes comes from the work of Jack Miner and his family.

The sanctuary is located on the great central flyway; this protected region of 300 acres is used by waterfowl, including an estimated 30,000 geese, during their seasonal migrations to and from breeding grounds in the Hudson Bay area. The most dramatic time to visit the sanctuary is late March and late October/early November, when you can also catch glimpses of a large variety of songbirds. Try to visit at feeding time, between 3:30 and 5 PM every day. It is open to the public all year from daylight to dusk, daily except Sundays. No admission charge.

For the best lunch served for miles around, try the *Rose and Thistle Tea Room.* Open 10 AM to 5 PM; closed Mondays (64 Main St. E.; phone: 519-733-5228).

Immediately south of Kingsville and west on Route 18A are two beautiful sandy beaches on Lake Erie. Linden Beach has about 2,640 feet of shoreline; Cedar Beach has about 413 feet. They are free and excellent for swimming and sunning; neither beach maintains a lifeguard.

En Route from Kingsville – Follow Route 18 east from the bird sanctuary for 3 miles (5 km) to the turnoff going north (about 5 minutes' driving time) to the tiny village of Ruthven on Route 3.

The Colasanti Cactus Garden and Farm at Ruthven is a major attraction for plant lovers. Acres of greenhouses feature one of the largest North American displays of tropical house plants. If you have a weakness for cacti, you'll be in your element here, and you may be compelled to make a purchase or two. The plants have been cleared for customs and may be taken to the US. Parrots and tropical birds are also on exhibit. The farm is famous for its oranges, lemons, bananas, and grapefruit. In the fall, they serve up apple cider and donuts. Open daily, all year except Christmas, New Year's, and Easter (phone: 519-326-3287; or in Detroit, 313-963-6654).

From Ruthven, continue east on Route 3 to Leamington, at the junction of Routes 18 and 77.

LEAMINGTON: Billed locally as the "tomato capital of Canada," this canning center almost floats in a sea of surrounding vegetable fields.

The keystone of Leamington's economy is the H. J. Heinz Company of Canada, which has been processing food for worldwide markets from its Leamington plants since 1914. Tours of the plant are available through the Tourist Information Center on Main Street. (You can't miss this booth maintained by the chamber of commerce: it's in the shape of a huge tomato, painted a vivid red.)

The *Thirteen Russell Street Steak House* (13 Russell St.; phone: 519-326-8401) is a charming restaurant, built at the turn of the century by Adolphus D. Broun. The *Dock Restaurant,* built on the edge of the wharf at the end of Erie St. S., offers a great view of the sea (phone: 519-326-2697).

POINT PELEE NATIONAL PARK: Located on the southernmost tip of contiguous Canadian land, the park is a 4,000-acre sandspit, supporting trees, grass, and some small animal life — and 14 miles of beaches. Though the park has no camping facilities, it is thoroughly crisscrossed with trails and boardwalks for viewing all year (some services are closed in winter).

PELEE ISLAND: Floating between Ontario and Ohio, Pelee is the largest Lake Erie island, with 10,000 acres of farmland. The island is a popular summer resort, with sandy beaches, cottage rentals, and the famous International Pheasant Hunt. Only a limited number of hunters — US and Canadian — are allowed a crack at the 18,000 pheasants released each fall (late October to early November; contact the township clerk for information, 519-724-2931). The island is accessible by boat from Leamington (for schedule and information, call *Pelee Island Ferry Services* (phone: 519-724-2115).

It's only about 85 miles (137 km) on Route 3 to St. Thomas, following Lake Erie's north shore.

WHEATLEY: The village of Wheatley claims to have the largest freshwater fish processing plant in the world, operated by Omstead Foods. You can photograph the picturesque harbor and chat with fishermen. There's also a mile of sandy beach, picnic grounds, a nine-hole golf course, and nearby Wheatley Provincial Park, with 270 wooded campsites.

En Route from Wheatley – There are several picturesque commercial ports along Route 3, but dominating any traveler's attention are the area's splendid fruit orchards and crops — corn, tomatoes, soybeans, and wheat — which represent a gross annual return of several million for the area. Roadside stands are numerous, and you could do worse than stop to savor some of the sun-ripened pears, peaches, plums, and apples.

DIRECTIONS / Ontario 515

For a pleasant break, drop in at *Monastery Crafts* (114 Chatham St., North Blenheim), where Art Pegg displays pottery, leather, and weaving.

ERIEAU: Another stop is the village of Erieau, a renowned center of commercial and recreational fishing with a fabulous 1,900-foot beach. (From Route 3 take County Road 12 southeast to Erieau.) Here, *Rondeau Charter Service* supplies houseboat rentals, fishing charters, and both day and moonlight cruises on Lake Erie. Tiny Erieau, fronting on both Lake Erie and Rondeau Bay, has swimming, boating, and excellent fishing for muskie, pike, coho salmon, bass, perch, and smelt during the runs in April.

RONDEAU PROVINCIAL PARK: Accessible from the junction of Routes 3 and 51, this park is another of Lake Erie's famous sandy spits and is Ontario's second oldest park (1894). It encloses sheltered, 9-mile Rondeau Bay. Located within an 80-mile radius of 5 million people, the park is a major preserve for birds, reptiles, whitetail deer, and Carolinean forest. There are sandy beaches, a swimming area, nature and hiking trails, picnic grounds, tennis courts, a riding stable, bicycling, miniature golf, a fishing dock, a store, and interpretive programs. During the fall, hunting of waterfowl is allowed, and winter activities include skating, icefishing, and iceboat racing.

En Route from Rondeau Park – From Rondeau, for a distance of about 30 miles (48 km), Route 3 continues to parallel the north shore of Lake Erie and leads to another park.

John E. Pearce Provincial Park has the appeal of secluded picnic sites, a woodland hiking trail, and a superb view over Lake Erie. Situated at the top of steep clay cliffs, there is no shoreline for swimming. But if you happen to be there during migration season, you can see (and photograph) a variety of hawks. For day use only.

Before you have traveled much farther along Route 3, you will notice the frequency of the name Talbot in Elgin County.

In 1791, Colonel Thomas Talbot became a member of Lieutenant-Governor John G. Simcoe's staff. The two men traveled throughout western Ontario, and Talbot was deeply impressed by the fertile land that lay between Lake Erie's north shore and the Thames River. He left Canada in 1794 to serve in the Napoleonic Wars, but the memory of the land stayed with him, and he returned in 1800. At the Colonial Office he insisted that the departed Simcoe had promised him 5,000 acres of this rich farmland. Finally, the office yielded to his persistence, and he received the land on the condition that he would divide it into 50-acre farms for settlement. Talbot drove a hard bargain, demanding an additional 200 acres for himself for every settler he located. Ultimately, he controlled 60,000 acres of Ontario's finest agricultural land and became known as the "pasha of the wilderness," in part because of his quarrelsome and difficult disposition. In all, he managed to organize 27 townships from Long Point to the Detroit River. Talbot's settlement project began May 21, 1803, in the Port Talbot area. Conveniently, he chose Iona Station as the site of a grandiose log cabin, which he called Malahide, after his ancestral castle in Dublin. It was here that the settlers applied for their land grants, and Talbot was far from gracious in fulfilling their needs — especially with the Scots, whom he despised for their frugality.

At Talbotville Royal, you can take Route 4 either north to London or south to St. Thomas and Port Stanley for a delightful diversion.

ST. THOMAS: Set in the gently rolling landscape of Elgin County's tobacco belt, St. Thomas is one of the prettiest cities in southwestern Ontario. It was the capital of the Talbot settlement and seems to have been named in honor of the cantankerous colonel, though one might be justified in reading a touch of irony into the naming.

The city is well known for its examples of fine architecture, which date back some 120 years. One of the most interesting of these early buildings is the Elgin County Courthouse, which took over a year to build. For this lovely old building, the pioneer taxpayers absorbed a construction charge of double the $20,000 estimate! Forty-four years later, on Dominion Day, 1898, a fire destroyed all but the ediface of the building. Within 12 months, the citizens of St. Thomas began rebuilding. They managed to incorporate the front of the old structure, with its Grecian columns, into the new building, and it now stands as a testimony to the perseverance and Victorian sensibilities of Ontario's pioneers.

Another example of early architecture is the St. Thomas Anglican Church. This white clapboard building, with its quaint covered entrance gate, was built in 1824 on a plot deeded by Captain Daniel Rapelje, founder of the city and a descendant of Huguenots from New England. The bell in the old steeple still summons the faithful to evensong.

Also of interest is the *Elgin County Pioneer Museum* (32 Talbot St.). This beautiful old home, built in 1848 and 1849, was the residence of a pioneer physician, Dr. Elijah Duncombe. The displays here relate to the early development of the community, with exhibits of numerous pioneer tools and crafts. A special section is devoted to Colonel Thomas Talbot, and the *Native Room* has a fascinating display of regional birds. The museum is open daily, except Mondays, February to December.

St. Thomas's 100-acre Pinafore Park at Elgin and Elm streets features a wildlife sanctuary, picnic area, tennis courts, baseball diamond, and, on weekends, a genuine steam locomotive that rides on a narrow-gauge railway. If you are in St. Thomas the first Sunday of the month, stop at the *St. Thomas Memorial Arena* to take in the antiques show.

PORT STANLEY: On the north shore of Lake Erie, no more than a 15-minute drive south on Route 4, is Port Stanley. This picturesque fishing village of 1,700 warrants at least a few photographs along the waterfront. The port is renowned as a boaters' haven, and you'll find pleasure craft of all sizes and types.

If you happen to be an enthusiastic angler and are out on the pier at an early hour, you could catch a tasty perch or two for breakfast as well as a prize-winning photograph of the fishing trawlers heading out onto Lake Erie for their daily commercial harvest.

Port Stanley holds a summer festival called *Calipso* (the name stands for Come and Live in Port Stanley, Ontario), in early August, featuring bonfires, an outdoor market, a boat parade, and dancing to a steel band. In late October, the apple harvest is celebrated during *Ciderfest,* with lots of hot apple cider and apple pies.

The town also boasts the only privately owned passenger train service in Canada. Run by volunteers, the 45-minute round trip links Port Stanley and Union. The service operates afternoons, Wednesdays through Sundays, from May to October.

Follow Route 24 along the north shore of Lake Erie to Port Bruce, where the road connects with Route 73. In another 15 minutes you'll reach the tobacco town of Aylmer.

AYLMER: Located in the heart of a thriving agricultural area, the heavily fertilized and irrigated fields of sandy soil are prime for the production of flue-cured tobacco. From early spring to mid-August, when the tobacco leaves are harvested, whole families work in the fields. At harvesttime, leaves must be picked, tied in bundles, and hung in the drying sheds. Regulated heat dries them at the proper temperature, which is the crucial step in the production of flue-cured tobacco. Aylmer also plays host to some 60,000 whistling swans who stop here on their yearly migration to the Artic during April and May.

Take Route 3 west back to its junction with Route 4 at St. Thomas, and follow Route 4 (joined by Rte. 2) until it becomes Wharncliffe Road, inside London.

LONDON: This city sits at the fork of the north and south branches of the Thames River. The river, originally called Aspensippi by the Indians, reminded Governor Simcoe of the English Thames, and, with his usual disregard for the established, he promptly changed its name. The Thames, capable of sudden floods, meanders through the heart of London, passing commercial enterprises and gracious old homes on quiet, tree-lined streets.

London is known as the "Forest City," the product of a far-sighted and extensive tree-planting program undertaken almost a century ago and continued today. The city still plants 1,000 trees in its civic squares, 1,500 acres of parkland, and along busy thoroughfares every year. As you stroll along these shady streets, you'll discover museums, art galleries, antiques shops, specialty stores, some excellent restaurants and hotels, and, of course, like its namesake, a surprising variety of parks.

Springbank Park, with 350 acres on the banks of the Thames, is a source of justifiable pride to London. There are broad expanses of lawn, colorful flower beds, a careful selection of trees, picnicking facilities, and Storybook Gardens, a theme park designed especially for children, with the Old Woman in a Shoe, Old McDonald's Farm, the Three Bears, a Climb to the Top of the Tree House, a thrilling slide down the slippery throat of Willie the Whale, and bells ringing in the Children's Peace Chapel. From the dock, you can take a summer cruise along the Thames River on the paddlewheeler *Storybook Queen* or a 20-minute ride on the *Tinkerbell* (open daily, May to September; boat schedules vary).

Reservoir Park, on the highest point of land in London, offers a beautiful vista of the Thames Valley and the downtown area. As natural woodland, the park represents one of the finest stands of native trees within the urban limits. Historically, it was the site of the city's original water reservoir (1878). At that time, residents were drinking spring water that was piped up the hill from Springbank Park and pumped by a water-driven wheel.

Fanshawe Park, operated by the Upper Thames Conservation Authority, was established to combat the traditional problem of flooding in the Thames's watershed. The dam and reservoir, built in 1953, remain the largest flood control structure in Ontario. The lake, although normally used at its low level for recreational activities, is capable of holding 38,880 acre-feet of water in emergencies. While functioning as flood control protection for downstream communities, the 4-mile lake and park area provide beaches, swimming, sailing, fishing, hiking, picnicking, campgrounds (May 1–September 30), an 18-hole golf course, and Fanshawe Pioneer Village. This museum complex authentically reproduces a typical crossroads Canadian community in the pre-railway era of the 19th century. Buildings include early log cabins, a barn, blacksmith's and weaver's shops, carriage makers, a general store, a Presbyterian church, and a replica of the original Free Press Building. Open daily late May to September; weekdays only September through December; off Clarke Road in London; phone: 519-451-2800.

Sifton Bog is a 15,000-year-old black spruce floating bog that contains rare specimens of orchids and certain medicinal plants; the round leaves of the sundew, for instance, can be dried and powdered for use as a cold medication. There are huge masses of bright green sphagnum moss, 60 feet deep in places, floating in the bog; the moss was used by Indian mothers as a disposable diaper, by medicine men as an antiseptic, by World War I medics as a field dressing. The center of the bog can be reached on a boardwalk, from which the bottom is visible through crystal-clear water. Carnivorous plants seem to do well around the edges of the area, and attentive bog-watchers may spot lemmings (on Oxford St., east of Sanitorium Rd.).

The *Royal Canadian Regiment Museum* has a spectacular collection of weapons, uniforms, and personal memorabilia from Canada's oldest regular infantry regiment. Closed Mondays and holidays (Wolseley Hall; phone: 519-679-5102).

The *London Regional Children's Museum* is the ultimate kids' playground — a place where they can climb down a manhole and see underground telephone cables, or study the stars, or rummage through a huge box of props and come up dressed as a Roman soldier or North American Indian. Open 10 AM to 5 PM Mondays through

Saturdays, 10 AM to 8 PM Fridays, 1 to 5 PM Sundays and holidays (21 Wharncliffe Rd. S.; phone: 519-434-5726).

The *Museum of Indian Archaeology and Pioneer Life,* on a bluff overlooking Snake Creek and the Medway River, shows life as it was for the Indians before the explorers and settlers arrived. Open daily (1600 Attawandaron Rd.; phone: 519-473-1360).

The *London Regional Art Galley* is an architectural gem in a superb natural setting. It features the works of leading national and international artists, plus a permanent collection of more than 2,000 historical and current works. Open from noon daily, from 10 AM on Saturdays (421 Ridout St.; phone: 519-672-4580).

The *Guy Lombardo Museum* traces the story of Mr. New Year's Eve and his Royal Canadians. Born in London, Guy, along with his brothers and sisters, formed a band that played for presidents at the White House and became synonymous with "Auld Lang Syne" and ringing in the New Year. Open May through September, 10 AM to 8 PM (205 Wonderland Rd. S.; phone: 519-473-9003).

London's pride and joy is its *Grand Theatre.* Restored to its turn-of-the-century glory in 1977 at a cost of $5 million, its professional productions range from serious drama to comedy and musical theater (471 Richmond Street; phone: 519-672-8800).

Those who enjoy a nice walk should avail themselves of the four walking tours prepared by the historians of London's public library. Check with the Visitors Bureau at City Hall, on the corner of Wellington Street and Dufferin Avenue, or the library, at 305 Queens Avenue. Less active people can catch the double-decker English bus from City Hall, which runs 7 days a week (phone: 519-672-1970).

Shopping in London is bountiful; the city is reputed to have a larger shopping area per capita than any other Canadian metropolis. Stop into the *Antiquarian* (corner of Richmond and Horton), famous for its antiques and wide variety of figurines unavailable elsewhere. The *Wicked Wick Candle Shop* (478 Richmond St. near Queens Ave.) claims to stock the largest array of handcrafted candles in North America. For something special for the kids, try the *Toy Chest* (255 Dundas St., near Wellington St.); then go over to the *Covent Garden Market,* just off Market Lane in the center of London, for some fresh fruit, a block of cheese, perhaps some still-warm, crusty bread, and homemade cookies to round it off. If you plan to relax after dinner one evening, pick up something interesting at *The Country Mouse,* London's favorite bookstore (621 Richmond St.).

This same part of downtown London teems with good restaurants of all kinds. There are family- and country-style cooking at *Mr. Abernathy's* (299 King St.) and traditional Canadian meals in the *Friar's Cellar II,* formerly the *Friar's Cellar* (267 Bathurst St. at Wellington), noted for its good service and quiet atmosphere. The buffet at *The Garage* (73 King St.) can be a real lifesaver, soothing strained appetites after a long day of shopping.

In the Longwoods Road Conservation Area, is Ska-Nah-Doht Indian Village (Oneida for "a village stands again"). Here, reconstructed with longhouses of cedar and elm bark, a village is perched on a sandy bluff overlooking the forks of a stream. The Attawandaron tribe occupied this area 400 years ago. An agricultural band, they were as rooted to this place as their carefully tended fields and refused to become involved in the Iroquois-Huron conflict. They became known as the Neutrals, and, like neutrals in so many wars, they traded their skillfully made flint tools and weapons to combatants throughout the area. Ska-Nah-Doht strives to recreate faithfully the activities of the entire village. Crops of corn and squash are planted and harvested on plots cleared by felling trees and burning out the stumps. A stockade encircles the central village, complete with a sweat lodge (similar to a sauna), council chamber, fish-drying racks, and the special dwelling belonging to the shaman, the tribe's spiritual leader. Open daily, late May to Labor Day; other times by appointment. The park area is open year-round and located 12 miles (19 km) west of London, off Route 2.

Depending on where you're staying in London, take either Route 4 (from the west side of town) north to its junction with Route 7 at Elgenfield and follow Route 7 into Stratford, or Route 90 or Route 2 east from downtown London as far as Ingersoll, where Route 19 leads north into the Stratford area. Routes 7 and 19 intersect outside of Stratford and enter the festival city as one road.

STRATFORD: Scottish novelist John Galt, dispatched to Canada in 1820 to deal with claims arising after the War of 1812, cast his eye on the undeveloped lands held as "clergy reserves" in then Upper Canada and saw a wealth of possibilities. He recommended that the Canada Company be set up to buy these churchlands and resell them to British settlers. The Anglican clergy fought this plan in court and achieved only one small victory: The terms of Canada Company's charter provided that one-third of the profits be earmarked for the building of roads, bridges, and schools to further the area's growth. The company acquired 1 million acres of Huronia's prized farmland at the rate of 3 shillings an acre and sold the kingdom of the Huron Nation for double the price.

Galt hired a fellow Scot, Dr. William ("Tiger") Dunlop, to survey the land, by then called the Queen's Bush or the Huron Tract, and plan the roads. Dunlop, a fiery redhead with a distinct liking for a "wee drap," rapidly became as enchanted with the area as Galt had been, and he took a millsite on a small tributary of the Thames as payment for laying a trail from Guelph to Goderich — now parts of Routes 7 and 8. The area around Dunlop's mill site soon became known as Little Thames. Around 1830, William Sargint, proprietor of the local inn, hung a sign bearing the likeness of William Shakespeare over his doorway, and, in the English custom, it soon became the Shakespeare Inn. That sign caused the community, which included a post office by 1835, to change its name to Stratford. The small river, dammed to power Dunlop's grist mill, was named the Avon.

It wasn't until the early 1900s that a Stratford citizen, R. Thomas Orr, convinced the town's council to replace the old wooden dam and clean out the marsh created by the brackish water it retained, turning the area into a 175-acre park and the clear waters of Lake Victoria. The new dam is named for this civic-minded individual.

Shortly after World War II, journalist Tom Patterson of Stratford initiated his plan to establish a counterpart of Britain's Stratford-on-Avon in Ontario. With the help of Sir Tyrone Guthrie, the first Stratford *Shakespearean Festival* opened in July 1953. The temporary tent enclosing the permanent stage was 98% filled the first season, and the festival's popularity has increased steadily. In 1957, John Fairfield designed a permanent theater along the lines of the familiar tent; it won him the Massey Gold Medal for Architecture.

From the beginning, the festival has followed a policy of casting regional talent as well as international stars in its productions. The festival stages numerous plays each season (June to October), not exclusively Shakespeare's, taxing the actors' talents as they perform in two or three revolving programs while learning two more roles for later in the summer. The 1963 addition of the *Avon Theatre,* a converted movie house, allowed the festival to expand its schedule. It also sponsors Shakespeare seminars, discussions, lectures, and an experimental theater workshop; contact the Stratford Festival, Box 520, Stratford, Ontario N5A 6V2 (phone: 519-273-1600) for details on these activities and play schedules. Although the festival sells out regularly, "rush reserved seats" are sold at 9 AM the day of each performance.

Queens Park, within sight of the *Festival Theatre,* is a tranquil place to pass a few hours between picking up your tickets and showtime. Picnic with the ducks by the shore or take a canoe or paddleboat for a brief outing. West of the theater is a footbridge leading over some train tracks to Confederation Park, where an attractive brick building houses *The Gallery,* a continually changing series of art and sculpture exhibits (54 Romeo St. N.; open daily in summer, closed Mondays from September to May).

Staging and establishing a sense of time and place in Stratford are not limited to the theaters. *The Church* (70 Brunswick St.; phone: 519-273-3424) is a century-old church converted into a restaurant serving French food; allusions to the church's past are sensed in the staff's religious dedication to Old World serving traditions. Overlooking the dining area is a new lounge bar called, naturally enough, the *Belfry*. The *Old Prune* (151 Albert St.; phone: 519-271-5052) is a fairly small restaurant in a beautifully renovated home serving the best and freshest of this farmland's produce in a variety of light, tasty, and well-prepared dishes including fresh fish, quiches, and soups. Dinners are on a fixed-price basis. In addition to the fine service in its dining area, *Rundles* restaurant (9 Cobourg St.; phone: 519-271-6442) will also prepare box lunches during the festival, ranging from the most basic fare to dinners of fresh salmon with watercress *mousseline*, fresh bread, cheese, and pâté. Bring your own *Rubaiyat* and turn a picnic on the Thames into an occasion.

From here, it's a 95-mile (153-km) drive to Toronto.

BEST EN ROUTE

If you're traveling during the summer, make reservations as early as possible; good places are booked far in advance. Fortunately, there is no shortage of good motels and campgrounds in this area, and you can expect all creature comforts to be available — this isn't the North Woods. The moderate price range ($42 to $60 per night, double occupancy) covers the vast majority of establishments, even most of the better inns; many places that offer excellent accommodations are inexpensive (under $42 per night for two people). In the expensive range (over $60 per night for two) you can expect the best in the house. All prices are quoted in US dollars.

WINDSOR

Holiday Inn – A 251-room motel overlooking the Detroit River that offers standard accommodations and many facilities, including a heated outdoor pool, air conditioned rooms, color TV sets, radios, phones, wheelchair access, and golf nearby. There's a dining room and a coffee shop that serves a good Sunday morning buffet. 480 Riverside Dr. W., just east of the Ambassador Bridge (phone: 519-253-4411). Expensive.

Red Oak Inn – This downtown property has 150 pleasant air conditioned rooms, color TV sets, radios, and phones. There's also a dining room, a heated indoor pool, and a sauna. 430 Ouellette Ave. (phone: 519-253-7281). Expensive.

Cadillac Motel – The 47 rooms (including bridal suites) here have water beds. There's also a heated pool, whirlpool bath, and babysitting service available. 2498 Dougall Ave. (phone: 519-969-9340). Moderate.

National Traveller – Near the entrance to the Windsor-Detroit tunnel, you'll find 110 pleasant, well-equipped rooms, dining room, and entertainment lounge. Popular with business people. 675 Goyeau (phone: 519-258-8411). Moderate.

Relax Plaza – A pancake house and indoor pool make this 150-room hotel an appealing place for families. 33 Riverside Dr. E. (phone: 519-258-7774). Moderate.

Ivy Rose – Reasonable prices make this 69-room motel a good place for families. The setting is landscaped and quiet; the rooms, spacious and pleasant. Facilities include water beds, air conditioning, color TV sets, radios, phones, a heated outdoor pool, playground, and a dining room. 2885 Howard Ave., opposite the Devonshire Shopping Mall (phone: 519-966-1700). Moderate to inexpensive.

Windsor South KOA – This 25-acre site has 145 campsites (89 with electrical and water hook-ups), a dumping station, flush toilets, showers, fireplaces, a shelter, a store, ice, and a pool. Laundry, restaurant, and golf course are all within a mile of the campground. Reservations are accepted. Seven miles (11 km) south on Howard Ave., west off Rte. 401 (phone: 519-726-5200). Inexpensive.

AMHERSTBURG

Duffy's – This attractive 2-story motel overlooking the Detroit River has 17 air conditioned rooms and TV sets. There's a heated swimming pool, complete marina facilities, and good dining in the *Marine Room*. 296 Dalhousie St. (phone: 519-736-2101). Moderate.

Blue Haven – Facing the Detroit River, this motel has 16 air conditioned units with balconies and 425 feet of beach on a protected bay where guests can swim and fish. Babysitting service is available. 680 Front Rd. S. on Hwy. 18 (phone: 519-736-5404). Inexpensive.

Holiday Beach Provincial Park – On the shores of Lake Erie, this campground has a lovely 2,000-foot sandy beach, 46 campsites, a dump tank, flush toilets, fireplaces, a store, a shelter, and a boat launching ramp; no hook-ups. There's a restaurant nearby. Motorbikes are not allowed. Nine miles (14 km) south of Amherstburg off Rte. 18 (phone: 519-736-3772). Inexpensive.

KINGSVILLE

Adams Golden Acres – The 27 rooms and efficiency units are laid out on grounds set back from the road. All are air conditioned and have TV sets and radios. There's also a playground and a golf course nearby. One mile (1.5 km) west on Rte. 18 (phone: 519-733-4496). Inexpensive.

Lakeshore Terrace – Set on the shores of Lake Erie, this hotel has 40 rooms with air conditioning and TV sets. There's a golf course nearby. 85 Park St. E. (phone: 519-733-4651). Inexpensive.

Pleasant Valley Trailer Park – This campground on Lake Erie has 125 sites with electrical and water hook-ups, fireplaces, a dump station, flush toilets, showers, a shelter, and a swimming pool. Within a mile there's a laundromat, restaurants, riding, hiking trails, and golf. One mile (1.5 km) west on Rte. 18 (phone: 519-733-5961). Inexpensive.

LEAMINGTON

Sun Parlor – A quiet motel that has 17 units, 6 with kitchens, and all with air conditioning, TV sets, and phones. Water beds are a new feature. 135 Talbot St. W. (phone: 519-326-2214). Inexpensive.

Pelee – Amenities at this 60-room motel include a sauna, whirlpool bath, indoor pool, coffee shop, dining room, beach, and nearby golf course. Just a few minutes' drive south of town on Rte. 33 (phone: 519-326-8646). Moderate

Wigle's – Set on spacious, landscaped grounds, this attractive motel has 24 air conditioned units, color TV sets, phones, and a playground. There's a coffee shop and dining room. 135 Talbot St. E. (phone: 519-326-3265). Inexpensive.

PELEE ISLAND

Brown's Beach – These secluded modern cottages are on a sandy beach on the east side of the island. Boat rentals are available. For information and reservations: 12500 Edgewater Dr., Cleveland, Ohio 44107 (phone: 216-228-7582). On East Side Rd. (phone: 519-724-2094). Moderate.

Pelee Island – Right on the lakefront, this 2-story hotel has its own beach for swimming and fishing, a pleasant dining room and lounge, and a dock a few steps down the beach. The dining room serves breakfast specials, a buffet lunch, and full-course dinners. The family rooms have TV sets and showers. Closed during the winter. At the West Dock (phone: 519-724-2912). Moderate to inexpensive.

Westview – Next door to the *Pelee Island* hotel, this small motel has 5 comfortable rooms with TV sets and 1 cottage with 3 bedrooms, a living room, dinette, kitchen, and bath. Open year-round. West Dock on the west side of the island (phone: 519-724-2072). Moderate to inexpensive.

Anchor and Wheel – This inn has 6 rooms, 5 motel units, and a campground with showers, plus boating, swimming, fishing, and golf. Closed winters. Special rates for large groups. On the northwest end of the island (phone: 519-724-2195). Inexpensive.

BLENHEIM

Rondeau Provincial Park – There are 226 campsites here, but only 12 have electrical hook-ups. Other facilities include flush toilets, fireplaces, a store, shelter, sanitary dump, launching ramp, and a natural beach. There are restaurants, boat rentals, a marina, hiking trails, and riding nearby. Four miles (6.4 km) south on Rte. 51 (phone: 519-674-5405). Inexpensive.

Queen's – Though small (17 rooms), this motel has been receiving high ratings. All units have air conditioning and TV sets; a restaurant, playground, and golf course are nearby. On Hwy. 3, a mile west of Blenheim (phone: 519-676-5477). Inexpensive.

ST. THOMAS

Dalewood Conservation Area – This 130-acre conservation area has 100 sites, 40 with electrical, water, and sewer connections; flush toilets, showers, fireplaces, shelter, laundry, launching ramp, swimming, fishing, picnicking, and walking trails. Three miles (5 km) north on Dalewood Rd. (phone: 519-631-1270). Inexpensive.

Sleepy Time – A good choice for budget-minded families. All 11 rooms have air conditioning, TV sets, and free in-room movies. Miniature golf on the grounds. Babysitting service. Exit Hwy. 401 at 177A, then 5 miles (8 km) on Hwy. 4 (phone: 519-633-0471). Inexpensive.

PORT STANLEY

Kettle Creek Inn – Here is an award-winning dining room in a 10-room inn, established in 1849. Maine St. (phone: 519-782-3388). Moderate.

Invary Heights Trailer Park – On this hilltop overlooking Lake Erie are 79 campsites, 42 with electricity and water hook-ups; a dumping station, flush toilets, showers, fireplaces, and a beach. Nearby there's a laundry, restaurants, boat rentals, a marina, and riding. Off Rte. 4 (phone: 519-782-3441). Inexpensive.

AYLMER

Aylmer – These 17 rooms have air conditioning and TV sets. There's also a coffee shop, an adjacent restaurant, and a municipal park and swimming pool 1 block away. 300 Talbot St. W. (phone: 519-773-3262). Inexpensive.

Red Oak Trailer Park – A 30-acre campground with 100 campsites, most of which are equipped with water hook-ups and electrical connections and 23 with sewer hook-ups. Other facilities include flush toilets, showers, fireplaces, a store, ice, a shelter, and a pool. There's a laundromat, restaurant, and hiking trails within a mile. Nine miles (14½ km) east on Rte. 3 (phone: 519-866-3504). Inexpensive.

LONDON

Motor Court Motel – Facilities here include water beds, air beds, and family and honeymoon suites. 1883 Dundas St. E., near the airport (phone: 519-451-2610). Expensive to moderate.

Golden Pheasant – All 41 rooms come with extra-long beds, air conditioning, TV sets, phones, and radios. Other amenities include facilities for the handicapped, a heated outdoor swimming pool, playground, restaurant, and coffee shop. Rte. 22, 1 mile (1.6 km) west of Rte. 4 (phone: 519-473-4551). Moderate.

Hyland – Set on spacious landscaped grounds, this motel has 33 air conditioned rooms, satellite TV, phones, and baths. There's also a heated pool and a playground; a restaurant is adjacent. 750 Wharncliffe Rd. S (phone: 519-681-5901). Moderate.

Fanshawe Park Conservation Area – This 1,500-acre park has lovely wooded areas and a large manmade lake. There are more than 660 campsites, 400 with electrical hook-ups and 475 with water. There are also flush toilets, showers, ice, fireplaces, a store, a shelter, launching ramps, and a beach. Nearby are boat rentals and hiking; pets are allowed. 691 Ontario St. (phone: 519-451-2800). Inexpensive.

Happy Hills – On 175 acres there are 320 sites, 200 with electrical and water hook-ups; a dumping station, flush toilets, showers, ice, fireplaces, a shelter, and a pool. Motorbikes are not allowed. From Rte. 7 take Embro Rd. 11 miles (18 km) southwest (phone: 519-475-4471). Inexpensive.

The Heritage Highways

The Heritage Highways are a network of roadways originating at the popular border-crossing of Niagara Falls, skirting Lake Ontario, and extending along the banks of the St. Lawrence River to the tip of the Gaspé Peninsula in Quebec. These highways follow the trails and byways developed from the Indian paths used by early explorers and settlers.

There are 377 miles (607 km) of these historical highways in Ontario, both high-speed express routes and meandering roadways. From Niagara Falls, the route takes you quickly back to Ontario's past, into the 1800s village of Niagara-on-the-Lake, home of the *George Bernard Shaw Festival*. It then traverses the extensive wine- and fruit-producing district spanning the Niagara peninsula.

The metropolitan areas of Hamilton, with its impressive Burlington Skyway Bridge, and Toronto are on the route as it rounds the western end of Lake Ontario and proceeds along the north shore toward Quebec. The outlying areas of Toronto are filled with beautiful old homes and estates that once belonged to early settlers and later to rich industrialists.

Whatever your interest — historic homes, battlefields of the War of 1812 and the French and Indian Wars, stone fortresses, sand castles — it is here on the shores of Lake Ontario.

The Isle of Quinte, in the eastern part of the Great Lake, has four beachparks: Sandbanks Park is a gigantic 894-acre sandbar. From here it's only a short hop to Kingston, guarding the passage between Lake Ontario and the St. Lawrence River as it has since Count Frontenac first established his trading post here in 1673. Fort Henry, erected to protect the sanctity of Canada's borders against thieves during the War of 1812, has been restored; it overlooks one of the world's most impressive shipping routes. At the narrows of the river, just past its juncture with Lake Ontario, lie the beautiful Thousand Islands, where the Indians came to "the place of good health" for peaceful relaxation. And beyond is the oft-challenged war zone of Canada's southern border: Across this river the Americans attempted time and again to strike out at their British adversaries through colonial Canada.

All of this transpired in the footsteps of the pioneers who first opened this countryside to settlement in their search for furs and precious metals. By traveling in their paths, the development and history of this country will come alive.

Population growth and herd depletion have limited hunting in the coastal areas to deer and small game, but game is more prevalent in the North. The fishing, on the other hand, couldn't be better: northern pike, muskie, walleye, smallmouth and largemouth bass, brown bullhead (catfish), and rainbow, lake, and brown trout all fill the lakes and rivers throughout southeastern Ontario. Small wonder that this varied countryside is immensely popular with residents and visitors alike.

NIAGARA FALLS: Canada's most famous border city, big and bawdy Niagara Falls, generally makes things seem larger than life. Even though its commercialism is more seedy and annoying than that of other areas in Canada, most residents of the American side will grudgingly but honestly admit that the Canadian side is more pleasant (meaning less commercial). The falls are formed as the waters of Lake Erie race downhill to join Lake Ontario, becoming the Niagara River en route. The river gathers strength and power in the narrows, then plunges almost 200 feet over the limestone cliffs at the rate of 34 million gallons a minute, creating the world-famous falls. A small island on the river splits the whitewater juggernaut at the point of its mighty dive, dividing it into two falls: the straight-crested American Falls — 182 feet high and 1,076 feet wide; and the Horseshoe (Canadian) Falls — 176 feet high and 2,100 feet wide. A smaller falls, Bridal Veil, lies on the American side.

The little island responsible for parting these rushing waters is New York's Goat Island, named for its former residents. Its 70 acres are a prime viewing location, making it a popular attraction. In addition to scenic walks almost to the brink of the falls, the island features a heliport for sightseeing "copter rides" and an elevator to the base of the falls. From here the fearless may don the heavy-weather gear provided by tour leaders and walk along a path just behind the wall of water — as drenching as it is deafening. The Indians originally christened the falls Onigara, "thunder of waters," and sacrificed at least one beautiful maiden over the falls. This gave rise to the legend of a "maid in the mist," whose image is sometimes visible in the spray.

It is ironic that the single most devastating threat to the future of the falls comes not from the abuses of man but from a weakness in nature. The shale and limestone foundations of the riverbed are slowly being washed away by the sheer force of the plunging water. As this erosion continues, the falls will be forced backward until they flatten out entirely, becoming just a series of rapids in the river.

If you can dream up an off-beat angle from which you'd like to view the falls, chances are someone has already thought of it and has turned it into a prosperous business. The *Horseshoe Falls Incline Railway* provides transportation up and down the escarpment in twin cable rail cars. Would you like an aerial view? Take your choice: *Niagara Spanish Aerocars* (cable cars that make a dizzying 1800-foot trip over the Whirlpool

Rapids), helicopter rides, or any of several observation towers. The two best viewing towers are on the Canadian side on a 250-foot bank across from the falls. The taller one is the 524-foot Skylon Tower (viewing height about 770 feet above the base of the falls), complete with a revolving dining room, a lounge, and an indoor/outdoor observation deck all housed on three levels atop its structural base. A variety of shops and an amusement area are located below. The shorter one, the 416-foot Minolta Tower (viewing height of about 665 feet), features the *Top of the Rainbow* restaurant.

At ground level there are any number of ways to approach the falls. People Movers are miniature trams that run a 30-minute course between Prospect Point and Goat Island, allowing passengers to get on and off at any of several stops. Of the various boat trips, the *Maid of the Mist* is the most famous. (Actually, there are four sightseeing boats named *Maid of the Mist,* so you won't have too long to wait.) Wearing hooded raincoats (supplied), you can enter the Table Rock Scenic Tunnels to view points behind the falls. There's also a viewing station halfway down the cliff; expect to feel the spray in your face. Open daily, year-round. Queen Victoria Park. Admission charge.

And don't forget night viewing. The Horseshoe Falls is lighted by 4 billion candlepower in rainbow colors every night.

Rainbow Bridge crosses the river just below the falls and makes an excellent vantage point. From the foot of the bridge, parallel to the falls area, a mile-long stretch of parking lots and flower gardens extends past the American Falls to the viewing towers near Horseshoe Falls.

The commercial area in the immediate vicinity of the falls tends to get congested at times. In the first few blocks occupying the hillside opposite the falls, beginning near the foot of the bridge and extending a block or two on either side of the main road, are the *Niagara Falls Museum* (5651 River Rd.), including the Daredevil Hall of Fame, honoring the greats who challenged the falls in barrels and on rafts (some made it, others perished). There's also a collection of Egyptian mummies; *Ripley's Believe It or Not Museum* (4960 Clifton Hill); *Louis Tussaud's Waxworks Museum* (4915 Clifton Hill), with life-size statues of kings, presidents, and other notables and nasties; and the *Houdini Museum* (4983 Clifton Hill). Marineland offers popular daily shows featuring whales, dolphins, and sea lions. The admission price also includes access to an adjacent game farm and midway (boasting the world's largest roller coaster). 7657 Portage Rd. Open daily, except Fridays mid-December to mid-March, year-round.

Gift stores in the area get plenty of business, although prices are sometimes out of line. Either wait until you've had time to check prices at other shops or postpone your shopping for one of the smaller towns along the route: those little pillows, key rings, medallions, and other prized items with NIAGARA FALLS emblazoned on them are available for miles around. Use care in selecting choice import items like English china, Scottish plaids, Irish woolens, and Inuit soapstone carvings (native Canadian, but foreign to this area).

A new attraction is the *Niagara River Boat Company*'s cruises aboard the *Senator,* an elegant Edwardian-style cruise ship with brass railings, plush carpeting, and rich mahogany trim. The ship offers moonlit dances, champagne brunches, and pre-theater dinners, as well as daily sightseeing trips. Sails May through October from the Olde Boatworks (phone: 416-468-4219 or 416-468-5154).

En Route from Niagara Falls – The Niagara Parkway parallels the river northward toward Lake Ontario, running through a delightful system of parks and historic sites on its 18-mile (29-km) route to Niagara-on-the-Lake.

Plan on spending at least a half-hour at the Niagara Parks Commission's School of Horticulture, among the acres of magnificent flowers and gardens. Beyond the school at Sir Adam Beck Generating Station is the Floral Clock, a working timepiece some 40 feet across comprised of thousands of brilliantly colored plants that bloom from early spring to the first frost.

Queenston Heights Park at Queenston, just a few miles north of Niagara Falls, marks the slopes where the British eventually defeated American troops attempting to overtake Queenston in October of 1812. British General Sir Isaac Brock, one of Upper Canada's most prominent war heroes, died here while leading the first counterattack against American soldiers.

Nearby, in Queenston Village, is the Laura Secord Homestead, a restored 1800s dwelling. Laura Secord became a heroine during the War of 1812 by walking 19 miles to reveal the plans of an American attack to a British officer. Although the officer knew of the attack already from other sources, her courage in defying the soldiers who had occupied her home was rewarded in later years by the Prince of Wales (later Edward VII). Open daily, mid-May to mid-October.

NIAGARA-ON-THE-LAKE: This historic village (1781), on the west bank of the Niagara River at its mouth on Lake Ontario, was one of the earlier settlements in southern Ontario. Originally called Butlersburg, its name was changed to Newark in 1792 when it became the first capital of Upper Canada (as Ontario was then called). During this period, Fort George, the principal British outpost on the Niagara frontier, was erected nearby. The town was occupied by American soldiers during the War of 1812, and both the town and Fort George were destroyed in 1813 when the troops abandoned the area.

The town was rebuilt and is an excellent example of 19th-century architecture. Stately homes with wide doorways adorned with decorative transoms and sidelights line avenues shaded by ancient trees. The revived community, the point of entry to Canada for many Mennonite and Amish settlers, was dubbed Niagara-on-the-Lake in 1906. Today the main street, Queen Street, houses several crafts shops selling quilts, handcrafted furniture, and other period items. *McClellands* store has been serving the community since 1835, and *Greaves Jam* (staffed by its fourth generation of cooks) still produces jam in the small kitchen behind the store. The *Old Apothecary Shop* no longer dispenses the medicaments on its shelves but merely displays them as a living museum. The bank, which does function, is staffed by women wearing long gingham gowns.

Fort George, on the outskirts of town, was rebuilt in 1815, and it was reconstructed as a tourist attraction in the 1930s after a period of disuse. Now it is manned by colorfully dressed troops who regularly display their expertise. The fort is open all year, from 9 AM to 6 PM in summer, shorter hours in early spring and late fall, and tours only by appointment during the winter (phone: 416-468-3938).

The town's biggest attraction, which draws theater-lovers from all over and presents top-name talent in several productions, is the annual *George Bernard Shaw Festival* held at the *Festival Theatre* late April through October; group packages for 20 or more are available (phone: 416-468-2172). The acclaimed mime group *Theatre Beyond Words* performs at the *Royal George Theatre* on Queen Street in December and January (phone: 416-468-3964).

The *Prince of Wales* hotel is a restored 1864 structure with period furnishings in its dining area and guest rooms (6 Picton St.; phone: 416-468-3246), and the *Oban Inn* (for more information on both hotels, see *Best En Route*), considered by residents a guide by which other restaurants are measured, lives up to its reputation for style and taste in both appearance and food (160 Front St.; phone: 416-468-2165).

En Route from Niagara-on-the-Lake – The Queen Elizabeth Way, a high-speed auto route, is easily accessible via the Stone Road (Rte. 55) about 7 miles (11 km) southwest of town. The QEW leads into St. Catharines and then follows the shore of Lake Ontario toward Hamilton.

The Scenic Blossom Route (Rte. 87) follows the lakeshore west from Niagara-on-the-Lake through a broad fruit-growing area where roadside stands sell the season's crop at favorable prices. Small towns, many of them founded by German settlers, appear almost as frequently as the fruit stands. The area is well known among antiques collectors searching for unusual pieces. Canal Road leads right into St. Catharines, about 16 miles (26 km) from Niagara-on-the-Lake.

ST. CATHARINES: Located among the vines and orchards of Ontario's prime fruit- and wine-producing district, St. Catharines has been nicknamed the Garden City. A visit to the Farmer's Market (outdoors near the city hall and federal buildings; Tuesdays, Thursdays, and Saturdays) demonstrates how well the town and region have earned their name and claim to unusually abundant harvests. Settled by English Loyalists before the American Civil War, the city was an important terminal of the Underground Railroad. Today it is a major stop for travelers to the many festivals in the area.

The *Niagara Grape and Wine Festival,* in late September, celebrates the ripening of the grapes in true bacchanalian style, with 10 days of eating, drinking, parades, and contests of strength and skill. The Bright's–St. Michelle Winery gives tours of the plant and product tastings Mondays through Saturdays, 10 AM, 1 PM, and 3 PM; reservations required for groups of 15 or more. (120 Ridley Rd.; phone: 416-641-8770).

Second only in size to the famous regatta in England, the Royal Canadian Henley Regatta in August attracts champion rowers from all over the world. It celebrated its 100th anniversary in 1982. Local newspapers provide details on the best vantage points for spectators.

The Welland Canal facilitates passage to and from inland ports of ships unable to negotiate the Niagara River (and Falls). Originally built between 1824 and 1829, the canal cuts across the peninsula from Port Weller on Lake Ontario to Port Colburne on Lake Erie. A series of locks compensate for the 326-foot variation in water level between the two lakes. The present canal was opened in 1933. An observation platform, near Lock 3, provides a close look at the lock as seagoing freighters rise and fall with the water level (take the Glendale Ave. exit from the QEW eastbound or Niagara St. exit westbound and follow signs).

A pleasant and reasonably priced family eatery (*Peter D's*) is on Louth Street, near Bright's winery, and a wide variety of restaurants are on Ontario Street: *The Parkway* and *Berto's* are good bets.

En Route from St. Catharines – Use Canal Road to get back onto Route 87, the Scenic Blossom Route, and continue west along Lake Ontario, bypassing several boat launching areas and beaches. To go swimming, try one of the smaller lakes on the north shore; Lake Ontario has a well-earned reputation for being cold. Near Henley Island, Route 87 becomes Route 34 and turns south to intersect Route 81/8. Follow Route 81/8 for a side trip to Jordan, a few miles inland.

JORDAN: Before the construction of the canal, Jordan was an important shipping center, providing access to Lake Ontario through Twenty Mile Creek. The area's economy is now based on its prominence as a wine-producing center. A group of early structures is part of the *Jordan Historical Museum of the Twenty,* named after the creek responsible for the settlement's growth. The Vintage House (c. 1840) and the Jacob Fry House (c. 1815) display many items used by the early Mennonite settlers, including a wedding dress, and several of the patterns and equipment used by Samuel Fry, a weaver. There are other period pieces like Franktur paintings and a primitive wine press.

The Balls Falls Conservation Area, just off Route 8, features two medium-sized waterfalls, the larger about 90 feet high, and an 1809 grist mill. The Bruce Trail, one of the original routes through the peninsula, cuts across the Balls Falls area on its 430-mile (692-km) stretch from Niagara Falls to Lake Huron.

En Route from Jordan – Return to Route 818 and continue along the lakeshore toward Hamilton.

The highlight of Vineland, a tiny vacation community, is Tivoli-on-the-Lake, a miniature village featuring replicas of world-famous landmarks (St. Peter's Basilica, the Eiffel Tower, the Tower of Pisa, and the Kremlin) in perfect 1:50 scale. Besides being an excellent way to visit these diverse places at once, think of the fun you can have with your photos.

The town of Grimsby is situated in farmland about 10 miles (16 km) farther, a total of 17 miles (27 km) from Jordan. There are several historical buildings, including an 1800s blacksmith shop, which houses the *Stone Shop Museum* (271 Main St. W.). An early railroad station (99 Ontario St.), now a restaurant called *The Village Depot,* makes a delicious lunch stop.

From here, take the high-speed Queen Elizabeth Way on to Hamilton, about 10 miles (16 km) west.

HAMILTON: History credits United Empire Loyalists with selecting this site in 1778, but not until businessman George Hamilton laid out a pattern of lots and roadways in 1813 did the city begin to sprout. Shortly after a canal was cut through the sandbar (which had landlocked the city's most usable port area), Hamilton rose to prominence as a Great Lakes shipping port and the largest steel-producing city in Canada. If you've never seen steel being made, you should arrange a tour of either the Dominion Foundries (phone: 416-544-3761) or the Steel Company of Canada (phone: 416-528-2511) plant. Both advise that you make reservations at least 2 or 3 weeks in advance; no one under 16 is admitted.

Dundurn Castle — built in 1832 by Sir Allan MacNab (later prime minister of pre-confederated Canada) and named for his ancestral homeland in Scotland — is a 36-room Regency villa restored in 1967. The mansion and grounds, overlooking Hamilton Harbour, were then opened to the public for concerts and other outdoor events. The gatekeeper's cottage has been converted into a museum detailing local involvement in the War of 1812, the Fenian Raids of the 1860s, and other military activities. Open 10 AM to 5 PM daily from mid-June through September; 1 to 4 PM the rest of the year (phone: 416-522-5313). A short distance northwest are the Royal Botanical Gardens, with over 2,000 acres of gardens and special plantings and a 1,200-acre wildlife sanctuary among the marshes and woods just outside town. The Lilac Garden blooms in May and June; Hendrie Park, dedicated to roses, blooms later in the summer, and in the fall Coote's Paradise, the wildlife area, blazes brightly. The *Sugaring-off Festival,* held in March, is a 2-week celebration of maple syrup making and pancake eating. The park is open daily all year.

Whitehern, the home of the McQuesten family, was built in the 1840s and purchased by Dr. Calvin McQuesten in 1852. It remained in the family until it was given to the city in 1959, and it now serves as a fine example of Canadian-Georgian architecture. Open 10 AM to 5 PM daily from June through September; noon to 4 PM daily from September through June (41 Jackson St. W. at McNab; phone: 416-522-5664).

En Route from Hamilton – Take the Queen Elizabeth Way east across Hamilton Harbour on the Burlington Skyway Bridge, heading toward Toronto, 44 miles (71 km) northeast. You are now entering the heart of Ontario's economy, the Golden Triangle, which stretches from Hamilton to Oshawa (on the far side of Toronto). Try to avoid driving through this congested area during afternoon rush hour. Take time out in Burlington, if possible, to visit the *Joseph Brant Museum,* a tribute to one of the most powerful Indian chiefs. It is housed in a replica of the cedar home built for him about 1800 (open daily; 1240 North Shore Blvd. E.). In mid-July, check out the *Highland Games,* a week-long festival including bagpipe contests, dancing, and the traditional throwing of the caber.

Halfway between Hamilton and Toronto is the community of Oakville, filled with beautiful parklands and the homes of the wealthy. The *Glen Abbey Golf Course,* designed by Jack Nicklaus for championship play, is the permanent site of the Canadian Open, held every June. Its clubhouse is a former monastery. Gairlock Gardens, a fashionable 1922 residence on the lake, houses an art gallery.

On the grounds is a wild bird sanctuary (open weekends, year-round; 1306 Lakeshore Rd. E.).

Nearby Bronte Provincial Park will please children after a day of looking at "old houses," since it contains a special children's farm full of animals waiting to be played with; a collection of farm implements adds to the fun (open all year, although hours are limited in winter).

The *Continental Pastry Shop* (170 Lakeshore Rd. E.) sells terrific European pastries and serves tea and luncheon.

In Toronto over a weekend? Look for Canada's largest year-round indoor flea market, held Sundays in Dixie Plaza in Mississauga (a suburb of Toronto). The plaza is right off the south side of the QEW.

If you stop over in Toronto, continue on the QEW to the Gardiner Expressway and take the Yonge Street turnoff into the downtown area. Otherwise, take Route 427 north from Mississauga to Route 401, which cuts across the northern part of Toronto much more efficiently, bringing you right to Oshawa.

TORONTO: See the *Toronto* chapter in THE CITIES.

En Route from Toronto – From downtown Toronto, take the Gardiner Expressway east from Yonge Street and pick up the Don Valley Parkway north to the MacDonald Cartier Freeway (Rte. 401) toward Oshawa. From the north end of town, you can pick up Route 401 directly. Either way, you will find yourself traveling through a broad district of suburban housing, a sign of Toronto's growth. At the Pickering Nuclear Power Station, 22 miles (35 km) from Toronto, visitors are welcome. Displays explain the conversion processes in words and pictures (use the Brock Rd. exit from Rte. 401; open daily; phone: 839-0465). Oshawa is 13 miles (21 km) beyond the plant.

OSHAWA: Called Canada's Detroit, Oshawa is the center of the Canadian automobile industry. The McLaughlin Carriage Company (1867) was one of the largest in the British Empire. In 1907, the same family founded the motor car factory that produced the McLaughlin Buick; it was later sold to GM in 1918. A third of the city's workforce is employed by General Motors and thousands more work in associated industries. The McLaughlin mansion, Parkwood, is open to public viewing of the formal gardens and the household furnishings, most of which are rare antiques (270 Simcoe St. N.; open Tuesdays through Sundays, June through August; open afternoons on Wednesdays and Sundays, September through November and April and May; winter months by appointment only).

The *Canadian Automotive Museum* contains exhibits of the town's history and economy and an interesting collection of early Canadian automobiles, including an 1898 Redpath runabout (99 Simcoe St. S.; open daily).

En Route from Oshawa – Continue driving east on Route 401, passing through the outer ring of Toronto suburbs and into the Great Pine Ridge Tourist Area, the 64-mile coastline between Oshawa and Trenton. This area, used heavily by residents, is filled with weekend vacation spots, camp grounds, picnic areas, and small, quiet communities. The Darlington Provincial Park, just off the roadway, is fine for camping or picnicking and has a beach for swimming and boat-launching ramps. About 9 miles (14 km) from Oshawa is the cutoff to Mosport, Canada's Grand Prix racing track (Exit 75 from Route 401; events are scheduled between April and October).

Port Hope, a small town on Lake Ontario, dates back to the 1700s, when French missionaries began frequenting the area. In the past, leather and woolen goods, iron, and whiskey were produced here; now it's just a quiet little community with several historic buildings, a good place to relax from driving.

Cobourg, just 7 miles (11 km) past Port Hope, has become a popular resort area over the years, aided by the town's typical Canadian flavor. Ancient maples along the avenues enhance the beauty of the 19th-century homes and traditional churches. An important transportation center during the 1800s — when lake steamers docked here and coaches on the Toronto-Montreal roadway stopped to change horses and allow passengers to refresh themselves — none of the town's beauty or appeal has faded.

The *Marie Dressler House*, a restored 1830s house and the former home of the actress, has been converted into a restaurant with excellent results. The furnishings are mostly period antiques, and you can dine on an outdoor terrace in warm weather (212 King St. W.; phone: 416-372-5243; open daily except Tuesdays).

From here toward Trenton you can either remain on Route 401 or take the older (and more pastoral) Route 2, running closer to the waterfront. The Presqu'ile Provincial Park at Brighton, just outside Trenton, has 500 sites for camping among its 2,000 acres of woodlands, plus a small natural history museum (in an old lighthouse) and a wildlife sanctuary for the migratory birds who make this an annual stop.

If you approach Trenton on Route 401, take Route 33 south into town; if you're on Route 2, it will bring you right into Trenton.

TRENTON: This town sits astride the Trent River at the southern terminus of the Trent-Severn Waterway, a 240-mile recreational inland waterway system cutting diagonally across the narrow neck of this huge peninsula (which separates Lakes Ontario, Erie, and Huron) to Port Severn, on an inlet of Lake Huron's Georgian Bay. The waterway follows the original Indian route — later used by fur traders — along the Trent River and across Lake Simcoe (and several other rivers and lakes). Today it is augmented by canals, locks, and even a rail line to make travel and portage easier for 20th-century voyagers. Samuel de Champlain used the route in 1615, when he traveled from Port Severn to attack the Iroquois at Oswego, New York.

Trenton also marks the southwestern end of the Bay of Quinte, separating the Isle of Quinte, a peninsular extention lying in Lake Ontario. Route 33, providing access to this beautiful area, runs along its coastline to bring us back to the mainland near Bath, just south of Napanee. The island deserves a full day's exploration, but if you must hurry east (toward Kingston and Quebec), stay on either Route 2 or 401 rather than taking Route 33 south to Trenton and Quinte's Isle.

QUINTE'S ISLE: Route 33 travels south onto Quinte's Isle and down to its southern coast before swinging east toward Glenora and the Adolphustown peninsula, which extends west from the mainland. An island tour is a peaceful and relaxing day's drive through several of the area's oldest settlements. The nomads of the Laurentian Group are thought to have roamed the island around 1000 BC, and the Point Peninsula culture occupied the area from about that same time until AD 1000. Europeans started to come during the early 1600s, and groups of United Empire Loyalists began to farm the island during the late 1700s (many of their descendants still farm the land). The general impression of the island is of a land unchanged by the years, of a more restful way of life than most of us know.

The island is one of the largest vegetable- and fruit-growing areas in Ontario, with roadside stands everywhere. Route 33 passes through Carrying Place (about 4 mi/6 km south of Trenton). A secondary roadway, Route 19, leads 6 miles (10 km) east toward Ameliasburgh.

The *Ameliasburgh Museum* is a collection of early settlement structures — an 1868 church, two more recent barns, and a reconstructed log cabin, all complete with crude furnishings. Indian and pioneer relics, such as blacksmithing tools, are on view in most of the buildings (open Tuesdays through Sundays during July and August; weekends only from *Victoria Day* through *Thanksgiving* — early October). Return to Route 33 and head south to the southwest corner of this little island and North Beach Recreation Area, a small beach for swimming and sunning (no camping).

Just below North Beach, about 22 miles (35 km) south of Trenton, Route 33 turns sharply east and traces the coast toward Bloomfield.

There are four provincial parks on the island. The two on the western coast boast the most beautiful sand dunes in Ontario. Take the marked secondary roads, Route 12 to Sandbanks and Route 18 to Outlet.

Sandbanks Provincial Park consists of an 894-acre sandbar extending 5 miles (8 km) across a wide bay to create West Lake under its sheltering wing. The dunes decorating the sandbar are spectacular. (There are boat rentals and designated swimming areas.) Camping available at 411 campsites.

In the morning, return to Route 33 near Bloomfield to continue to the mainland.

PICTON: Located on Route 33 about 8 miles (13 km) east of Bloomfield is the island's major town, Picton. Sir John A. Macdonald, Canada's first prime minister, grew up and successfully defended his first case here, in the District Courthouse and Gaol. Built in 1832, it is still used as the county courthouse and is, therefore, open to the public weekdays, year-round. Although it's the commercial center of the island, Picton is by no means big or bustling; it's quite peaceful and has attracted many fine craftspeople in a variety of fields. A brief walk about town is sure to end in front of somebody's studio, where a fine bit of leatherwork or silverwork or a painting catches your eye. The *Inn on the Bay* restaurant and tavern (73 Bridge St.) is an early 1800s house made over just slightly to become one of the best restaurants on the island (closed Mondays during the winter; to make reservations during the summer call 613-476-3113).

En Route from Picton – Your direction of travel will depend on what you want to see. North on Route 49 toward the mainland takes you past the 1,700-acre Tyendinaga Indian Reserve, with several native craft centers. About mid-May, an annual reenactment of the Mohawk landing is staged, complete with full battle array and traditional costumes. From here it's possible to continue north on Route 49 to either Route 2 or 401, both of which pass through the historic town of Napanee en route to a reunion with Route 33 at Kingston.

Route 33 east brings you to the Lake on the Mountain, a little lake 200 feet above Lake Ontario that local legend holds is fed by an underground connection with Niagara Falls, about 120 miles (193 km) away. The view from this little mountain is worth the short drive.

Route 33 continues east for a short distance to Glenora, where a free ferry takes you across the Adolphus Reach to Adolphustown on the mainland. The stone mills seen around the docks in Glenora were built in the 1800s as flour and carding mills by Sir John A. Macdonald's father. They're now the Fisheries Research Station. On the mainland, Route 33 travels 32 miles (52 km) along the shore toward Kingston, passing through Adolphustown and Bath, bypassing Amherst Island.

The origins of Adolphustown are evident in the Loyalist Memorial Church (1822) and in the *United Empire Loyalist Museum,* which describes the influx of Loyalist settlers in great detail. The Hay Bay Church (1792) is the oldest Methodist church in Upper Canada; even older are the Quaker Burying Grounds at Hay Bay (both about 2½ mi/4 km north of Adolphustown proper), established by some of the town's original settlers.

NAPANEE: For those traveling east on Routes 2 and 401, Napanee — just 7½ miles (12 km) east of the Route 49 junction — is a natural stop. A grist mill (1786) became the basis of the settlement's economy, and Scotsman Allan McPherson (who made a nice profit on the milling) built a magnificent home with the proceeds. The house (on Elizabeth St.), overlooking the Napanee River, has been restored to the state McPherson himself demanded in the early 1800s. Open Tuesdays through Sundays, *Victoria Day* (late May) to *Thanksgiving* (early October), and the first week in December for a Victorian Christmas.

Whether you take Route 2 or 401, it's still only 20 miles (32 km) east to Kingston.

KINGSTON: French fur traders quickly realized the importance of this point of land at the mouth of the Cataraqui River, where Lake Ontario meets the St. Lawrence River. An outpost was established here in 1673 by Louis de Buade, the Count of Frontenac, to control the fur trade with the Indians of the North and West who came down the Ottawa River as well as those of the Lake Huron and Ontario areas. A marker in the archway of the Tête de Pont Barracks (at the west end of Cataraqui Bridge) commemorates the site of the original Fort Frontenac (as the fortified trading post was called) and its later rebuilding under explorer and fellow fur trader Robert Cavelier, Sieur de La Salle.

Long before the French came, the site had been used as an Indian trade center. A small Iroquois village stood nearby. Fighting between the Iroquois Confederacy and the Huron Nation kept French traders from dealing with area tribes, but this outpost, established during a peace that lasted from the late 1660s until 1680, gave the French a strong foothold from which to trade with the interior. The profitable trade alliances of the French and the Huron on the one hand, and of the English and Dutch in New England and New York with the Iroquois of Upstate New York on the other, aggravated hostilities between the Indian groups. Fort Frontenac stood in the midst of the fighting. Shortly before the Treaty of Paris put an end to both the century-long series of French and Indian wars and the larger British-French conflict over the possession of Canada, a force of 3,000 British-American colonials and their Iroquois allies destroyed the fort and took control of Lake Ontario. Quebec was taken the following year.

Count Frontenac, crusty, autocratic, and likable from all accounts, did not live to see his fortress's demise. He died in 1698 at 76, 2 years after successfully leading a force of Hurons and fur traders against the Oneida and Onondaga tribes of the Iroquois Confederacy to relieve hostile Indian pressure on French holdings in the area.

Many structures date back to the period following the 1763 treaty, when United Empire Loyalists began to resettle in British-occupied Canada, fearing the loss of British control over the American colonies they inhabited. Brock Street, the main thoroughfare of Kingston (as the British christened the settlement), still lives as a commercial center, with many of the original stores still transacting business in the old manner. A century of aging has enhanced the color and depth of the locally quarried limestone used to build these buildings. A stroll down this street is a step into the past. Turn left at the foot of the street, along the waterfront and Ontario Street, to get to the site of Frontenac's original structure.

One of the city's highlights is Old Fort Henry, a reconstructed fort erected during the War of 1812 as the key defense of the southern end of the St. Lawrence River. The original Fort Henry fell into disrepair in the late 1890s after it was abandoned in the interest of Canadian-American cooperation. Nowadays the fortress is staffed by a fife and drum corps, tour guides, and a small detachment of gunners who fire salutes to match the precision of the drill team on the parade field. The Sunset Retreat Ceremony, performed each Monday, Wednesday, and Saturday at 7:30 PM during July and August, weather permitting, is impressive. The fort is located east of town, on the far side of both the harbor and Navy Bay (open daily, mid-May to mid-October). On Point Fredrick, which separates Navy Bay from Kingston Harbour and the mouth of the Cataraqui River, stands the circular Martello Tower of Fort Fredrick, one of the early fortifications protecting Kingston. Now the tower houses the *Royal Military College Museum* and the *Douglas Small Arms Collection* (open daily, June through *Labor Day*). Another stone Martello Tower, located at the corner of Barrie and King streets facing Lake Ontario, is the Murney Redoubt, which also contains a museum of pioneer artifacts and military history (open 10 AM to 8 PM July and August, 10 AM till dusk from mid-May through mid-October).

The importance of Kingston, Fort Frontenac, and Fort Henry to Canadian history is documented by numerous plaques about town detailing the contributions of individuals and the histories of many of the older buildings. The 1840 *Firehall* has been restored and is now a privately run restaurant offering lunch and dinner daily, and Sunday brunch. There are several dining areas within the structure, but everything is geared toward local history and culture. Even the menu is based on local produce and regional dishes, such as Wolfe Island pheasant (251 Ontario St.; phone: 613-548-8888.)

From Kingston Harbour, cruises north into the Thousand Islands area can be arranged through *Thousand Islands Cruises* (phone: 613-549-1123) from their dock about 5 miles (8 km) east of the town off Route 2.

Take Route 2 eastbound about 18 miles (29 km) to Gananoque, the "gateway to the Thousand Islands."

GANANOQUE: Although a plaque by the Town Hall of Gananoque credits United Empire Loyalist Joel Stone as its founder, it's likely the Indians were responsible for establishing this beautiful resort overlooking the fabulous Thousand Islands area. Their names for this coast, "place of good health" and "land that slopes toward the water and disappears under it," are both embodied in its anglicized name, pronounced Gan-non-*ock*-way.

The *Gananoque Historic Museum* (10 King East St.; open 2 to 5 PM, Mondays through Saturdays from June to September, with evening hours from 7 to 9 PM during July and August) contains many Indian relics discovered nearby and a large number of military items from the War of 1812 to World War II. Several historic plaques, placed around town by Ontario's Heritage Foundation, tell of the area's past — of Pirate Johnston (who attacked British shipping in the 1830s), and of the September 21 attack on the city by American soldiers during the War of 1812, to name two.

■**EXTRA SPECIAL:** It's not history that attracts hundreds of visitors to this bank of the St. Lawrence each year, it's the islands. Legend has it that a French explorer (unnamed) first called this area Thousand Islands, although there are actually about 1,700 separate bits and pieces of land in the chain. They vary in size from a few square feet to a few hundred square feet. Houses on these islands are prized for their beauty and privacy, and many of the stone dwellings date back to the early 1800s.

On Heart Island stands Boldt Castle, begun in the late 1890s by George Boldt (owner of the Waldorf-Astoria) as a gift for his wife. She died, the castle was never completed, and the magnificent stonework fell into disrepair. The castle has been renovated, and the charm and scale of Boldt's undertaking can be easily appreciated.

Cruises of the Thousand Islands can be arranged through *Gananoque Boat Line* and *International Boat Cruises,* both in Gananoque; *Kingston Excursions,* in Kingston; and through several smaller lines on both sides of the St. Lawrence. (Not all cruise boats stop at Heart Island.)

Two fine restaurants in Gananoque offer a true 19th-century atmosphere: the *Golden Apple Inn* (45 King St. W.; phone: 613-382-3300), in an 1830s farmhouse, and the dining room of the *Athlone* motor inn (250 King St. W.; phone: 613-382-2440), in an 1874 home. *The Golden Apple* specializes in prime ribs and seafood and does all its own baking. Open April through December 31.

En Route from Gananoque – Take Route 2, the Heritage Highway, east toward the Quebec border. The village of Ivy Lea and the Thousand Island Bridge to New York State are about 10 miles (16 km) away. *Skytown,* a combination viewing tower and entertainment complex, stands 400 feet above Hill Island, the central support for the bridge. This mid-river platform, Hill Island, also houses duty-free shops for travelers and Never-Never Land, a children's park with a fairy tale and nursery rhyme theme. Cruises of the islands are available from the docks at Ivy Lea through *Snider Thousand Island Boat Tours.*

At Mallorytown Landing, just 9 miles (14 km) beyond Ivy Lea, the St. Lawrence Islands National Park, comprised of 18 scattered areas, maintains a 97-acre visitor center on the mainland with visual displays of the history of the Thousand Islands and a War of 1812 gunboat, the HMS *Radcliff,* part of which is open to visitors.

BROCKVILLE: The industrial center of Brockville, 32 miles (52 km) east of Gananoque, marks the eastern end of the Thousand Islands area. While the town is worth a quick stop, there are few sightseeing highlights: Even the historical markers are less than inspiring. One marks the site of Canada's oldest railroad tunnel (just south of Town Hall) and a second reminds all visitors of the night of February 6, 1813, when the town was raided by Americans under the command of Major Forsyth (on the waterfront of Blockhouse Island). One good reason to see Brockville is the *Towne Haus* tavern (32 Apple St.; phone: 613-345-1182), in a building dating back to "sometime before 1826." The catch-of-the-day is the high point on an excellent menu. Open for lunch Mondays through Fridays, and dinner, Mondays through Saturdays.

The small town of Prescott lies 32 miles (52 km) farther east along Route 2.

PRESCOTT: One of the few deepwater ports along this section of the river, Prescott has risen in importance as a port over the last 100 years. Its principal fortification, Fort Wellington, overlooking the St. Lawrence River, played a crucial part in the War of 1812 when both Canadians and Americans vied for control of the valuable waterway. It was also involved in the fighting during the 1837 Rebellion and the Fenian Raids of the late 1860s. The fort, restored to its original condition, hosts a military pageant each July, with Canadian, British, and American troops dressed in period uniforms (right off Rte. 2; open daily from mid-May through mid-October; weekdays November to mid-May, by appointment only; phone: 613-925-2896).

En Route from Prescott – The banks of the St. Lawrence between here and Montreal, in Quebec, are dotted with small communities that date back to the early days of French exploration of the lands beyond the fortress of Mont Royal. The land has lost none of its appeal and beauty. When the village of Iroquois, 6 miles (10 km) from Prescott, was partially relocated to allow the construction of the St. Lawrence Seaway, many of the old homes were reconstructed in fine detail. One of the dwellings on its original site is the Carman House, thought to have been built in 1825 (Carman Rd., off Rte. 2, en route to the seaway locks; open 1 to 8 PM daily, June 28 to September 2).

MORRISBURG: Located 8 miles (13 km) closer to Montreal, this town was also settled in the early 1800s. About 40 of the best-preserved pioneer dwellings were restored when the town was moved to accommodate the rising waters of the St. Lawrence Seaway. A choice cross section of the early-19th-century buildings have been grouped together, 7 miles (11 km) east of the newly positioned Morrisburg, to form a typical, almost self-sufficient, 1850s community. The houses, mills, taverns, and shops are joined with hand-forged nails and dowels; the shingles have been split by hand, and the corduroy road is comprised of trees cut and dragged into place manually. Upper Canada Village (in Crysler Battlefield Park; open daily, mid-May through mid-October; phone: 613-543-2911), as this working settlement is called, is inhabited by a group of talented craftspeople keeping the old trades alive: Flour is ground with stone; an 1840 water-powered mill is the closest thing here to "mechanized"; women hook rugs and weave blankets by hand; and bread is baked in wood-fired ovens.

Crysler Battlefield Park is also the site of one of the most decisive battles of the War of 1812, a major turning point in Canadian history. Here about 800 British and Canadian civilians and soldiers and Indians battled over 4,000 American troops and forced their withdrawal on November 11, 1813. This defeat, coupled with another loss at Châteauguay, destroyed American hopes of capturing Canada.

En Route from Morrisburg – If you want to fish in an area where you have the advantage over the fish, then stop in the village of Ingleside or Long Sault, about 15 miles (24 km) from Morrisburg on Route 1: 11 islands, formed by the expanded St. Lawrence Seaway (and the dam at Cornwall), create an angler's heaven. The islands are linked by bridges and causeways, allowing easy access to almost any point in the group. A wildlife sanctuary and Canada goose compound are located on nearby Nairne Island. The whole area, with its beautiful river views and secluded inlets, is perfect for picnicking and camping.

CORNWALL: The St. Lawrence Seaway, with its extraordinary system of dams and power plants, was created to ease navigation through hazardous parts of the 800-mile St. Lawrence River and to harness the power of this tremendous river more efficiently. The headquarters of the Seaway Authority is located here in Cornwall, where Thomas A. Edison first installed a plant for lighting an entire factory by electricity. Today, the Robert H. Saunders–St. Lawrence Generating Station, a $6 billion section of the US-Canadian hydroelectric power system, is open for tours Sundays through Thursdays during the summer. A plaque at Lakeside Park, just outside of Cornwall proper, is a sad reminder of the numerous small communities and historic homes submerged by the altered watercourse.

Among the old structures that survived the flood are St. Andrew's Church, one of the oldest remaining stone buildings in Ontario (now used as the parish hall of the current church); the District Courthouse and Gaol, completed from the early 1830s; and the "Wood House," which serves as the *United Counties Museum,* with a collection of Canadian artifacts and some of the original electrical equipment Edison used in the Canada Mills plant (731 2nd St. W.; open 10 AM to noon and 1 to 5 PM, Mondays through Saturdays; Sundays, 2 to 5 PM only; May through October.)

The boundary of Ontario is just 20 miles (32 km) beyond Cornwall, and Routes 2 and 401 both continue eastward, toward Montreal, Quebec, and the Atlantic.

BEST EN ROUTE

Due to the high volume of tourist traffic flowing through the province, most hotel accommodations tend to fall into an average price category. While you're not going to find many rooms at bargain rates, very few hotels exceed the going rate except when premium services or especially desirable rooms are involved. Any establishment charging under $47 per night for two occupants is listed as inexpensive, and those with rates over $64 per night (double occupancy) are considered expensive. The majority of hotel space falls into the moderate ($47 to $64 per night) range. These rates apply to the summer high season. Reservations are advised at all times and should be made weeks in advance during the summer and fall. Recent developments in the Ontario park system allow (and encourage) advance registration for camping areas, and it is advisable to plan your trip accordingly. All prices are quoted in US dollars.

NIAGARA FALLS

Ameri-Cana – About 4 miles (6 km) outside the hustle and bustle of downtown, amid spacious grounds with a play area, this motor inn has 110 rooms, including honeymoon suites, as well as several efficiencies and kitchen units. A good base of operations if you've got a small mob with you. 8444 Lundy's La. (phone: 416-356-8444). Expensive.

Brock – Probably the best-known and most popular hotel in town, with a good view of both sets of falls from many of its 238 rooms. Dining room. 5685 Falls Ave. (For reservations call 800-263-7135). Expensive.

Foxhead Inn – Slightly closer to the falls than its neighboring cousin, the inn has over 400 modern rooms, many of which overlook the falls, and a full range of features — pool, excellent dining room, sports complex, and facilities for the handicapped. 5875 Falls Ave. (For reservations call 800-263-7135). Expensive.

Michael's Inn – A comfortable motor inn overlooking the river and gorge, it has a pool and dining facilities. Many of the 130 rooms offer good falls views from their balconies. 5599 River Rd. (phone: 416-354-2727). Expensive.

Parkwood – All 32 rooms have air conditioning and color TV sets; most have refrigerators. Outdoor pool. 8054 Lundy's La. (phone: 416-354-3162). Moderate to inexpensive.

Niagara Falls KOA – An appealing mixture of primitive and modern comforts, this campground has many wooded areas and grassy tent sites as well as RV facilities; it also has miniature golf and a pool. If you like tent camping, this is the one. One mile west of QEW on Rte. 20 (phone: 416-354-6472). Inexpensive.

NIAGARA-ON-THE-LAKE

Angel Inn – Originally built as a three-room log cabin in 1779, the inn has always been a center of local history and politics. Let one of the staff members fill you in on the events that took place here. It has been a hotel since 1823 and is full of authentic colonial pieces and collector's items. The beds in all 12 rooms are canopy-style, embellished with petit-point. Queen St. at Regent (phone: 416-468-3411). Expensive.

Oban Inn – Erected in 1824, it wasn't until a few years later that the 23-room *Oban* became a hotel and began a tradition of excellence which has made it one of the town's landmarks in terms of both grace and beauty. 160 Front St. (phone: 416-468-7811). Expensive.

Pillar and Post – There are fireplaces in half of the 90 rooms of this interesting hotel, and a sauna, whirlpool bath, and an outdoor pool for creature comforts, plus a dining room and a crafts and antiques shop. King and John Sts. (phone: 416-468-2123). Expensive.

Prince of Wales – A truly magnificent restored inn highlighted by a royal suite (and bed) occupied by the Prince of Wales in the 1920s. The other 103 rooms have yet to be blessed. 6 Picton St. (phone: 416-468-3246). Expensive.

ST. CATHARINES

Parkway Inn – An attractive and convenient downtown hotel, with 125 rooms and enough amenities to satisfy anyone: sauna, whirlpool bath, bowling, indoor pool, and good dining facilities. 327 Ontario St. at QEW (phone: 416-688-2324). Expensive to moderate.

Highwayman – Noted for its cozy atmosphere, this inn has 50 rooms with TV sets, and an outdoor pool. Winery tours can be arranged. 420 Ontario St. (phone: 416-688-1646). Moderate.

Lorenzi's Motor Inn – Minutes from Niagara Falls and the famous Seaway twin locks, this place has 27 pleasant, well-furnished rooms and a dining room. Exit 406 at Glandale Ave. W. to Merritt St. (phone: 416-227-1183). Moderate.

PICTON

Fireside Inn – Located right on Picton Harbour, this property has 30 large rooms, entertainment, a heated pool, and its own dock. 35 Bridge St. (phone: 613-476-2156). Moderate.

Tip of the Bay – Overlooking Picton Bay, the hotel has 28 rooms and 2 dining rooms. Docking facilities and fishing packages available. 35 Bridge St. (phone: 613-476-2156). Moderate.

KINGSTON

Confederation Place – Kingston's newest hostelry and a member of the Howard Johnson family, this modern, 101-room hotel is in the heart of downtown, overlooking the harbor. In fact, the Thousand Islands boat tours dock right here. 237 Ontario St. (phone: 613-549-6300). Expensive.

Seven Oakes – Just outside Kingston, this motel offers about the best accommodations, dollar for dollar, in the area. The 40 units occupy about 2 acres of the motel's 11 acres, so there's plenty of space for kids to play in addition to the Olympic-size pool. Also, the owners will arrange charters for fishing or just cruising the lake, and morning coffee is free. 2331 Princess St. (phone: 613-546-3655). Expensive to moderate.

Highland – Near historic Fort Henry, this 44-room establishment has spacious grounds, a heated pool, and tennis courts. Rte. 15 at Rte. 2, RR 1 (phone: 613-546-3121). Moderate.

Beaver – Some of the 22 clean, quiet rooms have a scenic view, and there's an outdoor pool, a playground, and babysitting service. Just off Hwy. 401 on Rte. 15 (phone: 613-546-6674). Moderate.

GANANOQUE

Country Squire Family Inn – An activity-oriented resort with everything from tennis to a trampoline to an 85-foot indoor pool. Fifteen cottages are available as well as 51 motel rooms. The honeymoon suites have fireplaces. Open April through November. 715 King St. E. (phone: 613-382-3511). Expensive.

Glen House – This resort lodge lies right on the St. Lawrence and has a beach, an indoor pool, 72 rooms, and 4 cottages. The view of the river from the dining room is excellent. Open February through November. On the Thousand Island Pkwy., Box 10 (phone: 613-659-2204). Expensive.

1000 Island – Clean and cozy motel, with honeymoon suites and suites with Jacuzzis, water beds, and an outdoor pool. Babysitting available. Tickets for the 1000 Island boat tour available here. 550 King St. E. (phone: 613-382-3911). Expensive to moderate.

IVY LEA

Ivy Lea Inn – Set on 35 acres, with 1,700 feet of St. Lawrence River shoreline, the inn has 23 rooms, 8 cottages, a pool, tennis courts, a fishing pier, and a yacht harbor. One mile (1.6 km) west on Thousands Island Parkway (phone: 613-659-2329). Expensive.

Caiger's – This quiet resort with 35 rooms is fully dedicated to the fine art of relaxing and casting a few fishing lines. They will arrange everything from boats and guides to licenses and bait. There's a beach area and a pool, and good dining facilities. Thousand Islands Pkwy. (phone: 613-659-2266). Moderate.

The Western Lakeshores

The 660-mile (1,063-km) route follows almost mile for mile — with a few inland departures — the spectacular shoreline of Lake Huron and Lake Superior, one of the most scenic drives in Canada. Less than 20 years ago, this wilderness area of thick forest, gorges, fjords, lakes, and rivers was passable only by rail, canoe, or air (bush pilots served various fishing and hunting lodges throughout the area). Today a road stretches from Owen Sound, on the peninsula of land that divides Georgian Bay and Lake Huron, to Nipigon on the southern shore of huge Lake Nipigon. At Nipigon the road joins Yonge Street, the long road from Toronto that is discussed in the following route.

This is a land of rushing rivers, untamed waterfalls, vast deposits of mineral wealth, thickly wooded bush, and deep forests. It is a tortuous landscape of canyons and gorges punctuated by tiny crystal lakes, with the mighty inland sea forever washing its shores. It is the country of the backpacker, canoeist, camper, camera enthusiast, rockhound, skier, angler, hunter, and anyone who enjoys unspoiled nature in its full beauty. For the adventurous, rough feeder roads along the route lead deeper into the wilderness, to remote fishing spots and wildlife habitats. It is, however, no place for a novice alone.

The many moods of Lake Superior dictate weather conditions deep into the surrounding interior. Fog is common, and the weather is changeable. The nature lover will find all its moods impressive, but there is a special purity to the vast expanse of azure blue on a sunny summer day. Winter comes early and stays late, and on occasions the overnight temperatures drop to the freezing mark as early as mid-August. On the other hand, daytime temperatures can reach the 90s F (30s C) in midsummer. And summertime visitors should include a good insect repellent in their luggage.

Hidden in the massive rock formations that line Lake Superior's shores are the Indian petroglyphs that influenced Longfellow when he wrote *Hiawatha,* and there are indications that the Indians who lived along the coastline were making copper tools long before Europeans visited this part of the country.

The original native American inhabitants were the Ojibwa Indians; they were joined by French fur traders in the early 1700s in a few locations around the lake, and soon after, British fur traders also discovered the area and established communications with the Ojibwa. The three cultures existed side by side (dominated by the Ojibwa, who far outnumbered the scattered French and British) for almost 100 years, until prospectors discovered the region's vast lode of mineral wealth — copper and silver, some gold, and heavy concentrations of iron ore — in the early 1800s.

That ended the halcyon days of the fur trade and brought the decline of the Indian culture. Between 1845 and 1870 mining was extremely heavy, focusing primarily on copper and silver. With the mines came the railroad, and the wild region began to open up. (Mining remains a significant part of the area's business, with uranium the most recent discovery.)

Visitors will be more interested in one particularly significant aspect of the region. Ontario's Great Lake shoreline is part of the transitional zone between northern and southern life forms. The Great Lakes–St. Lawrence Forest Region extends to just south of Wawa, where it begins to merge into the Boreal Forest Region of the North, thus representing a transition between northern and temperate climates. In the southern region the mixed hardwood forest is composed of sugar maple, yellow birch, and a mixed forest cover of conifers, white birch, and mountain ash. The northern sector of boreal mixed forest has birch, spruce, aspen, and balsam fir. On the floors of deep canyons of this region, where little sunlight falls, Arctic flowers, mosses, and lichens, normally found only in the extreme North, maintain a precarious existence.

The Owen Sound–Nipigon route is doubly delightful; conscientious observers of nature will be fascinated by the combinations of northern and southern life forms in the area. And you need no special knowledge to be awed by the massive rock formations along the lake; the cascades of waterfalls and necklace braids of lakes that lace the area's forests; the gorges and fjords chiseled out of the rocks; and the inpenetrable silence of the woods. From Owen Sound on the Bruce Peninsula, the route crosses the mouth of Georgian Bay to Manitoulin Island, where an annual Indian powwow is held. On the mainland, Route 17, part of the 5,000-mile Trans-Canada Highway, continues along the shoreline to the great locks at Sault Ste. Marie, which connect Lake Huron with Lake Superior.

Beyond "the Soo," as Sault Ste. Marie is known, most of the highway has only two lanes, and the stretch between Lake Superior Park (85 mi/137 km from the Soo) and Marathon (124 mi/200 km east of Nipigon) wasn't even built until the 1960s. In some places the road slices 60 feet into the crest of a mountain in an effort to climb over the top, and pits 80 feet deep had to be filled to provide footing for the road. This highway is one of the few in the world traveled not as a means of getting from one point to another but for the pure joy of the trip.

OWEN SOUND: This attractive community on its own inlet just within Georgian Bay is 74 miles (119 km) west of Barrie, Ontario, and 116 miles (187 km) northwest of Toronto. On the fringes of the historic Huron Indian district, its original population was nonetheless Ojibwa Indians, who were deeply influenced by the agricultural successes of the Hurons (one of the few Canadian Indian tribes to farm rather than hunt). Today, Owen Sound has a fine museum of local native history. The three buildings of the *County of Grey and Owen Sound Museum* (975 Sixth St. E.) date from a period of white settlement early in the 19th century. The museum not only has exhibits from that period and the era of the Ojibwa, but also presents even more interesting "living history" — demonstrations on spinning and weaving, the cooking styles of both Indians and early settlers, and blacksmithing. The museum staff has made a special study of the technology of Algonquin birchbark canoe construction, and you can see the 26-foot "express" canoe — built for speed, the kind used by Indians and voyageurs in the fur trade — that was built by the museum. Open Tuesdays through Fridays, 9 AM to 5 PM, and on weekends from 1 to 5 PM. During July and August, open daily from 9 AM to 5 PM, except on Sundays, 1 to 5 PM (phone: 519-376-3690).

Owen Sound is something of a bonanza for kids. If the demonstrations at the museum don't tickle their fancy, there are two "fairy tale" parks nearby — Sunny Valley Wildlife Park (6 mi/10 km south of town on Rte. 10 — also numbered Rte. 6) and Story Book Park (on the same road only 2 mi/3 km south of town). The wildlife park has various furry and feathered creatures from llamas to ducks for kids to pet; Story Book Park has animals, too, but the real attraction is favorite storybook characters who gambol about.

For a calmer end to the day, the *Tom Thompson Memorial Art Gallery* (840 First Ave. W.; closed Mondays), dedicated to one of Canada's most innovative landscape painters, displays Thompson's work as well as that of his well-known contemporaries, the Group of Seven, and others. Thompson spent his boyhood here, and the colors of the area's farms and countryside and the views of Georgian Bay heavily influenced his work.

En Route from Owen Sound – From Route 7, pick up Route 6 north and west of Owen Sound, leading out the Bruce Peninsula separating Georgian Bay (on your right) from Lake Huron (on your left). About 40 miles (64 km) from Owen Sound, just beyond Wiarton and its bustling shopping districts, is the Cape Croker Indian Reserve. Here, a reconstructed Indian fortress still guards the Ojibwa village on Georgian Bay; the village and fortress are open year-round, and campsites on the shore are available during the summer. Fishing in the bay once supported the community and is still too good for most anglers to resist. Many of the shoreline villages — on both shores — have developed into fishing-oriented resorts; two of the best are Lions Head and Tobermory.

TOBERMORY: At the very tip of the Bruce Peninsula, Tobermory is, first and always, a fishing village. Its wood-frame homes and harbors are quite peaceful, but it is a busy resort center. Whether you're fishing for rainbow trout, fighting northern pike, walleye, or bass in Lake Huron or Georgian Bay, or scuba diving for a glimpse of one of the 50 or so known wrecks that lie in nearby waters, charter boats are available in Tobermory's twin harbors. Water taxis will always take you out to fantastic Flower Pot Island, about 4 miles offshore, where wind- and water-carved rock formations look like giant flower pots in the distance. Also on the island are caves that you could explore for hours and a campground so you can spend some time here comfortably.

En Route from Tobermory – The Manitoulin Island car ferry crosses the main channel of Georgian Bay's mouth onto Lake Huron, passing among the beautiful Georgian Bay Islands. The crossing takes about 2 hours and operates daily, May–October. Make reservations during the summer (Owen Sound Transportation Company, 1101 1st Ave. W., Owen Sound; phone: 519-376-6601). There is a charge for the ferry.

MANITOULIN ISLAND: Stretching west from the mouth of Georgian Bay toward the mainland, the island forms part of the landmass that actually separates Georgian Bay from Lake Huron and makes it a distinct body of water. From its first habitation, the history of Manitoulin Island has been inextricably bound to its surrounding waters. Early Indian residents lived by fishing; current residents live primarily by fishing or the tourists that fishing attracts. At the South Baymouth Fish Research Station, north of South Baymouth off Route 68, and at the Sandfish Hatchery, 22 miles (35 km) northwest of South Baymouth, you can get a close view of the modern fishing industry. And just as fishing has always been a part of island life, Manitoulin is still very much an Indian area as well.

Time your visit to coincide with the *Wikwemikong Indian Powwow* (the first weekend in August), when the Manitoulin Indians host a conclave of some 18 tribes of six distinct Indian Nations. It's a spectacular colorfest of dancing, craft shows, and traditional tribal ceremonies. For information, contact the Wikwemikong Band Administration Office, Wikwemikong Unceded Indian Reserve, Wikwemikong (phone: 705-859-3122).

Take time to tour the quiet communities that line the island shores. Little Current, in the northeast corner, began as a Hudson's Bay Company trading post; just outside town is McLean's Mountain (1,075 ft.), and the views of the bay from there are eye-popping. Gore Bay, also on the north shore, is a major shopping stop for residents and visitors alike, but the calm and quiet of its old-fashioned streets keep that aspect in the background. On the south shore, opposite Gore Bay, is the long sandy beach of Providence Bay. At Meldrum Bay, on the western tip of the island, the Mississaugi Strait Lighthouse Museum has been guarding the hazardous strait since 1874. La Salle's ship, the *Griffin*, shipwrecked here in 1670, and relics are displayed in the old lighthouse.

En Route from Manitoulin Island – By a series of bridges and causeways, Route 68 leads across the Bay of Islands from Little Current to the industrial hub of Espanola on the mainland. If mining or geology are among your interests, drive east one hour on the Trans-Canada Highway to Sudbury, one of the country's biggest mining towns and home to the Science North exhibition center.

SUDBURY: Was it a meteorite or volcanic explosion that created the Sudbury Basin? Expert opinion is divided. Whatever the answer, this phenomenon — measuring 37 by 17 miles — is the largest source of nickel in the world, and Sudbury is the site of the world's largest integrated nickel mining, smelting, and refining complex. The region has other mineral wealth, too: platinum, copper, cobalt, silver, and gold. Its natural treasures include beautiful lakes — some within the city limits — and forests. But most visitors make the trip to Sudbury to check out Science North, a $28-million science center opened by the Queen in 1984. Perched on a rock outcropping on the shores of Lake Ramsey, one mile south of the Trans-Canada, the snowflake-shaped structure is set over a cavern blasted out of the rock to represent the probable creation of the Sudbury Basin. In a vast rock cavern, a stunning wilderness film is projected in 3D, and in the weather station, visitors can see the earth from 23,000 miles up and count lightning strikes during a storm. Science North has a restaurant, lounge bar and cafeterias. Open year-round, with extended hours in the summer (phone: 705-522-3700).

En Route from Sudbury – Backtracking west on the Trans-Canada leads to Elliot Lake, a modern boom town, created in 1954 by industries attracted to the spectacular lake district by the discovery of uranium. Limited tours of the facilities are available by contacting the Corporation of the Town of Elliot Lake (phone: 519-848-2888), Mondays through Fridays, July and August only. The town of Blind River, west on Route 17, is nestled at the mouth of the Mississaugi River in a way that hid it from lake travelers during the violent early years of exploration. The westernmost island of the Manitoulin group is accessible over a toll-free bridge from Route 17. An early British fort of the same name as the island, St. Joseph, has been reconstructed (it was burned by Americans in 1814), and parts of the large trading center here are in operation (May–September, daily). Route 68 ends at Espanola, where it joins Route 17 for the 143-mile (230-km) drive west to Sault Ste. Marie.

SAULT STE. MARIE: At this narrow point of land separating Lakes Huron and Superior, the rapids of the St. Mary's River separate the twin cities of Sault Ste. Marie — one in the US, the other in Canada. A settlement was established by Jesuit missionaries at this crucial juncture in 1668, and the British and French clashed over possession of the site several times. The Soo (as the city is known, because *Sault* is pronounced *soo*) is currently Canada's second biggest steel producer, its mills fed directly from the mines just north of here. The giant freighters that sail the Great Lakes to and from the port of Thunder Bay must pass through the locks here on either side of the St. Mary's River, making the Soo Locks among the busiest on the St. Lawrence Seaway. You can view these oceangoing ships from shore or take a cruise through the locks yourself. Contact *Chief Shingwauk Cruises* (phone: 705-253-9850), daily from June to October. The locks operate only from April to December due to the winter freeze.

The biggest attraction of the area is the day-long excursion train trip into wild Agawa Canyon, 114 miles (184 km) north of the city. The Algoma Central Railway takes you deep into the unspoiled Ontario wilderness, crossing gorges on trestle bridges and dipping into wide river valleys. The tracks wind around lakes and mountains where no roads exist. The 9-hour round trip to Agawa Canyon includes 2 hours to explore this beautiful area, which has ample opportunities for picnicking, fishing, and photography. Advance reservations are not accepted, but tickets may be purchased at the depot one day in advance. The train leaves the Algoma Central Railway Terminal (129 Bay St.; phone: 705-254-4331) daily at 8 AM from early June to mid-October. A special Snow Train — a cross-country ski special — runs between January and March, Saturdays and Sundays only, leaving the Soo at 8:30 AM and returning at 5:30 PM (call 705-254-4331 for reservations).

In Sault Ste. Marie, visit the Old Stone House, built in the early 1800s by Charles Ermatinger, a fur trader with the Northwest Company, for his Indian princess wife.

The restored first story is furnished as it was when the house was originally built, and the second floor has been turned into a museum. Ermatinger's house is the oldest extant dwelling in northwest Ontario (open daily, May to mid-October, 831 Queen St. E.).

The Soo waterfront is the berth of the last overnight passenger cruise ship built on the Great Lakes, the MS *Norgoma,* and the headquarters of the Firebirds, the aerial firefighters who protect the vast timberlands around Sault Ste. Marie. At the headquarters, you can inspect the planes and see some of the gear vital to their work. The headquarters is open to the public Tuesdays and Fridays from 2:30 to 4 PM during July and August only.

The Great Lakes Forest Research Station (1219 Queen St. E.), one of six around the country, conducts research programs to solve forestry problems. Tours of the facilities are free and are offered weekdays between 10 AM and 2 PM from June to September.

The King's Table, decorated in old English fashion, is an excellent beef and seafood restaurant in the *Royal* hotel (2 Queen St. E.; phone: 705-254-4321). For less formal occasions, try *Guffin's Chaw-Chew and Steer Stop* (Bay St. at the Algoma Central Railway Station; phone: 705-942-1535); an interesting mix of railroad and western themes with the overtones of a delicatessen.

En Route from Sault Ste. Marie – Take Route 17 for 133 miles (214 km) north toward Wawa. Population centers will dwindle as you draw away from the influence of the city, but tiny communities are scattered along the way as far as Montreal River Harbour (65 mi/105 km from the Soo), which is close to the boundary of Lake Superior Provincial Park. These small towns generally are able to provide basic services — gasoline, food, and lodging. Once you enter the park area, however, there are very few services, and accommodations are limited to government campgrounds.

Just north of Sault Ste. Marie, the Algoma Central Railway passes over the highway as it winds 236 miles (380 km) north to Hearst (on Route 11) to join the Canadian National Railway. The Algoma Central was a key tool in opening up the area.

If you are in the mood for some wilderness camping, leave Route 17 at Heyden, about 8 miles (13 km) north of the Soo, for Route 556, which leads to the Ranger Lake Game Preserve deep in the Ontario interior. Paved part way, most of Route 556 is gravel. Camping is primitive, and you will need to bring your own supplies.

Continuing 8 miles (13 km) beyond Heyden on Route 17 is the Goulais River turnoff. After a short drive along a gravel road on the left (toward Lake Superior), you could find a large swamp; if you are quiet and patient, you have a good chance of spotting moose here. There are also numerous waterfowl and some rare swamp orchids in the area. The spotted coral root (about 12 inches tall), which grows only in the Lake Superior region, is also found here.

By the time you reach Batchawana Bay on Route 16, you will really begin to experience Lake Superior. As the land starts to rise, large portions of the lake are visible. The rocks of the Canadian Shield become apparent, and the forest is thicker as you follow the lake shoreline for 50 miles (81 km). From here on, the coastline offers many deserted picnic and swimming spots. At Batchawana Bay itself there is a beautiful stretch of beach, once a government-run campground, now open for day use only.

BATCHAWANA BAY: The Batchawana Bay area is a huge bay encompassing both Havilland and Marmony bays. Its name comes from the Indian *Obajewunung,* which means "narrows and swift waters there," an appropriate description of the swift waters that pour through the narrow mouth of the bay when a strong wind whips across Lake Superior. The village of Batchawana was once an Ojibwa settlement, and Indians still live here, though they are now outnumbered by non-Indians working the local copper mines, logging operations, and a growing tourist industry.

On nearby Batchawana Island, off the mouth of the Batchawana River, a trading post was established in 1824, and it remained in operation for 70 years. The waters of the bay here are the warmest on Superior's east coast, and the rivers that empty here offer good access to the fishing and hunting areas inland.

En Route from Batchawana Bay – Just a few miles north, hidden by forests of black spruce, lies Pancake Bay. The bay was named by a party of fur traders who stayed only long enough to cook breakfast near the mouth of Pancake River. A small park (1,500 acres and 50 campsites) allows you to do the same. Before the railroads began laying track through here, all supplies came via the lake; from December freeze-up to April thaws, settlers were isolated by the winter ice. Pancake Bay is rough country and has rough waters: a lighthouse just north of the bay marks the loss of one lake freighter that went down here in 1902; it was not alone. From here the road stays close to Superior's irregular shore, passing the commercial fishing fleets at Hibbard Bay and the site of Indian copper mines at Point Mamainse, where the "Old Copper" Indians may have worked these mines as early as 6000 BC; commercial mining began here in 1889 and lasted only 5 years.

North of Hibbard Bay the terrain changes drastically — volcanic lava coated the surface a billion years ago, and when it hardened, trapped air bubbles became natural collection points for agates and copper. It is rockhound heaven, and you can collect interesting samples almost anywhere along the road simply by pulling over and looking.

The Montreal River powers four hydroelectric generating stations before draining into Lake Superior. Its 65-mile course winds through some of the most dramatic country in the region and has been painted from several different perspectives by artists of the Group of Seven.

Uranium was discovered in this area in 1847, but apparently the vein was lost soon after because it was "discovered" again in the 1950s, when a mining operation was set up. The Ranwick Uranium Mine, 3 miles (5 km) north of Montreal River Harbour on Route 17, permits public tours of its site from mid-May to mid-October.

LAKE SUPERIOR PROVINCIAL PARK: Established in 1944 to preserve this spectacular shoreline and the surrounding area, this park is 601 square miles of shore, forest, and rising hills. Its highest point, 1,950 feet, is about halfway through the park on Route 17 near Gamitagama Road. Except for the 50-mile ribbon of Route 17 that cuts through the park, this is a natural environment, established for hiking, boating, and camping. One of the newer trails leads into spectacular Agawa Canyon, but it's a pretty rough hike. The Agawa Bay section of the park, part of the shoreline around which the park was formed, is protected by several rocky hills. The curved beach is dotted with multicolored pebbles worn smooth by sand and waves.

A little farther into the park, Route 17 crosses the Agawa River and climbs to the Agawa Bay Lookout high over Lake Superior. Just a mile beyond here are the Agawa Rock Pictographs, a place of eerie and awesome proportions, which has been recognized for ages as a site of religious and spiritual significance. The 35 paintings around the cliff base include fish, mythical serpents, canoes, caribou, bears, and a turtle.

There is no real evidence of the age of these paintings, but they appear to span a broad period of time. By a curious and unlikely series of events, the stories told by the pictographs became the basis of Henry Wadsworth Longfellow's epic *Hiawatha* without the poet knowing where they were. In 1851, a government Indian agent named Henry Schoolcraft wrote down various myths and legends told by local Indian tribes. The stories actually came from the pictographs, but Schoolcraft knew nothing of their existence. A copy of Schoolcraft's version of the tales came to Longfellow, who was inspired to write *Hiawatha*. Unfortunately, no one mentioned *where* the pictographs were, and not until 1958 (12 years after the park was established) did Selwyn Dewdney end a 14-month search when he directed his canoe toward the massive rock point on which they appear.

En Route from Lake Superior Provincial Park – There are additional park facilities north of the pictographs and picnic grounds near the mouth of the Michipicoten River. This intersection of a water route leading north with the principal east-west access of the Great Lakes was the site of a trading post — erected by the French in 1725 — fought over by the Hudson's Bay Company and its economic rival, the Northwest Company. Ownership of the post was disputed constantly until the firms merged in 1821. The trading post was closed in 1904 and has since been reconstructed.

Take Route 101 east into Wawa, just a few miles away. At the intersection of Routes 101 and 17 stands the Wawa Goose — a 28-foot-tall, 22-foot-long steel sculpture of a goose weighing in at over 2 tons. You can't miss it.

WAWA: On the western shore of its own lake, also called Wawa (Ojibwa for "wild goose"), is this annual stopping place for flocks of Canada geese during migration. Although hunters have followed the geese here for ages, the town wasn't established until the accidental discovery of gold in 1896. Since that time Wawa has experienced two more gold rushes, all three of which burned out quickly. Today, iron mining is the basis of local industry, but you're welcome to try starting a fourth gold rush: Just explore the Old Gold Mine Road that lies between Routes 17 and 101. The town is very popular with waterfowl and big-game hunters and sport fisher folk as a starting point for treks and fly-in trips to the Ontario interior wilds, and a variety of shops, provisioners, guides, and accommodations are nearby.

En Route from Wawa – Back on Route 17, turn right at the Wawa goose and head for Nipigon, in Lake Superior's northwest corner. It's a fairly long trip — 220 miles (354 km) — on a road that didn't even exist until the 1960s. The highway curves inland, and the lakeshore lies far to the west, beyond reach except by foot; it is still as wild and desolate as ever. Part of this coast is included in the Pukaskwa Park (Puk-o-saw), Ojibwa for "place for the cleaning of fish." Even the park area is only accessible either from Lake Superior or overland by foot, since the streams leading in are mostly impassable even by canoe except during the spring thaws. It's the patient backpacker who really benefits from this park. One of Ontario's tallest mountains, 2,120-foot Tip Top, is deep in the park, and there are a couple of small herds of woodland caribou in the area.

As the land begins to flatten out, muskeg, bog, and swamp break up the forests, creating a virtual playground for beaver, waterfowl, and moose. Except for isolated communities and a few Indian reservations, this area is uninhabited and is beautiful beyond belief. Fungus Lake, excellent for pike and walleye, and Obatanga Park, a 36-square-mile primitive park, are accessible from Route 17, as are Bogh, Hammer (another pike hot spot), and Marion lakes. The patches of bright lavender and pink flowers that you see everywhere are fireweed; they spring out of the earth scorched by a forest fire in the late 1950s.

WHITE RIVER: Ever since that day in 1935 when the mercury hit 72F *below* freezing (−22C), White River has been known for its cold winters. But the locals get upset at claims that it's consistently the coldest spot in Canada. In any case, they argue (correctly), the dry cold is much more comfortable than the humid, higher temperatures near lakes and rivers. What the place should be known for, they say, are the pollen-free summers (it's a haven for those with hay fever), the magnificent scenery, and the abundance of game: black bear and moose, pike, walleye, lake trout, and whitefish. The *White River Trading Post* (106 Superior St.; phone: 807-822-2366) can equip hunters for expeditions, arrange for fishing licenses, and keep fish on ice. The store now has a deli and laundrette. Rates for the Trading Post's popular 5-day canoe trips start at about $68 a day, including all equipment. Guides are available. *White River Air Services* (phone: 807-822-2222) flies hunters into camps.

En Route from White River – Alongside this still-recent roadway are the tracks of the Canadian Pacific Railway, the first lifeline into this wild area. The small communities that huddle around the tracks testify to the importance of this steel network to the development of the land.

Most of the lakes visible from the road are nameless, just secluded places where you can take a break or cast for the "big one" hiding on the bottom somewhere. Route 17 runs right past the Mobert Indian Reservation, and the White Lake Provincial Park lies about 6 miles (10 km) beyond Mobert. The lake itself is pretty big, and if rumors are to be believed, it supports enormous walleye. Settle for a couple of 8- or 10-pounders. If fishing bores you, try some of the hiking trails or just stretch out on the lake's sandy beach.

About 10 miles (16 km) west of the park on Route 17 is the intersection of Manitouwadge Corners. Here Route 614 extends 36 miles (58 km) north to Manitouwadge, or "cave of the Great Spirit," a small mining town hidden in the bush. An Ojibwa Indian guided prospectors here in 1931, and they found copper, gold, zinc, silver, lead, and cadmium. By the mid-50s a town had grown around the hastily erected camps. So far there are four mines here, and engineers are still "sounding out" the area.

Over the next 20 miles (32 km) the landscape becomes hilly, and the Black River cuts a rocky path along the highway in its rush to Lake Superior. Route 17 also runs toward Lake Superior, through hills of pink granite as old as the river.

Here the Pic River crosses the highway to empty into the lake, and a small roadway, Route 627, leads south along the shore to the Pic River Indian Reservation. The reservation was the site of an 18th-century trading post, and it is the closest thing to "access" to Pukaskwa National Park, which lies south of here on the far side of the White River. Be sure to check with the tribal chief or administrator about arranging guide services or right-of-way passage through their lands if you go to the park overland.

MARATHON: When you see thousands upon thousands of logs piled on the waterfront, you'll be in Marathon, a fairly large town founded recently in connection with the lumber industry.

On a broad peninsula 20 miles (32 km) west of Marathon are the sandy beaches of Neys Provincial Park, some of the most beautiful on Superior's north shore, but too cold for swimming most of the time. Fishing in this area is excellent, though, and the park shelters a herd of woodland caribou who feed (partially) on the wild blueberries that grow here. During World War II, the park was used as a prisoner-of-war camp because of its almost escapeproof location.

En Route from Marathon – Continuing west on Route 17, with the offshore islands of Lake Superior on the left and a mountain ridge on the right, an unfortunate scene offends all who pass — the sight of a foaming, chemically polluted river making its way to the lake, a dumping ground for the paper processing industries in the area.

About 50 miles (81 km) west of Marathon is Terrace Bay, whose road winds among the coastal hills that surround Lake Superior.

TERRACE BAY: When the glaciers formed Lake Superior, the ice also cut a series of sand and gravel terraces into the shoreline. The exposed sides of these steps are full of amethyst, opalite, quartz, and other minerals, all of which are visible from Terrace Bay's Centennial Park, where a plaque describes the geological process that gave birth to these brilliant glacial scars. The town's main industry is a pulp mill, supported by the region's abundant forests. A few miles offshore are the twin Slate Islands, shelter for a herd of caribou.

En Route from Terrace Bay – Less than a mile west of town, off Route 17 on a marked access road, is the Aguasabon Falls and Gorge. The Aguasabon

River cascades over the edge of a 100-foot drop, plunging into a deep gorge as it courses toward nearby Lake Superior. Schreiber is only 9 miles (14 km) farther.

SCHREIBER: If you start seeing double, pull over and check — you're probably in Schreiber. The town has gained a certain notoriety for the incredible number of twins born here. A few years back there were 28, which doesn't include broken sets — some twins have moved away because of the absurdity of it all. There's no way of explaining this phenomenon.

En Route from Schreiber – At the scenic Lookout Point about 6 miles (10 km) west of town is a plaque telling a small part of a very large story. During the 1800s, the lands of the Hudson's Bay Company, originally granted by the Crown, were given over to the Dominion of Canada. Fearing that this voided their agreements with the company, many Métis, trappers, and Indians who occupied the Northwest Territories and Saskatchewan rebelled against the government and white settlers. The open fighting that broke out on the frontier contributed to the unwillingness of the railroad companies to run lines into this area. It also fueled the French-English antagonism within the country because many eastern French Canadians supported the leader of the rebellion, Louis Riel, in his claims for the rights of the Métis. Riel was executed in November of 1885. The use of rapid transit rail systems, relatively new in this area at the time, was crucial to the government's defeat of Riel's forces. In this area the rail line was incomplete, and the troops had to make a forced march across it to reach the fighting farther west. Their march is commemorated in the Lookout Point plaque.

Rainbow Falls Provincial Park, just outside Rossport, has a lovely set of falls, white sand lakes, and fishing and swimming facilities. From Rossport to Nipigon, then down a few miles toward Thunder Bay, the sheltered waters of Nipigon Bay are separated from Lake Superior by St. Ignace Island, just across the mouth of the bay.

Skirting the bay, Route 17 passes through Cavers, Gravel, and Dublin to Kama Lookout, 17 miles (27 km) east of Nipigon, where the view of the bay is considered to be the best on the shoreline. Here a plaque tells travelers about the "Old Copper" Indians, who by all evidence were making metal tools long before Europeans began exploring the New World.

At Nipigon, Route 17 intersects Yonge Street (Rte. 11) as it curves southward from its path across the northern frontier toward Thunder Bay, farther south and west. Yonge Street crossed Route 17 at North Bay as it climbed to Cochrane before bearing west, paralleling Route 17 on its journey through Ontario. See the *Yonge Street: Toronto to Thunder Bay* route for a complete report on Nipigon and Routes 11 and 17 (which run concurrently through Thunder Bay).

BEST EN ROUTE

Since this route covers such a varied area, there are wide discrepancies in the prices listed for any given location. In many areas you're actually comparing rates that include guide services, fishing permits, and equipment in addition to the rooms themselves. The bulk of the establishments fall into the moderate category, $35 to $50 per night, double occupancy. Those charging more than $50 per night for two are listed as expensive, and places charging under $35 per night for two are considered inexpensive. All prices are quoted in US dollars.

The price ranges cannot reflect the level of service, so be sure of what you're buying when you call to make reservations. Make your plans as far in advance as possible, and don't expect to find many vacancies; hotel and even camping space can be scarce in the summer.

SUDBURY

Journey's End Motel – Canada's largest motel chain (122 in Ontario alone) has a very good reputation for cleanliness and comfort. Morning coffee and newspaper are complimentary, and the must-see Science Center is 5 minutes away by car. 2171 Regent St. S., off Hwy. 69 (phone: 705-522-1101). Moderate.

SAULT STE. MARIE

Holiday Inn – Overlooking St. Mary's River and conveniently located near shopping and the Algoma Central depot, this large inn provides 200 standard rooms, an indoor pool, sauna, dining room, and a lounge. 208 St. Mary's River Dr. (phone: 705-949-0611). Expensive.

Ramada Inn – On the city's "golden mile" of shopping centers, the Ramada has 218 rooms and just about every facility you can think of — including a bowling alley and a new indoor *Wilderness* miniature golf course. 229 Great Northern Rd. (phone: 705-942-2500). Expensive.

Water Tower Inn – This modern 5-story member of the Best Western chain is part of Water Tower Place, a complex containing the inn and several good restaurants and lounges. The 180 rooms are large and impeccably clean; furnishings are contemporary, and each room has an original batik on the wall. Among the restaurants here is *Jimmie John's,* which specializes in seafood, steaks, and shish kebab. The new cocktail lounge is *Ripples.* Facilities include indoor and outdoor pools and whirlpool baths, a wading pool, sauna, and exercise room. In the winter, the hotel offers special ski packages for Search Mountain (20 mi/32 km away) and the many cross-country trails in the area. Rte. 17B at junction of Rte. 50 (phone: 705-949-8111). Expensive.

Empire – The area is noted for its many reasonably priced motels, and this is one of them. With 120 rooms, indoor pool, and sauna, it's the largest and best-equipped. 320 Bay St. (phone: 705-759-8200). Expensive to moderate.

Bar X – A 40-site tent and trailer park that has all electrical, water, and sewer connections, and swimming. Allen's Side Rd., just off Third Line near Rte. 17N (phone: 705-253-9751). Inexpensive.

WAWA

Normandy – This wilderness resort has 4 rooms and 10 cottages, a dining room, fly-in services, and hunting and fishing guides. Rate includes meals. Open from May to November. Rte. 17, 30 miles (48 km) north of Wawa. (phone: 705-856-2644). Expensive.

Wawa – A motel with 70 rooms and 18 secluded rustic log cabins, all with fireplaces. There's also an indoor pool, sauna, dining room, and exercise room. Rte. 101, 1 mile east off Rte. 17 (phone: 705-856-2278). Expensive (cottages) to moderate (rooms).

Kinniwabi Pines – Its 12 rooms and 3 two-bedroom chalets are set in an attractive wooded location; some have a river view. There's fishing, a restaurant across the road, and boat rentals nearby. Open from May to October. Rte. 17, 4 miles (6 km) south of town (phone: 705-856-7302). Moderate (chalets) to inexpensive (rooms).

Camp High Falls – Ten units, including 7 cottages with fireplaces and 3 air conditioned motel rooms, set back from the highway in a grove of trees. Open from May to October. Hwy. 17, 2 miles (3 km) south of town (phone: 705-856-4496). Inexpensive.

WHITE RIVER

Continental – Open year-round, this motel has 33 clean rooms with color TV sets, radios, and phones. There's a restaurant across the road. Rte. 17 (phone: 807-822-2500). Inexpensive.

MARATHON

Pic – Overlooking Lake Superior, this motel has 23 large, clean rooms with color TV sets. There's a two-level dining room; the top area serves full meals, and the bottom is a more informal disco serving pizza and subs. A golf course is nearby. Marathon Rd. off Rte. 17 (phone: 807-229-0130). Moderate.

Peninsula – Set back from the highway, this 21-unit inn is open year-round. Rte. 17 (phone: 807-229-0651). Moderate.

TERRACE BAY

Imperial – Overlooking Lake Superior, this in-town motel has 21 units and a dining room. Golf course nearby. Open year-round. Rte. 17 (phone: 807-825-3226). Moderate.

Red Dog – In the center of town, this inn has 40 large rooms with color TV sets, and a licensed dining room. It offers tennis on the spot and golf nearby. Open year-round. Rte. 17 (phone: 807-825-3286). Moderate.

SCHREIBER

Nor-West – This quiet motel is set well back from the highway. The 11 rooms (including some kitchenettes) have color TV sets, and there's an adjacent restaurant. Open year-round. Rte. 17 just west of town (phone: 807-824-2501). Moderate.

Circle Route – Some of the 31 rooms in this motel have kitchenettes. There is also a dining room, and a laundromat. Open year-round. Rte. 17 (phone: 807-824-2452). Inexpensive.

Yonge Street: Toronto to Thunder Bay

Toronto's Yonge Street, listed in the *Guinness Book of Records* as the longest street in the world, runs 1,142 miles (1,839 km) from downtown Toronto on Lake Ontario to the province's far southwestern border with Minnesota and Manitoba. It is a trip from urban sophistication to an almost frontier-like austerity, through the rich farmland of southern Ontario's "English counties," across the harsh, mineral-rich mining districts of the Canadian Shield, and through the trapping and fur country north of the Great Lakes. Called Route 11 once it leaves Toronto, Yonge Street cuts like a surgeon's knife across the width of southern Ontario, touching all the features that have forged Ontario's special culture. It is one of the major factors that knitted this diverse province into a political entity.

Lieutenant-Governor John Simcoe began planning the route in 1793, and construction of the roadway began the following year. Its original purpose was to provide a rapid military and commercial route to northern Ontario and the Upper Great Lakes; it became a major force in the settlement of Ontario.

The road grew as Ontario grew. Built along traditional Indian paths used long before Europeans came to Canada, the first leg of the road crossed the fertile lands of the southern Ontario peninsula, reaching from Lake Ontario to what was called the lakelands, near Georgian Bay. It served the fur trading routes, for voyageurs could bring furs from the west to be transported overland. But as people poured into the area, the rich mineral deposits of the Canadian Shield, north and west of the lakelands, became known, and the road was pushed northward, past Lake Nipissing. It crossed the "height of the land," the central crest of the Canadian Shield, past lumber and mining towns like Cobalt and Kirkland Lake, where the main street is called the Golden Mile because the roadbed is filled with raw gold ore. Most of the towns in this area were side effects of discoveries of gold or silver or offshoots of the lumber trade, and the growth of these industries brought first railroads and later settlers. As Ontario's development pushed back the frontiers, Yonge Street grew segment by segment.

At its western end, Route 11 cuts south, skirting the shores of Lake Nipigon to reach the city of the same name, on the far northwest corner of Lake Superior. Nipigon and the twin cities of Fort William and Port Arthur (now united as Thunder Bay) had been major trading posts and gateways to the lands of western Canada. Here are the spectacular rock carvings of nature — Sleeping Giant Mountain and Ouimet Canyon. This section of Ontario is pure heaven for hunters, anglers, and rockhounds.

Everything past North Bay is outdoors territory, for here Yonge Street is nothing more or less than a thin line through which hunters, miners, trappers, loggers, and others maintain contact with the outside world.

TORONTO: This active international business and cultural center is a highlight of any vacation or business trip. For a detailed report on the city, its sites, hotels, and restaurants, see *Toronto,* THE CITIES.

En Route from Toronto – The 60-mile (96-km) journey to Barrie, on the shore of Lake Simcoe, begins on Yonge Street (Rte. 11) going north. About 13 miles (21 km) from downtown Toronto is suburban Richmond Hill, known as Mt. Pleasant until the Duke of Richmond renamed it in 1819. Yonge Street runs right by Town Hall, where a marker recalls this period of Richmond Hill's history. On the grounds of the *Summit Golf and Country Club,* 11901 Yonge Street, about 2 miles (3 km) north of town, a marker names Lieutenant-Governor John G. Simcoe as the planner of this extensive roadway. A nearby historical plaque tells of the efforts of French Royalists to establish the De Puisaye settlement here.

Newmarket, just 11 miles (18 km) beyond Richmond Hill, is the site of a Quaker meetinghouse, the first church erected in the lands north of Toronto; it has stood on the west side of Yonge Street since 1810. Another early 1800s structure, also built by Quakers, has been incorporated into the Pine Orchard Union Church (RR 3, Newmarket). The history of Newmarket's settlement is detailed in the Whitchurch-Stouffville Museum, located slightly southeast of the town on Vivianside Road, near Woodbine Avenue (open May through September, Wednesdays through Sundays, holidays from 10:30 AM to 5 PM; or by appointment).

Continuing on Yonge Street, the route leads toward the Holland River, with its thousands of acres of rich, black farmland that were reclaimed by patient Dutch farmers during the early 1930s. The broad swath of bottomland opening to view as the road approaches is Holland Marsh. Careful management of this once unproductive swamp and flood plain by residents of this still very Dutch district has resulted in one of Ontario's prize vegetable-growing areas. The view is breathtaking, but don't get so engrossed that you miss the turnoff to Holland Landing at the foot of the hill.

HOLLAND LANDING: A little over 25 miles (40 km) from Toronto, here was the original terminus of Simcoe's Yonge Street. From the settlement of Holland Landing, soldiers and settlers would follow the route of the early trappers to Georgian Bay by taking the Holland River to Lake Simcoe and connecting with the Severn River to the north. This water route comprises the upper section of the Trent-Severn Waterway, which begins on Lake Ontario at Trenton. Before leaving Holland Landing, visit the hamlet of Sharon, about 1 mile (1.5 km) east. This settlement was established by a Quaker splinter group known as the Children of Peace, or Davidites, so named because they were led by one David Willson. Central to the community was the Temple of Peace, erected from the late 1820s to early 1830s and designed to reflect in its architecture aspects of the sect's beliefs. The structure fell into disrepair following Willson's death in 1866, when the sect began to wane. It has been partially restored and is now a museum of local history (open daily, except Tuesdays, 10 AM to 5 PM during the summer, weekends only during the fall).

   En Route from Holland Landing – Bradford, the commercial hub of Holland Marsh, is only 6 miles (10 km) beyond the Holland Landing turnoff. Yonge Street goes through the town, passing acres of the fertile black muck that in its manicured form produces such beautifully precise rows of fruits and vegetables.

   Beyond Bradford, the road crosses a series of river valleys that carry just a hint of the northern highlands to come; you will see occasional glimpses of distant Lake Simcoe as the road nears Barrie. This region, between the Toronto suburbs and the resort areas of Lake Simcoe–Huronia, contains clusters of hardwood forest, small dairy and cattle farms, and a few rural villages.

BARRIE: This gateway to Ontario's pleasant lakeland district, a year-round tourist center, is on Kempenfeldt Bay, an inlet of Lake Simcoe, Ontario's sixth largest lake. As you would expect, summers in Barrie are devoted to sailing, swimming, water skiing, and just about every other water sport, but the attraction doesn't end with the summer sun. Winters are given over to snowmobiling and alpine and crosscountry skiing as well as ice fishing on the lake. Smallmouth bass and lake trout live in Lake Simcoe, and they are just as likely to bite in winter as summer.

An afternoon stroll through downtown Barrie is bound to lead to one of the town's many craft shops. *Artifact* (123 Dunlop St. E.) offers custom weaving and embroidery, as well as a collection of work by skillful local artisans.

If you'd like a look at old Barrie — circa 1840 — the *Simcoe County Museum and Archives* has a replica of an 1840s street, with shops and buildings carefully reconstructed. Several restored pioneer buildings and other exhibits detail changes in the area from 2000 BC until today. The museum is 5 miles (8 km) north of town on Route 26 and is open daily; the Archives is open Tuesdays through Saturdays. (phone: 705-726-9300).

Springwater Provincial Park and the adjacent Midhurst Forest Station comprise an area aimed at preserving the natural environment that created this resort area a century ago. Some of the park's animals roam free, but for visitors' safety others are caged. The beaver dam, continually being expanded and improved by its residents and architects, is one of the most interesting sights (6 mi/10 km west of town on Rte. 26; the park is open daily; the forest station is open weekdays from April to October).

The *Canadian Forces Base Borden Military Museum,* incorporating six collections of military hardware ranging from small arms to heavy artillery and tanks, contains equipment dating back to the "Big War" (World War I). The base is 10 miles (16 km) west of Barrie on Route 90, near Angus. Look for signs with a simple military "M," for museum. Open Tuesdays through Fridays; afternoons only, Saturdays and Sundays. Proof of vehicle ownership and insurance is required to enter Base Borden.

Maude Koury's Steak House (126 Collier St.; phone: 705-726-6030) is one of the best restaurants in Barrie. Housed in one of the town's fine old structures, *Maude's* specializes in honey ribs and is open daily. Head for Bayfield St. for the best selection of restaurants. Barrie's other favorite nightspot is the *Raceway* (Essa Rd.), rebuilt in 1985 after being flattened by a tornado. Track facilities, including a dining room, are all top-notch, and the grandstand is completely glass-enclosed for year-round viewing. The track usually runs ten harness races per program, Wednesdays and Saturdays.

MIDLAND: In the early years of Canada's development, Jesuit missionaries established one of the first inland European settlements in the heart of the Huron Nation. The town of Midland, 24 miles (39 km) northwest of Barrie on Route 27, was established in the 1630s, when French Jesuits made it their headquarters for spreading Christianity through Canada. During the Iroquois Wars against the Hurons and their French allies in the 1640s, half a dozen Jesuits were killed by the Iroquois: Fathers Jean de Brebeuf and Gabriel Lalament, put to the torture fires at St. Ignace in March 1649, are buried here at the Martyrs' Shrine. The shrine commands a spectacular view of Georgian Bay and the Wye River and overlooks the mission of Ste. Marie-among-the-Hurons. The mission, completely rebuilt with a museum, illustrates the lives of the Indians and their Jesuit guests. (Both are on Route 12, about 3 mi/5 km east of Midland, on opposite sides of the highway. Hours are from 10 AM to 6 PM, late May through *Labor Day,* until 8 PM during July and August; *Labor Day* to *Thanksgiving* (early October), 10 AM to 5 PM. The shrine holds Mass daily for pilgrims.)

Across from the shrine is the Wye Marsh Wildlife Center, 2,500 acres of forests, fields, and marsh, with an interpretive program detailing the importance of this varied terrain to the development of the area, past and future. There are boardwalks, an observation tower, and even an underwater window, all of which are explained in a program of movies, slides, displays, and explanations by the guides. The center is open from late May to mid-October; by appointment at other times (phone: 705-526-7809).

To explain and describe something of the Hurons' life before and after the coming of the French, Midland has reconstructed a 1615 Huron village in Little Lake Park (King St. S) and an accompanying *Huronia Museum;* together they provide an excellent picture of both early Indian and fur trader life.

En Route from Midland – Back on Route 11, Yonge Street traces the shore of Lake Simcoe for 19 miles (31 km) to the narrows that separate it from Lake Couchiching to the north. In Samuel de Champlain's notes, he tells of this place, called Michekum by the Indians, meaning "fence." The fence consisted of a series of stakes driven into the lake bottom, almost closing the passage, much like a vertical dam. The Indians set fishnets in the breaks, capturing Lake Simcoe's fish bounty. This particular weir, recorded by Champlain, resulted in the lake being called Lac aux Claies (Lake of Sticks) or simply Le Clie until Governor Simcoe renamed it in honor of his father.

ORILLIA: Known as both an industrial city and a summer resort, Orillia has grown considerably since its days as an Indian homeland. A plaque at Couchiching Park relates the story of Chief William Yellowhead's Mississauga tribe of Ojibwa Indians (called Chippewa in the US), who fought with the British during the War of 1812 and settled in the Orillia area in 1830, at the traditional fishing grounds. White settlers came to Orillia less than a decade later, however, and forced the Indians to abandon their lands at the juncture of Lakes Simcoe and Couchiching (now called Atherley Narrows) and relocate at Rama Indian Reserve.

The city has made two important contributions to Canada's cultural heritage: Painter Frank Carmichael (the youngest artist of the original Group of Seven) was born and raised in Orillia, and Stephen Leacock (well-known humorist and Canada's favorite writer, who has more books in print than any other Canadian author) lived in the Lake Simcoe area from the age of 6, and built a 19-room mansion on Old Brewery Bay in 1908. Here he spent some of the most productive years of his life, writing his most famous works. On display at the Leacock home are the author's letters, notes, manuscripts, fishing rod, desk, and other memorabilia. In all likelihood, Leacock's *Sunshine Sketches of a Little Town* is based on life in Orillia. Open daily, late June to *Labor Day;* tours by appointment from May to mid-June and *Labor Day* to *Thanksgiving* — early October (phone: 705-326-9357).

Orillia's *Ossawippi Express* (210 Mississauga St. E.; phone: 705-325-1559) is a special restaurant in antique and turn-of-the-century railway cars (complete with brass fittings and Tiffany lamps); it has a marvelous view of Lake Couchiching and continental dishes. Closed Sundays. A good way to get an overview of the entire Lake Simcoe area is to take one of the sightseeing flights available from *Orillia Air Services* (phone: 705-325-6153); the company also runs two fishing camps on nearby lakes and will fly passengers in for 1-, 2-, or 5-day stays. For those who feel squeamish about flying around in small planes, the *Sir William Mac* cruises through 25 miles of islands in and about Lake Couchiching. Both 1½- and 3-hour cruises leave from the dock at the foot of Mississauga St. (phone: 705-325-5252 or 705-326-2379). Golden Creek Game and Bird Farm features exotic and domestic birds, with flight demonstrations by falcons and hawks on summer weekends. South Sparrow Lake Rd. Exit Highway 12 at Concession Road 12. Open daily mid-May to early September.

En Route from Orillia – The scenery begins to change north of Orillia — farms grow smaller, fewer, and farther apart as rocky outcroppings become more frequent and wooded hills, rivers, and streams tumble after one another in surprising profusion. It's an easy 23 miles (37 km) along Route 11 to Gravenhurst, at the southern tip of Lake Muskoka.

GRAVENHURST: This town began as a hard-working and rambunctious lumber town, but it became a favorite summer home and resort area during the early 1900s. Rumors persist that its name originated in Washington Irving's *Bracebridge Hall* (which indulges in some mischievous and fictitious geography), but its appeal to those seeking a quiet corner of the world is very real. It is the doorway to the fall foliage route, the Cavalcade of Color, when the changing season paints the trees of Muskoka's lakeside district a blaze of reds and oranges. The northern tip of the great forests of southern Ontario, filled with deciduous trees like birch and maple, extends only a few miles farther north before being replaced by firs and pines, and so the autumnal change begins early here — accompanied by dances, country fairs, parades, and firework displays to match the bright colors of the leaves. Take one of the *Lady Muskoka* cruises around the lake to see summer cottages built in the days when a "cottage" had a dozen rooms and servants' quarters. (*Muskoka Excursions,* Muskoka Wharf, Sagamo Dr.; phone: 705-687-9924; daily cruises during July and August, other times by charter only.)

Gravenhurst's favorite son is Norman Bethune, a doctor who became famous as the medical officer with the Chinese Communists. Mao dedicated an essay to Bethune after the Revolution, and his home is a destination for Chinese diplomats to this day. Bethune Memorial House, a former church manse where Bethune was born, has been restored to its original 1890 appearance and contains exhibits depicting Bethune's life and accomplishments (235 John St., open daily, except legal holidays in winter).

Sloanes restaurant (155 Muskoka St.; phone: 705-687-4611) is as much a historic landmark as it is a benchmark by which other area restaurants are judged, and none in town surpasses it. *Sloanes* serves delicious meals in the old-fashioned manner — even the breads, rolls, and cakes are homemade (and available for sale separately).

En Route from Gravenhurst – Only 10 miles (16 km) north of Gravenhurst, on the east side of Lake Muskoka, lies Bracebridge, which may (or may not) have also derived its name from Washington Irving. A highway sign claims the town is "halfway to the North Pole," and a Santa's Village theme park capitalizes on the idea. Children can ride a paddlewheel boat or miniature train, see Santa and his helpers, and play with a farm full of animals (west of town, on Santa's Village Rd., open mid-June through August, daily from 10 AM to 6 PM; weekends only from late May to mid-June and September to mid-October; closed *Labor Day* and *Thanksgiving* (celebrated in Canada in early October).

Instead of heading straight to Huntsville, take Highway 169 to Parry Sound and enjoy a real treat — a sightseeing cruise aboard the *Island Queen*. The navigational skills of the crew in some tight and spectacular rocky channels are as breathtaking as the scenery. A snack bar and washrooms are available on board. The ship makes trips from from June 1st to mid-October. From Parry Sound, take Hwy. 141 to Rosseau and then Hwy. 3 to Huntsville (phone: 705-746-2311).

HUNTSVILLE: Twenty-two miles (35 km) beyond Bracebridge on Yonge Street, Huntsville is located between the Lake of Bays and Lake Vernon and serves as the western entrance to Algonquin Provincial Park and as a resort center for this watershed area. Anglers can try their skill on lake, rainbow, and brook trout, which are plentiful in these waters, and hunters will find some moose and deer in the woods but may have better luck going after waterfowl. (Check the regulations before you hunt or fish; hunting regulations are more stringent than the fishing rules, and seasons are often short. See *Hunting,* DIVERSIONS.) In mid-January, Huntsville hosts the largest one-day cross-country ski race in Canada.

ALGONQUIN PROVINCIAL PARK: Created in 1893 as a wildlife sanctuary to protect the headwaters of five major rivers, Algonquin is a natural environment park, and, as such, it is one of the most varied recreational areas in the province. Only one road, Route 60 (which intersects Route 11 at Huntsville) actually runs through the park, although other access roads lead to the park grounds. The southern third of the park, those parts closest to the highway, are fairly heavily developed, with a logging museum, visitor center, tent and trailer sites, and basic sanitation facilities. The remaining sections of this 2,910-square-mile park are dedicated to hikers and canoeists and are crossed by two major hiking trails and 1,000 miles of canoe routes over calm lakes, rushing rivers, and an occasional portage over rough ground. No motor vehicles are allowed in the back country. Information on outfitters associated with the park, the lodges and campgrounds along Route 60, and seasonal activities is available from the Park Superintendent, Algonquin Provincial Park, Ministry of Natural Resources, Whitney, Ontario K0J 2M0.

En Route from Huntsville – Yonge Street, Route 11, continues for a little over 74 miles (119 km) north into the hills of the Canadian Shield toward North Bay on Lake Nipissing. Burk's Falls, on the **Magnetawan River**, is about 24 miles (38 km) from Huntsville; Sand Lake, a few miles east of town, is within canoeing distance of the backwaters of Algonquin Park. Sundridge, 12 miles (19 km) farther north, also provides a water route (from Bernard Lake) into the park area. The lakes that surround South River, 6 miles (10 km) past Sundridge, are filled with sheer joy for fishing enthusiasts and are excellent testing grounds for more rigorous expeditions into the Great North.

NORTH BAY: Popular with hunters, trappers, and anglers as a staging area for expeditions into the northern and western reaches of Ontario, North Bay began as a camp along the portage used by the Indians, explorers, and fur traders between the Ottawa River and Georgian Bay. Nearby Mattawa, 40 miles (64 km) east of North Bay at the junction of the Mattawa and Ottawa rivers, began as a Hudson's Bay Company trading post. This marked the turnoff point of the canoe-trade routes leading west rather than due north.

Today you can trace one of these routes aboard an excursion boat across Lake Nipissing to the French River, then down to the Dokis Indian Reserve. *Ontario North-*

land Marine Services (phone: 705-472-9530) will organize the trip for you. Departures are from the Government Dock off Main Street, North Bay, Sundays through Fridays from late May until early September.

North Bay's popularity with travelers of long-ago is probably due to the mile-long sand beach, around which the community grew, as well as the excellent fishing. And, lest the overabundance of trout in these waters begins to wane, the North Bay Fish Hatchery raises hundreds of brookies, lakers, and rainbows to keep the population up — and give sport fishers an even chance.

MARTEN RIVER PROVINCIAL PARK: Once past North Bay, the Bunyanesque proportions of the Ontario that lies beyond the urban and even rural areas begins to reveal itself. The Yonge Street route literally defines the limits of organized society in the province. Along its path towns become infrequent, roadways leading north trail into nothing, and travel into the backcountry is either by rail or more often by air. Viewed in these terms, Marten River Park, only 36 miles (58 km) "up the road," could easily be considered close to North Bay. The park lies in a transitional zone where the yellow birch of the southern forests (used by the Indians for canoe building) merges with the northern black spruce, balsam fir, and pines. Displays of logging tools and tales of the lives of lumberjacks comprise an accurate history of the park area, a story told at the *Northern Ontario Trappers Museum,* a few miles north on Route 11. The museum, built around a trapper's cabin, contains among other things exhibits of pelts and trapping gear. It is open daily from May to mid-October.

En Route from Marten River – Route 11 enters the Temagami Forest Reserve, traveling through its 4.2 million acres of protected forests, lakes, and rivers. This is the entrance to northeastern Ontario's mining and timber resources, and many of the towns on the route were founded in connection with the development of these industries.

TEMAGAMI: The town of Temagami appears out of the wilderness about 60 miles (97 km) past North Bay on the outstretched arm of Lake Temagami (which means "deep lake"). This oddly shaped lake, which extends long fjords and bays in every direction, encompasses some 1,600 islands and 370 miles of shoreline and varies from treacherous shallows to depths of 1,500 feet, making it closely akin to heaven for boaters, canoeists, and fisherfolk.

Temagami began as a fur trading post and grew as trapping and fishing, and later lumbering and then mining operations, started harvesting the wealth of the Canadian Shield. At the Sherman Mine, the largest in this area, visitors see first hand how iron ore is extracted from the four open-pit mines that began production in 1968. Although the iron is of a fairly low grade, only 25%, the ore — in red and black bands — is unusually beautiful, and tourists are invited to take home samples. Tours run Mondays through Fridays from May through August, and reservations are a must; other times by appointment; children under 14 must bring parents with them. Visitors without reservations are limited to a lookout point from which they can see the pit and some mine buildings. Inquire at Northland Traders, in town, for details.

En Route from Temagami – From the prosaic industrial iron ore at Temagami to the glamorous richness of the silver ore at Cobalt is a brief drive of 18 miles (29 km) on Route 11 to the 11B Bypass, then a few miles farther on Route 11B. Slightly south of the 11B cutoff is the *Highway Bookshop.* In addition to carrying a variety of area maps and guides, and works by Canadian and Indian authors, the shop stands squarely on the portage between the Montreal River, heading west, and Lake Timiskaming, on the route down the Ottawa River toward Montreal.

COBALT: Fate often dictates "strange happenings" that produce spectacular results, and one night in September 1903 a rather unusual chain of "happenings" led blacksmith Fred LaRose to throw his hammer at (he thought) the glittering eyes of a fox

— striking the world's richest silver vein. At least two lumberjacks made similar discoveries before a provincial geologist examined the area; he found traces of cobalt (hence the name) mixed into the wealth of silver, and miners flocked to the site. The mining boom died out in the 1930s but revived in the late 40s, when newer methods made additional silver extraction feasible, and the cobalt ore, once discarded as waste, became important for medical, military, and manufacturing uses.

Cobalt's birth as a boom town and its existence as a modern frontier community is outlined in the town's cobalt- and silver-filled *Mining Museum* (24 Silver St.), where tours can be arranged of area mines from May to October, daily.

The frontier lifestyle that characterized Cobalt's origins are remembered in the *Miner's Festival* (first week each August) with rock-breaking, canoeing, and fiddling contests, flea markets, French-Canadian step dancing, a parade, and a beauty contest.

En Route from Cobalt – If you continue north on the Route 11B Bypass to its reunion with Route 11 just past New Liskeard, you'll pass the beaches of Lake Timiskaming at Haileybury and go through the dairy farms of New Liskeard — a bit unusual in these chilly northern woods. It's about 70 miles (113 km) from Cobalt to Kirkland Lake, a short distance east of Route 11 on Route 66.

KIRKLAND LAKE: The legendary "streets paved with gold" sought by the Old World explorers are almost true here: The road construction crew accidentally used rock from the piles of gold ore rather than waste rock when filling in the roadbed of Kirkland Lake's main thoroughfare — Government Road, otherwise known as the Golden Mile. By the time they knew what had happened, it would have cost more than the value of the ore to recover the gold. Since the discovery of gold in 1912, the Kirkland Lake district has yielded over a billion dollars of the prized metal, and the three area mines are rated among Canada's largest. The chamber of commerce can arrange tours of the mines for you, but tours and schedules are limited, so plan this visit as far ahead as possible (contact the Kirkland Lake Chamber of Commerce, 20 Duncan St. N., Kirkland Lake, Ontario P2N 3L1; phone: 705-567-5444).

The old mining assay office has been converted into a museum and contains a variety of Eskimo and Indian carvings, weapons, and clothing, plus some interesting pieces of old mining gear.

En Route from Kirkland Lake – Double back (westbound) on Route 66 to Route 11, then travel about 9 miles (14 km) north to the signpost that marks the crest of the Arctic watershed. You'll recognize the spot easily: From here on, all the lakes and rivers flow *north* toward James and Hudson bays. A little fancy footwork on the nearby slopes puts you in position to photograph incredible expanses of countryside and streams flowing away to the north or the south in whichever direction you look. The area is rugged and rocky, another rich mineral stockpile of the Canadian Shield, producing silver, zinc, nickel, copper, lead, tin, cadmium, and more gold than any other source in North America. This region, known as the Porcupine-Timmins district, is also popular for big-game hunting, fishing, swimming, golf, and other outdoor activities. It is a little over 27 miles (43 km) on Yonge Street from the Route 66 intersection to the Route 101 access into Timmins.

TIMMINS: Europeans explored and traded in this area during the 1700s, but it was the discovery of gold in 1909 that created the Porcupine Gold Rush and drew settlers to the site. A forest fire, which took over 70 lives and destroyed more than 500,000 acres of timberland in 1916, dampened the miners' enthusiasm only slightly, and today over 40,000 people live and work in the area. The town is quite proud of its importance as a major mineral-producing center, and the chamber of commerce will be happy to arrange tours of various locations (Timmins-Porcupine Chamber of Commerce, PO Box 985, Rte. 101, Timmins, Ontario P4N 7H6; phone: 705-264-4321).

Kettle Lakes Provincial Park, on the Route 101 access east of town, is a beautiful area for camping, hiking, canoeing, and fishing — and blueberry picking. To maintain the park's environment, no motorboats are allowed.

En Route from Timmins – Take Route 610 east to Route 67 to return to Yonge Street; stop at the plaque marking the site of a 1700s Hudson's Bay trading post on Barber's Bay. The fur trade started its growth here and modern mining operations continually explore the area, but timber has remained the constant in the economy. Canada's forests cover about 1.25 million square miles (half the country's surface area), and Ontario's timber industries employ some 75,000 people. Many of the area mills welcome visitors, and the pulp- and paper-making process, converting the tall forests into broad sheets of high-grade paper, is really something to see.

IROQUOIS FALLS: It's a little startling, to say the least, to find a planned community, with parklands and broad avenues, in the midst of these forests and hills. Nonetheless, here it is. This mill town has been carefully planned as a model community and is quite interesting to visit, especially because of its contrast to the surrounding wilds. One of Ontario's newsprint producers, Abitibi Paper Company, was founded here in 1912 and conducts a 7½-hour tour, including a 40-mile (64-km) bus trip to its functioning logging camp, a lunch of true lumberjack fare at the camp, then a tour of the mills themselves as the logs are processed into paper. Reservations are advised; ask about current admission prices. The tour is offered Tuesdays, Wednesdays, Thursdays, and Fridays in July and August. Children under 8 are not allowed on the tour, but babysitting service is available. Contact Les Snook, Abitibi Paper Company (phone: 705-258-3410).

En Route from Iroquois Falls – Yonge Street continues north toward Cochrane, some 30 miles (48 km) from the Iroquois Falls access road. Route 11 has begun to arch slightly west ever since New Liskeard, but here it takes a definite turn and begins its journey across the frontiers of western Ontario.

COCHRANE: A major industrial, mining, lumbering, and rail center, Cochrane was established at the turn of the 20th century in the opening days of the area's mineral discoveries. It was the railroad that made, and still makes, Cochrane an important jumping-off point for mineral exploration and for hunting and fishing expeditions into the Far North and the Hudson Bay region.

The Polar Bear Express still crosses the wide Arctic watershed from Cochrane to the remote community of Moosonee, near the mouth of the Moose River on James Bay. Here, on a river island called Moose Factory, a lone fortress was erected in the early 1670s, the second such "trading post" under the auspices of the Hudson's Bay Company. A plaque near the site of the original post, which was destroyed in the closing days of the century, commemorates English explorer Henry Hudson, who first sailed into Hudson Bay — and was set adrift here with his sons. Several early buildings, including a smithy and a gunpowder magazine, are grouped together with a museum describing the post area's growth over the centuries. St. Thomas Church, on the small island, has floor "plugs" that are released during periods of flooding to prevent the rising waters from floating the church away. Inside are prayer books in Cree. Another aspect of the area's history is explained on the riverbank in Moosonee at the *Révillon Frères Museum* (Hudson's Bay Company's French rivals). The British-French conflict for control of the New World focused on the choice territory around this extensive inlet more than once; the museum describes much of the conflict. Only the tracks of the *Ontario Northland Railway* share the immense territory around Moosonee with the prints of moose, bear, caribou, deer — and an occasional person.

This excursion into Ontario's — and Canada's — heritage can be packed into one day; overnight accommodations can also be arranged at the isolated camp. It's a long walk back (186 mi/299 km from Moosonee to Cochrane), so contact the Ontario Northland Railway, Passenger Service Department, North Bay, Ontario P1B 8L3 (phone: 705-472-4500), well in advance of your trip. A "local" train, which stops anywhere upon request by trappers, hunters, or campers, takes a full day in each direction; the express runs 3 days a week in winter, and daily, except Fridays, in summer. Group fares for families available.

In keeping with Cochrane's background as a rail center, a locomotive and several cars dating back to the days of the railway construction have been set aside and filled with memorabilia of the era. In forthright frontier style, the *Railway Museum* is on a spur track at Union Station in Cochrane. Another aspect of Cochrane's development is a specialized facet of Ontario's timber industry — one of Canada's largest plywood plants. If you think that changing giant trees into newspaper took some incredible machinations, just wait until you see how these magicians turn tall trees into broad sheets of plywood (Cochrane Enterprises Plant, Railway St., PO Box 1059; phone: 705-272-4321; open July–*Labor Day,* Mondays, Wednesdays, and Fridays).

En Route from Cochrane – Yonge Street wheels westward at Cochrane, tracing 285 miles of thinly settled frontier outlining the Hudson Bay lowlands to the north and the fringes of the population centers around the westernmost Great Lake, Superior, to the south. The small towns along Route 11, such as Smooth Rock Falls, Kapuskasing, Mattice, Hearst, Longlac, and Geraldton, all cater to the camper, sport fisher, hunter, and canoeist. For a truly memorable experience, thousands of miles of unspoiled rivers and untrampled forest await an adventurous vacationer. And those who prefer a little less strenuous adventure will find innumerable fly-in hunting and fishing camps operated by experienced outfitters. Some of the best of these are operated by the Cree Indians in the James and Hudson bays areas, where the fall goose and duck hunting is superb.

Take advantage of the half-dozen provincial parks along the way; they encompass a wide variety of terrain and geographical oddities. A quick survey includes the following:

Greenwater Park – Centered on a 200-foot esker ridge (glacial gravel deposit) formed over 15,000 years ago, 26 small lakes are all filled with trout (20 mi/32 km west of Cochrane).

Remi Lake Park – In the midst of a belt of clay earth, this oasis of fertile land in the rocky Canadian Shield has good beaches. It is 45 miles (72 km) from Greenwater Park.

Fushimi Lake Park – The clay belt extends here from Remi Lake, but the cooler climate keeps the growing season too short for farming. The fish, however, seem to thrive.

Nagagamisis Park – South of Route 11 at the lake of the same name, offering boating, fishing, swimming, and a bit of history, the lake area was the site of an Indian camp. It is 25 miles (40 km) beyond Fushimi Lake, off Yonge Street via Route 631.

Klotz Lake Park – A 30-mile canoe trip down the Flint River begins here at the river's headwaters and courses north through an area where the banks are lined with flint, used by the Indians for arrowheads. It is 60 miles (97 km) west of the Nagagamisis Park access road.

Macleod Park – On the shores of Kenogamisis Lake, an extremely popular park for swimming and boating; the numerous islands and inlets around the lake harbor pike and pickerel, whitefish and yellow perch. It is 45 miles (72 km) from Klotz Lake Park, on the eastern outskirts of Geraldton.

GERALDTON: This small timber and mining community was founded in the wake of gold discoveries in the 1930s; Geraldton today is the western starting point for expeditions into the James Bay area. Here, Yonge Street begins to curve toward the western extremity of Lake Superior and its coastal towns and cities.

En Route from Geraldton – Originally a divisional point for rail lines leading north from the Thunder Bay tributary into the James Bay–Hudson Bay region,

Jellicoe, about 30 miles (48 km) west of Geraldton, later became a mining town for a short time. Semiprecious gemstones like agate and jasper can often be picked up beside the highway by sharp-eyed rockhounds between here and Beardmore, some 16 miles (26 km) west and south on Route 11. The timber and gold resources of Beardmore, on the southeast shore of Lake Nipigon (the largest inland lake in Ontario), preceded the town's current industries — hunting and fishing outfitting and tourism.

Yonge Street continues south from here, along the shore of Lake Nipigon through Macdiarmid, Orient Bay, Reflection Lake, and Gorge Creek. It's about 50 miles (81 km) to Route 11's juncture with Route 17 at Nipigon, on the northwest shore of Lake Superior. Between Beardmore and the fisheries at Macdiarmid, Lake Nipigon becomes visible to the west, and the tall palisades of the Pijitawabik region peer down upon the highway from the eastern side.

BLACKSAND PARK: Overlooking Pijitawabik Bay on Lake Nipigon, the beach of black sand that gives the park its name lies across from the legendary nesting place of the Thunderbird. Ojibwa stories tell of the wrath of the Thunderbird, who abandoned his home and destroyed his secluded mountaintop retreat as whites began invading the remote territory. Occasionally he still vents his rage through summer thunderstorms.

En Route from Blacksand Park – The area around the lakeshore of Nipigon and farther south to Lake Superior and the Minnesota border has yielded Indian artifacts (mostly pre-Ojibwa, or pre-Chippewa) and enough archaeological evidence to substantiate the presence of Norsemen — Vikings — in the Minnesota–Thunder Bay lands around Lake Superior.

NIPIGON: Spread across three terraces created by glacier-wrought changes in the water level, the city lies at the mouth of the Nipigon River on Nipigon Bay. The river has always been a major route inland, and this sheltered area near the river mouth was inhabited by the Ojibwa for ages before the European fur traders turned Nipigon into the first year-round white settlement on Superior's north shore. The fur trade no longer draws explorers, but the opportunity to hook a champion trout beckons many. The world's largest brook trout, a 14-pound, 8-ounce monster, was taken here.

The *Nipigon Museum,* incorporating the *L. M. Leim Gallery of Archaeology,* has displays of native cultures, logging and timber industries, and a history of the area. Nipigon's earliest history is told by the intriguing rock formations and the structure of the area itself. Open daily mid-June to September (Newton St. at Second). East of town, along Route 17, markers designate some of the formations, like the Kamahill Mesa, that fringe the Nipigon Bay–Lake Superior shore. The marker at the Kama Bay Lookout relates the history of the "Old Copper" Indians, who were making metal tools here long before the first European explorers arrived.

En Route from Nipigon – The 64 miles (103 km) explored by Routes 11 and 17 between Nipigon and Thunder Bay are filled with the fantastic rock formations that characterize the area. Red Rock Cuesta, a wall of red cliffs south of the roadway, is 2 miles long and about 700 feet high. The red hue is caused by horizontal layers of limestone tinted by hematite.

Ouimet Canyon is an amazing earth carving 500 feet wide, almost 2 miles long, and 300 to 500 feet deep into volcanic rock and red mudstone. Several tall columns have broken away from the sheer cliff walls and stand by themselves. One of these is called Indian Head because of its classic profile; other columns have tumbled, breaking into huge boulders hundreds of feet below. There are few guard rails, and if you happen to venture to the edge and peer straight down, you'll see large cracks in the canyon floor. No one knows which section will break free next.

The canyon floor is an environment all its own. Little sunlight warms these depths, and the cold holds back the flowering and greening of spring until late summer. In deeper areas, where even the summer sun brings no warmth, snow and ice cover the ground most of the year, and Arctic plants like firs, Arctic moss, and a type of liverwort thrive miles south of their southernmost growing areas.

This is not a place to allow children to run around unsupervised, and many adults may find some of the canyon trails a little hair-raising, especially when it comes to stepping over crevices that seem to extend to the canyon floor. From the trail along the canyon's south rim Lake Superior is visible in the distance, its surface dotted with tiny islands. At this point, Superior's Black Bay lies opposite, formed between Nipigon Bay's sheltering southern peninsula and Thunder Bay's northern Sibley Peninsula.

The Dorian Fish Hatchery, just off Route 17/11 near Ouimet, breeds speckled and lake trout to keep area population levels high. A few miles farther is the Thunder Bay Amethyst Mine (about 35 mi/56 km northeast of Thunder Bay or 30 mi/48 km south of Nipigon, 5 mi/8 km off Route 17/11 on E Loon Rd.; open daily May–October), uncovered by a crew cutting a logging road into the woods. You can climb into the pits and collect your own stones or purchase samples for about 65¢ a pound. Route 587 travels the length of Sibley Peninsula from the village of Pass Lake, on Route 17/11, to Sibley Provincial Park.

SIBLEY PROVINCIAL PARK: Although the park lies outside the town's boundaries, the port of Thunder Bay claims Sibley Park's most visible and memorable landmark as its own — the Sleeping Giant. The natural sculpture is as perfect as anything created by man, carved into exposed surfaces of the Canadian Shield over a span of centuries. Ojibwa legends, however, tell of the Son of the Great West Wind, Nanibijou (or Nanabozho), a giant demigod who had led the tribe north of Lake Superior in search of sanctuary from a violent tribe of the Sioux Nation. While exploring the peninsula, Nanibijou (who dwelled on the peak of nearby Mt. McKay, from which he could survey the entire region) discovered a rich vein of silver. He warned the tribe not to reveal the metal's presence to anyone, saying that if a white man were to learn of it, the tribe would perish and he would turn to stone. The silver was buried on a tiny island at the far end of the peninsula and the tribe sworn to secrecy; nevertheless, one warrior made himself silver weapons that fell into the hands of the Sioux. Nanibijou spotted the Sioux bringing white traders as they approached Sibley Peninsula across Lake Superior and caused a windstorm to sink their canoes, drowning both the Sioux and the whites. Fulfilling his own destiny, Nanibijou was turned to stone by the Great Spirit, and the next morning the Ojibwa tribe looked out upon him, transformed into the 1,000-foot-tall, 7-mile-long mountain peninsula called the Sleeping Giant.

It wasn't until 1868 that someone stumbled onto the Indian silver cache on Silver Islet, an island barely large enough to be worthy of notice. A haphazard pick stroke exposed $10,000 worth of silver, and a 14-year boom began. During that time, many lives were lost as miners were trapped in frequently flooded shafts, and even more were lost in Lake Superior's sudden storms. Today, a causeway built in the 1930s makes access to the isle a lot safer, and the island's century-old houses, general store, and rare photographs of the desperate miners and their families are an interesting adjunct to the park and its legend.

En Route from Sibley Park–Silver Islet – Back on Yonge Street, Route 17/11, it's about 24 miles (39 km) to Thunder Bay, traveling along the bay's shoreline under the watchful eyes of Sleeping Giant Mountain.

THUNDER BAY: Created when two separate communities sheltered by Sibley Peninsula merged in 1969, Thunder Bay is one of Canada's largest and busiest ports and one of the best harbors on the Great Lakes. Route 17/11 approaches from the northeast, through the gentle hills above the city; Lake Superior and the massive grain elevators that characterize the lakehead dominate the city's south; and Mt. McKay stands, taller than its fellow mountains, toward Thunder Bay's southwest corner. The Kaministikwa

River, which runs past Mt. McKay, empties into the harbor through a broad delta divided into three navigable channels.

This sheltered river mouth was the meeting place, the Great Rendezvous, of Indians and fur trappers bringing their skins to barter with the fur buyers carting European goods up the St. Lawrence. A French outpost, Fort Kaministquia, was erected here in the 1670s; in 1801 the British (who had assumed control of the area) built Fort William, the main supply post for the Northwest Company after the settlement of the US-Canadian boundaries showed the company's earlier headquarters to be in US territory. For the next 20 years, all of the Northwest Company's goods moved through this point until it merged with the Hudson's Bay Company. Each summer, more than 2,000 voyageurs gathered here.

The famous old fort has been extensively rebuilt on the bank of the Kaministikwa River, 9 miles (14 km) upstream from the original site, together with an entire village of about 50 buildings and an Ojibwa camp. The active trading center is staffed with a full complement of trappers, voyageurs, traders, and Indians, all going about as if it were still the early 1800s. There are demonstrations of Indian crafts, blacksmithing and tinsmithing, even a cooper (barrel and wheel maker), and boatbuilders making Indian birchbark canoes and European split-wood hulls. In late June and early July, the *Great Canadian Rendezvous* is celebrated with a week-long festival.

A 140-acre section of Thunder Bay North is devoted to Centennial Park, a wooded area with trails along the Current River and a working 1910 logging camp. The camp and some other facilities are open in summer only, but in winter there's day and night skiing and sleigh rides. The peak of Mt. McKay lies in the Fort William Indian Reservation, where the Ojibwa tribe operates a ski resort on the 1,800-foot mountain. There are six ski areas, including Mt. McKay, in the mountains of this compact alpine ski region, all just a short drive southwest from downtown Thunder Bay.

Cruises of the harbor, or of the whole area including Sleeping Giant and Old Fort William, can be arranged through *Welcomship Ltd.* (467 Parkwood Dr.; phone: 807-344-2512 or 807-577-7875) or *"Mary Ethel" Cruises* (467 Parkwood Dr.; phone: 807-577-7875).

Thunder Bay does have its own waterfall, Kakabeka Falls, and it is spectacular — but only on weekends! A hydroelectric dam on the Kaministikwa River controls the water flow, and during the week the fall is usually no more impressive than a drainpipe in a drought. Locally, the fall is called "Only on a Sunday Falls," because that's when it is let loose in full force (or almost), and the water tumbles over the 128-foot-high, 225-foot-wide ledge into the gorge below. In the days before the dam, according to legend, an Ojibwa princess captured by a band of Sioux was forced to lead her captors to her tribe. Instead, she guided the Sioux warriors over the falls, and all were killed. Her spirit is said to be visible in the spray, although the dam has probably cut down the frequency of her appearances (Kakabeka Falls Park is 18 mi/29 km northwest of Thunder Bay on Route 17/11).

There's no lack of variety in Lakehead restaurants. *Hoito's* (314 Bay St.; phone: 807-345-6323) has excellent Finnish food, while *Chan's* (130 May St. N.; phone: 807-622-2601) is the place to go for Chinese. Both are open daily and are easy on the budget. The *Circle Inn* (686 Memorial Ave.; phone: 807-344-5744) is moderately priced and offers good fare, including Sunday brunch, in pleasant surroundings. Open daily.

One of Thunder Bay's most popular camping-activity areas is Chippewa Park, 300 wooded acres with a beach, a small zoo, several rides for children, and a wide variety of facilities for travelers (south of town, off Rte. 61, on access road 61B; open mid-May to early September).

En Route from Thunder Bay – From the Lakehead to the US border at Rainy River, it is about 270 miles (435 km) through territory ideal for canoeing and fly-in hunting and fishing. Routes 17 and 11 travel together as far west as Shabaqua, about 25 miles (40 km) from Thunder Bay. Route 17 bears off to the northwest, past the tip of the Lake of the Woods and on into Manitoba. Yonge Street, Route 11, parallels the international border until it finally crosses into the US at Rainy River, Ontario–Baudette, Minnesota.

BEST EN ROUTE

Yonge Street covers a lot of territory, and along its route there's a wide range in hotel prices. In the northern areas you may well be comparing rates that include guide services, fishing permits, and equipment in addition to rooms. Accommodations farther north tend to be a little less fashionable and more rustic than in southern Ontario. After all, most visitors to this area are outdoor people, on their way to or from a moose hunt or fishing trip. In the stretch between Hearst and Geraldton, virtually the only places to stay are park campgrounds.

The price ranges cannot reflect the level of services, so be sure of what you're buying when you make reservations. Don't plan on finding any vacancies on the road in summer; hotel and camping space can be scarce then. Any establishment charging less than $43 per night, double occupancy, is listed as inexpensive; those charging over $60 per night for two are considered expensive. The moderate category covers the $43 to $60 per night range. All prices are quoted in US dollars.

Ontario offers advance registration for camping in provincial parks and makes only 40% of its campsites available for those with no reservation, so it's a good idea to plan your trip as far ahead as possible. Contact the Provincial Parks Branch, Ministry of Natural Resources, Whitney Block, Room 3321, Queen's Park, Toronto M7A 1W3, to obtain advance registration forms and a listing of those areas for which you must register.

BARRIE

Continental – This very comfortable inn and hotel has 124 rooms, a heated pool, whirlpool bath, tennis courts, and a fireplace in the lounge area. At the Dunlop St. interchange (phone: 705-726-1834). Expensive.

Journey's End – Sixty rooms offer air conditioning, TV sets, and all the comforts you'd expect from Canada's largest motel chain. Exit Hwy. 400 at Dunlop St. to Hart Drive (phone: 705-722-3600). Moderate.

Willow Creek Trailer Park – In addition to 175 campsites, there are showers, flush toilets, fireplaces, a pool, and a store. In Spring Water Park (phone: 705-726-0817). Inexpensive.

ORILLIA

Fern – A family-oriented resort with 72 rooms and 31 cabins that has something for everybody — fishing, water skiing, a sauna, lake swimming, 3 pools (one indoors), programs for adults and for kids, a babysitting service, and conference facilities. In winter, there is snowmobiling and skiing. Rate includes meals and complimentary coffee 24 hours a day. Rama Rd. (phone: 705-325-2256). Expensive.

Sundial – This is a popular motor hotel with 94 rooms and a view of Lake Simcoe. Pool and tennis courts on the grounds and a golf course nearby. 600 Sundial Dr. (phone: 705-325-2233). Expensive to moderate.

Friendship Knight's Inn – "Friendliness and cleanliness" is the motto here. All 40 rooms are air conditioned and have TV sets. Pets allowed. 265 Memorial Ave. (phone: 705-326-3554). Moderate.

GRAVENHURST

Pine Dale – A pleasant resort surrounded by pine groves on the shore of Gull Lake, the inn has a beach and a dock and will arrange fishing or water skiing on the lake. 21 efficiency units, 1 cabin. Pinedale Rd. (phone: 705-687-2822). Moderate.

BRACEBRIDGE

Aston Villa – This is a comfortable 67-room resort with a dock and a beach on Lake Muskoka for fishing, free windsurfing and water skiing, or just sunning and swimming. It also has an outdoor pool, and golf and tennis (with instruction), for the dry-land set. Rate includes breakfast and dinner. No-tipping policy. Open June to October. Off Rte. 118 (phone: 705-764-1111). Expensive.

Bangor Lodge – Six tennis courts, private 9-hole golf course, and an outdoor pool go with 98 fully equipped rooms and 5 cottages. Open June to September. Golden Beach Rd. (phone: 705-645-4791). Expensive.

HUNTSVILLE

Deerhurst Inn – This northern inn has been catering to the whims of summer guests for almost a century, and it does an equally good job summer and winter. It has an indoor pool, an outdoor pool, and nearby Peninsula Lake for every conceivable water activity — sailing, boating, canoeing, fishing; two types of tennis courts (clay and asphalt); a sauna and whirlpool bath; an 18-hole golf course; a billiard table; and fireplaces galore to warm skiers' frozen limbs. Choice of 122 rooms or 14 cottages. Muskoka Rd., PO Box 1950 (phone: 705-789-5543). Expensive.

Hidden Valley – It's a lot more like a family inn than part of a hotel chain. In the center of the skiing area, surrounded by a lake and golf course, the 100-room hotel offers racquet sports, sauna, indoor pool, and a whirlpool bath. It also has an outdoor pool, beachfront, dock, boats for water skiing or fishing, and snowmaking facilities. Hidden Valley Rd. (phone: 705-789-2301). Expensive.

Highland Court Motel – Located at the west end of town, it offers spotless, well-furnished accommodations, including 15 rooms and 2 cottages, each room equipped with a small refrigerator, a kettle, and coffee. 208 Main St. W. (phone: 705-789-4392). Moderate to inexpensive.

Algonquin Park – The Route 60 corridor provides access to the park's 8 campgrounds. *Lake of Two Rivers Campground* (243 sites) has the most facilities, including showers, a store, a laundry area, and fireplaces. (phone: 705-633-5572). Inexpensive.

NORTH BAY

Ramada Inn – One of the best of the far north, it has 130 rooms, a heated indoor pool, sauna, a good restaurant, and a coffee shop. Arrangements can be made for guests to play on a nearby golf course. 700 Lakeshore Dr. (phone: 705-474-5800). Expensive.

Ascot – Considered a high-quality inn, the *Ascot*'s 31 rooms have air conditioning and TV sets, and there's a also a sauna. Central location to bus, rail, beaches, sports, shopping, and entertainment. 255 McIntyre St. W. (phone: 705-474-4770). Moderate.

Champlain Trailer Park – A full range of services is available, including electrical hook-ups at many of the 56 sites, showers, flush toilets, fireplaces, and a store, all set on Lake Nipissing. 1202 Premier Rd. N. (phone: 705-474-4669). Inexpensive.

MARTEN RIVER

Land O'Lakes – In addition to a cluster of campsites around a store, a swimming pool, showers, toilets, a beach, boats, and space for fishing, there are 13 cottages. The season runs from May to October. On Rte. 11 (phone: 705-892-2206). Moderate to inexpensive.

COBALT

Marsh Bay – On beautiful Marsh Bay on the Montreal River, this establishment has housekeeping cottages, campsites, boat rentals, and guide services. Marsh Bay Rd., off Rte. 11 (phone: 705-679-8810). Moderate.

KIRKLAND LAKE

Commodore – This is Kirkland Lake's smaller establishment, with 27 rooms, but it's quite up to the standards of most people. There's a coffee shop and a tennis court. 1 Duncan Ave. N. at Government Rd. (phone: 705-567-9386). Inexpensive.

Esker Lake Park – About a half-hour from town, the park lies just within the Arctic watershed on Panagapke Lake. One-third of the 106 campsites have electric hookups. There is a store, and boat rentals are available in the park. Access from Rte. 66 (no phone). Inexpensive.

TIMMINS

Best Western Colonial Inn – Set on the Mattagami River, near cross-country and downhill skiing, the inn has 27 well-equipped rooms, a coffee shop, and a 24-hour restaurant. 1212 Riverside Dr. (phone: 705-264-1296). Moderate.

Ramada – Special attractions in this 116-room hotel include an indoor pool, nearby golf, free local phone calls, and rooms with king-size beds and refrigerators. There's a good dining room and a bar with a 6-foot video screen. 1800 Riverside Dr. (phone: 705-267-6241). Moderate.

COCHRANE

Westway – There are 42 units with color TV sets and air conditioning and a mini-putt course next door. 21 First St., on Rte. 11 (phone: 705-272-4285). Moderate.

Greenwater Provincial Park – You should have no trouble getting one of the park's 135 sites since this fairly remote area is not one of Ontario's busiest. All the basic facilities are here, including showers, a laundry, and a beach. Access from Rte. 636, off Rte. 11 (no phone). Inexpensive.

KAPUSKASING

Apollo – A popular place, with 38 large rooms, 9 housekeeping cottages, heated indoor pool, and a sauna. Rte. 11 (phone: 705-335-6084). Inexpensive.

Two Bridges – En route to the spectacular Polar Bear Express train ride, this motel has 23 rooms, some of which are housekeeping units. Refrigerators in rooms and complimentary morning coffee and newspaper, plus use of the mini-putt course. Rte. 11 (phone: 705-335-2281). Inexpensive.

GERALDTON

Park Bay View – Twenty rooms are equipped with all the necessities, and there are a dining room and coffee shop and a beach picnic area. A centralized video system, from which you can order movies, is also available. Golf nearby. Open May to October. Rte. 11 (phone: 807-854-1716). Moderate.

Wild Goose Lake Resort – Twelve cottages on 600 feet of private lakeshore, with boat rentals and hunting and fishing packages. Two fly-in cabins are available for some incredible fishing trips. Rte. 11 (phone: 807-854-0482). Moderate to inexpensive.

NIPIGON

Chalet Lodge – Nineteen rustic chalets are set among the trees. Dining room. Hunting and fishing packages. Open May to October. Hwy. 17 (phone: 807-887-3030). Moderate to inexpensive.

THUNDER BAY

Airlane – South of the town itself, close to the airport, this is one of Thunder Bay's top two hostelries. The hotel has 170 rooms and a full array of creature comforts, including a heated indoor pool, a sauna, a whirlpool bath, and a fine dining room. Complimentary limo service to the airport. 698 Arthur St. W. (phone: 807-577-1181). Expensive.

Landmark – The other half of Thunder Bay's pair of aces, this metropolitan hotel, with 106 rooms, matches any other in its range of amenities and excellence of service. Close to the shopping areas. Dawson Rd. and Thunder Bay Expy. (phone: 807-767-1681). Moderate.

Prince Edward Island

This crescent-shaped island in the gulf of the St. Lawrence River attracts over half a million visitors every summer. Unspoiled by modern freeways and heavy industry, Prince Edward Island is called the Garden of the Gulf. Visitors constantly remark on the island's charming appeal — its ubiquitous farmlands and cliffs, rich red soil, its evergreen forests, its views of the sea, its southern red sand beaches, its long-legged blue herons along the shores, its northern fishing villages, its community lobster suppers, and its lovely Cavendish area described in Lucy Maud Montgomery's fictive *Anne of Green Gables*. In short, for visitors seeking an enchanting, uncrowded, unhurried land, Prince Edward Island is a small utopia.

Once described humorously as two long beaches with potato fields in between, Prince Edward Island is the tiniest of Canada's ten provinces. Some 128,000 people live in the province, which encompasses 2,184 square miles. In 1864 Charlottetown, its seat of government, was the site of the first discussions on the Canadian Confederation (Canada was confederated in 1867; PEI entered the Confederation in 1873). Outside the capital, rural Prince Edward Island is noted for its peaceful landscape, across which the provincial government has mapped out many scenic drives.

Over half the island is tidily cultivated farms, the soil famous for its rich, red clay color. Northern evergreen and hardwood forests are cut by excellent clam-digging inlets and stretches of abandoned beaches. Wild blueberries ripen along roadsides during the month of August. The island has several picturesque inland and coastal villages, and exploring its period churches alone has occupied more than one photographer.

Accessible to motorists by two ferry routes across the Northumberland Strait (just 1½ hours from Caribou, Nova Scotia, to Wood Islands; 45 minutes from Cape Tormentine, New Brunswick, to Borden), the island stretches 140 miles long and from 4 to 40 miles wide. It is served almost entirely by one-lane roads (which make for wonderful car or bicycle expeditions).

It is hard to know exactly how to describe the shape of Prince Edward Island; looking at it on the map, it seems not so much one piece of land as three small islands that drifted together — barely — in a moment of forgetfulness. Most touring on the island starts at Charlottetown, the provincial capital, in the southern corner of the center "island." From there, travelers have two major choices: to go east, spanning the Hillsborough Bridge and the river that almost splits the island, along the Kings Byway Drive; or to go north and west along the Blue Heron Drive. The third alternative, from Kensington about three-quarters along the Blue Heron Drive, is to explore the westernmost section of the island, a route known as Lady Slipper Drive.

Information: Prince Edward Island Department of Tourism, Tourist Services, Box 940, Charlottetown, PEI C1A 7M5 (phone: 902-368-4444). Or from eastern US, phone 800-565-9060. From Nova Scotia and New Brunswick, phone 800-565-7421.

Blue Heron Drive

The Blue Heron Drive leads north and east out of Charlottetown to the island's northern shore, a stretch of 25 miles (40 km) of national park beaches and red sandstone capes, ending at the tourist town of Cavendish. Just beyond is New London Bay, the home of the beautiful blue herons for which the route is named. From here the drive begins turning south toward the southern shore of the island to return to Charlottetown. This route, which forms a loop that begins and ends at Charlottetown, circles the island's center and is 110 miles (177 km) long. At Kensington is the turnoff west that opens the third PEI route — Lady Slipper Drive — for exploration of the island's western third.

CHARLOTTETOWN: The provincial capital is just 38 miles (61 km) from the ferry landing at Wood Islands and 34 miles (55 km) from the ferry landing at Borden. Charlottetown's downtown area features beautiful tree-lined streets and rows of wood-frame houses. The city, concerned about preserving the character of its central core, has passed an ordinance restricting the demolition of its historic buildings. The only incorporated city in the province, Charlottetown still retains its original colonial seaport feeling despite a full array of 20th-century conveniences.

The French, under Comte St. Pierre, originally settled Port la Joie across the harbor from Charlottetown in 1720. In 1758, the British took control of the fort at Port la Joie and, as was the custom, renamed the island St. John's Island. Charlottetown became its capital in 1768 but grew slowly, even with an influx of British Loyalists at the close of the American Revolution. Today, Greater Charlottetown's population stands at 29,000, roughly one-fourth of the island's entire population.

The *Confederation Centre of the Arts* is the city's focal point. Built in the mid-1960s on the location of the original city market, this national museum, art gallery, and theater makes up for its stark architecture (acres of concrete) with its impressive exhibits and acclaimed theater.

In the foyer of *Confederation Centre,* you can pick up a free map of the city, which you can then study over a bowl of clam chowder at the indoor restaurant.

Theatergoers should plan to see the *Confederation Centre*'s annual summer festival performance of *Anne of Green Gables.* The touching story of a freckled, pigtailed orphan growing up in the splendor of rural Prince Edward Island is one of the world's most popular children's tales. The play, adapted from the Lucy Maud Montgomery novel, has been translated into 17 languages. Bordering the *Confederation Centre* is the city's downtown shopping district. Some of Charlottetown's oldest retail stores now form part of the Confederation Court Mall. Nearby is the century-old, red-brick city hall, with its mansard roof and 66-foot tower, which has retained most of its historic character in spite of renovations and modernization. A visitors' information center is located on the ground floor.

Just behind *Confederation Centre* is Province House, built from Nova Scotia sandstone in the 1840s. In 1864, this Georgian building was the site of the discussions that led to Canadian Confederation and the establishment of the Dominion of Canada in 1867. Ironically, Prince Edward Island did not join the dominion until pressured into it in 1873. Visited by thousands of people every year, Province House contains in its second-floor Confederation Chamber the original chairs and table around which the founders of Canada sat 125 years ago, along with other mementos of island history. Province House is now the home of the provincial legislative assembly and is a national historic site.

Guided walking tours of the city depart each daylight hour during summer from in front of Province House. People who wish to explore the city on their own can begin with a walk down Great George Street. Its old brick and wooden buildings have been restored, and the street is lined handsomely with old-fashioned lanterns. (To purchase a variety of crafts and artifacts made on the island, visit the *Island Crafts Shop,* 156 Richmond St., which is operated by the PEI Craftsmen's Council. Closed Sundays.)

One block beyond on the opposite side of the street is St. Dunstan's Basilica, the seat of the province's Roman Catholic diocese. Charlottetown has several other churches worth exploring: St. Paul's Anglican Church (Richmond St., one block east of Province House), established in 1747 and the oldest Protestant church on the island; St. James Presbyterian Church (Pownal and Fitzroy streets), with impressive stained glass windows and relics of Iona, Scotland; and St. Peter's Anglican Church (Rochford and Fitzroy streets), with murals by Canadian painter Robert Harris.

At the very bottom of Great George Street, on Water Street, lies the section of the city known as Old Charlottetown. Historic wood and brick buildings have been renovated as part of a major waterfront restoration called Project Harbourside.

Along Water Street is the *Prince Edward Hotel and Convention Centre* and the Sir Louis Henry Davies Law Courts. Below the courthouse is the *Charlottetown Yacht Club.* The *Root Cellar* (34 Queen St.) is one of the best natural foods stores in eastern Canada. The island's alternate-lifestyle community likes to chat with owners Joe and Gail Kern, to browse through the books, and to enjoy the good food. Island products sold here include fresh eggs, goat's milk, cheese, organic grains, and honey.

No stay in Charlottetown would be complete without a stroll through beautiful 40-acre Victoria Park, overlooking the harbor. At suppertime, islanders play softball (virtually every thriving business in Charlottetown has a team in the league) or ramble through the white birch woods. (Watch for raspberry canes along the pathways during early August.) Along the southern shore, you'll pass the old cannons guarding the harbor; from here you can see the city's striking silhouette.

Bordering the grounds of Victoria Park is Government House (1835), the official residence of the province's governors. Directly ahead at the corner of West Street is Beaconsfield, an old wood-frame house with an expansive porch, the current home of the Prince Edward Island Heritage Foundation.

Charlottetown has two movie theaters, an 18-hole golf course, and many good restaurants and lounges. The *Lord Selkirk Room* at the *Prince Edward* hotel (18 Queen St.) is the city's most formal and expensive dining room. The menu features salmon, lobster, chateaubriand, and seasonal dishes like quail, rabbit, and roast duckling. Less formal and more moderately priced, but also highly regarded, is the *Queen Street Café* (52 Queen St.), operated by one of the city's finest chefs, Larry Wilson. The *Griffon Room* at the *Dundee Arms Inn* (200 Pownal St.) is expensive, but the menu justifies the prices: lobster, scallops, and pepper steak are among the most popular entrées. *Pat's Rose & Grey Room* (132 Richmond St.) has a restaurant and bar, with mahogany-stained walls and leaded-glass windows. This establishment, which specializes in Italian food, steaks, and salads, is operated by the Kenny family, who also own *M. P. Hogan's* (134 Richmond St.), the city's most attractive nightspot. Here, wide pillars and archways separate a long bar from a table and dance floor area. Another pleasant establishment is *Chaplin's* (160 Richmond St.), a restaurant that serves mainly seafood. The *Off Broadway Café* (125 Sydney St.) is also inexpensive and features seven kinds of crêpes, Acadian meat pie, and rich desserts. In the wee hours, *Cedar's* (81 University

Ave.) has low-priced, hefty sandwiches and Lebanese food; open until 2 AM daily, except Sundays.

En Route from Charlottetown – Take Route 2 north 5 miles (8 km) to Marshfield. Turn left on Route 25 to York. Jewell's Gardens and Pioneer Village is a restored early-19th-century village surrounded by floral gardens, a natural pond, and rolling lawns. Admission charge. From York, take Route 220 to Grand Tracadie and turn left to Prince Edward Island National Park.

PRINCE EDWARD ISLAND NATIONAL PARK: Here are miles and miles of dunes, fronted by the sea, backed by salt marshes and beach grass, cliffs and sea-torn rock formations, and more than 200 species of birds, the most compelling and commanding of which are the great blue herons, those exquisitely gangling beasts of the wetlands. Like the Cape Cod National Seashore, this 25-mile stretch of shoreline — one of the most popular tourist destinations in Canada, though never as crowded as the great national parks in the US West are at high season — is at once delicate and durable, a wonder of ecology and balance. The park begins at Tracadie Bay and Dalvay Beach and ends at Cavendish Bay. The herons are easiest to find at Rustico Island and New London Bay.

DALVAY BEACH: This is the least crowded area of the national park. It has only one bathhouse and a sheltered cooking facility. Nearby, on the shores of Dalvay Lake, is the stately *Dalvay by the Sea* hotel, built almost a century ago as the summer residence of a business associate of John D. Rockefeller (see *Best En Route*). Along the Gulf Shore Road, watch for the nature trail, with a bubbling spring, pioneer cemetery, and log bridge. (Don't try the nature trail in the summer without a liberal application of insect repellent.) From Dalvay Beach, walk 2 miles (3 km) east along the shoreline to the Tracadie Harbour area, where you may be able to talk a local boater into taking you water skiing.

STANHOPE BEACH: Over three dozen cottage operations, many of them along Gulf Shore Road, provide ample accommodations for the thousands of visitors who spend summers here. Weekly housekeeping rates range from $170 to $340. For those on more modest budgets, the 25-acre national park campground, cut out of a spruce forest, has 104 campsites and 14 sites for trailers. Roadside shopping, laundry facilities, and bicycle rentals are available in the area.

BRACKLEY BEACH: The area has a wide range of cabins, farm tourist homes, and campgrounds. *Shaw's Hotel & Cottages,* located next to the national park on Route 15, has been under the same family management since 1860 (see *Best En Route*). The national park campground at Rustico Island is just west of Brackley Beach on the Gulf Shore Road. Overlooking beautiful Rustico Bay are 148 campsites set in 113 acres of evergreen forest.

En Route from Brackley Beach – Follow Route 6 west to Oyster Bed Bridge. On your right at the Route 223 intersection is a drag strip, popular with young people on summer weekends. For a pleasant, short side-trip, take Route 251 to the picturesque community of Wheatley River. Just 100 yards before the crossroads at Wheatley River is *The Weathervane* antiques store. Lynn and Cynthia Foley are among the most knowledgeable antiques dealers on the island and are always willing to give helpful tips to visiting antiques hunters.

On the drive between Oyster Bed Bridge and North Rustico, you will see blue herons along the inlets formed by the Wheatly and Hunter rivers. These long-legged birds have spearlike beaks and resemble cranes, though they aren't related; the herons can usually be seen wading near the shore in search of small fish. They are alert and wary of intruders; they are best viewed through binoculars and photographed using a telephoto lens.

NORTH RUSTICO: This fishing village has the reputation of being one of the most picturesque on the island; it isn't, but it is worth a look in passing. The Prince Edward

Island Wildlife Park is a popular children's attraction (don't miss Santa in Santa's Woods). Deep-sea tuna fishing charters can be arranged from here.

CAVENDISH: Native author Lucy Maud Montgomery set her novel *Anne of Green Gables* in this area. Some of the rustic paths that the fictional Anne explored have been turned into a golf course, but visitors can still see the Lover's Lane, the Babbling Brook, the Haunted Woods, and the Lake of Shining Waters. "Green Gables," the country farmhouse immortalized in the children's classic, is open daily. No admission charge.

Cavendish Beach is the busiest of all Canada's national park beaches, and Route 6 between Cavendish and Stanley Bridge has numerous motels, lodges, and summer cottages as well as a variety of roadside shopping and attractions for children.

En Route From Cavendish – Route 6 leads to Stanley Bridge, an area famous for its beautiful inlets and excellent inland fishing on the Stanley and Trout rivers. This part of Prince Edward Island has a tradition of community lobster suppers, held nightly during the summer, which has become a cherished part of island life. The tradition began in the community and parish halls of New Glasgow, St. Ann's, and New London, and is still going strong today. For about $15, lucky guests have a choice of hot or cold lobster, New York steaks, or pork chops, accompanied by seafood chowder, several styles of potatoes, corn, coleslaw, and rolls, finished off with three varieties of pie and ice cream. Call St. Ann's at 902-964-2351 or look for the signs pointing the way.

From Stanley Bridge, you can take a short side trip south on Route 254 to Devil's Punch Bowl Provincial Park. According to tradition, in 1771 a liquor transporter encountered the devil here (perhaps he was sampling his wares) and was so startled that his liquor fell off the wagon, creating this crater in the earth.

Route 6 leads to New London, Lucy Maud Montgomery's birthplace. The house in which the author was born contains her wedding dress, veil, shoes, and personal scrapbook. Open daily. Admission charge (phone: 902-886-2596).

Along Route 20 is the *Anne of Green Gables Museum* at Park Corner. Located in a house where Lucy Maud Montgomery lived at various times during her life, the museum contains the island's largest collection of Montgomery memorabilia, including autographed copies of the first edition of her world-famous novel. The museum has a gift shop, and outside a playground for children. Open daily. Admission charge (phone: 902-886-2884).

SOUTH SHORE: The Dunk River, near Ross Corner on Route 1A, is the best salmon and trout river on the island. The ferry landing from New Brunswick is at Borden Point, on Route 10 on the south shore. Follow Route 10 and then Route 1 to Victoria, a quaint seaside village. The *Victoria Village Inn,* on Main St., is a restored, century-old sea captain's house with comfortable guestrooms and a licensed dining room specializing in home cooking. Next door is the *Victoria Playhouse,* which stages local productions. *Time Was,* on River St., is one of PEI's most interesting antiques shops. Proprietors Gary and Jo Friesen restore antique clocks and go on annual buying trips to Europe.

En route from Victoria – Turn off Route 1 onto Route 19 at DeSable for a picturesque drive along the south shore. At Rocky Point, Fort Amherst is the site of the first French settlement on the island (1720). Only the earthworks built by the British after they captured the settlement in 1758 remain today, and the site has now been turned into a national historic park with a museum and picnic area. Open daily. No admission charge.

At Meadowbank, *McCrady's Green Acres* (see *Best En Route*) is a motel set among 34 acres of pastoral farmland. Its restaurant is known for home-cooked meals and English-style cream teas. From Meadowbank, Route 19 returns to Route 1, which leads back to Charlottetown.

BEST EN ROUTE

Prince Edward Island has an ample supply of accommodations of every sort: hotels, motels, bed-and-breakfast establishments, farms that take visitors, cottages, and lodges. Along the Blue Heron Drive, because of the national park, there is a preponderance of small cottages and tourist homes which are available for rental; and they should be booked early for July and August. They are listed in the comprehensive *Visitors Guide,* available free from the Department of Tourism, PO Box 940, Charlottetown, PEI C1A 7M5.

Listed below are our suggestions for accommodations. Expect to pay $50 and up for two in any place in the expensive category; $30 to $50 in the moderate range; and under $30 in the inexpensive range. All prices are quoted in US dollars.

CHARLOTTETOWN

Dundee Arms – Some of the rooms in this 80-year-old refurbished house have antiques and brass beds and are slightly less expensive than the modern rooms. Try to get one. The *Griffon Dining Room* serves excellent food. 200 Pownal St. (phone: 902-892-2496). Expensive.

Prince Edward – Overlooking the waterfront, this 10-story Canadian Pacific hotel is Charlottetown's finest, with 2 restaurants, a lounge, heated indoor pool, saunas, and fully equipped exercise room. The hotel is joined to a convention center and a small indoor shopping plaza, where visitors can purchase everything from men's and women's clothing to imported chocolates, antiques, paintings, crafts, and gift items. 18 Queen St. (phone: 902-566-2222). Expensive.

Duchess of Kent Inn – An antique clapboard-and-shingled house, just a block and a half from the center of the city. The spacious rooms have period furnishings and hardwood floors, and kitchen facilities are available. Continental breakfast is provided on request. 218 Kent St. (phone: 902-566-5826). Inexpensive.

DALVAY BEACH

Dalvay-by-the-Sea – A lovely resort hotel on Dalvay Lake with tennis courts, lawn bowling, and rowboats. Its dining room serves French and English dishes. Rte. 6, near Dalvay Beach. Winter address: PO Box 8, Little York (phone: 902-672-2048, in summer). Expensive.

BRACKLEY BEACH

Shaw's – The Shaw family has been welcoming guests to its hotel for 130 years. Adjacent to the national park, the hotel has 23 rooms and 11 cottages. Rates includes two meals a day. Licensed dining room and lounge on the premises. Sailboats and windsurfing available. Rte. 15 (phone: 902-675-2022). Expensive.

RUSTICO ISLAND

Rustico Island Campground – This 113-acre parkland with small fir trees overlooking Rustico Bay has more secluded campsites than any other campground in the area. There are 148 campsites only a short distance from Brackley Beach. It is administered by the park, at PO Box 487, Charlottetown, C1A 7L1 (phone: 902-672-2211). Inexpensive.

SOUTH SHORE

McCrady's Green Acres – A small motel overlooking the West River, the dining room serves home-cooked food, right down to rolls and dessert. Rte. 19, at Meadowbank (phone: 902-566-2814). Moderate.

Lady Slipper Drive

The westernmost third of Prince Edward Island is an odd piece of geography. Attached to the rest of the island by a small umbilical cord of land at Summerside and twisted into right angles like a bent paper clip, it appears to be doing its best to wriggle away from the rest of Prince Edward Island altogether, like an eel or a snake just disappearing. But for all its apparent reluctance, it shouldn't be missed. This is Acadian country, home of the island's French-speaking population, the descendants of the early French settlers who established villages here before the British took over in 1758. Two Acadian museums along the 171-mile (275-km) Lady Slipper Drive route recreate the way of life of the French settlers.

Although Lady Slipper Drive really begins at Summerside, most travelers will reach that point from Kensington if they have been on the Blue Heron Drive just described or from Borden, if they have taken the ferry from Cape Tormentine, New Brunswick. From Summerside, the route drops south to Cape Egmont and the Acadian Pioneer Village, then shoots north to the fabulous fishing centers of Tignish and Alberton on the northwestern cape. Tons of tuna, lobster, and cod are caught every year in the Gulf of St. Lawrence. It was near Alberton that Jacques Cartier landed in 1534, naming the whole island Isle St. Jean. Farther down the coast is Malpeque Bay, where oyster beds produce the famous Malpeques. Making a large loop, the route returns to Summerside.

SUMMERSIDE: This town of well-kept residential streets and wood-frame houses is sometimes referred to as Prince Edward Island's western capital. Residents (pop. 8,000) are mainly employed in fishing, farming, and at a nearby military installation. Town Hall (1886), with a fine old clock tower, makes the perfect starting point for a walking tour of the neighborhood, where every house looks like a stately château. *The Eptek Centre* in the Waterfront Mall features art and other exhibits open to the public. The building also houses the island's Sports Hall of Fame. Nearby, the yacht club offers a view of Bedeque Bay and Holman's Island, the site of a 125-room hotel destroyed by fire in 1904. *The Brothers Two* (618 Water St.) is the town's best steak and chop house. The *Summerside Lobster Carnival* in mid-July is the town's popular annual festival.

En Route from Summerside – Follow Central Street to Route 2. A left turn will take you through suburban St. Eleanor's and past the Canadian Forces Base, which employs many residents. At Miscouche, the *Acadian Museum* displays antiques from the early 19th century, including a collection of farm implements, trade tools, and portraits.

For 6 miles (10 km) beyond Miscouche, Route 2 cuts through a barren stretch of swamp and scrub. A left turn on Route 124 brings you to Mont Carmel.

MONT CARMEL: Overlooking Egmont Bay and dominated by the two black spires of Notre Dame Church, this city might serve nicely as the gateway to Acadian Prince Edward Island. Certainly Mont Carmel and its surrounding villages are staunchly French Canadian (and French-speaking). A favorite way to tour the whole area is by bike, tooling along the little roads between villages like a French curé visiting parishioners. Photographers should note the cemetery adjacent to Notre Dame, with several ornate statues standing on stone pillars.

Cape Egmont, just 3 miles (5 km) west of Mont Carmel on Route 11, is the site of the Acadian Pioneer Village, a re-creation of an early-19th-century log cabin settlement, with a church, common house, blacksmith shop, school, and water well. *Etoile de Mer,* in a spacious log building, is the island's most authentic Acadian restaurant. Its dishes include meat pies and *rapure,* a dish of grated potatoes wrapped around pork, then steamed or fried.

En Route from Mont Carmel – Follow Route 11 north for 14 miles (23 km) to Route 2 at Mt. Pleasant. Take Route 2 to Route 14 at Carleton, and proceed south to West Point. This drive around Egmont Bay takes you to Prince Edward Island's westernmost shore. Cedar Dunes Provincial Park at West Point has 33 campsites, 10 sites for trailers, and a beach on the bay. Route 14 follows the shoreline north to Cape Wolfe, named after General James Wolfe, who stopped here in 1759 on his way to lay siege to Quebec.

From Cape Wolfe to Christophers Cross, the island's western shore is dotted with small fishing villages and provincial parks. If you want to "get away from it all," the campgrounds and beaches here are uncrowded even at the height of summer. Seacow Pond on North Cape is named after the seacow, or manatee, which at one time lived here in great numbers.

The Atlantic Wind Test Site, at North Cape, is Canada's national laboratory for testing wind energy systems. Testing is done on traditional turbines with propeller blades and vertical "eggbeater" models. Visiting hours are 10 AM to 6 PM, daily (phone: 902-882-2746).

TIGNISH: The western terminus of the Canadian National Railway, Tignish is a busy fishing village from which large quantities of cod and lobster are shipped every year. The massive red brick Tignish Parish Church is the focal point of town life.

ALBERTON: Years ago this quiet little town was the center of Prince Edward Island's silver fox trade; today the remnant of that prosperous era is a heritage of tree-lined streets fronting large, lovely homes.

From Alberton, Route 12 winds south through rolling farm country. At Route 172, turn right to Route 162, along the banks of the Mill River.

MILL RIVER RESORT: This 500-acre park and camping area has facilities similar to those at Brudenell, including swimming, a pool, tennis courts, and an 18-hole golf course. River Resorts, an Atlantic Canada chain, has recently completed an 80-room hotel adjacent to the park.

MILL RIVER FUN PARK: On Route 2 at Woodstock, this park is especially worth visiting if you're traveling with children. Highlights include an outdoor pool and water slides, miniature golf, paddle and bumper boats, a petting zoo, and a 650-seat amphitheater for daytime entertainment. Admission charge (phone: 902-859-2071).

En Route from Mill River – Route 12 winds around the north shore. Lennox Island, accessible from Route 163, is the site of the island's largest Indian reserve, where many of the island's 350 surviving Micmac Indians live. At Bideford, government biologists work with oysters at the Ellerslie Research Station. The oyster beds in Malpeque Bay have made Prince Edward Island famous for bivalves. Nearby Green Provincial Park is perhaps the island's most beautiful camping spot. On the way into the park, the road winds through spruce and white birch forests and open fields. From here the route returns to Summerside.

BEST EN ROUTE

The western section of Prince Edward Island is sparsely populated, except for Summerside. Many smaller accommodations are listed in the *Visitors Guide,* available free from the Department of Tourism, PO Box 940, Charlottetown, PEI C1A 7M5. For the places we list as expensive expect to pay $50 and up for two; for moderate, $30 to $50; and for inexpensive, less than $30. All prices are quoted in US dollars.

There are many places to camp, including provincial parks along the shore. It usually costs $6 to $13 per night for campsites.

PORT HILL

Senator's House – Formerly the home of a Canadian senator, this turn-of-the-century mansion has 8 guestrooms, a dining room, and is just over a mile (2 km) from Green Provincial Park. Open year-round. Rte. 12 (phone: 902-831-2071). Inexpensive.

SUMMERSIDE

Linkletter Inn – Summerside's largest motel has 82 rooms, a licensed dining room, and a comfortable lounge. 311 Market St. (phone: 902-436-2157). Moderate.

Silver Fox – On a residential street, this is another restored house that's decorated with antiques — it's one of PEI's nicest inns. There are 6 rooms with private bath; rates include a continental breakfast. Open year-round. 61 Granville St. (phone: 902-436-4033). Moderate.

TYNE VALLEY

Doctor's Inn – About 20 miles (32 km) west of Summerside is this fine example of a traditional PEI country home. Owners Paul and Jean Offer operate a 7-acre market garden and have just 2 rooms available on a bed-and-breakfast basis. The owners are excellent cooks and will serve guests and others with reservations a delicious dinner in the dining room. On Rte. 167 off Rte. 12 (phone: 902-831-2164). Inexpensive.

WOODSTOCK

Rodd's Mill River – This resort, about 35 miles (56 km) west of Summerside, is considered one of the most scenic in Atlantic Canada. Among the amenities are tennis courts, an 18-hole championship golf course, a heated indoor pool, a dining room, and a lounge. Off Rte. 2 (phone: 902-859-3555). Expensive.

The Kings Byway

The eastern portion of Prince Edward Island is almost detached from the rest of the island by the Hillsborough River. Most of this 220-mile (354-km) drive transverses Kings County, from which it takes its name.

The Kings Byway starts in the strawberry fields across the river from the provincial capital of Charlottetown (pick an armload of berries for next to nothing). It turns south to the original Scottish settlement founded by Lord Selkirk at Eldon, then cuts across the island's hilly interior tobacco-growing region to the eastern shore. At Moore's Migratory Bird Sanctuary you can observe Canada geese, blue geese, and black ducks in their natural habitat or test your angling skills in the Sturgeon River for rainbow and speckled trout.

The many provincial parks along the route have facilities for camping and swimming; the largest is Brudenell Park, with 90 campsites. The adjacent 1,700-acre *Brudenell Resort* is also the home of the best golf courses on Prince Edward Island.

Route 16 follows the coastline of PEI to North Lake, the "tuna capital of the world," from which several companies offer chartered boats for deep-sea tuna fishing. Catches of 1,000-pound bluefin tuna are common. From North Lake, the Kings Byway returns to the Charlottetown area along the island's rugged northern coast through several tiny coastal fishing villages.

En Route from Charlottetown – For a detailed report on Charlottetown, see the *Blue Heron Drive,* the first Prince Edward Island route. Follow Grafton Street east over the Hillsborough Bridge to the village of Southport. Take Route 1A approximately 2 miles (3 km) to the top of Tea Hill for a spectacular view of Hillsborough Bay. Tea Hill and Alexandra are noted for their neatly kept country houses and thriving berry farms. During July, self-pick farms in this area sell strawberries and raspberries for about 65¢ per pound. Free picking boxes are provided; you do the work and reap the benefits.

Continue along Route 1A for 8 miles (13 km) beside Pownal Bay and take the Trans-Canada Highway (Rte. 1) east at Mt. Mellick. Proceed 6 miles (10 km) east to Orwell.

ORWELL CORNER: This tiny restored farm village depicts the life of the early settlers on PEI. The pioneer mood and setting of the mid-19th-century village are recreated by the historic site's store, post office, keeper's house, church, and barn. Open daily. Admission charge.

Campers visiting Orwell Corner can pitch a tent up the road at Sir Andrew MacPhail Provincial Park. MacPhail, a well-known writer born on PEI, was associated for years with McGill University, and his home is at the end of a magnificent tree-lined drive. The 24-site campground is located just opposite in an open field circumscribed by woods. The park has no facilities for trailers.

From MacPhail's home, walk back to the red clay road past the park entrance. In the valley below, a stream runs beneath a grassy mall — a perfect place for a picnic.

ELDON-BELFAST: These two tiny villages lie 6 miles (10 km) south of Orwell on Route 1. Lord Selkirk of Scotland led 800 Highlanders to settle the area in 1803. The small settlement at Eldon has remained a farming village through the years. On the opposite side of Route 1, Lord Selkirk Provincial Park overlooks Orwell Bay. There is a pioneer cemetery in the park, but unfortunately only a few memorials remain, their inscriptions all but indecipherable.

From Eldon take Route 207 east for the half-mile drive to Belfast, originally a French settlement called La Belle Face ("the beautiful face"), whose name was deeply distorted by the influx of Highlanders. Here, Selkirk settlers who moved inland built St. John's Presbyterian Church with timbers dragged uphill and squared with a broadax. Inside the church are memorials to Mary Douglas, the only daughter of Lord Selkirk, and to the Reverend John MacLellan, the church's first pastor.

Belfast was the site of an election day riot on March 1, 1847. Anxious for their respective candidates to win at the polls, Scottish and Irish factions exchanged words and then blows. Several men died during the fight, and the polls had to be reopened later under military supervision. A stone in the village cemetery marks the grave of Malcolm MacRae, the only Scot killed in the riot.

En Route from Belfast – Route 2 continues southeast along the shoreline to the Nova Scotia ferry landing at Wood Islands. Route 206 inland from Belfast meanders through the island's profuse tobacco district. At the intersection of Route 24, you have the choice of proceeding east on Route 316 or turning right through a stretch of hardwood forest to Caledonia and Murray River. Farther east, at the intersection of Routes 4 and 317, is Milltown Cross. Nearby is Buffaloland, with real buffalos, and Moore's Migratory Bird Sanctuary, with good freshwater fishing.

Panmure Island, 7 miles (11 km) farther east on Route 347 off Route 17, has one of the island's finest white sand beaches. In all, the drive from Belfast to the east coast is only 20 miles (32 km).

MONTAGUE: On the scenic Montague River, this town has a notable seafood restaurant, the *Lobster Shanty North,* which features lobster, scallops, and many other fish dishes. Be sure to glance through the guest book, in which the names of Queen Elizabeth II and Prince Philip are written, dated July 1, 1973.

At Poole's Corner, 3 miles (5 km) north on Route 4, stop at the Kings Byway Interpretive Centre. The center is a multimedia encapsulation of Kings County history and culture and worth some time to enhance the drive. Turn right on Route 3 to the Brudenell Provincial Park.

BRUDENELL RESORT: This 1,700-acre resort (see *Best En Route*) is the perfect spot to spend a few days relaxing. The resort has 50 chalets, including 36 overnight and 14 housekeeping units. *Brudenell* has the island's best 18-hole golf course, two tennis courts, open playing fields, and a small-craft marina on the river. The resort is family-oriented, with scheduled activities for children.

Nearby is the Brudenell Provincial Park, with 90 campsites (some with services for trailers). Guests staying in the park are entitled to use the resort's facilities.

Although the red sand bank of the Brudenell River offers only mediocre swimming, its placid inlets are ideal for canoeing and rowing (rentals are available at the marina).

GEORGETOWN: Once PEI's most thriving seaport, this town has fallen on hard times in recent years. While its shipyard and fish plant are still active, the future may rest on its tiny theater, on the main street. The *King's Playhouse* features local amateur productions.

En Route from Brudenell – For a picturesque drive through rural Prince Edward Island, follow Route 311 through Cardigan along the shore of the Boughton Peninsula. At Launching, its eastern point, you can very easily walk, at low tide, across to Boughton Island. At the western end of the island, look for Boughton's Natural Armchair, a freak of nature where the tide has cut an area out of rock at the foot of a cliff.

At Dundas, scene of the province's annual plowing match in late August, turn right on Route 310 along the north shore of Boughton Bay to Annandale. Named after a pioneer shipbuilder who established a business here in 1855, Annandale has a beautiful harbor — one of the few on PEI that does not freeze during winter.

From Annandale, follow Rte. 310 north to Souris.

SOURIS: This town got its name from the French word for "mice" after an invasion of these rodents early in the province's history. (The mice were passengers on ships bringing provisions to Prince Edward Island and, because they had no natural enemies, they multiplied with frightening speed.) A small park with beach access has been built just off Route 2 as you enter Souris. Some of the island's finest white sand beaches are found on the 9-mile (14-km) stretch between Souris and Bothwell. The town's *Bluefin Restaurant* (10 Federal Ave.) has good homemade fish chowder.

Souris is the jumping-off point for a side trip to the French-speaking Magdalen Islands, located 84 miles (135 km) north of Prince Edward Island in the Gulf of St. Lawrence. The Magdalens, part of Quebec, can be reached by ferry from a pier just beyond the outskirts of Souris.

En Route from Souris – Nearby Red Point Provincial Park has 26 campsites nestled behind a small woods close to the shore. The park has a picnic area, a large children's playground, and an excellent beach.

The *Basin Head Fisheries Museum* is nearby, with exhibits on the history of fishing in the province — and in many respects the history of fishing is the history of the province. The museum is open daily from June to September. Admission charge. There are shacks along the shore, an old lobster canning factory on the wharf, and a fine white sand beach below the museum.

At East Point, so named because it is the most easterly tip of the island, a lighthouse is stationed on a cliff overlooking the gulf, and Nova Scotia can be seen on a clear day. From East Point, Route 16 follows the north shore for 6 miles (10 km) to North Lake, which is both a lake and a seaport on the Gulf of St. Lawrence and Prince Edward Island's deep-sea tuna fishing center.

NORTH LAKE: Bluefin tuna are attracted to the seas of the Gulf of St. Lawrence by huge schools of herring and mackerel; men are attracted to the same seas by the bluefin tuna. Good charter fishing boats are available at the piers of North Lake for one to six people at about $210 per day. Charters should be booked in advance by calling *North Lake Tuna Charters* at 902-357-2044. The bluefin in these seas are big — spelled BIG — and the fishing can be physically demanding: Tuna weighing more than 1,200 pounds have been caught off North Lake. Bringing a tuna to gaff can take as long as 10 hours.

En Route from North Lake – The coastline along Route 16 turns rugged as it winds back toward Charlottetown. Fishermen in the tiny village of Naufrage, 15 miles (24 km) west of North Lake, harvest a unique product — Irish moss, a red algae used as a thickening and emulsifying agent, and a common ingredient in many food products under the better-known name of its extract, carrageenain.

Route 16 runs into Route 2 at St. Peters, from which you can return to Charlottetown or join the Blue Heron Drive on Route 6.

BEST EN ROUTE

While there are few large accommodations along this route, you will find many lodges and cottages with no more than five rooms all along the drive. Many of these are listed in the *Visitors Guide,* available free from the Department of Tourism, PO Box 940, Charlottetown, PEI C1A 7M5. For places we list as expensive, expect to pay $50 and up for two; for moderate, $30 to $50; and inexpensive, under $30. All prices are quoted in US dollars.

PANMURE ISLAND

Partridge's – About 15 miles (24 km) east of Montague, is this small guesthouse with 7 rooms (4 with private bath), within walking distance of white sandy beaches. Gertrude Partridge runs the place and has bicycles and canoes to rent. Route 2 (phone: 902-838-4687). Inexpensive.

ROSENEATH

Brudenell Resort – This resort is just west of Georgetown. The 1,700-acre park and resort area has 50 one-room chalets, each equipped with phone, television, and bath. The property has the island's best golf course, 2 tennis courts, a small-craft marina on the Brudenell River that meanders through park and resort, and a swimming pool — really preferable to swimming in the river. Open mid-May to mid-October. For information, write the Brudenell Resort, c/o Rodd Inns, PO Box 22, Cardigan, PEI C0A 1G0 (phone: 902-652-2332); in winter, Rodd Inns, PO Box 432, Charlottetown, PEI C1A 7K7 (phone: 902-892-7448). Expensive.

KINGSBORO

Sea Breeze – Overlooking Basin Head Harbour, 7 miles (11 km) east of Souris, this motel is an ideal overnight spot for tuna fishermen. There are 13 rooms and 3 housekeeping units, and fine home-cooked meals. Open all year. Mailing address: Souris RR2, PEI C0A 2B0 (phone: 902-357-2371). Moderate.

Quebec

Known as "La Belle Province," Quebec is the bastion of French nationalism and culture in Canada. At one time Quebec was part of New France — an area extending from the Hudson Bay to the Gulf of Mexico, and from the St. Lawrence nearly to the Rockies — which Louis XIV made into a French colony in 1663. In spite of a long battle to protect the French colony and its fur trading companies, in 1759 the British defeated the French and officially gained the land through the Treaty of Paris of 1763. To appease the French Canadians, the Quebec Act of 1774 was passed, allowing the French to maintain their feudal system, along with their language, religion, legal system, and other customs. But after the American Revolution many British Loyalists settled in Quebec, and by 1791 the British government had divided the colony into two regions — Upper and Lower Canada. The first elective assembly was also formed, but it provided little actual power for French Canadians. What followed was a revolt headed by Louis Papineau in 1837. The British defeated the French, but the uprising ultimately led to the creation of a truly self-governing body for Canada. Upper and Lower Canada were reunited and Canada East was made the province of Quebec. Under the new Canadian constitution, English and French were made the official languages of both Quebec and the Canadian Parliament. In 1974, though, French became the only official language of Quebec. Today, still, Quebec proudly maintains its French heritage. As the largest Canadian province, Quebec covers 594,860 square miles. More than 80% of the province's 6,580,000 residents are French Canadians. Its capital, Quebec City (pop. 580,000), one of the most beautiful cities in North America, is its second largest city; Montreal (pop. 2,862,000) is the first. (For individual reports on Quebec City and Montreal, see the appropriate chapters of THE CITIES.) Outside these urban centers, the terrain consists of hilly agricultural land in the south along the banks of the St. Lawrence River and rocky, barren mountains in the north. Quebec's summers are hot, on the humid side, and relatively brief. Winters are long and cold.

We have divided Quebec into six driving routes: the Eastern Townships, Beaupré/Charlevoix and Saguenay, the North Shore, the Laurentian Mountains, the Gaspé Peninsula, and the islands called Iles de la Madeleine.

The Eastern Townships consists of a fertile region between Montreal and New England that is dotted with ski resorts, glacial lakes, and country inns. From Montreal, our route follows Autoroute 10 or the slower, more scenic, Route 112 to Granby, which has a worthwhile zoo and, every October, a 26-day-long food festival. Bromont, a few miles south of Granby, is one of Canada's top ski resorts. Not far from Bromont is Cowansville, with a popular nature center. A detour west from Cowansville leads to Farnham, which boasts an interesting church and art collection. Backtracking east through Cowansville, the route goes to Sutton, which offers great downhill skiing and plenty of cross-country ski trails. Cottage country spreads along the shore of Lac Brome, which has a museum, and a renown for raising ducklings that make good eating. Swimming, picnicking, and regular boat tours are among the summer diversions possible at nearby Lake Memphremagog. Mont Orford, farther along this route, is both a good winter and summer holiday destination. Mont Orford Ski Area has everything for snow-lovers, and the *Orford Arts Center* hosts an ambitious music festival every summer. Summer theater and three well-known inns are found in North Hatley, on Lake Massawippi. The route ends in Sherbrooke, the industrial center of the Eastern Townships, with another ski resort (Mont Bellevue), a university, galleries, and museums.

The Beaupré/Charlevoix and Saguenay route takes you from Quebec City, northeast along the banks of the St. Lawrence River and finally to the Laurentian Mountains. You will pass the historic French villages of Giffard, Beauport, Courville, Montmorency Falls, Ile d'Orléans, and the shrine of Ste. Anne de Beaupré. From a detour to Parc du Mont-Ste.-Anne — where you can ski during the winter and visit the Ste. Anne Falls in spring, summer, and fall — the road continues to St. Tite des Caps, a mountain village; past Baie St. Paul; to St. Joseph de la Rive, where you can ferry to Ile aux Coudres. Along the way, you will drive through La Malbaie, a popular fishing area, and Cap à l'Aigle, where eagles nest. The wilderness begins at Havre St. Pierre, on the North Shore, and for those who prefer festivals, the friendly town of Chicoutimi is the site of an annual winter carnival.

The North Shore exploration picks up the route at Tadoussac and runs past Saguenay fjord along the St. Lawrence River toward Labrador. This is a sparsely settled area (five inhabitants per square mile along the coast and only one person per square mile inland) of mountains, trout-filled lakes, and forests full of bear, caribou, and moose. The route takes you through the lakes and farms of Petits Bergeronnes to Ilets Jérémie, a former Hudson's Bay Company trading post; past the hydroelectric plant and wildlife reserve Baie Comeau; through the fishing village of Franquelin at the foothills of the Laurentians; and alongside the rivers and lakes of Port Cartier and Sept Iles.

The Laurentian Mountains lie along the southern boundary of the glacial formation known as the Canadian Shield between the Ottawa and Saguenay Rivers. It is a region made up of parks, reserves, and resorts. The first route begins at Trois Rivières, halfway between Montreal and Quebec at the mouth of the St. Maurice River, and takes you to La Mauricie National Park, St. Maurice Reserve, and La Tuque Park. Another route runs north from Quebec to Laurentides Park, a camping and canoeing area; or, from north of Montreal to the ski slopes and resorts of St. Sauveur and Ste. Agathe des Monts, and on to St. Jovite and Mont Tremblant. A third route runs from the town of Hull through the Gatineau Valley to La Vérendrye reserve at the western end of the Laurentian range, where you can hunt moose and fish for trout.

One of the oldest landmasses on earth, the Gaspé Peninsula is an area of old-fashioned fishing settlements where people still cast with homemade nets. The route leaves Quebec City along the south bank of the St. Lawrence and encircles the peninsula, ending at Ste. Flavie and Mont Joli. You will pass St. Jean Port Joli, a handicrafts center; Rimouski, a deep-sea and river fishing port; Matapédia Lake, a salmon fishing center; the Micmac Indian reservation cooperative in Maria (where handmade snowshoes are sold); Port Daniel Park; Percé, home of Percé Rock; the town of Gaspé, where wildlife enthusiasts gather to observe animals and birds; and the salmon hatchery at Ste. Anne des Monts.

The section on Iles de la Madeleine in the Gulf of St. Lawrence, 180 miles (290 km) east-southeast of the Gaspé Peninsula, describes a remote archipelago of about 12 islands, only 7 of which are inhabited. The residents make their living from fishing: Herring, mackerel, scallops, cod, halibut, and lobster are the main catch. In spring and fall, naturalists observe migratory birds and animals. During the summer, many vacationers make their way to these islands via the Cap Tourmentine ferry and Borden, PEI.

Information: Ministère du Tourisme du Québec, CP 20,000, Quebec City, Quebec G1K 7X2 (phone: 800-361-5405 in Quebec; 514-873-2015 from Montreal and elsewhere; 800-361-6490 from Ontario and the Maritimes; 800-443-7000 from the eastern US).

The Eastern Townships

Sometimes called Quebec's best-kept secret, this scenic area of woods and glacial lakes, in the upper reaches of the Appalachian range, is just an hour's drive from Montreal. Long a popular vacation cottage area among Montrealers, the Eastern Townships region has gained an enthusiastic new following during the last 15 years. Now a busy resort area, it features such popular diversions as horseback riding, swimming, sailing, and festivals galore in summer; brilliant foliage worth biking or hiking through and cider mills fragrant with fresh-pressed apples in the fall; and alpine (downhill) and Nordic (cross-country) skiing, snowmobiling, and snowshoeing all winter. Winter facilities have grown to meet the increased demand: There are now some 14 alpine ski centers (such as Bromont, Orford, Owl's Head, and Sutton), more than 800 miles of cross-country ski trails, and close to 100 miles of snowshoeing tracks. (For more details, consult *Downhill Skiing* in DIVERSIONS.) It is also prime snowmobile country. The vehicle was invented in this area, and every February in the village of Valcourt an international snowmobile festival celebrates this sport. The townships' proximity to the American border states of Maine, New Hampshire, and Vermont, just across the road in some cases, makes it a favorite stopping-off place for New Englanders on their way to Montreal, and for Montrealers traveling in the opposite direction.

The Eastern Townships gets its name by virtue of its location east of Montreal. It was largely settled and developed by former New Englanders — known in Canada as United Empire Loyalists — who poured over the nearby border between 1774 and 1840 to escape, first, the American Revolution and, later, the government of the independent United States of America. Loyal to the King of England, settlers came to British North America and set up farms similar to their former homes south of the US-Canada border.

Prior to this influx, the earliest townshippers were the Abnaki Indians and other, smaller tribes who gave the region its romantic place names: Coaticook, Massawippi, Megantic, and Memphremagog. When Quebec was New France, a portion of the region known as Haut Saint-François was a trapping area that remained undeveloped until the Loyalists arrived. Town names like Granby, Sherbrooke, and Waterloo attest to the region's British heritage. However, following the construction of a rail network in 1852, increasing numbers of French-speaking Quebecois were drawn to this fertile land. Today, the area's residents are practically 95% francophone, and they refer to their home as "Estrie," a combination of the word "est" meaning east and "patrie" for homeland.

The region extends north and west from the New England border states and is flanked by the Yamaska and Chaudière rivers on either side. It begins at the town of Granby in the west, embracing Richmond and Asbestos to the north and Lac-Mégantic and Thetford Mines to the east. Although small compared to other vast spaces in the province, the townships make up for their diminutive size with spectacular scenery and a surplus of activities. Sherbrooke, the eastern terminus of this route, is 100 miles (160 km) from Montreal, so exploring the area is an easy day or weekend excursion from there.

> **En route from Montreal** – Head east from Montreal on either the high-speed Eastern Townships Autoroute, Route 10, or the winding (and far more scenic), older Route 112. The latter passes through Rougemont, a small town often considered a suburb of Montreal, known for its apple orchards and cider mills. If you follow this route in the fall, it is a great place to pick, buy, and eat apples, and to watch them being pressed into cider; you can purchase apple products, breads, and crafts all year. The town's apple interpretation center (488 Principale St.; phone: 514-469-3600 or 469-3967), in a former refrigerated warehouse, has an audiovisual presentation on the fruit's cultivation and arranges apple-picking excursions in the fall. Open May through October. Closed Mondays.
>
> **Granby:** The townships truly begin in Granby, on Route 112, just off the autoroute. Formerly known for its zoo, Granby has more recently been dubbed the Gastronomic Capital of Quebec, thanks to a month-long food festival staged here every October; regional specialties and dishes are created by guest chefs for visitors to sample at a number of restaurants, hostelries, and community centers in town (phone: 514-372-7272). Granby's zoo — in addition to 1,000 animals, a children's petting section, plenty of rides, and a picnic area — claims to have the only reptile farm in Canada. Located at 347 Bourget St. (phone: 514-372-9113), the zoo is open from May through October. The Lac Boivin nature preserve, at 700 Drummond St. (phone: 514-375-3861), features a collection of European fountains and nature trails. Nearby Yamaska Provincial Park, on Rural Route 2 (phone: 514-373-3204), is worth a short detour for its swimming, windsurfing, hiking, and picnicking facilities. A few miles south of Granby, just off the autoroute, is Bromont, one of a quartet of major mountains developed for skiing in the Eastern Townships.
>
> **Bromont:** This resort area is most popular during the winter, thanks to the Station Touristique Bromont, which has the longest illuminated night ski runs in Canada. There are 26 slopes in all, 12 of which operate at night, plus a ski school, rental shop, and restaurant. The entrance to the ski center is at 150 Champlain St. (phone: 514-534-2200). During the summer, Bromont's visitors take to its alpine water slides, also at the tourist station, or enjoy the lake's fine swimming and sailing. Bromont is also a great

place for horseback riding at *Centre Equestre Bromont* (100 Laproirie St.; phone: 514-534-3255). The *Bromont Equestrian Festival* in mid-July is one of the top events of the summer.

En route from Bromont – Hwy. 241 South goes to Cowansville and its nature center (corner Church and McKinnon streets), where water lovers can sail, windsurf, kayak, or swim on Lake Davignon from mid-June to *Labor Day* (phone: 514-263-4311). A detour west from Cowansville — via Jean-Jacques Bertrand Blvd. to the junction of Hwy. 104 West — leads to Farnham, worth a stop to visit Saint-Romuald Church (1904) and its collection of works by Quebec painter Ozias Leduc. From Cowansville, a short drive east on Route 104 to the junction of routes 139 and 215 puts you in Sutton, virtually in sight of the Vermont border. Some of the best skiing in eastern Canada can be enjoyed at Mont Sutton, which has a 1,500-foot vertical drop and 54 downhill trails. The woods and meadows surrounding the ski area have extensive cross-country trails as well. During warmer seasons, the public market, held every Saturday morning, harkens back to the farm life of an earlier time. From Sutton, head north on Route 215 to the town of Lac Brome, formerly Knowlton (and still called that by many locals).

Lac Brome: A choice vacation spot, this cottage country sprawls along the shore of Lac Brome, made famous by its delicious ducklings. Summer activities center around the lake, and during the winter there is skiing at nearby Mont Glen. The *Brome County Historical Museum* (130 Lakeside Rd.; phone: 514-243-6782) is housed in buildings dating back to the turn of the century, and its exhibits of furnishings and tools re-create the life of the Loyalist settlers. Open mid-May through September.

En route from Lac Brome – Stay on Route 215 north — past the autoroute — until you reach Waterloo, a little valley village set against the rolling Eastern Townships mountains. Founded by Loyalists during the 1790s, Waterloo claims to be the mushroom-growing capital of Canada. It is also the site of North America's only hunting museum, the *Musée Québécois de la Chasse* (45 Horizon Rd.; phone: 514-539-0501), which features a large taxidermic collection. Open from late-May to mid-September. From Waterloo, hop on the autoroute and head west about 15 miles (24 km) to the Magog-Orford area.

Magog: Pronounced *Ma*-gog, from a corruption of the Abnaki term Memrobagak, meaning "great expanse of water," this town lies at the northernmost tip of Lake Memphremagog. It is busy all summer long with tourists and seasonal residents, who often picnic and swim at the public beach on Merry Point. The motor launch *Adventure II* makes regular tours of the lake, while the International Swim Marathon attracts thousands of spectators in August. To celebrate the turning of the leaves each fall, the town hosts the *Magog Festival of Colors. Auberge de l'Étoile,* right in the heart of town (1133 Principale W.; phone: 819-843-6521), is an excellent spot to sample the area's Lac Brome duckling.

Mont Orford: Both exits 115 and 118 off the autoroute lead to Mont Orford, known for its ski center, scenic Stukely Lake, a provincial campground, and an ambitious summer music festival. The highlight here is the 2,600-foot peak of the Mont Orford Ski Area (phone: 819-843-6548), which has 32 trails traversing its 1,772-foot vertical drop. Mont Orford Provincial Park is much more than just a summer sports paradise: Since 1951, it has also been the site of a leading Canadian art center. A 500-seat concert hall, surrounded by scattered chalets hidden amid the trees, is the focal point of the Orford Arts Center, which is the scene of *Festival Orford.* One of Canada's best-known annual music festivals, this event begins in early July and concludes at the end of August. The summer home of the country's national youth orchestra, *Les Jeunesses Musicales,* the Orford hills come alive daily with the sound of classical, jazz, and popular music at both indoor and outdoor locations, including Victoria, Blanchard, Jacques Cartier, and Camirand parks. (The festival's Sunday brunch and supper concerts are extremely popular.) Students from all over the world attend the center's summer music school, and the public is invited to listen in on some of the master classes. The *Orford Arts Centre* is just off the Eastern Townships Autoroute, exit 118 on Route 141 North (phone: 819-843-3981).

The area also includes an 18-hole public golf course, open May to mid-October (phone: 819-843-5688), summer chairlift rides (phone: 819-843-6548), and a number of resorts. The Orford fishing center, 555 Alfred-Desrochers St., allows unlicensed angling for speckled and rainbow trout and provides picnic grounds on the site.

En route from Mont Orford – The autoroute goes directly to Sherbrooke, the heart of the Eastern Townships, but a more scenic circular route involves a quick backtrack to Magog to pick up Route 141 to Ayer's Cliff, then to Hwy. 143, around the jagged shoreline to Lake Massawippi and its resort community, and lastly to North Hatley. Ayer's Cliff, on the lake's southern banks, offers a wide range of summer and winter facilities and equipment, including cottages, pedal boats, kayaks, rowboats, and fishing tackle. It is home to the *Ripplecove Inn,* an old-fashioned resort complex of cottages and a main house overlooking the water. Montrealers don't seem to mind driving an hour or so just to enjoy the hostelry's award-winning food; guests also make good use of the pool, tennis and shuffleboard courts, and the sailboats and paddleboats (phone: 819-838-4296). The town has a public beach and a number of antiques stores.

North Hatley: One of the area's most popular destinations, the village is spread out along the northern banks of the lake. This is the site of two of the Eastern Townships' better-known inns and a summer theater. The *Piggery Theatre,* Quebec's only English-language summer theater, has a wide-ranging repertoire, from Broadway hits to Canadian productions. The theater's restaurant serves tasty country suppers prior to curtain time at 8 PM. The *Piggery* is off Autoroute 10 at exit 21 (phone: 819-842-2191). Both *Hovey Manor,* with its art gallery, and the *Auberge Hatley* (see *Best En Route* for both hotels), a member of the Relais & Châteaux group, are in North Hatley, as are a number of craft studios and galleries. The *Lake Massawippi Festival,* held from mid-June to mid-August, is highlighted by organ recitals at St. Barnabas Church and Sunday brunch "Sons et Brioches" concerts at the United Church.

Sherbrooke: Often called the Queen of Estrie, Sherbrooke is the area's industrial and cultural center. With just over 100,000 inhabitants, this small city, dating back to 1791, is home to the University of Sherbrooke. It is also the site of a number of art galleries and museums, such as the *Sherbrooke Museum of Fine Arts* at 86 Wellington St. (phone: 819-821-2115), which features a collection of 19th-century art inspired by local scenery. The town also has an imposing cathedral and an old seminary. During the winter, Sherbrooke is served by its own alpine and cross-country skiing facilities in several scenic municipal parks and at Mont Bellevue, a mountain just blocks from the downtown core. The city also takes advantage of activities at nearby Mont Orford — roughly 20 miles (32 km) east — with its ski slopes, cross-country runs, and summer festival.

The neighboring small town of Lennoxville, south of Sherbrooke on Route 143, is the site of one of Canada's leading universities, Bishop's (1843). The buildings that spread over the peaceful little campus were inspired by the architecture at Oxford University in England; visitors to both institutions have remarked on their similarities. Lennoxville's main street harbors a number of well-stocked antiques shops, while the *Lennoxville-Ascot Museum,* housing displays relating to the area's history, stands at 50 Park St. (phone: 819-569-1179; or 562-4949 in summer).

BEST EN ROUTE

The area is known for its excellent inns, but there is also a variety of accommodations in resort hotels, motels, and bed-and-breakfast establishments. The hostelries listed here all feature basic services and amenities. Prices vary with the fluctuation of exchange rates and the season. Expect to pay over $70 for a double room in the expensive range, $55 to $75 in the establishments listed as moderate, and under $55 in the inexpensive category. All prices are quoted in US dollars.

GRANBY

Bon Soir – Within walking distance of most Granby restaurants, this 44-unit motel has a pool but no dining room. 1587 Principale St. (phone: 514-378-7947). Moderate.

Le Castel de l'Estrie – This comfortable, 137-unit motel has kitchenettes and a satisfactory dining room. 901 Principale St. (phone: 514-378-9071). Moderate.

Motel du Lac – Here is a 36-unit motel with full-service restaurant. Bargain ski packages are available in the winter. Swimming pool. 255 Denison St. E. (phone: 514-372-5930). Inexpensive.

BROMONT

Auberge Bromont – An inn with motel units (55 rooms, all told) close to ski slopes, cross-country ski trails, and a golf course. It has an outdoor pool and a fairly good restaurant. 95 Montmorency St. (phone: 514-534-2200). Expensive.

Loft Acres – A country inn in an old farmhouse is the centerpiece of this complex. Around it is a condominium community with studio and 1-bedroom units available for overnight lodging. Popular bar and restaurant. Near Bromont and Mont Sutton. Rte. 139, West Brome (phone: 514-263-3294). Expensive.

La Petite Auberge – A 6-room inn, near ski hills, with very good dining. 360 Pierre La Porte Blvd. (phone: 514-534-2707). Inexpensive.

SUTTON

Centre Paulette Hiriart – Close to downhill and cross-country skiing, this 9-room establishment has a dining room and a pool. McCullough Rd. (phone: 514-538-2903). Expensive.

La Paimpolaise – This 28-room hotel is close to ski slopes and has good guest services and a fair dining room. In the summer, tennis and swimming are available. Chemin de Ski (phone: 514-538-3213). Moderate.

Horizon – A modern place with 48 rooms, an indoor pool and sauna, and a dining room that features old-fashioned roast pig every Thursday night. Cross-country ski trails ribbon the property. Chemin Mont Sutton (phone: 514-538-3212). Inexpensive.

MONT ORFORD

Auberge Chéribourg and Villas – This 42-room hotel has an outdoor pool and first-rate dining room. 2603 Chemin du Parc (phone: 819-843-3308). Expensive.

Auberge Estrimont – The best place to stay in the area, this 46-unit resort features rooms in the main house or accommodations in 50 completely equipped chalets with fireplaces and kitchens. The main house has a good dining room. Squash and racquetball courts, 2 golf courses, a sauna, and a swimming pool round out the facilities. Exit 118 off the Eastern Townships Autoroute. 44 l'Auberge Ave. (phone: 819-843-1616). Expensive.

Auberge du Parc Orford – Right in the park, with 42 units equipped with kitchenettes. There is also a restaurant, café, swimming pool, and grocery store on the premises. 1259 Montagne Rd. (phone: 819-843-8887). Moderate.

NORTH HATLEY

Hatley Inn – A member of the Relais & Châteaux group, this country inn was built in 1903 as a summer house on a beautiful piece of property overlooking Lake

Massawippi. The 23 colonial-style rooms are comfortably furnished with antique pieces; some have fireplaces. Sports include swimming in the pool or lake, sailing, golf, and riding. Award-winning chef Guy Bohec oversees the excellent dining room. On Magog Hwy. (phone: 819-842-2451). Expensive.

Hovey Manor – Formerly a private estate, this manor house is furnished with antiques. Most of the 35 rooms have views of Lake Massawippi and special suites feature wood-burning fireplaces, whirlpool baths, and private balconies. Water sports and tennis are available all summer. The inn's dining room is highly regarded, rating "four forks" from the Quebec government's tourism department. Hovey Rd. (phone: 819-842-2421). Expensive.

AYLER'S CLIFF

Ripplecove Inn – Situated at Lake Massawippi, this intimate 27-room country inn is just minutes away from five major alpine ski centers. It has one of the best restaurants in the entire region. 700 Ripplecove Rd. (phone: 819-838-4296). Expensive.

For more details on either the *Hatley Inn* or the *Hovey Manor,* see *Canada's Special Havens* in DIVERSIONS.

Beaupré/Charlevoix and Saguenay

The Beaupré/Charlevoix coast is the section of the St. Lawrence River shoreline that stretches from Quebec City north to Tadoussac, the former Indian trading post at the mouth of the Saguenay River where it pours into the St. Lawrence. This is the St. Lawrence at its most pristine, skirting the foothills of the Laurentian Mountains (called the Laurentides by French Canadians) to the west, growing ever wider as it gets nearer the Gulf of St. Lawrence, lined with fishing villages and farms, small houses and ancient estates, 18th-century churches and long vistas of unparalleled beauty. The 130-mile (209-km) road between Quebec City and Tadoussac faithfully follows the northern shore of the St. Lawrence. At Tadoussac the route turns inland to follow the Saguenay River for 70 miles (113 km) along Route 172 to Chicoutimi, near Lac St. Jean; it returns to Quebec on Route 175 through Laurentides Provincial Park. Along the way, several alternative routes can extend or shorten the journey, including a driving route around Lac St. Jean or a continuation of the drive along the northern bank of the St. Lawrence — see *The North Shore* — as far as Harve St. Pierre, after which the roads degenerate to unpaved and irregular tracks that may not be passable. Along this stretch, coastal transport is usually via all-terrain vehicles, small boats, or light aircraft.

This route covers a wide variety of terrain. North of Quebec City, beyond the gentle meadows of the St. Lawrence River valley, the land becomes hilly and turns mountainous inland along the Saguenay River. Lac St. Jean is a huge mountain pond, a basin among the peaks. The return cuts across one of the world's oldest mountain ranges, the magnificent glacier-ravaged Laurentian Mountains. Within Laurentides Provincial Park alone, the earth's convulsions have created more than 1,500 lakes and 700 streams.

The Saguenay fjord, carved into the mountains by glacial activity, is a rarity outside the frozen northlands of Alaska and Scandinavia. A giant crack in the earth's crust — the largest fjord in eastern North America — it cuts a narrow but deep tributary through the mountains from Lac St. Jean to the St. Lawrence. Saltwater tides from the Gulf of the St. Lawrence, channeled through the St. Lawrence River, gush into the mouth of the Saguenay with tremendous force. Greenland sharks and other ocean-dwellers are found in its waters as far as 60 miles (97 km) upstream. This junction of the two rivers is also a playground for whales, often seen cavorting in late July and August.

The Beaupré/Charlevoix region, Lac St. Jean, and the Saguenay River area are extremely popular with sportspeople and nature-lovers alike. The coastal marshes harbor many varieties of edible fowl in such abundance that bag limits are usually generous. Numerous sanctuaries help preserve the large flocks and provide natural viewing environments.

Sensible wildlife management programs limit the hunting of bear, moose, and caribou in the populated shoreline areas along the St. Lawrence, but farther north, in Nouveau Quebec, they are fair game. Guides/outfitters are mandatory — and dictated by common sense. But anglers need not travel the least bit out of their way. Not only are many of the rivers of this province known for their challenging Atlantic salmon fishing (considered one of the hardest-fighting gamefish), but the large speckled trout seem to be just waiting to be coaxed out of the water.

The French navigator and explorer Jacques Cartier, discoverer of Canada, first traveled this coast in 1534–1535. His exclamation "Quel beau pré!" ("What a lovely meadow!") was the source of the name of this pastoral coast between what is now the eastern edge of Quebec City and Cap Tourmenté (about 25 mi/40 km north). The borders of the Charlevoix region — named after the Jesuit historian the Reverend Pierre Francois Xavier de Charlevoix, who traveled the St. Lawrence and Mississippi rivers between 1719 and 1722 — extend from here to the Saguenay River area.

The first Europeans to inhabit the area were mostly French as well as English and Scottish; they settled during the late 1500s and early 1600s. These settlers lived in isolated communities, struggling to survive in much the same way as the Abnaki and the Algonquin Indians who preceded them — by trapping, hunting, fishing, and farming the fertile valley of the St. Lawrence River. The means of survival have changed little here. The Saguenay fjord area wasn't settled until the late 18th century, and it was not until the mid-19th century that settlers made their way up the Saguenay River to Chicoutimi, now the capital of the region, and farther north to Lac St. Jean. Only recently have tourists had easy access to these remote parts of the province and their distinctive French North American culture.

En Route from Quebec City – Traveling northeast from Quebec City, Route 138 passes through the historic villages of Giffard, Beauport, and Courville — all of them being swallowed by Quebec's expanding suburbs. Giffard (once part of Beauport) has a group of 18th-century structures. Two of the best known are the Côté House (3200 Royale Ave.) and the Parent House (2040 de Lisieux St.). Within Beauport itself are the Aimé Marcoux House (Rue de l'Academie) and the Bellanger-Girardin House (600 Ave. Royale). The Marcoux house is a 4-story mill in which one room has been restored in 19th-century style; it also houses an artisans' boutique, art gallery, theater, and *boîte à chansons* (cabaret). Open daily except Mondays, May to September. Once in Courville (7 mi/11 km from Quebec City), stop by the *Manoir Montmorency*. Originally built as the Kent House in 1781 and occupied by the Duke of Kent between 1791 and 1794, its lookout provides a spectacular view of Montmorency Falls and the river gorge and its restaurant provides a pleasant lunch. The site includes picnic grounds, a handicrafts boutique, and a tourist information center. Then drive back to Route 138 and the falls.

MONTMORENCY FALLS: About 9 miles (14 km) outside of Quebec City on Route 138, Montmorency Falls appear to the left and Ile d'Orléans (Island of Orléans) to the right. The falls cascade 274 feet to their base, considerably farther than Niagara's 193 feet. A terraced lookout (and some rain gear) allows visitors to get within 100 feet of the falls. During the winter, the water spray freezes into a gigantic cone that grows to 100 feet in diameter before the spring thaw. The cone is called *pain de sucre* (sugar loaf). From here, hop across to Ile d'Orléans on Route 368.

ILE D'ORLÉANS: Until the bridge was built in 1935, the only access to this picturesque isle was by boat in the summer and across a precarious ice bridge in winter. Cartier called the island Bacchus because of the abundance of wild grapes in the rich soil. Later the island was renamed for the Duke of Orléans, but the apples, strawberries, raspberries, and other fruits and vegetables that grow here still seem to be blessed by a god of fertility. Roadside stands and village shops sell local produce as well as quilts, blankets, and other items made on the island. The long isolation of Ile d'Orléans added to the strength of local legends of Loup-Garou and Feux-Follets. The Old Ones of the island believed (and taught) that the howling of the winter winds was the cry of supernatural wolves and that the lights that danced on the river waters at night (caused by phosphorus) were spirits. A circular tour of the 5½-by-21-mile island covers about 42 miles (68 km) and takes about 2 hours.

Turn right onto the road at the foot of the bridge (traveling counterclockwise), and go along the cliff to the village of Ste. Pétronille. Its wharf affords one of the best views of Quebec City and Cap Diamond. The village is the departure point for cruises to Quebec City. Island walking tours along Chemin Royale leave from the Ste. Pétronille wharf at 2:30 PM Tuesdays, Thursdays, Saturdays, and Sundays, May 1 through October 31. Be sure to visit the orchards — especially in late summer, when the apples ripen in the warm sun — before going on to St. Laurent, where the strawberries grow as large as small apples and taste heavenly. Just past St. Laurent's village church, which hosts regular folk and classical music concerts from July through September, is *Le Moulin St. Laurent* (phone: 418-829-3888), a fine French restaurant in a renovated mill, open during the summer. Reservations necessary for this special place; ask to be seated at a table near the cimballa, which is a horizontal harp, sort of a cross between a pedal-steel guitar and a vibraphone.

The village of St. Jean and its boatyards lie at the halfway point of the island's southern shore. Not only has St. Jean been involved in the construction of boats since the French first settled the island, but many of the villagers became captains and navigators on the St. Lawrence waterway. Walking tours of St. Jean leave from the church daily, except Mondays, at 2:30 PM, from May 1 to October 31. The *Mauvide-Genest Manor*, one of Quebec's most beautiful rural estates, has been converted into a private museum and a fine restaurant (phone: 418-829-2915). Also on the grounds is the *Théâtre Paul-Hébert*, which hosts French productions. (For summer reservations, call 418-829-2202.) The museum, restaurant, and theater are open May to October.

St. François, with its scenic church (1735), old schoolhouse, and picturesque little cemetery, occupies the eastern tip of the island, overlooking the smaller islands of the Orléans archipelago as well as the coast of Charlevoix County. Here salt water from the Gulf of St. Lawrence 600 miles (966 km) away taints the freshwater river and the tide achieves its greatest height of 25 feet.

Continue through the village of Ste. Famille to St. Pierre. The village church (1718) is a historical monument open to visitors, and the presbytère is a museum filled with household artifacts from the 18th century. St. Pierre is the home of well-known singer Felix LeClerc. The *Théâtre de l'Île* (phone: 418-828-9530) presents summer theater (in French) and entertainment. *Les Ancêtres de la Petite Canadienne* (391 Chemin Royal) is an excellent restaurant in an old farmhouse, but it is open to tour groups only. The cook specializes in Quebecois dishes. From here, it's back across the bridge and onto Route 138 through Château-Richer toward Ste. Anne de Beaupré.

STE. ANNE DE BEAUPRÉ: Local legend holds that this world-renowned Roman Catholic shrine began as a chapel built by a grateful group of Breton sailors. Caught in a violent storm, the sailors vowed to build a chapel upon reaching land safely. Three survived to start the project, and the chapel became an object of devotion even before it was completed when a crippled parishioner working on it was miraculously cured. The original wood chapel was replaced in 1676 with a stone church. By 1700 thousands of pilgrims were journeying to the shrine, and numerous cures were documented. That first stone church no longer exists, although a replica, incorporating material from the old church, serves as a Memorial Chapel. Both the Memorial Chapel and the newer Basilica, inaugurated in 1934, contain 18th-century art and silverwork. The wax museum near the Basilica illustrates the sanctuary's history (phone: 418-827-3781).

En Route from Ste. Anne de Beaupré – Parc du Mont-Ste.-Anne (phone: 418-827-4561), host to the Du Maurier International-Skiing Competitions in 1966, catapulted into the skiing public's eye only a year after its opening and has been the site of skiing competitions ever since. The park now boasts 40 ski trails and 14 lifts as well as the province's only gondola lift, and $8 million worth of new snow-making equipment keeps the slopes operating from early November through May. In summer, you can ride along the park's scenic bicycle path or play golf on its 18-hole course. Just 4 miles (6½ km) from the ski resort, there is a 166-site campground open from mid-June through *Labor Day*. The *Château Mont-Ste.-Anne,* a luxurious, 258-room property at the foot of Mont-Ste.-Anne, is considered by many to be the best winter resort hotel in the region (see *Best En Route*). It is accessible from Route 138 via Route 360, about 3 miles (5 km) northeast of Ste. Anne de Beaupré.

A well-marked secondary road off Route 138 just beyond the park access leads to St. Joachim and Cap Tourmente. This fertile area, the first portion of the Beaupré coast to be settled, lies within a triangle formed by two arms of the Laurentian range (known as Les Caps) and the St. Lawrence River. The first buildings erected here in 1626 were destroyed during the French-British conflicts; however the Petit Cap, built in 1777, remains, as do two other structures: the Château Bellevue and its chapel. Except for a later addition (1870), these buildings have not changed since they housed seminary students during their summer vacations 200 years ago.

The Cap Tourmente National Wildlife Reserve (phone: 418-827-4591) in the migratory path of greater snow geese (or white geese), is a haven for geese and other birds. Each spring and fall, the Petit Cap offers a fine view of about 150,000 white geese looking like a bed of live snow floating on the river. The Reserve's interpretative center offers guided tours from mid-April through October.

The 213-foot Ste. Anne Falls are located on a small road leading north from Route 138.

Outside St. Joachim, Route 138 climbs sharply, bypassing the village of St. Tite des Caps as it traverses the 2,300-foot crest of one of Les Caps. This vantage point, with a fantastic view of the river, marks the official boundary between the Beaupré region and Charlevoix County. Baie St. Paul, 26 miles (42 km) away, is barely visible from the peak through the spruce-forested hills.

BAIE ST. PAUL: This shallow, sheltered bay, guarded by tall promontories to the southwest and northeast, and Ile aux Coudres offshore in the St. Lawrence, has been a favored port since it was first settled in 1678. Many of the homes here are more than 200 years old. Just inland, outlining its valley of farms, are the highest mountains of the Laurentian Range (4,000 ft.). The mountain peaks and the rivers flowing into their valleys — notably the du Gouffre and du Bras — irrigate the soil and beautify the town's setting. The Bas-de-la-Baie Falls are a popular attraction, as are the lookouts at Cap-aux-Corbeaux and Rang Ste.-Catherine, with their stunning views of the bay. The cliffs and beach draw hang-gliding enthusiasts all summer. Many artists, drawn by the calm, colorful scenery, live here; others visit. Their numbers and talents account for the quality and quantity of art available at the town's many galleries. The *Clarence Gagnon Art Gallery* at 61 St. Jean-Baptiste St. (named for famous Quebec painter Clarence Gagnon, 1881-1942) is one of the better ones (phone: 418-435-2428). The *Centre d'Art Baie St. Paul* shows off Quebecois works at 4 Fafard St. (phone: 435-3681).

The 18th-century *César Mill,* 730 Rang St.-Laurent (phone: 435-5340), houses a workshop and sculpture gallery used by Quebecois sculptor Lucien Bouchard and others. Turning right onto Route 362 upon entering Baie St. Paul via Route 138, follow it through town to a secondary road, Rang St. Laurent. The mill is a little over 1 mile (1.5 km) from Route 362. Both the de Rémi Mill (1826) and the Michel Perron Mill (c. 1770), on the Rémi River and Michel Brook, respectively, still operate, but visitors are not allowed inside.

Every summer, in late July or early August, the town erupts into the *Baie St. Paul Folk Festival,* with dancing in the streets, shows of horsemanship, and sales of handmade woven goods, ceramics, and of course paintings and sculpture.

En Route from Baie St. Paul – Upon entering Baie St. Paul, Route 138 turns inland. The driving time from here to La Malbaie (25 mi/40 km) is less than 1 hour. Route 362, the old coast road, winds through town and then on to the villages of Les Eboulements, Cap aux Oies, and St. Joseph de la Rive. The route is hilly and some of the hairpin turns are tight. This area served as the backdrop for the popular French-language Radio-Canada television show, "Le Temps d'une Paix." One of the spots where scenes were shot — the forge in Les Eboulements — is open to visitors.

The name Eboulement means "landslide," and one occurred here in 1663 after an earthquake. This is another Quebec village noted for its period architecture that contains an array of art galleries and handicraft shops. The village church, from its elevation of 1,204 feet, offers a good view of Ile aux Coudres. Past the village, a dirt road leads to the Cap aux Oies lighthouse. From here you can see schools of porpoises playing in the St. Lawrence.

Also in Les Eboulements is a small, unnamed paved road to St. Joseph de la Rive, steep and treacherous when wet. About 300 people live in St. Joseph all year. The altar in the renovated Old Church is mounted on four sea anchors and the baptismal fonts are made of seashells. The St. Giles paper mill, which uses few machines, produces a luxurious parchment comparable to the finest of China, Japan, and France. The Ile aux Coudres ferry docks at a wharf lined with people year-round, fishing for the many varieties of smelt in the St. Lawrence. There are three small motels and one inn in St. Joseph de la Rive.

ILE AUX COUDRES (HAZELTREE ISLAND): Christened by Cartier for its thick copses of hazel trees, it was here in 1535 that the first Mass was celebrated on Canadian soil. The early settlers on the island were whalers and shipbuilders. Now the mining of peat moss, 20 feet thick in some areas of its vast bogs, is the principal industry of this island's 1,600 inhabitants.

Until the recent establishment of a year-round ferry, ice floes in the river cut off the island from the mainland in winter. By necessity, island people, seafarers like most island dwellers along the St. Lawrence, mastered the art of ice canoeing, now a competitive team sport at Quebec City's *Winter Carnival.*

This romantic island — just 35 miles in circumference — attracts many visitors lured by its isolation and scenery. The *Centre Artisanal de l'Île aux Coudres* (Artisans' Center) sells a wide range of pottery, leatherwork, sculpture, painting, knitted clothing, quilts, blankets, and other items crafted by the islanders. The *Leclerc House* (114 Principale St., La Baleine; phone: 418-438-2240), one of the island's first, also sells such arts and crafts. In addition, it now displays a collection of regional antiques and objets d'art. Open daily from June 24 to *Labor Day.*

The Moulin de l'Ile aux Coudres and windmills (du Moulin Road) are open for guided tours from June to September. An interpretative center, the *Musée Les Voitures d'Eau,* or "ship museum" (203 des Coudriers Rd. phone: 418-438-2208), explains the history of the area and its fabled schooners through a slide show, exhibitions, and tour of the boats, or *goélettes* as they are called here. Tours of the schooner *Mont-St.-Louis* are given June through September.

En Route from Ile aux Coudres – After the ferry returns you to St. Joseph de la Rive, drive up the hill to Les Eboulements and turn left onto Route 362. A secondary road leads inland to St. Hilarion and Route 138, but Route 362 continues along the coast to the resort area of Pointe-au-Pic, passing through the village of St. Irénée, the birthplace of Adolphe Routhier, composer of the Canadian national anthem.

The *Manoir Richelieu* (see *Best En Route*) has dominated this international resort area for over 60 years. Set high on a cape overlooking the St. Lawrence, the 400-room gray stone hotel has hosted such dignitaries as former US President William Howard Taft (who had a summer home nearby) and Senator Robert Taft, and many Canadian and American luminaries own or rent summer villas here. The rooms of the hotel, renovated in 1975, retain their traditional atmosphere. There is a golf course at the manor, another at the *Murray Bay Club.* The manor also has tennis, horseback riding, swimming, and facilities for shooting clay pigeons. There is also summer theater. For first class dining, try the classic French cooking at the *Les Trois Canards* hotel-motel on Côte Bellevue, or the French and regional dishes at the relatively new *Des Falaises* (18 des Falaises Blvd., Pointe-au-Pic), an inn with a stunning view of Malbaie.

LA MALBAIE: Ideally located at the mouth of the Malbaie River, with the summer resorts of Pointe-au-Pic (southwestern) and Cap à l'Aigle (northeastern) on either side, this town has attracted summer visitors and anglers since the 1760s. Champlain dropped anchor in this bay one evening in 1608. The morning low tide left him nearly beached on the clay flats, hence the name Malbaie ("bad bay"). The area's great forests of cedar and white pine have been gradually depleted since the establishment of a sawmill here in 1672. In 1759, two officers of General Wolfe's invasion force landed here, presumably to raze the town, but they decided to settle instead. Their attempt to rename the town and river in honor of their commanding officer General Murray (Wolfe's successor) failed, but unofficially the area is called Murray Bay by both French- and English-speaking people. The town is home to the *Laure-Conan* regional museum (30 Patrick Morgan St.; phone: 418-665-4411) which contains the recreated Victorian parlor of Quebec's first author; periodic art and history exhibitions are presented year-round.

En Route from La Malbaie – Follow Route 138 northeast toward Tadoussac and the Saguenay River, about 75 miles (121 km) away. There are fewer villages along this section of the coast.

Five miles (8 km) beyond La Malbaie is the tiny resort of Cap à l'Aigle, named by Samuel de Champlain in 1608 for the many eagles nesting on the rocky cape. These magnificent birds are still here, their numbers sadly reduced. Though a tiny village, Cap à l'Aigle is home to *La Pinsonnière,* one of only five members of the prestigious Relais & Châteaux group of fine country inns in Quebec (see "Special Havens," *DIVERSIONS*).

At the village of St. Siméon, you may turn left onto Route 170 and go north (and west) to Chicoutimi, but this means skipping Tadoussac and the mouth of the Saguenay River, which are well worth seeing. One of the several ferries on the St. Lawrence crosses from here to Rivière du Loup on the south shore. Ste. Catherine, at the edge of the mountains, marks the border of Charlevoix County. On the clay flats of this village, Champlain met with representatives of the Huron tribes and other inhabitants of the northern shore of the St. Lawrence to form an alliance. This put the French into direct conflict with the Iroquois Nation, the traditional enemies of the northern tribes. Eventually this treaty helped cause the downfall of New France because it was used by the British to funnel the hostilities of the violent Iroquois Nation against the French and their allies. The northern tribes, no match for the Iroquois, were decimated.

TADOUSSAC: This village, one of the oldest settlements north of Mexico, dates to when Cartier visited the site in 1535 and pronounced it the "gateway to the Kingdom of Saguenay," a land of precious metals and stones. In 1599 Pierre Chauvin became the first Frenchman to build a house in Canada by erecting a trading post here. Chauvin, a fur trader, arranged for 16 men to remain at the site during the winter of 1600-1601. As a colony, the attempt failed, but as a trading post, business boomed. By 1603, when Champlain stopped here on his way up the St. Lawrence, Tadoussac ("rounded hillock," or "knoll") was the supply port for ships traveling to and from Europe. The *Chauvin Museum* (157 du bord De L'eau St.), an exact replica of that first house, was constructed from a description written by Champlain. Open daily, mid-June to mid-September, 9 AM to 9 PM (phone: 235-4657). Next to it stands Quebec's oldest wooden church, a chapel that dates from 1747 (open all summer). The brothers Kirke (David, Lewis, and Thomas), British merchant-explorers commanding a fleet under royal patent to expel the French from Canada and establish their own trade monopoly, captured the post in 1628.

Tadoussac owes part of its growth to its location at the mouth of the Saguenay, which flows 471 miles (758 km) from Lac St. Jean, which connects with several other rivers to the north, creating a network of waterways. From Tadoussac, it was possible to establish trade with trappers and Indians halfway to Hudson Bay. The traders and explorers may have been attracted to the site because the Saguenay fjord is a deepwater channel (750 ft.), wide enough to sail, or because of the whales (belugas, blue, and finback) that congregate in the St. Lawrence during late July and early August. The blue are the largest, averaging 99 feet long and weighing 118 tons. The recently refurbished *Tadoussac* hotel (see *Best En Route*) arranges boat trips upriver to see the whales, as well as cruises on the *Marie Clarisse,* a tall ship plying the river during the summer. Film buffs will be interested to know that the hotel was one of the settings for the movie *Hotel New Hampshire.*

Tadoussac is prime hunting and fishing territory. The forests are filled with moose, and farther north, with caribou, grouse, ptarmigan, and small game. The waters are rich with pike, walleye, landlocked salmon, and speckled trout. For music lovers, the town bursts into song in mid-August when it presents the *Festival De La Québécoise* for North Shore and Quebec composers and singers. It is centered around the *Café du Fjord* (152 Bateau-Passeur; phone: 418-235-4372 or 235-4626), which also holds art exhibitions.

En Route from Tadoussac – At a strategic point on the river, Tadoussac can be the final goal, midpoint, or jumping-off spot for any vacationer. From here it is possible to follow Route 138 along the north bank of the St. Lawrence (see *The North Shore*) to Havre St. Pierre, where the road ends. Beyond that is wilderness. North and west from Tadoussac is Lac St. Jean, source of the Saguenay. Beyond that, light aircraft and an outfitter-guide are necessary to hunt and fish the wilds that extend toward Hudson Bay. A ferry at Escoumins, 24 miles (39 km) past Tadoussac, goes to Trois Pistoles on the south shore. Our choice is to take Route 172 north and west to Chicoutimi (70 mi/113 km) and on to Lac St. Jean; the turnoff is about 6 miles (10 km) outside Tadoussac.

The drive from Tadoussac takes in wild and splendid scenery, but the fjord is not visible from the highway. About 43 miles (69 km) north of Tadoussac, a road leads down a cliff to Ste. Rose du Nord, near the Chicoutimi Reserve. The road is quite tricky, but the town has an awe-inspiring view of the high cliffsides of the fjord and the rushing waters beneath. Every year hordes of photographers and artists flock to this spot for a glimpse of these near-vertical walls torn from the mountainous earth by glaciers countless years ago. There is a rest area, a few services, a wharf and a camping area (*Campground La Descente des Femmes;* phone: 418-675-2348), and little else — no hotels or motels.

About 30 miles (48 km) past the Ste. Rose du Nord turnoff is the village of St. Fulgence and the small park/rest area of Mont Valin, with a 3,000-foot crest (one of the tallest peaks in Quebec), offering a breathtaking view of the Saguenay fjord.

CHICOUTIMI: Chicoutimi means "as far as it is deep" in the language of the Montagnais Indians who inhabited the area; beyond this point the fjord was unnavigable. Peter McLeod, a Scottish settler, founded this thriving community on August 24, 1842. Shipbuilding was a major industry of the time, wood its principal material. McLeod brought a small group to this forested land to open a sawmill. From this venture grew one of the province's largest cities (pop. 60,000). A major convention city, it abounds with good Quebecois dining, generous watering holes, and, as befits this still-young frontier town, an active nightlife. Two large shopping centers, Place du Saguenay and Place du Royaume, are both on Racine Street.

The *Lac St. Jean Museum* provides a good introduction to the region's history and geography (534 Jacques Cartier E.; phone: 418-545-9000), and the Old Pulp Mill has displays on the city's industrial origins.

In mid-February the city hosts a week-long *Winter Carnival,* with skiing and snowshoe races, tobogganing, and singing, dancing, and riotous partying to rival the *Quebec Carnival* for excitement. In summer, there's the International Swimming Marathon and a series of regattas in July. And all summer the *Marjolaine II* (phone: 418-543-7630) leaves from the Chicoutimi dock for cruises along the Saguenay.

En Route from Chicoutimi (the Lac St. Jean circle) – If your time is limited, take Route 175 back to Quebec City (120 mi/193 km; driving time less than 3 hours). If you have time, however, continue north and west on Route 172 toward Lac St. Jean through a small agricultural district to the industrial town of Alma. Alma stands in the midst of several smaller lakes and rivers at the headwaters of the Saguenay River, its back to Lac St. Jean. Aluminum, pulp, and paper are the town's major industries.

The cruise ship *La Tournée* departs daily during the summer from the town's marina for tours of the Saguenay. At Alma, Route 172 intersects Route 169, which circles Lac St. Jean; bear to your right, traveling counterclockwise, and head north and west on Route 169.

Péribonka, 30 miles (48 km) from Alma, was the home of Louis Hémon (1880–1913), author of *Marie Chapdelaine.* A Marie Chapdelaine museum is located in the house Hémon occupied, 3 miles (5 km) east of the village. On the first Sunday in August there is a swimming race across the lake starting at the town's waterfront.

Twelve miles (19 km) farther around the lake, on the bank of the river of the same name, is Mistassini — "big rock" in Cree. The village holds a *Blueberry Festival* the first week of August, with contests for such local specialties as blueberry wine and blueberry pie. Across the river is a monastery of the Trappist fathers (phone: 418-276-0491); a slide presentation about the monastic lifestyle is available to visitors, but no guests are permitted in the monastery itself. Ask for Père Marcel Carrier.

At the far end of Lac St. Jean is St. Félicien. Here, on Chamouchouane Island, in the Saumon River, is the most beautiful zoo in the province, open from June to September. More than 2,600 animals representing 130 different species roam the open area. From St. Félicien, Route 167 leads to the Chibougamau Reserve and beyond it the Mistassini Reserve. These areas attract many hunters and anglers. Route 169 bears south and east here, beginning its swing back toward Alma.

Roberval, the first parish settled on Lac St. Jean (1855), is about 25 miles (40 km) beyond St. Félicien. It is now a small commercial center, providing access to the Pointe-Blue Indian Reserve and its Amerindian museum 3 miles (5 km) away on the lakeshore at 407 Amishk St. (phone: 418-275-4842). In late July, the town hosts 8 days of entertainment and sporting events culminating in a marathon swim from Péribonka the last Sunday of the month.

Six miles (10 km) from Roberval is Val Jalbert, erected as a company town servicing the paper, pulp, and lumber industry in 1901. It failed when the company went bankrupt in 1927. The site remained vacant until 1960, when it was turned into a park and historic museum (open late May to *Labor Day;* phone: 418-275-3132). A terrace café and a handicraft center operate out of the old mill. About 35 miles (56 km) outside Val Jalbert, Route 169 abruptly turns south toward Quebec and intersects Route 175 (from Chicoutimi) in the middle of the Laurentides Park. This final leg of the route, about 120 miles (193 km), takes about 3 hours to drive.

BEST EN ROUTE

Outside Quebec City and Montreal, the province's accommodations take on a rural flavor. Although services may be limited, all the necessities and the niceties of life are available. The hostelries listed here have services and amenities enough for any traveler. Prices, of course, fluctuate with exchange rates and the season. If your budget is tight, check before departure. These listings are based upon a range of over $55 (double occupancy) as expensive; $40 to $55 as moderate; and under $40 for two as inexpensive. All prices are quoted in US dollars.

ILE D'ORLÉANS

Auberge Le Chaumonot – This plush 8-room inn is about 18 miles (29 km) from the bridge, on an isolated stretch of waterfront. There is a heated pool, a bar, and the rooms are very comfortable. The French restaurant on the premises is quite good. Open April to October. 425 Chemin Royal, St. François (phone: 418-829-2735). Expensive.

STE. ANNE DE BEAUPRÉ

Château Mont-Ste.-Anne – Sitting right at the foot of Mont-Ste.-Anne and facing the hill, this hotel is the best winter resort in the region. Of its 258 air conditioned rooms, 18 have fireplaces and 50 are split-level suites. All have just been redecorated and offer cable and pay TV. The property also features 2 restaurants and a formal dining room. Ski week packages, as well as transportation from the airport, are available. 500 Blvd. Beaupré (phone: 418-827-5211 or 800-463-4467). Expensive to moderate.

BAIE ST. PAUL

Auberge La Pignoronde – A popular bayside hotel with 27 rooms, a swimming pool, and fine dining room. 750 Blvd. Mgr-de-Laval (phone: 418-435-5505). Expensive.

Belle Plage – As its name suggests, this small hotel with a restaurant is located at the water's edge. 192 Ste. Anne St. (phone: 418-435-3321). Expensive.

Maison Otis – A 28-room inn that has a highly rated restaurant and comfortable accommodations. 23 St.-Jean-Baptiste St. (phone: 418-435-2255). Expensive.

ILE AUX COUDRES

Auberge de la Roche Pleureuse – At the eastern tip of the island, this 90-room motel has a good restaurant, tennis courts, and a pool. Closed in winter. La Baleine, 238 Route Principale E. (phone: 418-438-2232). Expensive.

Cap-aux-Pierres – This is a hotel-motel with 60 motel units and 35 rooms in the main house, as well as a swimming pool, tennis courts, and special facilities for the handicapped. Canadian and international folk dancing shows are staged here on Saturdays, and the hotel runs a lively *boîte à chanson* (cabaret) from June to September. 220 Rte. Principale E. (phone: 418-438-2711 or 800-463-5250). Expensive.

St. Bernard – Here are 14 basic, comfortable rooms and a dining room. 45 Rue Royale E., St. Bernard (phone: 418-438-2261). Moderate to inexpensive.

POINTE-AU-PIC

Manoir Richelieu – One of the most popular resorts in the province, with very accommodating service, it has golf, tennis, pool, deluxe dining room, bars, and 390 traditional rooms. Make early reservations. 181 Manoir Richelieu Ave. (phone: 418-665-3703 or 800-463-2613). Expensive.

Auberge Les Trois Canards – Here is a small, comfortable 44-room hotel, known for its fine French and Quebecois food. Tennis and swimming. 49 Côte Bellevue (phone: 418-665-3761). Expensive.

Auberge Au Petit Berger – This comfortable inn with just 20 rooms dispenses especially good and reasonably priced food. 1 Côte Bellevue (phone: 418-665-4428). Expensive.

LA MALBAIE

Auberge Charlevoix – An attractive, 42-room inn with a restaurant, tennis courts, and a pool. 1030 St. Etienne St. (phone: 418-665-4413 or 800-463-5776). Expensive.

TADOUSSAC

Tadoussac – This popular hotel — the largest in town — has a dining room and full services; the management organizes various expeditions, including summer whale-watching trips on the Saguenay River. Totally renovated by the Famille Dufour Cap-aux-Pierres hotel group during the mid-1980s, the property has retained the charm of an old-fashioned summer resort. Summer theater and other entertainment are offered every evening during the summer. 165 Bord de l'Eau St. (phone: 418-235-4421/4343 or 800-463-5250). Expensive.

Georges – A small hotel-motel that offers 18 comfortable units and complete restaurant services. 135 Du Bateau-Passeur St. (phone: 418-235-4393). Inexpensive.

CHICOUTIMI

Auberge des Gouverneurs – This plush hotel, just outside town, has a pool, good restaurant, bar, and fine service. 1303 Talbot Blvd. (phone: 418-549-6244). Expensive.

Universel – A 119-room complex, with a pool and good restaurant; it is a member of the Quebec chain of efficiently run lodgings. 250 Des Sagueneens St. (phone: 418-545-8326). Expensive to moderate.

Chicoutimi – Centrally located, this older 99-room hotel features a dining room and full services. 460 Racine St. (phone: 418-549-7111). Moderate.

Le Montagnais – This large, modern complex has 222 rooms plus exhibition and conference halls. There are also 2 swimming pools (indoor and outdoor) and a restaurant. 1080 Talbot Blvd. (418-543-1512). Moderate.

ALMA

Universel – A pleasant place close to the lake, it has 60 rooms. 1000 Cascades Blvd. (phone: 418-668-5201). Expensive to moderate.

Cascades – This comfortable hotel-motel has 58 rooms and a decent restaurant. 140 du Pont Nord Ave. (phone: 418-662-6547). Moderate.

Dequen – A 56-unit motel with a dining room serving local dishes. 800 du Pont Nord Ave. (phone: 418-662-6649). Inexpensive.

The North Shore

The North Shore route explores the edge of that immense, remote region extending east from Tadoussac and the Saguenay fjord along the north bank of the St. Lawrence River toward Labrador.

The principal overland access, Route 138, extends to Havre St. Pierre, on the bank of the Gulf of St. Lawrence opposite Ile d'Anticosti. Previously, this blacktop highway went only as far as Moisie, augmented by an irregular series of unpaved (and periodically impassable) roads linking the tiny villages along the rugged coast. Route 138 runs for 385 miles (620 km), from Tadoussac to its end at Havre St. Pierre, along a sandy seashore wedged between capes and mountains and through fewer and ever more remote villages.

Beyond Havre St. Pierre, the coast is accessible only by small boats or light aircraft. North, into the immense wilderness of the province toward Hudson Strait, small aircraft are necessary for efficient, long-distance transportation, although all-terrain vehicles manage some of the logging roads and dirt trails through some areas.

The isolation, the abundance of fish and game, and the enormous volume of natural resources that have attracted hunters, anglers, and explorers for more than two centuries continue to dominate life in this vast land of mountains, lakes, and forests. The scarcity of settlements along the St. Lawrence is compounded by the lack of natural population centers beyond it. The population density ranges from five people per square mile near the coast to roughly one per square mile inland. There are only a handful of interior settlements in this area, and, for the most part, those that exist are either by-products of industrial exploration or modern equivalents of the 17th-century Hudson's Bay trading posts, outposts in the wilderness to which hunters and anglers journey in search of legendary prizes. Large portions of land just beyond the coastal strip are open to hunters, although outfitter services are necessary. Moose, caribou, and even bear can be taken in the forests of Nouveau Québec, as the northern area is called. Speckled and Quebec Red trout dominate the river waters. Commercial exploration has led to the recent opening of this isolated frontier, with expansion of the coastal settlements encouraged by the growth of mining, fishing, lumber, and hydroelectric power companies tapping the resources of the Canadian Shield. For example, the recently-completed power project at James Bay has created 1,000 miles of roads and three power stations.

Travel arrangements in this region must be made in advance. Because of the rapid industrial growth, service facilities (particularly lodging, guides and outfitters, and aircraft and boat transportation) may be strained by the flow of traffic in coastal villages used as jumping-off points for hunting and fishing as well as construction and exploration expeditions. There are three major charter services to the North Shore: *Air Inuit* from Montreal (phone: 514-636-9445), *Québec Aviation Ltée* from Quebec City (phone: 418-872-1200), and *Nordair* to Radisson (phone: 514-286-1212). Others can be picked up at Kuujjuak, Val d'Or, Schefferville, Fermont, La Sarre, and Sept Iles.

At Tadoussac, the massive Saguenay fjord, its cliffside walls rising 1,500 feet, joins the St. Lawrence River, where ocean-dwelling giants like the blue whale play in the river waters every summer just as they did when the Basque whalers hunted them during the 15th and 16th centuries. The route crosses the mountains and forests stretching along the St. Lawrence's edge toward Labrador, a cold barren tract often called the Land of Cain. This trip has just a taste of the extraordinary beauty and overpowering size of the land beyond the northern horizon. It will alter your conception of size and distance.

En Route from Tadoussac – Take Route 138 northeast from Tadoussac through a lovely area filled with lakes into the farming valley of Petits Bergeronnes. The village of Grandes Bergeronnes is about 15 miles (24 km) from Tadoussac; a secondary road on the far side of the tiny village leads to Bon Désir Bay. The bay (now a park) had been a meeting place for whalers and seal hunters. On nearby Anse à la Cave (Hollow Cove), remains of 16th-century furnaces used by Basque whalers to boil animal fat have been found. Les Escoumins, a town by comparison, is 9 miles (14 km) farther on Route 138. Champlain examined the site in 1603 and noted in his log, "This is the place where the Basques go whaling." Evidence of a Basque whale oil processing furnace has been found on (and since removed from) Pointe Escoumins. The first European to settle here, around 1825, was Joseph Moreau, a Hudson's Bay Company employee. Not until 1845 was a village established, in conjunction with the expansion of the timber industry into the area. Now the village is the point where inbound ocean ships pick up river pilots to navigate the hazardous waters of the St. Lawrence.

A ferry connects Les Escoumins with Trois Pistoles on the south shore from mid-May to December.

The 60-foot waterfall of the Sault au Mouton River is the principal attraction of the village bearing the same name, 16 miles (26 km) from Les Escoumins on Route 138 (a total of 40 mi/64 km from Tadoussac). Exactly who named the river (and village) and when is unknown, but it appeared on maps as early as 1611. In

1860 the area was developed by John Edmund Barry, who established a lumber business.

FORESTVILLE: Forestville is a born-again industrial center. Originally settled in 1844 as Sault au Cochon, a lumber camp with a sawmill, the town died during a decline in the lumber trade at the turn of the century. It was revived by a timber boom in 1937 and renamed Forestville in honor of Grant Forest, who had managed private lumber interests here before the decline. The dam and 1837 forest house are open to the public.

Route 385, paved as far as Labrieville, leads north to the Forestville and Labrieville park/reserves.

En Route from Forestville – On Route 138 eastbound about 2 miles (3 km) outside of Forestville is a turnoff toward Colombier. The town, which has an excellent beach at Anse à Norbert, is about a mile from the highway. Return to Route 138 and continue through the tiny hamlet of Ilets Jérémie. Like many of these villages, this began as a Hudson's Bay trading post (established by Joël-Jérémie de la Montagne). Peter McLeod, founder of Chicoutimi, was stationed here during the late 1820s and Napoleon-Alexandre Comeau, a well-known North Shore personality and naturalist, was born here in 1848. East of the Bersimis River, Route 138 skirts the Betsiamites Indian Reservation. The Montagnais Indians who inhabit the reservation are self-governing, manage their own logging and sawmill operation, and, with the consent of the tribal chief, organize and guide hunting and fishing trips on reservation land. During the summer, the Indians also operate a handicrafts boutique and a gallery with a permanent collection of Amerindian work (29 de la Réserve; phone: 418-233-3096). Less than 20 miles (32 km) from the reservation is the town of Chutes aux Outards and the Manicouagan Peninsula. The peninsula has several fine sandy beaches.

The city of Baie Comeau-Hauterive, including the ruins of its predecessor, the industrial village of St. Eugène de Manicouagan, 8 miles (13 km) east of Chute aux Outardes on Route 138, is another born-again community.

BAIE COMEAU: Enthusiasts of great technological achievements will enjoy Baie Comeau. Established by *Chicago Tribune* publisher Colonel Robert R. McCormick during the 1930s, the city (ten times the size of most coastal communities) began on this isolated site with the construction of a pulp and newsprint plant. The highway (Route 138) was built later as was the Hydro-Quebec Highway (Route 389), which leads to a series of giant hydroelectric dams. A Hydro-Quebec reception center at the intersection of Routes 138 and 389 arranges visits to the installations during July and August. This service road (Route 389) of 135 miles (215 km) is partially paved; the remainder is well-maintained gravel. There is a campground near the Manic 2 dam — about 15 miles (24 km) from Baie Comeau — as well as a forestry museum that's open from late June to *Labor Day*. Manic 5, the Daniel Johnson Dam, is considered one of the world's largest multiple-arch structures (4,310-foot crest length). The *Baie Comeau Museum* (43 Mance St.; phone: 418-296-9690) has regular art and cultural exhibitions during the summer. The museum is part of the town's Centre-Socio-Culturel, which also houses the *Baie Comeau Summer Theater;* the season runs from July 1 to September 5.

The Hydro-Quebec Highway (Route 389) also provides access to the Baie Comeau-Hauterive Reserve. The town, honoring the naturalist and favorite son of the North Shore, Napoléon-Alexandre Comeau, is 123 miles (198 km) from Tadoussac. The harbor serves more than 700 ships per year, and a ferry links this industrial town with Matane on the south shore.

En Route from Baie Comeau – Even with 20th-century transportation and communications, the isolation of this land becomes readily apparent after you leave Baie Comeau. The tiny fishing village of Franquelin, nested amid slopes of the Laurentian Mountains on three sides and the St. Lawrence River on the fourth, is 20 miles (32 km) beyond Baie Comeau on Route 138. During the early 1900s, the village grew with the logging industry. Following the construction of the highway from Baie Comeau to Sept Iles, both the industry and the population moved eastward. About 600 inhabitants remain in this village. Continue on Route 138 through the village cemetery to Godbout.

Route 138 crosses the Godbout River and swings north, but an access road leads east into one of the most beautiful sites on the North Shore. Embracing the east bank of the Godbout River on one side and extending to the promontory of Pointe des Monts on the other, with an enticing bay on the St. Lawrence, the village of Godbout began as a trading post in the mid-1600s. The river and village honor Nicholas Godbout, a sailor and river pilot, who lived on Ile d'Orléans in the 1670s. Godbout has an Indian and Inuit museum containing a number of artifacts; open daily, June through September, from 9 AM to 10 PM (phone: 418-568-7724). There's also a nearby beach and picnic area.

A secondary roadway 18 miles (29 km) past Godbout leads to the tiny village of Pointe des Monts, 7 miles (11 km) off Route 138 on a point jutting into the Gulf of St. Lawrence. This spot, where the bank of the St. Lawrence abruptly widens to the gulf, was the first harbor in the gulf. The lighthouse, reputedly the oldest in Canada (1830), was recently declared a historical landmark and is now an interpretation center, open daily, 10 AM to 8 PM, from late June to late September. A bar and restaurant were recently added. Before the lighthouse's construction (and occasionally since), the rocky coves and inlets on the eastern face of the shore saw numerous shipwrecks, inbound vessels blown by ocean storms onto the unseen rocks. Picnic grounds are also on the site, and an outfitter's service can provide fishing gear.

Return to Route 138 and proceed north to the village of Baie Trinité, which includes the hamlets of Pointe à Paulin, Petit Mai, and Ilets Caribou. Cartier supposedly christened the river when he visited here on Trinity Sunday, 1536, but this may be inaccurate. Regardless, the names Trinité River and Baie Trinité appear on maps dated 1682. These hamlets, settled in the late 1830s, were active in the lumber trade during the late 1920s. This entire area was once known for caribou hunting, but the wildlife has been greatly depleted, and the small islands that once sheltered game are now barren sand dunes. Recently, however, the government has converted some 200 square miles of territory bordering on the Grande- and Petite-Trinité rivers into a salmon fishing reserve. Baie Trinité has two campgrounds and cottages right on the bay.

Pointe aux Anglais, 20 miles (32 km) from Baie Trinité, was founded by a group of French settlers in 1873, who were joined by about 15 Acadian families from Anticosti Island 20 years later. The settlement followed the construction of a lighthouse (which remains) in 1870 on nearby Ile aux Oeufs. This point marks the spot where, on August 22, 1711, part of Admiral Walker's fleet was wrecked en route to laying siege to Quebec. A collection of salvaged cannons are on display, and occasionally an addition is brought to the surface.

PORT CARTIER: Incorporated in 1958, Port Cartier is a lumber community with a good deepwater harbor. The lumber industry gave the area its start in 1915, when Colonel McCormick ventured to the outpost known as Portage des Mousses (and later Rivière aux Rochers), renamed it Shelter Bay, and established a sawmill. The city, 228 miles (367 km) from Tadoussac, borders on the Port Cartier-Sept Iles Reserve. This entire region is known for its rivers and lakes. Moose, bear, wild duck, and partridge are plentiful, and speckled trout is the most popular attraction for anglers. Access to the reserve is via a 17-mile (27-km) secondary road. During the summer, the beaches on the east bank of the Ste. Marguerite River are excellent swimming areas.

En Route from Port Cartier – It is only 22 miles (35 km) along Route 138 to Clarke City, a suburb of Sept Iles. Established as a pulp mill by the Clarke brothers — William, James, John, and George — in 1908, the next generation of Clarkes expanded into gulf and North Shore shipping. The city of Sept Iles is 18 miles (29 km) farther.

SEPT ILES: In the northwest corner of the Gulf of St. Lawrence, the Baie des Sept Iles provided a perfect location for Basque fishing vessels and French explorers seeking refuge from the rough waters of the Atlantic and the Gulf of St. Lawrence. Pointe Noire, on the western side of the harbor, curves to form a breakwater on the west and south sides of the bay, while a protruding point forms the east side of the harbor mouth. The seven small islands that named the bay (and city) protect this passage. A trading post and mission were established here during the 1650s, but the first settlers were the Smith, Brochu, and Levesque families shortly after 1860.

Camping is allowed at rustic sites on one of the islands at the mouth of the bay (contact *Club Caravan Côte Nord;* phone: 418-583-2710), as is coastal (saltwater) fishing for cod, mackerel, and halibut. Inland, speckled trout and ouananiche (land-locked salmon) are the angler's game; and moose, bear, wolf, hare, partridge, wild duck, and goose attract hunters. Two airports and a seaplane base make this a good takeoff point for expeditions farther into the wilds. The original trading post, *Le Musée Vieux Poste,* has been reconstructed on a bank of the Vieux Fort River (with a restaurant added). Open daily, summer only, from 9 AM to 5 PM (phone: 418-968-2070).

En Route from Sept Iles – From Sept Iles to Havre St. Pierre is about 140 miles (225 km) via Route 138, which is now paved for its entire length. Air or sea transport is more suitable than the coast road for any travel farther into this region.

Beyond Sept Iles lies the coastal area known as the Mingan Coast and the coastal Iles de Mingan. The San Sebastian Basque whalers who visited these islands during the 16th century named one long island Min Gain ("tongue of land"). Five dry-stone ovens and assorted utensils for the preparation of whale oil have been found on two of these islands. The coast was the site of bloody border wars between the Inuit people from the north and the Iroquois, and later Montagnais, Indians who occupied the area to the south. The region was bought by Parks-Canada and is now a federal national preserve. A welcome center at Havre St. Pierre has audiovisual presentations on the Mingans and arranges guided tours (phone: 418-538-2512 or 538-2717).

BEST EN ROUTE

Even though Quebec is visited by more people than any other Canadian province, accommodations outside the larger towns are sometimes limited. Although there are enough places that provide all the amenities, deluxe accommodations are few and far between. Most of the hotels listed here fall into the moderate price range — $40 to $50 per night, double occupancy, with no meals. Those that cost more than $50 are listed as expensive, and those under $40 are considered inexpensive. Off-season rates are lower, and sometimes they're cut in half. All prices are quoted in US dollars.

ESCOUMINS

Complexe Hôtelier Pelchat – A comfortable 25-unit motel with a restaurant. Rte. 138 (phone: 418-233-2401). Moderate.

Gagnon – This family-run hotel has 14 rooms, a comfortable atmosphere, and home cooking. 87 Marcellin St. (phone: 418-233-2010). Inexpensive.

FORESTVILLE

Danube Bleu – A modern hotel-motel with excellent services and a restaurant. Rte. 138 (phone: 418-587-2278). Expensive to moderate.

L'An 2000 – The basic 20-unit motel has air conditioning and a TV set in every room. No dining room, but a restaurant is across the street. 164 Principale St. (phone: 418-587-4431). Inexpensive.

BAIE COMEAU

Le Manoir – A plush stone manor house in a beautiful garden setting, overlooking St. Lawrence. It offers one of the best tables on the North Shore, with French specialties and seafood. 8 Cabot St. (phone: 418-296-3391). Expensive to moderate.

Caravelle – On a hill overlooking town, this modern hotel-motel has an indoor swimming pool and sauna, plus a restaurant and a bar with dancing. 202 La Salle Blvd. (phone: 418-296-4986).Moderate.

PORT CARTIER

Château – A nice hotel-motel that includes a restaurant and sauna. 30 Elie Rochefort St. (phone: 418-766-3444). Moderate.

SEPT ILES

Auberge des Gouverneurs – This is a luxurious 124-room inn with all services, a good restaurant, and pool. 666 Laure Blvd. (phone: 418-962-7071). Expensive.

Sept Iles – A large establishment with a satisfactory restaurant. 451 Arnaud Ave. (phone: 418-962-2581). Moderate.

The Laurentians

The Laurentian Mountains, with extensive parks and wildlife reserves, play a crucial role in maintaining the high quality of Canadian life. They are at once a magnificent playground, a bulwark against misuse of the land, and a vital part of the heritage of Canada.

The Laurentians are the wilderness backyard of the populated section of the St. Lawrence shoreline. Cutting a broad swath across southwestern Quebec, this group of modest but ancient mountains provides huge areas of lakes and rivers for outdoor activities; the slopes closer to Quebec and Montreal have become world-famous ski resorts. There are 26 alpine ski areas within a 40-mile radius capable of handling up to 100,000 skiers per hour. The mountains comprise a natural reserve, their rugged slopes having deterred inquisitive explorers and thwarted industrial developers. As the coastal settlements became cities and wildlife began to take refuge deeper and deeper in the mountains, great sections of the Laurentians were made game reserves. Many of the area's parks are based on the historical boundaries of the Crown lands established as early as the 1600s; others have been created in response to recent trends in land use.

Carefully controlled hunting is permitted in some reserves and in certain areas is often restricted either to native Indian tribes or to Quebec residents. Although large sections of the Laurentian Mountains have been set aside as parks and reserves, there are also commercial skiing centers and private (owned or leased) hunting and fishing grounds. All wildlife is carefully monitored, and hunting and fishing guidelines are established to ensure that no species is threatened. With equal care, development in and around the parks and wooded areas is controlled to preserve this pristine environment where harried victims of modern life can retreat to mend soul and body.

The Laurentians are one of the oldest mountain ranges in the world, skirting the southern boundary of the part of the Canadian Shield that lies between the Ottawa and Saguenay rivers in Quebec. The Shield, formed by the first permanent rise of the North American landmass during the Precambrian era, outlines the Hudson Bay watershed. The glaciers that followed it carved out thousands of lakes and rivers and helped shape Hudson Bay itself. Continuous upheaval and erosion gradually defined the fringe of this U-shaped plateau into the low-level mountains of today. Few Laurentian peaks exceed 2,500 feet; the famous ski resort of Mont Tremblant is a relative giant at 3,000 feet. The mountains rise within sight of the St. Lawrence River in many places, and nowhere are the Laurentians more than 100 miles from the river, making this immense recreation area easily accessible from any of the metropolitan sections along the shoreline.

If you're planning to do any hunting other than in parks, the help of an outfitter is recommended. Because of the unique service and the close interaction between hunter (or angler) and outfitter, much of your enjoyment of the trip depends upon personalities; it's wise to talk to one or two outfitters before making arrangements. The *Quebec Outfitters Association Directory* (phone: 514-687-0041) details names and numbers according to region, so make a few calls.

CENTRAL QUEBEC: THE ST. MAURICE VALLEY

One of Quebec's major industrial cities, Trois Rivières, halfway between Montreal and Quebec, straddles the mouth of the St. Maurice River. The city's French name is based upon the three channels formed by the islands in the river delta where it meets the St. Lawrence. The Indians had called the river Métabéroutine, "sheet of water exposed to all winds." It was renamed for Maurice Poulin, who was granted control of the valley in 1668. The rich timberlands, providing the logs, and the river, providing transportation and power, were a vital combination in the creation of this busy city. It is fitting that this hectic industrial and shipping center with a past as old as Canada itself — Cartier toured the St. Maurice River Valley in 1535 and Champlain erected a trading post here in 1615 — should guard the entrance to one of the most beautiful sections of Quebec.

Trois Rivières: This prosperous industrial city warrants at least an afternoon's stop to tour its much-improved historic district, which is toward the river. The tourist information center is housed in the beautifully restored Manoir Boucher de Niverville (168 Bonaventure St.; phone: 819-375-9628), a 1730 house that was once home to the first *seigneurs* of the town. It also features two rooms of antique French Canadian pine furniture and artifacts. Guided tours of the city begin here, June to *Labor Day*. Maurice Duplessis, controversial premier of Quebec from 1936 to 1939 and again from 1944 to 1959, is Trois Rivière's most famous native son, and he is honored with a statue in the square adjacent to the Manoir Boucher de Niverville. Another attraction is the archaeology museum at the University of Quebec (3351 des Forges Blvd.; phone: 819-376-5032). From the end of June to mid-July the city stages a cultural festival — *Festival* *des Trois Rivières* — with concerts, shows, historical tableaux, and art exhibitions. These events take place at Champlain Park, Place Niverville, and Place d'Armes; for information, call 819-372-4610/4614.

En Route from Trois Rivières – Take Route 55 north about 25 miles (40 km) to Grand Mère, where the road becomes Route 155, or bypass Trois Rivières via Route 153 if you're approaching along the coast from Montreal or via Route 159 if you're coming from Quebec.

The growth and development of the St. Lawrence shoreline contrasts sharply with the rural atmosphere of this valley. Although many of the towns are industrial centers drawing upon neighboring resources, they maintain a deep and protective respect for their roots. They are dedicated to preserving the forests and rivers that surround them as part of a life of outdoor activity and a relaxed pace.

Most of the route runs past small farms or through forests, with the river rarely out of sight. It is not unusual to see logs, a staple of local industry, floating down toward the sawmills. You may see a logjam — thousands upon thousands of uniformly cut logs piled every which way until the river is covered with a floor of pine, not a glint of blue water to be seen. When an explosion clears the blockage, thousands of logs break loose and are swept downriver by the current. It's a sight you'll never forget.

The southeast entrance to La Mauricie National Park is a secondary road from St. Jean des Piles, about 8 miles (13 km) from Grand Mère.

LA MAURICIE NATIONAL PARK: Encompassing some 200 square miles of glacier-torn mountains, including 60 lakes and an untold number of rivers, the park is currently being enlarged to accommodate increasing numbers of visitors. There are now 124 campsites near the park entrance at Lac la Pêche as well as 218 at Lac Wapizagonke and 91 at Mistagance; perhaps a dozen wilderness sites, accessible only by boat, surround the lake. Beyond this small area, a canoe is the only feasible means of transportation to the many wilderness campsites in the backcountry. It is necessary to portage both canoe and gear about 1¼ miles to reach the next lake, and frequent portages are required to explore the area. Canoe rentals are available in the park along with detailed maps indicating 3-, 4-, and 5-day canoe-camping trips through the area. A license is necessary if you plan to catch trout dinners while you camp — a 4-day food supply can be heavy. Hunting is not permitted. Even if you don't spend your vacation tramping through the woods, take a day trip (by canoe) on Lac la Pêche. At the north end of the lake is half a mountain, sheared away by a passing glacier, with its solid rock interior exposed. There are several sandy shores along the lake where you can beach your canoe and walk in distant forests. But paddle close to the exposed mountainside, look straight up its rocky wall, and try to imagine the force that cut through it. Then back away and try to take a picture of this cliff, from water level to forested peak and end to end; capturing a bear with your hands would be easier. Lac Wapizagonke lies between two such rocky walls 8 miles long. Exploration has revealed Indian pictographs on these cliffs, but their origins are unknown. The park is open year-round, and there is an admission charge of $2.50 ($3 CN) per car (phone: 819-536-2638).

If this area is too tame or confining for your taste, bear in mind that it borders on the wilder reserves of St. Maurice (to the north) and Mastigouche (to the west).

ST. MAURICE RESERVE: If it's really untamed woodland you're looking for, this is a fine place to start. For 150 years, hunters and fishermen from Quebec, Ontario, and the US have come here to engage in their favorite outdoor pursuits. The reserve covers 617 square miles of wild mountains, rivers, and woods. There is no access road; you must take a ferry across the St. Maurice River at Matawin — about 42 miles (67 km) from Grand Mère — then proceed by jeep and boat to your campground. Some cottages (hunting lodges) are available, but tents may be necessary in some areas. A guide is recommended but not required. Small-game hunting is permitted (moose are controlled for residents), although it's really not feasible to hunt in this area without a guide, and the abundance of speckled trout almost takes the challenge out of fishing. Canoeing is encouraged, but only a few rentals are available in the park. The area has been leased to local hunting and fishing clubs, which have kept development (like roads) to a minimum. Line up an outfitter and let him direct you to non-park lands where moose and bear can be hunted.

LA TUQUE: Some 75 miles (121 km) from Grand Mère along Route 155, this town provides its own *Domaine Touristique de La Tuque* (public tours of La Tuque; phone: 819-523-2304), with seven camps where hunting and fishing are *the* activity (depending on the season). The park is relatively small — 40 square miles — but with 18 outfitters controlling 138 additional camps and lodges, there are places for almost everyone. Area game includes moose, deer, and bear, plus rabbit and various fowl. From here, Lac St. Jean is 82 miles (132 km) north, past the huge St. Maurice Reserve; the Chibougamau Reserve's access roads are only a short distance away.

NORTH OF QUEBEC CITY: RÉSERVE FAUNIQUE DES LAURENTIDES

En Route from Quebec City – Take Route 175 north from downtown for the 30-mile (48-km) drive to Laurentides' southern entrance.

RÉSERVE FANIQUE DES LAURENTIDES (LAURENTIANS): The 5,637 square miles of Laurentides Réserve began as a Montagnais hunting ground until infringement by Huron tribes turned the peaceful mountains into a battleground. When the fighting died down in 1895, the Quebec government opted to use the land as a park to preserve the natural forests and wildlife of this area as much as possible, but the caribou that once dominated the region have been severely depleted. The park is currently used to reacclimate animals from other areas and to encourage breeding to rebuild the herds. Only moose hunting is permitted (under controlled guidelines), but fishing is easily arranged. Several cottages are available summer and winter. There are two camping areas totaling 258 sites at Belle Rivière and Lac Loutre, plus a wilderness camping-canoeing area in the Jacques Cartier Valley. Guides are mandatory in many areas.

The reserve covers a wide variety of terrain, with the eastern peaks averaging between 3,120 and 4,025 feet. The western area is considerably less mountainous. All sectors are reasonably accessible, thanks to the network of roads serving the park. Route 175 travels a north-south path through the park. The southern entrance is only 30 miles (48 km) north of Quebec, the northern entrance only 13 miles (21 km) south of Chicoutimi. Route 169 from Alma, east of Lac St. Jean, leads to the park entrance only 24 miles (39 km) south and intersects Route 175 in the middle of the park.

NORTH OF MONTREAL: SKI COUNTRY

En Route from Montreal – Two routes lead north toward the entrance to Mont Tremblant Park. One leads into the heart of the Laurentian ski country, the other into more of a hunting area, although the skiing is equally good there.

Take either Route 117 or the high-speed Route 15 north from Montreal into the Laurentian foothills. The small city of Rosemere is only 15 miles (24 km) from the metropolitan area, yet the timeless peace of the mountains is apparent in the 2,800-acre forest in the heart of the town. Several of the houses in the area were built in the 17th and 18th centuries. The city of St. Jérôme, the gateway to the Laurentians, is only 15 miles (24 km) away. Farther north and east, along Route 125, is Canadiana Village (phone: 514-834-4135), a reconstructed 19th-century farm community in the Lanaudière region, a scenic area about 45 minutes northeast from Montreal that is also the site of the *Wilfrid Laurier National Park and House,* the former home of Canada's seventh Prime Minister and now a museum (phone: 514-439-3702). In the town of Joliette, the heart of the region, the annual Lanaudière summer festival fills local parks, theaters, and churches with the strains of classical music and jazz from June until late August. The event has attracted such performers as Oscar Peterson and Marilyn Horne. Most venues charge admission (phone: 514-759-7636). Tourisme Lanaudière (phone: 514-834-2535) can provide more details on the area's attractions and the summer-long music festival. For information on the Laurentians, stop at the tourist center at exit 39 off Route 15 or at the junction of Route 117 and 158 (phone: 514-436-8532).

ST. JÉRÔME: St. Jérôme was established in 1830, its development greatly aided by Curé Labelle, who attracted settlers to this community and others during the latter half of the 1800s. He is also credited with bringing the rail line to St. Jérôme and as far north as Mont Laurier. His fervent efforts to open the wild lands of Canada's North and West and his explorations to establish new communities made him a well-loved folk hero throughout the country. Many ski areas and summer resorts are hidden in the mountains just north of here.

St. Jérôme's de la Durantaye Park is the site of outdoor concerts from late June to mid-August. The art gallery in the Vieux Palais, or Old Courthouse (185 du Palais St.; phone: 514-432-7171), is open year-round.

SHAWBRIDGE: The Shawbridge resort area begins only 37 miles northwest of Montreal. It was here, in 1928, that Jack Rabbit Johanssen, considered the father of Laurentian skiing, laid out the slalom run that started it all. The famed Maple Leaf Trail, covering 60 miles (97 km) of cross-country trails from Shawbridge to Mont Tremblant, was established by Johanssen during the early 1930s.

Together with Piedmont, just 5 miles (8 km) away, and nearby Ste. Adèle, this area comprises a convenient change of pace. There are 21 ski runs at Morin Heights (Bellevue, Chemin du Lac Echo) and 20 at Mont Gabriel (Mont Gabriel, Auberge Mont Gabriel), plus 2 resorts in the area of Ste. Adèle, with a total of 27 slopes. *Le Chantecler* (phone: 819-229-3555) is the largest (see *Best En Route*), and *Cotes* (phone: 514-229-2921) follows. Around Piedmont are Alpine-style slopes at Monts Avila (Avila) and Olympia (Mont Olympia), and more than two dozen cross-country trails. At St. Sauveur, 4 ski resorts provide some 42 slopes, with maximum vertical drops averaging 530 feet. The largest is Mont St. Sauveur (Rue St. Denis; phone: 514-227-4671), with 22 slopes, followed by Mont Christie (Christieville, St. Sauveur) with 12 and Mont Habitant (12 Blvd. des Skieurs) with 8. St. Sauveur is also a prime area for nighttime activites, thanks to its many fine restaurants and discos.

Although the village of Piedmont has existed since 1853, it is gradually becoming associated with a broad resort area called St. Sauveur-des-Monts, which also includes Mont Gabriel and several other communities. During the summer months, golf courses bloom near many of these resorts (18 holes at Piedmont, Ste. Adèle, and Mont Gabriel respectively; 9 holes at Shawbridge), and there are dozens of private campgrounds. In Bellefeuille, just south of Shawbridge, are the Lac Claude (phone: 514-438-7532) and Lac Lafontaine (phone: 819-431-7373) campgrounds, with 75 and 250 sites respectively. The 150-site Au Pin d'Erable grounds (phone: 819-436-8319) and the 47-site De l'Iris grounds (phone: 514-563-2790) are located in St. Hippolyte. This area's popularity has attracted (and has been helped by) several excellent dining establishments. The *Alpine Inn* hotel (phone: 819-229-3516) in Ste. Marguerite Station and the *Estérel* (phone: 514-228-2571) rate among the best (see *Best En Route*).

Mont St. Sauveur has a water-slide park, the Parc Aquatique (phone: 514-227-4671), which includes a pool with 4-foot waves. The village's main street, dominated by the white church steeple, is lined with boutiques, crafts shops, and good restaurants — all favorites with Montrealers out for a weekend drive. On summer Tuesday evenings, music lovers flock to the classical concerts held at the church (call 514-227-2663 for information).

STE. AGATHE DES MONTS: The Val Morin and Val David sport centers are less than 20 miles (32 km) away, and the city of Ste. Agathe des Monts, on Lac des Sables, is the hub of this resort area (60 mi/97 km from Montreal), which dates back to the 1850s. There are 11 slopes at Alta (2114 Rte. 117), and another 12 at Vallée Bleue, all in Val David; Belle Neige (6820 Blvd. Labelle) also has 10 slopes, and Mont Sauvage (2nd Ave.) has 9, bringing the village of Val Morin's total to 19. Nearby, in St. Adolphe d'Howard, L'Avalanche (not exactly a choice name) has 7 slopes (phone: 819-327-3232). As popular for its tables as its slopes is Val David, which takes the culinary awards for this area. Leading the way is the restaurant of *La Sapinière* hotel (phone: 819-322-2020; see *Special Havens* in DIVERSIONS and *Best En Route*). St. Adolphe d'Howard's *Auberge La Soupière* (1944 Chemin du Village; phone: 819-327-2525) and *La Légende* (1510 de l'Avalanche Rd.; phone: 819-327-2055) are also highly regarded dining establishments.

For summer activities, there are campgrounds at Val David (La Belle Etoile, 100 sites, phone: 819-322-3207; Laurentian, 42 sites, phone: 819-322-2281; and Le Montagnais, 35 sites, phone: 819-322-2921), as well as a massive municipal campground (263 sites) in Ste. Agathe des Monts (phone: 819-326-5577). *Alouette Boat Tours* of Lac-des-Sables (phone: 819-326-0457) leave from the dock in the center of town daily during the summer.

En Route from Ste. Agathe des Monts – The village of St. Faustin, 14 miles (23 km) north on Route 117, marks the location of one access road to the giant Mont Tremblant Park. This small resort area is popular with hunters; Mont Blanc, with 24 ski slopes, is equally attractive to skiers (Mont Blanc). St. Jovite, a major resort area, is 6 miles (10 km) farther on Route 117.

ST. JOVITE: Three ski centers provide a total of over 50 slopes in the St. Jovite/Mont Tremblant area: Station Mont Tremblant Lodge (phone: 819-425-8711 or, from anywhere in the US except Massachusetts, 800-567-6761) is the biggest, with 34 slopes and a maximum vertical drop of over 2,100 feet, and Gray Rocks (phone: 819-425-2771) follows, with 18 slopes. For more complete information on skiing in this region, see *Downhill* and *Cross-Country Skiing*, DIVERSIONS.

Camping in the area is plentiful, with a 242-site provincial campground at Mont Tremblant, in the Lac Monroe district, and backed up with 158 sites in the private Vert et Blanc area (phone: 819-425-2018), and 93 sites in the Domaine Desjardins (phone: 819-688-2179) in St. Faustin. For serious diners, there are excellent choices: the *Gray Rocks Inn* (Lac Ouimet, phone: 819-425-2771) and the *Tremblant Club* (Lac Tremblant, phone: 819-425-2731), both in Mont Tremblant (see *Best En Route*). From St. Jovite, Route 117 runs northwest to La Vérendrye Reserve, 94 miles (151 km) away.

An alternate approach to Mont Tremblant Park is via Route 125, through the villages of Chertsey and St. Donat, a total of 83 miles (134 km). This route also provides access to the Joliette Park, and although there are 5 ski centers — the 2 major hills of Mont La Reserve with 13 slopes and Mont Garceau with 12 — in St. Donat, the area is definitely better outfitted for hunting and fishing. *La Corniche,* on Route 329 in St. Donat (phone: 819-424-2714), takes top table honors in the area, but there's a special satisfaction to a meal prepared over an open fire in the woods, especially if you caught (or shot) dinner yourself. Make arrangements with one of the many outfitters in the area to start hunting or fishing expeditions from here.

MONT TREMBLANT PARK: Created in 1894 as a recreation center for residents of Quebec Province, this park is used almost all year. Skiing, snowmobiling, and snowshoeing are the principal winter activities, with camping, canoeing, and moose hunting in season. (The park harbors some 30 animal species. Bear, deer, marten, mink, and porcupine are easily visible if you travel some of the more remote trails.) Only 22 cottages are available for rent, but provincial campgrounds at Lac Monroe, Lac Chat, and Lac Lajoie provide plenty of space for camping.

JOLIETTE: This small reserve is primarily devoted to fishing and small-game hunting, and the bear, deer, and moose you'll see wandering about appear to *know* this. There are cottages available around most lakes to make your hunting or fishing comfortable, but there are no canoe rentals in the park.

NORTH OF HULL: THE GATINEAU VALLEY AND LA VÉRENDRYE

Fur trader Nicholas Gatineau from Trois Rivières explored this valley in 1650. Lumberjacks and hunters followed his lead, opening a broad pathway to the north for settlers. The city of Hull, its sawmills fed with timber floated down the Gatineau River, grew quickly in what had been Indian hunting grounds.

A large group of Americans, including Philemon Wright from Massachusetts, settled the town in 1800. Wright is credited with establishing the first commercial enterprise in town, and another American, Ezra Eddy, started the match factory that made Hull known throughout the world in the 19th century.

Route 105 leads from Hull through the valley to La Vérendrye Reserve, 110 miles (177 km) north.

En Route from Hull – The Gatineau Park, which preserves part of the hunting grounds of the Iroquois and Algonguin Indians, is just outside Hull. There are four principal lakes and ten times that number of smaller ones. Although hunting is prohibited, fishing is allowed in all lakes and rivers, and canoe rentals are available. Protected wildlife — easily spotted while walking the trails — include deer, mink, marten, porcupine, beaver, and an occasional bear. Lac Philippe has an attractive campground with 306 sites (phone: 819-456-3016) as well as a large public beach, picnic tables, and boat rentals.

Also in the park is Moorside, the 575-acre summer estate of former Canadian Prime Minister William Lyon Mackenzie King, which he willed to the public. On the grounds is an interesting and impressive collection of ruins brought here by King, such as parts of the Canadian and British houses of parliament. Open May through mid-October. In the park, just off the Gatineau Pkwy.

Gracefield, Bouchette, and Messine, grouped together about 60 miles (97 km) from Hull, constitute a staging area for hunting and fishing trips. Approximately 30 outfitters based around these towns can point out the best spots for hunting moose, bear, deer, rabbit, partridge, fox, and duck. Fishing will bring in rainbow, speckled, brown, and lake trout, pike, and walleye. A secondary roadway from Gracefield leads to the Pontiac Reserve.

MANIWAKI: Set up as a Hudson's Bay Company trading post, this town is now a major hunting and fishing center. There are many outfitters in the surrounding area, controlling 642 campsites, chalets, and lodges, ranging from primitive to luxurious. A seaplane base is a jumping-off point for expeditions far north. The rustic feel of this community belies its location only 85 miles (137 km) from Hull and the 20th century.

En Route from Maniwaki – Continue on Route 105 to its end at Grand Remous, 20 miles (32 km) north, where Route 117 from Mont Laurier intersects and leads west into the La Vérendrye Reserve. There are about 100 hunting and fishing camps in the immediate area, served by 13 outfitters. Consult the *Quebec Outfitters Directory* or call 819-771-4840.

LA VÉRENDRYE: Established in 1939 to protect wildlife from the onslaught of hunters invading this area, the park preserves the natural habitat of moose, bear, wolf, mink, beaver, marten, rabbit, loon, and many other species. Route 117 travels through the heart of the 5,174-square-mile expanse. Hunting is limited to moose (for residents only), but fishing is encouraged because even these extensive waterways can support only so many pike, walleye, smallmouth bass, lake, and speckled trout. Contact Le Domaine, Reserve La Vérendrye (phone: 819-435-2216 or 438-2017), for details and access rights. Limited numbers of canoe rentals and cottages are available, and there is one inn within the park: *Auberge de Domaine* (phone: 819-435-2541). The reserve is located in the western extremity of the Laurentian Mountain Range.

BEST EN ROUTE

The Laurentians have some of the most pleasant and some of the most rustic accommodations in Canada. In the ski resort areas north of Montreal — around Val David, for instance — are several of the best hostelries in the country; in the backcountry, facilities are little more than basic, and prices are quite reasonable.

The selection below singles out the best in any given area, though not necessarily the least expensive. If your budget is tight, avail yourself of one of the many inexpensive roadside motels, but be prepared for less than perfection. For the hotels that follow, inexpensive refers to places in which a double-occupancy room goes for less than $35; moderate runs from $35 to $55 for two; and expensive, anything over $55 per day. In the prime ski resort areas, seasonal prices can be as high as $170 per day for two but may not include extras, like skis and lifts. Check to see what is included before making reservations. Note that Mont Tremblant has a central reservation service (phone: 819-425-8681 or 800-567-6760) for booking rental accommodations at any of its chalets or condomininiums, or lodgings at a select number of other area hotels. All prices are quoted in US dollars.

SHAWINIGAN

Auberge L'Escapade – An excellent place to stay — good facilities, comfortable, and conveniently located. Dining room. 3383 Rue Garnier (phone: 819-539-6911). Moderate.

LA TUQUE

Le Gîte – A good place to recover from the woods. Well-appointed rooms and good motel services, though the dining room tends to detract a little. 1100 Blvd. Ducharme (phone: 819-523-9501 or 800-361-1155). Moderate.

STE. ADÈLE

Altitude – This attractive 55-unit complex includes 22 rooms with fireplaces. A congenial ski resort, it also features indoor and outdoor pools and a hospitable dining room. Route 117 (phone: 514-229-6616 or 800-363-3683). Expensive.

Le Chantecler – Recently expanded, this resort has 224 well-appointed rooms, as well as squash and racquetball courts, saunas, and a whirlpool bath. It provides a full schedule of summer and winter sports. Lac Rond, Chemin du Chantecler (phone: 819-229-3555). Expensive.

STE. MARGUERITE STATION

Alpine Inn – A fairly large resort facility with a wide variety of extras — including tennis, swimming, and skating. Chalets are also available. (phone: 514-229-3516). Expensive.

VAL DAVID

Hôtel La Sapinière – An hour's drive from Montreal, this is one of the exceptional inns of eastern Canada and the first Canadian member of the association of international country hotels, the Relais & Châteaux group. Its primary distinction is its kitchen, run by Chef Marcel Kretz, who with pastry chef Jean-Pierre Monjon rules the roost. Plan to reserve a few weeks in advance for weekend dining. For more details, see *Special Havens* in DIVERSIONS. Val David, Rte. 117 (phone: 819-322-2020 or 866-8262, in Montreal). Expensive.

STE. AGATHE DES MONTS

Raymond – Although this comfortable 37-unit motel hasn't any dining facilities, all rooms have kitchenettes, and it does have a swimming pool and a pleasant view. 30 Blvd. Morin (phone: 819-326-3626). Moderate to inexpensive.

L'ESTEREL

L'Esterel – Near Ste. Marguerite Station, this hotel offers very good services, 135 redesigned rooms, a new indoor sports complex, and convention facilities. Pool, sauna, golf, tennis, fishing, and boating. Fridolin Simard Blvd. (phone: 819-228-2571 or 866-8224, in Montreal). Expensive.

MONT TREMBLANT

Tremblant Club – This 32-room inn faces Mont Tremblant, the highest peak in the Laurentians, and has "one step from the door" access to some of the best ski slopes in eastern Canada. The inn, which also has condominium units, sits on Lac Tremblant and is a year-round center of activities — cross-country and downhill skiing in winter; swimming, sailing, fishing, golf, tennis, and riding in summer. It is part of a dining exchange program with the other excellent inns in the area should you tire of its award-winning kitchen, an unlikely event. Mont Tremblant (phone: 819-425-2731). Expensive.

Auberge Villa Bellevue – The Dubois family has owned this 80-room lodge for three generations. Luc Dubois, head coach of the Canadian ski team from 1973 to 1976, is now director of the hotel ski school, while the rest of the family concentrates on keeping the accommodations cozy and comfortable and maintaining the restaurant's very high standards. On Lac Ouimet (phone: 819-425-2734 or 800-567-6763). Expensive.

Station Mont Tremblant – Skiing is serious business here, with bars, boutiques, and excellent food to enliven après-ski. On Lac Tremblant, the lodge is open summer and winter; closed about a month between seasons. Mont Tremblant (phone: 819-425-8711 or 800-567-6761). Expensive.

ST. JOVITE

Gray Rocks – Accommodations include rooms in the main inn or in intimate, romantic cottages. The resort has 18 ski runs and a well-known ski school. Also on a lake — Lac Ouimet — with canoeing and swimming and sailing and other summer delights. *Gray Rocks* also has a complete fitness center in the main lodge featuring a heated indoor pool, gym, and jogging facilities. (phone: 819-425-2771). Expensive.

Le St. Jovite – An excellent service staff, a good dining room, and newly added units transform the basic facilities here into a pleasurable place to stay. 1011 Rue Ouimet (phone: 819-425-2751). Moderate to inexpensive.

GATINEAU-LA VÉRENDRYE

Auberge Le Domaine – Being right in this vast park gives this inn a special air; and a good level of services takes it out of the realm of "camping on cots" into one of a true hostelry. Rte. 117 (phone: 819-435-2541). Expensive to moderate.

The Gaspé Peninsula

The southern shore of the St. Lawrence River ends at a peninsula of land that looks like a small child's fist thrown out against the Gulf of St. Lawrence. This is the Gaspé Peninsula. To the west is the ever-widening St. Lawrence River as it enters the gulf; to the north and east, the gulf itself and Anticosti Island; to the southeast, the Baie des Chaleurs (Bay of Warmth), which separates Gaspé from New Brunswick. The peninsula extends about 175 miles along the river, from the valley of the Matapédia River to its cape-edged shore on the gulf. The entire southern shoreline of the St. Lawrence is shaped something like a large, curved letter *P,* and the Gaspé Peninsula forms the large loop at the letter's top.

The peninsula is considered one of the oldest landmasses on the planet, with life forms that have long since disappeared from other areas. The Chic-Chocs Mountains, called Sigsoon, or "rocky mountains," by the Micmac Indians, create a high-altitude sanctuary for the centuries-old alpine fir and the rangifer, or wood caribou, which is virtually extinct elsewhere. The heavily wooded valleys and highland regions rate among the world's best for moose, deer, and upland game-bird hunting, and the Chic-Chocs are the source of some of the finest Atlantic salmon rivers.

When Cartier first sailed through the Strait of Belle Isle and entered the Gulf of St. Lawrence, the lands of Labrador and Newfoundland were thought to be cold, barren, and forbidding — fit for fisheries and little else. After cruising the western shore of Newfoundland and discovering the Iles de la Madeleine, he entered the Baie des Chaleurs. The more tolerable climate and fertile lands prompted him to explore the peninsula, called Gespeg by the resident Micmac Indians. Before returning to France, he sailed in the summer of 1534 from the Baie des Chaleurs around the rugged shoreline of the Gespeg ("land's end" or "extremity") and across the mouth of the St. Lawrence River to Ile d'Anticosti. During his next voyage he explored the river, hoping it would provide the route to the spice lands of the East — the Northwest Passage. His reports of the beautiful and fertile lands of the *gaspé* (the European influence rapidly corrupted the language of the Indians) and visions of the wealth of resources yet undiscovered attracted settlers to New France.

The massive scale of this primitive area is illustrated by the unique Percé Rock; 1,420 feet long (plus a little extra for the piece that stands apart) and 288 feet tall, its weight is estimated at 400 million tons. It stands silent and alone just off the Gaspé coast. During his voyage, Cartier anchored his three ships in its protective shadow.

Given the accessibility of the Gaspé, it is surprising that the region remained so completely undeveloped. When Cartier arrived, the Micmac and Malecite tribes occupied the peninsula, but the Indians of the East Coast were restless peoples and rarely colonized areas they roamed. The land was crossed many times by the Abnaki, Montagnais, and Huron and war parties of the Iroquois. All these tribes contributed words, place names, and bits of history to its culture. Long before Cartier, the Basques had left their mark on the coast of this "tongue of land" and the seafaring Vikings had preceded them. But these groups were not colonists, and none built dwellings or bound themselves to any one place. They were explorers, hunters, sailors, travelers.

The coastal fishing settlements established by the French and other Europeans began as isolated, independent villages relatively oblivious to one another. In some sense this isolation is an abiding characteristic of Gaspé life. Few of the original inland villages have grown much, since most settlers arriving in successive waves followed the St. Lawrence farther inland, skipping the rugged peninsula in search of unexplored lands to the west. The extensive mountains of the peninsula — part of the Appalachian chain — may have seemed too difficult for settlers. In any case, growth in this part of the province has always been slow. The principal highway, Route 132, was completed in 1928 and runs through the Matapédia River valley, following the rocky coastline and the shoreline of the St. Lawrence; commercial growth has been largely limited to tourist services. Because of competition from already developed areas of the province, industry has overlooked Gaspé. Visiting the Gaspé is like stepping backward in time. Most of the villagers continue to depend upon the sea for their livelihood, in many places still using the same methods and equipment as their grandparents. Sails and nets are still mended by hand, and salted fish, like cod and herring, are dried in open racks.

There is more to the Gaspé than the small fishing villages with their century-old dwellings, the handmade sails mounted on wooden fishing boats, and the stories of shipwrecks and ghosts. There is the unspoiled beauty of the forests; glimpses of moose, bear, and caribou in the underbrush; trout leaping from mountain streams; and the mountains themselves, which color the air with their ancient aura — the feeling of indomitable, massive power defying age. All this makes a most attractive vacation for hunters, anglers, naturalists, artists, and latter-day explorers.

The route originates across the river from Quebec City, and jumps quickly to Rivière du Loup, a distance of 123 miles (198 km) along the south bank of the St. Lawrence on Route 132. Route 20, the Trans-Canada Highway, can cut down on your travel time between the two cities, or take one of the many ferries from the north shore (see the *Beaupré/Charlevoix* route and the *North Shore* route). From Rivière du Loup the route follows the St. Lawrence on Route 132 and circles the peninsula. Since a large number of visitors drive this route (circling clockwise), we suggest you circle counterclockwise to avoid congestion. Rather than continue on Route 132 all the way up the south shore, turn right at Ste. Flavie and explore the Matapédia Valley to the Baie des Chaleurs, via Route 132, then follow the road as it traces the route of Cartier's exploration of the region — from south to north along the coast and up the St. Lawrence River. The journey covers some 220 miles (350 km), beginning at Quebec City and ending at the Ste. Flavie–Mont Joli area. Rather than return to Quebec on a familiar route, combine this with the Beaupré/Charlevoix and North Shore routes and cover fresh ground.

QUEBEC CITY: This beautiful bit of history is more than a commercial hub and the travel center of eastern Canada: It embodies the soul of French Canada. Unless you have visited the city before, it is a necessary introduction to this unique province. For a detailed report, see *Quebec City,* THE CITIES.

En Route from Quebec – The pont de Québec (Quebec Bridge) leads to both Routes 20 and 132, so you can choose whether to take the newer highway, reaching Rivière du Loup in 2½ hours, or drive the more scenic Route 132. Either way, it is about 123 miles (198 km) and, although Route 20 does have rest areas, it is necessary to get off the Trans-Canada and onto Route 132 for food and gas.

LÉVIS: Shortly after leaving Quebec City (6 mi/10 km), Route 132 passes through Lévis. It was here, in 1648, that Father Pierre Bailloquet celebrated the south shore's first Mass. From terraces overlooking the river, the city of Quebec unfolds in a magnificent panorama. Pointe Lévis, directly opposite Quebec City, was used for a variety of purposes over the years, including the defense of the walled city. On April 18, 1793, Marie-Josephe Corriveau was hanged near the Plains of Abraham (outside Quebec) after being convicted of murdering her second husband with an ax. This may have been the finale to a long string of murders she committed, and after being hanged, the body of La Corriveau, as she was nicknamed, was displayed in an iron cage on Pointe Lévis — in view of Quebec City — until May 25. The cage itself was recovered during the 1850s, and La Corriveau was immortalized as a female Jack the Ripper.

The *Alphonse-Desjardins House,* built in 1882–1884, at 8 Mont-Marie St. is now a museum commemorating the founder of North America's first savings and loan institution, Les Caisses Populaires Desjardins, which began in 1901 in the kitchen (phone: 418-853-2090).

En Route from Lévis – A little farther northeast is the city of Montmagny and the South Shore Archipelago — a group of seven small islands that are prime hunting ground for waterfowl. Each fall thousands of white geese and other migrating birds invade the shoreline flats of Ile aux Grues while hunters ferry from the mainland for the occasion. The mud flats also connect Ile aux Grues to Ile aux Oies. In 1655, this island was subjected to one of many Iroquois raids against French settlers, and the two daughters of farmer Jean-Baptiste Moyen were captured (the rest of the family was killed). Raphael Lambert Closse, acting governor of Montreal, saved both girls from the Indians and then married one. After his death (during a skirmish with Indians in 1662), the girls entered the Order of the Hospitalières de Québec, and part of the island was given as their dowry. Although the Order acquired the remainder of the island in 1713, a British regiment raided the island, killed the inhabitants and their stock, and burned all the buildings and farms in 1759. Only two nuns escaped the carnage. The island was sold to private interests in 1964.

ST. JEAN PORT JOLI: Just 60 miles (97 km) from Quebec City, St. Jean Port Joli, known as the handicraft capital of the region, is well worth visiting. Just before entering the village, Route 132 passes a large group of wood sculpture and craft shops — the greatest concentration of handicrafts in the province. The Bourgault family, known through the region, provided the impetus for this loose association in 1936 by bringing their own shop and personal artistry in wood carving to the area. Soon they were joined by craftspeople working in an assortment of materials. An unrestored (1776) church, classified as an historic landmark, stands alongside the roadway at the edge of the village. Its sculptured wooden detail is exquisite. The *Musée des Anciens Canadiens* (352 Gaspe Ouest Ave.; phone: 418-598-3392) contains works of well-known woodcarvers. In town, try *Auberge du Faubourg* (phone: 418-598-6455) on Gaspé Avenue for lunch.

RIVIÈRE DU LOUP: The town's name is derived from the *loups-marins* — seals — that at one time made frequent appearances in the St. Lawrence at its junction with the du Loup River. Although the seals are rarely seen nowadays, the town has kept the name — except for the period from 1850 to 1919, when it was called Fraserville. With its back to the northern slopes of the Notre Dame Mountains, this terraced town provides excellent views of the St. Lawrence River and three small islands. Each spring, a number of eider ducks nest on the easternmost isle of the group, Ile Blanche.

The town is a popular gathering spot for hunters and anglers preparing to enter the Gaspé. Guides point out the best nearby places to start. If you're hungry, stop at the dining room of the *Château Grandville* (94 Lafontaine St.; phone: 418-862-3551).

En Route from Rivière du Loup – It is possible to ferry across the St. Lawrence River from St. Siméon on the north shore to join the route (or leave it during the return) at this point. The ferry runs from May to October (with some crossings from November to January) and usually makes several trips daily, depending upon demand (phone: 418-862-5094). It is also possible to take Route 185 southeast from Rivière du Loup toward New Brunswick and the northeast tip of Maine. The Gaspé region lies ahead on Route 132, 83 miles (134 km) away, at the town of Ste. Flavie. The newer highway, Route 20, has not been extended much past Île verte as yet, which increases the traffic on Route 132 into the Gaspé.

TROIS PISTOLES: A brief drive of 29 miles (47 km) beyond Rivière du Loup leads to the fishing village of Trois Pistoles. The town's name has been traced back to a legendary incident in 1621, when oarsmen crossing one of the many rivers in the area dropped a silver cup worth three "pistoles," the currency of the day, into the water. Their cry of "Voilà trois pistoles perdues!" ("There go three pistols!") gave rise to the town's name. Today, the town is known for its fish. The size and number of catches made by fishermen on the commercial craft available continue to draw anglers to the city. The town hosts the ten-day *Festival des Iles* (Island Festival) in mid-July, with 50 outdoor activities, entertainment, and games. Also worth a visit is a restored notary's house dating to 1842 at 162 Rue Notre Dame E. (phone: 418-851-1656). It is a good example of the area's Kamouraska style of architecture and adjoins a handicraft shop and a bakery, all three of which are open year-round. One of its offshore islands bears the name Ile aux Basques, and three Basque whale oil furnaces have been reconstructed on the island. Along with the twin Iles Razades, these islands provide sanctuary for numbers of birds and are administered by the Provancher Society (a cousin of the Audubon Society). Check with the visitor center for permission to visit the Basque furnaces (phone: 418-851-2959/3698). The islands are also visited each spring by schools of dolphins, easily seen from the shore, and whales visit from July to September when whale-watching cruises leave from Trois Pistoles' dock. (For more information phone the Association Touristique du Bas-St. Laurent at 418-867-1272).

A ferry connects Trois Pistoles with Les Escoumins on the north shore from mid-May to mid-October (phone: 418-851-3099). *Le Marmiton* (70 Notre Dame St.; phone: 418-851-3202) is a good place to eat, whether you're waiting for a ferry or just passing through.

BIC: The small town of Bic, 25 miles (40 km) from Trois Pistoles, is a beautiful place to stop. The story told by most people around here is that during the creation of the earth, an overworked angel in charge of mountains and islands decided to end his day right there and unloaded everything at his disposal in and around Bic. They may be right, because the town is surrounded by heavenly hills and islands and 15 good walking and bicycle tours.

Bic was also blessed, perhaps by the same angelic gesture, with a deepwater harbor, making it a natural military port. During the British-French conflict, General Wolfe anchored his fleet here on his way toward Quebec, and during the American Civil War, fear of an American invasion prompted the British to dispatch the cutter *Persia* and a regiment of troops to the port city to prepare the defense of the Canada-Maine border. One of the offshore islands bears the gruesome name Ile du Massacre, and, beautiful as the island is, the name is accurate. In 1533 a band of about 200 Micmac Indians were driven from shelter in a cave and murdered by a party of Iroquois raiders.

There are two camping grounds in the area: *Bic* (phone: 418-736-4711) and *Delavoie* (phone: 418-736-4730), both directly off Route 132. Prices are reasonable. Route 132 leads to Bic Park and its nature center, inn, campground, and activities — clam-digging in summer, cross-country skiing in winter.

RIMOUSKI: Situated midway between Quebec City and Gaspé, this city, with a population of about 30,000, rates as one of the urban centers of the region. It is beginning to show signs of extraordinary development as a year-round shipping center. Almost 25% of the city was destroyed by fire in 1950, which provided space for the growth of many of the more modern facilities and subsequently attracted people and industry.

As the route enters the Gaspé, hunting and fishing improve, and the city of Rimouski is no exception. For river fishing, contact the Association de Chasse et Pêche de Rivière-du-Loup (phone: 418-862-5890), or the provincial fish and game office (phone: 418-722-3830); to arrange hunting, check the Lechasseur Club (phone: 418-775-3655) in nearby Mont Joli or make arrangements at the government-run Rimouski Reserve, which allows deer and small-game hunting. Although moose may not be hunted most of the year, bear in mind that the name Rimouski means land of moose, and these prize animals *can* be hunted (one per person) during late October, but check for the exact dates (phone: 418-722-3830). The season lasts only 1 or 2 weeks.

The city has a regional art museum (phone: 418-724-2272) open all year and an intriguing sea museum at Pointe-au-Père, 6 miles (10 km) from Rimouski (open mid-June to September) with displays on the area's maritime history. From late September to mid-October, the city stages a lively fall festival of arts and crafts displays, street fairs, concerts, and sporting events.

En Route from Rimouski – Rimouski and its suburbs spread along the coast, so it can be difficult to differentiate between localities sometimes. You'll have no trouble, however, in recognizing the sandy beaches of Ste. Luce, an old whaling village that has grown into a popular water sport resort. Go right over to the village wharf and charter a boat for deep-sea fishing. In the village of Ste. Luce sur Mer (a separate but indistinguishable entity) there is a French restaurant in the *Auberge Sainte-Luce* (see *Best En Route*) at Pointe-au-Père, 6 miles (10 km) from Rimouski, which also provides the best accommodations in town (open in summer only). About 12 miles (19 km) from Rimouski, Route 132 splits and circles the peninsula in each direction. Since most traffic goes clockwise around the Gaspé, we've mapped a counterclockwise route to avoid crowds and aggravation.

The drive from Ste. Flavie to Matapédia, at the Restigouche estuary on the Baie des Chaleurs, just under 100 miles (161 km), can be negotiated in about 2½ hours, but don't rush. The route follows an old Indian trail through the valley of the Matapédia River, which has some of the most beautiful scenery in the world. The valley is formed by the steep slopes of the central highlands paralleling the coast between Quebec and Ste. Flavie and the beginning of the Chic-Chocs Mountain Range. Between these two rocky masses, and fed by streams that run down their slopes, is the Matapédia River, aptly nicknamed "river of the 222 rapids."

Bypass the industrial town of Mont Joli and head inland through the farming and hunting villages of Ste. Angèle de Mérici and St. Moise to Sayabec, at the head of Matapédia Lake. In the village forestry museum is the trunk of a 700-year-old cedar tree and a fir tree growing within a cedar.

Val Brillant has the good fortune of sprawling along the western side of Matapédia Lake with a really fine beach. Take a few minutes to stop and relax. Amqui, at the confluence of the Matapédia and Humqui rivers, is the county seat.

It's named after the Humqui River, which means "place of playful waters," but the spelling was altered in recent times. A secondary road from the town leads to the Matapédia wildlife reserve, a park encompassing 66 square miles of rivers, small lakes, and mountains.

Lac au Saumon, dominating a small lake formed by a widening of the Matapédia River, was originally settled by a group of Acadians from the Iles de la Madeleine. The area around it is filled with trout streams and small waterfalls, a favorite of many freshwater anglers. A few miles downstream is Causapscal, an industrial town by the standards of this region. With a population of 3,000, it is second by only a few hundred people to the county seat at Amqui. Built at the junction of the Matapédia and Causapscal rivers, it was once called Les Fourches ("the forks"). With two sets of riverbanks on which to draw, the scenery runs a close second to salmon fishing as favorite pastime. There are six fishing zones, four of which do not require reservations, so it's possible just to stop off and fish for a spell. Try your luck and skill because the Atlantic salmon that run in the river are considered one of the toughest fighting fish in the world. Those who prefer to watch can visit the Domaine Matamajaw, at 48 St.-Jacques St. (phone: 418-756-3752), an interpretative center that recounts the history of salmon fishing. Observant visitors may also take in the sport along the Les Fourches Trail, where the Matapedia and Causapscal rivers meet. Local fishing guides can be hired for visiting anglers by calling Zec Casault, phone: 418-756-3670.

After you've taken your limit (check the fishing regulations for open season and limits), continue through the small farming village of Ste. Florence on to Routhierville. The only access to the village is across the old 259-foot covered bridge. The road to Routhierviell winds around the river, giving panoramic views of the rushing water below. There are a number of scenic rest areas en route. From here to Matapédia, 24 miles (39 km) south, there is little but farmland and river ... and good fishing.

MATAPÉDIA: This small village is at the juncture of the Restigouche and Matapédia rivers; the Ristigouche flows on from here into the Baie des Chaleurs. The delta itself is a major salmon fishing area as well as a historical area. First settled by a group of Loyalists in 1808, the village was bolstered by the arrival of Irish immigrants in 1832 and Acadians in 1860. By 1872, population growth warranted the construction of a rail link with the northern and eastern regions of the peninsula.

On July 9, 1760, in a sea battle between the French and British, the ships *Machault* and *Bienfaisant* were scuttled in the north channel of the river delta, and a third French ship, the *Marquis de Malauze,* burned to its waterline. The hull of the *Marquis de Malauze* was refloated in 1939, and divers have recovered many artifacts from all three ships, including complete sets of dishes, kitchen utensils, and pieces of equipment.

En Route from Matapédia – If you are planning to visit New Brunswick or Prince Edward Island, this is an excellent approach. To see the Gaspé, however, stay on Route 132 as it bears east and begins to follow Cartier's route along the south coast of the peninsula. Restigouche, built on the site of a 17th-century Capuchin mission, is just a few miles away. The Bataille-de-la-Ristigouche National Historic Park at Pointe-a-la-Croix (open mid-June to early September), which commemorates the last naval battle between France and England in 1760, is where you can see the hull of the *Machault* and many of its recovered artifacts. The Historical Sites Commission is working to salvage as many artifacts as possible. A monument in front of the Church of St. Anne commemorates the conversion of a Micmac tribe to Christianity in 1610.

The parish of Notre Dame de la Garde, part of the village of Escuminac, is dedicated to a French officer, Donat de la Garde, who distinguished himself during the naval encounter in the Restigouche estuary in July 1760. Escuminac itself, a little farther east, lies on a high rise and dominates the roadstead of the estuary. Although the earliest settlers in the area were Loyalists, the parish of Notre Dame de la Garde was an outgrowth of a colony established in 1758 by Acadians who fled Nova Scotia to avoid deportation by the British.

A secondary road beyond Escuminac leads south onto a point occupied by the town of Miguasha, which is being transformed into a natural sciences park. The cliffs supply specimens of plant and fish fossils to museums all over the world; fossils that have accumulated here date back 365 million years. The point, and the city of Dalhousie on the New Brunswick opposite shore, mark the beginning of the Baie de Chaleur and the end of the Restigouche estuary.

CARLETON: This city is an excellent example of the bicultural heritage of the Gaspé. Originally established in 1756 by Acadians forced from their homes by the British and named Petite-Tracadie, it was later renamed Carleton in honor of the British governor-general of the province by Loyalists who relocated here after the American Revolution. The city is still French-speaking, however, and the Notre Dame Oratory on Mont St. Joseph still dominates the town. From this point, almost 2,000 feet above the bay, you can see the mountains of the Gaspé to the east, north, and west and the shore of New Brunswick across the bay to the south. A minibus makes scheduled trips up the mountainside.

When you come down from the mountain, check into the provincial campground if possible. It's on a ridge overlooking the sea, and the sunrise makes it worth getting up early to watch. Then go down to the water and swim. Cartier named this the Bay of Warmth for good reason; the water is warm enough for swimming even when it's chilly in surrounding areas. And if you are an early riser, look for reflections in the water from pieces of agate. The beach is loaded with them. Of course, the water here is loaded with other things, too, like mackerel, smelts, and flat fish that can be caught right from the wharf; charter boats are available for deep-sea fishing — sea trout, cod, and halibut. If you'd rather watch the animal life than mount it on your wall, just wander along the beaches and observe the sea terns, herons, and gannets that congregate here. Cultural offerings can be found along Perron Boulevard, site of a 120-year-old convent that has been converted to an art gallery, and the unusual Penouil Ornithology Center, which sells models of Gaspé birds made from fish bones and shells.

If you fail to catch dinner or would rather not try, stop into the *Baie Bleue* hotel (see *Best En route*) at 482 Derron Boulevard (phone: 418-364-3355) for an excellent French dinner (or lunch for that matter).

MARIA: About 15 miles (24 km) east of Carleton on the area's only highway (Rte. 132), this city is the site of one of the two Micmac Indian reservations on the Baie des Chaleurs. A roadside cooperative operated by the Indians sells snowshoes and hand-woven baskets produced by the tribe. The Indian village, open to visitors, features a church in the shape of a teepee. Access is via a secondary road to the right of the crafts stand. Like many other communities in this area, Maria was originally settled by French-speaking people (who named the village Baie Ste. Hélène) before the British conquest of Canada forced a name change. The newer name honors Maria Effingham, who became Lady Dorchester, wife of Governor-General (Sir Guy) Carleton, during his second term as British governor of the territory.

Stay on Route 132 across the Cascapédia River (and past Route 299, which cuts north across the peninsula) to Bonaventure, a distance of 25 miles (40 km). Casgapegiag was the Micmac name for the river — "large body of water."

BONAVENTURE: A popular resort on the south shore of the Gaspé, Bonaventure was named after one of the many ships that carried French nobles on tours of the region during the late 1500s. The village was a fishing port burned by the British after the battle of the Restigouche estuary. A group of Acadians rebuilt the village in the same year, following their forced exit at the hands of the British from the Nova Scotia colony.

The *Acadian Museum,* in an original wooden structure at 97 Port-Royal Ave., contains many period pieces, including kitchen utensils, looms, furniture, and a fossil collection (phone: 418-534-2550). Open June to early September. The Gaspé Zoo, off Route 132, has some 250 animals, most native to the area. The zoo is open daily from 9 AM to 7 PM, June 1 to early September.

En Route from Bonaventure – Many of the villages on this part of the coast were settled by British Loyalists about the time of the American Revolution; others were established by Acadians fleeing the British in Nova Scotia. The fact that groups of such polarized individuals were able to settle within a few miles of each other and not fight is amazing — especially considering the frequency of conflicts between the two countries. Hope Town, just 21 miles east (34 km) of Bonaventure, is an example of British influence in the area. Established by Loyalists in 1786, and named for British Lieutenant-Governor Henry Hope, the village remains almost purely English in its outlook.

PORT DANIEL AND PORT DANIEL PARK: Port Daniel is at the end of the beach-lined, deepwater bay where Cartier anchored his ships for a week during his explorations. He called it Conche St. Martin (St. Martin Cove), but it was renamed for one of the many sea captains who later visited the area. Whether Cartier explored the Port Daniel River and the mountains from which it runs is unknown, but the river and surrounding peaks are some of the most splendid scenery in Gaspé. The park, 8 miles (13 km) north on a small secondary road, encompasses 18 separate trout lakes as well as the Port Daniel River, known for Atlantic salmon fishing. The mountains in the north end of the park average 900 feet, and their wide range of climate, from cold and mountainous to almost temperate, supports an interesting variety of foliage.

En Route from Port Daniel – It is only about 52 miles (84 km) from Port Daniel to Percé, an active travel center and the entrance to the beautiful L'Ile Bonaventure Park, but allow time for a few stops on the way.

This part of the coast, facing east into the Gulf of St. Lawrence, has seen many shipwrecks, and the coastal villages are filled with tales of ghosts, phantom ships, and treasure. Anse aux Gascons, a few miles east of Port Daniel, for example, was the scene of the wreck of an English ship during the 19th century. The villagers were able to rescue a few survivors (burying the rest) and took the cargo of 40,000 gold louis for their pains. True to storybook fantasy, one of the sailors later married the daughter of the fisherman who saved him. Although it is unlikely that a search of the coastal rocks will turn up any of the treasure, the shore is filled with pieces of agate.

At the villages of Grande Rivière and Ste. Thérèse de Gaspé, the villagers still hold pretty much with the ways of their ancestors, using open-air, cod drying racks to prepare their daily catches. Cap d'Espoir, 42 miles (68 km) from Port Daniel, is haunted, according to legend, by the ghost of a stray ship from Admiral Walker's fleet, which crashed into the rocks in 1711 and can sometimes be seen on summer nights, crashing onto the rocky cape. Try to arrive here around dusk and wait for it to reappear, then go on to Percé to watch the sun rise behind the immense rock that guards the town.

PERCÉ: With a population of over 5,500, this qualifies as a major town in the Gaspé, but it's just a small fishing village with many attractions for visitors. Primarily, there's Percé Rock, a natural wonder that defies accurate description. The rock rises 298 feet out of the sea, 1,420 feet long, and 300 feet wide with a natural arch, 50 feet high, in its eastern end. A few feet from this monolith stands a natural stone tower, all that is left of a second arch in the rock that collapsed in 1845. There is splendid silent power — a testament to obdurate, unyielding, inhuman endurance — in the rock, but at dawn, when the sun rises *through* the arch, the entire stone changes from something inorganic to a presence filled, if not with intelligence, at least with luminescence and the suggestion of intent. It certainly rates as one of the natural wonders of the world. There's a particularly good view of it from Percé Natural History Center (phone: 418-782-2240) on the road to Petite Irlande. During low tide, you can walk out to the rock on a convenient sandbar at the foot of Mont Joli (be sure to check on when the tide will come *in*) to inspect the fossils (Devonian period, the fourth phase of the Paleozoic Era, just before trees began to appear on the East Coast of North America) on the sides of the monolith.

The village is laid out in a semicircle surrounding two bays, with capes between and within a larger semicircle created by the slopes of the mountains that isolate it from the rest of the peninsula. The peak of Mont Ste. Anne, used by the Micmac Indians in their sun-worshiping ceremonies, is accessible by walking up the dirt road near the church. The road is drivable only partway, but the weak of flesh can rent carts rather than make the 2½-to-3-hour hike. Not only is the peak historical (by virtue of the Micmac ceremonies), but its 1,230-foot height makes an ideal viewpoint for planning your explorations. From here, you can see Percé Rock, Bonaventure Island, and the entire village at a glance. A trail behind the church leads to a small waterfall.

In the town itself, the Percé Wildlife Interpretation Center (phone: 418-782-2240) can give a good idea, through dioramas and a filmstrip, of the stages of development that produced Percé Rock and the irregular coastline of the peninsula (it explains why the mouth of the Restigouche River is considered "drowned" in the Baie des Chaleurs). Open daily, June through *Labor Day,* from 10 AM to 5:30 PM; small admission fee.

Aside from its geography, Percé's other attraction is food. More than two dozen establishments serve excellent seafood and French dishes, and two of the best (both expensive) are the *La Normandie* hotel-motel (phone: 418-782-2112), on Route 132 at 222 Route des Failles (phone: 418-782-2852), and *Restaurant de l'Auberge du Gargantua,* about a mile off Route 132 toward the mountains (open May to October). But don't limit yourself; the food here is half the trip.

From the wharf at Percé, take any of the many boat tours available to Bonaventure Island. Once the home of a community of fishermen-farmers, it now belongs exclusively to the birds. The dominant species — gannets — number about 50,000, although there are also kittiwakes, gulls, razor-billed auks, murres, and occasional sea pigeons and sea parrots. Most of the island's new residents have established nests along the cliffs that line the shore and can easily be photographed. The island is a sanctuary under the control of the Tourism, Fish, and Game Commission.

En Route from Percé – From Percé to Gaspé is a comfortable morning's drive — just under 50 miles (81 km) — through countryside that varies from cliffs to sandy beaches. The tiny village of Coin du Banc lies in a small pass that marks your exit from the guardian mountains of Percé and the entrance to the northern sectors of the peninsula. Its beach attracts avid windsurfers. To rent sailboards, call 418-645-2517.

AUBERGE FORT PRÉVEL: The resort center of Auberge Fort Prével, about 25 miles (40 km) from Percé, attracts diners and food fanatics from all over the world. The settlement began after a British sailor, George Prével, somehow floated onto a nearby shore — either swept overboard or shipwrecked — married a local girl, and set up housekeeping. During World War II, coastal guns were installed and barracks erected. These buildings, extensively redecorated, comprise the heart of the resort. The *Relais Gastronomique,* inside the fort, is one of the top restaurants in the province — and with good cause. Besides drawing upon the waters of the gulf to supply the freshest fish possible, it is also a government training school from spring to early autumn catering to the hotel-restaurant trade. The inn also has a golf course.

GASPÉ: This industrial hub of the peninsula is a deepwater port and the railhead of the region, linking the city with Montreal, Quebec City, and Matapédia. It fronts the Baie de Gaspé, which receives the waters of three of the region's major Atlantic salmon rivers — the Dartmouth, York, and St. Jean — all of which originate high in the mountains. Station Piscicole de Gaspé, a fish hatchery near the mouth of the York River (5 mi/8 km on Route 198), provides almost 2 million salmon and trout to stock lakes and rivers all over the province. Open to the public daily, with guided tours offered during the summer (phone: 418-368-3395). You can go after the grown ones in all three rivers (within the limits set by law) as long as you make arrangements in advance with the lower Saint-Laurent and Gaspé government office (phone: 418-722-3830, or check limits in the current *Fishing, Hunting and Trapping Guide,* available at tourist offices); reservations are needed 48 hours ahead of time since the number of anglers is controlled. You may be able to get a space on only 24 hours' notice, but don't count on it.

The *Gaspé Museum* (Gaspé Blvd.) holds periodic exhibitions during the summer (phone: 418-368-5710), while the Manoir Le Boutillier (phone: 418-892-5150) at Anse-au-Griffon on Route 132 recalls the Gaspé's proud fishing heritage.

En Route from Gaspé – About 10 miles (16 km) outside Gaspé, Route 132 takes a sharp turn eastward, outlining the peninsula containing Forillon Park, while Route 197 cuts across the western end of the park, joining Route 132 on the other side. The park, encompassing some 92 square miles of the most varied landscape and vegetation, is a wonder in itself. It occupies almost all of the small peninsula; its low areas are almost marine (saltwater plants, sand dunes, grottoes, and occasional seals), while the mountains in the center nurture a variety of alpine vegetation, including species of plants which have survived since the Ice Age. Altogether, there are nine different levels of climatic variation and a spectacular array of wildlife — moose, black bear, whitetailed deer, fox, lynx, mink, otter, muskrat, and others. Scuba diving and nature walks are among the park's varied activities. The park's reception center in Penouille is open daily, 8 AM to 7 PM July to August 1 (phone: 418-368-5505). Three private campgrounds in the park area provide most facilities.

On the south coast of this peninsula, along Route 132, is the village of Penouille. It is believed a Viking outpost may have been established here during the 11th century, and that Freydis (Eric the Red's illegitimate sister) may have visited the site — which would make her the first white female to set foot in Canada. The difficulty in proving this has been compounded by the destruction of the French settlements on this site by English troops on three separate occasions (1690, 1711, and 1759). The village of Cap aux Os, a few miles farther on, was named for the whale bones found here by the earliest settlers. While this does not prove that Vikings actually landed on this shore, it adds credence to the theory.

The Forillon Park draws its name from *pharillon,* or "little lighthouse," the name given to one of the tall towers of rock at the eastern tip of the peninsula, the site of signal fires to warn sailors off the rocky cape. The north side of the peninsula, Cap des Rosiers, is said to be the site of more shipwrecks than any other point on the Canadian coast. Its lighthouse, built in 1858, is a historic monument open 9 AM to 7 PM, from early June until late August (phone: 418-892-5613 or 368-5710).

Routes 132 and 197 reunite near Rivière au Renard, where descendants of a group of Irish sailors, shipwrecked at Cap des Rosiers, comprise a large part of the population. Route 132 continues along the north coast toward Grand Etang, 18 miles (29 km) west. Just past Grand Etang is tiny St. Yvon, where the remains of a German torpedo, which missed its target and exploded against the rocks, are kept in a shed. It is only 48 more miles (77 km) to Anse Pleureuse, where Route 198 leads to Gaspé Park, about 25 miles (40 km) inland. (This is the only entrance to the park. For details, see the section under Ste. Anne des Monts.)

Between Anse Pleureuse and Ste. Anne des Monts are 42 miles (68 km) of irregular roadway, running so close to the water in places that spray splashes the cars, then climbing 1,200 feet over a rocky cape. Stop at the village of Mont St. Pierre, and take an hour to climb the mountain itself or drive up the Jeep trail. From its peak, you can look out over the vast Gulf of St. Lawrence or face slightly westward and strain to see Pointe des Monts, at the base of the gulf on the north shore. The *Mont St. Pierre* hotel-motel, serving good food at inexpensive prices, makes a timely stopping place (see *Best En Route*) at 60 Rue Prudent Cloutier (phone: 418-797-2850).

As you pass through the village of Tourelle, 37 miles (60 km) from Anse Pleureuse, keep an eye out for falling rocks as you approach from the east; the highway runs between the beach and the mountains, and in 1963, part of the village was wiped out by a landslide.

STE. ANNE DES MONTS: When you arrive at Ste. Anne des Monts, get off Route 132 and take the old road along the shore. Most of the older buildings were destroyed by fire in 1925, but the Theodore Lamontagne Residence (phone: 418-763-2524) still watches over the bay, and it's worth the 5-mile (8-km) drive to see the house and grounds and to try out its new restaurant. The road crosses the Ste. Anne River (where salmon fishing is allowed under government guidelines; see the current *Fishing, Hunting and Trapping Guide*). Between the hatchery upstream and the fish coming from the St. Lawrence, it is a good spot to land a salmon. If you're in the area for dinner, try *Auberge Gîte du Mont Albert* (phone: 418-763-2288) in Gaspé Park. Route 299, through the middle of the park, runs right past it. The inn specializes in classic French cooking as well as regional dishes of the Gaspé and Quebec Province; it has been awarded high marks for service by gastronomes from all over the world. During the academic year, students from the Quebec Institute of Tourism and Hostelry show off their know-how for guests. Telephone for reservations and information before heading into the park (phone: 418-763-3039 or 392-5388). See *Best En Route*.

PARC DE LA GASPÉSIE: The park can be reached from Ste. Anne des Monts via Route 299 (12 mi/19 km), from Anse Pleureuse via Routes 198 and 1000 (25 mi/40 km), or from New Richmond on the south shore of the Gaspé Peninsula (85 mi/137 km).

The Parc de la Gaspésie covers almost 500 square miles of magnificent mountainous land, preserving for all time a portion of the natural beauty that prompted Cartier's praise of the area called Gaspé in New France. This is one of the few places in the province where herds of caribou, moose, and deer still roam in the same area. The highest peaks of the Chic-Chocs Mountains preserve alpine vegetation that exists nowhere else at such a southern latitude.

The Chic-Chocs Mountains, an arm of the Appalachian chain, run the length of the park and most of the peninsula, from the Matapédia Valley to the eastern capes. They average 3,500 feet, and the highest peaks — like the McGerrigle — scrape the skies at 4,100 feet. It was the height of these slopes that kept the alpine flora from dying out during the last (Wisconsin) ice age, which lasted from about 15,000 to 5,000 BC. The alpine fir, representative of the period, rarely grows more than 8 feet tall. Mont Jacques Cartier has the largest concentration of these plants. Both Mont Jacques Cartier and the McGerrigle are frequented by herds of caribou most of the year. In the summer they remain in the cool of these peaks, venturing down to the lower region only during winter.

The vegetation of the park changes with the altitudes: Peat bogs on the valley floor give way to forested slopes, then to lichen, moss, and low shrubs on the windblown crests. Mont Albert is a naturalist's dream. Its base is lined with conifers (cone-bearing trees) such as firs and spruces, which gradually mix with subalpine forests of stubby alpine firs. Toward the peak, the trees thin out and are replaced by alpine tundra and

Arctic vegetation — shrubs and moss — and in the barren areas, the intense cold and frost shatter massive chunks of exposed rock into gigantic boulders.

The park is crisscrossed by a network of hiking trails and drivable roads. Most conveniences are available in the park area. Trail guides and trained naturalists are on duty on an irregular basis, and many activities can be arranged with the help of the staff. Although hunting is strictly prohibited, the park's lakes and rivers yield speckled, sea, and Quebec red trout as well as hard-fighting Atlantic salmon. During the winter months, these slopes attract cross-country skiers from all over the world. This is still very much an untamed forest; the animals (including black bears) have rights to the area, and it does get dark quickly in the mountain forests. Be sure to *return to your campsite or car before dark* or you may get lost. The parks use a check-in, check-out system designed to keep track of all those wandering in the forest, but it might take a few hours to locate you.

This park is bordered by the Matane and Dunière parks, extensions of the Parc de la Gaspésie in geography and content but under a separate administration. The principal access to these areas is via Route 195 from Matane.

Continue eastbound on Route 132 along the south bank of the St. Lawrence River for 55 miles (89 km) to Matane.

MATANE: This industrial town was originally settled in 1795, but it remained basically a Micmac Indian village until 1845. During the mid-19th century, the town began to evolve into a river pilot station and grew with the lumber trade. Its name is based on the Indian word for "beaver pond." Ferries connect Matane with Godbout and Baie Comeau on the north shore of the St. Lawrence River (a good place to pick up the *North Shore* route for your return to Quebec). Atlantic salmon fishing in the Matane River is excellent. A stopover at Le Barrage Mathieu-D'Amours fish ladder, a short walk from the *Auberge des Gouverneurs,* is where the vicarious angler observes the salmon both above and below water as they struggle upstream in Des Iles Park.

JARDENS DE MÉTIS PARK: If you are returning toward Quebec on the south shore, be sure to see Jardens de Métis Park. It is 32 miles (52 km) from Matane, and 6 miles (10 km) from Ste. Flavie, the turnoff for heading south across the Matapédia Valley through which the route passed much earlier. The park began as a private estate, one of many English-style manors established during the Victorian era. The formal gardens have been adapted to include approximately 4,000 species of plants of many different climates. There are alpine 500 species of shrubs, annuals and perennials, and experimental plantings of a group of aquatic plants. The success of these plantings is a tribute to Elsie Reford, who began the gardens in 1922. Villa Reford — her former home — is the centerpiece of the park and houses a museum, restaurant, and craft shop. Open daily, 8:30 AM to 8 PM, mid-June to mid-September. Admission charge.

BEST EN ROUTE

The range of lodgings on the Gaspé Peninsula is especially wide, with inns that have kitchens of provincewide reputation in several parks and rustic, simple motel-hotel or even campground accommodations elsewhere. Expect to pay $65 or more for a double in the places listed as expensive; between $45 and $65 in those categorized as moderate; and under $45 in the inexpensive choices. These prices are valid for the summer season; off-season, rates are halved. All prices are quoted in US dollars.

RIVIÈRE DU LOUP

Auberge de la Pointe – A good hotel at a very reasonable price. Good dining and comfortable rooms with all services. Autoroute 20, exit 507 (phone: 418-862-3514). Moderate.

Lévesque – Not so plush, but comfortable, with 89 rooms and an excellent dining room. French and Canadian foods. 171 Fraser St. (phone: 418-862-6927). Moderate.

Universel – A large 119-room motel in the center of town, offering all the facilities of most large hotels. The rooms are comfortable and the service excellent. Restaurant and a nice bar. 311 Hôtel de Ville Blvd. (phone: 418-862-9520). Moderate.

Château Grandville – This is a smaller but comfortable hotel, with 47 rooms and a fair restaurant. 94 Lafontaine St. (phone: 418-862-3551). Inexpensive.

RIMOUSKI

Auberge des Gouverneurs – Comfortable and modern, this 166-room hotel has excellent service, average dining room. 155 René Lepage Blvd. E. (phone: 418-723-4422). Expensive.

Auberge Wandlyn Le Brasier – A small-scale version of a full-service hotel, with 63 rooms. 130 Rue St. Barnabé (phone: 418-724-6944). Moderate.

STE.-LUCE-SUR-MER

Auberge Ste. Luce – This small motel (29 rooms) is open in summer only. It is known mostly for its good restaurant. 52 Rue Bord du Fleuve (phone: 418-739-4955). Inexpensive.

MATAPÉDIA

Restigouche – Located along the banks of the Restigouche and Matapédia rivers, this 40-room motel is a popular spot among salmon fishermen. Comfortable, although not plush, with most rooms overlooking the bay; a good dining room. Rue du Saumon (phone: 418-865-2155). Moderate.

CARLETON

Baie Bleue – An 85-unit hotel-motel with a color TV set in each room. Guests have access to the heated pool and beach. The *La Baie Bleue* restaurant is the best in the area, with fine French and Canadian dishes and seafood. 482 Perron Blvd. (phone: 418-364-3355). Expensive to moderate.

Shick Shock – This 35-unit motel has comfortable rooms, a dining room, and a bar. 1746 Perron Blvd., East Carleton (phone: 418-364-3288). Inexpensive.

BONAVENTURE

Auberge Le Château – A decent hotel-motel with a restaurant. 98 Port Royal Ave. (phone: 418-534-3336). Moderate.

CHANDLER

Fraser – French and Canadian specialties and seafood are served in the restaurant at this 40-unit motel. Rte. 132 (phone: 418-689-2281). Moderate.

St. Laurent – This is an older hotel with comfortable rooms, good service, and a fair dining room. 499 Réhel St. (phone: 418-689-3355). Moderate to inexpensive.

PERCÉ

Le Bonaventure sur Mer – An 88-room, 36-unit hotel-motel offering grand accommodations, a bar, and a good restaurant. Rte. 132 (phone: 418-782-2166). Expensive to moderate.

Pic de l'Aurore – Overlooking Percé Rock, this 18-unit motel has a fair dining room. Rte. 132 (phone: 418-782-2166). Expensive to moderate.

Auberge du Gargantua – A motel with 11 units overlooking Percé Rock, it is known for its fine restaurant, with French dishes and seafood. 222 Rte. des Failles (phone: 418-782-2852). Moderate to inexpensive.

Bleu-Blanc-Rouge – Here is a comfortable 13-room hotel-motel with a good dining room featuring seafood and French cooking. Rte. 132 (phone: 418-782-2142). Moderate to inexpensive.

Manoir Percé – A 38-unit establishment with a nice dining room. Rte. 132 (phone: 418-782-2022). Moderate to inexpensive.

FORT PRÉVEL

Auberge Fort Prével – This is a comfortable 54-unit motel and resort area built from World War II army barracks. It features a 9-hole golf course and an excellent restaurant which capitalizes on fresh seafood and French recipes. Closed in winter. Rte. 132 (phone: 418-368-2281). Moderate.

GASPÉ

Auberge des Commandants – Certainly the best hotel on the Gaspé Peninsula, it has 44 rooms and overlooks the bay. 178 Rue de la Reine (phone: 418-368-3355). Expensive to moderate.

Adams – A 98-unit motel overlooking the ocean. Nice rooms, good service, and a dining room offering seafood and French dishes. Rte. 132, 2 Adam's St. (phone: 418-368-2244). Moderate.

GRANDE VALLÉE

Frigault – This 21-unit motel has a fairly good French and seafood restaurant. Large rooms and good service. Rte. 132 (phone: 418-393-2720). Moderate.

MONT ST. PIERRE

Mont-St.-Pierre – Small motel on the ocean shore with a good restaurant. Prudent Cloutier St. (phone: 418-797-2202). Moderate to inexpensive.

STE. ANNE DES MONTS

Monaco des Monts – The dining facilities are good for the area; the guest services are average. 90 Ste.-Anne Blvd. W. (phone: 418-763-3321). Moderate.

PARC DE LA GASPÉSIE

Gîte du Mont Albert – Besides 21 rustic rooms, this hotel-motel has a very famous restaurant. Open only during the summer. Rte. 299 (phone: 418-763-2288). Moderate.

MATANE

Auberge des Gouverneurs – Here is an elegant hotel with 48 large, comfortable rooms. Good dining room and excellent service. 250 du Phare Ave. E. (phone: 418-566-2651). Expensive to moderate.

Iles de la Madeleine

The Iles de la Madeleine (Magdalen Islands) — anchored in the Gulf of St. Lawrence about 180 miles (290 km) east by southeast of the Gaspé Peninsula, about 55 miles (89 km) northeast of the tip of Nova Scotia's Cape Breton

Island, and 70 miles (113 km) east of Prince Edward Island — are an unusual and satisfyingly remote getaway spot.

Only seven of the dozen or so islands, islets, and reefs in this archipelago are inhabited, so that even as travelers discover them, it is easy to find a dune-lined beach where you can be alone with the sea. The major islands of the Madeleines cluster together and are connected by causeways, forming one long strip of islands and bays. They are Ile du Cap aux Meules, the centerpiece of this string, the largest of the Madeleines, and the starting point of most tours (at its community Cap aux Meules); Ile de Havre aux Maisons, Ile aux Loups, La Grosse Ile, and Ile de la Grande Entrée to the northeast; and Ile du Havre Aubert to the southeast. Accessible only by ferry is Ile d'Entrée. Because most of these islands are connected by causeways and are themselves divided into smaller sections also called islands, it only takes a quick glance at a map to make the geography of the islands perfectly comprehensible. Most of the coastal rocks are a soft grayish red, laced with sandstone and gypsum (hints of volcanic ancestry), stained ocher by the sea water and salt air, and carved for centuries into weird formations. Tall pillars overlook chasms and the crashing ocean. Atop overhanging ledges are picnic sites with panoramic views of neighboring islands and the sea; below are enchanting caves. These natural formations, the fine sandy beaches with their dunes and warm waters, make this quiet archipelago a summer destination of some romance and mystery.

The life-style of the Madelinot villagers reflects the quietude of the islands, affected most by the surrounding sea. Lobster, herring, mackerel, scallops, cod, and halibut are the mainstays of their economy, and most of the people belong to island-based cooperatives that freeze, can, smoke, and ship as well as market their catch. Until recently, the annual seal hunt (in March and April) was the second component of the economy, with most of the islanders taking part, but because of popular indignation and the depletion of the seal herds, attempts are under way to develop other resources to replace seal hides in the marketplace.

The Madelinots inherited the seal-hunting tradition from the Basque sailors who hunted and fished in these waters 4 centuries ago, although most of the islanders are of Acadian origin. The Acadian colony, based in Nova Scotia, was destroyed twice (in 1613 and in the 1750s), and each time many of the colonists resettled on these secluded islands. Of the 15,000 inhabitants occupying this 55,000-acre haven, about 1,000 are of Scottish ancestry; many others descend from shipwrecked sailors of all nationalities.

These attractive little islands have been prized ever since Cartier first explored them in June 1534. In his enthusiasm he named one isolated island Île de Brion, after the grand admiral of France, Phillipe Chabot, Sieur de Brion (probably hoping the admiral would let him keep the rest for himself). The name Madeleine is derived from Madeleine Fontaine, wife of François Doublet, first seigneur of the islands. Doublet made the settling of the archipelago his life project. Sir Isaac Coffin, after being promoted to admiral of the British navy in 1814, was awarded the Iles de la Madeleine in 1815 as a reward for public service; on English maps Ile de la Grande Entrée is referred to as Coffin Island.

The relative isolation of the islands, even from each other, has allowed communities established by early settlers to retain their individuality — for example, Scottish communities concentrated on Grosse Ile and Ile d'Entrée. "Magdalen Islands" or "Grindstone" (English for Cap aux Meules) appears on many local fishing vessels, and even French maps of the islands are strewn with such names as Old Harry, Leslie, and Cap (Cape) Alright.

During the spring and fall migrations, the Iles de la Madeleine become a bird-watcher's haven. More than 50 species of waders, ducks, alcids (a family of diving birds), and other waterfowl, plus many varieties of land birds, take sanctuary here. In summer, the seas around are like fields for harvest. The deep-sea fishing for bluefin tuna is as good as anywhere in the world. The early days of summer are reserved for lobsters taken fresh from the gulf (you can buy them at wharves) and cooked on the beach. And the later summer months are perfect for swimming and long afternoons of basking on the dunes. Winters here are beautiful in their solitude, but few (except the seals) appreciate them.

Since the summer days are apt to attract many travelers, and since there are less than 200 hotel rooms — and about the same number of campsites — available, it is advisable to make arrangements far in advance. The best approach to Iles de la Madeleines is by air: *Inter-Canadian* flies from both Montreal (phone: 800-361-0200) and Quebec City (phone: 418-692-1031) to Havre aux Maisons (phone: 418-969-2764), with stops at Mont Joli and Gaspé; *Canadian International* has daily service from Montreal (phone: 514-286-1212) that connects with other flights to the island via Halifax Airport. Both *Inter-Canadian* and *Canadian International* schedule daily flights during the summer. Many travelers prefer to drive to Cap Tormentine, New Brunswick, and take a ferry to Prince Edward Island. From the wharf at Borden, PEI, they drive across the island to Souris for the MV *Lucy Maud Montgomery* ferry to Cap aux Meules. Between Cap Tormentine and Borden, PEI, there is continuous service and little waiting. At Souris this is not the case. The trip from Souris to the Madeleines takes 5 hours, with only one departure daily (at 2 PM, except Tuesdays when it leaves at 2 AM; in high season, a daily 2 AM ferry is added). It's first-come, first-served, so many people set up camp while waiting. *If you take the ferry:* Be sure to make your reservations for the return trip 7 days in advance. Check current schedules before you reserve. For information about the ferry, call 902-687-2181 (in Souris) or 418-986-6600 (in Cap aux Meules). Visitors can also travel by ship on the *M.V. Voyager,* which transports cargo and up to 12 passengers from Montreal to the Iles de la Madeleine. The ship departs on Fridays and returns on Sunday afternoons; return trips depart on Wednesdays and arrive in Montreal on Fridays. Round-trip fare, including meals and cabin accommodations, is approximately $630; cars are an additional $135. For more information, call 514-257-0323.

To get to Cap Tormentine from Montreal or Quebec, take Route 20 east along the south shore of the St. Lawrence River to Rivière du Loup, then pick up Route 185 across the Gaspé and into New Brunswick, where it encounters Route 2 to Moncton. Cap Tormentine is just a short distance away from here via local roadways. From New England, pick up US 1 from US 95 in Portland, Maine. It leads into Canadian Route 1, which goes through Saint John, New Brunswick, where it intersects Route 2 toward Moncton. Another option is available for those who want to take their cars but don't want to make the long drive: A freighter makes the 3-day voyage from Montreal to Cap aux Meules once a week. The schedule, which is subject to change, calls for departure from Montreal (phone: 514-866-8066) on Mondays and arrival at Cap aux Meules (phone: 418-986-4224) on Wednesdays from April through December, with returns departing on Fridays from the island port, reaching Montreal on Mondays. Reserve two months in advance.

The relaxing atmosphere of the Madeleines permeates the air among those awaiting the ferry from Souris. The wharf is on the outskirts of the town, and many people, braced for the long wait for either the 8 PM or 8 AM run, set up their tents, explore the area, or start parties. With a restaurant and bar aboard the ferry, the 8 PM, 5-hour voyage often turns into an all-night international summer festival.

Whether you arrive at 8 in the morning or the evening, the first view of Ile d'Entrée (Entry Island) is astounding: a large grassy hillock protruding from the sea. Passing Cap Rouge and Pointe du Sud-Ouest, look for the hiking trails that lead along the cliffs and try to pick a spot among the red rock formations to visit later. The ferry docks at Cap aux Meules in a sheltered bay full of small fishing vessels and visiting sailing sloops. Local ferry service to Ile d'Entrée and Havre Aubert (phone: 418-986-6600) originates here. A tourist information booth is located at the exit for the ferry dock. To the left of the wharf is the formation known as Gros Cap. Ile du Cap aux Meules, the largest island in the archipelago, is the most heavily populated. Three municipalities are centered here: Cap aux Meules (a small district on the eastern shore of the island); Fatima (encompassing the north end of the island and a long beach and reef extending north from the perimeter), and Etang du Nord (occupying the southern end of the island).

Items made by the islanders are sold at reasonable rates in Cap aux Meules at a shop run by the *Coopérative d'Artisanat des Iles*. Cold, lonely winters provide many hours for exacting, detailed work. Carved pieces of whale bone and seal fur items are among the popular choices. The fishwells, where freshly caught fish and lobsters are kept ready for shipment, may be visited to see how these people pursue their arduous living from the sea (open to visitors Tuesdays and Fridays, all year). There is an excellent marina on the Gulf of St. Lawrence, with some interesting specimens on display. Check with the tourism office near the wharf (20 route du Quai) for details on season and hours. Nine-meter sailboats with a captain can be rented, and fishing trips are scheduled daily, weather permitting. Check with Fédération de Voile du Québec (phone: 514-252-3000) about rentals and schools, and call the Association Touristique des Iles (phone: 418-986-2245) for information on sailing and fishing excursions, or drop by the island sailing school, *Centre Nautique des Iles*, at Havre-aux-Maisons (phone: 418-969-2571), for charters and rentals.

Chemin du Gros Cap leads to the Gros Cap Scenic Area, which lies in the Etang du Nord district. A provincial campground with 38 sites is located just past Cap Rouge, about 4 miles (6 km) from the wharf. This point, like most of these exposed hills and cliffs, is subject to the 20-mph winds that created the rock carvings, so dress appropriately — wear a sweater and/or windbreaker on the windier days. The same road, Chemin du Gros Cap, curves inland toward La Vernière, with a beautiful old wooden church near Butte du Vent, the highest point on the islands. The entire archipelago may be seen from this summit. And on a clear day you can see Cape Breton Island, almost 60 miles (97 km) away.

Route 199, the connecting highway that links most of the islands into a cohesive landmass, leads south from La Venière through the Plage de la Martinique (Martinique Beach) and across a causeway to Ile du Havre Aubert. A similar connecting beach links the western sides of these two islands, creating a lagoon called Havre aux Basques (Basque Harbor). Along this western leg of Ile du Cap aux Meules, in the Etang du Nord district, you may see in the shallow offshore waters the remains of several wooden ships among the many wrecked here. The roadway bears east and follows the beach of Ile du Havre Aubert to the village of Havre Aubert. This busy harbor looks much like the bay at Cap aux Meules, populated by Madelinot fishers and fisheries, with the sea dominating everything. The fishwells (and a sales counter) are open to visitors weekdays from April through mid-October. The *Musée de la Mer* (Marine Museum) not only records the history of the archipelago, but also portrays the history of sailing and fishing. There is a tourist office at the museum (phone: 418-937-5711) and a reconstructed Madelinot village nearby. Two of the five campgrounds in the islands are located on the southern coast, near the village of Bassin. *Belle Plage* (phone: 418-937-5408) has 28 sites and *Plage du Golfe* (phone: 418-937-5224) has 72 sites. Check the *Quebec Camping* booklet for facilities available at each.

If you drove from Ile du Cap aux Meules on Route 199, then you should certainly return along the Plage de l'Ouest (West Beach). Try to keep an eye out for the shipwrecks in the gulf on your left and be sure to glance over at the waters of the lagoon to your right.

When you arrive at Ile du Cap aux Meules, take the road leading north through the village of Etang du Nord and toward Fatima. A private 32-site campground, Mon Rivage (phone: 418-986-3786), overlooks the northwest shore. This district on the northern end of the island extends the Dune du Nord, a long, wide, sandy arm of dune-filled beach that connects with the outstretched southerly arm of Grosse Ile. At various points this elongated beach is called Plage de l'Hôpital and Plage de la Pointe au Loup. Here, too, a second arm paralleling the first (the northern extension of Ile du Havre aux Maisons) forms a lagoon between these two beaches.

Route 199, which runs along the east side of the lagoon south of Ile du Cap aux Meules and onto Havre aux Maisons, crosses this lagoon (north of Ile du Cap aux Meules) and runs along the west side on the Dune du Nord beach. The Grosse Ile district occupies two islands that form a severe V shape, pointing north. The western side is Grosse Ile; the other, obviously, is Ile de l'Est. Not so obvious is exactly where one island ends and the other begins. Route 199, traveling north along the west side of this question, passes through the village of Leslie, which was settled by Scots. To a large extent, their language has been lost in the French, but some of the customs of the families date back to early Scotland. Spend a little time in the village and try to get a taste of the Scottish-Madelinot atmosphere. The highway turns sharply south across the mouth of the bay (Baie Clarke) that forms the northern tip of the lagoon and continues in the direction of Old Harry on Ile de l'Est. The entire northern section, to your left if you're on Route 199 traveling clockwise, is comprised of two beach shorelines, the Plage de la Point l'Est (from Grosse Ile along the western side of the V) and the Plage de la Grande Echouerie — perhaps one of the most beautiful beaches in the world (along the eastern side of the island). The panorama of Ile de Brion to the north, over the dunes and the sea, is magnificent; and the southern view of the lagoon is equally so, especially at sunset.

Route 199 goes into the village of Old Harry, where the Anglican chapel is located, and on through to Ile de la Grande Entrée.

Ile de la Grande Entrée is a peninsula extending south from Ile de l'Est, helping to form the Lagune de la Grande Entrée, to a large bay, known as Havre de la Grande Entrée. A processing plant (equipped to handle lobster, herring, cod, or whatever the catch) is open to visitors weekdays from April to September. The huts used for smoking herring are also open from the beginning of May until the end of July. Camping space on the island is limited to the 38-site provincial park (phone: 418-985-2833); there is no other lodging at this end of the archipelago.

Since the highway does not jump across the mouth of the lagoon, the Chenal de la Grande Entrée, to the northern extension of Ile du Havre aux Maisons, the Plage de la Dune du Sud, the return trip means retracing steps through Leslie and the Dune du Nord.

Halfway south on the Dune du Nord, take Route 199 across a causeway to Ile du Havre aux Maisons. This island comprises most of the eastern shoreline of the archipelago, so it's not so odd that the majority of the shipwrecks occurred on its shores as the boats sailed west to the New World. The northern section of the island is relatively barren, but the southern end is well settled. Be sure to visit the lighthouse at Cap Alright and the shipwreck at nearby Pointe Basse.

From here to Cap aux Meules is a quick ride west and south — across a short causeway and down the west coast of the island.

A short visit to Ile d'Entrée makes for a pleasant day — just rock formations, birds, and its own fishing port, of course.

For general information call the Iles de la Madeleine tourist board (phone: 418-986-2245).

BEST EN ROUTE

Although the islands are not exactly overflowing with hotel space, a few places can handle guests very nicely. Fluctuating exchange rates, inflation, and seasonal demand make prices difficult to predict, but most establishments are priced moderately; none can be called expensive. In those places listed as moderate, plan on spending $45 to $65 for two, and in places listed as inexpensive, rates are under $45 for double occupancy. Note that the provincial family vacations network also offers accommodations in private homes at Etang du Nord (phone: 418-658-0576, for information). All prices are quoted in US dollars.

HAVRE AUX MAISONS

Des Iles – Fairly large by island standards (28 rooms) and a relaxing place to stay (phone: 418-969-2931). Moderate.

Thériault – An excellent motel, with 20 units and a restaurant. Dune du Sud (phone: 418-969-2955). Moderate.

Au Vieux Couvent – A 12-unit hotel in a convent. The rooms are spartan, but the bar gets a crowd almost every night; the newly added restaurant specializes in serving island mussel dishes. Rte. 199 (phone: 418-969-2233). Inexpensive.

CAP AUX MEULES

Château Madelinot – Some of the 56 units in this motel have kitchenettes, and there's wheelchair access. Rte. 199 (phone: 418-986-3695). Expensive.

Bellevue – In the main village, atop a hill overlooking the sea, is this establishment with 28 comfortable rooms and a restaurant. 40 Rue Principale (phone: 418-986-4477). Moderate.

■ **Note:** In addition to the campgrounds mentioned in the text, camping is allowed almost anywhere. Just follow basic rules of courtesy and ask permission before setting up; don't camp on anyone's front lawn.

Saskatchewan

Saskatchewan's southern grasslands and vast farmlands can be deceiving, giving the impression that it is completely a prairie province, but, in fact, trees cover much of the province's 251,700 square miles. In the northern areas the terrain changes, most noticeably at Prince Albert National Park, the forested entrance to Saskatchewan's wilds. And, once you've passed Prince Albert, traveling by air is a virtual necessity. Many roads have only gravel surfaces, and service stations are rare. Despite this inconvenience, campers, hikers, and fishermen make their way to the region's remote camps and lodges.

Although best known for its wilderness and prairies, Saskatchewan has been in the forefront of political innovation ever since it elected the first socialist government in North America in 1944. The socialists initiated a series of programs that changed many people's lives. They established government-owned businesses, modernized schools, and brought electricity to 99% of Saskatchewan's farms through the Saskatchewan Power Corporation.

These accomplishments have not altered the nature of life in the province, however. With a population of about 1 million pretty evenly divided between city and country, it is still sparsely populated. Farming and wheat production are the leading industries, followed by oil production. Longtime residents remain aware of their frontier heritage. Branches of the *Western Development Museum* dot the province, each focusing on a different historical perspective. The museum in North Battleford, for instance, emphasizes the 1800s pioneer life, complete with an outdoor village duplicating the look and feel of the era. Museums around the province also reflect the long-standing presence of the Royal Canadian Mounted Police, especially in the capital, Regina (pop. 179,000), the group's original headquarters.

In the following pages we offer three itineraries across Saskatchewan: east to west on the Trans-Canada Highway, slicing through the heart of the rich prairie farmland in the province's southerly quarter; south to north, from the US North Dakota border at Estevan through Saskatoon to splendid Prince Albert National Park, poised on the edge of the vast wilderness stretching to the Northwest Territories; and east to west across the very center of the province on the Yellowhead Highway, Saskatchewan's richest historical area, where the memory of the early frontier is strongest. At several points these routes meet, cross, and can be combined for even longer tours. A map of Saskatchewan and a detailed guide may be obtained from Saskatchewan Tourism (address below). Both documents may also be obtained from the Canadian Government Office of Tourism in major US cities.

Information: Tourism Saskatchewan, 1919 Saskatchewan Drive, Regina, Saskatchewan S4P 3V7 (phone: 800-667-7191).

The Trans-Canada across Saskatchewan

The Trans-Canada Highway (Rte. 1), running 370 miles (596 km) through Saskatchewan's southern prairies and wheatfields, offers a good way to see much of the province. This road, passing through the cities of Regina and Swift Current, is best used as a principal east-west path from which to take side trips to the many other interesting sights on secondary roads to the north and south. Moose Mountain Provincial Park, near the eastern border, contradicts the notion that Saskatchewan can't be green and glamorous. Farther on, the Qu'Appelle Valley is rich in history and contains beautiful parkland. Regina offers the full range of urban pleasures and is the home of the Royal Canadian Mounted Police training center. Moose Jaw numbers among its attractions a wild animal park and an important historical museum. A side trip will take you to an ancient Indian settlement and to an important point in Canada's frontier history. Near the western border, Cypress Hills is a welcome stretch of pine-covered hills and high plateaus, and Fort Walsh Historical Park features a reconstruction of one of the earliest RCMP forts. And all along the way there are spots for swimming, fishing, and hunting. The Trans-Canada road is excellent, and most of the secondary roads are quite good. The roadbed frequently dips to break the tedium of driving through flat country.

En Route from Manitoba – Route 1 enters Saskatchewan from Manitoba in the east, passing through a series of small communities. At Whitewood, 41 miles (66 km) from the Manitoba border, turn south on Route 9 for Moose Mountain Provincial Park, one of the most popular of Saskatchewan's parks, a 38-mile (61-km) drive. In Whitewood, stop at *Old George Collectibles* for prairie Victoriana.

MOOSE MOUNTAIN PROVINCIAL PARK: The park, with Kenosee Lake at its center, consists of rolling terrain covered with aspen, white birch, and spruce. The park's origins go back to 1906, when R. B. Clark established a resort beach along Lake Kenosee. The present park's chief building is a chalet-like, stonework field house. First built in 1930, the building was damaged by fire and reconstructed as a relief project by men thrown out of work by the Depression. Today, besides functioning as headquarters for park operations, it contains meeting rooms, a dining room, and a kitchen. Park accommodations range from cabins to a modern motel. In addition, there are about 329 campsites.

Recreational facilities include an 18-hole golf course, beaches for swimming, privately operated riding stables, biking and hiking trails, tennis courts, water slide, and supervised children's activities. In addition, there is good lake fishing for pike, pickerel, and perch. A 15-mile (24-km) gravel road stretches into the forest area, where one may see moose or elk grazing in the early morning or early evening. The park, which houses some 450 beaver lodges, is also a nesting place for geese and a wide variety of birds ranging from wood ducks to blue herons and vultures.

Adjoining Moose Mountain Park is Cannington Manor Historical Park, site of a

19th-century venture in community-building. In 1882, Captain Edward Mitchell Pierce and his son came here to establish a traditional English manor system in the New World. The middle class Pierce, hoping to lead the life of an aristocratic Victorian squire on this land, established five tenant homestead farms, a wagon shop, a paint business, and sawmills. The colony lasted 15 years. The inherent impracticality of the scheme, coupled with Pierce's costly indulgence in horse racing, caught up with the community and the effort was gradually abandoned. Today, visitors can see the original church and reconstructions of the blacksmith and carpenter shops. The original schoolhouse has been turned into a museum of memorabilia from the colony.

En Route from Moose Mountain – Go north on Route 9 to Whitewood, and rejoin Route 1 heading west through Saskatchewan's prairies and farming communities. After 68 miles (109 km) you will reach the town of Indian Head, where you can tour the Canada Agricultural Experimental Farm and examine its landscaping and its demonstration gardens of grain, vegetables, flowers, and trees. Turn north on Route 56 to tour the Qu'Appelle Valley area.

THE QU'APPELLE VALLEY: The valley, forming the shores of Qu'Appelle Lake, is another pocket of timberland in the Saskatchewan prairie. The valley's ready supply of wood for fuel and building made it attractive to the pioneers, and it thus became an early stop on the fur trade route and a haven for the area's first white settlers. It is significant in Indian history because a portion of the Sioux nation, fleeing north after the Battle of Little Big Horn, sought refuge here. In addition, Pauline Johnson, the popular Indian poet of the 1890s and early 1900s, commemorated the valley in several poems. The valley is now known for its parks and its arts and crafts.

Route 35 merges with Route 10 and leads to the town of Fort Qu'Appelle, 20 miles (32 km) north of the Trans-Canada. In Fort Qu'Appelle, *Qu'Appelle Crafts* and the *Hansen Ross Pottery Studio,* have local handicrafts and pottery. A short ride south on Route 56 takes you to Katepwa Provincial Park, whose name in Cree means "river that calls." Katepwa is a lakeside park designed primarily for day use and family activity. Traveling west from Fort Qu'Appelle, you will quickly reach Echo Valley Provincial Park, another lakeside park that specializes in swimming and fishing. Between Fort Qu'Appelle and Echo Valley is the small townsite of Fort San, home of the Saskatchewan Summer School of the Arts, which presents concerts and shows of student work all summer.

The simplest return route is to follow Route 10 southeast 30 miles (48 km), from Fort Qu'Appelle. Rejoin the Trans-Canada at Balgonie, 16 miles (26 km) from Regina.

REGINA: Saskatchewan's capital began in 1882 as a small frontier settlement near a spot named Pile of Bones for its large number of buffalo skeletons. Feeling the need for another name, the residents christened the new town Regina, in honor of Queen Victoria. Today, it is a modern city, with a full range of urban facilities — not exactly a mecca for vacationers, but visitors will find a number of entertaining attractions in town. Perhaps the most interesting is the *Royal Canadian Mounted Police Museum and Training Academy* (off Dewdney Ave. on the west side of the city), which offer one of the best opportunities to view the past and present of the RCMP. The nation's major display of Mountie history, its exhibits focus on the history of the Northwest Mounted Police in the Old West. The collection includes uniforms and weapons, models of forts, photographs, and pictorial representations of historical moments. In addition, there are more unusual exhibits: the crow's nest of the *St. Roch,* a ship instrumental in the establishment of a Northwest Passage; the tobacco pouch that Sitting Bull brought with him when he fled to Canada; and, since Saskatchewan was the center of the Riel Rebellion of the 1880s, the crucifix Louis Riel carried to his execution. The museum also devotes considerable space to the culture of the Plains Indians. And, with an appropriate touch of whimsy, a corner of the museum is given over to photographs of Jeannette MacDonald and Nelson Eddy.

The training academy, the RCMP's national center for basic training of recruits, is open to visitors, who may observe recruits exercising and drilling. Tours are largely do-it-yourself, although guided tours can be arranged. As you would expect, basic training is basic training, so there's little difference between the regimen here and that in armies and police forces elsewhere. More picturesque are the ceremonial drills, in which the Mounties march in their red-coated uniforms. The sergeant majors' parade is Mondays through Fridays at midday.

Many of the other places to visit are located in Wascana Centre, a 2,300-acre, manmade park built around Wascana Lake in the southern part of town. Here are the Legislative Buildings, the provincial seat of government, and the main campus of the University of Regina. On the center's north side, off College Avenue, are the *Museum of Natural History* (phone: 306-787-2815) and the *Norman Mackenzie Art Gallery* (phone: 306-779-4771). The museum concentrates on the flora and fauna of Saskatchewan largely through dioramas and paintings. Other sections are devoted to Native American life. The museum, enjoying a high reputation, sponsors a number of conservation and archaeological projects throughout the province, the results of which are on exhibit. The art gallery is a traditional museum featuring European art from the Renaissance onward and contemporary Canadian and US work. Also on the center's grounds is the Diefenbaker Homestead. Relocated here from Borden, Saskatchewan, this is the family home of John Diefenbaker, Canada's prime minister from 1957 to 1963. Even if you're not interested in Canadian politics, you may find a visit to the homestead interesting since it is furnished in an authentic pioneer manner. In the middle of Wascana Centre, the Saskatchewan Centre of the Arts houses a 2,000-seat theater that accommodates touring productions. Near the arts center, on the lakeshore, is a wild bird sanctuary. From an observation point on the opposite bank you have an excellent opportunity to view Canada geese, ducks, swans, and other shore birds.

The City Centre, in the middle of the city, is the headquarters of municipal government and services. In the public library (12th Ave. and Lorne St.), the Prairie History Room exhibits documents on local history and the Dunlop Art Gallery shows the work of local artists. On 11th Avenue, in the old City Hall, is the *Globe Theatre,* Regina's professional company. The historical drama *The Trial of Louis Riel* is staged each summer in Government House. Also worth your attention are the *Queensbury Downs* a few blocks west of City Centre. *Buffalo Days,* the annual summer fair, is held here each August, and the *Agridome,* a multipurpose, 7,000-seat complex, may well be housing an attraction at any time. As for sports, there's horse racing at the *Queensbury Downs* track; golf at nine courses encircling the city; and football at Taylor Field (at Albert St. and Dewdney Ave.) featuring the Saskatchewan Roughriders.

There are several interesting places to dine in Regina. *Bartleby's* (1920 Broad St.) creates an Old West atmosphere with a stand-up bar, player piano, and antique decorations. The food is reasonably good, too. The *Elephant & Castle* is an English-style pub serving beer and good food (11th Ave. at Scarth St.). *Mieka's* (11th Ave. and Smith St.) has a contemporary decor, an ever-changing menu of continental and vegetarian fare, and moderate prices. *C.C. Lloyd's Dining Room* in the *Chelton Inn* (1907 11th Ave.) offers fine continental fare.

From Regina, it is only 44 miles (71 km) to Moose Jaw via Route 1. On the way, you can take an interesting side trip by turning north on Route 301 just before you reach Moose Jaw.

BUFFALO POUND PROVINCIAL PARK: A 13-mile (21-km) drive brings you to Buffalo Pound Provincial Park, where 260 acres of fenced-in land provide a grazing area for a herd of buffalo. The park is an excellent place to observe these animals in something close to a state of nature. Outside the buffalo pound, the park offers horse rentals and guided trail rides along old paths through some interesting scenery. Fishing is permitted in Buffalo Pound Lake, and there are tennis courts and a swimming pool.

The park has a cafeteria, a grocery store, and 248 campsites. During the winter, the park operates the White Track Ski Resort and offers tobogganing, cross-country skiing, and ice fishing.

Upon leaving the park, you can return south on Route 301 and rejoin Route 1 heading west to Moose Jaw.

MOOSE JAW: Moose Jaw (pop. 36,000) is an industrial city set in the heart of wheat country. Of greatest interest is the Moose Jaw Wild Animal Park, open year-round. This full-fledged zoo features animals from all over the world, perhaps a welcome change of pace from moose and buffalo. The children's section emphasizes Saskatchewan wildlife. At the junction of Routes 1 and 2, one of Saskatchewan's four Western Development museums provides a visual record of the area's growth of culture and technology from pioneer days onward. The Moose Jaw branch specializes in the history of transportation, the exhibits running from horse wagons and dogsleds through trains and airplanes.

Apart from the zoo and the museum, most of Moose Jaw's attractions are annual events: the summer fair the first week in July; the Saskatchewan Air Show in mid-July, which features demonstrations of both antique and modern planes; and the *Kinsmen Band Festival*, a mid-May competition that draws marching bands from all around North America. The 82-room *Park Lodge Motor Hotel* (on Hwy. 1 at the junction of Hwy. 2) has a dining room and bar.

> **En Route from Moose Jaw** – If you're interested in history, you may want to make a somewhat lengthy side trip south to see the St. Victor petroglyphs and the reconstructed fort at Wood Mountain. Follow Route 2 south from Moose Jaw for 88 miles (142 km); a side road takes you a few miles farther to the park.

ST. VICTOR PETROGLYPHS HISTORIC PARK: The petroglyphs are carvings made in a sandstone rockface by Indians in prehistoric times. Pictured are animal and human figures and totemistic renderings of human faces. Getting to the carvings is a somewhat strenuous venture; you have to follow a path to the foot of the cliff, then climb a series of stairs to get to the ledge. Also, since the figures have faded through erosion, they are best seen when the sunlight is not directly on them.

Returning to Route 2, head south for a short distance to an unpaved road leading to Route 358, about 10 miles (16 km) west.

WOOD MOUNTAIN HISTORIC PARK: Following Route 358 south to the junction with Route 18 brings you to the entrance road to Wood Mountain Historic Park, with two reconstructed buildings from the Northwest Mounted Police post that existed here from 1874 to 1918. The buildings feature photographs and artifacts relating to the history of the fort, especially the fort's most memorable episode: Sitting Bull brought the Sioux Nation north from Montana following the Battle of Little Bighorn to settle for several years in the vicinity of Wood Mountain.

> **En Route from Wood Mountain** – From Wood Mountain follow Route 18 west to Valmarie in Grasslands National Park. Then take Route 4 north to Route 1 and the town of Swift Current.

SWIFT CURRENT: A town of 16,000, Swift Current preserves an Old West spirit, although you'll find all the modern amenities. Its pioneer tradition is particularly expressed in the *Frontier Days* celebration and rodeo, held annually around July 1, and the amateur fiddling contest in late September. Swift Current is convenient for an overnight stop since there are plenty of hotels. Major attractions are not plentiful, but there are interesting exhibits on pioneer history at the *Swift Current Museum* and artwork at the National Exhibition Centre, downtown.

> **En Route from Swift Current** – Before heading west on Route 1, you may want to drive north on Route 4 to Saskatchewan Landing Provincial Park, 24 miles (39 km) away. A historical marker pinpoints the spot where generations of pioneers had to ford or ferry across the South Saskatchewan River to reach the Battlefords

Trail and the route into northern Saskatchewan. Indian gravesites and teepee rings can be found in the hills throughout the park. And there is the Victorian Goodwin House mansion, built of fieldstone in 1900.

West from Swift Current on Route 1, you head deeper into ranching country. To the north of the highway are the Great Sand Hills, an open area of dunelike hills harboring an abundance of wildlife. You can get a closer look by turning north on Route 37 at Gull Lake, 34 miles (55 km) west of Swift Current.

Continuing west, Route 1 intersects Route 21 after another 44 miles (71 km). Turning south on Route 21 quickly brings you to Maple Creek, with a couple of small, local museums along the main route. The *Old-Timers Museum* concentrates on local history. About 22 miles (35 km) directly south of Maple Creek on Route 271 is Cypress Hills Provincial Park.

CYPRESS HILLS PROVINCIAL PARK: The Cypress Hills are a singular twist of nature — hilly, high-level plateaus covered with rich forests set in the midst of flat, dry, low-scrub prairie. Scientists believe that 30 million years ago, a river flowing eastward left a deposit of cobblestone in the area that was gradually lifted into prominence by the erosion of the surrounding strata. Later, when the Wisconsin glacier moved across Canada, it bypassed the 80 square miles that today form the summit of the hills.

Cypress Hills is a relief from monotonous prairies. It is filled with buttes, ridges, and plateaus, with huge areas of rolling ranchland in between. There's a manmade lake with a chalet, condominiums, and cabins on the shoreline. This main area has a nine-hole sand greens golf course, tennis courts, a swimming pool, and a beach. Hiking trails lead around the park; the trail to Bald Butte promontory is especially scenic. You can drive through cattle country and see curiously shaped rock formations and the impressive Conglomerate Cliffs. And the woodland is a good place to observe deer, moose, and other wildlife. During the winter, the park offers downhill and cross-country skiing, snowmobiling, skating, and tobogganing. In addition to cabins, the park has 200 camping spaces.

FORT WALSH NATIONAL HISTORIC PARK: Directly west of Cypress Hills, Fort Walsh can be reached from the park if you don't mind some rougher-than-usual driving. A road from Maple Creek also leads directly to Fort Walsh. Fort Walsh was the original headquarters of the Northwest Mounted Police. In May 1873, a battle took place in the Cypress Hills area between US and Canadian traders and the Assiniboine Indians. The traders lost badly, followed by a hue and cry resulting in the establishment of the Mounties. Fort Walsh, built in 1874, served as the main patrol center until 1882. The old fort has been duplicated at its original site, with original artifacts lending authenticity. Horses are kept at the fort, but there are no historical reenactments or Mounties in period uniforms. For the visitor, what distinguishes Fort Walsh from other Mountie reconstructions is the isolated setting evocative of a bygone age. Nearby is *Farwell's Trading Post,* restored to 1872 conditions, staffed with costumed guides.

En Route from Fort Walsh – The trip back to Maple Creek returns you to Route 21 and from there to Route 1. Heading west on Route 1 for 25 miles (40 km) takes you into the province of Alberta.

BEST EN ROUTE

Since the Trans-Canada is a principal highway, there is no trouble in finding adequate hotels, motels, or campgrounds. Some of the Regina inns are elaborate, with on premises entertainment and recreational facilities. Elsewhere, the motels tend to be functional, clean, and modern. Rates for hotels and motels are generally reasonable. Expect to pay $60 or more per night for a double room in the expensive range, $35 to $60 in the moderate range, and $20 to $35 in the inexpensive range. All prices are quoted in US dollars.

MOOSE MOUNTAIN PROVINCIAL PARK

Fish Creek Campground – This government-operated campground has 333 campsites, 131 with electricity. Showers, flush toilets, firewood, laundry, and a grocery store are on the premises. Open mid-May to early September. Just 4 miles (6.4 km) west of the park entrance (phone: 306-577-2155). Inexpensive.

Moose Mountain Park Cabins – There are 30 cabins of deluxe, modern, and semi-modern style. Open mid-May to September. Inquiries to Park Superintendent. Box 100, Carlyle, Saskatchewan S0C 0R0 (phone: 306-577-2155). Inexpensive.

REGINA

Landmark – The inn's 188 units are distinctively furnished and have air conditioning. Heated indoor pool, sauna, and whirlpool bath. Bar and restaurant. 4150 Albert St. (phone: 800-667-8191). Expensive.

Regina Inn – The best business hotel in the center of town. All 237 rooms, the convention floor, and main level have been newly renovated. Outdoor whirlpool bath, indoor pool with sauna, and exercise room. Two restaurants and a cocktail lounge. 1975 Broad St. (phone: 306-525-6767). Expensive.

Sheraton Centre – All 251 units have air conditioning. Heated pool, indoor waterslide, and a restaurant. Victoria Ave. and Broad St. (phone: 800-325-3535 or 306-569-1666). Expensive.

Imperial 400 – A motel with 200 rooms and dining, convention, and entertainment facilities, as well as a sauna, whirlpool bath, and indoor pool. 4255 Albert St. (phone: 800-667-0400 or 306-584-8800). Moderate.

Seven Oaks – Another motel, this one has 105 air conditioned rooms, a heated pool, dining room, and coffee shop. 777 Albert St. (phone: 800-667-8063 or 306-757-0121). Moderate.

Travelodge – The expanded inn now has 164 rooms. There is also a 3-story waterslide and a restaurant and bar complex on the mezzanine. 4177 Albert St. (phone: 306-586-3443). Moderate.

Sandman Inn – This hostelry has 181 units with air conditioning and TV sets; also a dining room, cocktail lounge, indoor pool, and whirlpool bath. 4025 Albert St. (phone: 800-663-6900 or 306-586-2663). Moderate to inexpensive.

MOOSE JAW

Best Western Downtown – A lodge that has 28 units with an adjacent restaurant. 45 Athabasca St. E. (phone: 306-692-1884). Moderate.

Best Western Heritage Inn – In addition to 90 units, facilities include an indoor pool, whirlpool bath, dining room, and cocktail lounge. 1590 Main St. N. (phone: 306-693-7550). Moderate.

Harwood Moose Jaw Inn – There are 89 rooms with air conditioning, a heated pool, wading pool, and sauna. Also a coffee shop, dining room, and cocktail lounge with nightly entertainment. 24 Fairford St. E. (phone: 306-692-2366). Moderate.

SWIFT CURRENT

Horseshoe Lodge – There are 49 units with a good view of the countryside. Air conditioning, heated pool, dining room, cocktail lounge. Hwy. 1E on N. Service Rd. (phone: 306-773-4643). Moderate.

Imperial 400 – A motel with 142 air conditioned units, indoor pool, sauna, dining room, and lounge. 1150 Begg St. E. (phone: 800-667-0400 or 306-773-2033). Expensive to moderate.

MAPLE CREEK

Maple Grove – It's got 14 rooms and 6 serviced trailer sites, so one may be a guest or park a recreational vehicle. Hwy. 21 and 1st Ave W. (phone: 306-662-2658). Moderate to inexpensive.

Estevan to the Northern Lakes

A south-north trip through Saskatchewan is a long journey. The distance from Estevan, near the North Dakota border, to Prince Albert, the northernmost city, is 363 miles (584 km). And if you choose to head farther north or to make side trips in the southern part of the province, you could double that. The southern part of the journey can be arranged so that you pass through Regina and Saskatoon, Saskatchewan's two major cities, and so that you can see many of the province's most interesting attractions. The route can appeal to your sense of adventure, since it takes you partway into Saskatchewan's great northern wilderness. Less than half of Saskatchewan is populated; the entire northern portion is open forest country filled with lakes and dotted with only a few settlements. This north country offers some of the finest fishing anywhere; for others, it is a chance to observe open, undisturbed nature. While many sites are accessible only by airplane, roads do lead a fair distance into the wilderness. If you choose, you may end your northward trek at Prince Albert National Park, which gives you a taste of the wilderness close to civilization.

En Route from North Dakota – There are 13 points at which the border may be crossed from the US into Saskatchewan. North Dakota's Route 52 brings you to the border at North Portal. Once across, you can follow Route 39 to Estevan, 18 miles (29 km) to the northwest. Shortly after setting out on Route 39, you may want to stop at Roche Percée to view the badlands rock formations inscribed with Indian carvings and the signatures of early explorers.

ESTEVAN: A small city of 10,000, Estevan is a major center for oil and coal resources. Boundary Dam, just south of town on Route 47, is the largest lignite coalburning power station in Canada; it is open for tours. Southeast, Woodlawn Regional Park houses a reconstruction of a Northwest Mounted Police barracks from the 1870s. The Estevan Brick Wildlife Compound displays a collection of area animals.

En Route from Estevan – The entire southern edge of Saskatchewan has a lot of badlands territory, but if you want to see more spectacular badlands terrain, take a side trip west on Route 18 from Estevan for 73 miles (117 km) to the edge of the Big Muddy Badlands. You can then head north on Route 6 for 66 miles (106 km) to Regina.

If the prospect of more badlands does not excite you, leave Estevan, heading northwest on Route 39. You will find more than enough semi-arid terrain along this route. After 53 miles (85 km) you will arrive at the next major town, Weyburn. Here the *Soo Line Historical Society Museum* is devoted to exhibits on local history, and there is a small art gallery in the town library. Forty-four miles (71 km) farther northwest, Route 39 joins Route 6 at the village of Corinne. Although you will want to take Route 6 north to Regina, staying on Route 39 a few miles past the intersection brings you to Wilcox, site of Notre Dame College, founded by Father Athol Murray. The Tower of God, a place of worship on campus, is open 24 hours a day. Backtracking to Corinne, head north on Route 6 to Regina, 28 miles (45 km) away.

REGINA: For a full account of Regina and its attractions, see *The Trans-Canada across Saskatchewan,* the preceding route.

En Route from Regina – The best route north from Regina is Route 11, a divided highway all the way to Saskatoon. The 154-mile (248-km) drive can be made quickly, but one lengthy side trip is recommended — to Gardiner Dam at Lake Diefenbaker. You can reach the dam by turning west on Route 44 at Davidson, about halfway between Saskatoon and Regina. After 31 miles (50 km), Route 44 crosses Route 19. Turn north on Route 19 and you will shortly see a turnoff heading west to the dam, 10 miles (16 km) away.

GARDINER DAM: The largest rolled-earth dam in Canada, Gardiner is an impressive sight. Over 3 miles long and 5,300 feet wide at its base, the dam rises to a height of 210 feet. It lies across the South Saskatchewan River, its backwash turning a 140-mile portion of the river into Lake Diefenbaker. Danielson Provincial Park, established around the dam, provides for camping, swimming, fishing, and boating. A visitor pavilion shows the workings of the dam, and tours are available. Farther south along the lakeshore on Route 19 is Douglas Provincial Park, which also offers a full range of lake activities adjacent to the smaller Qu'Appelle Dam. Just north of Douglas on Route 19, the museum in the community of Elbow contains a pioneer sod house and a portion of a sacred Indian rock, Mistusinne. The original 400-ton glacial boulder was used by the Plains Indians for their offerings to the spirit Manitou. The museum is open during the summer months.

En Route from Gardiner Dam – Return to Route 19 and head north for 14 miles (23 km) until the road intersects Route 15. Turn west on Route 15, and another 14 miles (23 km) returns you to Route 11 at Kenaston. Continuing north on Route 11, another 25 miles (40 km) brings you to a turnoff for Blackstrap Provincial Park, which boasts a manmade mountain. When Saskatoon was asked to stage the Canadian Winter Games in 1970, a demand was made for a ski hill. An extra 150 feet was added to a hill overlooking the lake at Blackstrap, giving skiers a run of 300 feet onto the ice. In addition to this somewhat treacherous hill, Blackstrap has fishing, swimming, and a campground. From here, it is 20 miles (32 km) to Saskatoon.

SASKATOON: For a full account of Saskatoon and its attractions, see *The Yellowhead Highway* route, which follows.

En Route from Saskatoon – Continuing north on Route 11 brings you to an area of considerable historical interest. Three historical sights lie off Route 11 about 40 miles (64 km) north. The first of these, Batoche National Historic Park, may be reached by turning east on Route 312 at Rosthern, traveling 10 miles (16 km), then turning north on Route 225 for 6 miles (10 km). At Batoche, a decisive battle took place in 1885 between Louis Riel and his Métis forces and General Middleton and his NWMP troops. The Métis were Canadians of European-Indian heritage who were largely neglected by the Canadian government, and their sense of injustice spilled into armed revolt. But the defeat of their leader, Riel, at Batoche marked the end of their war. Although one more battle took place at Steele Narrows, the Riel Rebellion was over. Most of the signs of the battle have disappeared, but you can still see some bullet scars on the walls of St. Antoine de Padoue Church rectory. Inside the building, photographs and displays commemorate the battle, and the graves of slain Métis are nearby. By returning east on Route 312 a few miles, then heading south on an unpaved road for 11 miles (18 km), you can see the Fish Creek Battlefield, where the rebellion began.

Returning by Route 312 to Route 11, a brief drive north brings you to *Duck Lake Historical Museum.* The recently opened museum includes exhibits on the Riel Rebellion, a jail that once housed the Indian rebel Almighty Voice, and material relating to the Indian community at Duck Lake. From Duck Lake, a trip 18 miles (29 km) west on Route 212 takes you to Fort Carlton Historic Park. Fort Carlton, partially reconstructed, was an early Hudson's Bay Company outpost. Inside the fort is a replica of an early Hudson's Bay store, and several other buildings have been furnished in period decor.

Returning to Route 11, head north 35 miles (56 km) to Prince Albert.

PRINCE ALBERT: The city of Prince Albert is considered the gateway to the north, the point where the rolling prairies give way to the heavily treed, lake-dotted parklands. The *Prince Albert Historical Museum* in Bryant Park is housed in a log church built in 1866. Exhibits relate to area history and the inevitable artifacts from the NWMP. Adjacent to the church is a blockhouse dating from the Riel Rebellion. Lund's Wildlife Exhibit, on the shore of the North Saskatchewan downtown, contains an excellent collection of North American animals. Both are open only during the summer.

There is also some chance to sample art in Prince Albert. *The Little Gallery* presents art shows in a building that was once an opera house. The *Prince Albert Art Centre* presents work of local, national, and international artists. And the public library on 12th Street houses a small art and crafts gallery.

The most interesting annual event is the winter festival held in February, with dogsled races and king trapper competitions, in which contestants try to duplicate legendary pioneer acts of strength by lifting 600-pound loads onto their backs, cutting wood at great speed with different kinds of saws, and cooking traditional Indian dishes. The more conventional summer fair is usually held the first week in August.

As a jumping-off point for expeditions farther north, either by road or by air, Prince Albert offers a bewildering number of routes from which to choose. However, one trip not to be missed is the relatively short journey north to Prince Albert National Park. Head north from Prince Albert on Route 2. After 19 miles (31 km), a turnoff west onto Route 263 will shortly take you into the park; travel 26 miles (42 km) north through the park to the main townsite at Waskesiu Lake.

PRINCE ALBERT NATIONAL PARK: Here is an excellent introduction to Saskatchewan's northern wilderness. Characteristic of the north country, the 960,000-acre park is filled with lakes, ponds, and streams formed thousands of years ago by receding glaciers. The terrain is hilly and forested, with white spruce, black spruce, poplar, and birch prominent. Animals, including elk, moose, deer, and bear, are abundant. Waskesiu Lake, with the park's townsite on its shores, is the main center of water activity, but Crean and Kingsmere, two other large, neighboring lakes, are also popular, as are the smaller Namekus, Hanging Heart, and Sandy. There are also many less crowded lakes and streams and hiking trails.

The Waskesiu townsite has several motels, cabins, and hotels, and campgrounds in and around the park offer 500 camping sites. Most of the recreational facilities are based at Waskesiu Lake townsite: tennis courts, an 18-hole golf course, riding stables, lawn bowling greens; rentals of houseboats, motorboats, rowboats, and canoes; a boat launch, if you've brought your craft; and a paddlewheeler tour boat that makes excursions on the lake. Most other lakes are accessible by road, but Crean and Kingsmere can be reached only by boat from Waskesiu. The fishing for lake trout is particularly good at Crean and Kingsmere. From the boat dock on the northwest shore of Kingsmere, a long hike leads to the home of Grey Owl, an Englishman adopted by the Ojibwas who became one of Canada's greatest naturalists.

Though the park is open year-round, many motels, campgrounds, and park facilities close in early October. The *Lakeview* hotel, with 44 modern rooms, is one way to enjoy the off-season; another is to make use of the 16 winter campsites, all with electric hook-ups. Cross-country skiing, ice fishing, and skating are available, with more winter activities planned.

En Route from Prince Albert National Park – Prince Albert Park can mark the terminus of your northward journey. But if you want a further taste of the wilderness or if you are interested in serious fishing, head north to La Ronge. Leaving the park by the Waskesiu Lake gate, Route 2 north, after 92 miles (148 km) through unpopulated countryside, takes you to La Ronge.

LA RONGE and vicinity: The town sits on the southwest shore of Lac La Ronge, a large lake surrounded by a myriad of smaller lakes and streams. It is a good fishing spot in its own right and serves as a launching point for trips to resorts deeper into the wilderness, either by car on the Route 102 continuation of Route 2 or by plane from La Ronge's small airport. In town are a few motels, some resorts, and a small campground. And on the north shore of the lake, another 13 miles (21 km) on Route 2, is Lac La Ronge Provincial Park, where camping, more or less in the rough, is permitted.

Lac La Ronge is a good place to catch lake trout, and the Churchill River, just to the north, is plentiful in walleye and pike. While it is certainly possible to fish entirely on your own here, especially if you've brought your own boat, resorts in the area provide guides. *Kikinahk* hostel, *Red's Camps,* and *Camp Kinisoo* are resorts accessible by road and licensed as fishing outfitters. If you want to stay or use the facilities of a resort, it will be necessary to make reservations several months in advance. Even if you wish simply to rent a boat, you will do well to inquire ahead. The fishing season is short — from May to October — and resorts get booked up fast.

If you're not interested in fishing, Lac La Ronge and Churchill River are excellent for canoeing. The Saskatchewan Tourism Office, in a drive to promote canoeing, has worked out 56 canoe routes in northern Saskatchewan, several of them in the La Ronge area. A brochure detailing the routes is available on request from Tourism Saskatchewan, 1919 Saskatchewan Dr., Regina. If nothing else, the La Ronge area is interesting as a place in which to get a stronger feel of the wilderness.

En Route from La Ronge – Fishermen can continue the eternal search for perch, pike, walleye, and lake trout farther north by road; wilderness buffs can use the same route to satisfy their sense of adventure. Just beyond the provincial park, Route 2, which became a gravel road several miles back, changes its designation to Route 102; the gravel road continues northeastward. For about 58 miles (93 km), it passes a series of smaller lakes, such as McLennan and Brabant, with a number of small, primitive campgrounds along the lakeshores. While roadside facilities are being developed and an occasional gas station can be found, it is wise to leave La Ronge with a full tank of gas and to keep your eye on the fuel gauge. Shortly past Brabant Lake, the road forks. Route 102 continues on for 27 miles (43 km) to the southern shore of large Reindeer Lake, where there is a small campground. The new Route 905 heads north for the long trip to Wollaston Lake. The Wollaston Lake camps all offer fly-in packages, and the most prominent, *Wollaston Lake Lodge,* is almost exclusively a fly-in operation. Route 905 ends west of Collins Bay at Wollaston Lake. Be sure to have a full tank of gas, a good spare tire, and to drive very carefully on the gravel surface.

Saskatchewan maintains a list of fishing resorts and outfitters. The list, available from the Tourism Saskatchewan, 1919 Sasketchewan Dr., Regina, should be consulted by anyone seriously planning a fishing trip. You can also get further details on fishing by checking *Fishing in Canada,* DIVERSIONS. Again, reservations at fishing camps should be made months in advance.

An alternate fishing route from La Ronge is to backtrack south on Route 2 to the intersection with Route 165, 12 miles (19 km) south of town. Heading east on Route 165 through open country for 60 miles (97 km) brings you to the shores of Deschambault Lake, a good spot for pike. Just before Deschambault, the road changes its designation to Route 106, and *Northern Lights Lodge* and *Deschambault Lake* resort are both accessible from the highway. Route 106 turns northeast, and another 20 miles (32 km) brings you to the intersection with Route 135. Turning north on Route 135 quickly brings you to Jan Lake, famous for its pike fishing. There are five licensed outfitter lodges here, of which *Jan Lake Lodge* and *Martin's Cabins* are the most elaborate. Following Route 135 north for 25 miles (40 km) brings you to Pelican Narrows, another excellent fishing spot.

From the city of Prince Albert, it is possible to take a 155-mile (249 km) drive northeast via Routes 3, 55, and 924 to Dore Lake for fishing. And the city serves as a base for fly-ins to remote camps, such as Reindeer Lake, Cree Lake, and Wollaston Lake.

BEST EN ROUTE

Although only a few motels and campgrounds are listed here, you'll find a steady supply along this route. The greatest number — and most comfortable — are in Regina and Saskatoon, and these are discussed in the previous and following *Best En Route* sections. Otherwise, no accommodations along this route can be classified as expensive. Expect to pay $40 to $60 in the moderate range and under $40 in the inexpensive range. All prices quoted are in US dollars.

WEYBURN

Weyburn Inn – In addition to the 70 rooms, there is a coffee shop, dining room, and cocktail lounge. 5 Government Rd. (phone: 306-842-6543). Moderate.

REGINA

For a list of Regina's accommodations, see *The Trans-Canada across Saskatchewan*, the preceding route.

SASKATOON

For Saskatoon accommodations, see *The Yellowhead Highway*, the following route.

PRINCE ALBERT

Imperial 400 – In addition to its 137 units, this motel has a heated pool and coffee shop. 3580 Second Ave. W. (phone: 306-764-6881). Moderate.

Marlboro Inn – A 112-unit hostelry with an indoor pool, a dining room specializing in smorgasbord, and a cocktail lounge. 67 13th St. E. (phone: 800-667-0400 or 306-763-2643). Moderate.

Coronet – There are 100 units, an indoor pool, whirlpool bath, sauna, dining room, and cocktail lounge with entertainment. 3551 Second Ave. W. (phone: 800-667-0400 or 306-764-6441). Moderate to inexpensive.

PRINCE ALBERT NATIONAL PARK

Northland – There are 13 units in this Waskesiu Lake townsite. Open April 15 to mid-October. Reservation deposit required. Box 57, Waskesiu (phone: 306-663-5322). Moderate.

Skyline – A 21-unit motel in Waskesiu. Reservation deposit required. Box 22, Waskesiu (phone: 306-663-5461). Inexpensive.

Beaver Glen Campground – The campground has 213 sites. Showers, flush toilets, dump station, and firewood. Operated by Parks Canada; open mid-May to mid-September. Near townsite (phone: 306-663-5322). Inexpensive.

The Yellowhead Highway

The Yellowhead Highway describes a connected series of east-west routes through Canada's four western provinces. A promotional effort by the municipalities and businesses along the route, it calls attention to attractions that might otherwise be bypassed. The Yellowhead crosses central Saskatchewan, entering from Manitoba just east of Langenburg on Route 16, and heads northwest through Yorkton, Saskatoon, and North Battleford, entering Alberta at Lloydminster. The length of the Yellowhead in Saskatchewan is 433 miles (697 km). As a basic route, the Yellowhead gives you a fairly good view of Saskatchewan if you make side trips. The route is rich in reminders of the frontier of the late 1800s: three of Saskatchewan's Western Development museums, at Yorkton, Saskatoon, and North Battleford; fort sites at Fort Battleford Historic Park and Fort Pitt Historic Park; and battle sites at Cut Knife and Steel Narrows. Saskatoon is a large, modern city. Several provincial parks offer scenery, hiking, swimming, and fishing.

En Route from Manitoba – After entering Saskatchewan on Route 16, you pass quickly through the small communities of Marchwell and Langenburg. At Churchbridge, 18 miles (29 km) west of the border, you have your first opportunity for a side trip. Head north on Route 8 for 48 miles (77 km) to Kamsack, turn east for a few miles on Route 5 to Duck Mountain Provincial Park.

DUCK MOUNTAIN PROVINCIAL PARK: One of Saskatchewan's most picturesque parks, Duck Mountain is set in highlands formed over 10,000 years ago when glaciers halted their progress southward, melting where they stood. Tons of silt, sand, and gravel fell from the ice to form a hummocky moraine, "knob and kettle" topography. The center of the park is Madge Lake. Small and relatively shallow, it is a source of good perch, pickerel, and pike. Tall aspen cover the countryside. Whitetail deer and moose are abundant as are black bear and many fur-bearing animals; on occasion, golden and bald eagles can be seen. The *Ministik Inn* is near the main beach, and there are also cabins and condominiums for rent. Recreational facilities include an 18-hole golf course and bicycle and hiking trails. Because of its higher elevation, the park is cooler and rainier than the surrounding plains.

En Route from Duck Mountain Park – Wend your way back to the Yellowhead through interesting countryside. If you head west on Route 5, you will find many signs of Ukrainian culture in this grain farming area. Most visible are the silver-domed Ukrainian Orthodox churches. At the village of Verigin, 13 miles (21 km) west of Duck Mountain Park, the *Museum of the Society of Doukhobors* is devoted to traditional Russian culture. At Canora, 28 miles (45 km) west of Duck Mountain, you can see the area's finest example of a Ukrainian church. Turn south onto Route 9 to rejoin the Yellowhead Highway at Yorkton.

GOOD SPIRIT LAKE PROVINCIAL PARK: Along the way, you will pass Good Spirit Lake Provincial Park, a translation of the Indian Kitchimanitou. A Hudson's Bay Company trading post in the 1880s, the site was established as a provincial park in 1931. It may be reached by unpaved roads from Canora or you can travel a few miles south on Route 5 and turn west on Route 229 for a short drive to the southeast entrance. Sand dunes stretching for 3 miles from the lakeshore reach heights of 18 feet.

The shallow, sandy water makes for an easy swim. The park, heavily treed with poplar, offers 157 secluded, tree-lined campsites, each with its own fireplace and picnic table.

From the park, continue south on Route 5 to Yorkton, 31 miles (50 km) south of Canora.

YORKTON: A city of 16,000, Yorkton is a commercial center for the surrounding farming area. Its branch of the *Western Development Museum* (Western Development museums record daily life and industry in the late 19th and 20th centuries) focuses on Saskatchewan's ethnic groups and the development of agricultural technology. There are rooms furnished in the manner of the English, French, Ukrainian, and Swedish; the Plains Indians are represented by a teepee and bark canoe. The agricultural exhibits include a collection of old and new farm machinery. Most intriguing are the specimens of early tools. The museum, on the western portion of Route 16, is open all year.

The Yorkton Art Council (Smith St.) houses visiting art shows as well as a small permanent collection, and *Norinne Creative Hands,* on Broadway downtown, sells local handicrafts. A winter fair is held in February, a multicultural festival in June, and a summer fair in August. A Pioneer Thresherman's show is held in late summer. The *Yorkton Short Film/Video Festival,* which attracts entries from around the world, is held every fall.

En Route from Yorkton – Go west on the Yellowhead, Route 16, through more farming country, to the town of Wynyard, 90 miles (145 km) northwest of Yorkton near the famous Quill Lakes. On one of the principal migration flyways for birds, the lakes provide 100 miles of shoreline for waterfowl nesting. A short drive north from Wynyard on an unpaved road will take you to the lakeshore, excellent for waterfowl hunting or a beautiful view. Continue west from Wynyard on Route 16 to Lanigan, another 37 miles (60 km). The area from here west toward Saskatoon contains a number of potash mines. Unfortunately, none offer public tours. From Lanigan it is 77 miles (124 km) to Saskatoon.

SASKATOON: A city of 177,600 on the banks of the South Saskatchewan River, Saskatoon is known as the City of Bridges. The riverfront and its many parks are a skillful blending of urban design with the work of nature. The *Bessborough* hotel, built by the Canadian National Railroad in the 1930s, is a riverfront landmark downtown. On the opposite shore is the campus of the University of Saskatchewan.

Saskatoon's *Western Development Museum* (on Lorne Ave. in the southern part of the city) features Boomtown 1910, an indoor reconstruction of a frontier main street and stores a city block long. There are no false fronts; all the buildings are complete and fully furnished with material from the early 1900s. Footsteps echo on the wooden sidewalks as people roam the frame buildings. Cars and buggies are parked on the street, and a railway station is at one end of town. Some of the buildings include a barbershop, hotel, print shop, fire hall, town hall, dry goods store, drugstore, bank, school, and a church brought to the museum from a small village. The old-fashioned *Palace Theatre* shows silent movies and historical films. The balcony on the Saskatchewan Hotel is a good place from which to observe the Boomtown. Other exhibits include collections of vintage cars, farm machinery, and small planes. Some of the old farm machinery is used in threshing competitions during the fair at the nearby exhibition grounds during the third week of July.

The *University of Saskatchewan Museum of Anthropology and Archaeology,* in the Arts Building, devotes much space to the life of Saskatchewan Indians before the coming of the white man. A small, privately operated Ukrainian museum is open during the summer. The *Ukrainian Museum of Canada* (910 Spadina Crescent, E) houses exhibits of traditional clothing and handicrafts and is open Tuesdays through Saturdays from 1 to 4 PM.

The *Mendel Art Gallery and Conservatory* (on Spadina Crescent on the riverfront) houses visiting exhibitions; its permanent collection includes Canadian, European, and

Eskimo art. *Herold's Art Studio* (404 32nd St. W.) features native and local paintings. The *Photographer's Gallery* (236 Second Ave. S.) also emphasizes local work. Handicrafts are available at the *House of Treasures* (1416 22nd St. W.), *Past and Present Antiques* (327 21st W), *Prairie Pottery* (35-158 Second Ave. N.), and at the *Trading Post* (226 Second Ave. S.). On the east side of town, off 115th Street, Forestry Farm Park exhibits 300 live animals from the Saskatchewan region and has picnic areas on the grounds.

Saskatoon's isolation hasn't hindered its residents' interest in food. Its restaurants include the *St. Tropez Bistro* (243 Third Ave. S.), which serves French fare; *Cousin Nik's* (1110 Grosvenor), a top-quality prairie steakhouse; and *Lucci's* (117 Third Ave. S.), a somewhat more formal restaurant with an elaborate haute cuisine menu.

The city's annual events include a Ukrainian festival in mid-May, *Louis Riel Day* and the annual exhibition in July, and a multicultural festival in August.

En Route from Saskatoon – If you want a day's run from Saskatoon, two small parks are within easy reach. Pike Lake Provincial Park, 19 miles (30 km) south, can be reached by taking Route 7 out of Saskatoon and going south on Route 60. Blackstrap Provincial Park lies 22 miles (35 km) to the south just off Route 11. Both have sandy beaches, boating, and fishing. From Saskatoon, the Yellowhead continues northwest 86 miles (138 km) through more farming country to North Battleford.

NORTH BATTLEFORD: This city and an adjacent smaller town, Battleford, are of interest for Fort Battleford National Historic Park and for the *Western Development Museum* featuring an outdoor reconstruction of a pioneer village. In contrast to Saskatoon's Boomtown, this village emphasizes home life, pioneer virtues, and the area's ethnic diversity. The village, comprised of 26 buildings, includes homes furnished in the manner of Ukrainian and French-Canadian settlers, a railroad station, a barbershop, and a schoolhouse. The indoor exhibits concentrate on the history of agricultural technology and include examples of new and old machinery and tools. The museum is located at the junction of Routes 16 and 40.

Fort Battleford National Historic Park, across the North Saskatchewan River just off Central Avenue in Battleford, commemorates the Mountie post established here in 1876, which served as the capital of the Northwest Territories and played an important part in the Riel Rebellion. Five of the original buildings still stand; they are restorations, not reconstructions. Most impressive is the commanding officer's house, furnished with authentic Victorian furniture and rugged pioneer necessities like washbasins and wood stoves. The other buildings, including two barracks, a guardhouse, and the government house, display artifacts and other material.

In North Battleford, exhibits can be seen at the *North Battleford Arts Centre* (1301 104th St.) and at the *Western Development Museum* (junction of Hwys. 16 and 40). For handicrafts in Battleford, your best bet is the *Saskatchewan Handcraft Festival,* held annually in mid-July.

Due west on Route 40, 128 miles (206 km) to the town of Cut Knife, is the Cut Knife Battlefield Historic Site, where plaques commemorate an 1885 battle between the Indians and the NWMP. In town, the *McLain Memorial Museum* is a private operation with more exhibits on the battle and on pioneer and Indian life.

En Route from North Battleford – At this point you may follow Route 16 to the Alberta border, but if you still wish to see Saskatchewan scenery and historic sites, a trip north from the Yellowhead route will be rewarding. Taking Route 4 north from the Battlefords for 25 miles (40 km) brings you to Battlefords Provincial Park, geared for the camper with 413 camping sites, 68 of which have electricity. The golf course is the main attraction, and fishing is popular. Jackfish Lake is ideal for swimming. If you double back a short distance from the park, Route 4 will intersect Route 26 heading northwest. A drive up Route 26 will begin to introduce you to Saskatchewan's northern lake country, and after 71 miles (114 km) will bring you to the Steele Narrows Historic Park, the site of the 1885 battle that led to the final defeat of Louis Riel and the rebels. With the exception of some historic markers, the battlefield is the same as it was nearly a century ago.

Another 27 miles (43 km) north on Route 26 brings you to Meadow Lake Provincial Park.

MEADOW LAKE PROVINCIAL PARK: Meadow Lake, a large park centered around a series of lakes, sits on the edge of Saskatchewan's northern wilderness, yet it includes enough facilities so that the visitor never seems to be roughing it. The park offers a slight taste of wilderness free of commercialism, with no restaurants, bars, golf courses, tennis courts, or riding stables. But there are cabins for rent and 654 camping sites. Canoes can be rented, and fishing for pike and perch is good in all the lakes. Hunting is permitted in certain areas; check for signs. Cross-country skiing and power tobogganing are popular in the winter. The park is full of wildlife, with plenty of black bear and moose and pockets of elk, wolves, foxes, and coyotes.

En Route from Meadow Lake Park – Route 21 leads south from the western end of the park. But it is a rough road and you may find it easier to retrace your drive on Route 26. At St. Walburg, turn west on Route 3. After 17 miles (27 km) you will see a turnoff heading north; it's a short drive to the village of Frenchman Butts, where you can still see rifle pits left from the Riel. After returning to Route 3, another 10 miles (16 km) brings you to Fort Pitt Historic Park. An early Hudson's Bay Company post (1829) later figured in the Riel Rebellion. In the park, exhibits and reconstructions retrace this history. Fifteen miles (24 km) beyond Fort Pitt, Route 3 intersects Route 17, which runs along the Saskatchewan-Alberta boundary. Heading south on Route 17 for 16 miles (26 km) will bring you to Lloydminster and the Yellowhead Highway.

LLOYDMINSTER: Straddling the Saskatchewan-Alberta border, Lloydminster was founded in 1903 by the British Barr colonists. Most of the interesting sights in town are located in the *Barr Colony Museum* complex in Weaver Park. The museum's buildings contain exhibits on the Barr Colony, the RCMP, and area history. *Fuch's Wildlife Museum*, in the complex, features preserved animals in settings duplicating their natural habitat. Also on the grounds is a gallery featuring more paintings by Berthold Imhoff. From Lloydminster, continue on the Yellowhead into Alberta.

BEST EN ROUTE

The best hotels and the widest range of accommodations are found in Saskatoon. But Yorkton and Lloydminster also offer a good selection of inns, and all along the route are motels for overnight stops. The best bets if you're camping are the government-operated Yellowhead Highway campgrounds and provincial parks campgrounds. Apart from Saskatoon, motel and hotel rates are not high. Expect to pay $60 to $90 per night for a double room in the expensive range, $40 to $60 in the moderate range, and under $40 in the inexpensive range. All prices are quoted in US dollars.

YORKTON

Holiday Inn – This motor inn has 91 units, with a heated indoor pool, a wading pool, sauna, and a whirlpool bath. Also a restaurant specializing in Russian cuisine and a nightclub. 110 E. Broadway (phone: 800-667-1585). Expensive to moderate.

SASKATOON

Holiday Inn – Adjacent to a shopping mall and the *Centennial Auditorium,* this 187-unit motel has a heated indoor pool, restaurant, and cocktail lounge with entertainment. First Ave. and 22nd St. E. (phone: 800-465-4329). Expensive.

Ramada Renaissance – A 300-room hotel in an 18-story downtown tower. It has 14 luxury suites with extension phones and wet bars. There are two super waterslides in the recreation complex, which also has a sauna, whirlpool bath, and an indoor pool. Satellite TV and nightly entertainment. 405 20th St. E. (phone: 800-667-3020). Expensive.

Saskatoon Inn – This establishment, 2 minutes from the airport, features a central courtyard with tropical plants. Each of its 257 rooms has a queen-size bed, and there is a sauna, whirlpool bath, indoor pool, and nightly entertainment. Lounge, coffee shop, and licensed restaurant. 2002 Airport Dr. (phone: 800-667-8789). Expensive.

Sheraton-Cavalier – The inn has 250 units, a pool, sauna, and a whirlpool bath. A restaurant-nightclub overlooks the river. 612 Spadina Crescent E. (phone: 800-325-3535). Expensive.

Holiday House – These 107 units are complemented by a heated outdoor pool, dining room, and cocktail lounge with entertainment. 2901 Eighth St. E. (phone: 306-374-9111). Expensive to moderate.

Will Inns Saskatoon – Centrally located, with 171 modern rooms, convention facilities, free parking, nightly entertainment, indoor pool, and sauna. 806 Idylwyld Dr. N., on Yellowhead Hwy. 16 (phone: 800-661-1331). Expensive to moderate.

Parktown – A 109-unit hotel, with a heated indoor pool, sauna, whirlpool bath, restaurant, and disco. 924 Spadina Crescent E. (phone: 800-667-3999). Moderate.

Relax Inn – Close to the airport, this motel has 192 rooms and special accommodations for the handicapped. Other amenities include a licensed restaurant, pool, and satellite TV. Corner of Airport and Circle Drives (phone: 800-661-9563). Moderate.

TraveLodge – Near the airport, with 221 units, an indoor pool with a waterslide, sauna, whirlpool bath, exercise room, and dining room. 106 Circle Dr. W. (phone: 306-242-8881 or 800-255-3050). Moderate.

King George – Centrally located, the hotel has 104 rooms and extensive indoor shopping in an underground arcade. 157 Second Ave. N. (phone: 306-244-6133). Moderate to inexpensive.

Patricia – A small, quiet, 48-room hotel with a restaurant and a pub, near downtown shopping malls. 345 Second Ave. N. (phone: 306-242-8861). Inexpensive.

BORDEN

Borden Bridge Campground – Of 29 campsites, 12 have electricity. Pit toilets, dump station, firewood. Government-operated; open mid-May to early September. Rte. 16 in Borden, between Saskatoon and North Battleford (phone: 306-933-6240). Inexpensive.

NORTH BATTLEFORD

Capri – There are 97 rooms (47 more in the adjacent sister motel), a dining room, nightclub. 992 101st St. (phone: 306-445-9425). Moderate.

Battlefords Provincial Park South Beach Campground – Of 167 sites, 25 have electricity. Showers, laundry, flush toilets, dump station, and firewood. Government-operated; open year-round. Off Rte. 4, northwest of the park gate (phone: 306-386-2212). Inexpensive.

MEADOW LAKE PROVINCIAL PARK

Kimball Lake Campground – A government-operated campground that has 205 sites, 75 with electricity. Showers, laundry, flush toilets, dump station, firewood. Grocery store, beach, playground, boat launch. Fourteen other campgrounds are in the park. Open late May to early September. Off Rte. 26, inside the park (phone: 306-236-3382). Inexpensive.

LLOYDMINSTER

Tropical Inn – This hostelry has an indoor pool with water slide, children's play area, and 72 rooms. 5621 44th St. (phone: 403-875-7000). Expensive to moderate.

Capri – A 60-room inn with a restaurant and bar. 4615 50th Ave. (phone: 403-825-5591). Moderate.

Imperial 400 – Recently built with 100 rooms, it can accommodate guests in wheelchairs. 4320 44th St. (phone: 800-667-0400). Moderate.

Voyageur – Very basic economy motel with 31 rooms. 4724 44th St. (phone: 403-825-2248). Moderate.

Wayside Flag Inn – Offered here are 99 rooms, a poolside restaurant, executive suites, and nightly entertainment. Hwy. 16, 2 blocks west of the Saskatchewan-Alberta border (phone: 403-875-4404). Moderate.

Cedar Inn – Only 6 years old, this small (50 rooms) motel offers queen-size beds and complimentary coffee. 4526 44th St. (phone: 403-825-6155). Inexpensive.

The Yukon Territory

> There are strange things done in the midnight sun
> By the men who moil for gold;
> The Arctic trails have their secret tales
> That would make your blood run cold.
> — Robert Service,
> "The Cremation of Sam McGee"

For thousands of years only the Indians lived in the Yukon; then, in the 19th century, as part of its constant search for fur, the Hudson's Bay Company began to push north and west. Under the auspices of the company, Robert Campbell and John Bell explored the upper watercourse of the Yukon River and the northern sections of the territory in the 1840s. Trappers and traders followed the trail of Hudson's Bay trading posts, and in 1869 the Alaska Commercial Company moved in, extending the system of trading posts. Prospectors began drifting into the area as early as 1863, encouraged by finds of gold traces along the course of the Yukon River.

The land, acquired from the Hudson's Bay Company in 1870, became a provisional district in 1895. At that time less than 1,000 Caucasians lived among the Indians. By 1898, they had mushroomed to more than 60,000, nearly all living in decadent splendor and desperation in this vast, wild land 4,000 miles from the nearest city of any consequence.

An epic human drama, the Klondike Gold Rush of 1898 lasted less than 5 years and changed forever the face of Canada's virgin, 207,000-square-mile Yukon Territory.

Approximately 100,000 people, mostly Americans, scrambled madly in pursuit of a fortune in gold, enduring hardships for which they were ill prepared, driven by "Klondicitis" — gold fever. Their materialistic quest resembled a mass pilgrimage or a holy war, as they crept over treacherous mountain passes like a stream of ants, each hauling a ton or more of supplies. Less than half even reached the fabulous gold fields, and of these, perhaps 20,000 actually panned for gold. Only 4,000 found anything of value. Ironically, few of the successful seekers could call themselves wealthy; the richest claims had been staked long before the hordes reached the fabled creekbeds. And for most of those who did make small fortunes, their new wealth slipped through their fingers as quickly as it had appeared in their gold pans. This is the dominant thread in the Yukon's brief historical tapestry.

Miners' tales are like fish stories — there's always a big one that got away, a spot left barren where somebody else got a strike. The incident that caused the Klondike Gold Rush, created several millionaires, and ruined the lives of hundreds stands as one of the toughest hard-luck stories of all time.

A miner named Robert Henderson found a river of gold, or at least knew where it was, and told fellow prospector George Washington Carmack. Carmack, a white man whose wife was a Stick Indian, was a rare individual for that place in those days — a well-educated man. He maintained a library and kept an organ in his Yukon home. Henderson, who apparently didn't care for Indians, may have antagonized Carmack. After learning the location of the gold from Henderson, Carmack and his two Indian brothers-in-law began to work the juncture of the Klondike and Yukon rivers. On August 17, 1896, Carmack found the large nugget that sparked it all. Carmack, Skookum Jim, and Tagish Charley (his brothers-in-law) laid claim to the area once called Rabbit Creek where it met the Eldorado Creek, and later known as Bonanza Creek. Henderson was never told, losing the chance to stake a claim to one of the biggest strikes in the Klondike. He established a claim on another rich section, but failing health prevented him from working it himself. He sold it for $3,000 to another miner, who took an estimated half million in gold from the claim. In his later years, Henderson was awarded a government pension as co-discoverer of the Klondike gold fields, but he died a poor man in Vancouver.

Rather than trace this intriguing yarn down murky museum hallways, travel the "Trail of '98" yourself. Follow the actual path of the gold-crazed hordes — stampeders, as they were called. Take advantage of a unique opportunity to step back in time and retrace history where it happened, adding substance and a sense of adventure to a Yukon trip.

The Yukon Territory is shaped like a right-angle triangle — wide at the bottom and tapered at the top. Its base rests on the 60th parallel, which also marks the northern boundary of British Columbia; the upright, western edge leans against Alaska. The northern end, lying within the Arctic Circle, opens on Beaufort Sea. The jagged eastern border of the Yukon is shared with the Northwest Territories.

When the gold rush started, most of the boundary lines between these states and nations hadn't even been conceived. The vast majority of the miners sailed from West Coast ports, cutting through the offshore islands to gain access to the Lynn Canal, which leads past Juneau to a point of land formed by the mouths of two rivers, the Skagway and the Taiya. Both these rivers arise in the southwest corner of the Territory from the St. Elias Mountains, a component of the chain of coastal mountains that extend along the Pacific from Alaska to the Baja.

They docked at one of two settlements, Dyea or Skagway, where they prepared for the overland trek to the headwaters of the Yukon River. The Yukon headwaters are just 30 miles from the Pacific Ocean, yet it flows north almost 500 miles (850 km) to Dawson, turns west into Alaska, and cuts completely across it before emptying into the Bering Sea, traveling a total of more than 2,000 miles.

The task of crossing the mountains in time to reach the Yukon River before freeze-up — when the river would ice over and curtail travel to the gold fields — drove the stampeders to desperation. Two passes were found through the mountains, the Chilkoot and the White. The Chilkoot, which parallels the Taiya River into the mountains, is 32 miles long, and the White, which follows the Skagway River for a distance, is 41 miles long. The two passes meet on the shores of Lake Bennett, at the headwaters of the Yukon River.

At this point, the stampeders could load their goods on boats and float to the fields. The camps they established and the trading posts they patronized grew into towns, forming a thin lifeline into the wilderness.

Although the 1898 gold rush, the building of the Alaska Highway in 1942, and other encroachments of civilization have taken a toll on Canada's last frontier, the Yukon remains largely untamed wilderness. Just 28,000 people live in this 207,000-square-mile area, and more than half of them are concentrated in the capital of Whitehorse, which sprawls over 12 square miles. Faro (pop. 1,300) is the next largest community. The remaining inhabitants live in small, isolated communities.

An excellent transportation system allows them to share this bounty with the estimated 300,000 people who visit the Yukon each year.

For air travel: Canadian Airlines International (Whitehorse International Airport, Whitehorse, Yukon; phone: 403-668-3535), Alkan Air (Box 4008, Whitehorse, Yukon; phone: 403-668-6616), and Air North (Box 4998, Hanger A, Whitehorse International Airport, Yukon; phone: 403-668-2228); a number of smaller carriers provide charter service from the outside as well as between distant points within the territory.

Buses: *Whitepass & Yukon Route* (300 Elliot Ave. W., Seattle, WA; phone: 206-281-0576), *Atlas Tours, Ltd.* (Box 4340, Whitehorse, Yukon; phone: 403-668-3161), *Atlin Express* (Box 175, Atlin, B.C.; phone: 604-651-7617), *Greyhound of Canada* (3211A Third Avenue, Whitehorse, Yukon; phone: 403-667-2223), *Norline Coaches* (3211A Third Avenue, Whitehorse, Yukon; phone: 403-668-3355), *Watson Lake Bus Lines* (Box 469, Watson Lake, Yukon; phone: 403-536-7381), *Westours, Ltd.* (Box 4197, Whitehorse, Yukon; phone: 403-668-3225 or 443-403-4494), and *Whitehorse Transit* (110 Tlingit St., Yukon; phone: 403-668-2831) create a bus network linking most of the towns in the area.

Package tours can be arranged through *Atlas Tours, Ltd.* (PO Box 4340, Whitehorse, Yukon Y1A 3T5; phone: 403-668-3161), *Princess Tours* (2815 Second Ave., Suite 400, Seattle, WA 98121; phone: 206-728-4202), *Greyline Yukon/Westours* (300 Elliott Ave. W., Seattle, WA 98119; phone: 206-281-3535) and *Gold City Tours* in Dawson (PO Box 846, Dawson City, Yukon; phone: 403-993-5175).

For backcountry expeditions in the Yukon, 75 outfitters arrange wilderness encounters, outdoor adventures, and hunting and fishing trips. Two are *Rainbow Tours* — wilderness boating, camping, and backpacking trips (3089 Third Ave., Whitehorse; phone: 403-668-5598); *Kluane Wilderness Lodges* — by air to Welsley Lake and beyond for fishing expeditions (PO Box 1268, Station A, Kelowna, BC; phone: 604-764-2133).

Before making up your mind, ask the Department of Tourism for a complete list of services. Also request the latest copy of the hunting and fishing regulations and a list of outfitters. Careful wildlife management is needed to prevent depletion of herds, so the territory is divided into 20 active registered guiding areas; one outfitter has sole rights to guiding and outfitting in each. Any hunter from beyond the Yukon's borders must be accompanied by a licensed guide. Grizzly, black, and brown bear, Dall's and stone sheep, woodland and barren-ground caribou, moose, and mountain goat are abundant, and so are white-tailed ptarmigan, rock ptarmigan, four types of grouse, and various ducks and geese. Bag limits are more than generous.

Anglers who fish the waters of the Yukon Territory had better start thinking of new ways to describe "the one that got away," because no one's ever going to believe it. The fish up here, like the mountains, are big. The largest lake trout taken in recent years was 87 pounds, and catches of 20 to 30 pounds are common. With a daily limit of five each for northern pike (average 3 to 4 feet), Arctic grayling, Dolly Varden, rainbow trout, steelheads, and salmon (with a 2-day limit in your possession at any one time), you know the fish are striking. And there is no closed season. Guides are not required for fishing trips, but they're recommended.

Hunting season starts in early spring and extends into late fall, but the principal tourist season runs from mid-May to mid-September. Summer temperatures often soar to the high 80s F (30C), but average July temperatures are in the high 60s F(20C). Yukon winters, with readings as low as −50F (−45C), are no time to tour. Some roads, like the Taylor or Top of the World Highway, are closed to winter travel. Travel arrangements, especially hotel reservations, should be made as far in advance as possible or you may find yourself shut out. Expect to book at least 90 days ahead. Even dining reservations at popular restaurants should be made in advance.

A few quick notes about traveling in the Yukon:

About 20% of the route is on gravel roads, and though these are generally well maintained, it's a good idea to put protective covers over your headlights and screens on windshields to protect them from flying rocks and stones.

Lengthen your following distances, especially behind large trucks or buses, because dust obscures your vision. If you require unleaded gas, it's available nearly everywhere in the Yukon. However, gas is quite a bit more expensive in the Yukon than in other parts of Canada. The roads are patrolled thoroughly, and services are spread along most highways, but spare tires and changing equipment are a must. First-aid kits and some dehydrated foods aren't a bad idea either, and if you must travel during winter, they're a necessity. The same is true of a camp stove, to provide heat in case of emergency.

If you're camping or just cooking on the side of the road, avoid foods that are highly aromatic since most animals are sensitive to smells. Caribou, moose, and grizzly, black, and brown bears abound. Do not be alarmed by them, but remember they are wild, and lives have been lost through unnecessary and (usually) foolish acts. *Do not try to corner a bear* or in any way force him to move against his will. Don't create a bad situation by feeding bears or any other animals, and be sure to burn all waste and foodstuffs when you're through. If you are confronted by a bear, the best policy is simply to back away slowly and quietly. Do not run, yell, or scream. Remember that the wilderness of the Yukon is not an inherently frightening place. Common sense and caution will carry you through almost anything new.

The Yukon is outdoor country and Yukoners usually dress casually. Caribou and grizzlies, after all, aren't impressed with the latest fashions. Nevertheless, it's a good idea to bring along a nice outfit for nights on the town. You won't need a heavy-duty parka during the summer, but a sweater or jacket will be useful.

Today, you can follow the footsteps of the stampeders of '98. In this chapter we trace two routes through the territory. The Dawson Circle Route, which explores the contemporary Yukon, begins and ends in the capital, Whitehorse, traveling the highways through the mining areas of the Yukon and crossing into nearby Alaska. The Trail of '98 actually follows the path used by most of those hopeful prospectors as they crossed the Chilkoot Pass through the St. Elias Mountains and then rafted 500 miles north on the Yukon River to the gold fields at Dawson. Today that same trip is no less difficult for any traveler who attempts to challenge the mighty river. Either way, exploring the Yukon Territory is an experience not soon forgotten.

Information: Tourism Yukon, Box 2703, Whitehorse, Yukon Territory Y1A 2C6 (phone: 403-667-5340).

The Dawson Circle Route

For a broader view of the Yukon Territory, travel the Dawson Circle Route, 333 miles (536 km) northwest from Whitehorse to Dawson via the Klondike Highway (Rtes. 1 and 2) and return to Whitehorse by way of Alaska. Hook up with the Alaska Highway (Rtes. 9 and 1) to Tetlin Junction, Alaska, a distance of 170 miles (274 km). The Circle Route, about 1,125 miles (1,811 km), provides an excellent overview of the area. Cameras and binoculars are a must.

Allow at least 6 days and 5 nights to travel the circle from Whitehorse past Dawson, through Alaska, swinging back to Whitehorse. If you dabble in fishing or would like to hike in Kluane, the trip may happily be extended.

WHITEHORSE: Between a 200-foot clay escarpment and the banks of the Yukon River lies Whitehorse. The Yukon's capital since 1953, this city had its origins in the Klondike Gold Rush. In the spring of '98 thousands of stampeders drifted down the Yukon River through Miles Canyon only to encounter the treacherous Squaw and White Horse Rapids, whose frothing white foam resembled white horses leaping through the air. After the first few boats were wrecked and men drowned, the stampeders constructed a wooden tramway system around the canyon and the rapids. A small settlement developed at the northern end of the tramway, where the stampeders stopped to get their second breath before continuing downriver. This settlement, on the opposite side of the river from the present city, was called White Horse.

The White Horse Rapids were tamed by the construction of a power dam. From June until mid-September, you can take a 2½-hour cruise through Miles Canyon aboard the MV *Schwatka*. A running commentary details the history of the canyon and the rapids. Transportation to the dock on Schwatka Lake is available from all hotels and most RV parks. For tickets and additional information, contact *Atlas Travel Tours* (208 Steele St.; phone: 667-7823) or *Yellow Cab* (Second Ave.; phone: 668-4811).

Take the South Access Road from Whitehorse to Miles Canyon if you'd rather drive. Turn left just before the railroad tracks and follow the road around the west side of Schwatka Lake. The canyon can also be reached via an access road from Kilometer

1470 of the Alaska Highway. A suspension footbridge spans the canyon, leading from the parking area to a trail on the opposite side. The site of Canyon City, where the stampeders built the initial stage of a tramline above the rapids, is off to the right about 7 miles (11 km). Although little remains of Canyon City, the walk is a pleasant one and the path easy. Even if you don't feel up to walking the full distance, the area is excellent for picnics.

Between 1898 and 1900, construction of the White Pass and Yukon Railway was carried out simultaneously from Whitehorse and Skagway, Alaska, until the two lines met at Carcross in 1900. The northern terminus of the railroad was on the west bank of the Yukon River. The original town of White Horse moved across the river also. This new settlement was called Closeleigh, after English stockholders in the railway. However, people soon started calling the settlement Whitehorse again, and the name stuck.

During the gold rush years Whitehorse was a busy place. As the trains rolled into the station, sternwheelers docked along the riverbank and filled with people and cargo destined for Dawson. You can still see the old wooden pilings protruding from the river behind the White Pass station on First Avenue.

Ironically, the rail link from Skagway was completed about a year after the gold rush ceased. Subsequently, Whitehorse's population decreased drastically. Copper mining sustained the town for a while, but by the 1920s this proved unprofitable and the population dwindled to less than 400.

By the river, at the end of Second Avenue, rests the SS *Klondike,* a restored sternwheeler. Magnificent boats such as this were once a common sight as they plied their way downstream toward Dawson. Long after the gold rush, sternwheelers retained their position as a major means of transportation. The SS *Klondike,* built in 1936, carried ore concentrates from the silver mine at Mayo to freight cars at Whitehorse until 1955. Daily tours of the ship, in summer, are free.

You'll probably want to spend a day or two browsing around and shopping in Whitehorse. Since the downtown area is compact, you can walk to most of the stores. Typically northern items, such as gold nugget jewelry and Eskimo carvings and prints are available. *Northern Images* (Fourth Ave. and Jarvis St.) has a beautiful, if expensive, collection of soapstone carvings. *Murdoch's Gem Shop* (Main St.) is another good but fairly expensive place. Yukon items such as mukluks, parkas, and beaded jewelry can be purchased at the *Yukon Native Products* (4230 Fourth Ave.); *Conspiracy* (4129 Fourth Ave.); *McFarlane Trading Co. Yukon* (309 Main St.); *Yukon Gallery* (in the *Westmark* hotel on Steele St.); or *Mac's Fireweed Books & Gifts* (305 B Main St.); *Books on Main* (203 Main St.).

Relics from the gold rush period can be seen at the *MacBride Museum* (First Ave. and Wood St.). Open daily May through September, the admission fee is nominal. As well as containing the first telegraph key used in the Yukon during the gold rush and one of the original engines used on the White Pass and Yukon Railway, the museum has a collection of mounted Yukon wildlife, such as wolves, Dall's sheep, and grizzly bears.

You'll feel as though you're back in the gold rush days with the 1898 gaslight decor at *Charlie's* in the *Westmark Klondike Inn* (see *Best En Route*) at 2288 Second Ave. Other good bets for dinner include the *Versailles* restaurant (202 Strickland St.), which serves continental dishes; *Golden Garter* (210 Main St.), which serves European dishes; or *the Parthenon* (204 Main St.), specializing in Greek and European cuisine. An outdoor barbecue at the *Westmark Whitehorse* hotel on Second Ave. and Wood St. can be fun (see *Best En Route*).

The big evening show in Whitehorse is the "Frantic Follies" at the *Westmark Whitehorse* hotel. It's a gold rush vaudeville stage show with whooping cancan dancers and honky-tonk piano music. There are two shows nightly, from mid-June until mid-

September. Get your tickets during the day rather than take a chance in the evening.

The 1898 atmosphere of the *Golden Garter* carries a heavy tariff, but the quality is well worth the cost.

En Route from Whitehorse – It is possible to drive directly to Dawson — 333 miles (536 km) — in one day, but if you wish to visit Faro, allow a full day just for this side trip. Carmacks is just over 100 miles (161 km) away and marks the Faro turnoff.

Take the Alaska Highway (Route 1) north out of Whitehorse for about 7 miles (11 km) to the Klondike Highway turnoff, and follow Route 2 toward Carmacks. A secondary roadway, the Takhini Hot Springs cutoff, is 3½ miles (5.5 km) north and leads to the Hot Springs area 6½ miles (10.5 km) off the main highway. A cement pool holding the naturally hot spring waters is open from 8 AM to 10 PM, for swimming. Swimwear can be rented at the springs, and the cost of swimming is nominal. There are also dining facilities available, featuring German food.

Return to the Klondike Highway and continue northward to *Braeburn Lodge,* 55 miles (89 km) away. Here you get the largest servings of food anywhere in the Yukon — and at good prices. One of the most popular items on the menu is the Braeburn cinnamon bun, about a foot in diameter. On opposite sides of the highway, Twin Lakes is only 16 miles (26 km) from Braeburn. These two small lakes and the surrounding picnic sites are great places to stop. If the pike and grayling cooperate, you can catch lunch or dinner on the spot.

CARMACKS: Named after George Carmack, whose discovery of gold sparked the Klondike Gold Rush, Carmacks is a small, predominantly Indian settlement. About 400 people live at this one-time sternwheeler port. Stop for a cold beer or coffee at the *Carmacks* hotel, and gas up your vehicle.

En Route from Carmacks – From Carmacks it's only 2 miles (3 km) to the Robert Campbell Highway (Rte. 4) and the turnoff to Faro. The highway follows roughly the same route taken by Robert Campbell, the Hudson's Bay Company employee who explored the Territory in the mid-1800s. It's a 112-mile (180-km) trip east to Faro. One place to stop for gas, rest, or a bite to eat is 78 miles (126 km) along the road at *Little Salmon Lodge.* Dawson is 224 miles (361 km) north of Carmacks on the Klondike Highway.

FARO: This young town, named after the card game, is the fourth largest settlement in the Yukon (pop. 1,300). Built in 1969, Faro is primarily a company town servicing the Curragh Resources lead-zinc mine. The devastation caused by forest fires in the 1960s is still visible here.

If you turn off the Campbell Highway onto the access road to Faro and continue for 14 miles (23 km) past Faro, you'll come to the Anvil mine operated by Curragh Resources. The mine reopened in early 1986, and tours are available from mid-June through mid-September by phoning 403-994-2600.

While there are many more beautiful spots in the Yukon, the town of Faro and its mine represent an integral part of Yukon life. Perhaps you'll better appreciate the uncivilized and natural side of the Yukon all the more for having seen Faro.

En Route from Faro – You may camp overnight in one of the three government campgrounds along the way rather than drive back to Carmacks. There's a campground 26 miles (42 km) from Faro at Little Salmon Lake, where you might catch some pike, grayling, or trout to fry up for a good dinner. You can dine as fashionably late as you like during the long summer days. There's an average of 20 hours of daylight in the Yukon during July. (The days get longer the farther north you travel.)

If you want to put a few more miles behind you before bedding down, there's another campground 81 miles (130 km) from Faro and only 31 miles (50 km) from

Carmacks. This is the Frenchman Lake campground, 5 miles (8 km) off the main highway. You can fish here as well.

Unless you want to camp along the way, there's not much more to detain you en route to Dawson. But that's not to say the drive is uneventful, for, as on any Yukon highway, you'll find yourself absorbed in the beauty that surrounds you. You'll pass over dome-shaped mountains and wend your way along forested lakeshores.

From Carmacks to Stewart Crossing, your next food and gas stop, is 111 miles (179 km). Just 14 miles (23 km) north of Carmacks are the Five Fingers Rapids. Although not comparable to the dangerous White Horse Rapids, they posed some problems for the old sternwheelers. Ringbolts, through which heavy cables were threaded to pull the riverboats upstream, are still embedded in the rocks of Five Fingers. This is a good spot to pull over and gaze upon the Yukon River flowing steadily 500 feet below you.

In another 52 miles (84 km) you'll come to Pelly Crossing, a small native community of about 100. Facilities include the Ft. Selkirk Trading Post, a gas station, and a store with groceries and native handicrafts. *North Tuchone Tours & Outfitting* (General Delivery, Pelly Crossing, Yukon) provides 1- to 7-day guided tours that explore historical sites in the Minto, Ft. Selkirk, and Pelly Crossing areas. Enjoy trophy fishing here or listen to native elders interpret and demonstrate traditional crafts and ways of life. Drive another 45 miles (72 km) to reach Stewart Crossing, where there is a lodge with a café and tavern as well as a service station. Leaving town, you'll cross the Stewart River Bridge, turn left, and continue toward Dawson. Just 15 miles (24 km) beyond Stewart Crossing is the *Moose Creek Lodge,* with five rustic cabins and a café featuring hearty, homemade food such as sourdough pancakes and mouthwatering pastries. The lodge is open from mid-May through mid-September. From this point, you have just 98 miles (157 km) to go before reaching Dawson.

Eighty-seven miles (140 km) from Stewart Crossing you'll come upon the *Klondike River Lodge* and the Dempster Highway turnoff. Once again you can gas up and get a bite to eat at the lodge. Then, if you want to see virgin wilderness rather than heading into Dawson, you can travel the Dempster Highway for 45 miles (72 km) due north until you come to *Tombstone Mountain,* a government campground near the north fork of the Klondike River. There are very few services along this newly constructed road, built to connect Yukon communities with Fort McPherson and Inuvik in the Northwest Territories.

From the Dempster Highway turnoff to Dawson City is only 28 miles (45 km). A mile before you reach Dawson, the Bonanza Creek Road on your left will take you to the historic creeks of the gold rush and George Carmack's Discovery Claim, which started it all. The road winds through 11 miles (18 km) of tailings left behind by the gigantic gold dredges that soon replaced the 1898 prospector with his pick, shovel, and gold pan. Some of the claims are private property, but if you wish to do a bit of gold panning, you can do so at Guggieville, about a mile from the Dawson city center on the Bonanza Creek turnoff (phone: 403-993-5008).

After seeing the creeks, you've only a mile to go before reaching Dawson.

DAWSON: For one brief year this former moose pasture at the confluence of the Klondike and Yukon rivers was hailed as the San Francisco of the North. This transformation had been brewing for 2 years, ever since that August day in '96 when George Carmack plucked from the bed of Bonanza Creek a gold nugget, reputedly the size of his thumb.

The first eager stampeders arrived in Dawson during the late fall of '97, many of them having slipped into the Yukon with inadequate supplies of food. Later, Canada insisted that each person bring a year's supply of food and clothing. There were already 3,500 people in Dawson at that time, many of them old-time prospectors who had been panning the creeks of the North for years. But there was no food to be bought in Dawson that fall. The supply ships didn't make it through before the water froze. Warnings were given — and fortunately heeded by some — to evacuate Dawson and head for the nearest outpost, 350 miles away. Only this evacuation prevented a full-fledged disaster. While those who remained did not die of starvation, scurvy was prevalent. Food was so scarce that, for a sack of flour, one man traded a mountain sheep.

Finally, in the spring, the stampeders arrived with all their goods. The law of supply and demand operated in a classic fashion. One man lugged 200 dozen eggs over the trail and sold them for $18 a dozen. Within an hour he'd dispensed of them all for a total of $3,600. By the week's end, with thousands arriving daily, the market was so saturated with eggs that the price dropped to $3 a dozen.

In the early summer of '98, the many thousands who had been waiting impatiently on the shores of Lindeman and Bennett lakes started arriving in Dawson only to discover that the richest claims they had so fanatically sought had been staked even before anybody outside had heard of the Klondike. Supplies these men had laboriously transported over the mountains were sold at any price to raise the fare home. The muddy streets of Dawson took on the appearance of a huge marketplace. While certainly not the streets of gold so many expected, an air of decadent extravagance permeated the city of 23,000. Dance hall queens bathed in champagne, and butlers were installed in a few of the gloomy, one-room cabins of prospectors living along the hillsides and creeks.

Posh hotels complete with chandeliers, Persian carpets, and Turkish baths sprang up along Front Street. In their dining rooms, these establishments served such delicacies as lobster Newburg, cold tongue, and Bengal Club chutney prepared by San Francisco chefs. The luxuries were brought to Dawson because the Klondike Kings, the men who first staked the creekbeds in 1896 and 1897, invested their fabulous fortunes in hotels, dance halls, and numerous shipping companies. Thus, ships laden with Paris fashions and fresh oysters docked continuously at Dawson's shore during the summer of '98.

One of the wealthiest of the original prospectors was "Big Alex" McDonald. He owned many claims, and from one of his richest he panned $5,000 a day. "Big Alex," who died penniless, was soon known throughout the world as the King of the Klondike. Such was his fame that while in Rome he was granted an audience with the Pope. Curiously, Big Alex exhibited a distinct contempt for gold. He left bowls full of nuggets on his sideboard and urged guests to help themselves, explaining he had no use for the things.

Big Alex's attitude was shared to some extent by the stampeders of '98. Few hoarded the precious metal they had sought; these men had their values tempered on the trail. They were no longer the naive young men who had set off in 1897, oblivious to the trials awaiting them. No, these men had been forced to struggle daily for their very existence. They had walked the fine line between life and death, never knowing from one minute to the next what hardship would befall them. But they had survived, and they came to Dawson wiser yet all the more foolish for that. They spent their days either frantically panning the creeks seeking their own bonanza or working for wages on the rich claims of men like Big Alex. Collecting a supply of nuggets and dust, they rushed down to Dawson's dance halls and frantically dispensed of their riches.

The dance halls lining Front Street were like fun houses at a carnival. There was a room for drinking, a room for gambling, and upstairs, numerous rooms where the dance hall queens entertained their guests in private. There was also a theater, complete with balconies, from which the Klondike Kings gazed down upon the plebeian masses who gathered to enjoy vaudeville and the plays. When the show was over, the theater turned into a large dance floor that shook with the stomping of feet until dawn. A man had to pay to dance with one of the women and some paid dearly.

But even more popular than the dance halls were the gaming rooms, for these were men who had gambled from the beginning. On the trail they'd learned to play for stakes that were higher than gold. Their experiences crossing the passes and shooting the rapids had imbued in them a deep understanding of the gambling maxim — winner takes all, loser gets nothing. So fortunes were won and lost in these dimly lit back rooms. The stakes were high, the pot in one poker game amounting to $150,000. And not only gold was laid on the line; the ownership of the dance halls themselves came up for bid, and as often as not the establishment changed hands with the flick of a card. So pervasive was gambling that two men are reported to have actually wagered $10,000 in a spitting duel. The city's brief life was a carnival gone mad, a grotesque ball unmasked during the summer of 1899.

Rumors of a new gold find near the mouth of the Yukon River were confirmed in August of '99. The fever set in once again. In one week alone, 8,000 people left Dawson for Nome, Alaska. Some, however, chose to remain in Dawson and make it their home. But the Dawson they created was a far cry from the San Francisco of the North. An air of respectability prevailed while Dawson served as the territory's capital until 1953. The digging for gold continued, but the individual prospector was quickly replaced by companies of men using massive dredges. The damage these huge machines did to the creekbeds and hillsides is still apparent (the dredging continues today).

Today, about 1,650 people live in Dawson through the long, cold, dark winters. Most residents are either government employees or involved in the summer tourism industry. The city has been designated a historical complex, and in the summer of 1977 the Canadian government announced that $20 million would be spent to restore some of the buildings and mining sites. Apart from these areas of employment, there are still many who live along the creeks, mining for gold.

Although the elaborate display of wealth is gone, the memory of those golden days remains. You can almost hear the carousing as you stroll down wooden sidewalks past old and empty buildings. Unfortunately, numerous fires during 1898 destroyed all but a few of the structures from that period, and the derelict buildings you see today date back to the 1900s. One 19th-century survivor is Arizona Charlie Meadows's *Palace Grand Theatre*. Meadows, a one-time American Indian fighter, built the theater from two steamboats he purchased and demolished for the purpose and opened it in July 1899. It sat in ruins until 1962, when it was rebuilt by the Canadian government. You may tour the theater during the day; at night you can enjoy an authentic 1898 vaudeville production, the *Gaslight Follies*. Performances are held nightly except Tuesdays. Advance tickets can be purchased at the Dawson City Visitor Reception Center on Front Street, or at the theater (King St. and Third Ave.), which is operated by the Klondike Visitors' Association (phone: 403-933-5575).

A pleasant way to spend a few hours in the afternoon is to take the Yukon River Cruise aboard the *Yukon Lou*. The cruise departs at 1 PM daily, and coffee and muffins are served. Along the way, you may catch a glimpse of the sternwheeler graveyard ashore. The *Yukon Queen* also makes day trips from Dawson to Eagle, Alaska.

You should also try your luck at *Diamond Tooth Gertie's Gambling Hall* (Fourth Ave. near Queen St.), named for one of the dance hall queens of '98. This is the only full-time legalized gambling hall in Canada. The stakes may not be as high as before, but people have been known to walk out richer than when they arrived — and also poorer. There's a bar at *Gertie's* and three floor shows each evening featuring colorful cancan dancers and a singer-hostess — Gertie herself! *Gertie's* is open nightly except Sundays from 8 PM to 2 AM. Admission is about $2.50 at the door.

Another attraction in Dawson is the daily poetry reading by the "ghost" of Robert

Service (the Yukon's gold rush bard). The free readings are done on the lawn or inside Service's log cabin (Eighth Ave. near Church St.) at 10 AM and 3 PM, June 1 through September 15.

Many visitors like to test their skill at gold panning. This can be done at Guggieville, at the Bonanza Creek turnoff (phone: 403-993-5008), which is also a campground with showers and hook-ups, a gift store, and car wash. You can also see George Carmack's original claim and the largest wooden-hulled gold dredge in the world. Transportation to the gold fields is available; contact the Tourist Information Centre (First Ave.) for a schedule.

You may want to plan your trip to coincide with Dawson's Discovery Days celebration, held the weekend of the third Monday in August. Raft races, handicraft displays, and a parade are among the many activities. Dawson also is the site of its own *Labor Day* weekend craziness, with annual Outhouse Races in which contestants pull and push brightly colored outhouses (with one person sitting inside) through the city streets.

En Route from Dawson – It's a long drive from Dawson to Beaver Creek, 20 miles (32 km) inside the Yukon border near the southwestern corner of the territory, through a bit of Alaska and along one of the most impressive roads in the world — the Top of the World Highway. You'll climb up, winding your way on mountaintops from which you can gaze at the splendor around and below you. Snow hoods the distant peaks as the wind howls through the grass and mountain flowers bow to its passing. Then you'll descend to the lush valleys below.

Go 67 miles (108 km) west from Dawson to the US-Canadian border, where the crossing is open from 9 AM to 9 PM (Yukon time). There are no services between Dawson and the border, so plan accordingly. The village of Boundary, Alaska, is just 4 miles (6 km) into US territory, and services are available here. From Boundary, it's 112 miles (180 km) south to Tetlin Junction and another 100 miles (161 km) to Beaver Creek, Yukon. The border crossing here is open 24 hours a day.

BEAVER CREEK: This "town" has the distinction of being the most westerly community in all of Canada. With a population of about 100 people, it is a by-product of the Alaska Highway construction. It was created to provide highway services. Three motels with lounges and cafés do an admirable job. A KOA campground is located at the *Westmark Alas Kan Border Lodge,* and a government campground with 20 sites (and great fishing) is at Snag Junction, 13 miles (21 km) beyond Beaver Creek.

En Route from Beaver Creek – Burwash Landing is a tiny, predominantly Indian village of about 80 people some 109 miles (175 km) from Beaver Creek. Virtually all the homes and cabins are heated by wood fires, and most look out over Kluane Lake. *Burwash Landing* resort, one of the nicest spots in the Yukon, is hidden on this shore (see *Best En Route*). While in Burwash, explore the *Kluane Museum of Natural History* and handicraft shop. Visitors should remember that this is home to the native residents and they may not appreciate being examined through the end of a camera lens. A bit of consideration can go a long way. Destruction Bay, another small community created by highway construction, lies 10 miles (16 km) from Burwash. Kluane Lake is 46 miles long, covers 153 square miles, and is filled with trout, grayling, steelfish, and pike. The trout can weigh up to 40 pounds, so be prepared.

After driving only 23 miles (37 km) from Destruction Bay, you'll probably want to stop at Slim's River Bridge. Crossing an ancient glacier moraine at the head of Kluane Lake, the bridge offers amazing views. Sheep Mountain borders the highway near this spot and, with an alert eye, you can often see the proud Dall's sheep on the hillside. There is also a new interpretive center at Sheep Mountain. Remember, Kluane is a national park; walking over spring vegetation could damage the animals' winter supply of food.

Drive another 6 miles (10 km) and take the short side road to the ghost town of Silver City. These old wooden buildings are the remains of a stopover point on the wagon road between Whitehorse and the Kluane gold fields.

The headquarters of Kluane National Park lie 35 miles (56 km) down the highway, only 3 miles (5 km) north of Haines Junction. Make a point of stopping here and finding out details about the hikes, slide shows, and overnight trips park personnel conduct for visitors. Kluane was set aside as a national park in 1972; many of the trails are marked, and maps are available. Experienced climbers who want to attempt the mountains and glaciers must first report to the park warden at headquarters.

KLUANE NATIONAL PARK: Most of the 186-mile (299-km) drive from Beaver Creek to Haines Junction will be within sight of the 8,500-square-mile Kluane National Park. This magnificent area is characterized by soaring snowcapped peaks that rise through the clear blue skies, piercing billowy white clouds as they tease the sun. The world's largest ice fields outside of the polar regions are within the park, and Canada's highest peak, Mt. Logan (19,520 ft.), rises majestically from these fields.

The 8,000-foot mountains that border the highway for 80 miles (129 km) are draped in white spruce, aspen, and balsam poplar until the treeline is reached at about 4,000 feet. Above, colorful Arctic and alpine flowers dot the mountainsides as do stunted species of shrubs. The jagged mountaintops are crowned in wreaths of snow. Check in with park authorities at park headquarters in Haines Junction.

HAINES JUNCTION: This community of about 575, in the shadow of the park, came into being with the construction of the Alaska Highway in 1942. Kluane National Park has a visitor information center in town featuring a very good six-projector slide show on the park. You'll probably want to stay in one of the town's handful of hotels while you visit the park by day. If you prefer to camp, there is a government campground at Pine Creek, just 3 miles (5 km) east of Haines Junction.

En Route from Haines Junction – From here it's only a 98-mile (158-km) drive to complete the circle back to Whitehorse. Forty-one miles (66 km) from Haines Junction you'll pass through the almost deserted trading post of Champagne. At one time, this post serviced the Dalton Trail, which ran from Pyramid Harbor on the Lynn Canal to the Yukon's interior. Frontiersman Jack Dalton cut the trail, and 2,000 head of beef cattle were successfully driven across it in 1898. From the trading post, it's only 57 miles (92 km) to the lights of Whitehorse.

BEST EN ROUTE

So many travelers are attracted to the Yukon each year, it is necessary to reserve hotel rooms as far in advance as possible. Book your June vacation in January if you want to get first crack at top accommodations. Plan on spending between $40 and $50 for a moderately priced double room, a minimum of $30 for an inexpensive room, and over $50 for expensive accommodations. Reservations must be accompanied by a guaranteed deposit, usually the equivalent of one night's stay. Also try the Yukon Bed and Breakfast Association, 102-302 Steele St., Whitehorse, Yukon (phone: 403-633-4609), which has accommodations in several communities. Private campground charges, based upon facilities, range from $4 to $8.50 per site. Government campground rates are about $4 per night, or about $20 annually, and are given out on a first-come, first-served basis. All prices are quoted in US dollars.

WHITEHORSE

Goldrush Inn – Behind its chalet-like front are 87 units, with a gift shop, cable TV, a laundromat, lounge, and a dining room. 411 Main St. (phone: 403-668-4500). Expensive.

Westmark Klondike Inn – This inn has 98 rooms, a coffee shop, restaurant and lounge, 2 saunas, and a hair salon. 2288 Second Ave. (phone: 403-668-4747). Expensive.

Westmark Whitehorse – This popular hotel for businessmen and tourists has 181 rooms, a café, dining room, lounge, gift shop, barbershop, art gallery, and travel agency (*Atlas Travel Tours*). 201 Wood St., PO Box 4250 (phone: 403-668-4700). Expensive.

Regina – The lobby of this 53-room hotel is stocked with Yukon memorabilia. Amenities include cable TV and a dining room. 102 Wood St. (phone: 403-667-7801). Expensive to moderate.

MacKenzie's Campground – A new campground at Kilometer 1476 on the Alaska Highway, 6 miles (10 km) north of downtown Whitehorse. There are 54 serviced and 20 unserviced sites, free gold panning, a general store, video games, showers, and a laundromat. Open year-round (phone: 403-633-2337). Inexpensive.

Pioneer Trailer Park – At Kilometer 1,465 of the Alaska Highway, this campground is 5 miles (8 km) south of Whitehorse. There are 125 camping spaces; 73 full and 16 partial hook-ups, and 36 wooded areas; a laundromat, showers, restrooms, store, rec hall, and RV wash. Open May 15–October 1. PO Box 4056 (phone: 403-668-5944). Inexpensive.

Robert Service Campground – A popular private campground on the banks of the Yukon River, it has 40 tents-only campsites as well as restrooms, picnic tables, a firepot, and nature trail. Open mid-May through mid-September. On the South Access Road, one mile from downtown. Information: City of Whitehorse, Parks & Recreation Department, 2121 Second Ave. (phone: 403-667-6401). Inexpensive.

Sourdough City RV Park – This campground features 103 fully serviced sites and 42 sites with electricity only, a laundromat, showers, gift shop, and dump. Open May 1 through mid-September. Second Avenue north of Ogilvie, at Second Avenue Chevron (phone: 403-668-7938). Inexpensive.

Wolf Creek Government Campground – If you don't want to pay for all the amenities, Wolf Creek, 12 miles (19 km) south of Whitehorse on the Alaska Highway (Kilometer 1,459), is a good spot. It has 50 outdoor sites and free wood. Open mid-May to mid-October. Inexpensive.

DAWSON

Downtown – Features VIP suites, 60 units, Jacuzzi, conference room, and the *Jack London Grill*. Open year-round. PO Box 780 (phone: 403-993-5346). Expensive.

Eldorado – There are 53 units, VIP suites, and the *Bonanza* dining room. Open year-round. PO Box 338 (phone: 403-993-5451). Expensive.

Westmark Dawson City – A modern motel with 52 rooms, a gift shop, coin laundromat, travel agency and tour office (*Gold City Tours and Travel Limited*). PO Box 420 (phone: 403-993-5542, mid-May through mid-September; 403-668-4700, balance of year). Expensive.

Yukon River Campground – A good government campground across the Yukon River from Dawson with 97 sites, 9 for tents, the rest for RVs. A ferry service is operated daily during the summer. For more information phone Parks and Outdoor Recreation, Government of the Yukon, at 403-667-5905.

Guggieville – Just about a mile from downtown at the Bonanza Creek turnoff, this campground has showers and hook-ups along with a gift shop, car wash, and a gold panning operation. PO Box 311 (phone: 403-993-5319).

BEAVER CREEK

Alas/Kon Border Lodge – This is a good modern facility with 179 rooms, a dining room, gift shop, recreation area, and lounge. To be safe, reservations should be made before you depart Whitehorse. Open May 15–September 28. Km 1,934, Alaska Highway (phone: 800-544-2206, in US, 206-281-0576, collect, in Canada). Expensive.

Customs Campground, Beaver Creek, Yukon – Here are 69 serviced campsites, showers, laundromat, small store, and dump, with a lounge and restaurant nearby. Open June through mid-October. Write care of General Delivery, Beaver Creek (phone: 403-862-7418).

BURWASH LANDING

Burwash Landing – An old lodge on Kluane Lake, it has 32 units, a bar restaurant, wildlife museum, and 14 sites with hook-ups. Staff can arrange glacier flights and fishing and boating trips. Reservations necessary well in advance. Open year-round. Km 1,759, Alaska Highway, Yukon Territory (phone: 403-841-4441). Moderate.

HAINES JUNCTION

Kluane Park Inn – This popular spot, directly across from Kluane National Park, has 20 units with color, satellite TV, a cocktail lounge, and rec room. Reservations should be made prior to departure from Whitehorse. Open year-round (phone: 403-634-2261). Moderate.

The Trail of '98

It is estimated that more than 100,000 people stormed the Yukon Territory during the boom years between 1896 and 1900. Perhaps 60,000 sailed up the Lynn Canal, cutting north across what is now the Alaskan panhandle, past Juneau, from the Pacific Ocean to the head of the canal, and docked at either Skagway or Dyea, Alaska. From there they struggled across the St. Elias Mountains of the Coast Mountain Range through the Chilkoot or White Pass to reach the settlement of Bennett, British Columbia, on the south shore of Lake Bennett just below the present Yukon boundary line. The tandem mountain lakes of Lindeman (which feeds north into its sister lake) and Bennett form the headwaters of the Yukon River. Here they built or boarded boats and rafts for the journey downriver, past Whitehorse, all the way to the gold fields at Dawson.

The 32-mile (52-km) Chilkoot Pass was the primary route of the earliest travelers into the region. It had been established by the Chilkat Indian tribe, who held a monopoly on trade between the seacoast and the Stick Indian tribe on the far side of the mountains. The Indians guarded their trade link violently, exacting a heavy toll from those who wished to cross the pass and occasionally killing a disagreeable traveler. A show of arms by a US gunboat convinced the tribe to make other arrangements. Thereafter, prospectors and explorers paid the Indians as guides and packers as a prerequisite for use of the trail; even an 1883 US Army expedition followed this practice.

During the pre-gold rush years, about 1,000 people took this route into the newly opened area, and interest in the unexplored lands began to grow. As more people flocked to the Yukon, the Indians lost control of the pass; soon only those affluent travelers who could afford their assistance paid the Chilkats as packers. Most of the stampeders carried their own goods along the well-worn trail. During the early stages of the rush, Canadian authorities required each stampeder to bring with him a year's supply of food, clothing, and equipment in an effort to stem deaths due to starvation and exposure. A Canadian surveying expedition discovered the White Pass, just a few miles east. Captain William Moore, a 74-year-old retired sea captain who was part of the expedition, felt that a rail line could be laid through this pass into the Yukon Territory; he was also sure that the trail of gold he had traced up from South America would lead to a massive strike in the North.

SKAGWAY AND DYEA: In 1887, Moore erected a cabin and a wharf on a point of land at the mouth of the Skagway River on the eastern side of the head of the Lynn Canal. On the west side of the canal stood the settlement of Dyea, at the mouth of the Taiya River, in a direct line with the Chilkoot Pass. Moore foresaw that with a railroad through White Pass, more facilities would be needed. He fully expected to found the town of Skagway as it grew around his homestead.

When news of the gold strike at Bonanza Creek reached the outside world, the flow of travelers that Moore had expected turned into a flood, forcing him to abandon his plans. The gold-crazed mob tore him from his cabin and took over his wharf. A city of tents and temporary buildings sprang up, obscuring Moore's claim. (His cabin still stands, just off Skagway's main thoroughfare, Broadway Street, behind *Kirme's* jewelry store.) Several years later, Moore took the matter to court and received some compensation for his losses. Eventually, his dream of a railroad through White Pass was realized, but by that time the Chilkoot Pass had become symbolic of the courage, determination, and recklessness of the stampeders.

An attempt to cross the White Pass during the late fall of 1897 was disastrous. Fully 5,000 people embarked on a 41-mile trek that became a continuous frozen hell. Men and horses died under the strain of their loads, and animals who could no longer walk were shot or abandoned as their owners trudged onward. It was a desperate fight for survival, a battle against time and the elements, and often against other men. Some were appalled by the horrors they had seen, others were hardened by the experience, but no one was untouched. Early rains and rocky trails created a morass that seemed to swallow men and horses whole, slowing the pace to a crawl and holding them captive until the winter snows caught them exposed in the mountains. Only a few of the hardiest made it through to the Yukon River before the winter freeze-up. Some returned to Skagway to await the spring thaw; many died on the path named Dead Horse Trail. Bits and pieces of their goods and equipment still line the trail in mute testimony.

Weary, frustrated men returned to Skagway. As tensions grew, the sound of gunfire became commonplace. With no laws to constrain them, mobs ruled the small town of tents and impromptu buildings. By midwinter, Skagway's population hovered around 5,000. Not all of them were bound for the Klondike: Their fortunes lay in providing entertainment for those en route to the gold fields. Saloons as well as gambling and dance halls crowded Skagway's already congested streets. The chaos of those early days was made to order for a particular type of businessman — the con artist.

Soapy Smith was an expert at his trade — the ultimate professional con artist. With a group of felons, thugs, and whores to back him, Soapy set out to dominate the town of Skagway. Card games were rigged, pokes stolen, greenhorns shot in the back, and outright robbery was the prevailing order as Smith penetrated every area of Skagway's vulnerable social fabric. Posing as a civic-minded member of the business community, he convinced the chamber of commerce of the righteousness of his activities, and the false-fronted buildings that lined the streets of Skagway camouflaged his numerous bogus business dealings. In fact, when an avalanche killed about 60 people on the

Chilkoot, Smith, appointed coroner for the occasion, set up a tent into which the victims were brought for identification — and stripped of all valuables.

By February 1898, the people around Skagway decided that Soapy Smith had gotten out of hand and requested that US troops take charge of the town. Legend has it that in July of that year, Soapy robbed a prospector of over $2,000 in gold dust. The man refused to accept this as a matter of course, and word spread among the community that if the money wasn't returned, other prospectors would avoid the town. Faced with a loss of income, the citizens formed a vigilante committee to force Smith to return the money. Smith refused and, after getting drunk (remember, this is a legend), went out to face the mob. It seems that Smith had already fought with Frank Reid earlier that day and had challenged Reid to return "with a gun." The first man Smith encountered that night was Reid. Shots were fired and both men fell. Reid was taken to a doctor and lasted 2 weeks before dying; Soapy Smith was left dying in the street. Rumors persist that Reid couldn't have fired the fatal shot, but no one ever took credit for the deed. The two men lie buried, side by side, in the Gold Rush Cemetery. Soapy's former mistress was the only mourner at his funeral; the gang members had been rounded up and shipped out of town. Reid's funeral was the largest in Skagway's history.

Although Dyea was certainly not a quiet or conservative community, it never sank to the depths of squalor and degeneracy that permeated Skagway. Since the Chilkoot Pass was always open, the flow of traffic was steady. Prior to the summer of 1897, Dyea consisted of a trading post and village of about 125 Indian guides and packers. By the spring of '98, there were 4,000 people, several hotels, and even a newspaper. Shortly after the railroad construction began, the town started to evaporate, until only one resident remained in 1906.

En Route from Skagway – The most natural way to explore the Yukon is just to follow the route taken by the first travelers into the region: Sail up the Lynn Canal to Skagway, hike the Chilkoot Pass to Bennett, BC, then raft down the Yukon to Dawson. It's possible to cruise into Skagway aboard the Alaska Marine Highway System from Seattle. Ferries carry passengers and vehicles. Many travelers enjoy cruising one way and driving back the other (Pouch R, Juneau, AK 99811; phone: 907-465-3941).

The Skagway-Carcross road makes it possible to drive down from Whitehorse during the summer months, and airports in both Skagway and Whitehorse make travel into the Yukon easier than any trailhand ever expected. Unfortunately, the White Pass and Yukon Railway, completed in 1900 just after the gold rush, has closed down. It was a fascinating means of transportation here since the tracks follow closely the route of those stampeders who fought their way from Skagway to Bennett in the fall of 1897, then parallel the watercourse as far north as Whitehorse. Now you can hike the Chilkoot as far as Bennett and then boat down the Yukon River to Whitehorse or Dawson, instead of taking the train. (Some bus service is also available at the trailhead in Dyea and near the trail's end; check schedules and pick-up points before starting out.)

CHILKOOT PASS: The most dramatic event in the history of the gold rush was the assault by thousands of stampeders upon the 3,739-foot summit of the Chilkoot Pass during the winter of 1897-98. Bent under the weight of their packs, sweat freezing upon their brows, these men trudged up a 40° slope for more than 6 hours while temperatures fell to $-60F$ ($-51C$) to find themselves a mere 1,000 feet from where they had begun. Only a fanatical devotion to the gold they believed lay beyond enabled them to persevere. Finally reaching the summit and depositing their goods, often losing them in the 70 feet of snow that fell that winter, the weary men slid back down to strap on another pack and make the climb again. For the average stampeder, who could pack only 50 pounds at a time, it took 30 trips to bring his required ton of supplies to the peak.

During that winter, 1,500 steps were hacked out of the ice and snow by a few industrious stampeders. A rope, for balance, was strung beside these Golden Stairs that rose to the summit, providing some small assistance to the climbers. For the 22,000 people who crossed the Chilkoot Pass that winter, the experience invariably overshadowed all other memories of their gold rush days. Other trails lay ahead, but having conquered the pass, no longer were they *cheechakos* (naive newcomers to the North).

Necessity being the mother of invention, the first tramway was constructed from the base of the summit to the top in December 1897. Five such tramways were in operation by the spring of '98. The most effective one transported goods from Canyon City, 8 miles north of Dyea, to the summit, a distance of about 8 miles, at a rate of 9 tons per hour. But as was the case with the Indian carriers, not all the stampeders could afford the tramways. They trudged along while goods whisked by overhead. It took the average stampeder 3 months to lug his supplies 32 miles across the pass from Dyea to Lake Bennett.

Most hikers traveling the Chilkoot Pass now allow 4 days for the trip from Dyea to Bennett. The trail is well marked and patrolled daily by park rangers. They are stationed at Sheep Camp (Mile 13) on the American side and at Lindeman (Mile 25.5) on the Canadian side. Cabins at three points along the trail are open to hikers, but don't bet on finding a vacancy. Plan to sleep under canvas. While the trail is not too difficult, remember that it is not a Sunday stroll through the park. Don't even attempt it unless you're in good physical condition. Take the bus instead.

In addition to maps and information available from the Yukon Territory Department of Tourism and the Skagway, Alaska, Visitor Information Bureau on the pass, Archie Satterfield's *Chilkoot Pass* (Alaska Northwest Publishing Co., Box 4-EEE, Anchorage, AK 99509, 1973) is an excellent and entertaining guide. You'll find it a welcome traveling companion.

Your hike up the Chilkoot actually begins near Dyea, 8½ miles (14 km) west of Skagway. If you don't feel like walking to the starting point, it's possible to take a taxi from Skagway right to the trailhead at the south end of the Taiya River Bridge. A row of old pilings and a few rotten timbers about a mile away mark the old Dyea townsite. The nearby Slide Cemetery contains the graves of about 60 people killed in the Palm Sunday Avalanche of April 3, 1898. These stampeders were trapped under 30 feet of snow, and many of the bodies weren't recovered until months later.

The trek commences as you depart Dyea. Except for the initial one-quarter mile, which is very steep, the first 7 miles are fairly easy, through level then gently rising and falling terrain. The trail cuts through thick timber, opening at times to enable you to peer out at the 5,000-foot (and higher) St. Elias and Coastal Mountain ranges ahead.

As you continue, the trail drops to the bank of the Taiya River. Across its banks can be seen the magnificent blue-green glaciers whose icy streams tumble noisily into the Taiya. Eventually the path rises over a trail of boulders and scrambles down to cross an old moss-and lichen-covered glacial moraine. Stunted conifer trees and wild flowers decorate the area. The Canyon City shelter, at Mile 7.75, will startle you with its sudden appearance. The one-room cabin has a wood-burning stove, a table, and benches. Forget about using the stove, and unless there's a storm brewing, you'll probably be more comfortable outside the cabin than in. A stream flows past the shelter, invigorated by a series of small waterfalls a short distance upriver. Many campers break at the Canyon City shelter area, so you may wish to go a little farther to secure some privacy.

About a half-mile up the trail, an old suspension bridge across the Taiya River leads to the original Canyon City site. At one time there were hotels, saloons, and stores here. Now it is rotting wood and rusting equipment. An old steam boiler, some rusty cooking utensils, half-rotten cabins, and a garbage dump are all that remain of the boom town.

Traveling north, the trail runs through some mildly hilly ground, as it crosses several streams that feed into the Taiya River. A handrail has been installed along the one steep climb about a mile beyond the bridge. Camp Pleasant, at Mile 10, is a beautiful place.

Since the Sheep Camp Shelter is only 3 miles farther, not as many people stop here as at either Canyon City or Sheep Camp.

In its heyday, Sheep Camp had a population of about 1,500. It was then, and remains today, the last suitable place to camp before assaulting the summit. Park rangers stationed here enforce this dictum. A cabin, similar to the one at Canyon City, is open to hikers, and there are several campsites in the vicinity. The remains of Sheep Camp, in poor condition, are on the opposite bank of the Taiya, which can be crossed easily at this point since it is a small stream here. These slopes are the origin of the river.

In addition to the wagon wheels and other parts of their lives that the stampeders abandoned along this trail, glaciers and waterfalls abound. It's a rare moment when some antique object or glimpse of beauty doesn't catch your eye. Because of the altitude, snowstorms can occur at any time, even in the middle of summer, and winter snow often remains through June. Use extreme care in crossing any unbroken area of snow; you can't tell what's underneath.

The upward climb starts here, and the trail rises about 1,000 feet in the next 2 miles. You break through the treeline at about 1,900 feet, a mile outside of camp, so it's loose rock from here on up. Markers are placed daily along the safest path by rangers, but if they're down for any reason, just keep heading up. Ruins of a tramway tripod and an old building are on a flat bit of land near Mile 15.5. A short way from here, beyond an undulating progression of rocky ridges, is a deep depression. Cupped within its half-moon shape, formed by mountains on three sides, are the remains of cabins, machine parts, tools, equipment, and even bits of clothing. Here packs were retied, goods to be hauled by tram were weighed, and stampeders tightened their belts for the final ascent. This point, at Mile 16, is known as the Scales.

The half-mile from the Scales to the summit is virtually straight up, roughly 1,000 feet, to the notch in the peak that marks the Chilkoot Pass. The mountaintops resemble mounds of boulders and rocks piled higher and higher atop each other to form this barrier. Here, looking up at the crests, the Chilkoot lies between two such mounds, a shallow break in the ridgetop. As you climb toward the top, Chilkoot bears off slightly to the left. A second trail, which tends to be unsafe, leads to the right until it crosses the peak, then cuts back to the left. Avoid this route since the rocks may break loose. People can get hurt here. It can happen on the Chilkoot, too, but this trail is more dangerous. Climbers should allow extra space between each other while going through this area, since even small rocks can injure climbers too close below to avoid them. Also, remember to keep an eye on the hiker ahead of you at all times; unless you're the lead person, never turn your back on the slope. If you're in doubt about which trail to take, look for tramway cables on the ground — that's the Chilkoot.

When you reach the top, turn around for a spectacular view of the trail back to Alaska that you've just hiked. You'll have a satisfying sense of accomplishment as you gaze at these peaks. They are invariably covered with a coating of snow, which enhances their beauty. Then face north again and gaze off into Canada. If you're fortunate enough to make the crossing on a clear day, you'll be greeted by the sight of soaring mountains, immense glaciers, and unbelievably blue lakes.

The snow that blankets the peaks extends almost a mile down the reverse slope, right to the shores of Crater Lake at Mile 17.5. The lake is a volcanic crater, filled with icy glacial waters that tumble into the basin from the surrounding slopes. The lake was a major staging area for the stampeders; they hauled load after load of supplies to the crest of the pass, then brought the loads down to these shores, where they were ferried across the lake, then loaded again for the hike to Long Lake, about 4 miles away. Many stampeders set up camp here, and relics are lying about in several places. The trail from Crater Lake to Long Lake winds its way through mountain flowers, heather, and colorful varieties of moss and lichen. You'll pass another waterfall near the entrance to a canyon that opens on Long Lake. The waterfall, formed by Coltsfoot Creek, waters the first trees you see since breaking the treeline on the American side of the pass. This area, at Mile 21.5, is called Happy Camp. From here down to the lake is a rocky trail, but the land near Long Lake is a masterwork of natural gardening. The trail gently crosses back and forth to and from the bank of the lake, winding among a number of tarns and waterholes carved into the ground by glaciers and filled with freshly melted snow. Alpine firs and hemlocks, their growth stunted by the harsh weather, turn the wild expanse into a vast garden of Japanese miniatures.

A stream on the far shore drains the mountain waters of Long Lake into Deep Lake at Mile 23. Atop the cliffs overlooking Deep Lake are several beautiful campsites. More than one waterfall tumbles over the edge into the lake below. There are many islands in Deep Lake, and the north end, which feeds into Lake Lindeman, is a hazardous stretch of rapids. As the trail parallels the flow of water toward Lindeman, you cross back through the timberline into a well-forested area.

The trail emerges from the forest at the head of Lake Lindeman, at Mile 25.5. The Canadian ranger station and a cabin for hikers are both located here. The lake makes a good resting spot if you have the time; the stampeders who arrived too late to float down the river that winter set up a city here. The remains of several buildings can easily be seen, and there are rusty tools and pieces of equipment everywhere. A second cabin is located at Mile 26, along the side of the lake. The Chilkoot Trail ends at the head of Lake Bennett, at Mile 32.

BENNETT: Since the stream that connects Lindeman and Bennett lakes is large enough to be navigated and rocky enough to be dangerous, many of the stampeders built boats at Lindeman during the winter and tried to sail down to Lake Bennett after breakup. Some of them made it; others wrecked on the rocks. A larger camp was established at Bennett, and following breakup on May 29, 1898, over 7,000 small boats left for the gold fields at Dawson. Within a matter of days the camp was vacated.

   En Route from Bennett – If you really want to duplicate the Trail of '98 experience, you'll have to build a boat before continuing. It's more feasible, however, to arrange canoe rentals for the remainder of the journey. If you're an experienced canoeist, you already realize the importance of having the correct gear and accurate maps; if not, don't try it without a guide.

   The Carcross-Skagway road will provide car and bus access to Bennett.

   Be sure to make time to stop off in Carcross, at the north end of Lake Bennett.

CARCROSS: This quiet community of less than 300 lies in a mountain-rimmed valley with a sandy shore opening on the lake. Just 26 miles (42 km) from Bennett, it's not a difficult day's work if you're canoeing.

If you're staying in Whitehorse and choose not to take the Trail of '98, it's also easily reached by car via Route 2, a distance of about 45 miles (72 km). Driving south, on your left you'll pass the Carcross desert, reputed to be the smallest desert in the world. Emerald Lake, named for its shimmering green waters, is also along this roadway.

Prior to the gold rush, Carcross was known as Caribou Crossing; when the migrating herds of caribou came here to cross the narrows between Lake Bennett and Nares Lake, the Tagish Indians would camp in the area to hunt. It was here, in 1900, that the two sections of the railroad, one coming south from Whitehorse and the other north from Skagway, were linked with the traditional golden spike.

Stop at the Carcross Visitor Center, where you can hear the history of the S.S. *Tutshi*, a 1917 sternwheeler that until 1955 plied the headwaters of the Yukon River. The boat, now docked beside the center, has been restored and is open to the public May 15 through September 20 (phone: 403-821-4431). Nearby sits the Duchess, an old White Pass and Yukon Railway engine, and next to her, a mail wagon from the early 1900s.

Another enjoyable diversion is the lively lunchtime show at the *Riverboat Warehouse Luncheon Theatre* (PO Box 144). The site is a riverside warehouse that was once important to the British Yukon Navigation Company. Shows start at 11:30 AM daily, mid-May to mid-September (phone: 403-821-4591).

Watson's general store, built by Matthew Watson in 1911, is also an intriguing place. It is still heated by a wood-burning Yukon barrel stove, as is the *Caribou* hotel's tavern.

After stopping in Carcross, continue the journey to Whitehorse, or steer your canoe down the Yukon River to Whitehorse or all the way to Dawson.

YUKON RIVER: It's 500 miles (805 km) to the gold fields at Dawson, and there's no better way to tour the Yukon Territory than riding on the river that gives this wild land its name. The rapids, once greatly feared by the Klondikers, have been tamed by the construction of a power dam necessitating the only portage on the entire route.

Once past Whitehorse and Miles Canyon, you'll be hard pressed to find an experience comparable to the serenity that envelops you as your canoe floats lazily through the heart of this vast land. Perhaps you'll spot a cabin or two along the riverbank, but more likely the only signs of life you'll encounter will be an occasional moose or bear taking a swim or standing on the bank drinking the cool water. Set up camp on a deserted bank and watch as the summer days stretch into the night. If you stay awake long enough, you can detect subtle hues of pink permeating the night sky as the sun rolls over in its sleep at 1 or 2 in the morning. Eventually you'll turn a bend in the river and there, on the right bank, stands the tarnished ghost of Dawson, the city of gold.

BEST EN ROUTE

Again, so many travelers are attracted to the Yukon each year that it is necessary to make hotel reservations as far in advance as possible. Book your June vacation in January if you want to get first crack at the top accommodations. Plan on spending between $50 and $60 for a moderately priced room for two, a minimum of $40 for an inexpensive room, and more than $70 for expensive accommodations. Reservations must be accompanied by a guaranteed deposit, usually the equivalent of one night's stay. Charges at privately owned campgrounds range between about $6.50 and $10 per site, depending upon facilities. Government-operated camping areas charge $4 per night, or $20 for an annual pass. Goverment campground sites are given out on a first-come, first-served basis. Since this is an outdoor route, you'll be sleeping under canvas or in cabins operated by your outfitter-guide. Detailed maps of the Yukon watercourse are available from the Alaska Northwest Publishing Company, Box 4-EEE, Anchorage, AK 99509. Even if you don't make the trip, the catalogue is worth reading. All prices are quoted in US dollars.

For information on Whitehorse and Dawson, see the relevant parts of the *Dawson Circle Route*.

SKAGWAY, ALASKA

Golden North – All of the 33 rooms in this lovely hotel are furnished with period antiques, each room dedicated to an 1890s character. There's an 1898 bar, a beauty shop, restaurant, and car rental and sightseeing services. PO Box 343 (phone: 907-983-2451). Moderate.

Sgt. Preston's – Bordering on Skagway's historic district, each of this hotel's 23 rooms has street-level access and cable TV. Sixth St. between Broadway and State. PO Box 473-AT (phone: 907-983-2521). Moderate.

Skagway Bed & Breakfast Inn – An intriguing and friendly guesthouse, the atmosphere here is totally 1898. In fact, the core of the building dates back to the gold rush, when this warm and respectable inn was, of all things, a home operated by "ladies of the night." With only 12 rooms it is small, but very popular. *Miss Suzanne's Tea Room,* serving dishes such as halibut and rack of lamb for lunch and dinner, has recently been added. PO Box 13 (phone: 907-983-2289). Moderate.

Irene's Inn – The 10 rooms in this gold-rush-era building are newly remodeled and straightforward. Some rooms share a bath. The restaurant serves steak, local seafood, homemade bread, soups, and pies for lunch and dinner. Sixth and Broadway. PO Box 5385-AT (phone: 907-983-2520). Moderate to inexpensive.

INDEX

INDEX

Index

Acadian Festival (Caraquet, NB), 326
Acadian Trail, NB, tour, 425–30
  hotels, 429–30
Acadian Village, NB, 428–629
Accommodations, 49–50, 83–86, 336–45
  bed-and-breakfast, 85–86
  budget, 85
  costs, calculating, 49–50
  home exchange, 86
  overbooking, 84–85
  reservations, 84
  special, 336–45
  See also hotels *entry under names of individual cities*
Airplane travel, 16–29
  bartered travel sources, 27–28
  charter flights, 24–26
    booking, 25–26
  consumer protection, 28–29
  default and/or bankruptcy insurance, 57
  discount travel sources, 26–27
  flight insurance, 57–58
  hints for handicapped travelers, 66
  hints for traveling with children, 21, 75
  hints for traveling with pets, 78–79
  net fare sources, 27
  scheduled flights, 16–24
    airline clubs, 23–24
    baggage, 23
    delays and cancellations, 22–23
    fares, 17–19
    getting bumped, 21–22
    meals, 21
    reservations, 19–20
    seating, 20–21
    smoking, 21
    tickets, 16–17
  trip cancellation insurance, 56–57
Albany Watershed (north of Geraldton, Ontario), 298
Alberta, exploring, 355–75
Alberton, PEI, 572
Algoma Region (north of Sault Ste. Marie, Ontario), 285

Algonquin Golf Course (St. Andrews, NB), 292
Algonquin Hotel (St. Andrews-by-the-Sea, NB), 337
Algonquin Provincial Park (near Huntsville, Ontario), 318, 553
Allen's Holiday Farm (Port Elgin, NB), 347–48
Alma, Quebec, hotels, 594
Alpine Club of Canada (Banff, Alberta), 312
Amherst, Yarmouth to, NS, tour, 482–92
  hotels, 491–92
Amherst around Cape Breton Island, NS, tour, 500–508
  hotels, 506–8
Amherstburg, Ontario, 512–13
  hotels, 521
Anderson's Holiday Farm (Sussex, NB), 348
Antigonish, NS, 502
  hotels, 506
Antigonish Highland Games (Antigonish, NS), 327
Apex-Alpine (Kelowna, BC), 280–81
Appalachian region, 9–10
Arctic Red River, NWT, 474
Aroostook, NB, hotels, 444
Arowhon Pines (Algonquin Park, Ontario), 338–39
Ashcroft, BC, hotels, 392
Aspen Ridge (Clear Lake, Manitoba), 347
Athabasca, Alberta, 374–75
  hotels, 378
Atlantic Yachting Academy (Dartmouth, NS), 306–7
Auberge Fort Prével, Quebec, 616
  hotels, 621
Auberge Handfield (St. Marc-sur-Richelieu, Quebec), 342–43
Auberge Hatley (North Hatley, Quebec), 342
Automobile clubs, 32–33
Automobile insurance, 32, 58–59
Auyuittuq National Park (Baffin Island, NWT), 315, 331–32

670 Index

Avalon Peninsula, Northern, Newfoundland, tour, 459–63
  hotels, 463
Avalon Peninsula, Southern Shore, Newfoundland, tour, 446–49
  hotels, 448–49
Aylmer, Ontario, 516
  hotels, 522

Backpacking and Hiking, 43, 315–19
Baddeck, NS, 504
  hotels, 507
Baie Comeau, Quebec, 596–97
  hotels, 599
Baie St. Paul, Quebec, 588
  hotels, 593
Bally Haly Golf and Curling Club (St. John's, Newfoundland), 292
Balmoral Mills, NS, 501
Banff Alpine Guides School of Moutaineering (Banff, Alberta), 312
Banff and Jasper National Parks, Calgary to, Alberta, tour, 361–78
Banff National Park (Banff, Alberta), 315, 333, 363–65
Banff Springs Golf Club (Banff, Alberta), 294
Banff Springs Hotel (Banff, Alberta), 323, 343
Barkerville, BC, 391–92
Barrie, Ontario, 550–51
  hotels, 561
Barrington, NS, 494
Bartered travel sources, 27
Batchawana Bay, Ontario, 542–43
Bathurst, NB, 429
  hotels, 430
Bay Bulls, Newfoundland, 447
Bay of Quinte (Ontario), 304
Bear River, NS, 487
Beaupré/Charlevoix and Saguenay, Quebec, tour, 584–94
  hotels, 592–94
Beaver Creek, Yukon Territory, 656–57
  lodge, 658
Benmiller Inn (Goderich, Ontario), 339
Bennett, Yukon Territory, 664
Bic, Quebec, 611–12
Big White (Kelowna, BC), 280–81
Biking, 43–44
  choosing a bike, 44
  road safety, 44
  tours, 44

Bird Island, Newfoundland, 448
Black Cat Guest Ranch (Hinton, Alberta), 350
Black Feather Wilderness Adventures (Ottawa, Ontario), 319
Blacksand Park, Ontario, 558
Blenheim, Ontario, campsites, 522
Blue Heron Drive, PEI, tour, 566–70
  hotels, 570
Bonaventure, Quebec, 614–15
  hotels, 620
Bonavista Peninsula, Newfoundland, 451–52
Borden, Saskatchewan, campsites, 644
Border crossings, 59–60
  duty and customs, 59–60
  entry requirements, 59
  reentering, 60
Bouctouche, NB, 426
  hotels, 430
Bowron Lakes Provincial Park (near Barkerville, BC), 310
Brabant Island (Mackenzie River, near Hay River, NWT), 301
Bracebridge, Ontario, hotels, 562
Brackley Beach, PEI, 568
  hotels, 570
Brandon, Manitoba, 411
  hotels, 413
Bridgetown, NS, hotels, 492
Bridgewater, NS, 495
  hotels, 499
Brier Island, NS, 486–87
Brightwood Golf and Country Club (Dartmouth, NS), 292
Brigus, Newfoundland, 462
British Columbia, exploring, 379–404
Broadleaf Farm (Hopewell Hill, NB), 348
Brockville, Ontario, 534
Bromont, 580–81
  hotels, 583
Brooklyn, NS, 495
Brooks, Alberta, hotels, 373
Bruce Trail (near Hamilton, Ontario), 318
Brudenell Resort, PEI, 575
Brudenell River Provincial Golf Course (Roseneath, PEI), 293
Buffalo Pound Provincial Park, Saskatchewan, 631–32
Burin Peninsula, Newfoundland, 452
Burwash Landing, Yukon Territory, lodge, 659

Bus, touring by, 31
  accommodations and fares, 31
  booking, 31
  hints for handicapped travelers, 67
  hints for traveling with children, 73–77
  services, 31
  suggestions for comfortable travel, 31
  tours, 31
Business hours, 88–89
Butchart Gardens, Vancouver Island, BC, 383

Cache Creek, BC, 390
Calgary, Alberta, 135–44
  climate and clothes, 140
  essay, 135–37
  hotels, 142–43
  local transportation, 140
  museums, 141
  music, 142
  nightclubs and nightlife, 142
  restaurants, 143–44
  shopping, 141
  sights and activities, 137–39
    downtown, 137–39
    suburbs, 139
  special events, 140
  sports, 141–42
  theater, 142
  tipping, 140
  tourist information, 140
Calgary, Lethbridge to, via Waterton Lakes National Park, Alberta, tour, 356–61
  hotels, 360–61
Calgary Exhibition & Stampede (Calgary, Alberta), 329
Calgary to Banff and Jasper National Parks, Alberta, tour, 361–78
Calvert, Newfoundland, hotels, 449
Camera and equipment, 98–101
Campbell River, Vancouver Island, BC, 385
  hotels, 386
Campers, camping vehicles, *see* Recreational vehicles
Camping, 41–43
  locations, 41–42
  necessities, 42
  organized trips, 42–43
Campobello Island, 434
Canadian Mountain Holidays (Banff, Alberta), 283

Canadian National Exhibition (Toronto, Ontario), 328
Canadian School of Mountaineering (Canmore, Alberta), 313
Canadian (or Precambrian) Shield, 10–11
Canmore, Alberta, hotels, 366–67
Canoe and raft routes, 307–11
Cap aux Meules, Quebec, hotels, 627. *See also* Iles de la Madeleine
Cape Breton Highlands National Park (near Ingonish Beach, NS), 332, 503–4
Cape Breton Island, Amherst around, NS, tour, 500–508
  hotels, 506–8
Cape Ray, Newfoundland, 455
Cape Spear National Historic Park, Newfoundland, 446–47
Car, driving own, 31–38
  automobile clubs, 32–33
  breakdowns, 35
  gasoline, 36
  hints for handicapped travelers, 67
  hints for traveling with children, 75
  hints for traveling with pets, 78–79
  insurance, 32, 58–59
  maps, 34
  mechanics and car care, 35
  oil company credit cards, 34
  preparing car, 34–35
  renting, 36–38
  speed, 35–35
  See also Car rentals
Caraquet, NB, 428
  hotels, 430
Carcross, Yukon Territory, 664–65
Cardston, Alberta, 357
  hotels, 360
Cariboos (BC), 287–88
Carleton, Quebec, 614
  hotels, 620
Carling Lake Golf Club (Lachute, Quebec), 294
Carmacks, Yukon Territory, 652
Car rentals, 36–38
  cost and requirements, 37–38
  fly/drive packages, 38
Cavendish, PEI, 569
Cedar Lakes (near Messines, Quebec), 299
Chapleau Area (Chapleau, Ontario), 319–20

Charlevoix/Beaupré and Saguenay, Quebec, tour, 584–94
  hotels, 592–94
Charlottetown, PEI, 566–68
  hotels, 570
Charlottetown Festival (Charlottetown, PEI), 328
Charter flights, 24–26
Château Lake Louise (Lake Louise, Alberta), 344
Chatham, NB, 427
  hotels, 430
Chester, NS, 497
  hotels, 500
Chéticamp, NS, 503
  hotels, 507
Chicoutimi, Quebec, 591–92
  hotels, 594
Chilcotin River (BC), 309–10
Children, hints for traveling with, 73–77
  accommodations, 76–77
  by bus, 76
  by car, 75
  family trips, 76
  packing, 74
  by plane, 75
  planning, 73–77
  by train, 76
  transportation, 74–76
Chilko Lake Wilderness Ranch (Williams Lake, BC), 350–51
Chilkoot Pass, Yukon Territory, 661–64
Chilkoot Trail (from Dyea, Alaska, to Bennett, BC), 316
Churchill, Manitoba, 421
  hotels, 423
Church Point, NS, 484
Claresholm, Alberta, hotels, 361
Clark's Harbour, NS, 494
Clearwater Lake Provincial Park, Manitoba, hotels, 422–23
Clevelands House (Minett, Ontario), 290
Climate, 14–15
  British Columbia, 15
  Central Canada, 14
  Maritimes, 14
  North, 15
  packing hints for, 61–62
  Prairies, 14
  See also climate and clothes *entry under names of individual cities*
Climbing, mountain, 312–15
Clinton, BC, 390

Clyde River (near Barrington, NS), 494
Cobalt, Ontario, 554–55
  hotels, 563
Cocagne, NB, 426
Cochrane, Ontario, 556–57
  hotels, 563
Columbia Ice Field (near Jasper, Alberta), 314–15
Contemporary Canada, 119–22
  and separatism, 123–31
Corner Brook, Newfoundland, 456
  hotels, 459
Cornwall, Ontario, 535
Costs, calculating, 47–50
  determining a budget, 47–49
  hotel/restaurant, 49–50
  transportation, 49
Courtenay, Vancouver Island, BC, 385
Cowichan Bay (near Duncan, BC), 383–84
Credit cards, 82–83
Cross-country skiing, 284–88
Cultural events, 15
Culture, contemporary Canadian, 129–31
Curling, 95
Customs, duty and, 59–60
Cuttle's Tremblant Club (Mont Tremblant, Quebec), 340–41
Cypress (Vancouver, BC), 282
Cypress Hills Provincial Park, Saskatchewan, 369, 633
Cypress Hills Provincial Park to Edmonton via Dinosaur Country, Alberta, tour, 368–73
  hotels, 373

Dalvay Beach, PEI, 568
  hotels, 570
Dalvay-by-the-Sea (Dalvay Beach, PEI), 340
Dauphin, Manitoba, 419–20
Dawson Circle Route, Yukon Territory, tour, 650–58
  hotels, 657–58
Dawson City to Inuvik, NWT, tour, 472–75
  hotels, 475
Dawson Creek, BC, hotels, 404
Deerbank Farm (Morris, Manitoba), 347
Deerhurst Inn and Country Club (Huntsville, Ontario), 290, 339
Deer Island, 434

Default and/or bankruptcy insurance, 57
Digby, NS, 485
  hotels, 492
Dining, see Restaurants
Dinosaur Country, Cypress Hills Provincial Park to Edmonton via, Alberta, tour, 368–73
  hotels, 373
Dinosaur Provincial Park, Alberta, 370–71
Discount travel sources, 26–27
Discovery Passage (Quadra Island, near Campbell River, BC), 300–301
Doaktown, New Brunswick, hotels, 430
Dobson Trail (near Moncton, NB), 317–18
Don Valley Golf Course (Toronto, Ontario), 293
Downhill skiing, 284–88
Drinking and drug laws, 91–92
Drumheller, Alberta, 371
  hotels, 373
Duck Mountain Provincial Park, Manitoba, 640
Duncan, Vancouver Island, BC, 383–84
Duty and customs, 59–60
Dyea, Alaska, 660–61

Eagle Lake (near Vermilion Bay, Ontario), 299
Eagle River (near Goose Bay, Labrador, Newfoundland), 297–98
Eastern Townships (Estrie) (Montréal, Quebec), 277–78, 579–84
  hotels, 582–84
Edmonton, Alberta, 145–54
  climate and clothes, 149
  essay, 145–47
  hotels, 151–52
  local transportation, 149
  museums, 150
  music, 151
  nightclubs and nightlife, 151
  restaurants, 152–54
  shopping, 150
  sights and activities, 147–49
    downtown, 147–48
    suburbs, 148–49
  special events, 150
  sports, 150–51
  theater, 151
  tipping, 149
  tourist information, 149

Edmonton, Cypress Hills Provincial Park to, via Dinosaur Country, Alberta, tour, 368–73
  hotels, 373
Edmonton to Slave Lake and Peace River, Alberta, tour, 373–78
  hotels, 378
Edmundston, NB, 443
  hotels, 444
Edmundston Golf Club (Edmundston, NB), 290
Eldon-Belfast, PEI, 574–75
Electricity, 90
Elgin House (Port Carling, Ontario), 289–90
Elk Island National Park (near Edmonton, Alberta), 334
Entry requirements, 59–60
Erieau, Ontario, 515
Escoumins, Quebec, hotels, 598
Estevan to the Northern Lakes, Saskatchewan, tour, 635–39
  hotels, 639
Étang du Nord, Quebec, see Iles de la Madeleine
Exploits River (near Grand Falls, Newfoundland), 297

Fairmont Hot Springs Golf Club (Fairmont Hot Springs, BC), 294
Fairmont Hot Springs Resort (Fairmont Hot Springs, BC), 344
Fairs and celebrations, 16, 326–30
Falcon Beach Golf Course (Whiteshell Provincial Park, Manitoba), 295
Falcon Lake, Manitoba, 407
Farm and ranch vacations, 345–51
  family farms, 346–49
  guest ranches, 350–51
  working ranches, 349–50
Faro, Yukon Territory, 652–53
Ferryland, Newfoundland, 447
Festival by the Sea (St. John, NB), 326
Festival du Voyageur (St. Boniface, Manitoba), 330
Festival of Spring (Ottawa, Ontario), 327–28
Festivals and fairs, 16, 326–30
First aid, 79
Fishing, 95, 296–302
Five Islands, NS, 490
Flat Rock, Newfoundland, 462
Flight insurance, 57–58

Flin Flon, Manitoba, 420–21
  hotels, 423
Football, 95
Foreign exchange, 82–83
Forestville, Quebec, 596
  hotels, 599
Forillon National Park (Gaspé Peninsula, Quebec), 333
Fort Anne National Historic Park, NS, 487
Fort Hope, wilderness around (near Nakina, Ontario), 320
Fort Macleod, Alberta, 358–59
  hotels, 361
Fort McPherson, NWT, 473–74
Fort Nelson, BC, hotels, 404
Fort Prével, see Auberge Fort Prével
Fort Providence, NWT, 466–67
Fortress of Louisbourg, NS, 505
  hotels, 507
Fort St. John, BC, 402–3
  hotels, 404
Fort Simpson, NWT, 471
  hotels, 472
Fort Smith, Hay River to, NWT, tour, 475–80
  hotels, 480
Fort Walsh National Historic Park, Saskatchewan, 633
Fraser River (BC), 309–10
Fraser River, BC, tour, 387–92
  hotels, 392
Fredericton, NB, 440–41
  hotels, 443
Frelo Farm (Angusville, Manitoba), 347
Fundy Coast, tour, NB, 431–38
  hotels, 436–37
Fundy Isles, 433–34
Fundy National Park (near Alma, NB), 331, 436
  hotels, 438
Fushimi Lake Park, Ontario, 557

Gananoque, Ontario, 533
  hotels, 537
Gander, Newfoundland, 450–51
  hotels, 453
Gander River (near Gander, Newfoundland), 297
Gardiner Dam, Saskatchewan, 636
Gaspé, Quebec, 616–17
  hotels, 621

Gaspé Peninsula, Quebec, tour, 608–21
  hotels, 619–21
Gatineau Park (near Hull, Quebec), 318
Gatineau Valley and La Vérendrye, Quebec, 605–6
  hotels, 607
George River (northeast of Schefferville, Quebec), 299–300
Georgetown, PEI, 575
Georgian Bay (north of Midland, Ontario), 298–99, 304
Georgian Bay Islands National Park (near Honey Harbour, Ontario), 332
Geraldton, Ontario, 557–58
  hotels, 563
Gimli, Manitoba, 415–16
  hotels, 417
Glacier National Park (near Rogers Pass, BC), 317, 334, 397
Glen Abbey Golf Course (Oakville, Ontario), 528
Glenalby Farms (New Hamburg, Ontario), 348
Glenboro, Manitoba, hotels, 413
Glen Lawrence Golf and Country Club (Kingston, Ontario), 293
Golf, 95–96, 291–95
Good Spirit Lake Provincial Park, Saskatchewan, 640–41
Granby, 580
  hotels, 583
Grand Codroy River, Newfoundland, 455–56
Grande Prairie, Alberta, 377
  hotels, 378
Grande Vallée, Quebec, hotels, 621
Grand Falls, NB, 443
  hotels, 444
Grand Lake, NB, 440
Grand Manan Island (near Black's Harbour, NB), 433
  hotels, 437
Grand Pré, NS, 489
Gravenhurst, Ontario, 552–53
  hotels, 562
Gray Rocks Golf Club (St. Jovite, Quebec), 294
Gray Rocks Inn (St. Jovite, Quebec), 342
Great Barren Ground Rivers (NWT), 311
Great Bear Lake (north of Yellowknife, NWT), 301

Great Plains, 12
Great Slave Lake (near Yellowknife, NWT), 301–2
Green Gables Golf Course (Cavendish, PEI), 293
Greenwater Park, Ontario, 557
Gros Morne National Park (Newfoundland), 331, 456–57
  hotels, 459
Grouse Mountain (Vancouver, BC), 282
Gwynalta Farm (Gwynne, Alberta), 346–47

Haines Junction, Yukon Territory, 657
  hotels, 659
Halifax, NS, 155–65
  climate and clothes, 160
  essay, 155–57
  hotels, 162–63
  local transportation, 160
  museums, 160
  music, 161
  nightclubs and nightlife, 162
  restaurants, 163–65
  shopping, 160–61
  sights and activities, 157–59
    downtown, 157–58
    suburbs, 158–59
  special events, 160
  sports, 161
  theater, 161
  tipping, 159
  tourist information, 159
Hamilton, Ontario, 528–29
Handicapped travelers, hints for, 63–68
  by bus, 67
  by car, 67
  by plane, 66
  planning, 63–66
  tours, 67–68
  by train, 67
Hanson Lake Road area (near Saskatchewan), 302
Hantsport, NS, 489
Harbour Grace, Newfoundland, 462–63
Harrison Hot Springs Resort Hotel (Harrison Hot Springs, BC), 344–45
Havre aux Maisons, Quebec, hotels, 626–27. *See also* Iles de la Madeleine
Hay River to Fort Smith, NWT, tour, 475–80
  hotels, 480

Hay River to Yellowknife, NWT, tour, 465–69
  hotels, 469
Health hints, 79–80
Hecla Provincial Park, Manitoba, 416–17
  hotels, 417
Helicopter skiing, 282–84
Heritage Highways, Ontario, tour, 523–37
  hotels, 535–37
Hidden Valley Resort Hotel (Huntsville, Ontario), 290
Highlands Golf Links (Cape Breton Highlands National Park, Ingonish Beach, NS), 292
High River, Alberta, 139, 359–60
Hiking, 43, 315–19
  guided trips, 318–19
History, short, of Canada, 105–31
  American Revolution, 111–13
  British Canada, 113–15
  coming of Europeans, 106–8
  contemporary Canada, 119–22
  Dominion of Canada, 116–17
  French and English wars, 108–11
  late-nineteenth-century development, 117–18
  mid-nineteenth-century development, 115–16
  separatism, 123–31
  WWI and its aftermath, 118–19
Hockey, 96
  museums, 324–25
Hockey Hall of Fame and Museum (Toronto, Ontario), 325
Holidays, national and provincial, 89
Holland Landing, Ontario, 550
Hope, BC, 388–90
Horse racing, 96
Hostellerie Les Trois Tilleuls (St. Marc, Quebec), 343
Hôtel la Sapinière (Val David, Quebec), 343
Hotels, 83–86
  bed-and-breakfast, 85–86
  budget, 85
  costs, calculating, 49–50
  home exchange, 86
  overbooking, 84–85
  reservations, 84
  special, 336–45

Hotels (cont.)
See also hotels entry under names of individual cities
Hovey Manor (North Hatley, Quebec), 341–42
Hubbards, NS, 497
  hotels, 500
Humber River (near Corner Brook, Newfoundland), 297
Hunting, 319–22
Huntsville, Ontario, 553
  hotels, 562
Huron, Lake, see Western Lakeshores, Ontario's, tour

Ice skating, 322–25
Ile aux Coudres (Hazeltree Island), Quebec, 588–89
  hotels, 593
Ile aux Grues (Crane Island, near Quebec City, Quebec), 320
Ile d'Orléans, Quebec, 586–87
  hotels, 592
Ile Notre Dame, Montréal, 176
Ile Ste. Hélène, Montréal, 176–77
Iles de la Madeleine, Quebec, tour, 621–27
  hotels, 626–27
Ingonish and Ingonish Beach, NS, hotels, 507
Inn and Tennis Club at Manitou (McKellar, Ontario), 290
Inns, see Hotels
Insurance, 55–59
  automobile, 32, 58–59
  baggage and personal effects, 55–56
  combination packages, 59
  default and/or bankruptcy, 57
  flight, 57–58
  personal accident and sickness, 56–57
  trip cancellation and interruption, 56–57
Interlake, Manitoba, tour, 414–18
  hotels, 417–18
Interlake Region (between Lake Manitoba and Lake Winnipeg, Manitoba), 321–22, 414–18
  hotels, 417–18
International Hockey Hall of Fame and Museum (Kingston, Ontario), 324–25

International Peace Garden, Manitoba, 412–13
Inuvik, Dawson City to, NWT, tour, 472–75
  hotels, 475
Inverness, NS, hotels, 506
Iroquois Fall, Ontario, 556
Ivy Lea, Ontario, hotels, 537

James and Hudson Bay (near Moosonee, Ontario), 320
Jardens de Métis Park, Quebec, 619
Jasper and Banff National Parks, Calgary to, Alberta, tour, 361–78
Jasper Climbing School and Guide Service (Jasper, Alberta), 313
Jasper National Park (Jasper, Alberta), 315–16, 334, 365–66
Jasper Park Lodge Golf Course (Jasper, Alberta), 294
Jasper Park Lodge (Jasper, Alberta), 289, 344, 367
Joliette, Quebec, 604–5
Jordan, Ontario, 527–28

Kamloops, BC, 393–94
  hotels, 395
Kananaskis Country, Alberta, 363
  hotels, 367
Kapuskasing, Ontario, hotels, 563
Kejimkujik National Park (near Maitland Bridge, NS), 332
Kelowna, British Columbia, hotels, 395
Keltic Lodge (Cape Breton Island, NS), 337
Kentville, NS, 488
Kilmuir Place (Cape Breton Island, NS), 337–38
Kimberley (Kimberley, BC), 281
Kingsboro, PEI, hotels, 576
Kings Byway, PEI, tour, 573–76
  hotels, 576
Kings Landing, NB, 441–42
Kingston, Ontario, 532–33
  hotels, 537
Kingston Peninsula, NB, 439
Kingsville, Ontario, 513–14
  hotels, 521
Kirkland Lake, Ontario, 555
  hotels, 563
Kitchener-Waterloo Oktoberfest (Kitchener, Ontario), 327

Index 677

K J 5 Ranch (Rapid City, Manitoba), 349–50
Klondike Days (Edmonton, Alberta), 149, 329
Klotz Lake Park, Ontario, 557
Kluane Lake, Yukon Territory, 657
Kluane National Park (near Haines Junction, Yukon Territory), 335–36
Knight Inlet (Minstral Island, near Campbell River, BC), 300
Kokanee Glacier Provincial Park (near Nelson, BC), 317
Kootenay Lake (BC), 305–6
Kootenay National Park (Radium Hot Springs, BC), 334, 397–98
hotels, 398
Kouchibouguac National Park (Kent County, NB), 331, 426–27

Labrador Coast, from Newfoundland, 458
Lac Brome, 581
Lac La Hache (near 100 Mile House, BC), 329
Lac La Ronge area (near north central Saskatchewan), 302
Lacrosse, 96
Lady Slipper Drive, PEI, tour, 571–73
hotels, 572–73
Ladysmith, Vancouver Island, BC, hotels, 386
La Ferme des Érables (Aroostock, NB), 347
Lake Louise (Banff area, Alberta), 365
hotels, 367
Lake of the Woods (Ontario-Manitoba), 304–5
Lake Okanagan Resort (Kelowna, BC), 289
Lake Superior Provincial Park, Ontario, 543–44
Lake Winnipeg (Manitoba), 305
La Malbaie, Quebec, 589–90
hotels, 593
La Mauricie National Park (near Shawinigan, Quebec), 333, 601
L'Anse aux Meadows, Newfoundland, 458
La Pinsonniére (Cap á l'Aigle, Quebec), 340
La Ronge and vicinity, Saskatchewan, 638–39

La Tuque, Quebec, 602
hotels, 606
Laura Second Homestead (Queenston Village, Ontario), 526
Laurentians (Les Laurentides) (near Montréal, Quebec), 177, 276–77, 285–86, 290–91, 323–24, 602
Laurentians, Quebec, tour, 599–607
hotels, 606–7
La Vérendrye and Gatineau Valley, Quebec, 605–6
hotels, 607
Lawrencetown, NS, 488
Leamington, Ontario, 514
hotels, 521
Le Chantecler Golf Club (Ste. Adèle, Quebec), 294
Le Chateau Montebello (Montebello, Quebec), 294, 341
Legal aid, 91
L'Esterel, Quebec, hotels, 607
Lethbridge to Calgary via Waterton Lakes National Park, Alberta, tour, 356–61
hotels, 360–61
Lévis, Quebec, 610
Lewin's Cove, Newfoundland, hotels, 454
Liard Highway, 470–71
Liivam Farms (Eckville, Alberta), 346
Lingan Country Club (Sydney, NS), 293
Liscomb Mills, NS, hotels, 500
Liverpool, NS, 495
hotels, 499
Lloydminster, Saskatchewan, 643
hotels, 645
Lobster Carnival and Livestock Exhibition (Summerside, PEI), 328
Lockeport, NS, 495
Lockport, Manitoba, 415
London, Ontario, 516–19
hotels, 523
Louisbourg, NS
Fortress of, 505
hotels, 507
Lundar, Manitoba, hotels, 418
Lunenburg, NS, 496

Mackenzie, BC, hotels, 404
Mackenzie Mountains (near Norman Wells, NWT), 322
Macleod Park, 557
Mactaquac Provincial Park, NB, 441

Magdalen Islands, *see* Iles de la Madeleine
Magog, 581
Mahone Bay, NS, 496
Mail, 89
Manitoba, exploring, 405–23
Manitoba, North, tour, 418–23
  hotels, 422–23
Manitoba Narrows, 417
Manitoulin Island, Ontario, 540–41
Maniwaki, Quebec, 605
Manning Provincial Park (Manning Park, BC), 317
Manoir Richelieu Golf Club (Pointe-au-Pic, Quebec), 294
Marathon, Ontario, 545
  hotels, 548
Marathon Inn (Grand Manan Island, NB), 336
Marble Mountain Ski Resort, Newfoundland, 456
Margaree Forks, NS, hotels, 506–7
Maria, Quebec, 614
Marmot Basin (Jasper, Alberta), 280
Marshlands Inn (Sackville, NB), 336–37
Marten River Provincial Park, Ontario, 554
  campsites, 563
Marystown, Newfoundland, 452
Matane, Quebec, 619
  hotels, 621
Matapédia, Quebec, 613–14
  hotels, 620
Meadow Lake Provincial Park, Saskatchewan, 643
  campgrounds, 644–45
Medical help, 90–91
Medicine Hat, Alberta, 369–70
  hotels, 373
Meductic, NB, 442
Meteghan, NS, 484
Metis Park, Quebec, 619
Metric systems, *see* Weights and measures, table of
Midland, Ontario, 551
Mike Wiegele Helicopter Skiing (Banff, Alberta), 283
Milford House (South Milford, NS), 338
Millcroft Inn (Alton, Ontario), 338
Mill River Fun Park, PEI, 572
Mill River Provincial Park Golf Course (Woodstock, PEI), 293

Mill River Resort, PEI, 572
Miramichi Folk Song Festival (Newcastle, NB), 326
Miramichi River (near Fredericton, NB), 296–97
Miscou Island, NB, 428
Moldenhauers (Allan, Saskatchewan), 349
Moncton, NB, 436
  hotels, 438
Montague, PEI, 575
Mont Carmel, PEI, 571–72
Montmorency Falls, Quebec, 586
Montreal, Quebec, 166–89
  climate and clothes, 177–78
  essay, 166–69
  hotels, 183–85
  ice skating, 324
  local transportation, 178
  museums, 179–80
  music, 182
  nightclubs and nightlife, 182–83
  restaurants, 185–89
  shopping, 180–81
  sights and activities, 169–77
    old Montreal, 172–73
    underground Montreal, 170–72
  ski areas, 602–3
  special events, 178–79
  sports, 181–82
  theater, 182
  tipping, 177
  tourist information, 177
Mont Ste. Anne (near Quebec City, Quebec), 618
Mont Ste. Marie Resort and Conference Center (Lac Ste. Marie, Ste. Marie, Quebec), 291
Mont St. Pierre, Quebec, hotels, 621
Mont Tremblant Parc, Quebec, 604
  hotels, 607
Moose Jaw, Saskatchewan, 632
  hotels, 634
Moose Mountain Provincial Park, Saskatchewan, 629–30
  hotels, 634
Morden, Manitoba, hotels (farms), 414
Morrisburg, Ontario, 534–35
Mountain Canada (Golden, BC), 284, 312
Mountain climbing, 312–15
  schools, 312–13
Mountains, western, 12–13

Index 679

Mt. Assiniboine Provincial Park (near Invermere, BC), 316–17
Mt. Carleton Provincial Park, NB, 442
Mt. Edith Cavell (near Jasper, Alberta), 314
Mt. Lefroy (next to Lake Louise, Alberta), 313–14
Mt. Orford, 581–82
   hotels, 583
Mt. Revelstoke National Park (near Revelstoke, BC), 334–35, 396–97
   hotels, 398
Mt. Robson (near Jasper, Alberta), 314
Mt. Temple (next to Lake Louise, Alberta), 313–14
Mt. Victoria (next to Lake Louise, Alberta), 313–14
Muncho Lake Provincial Park, BC, 403
Murray Municipal Golf Club (Regina, Saskatchewan), 295
Museums, hockey, 324–25. *See also* museums *entry under names of individual cities*
Music, *see* music *entry under names of individual cities*
Muskoka Winter Carnival (Bracebridge, Gravenhurst, and Huntsville, Ontario), 327

Nagagamisis Park, Ontario, 557
Nahanni National Park (near Fort Simpson, NWT), 335, 470–72
   hotels, 472
Nakiska at Mount Allan (Kananaskis Village, Albert), 279–80
Nanaimo, Vancouver Island, BC, 384
   hotels, 386
Napanee, Ontario, 531–32
Naramata, BC, hotels, 395
National parks, 15, 330–36
National Ukrainian Festival (Dauphin, Manitoba), 330
Net fare sources, 27
Netley Marsh, Manitoba, 415
New Brunswick, exploring, 424–44
Newcastle, NB, 427–28
Newfoundland, Central, tour, 449–54
   hotels, 453–54
Newfoundland, exploring, 445–63
Newfoundland, West Coast, tour, 454–59
   hotels, 459
New Glasgow, NS, 502
New River Beach, NB, 434

Niagara Falls, Ontario, 230–31, 524–26
   hotels, 535–36
Niagara Grape and Wine Festival (St. Catherines, Ontario), 328
Niagara-on-the-Lake, Ontario, 526–27
   hotels, 536
Nightclubs and nightlife, *see* nightclubs and nightlife *entry under names of individual cities*
Nipigon, Ontario, 558–59
   hotels, 564
North Battleford, Saskatchewan, 642–43
   hotels, 644
North Bay, Ontario, 553–54
   hotels, 562
North Channel (near Little Current, Ontario), 298, 304
Northern Lakes, Estevan to, Saskatchewan, tour, 635–39
   hotels, 639
Northern Manitoba Trappers Festival (The Pas, Manitoba), 330
North Hatley, 582
   hotels, 583–84
North Lake, PEI, 299
North Rustico, PEI, 568–69
Northwest Territories, exploring, 464–80
Notre Dame Bay, Newfoundland
   East, 450
   West, 449–50
Nova Scotia, exploring, 481–508
Nueltin Lake (north of Thompson, Manitoba), 301
Num-Ti-Jah Lodge (Bow Lake, Alberta), 343

Oakfield Golf and Country Club (Grand Lake, NS), 292
Oak Island, NS, 496–97
Okanagan Orchard Country, BC, tour, 393–95
   hotels, 395
Okanagan Valley (Big White Ski Village, Apex-Alpine, Silver Star) (Kelowna, BC), 280–81
Older travelers, hints for, 70–73
   discounts, 71–73
   health, 71
   package tours, 71–73
100 Mile House, BC, 390–91
   hotels, 392
108 Golf Course (100 Mile House, BC), 294–95

Ontario, exploring, 509–64
Ontario's Western Lakeshores, tour, 537–49
  hotels, 546–49
Orilla, Ontario, 551–52
  hotels, 561
Orwell Corner, PEI, 574
Oshawa, Ontario, 529–30
Ottawa, Ontario, 190–202
  climate and clothes, 196
  essay, 190–92
  hotels, 199–200
  ice skating, 323
  local transportation, 196
  museums, 197
  music, 198
  nightclubs and nightlife, 199
  restaurants, 201–2
  shopping, 197
  sights and activities, 192–95
    downtown, 192–94
    suburbs, 194–95
  special events, 197
  sports, 197–98
  theater, 198
  tipping, 196
  tourist information, 195–96
Ottawa River (near Pembroke, Ontario), 309
Outaouais (Ottawa Valley) (near Ottawa, Ontario, and Hull, Quebec), 276
Owen Sound, Ontario, 539–40

Pacific National Parks, BC, tour, 396–98
  hotels, 398
Pacific Rim National Park (near Ucluelet, Vancouver Island, BC), 317, 335
Package tours, 38–41
Packing hints, 60–63
Panmure Island (prince Edward Island), hotel, 576
Parc de la Gaspésie, Quebec, 618–19
  hotels, 621
Parks, national, 15, 330–36
Parksville, Vancouver Island, BC, hotels, 386
Parrsboro, NS, 490
  hotels, 492
Pas, The, Manitoba, 420
  hotels, 422

Peace River, Edmonton to Slave Lake and, Alberta, tour, 373–78
  hotels, 378
Peggy's Cove, NS, 159, 497–98
Pelee Island (in Lake Erie, Ontario), 320
  hotels, 521–22
Penticton, BC, 394
  hotels, 395
People and provinces, Canadian, 124–28
Percé, Quebec, 615–16
  hotels, 620–21
Petersfield, Manitoba, hotels, 417
Pets, hints for traveling with, 77–79
Picton, Ontario, 530
  hotels, 536
Pictou, NS, 502
Pinawa, Manitoba, 408
Pincher Creek, Alberta, hotels, 361
Pines Golf Club (Digby, NS), 292
Pinestone Inn and Country Club (Haliburton, Ontario), 339
Placentia, Newfoundland, 448
  hotels, 449
Plains and prairies, 12
Planning a trip, 50–52
  hints for traveling with children, 73–77
  hints for handicapped travelers, 63–66
Pointe-au-Pic, Quebec, hotels, 593
Point Pelee National Park (near Leamington, Ontario), 332, 514
Poplar Bluff Stock Farm (Chauvin, Alberta), 349
Portage la Prairie, Manitoba, 410
Port Alberni, Vancouver Island, BC, 384–85
Port au Choix, Newfoundland, 458
Port au Port Peninsula, Newfoundland, 456
Port aux Basques, Newfoundland, hotels, 459
Port Cartier, Quebec, 597–98
  hotels, 599
Port Daniel and Port Daniel Parc, Quebec, 615
Port-de-Grave Peninsula, Newfoundland, 462
Port Hastings, NS, hotels, 506
Port Hawkesbury, NS, hotels, 508
Port Hill, PEI, hotels, 573
Port Royal National Historic Park, NS, 487–88

Port Stanley, Ontario, 516
  hotels, 522
Portugal Cove, Newfoundland, 462
Pothole Country (from Minnedosa to Saskatchewan River, Manitoba), 322
Pouch Cove, Newfoundland, 462
Prescott, Ontario, 534
Prince Albert, Saskatchewan, 637–38
  hotels, 639
Prince Albert National Park (Prince Albert, Saskatchewan), 335, 637–38
  hotels, 639
Prince Edward Island, exploring, 565–76
Prince Edward Island National Park (near Charlottetown, PEI), 333, 568
Prince George, BC, to the Yukon, tour, 401–4
  hotels, 403–4
Prince George to Prince Rupert, BC, tour, 398–401
  hotels, 400–401
Prince Rupert, Prince George to, BC, tour, 398–401
  hotels, 400–401
Prince William, hotels, 443
Provincial Tourist Offices, 94–95
Pugwash, NS, 501
Pukaskwa National Park (near Marathon, Ontario), 332–33
Purcells (BC), 284, 288

Quadra Island, Vancouver Island, BC, hotels, 387
Qualicum Beach, Vancouver Island, BC, hotels, 386
Qu'Appelle Valley, Saskatchewan, 630
Quebec, exploring, 577–627
Quebec, North Shore of, tour, 594–99
  hotels, 598–99
Quebec City, Quebec, 203–20
  climate and clothes, 212
  essay, 203–6
  exploring, 577–627
  hotels, 216–18
  ice skating, 324
  local transportation, 212–13
  museums, 214
  music, 215–16
  nightclubs and nightlife, 216
  restaurants, 218–20
  shopping, 214
  sights and activities, 206–11
    old lower town, 207–8
    old upper town, 208–10
    Parliament Hill and Plains of Abraham, 210–11
    Ste. Anne de Beaupré, 210–11
    suburbs, 211
  ski areas, 278, 286
  special events, 213–14
  sports, 214–15
  theater, 215
  tipping, 212
  tourist information, 212
Quebec Winter Carnival (Quebec City, Quebec), 329
Queen Charlotte Islands (off coast of BC), 321
Quilchena, BC, hotels, 395
Quinte's Isle, Ontario, 530–31

Rae-Edzo, NWT, 467
Raft and canoe routes, 307–11
Rafter Six Ranch (Seebe, Alberta), 350
Ranch and farm vacations, 345–51
  family farms, 346–49
  guest ranches, 350–51
  working ranches, 349–50
Recreational vehicles (RVs), 45–46
  gas consumption, 46
  renting, 46
  self-propelled, 45–46
  towable, 45
Red Deer, Alberta, 372
  hotels, 373
Red Mountain (Rossland, BC), 281–82
Regina, Saskatchewan, 630–31
  hotels, 634
Religious services, 92–93
Remi Lake Park, Ontario, 557
Rennie, Manitoba, hotels, 409
Resorts, *see* Hotels
Restaurants, 86–88
  costs, calculating, 49–50
  reservations, 88
  See also restaurants *entry under names of individual cities*
Revelstoke, BC, 396–97
  hotels, 398
Rexton, NB, 426
Rideau Canal (Kingston to Ottawa, Ontario), 309

Rideau Trail (at Kingston, Ontario), 318
Riding Mountain National Park (near Wasagaming and Dauphin, Manitoba), 317, 335, 419
  hotels, 422
Rimouski, Quebec, 612–13
  hotels, 620
River of Ponds (near River of Ponds, Newfoundland), 297, 457–58
Riverport, NS, 495–96
Rivière du Loup, Quebec, 610–11
  hotels, 619–20
Rocky Mountains (western Alberta), 12–13, 286–87
Roewood Farm (Wallenstein, Ontario), 348–49
Rondeau Provincial Park, Ontario, 515
Roseneath, PEI, hotels, 576
Rossmount Inn (St. Andrews-by-the-Sea, NB), 337
Rothesay, NB, hotels, 438
Rustico Island, PEI, campgrounds, 570

Sackville, NB, hotels, 438
Saguenay, Beaupré Charlevoix and, Quebec, tour, 584–94
  hotels, 592–94
Sailing, 302–7
  schools, 306–7
St. Albert, Alberta, 374
St. Andrews, NB, 432–33
  hotels, 437
St. Anthony, Newfoundland, 458–59
  hotels, 459
St. Bernard, NS, 484–85
St. Catharines, Ontario, 527
  hotels, 536
Ste. Adèle, Quebec, hotels, 606
Ste. Agathe des Monts, Quebec, 603
  hotels, 607
Ste. Anne de Beaupré, Quebec, 211–12, 587–88
  hotels, 592–93
Ste. Anne des Monts, Quebec, 618
  hotels, 621
Ste.-Luce-sur-Mer, Quebec, hotels, 620
Ste. Marguerite Station, Quebec, hotels, 606
St. Jean Port Joli, Quebec, 610
St. Jérôme, Quebec, 603
Saint John, NB, 434–35
  hotels, 437
St. John River, NB, tour, 438–44
  hotels, 443–44
St. John River System (NB), 303
St. John's, Newfoundland, 460–62
  hotels, 463–64
St. Jovite, Quebec, 604
  hotels, 607
St. Lawrence Islands National Park (near Mallorytown Landing, Ontario), 332
St. Lawrence Lowlands and Lakes Region, 11–12
St. Leonard, New Brunswick, 443
St. Martins, New Brunswick, hotels, 437
St. Maurice Reserve, Quebec, 601–2
St. Maurice Valley, Quebec, 600–602
St. Peter's, NS, 505–6
St. Pierre Island, Newfoundland, 452–53
  hotels, 454
St. Stephen, NB, 431–32
  hotels, 437
St. Thomas, Ontario, 515–16
  hotels, 522
St. Victor Petroglyphs Historic Park, Saskatchewan, 632
Sandy Cove, NS, 485–86
Saskatchewan, exploring, 628–45
Saskatoon, Saskatchewan, 636–37, 641–42. *See also* Yellowhead Highway
  hotels, 639, 643–44
Sault Ste. Marie, Ontario, 541–42
  hotels, 547
Schreiber, Ontario, 546
  hotels, 548
Sealand, Vancouver Island, BC, 383
Selkirks (BC), 284, 288
Separatism, contemporary Canadian, 123–31
Sept Iles, Quebec, 598
  hotels, 599
Shawbridge, Quebec, 603
Shaw Festival (Niagara-on-the-Lake, Ontario), 327
Shawinigan, Quebec, hotels, 606
Shaw's Hotel (Brackley Beach, PEI), 340
Shediac, NB, 426
Shediac Lobster Festival (Shediac, NB), 326–27
Sheet Harbour (near Tangier, NS), 498
Shelburne, NS, 494–95
  hotels, 499
Sherbrooke, NS, 498–99

Index

Sherbrooke, Quebec, 582
Shippegan, NB, 428
Shopping, see shopping *entry under names of individual cities*
Sibley Provincial Park, Ontario, 559
Silver Star (Kelowna, BC), 280–81
Single travelers, hints for, 68–70
Skagway, Alaska, 660–61
   hotels, 665–66
Skating, ice, 322–25
Skiing, 96, 275–88
   cross-country, 284–88
   downhill, 275–84
   wilderness, 282–84
Skyline Hikers of the Canadian Rockies (based in Calgary, Alberta), 318
Slave Lake and Peace River, Edmonton to, Alberta, tour, 373–78
   hotels, 378
Snowmobiling, 96–97
Soo Line Historical Society Museum (Weyburn, Saskatchewan), 635
Souris, Manitoba, 411–12
Souris, PEI, 575–76
Southern Alberta Hostelling Association (Calgary, Alberta), 313
South Milford, NS, hotels, 492
South Nahanni River (southwestern NWT), 310–11
South Shore, PEI, 569–70
   hotels, 570
Spatsizi Plateau (near Kinaskan, BC), 321
Special events, see special events *entry under names of individual cities*
Spencer's Island, NS, 490–91
Sports, 15, 95–97
   curling, 95
   fishing, 95, 296–302
   football, 95
   golf, 95–96, 291–95
   hockey, 96
   horse racing, 96
   hunting, 319–22
   ice skating, 322–25
   lacrosse, 96
   sailing, 302–7
   skiing, 96, 275–88
   snowmobiling, 96–97
   tennis, 97, 288–91
   See also sports *entry under names of individual cities and specific sports entries*
Springdale, Newfoundland, hotels, 453
Springhill, NS, 491
Spruce Wood Provincial Heritage Park, Manitoba, 410–11
   campgrounds, 413
Stanhope Beach, PEI, 568
Station Mont Tremblant (Mont Tremblant, Quebec), 341
Steinbach, Manitoba, 406
   hotels, 408
Stellarton, NS, 502
Stoney Indian Reserve, Alberta, 362–63
Strait of Canso, NS, 502–3
Strait of Canso, Yarmouth to, NS, tour, 493–500
   hotels, 499–500
Stratford, Windsor to, Ontario, tour, 510–23
   hotels, 520–23
Stratford Shakespearean Festival (Stratford, Ontario), 328
Strathcona Park Lodge (near Campbell River, BC), 318–19
Students, hints for, 70
Sudbury, Ontario, 541
   hotels, 547
Summerside, PEI, 571
   hotels, 573
Sunburn, 79–80
Sundance Guest Ranch (Ashcroft, BC), 350
Superior, Lake, *see* Western Lakeshores, Ontario's, tour
Sussex, NB, hotels, 438
Sutton, Quebec, hotels, 583
Swift Current, Saskatchewan, 632–33
   hotels, 634
Sydney, NS, 504–5

Table Mountain, Newfoundland, 455
Tadoussac, Quebec, 590–91
   hotels, 593
Tangier, NS, 498
Tatamagouche, NS, 501
Telephone, 89–90
   emergencies, 90
   hotel surcharges, 90
Temagami, Ontario, 554
Tennis, 97, 288–91

Tennis vacations, 288–91
Terrace Bay, Ontario, 545–46
　hotels, 548
Terra Nova National Park (near Glovertown, Newfoundland), 331, 451
　hotels, 453
Theater, *see* theater *entry under names of individual cities*
Thompson River (BC), 309–10
Thousand Islands and Bay of Quinte (Ontario), 304
Thunder Bay, Yonge Street: Toronto to, Ontario, tour, 548–64
　hotels, 561–64
Tignish, PEI, 572
Time zones, 88
Timmins, Ontario, 555–56
　hotels, 563
TL Bar Ranch (Trochu, Alberta), 349
Tobermory, Ontario, 540
Tod Mountain (Kamloops, BC), 280
Toronto, Ontario, 221–41, 529
　climate and clothes, 231
　essay, 221–24
　hotels, 235–38
　ice skating, 320
　local transportation, 231–32
　museums, 232
　music, 235
　nightclubs and nightlife, 235
　restaurants, 238–41
　shopping, 232–33
　sights and activities, 224–31
　　downtown, 225–29
　　Niagara Falls, 230–31
　　outdoors, 229
　　suburbs, 229–30
　special events, 232
　sports, 233–34
　theater, 234–35
　tipping, 231
　tourist information, 231
　See also Yonge Street: Toronto to Thunder Bay, tour
Tourist information, 94–95. *See also* tourist information *entry under names of individual cities*
Tours
　biking, 44
　bus, 31
　for handicapped travelers, 67–68
　hiking, 318–19

　for older travelers, 53–54
　package, 38–41
　train, 30
Tracadie, NB, 428
Trail of '98, Yukon Territory, tour, 659–66
　hotels, 665–66
Train, touring by, 29–30
　accommodations and fares, 29–30
　baggage, 30
　booking, 30
　hints for handicapped travelers, 67
　hints for traveling with children, 76
　tours, 30
Trans-Canada Highway across Saskatchewan, tour, 629–35
　hotels, 633–35
Transportation, local, *see* local transportation *entry under names of individual cities*
Transportation costs, calculating, 49. *See also* Airplane travel; Bus, touring by; Car, driving own; Car rentals; Train, touring by
Travel agents, how to use, 52–54
Traveler's checks, 81–82
Trenton, Ontario, 530
Trepassey Barrens, Newfoundland, 447–48
　hotels, 449
Trinity, Newfoundland, hotels, 454
Trip cancellation and interruption insurance, 56–57
Trois Pistoles, Quebec, 611
Trois Rivières, Quebec, 600–601
Truro, NS, 490
　hotels, 492
Tunelik River (near Kuujjuaq, Quebec), 299
Turtle Mountain Provincial Park, Manitoba, 412
　campgrounds, 414
Tweedsmuir Provincial Park, BC, 316, 400
Twillingate, Newfoundland, 450
　hotels, 453
Tyne Valley, PEI, hotels, 573
Tyne Valley Oyster Festival (Tyne Valley, PEI), 328–29

Ungava (near Fort Chimo, Quebec), 320
Uplands Golf Club (Victoria, BC), 295

Upper Canada Golf Course (near Morrisburg, Ontario), 293
Upper Sustut and Finlay Watersheds (northwest of Fort St. John, BC), 301

Val David, Quebec, hotels, 606
Vancouver, BC, 242-60
 climate, 250
 essay, 242-45
 hotels, 254-56
 ice skating, 323
 local transportation, 250-51
 museums, 251
 music, 254
 nightclubs and nightlife, 254
 restaurants, 256-60
 shopping, 251-52
 sights and activities, 245-48
  downtown, 246-47
  suburbs, 247-48
  Vancouver Island, 249-50
 ski areas, 282
 special events, 251
 sports, 253
 theater, 253-54
 tipping, 250
 tourist information, 250
Vancouver Island, BC, tour, 249-50, 381-87
 hotels, 385-87
Vernon, BC, hotels, 395
Vernon Winter Carnival (Vernon, BC), 330
Victoria, Vancouver Island, BC, 381-83
 hotels, 385-86
Victoria Golf Club (Victoria, BC), 295

Wallace, NS, 501
Wasagaming Golf Course (Riding Mountain National Park, Wasagaming, Manitoba), 295
Waskesiu Lake Golf Club (Waskesiu Lake, Saskatchewan), 295
Water safety, 80
Waterton Lakes National Park (near Cardston, Alberta), 315, 333-34, 357-58
 hotels, 361
Waterton Park Golf Club (Waterton Park, Alberta), 294

Wawa, Ontario, 544
 hotels, 547
Weights and measures, table of, 97-98
West Coast Trail (Vancouver Island, BC), 317
Western Lakeshores, Ontario's, tour, 537-49
 hotels, 546-49
West Hawk Lake, Manitoba, 407-8
Weyburn, Saskatchewan, hotels, 639
Weymouth, NS, 485
Wheat Belt, Manitoba, tour, 409-14
 hotels, 413-14
Wheatley, Ontario, 514-15
Whirlpool Golf Course (Niagara Falls, Ontario), 293
Whistler Resort (Whistler, BC), 282
Whitehorse, Yukon Territory, 650-52
 hotels, 657-58
White River, Ontario, 544-45
 hotels, 548
Whiteshell, Manitoba, tour, 405-9
 hotels, 408-9
Whiteshell Provincial Park, Manitoba, 406-7
 hotels, 408-9
Wilderness around Fort Hope (near Nakina, Ontario), 320
Wilderness Mountain Skiing in Purcells and Selkirks (BC), 284, 288
Williams Lake, BC, 391
Willmore Wilderness (north of Jasper National Park, Alberta), 321
Windermere House (Muskoka, Ontario), 339-40
Windsor, NS, 489-90
Windsor to Stratford, Ontario, tour, 510-23
 hotels, 520-23
Winnipeg, Manitoba, 261-63
 climate and clothes, 266
 essay, 261-63
 hotels, 268-69
 local transportation, 266
 museums, 267
 music, 268
 nightclubs and nightlife, 268
 restaurants, 270-72
 shopping, 267
 sights and activities, 263-65
  downtown, 264
  suburbs, 264-65

Winnipeg (*cont.*)
  special events, 266–67
  sports, 267–68
  theater, 268
  tipping, 266
  tourist information, 265–66
Winnipeg River (Kenora, Ontario), 305
Winterlude, Ottawa, Ontario, 327
Wolfville, NS, 488
  hotels, 492
Women travelers, hints for, 70
Wood Buffalo National Park (near Fort Smith, NWT), 334, 478–79
Wood Mountain Historic Park, Saskatchewan, 632
Woodstock, NB, 442
  hotels, 444
Woodstock, PEI, hotels, 573
World Champion Bathtub Race (Vancouver to Nanaimo, BC), 329–30
World Championship Outhouse Race and Lac La Hache Winter Carnival (Lac La Hache, BC), 329

Yarmouth to Amherst, NS, tour, 482–92
  hotels, 491–92
Yarmouth to Strait of Canso, NS, tour, 493–500
  hotels, 499–500
Yellowhead Highway, Saskatchewan, tour, 640–45
  hotels, 643–45
Yellowknife, Hay River to, NWT, tour, 465–69
  hotels, 469
Yoho National Park (Field, BC), 316, 334, 397
  hotels, 398
Yonge Street: Toronto to Thunder Bay, Ontario, tour, 548–64
  hotels, 561–64
Yorkton, Saskatchewan, 641
  hotels, 643
Yukon, Prince George, BC, to, tour, 401–4
  hotels, 403–4
Yukon River, Yukon Territory, 665
Yukon Territory, exploring, 646–65

GET YOUR TRAVEL ADVICE AND GO!

Stephen Birnbaum gives you the very best travel advice in the world, in his series of travel guides. Each is revised annually, to provide you with accurate information available, on vacations destinations around the world.

Canada 1990	$12.95
Caribbean, Bermuda and the Bahamas 1990	$14.95
Europe 1990	$14.95
France 1990	$12.95
Great Britain 1990	$13.95
Hawaii 1990	$12.95
Ireland 1990	$12.95
Italy 1990	$12.95
Mexico 1990	$12.95
South America 1990	$13.95
Spain and Portugal 1990	$12.95
United States 1990	$13.95

Stephen Birnbaum brings you unforgettable business travel at extra large, single prices:

USA for Business Travelers 1990	$9.95
Europe for Business Travelers 1990	$9.95

Available at bookstores everywhere, or send check, (no cash), or money order, for the total listed plus $1.50 for shipping and handling (NY, NJ. applicable) Allow 4 weeks for delivery.

Travel Guides, Department G1,
Houghton Mifflin Company,
Park Street, Boston, MA 02108

Travel agencies receiving discounts of 10% for purchases of

Houghton Mifflin Company
Park Street, Boston, MA 02108

GET YOUR TRAVEL ADVICE AND GO!

Stephen Birnbaum brings you the very best travel advice in the world in his series of travel guides. Each is revised annually, to provide the most accurate information available on vacation destinations around the world.

Canada 1990	$13.95
Caribbean, Bermuda, and the Bahamas 1990	$13.95
Europe 1990	$14.95
France 1990	$13.95
Great Britain 1990	$13.95
Hawaii 1990	$13.95
Ireland 1990	$13.95
Italy 1990	$13.95
Mexico 1990	$13.95
South America 1990	$13.95
Spain and Portugal 1990	$13.95
United States 1990	$13.95

Stephen Birnbaum brings you indispensable business travel advice in two unique guides.

USA for Business Travelers 1990	$8.95
Europe for Business Travelers 1990	$8.95

Available in bookstores everywhere. Or, order directly by mail. Send your check or money order for the price listed plus $1.50 for shipping and tax (where applicable). Allow 4 weeks for delivery:

    Travel Guides Department GG
    Houghton Mifflin Company
    2 Park Street, Boston, MA 02108

Direct inquiries regarding discounts on bulk purchases to:

    Special Sales Manager
    Houghton Mifflin Company
    2 Park Street, Boston, MA 02108